1713   Treaty of Utrecht ending War of Spanish Succession: French threat to balance of power checked

1721   Treaty of Nystadt ending Great Northern War: rise of Russia under Peter the Great

1740   Accession of Maria Theresa in Austria and of Frederick the Great in Prussia; outbreak of War of Austrian Succession

1756   The Diplomatic Revolution; outbreak of Seven Years' War

1776   American Declaration of Independence
Adam Smith's *Wealth of Nations*

1787   United States Constitution drawn up

1789   Onset of the French Revolution

1799   (November 9–10) *Coup d'état* of Brumaire: Napoleon in power in France

1815   Vienna settlement reshapes Europe after Napoleonic Wars

1823   Monroe Doctrine: U.S. opposed to European intervention in New World

1830   Revolutions in France, Belgium, Poland

1832   First Reform Bill in Britain: victory of middle-class liberalism

1846   Repeal of British Corn Laws: victory of new industrial classes

1848   Wave of liberal and nationalist revolutions in Europe
Communist Manifesto by Marx and Engels

901
B77m

94707

ERN

ION

MODERN

CIVILIZATION

CRANE BRINTON

McLean Professor of Ancient and Modern History, Harvard University

JOHN B. CHRISTOPHER

University of Rochester

ROBERT LEE WOLFF

Harvard University

A History of the Last Five Centuries

Englewood Cliffs, New Jersey
PRENTICE-HALL, INC.

PRENTICE-HALL HISTORY SERIES

Donald C. McKay, Editor

Amherst College

Grateful acknowledgment is made to the following publishers for granting permission to use the material quoted on the pages indicated: *James Clarke & Co. Ltd.*, 92; *E. P. Dutton & Co., Inc.*, 43, 341, 342, 369; *Harcourt, Brace and Company, Inc.*, 60; *Alfred A. Knopf, Inc.*, 775; *The Macmillan Co.*, 409, 418; *Oxford University Press (London)*, 77, 78, 79, 94, 731; *Random House, Inc.*, 44, 45; *St. Martin's Press, Inc.*, 198; *Charles Scribner's Sons*, 521.

"The White Man's Burden" on p. 571 is from "The Five Nations" by Rudyard Kipling. Copyright 1903 by Rudyard Kipling, reprinted by permission of Mrs. George Bambridge, Doubleday & Company, Inc., and Methuen & Co. Ltd.

Tenth printing.........January, 1965

Printed in the United States of America

59008–C

Acknowledgments

In a book of this magnitude it would be quite impossible to make adequate acknowledgment of all our collaborators. They begin, of course, with all those who have written, or made, history in the past. On a far more modest scale, it would be very difficult even to assemble the names of all those who have contributed in a very immediate way, through suggestion or criticism. Readers of our two-volumed *A History of Civilization* (Englewood Cliffs, N.J.: Prentice-Hall, Inc., 1955), which is the parent of the present work, have sent in useful comments. We should particularly like to express our gratitude to Donald C. McKay, of Amherst College, who has contributed both guidance and enthusiasm, and to the members of the Prentice-Hall staff, who have given their skills and energies without stint in seeing this book through all its complicated processes.

Crane Brinton

John B. Christopher

Robert L. Wolff

A Note
on the Endpapers

Some day psychologists may be able to tell us just what and how to remember. But at present we know little more than this: though a few exceptional people can absorb and tap at will large stores of systematically arranged facts—say the list of popes from St. Peter on—most human beings cannot remember great systems of facts for very long unless they make fairly regular use of them. Indeed, if we never did any figuring at all, most of us would forget the multiplication table. Few of us make any regular use of history. Fortunately, the modern world is admirably supplied with works of ready reference that can free our minds for more useful work than just memorizing. The engineer, for example, does not need to keep in mind all the formulas and equations he might need; he has his engineer's handbook. So anyone using history has a host of reference books available in libraries, and on his desk he may have for immediate use such a storehouse of information as the one-volume *Encyclopaedia of World History* (Boston: Houghton Mifflin Company, 1948), edited by W. L. Langer.

Yet we do need something like a historian's equivalent of the multiplication table, if only to give us a frame of reference. The trouble with most historical tables, however, is that they are much too long and contain far too many facts for the average person. It is as if our multiplication table, instead of stopping with twelve times twelve, or even ten times ten, went on to fifty times fifty. The list of dates in the endpapers of this volume is an attempt to construct the modern historian's equivalent of the multiplication table. It is a simple list of a few dozen dates, a rough map of historic time over the past five centuries. It does not necessarily include all the great dates since 1450, but it attempts to show some of the key dates—the chronological turning points—in the history of the modern world. It is worth mastering bit by bit and keeping in memory.

A Note
on the Reading Suggestions

A list of reading suggestions is appended to each chapter of this book. Almost all historical bibliographies nowadays begin apologetically with the statement that they are highly selective and do not, of course, aspire to be exhaustive. This apology is hardly necessary, for the fact is that in most fields of history we have outrun the possibility of bringing together in one list all the books and articles in all languages on a given topic. There are for the wide fields of this book, and in English alone, thousands of volumes and hundreds of thousands of articles in periodicals. The brief lists following each chapter are simply suggestions to the reader who wishes to explore a given topic further.

Each list attempts to give important and readable books for each chapter. Special attention has been paid to listing inexpensive editions, often paper-backed, in such series as Mentor Books (published by the New American Library, New York), Penguin and Pelican Books (published at Harmondsworth, England), Anchor Books (published by Doubleday & Co., Garden City, New York), the Teach-Yourself-History Library (published in New York by The Macmillan Company), Vintage Books (published by Alfred A. Knopf, New York), and the Berkshire Studies (published by Henry Holt and Co., New York). A useful guide to paper-backs is *Paperbound Books in Print*, appearing twice a year (New York: R.R. Bowker Co.).

Good readings in original sources, the contemporary documents and writings of an age, are sometimes listed, though the reader can supplement these listings from the text itself and from the references in footnotes to the source of quotations. In addition, there are many good collections of sources for European history, notably the two-volume *Introduction to Contemporary Civilization in the West* (1954), prepared by faculty members at Columbia University; this begins with the Middle Ages and gives much longer selections from the sources than such compilations usually do. Other good collections are to be found in the Viking Portable Readers (published in New York by the Viking Press). There are also books on central problems in European history. A good recent example is K. M. Setton and H. R. Winkler, eds., *Great Problems in European Civilization* (Englewood Cliffs, N.J.: Prentice-Hall, Inc., 1954).

Our lists also include historical novels and, occasionally, dramas. Professional historians are likely to be somewhat severe in their standards for a historical novel. They naturally want its history to be sound; and at bottom they are likely to be somewhat prejudiced against the form as a painting of their lily or a sweetening of their pill. The historical novels listed here are all readable and all reasonably good as history. But note that historical novels, like historical films, though accurate on such material matters as authentic settings and appropriate costumes, often fail to capture the immaterial aspects—the psychology, the spirit—of the age they are written about. Many such novels motivate their characters, especially in love, as if they were modern Europeans and Americans. Exceptions to this rule are noted in the lists.

It is not hard to assemble more material on a given topic than is furnished by our reading lists. American libraries, large and small, have catalogues with subject and title listings, as well as a section of reference books with encyclopaedias and bibliographies. Many libraries have open shelves where, once a single title is discovered, many others may be found in the immediate area. Perhaps the first printed list of books to be consulted is *A Guide to Historical Literature* (New York: The Macmillan Company, 1931), discussed below on page 31. For more recent books one can turn, for American history, to the *Harvard Guide to American History* (Cambridge, Mass.: Belknap, 1954), edited by O. Handlin and others. And for the history of Europe and other areas there are many good bibliographies; see, for example, those in the volumes of "The Rise of Modern Europe" series edited by W. L. Langer and published by Harper & Brothers; in the multi-volumed *Oxford History of England;* and in the bibliography, unusually full, of R. R. Palmer and J. Colton, *A History of the Modern World* (New York: Alfred A. Knopf, Inc., 1956). For historical fiction, one may consult two older specialized guides: E. A. Baker, *A Guide to Historical Fiction* (New York: The Macmillan Company, 1914) and J. Nield, *A Guide to the Best Historical Novels and Tales* (London: Elkins, Mathews, and Marrot, 1929). The more recent *Fiction Catalogue* (New York: H. W. Wilson Company, 1951) covers much besides historical fiction but does furnish keys to books that cover particular countries and particular historical eras.

What is much more difficult than assembling titles is securing an evaluation of individual books. For older books the *Guide to Historical Literature*, already mentioned, gives the most useful references to critical reviews of the titles it discusses. *The Book Review Digest*, a periodical published in New York by the H. W. Wilson Company, gives capsule reviews and references to longer ones. For current books the weekly book section of *The New York Times* and *The Times Literary Supplement* (published in London) usually provide informative reviews of historical works soon after they are published. Later—sometimes as much as three years later—full scholarly appraisals are published in the *American Historical Review*, its British equivalent the *English Historical Review*, and in many more specialized reviews, such as the *Journal of Modern History* and, for medieval studies, *Speculum*. By reading a few reviews of a book one can usually get an indication of its scope and quality. In the reading suggestions for this book we have tried, briefly, to give our readers comparable indications.

Contents

ONE

The Background of Modern Western Civilization   3

I: INTRODUCTION: THE NEW HISTORY AND THE OLD. II: THE FIRST MEN. *Prehistory. The Neolithic Revolution.* III: THE FIRST CIVILIZATIONS. *Our Own Beginnings: The Near East. Religious and Political Beginnings.* IV: GREECE AND ROME. *Some Greek "Firsts." The Style of Greco-Roman Culture. The Romans. The Roman Empire. Early Christianity.* V: THE MIDDLE AGES. *Geographic Divisions. The Dark Ages. The Franks. Transition to the High Middle Ages. Feudalism. Manorialism. The Towns and the Church. Our Medieval Origins. The Medieval Style. Summary.*

TWO

The Renaissance   32

I: INTRODUCTION. II: THE ECONOMIC BACKGROUND. *Trade. Industry. Banking. The Impact of Economic Change.* III: THE POLITICAL BACKGROUND. *The Italian States. The New Realism: Machiavelli. France. England. Spain.* IV: LITERATURE AND THOUGHT. *The Rise of the Vernaculars. Humanism. Later Humanism.* V: THE ARTS. *Painting. Leonardo, Michelangelo, Titian. Northern European Painting. Sculpture. Architecture. Music.* VI: SCIENCE. VII: RELIGION. VIII: CONCLUSION: THE RENAISSANCE STYLE.

THREE

The Protestant Reformation 75

I: PROTESTANT ORIGINS—LUTHER. *Luther and the Ninety-Five Theses. Luther's Revolt. The Reasons for Luther's Success. The Opposition to Luther. Knights' War and Peasants' Rebellion.* II: PROTESTANT ORIGINS—ZWINGLI, CALVIN, AND OTHER FOUNDERS. *Zwingli. Calvin. The English Reformation. The Anabaptists. Unitarianism.* III: PROTESTANT BELIEFS AND PRACTICES. *Common Denominators. Anglicanism. Lutheranism. Calvinism: Predestination. The Left Wing.* IV: THE CATHOLIC REFORMATION. *The Jesuits. The Inquisition. The Council of Trent.* V: THE PLACE OF PROTESTANTISM IN HISTORY. *Protestantism and Progress. Protestantism and Nationalism.*

FOUR

Dynastic and Religious Wars 100

I: INTERNATIONAL POLITICS—THE MODERN EUROPEAN STATE-SYSTEM. *The Competitive State-System. Dynastic State and Nation State. Diplomacy. The Armed Forces.* II: HABSBURG AND VALOIS. *The Italian Wars of Charles VIII and Louis XII. Charles vs. Francis: The First Round. Charles vs. Francis: The Second Round. The Peace of Augsburg. The Wars of Philip II. The Dutch Revolt. The End of Philip II. The Dutch Republic.* III: THE THIRTY YEARS' WAR. *Nature and Causes. The Danish Period, 1625-1629. The Swedish Period, 1630-1635. Swedish-French Period, 1635-1648. Effects on Germany. The Peace of Westphalia.* IV: THE NEW MONARCHIES—SPAIN AND FRANCE. *The "Age of Absolutism." Power and Limits of Spanish Absolutism. The Spanish Economy. The Spanish Style. The French Monarchy. The French Wars of Religion, 1562-1598. The Victory of Henry of Navarre. The Politiques.* V: THE NEW MONARCHIES—ENGLAND. *Henry VIII, 1509-1547. Tudor Parliaments. Religious Difficulties. Elizabeth the Queen. The English Renaissance.*

FIVE

The Expansion of Europe: Fifteenth Through Seventeenth Centuries

136

I: INTRODUCTION. *Ancient and Modern Expansion Contrasted. The Nature of Modern Expansion.* II: EAST BY SEA TO THE INDIES. *Prince Henry and the Portuguese. India. China. The Portuguese Empire.* III: WEST BY SEA TO THE INDIES. *Columbus. The Foundation of the Spanish Empire. The Balance Sheet of Latin-American Empire.* IV: THE LATE-COMERS—FRANCE, HOLLAND, ENGLAND. *Early French and English Activity. The Thirteen Colonies: Settlement. The Thirteen Colonies: Institutions. New France. The Indies, West and East. Africa. The Far East.* V: THE BEGINNINGS OF ONE WORLD. *The Black Side of the Record. The Economic Record. Effect of Expansion on the West. The One World of 1700.*

SIX

Divine-Right Monarchy — and Revolution

168

I: INTERNATIONAL POLITICS—FRANCE AS AGGRESSOR. *Before Louis XIV: Henry IV and Sully. Before Louis XIV: Richelieu and Mazarin. The Successes of Louis XIV. The Failures of Louis XIV. The Utrecht Settlement. French Aggression in Review.* II: THE FRANCE OF LOUIS XIV. *Divine-Right Monarchy. The Nobility. The Clergy. The Royal Administration. Mercantilism in Theory. Mercantilism in Practice: Colbert.* III: ENGLAND IN REVOLUTION. *The Constitutional Tradition. The Role of the Crown. Issues between Crown and Parliament. The Reign of James I (1603-1625). The Troubles of Charles I. The Road to Civil War, 1638-1642. The Civil War, 1642-1649. Cromwell and the Interregnum, 1649-1660. The Revolution in Review. The Restoration, 1660-1688. The Glorious Revolution of 1688-1689.* IV: THE CENTURY OF GENIUS. *Inductive Science. The Implications of Scientific Progress. The Classical Spirit. The Arts. Seventeenth-Century Culture in Review.*

SEVEN

The Eastern Outposts 208

I: THE HEIRS OF OTHER TRADITIONS. *The Ottoman Turks.* II: MUSCOVITE RUSSIA: FROM THE TARTAR DEFEAT TO 1682. *The Imperial Political Theory. Nobles and Serfs. The Reign of Ivan the Terrible. The Time of Troubles. The Role of the Zemski Sobor. The Role of the Church. The Expansion of Russia. Russia and the West.* III: THE ERA OF PETER THE GREAT (1682-1725). *Sophia: The Forerunner (1682-1689). Peter the Great: A Character Sketch. The Western Trip. Peter's Wars. The Machinery of Government. More Innovations. The Total Estimate.* IV: THE OTTOMAN SUCCESSOR-STATE, 1453-1699. *A Slave System. The "Four Pillars" of Administration. Weaknesses of the Ottoman System. Ottoman Expansion to 1566. Ottoman Decline, 1566-1699. The Subject Peoples.*

EIGHT

The Eighteenth Century:
The International Balance 246

I: INTRODUCTION: THE PROSPECT IN 1715. II: THE ECONOMIC REVOLUTIONS IN THE WEST. *The Commercial Revolution. The Mississippi and South Sea Bubbles. The Agricultural Revolution. The Beginnings of the Industrial Revolution.* III: THE WESTERN POWERS. *The Assets of Britain. The Liabilities of France. The Other Western States.* IV: ITALY AND GERMANY. *The Habsburg Domains. The Rise of Prussia.* V: WAR AND DIPLOMACY, 1715-1763. *Early Eighteenth-Century Diplomacy in Review. The War of the Austrian Succession, 1740-1748. The Uneasy Peace, 1748-1756. The Seven Years' War, 1756-1763.* VI: CONCLUSION: THE INTERNATIONAL BALANCE IN REVIEW.

NINE

The Eighteenth Century: The Enlightenment 274

I: BASIC PRINCIPLES AND TRAITS. *The Inheritance from Locke and Newton. Eighteenth-century Science. French Leadership.* II: THE REFORM PROGRAM OF THE PHILOSOPHES. *Laissez-Faire Economics. Justice. Education. Attitudes toward Religion. Political Thought: Montesquieu. Political Thought: Rousseau. Enlightened Despotism.* III: THE ENLIGHTENED DESPOTS. *Prussia: Frederick the Great. Austria: Maria Theresa and Joseph II. The Limitations of Enlightened Despotism.* IV: RUSSIA, 1725-1825. *The Fate of the Autocracy, 1725-1762. Nobles and Serfs, 1730-1762. Catherine the Great, 1762-1796. Paul (1796-1801). Alexander I (1801-1825). Russian Foreign Policy, 1725-1796.* V: THE CULTURE OF THE ENLIGHTENMENT. *Philosophy. The Evangelical Revival. Literature. Art. The Great Musicians.*

TEN

Revolution in America and France 313

I: GEORGE III AND THE AMERICAN REVOLUTION. *George III. Background of the Revolution. Implications of the Revolution.* II: THE CAUSES OF THE FRENCH REVOLUTION. *The First and Second Estates. The Third Estate. The Financial Crisis. The Estates General.* III: THE DISSOLUTION OF THE FRENCH MONARCHY. *Popular Uprisings (July-October, 1789). National Assembly (1789-1791). The Constitution of 1791. The Legislative Assembly, Oct. 1791-Sept. 1792.* IV: THE FIRST FRENCH REPUBLIC. *Gironde and Mountain. The Reign of Terror (June, 1793-July, 1794). The Record of the Terror. The Thermidorean Reaction.*

ELEVEN

Napoleon   341

I: THE RISE OF NAPOLEON. *The First Coalition (1792-1795). Napoleon's Early Career. Brumaire.* II: NAPOLEON AND FRANCE. *Napoleonic Government. Law and Justice. Education. Economics.* III: NAPOLEON AND EUROPE. *The War (1800-1807). The Empire at Its Height (1807-1812). The Continental System. The Downfall of Napoleon. The Legacy of the Revolution and Napoleon.* IV: THE ROMANTIC PROTEST. *Literature: The Revolt against Reason. Literature: the Return to the Past. Music. The Arts. Religion and Philosophy.* V: THE CONSERVATIVE OUTLOOK AND THE VIENNA SETTLEMENT. *The Congress of Vienna. The Quarantine of France.*

TWELVE

Revolution and Counter-Revolution
1815-1850   376

I: INTRODUCTION: THE PERSISTENCE OF REVOLUTION. II: THE REVOLUTIONS OF THE 1820's. *The Iberian States and Naples. The Greek War of Independence, 1821-1829. The Decembrist Revolt in Russia.* III: THE REVOLUTIONS OF 1830. *France: The July Revolution. Belgium. Poland. Italy and Germany. The Lessons of 1830.* IV: THE REVOLUTIONS OF 1848. *Common Denominators. France. Italy. Germany. The Habsburg Domains. The Lessons of 1848.*

THIRTEEN

The Impact of the Economic Revolutions   400

I: THE INDUSTRIAL REVOLUTION. *The Machine. Coal and Iron. Transport and Communication. The Timetable of Industrialization.* II: ECONOMIC AND SOCIAL CONSEQUENCES OF INDUSTRIALIZATION. *The Agricultural Revolution. Changes in Population. The Aspirations of the Middle Class. The Grievances of the Working Class.* III: THE RESPONSES OF LIBERALISM. *The Classical Economists. Utilitarianism: Bentham. Democratic Liberalism: Mill.* IV: THE SOCIALIST RESPONSE—THE UTOPIANS. *Saint-Simon and Fourier. Owen. The Early Utopians Appraised.* V: THE SOCIALIST RESPONSE—MARX. *Basic Principles. The Communist Manifesto. The Later Career of Marx.* VI: OTHER RESPONSES. *The Anarchists. Proudhon. The Christian Socialists. The Catholic Response.*

FOURTEEN

The Western Democracies in the Nineteenth Century   432

I: BRITAIN, 1815-1914. *The Process of Reform. Parliamentary Reform. The Two-Party System: Liberals and Conservatives. The Two-Party System: An Explanation. Reforms of the Utilitarians. Free Trade. The Improvement of Labor. Education. Chartism. Foreign Policy. Imperial Policy. The Irish Problem. The Threat to Free Trade. The Welfare State. The Labor Party.* II: FRANCE—SECOND EMPIRE AND THIRD REPUBLIC. *The Coup d'Etat of 1851. The Second Empire, 1852-1870: Domestic Developments. The Second Empire: Foreign Policy. The "Liberal Empire." The Birth of the Third Republic. The Constitution of 1875. Boulanger and Panama. The Dreyfus Case. The Republic after Dreyfus.* III: ITALY, 1848-1914. *Cavour and the Completion of Unification. Assets and Liabilities of United Italy.* IV: THE UNITED STATES. *The Federal Union. Civil War and Reconstruction. Economic and Social Development. The Myth of Isolation.*

FIFTEEN

Central and Eastern Europe: To the Outbreak
of World War I   469

I: GERMANY, 1850-1914. *Prussia and the German Confederation, 1850-1859. Bismarck Comes to Power. The Schleswig-Holstein Question, 1863-1865. War with Austria, 1866. The North German Confederation. Showdown with France. The German Empire. Domestic Developments, 1871-1878. Domestic Developments, 1878-1890. William II. Domestic Tensions, 1890-1914.* II: THE HABSBURG MONARCHY, 1850-1914. *Political Experiments, 1850-1867. The Dual Monarchy, 1867. The Czechs. Poles and Ruthenians. Other Minorities in Austria. Minorities in Hungary. Croatia. Bosnia-Herzegovina. Austrian Society and Politics, 1867-1914. Hungarian Society and Politics, 1867-1914.* III: RUSSIA, 1825-1914. *Nicholas I (1825-1855). The Crimean War. Alexander II and Reform. Russian Intellectual Life. Nihilism, Populism, Terrorism. Foreign Policy under Alexander II. The Reaction, 1881-1904. The Russo-Japanese War. The Revolution of 1905. The Dumas, 1906-1914.* IV: CONCLUSION.

SIXTEEN

The Intellectual Revolution   515

I: DARWINISM. *The Origin of Species. Darwin's Theories. The Effect on Theology. The Effect on Social and Economic Attitudes. Eugenics. "Racism." A New Historical Determinism.* II: LITERATURE AND THE ARTS. *The Victorian Age. The Realistic Novel. The Naturalistic Novel: Zola. The Literature of Pessimism and Protest. Poetry. Painting. The Other Arts. Music. The Arts In Review.* III: PHILOSOPHY. *Idealism and Realism. The Cult of the Will. The Revolt against Reason. The Chastened Rationalists. The Extreme Anti-rationalists.* IV: PSYCHOLOGY. *Pavlov. Freud. The Implications of Freudianism.* V: POLITICAL AND SOCIAL THOUGHT. *Pareto. Political Thought in Review.*

SEVENTEEN

Nineteenth-Century Imperialism

547

I: THE MOVEMENT IN GENERAL. *Imperialism, New and Old. The Economic Aspect. The Powers Involved. The Areas Involved.* II: THE BRITISH EMPIRE. *The Boer War and After. Egypt. The Rest of British Africa. Other British Spheres. India: Political Organization. India: "The Meeting of East and West."* III: THE OTHER EMPIRES. *The French: North Africa. The French: Tropical Africa. The French: Asia. The Germans. The Italians and Belgians. The Americans. The Japanese.* IV: THE DEBATE OVER IMPERIALISM. *Pro: The Argument from Social Darwinism. Pro: The Argument of Duty. Pro: The Defensive Argument. Con: Anti-Imperialist Arguments.* V: THE RESULTS OF IMPERIALISM. *The Results in General. The Colonies of Settlement. Canada: Background of Revolt. Canada: Durham and A New Status. The Extension of Dominion Status. The Commonwealth in Review.*

EIGHTEEN

The First World War

580

I: INTRODUCTION. II: CAUSES OF THE WAR. *The Shift in the Balance of Power. The Role of Public Opinion. German Aspirations. British Aspirations. The Other Belligerents. The Era of Bismarck, 1871-1890. Formation of the Triple Entente, 1890-1907. A Decade of Crises, 1905-1914. The Final Crisis, July-August, 1914. The Entry of Other Powers.* III: THE COURSE OF THE WAR. *Resources of the Belligerents. The Western Front: German Offensive. The Eastern Front. Balkan and Turkish Fronts. The Near East and the Colonies. The War at Sea. The Western Front: Allied Victory. Morale on the Fighting Fronts. The Home Fronts. The Role of Propaganda. Political Repercussions.* IV: THE PEACE. *The Aftermath of World War. The Fourteen Points. Opposing Hopes and Promises. The Process of Peacemaking. The Territorial Settlement. The Mandates. The Punishment of Germany. The Settlement Evaluated.*

NINETEEN

Communist Russia 1917-1941   620

I: INTRODUCTION. II: THE REVOLUTION OF 1917. *The March Revolution. The Provisional Government. Lenin and Bolshevism. The Coming of the November Revolution. The Constituent Assembly.* III: WAR COMMUNISM AND NEP, 1917-1928. *Civil War. Why the Counter-revolution Failed. NEP ("The New Economic Policy"). The Struggle for Power: Stalin versus Trotsky. The Struggle for Power: Stalin's Victory.* IV: STALIN'S SUPREMACY: INTERNAL AFFAIRS, 1928-1941. *Collectivized Agriculture. Industrialization. The Social Impact. The Purge Trials. The Authoritarian State. The Russian Thermidor?* V: SOVIET FOREIGN POLICY, 1918-1941. *Foreign Office and Comintern, 1918-1928. Stalin and the West, 1928-1939. Stalin and the Second World War.* VI: CONCLUSION.

TWENTY

The Rise of Fascism 1918-1939   660

I: INTRODUCTION. II: ITALY AND FASCISM. *The Setting. Mussolini: Early Career. Mussolini: Rise to Power. The "March" on Rome. The Fascist Dictatorship. The Corporative State. Other Fascist Domestic Policies. Fascist Foreign Policy and Its Consequences.* III: GERMANY AND THE WEIMAR REPUBLIC, 1918-1933. *The Impact of Defeat. Postwar Political Alignments and Activities. The Weimar Constitution, 1919. Right and Left Extremism, 1920-1922. Hitler: Early Career. The Inflation, 1922-1923. The End of Inflation, 1923-1924. Recovery at Home, 1924-1929. "Fulfillment" Abroad, 1925-1930. The Impact of the Depression, 1929-1931. The Republic in Danger, 1931-1932. Hitler: Rise to Power, 1932-1933.* IV: GERMANY UNDER HITLER, 1933-1939. *The Nazi Dictatorship. The "Blood Purge" of 1934. Racism. Legal and Economic Policies. Religion and Culture. The Bases of Foreign Policy.* V: THE FAILURE OF PARLIAMENTARISM IN SPAIN AND EASTERN EUROPE, 1918-1939. *Spain: The Background. Birth of the Spanish Republic. Crisis of the Republic, 1933-1936. The Spanish Civil War, 1936-1939. Eastern Europe. Austria. Hungary. Yugoslavia. Other Authoritarian Regimes. Fascism in Review.*

TWENTY-ONE

The Democracies 1919-1939   703
Domestic and Imperial Problems

I: INTRODUCTION. II: GREAT BRITAIN. *The Postwar Depression. The Conservative and Labor Programs. Postwar Politics. Settlement of the Irish Question. The Commonwealth of Nations.* III: FRANCE. *The Impact of the War. Social and Political Tensions. The Stavisky Case and the Popular Front. Divided France.* IV: THE UNITED STATES. *Isolationism. The Road to Internationalism. Boom—and Bust. The New Deal. Confident America.* V: THE LOOSENING OF IMPERIAL TIES. *Japan. China: The Revolution of 1911-1912. China between the World Wars. The Chinese Communists. Southeast Asia. India. The Middle East.*

TWENTY-TWO

The Second World War   736

I: INTERNATIONAL POLITICS, 1919-1932. *The "Era of Fulfillment." The Failure of "Fulfillment." The Aggressors.* II: THE ROAD TO WAR, 1931-1939. *The First Step: Manchuria, 1931. The Second Step: German Rearmament, 1935-1936. The Third Step: Ethiopia, 1935. The Fourth Step: The Spanish Civil War, 1936-1939. The Fifth Step: "Anschluss," 1938. The Sixth Step: Czechoslovakia Dismembered, 1938-1939. The Final Step: Poland, 1939. Democratic Policy in Review.* III: THE NATURE OF THE WAR. IV: EARLY SUCCESSES OF THE AXIS. *Polish and Finnish Campaigns. "Phony War" and Blitzkrieg in the West. "The Fall of France." The Battle of Britain. Mediterranean and Balkan Campaigns. The Invasion of Russia. American Policy. Pearl Harbor and After.* V: THE VICTORY OF THE UNITED NATIONS. *The Turning Points. The Battle of Supply. The Axis on the Defensive. The Defeat of Germany. The Defeat of Japan. The Allied Coalition. Political Issues.*

TWENTY-THREE

The Revolt Against Imperialism

771

I: INTRODUCTION: CAUSES AND NATURE OF THE REVOLT. II: ASIA. *Defeated Japan. Communist China. The Korean War. Southeast Asia. India and Pakistan.* III: THE MIDDLE EAST. *Political Changes. Oil. Communism. Israel. Arab Unity and Disunity.* IV: AFRICA. *"Black" Africa. "White" Africa. Kenya. South Africa. French North Africa.* V: THE BRITISH COMMONWEALTH. *Canada. New Zealand and Australia. The Nature of the Commonwealth.* VI: CONCLUSIONS.

TWENTY-FOUR

The Western World Since 1945

804

I: THE "COLD WAR"—THE INTERNATIONAL AFTERMATH. *The Aftermath of War. New Elements and Old. The Communist Bloc in Europe. Yugoslavia. China. Stresses within the Communist Bloc. Communists outside the Russian Bloc. The "Free World." The Neutrals. The United Nations. The Record of the United Nations. International Relations in Perspective.* II: THE POSTWAR HISTORY OF THE MAJOR AMERICAN AND EUROPEAN STATES. *The United States. Canada and Latin America. Western Europe. Great Britain. France. Other Western Countries. Soviet Russia. The Soviet Satellites.* III: THE TEMPER OF THE WESTERN WORLD. *The Prophets of Doom. The Optimism of the Enlightenment. Repudiation or Revision of the Enlightenment.*

Illustrations

844

Index

847

Maps *by Vaughn Gray*

The Ancient World about 180 A.D.	*15*
The Medieval Western World about 1250	*20*
Renaissance Europe about 1490	*40*
Religious Situation about 1600	*95*
Political Situation about 1560	*108*
Europe in 1648	*116-117*
Growth of Empires to 1715: 1529	*138*
Growth of Empires to 1715: 1715	*139*
India about 1715	*158*
Europe in 1715	*174-175*
Medieval and Early Modern Russia—1300 to 1725	*213*
Russia in Asia—1725	*224*
Growth & Decline of Ottoman Empire, 1300-1725	*242*
Growth of Prussia—1740 to 1795	*261*
North America and the Caribbean, 1763	*271*
Russian Expansion in Europe, 1725-1825	*301*
Partitions of Poland	*303*
Napoleonic Europe, 1812	*352-353*
Europe after 1815	*370-371*
Centers of Revolution, 1820-1830	*378*
Centers of Revolution, 1848-1849	*389*

Industrial Europe, 1860	*403*
Unification of Italy, 1859-1870	*456*
Growth of Continental United States and Southern Canada	*461*
Unification of Germany, 1866-1871	*471*
Nationalities in Central and Eastern Europe	*487*
South America, 1914	*550*
Asia and the Pacific, 1914	*554-555*
Africa—1914	*556*
Caribbean America, 1914	*559*
Diplomatic Alignments Before 1914	*587*
The "Sick Man" of Europe, 1725-1914	*590*
Europe and the Near East, 1914-1918	*596*
Europe and the Near East, after World War I	*612*
The World, 1914-1924	*615*
Russia in Revolution, 1917-1921	*631*
Europe on the Eve—Aug. 1939	*744*
World War II—European and Mediterranean Theaters	*752*
World War II—Asian and Pacific Theaters	*765*
Eurasia, 1957	*776-777*
The Middle East—1957	*787*
The World, 1957	*792*
Europe, 1957	*808-809*
The Soviet Union, 1957	*812*

MODERN

CIVILIZATION

CHAPTER ONE

The Background

of Modern

Western Civilization

1: Introduction: The New History and the Old

Only a generation or two ago, "history" meant something very clear-cut and simple in American schools and colleges. It meant a study of our own history, which was unashamedly called "American History," even though it told almost nothing about Latin Americans or Canadians. Outside American History, it meant the classic sequence of Ancient, Medieval, Modern, from the old states of the Near East through Greece and Rome to the origins and development of the states of modern Europe. Finally, "history" dealt almost wholly with "past politics," with wars, with the men—and women—who stood out in the making of national and international politics.

In the twentieth century, this old-fashioned concept of what the study of history should mean has come under severe attack. In fact, in our times, which have seen so many revolutionary changes, something like a revolution in the study, writing, and teaching of history has taken place. There have been three phases in this revolution: First, in place of the old concentration on our modern European-American states and their background in the Near East and the Mediterranean, a concentration attacked as a form of narrowness and indeed "self-worship," the newer historians propose the study of other great civilizations with historical pasts: those of China and other lands of the Far East, of India, of Central and South America; and, in so far as anthropology and archaeology permit, the study of the past of human groups all over the world. Second, some of the newer historians feel that the old sequence of Ancient, Medieval, Modern does violence to the real continuities of history, that it is a kind of hangover from the Age of Reason in the eighteenth century, with its shallow contempt for the so-called Middle Ages. Third, and most important of all, the newer historians insist that politics and war have made only part of the record of history, perhaps a less important part than has been made by economic activity, art, literature, religion, even the routines of daily living of ordinary men and women. The study of history, in short, is to be not so much the study of past politics as the study of "past everything."

Now no sensible person will deny that these newer interpretations have greatly enriched and deepened the study of history. On the other hand, this new history is much more complex, difficult, and unwieldy than was the old. To use a nice old-fashioned figure of speech out of the old "classical" education, adding China, India, the Aztecs, and a lot more in space, adding the centuries back to ancestral sub-humans in time, adding all the innumerable activities of all men to the dramatic activities of a few in politics and war—adding all this is piling Pelion on Ossa indeed. What happens,

of course, is that in the ordinary "introduction" to history more ground is now covered, but it is covered less thoroughly. We have what is sometimes wryly called a "gallop through the centuries."

Often, indeed, historians pile up even more material in a given space than did their predecessors. The result is sometimes a longer and more arid catalogue of details than the lists of kings, queens, presidents, consuls, generals, popes, and cardinals that used to fill the older histories. After all, a list of poets, or even of inventors, is not in itself very illuminating; and even a hasty epithet or two—"ethereal" Shelley, "sweet-voiced" Keats, "ingenious and laborious" Edison—adds very little.

The present book is in part—though only in part—a reaction against the attempt to cover all the past everywhere on earth. We hope to retain the best of the old and add the best of the new. As for space, we shall concentrate on the history of one part of the world, the Europe sometimes scornfully called a "small peninsula of Asia." We shall trace the expansion of Europe as Europeans explored, settled, colonized, and traded in all parts of the globe. But we shall be concerned with non-European peoples only as they and their histories impinged on the development of European cultures. We are not motivated by any "self-worship," by any contempt for Asians or Africans, but simply by a desire to get our own record straight. As for time, after this brief introductory chapter, we shall be concerned with the years since about 1450, the period we must still think of as "modern," if only as a matter of convenience and convention. Obviously, this is not all a good American citizen of the second half of the twentieth century needs to know about the past of *homo sapiens*. But it is an essential part of what he needs to know, probably the part he *most* needs to know if he is to face the problems of human relations on this planet. Now for the first time, as a result of modern transportation and com-

from a close study of these tools. Almost all the time man or manlike creatures have been on earth is known as the Paleolithic period (Old Stone Age), and for the first part of this time it seems clear that man did not shape his tools at all. Indeed the earliest implements, which the archaeologist calls *eoliths* ("dawn stones"), are hard for the lay observer in a museum to recognize as tools. Toward the end of Paleolithic time, twenty thousand years ago or so, the chipped stone tools, including actual knives of flint or obsidian, became very good indeed. And finally, in Europe and the Near East there appeared about ten thousand years ago polished stone implements. The archaeologist now speaks of a Neolithic period (New Stone Age), which, however, very soon becomes the Age of Bronze and, again soon, of other metals, notably iron.

The Neolithic Revolution

The Neolithic Age marks one of the great turning points—one of the "revolutions"—in human development. We do not know exactly where or when it happened, but somehow men learned to *produce* rather than *gather* what they needed for food and shelter. This *domestication* of plants and animals was slow in comparison with our "Industrial Revolution" of the eighteenth and nineteenth centuries, but it was incredibly fast compared with the slow improvements in fist-hatchets made by men of the Old Stone Age. Domestication meant more and better food and shelter, and more human beings here on earth.

With the Neolithic, or agricultural and stock-raising revolution, then, a given area could support many more human beings. Moreover, instead of wandering about, men could—indeed had to—settle down in one place, first in villages, then in towns or cities. Man had become a political animal; his apparatus of culture, backed up by the power of symbolic thought, had become so complex that it had to be *recorded*. Writing (not at first alphabetical, but ideographic) was not the least of his inventions in the age that saw the domestication of plants and animals, the wheel, pottery, and much else. And with writing came written

Two reindeer from cavern at Font-de-Gaume, France. Cave paintings probably more than 10,000 years old.

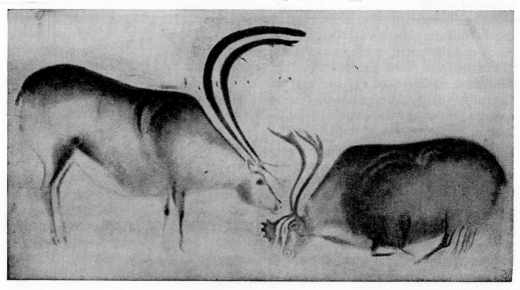

records, the basis for history as we know it, some five thousand years ago.

So far, we have limited ourselves to tracing culture in terms of its material remains. Toward the end of the Paleolithic we find graves, little statuettes (perhaps used as charms or fetishes), the famous cave-paintings of animals, which may have had religious or magical functions, all of which indicate that their makers had a life of ideas. We find jewelry, an indication that some of these people could afford fairly complicated desires and satisfactions. But we cannot know what their religious or magical ideas were, what ethical ideas they cherished, what sort of social and political life they had. We can be sure they had "culture," in the sense that they depended on the communication of symbolic thinking; and we can guess that the improvement of their material implements was accompanied by political and social "invention."

III: *The First Civilizations*

In the later part of the "Neolithic revolution" this political and social invention made it possible for men to live in cities, to hold together larger political units than had been possible in a hunting and food-gathering culture. These were the first "civilizations." Civilization is a term that social scientists have trouble defining, but it can be used roughly for human societies of the kind we are about to study, societies with some kind of writing, some "politics," and usually with cities, division of labor, social classes or castes—and organized armed forces.

Such civilizations apparently grew up independently in the lower valleys of the Tigris and Euphrates, in the valleys of the Nile, the Indus, and the Yellow River (Hwang Ho) in China, and in Peru and Central America. Each of these civilizations tended to "spread," for surrounding peoples learned from the civilized centers through trade, or other forms of contact. Very early, by the third millennium B.C., the civilizations of the Tigris-Euphrates (Mesopotamia) and of the Nile (Egypt) were in the kind of contact we now describe as "international relations"—trade, travel, diplomacy, war, and conquest. The other civilizations, until the beginnings of Europe's expansion only five hundred years ago, developed in relative isolation. It is true that there were some contacts among them. The Greeks and the Romans traded with India, and knew something about that subcontinent, but really very little. China was known vaguely to the westerners, a little less vaguely after the famous travels of Marco Polo in the thirteenth century A.D. And from the steppes of Central Asia nomads raided east to China and west to Europe. But the isolation of civilizations tended to be the rule until Da Gama, Columbus, and the other great explorers started us all on the way to One World. This is especially true of the American civilizations that grew up with centers in Peru and in Central America. Even if Leif Ericsson, the Viking leader, did reach North America about 1000 A.D., there was no real contact between the cultures of the "Red Indians" and those of Christian Europe until 1492.

Our Own Beginnings:
The Near East

From the beginnings of the civilizations of Mesopotamia and Egypt, however, we can speak of the continuity of a "western" civilization. Continuity, note, not identity. There has been much change, even among the human stocks that shared this civilization, though until with modern times western civilization began to spread around the world all have been what is loosely called "white." And the center of this civilization has moved, generally northward and westward from the ancient Near East. The sequence of leadership is easiest to trace in politics and war, though usually it can be traced in art and thought as well. It runs from the Near East to Greece to Rome and Italy to Western and Central Europe. That this leadership seems now in dispute between the United States and the Soviet Union, neither of which is geographically on what might be called the Babylon-Memphis-Athens-Rome-Paris-London axis of historical development, is but another indication that changes continue.

The awareness of some sort of common past is never quite broken in the five or six thousand years since the beginnings in the Near East. This awareness has not always been as strong as in our present history-conscious (some would say history-ridden) age. The main written languages of Mesopotamia and Egypt were forgotten, and had to be re-learned by modern scientists before the records, on clay tablets, stone, or papyrus, could be read. Two institutions—and the beliefs, the "values," even the "way of life" they meant to men—have been the main vehicles of this continuity of western civilization. These are formal education, especially higher education, which until very recently was patterned after the civilization of the Greeks; and the Christian churches, which preserved much of both Greco-Roman civilization, and, through its Jewish origins, that of the ancient Near East.

The number of "firsts" in our own western civilization to come from these Near Eastern river valleys is most impressive. Here we find for the first time what we can recognize as a "state," and with it law. The famous code of Hammurabi, from Mesopotamia about 1800 B.C., is clearly a true law code. Here first we encounter writing, and finally, from a people near or in Palestine, a true alphabet, the direct ancestor of our own. Here first a number of "practical" techniques in building, engineering, farming, and business were devised, and, for the most part, never quite lost. Surveying will do as an example. The need to delimit farm fields, to apportion "property" among individual or corporate owners, and, in Mesopotamia, the complex demands of an irrigation system, forced men to turn their attention to the practical matter of surveying the land. But note a characteristic that will hold through all western history: very soon men began to study such matters in other than a direct "practical" way. Some men became, not so much surveyors, as geometers, mathematicians, and astronomers. Here in the Near East—and *not* in Greece—we find the first scientists. And it seems likely that the origins of science were intertwined with age-old ideas and practices of magic.

Architecture, sculpture, painting (though very little painting has survived the rigors of time), and literature—art in its widest sense—are also firsts of this region. But here there is one significant exception, which makes us realize that we probably owe more to our Paleolithic ancestors than we can ever know. In France and Spain cave-paintings and drawings of animals have been found that are almost certainly at least ten or twelve thousand years old, far older than the pyramids of Egypt. The best of these paintings are striking not just as curiosities, but as works of art. These beasts look more like beasts as our modern artists see them than do the more stiff, formal creatures we first find in the art of the ancient Near East. Nevertheless, the arts as we have generally practiced them in the West do originate in the ancient Near East. The reindeer of the cave-painters look more natural to us than the lions of the Assyrian sculptors, but we

Sculptured head of Queen Nefertiti, wife of the Egyptian Pharaoh, Ikhnaton, about 1375 B.C.

plex than those of our earliest science. The completely orthodox "fundamentalist"— Jew, Christian, or Moslem—finds no problem in explaining the origins of his faith: his holy books tell him at what point in space and time his God made known to man the true religion. They also tell him that the Creation took place about 4000 B.C.

For the historian, however, the date 4000 B.C. was preceded by thousands of years of religion of which he has no record. So he faces a series of problems about the primitive religions of the Near East and their transformation into the "higher" religions. The earlier religions were almost certainly polytheistic; just how did polytheism develop into monotheism? Were the Jews the first monotheists, or was their Yaweh (in English traditional usage, Jehovah) just another private tribal god until very late— until, say, Egyptian and other influences had begun to work on those Jewish intellectuals we call the prophets? Is the real transition from a primitive to a higher religion less a matter of the number of gods than of the relation of the believer to his god or gods? Is it a matter of *ethics* rather than *theology*, of recognition by the individual of a "force not himself making for righteousness"? Do such terms as "sin" and "conscience" first begin to have real meaning for western civilization in the ancient Near East? The answer to this last query is almost certainly yes, but all these questions are still debated by specialists in religious history.

Another series of "firsts" is somewhat clearer than these problems of religion. Here in the Nile and Mesopotamian valleys, and in the "fertile crescent" that links them, we find the first recorded contacts among organized human groups, the first "international relations." Here first is the *drama* of recorded history, with the rise and fall of men and empires, with intrigue, aspiration, success and failure. Here too are what we may call the first case-histories for the modern social scientist. The tendency in international relations among many "sovereign

have nothing from the Stone Age that looks like a human being as the modern artist conceives him. In the bust of the Egyptian Queen Nefertiti, however, done more than three thousand years ago, we have one of the great works of our art.

Religious and Political Beginnings

Here in the Near East religions first take on forms that have been continuously alive in the hearts and habits of men ever since. The problems of our earliest religious history are even more com-

states" is for one to hold precariously a hegemony or leadership in a rough "balance of power." Then over the long run one imperial power upsets the balance and tends to dominate all the other states; at the end of the great period of the ancient Near East this power was the Persian Empire made famous by Cyrus, Darius, and Xerxes.

In sum, the long-dead Egyptians, Sumerians, Chaldaeans, Babylonians, Assyrians, Jews, Persians, and all the rest, though they lacked our modern command over power or energy—though they had only horses, oxen, and water-powered tools and no real machines—had almost everything else we have. They had cities, temples, armies, governments, schools, factories, stores, art, and all that these imply for men and women. Were they more like us than unlike us? It seems likely that they were very much like us, civilized men and women.

IV: Greece and Rome

Our great-grandfathers were taught to believe that the Greeks created, with no debt to earlier peoples, almost everything in our western culture, with the exception of the Old Testament of our Bible. This was to claim more for the Greeks than did most of their own writers, who acknowledged their debt to the Egyptians and other peoples. We now know that the ancient Greeks were northern barbarians speaking a language akin to our own and to most of the others of modern Europe—the so-called Indo-European group of languages. They came into the Aegean area in various bands probably from about the fifteenth century B.C. to the eleventh. We believe also that the Greeks found there a well-developed civilization to which has been given the name "Minoan," with its center on the island of Crete. This Minoan civilization probably was the first to depend on sea power and sea-borne trade; very likely the Minoans borrowed from Egypt and Palestine. Since the relatively few Minoan inscriptions have not yet been entirely deciphered, we still have to depend on artifacts for our knowledge of this civilization. Minoan art is full of life and movement; Minoan building, at least for the upper classes, provided plumbing and heating arrangements not to be equaled in medieval Europe. And the Greeks, though their war bands finished the destruction of Minoan civilization, learned much from their predecessors; indeed, the recently deciphered inscriptions seem to be in very early Greek.

Some Greek "Firsts"

About the ancient Greeks we know a very great deal. Though many Greek writings perished in the so-called Dark Ages that followed the breakdown of the Roman Empire in the fifth century A.D., a kind of basic library did survive. And of course there are surviving buildings, inscriptions, and statues. The narrative history of Greece from about 700 B.C. is reasonably clear.

As the tribal Greeks settled down in the Aegean area, a mountainous region with deep bays and little inland valleys, they developed a political form that seems to be an important historical "first." This was the city-state, which they called *polis*, and from which we take our word "politics." The city-state suggests the modern European nation-state, but in miniature. There was a walled city, often a harbor, and a surrounding countryside with farms. But the whole city-state—even the famous ones like Athens, Sparta, Thebes, or Corinth—was no bigger

than a smallish county in the eastern United States. These city-states were independent. There was no political entity that could be called Greece, any more than there is now a political entity that can be called Europe. A *citizen* of Athens had no higher political allegiance than to Athens. Indeed, since religion and the state were inseparable, the Athenian of the fifth century B.C. had no other major group-allegiance, save for family, than the *polis*. These independent city-states fought one another, made alliances, and in general created a pattern of international relations which in its broad lines resembles that of the modern West since about 1500. Although certain city-states, Athens, Sparta, and Thebes, won successively what is called, from the Greek word for leader, a *hegemony*, none succeeded in really uniting Greece. Still quarreling, these city-states fell easy victims in the second century B.C. to an Italian city-state, Rome, which succeeded in absorbing Greece into the Roman Empire.

In this last paragraph, one small word summarizes a very great achievement—*citizen*. We do not usually think of an Egyptian citizen, an Assyrian citizen, or even a Jewish citizen. But the Greek was a citizen of his *polis*, a voting, discussing, participating member of a commonwealth. In Athens, notably, in the great age of the fifth century B.C., he was proud of being a citizen of a *democracy*. The word is Greek, and so too is the political form itself. True, even in Athens there were slaves, and there was a group of resident aliens who were denied full citizenship. And these two groups together may have outnumbered the citizens. Nevertheless, for thousands of citizens this was a direct democracy, a kind of great New England town meeting. In both Greece and Rome, the citizen participated directly in government; nowhere in the ancient world was representative government, with elected deputies or representatives, really achieved.

Within the Greek city-states there was a lively devotion to almost the whole range of human cultural activity, from sport—the Olympic games were another Greek "first" —to high formal philosophy, also a Greek "first." If we extend the cultural history of Greece to include that of imperial Rome down to the fifth century A.D., then its range is extraordinarily complete, so complete that in the arts, in literature, in philosophy, and in religious thought it is difficult to find anything since that seems entirely new. Even in science and technology, and in economic life, the Greco-Roman world produced at least a foreshadowing of what we have since achieved. There were capitalists, bankers, factories—operated by human power for the most part—and, by 300 B.C., large political units, bureaucracies, and professionals of all kinds, including professional soldiers. There were even machines; the word itself is Greek. And later Greek scientists made steam engines, which they exhibited as museum pieces, a kind of toy. One of the obvious differences between the Greco-Roman world and our own is that the ancients never really applied their technical knowledge to harness *power* and thus extend the labor force. *Why* they did not is still a subject for debate. The easiest explanation, though probably incomplete, is that since they had slaves they did not feel the need for labor-saving devices.

The Style of Greco-Roman Culture

Any human group that gets at all established, even a family or a fraternity, comes to have what we shall here call its *style*. The style is a compound of many elements, tradition-cemented ways of going about the full round of living. The style of a great nation is complex, and is constantly changing and developing, or at least going through the cycle of youth, maturity, old age, and senility.

The Greeks, and even the more practical Romans, were at bottom *rationalists*, interested in trying to find out how things on this earth really ran, aware that immediate sense-impressions are often misleading, and also aware that they had inherited from their ancestors notions which, though sanctioned by religion, were in our own modern sense of the word, "myths." They freed their minds of these "myths" and "prejudices" and really tried to "reason things out." But they tended to rely too much on theory, on abstract speculation, and too little on detailed and undignified observation and experiment; and they tended to emphasize the finished, the complete, even to the point of holding that change, development, and evolution are illusions. Their great mathematical achievement was Euclidean geometry, which deals with finished, unchanging forms and laws; they were not great algebraists, and they did not come near finding the infinitesimal calculus. There is in their mythology a strong sense of the harshness, the repetitiveness, the treadmill aspect, of human life on earth—Sisyphus who rolled a stone uphill, only to have it roll back; the Danaïdes, who had to pour water into sieves; Niobe, perpetually weeping; the Augean stables, which could never be cleaned. It is true that Hercules did clean these stables by channeling two rivers through them, a suggestion that the ancient Greeks had glimpses of technological progress. Still, not really believing in growth, they did not turn their attention to economic growth, to trying to change a planet—and its inhabitants —that they believed were at bottom unchanging, and unchangeable.

All these generalizations about the Greco-Roman "style" are suggestive. But they have nothing like the precision that the modern natural scientist is used to, and they have numerous exceptions. For example, it is broadly true that the Greco-Roman intellectual did not get into a laboratory and dirty his hands—put more fairly, he was addicted to abstract "reasoning" after the Euclidean fashion from a few accepted postulates rather than from observation. Yet it is also true that the so-called Hippocratic school of medicine has left behind it concrete descriptions of symptoms of sick people, "case-histories" worthy of the best trained clinician of our own time.

Moreover, as the distinguished British scholar Gilbert Murray has suggested, the manner in which Greco-Roman culture was transmitted to us may have overweighted the elements of rational calm, measure, and

sobriety in their "style." What has been preserved of this cultural heritage, especially
the manuscripts of books, has been subjected
to the censorship of generations of schoolmasters and Christian monks. Naturally
these people preferred the tame to the wild,
the decent to the indecent, the finished to
the struggling and the growing. In terms the
reader will find more fully developed in
Chapters VI and XI, Murray claims that
the people who kept ancient culture alive
were moved by their very temperament and
calling to preserve the "classical" and let the
"romantic" perish. There may have been
more heaven-stormers, more wild strivers,
among Greek artists and thinkers than we
can ever know. Certainly the political record of the struggling city-states suggests
that the Greeks were not very reasonable
people.

The Romans

With the
Romans we
come to the last of the peoples who make
up conventional "Ancient History." They
were probably a mixed stock from various
groups established in the Italian peninsula,
including the Etruscans, an interesting people who are known to us, like the Minoans,
chiefly from archaeological remains. Rome
itself was probably "founded," in the sense
that American cities were often founded by
pioneers, at a date not far from 753 B.C., the
year of the traditional founding of the city
by the wolf-suckled Romulus and Remus.
The new city had a good strategic site at a
crossing of the Tiber, and it was centrally
located in Italy, though it had no good
natural harbor. Its inhabitants, some historians believe, showed the "hybrid vigor"
the biologist often finds in mixed stock.

At any rate, Rome, partly under the influence of Greek city-states in the south of
Italy which had been set up by colonists from
Greece itself, developed into a true city-
state based on the absorption of surrounding towns and villages in Latium (whence

Latin). The Romans began a process of expansion that at first sight was not very different from that undertaken by Athens and
Sparta. First the Italian peninsula was consolidated under Roman leadership, which
the divided Greek city-states of the south
were unable to resist. This expansion
brought Rome squarely up against her first
and most dangerous foe in large-scale international politics: Carthage, near what is now
the North African city of Tunis. Carthage
was originally a colony of Phoenicians from
the Palestinian region, and a very successful
merchant state that had expanded into Sicily
and Spain. (Note, by the way, that our
story is moving more and more into Europe.) In three wars, known from the Latin
adjective for the Phoenicians as the "Punic
Wars" (264-146 B.C.), the Romans broke
Carthage and annexed her empire, though
in the second war they were temporarily
beaten by one of the great generals of western history, the Carthaginian Hannibal.

Meanwhile, Rome was involved in the
politics of the Greek world around the
Aegean Sea. After the city-states of Greece
proper had worn themselves out in interne-
cine wars, a people on the northern fringes
of Greece, the Macedonians, under the leadership of two able kings, Philip and his son
Alexander, had moved in and put a temporary end to the squabbles of the city-states.
Though the Macedonians by no means
united Greece, Alexander was able to enlist
Greek soldiers, and with them and his Macedonians he started eastward in 334 B.C. on
an expedition that has ever since gripped
the imagination of the world. Alexander the
Great conquered the whole Near East, and
moved on into India; then he turned back,
but not until he had reached the Ganges
watershed. He died in 323 at Babylon, and
his empire, which he had had no real chance
to consolidate, fell apart at once.

Some traces of Greek culture—coins,
styles in sculpture—persisted in the East,
and even moved farther eastward, creating
one of the rare "contacts" between East and

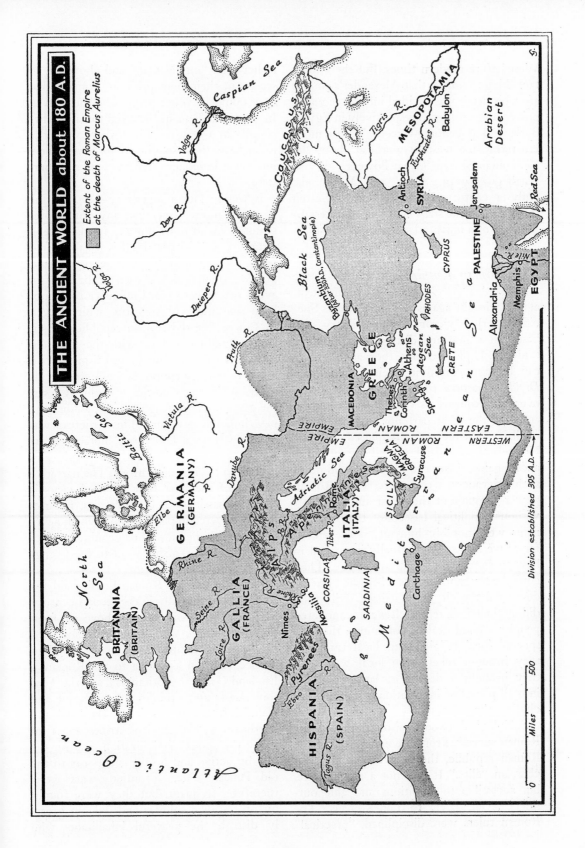

THE ANCIENT WORLD about 180 A.D.

☐ Extent of the Roman Empire at the death of Marcus Aurelius

Caspian Sea

Volga R.

Don R.

Dnieper R.

Volga R.

Caucasus

Black Sea

Byzantium (after 330 A.D., Constantinople)

MESOPOTAMIA

Tigris R.

Euphrates R.

Babylon

Arabian Desert

SYRIA

Antioch

PALESTINE

Jerusalem

Red Sea

Nile R.

CYPRUS

RHODES

CRETE

Aegean Sea

Memphis

Alexandria

EGYPT

GREECE

Athens

Corinth

Thebes

Sparta

MACEDONIA

EASTERN ROMAN EMPIRE

WESTERN ROMAN EMPIRE

Pruth R.

Vistula R.

Baltic Sea

North Sea

Danube R.

GERMANIA (GERMANY)

Elbe R.

Rhine R.

Adriatic Sea

Apennines

ITALIA (ITALY)

Rome

Tiber R.

Brindisi

SICILY

Syracuse

"MAGNA GRAECIA"

Mediterranean Sea

Alps

Seine R.

Loire R.

Rhône R.

GALLIA (FRANCE)

Nîmes

Massilia

CORSICA

SARDINIA

Carthage

BRITANNIA (BRITAIN)

Pyrenees

Ebro R.

HISPANIA (SPAIN)

Tagus R.

Atlantic Ocean

Division established 395 A.D.

0   500   Miles

West before modern times. But the important thing to note is that Alexander's empire after his death was divided into three major power-units, centered respectively in Egypt, Syria, and Macedonia-Greece. To use modern terms, the western world at about 200 B.C. contained five "Great Powers"—Rome, Carthage, Egypt, Syria, and Macedonia. Only a century later, Rome had beaten them all, and the stage was set for the establishment of a universal state in the West.

The Roman Empire

How did the Romans manage to win out against all their rivals? Specifically, their victory was a military one, based on a long and distinguished military tradition. Diplomatically, their achievement can be summarized in their own phrase: *Divide et impera* (divide and rule). Moreover, the Romans, as they expanded, managed for the most part not to make irreconcilable enemies of conquered peoples. No Ireland, no Poland, nursed eternal grievances against them; the Jews, who did nurse such grievances, were scattered by Roman power throughout the West and were left without a political base. Not that the Romans were notably humane, nor even, so far as we know, intellectually interested in how to acquire and hold an empire. They could be tough indeed, as when they utterly destroyed the city of Carthage. Still, they did on the whole tend to leave to conquered peoples a good deal of autonomy; they respected local religion and local tradition; they brought relief from local wars; and they brought a degree of law and order into all phases of international relations, including the economic.

Sociological reasons also accounted for Roman success. From the early days of the Roman republic, there developed a ruling class, an "élite." It was not a closed caste, but accessible to ambitious and able outsiders, even, later, to non-Romans. The Roman rulers were disciplined, "practical" rather than "intellectual," and above all, so secure in their own pride as Romans that they could let other peoples be themselves. In short, the Romans behaved toward other peoples in a way for which there was little precedent; they sought to *integrate* them into what in modern terms we call a "super-state."

It was in fact a super-city-state, for the Roman Empire never had any true representative institutions, nor any formal federal structure. The empire itself is usually dated from the reign of the first emperor (*imperator*, ruler, a title chosen deliberately to avoid *rex*, king, a word offensive to republican sensibilities), Augustus, which began in 31 B.C. The old Roman republican institutions could not cope with the manifold problems of the new imperialism. It had taken nearly a century of civil strife, culminating in the victories of Julius Caesar, the great-uncle of Augustus, to establish the new imperial structure. This structure was in many ways a faulty one, notably in its failure to establish a clear and simple succession to the imperial throne. The narrative history of the next four hundred years is full of assassinations, conspiracies, rivalries for the coveted imperial purple, which never became truly hereditary or genuinely "elective." The emperorship went to the strongest—or luckiest—claimant.

Nevertheless, the Roman Empire did for a time, and especially in the second century A.D., bring law, order, and, above all, freedom from major wars. The empire included the whole Mediterranean basin, modern France (known as Gallia to the Romans), England (known as Britannia), and the Teutonic lands up to the line of the Rhine and Danube. It was surrounded on the north and northeast by "barbarian" tribes eager to enjoy the spoils of civilization, and on the east by active and hostile successors to the old Persian state. "Frontier" wars were, therefore, frequent, but they were fought by professional soldiers and did not greatly disturb the peaceful inhabitants who lived in the interior parts of the empire.

The Roman Empire has always appealed to the imagination of the West. In a sense, as we shall see when we come to medieval history in the final section of this chapter, the West Roman Empire lived on long after the deposition in 476 A.D. of the last emperor in Rome itself. This old Roman One World has seemed especially successful to those who have lived through periods of grave international conflict like the present. Yet it had many serious weaknesses, and its full life was not long. There was always a large slave population, the bulk of which was never well off materially, and never seems to have felt itself part of the great empire. The imperial patriots were a small group, educated, and, as ruling classes go, conscientious and sometimes even kindly, but with no effective links with the masses. They formed the bureaucracy which along with the military leaders did the daily work of ruling, and they did hold the empire together. But they could not solve a whole series of political, social, and economic problems. The situation in Rome itself was typical. Here there was a population perhaps as great as a million, most of whom lived on a state dole and were entertained by the great free shows in the Colosseum and the Circus Maximus, and in the game rooms, libraries, and pools of the great public baths. Economically, Rome was a parasite on the empire, which had to feed it and the far-flung armies as well. Fairly early, the ruling class began to bend under its burdens, to lose faith in itself, and actually to cease to reproduce itself—the famous "lack of Romans." As the Germanic tribes pushed along into the empire, the decline became obvious. There were rallies, in one of which, early in the fourth century A.D., the emperor Constantine made of old Byzantium a new capital called after himself Constantinople, and set up a nucleus that did hold off the barbarians and became the Eastern Roman or Byzantine Empire (see Chapter VII). But the empire in the Roman West was doomed, and by the end of the fifth century had ceased to exist, at least in the shape it had held in its prime.

In the last paragraph, we have suggested part of an answer to the age-old problem: Why did the West Roman Empire fall? In concrete terms, it fell before a series of attacks from wandering German war bands. But did it fall from its own weakness or from the strength of the German attackers? *Both* factors were present, though modern opinion tends to stress the failure and decay of the empire rather than the strength of the barbarians. Many forces produced this decay—the falling birth-rate of the responsible ruling classes; the failure of taxes to pay for the armies; the unwieldy bureaucratic structure of the empire; the failure to make the masses true participants in the imperial enterprise; the distracting otherworldliness preached by the growing Christian faith, which is claimed to have made the Christians indifferent to the worldly fate of their society; the pressure of nomads from the steppes of Asia, which seems to have driven the Germans westward; and many more.

The Romans have left us a great deal. It is broadly true that in the arts, in literature, in philosophy they were imitators of the Greeks rather than originators. Yet they did preserve much of what the Greeks had done. In law, in engineering, both civil and military, and in architecture, what they did was never wholly lost to their European successors. Their language remained for over a thousand years after the fall of the empire the medium for all formal culture in the European West; above all, it remained the *lingua franca* of the Roman Catholic Church. Until only yesterday, Latin was an inescapable part of all higher education in the European West. Even now, it is embedded in all western tongues, even in German, and most certainly in English, as the carrier of most of our more general cultural ideas. We think as we do, in part at least, because of the way Caesar, Cicero, and thousands of forgotten Romans thought. And, heirs as we are of four hundred years of nationalistic and religious wars, we can never quite get the example of the Roman Peace out of our minds.

Early Christianity

One more element of great importance belongs chronologically in the history of the Greco-Roman world, though in that world it never fitted the ways of the ruling classes. Christianity began with the preaching of Jesus Christ in Palestine in the early days of the Roman Empire. Long persecuted or barely tolerated by the authorities of the empire, to whom it seemed a crude proletarian superstition, Christianity spread and won adherents until early in the fourth century the emperor Constantine himself was converted. By the fifth century, Christianity had become the established religion of the imperial government, and the old pagan faiths were dying out. As an established religion, it had to acquire the worldly apparatus of government and administration necessary to its success on this earth. By 500, its structure of government was substantially the one that was to prevail throughout the Middle Ages, the hierarchically organized Roman Catholic Church headed by the Bishop of Rome, the Pope, heir of the old Roman emperors—and of much, much more than the emperors.

For most of the time since the conversion of Constantine, men in the West, though they may have been very poor Christians in their daily lives, though they may have quarreled with their ecclesiastical superiors and thus become what are called heretics or schismatics, did not question the existence of God and all the rest of Christian fundamentals, including, emphatically, the Book of Genesis with its account of the Creation and the Flood. One of the best dividing lines between the medieval and modern history of the West is the rise, at first in the Renaissance of the fifteenth and sixteenth centuries, of a few men who questioned the whole Christian cosmology, to be followed in the eighteenth century by thousands who said openly they were not Christians.

Yet even in the twentieth century the vast majority of men and women in our western world would list themselves as Christians. To the historian the Church and the specific content of its faith have had a history—that is, they have changed and developed in time and space, as part of this changing world. But it should not be forgotten that some part at least of Christian faith must deny that history is all there is. The Christian must believe that a history dealing with this world cannot possibly explain the *ultimates* of Christian belief, which do not depend on process, on history, but are above them, unchanging and absolute.

Yet Christianity has never, like many oriental religions, denied the reality of this changing world of the senses, the world of history. It has never in its accepted forms attempted to extinguish all normal sense-life to achieve a kind of perpetual trance or ecstasy. It has never been indifferent to the choices between "good" and "evil" met in daily life. For over two thousand years, Christianity has displayed an amazing range of belief and behavior. Yet its general tendency has been to preserve in fruitful tension its concepts of this imperfect world and of the other perfect world, of the relative and the absolute. It has certainly never been what our modern cant phrase puts as "materialistic" in its cosmology; it has never, to put the matter with even more contemporary vulgarity—and clarity—countenanced the belief that "it's all chemistry, it's all physics." On the other hand, it has seldom denied that what the chemist is working with and on is real and important. To the absolutist temper, Christianity has compromised with this world of the senses. To most of us, it has rather accepted this shifting and unpredictable world of the senses as part of God's design, an indispensable complement of the unchanging and eternal.

V: The Middle Ages

The thousand years from the fall of the West Roman Empire to the end of the fifteenth century A.D. are known as the "Middle Ages," or the *medieval* period. The first four or five hundred years of this period were long known as the Dark Ages, the years when the lapse from the complex urban civilization of the Roman Empire into a self-sufficient rural economy was greatest. It is now more fashionable to avoid the value-judgment implied in the term "dark" by calling these centuries the "early Middle Ages." The eleventh, twelfth, and thirteenth centuries are then the "high" Middle Ages, and the fourteenth and fifteenth the "late" Middle Ages.

Actually the term "Middle Ages" is in itself as much a value-judgment as "Dark Ages." It was coined as the Latin *medium aevum* by a now forgotten seventeenth-century scholar named Keller, who like so many Germans of those days showed his respect for ancient tradition by Latinizing his name as Cellarius. Now Cellarius was merely putting into a neat—and very successful—phrase an opinion that has been held by most educated people since about 1500. This is the opinion that there was a great flowering of culture, a Great Age, in old Greece and Rome, and that another had begun in fifteenth-century Italy with the Renaissance (see Chapter II). In between were some ten centuries without distinction, without great achievement, which could therefore best be labeled simply as the years between, or in the middle. Thus by the seventeenth century we have the familiar division—Ancient, Medieval, Modern.

The scholars who popularized the term Middle Ages, and their immediate successors of the eighteenth-century Enlightenment (see Chapter IX), did not feel that these thousand years had been a mere blank. They felt that they had been positively evil, years when mankind pursued wrong ends, years of ignorance and barbarism, of monkish superstition, of poverty and unchanging tradition. For the architectural style of the great buildings of the Middle Ages that had survived, they used the term "Gothic," a synonym for "crude and barbarous."

The judgments implied in these terms have never quite yielded to the attacks that have since been made on them. They still color much American opinion, which, though it recognizes that the great Gothic cathedrals of Europe are worth the tourist's attention, still tends to see these thousand years generally as the bad old days—or, in a familiar vulgarism, "a thousand years without a bath." The Roman Catholic Church could hardly be expected to damn completely the centuries in which it had grown and flourished; and indeed a modern American Catholic writer has entitled a book *Thirteenth, Greatest of Centuries*. And as we shall see (Chapter XI) the writers of the Romantic Age, in the early 1800's, turned longingly toward the years when knighthood was in flower and there were no dark satanic mills. Yet the term Middle Ages has persisted, used now by friend and foe alike. Like all such terms, it is a convenient label, used by the symbol-making creature man to organize some small part of his vast experience. It is an arbitrary human division of time—but so too is a minute, an hour, a century.

Geographic Divisions

During the thousand years of the Middle Ages, the great cultural tradition, which began in the river valleys of the Near East and continues to the present day, split into three parts that are never

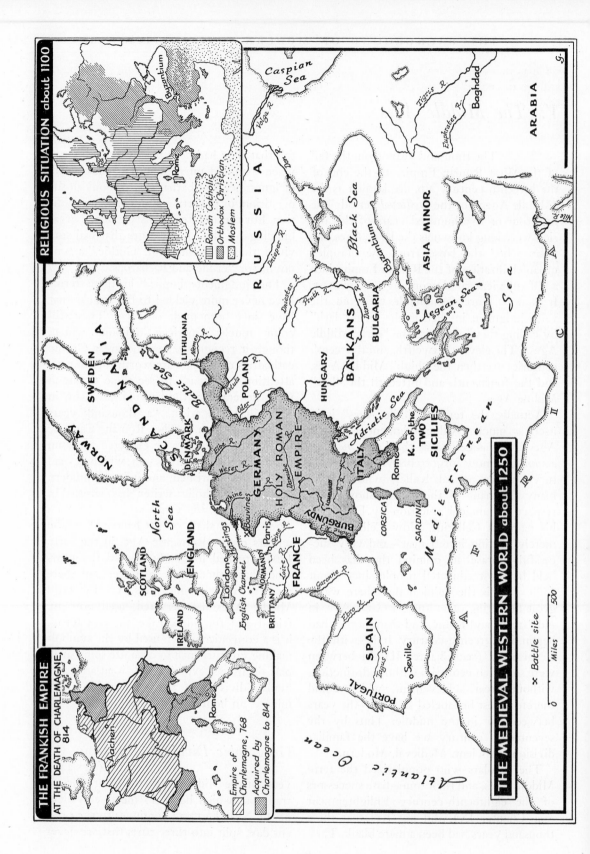

RELIGIOUS SITUATION about 1100

Roman Catholic
Orthodox Christian
Moslem

Byzantium

Rome

THE FRANKISH EMPIRE
AT THE DEATH OF CHARLEMAGNE, 814

Empire of Charlemagne, 768
Acquired by Charlemagne to 814

Aachen
Rome

THE MEDIEVAL WESTERN WORLD about 1250

× Battle site

0   Miles   500

Atlantic Ocean

IRELAND
SCOTLAND
ENGLAND
North Sea
London
×Hastings
English Channel
BRITTANY
NORMANDY
Paris
Seine R.
Loire R.
FRANCE
Garonne R.
Ebro R.
SPAIN
Tagus R.
PORTUGAL
o Seville

NORWAY
SWEDEN
SCANDINAVIA
Baltic Sea
DENMARK
Weser R.
Rhine R.
×Bouvines
GERMANY
Elbe R.
Oder R.
Vistula R.
POLAND
LITHUANIA
Nemen R.

HOLY ROMAN EMPIRE
Danube R.
BURGUNDY
LOMBARDY
ITALY
Rome
Adriatic Sea
CORSICA
SARDINIA
K. of the TWO SICILIES
Mediterranean Sea

HUNGARY
BALKANS
BULGARIA
Byzantium
Danube R.
Prut R.
Dniester R.
Dnieper R.
Don R.
Volga R.
RUSSIA
Caspian Sea
Black Sea
Aegean Sea
ASIA MINOR

ARABIA
Baghdad
Tigris R.
Euphrates R.
Nile R.

20

wholly without interrelations, but that can still be distinguished as sub-cultures. Foreshadowed as early as the fourth century A.D. by the emperor Constantine's division of his empire into eastern and western halves, there was a division between the eastern Orthodox culture centered in Constantinople, and the western Catholic culture centered in Rome. Then in the seventh century A.D. came the rise of the Arabs under Mohammed and the formation of another great sub-culture along an arc from Baghdad through North Africa to Seville in Spain. These great cultural areas were, especially toward the end of the Middle Ages, in very active contact. What we in the western European tradition call the Crusades (lasting from 1095 to the end of the thirteenth century) were a very thorough mixing up of all three. Nevertheless, when Americans talk of the "Middle Ages" they commonly mean the Middle Ages in Roman Catholic Christendom. This too is a convention we must accept. But we must not forget that both the Byzantines, and the Arabs who learned so much from them, preserved a good deal of the Greek heritage, notably in science and philosophy, when the West had lost it; that most of the vast area occupied now by Slavic peoples came first under the civilizing influence of Byzantium; that the Byzantine Empire acted for centuries as a shield to protect our West from the Moslems; that the stimulus of the Crusades was one of the factors that produced the modern West.

The Dark Ages

The overtones suggested by the old-fashioned phrase "Dark Ages" are not altogether misleading. With the breakdown of the western Roman Empire—which was a gradual process that lasted over several generations in any single region, such as Gaul—something real was lost, as we shall soon see. But there was nothing like a complete break; had there been, you could hardly be reading a book of this sort in the twentieth century. The basic gains of the Neolithic Revolution—agriculture, stock-raising, pottery, weaving, and many other arts and crafts—were by no means lost. There was even some improvement in techniques. The horse-collar, which gave the beast a better traction without shutting off his wind-pipe, is a "barbarian" invention of the Dark Ages. The Anglo-Saxons in England devised a heavier plow that broke rich, wet clays their predecessors, the Romano-Britons, had never tried to cultivate. At the higher levels of culture, the Christian religion, some essentials of Greco-Roman thought, some concept of imperial unity, survived.

What was lost was the political, economic, and intellectual techniques that enable men to live together in large territorial units, with extensive trade carried on by good sea and land communications. By the seventh century, what had once been great cities, even imperial Rome itself, had shrunk to towns at best, kept alive as administrative centers for the one great large-scale organization that did survive, the Roman Catholic Church. Most of the inhabitants of western and central Europe were country dwellers, living in small local units soon to be the bases of the feudal-manorial system. These local units were to a great degree autarkic, or self-sufficing. The villagers raised or made almost everything they used. Trade was reduced to a minimum, though it never vanished. Warriors, for instance, always had weapons, and indeed armor; and iron and steel are not commodities that can always be locally produced. Little money was needed, and it was impossible to maintain effective large-scale activities. The state as the Romans knew it had been transformed into a more rudimentary form.

The Germanic peoples had long been filtering into the empire, partly as individuals or families who were "immigrants" in almost our American sense, who took up farms or got jobs as soldiers, and partly, as the empire really began to go to pieces, as organized bands or tribes. These bands had names that history has made familiar—Goths, Vandals, Franks, Angles, Saxons, Burgundians, Longobards (Lombards). But their organization, as the very name "tribe" indicates, was politically primitive. The Germans had rubbed up against the imperial frontier for several centuries; they had absorbed some of the Roman material culture. And their leaders had developed an admiration for Rome. None the less, the Germans could not possibly take over and sustain so elaborate a politico-economic structure as the empire. We have seen what happened: The basic unit of group life became the almost completely self-sufficient agricultural village, with peasants, craftsmen, strong man or overlord, and village church. Yet some trace remained of a bigger territorial unit, the state, and we remember tribal names largely because so many of the tribal kings held together loosely those major units of the old empire that became the states of modern Europe. Britannia became England, land of the Angles; Gallia became France, land of the Franks. Two tribes gave names to later provinces that might well have become modern states, Burgundy and Lombardy. Italy and Spain have retained their old Latin names, in part an indication that Germanic blood and influence diminished toward the south, until in North Africa the passage of the Vandals has left us only a bad name for willful destroyers.

The Franks

Toward the end of the eighth century the Franks provided a leader under whom western Europe was briefly united. This was Charlemagne, king of the Franks—not of France, for France and Frenchmen did not yet exist. From his hereditary center at Aachen—now, incidentally, in Germany—Charlemagne led his troops on forays which brought under his name, though hardly under his control, much of the old empire in the West. It did not include the British Isles. Nor did it include Spain, southern Italy, and North Africa, which were largely under Moslem control. But it added Germany from the Rhine to the Elbe, which now first really comes into European narrative history. Charlemagne's achievement was recognized by the Pope when, on Christmas Day, 800 A.D., the Frankish king was crowned emperor by the Pope in Rome.

The rally did not last, for the *cultural* basis for so great a *political* institution did not really exist. Charlemagne's heirs divided the brief empire up into more manageable parts, forerunners of France, Germany, and smaller West European states. But the fascination of the imperial idea would not be banished from these northern minds. And in 962 another German ruler, Otto the Great, was crowned emperor by another pope, and the Holy Roman Empire of the German people started on a career that was not ended formally until 1806.

Charlemagne, who himself never quite succeeded in learning to write, nevertheless did his best to keep learning alive; and historians still speak of a "Carolingian Renaissance." Part of the real darkness of the Dark Ages is the loss of techniques in art and letters. Here again the loss is never total, even in the fine arts, which demand so much in continuity of the master-pupil relation over the generations, and which require so much economic support. Stone churches were built somewhere in western Europe in every century, and were decorated with some sculpture, and some paintings. But they were inferior to what had been done before, and was to be done again. Tombstones of the period, for instance, were crudely sculptured, especially in comparison with Greek and Roman work. Learning and higher education lapsed. The tradition was kept alive, but just barely. You are not likely to find today anything written during the Carolingian Renaissance on lists of the Great Books. Carolingian science can hardly be said to exist.

Transition to the
High Middle Ages

Moreover, after Charlemagne's rally northwestern Europe underwent a more serious attack than that of the German tribes in the fifth and sixth centuries. In the tenth century the last of the northern pagan barbarians, the Scandinavians, descended on the seacoasts and estuaries in their famous Viking ships, and harried and burned and murdered. The islands of Great Britain and Ireland and the Channel coast of France were particularly hard hit, but the Vikings went all the way from the Elbe to the Mediterranean, and even, some believe, to what is now known as New England. By the eleventh century the energies that drove the Vikings on had been exhausted, and those who stayed had begun the process of amalgamation with the peoples they had raided.

In these long five centuries or so, from the end of the fifth to the beginning of the eleventh, western historians have usually found the low point, the real "break" with the past, in the Germanic invasions. But a distinguished Belgian historian, the late Henri Pirenne, advanced the thesis that the real break came several centuries later, after the great conquests of the Arabs in the seventh century had cut western and central Europe almost wholly off from commerce, intellectual as well as economic, with the Mediterranean world that had been the center of the Greco-Roman civilization. According to this view, the modern western and central Europe we know was first thrown in on itself, began its "own" history, in the eighth century rather than in the fifth.

At any rate, by the eleventh century western European history is clearly being made. Politically, we can begin to see the outlines of the nation-states we know today. The English, of course, make much of their Anglo-Saxon period; but they really date their present ruling house from 1066, when William the Conqueror ascended the throne. And in France, when Louis XVI was put on trial by the triumphant revolutionists in 1792, he appears in the indictment not as king, but as "citizen" Louis Capet. His very distant ancestor, Hugues Capet, came to the throne in 987. Even war and international politics begin to look familiar. When William, Duke of Normandy, crossed the Channel in 1066 and won the battle of Hastings and the English crown, the struggle was not between the nation England and the nation France. But events move fast, and when in 1214 a battle is fought at Bouvines in modern Belgium, "cockpit of Europe," the participants are beginning to be recognizable as England, France, and Germany—the nations who were to meet again in battle in Belgium just seven hundred years later.

Yet we must not exaggerate the "modernity" of the high Middle Ages. The culture of the thirteenth century is not just an unfinished form of modern culture; it is not the child that becomes a man about 1500, and then puts away childish things. On the other hand, such metaphors as "seed-bed," "roots," and the like are not wholly misleading. The Middle Ages were *both* a culture unique in itself, with its own way of life, *and* a culture in which many institutions, many human attitudes and habits, prepare the way for ours today, are indeed ourselves when young.

Feudalism

The so-called "feudal system" was at once a way of life—or to use now fashionable sociological terms, a *structuring* of social, economic, and political life —and a preparation for the modern state. It was a transition from the self-sufficient agricultural units of the Dark Ages to the great bureaucratic states of modern times. Feudalism was not by any means, as so many students continue with their eighteenth-century ancestors to believe, simply chaos, anarchy, gangsterism glossed over by the absurd pretensions of "chivalry."

It is better not to use "feudalism" as a

blanket term to describe all group relations in the Middle Ages. More accurately, feudalism refers to the relations among individuals and families of a ruling class. These relations were hierarchical—that is, they constituted a chain of command from lesser authority to greater authority, much as among the officers of an army or the civil servants of a modern state. In theory, the chain ran from the knight, through barons and other nobles, to the king, to the emperor. But in comparison with modern chains of command, the feudal chain was incomplete and irregular in its workings. First of all, as the system developed out of the extreme localism of the Dark Ages, the individual feudal lords were not appointed by superiors, nor were they elected. They inherited their position, usually by primogeniture—that is, the eldest son inherited the father's post, or in feudal terms, his *fief*. Second, and perhaps the best single distinguishing mark of the European feudal system, the post of fief was not just a place or "job" that carried authority. It was almost always a piece of property, a tract of land worked by the lord's dependents; and the surplus from the land was sufficient to keep the lord and his family in the style to which they grew accustomed. Thus in the developed feudal system, ownership of land carried with it political authority. But because this authority implied definite obligations toward superiors and dependents, it was a less clear-cut and absolute "ownership" than we today associate with that word. We must not think of the feudal lord as an independent despot who could legally do what he liked in his domain. Of course, there were always some who acted illegally, and then as now the law did not always "catch up with them." By and large, however, the nineteenth-century English mill owner "owned" his mill in a way the thirteenth-century English earl could not own his fief.

The feudal lord's relations to other feudal persons in the system—his duties and privileges—were explicit. They were part of a feudal contract, were given the sanction of ritual, and were heavily reinforced by custom. In theory, the feudal order was a neatly arranged system of government; in practice, it departed widely from the ideal. Historically, the system grew out of an effort to find a substitute for the lost Roman techniques for holding together large territorial groups of human beings. The Roman techniques, like ours, depended on money payments to civil and military servants by central governments, which had to raise the money by taxation. Furthermore, these techniques depended on the ability of the central authority to keep in constant communication with its local agents, which the Romans did by means of their excellent roads and posting system. Then, with the barbarian invasions, the money economy, money taxation, and even the roads and posting system ceased to exist. Feudalism grew up, in a long and complex process, as a substitute in response to a need for something more than pure localism. This need was carried even to the barbarian leaders of the Dark Ages by that cultural inheritance we have traced from the ancient Near East.

At first, the very conditions to which feudalism was reacting—that is, lack of a money economy, lack of good communication—limited the degree to which it could "work." Moreover, as the years went on, and as deaths, marriages, and illegal seizures piled up, the chain of command, which had never been very neat, got hopelessly mixed up. For each fief there was a specific feudal relation—that is, each fief-owner swore allegiance to a specific overlord. But as time passed, Count A might hold a fief from Duke B and another from Duke C. By his feudal contract he was in duty bound to give military service to his overlords. But suppose—and this happened often enough—Duke B went to war with Duke C. What was Count A's duty? A conscious effort was made to cope with this very quandary. Where cross-allegiances developed, one superior was distinguished as *liege-lord*; the feudal inferior—known as the "vassal"—took a special oath to his liege-lord, which became his paramount obligation. This scheme, however, worked only imperfectly. Furthermore, unscrupulous and ambitious feudal lords could defy their superiors and indulge in "private" wars with their neighbors. But these wars were fought only by the feudal class, who were brought up as professional fighters. The peasants, the merchants, and the priests took no direct part in them, although peasants and their crops often suffered severely.

A great deal has been written about the medieval feudal class. Their way of life has been summed up under the word "chivalry," which is the French for "knighthood." Initiation into knighthood made one a member of the feudal class. This was not a rigorously defined *caste* to which only birth could give admission. Especially in the early days, the sturdy, ambitious, fighting young man of peasant stock might win his way to knighthood, and transmit his acquired membership in the feudal class to his heirs. Similarly, an intellectual lad from a humble background might become a priest, and then a bishop or an abbot. There was less social mobility toward the end of the Middle Ages, however. Chivalry was not the gentle, elegant, interesting way of life it seemed to the romantic lovers of Walter Scott's novels to have been. Nor on the other hand was it the violent, ignorant, cruel way of life it seemed to the eighteenth century. It did provide enough orderliness in daily life for Europe to rally from the losses of the Dark Ages.

Manorialism

The feudal class was only a small minority of the European population of the Middle Ages. The vast majority of men and women, probably nine out of ten, lived on and worked the land. They lived for the most part as dependents on the lands of a lord, in the typical village and surrounding farmlands we call the *manor*. But as dependents they were not, in the high Middle Ages, chattel slaves. Somewhere in the later Dark Ages the Greco-Roman institution of slavery disappeared in Europe, to be revived among Europeans only as they spread outside Europe in modern times and enslaved, as their Moslem predecessors had already done, African Negroes. Some, though not all, of the medieval workers on the land were *serfs*—that is, they could not, without the lord's consent, leave the manor. On the other hand, the lord could not sell them or otherwise dispose of them without the land.

The manorial system grew to be as complicated as the feudal system among the ruling class. Like the feudal system, it was a vast network of reciprocal rights and duties, preserved by the medieval respect for custom and tradition, for the way things have been done "time out of mind." Broadly speaking, the individual peasant families, whether free, part-free, or serf, worked plots that they kept in the family year after year, even if they did not "own" them as an American farmer owns his land. (We have seen above that neither did the feudal lord "own" the fief or manor in the modern sense of ownership.) Most of the peasants also worked on the lord's own farmlands, and the produce went to the family at the castle or manor house. In addition, they paid a complex set of fees for using the lord's mill or wine-press, and a lot of other dues, all minutely regulated, and all varying from manor to manor, to the delight of today's specialist in medieval history, and to the confusion of the rest of us. Indeed, as the centuries wore on, the users—or victims—of the system became badly confused by its top-heavy accumulation of rules and customs.

In summary, however, the manorial system seems to have protected the peasant in a semi-independent status rather than to have exposed him to the oppression of his lord. Of course an occasional lord of the manor could be a shocking tyrant, oppressing his tenants, violating their women, and doing other wicked things. Not even in England, the best and earliest organized area, were there courts or a judicial system that could wholly counter such violence. But usually the lord was as limited by the network of custom as were his tenants. The system's resistance to change, and its comparative, but not absolute inability to provide for enterprise and improvement, are more significant than its tyranny of lord over peasants, its great social inequalities.

The Towns and the Church

The towns did not readily fit into the increasingly complex structure of the feudal-manorial system. Town life, which was never quite extinguished, especially in the south of Europe, grew increasingly important as the slowly developing feudal-manorial system proved itself capable of sustaining more trade, more of a money economy, more specialization. But the inhabitants of a town or city (the latter term refers to seats of bishoprics; it does not necessarily indicate a bigger population) were likely to be restive in a feudal system. Townsmen tend to be, in a word the Middle Ages had not yet coined, more "progressive" than peasants. They needed, if only from their very numbers, a more elaborate and flexible political organization than feudalism afforded. And once they had a town government, with the ability to tax, they could use the tax money, as men have done since history began, to support an armed force of their own. At its height, the feudal system was so pervasive—the French lawyers even had a maxim, "No piece of land without its overlord"—that the towns were formally made part of the system. But they began to break loose quite early, and served as one of the great factors in the transition from medieval political conditions to the modern state. The kings soon bargained

with these towns, or "communes," for their alliance against the common enemy, the feudal nobility.

Nor did the Church fit very well into the feudal-manorial system. No doubt at the manorial level the village priest was usually a good servant of his overlord, essentially conservative in his influence. But, even though the lord controlled the appointment of the village priest, the priest by the very nature of his calling was not *just* a member of the manorial community. He was also a member of a great international organization with its own chain of command, an organization that could and did have economic and political interests directly conflicting with those of the lay feudal lords. And vastly more important, the village priest was for all medieval men an agent of God on earth, an agent whose powers were of a different nature from any earthly power. In western Europe there was as yet no organized rival church, no organized skepticism or "materialism." Men did indeed defy the Church, but in the high Middle Ages they took fearful risks in so doing.

Finally, the Church was more than the secular hierarchy from priest through bishop and archbishop to pope. It was also the great body of the regular clergy (from the Latin *regula*, rule), the monks and nuns organized in many different orders. Both in its secular and its regular branches, the Church owned vast properties, and was enmeshed in the complexities of the feudal-manorial system. The bishop was often a more effective political ruler than any count or duke. Both branches, and especially the regular clergy, carried on almost all of what we should call higher education, and many of what we should call the social services—organized poor relief, hospital care, and the like.

The Church, then, is central to all medieval history; if you could write a history of everything the Church touched, you would write a complete history of the Middle Ages. And the Church, like the towns, was a force that acted as a dissolvent of the feudal-manorial system. In the realm of ideas, the basic influence of the Church was no doubt to buttress the established order. Yet from the clergy came a whole series of reforming movements that questioned the relations of man to master, the distribution of wealth and power, and even, with Luther and Protestantism, the philosophic basis of the medieval outlook.

In the realm of institutions, the influence of the Church helped build the modern state. First, in a series of dramatic struggles in the twelfth and thirteenth centuries between popes and emperors, the popes successfully challenged the claims of the emperors to supreme power in Europe. Second, though within the embryonic nation-states the Church often resisted the centralizing work of the kings, over most of the West the Church helped the kings make the new states. The popes beat the emperors, but they could not beat the kings; therefore they sought to become allies of the kings.

Our Medieval
Origins

Let us sum up very briefly those aspects of the Middle Ages that seem in retrospect to be a preparation for modern times, ourselves when young. With the political and social order produced by the feudal-manorial system, there began an unmistakable economic growth, which as early as the thirteenth century had made possible real cities, trade, money, banking, an incipient middle class. Even population and food supply increased, though only slowly. In alliance with the growing towns—some of which were actually founded as "Newtowns" or "Villeneuves" or "Freiburgs," and most of which came to have a great degree of self-government—a line of princes gradually came to acquire substantial power of the kind we call royal. A new political central state began to form, with a treasury based on taxation, not just on feudal dues from feudal vassals; with obedient civil

servants, not just agents anxious to set themselves up in a nice feudal fief of their own; and with a paid army of professional soldiers willing and able to use even vulgar new weapons like gunpowder, not just feudal horsemen proud of their indiscipline.

The mention of new weapons reminds us that part of the process we are so briefly sketching is marked by new techniques, by slow but real material improvements in transportation, in mining, in agriculture, in industrial and mechanical arts. In fact, almost all the specific elements that have been listed as marks of the beginning of "modern" times—whether political, like the "new monarchy"; economic, like genuine large-scale trade or credit systems; social, like the breakdown of the old class of feudal nobles; intellectual, like the appeal to experience instead of to Aristotle's authority; or artistic, like the effort to achieve a three-dimensional look in a two-dimensional painting—all these go back to the 1300's and even earlier. We must admit that modern times do not start with any such neat date as 1450, 1500, or 1492; we must admit a long "transitional" period, amusingly reflected in one student's statement on an examination that Dante (1265-1321) was an Italian poet "with one foot in the grave of the Middle Ages and with the other saluting the rising sun of the Renaissance."

The Medieval Style

Yet it will not do to see the Middle Ages as nothing more than the awkward youth of our modern culture. The Middle Ages are also a complete culture, with a style of their own. The arts, especially architecture, give us a good symbol: a medieval cathedral can "stand for" the Middle Ages, just as an Egyptian pyramid, a Greek temple, a Roman aqueduct, a seventeenth-century palace, or a New York skyscraper can stand for their respective cultures.

For the Middle Ages were an Age of Faith. It was not a pious age in the sense

Cathedral of Notre Dame, Paris.

that most men and women were evangelical Christians in practice. But it was an age when almost all men and women believed that the broad outlines of the structure of the universe were known, and with them the broad outlines of human destiny on earth. The Bible, as expounded by the authority of the Roman Catholic Church, told the inquiring medieval youth how men had come into existence, told him of their relationship to God, told him that life on this earth is a transition, a probation, for an eternal life in Heaven or Hell. To put the matter negatively, the medieval man had no conception of *progress* or *evolution* as an orderly and inevitable process here on earth, no conception, for the most part, of what we call natural science as a systematic explanation of life on this earth, no *systematic* conception of what we call variously "planning," "invention," "innovation."

This last statement, which is very important, must not be misunderstood. The qualifying adjective "systematic," which might also be put as "philosophic" or "general," is crucial. In fact, as we have noted, in material command over the environment the centuries from the eleventh on do show progress. But these advances were in effect made in spite of this state of mind of medieval man. A concrete example is the growth of what we now call statute law, especially in England. The courts, particularly the High Court of Parliament that became the mother of modern legislatures, thought of law as something decreed from on high as part of the structure of the universe. Law was something men could *find*—and lose, if they were wicked or careless—but not something they could *make* or invent. The men behind so great an institutional change as Magna Carta (1215) thought of themselves as simply stating the basic rules of the English monarchy, not as making an innovation in the constitution.

The Middle Ages, save for a few exceptional intellectuals, could hardly have understood our modern conception of "experimentation." Why struggle painfully with observations, measuring, testing hypotheses, experimenting, when God has given you a mind that can, aided by Christian learning, get the right answer from the right books? The medieval mind simply did not feel what we call Nature to be impersonal, of a different stuff from that of the human mind. Both Man and Nature were immediately subordinate to an omnipotent and just God, but not a God whose ways were to be measured and established in any kind of laboratory.

The medieval man did not question the immediacy, the reality—*and the frequency* —of the supernatural, the miraculous. He did not believe that man makes himself and his history. God, he believed, has full control. God made the weather, earthquakes, volcanic eruptions, which were therefore in a sense miracles; the medieval man would hardly have understood the concept of a science of meteorology.

But just because medieval man did not believe that he could greatly improve his own state, let alone the state of the world, he could attain a kind of serenity that is hard to attain in the mid-twentieth century. He was by no means a fatalist, however; the moral struggle on earth was a reality, part of God's plan as he had told man in the Bible. But right conduct in that struggle, the medieval man believed, would insure for the individual eternal salvation; wrong conduct would insure eternal damnation. True, there was plenty of wrong conduct in the Middle Ages. Only the sentimental lover of things medieval will maintain that men and women behaved much better then than now. But it is just possible that fewer of them were neurotic than now. They hoped for so much less—at least here on earth— than we do that they were surely less often *frustrated* than we.

Summary

How much of the Middle Ages is really alive today? If we understand this question simply in the conventional terms of what institutions can clearly be shown to have medieval *origins*, a long list could be drawn up: our Common Law; our representative system of government; our language, certainly in its origins; most of our Christian sects; right on down to our college dormitories, which are often heavily Gothic, and our Anglo-American weights and measures, which are medieval indeed. But this is not really an answer to the question of "aliveness," which means if we revert to an example cited early in this chapter, do we do certain things because our medieval ancestors did them, as the house dog still turns round and round to flatten out a sleeping place? Most Americans would say no, both of the little things and of the big things. Most Americans, for instance, would say that since our country was lucky enough to have been founded fairly late, we have never had a "feudal" system, no overlords or nobility, no monarch, none of the class structure of the Middle Ages. Therefore, they would say, we really can practice and believe in equality and other modern ideas in a way the poor Europeans cannot.

Yet we all carry a little more of the burden of the medieval past—if it *is* a burden—than we commonly believe. May we not still have a particularly elaborate law of "real estate" just because landed property was the basis of medieval institutions? May we not worship the athlete in part because both the Greeks and the Middle Ages admired prowess in games and tournaments? May we not indeed, in spite of our American belief in the pursuit—and achievement—of happiness here on earth, sometimes revert for a moment at least to our medieval ancestors' belief that the universe was not designed as a vast gadget to serve the ends and immediate desires of *homo sapiens*?

Reading Suggestions on the Background of Civilization

J. Barzun and H. F. Graff, *The Modern Researcher* (N.Y.: Harcourt, Brace, 1957), is an admirable introduction to the study of history, as well as a practical manual for research in history and allied fields.

R. Sedillot, *History of the World in 240 Pages*, translated from the French by G. Hopkins (N.Y.: Mentor, 1953), is a remarkable attempt at compression, and surely the shortest survey of the field in existence.

H. Nicolson, *Good Behavior: Being a Study of Certain Types of Civility* (Garden City, N.Y.: Doubleday, 1956), is a brief and lively sampling of manners in various societies from ancient to modern times.

Authoritative synopses of each century since the birth of Christ are available in the latest edition of the *Encyclopedia Americana* under the alphabetical headings "First Century," "Second Century," on to the "Twentieth Century," all written by specialists and all brief.

H. G. Wells, *Outline of History* (many editions), though written by an old-fashioned liberal and biased against Christianity and conservatism generally, is still extremely readable, and if read cautiously and with common sense, a very good introduction, especially for the early history of mankind.

Will Durant's *The Story of Civilization* (N.Y.: Simon and Schuster, 1935-1953), is detailed, careful, well illustrated, and the work of a good popularizer, with much the same views as H. G. Wells, but chastened by another generation of experience. In five volumes Mr. Durant takes the story—of the world, not just the West—up through the Renaissance. Vol. I, Our Oriental Heritage; Vol. II, The Life of Greece; Vol. III. Caesar and Christ; Vol. IV, The Age of Faith; Vol. V, The Renaissance.

The scholar's multi-volumed history in English for this long period is still the two collaborative series published by the Cambridge University Press in England—the *Cambridge Ancient History* (12 vols. plus 5 vols. of plates, 1923-39) and the *Cambridge Medieval History* (8 vols. and 1 vol. of maps, 1911-36). There is a very useful two-volume abbreviated edition of the second, C. W. Previté-Orton, ed., *The Shorter Cambridge Medieval History* (1952).

The Oxford University Press has published a series of "Legacy" books, with specialists writing on their own fields. These books emphasize, as the title indicates, the ideas and institutions of the past that seem to their authors part of our own lives. They are: *The Legacy of Egypt*, ed. S. R. K. Glanville (1942); *The Legacy of Israel*, ed. E. R. Bevan and C. J. Singer (1927); *The Legacy of Greece*, ed. R. W. Livingstone (1921); *The Legacy of Rome*, ed. Cyril Bailey (1923); *The Legacy of the Middle Ages*, ed. G. C. Crump and E. F. Jacob (1926); *The Legacy of Islam*, ed. Sir Thomas W. Arnold and Alfred Guillaume (1931).

A. L. Kroeber, *Anthropology* (N.Y.: Harcourt, Brace, 1948), and W. Howells, *Back of History* (N.Y.: Doubleday, 1954), will put flesh on the bare bones of our outline of pre-history.

A. Senet, *Man in Search of His Ancestors: The Romance of Paleontology* (N.Y.: McGraw-Hill, 1956), is an excellent popularization of the subject.

M. Rostovstev, *The Ancient World*, 2 vols. (Oxford University Press, 1926-28), is beautifully illustrated, and a fine introduction.

For a general treatment of medieval history, see C. Brinton, J. B. Christopher, and R. L.

Wolff, *A History of Civilization* (Englewood Cliffs, N.J.: Prentice-Hall, 1955), Vol. I, chs. v-ix.

S. Painter, *Medieval Society* (Ithaca: Cornell University Press, 1951), and F. B. Artz, *The Mind of the Middle Ages* (N.Y.: Knopf, 1954), are very good surveys of important parts of medieval history.

For the reader who would like to see how far apart in interpretation historians can get, J. J. Walsh, *The Thirteenth, Greatest of Centuries* (N.Y.: Fordham Univ. Press, 1943), may be contrasted with Part III of H. E. Barnes, *Intellectual and Cultural History of the Western World* (N.Y.: Random House, 1937).

The problem of the Middle Ages as a historical "period" is provocatively treated in an essay, "Medium Aevum: Some Reflections on Medieval History and on the term 'The Middle Ages,'" in G. Barraclough, *History in a Changing World* (Oxford: Basil Blackwell, 1955). The whole book is recommended as an interesting modern discussion of a series of problems of historical interpretation.

Planned for publication in 1958 under the auspices of the American Historical Association, Washington, D.C., is a modernization of G. M. Dutcher and others, *A Guide to Historical Literature* (N.Y.: Macmillan, 1931). This new guide will be indispensable for all serious study of history. It will cover the books published through 1956. The 1931 volume is still useful for works through 1929.

The American Historical Review, a quarterly published by the American Historical Association, reviews all the current books of history it can, and lists all the pertinent periodical writings it can. The serious worker in history must consult it regularly to "keep up" with the field. There are many other historical periodicals in the languages of the West. Unfortunately, no such service of "abstracts" as the physicist, chemist, or biologist enjoys has ever been effectively established for the whole field of history, although a useful one now exists for the very modern period—*Historical Abstracts, 19th and 20th Century*, a quarterly journal.

CHAPTER TWO

The Renaissance

I: Introduction

In the fifteenth century, at the dawn of modern times, momentous political changes were taking place in Europe. In the East, the "second Rome," Byzantium, fell to the Ottoman Turks in 1453; meanwhile, the rulers of Moscow, the "third Rome," were slowly beginning to build a new Russian territorial state. In the West, the city-states of Italy reached the height of their power and prestige, and a new and most significant political institution—the national monarchy—was developing fast in England, in France, and in Spain. To the east of the national monarchies lay Germany, united in theory under the rule of the Holy Roman Emperor, but in practice divided into hundreds of particular states, whose ruling princes enjoyed almost complete sovereignty. Particularism was the dominant political force in Central Europe, and even the

Habsburg dynasty, which now filled the office of emperor, owed its strength not to the imperial title but to the extensive family lands centered in Austria along the middle Danube valley.

The details of this political map will be filled in as our account unfolds. Italy and the national monarchies are discussed in this chapter; the Germanies are treated in conjunction with the Protestant Reformation and the Habsburg wars (Chapters III and IV); and the Ottoman and Muscovite successors of Byzantium in Chapter VII, after the picture of the early modern West has been completed.

Politics alone did not make the fifteenth century memorable in western history. Far from it. This was also a time of cultural flowering, the midpoint in the great literary, artistic, and intellectual movement labeled the Renaissance. The label "Renaissance" immediately poses a problem of interpretation. The term itself means "rebirth," the rebirth of the classical culture of ancient Greece and Rome. But what in actual fact was the Renaissance? Was Greco-Roman culture truly reborn? What accounted for the remarkable productivity of the writers, the sculptors, the painters, and all the other artists of the Renaissance?

Two hundred years ago, most educated men would have offered simple answers to these difficult questions. The chief reason for the classical revival appeared to be the capture of Byzantium by the Turks in 1453 and the subsequent flight of Greek scholars to Italy. The Renaissance seemed to mark a return from Christian barbarism to the classical decencies, a blaze of light after the thousand years of unrelieved gloom that had enveloped the West following the disintegration of the Roman Empire. Today, however, no educated man accepts this polar contrast between medieval darkness and Renaissance light. A great Christian civilization had in fact come to maturity during the Middle Ages, and culture, even culture in the narrow sense of the heritage from clas-

sical antiquity, had never actually disappeared in the medieval West. We can, therefore, scarcely speak of a "rebirth" of culture at the close of the Middle Ages.

Nor can we any longer attribute such exaggerated importance to the fall of Byzantium. Well before 1453 knowledge of Greek writings was filtering into the West from Moslem Spain, from Sicily, and from Byzantium itself. Moreover, Greek influence was by no means the only decisive factor in promoting the Renaissance. The cutthroat economic and political competition of the Italian city-states schooled men in resourceful individualism; Italian men of affairs impressed upon the Renaissance the stamp of their own enterprise and materialism. Finally, the Renaissance owed a great debt to the Middle Ages themselves. The Renaissance was religious as well as materialistic, credulous as well as skeptical, caste-conscious as well as individualistic. It had a "style" of its own, in part medieval and in part modern. It was not the rebirth of the classical past, not the abrupt beginning of modern times, but a transition, sometimes gradual and sometimes swift, from the medieval to the modern.

This period of transition began in the 1300's; it came to an end during the 1500's and early 1600's, as Europe passed through the ages of the Reformation and of dynastic and religious wars. The first great writer to express the "style" of the Renaissance was the Italian poet, Dante, who lived at the turn of the thirteenth century to the fourteenth. The last great man of the Renaissance was Shakespeare, who lived three centuries after Dante, or perhaps John Milton, who came later still, in the mid-seventeenth-century England of revolution and civil war. The movement reached France, Germany, and the Low Countries as well as England, but its homeland was Italy, the Italy of aggressive and cultivated businessmen and politicians. Our account of the Renaissance begins with a survey of the economic and political background.

II: The Economic Background

Trade The prosperity of Renaissance businessmen depended, of course, on trade. Trade had started to revive several centuries before the Renaissance; western Europe had begun to emerge from the economic depression of the Dark Ages about the year 1000. To preserve food, for example, people in northwestern Europe had long imported salt from Spain, Italy, and Germany; to make food tasty, if it had begun to spoil in those unrefrigerated days, they had long sought the spices of the East. Since drafty medieval buildings made warm clothing essential, the furs of eastern Europe, the wool of England and Spain, and the woolen cloth of Flanders and Italy all commanded good markets. At the close of the Middle Ages supplies of palatable food and comfortable clothing were steadily increasing.

In sum, the difference between the trade of the later Middle Ages and that of the Renaissance was one of degree, not of kind. It was the difference between some commerce and more commerce, rather than between no commerce and a reborn commerce. At the onset of the Renaissance, the trade of the West was for the first time beginning to compare in volume and variety with that of imperial Rome and of other prosperous eras of the past. Merchants were developing more elaborate commercial procedures and organizations. The most useful case history of these developments is supplied by the great Italian trading city, the Republic of Venice.

By 1300, many of the Mediterranean cities were already thriving veterans of trade, toughened and enriched by their experience in the Crusades. In Italy, besides Venice, there were Genoa, Lucca, Pisa, Florence, Milan, and a dozen others; in southern France there were Narbonne, Montpellier, and Marseilles; and in Spain there was Barcelona. Venice, however, was not merely first among equals, not just Queen of the Adriatic, but the undisputed mistress of Mediterranean trade through most of the fourteenth and fifteenth centuries. She ran a highly centralized empire strung along the shipping route to Byzantium and the East, and consisting mainly of ports and islands on the Aegean and Adriatic seas.

The Venetian government not only defended trading routes and regulated trade in general but also operated merchant galleys and a great shipyard called the Arsenal. Records from the early fifteenth century show approximately forty-five galleys sailing from Venice annually, among them four to Flanders, four to Beirut on the Lebanon coast, three to the Black Sea, and three to Egypt. The Flanders galleys touched both at Sluys, the harbor of Bruges in Flanders, and at the English ports of London and Southampton. First sent out in 1317, and making an annual voyage thereafter, the Flanders fleet was a very important European economic institution. It provided the first regular all-water service between Italy and northwestern Europe, and made shipments between the two cheaper and more secure than they had been on the older overland route.

The state supervised the activities of these galleys from the cradle to the grave. The Arsenal undertook the systematic replacement of galleys that had worn out or had been sunk. And the captains of the Flanders galleys were directed to protect the health of the crew by enlisting a physician and a surgeon, to maintain the prestige of the city with two fifers and two trumpeters, to avoid "affrays and mischiefs" in English ports, even if the crew had to be denied shore leave, and, above all, to get to Bruges before the Genoese did. Officials

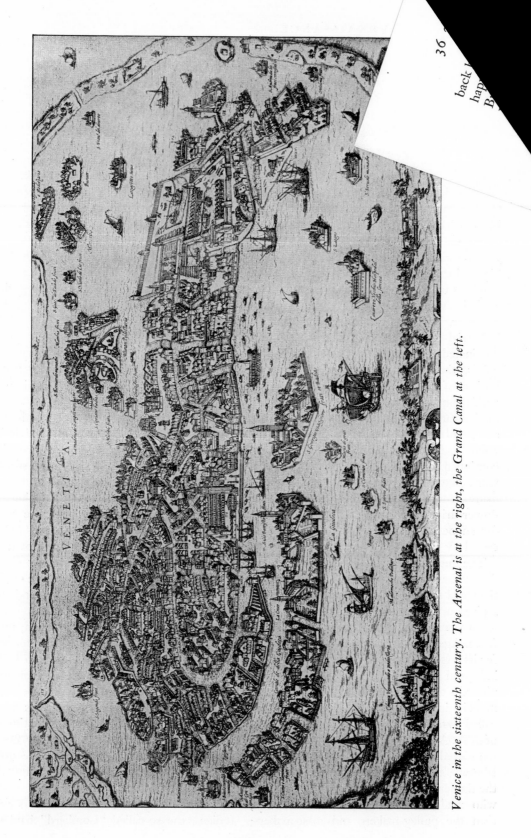

Venice in the sixteenth century. The Arsenal is at the right, the Grand Canal at the left.

home were furious when, as sometimes happened, merchants from Genoa did get to Bruges first and skimmed the cream off the Flemish market.

Industry

The expansion of trade stimulated the industries that furnished the textiles, metals, ships, and other commodities needed by the merchants. The towns of medieval Italy and Flanders had already developed cloth-weaving into something like big business, with a large production, large numbers of workmen, and large profits for a relatively few capitalists. The Renaissance, however, by no means experienced a true industrial revolution. Industries were often dominated, and sometimes retarded, by the guilds, the characteristic medieval organizations of tradesmen and of craftsmen. The guilds controlled the admission of new men to the various trades and crafts, set prices and standards, and sometimes regulated the volume of output as well. Manufacturing continued to be what the Latin roots of the word suggest—making by hand—though many hand tools were clever and efficient. Power-driven machines did not exist, except for an occasional experimental device operated by water.

The modern aspects of Renaissance industry lay chiefly in its rising output, in the trend toward mass production of standardized articles, and in the complementary trend toward the specialization of the labor force. Again Venice is a good case in point, for its Arsenal was perhaps the largest single industrial establishment in Europe. It employed a thousand men normally, and many more in time of emergency. These workmen, called *Arsenalotti*, formed a kind of pyramid of skills. At the bottom of the pyramid were the stevedores, helpers, and other unskilled laborers; then came the sawyers, who cut the timbers for the galleys, and the caulkers, who made the wooden hulls seaworthy; then the pulley-makers and mast-makers; and finally, at the top, the highly skilled ship carpenters, who did the all-important work of shaping the lines of the hull and determining the basic design of the galley. Supervisors checked to see that the *Arsenalotti* were manning their posts; anyone who reported late, after the Arsenal bell had ceased tolling its summons to work, forfeited a day's pay. By the sixteenth century the Venetian Arsenal was anticipating both the efficiency and the minute subdivision of labor characteristic of the twentieth-century assembly line. In 1570, the *Arsenalotti* completed and equipped in the space of two months a hundred galleys for a campaign against the Turks.

Banking

Industry and trade were two foundation stones of the Renaissance economy; a third, closely cemented to the other two, was banking. The origins of banking lay in the Middle Ages. The desire of successful merchants to invest the capital they had accumulated increased the supply of money available to borrowers. Although the risks of lending were great (kings in particular were likely to repudiate their debts), the potential profits were also very large. Florentine bankers were known to charge 266 per cent annual interest on an especially risky loan. The high rate of interest in turn reflected the demand for money. Kings, popes, and lesser rulers needed it for war and administration; businessmen needed it to finance trading voyages and other enterprises. In addition to being money-lenders, bankers were also money-changers. This was an indispensable function, for there were hundreds upon hundreds of different coins, fluctuating in value and reliability, and minted by every kind of governmental unit from the great monarchy down to the small city and the tiny feudal principality.

By 1300, the great European bankers were Italians, the so-called "Lombard" bankers, though many of them came not from Lombardy but from Florence, Siena, and other towns in Tuscany, to the south of Lombardy. The great Florentine banking families of the Bardi and the Peruzzi advanced large sums to the kings of England and France, and the beautiful gold florins minted by the city were the first gold coins made outside Byzantium to gain international currency. But the expenses of the Hundred Years' War led King Edward III of England to default on his debts to the Bardi and the Peruzzi, with the result that both firms failed in the 1340's. Although Florentine banking rallied in the fifteenth century under the dynamic Medici, Florence never regained her old fiscal leadership, for wealthy banks and rich bankers had appeared elsewhere.

From the little city of Bourges in France came one of the great millionaires of the time, Jacques Coeur (1395-1456). The son of an ordinary craftsman, Coeur made a fortune by trading with the Moslem Near East and by running a ship service for pilgrims to the Holy Land. King Charles VII of France sent him on diplomatic missions and made him the chief royal fiscal agent. Coeur, indeed, financed the French forces in the final campaigns of the Hundred Years' War. Meanwhile, aided by royal favor, he acquired textile workshops and mines, bought landed estates from impoverished nobles, lent money to half the dignitaries of France, and obtained noble husbands and high church offices for his own middle-class relatives. At Bourges he met the cost of embellishing the cathedral and built himself a private palace, one of the showplaces of France.

Coeur demonstrated dramatically the wealth and the power that a mere bourgeois could obtain. Yet it was all too good to last. Coeur's success seemed to threaten the established order of things; too many highly placed people owed him too much money. He was finally disgraced on the trumped-up charge of poisoning the favorite royal mistress.

House of Jacques Coeur, Bourges, France, fifteenth century.

Even richer and more powerful than Jacques Coeur in his prime was the Fugger family, who made the little Bavarian city of Augsburg an international financial center from about 1450 to 1600. The founder of the Fugger fortune was a prosperous linen-weaver. His sons and grandsons branched out into the merchandising of textiles and luxuries, began buying up mines, and in the late 1400's became bankers to the papacy and to the Habsburgs. With the Fuggers, as with Jacques Coeur, wealth bred more wealth, power, and eventual ruin. At the peak of their prosperity in the 1540's, the family fortune is estimated to have reached a figure worth about a quarter of a billion of our present-day dollars. But the Fuggers made the mistake of extending repeated loans to a very poor risk, the Habsburg Philip II of Spain (see Chapter IV), who did not honor his debts. In 1607, the firm went bankrupt.

Two quotations will convey something of the personality of these German bankers. First, there is the note of rugged individualism in the epitaph that Jacob Fugger composed for his own tomb in the early sixteenth century:

To the best, greatest God! Jacob Fugger of Augsburg, the ornament of his class and people, imperial councillor under Maximilian I and Charles V, who was behind no one in the attainment of extraordinary wealth, in generosity, purity of morals, and greatness of soul, is, as he was not comparable with anyone in his lifetime, even after death not to be counted among the mortals.[*]

The proud Fuggers were not just "robber barons," and so there is a note of philanthropy in the inscription at the entrance to the "Fuggerei," a charming garden village that they built for the poor of Augsburg:

Ulrich, George, and Jacob Fugger of Augsburg, blood brothers, being firmly convinced that they were born for the good of the city, and that for their great prosperity they have to thank chiefly an all-powerful and benevolent God, have out of piety, and as an example of special generosity founded, given, and dedicated 106 dwellings, both buildings and furnishings, to those of their fellow citizens who live righteously, but are beset by poverty.[†]

The Impact of Economic Change

Sixteenth-century Augsburg, with its special housing development for low-income families, begins to seem very much like a modern city; yet its total population probably never exceeded 20,000. In fact, neither Augsburg nor the other centers of international economic life five or six hundred years ago were really big cities at all. One set of estimates for the fourteenth century puts the population of Venice, Florence, and Paris in the vicinity of 100,000

[*] Quoted by Miriam Beard, *A History of the Business Man* (New York, 1938), 239–240.
[†] J. Strieder, *Jacob Fugger the Rich* (New York, 1931), 176.

each; that of Genoa, Milan, Barcelona, and London at about 50,000; and that of the biggest German and Flemish towns between 20,000 and 40,000. The great majority of the inhabitants of Renaissance Europe were rural.

The urban minority, however, profoundly affected the life of the rural majority. The ties between town and countryside tightened, particularly in the parts of Europe where towns were especially numerous—Lombardy, Tuscany, Flanders, the Rhine Valley, and northern Germany. Merchants often invested their wealth in farm properties, and peasants often moved to town as workmen or became part-time artisans on the farm itself. Rural laborers made prayer beads for German capitalists and spun woolen yarn for the guild masters of Florence.

Moreover, the growth of trade and the increased use of money partly transformed the social and economic institutions of western Europe. Many manors, no longer largely self-sufficient, now specialized in a single crop, like grain or wool; consequently, they had to purchase outside the manor the necessities that were no longer produced on it. The lords of these one-crop manors, depending increasingly on a monetary income, became capitalists, often very enterprising and ruthless capitalists. They wanted to sweep away what seemed to them inefficient medieval practices, like the peasants' traditional right to pasture livestock on the lands used in common by the farmers of the neighborhood. Thus the sheep-raising capitalists of sixteenth-century England were to secure the famous right of enclosure, of fencing former common lands in order to reserve them for their own flocks. In Spain, the great guild of sheep-raisers called the *Mesta* secured somewhat similar rights over vast tracts of territory. Businessmen, too, attacked medieval economic ways. They wanted property in a form that they might readily sell and buy, free from the complex restrictions of feudal landholding. And they wanted a labor force that they could hire and fire and move to new jobs at will, free from the restrictions of serfdom.

These new developments emancipated many individuals from outworn social restrictions; they blurred the lines between classes, weakening the famous medieval division of society into the first estate of the clergy, the second estate of the nobility, and the third estate of the commoners. At the top of the third estate the bourgeoisie, the middle class of capitalists, businessmen, and master craftsmen, was steadily growing in numbers and wealth. Further down in the third estate the ordinary man probably gained in economic status by becoming a wage-earning laborer instead of remaining a serf. Yet he also lost something. He lost the security, the inherited job, the right to certain lands, all of which he had possessed in the days of manorialism. Undercurrents of despair and discontent ran beneath the prosperous surface of the Renaissance.

The wealthy urban bourgeois helped to alter the medieval outlook on man and his potentialities. The epitaph of Jacob Fugger just quoted furnishes an extreme example of the worldly pride asserted by so many men of the Renaissance, though few medieval men would have been so presumptuous, so self-centered, so lacking in humility. Further, the Church was beginning to lose its medieval function of acting as the chief supporter of culture. The Fuggers, the Medici, Jacques Coeur, the well-to-do generally, were undertaking the monumental building and the patronage of art and learning that had for so long been almost identified with the Church. The palace or library of the rich individual challenged the monastery or the Church-dominated university as a center of education. Indeed, as we shall see, the Church itself, the very keystone of medieval civilization, threatened to crumble under the impact of the new economic forces and the new secularism.

III: *The Political Background*

In politics, too, the Renaissance was more businesslike than the Middle Ages had been. True, there had been plenty of hard-boiled kings in medieval Europe; but what set the politicians of the Renaissance most clearly apart from their medieval predecessors was the candor and the efficiency of their operations. Many of them were bluntly outspoken about their pursuit of power; they gave up the medieval pretense that they were doing God's work by executing the terms of a solemn feudal contract. They developed better instruments of power than medieval rulers had usually possessed, better soldiers, diplomats, bureaucrats.

The Italian States   Of all the rulers of the Renaissance the most businesslike were the despots of the Italian states. Despots had not always ruled in Italy, however. The great medieval struggle between popes and emperors had promoted the growth of independent communes or city-states, particularly in the north of the peninsula. In the twelfth and thirteenth centuries, the communes were oligarchic republics, dominated by the nobility and by the newly rich businessmen who were bluntly called the *popolo grasso* (fat people). The ruling oligarchies, however, were torn by the strife between the pro-papal Guelfs and the pro-imperial Ghibellines. Meantime, something close to class warfare arose between the *popolo grasso* and the small businessmen and wage-earners. In town after town, from the thirteenth century on, social and political dissensions grew so bitter that arbitrary one-man government seemed to be the only remedy. Sometimes a despot seized power;

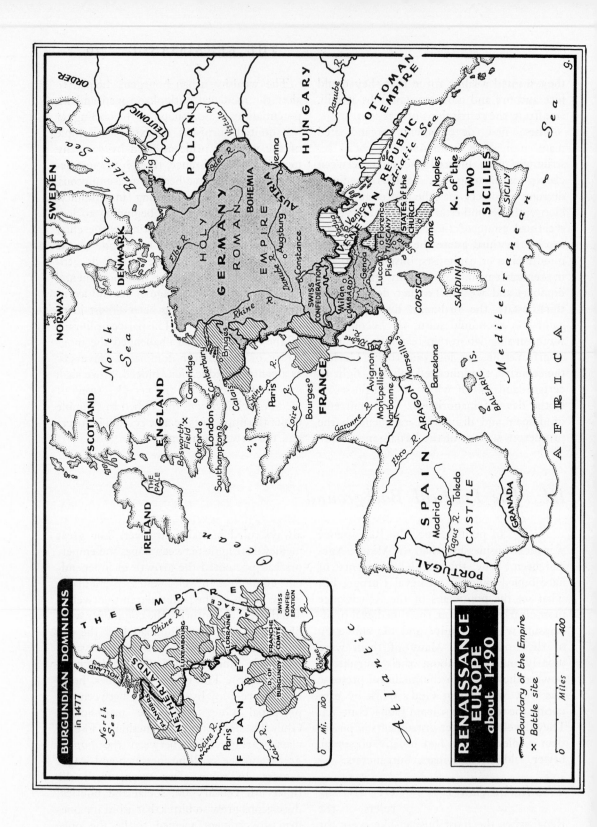

RENAISSANCE
EUROPE
about 1490

Boundary of the Empire
x Battle site

0   Miles   400

BURGUNDIAN DOMINIONS
in 1477

0   Mi.   100

sometimes he was invited in from outside by the contending factions. Often he was a *condottiere*, a captain of the mercenary soldiers whom the states hired to fight their wars.

By the fifteenth century, the fortunes of politics and of war had worked significant changes in the map of Italy. Many towns that had been important in the Middle Ages were sinking into political obscurity, victims of their stronger neighbors. The states that now dominated Italy were the Two Sicilies in the south, the States of the Church in the center, and Milan, Florence, and Venice in the north.

The Two Sicilies comprised the island of Sicily and, on the mainland, the Kingdom of Naples. In the twelfth and early thirteenth centuries these territories had been ruled by able Norman kings and German emperors and had become a great meeting point of the streams of eastern and western trade and culture. After the collapse of imperial power in the mid-thirteenth century, Naples went to the Angevin family from France, and the island of Sicily went to the dynasty of Aragon in Spain. In 1435, the King of Aragon, Alfonso the Magnanimous, took over the Angevin lands of Naples, thus forming the Kingdom of the Two Sicilies. On the death of Alfonso in 1458, Naples came under his illegitimate son Ferrante, or Ferdinand (1458-1494), an especially ruthless despot. Although the Renaissance by no means passed the Two Sicilies by, southern Italy never recovered the vigor and prosperity it had enjoyed in its great medieval days.

The States of the Church had likewise suffered a material decline. At the opening of the fourteenth century, the papacy had lost a great struggle with the French monarchy; the result was the "Babylonian Captivity," 1305-1378, when the papal capital was removed from Rome to Avignon in southern France. The Babylonian Captivity was followed by the Great Schism, 1378-1417, when there were two rival popes, one at Avignon, the other at Rome, and by the Conciliar Movement of the early fifteenth century, a serious though ultimately unsuccessful attempt to make the papacy a kind of limited monarchy by enlarging the powers of councils of church dignitaries at the expense of papal authority. These successive blows not only weakened the prestige of the papacy in religious matters but also weakened the temporal authority of the pope over Rome and the Papal States, a band of territory across central Italy. The city of Rome came under the control of princely families, and the outlying papal lands fell to local feudal lords.

After 1450, the popes once more concentrated their attention on central Italy. Beginning with the scholarly Nicholas V (1447-1455), the papacy was held by a series of able men, often highly cultivated, and often highly ambitious and corrupt. They restored Rome to its old importance as a center of art and learning, and they began the reconquest of the papal dominions. The Borgia pope, Alexander VI (1492-1503), greatly aided by his aggressive and unscrupulous son, Caesar, made notable progress in subjugating the feudal lords of central Italy and in breaking the power of the Roman princely families. Caesar employed almost any means—treachery, violence, assassination by poisoning—to gain his ends. The next pope, Julius II (1503-1513), commanded papal troops in person and consolidated further the temporal authority of the papacy. Soon, however, the double blow of the Reformation and the Habsburg-Valois Wars shattered the popes' political ambitions (see Chapters III and IV).

Throughout the Renaissance neither the Two Sicilies nor the States of the Church effectively challenged the supremacy of the three great North Italian states. Milan occupied a site of great strategic and economic value. Located in the midst of the fertile Lombard plain and within sight of the Alps, it was the terminus of trade routes through the Alpine passes from northern

Europe. It was also a textile and metal-lurgical center, famous for its velvets and brocades, its weapons and armor. Politically, medieval Milan had been a republic, run by the nobility in conjunction with a great council, in which all citizens of modest means could participate. This combination of aristocracy and direct democracy, how-ever, proved unworkable; it could not prevent the seizure of power by the noble Visconti family in 1277. These henchmen of the powerful Archbishops of Milan soon exceeded the promise of their name (which means "viscounts") by becoming hereditary Dukes of Milan. When the direct line of the Visconti died out in 1447, the ducal title was usurped by Francesco Sforza (1450-1466), an energetic *condottiere* who quickly over-came the efforts of a group of Milanese citizens to revive the old republic. Francesco continued the arbitrary rule of the Visconti but made it more tolerable by his soldierly efficiency and by his many public works.

The most famous of the Sforza Dukes of Milan was a younger son of Francesco, Ludovico Il Moro, 1479-1500 (Lewis "the Moor"). Il Moro assembled a retinue of out-standing artists and intellectuals, headed by the renowned Leonardo da Vinci, and made the court of Milan perhaps the most brilliant in all Europe. He had the reputation of being the craftiest diplomat of the age. All his craftiness and diplomacy, however, did not suffice to defend him against the armies of France and Spain (see Chapter IV). Driven from his throne by the French in 1500, Il Moro died in a French prison eight years later. The Duchy of Milan, after a brief restoration of the Sforza, came under direct Spanish rule in 1535 and remained under the control of Spain for nearly two centuries. The Sforza were thus true *con-dottieri*, soldiers of fortune who gained power—and lost it—almost overnight.

Not *condottieri* but bankers and mer-chants governed the Republic of Flor-ence. In this pioneer city of industry and banking, class conflicts largely determined the course of politics. The struggle between Guelfs and Ghibellines became a contest for power between the *popolo grasso* and the older feudal nobility. In the late 1200's, the Guelf plutocrats won out over the Ghibel-line aristocrats. The victorious Guelfs now revised the constitution of the Republic so that a virtual monopoly of key government offices rested with the seven major guilds, which were controlled by the great woolen masters, bankers, and exporters. They de-nied any effective political voice to nobles, Ghibellines, common laborers, or the small businessmen and shopkeepers of the four-teen lesser guilds. Feuds soon divided the dominant Guelfs, and factionalism con-tinued to torment Florence. The politically unprivileged wanted a voice in govern-ment and sought in vain to make the Repub-lic more democratic. The chronic unrest was aggravated first by the bank failures of the 1340's (see above, p. 37) and the con-sequent economic depression, and then, in the early 1400's, by a new rash of bankrupt-cies and a series of military reverses. In 1434, some of the leaders of the ruling clique were forced into exile, and power fell to a political champion of the poor, Cosimo de' Medici.

The Medici ran Florence for the next sixty years (1434-1494). Their championing of the poor had its ironic side, for they had large woolen and banking interests and were perhaps the wealthiest family in Italy; yet they introduced a "soak-the-rich" tax pro-gram and did a good deal to improve the status of the lower classes. The Medici were despots, but despots who operated quietly behind the façade of republican institutions. Cosimo kept himself in the background and seldom held public office. It was an old cus-tom that the municipal executives should be chosen every two months by a sort of po-litical lottery, by random selection from leather bags containing the names of eligible citizens. All the Medici had to do to con-trol the outcome of these "elections" was to arrange it so that only the names of their supporters got into the leather bags.

The most famous of the Medici was the grandson of Cosimo, Lorenzo the Magnificent, ruler of Florence from 1469 to 1492. Machiavelli, who came to hate some of the later Medici, drew an admiring portrait of Lorenzo:

It was throughout his aim to make the city prosperous, the people united, and the nobles honored. He loved exceedingly all who excelled in the arts, and he showered favors on the learned. . . . Lorenzo delighted in architecture, music, and poetry. . . . To give the youth of Florence an opportunity of studying letters he founded a college at Pisa, to which he had appointed the most excellent professors that Italy could produce. . . . His character, prudence, and good fortune were such that he was known and esteemed, not only by the princes of Italy, but by many others in distant lands. . . . In his conversation he was ready and eloquent, in his resolutions wise, in action swift and courageous. There was nothing in his conduct, although inclined to excessive gallantry, which in any way impaired his many virtues; it is possible he found more pleasure in the company of droll and witty men than became a man of his position; and he would often be found playing among his children as if he were still a child. To see him at one time in his grave moments and at another in his gay was to see in him two personalities, joined as it were with invisible bonds. . . . There had never died in Florence—nor yet in Italy—one for whom his country mourned so much, or who left behind him so wide a reputation for wisdom.*

Although Lorenzo possessed in abundance many of the qualities most admired in the Renaissance, he was not a perfect ruler. His neglect of military matters and his financial carelessness left Florence ill prepared for war.

The Medici story after Lorenzo the Magnificent is anticlimax. Following his death, the Florentines made two short-lived attempts to drive the Medici from power and to re-establish a genuine republic. In 1512 and again in 1530 the Medici returned, and presently converted the Florentine Republic, now a very minor state, into the Grand Duchy of Tuscany, with themselves as hereditary Grand Dukes.

In marked contrast to the turbulence of Florence and Milan was the political stability of the other great North Italian state, Venice. Once the Venetian constitution assumed its definitive form in the early fourteenth century, there were no upheavals, no sudden seizures or losses of power by rival factions or ambitious despots. All was calm, orderly, and forthrightly plutocratic.

The chief executive of medieval Venice was the elected doge or duke; the legislature was a general assembly of all the citizens. The Venetian merchants, however, feared that a powerful doge might establish a hereditary monarchy, and they found the assembly unwieldy and unbusinesslike. Accordingly, they relegated the doge to an ornamental role like that of a constitutional monarch today. Conveyed in a gorgeously outfitted barge, rowed by the pick of the Arsenalotti, attended by a host of citizens and foreign visitors, the doge annually cast a huge "wedding ring" into the Adriatic. He thus "married" the sea and paid yearly tribute to the source of Venetian wealth. Meanwhile, the merchants had seized the real instruments of political power. They made the old assembly into the Great Council, a closed corporation whose membership was limited to individuals whose names appeared in a special "Golden Book." Effective authority, however, rested with a series of smaller bodies, notably the secret Council of Ten, charged with maintaining the security of the Republic.

Under this system the rule was permanently restricted to the old merchant families listed in the Golden Book, about 2 per cent of the total population. The derogatory label, "Venetian oligarchy," has accordingly been pinned on any government that seeks to perpetuate the privileges and profits of the few. The oligarchs of Venice, however, while denying the many a voice in politics, did institute projects for

---

* Machiavelli, *Florentine History*, W. K. Marriott, trans. (New York, 1909), 359-360.

the general welfare, from neighborhood public fountains on up to the Arsenal. And they did pursue their business aims with single-minded efficiency for several hundred prosperous years. Seldom in history have political means been so perfectly adapted to economic ends as they were in Renaissance Venice.

The New Realism: Machiavelli

The classic defender of Renaissance power politics was Niccolo Machiavelli (1469-1527), an experienced Florentine diplomat and author of *The Prince*. This famous work praised the vigorous absolutism of Francesco Sforza, Lorenzo the Magnificent and, above all, Caesar Borgia. Actually, *The Prince* makes rather dull reading in spots, but in it may still be found the statements that have given the word "Machiavellian" its sinister significance. Machiavelli has a low opinion of human nature:

For it may be said of men in general that they are ungrateful, voluble, dissemblers, anxious to avoid danger, and covetous of gain; as long as you benefit them, they are entirely yours; they offer you their blood, their goods, their life, and their children, . . . when necessity is remote; but when it approaches, they revolt.*

The politics of *The Prince* follow directly from its estimate of human nature:

A prudent ruler ought not to keep faith when by so doing it would be against his interest, and when the reasons which made him bind himself no longer exist. If men were all good, the precept would not be a good one; but as they are bad, and would not observe their faith with you, so you are not bound to keep faith with them. . . .†

Accordingly, after surveying the bad faith and deception practiced by Caesar Borgia to

tighten his hold on the States of the Church, Machiavelli concludes:

I find nothing to blame, on the contrary, I feel bound . . . to hold him up as an example to be imitated by all who by fortune and with the arms of others have risen to power.*

This, then, is the celebrated Machiavellian doctrine that the end justifies the means. Its author had a very particular end in mind: Italy is "without a head, without order, beaten, despoiled, lacerated, and overrun," he wrote in the last chapter of *The Prince;* Italy must be strengthened to expel the French, Spanish, and Habsburg intruders who had swarmed in during the preceding decades (see Chapter IV for details). *The Prince* was a tract for the times, a drastic prescription against the political maladies afflicting Italy in the early 1500's.

Machiavelli wrote a second major political work, the *Discourses on the First Ten Books of Titus Livius* (the Roman historian Livy). Here he addressed himself not to the immediate Italian crisis but to the problem of building a lasting government, and he reached significantly different conclusions. To achieve lasting stability, *The Discourses* argue, the state requires something more than a single prince endowed with power, more power, and yet more power. In a chapter entitled "The People Are Wiser and More Constant than Princes," Machiavelli writes:

I say that the people are more prudent and stable, and have better judgment than a prince. . . . We also see that in the election of their magistrates they make far better choice than princes; and no people will ever be persuaded to elect a man of infamous character and corrupt habits to any post of dignity, to which a prince is easily influenced in a thousand different ways. . . . We furthermore see the cities where the people are masters make the greatest progress in the least possible time, and much greater than such as have always been governed by princes. . . .†

---

* *The Prince*, Ch. 17. This and the succeeding quotations from Machiavelli are from the Modern Library edition of *The Prince and the Discourses* (New York, n.d.).
† *The Prince*, Ch. 18.

* *The Prince*, Ch. 7.
† *The Discourses*, Bk. I, Ch. 58.

Then Machiavelli goes on to cite the examples of democratic Athens and republican Rome.

In *The Discourses*, Machiavelli thus presents both an estimate of human nature and a political program seemingly in conflict with the statements of *The Prince*. But the conflict is perhaps more apparent than real. *The Discourses* concerned people, like the Athenians and Romans of old, who had great civic virtues and were capable of self-government. *The Prince* concerned people, Machiavelli's Italians, who in his view had lost their civic virtues and therefore required the strongest kind of government from above.

More important, Machiavelli vigorously defended the new secularism of his age. His defense in its positive form foreshadowed the formidable modern doctrine of nationalism: the Italians were one nation, they should be unified in a single state strong enough to repel all invaders. In its negative form his defense of secularism questioned the political values of Christianity, as in this passage from *The Discourses*:

Reflecting now as to whence it came that in ancient times the people were more devoted to liberty than in the present, I believe that it resulted from this, that men were stronger in those days, which I believe to be attributable to the difference of education, founded upon the difference of their religion and ours. For, as our religion teaches us the truth and the true way of life, it causes us to attach less value to the honors and possessions of this world; whilst the Pagans, esteeming those things as the highest good, were more energetic and ferocious in their actions. . . . The Pagan religion deified only men who had achieved great glory, such as commanders of armies and chiefs of republics, whilst ours glorifies more the humble and contemplative men than the men of action. Our religion, moreover, places the supreme happiness in humility, lowliness, and a contempt for worldly objects, whilst the other, on the contrary, places the supreme good in grandeur of soul, strength of body, and all such other qualities as render men formidable. . . .*

* *The Discourses*, Bk. II, Ch. 2.

Further, Machiavelli accused the Christian institution of the papacy of responsibility for the ruin of Italy:

The Church, then, not having been powerful enough to be able to master all Italy, nor having permitted any other power to do so, has been the cause why Italy has never been able to unite under one head, but has always remained under a number of princes and lords, which occasioned her to so many dissensions and so much weakness that she became a prey . . . of whoever chose to assail her.*

Machiavelli believed that the purpose of government was not to prepare men for the hereafter but to make upstanding citizens of this world, ready to fight and die for their earthly country.

A generation before *The Prince* was written, the political realism that Machiavelli was to preach was already being practiced by the monarchs of three European states. In the late fifteenth century, Louis XI of France, Henry VII of England, and Ferdinand and Isabella of Spain were all briskly at work putting their respective states in order, laying the foundations of powerful modern nations, and attacking the problems that threatened their central authority.

France

The central problem in France was recovery from the heavy blows of the Hundred Years' War with England (1337-1453). France won the war, and England, which had long controlled sizable French territories, retained only the Channel port of Calais. But the victorious French king, Charles VII (1422-1461) of the House of Valois, badly needed to rebuild the royal prestige and to forge new instruments of royal power. The government of Charles could not maintain law and order in the countryside, which was ravaged by rebellious feudal nobles and pillaged by bands of French soldiers.

* *The Discourses*, Bk. I, Ch. 12.

In restoring the kingly authority, Charles VII had the invaluable support of the strong French monarchical tradition, for the kings of medieval France had created the institutions of an absolute monarchy. Partly because of dissensions among the vassals, partly because the monarchy had enlisted the towns and the new middle class on its side, partly because the prolonged English danger made opposition to the French king appear unpatriotic, no effective checks had developed on French absolutism. For the same reasons, the chief institution that might have checked absolutism, the central representative assembly called the Estates General, had become the docile servant of the Crown. In 1439, Charles VII secured from the Estates the important rights of maintaining a professional non-feudal army and of collecting a non-feudal tax levied directly on individuals by royal agents. With these instruments at hand, and with the financial aid of Jacques Coeur, Charles was able to build the forces that won the final campaigns of the Hundred Years' War.

Meantime, Charles had scored against another institution, the Church, that might have weakened the Crown. In 1438, he regulated Church-State relations by the Pragmatic Sanction of Bourges ("pragmatic sanction" is simply a name for a solemn royal pronouncement). This document laid down the policy known as Gallicanism, claiming for the Gallican, or French, church a virtually autonomous position within the Church Universal. It greatly limited papal control over ecclesiastical appointments and revenues in France and asserted the superiority of church councils over popes. Despite these achievements, however, when Charles VII died in 1461 rebellious vassals were still defying his authority in large areas of the kingdom.

Louis XI (1461-1483), the son of Charles, energetically pursued the unfinished business of his father. At his accession Louis was already a mature and practiced politician.

One of his aides, the statesman and historian Philippe de Comines (1445-1509), drew a notable portrait of the wily Louis:

. . . He was the wisest Prince in winding himself out of trouble and adversity, the humblest in words, the plainest in apparel, and greatest traveller to win a man that might do him service or harm that ever I knew. . . . Never Prince gave audience to so many men, never Prince was inquisitive of so many matters, nor desirous to be acquainted with so many strangers as he. . . . And by these virtues preserved he his estate, which stood in great danger at his first coming to the crown, because of the enemies himself had procured to himself.

. . . And I think verily he should never have wound himself out of those troubles had not his education been better than noblemen's commonly is in this realm, who are brought altogether in wantonness and dissoluteness, as well in their apparel as in their talk, they are utterly unlearned, there is not one wise man about them. . . .*

Louis XI forced his protesting subjects to pay higher taxes, then sweetened the dose, at least for the bourgeois, by granting them favors and giving them responsible posts in his administration. He enlarged the army bequeathed him by his father yet conserved its use for emergencies; he usually relied on diplomacy to gain his ends. And he countered the greatest single feudal force still threatening the French Crown.

Burgundy was that threat. The authority of its dukes reached far beyond the Duchy of Burgundy in eastern France and the adjoining Free County (Franche Comté) and encompassed a large portion of the Low Countries. This sprawling Burgundian realm almost deserved to be called an empire. But it was a divided empire: the two main territorial blocs in eastern France and the Low Countries were separated by the non-Burgundian lands of Alsace and Lorraine. And it was a personal empire, for Duke Philip the Good (1419-1467) had assembled it as

* *The History of Comines*, Thomas Danett, trans., Bk. I, Ch. X. Translation somewhat modernized.

much by good luck as by good management, inheriting some lands and acquiring others by conquest or negotiation. And it was also a menacing empire, which might have interposed itself permanently as a middle kingdom between France and Germany. Philip had made an alliance with England in the Hundred Years' War, and he could draw on the wealth of the Flemish and Dutch towns.

The decisive trial of strength between France and Burgundy took place under Philip's successor, Charles the Bold (1467-1477). Where Louis XI was plain, Charles was, in the words of Comines, "wonderful pompous, yea somewhat too excessive"; where Louis was cautious, Charles was bold to the point of folly. He determined to build a true middle kingdom by bridging the territorial gap between Burgundy and the Low Countries and seizing Lorraine and Alsace. But since Alsace in those days was a confused patchwork of feudal jurisdictions overlapping northern Switzerland, his designs threatened the largely independent Swiss confederation. Subsidized by Louis XI, who wanted allies to do his fighting for him, the Swiss defeated Charles three times in 1476 and 1477. In the last of the battles Charles was slain.

Since Charles left no son, his lands were partitioned. The Duchy of Burgundy passed permanently, and the Franche Comté temporarily, to France; the Low Countries went to Mary, the daughter of Charles. Thus Louis XI, though he shattered the prospect of a middle kingdom, was not able to keep all the Burgundian inheritance out of the hands of the future enemies of France. Mary of Burgundy married Maximilian of Habsburg, who later became Holy Roman Emperor; their son was to marry the daughter of Ferdinand and Isabella of Spain. The son of this latter union, the emperor Charles V, was to rule Germany, the Low Countries, and Spain, and to threaten the kingdom of France with hostile encirclement (see Chapter IV).

England

The problems confronting the Crown of England in the late fifteenth century were often strikingly like those facing the Crown of France. In England, too, the last phases of the Hundred Years' War produced plundering by an uncontrolled soldiery and a belated feudal reaction. The great nobles paired off into two camps led by the rival houses of Lancaster and York and contested the throne itself. The aristocrats slaughtered each other in droves during the dreary civil struggle named the Wars of the Roses, 1455-1485, after the red rose, badge of the House of Lancaster, and the white rose, badge of the House of York.

Some historians have maintained that this convenient self-liquidation of the aristocracy in the Wars of the Roses was why monarchy was to be more temperate and less despotic in England than on the Continent. In France and Spain the nobility resisted the royal authority so stubbornly that the kings pushed their power to great extremes in order to curb the feudal lords. It is well to remember, however, that England had a long tradition of constitutional monarchy. It was the realm where institutions had long checked the Crown, the country of Magna Carta and of Parliament.

Because the Norman conquerors of England were powerful rulers, the vassals of the king early recognized the need for uniting and presenting corporate opposition to the Crown if they were to avoid losing their rights. Out of the baronial opposition there emerged guarantees limiting the king: promises that were given on behalf of the great vassals, the barons, but that were always subject to broader interpretation. Here the classic example, of course, was Magna Carta, the great charter exacted from King John by the barons in 1215.

And out of the king's need to obtain assent for taxation, and out of the custom of consulting his vassals, there had emerged Parliament. This body differed in very important ways from its French counterpart, the Estates General. Although by the fifteenth century it had by no means acquired the sovereign powers it enjoys today, it was far from being merely the docile servant of the Crown, as were the Estates General. It was developing the beginnings of its law-making function and it exerted considerable control over royal finances through the power of the purse, the assent to new taxes. Most significantly, Parliament was not organized like the Estates General, where the three estates—clergy, nobility, commoners—sat as three separate and often warring houses. In Parliament the great nobles and prelates sat together in the House of Lords; the "knights of the shire" and the "burgesses" sat together in the House of Commons. The "burgesses" were indeed commoners, representatives of boroughs (towns), but the knights came from the class of landed gentry, the English counterpart of the lesser nobility on the Continent. This alliance of knights and burgesses, of the lower ranks of the second estate and the upper ranks of the third, so to speak, did not always operate smoothly, but it was unique in Europe, where the second and third estates were usually antagonistic.

Parliament, however, did not play a leading part in tidying up England after the Wars of the Roses. This task was undertaken by Henry Tudor, who brought the Wars of the Roses to an end by defeating Richard III, the last Yorkist king, at Bosworth Field. The battle gave England a new monarch, Henry VII (1485-1509), and a new dynasty, the Tudors (1485-1603). Henry was descended from a bastard branch of the Lancaster family, but his right to be king really derived from his victory at Bosworth and from his subsequent confirmation by Parliament. Shrewd and economical, able but far from heart-warming, Henry VII bore many resemblances to Louis XI of France.

Henry formally healed the breach between the houses of the rival roses by marrying Elizabeth of York, the niece of Richard III. He also saw to it that the nobles should not in the future find it so easy to make war: he forbade them to keep uniformed private armies or to interfere with royal justice. Henry enforced these measures against the great lords through an administrative court known as the Star Chamber, from the star-painted ceiling of the room in which it met. The Star Chamber was charged with the task of seeing that the apparatus of the law should not be used to back up local privileges, local abuses, local resistance to what Henry wanted. To make justice swift and implacable, the Star Chamber avoided using juries and the customary procedures of the common law. It could be arbitrary, could trample on the rights of defendants, and could engage in the other dubious practices which have made "star-chamber proceedings" a term of reproach, synonymous with the abuse of judicial authority. The court, however, did not fully acquire its bad reputation until the seventeenth century (see Chapter VI). During the reign of Henry VII and all through the Tudor rule, it is fair to say that the Star Chamber and the rest of the royal administration usually served purposes approved by the nation, or, more precisely, by Englishmen concerned with affairs of state.

The men who did Henry's work for him were for the most part men of the prosperous urban merchant class, or men who had worked their way up in the Church with royal assistance. The King and his advisers more than doubled the revenues of the central government, sometimes by using high-handed methods. But Henry thus avoided a clash with Parliament, because he seldom had to raise taxes requiring parliamentary sanction. Both the King's obvious efficiency and his commercial policy, moreover, won support in the business community. Since foreign vessels still carried the bulk of England's trade, Henry dared not revoke the special privileges of foreign merchants. But he used the threat of revocation to gain trading rights for English merchants abroad, especially in Italy. Henry VII left a well-filled treasury and a prosperous country; he had re-established law and order in an England weary of rebellion and civil war.

Spain

The accomplishments of Henry VII and Louis XI were eclipsed by those of their great Spanish contemporaries, Ferdinand and Isabella. Whereas Henry and Louis ruled kingdoms that had long been well-defined states with established central institutions, Ferdinand and Isabella inherited a disunited Spain and had to build a central government from the very foundations. The decisive event in the early medieval history of the Iberian peninsula was the Moslem conquest, by mixed groups of Arabs and North African Berbers, starting in the year 711. The whole peninsula came under Moslem control with the exception of the extreme north, where small independent Christian states survived. From the ninth century through the fifteenth the Christian states of the north gradually pressed south, recovering territory from the Moslems, until finally the Moslem remnant at Granada, in the extreme south, fell in 1492. This slow expansion by Catholic Spaniards has often been likened to a crusade five hundred years long. It was indeed a crusade, and the proud, militant, intolerant spirit of the crusader left a permanent mark upon the Spanish "style."

In the middle of the fifteenth century, when the reconquest was nearing completion, three Christian kingdoms dominated the Iberian peninsula. Castile, the largest and most populous, occupied the center of the peninsula and had assumed the leadership of the reconquest. The power of the Castilian kings, however, did not grow in proportion to their territory. The powerful sheep interests of the *Mesta* constituted a virtual state within the state. Both the nobility and the towns maintained many rights against the royal authority; both were represented in the Cortes, the medieval Castilian counterpart of the English Parliament and the French Estates General.

To the west of Castile, along the Atlantic coast, lay the kingdom of Portugal, a Castilian province that had won independence in the twelfth century. Though still retaining close links with Castile, the Portuguese were gradually maturing their own particular national interests, especially in seaborne trade (see Chapter V). The third kingdom, located in northeastern Spain, was Aragon, which was as much a Mediterranean power as a Spanish one. Its kings controlled the Balearic Islands and, as we have seen, had a large stake in southern Italy. In Aragon, as in Castile, the oldest established political institutions were those limiting the Crown—the Cortes, the nobility, and the towns, particularly the thriving city of Barcelona.

In 1469, Ferdinand, later King of Aragon (1479-1516), married Isabella, later Queen of Castile (1474-1504), and thus made the dynastic alliance that eventually consummated the political unification of Spain. The obstacles confronting them were immense. Not only was the royal power weak in both states; the inhabitants of Castile and Aragon did not even speak the same language, a difference still evident today in the distinction between the Castilian spoken in Madrid and the Catalan of the area of Barcelona. The one state looked toward the Atlantic, the other toward the Mediterranean. Finally, Ferdinand and Isabella themselves did not make a perfect political team. Ferdinand was a wary and skeptical realist of the stamp of Louis XI and an ardent promoter of Aragon's Italian ambitions. Isabella, on the other hand, was devout in religion, and in policy was wholly absorbed in consolidating her authority over Castile.

It is scarcely remarkable, then, that Ferdinand and Isabella failed to weld Castile and Aragon into a single nation. What is surprising is that they nevertheless managed to raise Spain to the rank of a first-rate power. This they achieved, above all, by creating a strong central government in Isabella's Castile. The Queen summoned the Cortes as infrequently as she dared and entrusted much executive power to a potent new instrument of absolutism staffed by royal appointees, the Council of Castile. She allied with the middle class against the nobles and drew military support more from town militias than from feudal levies.

Last and most important, Ferdinand and Isabella enlisted the aid of the Church. The Queen was pious, but she was also determined to bring the Church under royal discipline and prescribed a thorough purge of ecclesiastical corruption. The purified Spanish church was later to assume leadership of the Catholic Reformation (see Chapter III). The Spanish monarchs also obtained from the easygoing popes of the Renaissance the right to dispose of ecclesiastical appointments and part of the ecclesiastical revenue in their dominions. An individual and an institution cemented the alliance of Church and State in Spain. The individual was Cardinal Ximenes (1436-1517), the Archbishop of Toledo, who was the chief minister of Isabella. The institution was the Inquisition, a special kind of court developed by the medieval Church to prosecute heretics. The Spanish Inquisition was from the first a royal instrument; it sought to promote Spanish nationalism by enforcing universal Catholicism, to create loyal subjects of the Crown by obliging men to be obedient children of the Church.

The chief targets of Isabella and Ximenes were two important religious minorities— Moslems and Jews. Both groups had long enjoyed toleration and owned some of the most flourishing farms and businesses in Spain. In 1492, persecution of the Jews began; they were given the choice of immediate baptism into the Christian faith or immediate exile, with loss of their property. Ten years later, it was the turn of the Moslems. Many of the coerced converts from Judaism and Islam were no more than nominal Christians, conforming only because they feared the tortures and burnings which the Inquisition could prescribe if they wavered in their new faith.

The year 1492, then, is the great date in the whole history of Spain. It was the year when Ferdinand and Isabella seized the last fragment of Moslem Spain and Columbus laid the first stones of the great Spanish empire in the New World. But it was also the year when intensive religious persecution began. The new Spanish monarchy already showed the narrow and bigoted nationalism that was to be at once its strength and its weakness in the centuries to come.

IV: Literature and Thought

The writers, the thinkers, and the artists of the Renaissance expressed the new nationalism and the new materialism of their time. But they also continued the age-old human examination into the mysteries of nature and the personality of man. The world of culture, though never wholly separate from the workaday world of business and politics, is never wholly the same. Parallels between the two exist; we must find them, but we must never push them too far. Our inquiry into the culture of the Renaissance begins with the instrument of so many Renaissance writers, the vernacular languages.

The Rise
of the Vernaculars

In the western European countries the vernaculars arose deep in the Middle Ages as the spoken language of the people, then were extended gradually to popular writing and later to formal and official works. Many of the vernaculars developed from Latin; these were the Romance (that is, Roman) languages—Spanish, Portuguese, Italian, and French. The German vernacular, of course, was not a Romance language but a Teutonic one. English, a Germanic derivative with many borrowings from Norman French and Latin, came into its own during the fourteenth century with a series of popular works capped by *The Canterbury Tales* of Geoffrey Chaucer.

The rise of national vernaculars sometimes did, but as often did not, parallel the growth of political nationalism. Use of a common language undoubtedly aroused in Englishmen a common sense of national purpose and a common mistrust of the foreigners who did not speak the King's English. Yet the vernaculars maturing in Italy and in Germany did little to remedy the political disunity of both countries. The vernaculars quickened the emergence of distinctive national "styles" in England, in France, and in Spain. It is language in part that makes Shakespeare seem so English, Rabelais so French, Cervantes so Spanish. Yet the vernaculars did not divide western culture into watertight national compartments; translations kept ideas flowing across national frontiers.

Humanism

In the Renaissance the vernaculars did not fully displace Latin, which remained the international language of the Church and the academic world. Scholars worked diligently to perfect their Latin and, in the later Renaissance, to learn at least the rudiments of Greek. They called themselves humanists. Many avowed humanists both revered the classics and employed one of the vernaculars with great skill; this is but one example of the Renaissance transition, the old and the new side by side. Humanism, however, was far more than a linguistic term. The leading humanists studied the great men, the great ideas, the great art of the past, particularly of classical antiquity, and became eager students of humankind. In the Renaissance, humanism, interpreted most widely, meant what the terms "humanities" and "liberal arts" mean today.

The evolution of humanism may be traced most readily through the great writers of the Renaissance, starting with the earliest, Dante Alighieri (1265-1321). Much of Dante's work was firmly planted in the Middle Ages. Though hostile to the political ambitions of the papacy, Dante was no Machiavellian anticlerical but simply a good Christian who wanted the popes to keep out of politics. His *Divine Comedy*, recounting his journey through Hell, Purgatory, and Heaven, was the magnificent imaginative expression of the medieval Christian view toward the drama of the human soul.

Yet for the *Comedy* Dante deliberately chose the vernacular of his native Tuscany over the more respectable Latin, and he modeled his style after popular vernacular poetry rather than after the loftier epic verse of the classics. The personages of the *Comedy* include many classical figures, both real and mythological. The Trojan Hector, Homer, Vergil's Aeneas, Vergil himself, Euclid, Plato, Socrates, Caesar, and other virtuous pagans dwell forever in Limbo on the edge of Hell, suffering only the hopelessness of the unbaptized who can never reach God's presence. The lost souls are real people, from Judas through corrupt medieval clerics down to Dante's own political enemies in Florence. The concerns of this world are constantly with Dante in the other world. Moreover, Dante was not one of the medieval intellectuals who withdrew from society to the sanctuary of holy orders. He was deeply involved in practical politics and in the secular concerns of the guild of physicians and apothecaries. As a political refugee from Florence, he adopted the good Renaissance expedient of obtaining the patronage of the ruler of Verona.

The next great figure in the line of Italian humanists was Francesco Petrarca (1304-1374), better known as Petrarch, who devoted himself to collecting and copying the manuscripts of ancient authors. He so admired the past that he addressed a series of affectionate letters to Cicero and other old masters and composed a Latin epic in the manner of the *Aeneid*. Petrarch wanted desperately to win lasting fame, to rank with the great Romans to whom he addressed his "correspondence." He achieved fame, but, ironically, the writings of Petrarch most admired in modern times are not those he wrote in his beloved Latin but those that he himself esteemed the least, the beautiful vernacular love sonnets to his adored Laura.

Petrarch, indeed, had that deep feeling for the beauties of this world that characterized so many Renaissance humanists. His Laura was a living, human woman, not a disembodied chivalric ideal. Medieval men had apparently paid little attention to beautiful scenery; not so Petrarch. This is his account of reaching the summit of Mont Ventoux in southern France:

I looked around me: clouds were gathering below my feet, and Athos and Olympus grew less incredible, since I saw on a mountain of lesser fame what I had heard and read about them. From there I turned my eyes in the direction of Italy, for which my mind is so fervently yearning. The Alps were frozen stiff and covered with snow—those mountains through which that ferocious enemy of the Roman name once passed, blasting his way through the rocks with vinegar if we may believe tradition.*

Note here the classical allusions—to the Greek mountains, Athos and Olympus, and to the Carthaginian Hannibal, "ferocious enemy of the Roman name." But note, too, that at the end Petrarch's story takes a me-

* Quoted in E. Cassirer, P. O. Kristeller, J. H. Randall, Jr., *The Renaissance Philosophy of Man* (Chicago, 1948), 41.

dieval turn and leads to Saint Augustine, the great Christian philosopher of the early fifth century:

I admired every detail, now relishing earthly enjoyment, now lifting up my mind to higher spheres after the example of my body, and I thought it fit to look into the volume of Augustine's *Confessions*. . . . I happened to hit upon the tenth book of the work. My brother stood beside me, intently expecting to hear something from Augustine on my mouth. I ask God to be my witness and my brother who was with me: Where I fixed my eyes first it was written: 'And men go to admire the high mountains, the vast floods of the sea, the huge streams of the rivers, the circumference of the ocean, and the revolutions of the stars— and desert themselves.' I was stunned, I confess. I bade my brother, who wanted to hear more, not to molest me, and closed the book, angry with myself that I still admired earthly things.*

The episode suggests that Petrarch was both a humanist *and* a Christian, a complex Renaissance man who strove to keep a nice balance between the worldly and the otherworldly.

Not every humanist struck this balance, however, least of all Petrarch's friend and pupil, Giovanni Boccaccio (1313-1375). Boccaccio aided his master in the search for ancient manuscripts; he claimed indeed to have rescued copies of the famous Roman historian, Tacitus, lying "shamefully neglected" in the Benedictine abbey of Monte Cassino. The anticlerical touch here is significant. Boccaccio is, of course, synonymous with the *Decameron*, and the *Decameron* is synonymous with an un-Christian view of life.

The *Decameron* recounts the stories told by a gay company of seven young ladies and three men who fled from Florence in 1348 to escape the Black Death. Boccaccio reworks some of the vulgar tales of medieval France, mocks the hypocrisy of practicing Christians, and exposes the corruption of the Church. Perhaps the most un-Christian thing about the *Decameron*

* *Ibid.*, 44.

is not its obscenity or its revelations of immorality; it is rather Boccaccio's own light-hearted and matter-of-fact attitude. This is the gist of one of his stories:

You must know, then, that there was once in our city a very rich merchant called Arriguccio Berlinghieri, who . . . took to wife a young gentlewoman ill sorting with himself, by name Madam Sismonda, who, for that he, merchant-like, was much abroad and sojourned little with her, fell in love with a young man called Ruberto.*

Arriguccio discovers his wife's infidelity and gives her the beating of her life—or so he thinks. The beating occurs in a darkened room; Sismonda has directed her maid to take her place; and it is actually the maid whom Arriguccio has thrashed. He, ignorant of the deception, plays the wronged husband to the hilt and summons Sismonda's brothers to witness her disgrace. "The brothers,—seeing her seated sewing with no sign of beating on her face, whereas Arriguccio avouched that he had beaten her to a mummy,—began to marvel." Sismonda immediately accuses her hapless husband of "fuddling himself about the taverns, foregathering now with this lewd woman and now with that and keeping me waiting for him . . . half the night." The result: the brothers give Arriguccio a thorough beating. And Boccaccio's moral:

Thus the lady, by her ready wit, not only escaped the imminent peril but opened herself a way to do her every pleasure in time to come, without evermore having any fear of her husband.

Later Humanism

The humanists who came after Petrarch and Boccaccio may be divided into three fairly distinct groups. First there are the conservers of classical culture, the bookworms, scholars, cultivated despots

* This and the following quotations are from the eighth story of the seventh day, as translated in the Modern Library edition of the *Decameron* (New York. n.d.).

and businessmen, all the heirs of Petrarch's great enthusiasm for classical antiquity. Second come the writers of vernacular narratives, who take the path marked out by the *Decameron,* from Chaucer at the close of the fourteenth century down to Rabelais and to Cervantes in the sixteenth. And third there are the synthesizers, headed by Pico and Erasmus, who try to fuse Christianity, classicism, and much else into a universal philosophy of man.

The devoted antiquarians of the fifteenth century uncovered a really remarkable quantity of ancient manuscripts. They ransacked all the likely hiding places, particularly monasteries, and gradually pieced together the works of Cicero, Tacitus, and other Latin authors. Searchers for Greek texts did their work so thoroughly that virtually all the Greek classics we now possess reached the West before 1500. To preserve, catalogue, and study these literary treasures, the first modern libraries were created. In Florence, Cosimo de' Medici supported three separate libraries, and the humanist popes founded the library of the Vatican, today one of the half-dozen most important collections in the world.

The classicists of the fifteenth century made a fetish of pure and polished Latin. The learned composed elaborate letters designed less for private reading than for the instruction of their colleagues. Papal secretaries began to make ecclesiastical correspondence conform to what we should call a manual of correct style. At their worst, these men were not humanists but pedants, exalting manner over matter, draining vitality from the Latin language. At their best, they were keen and erudite scholars who applied to classical studies the kind of critical spirit that Machiavelli would bring to politics.

Our second group of humanists, the writers of vernacular narratives, illustrate once again the extraordinary variety of the Renaissance. Geoffrey Chaucer (c. 1340-1400), like Dante, belongs both to the

Middle Ages and to the Renaissance. His *Canterbury Tales* have a medieval setting; they are told by pilgrims on their way to the great shrine at Canterbury. The "Knight's Tale" of the mortal feud between two cousins over a girl whom they have barely glimpsed is a good mirror of feudal chivalry and its romantic view of love. Yet Chaucer writes in the English vernacular, and, when he has a commoner speak, even uses those "Anglo-Saxon monosyllables" which everyone knows and which only the very highbrow print nowadays. His "Miller's Tale" is a very good mirror of popular taste, a broad, farcical, bawdy tale, in which the jealous, stupid husband is properly cuckolded in the best traditions of folklore.

The medieval values still evident in Chaucer have disappeared when we come to the Frenchman, François Rabelais (c. 1494-1553), who contributed far more to culture than the pornography for which he is famous. Gargantua and Pantagruel, his great comic creations, are quite literally larger than life: they are giants, and everything they do is on the heroic scale. The abbey of Theleme, which Gargantua helps to found, permits its residents a wildly un-monastic existence:

> All their life was spent not in lawes, statutes or rules, but according to their own free will and pleasure. They rose out of their beds, when they thought good: they did eat, drink, labour, sleep, when they had a minde to it, and were disposed for it. . . . In all their rule, and strictest tie of their order, there was but this one clause to be observed,
> DO WHAT THOU WILT.*

Gargantua exhorts Pantagruel to learn everything. He is to master Arabic in addition to Latin, read the New Testament in Greek and the Old in Hebrew, and study history, geometry, architecture, music, and civil law. He must also know "the fishes, all the fowles of the aire, all the several

* Rabelais, *Gargantua and Pantagruel*, Urquhart trans. (New York, 1883), Bk. I, Ch. 57.

kinds of shrubs and trees," "all the sorts of herbs and flowers that grow upon the ground: all the various metals that are hid within the bowels of the earth." * Here is the mark of the Renaissance "style"—the immense curiosity, the zest for all knowledge and all experience.

Rabelais revived the Greek ideal of the individual sound in mind and body; our third group of humanists, the philosophers, resumed the old Greek quest for ultimate truth. The Platonic Academy, an informal intellectual club subsidized by the Medici, made Florence a center of philosophical studies in the late fifteenth century. The outstanding member of the Academy was Pico (Giovanni Pico, Count of Mirandola, 1463-1494). Pico would have delighted Gargantua, for he knew Arabic and Hebrew and studied Jewish allegory, Arab philosophy, and Christian medieval thought. His tolerance was as broad as his learning. In his short *Oration on the Dignity of Man*, he cited approvingly Chaldean and Persian

* *Ibid.*, Bk. I, Ch. 8.

Erasmus, by Dürer.

theologians, the priests of Apollo, Socrates, Pythagoras, Cicero, Moses, St. Paul, St. Augustine, Mohammed, and many others. In all the varied beliefs of this galaxy Pico hoped to find the common denominator of faith, the key to man and the universe. Naturally he failed. Yet there is something very appealing about the man who strove to capture the essence of all truth. He helped to found the great humane studies of comparative religion and comparative philosophy. And, though ambitious, Pico was disarmingly modest. "I have wished to give assurance," he wrote, "not so much that I know many things, as that I know things of which many are ignorant."

The "Prince of Humanists," Erasmus, brought to maturity the humanist endeavor to draw on all wisdom. Dutch by birth, Erasmus (1466-1536) was the foremost citizen of the Republic of Letters. He studied, taught, and lived at Oxford, Cambridge, and Paris, and in Italy, Switzerland, and Germany. He published a scholarly edition of the New Testament in its original Greek and compiled a series of *Adages* and *Colloquies* to give students examples of good Latin composition. But Erasmus never regarded elegance of style as an end in itself and assailed the pedantic humanists:

As for those stilted, insipid verses they display on all occasions (and there are those to admire them), obviously the writer believes that the soul of Virgil has transmigrated into his own breast. But the funniest sight of all is to see them admiring and praising each other,

trading compliment for compliment, thus mutually scratching each other's itch.*

The *Adages* and *Colloquies*, in fact most of his enormous output, contain penetrating comments on human weaknesses. Erasmus played no favorites; he satirized any group or class inflated by a sense of its own importance—merchants, churchmen, scientists, philosophers, courtiers, and kings. Therefore, Erasmus concluded, we must cherish particularly the few outstanding individuals who have led great and good lives. Christ heads his list of great men; Cicero and Socrates rank very high. Plato's account of the death of Socrates moved Erasmus so deeply that he almost cried out, "Pray for us, Saint Socrates."

Erasmus possessed almost all the main attributes of Renaissance humanism. He coupled a detached view of human nature with faith in the dignity of man; he joined love of the classics with respect for Christian values. But, though he always considered himself a loyal son of the Church, he nevertheless helped to destroy the universality of Catholicism. His edition of the Greek New Testament raised disquieting doubts about the correctness of Catholic Biblical interpretations. His attacks on the laxity of the clergy implied that the wide gap between the professed ideals and the corrupt practices of the Church could not long endure.

----

* Erasmus, *Praise of Folly*, H. H. Hudson, trans. (Princeton, 1941), 71-72.

V: *The Arts*

Humanism not only prepared the way for the Reformation but also helped to promote a revolution in the fine arts. Two of the great humanistic traits—the new interest in classical antiquity and the new emphasis on the secular world—carried over into the realm of art with most significant results. In the medieval West, architecture had eclipsed the other fine arts. Painting and sculpture had scarcely been independent but had been absorbed into the great enterprise of religious devotion and municipal pride which produced the Gothic cathedral. In the Renaissance, architecture gradually lost its old predominance, and sculpture and painting came into their own. Influenced by the classical revival, architects changed their style of building from the soaring Gothic to adaptations of the ancient Roman temple, emphasizing symmetry and the horizontal line. In the Renaissance, moreover, art was no longer quite so emphatically Christian as it had been in the Middle Ages. Painters and sculptors no longer devoted so much time to the decoration of ecclesiastical buildings; they often produced portraits and statues designed as independent works of art. Along with the usual Virgins, Christs, and saints, they also chose for subjects pagan gods and living, secular individuals. Leonardo da Vinci painted the profoundly religious Last Supper *and* the quite unreligious portrait of Mona Lisa.

The artists of the Renaissance produced both secular and sacred works; they both copied ancient classical models and launched bold new experiments in artistic expression; they took pride in their individual achievements, even boasted of them. They demonstrate the extreme limit of Renaissance complexity and individualism. Some of the very greatest were also the most versatile. Giotto, whom we shall encounter in a moment, painted, designed, and ornamented buildings, wrote verses, and did handsomely in business. Leonardo was a jack-of-all-trades and a master of many—painter and sculptor, musician and physicist, anatomist and geologist, engineer and plumber.

Painting

The art of the Renaissance began to emerge from the Middle Ages about 1300, and after a long development reached its zenith two hundred years later. The most celebrated names in painting—Leonardo, Michelangelo, Titian, Dürer —belong to the fifteenth and early sixteenth centuries. But the great forerunner of these masters was a contemporary of Dante, Giotto (c. 1270-1337). Up to Giotto's day, Italian painters had generally followed the lead of Byzantium. The work of these "Italian Primitives" was impressively religious and highly decorative, but it tended to be stiff and unnatural. Giotto, though not wholly deserting the Byzantine tradition, also experimented to obtain more lifelike effects. He learned much, it appears, from the realistic statues of Italian sculptors, who, in turn, were influenced by the striking sculptures decorating the portals of French Gothic cathedrals. Humanity and emotion stand forth from many of Giotto's paintings. In the Entombment of Christ, in the Arena Chapel at Padua, the mood of grief is intensified by the lamentations of the mourners on the ground, and still more by the angels flying above the dead Christ. They do not glide placidly but seem to be beating their wings in a transport of distraction and sorrow.

As a person, Giotto anticipated the proud and versatile man of the Renaissance bent on worldly success. He was no anonymous craftsman, but hungry for fame; and he was famous in his own day for his verses and his witty remarks as well as for his artistic accomplishments. His artistic commissions netted him a sizable fortune, which he augmented by lending money, running a debt-collection service, and renting looms (at stiff fees) to poor woolen-weavers. Giotto won the patronage of Roman cardinals, the king of Naples, and the guilds and millionaires of Florence, including the banking families of the Bardi and the Peruzzi.

Thus in the time of Giotto art was beginning to attract the patronage of secular individuals in addition to that of the churchmen who had been its chief sponsors in the Middle Ages. During the next two centuries, more and more despots, kings, popes, and merchant princes joined the ranks of patrons. This is one of the chief topics to follow in surveying the history of Renaissance painting. A second topic is the introduction of humanistic and secular themes into the world of art. A final topic is technical: the advances in the use of perspective, color, precise natural detail—all the techniques that made the medium more lifelike and gave it more expressive power.

By 1500, almost all the Italian states, and many states outside Italy, had their court painters. In Florence, the government, the guilds, the wealthy magnates, and the churches and monasteries had all been patronizing artists since the time of Giotto. Lorenzo the Magnificent subsidized a great painter like Botticelli as well as the humanists of the Platonic Academy. "Il Moro," the Sforza usurper in Milan, made Leonardo in effect his Minister of Fine Arts, Director of Public Works, and Master of the Revels. After the collapse of Il Moro's fortunes, Leonardo found new patrons in Caesar Borgia, the Pope, and the French kings, Louis XII and Francis I, ambitious rulers all. The popes employed Leonardo, Botticelli,

Michelangelo, and many other leading artists to adorn the Vatican and to design the great basilica of St. Peter's.

The painters of the Renaissance again and again chose to work on Madonnas, the Nativity, the Crucifixion, and all the rest of the grand Christian themes. But they interpreted them in their own individual ways, realistically or piously. And they applied equal skill to scenes from classical mythology, portraits of their secular contemporaries, and other subjects remote from the Christian tradition. The contrast between the sacred and the secular, however, was seldom clear-cut. In the Peruzzi Chapel at Florence, for example, Giotto placed around a religious fresco a border of medallions portraying the leading members of the sponsoring family. Giotto's successors often introduced into a sacred painting the person who had commissioned it, and they sometimes brought in the whole family (see the illustration on p. 61). Usually the patron assumed a duly reverent posture, but there

Botticelli, "Primavera" (Spring).

was often more than a hint of the acumen and ambition that had won him worldly success and permitted him to afford the luxury of commissioning a work of art. It is hard to tell whom such paintings were intended to honor more, God or the donor.

Masaccio, "Expulsion of Adam and Eve from Eden."

Ambiguities also clouded the treatment of pagan and classical themes in the Renaissance. When painters depicted gods and goddesses in a proper classical setting, sometimes in a proper pagan state of undress, the result was seldom fully pagan. For example, there is nothing crude or carnal in the exquisite paintings of Botticelli (1445-1510). Still another great figure in the almost endless file of great Florentines, Botticelli painted the famous *Primavera*, a pagan allegory of Spring. The figures in the *Primavera* are, from left to right, Mercury, the messenger of the gods; the lightly clad Three Graces; a more heavily draped Venus; the goddess Flora, bedecked with flowers; and Spring herself, blown in by the West Wind. They all have tiny feet; all are slender, youthful, almost dainty; and many of them have a detached and sweetly sad expression.

Indeed, it may be argued that Botticelli was to painting what the mystics of the Platonic Academy were to humanism. He seems to have moved in the circle of Pico della Mirandola at Florence, and his paintings often suggest an aspiration to some lofty Platonic realm. Botticelli also felt the drive of religious emotion. He rallied to the reforming friar, Savonarola, who briefly imposed a puritanical regime on Florence in the late 1490's (see below, p. 71). And when Savonarola prescribed the burning of all worldly "vanities," so the story has it, Botticelli threw some of his paintings of nudes onto the flames.

The most significant contributor to the advance of painting techniques in the fifteenth century was Masaccio (1401-c. 1428). A student also of sculpture and architecture, Masaccio strove to create the impression of three dimensions on the two-dimensional surface of a picture. In painting the expulsion from the Garden of Eden, he conveyed the shame and the sorrow of Adam and Eve both by their facial expressions and by the forlorn posture of their bodies. He intensified the dramatic impact of the scene by using somber colors appropriate to the tragedy. And he achieved a three-dimensional effect by employing bold contrasts of light and shadow on the bodies. Masaccio had the rare gift of stripping a situation down to its essentials and concentrating upon them.

Where Masaccio stressed human nature, other artists strove for the more faithful representation of the natural environment. A botanist can identify the plants and flowers in Botticelli's *Primavera*. Where Masaccio relied, as it were, on mass to achieve his artistic effects, some of his contemporaries and followers turned to line and to color. Uccello (c.1396-1475) in his battle

Leonardo da Vinci, "The Madonna of the Rocks" (Louvre, Paris).

scenes arranged soldiers and lances at the angles that would best create the illusion of depth. Botticelli was a superb colorist, and such a painstaking draughtsman that he seems to have brushed in every single hair on a human head.

Leonardo, Michelangelo, Titian

The major trends we have been following in patronage, subject matter, and technical proficiency reached a climax with Leonardo, Michelangelo, and Titian. Leonardo da Vinci (1452-1519) kept voluminous notebooks detailing his theories and activities. From them comes this statement of his aesthetic ideals:

. . . Since, as we know, painting embraces and contains within itself . . . whatever can be comprehended by the eyes, it would seem to me that he is but a poor master who makes only a single figure well.

For do you not see how many and how varied are the actions which are performed by men alone? Do you not see how many different kinds of animals there are, and also of trees and plants and flowers? What variety of hilly and level places, of springs, rivers, cities, public and private buildings; of instruments fitted for man's use; of divers costumes, ornaments and arts?—Things which should be rendered with equal facility and grace by whoever you wish to call a painter.

. . .

The painter will produce pictures of little merit if he takes the works of others as his standard; but if he will apply himself to learn from the objects of nature he will produce good results.*

Leonardo followed his own advice about studying nature afresh. From his intensive study of human anatomy he drew up rules for indicating the actions of human muscles and for establishing the proportions between the parts of the human body. He investigated plants, animals, and the earth itself. The result may be observed in the picture of Leonardo's illustrated on page 59, the Madonna of the Rocks. The plants and flowers have the accuracy of plates in a textbook. The arrangement of the figures in a pyramid, the foreshortening of the arms, the fineness of the hair, and the care-

---

* *The Notebooks of Leonardo da Vinci*, Edward MacCurdy, ed. (New York, n.d.), II, 256, 276

ful painting of the folds in the draperies show Leonardo's geometrical sense and his expert draughtsmanship. Beyond all this, Leonardo quietly insists on the religious beauty of the scene, as the angel (on the right) supports the infant Jesus and points to the young St. John, kneeling reverently.

While Leonardo got on reasonably well with his patrons, the strong-minded Michelangelo Buonarotti (1475-1564) had very poor luck. He quarreled violently and repeatedly with his most important backer, the imperious and wrathful Pope Julius II. Julius needed all his high-handedness to persuade Michelangelo to paint the ceiling of the Sistine Chapel. It was a prodigious piece of work. The area is approximately fourteen yards by forty, and Michelangelo covered it with 343 separate figures. He executed the whole in the space of four years, working almost single-handed, assisted only by a plasterer and a color-mixer, painting uncomfortably on his back atop a scaffolding, sometimes not bothering to descend for his night's rest, and arguing stormily with the impatient pope, who dared to complain of the painter's slow rate of progress. For this massive undertaking Michelangelo boldly chose not a simple subject but a series of the grandest scenes from Genesis —the creation of the sun and moon, God hovering over the waters, the creation of Adam and of Eve, the eating of the forbidden fruit, and the expulsion from Paradise. Throughout, the recurring form is that most appropriate to a great sculptor-painter, the human nude, particularly the male. In this vast gallery of nudes in all types of poses Michelangelo summed up all that Renaissance art had learned about perspective, anatomy, and motion.

Both Michelangelo and Leonardo received their artistic training in Florence; now we come to a Renaissance master who was identified with Venice. Titian (1477-1576) had in some respects the most remarkable career of any artist in that remarkable age. He produced an average of one picture a month for eighty years and in his nineties still retained much of the skill of his prime. Even a partial listing of the commissions he received underscores again the wide range and appeal of Renaissance painting. At the start of his career in Venice, Titian was hired to do frescoes for the headquarters of the German merchant colony. Then he undertook portraits for rich merchants, altarpieces and madonnas for churches and monasteries, and a great battle scene for the palace of the Doge. Titian became so famous that he received offers from half the despots of Italy and crowned heads of Europe. The Habsburg Emperor Charles V and Charles' son, Philip II of Spain, were his patrons.

Titian transferred to paint much of the flamboyance and pageantry identified with Venice. Rich, intense colors, particularly reds and purples, are his hallmark. And he accomplished wonders of design and characterization. When he painted the Assumption of the Virgin for a place high up in a church, he distorted the figures so that they would seem right to the viewers below and would at the same time direct their eyes upward. The Virgin herself was a majestic

Titian, "Vendramin Family in Adoration."

figure, ascending to Heaven effortlessly. A gallery of Titian's portraits would make a splendid introduction to the high politics, and politicians, of the sixteenth century. There is Paul III, one of the last of the Renaissance popes, ambitious and authoritative. And there is a *condottiere* from the successful family of the della Rovere, at once handsome and worn, cultivated and shrewd. Titian even accomplished the artistic miracle of making the undistinguished-looking Charles V seem reasonably imperial (see illustration on p. 80).

Northern European Painting

The fame and influence of Titian and many other Italians reached far beyond Italy itself and helped to stimulate the flowering of northern European painting in the sixteenth century. This northern Renaissance was centered chiefly in southern Germany and in the Low Countries. Its leading artists were Albrecht Dürer (1471-1528) and Hans Holbein (c.1497-1543), Germans both, and Pieter Breughel the Elder (c.1520-1569), who was born near Brussels.

The northern artists often shared Italian tastes in subject matter. Holbein executed handsome paintings and sketches of his contemporaries, notably Henry VIII, the second Tudor king (see illustration on p. 128). Dürer's realistic yet compassionate portrait of his aged and homely mother might almost have been taken from da Vinci's sketch book. Dürer, in fact, came close to being the Leonardo of Germany. He collected monkeys and other tropical specimens, painted the Virgin in the unusual pose of a Madonna with Many Animals, and, in the closing years of his career, wrote treatises on perspective and human proportions. On the other hand, Dürer also showed some of the differences between northern and Italian art. He worked not only with

paints but also with copper engraving and woodcuts, which permitted the reproduction of drawings in many copies. These new techniques brought Dürer closer than any Italian to the rapidly expanding public of readers; they made him in effect the first artist in history to become a "best-seller."

Two other traits set northern painting apart from Italian. Breughel illustrated one of them in his fondness for scenes of peasant weddings, dances, and festivals, executed with a Rabelaisian gusto. He also painted a series of lovely landscapes showing the cycle of farming activities during the various months of the year. Here Breughel was not striving deliberately to be popular, as Dürer sought popularity through the mass production of engravings and woodcuts; wealthy individuals commissioned most of Breughel's plebeian subjects. Lastly, northern art retained the old medieval fascination with the monstrous and supernatural. Dürer showed this Gothic strain in a series of sixteen woodcuts depicting the Four Horsemen and the other grim marvels of the Apocalypse. In Breughel, the strain appears over and over. His Tower of Babel is a decayed skyscraper, massive and somewhat unclean. And his bizarre Battle of the Angels and the Demons is full of "things" whose nearest relatives populate the science fiction and the surrealist art of the twentieth century—coats-of-arms that actually fight, shellfish that fly, hybrids with insect wings, artichoke bodies, and flower heads. Most of these fantasies were designed to teach a moral lesson; they were sermons in paint or ink, almost as the Gothic cathedrals had been sermons in stone.

Sculpture

The sculptors of the Renaissance, like the painters, took their art out of the church, turned to classical models and secular themes, studied human anatomy, and experimented with new techniques.

Some of these innovations stand forth clearly in the equestrian statue of General Gattemalata by Donatello (c.1386-1466), a Florentine, and the earliest of the great names in Renaissance sculpture. The subject was secular: the general was a famous *condottiere* of the fifteenth century. The treatment was classical: he was costumed as an ancient Roman and looked able to command a crack legion. When Donatello took sacred subjects, he approached these old problems and themes in new ways. In a masterpiece like the statue of Mary Magdalen, he transcended literal realism and heightened the dramatic and emotional effect by exaggeration. A critic has called the saint "an emaciated monster." Emaciated the figure certainly is, all skin and bone, lank hair and ragged clothing; but everything about it accents the vertical line and contributes to its extraordinary gaunt and haggard quality. Mary Magdalen is a saint who looks the part.

Half a century after Donatello, the genius of Michelangelo brought sculpture to the highest summit it had reached since the days of the Greeks, perhaps the highest in the whole record of the art. The man who painted the Sistine ceiling single-handed brought the same daring conceptions and concentrated energy to his sculptures. Early in his career, the government of Florence offered him the exacting task of creating something beautiful from an enormous chunk of marble that another artist had already attempted in vain. He produced a colossal statue of David, its ham-like hands and its tense and powerful muscles furnishing a great lesson in masculine anatomy. In portraying the Virgin grieving over the dead Christ (see illustration on p. 64), Michelangelo brilliantly solved the difficult technical problem of posing a seated woman with a corpse lying across her lap, and he triumphantly called attention to his feat by executing the work in highly polished marble. The face of Mary is sorrowful yet

Donatello, "Mary Magdalen," about 1455.

composed, and younger than that of the dead Christ. She is the eternal Virgin, Michelangelo explained, and so is always youthful and does not grieve passionately as an earthly mother would.

Architecture

In 1546, at the age of seventy, Michelangelo shouldered one more artistic burden: he agreed to be the chief architect of St. Peter's. Michelangelo died long before the great Roman basilica was finally completed in 1626, and his successors altered many of his details. But the great dome, the key feature of the whole structure, followed his basic design. St. Peter's shows most of the characteristics that separate the architectural style of the Renaissance from the Gothic of the High Middle Ages. Instead of great spires and towers, it has Michelangelo's dome, which rises 435 feet above the floor below, yet is dwarfed in mass by the immense building underneath. Gothic structures, with their great windows, pointed arches, and high-flung vaults, create an impression of strain and instability. St. Peter's, on the other hand, with its round arches, heavier walls, and stout columns, seems to have been built for eternity.

St. Peter's also has the symmetry so admired by Renaissance builders; everything about it fits into a tidy geometrical pattern. The balanced character of the whole edifice is enhanced by the magnificent pair of identical curving colonnades which were built in the early seventeenth century in the great square outside the basilica and which sweep the eye of the approaching visitor straight to the church of the pope himself. The architects of the Renaissance thus incorporated many elements used fifteen hundred and more years earlier in the buildings of

Michelangelo, "Pietà," in St. Peter's, Rome.

classical antiquity—domes, columns, round arches, geometrical symmetry. They seldom copied a classical building outright, however; what they really admired was the over-all conception of classical architecture, its grandeur, its balance, its huge dimensions.

The total architectural record of the Renaissance includes a large number of palaces, chateaux, villas, and other purely secular buildings. This conspicuous display of worldly wealth was partly a matter of the decline of medieval values and the rise of secular pride. But it was also a simple question of economics and security. The expansion of business gave private individuals the money to finance the construction of lavish residences. The gradual growth of effective government meant that, even in the country, a man's home could be a showplace and no longer had to be, quite literally, his castle.

In the Italian countryside elaborate symmetrical villas began to appear. In Venice palaces lined the Grand Canal, the chief thoroughfare, almost solidly from one end to the other. The scale and design of the Renaissance palaces thoroughly expressed the prevailing taste for the monumental. The Pitti Palace, erected in fifteenth-century Florence by a millionaire rival of the Medici, was 475 feet long and 114 feet high. Architects relieved the monotonous regularity of such buildings by decorative devices like pillars, pilasters, and cornices, and by using a different finish of stone for each story, with the roughest at the bottom.

The fame of Italian builders soon spread throughout Europe, even to distant Moscow, where Italian experts supervised the remodeling of the Kremlin. Most countries did not just copy the Italian style but grafted it onto the older native architecture. The resulting compound produced some very striking buildings, particularly the great chateaux of central France. The "chateau country" of the Loire Valley contains perhaps the most graceful and elegant private residences ever constructed. The tasteful combination of elements from the Gothic church, the feudal castle, and the Italian palace gives these chateaux the magic and the unreality of buildings in a fairy tale.

Music

The structure of music is often called architectural. A musical composition, like a building, has its basic skeleton or form, its over-all line, and also its surface decorations and embellishments. In the Middle Ages, sacred music had achieved very complex and elaborate combinations of form, line, and decoration. The center of this Gothic music was northern France and the Low Countries. By the fifteenth century, French and Flemish musicians were journeying to Italy, where a double set of influences came into play. The northerners took up the simple tuneful melodies of folk songs and dances; the Italians, in turn, added a strain of Gothic complexity to the austere plain-song that had long been the mainstay of their sacred music. The end-product of this interaction was the beautiful sacred music of the Italian composer, Palestrina (c.1525-1594), at once intricate in the northern manner and devout in the Italian.

Music was probably affected less than the other arts by the secularism and the individualism of the Renaissance. Yet the composers and performers of music showed the experimental bent of the Renaissance. They developed or imported new instruments— the violin, double-bass, and harpsichord; the organ, with a goodly complement of keyboards, pedals, and stops; and the kettledrum, which was adopted from the Polish army. The retinue of musicians became a fixture of court life, with the Dukes of Burgundy, Philip the Good and Charles the Bold, leading the way. Castiglione, an Italian authority on etiquette, thought music proper for every social station:

St. Peter's, Rome.

We may see it used in the holy temples to render laud and thanks unto God, and it is a credible matter . . . that He hath given it unto us for a most sweet lightening of our travails and vexations. So that many times the boisterous laborers in the fields, in the heat of the sun, beguile their pain with rude and carterlike singing. With this the unmannerly countrywoman, that ariseth before day out of sleep to spin and card, defendeth herself and maketh her labor pleasant. This is the most sweet pastime after rain, wind, and tempest unto the miserable mariners. With this do the weary pilgrims comfort themselves in their troublesome and long voyages.*

---

* Castiglione, *The Courtier*, T. Hoby, trans., modernized (1907), 77.

VI: *Science*

Science is a field of human endeavor where the term "Renaissance" must be used with special caution. A great upsurge of scientific activity did come in early modern history, but it came in the seventeenth century when the Renaissance had run its course (see Chapter VI). In the history of science, the fifteenth and sixteenth centuries were largely a time of preparation. Scientists absorbed and digested the body of knowledge handed down to them from the Middle Ages. By criticizing and modifying the earlier work they prepared the way for later achievements.

Leonardo da Vinci is a good example of both the shortcomings and the achievements of Renaissance science. On the one hand, he took notes in a random manner, quite unscientifically, and in a left-handed "mirror writing," which must be held up to a mirror to be read. He kept his famous notebooks as secret as a diary. In short, he did not have the modern scientist's interest in the systematic cataloguing of observations and the frequent publication of findings and speculations. On the other hand, Leonardo did have the true scientist's passion for investigation. Witness his engrossing concern with anatomy and proportion, with almost everything about man and nature. He had a real genius for invention. He perfected or projected pumps, lathes, war-machines, flying machines, and many other instruments and contraptions. Finally, Leonardo contributed to the major areas of Renaissance scientific activity—technology and invention, anatomy and medicine—with the one exception of astronomy. Our survey of Renaissance science will be centered on these areas, beginning with technology and invention.

In these applied sciences, it is difficult to settle on a few outstanding names. For instance, Gutenberg, the supposed inventor of movable type, has become the focus of a scholarly controversy that has largely "debunked" his old heroic reputation. The revolution in book production began when medieval Europeans imported paper from China and found it to be cheaper than the lambskin or sheepskin previously used by copyists. The next step came when engravers, pioneering in the methods later used by Dürer, made woodcuts or copper plates that could produce many copies of the same drawing. Then sentences were added to the cuts or plates explaining the sketches. Finally, almost certainly in Germany in the 1440's, Gutenberg or someone else devised movable type. Each piece of type was simply a minute bit of engraving; it could be combined with other pieces to form words, sentences, a whole page, and then salvaged to be used over and over again. Everywhere the printing press suddenly made literature available to large numbers of people who could never have afforded hand-copied manuscripts. Without the perfecting of printing, Erasmus might not have become the acknowledged arbiter of European letters. Without it, Luther could not have secured the rapid distribution of his anti-papal tracts, and the Protestant Reformation might not have shaken Christian Europe to its foundations.

Many other inventions and innovations ultimately exerted an influence of comparable magnitude. Gunpowder, for example, also brought from China to medieval Europe, was used in the fighting of the early 1400's, notably the later campaigns of the Hundred Years' War. The long, slow improvement of firearms and artillery doomed both the feudal knight and the feudal castle, for both were vulnerable to the new weapons. In navigation, the Venetians designed swift and relatively capacious galleys capable of sailing in the Atlantic. Important aids to navigation came into general use, particularly the magnetic compass and relatively accurate sailing charts. By the close of the fifteenth century, Europeans possessed the equipment needed for the oncoming age of world discovery and empire-building.

Medical knowledge advanced very unevenly during the Renaissance. Though anatomical studies moved ahead, the practical application of this knowledge to suffering humanity lagged, often very badly. Many so-called physicians were outright quacks; many teachers of medicine simply repeated for their classes ancient Roman demonstrations without attempting to test the validity of the findings. The physicians and scholars associated with the University of Padua in Italy, however, constituted a striking exception to the prevailing custom of accepting authorities unquestioningly.

In 1537, a young Belgian named Vesalius (1514-1564) took a teaching post at Padua. In 1543, he published *De Humanis Corporis Fabrica* (Concerning the Structure of the Human Body). In this great anatomical study Vesalius largely confirmed the teachings of older authorities, but he also pointed out some of their shortcomings. He prepared the work with admirable concern for accuracy and detail, and the elaborate woodcuts established a new standard of excellence in scientific illustration.

The year 1543 was a landmark in the history of scientific publication. Not only did it mark the appearance of Vesalius' treatise; it was also the year in which Copernicus launched modern astronomical studies with *De Revolutionibus Orbium Coelestium* (Concerning the Revolutions of Heavenly Bodies). Nicholas Copernicus (1473-1543) furnishes still another example of Renaissance versatility. Born in Poland, of German extraction, he studied law and medicine at Padua and other Italian universities, spent thirty years as canon of a cathedral near Danzig, and made his real career in mathematics and astronomy. His scientific work led him to attack the traditional hypothesis of the *geocentric* (earth-centered) universe derived from Ptolemy and other astronomers of antiquity. In its place, he advanced the revolutionary new hypothesis of the *heliocentric* (sun-centered) universe.

The concept of the geocentric universe generally accepted in the sixteenth century included an elaborate system of spheres. Around the stationary earth there revolved some eighty spheres, each, as it were, a separate sky containing some of the heavenly bodies, each moving on an invisible circular path, each transparent so that we mortals could see the spheres beyond it. This imaginative and symmetrical picture of the universe had already come under attack before the time of Copernicus. Now and again scientists had had trouble making it agree with the observable behavior of heavenly bodies. Copernicus apparently used both these earlier criticisms and his own computations in arriving at the heliocentric concept.

Once Copernicus had made the sun and the earth exchange roles, his universe retained many Ptolemaic characteristics. Its heavens were still filled with spheres revolving along their invisible orbits. Only they now moved about a stationary sun, instead of the stationary earth, and Copernican astronomy required only thirty-four of them, not eighty. The revolution in astronomy begun by Copernicus did not reach its culmination for a hundred and fifty years. The *circular* orbits of Copernicus had to yield to *elliptical* orbits; the scheme of thirty-four spheres had to be modified; and a theory explaining the forces that kept the universe together had to be put forward. And all these developments had to await the genius of Galileo and Newton, and the detailed observations that were made possible with the invention of the telescope.

VII: Religion

By the time Copernicus published, Christianity was split into the warring factions of Catholic and Protestant. This great religious crisis was the outgrowth of the unresolved religious problems accompanying the Renaissance. The Renaissance might never have led to the Protestant Reformation if the Catholic Church of the 1400's and early 1500's had been relatively strong and healthy, relatively free of corruption. But, except in Spain, the Church was nowhere strong or healthy. The ambitious popes of the Renaissance did little to restore to the Church the prestige and power it had lost in the Babylonian Captivity and the Great Schism. Powerful monarchs, meantime, had profited by ecclesiastical weakness to redefine the relations of Church and State, and always on terms advantageous to the latter, as in the Pragmatic Sanction of Bourges. Meantime, also, the Church had been obliged to contend with movements aiming at its reform, movements that were revolutionary in their implications. At the top there was the Conciliar Movement of the early fifteenth century, which vainly attempted to replace papal absolutism with a kind of constitutional monarchy; further down, at the roots, were the movements associated with John Wiclif and John Hus.

Wiclif, an Oxford scholar who died in 1384, advocated a church without property in the spirit of the early Christians; he called, too, for the abolition or weakening of many of the functions of the priest. He and his followers were responsible for the preparation and circulation of an English translation of the Bible—a significant instance of the growing strength of the vernacular and of nationalism in fourteenth-century England. Wiclif's views were heretical, for the Church had long insisted that the priest was the indispensable intermediary between man and God, and that the Bible should remain in its Latin version, the famous Vulgate. The ferment begun by Wiclif boiled over in the English Peasants' Revolt of 1381. The rebels were protesting against royal taxation and against the surviving remnants of serfdom, but one of their chief targets was clerical wealth. Although the forces of the English monarchy suppressed the Peasants' Revolt with great severity, the anticlericalism of the movement lived on.

John Hus (1369-1415), who absorbed Wiclif's doctrines when he was studying at Oxford, lived in Bohemia, the western province of modern Czechoslovakia. The Hussite movement which he led was a compound of religious and social aims, with a strong component of Czech nationalism. Hus wanted to end many clerical abuses, notably the domination of the Church in Bohemia by German prelates. He himself was condemned as a heretic by the Church Council meeting at Constance in 1415 and was burnt at the stake. His heresy, however, was merely driven underground to emerge once more in the age of the Protestant Reformation.

Few critics of the Church in the days of

humanism carried their attacks as far as Wiclif and Hus had carried theirs. Most critics simply cried out against those clerics who obviously fell short of the ideals that they had solemnly vowed to observe. The tone of the Renaissance was often anticlerical but seldom anti-Christian. If we look back over the varied aspects of Renaissance civilization, we find a good deal that can at least be reconciled to Christianity, comparatively little that cannot. Naturally, the materialism, the self-indulgence, and the power politics of the Renaissance could become truly anti-Christian if they were carried to extremes. Only the most ruthless *condottieri* of politics and business, men like the Fuggers and Caesar Borgia, reached the extreme, and even they remained nominal Christians. Perhaps Boccaccio and Rabelais were at bottom authentic enemies of the Christian spirit. Yet much of the fun in the *Decameron* and in the adventures of Gargantua and Pantagruel comes from the mocking of clerical misbehavior, which was certainly a proper object of satire. In any case, most humanists did not scoff at essential Christian values; Pico and Erasmus proposed to enrich or purify Christianity, not to subvert it.

In the religious crisis accompanying the Renaissance the Church was to some extent the innocent victim of great secular forces operating beyond its control, but it suffered in much greater measure from its own shortcomings. From top to bottom, the Renaissance Church exhibited a low moral tone. Pope Sixtus IV (1471-1484), for example, built for the Vatican the Sistine Chapel which bears his name; otherwise he used most of his power to promote the fortunes of his large family of nephews and nieces. Julius II (1503-1513), a nephew of Sixtus IV, undertook with ferocious energy wars, political expansion, and artistic patronage, but not the full execution of his ecclesiastical duties. Leo X (1513-1521), the son of Lorenzo de' Medici, transplanted to Rome some of the cultivated humanism of the Platonic Academy, but he, too, showed scant awareness of the fact that he was the Vicar of Christ.

The modern world owes to the patronage of the Renaissance popes the Vatican Library, the ceiling of the Sistine Chapel, and the Basilica of St. Peter. The debt is a large one. Yet the Roman Catholic Church might still be catholic in fact as well as in name if these *condottieri* and connoisseurs had not been elected to the See of Peter. Their magnificence cost immense sums of money and increased the burden of ecclesiastical taxation, and with it increased the resentment that higher taxes usually arouse. Their indifference to their spiritual functions enfeebled the Church at a time when it needed firm and dedicated control.

Further down the clerical hierarchy, conditions were little better. Many bishops—following good medieval precedent, it must be admitted—behaved as statesmen, not churchmen. Priests were often illiterate and uneducated, and sometimes immoral, too, quite unfitted to exercise their parochial duties. Some of the monks and friars on university faculties hardly qualified as teachers; they sought mainly to frustrate the new humanist studies that might have revitalized the intellectual life of the clergy.

Honorable exceptions to the prevailing backwardness and laxity of the clergy existed, but they were still only exceptions and did not exert a wide influence. The Brethren of the Common Life, founded in the Low Countries about 1375, revivified the high Christian ideal of service. This semi-monastic organization, partly composed of laymen, carried on educational and charitable works; its influence, however, did not extend much beyond the Low Countries. In the secular hierarchy, where the bishops exerted monarchical authority over priests and the pope over all, serious-minded clerics wanted to increase the powers of representative councils. But their attempts failed to overcome the papal opposition that had defeated the earlier Conciliar Movement. The most turbulent of the reforming currents, finally, the one set in motion by Savonarola, had the shortest course.

Savonarola (1452-1498) preached in the very capital of Renaissance culture, Florence, and demanded sweeping changes in Christian behavior. A Dominican friar, he won the favor of the Medici through the influence of Pico della Mirandola; his eloquent sermons and reputed gift of predicting future events soon made him the most popular preacher in Florence. Savonarola spared no clerics in his strictures on unChristian conduct:

You Christians should always have the Gospel with you, I do not mean the book, but the spirit, for if you do not possess the spirit of grace and yet carry with you the whole book, of what advantage is it to you? And again, all the more foolish are they who carry round their necks Breviaries, notes, tracts and writings, until they look like pedlars going to a fair. Charity does not consist in the writing of papers. The true books of Christ are the Apostles and saints, and true reading consists in imitating their lives. But in these days men are like books made by the Devil. They speak against pride and ambition and yet they are immersed in them up to their eyes. They preach chastity and maintain concubines. They enjoin fasting and partake of splendid feasts. . . . Only look to-day at the prelates. They are tied to earthly vanities. They love them. The cure of souls is no longer their chief concern. . . . In the Primitive Church the chalices were made of wood and the prelates of gold—to-day—chalices of gold, prelates of wood!*

Savonarola particularly abominated Pope Alexander VI, whom he cursed for "a devil" presiding over what he labeled a "harlot" Church.

In the political confusion resulting from the death of Lorenzo the Magnificent (1492), Savonarola rapidly gained power and prestige. He attracted many enthusiastic supporters, among them Botticelli and Michelangelo. By 1497, he was virtually dictator of Florence and organized troops of boys and girls to tour the city, collect all "vanities," from cosmetics to "pagan" books and paintings, and burn them on public bonfires. This high pitch of puritanism could not be sustained for long, however. Savonarola was excommunicated by Alexander VI and condemned for heresy; on May 23, 1498, he was hanged and his body was burnt. Savonarola perished not only at the hands of his enemies but also by his own uncompromising violence. Like most extreme puritans, he was more a fanatic than a saint; he was in a sense too unworldly to survive. But the Church that he sought to cleanse was too worldly to survive without undergoing the major crisis of the Reformation.

---

* Quoted by Piero Misciatelli, *Savonarola* (New York, 1930), 60-61.

VIII: Conclusion: The Renaissance Style

We have discussed the Renaissance in terms of its complexity and the versatility of its great men. To seek a distinctive Renaissance "style," then, may seem absurd. Neither one single masterpiece nor one single person was fully "typical" of the Renaissance; and yet there is something about them all that places them apart from the great works and great figures of other ages in history. That something is presented most sympathetically and disarmingly in a dialogue published in 1528, *The Courtier* by Castiglione.

A good solid book of etiquette sometimes reveals much about a whole way of life. Castiglione begins his delineation of the ideal courtier with a group of traits differing very little from those commended in the paladins of medieval chivalry:

I will have this our Courtier to be a gentleman born and of a good house. For it is a great deal less dispraise for him that is not born a gentleman to fail in the acts of virtue than for a gentleman.

I will have him by nature to have not only a wit and a comely shape of person and countenance, but also a certain grace, and, as they say, a hue, that shall make him at the first sight acceptable and loving unto who so beholdeth him.

I judge the principal and true profession of a Courtier ought to be in feats of arms, the which above all I will have him to practise lively.*

With Castiglione, however, chivalry is restrained by the Renaissance sense of balance and grasp of reality. In love, the perfect gentleman should adore in his lady "no less the beauty of the mind than of the body." In duels and private quarrels, he should be far more moderate than the medieval knight was ever supposed to be. He should excel in sport, like the knight of old, should hunt, wrestle, swim, "play at tennis." Then, again, Castiglione sounds the note of balance:

Therefore will I have our Courtier to descend many times to more easy and pleasant exercises. And to avoid envy and to keep company pleasantly with every man, let him do whatsoever other men do.†

The courtier should also receive a good education

. . . in those studies which they call Humanity, and to have not only the understanding of the Latin tongue, but also of the Greek, because of the many and sundry things that with great excellency are written in it. Let him much exercise himself in poets, and no less in orators and historiographers, and also in writing both rhyme and prose, and especially in this our vulgar tongue.**

---

* Adapted from Castiglione, *The Courtier*, T. Hoby, trans., modernized (1907), 21, 23, 26.
† *Ibid.*, 35.
** *Ibid.*, 70.

Here Castiglione is not simply writing a manual of good manners; he is advancing the celebrated Renaissance concept of the "universal man," the well-rounded individual skilled in all human pursuits.

Finally, when Castiglione praises beauty, he is putting into words, if anyone did, the style of the Renaissance:

Behold the state of this great engine of the world, which God created for the health and preservation of everything that was made: The heaven round beset with so many heavenly lights; and in the middle the Earth environed with the elements and upheld with the very weight of itself. . . . These things among themselves have such force by the knitting together of an order so necessarily framed that, with altering them any one jot, they should all be loosed and the world would decay. They have also such beauty and comeliness that all the wits men have can not imagine a more beautiful matter.

Think now of the shape of man, which may be called a little world, in whom every parcel of his body is seen to be necessarily framed by art and not by hap, and then the form altogether most beautiful. . . . Leave Nature, and come to art. . . . Pillars and great beams uphold high buildings and palaces, and yet are they no less pleasureful unto the eyes of the beholders than profitable to the buildings. . . . Besides other things, therefore, it giveth a great praise to the world in saying that it is beautiful. It is praised in saying the beautiful heaven, beautiful earth, beautiful sea, beautiful rivers, beautiful woods, trees, gardens, beautiful cities, beautiful churches, houses, armies. In conclusion, this comely and holy beauty is a wondrous setting out of everything. And it may be said that good and beautiful be after a sort one self thing. . . .*

A medieval man might also have coupled the good and the beautiful, but he would have stressed the good, the mysterious ways in which God led man to righteousness. Castiglione seemed to take God and religion rather for granted. Medieval man had had a vision of God's world. The age of Leonardo and of humanism, which Castiglione interpreted so eloquently, had a vision of nature's world and man's world.

---

* *Ibid.*, 348-349.

Reading Suggestions on the Renaissance

General Accounts

E. P. Cheyney, *The Dawn of a New Era, 1250-1453* (N.Y.: Harper, 1936); and M. Gilmore, *The World of Humanism, 1453-1517* (N.Y.: Harper, 1952). Two volumes in the important *Rise of Modern Europe* series edited by W. L. Langer; provide good introductory accounts and have full bibliographies.

W. K. Ferguson, *The Renaissance* (N.Y.: Holt, 1940), and *The Renaissance in Historical Thought* (Boston: Houghton, Mifflin, 1948). Respectively, a brief introduction and a stimulating special study by a sound modern scholar.

J. Burckhardt, *The Civilization of the Renaissance in Italy* (many editions). An old and very celebrated book; its interpretations are now accepted only with serious modification.

J. A. Symonds, *Renaissance in Italy* (N.Y.: Modern Library). Another old and famous work, as controversial as Burckhardt's.

Special Studies: The Material and Political Background

H. Heaton, *Economic History of Europe*, rev. ed. (N.Y.: Harper, 1948). An excellent survey.

F. C. Lane, *Venetian Ships and Shipping of the Renaissance* (Baltimore: Johns Hopkins Univ. Press, 1934). A highly interesting monograph.

M. Beard, *A History of the Business Man* (N.Y.: Macmillan, 1938). Contains good sketches of Renaissance millionaires.

H. Baron, *The Crisis of the Early Italian Renaissance: Civic Humanism and Republican Liberty in an Age of Classicism and Tyranny*, 2 vols. (Princeton: Princeton Univ. Press, 1955).

A. W. O. von Martin, *Sociology of the Renaissance* (N.Y.: Oxford Univ. Press, 1941). A helpful study of Italian society in the fourteenth and fifteenth centuries.

F. Schevill, *A History of Florence* (N.Y.: Harcourt, Brace, 1936), and *The Medici* (N.Y.: Harcourt, Brace, 1949). Useful studies by a modern American scholar.

G. F. Young, *The Medici* (N.Y.: Modern Library). Very readable but not very objective.

R. Sabatini, *Life of Cesare Borgia* (Boston: Houghton, Mifflin, 1924). A colorful account by the author of swashbuckling historical novels.

H. Butterfield, *The Statecraft of Machiavelli* (London: Bell, 1940) and J. H. Whitfield, *Machiavelli* (Oxford: Blackwell, 1947). Contrasting evaluations, Butterfield's rather unfavorable, and Whitfield's more indulgent.

C. W. S. Williams, *Henry VII* (London: Barker, 1937). A modern study of the first Tudor.

P. Champion, *Louis XI* (N.Y.: Dodd, Mead, 1929). A solid, popular account.

R. B. Merriman, *The Rise of the Spanish Empire*, Vol. II (N.Y.: Macmillan, 1918). Perhaps the best account of Ferdinand and Isabella in English.

Special Studies: Literature, the Arts, Religion

G. Highet, *The Classical Tradition: Greek and Roman Influences on Western Literature* (N.Y.: Oxford Univ. Press, 1949). A lively and scholarly account.

H. O. Taylor, *Thought and Expression in the Sixteenth Century*, rev. ed. (N.Y.: Macmillan, 1930). A sound and suggestive work.

F. Antal, *Florentine Painting and Its Social Background* (London: Kegan Paul, 1948). Seeks to relate art to economic and social currents.

E. Panofsky, *Studies in Iconology: Humanistic Themes in the Art of the Renaissance* (N.Y.: Oxford Univ. Press, 1939). By a great modern expert in art history.

H. Wölfflin, *Classic Art: The Great Masters of the Italian Renaissance* (London: Phaidon, 1952). Reprint of an old and famous work.

K. M. Clark, *Leonardo da Vinci*, 2nd ed. (Cambridge, England: Cambridge Univ. Press, 1952). By a learned and witty English authority.

O. Benesch, *The Art of the Renaissance in Northern Europe: Its Relation to the Contemporary Spiritual and Intellectual Movements* (Cambridge, Mass.: Harvard Univ. Press, 1945).

R. Wittkower, *Architectural Principles in the Age of Humanism*, 2nd ed. (London: A. Tiranti, 1952). A notable attempt to show the connection between humanism and architecture.

P. H. Láng, *Music in Western Civilization* (N.Y.: Norton, 1941), and C. Gray, *The History of Music*, 2nd ed. (N.Y.: Knopf, 1947). Two good general histories: Láng's an ambitious and detailed attempt to show relationships between music and other historical forces; Gray's a briefer, opinionated, lively book.

Special Studies: Science

F. S. Taylor, *A Short History of Science and Scientific Thought* (N.Y.: Norton, 1949). A useful introductory manual.

H. Butterfield, *The Origins of Modern Science, 1300-1800* (N.Y.: Macmillan, 1951). A work of major importance that has stirred up considerable controversy.

A. R. Hall, *The Scientific Revolution, 1500-1800: The Formation of the Modern Scientific Attitude* (Boston: Beacon, 1956). A sound general account.

L. Thorndike, *Science and Thought in the Fifteenth Century* (N.Y.: Columbia Univ. Press, 1929). An important study by a major historian of science.

Sources

E. Cassirer and others, eds., *The Renaissance Philosophy of Man* (Chicago: Univ. of Chicago Press. A Phoenix Book). Selections from the writings of Petrarch, Pico, and other humanists, with helpful editorial comments.

Three Renaissance Classics: Machiavelli's Prince, *Castiglione's* Courtier, *More's* Utopia. (N.Y.: Scribner's, 1953. Modern Student's Library).

Erasmus, *The Praise of Folly*, H. H. Hudson, trans. (Princeton: Princeton Univ. Press).

Rabelais, *Gargantua and Pantagruel*. The best translation is by Urquhart (many editions).

E. MacCurdy, ed., *The Notebooks of Leonardo da Vinci*, 2 vols. (N.Y.: Reynal and Hitchcock) and A. H. Popham, ed., *The Drawings of Leonardo da Vinci* (N.Y.: Reynal and Hitchcock). Fascinating records left by the great artist-scientist.

Historical Fiction

N. Balchin, *The Borgia Testament* (Boston: Houghton Mifflin, 1949). A fictional "autobiography" of Caesar Borgia.

W. Scott, *Quentin Durward* (many editions), and V. Hugo, *Notre Dame* (many editions). Two celebrated novels of the Romantic school, set in the France of Louis XI.

D. Merejkowski, *The Romance of Leonardo* (N.Y.: Modern Library). The best work of fiction dealing with the culture of the Renaissance.

C. Reade, *The Cloister and the Hearth* (many editions). Based on scholarly research and set on the Continent in the fifteenth century.

CHAPTER THREE

The Protestant

Reformation

I: Protestant Origins — Luther

In our usual scheme of breaking history up into periods, the Renaissance and the Reformation are closely linked, and are sometimes made to appear manifestations of some common spirit, such as individual freedom, democracy, modernity. And they are unquestionably related. Certainly in time they are roughly contemporary, though in space Protestantism never really got a foothold in the Mediterranean lands that were so important to the Renaissance. Through humanists like Erasmus the two movements meet. On the whole, it will make for clearer thinking if we consider the two movements as concerned with quite different aspects of man's cultural life, the Renaissance with the arts of living well, the Reformation with the problems of living as God wishes men to live. The thinkers and artists of the Renaissance were not for the most part anti-Christian, or even non-Christian, but their interests as Renaissance men were at least *tangential* to the central themes of Christianity. This is true even of the figures that

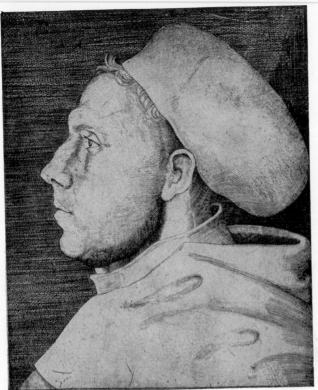

Martin Luther, by Cranach, 1521.

general council would consider the whole problem that Luther's activities had set.

Martin Luther (1483-1546), who began the Protestant Revolt, was a professor of divinity at the University of Wittenberg. His parents were peasants; his father became a miner and in time a prosperous investor in a mining enterprise. He sent Martin to study law, but in 1505 the young man had a shattering experience. Caught in a severe thunderstorm, the terrified Luther prayed to Saint Anne for help and pledged himself to become a monk. He joined the order of Augustinian canons in fulfillment of his pledge and then soon found himself in a major personal religious crisis.

The spiritual experiences of Luther inevitably look different to historians and biographers of different times and faiths. He was certainly a man capable of intense moral indignation; and he was probably a man afflicted in his early maturity by painful doubts about his personal salvation. Through his readings in the Epistles of St. Paul and the writings of St. Augustine, Luther at last found a positive answer to his anxiety. The answer was that man should have faith in God, faith in the possibility of his own salvation.

Fortified by his intense personal conviction of the great importance of faith, Luther questioned Catholic practices which in his view were abuses and tended to corrupt or weaken faith. He cast his questions in the form of the Ninety-Five Theses, as a challenge to academic debate. The specific abuse that Luther sought to prove un-Christian in the Ninety-Five Theses was the sale of indulgences, especially a current sale by a talented ecclesiastical fund-raiser named Tetzel. In our own language, Tetzel was conducting a "campaign" or "drive" for voluntary contributions of money to help fill the treasury of a great institution, an institution which like the state possessed taxing powers, but which like many modern states could not in fact extend those taxing

link the two movements together, men like Erasmus and other Christian humanists. The Protestants, however, were centrally concerned with the miraculous rule of God on earth; and their Puritanical wing simply refused to permit the devotion to the arts that was so central to the Renaissance.

Luther and the Ninety-Five Theses

The beginning of the Reformation can be precisely dated, in the sense that a "trigger event" like a battle can be said to begin a war. The beginning is October 31, 1517, when the Augustinian monk Martin Luther nailed his Ninety-Five Theses to the door of the court church at Wittenberg in the German state of Saxony. The actual term "protestant" dates from April 19, 1529, when a group of German princes professing Lutheran doctrines lodged a formal protest at the Diet of Spires against the annulment of an earlier imperial decree. This decree had promised that a

powers to keep up with the rising costs of an era of inflation and luxurious living. Tetzel was raising money to rebuild the great basilica of St. Peter's in Rome, and he had papal authorization for his sale of indulgences.

The theory of indulgences concerned the remission of some, at least, of the personal consequences of sin. The Church claimed authority to grant such remission by drawing on the Treasury of Merit, a storehouse of surplus good works accumulated by the holy activities of Christ, the Virgin, and the saints. Only the priest could secure for a layman a draft, as it were, on this heavenly treasury. Technically, indulgences were granted, not sold, but it was the practice for the recipient to make a monetary contribution to the Church when he received the indulgence.

The doctrine of indulgences was thus a complex matter, too complex for the ordinary layman to grasp completely. To the man in the street, it looked as though a sinner could obtain not only remission of punishment but also forgiveness of sin if only he secured enough indulgences. Men like Tetzel, by making extravagant claims for the power of their indulgences, strengthened this popular feeling. Luther objected not only to Tetzel's perversion of indulgences but also to the whole doctrine behind them. He phrased his objections with great vehemence in the Ninety-Five Theses:

20. The pope by his plenary remission of all penalties does not understand the remission of all penalties absolutely, but only of those imposed by himself.
21. Therefore those preachers of indulgences are in error who allege that through the indulgences of the pope a man is freed from every penalty.
22. For he remits to souls in purgatory no penalty which they had been bound, according to the canons, to pay in this life.
23. If any complete remission of penalties can be given to anyone it is sure that it can be given only to the most perfect; that is, to very few.
24. And therefore it follows that the greater

part of the people is deceived by this indiscriminate and liberal promising of freedom from penalty.*

At the highest level of formal theological thought, Luther's quarrel with his ecclesiastical superiors was over one of the oldest and most abiding issues of Christian thought, the issue of faith against good works. Now Christian practice usually insists on the need for *both* faith and good works. But at times of crisis some men pursue one extreme, others the other. In the years of crisis immediately after the posting of the Ninety-Five Theses, the challenged papal party stiffened into a resistance that in turn drove the Lutherans into further resistance.

Luther's Revolt   The Church was quick to sense the high importance of the issues that Luther had raised. In 1518, at Augsburg, Luther was summoned before a papal legate, Cardinal Cajetan, and was directed to recant some of his propositions on indulgences; Luther defied the legate. In 1519, at Leipzig, a learned theologian, John Eck, taxed Luther in debate with disobeying the authoritative findings of popes and church councils. Luther denied that popes and councils were necessarily authoritative and, carrying his revolt further, explicitly declared his adherence to teachings of Hus that previously had been declared heretical. In 1520, Luther brought his defiance to its highest pitch by publishing a pamphlet, *The Appeal to the Christian Nobility of the German Nation*, which stated in part:

There has been a fiction by which the Pope, bishops, priests, and monks are called the 'spiritual estate'; princes, lords, artisans, and peasants are the 'temporal estate.' This is an artful lie and hypocritical invention, but let no one be made afraid by it, and that for this reason: that all Christians are truly of the spiritual estate, and there is no difference among them,

* *Documents of the Christian Church*, Henry Bettenson, ed. (New York, 1947), 265, 270-271.

save of office. As St. Paul says (1 Cor. xii), we are all one body, though each member does its own work so as to serve the others. This is because we have one baptism, one Gospel, one faith, and are all Christians alike; for baptism, Gospel, and faith, these alone make spiritual and Christian people.*

Luther's adherence to justification by faith had now led him to deny totally the central Catholic doctrine of works, that only the priest had the God-given power to secure for the layman, through the "works" of penance, remission of punishment for sin. In *The Appeal to the Christian Nobility* he swept aside the distinction between clergy and laity and declared the "priesthood of all believers." The complete break between the rebel and the Church was now at hand. Late in 1520, Pope Leo X (1513-1521) issued a bull condemning Luther's teachings; Luther burnt the bull. In 1521, Luther was excommunicated and made an outlaw, the political equivalent of being excommunicated. The Emperor Charles V and the imperial diet passed the sentence of outlawry in a most dramatic session at Worms. Luther was asked, once again, if he would recant. His reply contained his most famous words:

Unless I am convicted of error by the testimony of Scripture or (since I put not trust in the unsupported authority of Pope or of councils, since it is plain that they have often erred and often contradicted themselves) by manifest reasoning I stand convicted by the Scriptures to which I have appealed, and my conscience is taken captive by God's word, I cannot and will not recant anything, for to act against our conscience is neither safe for us, nor open to us.
Hier stehe ich. Ich kann nicht anders. Gott helff mir. Amen. [On this I take my stand. I can do no other. God help me. Amen.]†

The empire and the papacy took their drastic actions in vain. Luther was already gathering a substantial following and becoming a national hero. He had the pro-

tection of the ruler of his own German state, the Elector Frederick the Wise of Saxony (1463-1525), and was soon to secure the backing of other princes. In the next few years he translated the Bible into vigorous and effective German and remodeled the church in Saxony according to his own views. His revolt was a success.

The Reasons for Luther's Success

More than theology was at issue in Luther's revolt. The Catholic Church that Luther attacked was, as many Catholic historians grant, at the time in one of its more worldly periods. Especially in its center at Rome, it had come under the influence of the Renaissance. New wealth had come to Italy, and new fashions of good living. The papacy, triumphant over the councils, had been drawn into Italian politics, for the States of the Church were a "sovereign" nation in the new context of international politics. The Rome Luther visited in his younger days was a shocking spectacle of intrigue, display, and corruption. Some part of Luther's success lies in the fact that he was attacking practices revolting to decent men.

There is a second great reason for his success: in the name of good Germans he was attacking the practices of Italians and Italianate Germans. Tetzel was in the eyes of Luther and his followers not only extending an abuse theologically and morally outrageous; the money he was raising was going to enrich Italy, and that was one more step in the exploitation of Germans by Italians. Unquestionably, this German propaganda exaggerated the burden of papal exactions, which were not of a crippling kind.

For Rome is the greatest thief and robber that has ever appeared on earth, or ever will. . . . Poor Germans that we are—we have been deceived! We were born to be masters, and we have been compelled to bow the head

---
* *Documents,* 274.
† *Ibid.,* 285.

beneath the yoke of our tyrants. . . . It is time the glorious Teutonic people should cease to be the puppet of the Roman pontiff.*

In terms that come natural to us today, the nationalistic and economic factors present in the Lutheran movement help explain its success. But a word of warning is necessary. These political and economic factors *help* explain Lutheran success; they do not in and of themselves wholly account for it. As always in human affairs, ideas and ideals worked together with material interests to move the men of the Reformation.

The princes who supported Luther stood to gain financially, not so much by the cessation of the flow of German money to Italy, but rather by the confiscation of Catholic property, especially monastic property, which was not needed for the new Lutheran cult. Luther gave them a new weapon in the eternal struggle against their feudal overlord, the emperor, who kept firmly to the Catholic side. The princes were also moved by Luther's German patriotism. Some, like Frederick the Wise of Saxony, sympathized with many of his ideas. Philip of Hesse found Luther helpful in a very personal problem of his relations with women: he had decided on the somewhat un-Christian and indeed unpromising solution of trying bigamy. Though Luther did not precisely like this solution, he condoned it, much to the salving of Philip's conscience.

Nor must Luther's personality be left out of account. It is true enough that what he started was soon taken out of his hands by the German princes who joined the reform movement in part to strengthen their political power against the emperor, and to strengthen their treasuries by confiscating the possessions of the Catholic Church. Yet Lutheranism without Luther is inconceivable, save perhaps to single-minded devotees of the economic interpretation of history. He wrote the pamphlets that did for this revolution what Tom Paine and the Decla-

ration of Independence did for ours. He put his *Appeal to the Christian Nobility of the German Nation* (1520) in the vernacular German, not the academic Latin, so that it became a "best-seller" overnight. His defiance of the papal legate Cajetan, of the papal champion Eck, and of the Pope himself—indeed all his actions—helped to focus German sentiments on what was, in spite of rather primitive techniques of communication, a mass movement. Luther's translation of the Bible made that book a part of German life, and made Luther's language one of the bases of modern literary German. His marriage to a former nun and his raising of a large family dramatized the break with Rome. And back of all this was Luther's passionate conviction that he was doing what he had to do: *"Ich kann nicht anders."*

The Opposition to Luther

A final reason for Luther's success lay in the relative weakness of the forces that opposed him. The opposition may be divided into the religious and the political, though the two were really inseparably connected. Clerical opposition centered in the top levels of the Catholic bureaucracy; Pope Leo X did not so much head it as prove its willing instrument. Moderate Catholics, anxious to compromise and avert a schism, existed both within the Church and on its margin among the humanist scholars of the Renaissance. It is tempting to agree with the great liberal Catholic historian, Lord Acton, that had there been at the head of the Catholic Church a pope willing to reform in order to conserve, willing to make concessions that did not destroy the basic position of the Church as God's chosen instrument on earth, even Luther might have been reconciled. Luther's ablest associate, Melanchthon, was a moderate. Yet the historian can hardly avoid comparing this revolution with other great modern revolutions, the English, the

---

* *Documents*, 278-279.

The Emperor Charles V, by Titian.

make it such a state in reality. The activities of Luther's princely German supporters seemed to him a threat to his hold over Germany, and might in themselves have sufficed to turn him against Luther. But Charles was by upbringing an unquestioning, indeed a passionate, Catholic, in no state of mind to throw his great influence on the side of the moderate group within the Catholic Church. He decided to fight—and had to fight the rest of his reign, thus gainsaying the famous epigram about his house.

Charles V entrusted the imperial government in Germany and the direct rule of the hereditary Habsburg lands in Central Europe to his younger brother Ferdinand, who formed alliances with Bavaria and other Catholic German states to oppose the Lutheran states. Thus began a long series of alliances and combinations within the Germanies, the fruits of which were the religious wars of the next few generations, and the territorial division of Germany into, roughly, a Protestant north and east and a Catholic south and west, which has endured to this day. The fact that Charles himself did not directly lead the fight in Germany suggests another reason for the success of the Protestant movement in breaking down the unity of western Christendom. Charles had too many other fights on his hands to concentrate on Germany. His huge inheritance was a threat to the only remaining great power on the continent, France. Four general wars between Charles V and Francis I of France, really one great war, prevented anything like the forcible suppression of the German Protestants by imperial Habsburg power (see Chapter IV).

French, the Russian, and noting that in all of them the moderates—gifted, numerous, and active though they were—could not hold up against the extremists. Once Leo X had excommunicated Luther in 1520, the way to compromise was probably blocked, for most of Luther's associates could have been won away from him only by concessions too great for a Catholic to make.

Politically, the opposition in these critical early years centered in the young Emperor Charles V, who came to the imperial throne in 1519. Charles of Habsburg was the fruit of a series of marriages that gave rise to the famous epigram: "Let others wage war; thou, happy Austria, marry." The combined inheritance of his Austrian father and Spanish mother made Charles ruler of the German Empire, the Low Countries, Spain, the Spanish Indies, Hungary, and parts of Italy. This looks on the map like the nearest thing to a real European superstate since Charlemagne, and Charles wanted very much to

The Lutheran Church

Thus far, Luther has appeared in the role of the great revolutionary. But on some issues he also took a fundamentally conservative stand. He did not, for example, push his doctrines of justification by faith and the priesthood of all believers to their logical extreme, which is a kind of religious anarchy, or complete absence of church government. If religion is a matter between each man and his maker, an organized church becomes unnecessary if not impossible. Reformers inspired by Luther, but more radical, attempted to apply these anarchical concepts to the churches of Saxony; the consequences were immense confusion and popular unrest. Luther and his moderate followers, who had no sympathy with such anarchistic experiments, intervened in Saxony. They organized a church that permitted its clergy to marry, but that did have ordained clergymen, ritual, dogmas, even some sacraments—a whole apparatus of good works.

And, most important for us to understand, the Lutherans did not found this church as an alternative to the Roman Catholic, but as the *one true church*. At first, where a Lutheran church was founded, a Catholic church ceased to be; indeed, the Lutherans commonly just took over the church building. Stimulated by Luther and his clerical and academic disciples, this process began among the people of Germany almost spontaneously, without the intervention of political leaders.

But very soon the lay rulers of certain of the half-independent, or rather nine-tenths independent, German states took a hand. In Saxony, in Hesse, soon in most of northern Germany, princes and their ministers superintended and hastened the process of converting the willing to Lutheranism, and evicting the unwilling. Here, as so often in any process of change, the formula "either . . . or" does not serve well for sensible interpretation. The Lutheran Church was not invented by Luther and the princes and foisted on the people; nor on the other hand was it the spontaneous work of the German people. *Both* people and princes had a share in the process. With time, the church of Luther was to become a national church for most of the people of northern Germany and of the Scandanavian peninsula.

Knights' War and Peasants' Rebellion

It was not only the great and near-great German princes who took advantage of the Lutheran movement to assert themselves. Just beneath the princes, lay and ecclesiastical, in the German social and political pyramid and like them a legacy of the Middle Ages were the knights, the lesser nobility. Some of them held a castle and a few square miles direct from the emperor. Many were younger sons, landless but still gentlemen, who could hardly have a career save that of arms. The class as a whole was caught in the squeeze of rising prices and the need for maintaining aristocratic standards of living. Luther's challenge to the established order, above all the chance it seemed to give for taking over ecclesiastical holdings, was too good an opportunity for many of these knights to miss. Under the leadership of Ulrich von Hutten and Franz von Sickingen, they rose in 1522 in the "Knights' War." They were put down by the bigger lords, but only after a struggle, and their rising added to the confusion of the time.

The really bitter social struggle of the early German Reformation was the Peasants' Rebellion of 1524-25. Now peasant risings were not unknown in the Middle Ages. In many ways, the German rising resembles the peasant revolts of the fourteenth century in England and France. In England, Wat Tyler's followers had this slogan:

When Adam delved and Eve span
Who was then the gentleman?

In France, similar revolts called *jacqueries* had seen embittered peasants burn and murder. Like these, the German revolt was directed against the burdens of the manorial system; like them, it lacked coordination and effective military organization and was cruelly put down by the possessing classes who did have command over military power. Like them, too, it was a rising, not of peasants who were in the very lowest state of oppression, but of peasants who were beginning to enjoy some gain from the slowly rising standards of living of medieval society, who had enough to know they wanted more. The German Peasants' Rebellion centered, not in those eastern parts of the country where serfdom was most complete, where the status of the peasant was lowest, but in the southwestern parts where the peasant had at least the beginnings of the status of a landowning farmer.

Luther's reaction to the Peasants' Rebellion was thoroughly conservative. He was horrified at what the peasants' leaders had found in the Bible he had translated into German so that they might read it. He turned against them, directing at them impassioned abuse that sounds even stronger than his abuse of the Catholics. From this time on, he turned definitely to the princes, and the church he founded became itself an established church, respectful toward civil authority. Luther indeed is quoted in his *Table Talk* as saying: "The princes of the world are gods, the common people are Satan."

Luther's conservative views on social and political questions had two important results. First, he won increasing support from kings and princes. By the mid-sixteenth century, Lutheranism had become the state religion in most of the principalities of northern Germany and in the Scandinavian kingdoms, Sweden and Denmark, together with the Danish dependency of Norway. Second, it is hardly surprising that after the Peasants' Rebellion the popular initiative in the Protestant movement passed into the hands of more radical leaders, leaders who wanted freedom from princes as well as from prelates. The radical impetus of Lutheranism was of brief duration indeed.

II: *Protestant Origins—Zwingli, Calvin, and Other Founders*

Many of the things that had troubled Luther had long been troubling his contemporaries in Germany, France, England, and elsewhere (see Chapter II). The great humanist Erasmus, the Englishman Thomas More (author of *Utopia*), and many others were in revulsion against the worldliness and corruption of the Church and against the oversubtleties of late Scholasticism, as the official philosophy of the medieval Church is called. They had been seeking in their writing and preaching for a renewal of evangelical Christianity, for a return to what most of them held to be an earlier and better faith that had somehow gone wrong in their day. Many of these reform-minded men wanted the Catholic Church to be reformed from within. They were shocked by Luther's intransigent revolt, and sought to tame the movement he had unloosed. Others, however, went on to a break even more complete in many ways than Luther's. Of these other founders of Protestantism the first in time was Zwingli and the first in importance was Calvin.

Zwingli   Almost contemporaneously with Luther's spectacular revolt, another German, Ulrich Zwingli (1484-1531), had begun in Switzerland a quieter reform, one that produced no great church but that nevertheless extended and deepened some of the fundamental theological and moral conceptions of Protestantism, and gave it a bent toward what came to be called "liberalism" or "modernism" in religion. Zwingli was a scholarly humanist trained in the tradition of Erasmus. Like Luther, he was aiming to destroy what seemed to him the perversion of primitive Christianity which made the consecrated priest an agent, indeed a sharer, of a miraculous power not possessed by the layman. But, where the doctrine of the priesthood of the true believer drove the emotional Luther to the edge of anarchism, the humanistic Zwingli saw that individuals might achieve a common discipline that would promote righteous living. This discipline would arise from the social conscience of enlightened and emancipated people led but not commanded by their pastors.

Zwingli believed in a personal God and in the miraculous origin of the Christian religion. He was by no means what we sometimes call a rationalist, but he did distrust what many Protestants feel is the continuous appeal of the Catholics to "superstition," to belief in saints, to the use of images, to incense and candles, and of course to indulgences. Zwingli began the process of making the church building an almost undecorated hall, of making the service a sermon and responsive reading, of abolishing the Catholic liturgy. He thus started on the way toward the puritanical simplicity of the later Calvinists.

A concrete example of Zwingli's attitude is his doctrine of the Eucharist. The Catholic doctrine of *transubstantiation* holds that by the miraculous power of the priest the elements, the bread and the wine, become in *substance* the body and blood of Christ, although their *accidents*, their make-up as far as chemistry or indeed common sense sees them, remain those of bread and wine. Luther stubbornly refused to eliminate the miraculous completely, and adhered to a difficult and confusing compromise doctrine called *consubstantiation*. Zwingli, however, went all the way to what is nowadays the usual Protestant doctrine that when we partake of the elements in communion we are indeed commemo-

rating Christ's last supper with his disciples, but only in a symbolic way. We are only reviving a memory of Christ on earth.

Calvin

Zwingli attracted adherents in the German-speaking parts of Switzerland. The independent French Swiss city of Geneva came under the domination of the French-born Jean Cauvin (1509-1564), better known in the Latin form of his name as Calvin. Under Calvin, the Protestant movement was shaped as a faith, a way of life, that gave it a European and not merely a German basis. The historian finds it useful to take Calvinism as the middle—to borrow a political term, the Center—of Protestant beliefs. In Germany and Scandinavia the Lutherans, and in England the Anglican Church, remained in doctrine what we may call to the Right of Calvinism. In England, the Low Countries, and Germany there grew up radical sects like the Anabaptists, to whom we shall shortly come, who were to the Left of Calvinism.

With the moral and theological ideas of Calvin we shall deal in the next section of this chapter. Here we may note that in his *Institutes of the Christian Religion*, published in 1536, he laid a firm doctrinal basis for a Protestantism that, like Zwingli's, breaks completely with Catholic church organization and with Catholic ritual. Calvin had been trained as a lawyer. His system had a logical rigor and completeness that gave it great conviction. He had also a base from which to work, a town that was to become a Protestant Rome, Geneva, where after a temporary rejection in 1538 he returned in 1541 to organize his City of God. To Geneva came Protestant refugees from many parts of Europe, there to receive indoctrination in Calvin's faith, and to return, sometimes at the risk of their lives, to spread the word in their own countries. Within a generation or two, Calvinism had spread to Scotland, where it was led by a great preacher and organizer, John Knox; to England, whence it was brought to New England; and even to Hungary and Poland.

In the Low Countries, Calvinism had by the second half of the sixteenth century taken hold in the northern parts we somewhat inaccurately call Holland (Holland is but the richest and most densely populated of the northern provinces that became the present Kingdom of the Netherlands). The southern part (which became present-day Belgium) was less affected by the Protestant movement, though some of the cities, particularly Antwerp, were for a time Protestant centers.

In France—where the intellectual classes have long been very serious-minded, and not at all as common opinion conceives Frenchmen, gay and irresponsible—concern over the worldliness of the Catholic Church was strong. Beginning with Jean Gerson, one of the leaders of the Conciliar Movement, Frenchmen had for a century been seeking ways of reform. Calvin's ideas found ready acceptance among many Frenchmen, and soon there were organized Protestant churches called Huguenot. But France was a centralized monarchy. King Francis I (1515-1547) was not anxious, as so many of the German princes were, to stir up trouble with Rome. In 1516, he had signed with the Pope the Concordat of Bologna, an agreement that increased the royal authority over the Gallican Church. In the mid-sixteenth century, only a very few intellectuals could even conceive of the possibility of citizens or subjects of the *same* political unit professing and practicing *different* religious faiths. Protestantism in France had to fight, not for toleration, but to succeed Catholicism as the established religion of Frenchmen. The attempt failed, but only after the long hard struggle of the French wars of religion, only after Protestantism had left its mark on the French conscience (see Chapter IV).

Classroom sketches of Calvin by one of his students.

The English Reformation

In strict chronology, the first great sixteenth-century religious overturn outside the Germanies was in England. The signal—though by no means the sole cause—for the English Reformation was a matter very different from the Ninety-Five Theses of Luther. It was the desire of King Henry VIII (1509-1547) to put aside his wife, Catherine of Aragon, who had given him no male heir, and to marry a lady of his court, Anne Boleyn. He rested his case on the fact that Catherine had been married to his deceased brother Arthur, and that marriage with a deceased brother's widow is against the canon law of the Church. Henry's case was hardly strengthened by the circumstance that he had taken nearly twenty years to discover the existence of an impediment. Moreover, Catherine was aunt to the Emperor Charles V, whom the

Pope could scarcely risk offending by granting an annulment. Nevertheless Henry tried hard, through his minister Cardinal Wolsey, who was dismissed in disgrace for his failure. Henry then put his case to universities in England and on the Continent, and got some favorable replies. Finally, he married Anne Boleyn, and Cranmer, the obliging Archbishop of Canterbury whom Henry had recently appointed, pronounced the divorce of Henry and Catherine. The Pope excommunicated Henry and declared the divorce invalid. Henry's answer was the Act of Supremacy in 1534, which set the king up as supreme head of the Church in England.

Much more than the private life of Henry VIII was involved in this English Reformation. Henry could not have secured the Act of Supremacy and other Protestant legislation from Parliament if there had not been a considerable body of English opinion favorable to the breach with Rome, particularly among the sizable and prosperous middle classes. Anti-papal sentiment, which was an aspect of English nationalism, had long existed; it had motivated fourteenth-century statutes limiting the right of the pope to intervene in the affairs of the English church. Anticlericalism went back to the the days of Wiclif; in the days of Henry VIII it was aimed particularly at the monasteries, which were still wealthy landowners but had become corrupt since their great medieval days. In the eyes of many Englishmen, the monasteries had outlived their purpose and needed to be reformed or indeed abolished. Moreover, the ideas of Luther and other continental Protestants quickly won a sympathetic hearing in England. Many English scholars were in touch with continental reformers; one of them, Tindal, studied with Luther and published an English translation of the New Testament in 1526.

Henry VIII sponsored measures in addition to the Act of Supremacy which found favor with Protestant opinion in England. Most important, he closed the monasteries, confiscated their property, and distributed much of the loot among the nobility and the country gentry. Thus Henry gave many influential subjects good reason to be grateful to him and to the Tudor dynasty. Moreover, this policy, by increasing the wealth of the landed aristocracy, amounted to a social and economic revolution. It is another illustration of how closely the religious and the secular threads were interwoven in the Reformation.

Yet Henry VIII did not really consider himself a Protestant. The church set up by the Act of Supremacy was in his eyes—and remains today in the eyes of some of its communicants—a Catholic body. Henry acted as a *schismatic*, not as a *heretic*. He hoped to retain Catholic doctrines and ritual, doing no more than abolish monasteries, conduct parts of services in English, and deny the pope's position as head of the Church in England. Inevitably, his policies aroused opposition. Part of that opposition was Roman Catholic, for some Englishmen greatly resented the break with Rome. And part, the more pressing and the larger part, was militantly Protestant. Hardly had Henry given the signal for the break with Rome when groups began even within the new Church of England to introduce such Protestant practices as marriage of the clergy, use of English instead of Latin throughout the ritual, abolition of auricular confession, abolition of the invocation of saints.

Henry used force against the Catholic opposition, and executed some of its leaders, notably Thomas More, canonized as St. Thomas More in 1935. He tried to stem the Protestant tide by appealing to a willing Parliament, many members of which were enriched by the spoliation of the Catholic Church. In 1539, Parliament passed the statute of the Six Articles, reaffirming transubstantiation, celibacy of the priesthood, confession, and other Catholic doctrines and ritual, and making their denial heresy.

By this definition, indeed by almost any possible definition, there were far too many heretics to be repressed. The patriotic Englishman was against Rome and all its works. England from now on was to be a great center of religious variation and experimentation, much (though not all) of it peaceful. The Church of England, substantially more Protestant than Henry had intended, became a kind of central national core of precarious orthodoxy.

The Anabaptists

One major item is left to consider in this survey of Protestant origins. Socially and intellectually less respectable than the soon-established Lutheran and Anglican churches, or the rapidly sobered Calvinists, was a whole group of radical sects, the left wing of the Protestant revolution. In the sixteenth century, most of them were known loosely as Anabaptists, from the Greek for "baptizing again." Some of Zwingli's followers had come to believe that the Catholic sacrament of baptism of infants had no validity, since the infant could not possibly be said to "believe" or "understand." Here again the connection with Luther's basic doctrine of faith as a direct relation between the believer and God is clear—only for the Anabaptist it is a relation of rational understanding on the part of the believer. The Anabaptists therefore in these early years "baptized again" when the believer could hold that he was voluntarily joining the company of the elect. Later generations were never baptized until they came of age, so the prefix "ana" was dropped, and we have the familiar Baptists of our own time.

The Anabaptists split under the pressure of persecution and with the spread of private reading of the Bible. Indeed, for some Catholic observers, the proliferation of Protestant sects seems due inevitably to the Protestants' practice of seeking in the Bible an authority they refused to find in the established dogmas of Catholic authority. The Bible is—from the historian's point of view—a complex record of several thousand years of Jewish history, and it contains an extraordinary variety of religious experience. Especially the apocalyptic books of the Old Testament and the Revelation of St. John the Divine of the New can be made to yield almost anything a lively imagination wants to find. Many of the leaders of these new sects were uneducated men with a sense of grievance against the established order. They were seeking to bring heaven to earth, quickly.

Their best-known early manifestation in the Reformation gave the conservatives and moderates as great a shock as had the German Peasants' Rebellion, in which these same radical religious ideas had also played a large part. In the mid-1530's, a group of Anabaptists under the leadership of John of Leyden, a Dutch tailor, got control of the city of Münster in Germany, and set up a Biblical Utopia. They were put down by force, their leaders executed, and the faithful dispersed. We know about them chiefly from their opponents, who certainly exaggerated their doctrines and practices. Still, even if we allow for the distortions of propaganda, it seems clear that the Anabaptists of Münster were behaving in ways that western traditions do not permit large groups to adopt. For one thing, they preached, and apparently practiced, polygamy. They pushed the Lutheran doctrine of justification by faith to its logical extreme in anarchism, or in theological language, *antinomianism*, from the Greek "against law." Each man was to be his own law, or rather, to find God's universal law in his own conscience, not in written law and tradition. They did not believe in class distinctions or in the customary forms of private property. They were disturbers of an established order that was strong enough to put them down.

The great majority of Anabaptists were very far from being such wild fanatics as the men of Münster. Many Anabaptist groups sought to bring the evangelical Christian life to earth in quieter and more respected ways. They established communities where they lived as they thought the primitive Christians had lived, in brotherhood, working, sharing, and praying together. These communities bore many resemblances to monasteries, though their members had taken no vows and did not observe celibacy. As we shall see in the next section of this chapter, some of the Anabaptist ideas—quietism, asceticism, the high sense of community—made a lasting contribution to the Protestant tradition. This sober majority of Anabaptists, too, met violent persecution in the sixteenth century. But their spirit lives on today in such diverse groups as the Baptists, the Quakers, the Hutterites of Canada, and the Mennonites and the Amish of the Pennsylvania "Dutch."

Unitarianism A Protestant strain close to Anabaptism was that of Unitarianism, the denial of the Trinity and of the full divinity of Christ. Today, Unitarianism is usually identified with the rejection of the Trinity on the grounds that it is an unreasonable concept and with the view that Christ was simply a particularly inspired human being. But this version of Unitarianism derives largely from the rationalistic Enlightenment of the eighteenth century. Sixteenth-century Unitarianism was a very different matter and much more mystical in outlook. Its most famous advocate, the Spanish physician Servetus (1511-1553), believed that though Christ was not eternal, he was indeed the Son of God. His concept made Christ, as it were, less removed from man but not more removed from God. Thereby Servetus hoped to make it easier for humanity to acquire a mystic identification with Christ and to achieve salvation.

Even this mystic doctrine of Unitarianism greatly alarmed not only Catholics but also many Protestants. Servetus was finally prosecuted for heresy at Geneva by Calvin himself and burnt in 1553. The doctrines of Servetus, however, contributed to the teachings of another Unitarian, Socinus (in Italian, Sozzini; 1539-1604). This far-traveling Italian theologian gained a considerable following among the peoples of eastern Europe, particularly in Poland, Hungary, and Transylvania. The Socinians, too, suffered vigorous persecution at the hands of both Catholics and Protestants, but they were never to be fully stamped out.

III: *Protestant Beliefs and Practices*

Common Denominators It is very difficult to establish a common denominator for Protestant beliefs. Henry VIII (who almost certainly never thought of himself as a Protestant), Luther, Zwingli, Calvin, John of Leyden, and Servetus make a most disparate group. Obviously they all repudiated the claim of the Roman Catholic Church to be the one true faith. They were all hostile to the Church of Rome.

One other generalization is almost as universally valid, if less obvious today. In these early days, each Protestant sect was convinced that it was the one true faith, that it and not Rome was the true successor of Christ and his apostles. Even the Antinomians, who believed that each man carried the truth in his own bosom, believed that if all the perversions that custom, education, and bad environment generally had set up as obstacles to the penetration of truth were swept away, each man would find the *same* truth in his bosom. Some early Protestants held that, though their own belief was the sole true belief, its ultimate prevailing on earth must be the slow process of educating men, of convincing them, of converting them. Others, however, could not wait for this slow process. Though they had once been persecuted themselves, they did not hesitate to persecute in their turn when they rose to power. Witness Calvin's condemnation of Servetus.

Finally, even the conservative established churches of the Reformation—the Anglican and the Lutheran—shared with the more radical Protestants certain reductions in ritual and other external manifestations of belief. All reduced or altered somewhat the traditional seven sacraments—baptism, confirmation, communion or the Eucharist, penance, extreme unction ("the last rites"), holy orders, matrimony. The usual Protestant minimum was to retain baptism and a symbolical communion and, of course, matrimony. But the Protestant theological justification of these sacraments could range very widely, from consubstantiation to the symbolic view of the Eucharist, from an almost Roman *acceptance* of the miraculous to an almost secularist *denial* of the miraculous. Veneration of saints, pilgrimages, rosaries, amulets, and such "papist" practices disappeared even among the right-wing Protestants; the left wing banished music, painting, indeed all the arts except the oratorical arts.

To these outward signs there corresponds an inner link that ties Protestantism together, loosely indeed, and often uncomfortably. All Protestants were rebels in origin. They had *protested* almost always in the name of an older, purer, primitive church, almost always maintaining that *Rome* was the real innovator, the wicked revolutionist. (This attempt of the rebel not to seem to be rebelling often recurs in western history.) The Protestants had appealed from an established order to a "higher law" not yet concretely established on this earth. That is to say, all Protestantism has at least a tinge of the Lutheran appeal from works to faith, in the terms of St. Paul, from the "letter" of the law to the "spirit"; it has at least a tinge of *individualism* based on the individual's inner judgment.

The divergent beliefs of the separate Protestant churches may most conveniently be arranged in order of their theological distance from Roman Catholicism, beginning with those nearest Rome. But it must be noted that the political and social distance is not always the same as the theological.

Anglicanism

The Church of England, as we have already noted, contains communicants who think of themselves as Catholics; they represent the "High Church" point of view. But the Church of England also includes members who take a "Low Church" view; they are more Protestant in outlook, and some come very close to being Unitarians. The Church of England keeps a modified form of the Catholic hierarchy, with archbishops and bishops, though of course without acknowledging the authority of the pope. On the other hand, it permits its clergy to marry and, although it has had, since the nineteenth-century "High Church" revival, orders of monks and nuns, it does not put anything like the Catholic emphasis on the regular clergy. Indeed, historically speaking, the Church of England has somehow managed to contain elements from almost the whole range of Protestant belief, though Anglicans have not been very cordial toward the more publicly demonstrative types of Protestantism, toward "holy rolling."

Perhaps the central core of Anglicanism has been a tempered ritualism, a tempered belief in hierarchy, in discipline from above, a tempered acceptance of this imperfect world—a moderate attitude really not very far from the Catholicism of St. Thomas Aquinas, the most influential medieval Catholic theologian. Indeed, Richard Hooker, who wrote a great defense of the Anglican Church in the 1590's (*The Laws of Ecclesiastical Polity*), relied heavily on Aquinas. It is significant, too, that Hooker is usually called "the judicious Hooker," because of his efforts to reconcile divergent points of view and adjust them to Anglicanism.

The Church of England assumed its definitive form during the reign of Henry VIII's daughter, Elizabeth I (1558-1603). The Thirty-Nine Articles enacted by Parliament in 1563 were a kind of constitution for the Church. They illustrate the essential conservatism of the Anglican Church and the compromises on which it is founded. The Thirty-Nine Articles rejected the more obvious forms of Romanism—the use of Latin, auricular confession, clerical celibacy, the allegiance to the pope. The thirtieth article took a firm Protestant stand on one of the great symbolic points at issue. The Church of England gave communion in both kinds, both wine and bread, to the layman, where the Catholic Church gave only the bread. Yet the articles also sought to compromise on some of the greater issues, and notably to avoid the anarchistic dangers of the doctrines of justification by faith and the priesthood of the believer.

The Church of England has always seemed to its enemies, and even to some of its friends, a bit too acquiescent in face of civil authority. In what was once a word of abuse, the Church of England has seemed *Erastian*. The term comes from the name of a sixteenth-century Swiss theologian and physician named Erastus (not to be confused with the Dutch humanist Erasmus), who by no means held the doctrine attributed to him. This doctrine in the abusive sense—and it has hardly any other—holds that the State is all-powerful against the Church, that the clergy are but the moral police force of the State, in short, that the

government in power is always right. This extreme statement is indeed a caricature of Anglican practice. But a touch of subservience to political authority, a modified Erastianism, does remain in the Church of England. It is evident in the English civil and religious struggles of the seventeenth century (see Chapter VI).

Lutheranism

The first section of this chapter has already presented the main beliefs of the other great conservative Protestant church, the Lutheran. Once it had become established, Lutheranism preserved many practices which seem to outsiders Catholic in origin, but which to Luther represented a return to early Christianity before the corruption by Rome. Lutheranism preserved the Eucharist, now interpreted according to the mysterious doctrine of consubstantiation. It also preserved the notion of hierarchy, bishops, gowns, and something of the plastic arts. The tradition of good music in the church it not only preserved but greatly fortified. Lutheranism had room for evangelical piety, for much of what we think of as the spirit of Protestantism; but it was never really "puritanical" or violently evangelical.

Luther, like so many others upon whom character and fate have thrust rebellion, was at heart a conservative, as we have seen. In his own lifetime he really wanted the forms of Lutheran worship to recall the forms he was used to. The Lutheran Church, like the Anglican, had its high or conservative party. Yet it also had a strong evangelical party and a tradition of Bible reading. To outsiders, the Lutheran Church has seemed even more Erastian than the Anglican. As the state church in much of North Germany and in Scandinavia, it was often a docile instrument of its political masters. And in its close association with the rise of Prussia—though Prussia's Hohenzollern rulers later became Calvinist—it was inevitably brought under the rule of the strongly bureaucratic Prussian state.

Calvinism: Predestination

The Protestant Center is Calvinism, and the main theological problem of Calvinism is not so much Luther's problem of faith against good works as the related problem of predestination against free will. The problem is an old one in Christianity. It arises from the Christian concept that God is all-powerful, all-good, all-knowing. If this is so, he must will, must *determine*, everything that happens. He must will that the sinner shall sin. For if he did not so will, the individual would be doing something God did not want him to do, and God would not be all-powerful. But there is a grave moral difficulty here —or at least a logical difficulty. If God wills that the sinner sin, the sinner cannot help himself, cannot be "blamed" for his sin. We seem to be at a dead end, where the individual can always say, no matter what he does, that he is doing what God makes him do. We seem, in short, to have cut the ground from individual moral responsibility. And—at least from their enemies' reports—that is just what John of Leyden and his Antinomians (see p. 86) did. When they took several wives at once, they argued that *God* must want them to, since *they* wanted to.

The dilemma is clear: if the individual can choose for himself between good and evil acts, if in theological terms he has *free will*—then it looks as if God were not all-powerful; if he has no such choice, if in theological terms he is subject to *predestination*—then it looks as if the individual were morally irresponsible. *Both* these conclusions are repugnant to the general nature of historical Christianity.

To an outsider, it looks as if most Christians most of the time solved the dilemma by embracing both horns at once—by holding that God determines every human **act**, and yet that human beings may do things God does not want them to do. Theologians do not of course put the matter this way. Most of their basic solutions preserve the moral responsibility of the individual by asserting the profound distance between God and man, a distance that the miracle of faith alone can, in a sense imperfectly, bridge. In terms of everyday life, this means that for the individual to claim that whatever he does is what God wants him to do is to make the incredibly presumptuous claim that he *knows* God's will, that his petty human understanding is on a par with God's. The individual can never be *certain* that what he wants to do is what God wants him to do. Therefore he should look about him and see what signs he can, limited though his vision be, of God's intentions. These he will find in Christian tradition and Christian history. To be concrete: if the individual is tempted to commit adultery, he will not follow the Antinomian and say that God wants him to do so; he will follow Christian tradition, and recognize the adulterous desire as an indication that he is being tempted to do wrong, and that if he does it he will not be saved, but damned.

Calvin himself, though he would not have put it this way, would have reached the same conclusion. But he was, as we have noted, a logician. Both his temperament and his environment led him to reject what he believed to be the Catholic emphasis on easy salvation by indulgences and the like. He put his own emphasis on the hard path of true salvation, on the majesty of God and the littleness of man. He evolved therefore a very extreme form of the doctrine of predestination.

In Calvin's system, Adam's original sin was unforgivable. God, however, in his incomprehensible mercy, sent Jesus Christ to this earth to make salvation possible for some of Adam's progeny, stained though they were by original sin. Very few indeed, the elect, could attain this salvation, and that through no merit of their own, and certainly not on the wholesale scale the Roman Catholic Church of the sixteenth century was claiming. The elect were saved, Calvin held, only through God's free and infinite grace, by means of which they were given the strength to gain salvation. Grace is not like anything else that touches human life on earth. It is not of a piece with law, morals, philosophy, engineering, and other human ways of relating man to his environment; to hold that it is, was to Calvin one of the errors of the Catholic. But it is not wholly divorced from these earthly relations —to hold that it is, is the error of the Antinomian. The elect actually tend to behave in a certain way, an identifiable way, a way not wholly misrepresented if it is called *puritanical*.

The preceding paragraph is not quite fair to Calvin. For all his harsh logic and rigorous theocratic rule, he was a man of God, and a skillful practitioner of the cure of souls. Here is the prayer with which he ordinarily began his sermons:

We invoke our good God and Father, praying that he deign to turn his face from the many faults and offenses by which we cease not to provoke his wrath against us: and, since we are too unworthy to appear before his majesty, that he deign to see us in the countenance of his beloved Son our Lord Jesus Christ, accepting the merit of his death and passion as recompense for all our faults, that thus we may be acceptable to him; that he may light within us through his Holy Spirit the true understanding of his Word, give us grace that we may receive this Word in true fear and humility, that we may be taught thus to put our trust in him, serve him and honor him to glorify his holy name all our lives, giving him the love and obedience that faithful servants owe their masters, and children their parents, since he has pleased to call us to the number of his servants and children.*

Note that Calvin says "love" as well as "obedience." Indeed love had to be there,

---

* C. O. Vignet and D. Tissot, *Calvin d'après Calvin* (Geneva, 1864), 443. Our translation.

or Calvinism would have remained a mere intellectual exercise.

The Left Wing

The sects of the Protestant Left were usually greatly influenced by Calvinist theology and by Calvinist example. The Anabaptists and the others generally arose among humble people. In these new sects, the congregation sometimes shouted and danced, and always sang hymns with great fervor. Preaching was even more important than in more conservative forms of Protestantism, and more emotionally charged with hopes of heaven and fears of hell. Many of the sects were wildly chiliastic —that is, they expected the Second Coming of Christ at once. Many were in aim, and among themselves in practice, economic equalitarians, communists of a sort. They did not share wealth, however, so much as the poverty that had seemed to St. Francis and now seemed to them an essential part of the Christian way.

Almost all of them had some beliefs, some goals, that alarmed many ordinary, conventional men and women. Many refused to take oaths. Most distrusted the state, regarding it as a necessary instrument operated by sinners to punish other sinners, an institution from which true Christians should hold aloof. What is most striking about these sects is the extraordinary range of their ideals and behavior. Some of them really behaved as badly—as insanely—as their conservative enemies have charged. John of Leyden, crowned at Münster as "King David" with two golden, jeweled crowns, one kingly, one imperial, with his "Queen Divara" and a whole harem in attendance, seems a mad parody of the Protestant appeal to the Bible. Yet the Anabaptists already scattered about northwestern Europe at the time were shocked by what went on in Münster; and if one examines their ideas and practices one finds, for the most part, pious and earnest pacifist

Christians, living simply and productively as do their modern successors, Mennonites, Baptists, and Quakers.

These left-wing sects often display an illogical and magnificent combination of pacifist principles and ardent combativeness (as long as the weapons are not physical ones, conventional means of inflicting bodily harm). These men are fighting to end fighting. Here is Jacob Hutter, who founded the Hutterite sect of Moravian Anabaptists, addressing the Governor-General of Moravia, Ferdinand of Habsburg, a good Catholic who was ruling the Germanies for his brother Charles V:

And now that you have with violence bidden us forthwith to depart into exile, let this be our answer. We know not any place where we may securely live; nor can we longer dare here to remain for hunger and fear. If we turn to the territories of this or that sovereign, everywhere we find an enemy. . . . We desire to molest no one, nor to prejudice our foes, not even Ferdinand the king. Our manner of life, our customs and conversation, are known everywhere to all. Rather than wrong any man of a single penny, we would suffer the loss of a hundred gulden, and sooner than strike our enemy with the hand, much less with spear, or sword, or halbert, as the world does, we would die and surrender life.

. . . .

Woe, woe! unto you, O ye Moravian rulers, who have sworn to that cruel tyrant and enemy of God's truth, Ferdinand, to drive away his pious and faithful servants. Woe! we say unto you, who fear that frail and mortal man more than the living, omnipotent, and eternal God, and chase from you, suddenly and inhumanly, the children of God, the afflicted widow, the desolate orphan, and scatter them abroad. . . . God, by the mouth of the prophet, proclaims that He will fearfully and terribly avenge the shedding of innocent blood, and will not pass by such as fear not to pollute and contaminate their hands therewith. Therefore, great slaughter, much misery and anguish, sorrow and adversity, yea, everlasting groaning, pain and torment are daily appointed you.*

_____

* J. T. van Braght, *Martyrology*, I, 149-153, quoted in R. J. Smithson, *The Anabaptists* (London, 1935), 69-71.

The mixture of professions of pacifism and threats of violence in this letter is extraordinary, even for the time. Yet these men did know how to die. They, too, were martyrs. And they were persecuted by the more moderate reformers with a violence as firm and principled as that which Protestant tradition attributes to the Catholic Inquisition.

Finally, some of these sectarians begin to formulate the ideal of religious toleration. That ideal, it is clear, did not inspire the early reformers—Luther, Calvin, Zwingli. It is probably true that western men were in practice driven to religious toleration by sheer exhaustion after vain efforts to make one form of religion universal in the West. It is also true that some part of the ultimately successful efforts to allow men to "belong to" different churches as they might belong to different clubs was the work of men indifferent to religion, men who belonged to no church in their hearts. But this is not the whole truth. We have religious toleration today in part because some very earnest believers in the truth of their own form of belief and worship came to hold that this truth could prevail only under conditions of free religious association, by the voluntary—and necessarily slow —process of education and conversion. To these men, even the word "toleration" had negative overtones, a suggestion of a sort of suspended threat of persecution, which they did not like. Religious freedom, variation in religion, became for them part of God's plan—a part that was not to be interfered with by men wielding secular power—or religious power either. In short, freedom of religion became for them one of the rights of men. But by the time such a belief was held *widely* in the West we are well out of the sixteenth century, are indeed in the Enlightenment of the eighteenth century. In this matter of toleration, as in so much else, "modern" begins and "medieval" ends in the eighteenth century rather than in the Renaissance.

IV: The Catholic Reformation

The dominant early Catholic response to the challenge of the Protestant Reformation was to stand pat and try to suppress the rebels. Such, basically, was the papal policy toward Luther. But the efforts of Catholic humanists and moderates to reform the abuses the Protestants had attacked were by no means vain. Within a long generation, the Catholic Church was to rally its spiritual and material forces, achieve a large measure of reform from within, and, by winning back areas in Germany, Bohemia, Hungary, and Poland, establish the territorial limits of Protestantism in the West substantially where they now are. This Catholic Reformation, in Protestant historical writing often called the Counter-Reformation, was no mere negative defense, but a positive spiritual renewal in its own right. It did not restore the medieval unity of Christendom, but it did preserve and reinvigorate fundamental Catholic beliefs and practice.

They were not preserved without the aid of the secular arm. Both the Catholic and the Protestant Reformations were inseparably tied up with domestic and international politics, as we shall see in detail in the next chapter. The powerful House of Habsburg, both in its Spanish and its German branches, was the active head of political Catholicism in the next few generations. The French monarchs, though their support was perhaps rather more political than religious, none the less helped greatly to preserve France as a Catholic land. In many parts of Germany and its Slavic borderlands, and in Italy, the reigning princes and their nobilities were powerful influences behind the old religion.

Nor were Catholic fundamentals preserved without special organization. Once more, as in the Middle Ages, this renewal of Catholic strength, this need to achieve in the name of the old something quite new, produced a series of new orders of the regular clergy, a revival and re-direction of the old monastic ideals of austere simplicity and social service. The reforming current was already gathering strength when the papacy was still in the lax hands of Leo X, Luther's opponent. During Leo's pontificate an earnest group formed at Rome the Oratory of Divine Love, dedicated to the deepening of spiritual experience through special services and religious exercises. In the 1520's, the Oratory inspired the foundation of the Theatines, an order aimed particularly at the education of the clergy. In the 1520's also, a new branch of the Franciscans appeared, the Capuchins, to lead the order back to Francis' own ideals of poverty and preaching to the poor. During the next decade or so, half a dozen other new orders were established.

The Jesuits

The greatest of these by far was the Society of Jesus, founded in 1534 by the Spaniard Ignatius Loyola (1491-1556). The founder, until he turned to religion after a painful wound received in battle, had been a soldier, and the Jesuit order was from the beginning the soldiery of the Catholic Church. Loyola set the rules for his order in his *Spiritual Exercises*. The following extracts bring out admirably two major characteristics of the Jesuits: first, the absolute (for once the word must be taken literally) obedience to higher authority, to the Catholic Church as embodied in its hierarchy; and second, the realistic, middle-of-the-road estimate of what can be expected of ordinary human beings in this world:

1. Always to be ready to obey with mind and heart, setting aside all judgment of one's own, the true spouse of Jesus Christ, our holy mother, our infallible and orthodox mistress, the Catholic Church, whose authority is exercised over us by the hierarchy.

13. That we may be altogether of the same mind and in conformity with the Church herself, if she shall have defined anything to be

Loyola.

black which to our eyes appears to be white, we ought in like manner to pronounce it to be black. . . .

14. It must also be borne in mind, that although it be most true, that no one is saved but he that is predestinated, yet we must speak with circumspection concerning this matter, lest perchance, stressing too much the grace or predestination of God, we should seem to wish to shut out the force of free will and the merits of good works; or on the other hand, attributing to these latter more than belongs to them, we derogate meanwhile from the power of grace.*

* *Documents of the Christian Church*, Henry Bettenson, ed. (New York, 1947), 363-365.

Born in controversy, the Jesuits have always been a center of controversy. To their hostile critics, who have been numerous both within and without the Catholic Church, the Jesuits have seemed unscrupulous soldiers of the pope. Though they have rarely been accused of the simpler vices common gossip has long alleged against the monk—fondness for food and drink, laziness, laxity with women—they have been accused of a subtler devotion to worldly power, to success in a quite unspiritual sense. They have been accused of preaching and practicing the doctrine that the end justifies the means, that as soldiers of the one true Church they may indulge in dirty fighting as long as such tactics seem likely to bring victory.

This is indeed a slander, for even at the purely worldly level, Jesuit devotion to Catholic tradition is too deep for them to make the mistake of underestimating the hold the moral decencies have on human beings. And the historical record leaves no doubt of Jesuit success in bolstering the spiritual as well as the material credit of Catholicism in these critical days of the sixteenth and seventeenth centuries. Jesuits were everywhere, in Hungary, in Poland, in England, in Holland, trying to win back lost lands and peoples from the Protestants. They were winning new lands and peoples on the expanding frontiers of the West, in India, in China, in Japan, in North America. They were martyrs, preachers, teachers, social workers, counselors of statesmen, always disciplined, never lapsing into the kind of fleshly worldliness that had been the fate of other monastic orders.

The Inquisition

The Jesuits were the chief new instruments of the Catholic Reformation. An old instrument of the Church was also employed—the Inquisition, a special ecclesiastical court which in its papal form began in the thirteenth century as part of the effort to put down heresy, and in its

Spanish form began in the fifteenth century as part of the effort of the new Spanish monarchy to enforce religious uniformity on its subjects (see Chapter II). Both papal and Spanish inquisitions were medieval courts, which used medieval methods of torture. Both were employed against the Protestants in the sixteenth century.

Protestant tradition sometimes makes both the Inquisition and the Jesuits appear as the promoters of a widespread and veritable reign of terror. Certainly the Jesuits and their allies made full use of the many pressures and persuasions any highly organized society can bring to bear on nonconformists. And the Inquisition did perpetrate horrors against former Moslems in Spain and against Catholics-turned-Protestants in the Low Countries. But the Inquisition does not appear to have been a really major force

in stemming the Protestant tide. It was most active in countries of southern Europe—Italy, Spain, Portugal—where Protestantism was never a real threat. And in the regions where the Catholic Reformation was most successful in winning back large numbers to the Roman faith—the Germanies, the Slavic and Magyar marches of the West—sheer persecution was not a decisive factor.

The Council of Trent   The Catholic Reformation was not a change of dogma, not a change of spiritual direction. If anything, revulsion against the Protestant tendency toward some form of the "priesthood of the believer" hardened Catholic doctrines into a firmer insistence on the miraculous power of the priesthood. Protestant variation pro-

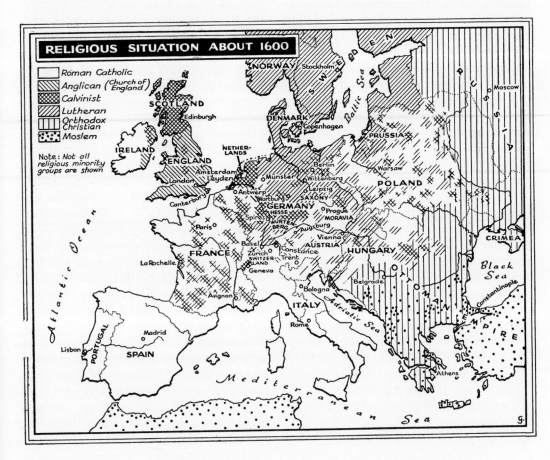

RELIGIOUS SITUATION ABOUT 1600

- Roman Catholic
- Anglican (Church of England)
- Calvinist
- Lutheran
- Orthodox Christian
- Moslem

Note: Not all religious minority groups are shown

moted Catholic uniformity. Not even on indulgences did the Church yield; interpreted as a spiritual return for spiritual effort, not as a money transaction, indulgences were reaffirmed by the Council of Trent. The work of this council ties together the various measures of reform, and illustrates clearly the fact that what the Catholic Reformation reformed was not doctrine but practice and spirit.

The Council of Trent was called in 1545 by Paul III (1534-1549), the first of a line of popes devoted to the task of combating realistically the inroads of Protestantism. To liberals—including liberal Catholics—it has seemed no true general council, but an instrument in the hands of the popes and the Jesuits, a mere rubber stamp. Certainly in conception it was meant to provide at least a chance for reconciliation with the Protestants. Leading figures in the more conservative Protestant groups were invited, but they never attended. The French clergy, with their Gallican tradition, did not cooperate freely, and indeed part of the work of the Council of Trent was not accepted in France for some fifty years. The Council was caught in the web of the religious wars and intrigues of high politics, and its work was several times interrupted. Nevertheless it continued to meet off and on for twenty years until it completed its work in 1564.

On matters of doctrine, the Council of Trent took a stand that ruled out all possibility of a compromise with the Protestants on the major issues separating them from Catholics. It reaffirmed the essential role of the priesthood, reaffirmed all seven sacraments, reaffirmed the great importance of *both* faith and works, reaffirmed that *both* the Scriptures and the spokesmen of the Church were authorities on theology. The Council of Trent insisted on the strict observance of clerical vows and on the ending of abuses. It took measures against the sale of church offices and against non-residence of prelates. It called for the establishment of seminaries to give priests better training. To promote discipline among the laity, it imposed censorship on a large scale, issuing the *Index,* a list of books that Catholics were not to read because of the peril to their faith. The *Index* included not only the writings of heretics and Protestants but also the works of such anticlericals as Machiavelli and Boccaccio.

Under Pius V, pope from 1566 to 1572, a standard catechism, breviary, and missal were drawn up to embody for purposes of instruction the codifying work of the Council of Trent. In short, the whole structure of the Church, both for the training of the priesthood and for the training of the layman, was tightened up, given a new spirit. The papal court was no longer just another Italian Renaissance court. It is true that, especially among the upper clergy in countries like France, a certain laxity had again crept in by the eighteenth century. But the scandalous and widespread corruption against which Luther and his fellows inveighed never again prevailed.

The strength of the Catholic Reformation is shown by the fact that, once it was launched, the Protestants made few further inroads. Within a century of Luther's revolt, the broad lines of the territorial division in the West between areas dominantly Catholic and areas dominantly Protestant were established much as they are today. England, Scotland, Holland, northern and eastern Germany (with a southward projection in Wurtemberg and Switzerland), and Scandinavia were predominantly Protestant. Ireland, Belgium, France, southern Germany (with a northern projection in the valley of the Rhine), the Habsburg lands, Poland, Italy, and the Iberian Peninsula were predominantly Catholic. But only predominantly. There were Catholic minorities in England, Scotland, and Holland, and the two faiths interpenetrated most confusedly in a greatly divided Germany; there were Protestant minorities in Ireland, France, and even in some of the Habsburg lands the Jesuits had won back.

V: The Place of Protestantism in History

Protestantism and Progress

Protestants and secularists sometimes interpret the Reformation as something peculiarly "modern," a decisive break with a "medieval" past, something forward-looking and even "democratic" as distinguished from the stagnant and status-ridden Middle Ages. This notion seems to gain support from the obvious fact that those parts of the West which in the last three centuries have been economically most prosperous, which have worked out most successfully democratic constitutional government, and which have made the most striking contributions to modern western culture, especially in the natural sciences, were predominantly Protestant. Moreover, the powers which, since the decline of Spanish power after 1600, have risen to a kind of preponderance of power and prestige in the West—namely France, the British Empire, Germany, and now the United States—have been with one exception predominantly Protestant. And the one exception, France, has had since the eighteenth century a strong, at times a leading element which, though not Protestant, is strongly secularist and anticlerical. Moreover, in modern France Protestants have had an influence in business and politics out of proportion to their numbers. It looks as if the nations that went Protestant also went modern and progressive.

This notion that Protestantism is somehow a cause or at least an accompaniment of political and cultural leadership in the modern West needs to be examined carefully. It has, of course, the kind of truth certain modern philosophers have called the truth of the "myth." That is, for a good many years a good many Protestants and secularists in these prosperous countries have believed that their Protestantism was a major part of what made them prosperous. To the average Victorian Englishman, for instance, at the height of British power and wealth, the fact that his country had gone Protestant in the sixteenth century was at least as important as Magna Carta—and the existence of good deposits of coal and iron—in producing the prosperous England of which he was so proud. The historian must record the acceptance of the myth; but he must also attempt to go back to the events that were used to construct the myth.

We find that Protestantism in the sixteenth century looks in many ways quite different from Protestantism seen from the nineteenth and twentieth centuries. First, as we have already noted, sixteenth-century Protestants were not rationalists. They were, to use an unfavorable word, almost as "superstitious" as the Catholics. Luther actually threw his ink bottle at the devil, or so they tell the tourists at the castle of the Wartburg; the Calvinists burned witches, or at any rate hanged them. To put the matter more favorably, the Protestants for the most part shared with their Catholic opponents very fundamental Christian conceptions of original sin, the direct divine governance of the universe, the reality of heaven and hell, and—most important—they had no more than did the Catholics a general conception of life on this earth as improving, as progressing to an even better life for coming generations.

Second, these early Protestants were by no means tolerant, by no means believers in the separation of Church and State. When they were in a position to do so, they used governmental power to prevent public worship in any form other than their own. Many of them persecuted those who disagreed with them, both Protestants of other sects and Catholics—that is, they banished them or imprisoned them or even killed them. The classic instance is Calvin's condemnation and execution of Servetus, and there are many other instances.

Third, these early Protestants were hardly democratic, at least in most of the senses that loose (but indispensable) word has for twentieth-century Americans. Logically, the Protestant appeal from the authority of the pope backed by Catholic tradition to the conscience of the individual believer fits in with notions like "individualism," "rights of man," and "liberty." Some historians have even found a correlation between the Protestant appeal to the authority of the Bible and the later characteristic American appeal to the authority of a written constitution. But most of the early Protestant reformers certainly did not hold that all men are created equal; they were not social and economic equalitarians. Rather, they believed in an order of rank, in a society of status. Lutheranism and Anglicanism were clearly conservative in their political and social doctrines. Calvinism can be made to look very undemocratic indeed if we concentrate on its conception of an elect few chosen by God for salvation and an unregenerate majority condemned to eternal damnation. And in its early years in Geneva and in New England Calvinism was in fact a theocracy, a rule of the "saints."

In the long run, however, Calvinism favored the domination of a fairly numerous middle class. The most persuasive argument for a causal relation between Protestantism and modern western democratic life does not proceed directly from the ideas of the early Protestants about men in society, but from the way Protestant moral ideals fitted in with the strengthening of a commercial and industrial middle class. This argument is developed in the work of the German sociologist Max Weber. He points out that Calvinist encouragement of hard work and discouragement of luxury and the arts encouraged saving for production—for "cap-

ital," in short.

Finally, among the Anabaptists and other radical sects, we do find even in the sixteenth century demands for political, social, and economic equality. But where these demands are made, they are cast in Biblical language and rest on concepts of direct divine intervention quite strange to us. Moreover, some of these sects tended not so much toward active social revolt to improve earthly standards of living as toward a peculiarly Protestant form of withdrawal from things of this earth, toward a pacifism and a mysticism quite compatible with leaving the unregenerate majority in possession of this unworthy sense-world.

The Protestant Reformation, then, did not create modern society single-handed. But it did challenge those in authority in many parts of Europe and did start all sorts of men, some of them in humble circumstances, thinking about fundamental problems of life in this world as well as in the next. It was one of the great destroyers of the medieval synthesis. Its most important positive action can best be traced through its part in forming the way of life of the middle classes who were to lay the foundations of modern western democracy.

Protestantism and Nationalism   One final big generalization about the Protestant Reformation is much less disputable than attempts to tie that movement with modern individualism, democracy, and industrialism. After the great break of the sixteenth century, both Protestantism and Catholicism became important elements in the formation of modern nationalism. Here again we must not fall into the trap of one-way causation. Much besides the Reformation goes into the formation of the modern state-system of the West and its cementing patriotism. "Frenchness" and modern "German-ness" perhaps began as far back as the ninth century, when Charlemagne's brief European unity broke up into embryo nationalities. But where a specific form of religion became identified with a given political unit, religious feeling and patriotic feeling each reinforced the other. This is most clear where a political unit had to struggle for its independence. Protestantism heightened Dutch resistance to the Spaniard; Catholicism heightened Irish resistance to the English-man. But even in states already independent in the sixteenth century, religion came to strengthen patriotism. England from Elizabeth I on has, despite the existence of a Catholic minority, proudly held itself up as a Protestant nation. Spain has with at least equal pride identified itself as a Catholic nation. In the great wars to which we must now turn, religion and politics were inextricably mixed.

Reading Suggestions on the Protestant Reformation

General Accounts

L. von Ranke, *History of the Reformation in Germany* (many editions). A very famous work, more than a century old.

P. Smith, *The Age of the Reformation* (N.Y.: Holt, 1920). A very readable account, now somewhat out of date.

R. H. Bainton, *The Reformation of the Sixteenth Century* (Boston: Beacon, 1952). By a sound Protestant historian, fully abreast of modern research.

G. L. Mosse, *The Reformation* (N.Y.: Holt, 1952. A Berkshire Study). A very brief account.

Special Studies

R. H. Bainton, *Here I Stand: A Life of Martin Luther* (N.Y.: Abingdon-Cokesbury, 1950). Sympathetic, scholarly, and readable.

H. Grisar, *Martin Luther, His Life and Works* (St. Louis: Herder, 1930). From the Catholic point of view.

H. Boehmer, *Luther and the Reformation in the Light of Modern Research* (London: Bell, 1930). An older, sympathetic account.

E. G. Schweibert, *Luther and His Times* (St. Louis: Concordia, 1952). Particularly useful for the setting and the effects of Luther's revolt.

S. M. Jackson, *Ulrich Zwingli: The Reformer of German Switzerland* (N.Y.: Putnam's, 1900). An old work, but indispensable.

G. Harkness, *John Calvin, The Man and His Ethics* (N.Y.: Holt, 1931). A good short introduction.

J. Mackinnon, *Calvin and the Reformation* (London: Longmans, Green, 1936); and W. Walker, *John Calvin, The Organizer of Protestantism* (N.Y.: Putnam's, 1906). Solid, longer studies.

T. M. Parker, *The English Reformation to 1558* (N.Y.: Oxford Univ. Press, 1950. Home University Library). Excellent short account.

F. M. Powicke, *The Reformation in England* (London: Oxford Univ. Press, 1941). A scholarly study.

P. Janelle, *The Catholic Reformation* (Milwaukee: Bruce, 1949). Sympathetic and balanced Catholic account.

L. Pastor, *History of the Popes from the Close of the Middle Ages* (St. Louis: Herder, 1923-1953). The classic account; in many volumes.

T. J. Campbell, *The Jesuits, 1534-1921* (N.Y.: Encyclopaedia Press, 1921). Written from the Catholic standpoint.

H. Boehmer, *The Jesuits* (Philadelphia: Castle, 1928). From the Protestant point of view.

M. Weber, *The Protestant Ethic and the Spirit of Capitalism*, T. Parsons, ed. (N.Y.: Scribner's, 1930). A famous and controversial work on the interrelationship of religion and economics.

R. H. Tawney, *Religion and the Rise of Capitalism* (N.Y.: Mentor Books). A modified English version of the Weber thesis, written by a leading intellectual associated with the Labor party.

E. Troeltsch, *Protestantism and Progress* (N.Y.: Putnam's, 1912). By one of the most important religious philosophers of modern times.

E. B. Bax, *The Peasants' War in Germany* (N.Y.: Macmillan, 1899). Badly outdated in interpretation, but the most complete account in English.

J. W. Allen, *Political Thought in the Sixteenth Century* (N.Y.: Dial, 1928). The best account of the subject in English, though not easy reading.

Sources

H. S. Bettenson, *Documents of the Christian Church* (N.Y.: Oxford Univ. Press, 1947). This admirably arranged compilation is particularly useful for the Reformation.

R. H. Bainton, *The Age of the Reformation* (Princeton: Van Nostrand, 1956. An Anvil Book). A comprehensive selection from the great men and great works of the period.

CHAPTER FOUR

Dynastic and
Religious Wars

I: *International Politics—*
The Modern European State-System

Historians have chosen a number of different dates to mark the watershed between "medieval" and "modern." Americans like to think of 1492 as the great date. In the kingdoms of western Europe, the historian singles out the appearance of strong and ambitious monarchs—1485, Henry VII in England; 1461, Louis XI in France; 1469, the marriage of Ferdinand of Aragon and Isabella of Castile. Some

historians feel that Luther's posting of the Ninety-Five Theses in 1517 is the real break with the Middle Ages. Others, focusing on what we now call international relations, choose a date obscure to most Americans— 1494. In that year, Charles VIII of France led his army over the Alps toward the conquest of Italy, in what some consider the "first modern war."

All such dates are of course somewhat

arbitrary. As we have seen in the chapter on the Renaissance, the watershed between medieval and modern culture cannot be placed in a single country or a single year. The dividing line stands out best in the field of international relations. But even here the later Middle Ages show the beginnings of modern developments—the ritual of formal diplomacy, the rivalries of territorial political units, the making and unmaking of alliances, the working of the "balance of power." With Charles VIII's descent on Italy, however, all these elements appear most clearly. Before we trace the course of these first major wars of early modern times, we must examine the bases of the international politics of which the wars were an expression.

The Competitive
State-System

First of all, there *was* a state-system, indeed in some senses a society of states. All political units whose citizens have frequent relations of any kind—trade, travel, study, sport, war—with citizens of other units are perforce members of the same state-system. Rome and China in 100 A.D. were not members of the same system, for though there are traces of some relations, some traffic across Asia between the two, these are slight indeed. But France, Spain, England, and indeed all the nations of Europe belonged to one system in the sixteenth century.

This state-system had no common central political or ecclesiastical institution. In theory, in the West during the Middle Ages, there was on earth but one Christian society, headed by Pope and Emperor, each wielding one of the swords of God. In practice, the eastern Orthodox Church was wholly separate from Rome; and the emperor never had any real hold on England, France, or, in the Middle Ages, the Iberian Peninsula. Medieval unity was an aspiration rather than a fact. Still, the pope was a fact, and Roman Catholic unity was a fact in the late Middle Ages. Protestantism and the rise of strong dynastic states made the later disunity, the lack of any central institutions, even more obvious.

The West, then, is in early modern times a group of states, big, middle-sized, and little, each striving to grow, usually in a quite concrete way by annexing others in whole or in part, or at least by bringing them under some sort of control. In practice, at any given moment some states are on the offensive, trying to gain land, power, and wealth; others are on the defensive, trying to preserve what they have. Historically, some few of these units have been so small, so self-contained, that they have never tried to expand. Yet even the model small democracies of the twentieth century, like Sweden and Denmark, have taken the offensive at some time in the past five hundred years.

The constituent units of this system of competing states may be called "sovereign" or "independent." There is never a perfect achievement of sovereignty or independence; since by definition the states are in competitive relations, no one can ever be unaffected by the behavior of the others. But we may roughly call a state sovereign if its rulers have an armed force they can use against others. In this sense, there has been since the height of feudal disintegration, perhaps in the tenth century, a continuous though irregular process of reducing the number of sovereign states, until today the whole world contains fewer than a hundred. If a feudal lord with his own armed retainers is called "sovereign," since he could and did make war on his own initiative, then the tenth-century West had thousands of such units. As we have seen in Chapter I, the situation was never quite so bad as this. The successor states of the Roman Empire in the West did preserve some kind of formal national or at least provincial unity. By the end of the Middle Ages, however, over large parts of the West the little feudal units had been absorbed into much bigger states and local wars had become impossible—or if they did occur, they were risings of barons against the big ruler, and were felt to be *civil wars*. The great but shadowy unity of western Christendom was destroyed at the end of the Middle Ages; but so too was the real disunity of numerous local units capable of organized war among themselves.

As the modern state-system began to shape up in the fifteenth and sixteenth centuries, the three well-organized monarchies of Spain, France, and England dominated the western part of Europe. The smaller states of Scotland, Portugal, and Scandinavia generally played a subordinate role. In Central Europe, the Holy Roman Empire, with its many quasi-independent member states, did not have the kind of internal unity enjoyed by the Atlantic powers. Yet, under the leadership of the Austrian Habsburgs, the Empire proved capable of taking a leading part in international competition. Between the French and Habsburg power centers lay a zone of fragmentation where Burgundian dukes of the fifteenth century had tried to revive the middle kingdom. Out of this zone have come the modern small nations of Holland, Belgium, Luxembourg, Switzerland, and the larger (but never quite major) power, Italy. To the southeast was a new factor in international relations, Turkey, the Moslem successor to the old Byzantine Empire, with European lands right up to and beyond the Danube. To the east, the great state of Russia was beginning to be formed, and Poland was already great, at least in size. But save for Turkey, which sought to expand northwestward, and which was therefore actively anti-Habsburg, the eastern and southeastern states of Europe were not yet really integrated into high international politics.

Save for the overseas expansion of Europe, we have here a picture that is not worlds apart from the present one. Italy is today one political nation instead of a dozen, the German power-unit is in normal times one unified nation instead of the decentralized Holy Roman Empire, and on the east Russia is a very great power indeed, Poland a lesser one. Still, on the whole, the European state-system has the broad lines it had five centuries ago.

This comparative stability has not been maintained without threats to destroy it. In succession, certain states have attempted to break it down—sixteenth-century Spain, the France of Louis XIV in the seventeenth century and of the Revolution and Napoleon at the turn from the eighteenth to the nineteenth, the Germany of the Kaiser and Hitler in the twentieth. They have tried to absorb the other states, or at the very least to control them to a point where they were scarcely "sovereign." Each time, the threatened units sooner or later joined together in a coalition that was able to beat the armies of the aggressive power and maintain the system. Each time, England, which after the late medieval venture of the Hundred Years' War with France never attempted to absorb lands on the Continent of Europe (save for the few square miles of Gibraltar), sooner or later intervened to bolster, often to lead, the coalition against the aggressor. To use a time-honored phrase, the system was maintained through the workings of the "balance of power." This principle is not primarily a moral one, though some writers have defended it as basically moral in the sense that it tends to preserve the independence of organized states. "Balance of power" is, rather, a descriptive principle, a thread through the intricacies of international politics in the modern West. We must take up this thread in 1494.

Dynastic State and Nation State

First, however, we must examine briefly the nature of the political units that make up the competitive state-system. It is the fashion to call them *dynastic* states up to about the end of the eighteenth century and *nation* states thereafter. The distinction is a good rough working one. In the early modern period, many states were loose agglomerations of formerly independent medieval units that were sometimes separated from each other by foreign territory, that sometimes spoke separate languages, and that were tied together almost solely by the ruling dynasty. The Habsburg realm is a good example. In war and diplomacy the dynastic ruler and his circle of nobles and bureaucrats were a team, but the different peoples in the state had relatively little sense of patriotism, of common national effort and ambitions. Early modern wars, perhaps excepting the wars of religion, were less than total wars. Except in their disastrous effects on government finances and on taxes, they scarcely touched the lives of the common people who were not actually in the way of contending armies. In the peace settlements, no one talked about "national self-determination of peoples," or worried greatly about transferring areas and populations from one ruler to another.

The distinction between dynastic and nation states must not, however, be exaggerated or oversimplified. Especially in the great monarchies of Spain, England, and France a degree of national patriotism existed as early as the sixteenth century. Even in divided Germany, Luther could count on Germans to dislike Italians. Hatred of the foreigner binds men together at least as effectively as love of one another. Nor does the custom, so strange to us, of transferring political units by marriage of ruling families really affect the basic similarity between the state-system of early modern times and our own. Perhaps the accidents of marriage account for the unusual combination under one ruler of Germany and Spain under Charles V; but for the most part the alliances and alignments of the sixteenth century conform extremely well to conditions of geography, resources, tradition, and culture.

By 1500, almost all these states possessed in at least a rudimentary form most of the social and political organs of a modern state. They lacked only a large literate population brought up in the ritual and faith of national patriotism. Notably they had two essential organs, a diplomatic service and an army, both professional, both usually controlled from a common governmental center.

Diplomacy

Some forms of diplomacy can be traced back into the Middle Ages, and indeed into ancient times. But the fifteenth and sixteenth centuries saw the full development of modern diplomatic agencies and methods. Governments established central foreign offices and sent diplomats on regular missions to foreign courts. Espionage and the secret services developed under the cover of open diplomacy. Formal peace conferences were held, and formal treaties were signed, to the accompaniment of the ceremony and protocol we now associate with such occasions. Finally, a set of rules governing all these formal relations began to take shape, a set of rules that can be called international law.

The apparatus of international politics developed most fully and soonest in Renaissance Italy, and found its classic expression in the admirably organized diplomatic service of the Republic of Venice. The detailed reports Venetian ambassadors sent back to the Senate from abroad are among the first documents of intelligence work. They are careful political and social studies of the personalities and lands involved rather than mere gossipy cloak-and-dagger reports.

In those days, the diplomat abroad was a most important maker of policy in his own right. With rapid travel impossible, his government could not communicate with him in time to prescribe his acts minutely, and he had often to make important decisions on his own responsibility. Good or bad diplomacy, good or bad intelligence about foreign lands, made a vital difference in a state's success or failure in the struggle for power.

The Armed Forces

The armed forces made still more difference. These early modern centuries are the great days of the professional soldier, freed from the limitations of feudal warfare and not yet tied to the immense economic requirements and the inhuman scale of our modern warfare. The officer class in particular could plan, drill, and campaign on a fairly large but quite manageable scale; they could do more than the interminable jousting of late medieval times. They could, so to speak, handle warfare as an art and sometimes as a pleasure. The common soldiers had a less agreeable life. But they too, for the most part, were paid professionals; indeed the word "soldier" comes from *solidus*, the Latin for a piece of money. Recruited usually from among the poor and dispossessed, sometimes by force, they became inured to many hardships and were on the whole rather more secure in food, clothing, and housing than their poorer civilian relatives.

The armed forces were the ruler's forces, no longer mere feudal levies. They were paid professionals, often trained to parade, to dress ranks, to keep discipline. They were whipped if they broke discipline, although threats of punishment did not always prevent desertions when pay was late or rations inadequate. Each regiment, troop, or unit commonly wore the same uniforms; whole armies, however, usually displayed such an extraordinary variety of costume that in battle recognition of friend and foe was not easy. Tactics and strategy in the field were under the control of a formal officer hierarchy that culminated in a general in command, who in turn was at least somewhat controlled by the central government

through a ministry of war. In short, though these armies would look anarchic to a modern professional of the spit-and-polish school, they were far better organized and better disciplined than feudal levies had been.

Armies on the march lived mostly off the land, even when they were in home territory. But they were beginning to develop the elaborate modern organization of supply and the modern service of engineers. Both the growth of military technology and differences of national temperament were reflected in the shift of military predominance from Spain to France about 1600. Spain, the great fighting nation of the sixteenth century on land, excelled in infantry, where the pike was a major weapon. France, the great fighting nation of the seventeenth and early eighteenth centuries on land, excelled in artillery, engineering, and fortification, all services that were more plebeian, less suited to the former feudal nobility than infantry and cavalry.

Meanwhile, the first modern navies were also growing up. In the later Middle Ages, Venice, Genoa, and Pisa had all begun to assemble fleets of galleys disciplined both in the running of each ship and in maneuvers as a fleet. In the Renaissance, Venice took the lead with its Arsenal and its detailed code of maritime regulations (see Chapter II). Naval organization, naval supply, the dispatch and handling of ships, all required more orderly centralized methods than an army. They could not tolerate the survival of rugged feudal individualism, indiscipline, and lack of planning. The officer class, as in the armies, was predominantly aristocratic, but it came usually from the more adventurous, the less custom-ridden part of that class. During the sixteenth century, naval supremacy passed out of the Mediterranean to the Atlantic, where it rested briefly with Spain, and thence passed in the seventeenth century to the northern maritime powers of England, Holland, and France.

II: Habsburg and Valois

The Italian Wars of Charles VIII and Louis XII

Charles VIII of France (1483-1498) inherited from his parsimonious father Louis XI a well-filled treasury and a good army (see Chapter II). He added to his kingdom by marrying the heiress to the Duchy of Brittany, which had long been largely independent of the French crown. Apparently secure on the home front, Charles decided to expand abroad. As the remote heir of the Angevins who had conquered Naples in the thirteenth century, Charles disputed the right of the Aragonese Ferrante (see Chapter II) to hold the Neapolitan throne. He chose Italy, however, not only because he had this tenuous genealogical claim but also because Renaissance Italy was rich, held romantic attractions for the Northerners, and was divided into small rival political units—it looked, in short, to be easy picking. So it was at first, for in the winter of 1494-95 Charles paraded through to Naples in triumph. But Charles' acquisition of Brittany had already disturbed his neighbors, and his possession of Naples threatened the balance of power in Italy. The French intrusion provoked the first of the great modern coalitions, the so-called Holy League of the Papacy (which, remember, was also an Italian territorial state), the Empire, Spain, Venice, Milan, and soon England. This coalition forced the French armies out of Italy without much trouble in 1495.

Charles was followed on the French throne by his cousin of the Orléans branch of the Valois family, Louis XII (1498-1515). Louis married Charles' widow to make sure of Brittany, and then tried again in Italy, reinforced by another genealogical claim, this time to Milan. Since his grandmother came from the dispossessed Visconti family,

Louis regarded the reigning Sforza dukes as simple usurpers; he proceeded to drive Il Moro from Milan in 1499. In this second French invasion, the play of alliances was much subtler and more complicated, quite worthy of the age of Machiavelli. Louis tried to insure himself from the isolation that had ruined his predecessor, Charles VIII, by allying in 1500 with Ferdinand of Aragon, with whom he agreed to partition Naples. Then, in 1508, Louis helped form one of those cynical coalitions that look on paper as though they could break the balance-of-power principle, because they are the union of the strong against a much weaker victim. This was the League of Cambray, in which Louis, Ferdinand, Pope Julius II, and the Emperor Maximilian joined to divide up the lands held in the lower Po Valley by the rich but militarily weak Republic of Venice.

The practical trouble with such combinations is that the combiners do not really trust one another, and usually fall to quarreling over the pickings. All went well for the despoilers at first, though the Venetians rallied and re-took their mainland stronghold of Padua. Then Ferdinand, having taken the Neapolitan towns he wanted, decided to desert Louis. The Pope, frightened at the prospect that France and the Empire might squeeze him out entirely, in 1511 formed another "Holy League" *with* Venice and Ferdinand, later joined by Henry VIII of England and the Emperor Maximilian, *against* France. Despite some early successes in the field, the French could not hold out against such a coalition, for they now had a war on two fronts. Henry attacked the north of France and won at Guinegate in 1513 a battle that has always been a sore spot with Frenchmen. It was called (by the English) the "battle of the spurs" from the speed with which the

French cavalry departed from the battlefield. In Italy too the French were defeated, and Louis XII, like Charles VIII, was checkmated.

Charles vs. Francis: The First Round

These two efforts were, however, merely preliminaries. The important phase of this first great modern test of the balance of power was to follow immediately, and to take a basically different form. For there were now really two aggressors: the French House of Valois, still bent on expansion, and the House of Habsburg. When the Habsburg Charles V succeeded his grandfather Maximilian as emperor in 1519, he was a disturber by the mere fact of his existence rather than by temperament or intent. As we have already seen, in Chapter III, he had inherited Spain, the Low Countries, Germany, and the preponderance in Italy. He apparently had France squeezed in a perfect vise.

The vise almost closed. The French king, Francis I, was badly defeated by the imperial—mostly Spanish—forces at Pavia in 1525. Francis himself was taken prisoner and held in Madrid until he signed a treaty giving up all his Italian claims, and ceding the Duchy of Burgundy. This treaty he repudiated the moment he was safely back on French soil. It is of course possible that Charles V would not have "eliminated" France entirely even had he been able to; it is possible that the soldiers and diplomats were against the complete crushing of an opponent if only on the professional grounds of keeping the game going. Certainly these people convey the impression of engaging in a kind of professional athleticism that was often bloody and unscrupulous but by no means without rules. The players sometimes changed sides. In fact, one of the imperial commanders at the battle of Pavia in which the French were so badly beaten was the Constable de Bourbon, a great French noble at odds with his king.

Two years after Pavia, an incident occurred that burnt deeply into the minds of contemporaries—the sack of Rome in 1527 by the Spanish and German mercenaries of the emperor, led by the Frenchman Bourbon. These mercenaries had become infuriated by delays in pay and supplies. In a sudden shift of alignment, Pope Clement VII, a Medici and a good Italian at heart, had turned against the foreign Charles, and had allied himself with Francis and the other main Italian powers in the League of Cognac in 1526. The siege of Rome was part of Charles' reply, but the sack was a horror that he had not planned, and that lay heavily on his conscience as a good Catholic. This was one of the horrors of war that outrage public opinion in all but the most hardened partisan circles.

Charles was now at the height of his power. By the end of the decade, he had made peace with the Pope and with Francis. In 1530, he was crowned by the Pope as Emperor and as King of Italy, the last ruler to receive this double crown, this inheritance of Charlemagne and the ages, with the full formality of tradition. But the western world over which he thus symbolically ruled was a very different world from Charlemagne's, and Charles was in fact no emperor, but a new dynast in a new conflict of power.

Charles vs. Francis: The Second Round

France was still in the vise between the Spanish and the German holdings of Charles, and Francis I was no man to accept for long so precarious a position—above all, a position in which he lost face. He used the death of the Sforza ruler of Milan in 1535 to reopen the old claim to Milan and to begin the struggle once more. Neither Francis nor Charles lived to see the end even of this particular phase of the Habsburg-Valois rivalry. Neither side secured decisive military victory. In 1559, the Treaty of Cateau-Cambrésis confirmed Habsburg control of Milan and Naples. It marked the failure of France to acquire a real foothold in Italy, but it also marked the failure of the Habsburgs to lessen the real strength of France. The vise had not closed.

It had not closed because France proved militarily, economically, and politically strong enough to resist the pressure. But the vise itself was a most imperfect instrument. Charles was not as stong as he looked on the map to be. His German arm was paralyzed by the political consequences of the Protestant Reformation. Even in the decade of the 1520's, when the power of Charles was at its height, the Protestant princes of Germany had formed the League of Torgau to resist him. All the rest of his life, Germany was to be in a state of civil war, marked by truces indeed, and by attempts to settle the religious question, but never permitting the Emperor to count on a united Germany.

The last phase of the personal duel between the aging rivals, Charles and Francis, is a concrete example of how many variables enter the play of balance of power. Francis, to gain allies, did not hesitate to turn to Charles' rebellious German subjects. Although head of a Catholic state, a "most Christian" king, he allied himself with the Protestant Duke of Cleves. He did not even stop with Protestants, but concluded an alliance with the Moslem Sultan Suleiman of Turkey, who attacked Charles in the rear in Hungary. At the death of Francis in 1547, his son Henry II continued the Protestant alliance.

The Peace of Augsburg

Charles V, beset by Protestants, French, and Turks, allowed in 1555 the very important German religious settlement known as the Peace of Augsburg. By this peace, the Protestants were formally recognized as established in the regions they had consolidated. Augsburg marks the formal end of the first great effort to keep the Empire Catholic. But it by no means established full toleration in the modern sense. Its guiding principle is in the Latin phrase *cuius regio eius religio*, freely translated as *whoever rules an area may establish the religion of that area*. The ruler of Saxony is Lutheran: then all Saxons are practicing Lutherans. The ruler of Bavaria is Catholic: then all Bavarians are practicing Catholics. To work, this settlement would have had to mean that all the many German states were self-sealed little blocks of one religion, which was quite impossible.

Two concrete failures of the Augsburg settlement made a renewal of religious strife almost certain. First, no solution was reached concerning "ecclesiastical reservation," the problem of what happened to the property of the Church in a given region if its ruler were a Catholic prelate who was converted to Protestantism. Second, by recognizing formally only the Catholic and Lutheran faiths, the settlement ignored the growing numbers of militant Calvinists who were bound to press for equal treatment. Still, with all its weaknesses, Augsburg made possible the permanent establishment of Protestantism on a peaceful footing in Germany. With the Treaty of Cateau-Cambrésis, it brought to an end the first great Habsburg effort to dominate Europe.

The Wars of Philip II

The second effort at domination of Europe was less Habsburg than Spanish. In 1556, Charles V abdicated both his Spanish and imperial crowns and retired to a monastery, where he died two years later. His brother, Ferdinand I (1556-1564), secured the Austrian Habsburg complex of territories and, by election, the Empire. His son, Philip II (1556-1598), got Spain and

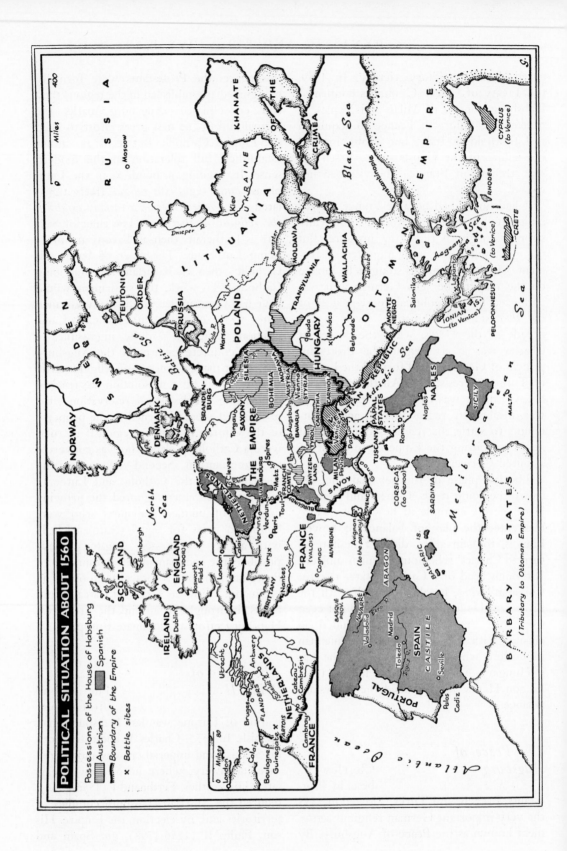

POLITICAL SITUATION ABOUT 1560

Possessions of the House of Habsburg
- Austrian
- Spanish
- Boundary of the Empire
- x Battle sites

108

the colonies, the Burgundian inheritance of the Netherlands, and the Italian holdings of Milan and Naples. Philip's realm was no mere national state; even without the Germanies, it was a supranational state threatening France, England, and the whole balance of power.

Like his father, Philip II found Protestantism and the concept of many separate Christian political units intolerable. He was a serious, hard-working administrator, and certainly no lover of war for its own sake. He saw Protestantism as an intolerable divisive force that must be wiped out by force if necessary. He was a doctrinaire chained to a past no one could restore, committed to a lost cause.

Philip's major points of involvement were: (1) Italy, which as long as it remained divided was to be a major source of difficulties—and opportunities for aggression—in the play of balance of power; (2) the Netherlands, where the revolt of his Dutch Protestant subjects was soon to involve Philip not only with them but with Protestant England; (3) France, where the second half of the century brought a series of civil wars of religion in which Philip was bound to appear as the Catholic champion; (4) the Mediterranean, where the Turks, now at the height of their naval power, threatened Spanish control. Finally, as we shall see in the next chapter, England and France were beginning to challenge the monopoly Spain and Portugal had tried to set up in the New World. Since this New World as well as the Old World was at stake in Philip's wars, there is some justification for considering these as in fact the first "world wars."

The Dutch Revolt

The dramatic focal point of these struggles is the revolt of the Netherlands. When the Burgundian inheritance had come to the Habsburgs, Charles V had made no attempt to absorb these provinces into a unified superstate. They were simply parts of a great dynastic holding, parts that were essentially autonomous, with their own complex of feudal privileges confirmed by their new ruler. They had medieval estates or assemblies, representing privileged groups, which raised taxes and armies. The southern provinces (roughly present-day Belgium) remained Catholic, but the northern provinces (roughly the present Kingdom of the Netherlands) had warmly espoused Calvinism.

Philip II was bound to antagonize his subjects in the Low Countries. Charles V had liked the Low Countries and had made Brussels his favorite place of residence, but Philip was thoroughly Spanish in outlook. For all his medievalism, he had up-to-date ideas about centralized, efficient rule, and he curtailed the political liberties of the Netherlands. Moreover, he hated all forms of Protestantism. Finally, the economic element was also present, for the Dutch were a seafaring commercial people, desirous of conducting a trade freed from the jealous restrictions of Spanish mercantilism. Under the complex of ideas known as "mercantilism," a dominant nation would seek to sell abroad more than it bought, thus gaining gold in the balance. And it would especially restrict foreigners and its own dependencies in their manufacturing and sea trade. Finally, it would seek to use its own dependencies as a source of raw materials.

This explosive mixture of religion, politics, and economics produced the revolt. Philip sent Spanish garrisons to the Netherlands, and attempted to enforce edicts against heretics. Opposition, which centered at first in the privileged classes who had been most affected by Philip's political restrictions, soon spread to the common people. Riots culminated in the destruction of Catholic churches and in the formation of a league against the Spaniards, which took on proudly the scornful name of "Beggars" that had been given them by a conservative. When in 1567 Philip dispatched to the Netherlands an army of twenty thousand

Spaniards headed by the unyielding, politically stupid Duke of Alva, the revolt had fully begun.

The Spanish infantry was in those days incomparably the best in Europe, and the Dutch were ill-armed and ill-prepared. The Dutch resistance, successful in the long run, was a heroic achievement against great odds, fully deserving the praise sympathetic historians have given it. It was, however, no extraordinary victory of weakness over strength, but rather a victory in full accord with what has until the twentieth century at least been a general rule of western political life—that no thoroughly disaffected population can be held down by force alone. Alva had the force, and he set up a Council of Troubles, which applied executions, confiscations, and severe taxation on a large scale. The Council has received from history the significant title of the "Council of Blood." Yet all that this repression accomplished was to unite opposition against Alva, for the Catholic southern provinces of the Netherlands now joined the Protestant northern provinces. Both the ordinarily quiet merchants and the great nobles like William the Silent, Prince of Orange, stood with the populace and with the adventurous "Beggars," who turned to a sort of naval guerrilla warfare. Alva gave up in despair in 1573, but it was not until the Duke of Parma was sent out in 1578 that Philip's policy showed signs of the essential element of statesmanship, a willingness to compromise in the face of facts.

Under Parma, the Catholic southern provinces at least were won back by political concessions to their old privileges of self-rule. But it was too late to win back the northern provinces, except perhaps by radical religious concessions which Philip was by temperament utterly unable to make. By the Union of Utrecht, the Dutch tightened their organization and in 1581 took the decisive step of declaring themselves independent of the Spanish Crown. They made

good that declaration by their courageous use of their now much better-organized land forces. But they were greatly helped by three facts. First, Philip, like most of the great aggressors, had been drawn into fighting on more than one front. He had to cope with the Turks, the French Protestants, and the anti-Spanish moderate French Catholics, as well as with grave internal economic problems. Second, fate gave the Dutch that invaluable spiritual aid, a martyr. And last and most important, they acquired a major ally.

The martyr was William the Silent, who was assassinated in 1584 by an individual moved either by religious hatred or by the reward Philip had set upon the outlawed Dutchman's head, or by both. William's death deprived the Dutch of the first great leader in their national history, but the assassination did not profit the Spanish cause. It made William, who was a western European nobleman without strong religious feeling, a Protestant and Dutch hero. The ally was England, now under Elizabeth I firmly Protestant and from the start sympathetic with the Dutch cause. Elizabeth, however, was no crusader, and her kingdom appeared to be no match for powerful Spain. She had been hesitant to come out openly on the Dutch side, the more since in the uncertain condition of French politics a Franco-Spanish alliance seemed by no means impossible. Here too Philip showed himself a poor diplomat. He permitted France to maneuver into neutrality, and provoked England by fomenting Catholic plots against Elizabeth. The English in turn, provoked Spain. For years they had been preying on Spanish commerce on the high seas, and Hawkins, Drake, and other English sailors had been raiding Spanish possessions in the New World. When an English army came to the aid of the Dutch in 1585, Philip decided to make formal war on England, though he still had the Dutch on his hands.

The End of Philip II   The great Spanish Armada of unwieldy men-of-war which he sent out to invade England was defeated in the English Channel in July, 1588, by a skillfully maneuvered lighter English fleet, and was utterly destroyed afterward by a great storm. The battle was the beginning of the end of Spanish preponderance, the beginning of English greatness in international politics, and the decisive step in the achievement of the independence of the Dutch Republic. These portentous results were not as evident in 1588 as they are now, but even at the time the defeat of the Armada was seen as a great event. Protestants everywhere were greatly heartened, and the great storm that finished the destruction of the Spanish fleet was christened the "Protestant wind."

Philip II died in 1598 after a long and painful illness, in the great, severe palace of the Escorial he had built near Madrid. He had ordered an open coffin put beside his bed, and a skull with a crown of gold. Save for the seven northern provinces of the Netherlands—and even these he had never officially given up—the great possessions with which he had begun to reign were still his. Indeed, he had added Portugal in 1580 at the death of the Portuguese Cardinal-King Henry and had made the whole Iberian Peninsula formally if briefly one. Yet he knew almost as clearly as we know that his life had been a failure. He left his kingdom, as we shall see, worn out, drained of men and money. And, whatever his aims in international politics had been, whether a Spanish hegemony, a revived western Empire, or merely the extinction of the Protestant heresy, he had realized none of them. Under his illegitimate half-brother Don John of Austria, the Spanish fleet had indeed participated in a great naval victory over the Turkish fleet at Lepanto in 1571. But Lepanto was at most a checking of Turkish expansion, not a great gain for the Spaniards. It was no balance for the loss of the great Armada.

The Dutch Republic   After Philip's death, the fighting went on in Holland in a desultory way until a truce in 1609 established the virtual independence of the United Provinces—or United Netherlands, as the Dutch Republic was termed. This independence was confirmed as part of international law by the Peace of Westphalia in 1648. In those days the Dutch were one of the great powers of Europe, a major factor in international politics (see Chapter VI), and the leaders in some highly significant developments. In religion, for instance, a wide toleration was practiced, and Holland became a refuge for persecuted Jews from Portugal and Spain and even from Poland and Lithuania. The government was controlled by a few thousand well-to-do merchants, but this northern counterpart of "Venetian oligarchy" also undertook a hectic yet fruitful experiment in decentralized government, in which each of the seven provinces enjoyed a measure of "states' rights."

In economic life, above all, the Dutch were the pace-setters of seventeenth-century Europe. They managed government finances as adroitly and efficiently as they managed their private businesses; the state borrowed money at 2½ per cent interest, an amazingly low figure for the time. They made life insurance into a big business by putting it on a firm actuarial basis, and in the Bank of Amsterdam they fostered a great commercial institution that went far to make Amsterdam the financial capital of Europe. Highly successful specialized industries grew up in the cities and towns of Holland —diamond-cutting at Amsterdam, shipbuilding at Zaandam, the distilling of gin at Schiedam, and around Haarlem the growing of tulip bulbs, which set off a wild financial speculation. Abroad, Dutch ships played a large part in the international carrying trade, and the Dutch East India Company assembled and exploited a commercial empire (see Chapter V). By 1700, however, the great days of Holland were coming to a close. The Dutch Republic remained generally prosperous and with a high level of civilization, but it was a small state without the manpower and the resources needed to sustain permanently the role of a great international power.

III: The Thirty Years' War

Nature and Causes

We have now reviewed two of the great conflicts of early modern times—the Habsburg-Valois struggle and the wars of Philip II. The third great conflict, the Thirty Years' War of 1618-1648, was fought largely in Germany and takes us a bit beyond the chronological limits of this chapter. But it was a war in which religion bore a part at least as great as it had in the wars of Charles and Philip, and its focus was still a Habsburg focus. The Austrian Emperor, Ferdinand II (1619-1637), scarcely aspired to universal rule, but he did make the last serious political and military effort to unify Germany under Catholic rule. The Thirty Years' War began as a conflict between Catholics and Protestants; it ended as an almost purely political struggle to reduce the power of the Habsburgs in favor of France and a newcomer to high international politics, Sweden. It was the last of the old and the first of the new wars.

As we have already noted, the Augsburg Peace of 1555 did not bring complete religious peace to Germany. It did not recognize Calvinism, to say nothing of the more radical Protestant sects, and it left unsettled the problem of ecclesiastical reservation. On this latter issue, an imperial decree provided that if a Catholic prelate were converted to Protestantism the property formerly under his control should remain in Catholic hands. But this was a one-sided proclamation; it had not been formally negotiated with the Protestants and it was naturally much resented by them.

By the opening of the seventeenth century, the religious situation in Germany was becoming increasingly unsettled. Incidents of violence between Catholics and Protestants, especially Calvinists, were multiplying. In 1608, Calvinist elements formed the Protestant Union, which in turn prompted the creation of the Catholic League in 1609. Thus Germany was split into rival camps a decade before the outbreak of war. From the start, moreover, both the Protestant Union and the Catholic League had political as well as religious ambitions. Both really represented the interests of German particularism—that is, of the individual German states—against those of the Empire, even though the Catholic League and its leader, Maximilian of Bavaria, were to ally with the Emperor Ferdinand.

The Bohemian Period, 1618-1625

The war broke out in Bohemia, now part of Czechoslovakia, then a Habsburg crown land, with a strong Protestant minority known as the Utraquists. This name brings up one of the main quarrels between Protestants and Catholics, that of the actual administration of the Eucharist. In Catholic worship, the layman receives the bread but not the wine; only the officiating priest takes the wine. The Utraquist, from the Latin for "both," took both the wine and the bread in communion. As with the Hussite movement two centuries earlier (see Chapter II), Utraquism was in part Bohemian nationalism. The nationalists wanted local independence from the rule of Germans and of Vienna, and they caused the incident that actually provoked war, the "defenestration of Prague" in 1618. Rebels headed by Count Matthias of Thurn seized control of the Bohemian capital city and in an excited conference threw two royal governors out of a palace window. Though the victims fell seventy feet, they landed on a pile of dung and escaped with their lives.

The emperor-to-be, Ferdinand II (he was formally elected in 1619), was not prepared for civil war. The rebels, aided by Protestant forces from Germany, gained control in Bohemia and deposed Ferdinand as King of Bohemia. To fill his place, an assembly of the Bohemian estates chose the youthful Frederick V, Elector of the Palatinate in western Germany, and head of the Protestant Union. Although Frederick was the son-in-law of James I of England and as a Protestant very popular there, England did not come to his aid, nor in effect did the Protestant Union. The Spaniards, however, did come in on the Catholic side and sent an army to the Palatinate, frightening the Union into a declaration of neutrality. In Bohemia, Frederick was defeated by the army of the Catholic League at the battle of the White Mountain (1620) and was forced to flee his new kingdom. The Protestant Union was dissolved, and small Protestant remnants were beaten by the imperial general Tilly.

The Danish Period, 1625-1629

At this low point in Protestant fortunes, a champion arose outside Germany proper in Denmark, where King Christian IV (1588-1648) took over the leadership of the Protestant forces. A vigorous and ambitious monarch, Christian had increased his royal power by taking full advantage of the increased authority that Lutheranism gave to the king. When he intervened in the war, he sought not only to defend his co-religionists but also to extend Danish political and economic hegemony over northern Germany.

Still another factor now entered the struggle, the famous—and infamous—private army of Wallenstein (1583-1634). This general, though born of a German Protestant family in Bohemia, was reared a Catholic, and fought on the imperial side. His army was recruited and paid by himself, and lived off the land by requisitions and plunderings, sometimes at the expense of imperial and Catholic sympathizers. Wallenstein was in fact a German *condottiere*, a private citizen seeking to become a ruling prince, perhaps even dreaming of a united German empire, no longer the old medieval successor to Charlemagne's empire, but a fine, new-model monarchy. He never came close to success, but his army was a major factor in the war at its most critical period. Tilly's and Wallenstein's armies were enough to dispose of Christian IV. They overran Christian's North German lands and pushed into the Danish peninsula.

Then, at the height of the imperial and Catholic success, Ferdinand and his advisers overreached themselves. By the Edict of Restitution and the Treaty of Lübeck in 1629, they sought to take the fullest advantage of their victories. The Edict of Restitution not only reaffirmed the Augsburg exclusion of the Calvinists and Protestant radicals from toleration but also demanded the restoration of all ecclesiastical estates that had passed from Catholic to Lutheran hands since 1551, three generations before. The Treaty of Lübeck allowed Christian IV to recover his lands, but it exacted from him a promise not to intervene in Germany. This seemed to the outside world a sign that the Habsburg power was actually spreading to the Baltic, to a region thoroughly Protestant and hitherto only on the margin of imperial control. The old pattern was, then, repeated. The Habsburgs on the wave of success went outside the bounds of their customary spheres of influence; those upon whose spheres they thus encroached fought back against the trespass; the trespasser was finally forced to withdraw.

The Swedish Period, 1630-1635

In 1630, at the height of Habsburg success, Gustavus Adolphus, King of Sweden (1611-1632), landed with a Swedish army on the North German coast. A new champion of the Protestants, a much stronger one than Christian of Denmark, had come out of the North. Once again, religious and secular motives were thoroughly intermixed. Gustavus was a strong Lutheran, who led an army of hymn-singing soldiers. In Sweden, as in Denmark, the coming of the Reformation had consolidated royal authority. Like Christian, Gustavus Adolphus had ambitions for political control in northern Germany, and he hoped, too, that Sweden might take over economic leadership there. He had already won territories along the eastern Baltic by waging successful wars against Russia and Poland. Significantly, his army, large and well equipped for so relatively poor a country as Sweden, was now in part paid for by subsidies received from the French monarchy through negotiations with its minister Richelieu, a cardinal of the Roman Catholic Church. For France, too, the great success of the old Habsburg enemy seemed a trespass, and those who guided French policy were quite willing to help Protestant Sweden beat Catholic Austria.

Gustavus Adolphus was a very skillful general whose intervention was to alter the whole course of the war. In the field, the Swedes won two decisive victories at Leipzig in 1631 and at Lützen in 1632.

Gustavus Adolphus was killed at Lützen, but his coming had turned the tide. Wallenstein withdrew into winter quarters, and began negotiations that have baffled historians ever since. Certainly he was trying to set himself up as a mediator between the Protestants and the extremist wing of the imperial party, the Court at Vienna, the wing that had called in the Spaniards. Perhaps he was at heart a great patriot, striving to unite divided Germany. Whatever he was planning was cut short by his assassination in 1634, an assassination almost certainly not directly planned by the Emperor Ferdinand, but from which he cannot be dissociated, since he rewarded the assassins.

Swedish-French Period, 1635-1648

Though the two great antagonists, Gustavus and Wallenstein, were dead, the war went on. Swedish affairs were in the able hands of the chancellor Oxenstierna, aided by two good generals, Baner and Torstenson. In 1642, the Swedes won a second battle at Leipzig and threatened the core of Habsburg power, the hereditary lands of Bohemia and Austria. But these Swedish successes had begun to seem more Swedish than Protestant and drew from Christian IV of Denmark, the recent champion of Protestantism, a response not uncommon in the history of balance-of-power politics. Now more fearful of the nearby Swedes than of the distant Austrians, Christian went to war with Sweden, and saw his lands once more successfully invaded.

Meanwhile, however, the ultimately decisive force was entering the bewildering struggle. The French had decided that subsidies ("economic aid") to German and Swedish opponents of the Habsburg power were not enough, and that they themselves would have to fight. French armies crossed the Rhine and struck at the imperialists through South Germany. Theirs was by no means a triumphal march, and bitter fighting took place in the last years of the war, from 1643 to 1648. In 1645, the Danes gave up and made a separate peace. In 1648, a series of peace conferences met in the north-western German region of Westphalia—the first of the great general peace conferences of modern times. The Habsburgs were the vanquished; the French and Swedes were the victors.

In its last years the Thirty Years' War had in fact become a general war. On the seven seas the French and Spanish were at odds. In Italy, the French had tried to split communication between the Austrian and the Spanish Habsburgs by controlling the Alpine passes. This general war had, how-ever, one striking difference from all others of modern times: the balance of power had to be achieved without one of its main fac-tors, England. England kept out of the war for the obvious reason that in all these years she was facing domestic crisis and civil war (see Chapter VI).

Effects on Germany

The defeat of the Habs-burgs in 1648, though it did not end in the sheer collapse of the defeated power, left the Germanies in a fearful state. Although the engines of destruction available to men in the seventeenth century were feeble in comparison with those available to us, it may well be that in terms of human suffer-ing and material destruction the Thirty Years' War was quite as disastrous to Ger-many as the last two world wars of the twentieth century. One obvious point: if we today can destroy more easily, we can also mend more easily. In the seventeenth century, the rebuilding of a destroyed town was a long process. On the human side, deaths from wounds, disease, and famine could not in the defective state of medicine and transport be effectively checked as they are today.

On the other hand, some recent his-torians have questioned the old thesis of the shattering effect of the Thirty Years' War on the Germanies. They think twentieth-century Germans have exaggerated these seventeenth-century sufferings in order to explain, like any neurotic, their subsequent "bad" behavior, their inability to produce a democratic modern state. As usual, there is no doubt something in this particular instance of historical "revisionism"; still, the fact remains that the Thirty Years' War was fought in Germany with disastrous and long-continuing results for the peoples of Germany.

The Peace of Westphalia

The reality of 1648 was that Germany had reached a low point of political and cultural disintegration. In the great settlements of Westphalia, though some of the separate German states came out well, Germany herself was a major victim. The French got bits of land toward their northeast frontier, notably a foothold in Alsace. Sweden got lands south of the Baltic, on the German mainland, and a real start toward her ambitious goal of con-trolling the Baltic area. Due compensations and adjustments were made among the major German states. In particular, Branden-burg, though damaged by the cessions to Sweden on the mainland, got valuable com-pensations in lands around Magdeburg, and in the next two centuries was to recover some of the cessions made to Sweden. Indeed, the beginning of the greatness of Brandenburg-Prussia is commonly dated from 1648.

Still more important, the Peace of West-phalia formally recognized the "independ-ence" of the constituent elements of the German Empire. From now on, the Ger-man states could enter into alliances with one another and with foreign powers, as long as they were not directed against the emperor. This last was a face-saving for the Habsburgs, but the fact that the constituent

EUROPE IN 1648

Brandenburg-Prussia
Austrian ⎫ Habsburg Lands
Spanish ⎭
Swedish possessions
Venetian possessions
Ottoman Empire
Boundary of the Holy Roman Empire
× Battle sites

20 15 10 5 0 5 10 15

55

NORWAY
Oslo

SCOTLAND
Edinburgh
Dunbar
Berwick

North Sea

DENMARK
Copenhagen
Lübeck
Hamburg
Bremen
Magdeburg
Berlin
BRANDENBURG

Stockh

Bal

50

ULSTER
IRELAND
Drogheda
Dublin
Wexford ×

Preston ×
Marston Moor ×
ENGLAND
Nottingham
Worcester ×
Naseby ×
London

TEXEL ×
UNITED NETHERLANDS
Osnabrück
Münster
WEST-PHALIA
Lützen ×
SAXONY

THE

Prague
BOHEMIA
SILE
MORA

Approximate division line between Puritans [ ] and Cavaliers in England, May, 1643

45

Atlantic Ocean

Seine R.

Paris
Nantes
Orleans
Loire R.

Verdun
Metz
Toul
PALATINATE
Heidelberg
ALSACE
Strasbourg
Danube
BAVARIA

EMPIRE

WHITE MT.
WHITE MT.
AUSTRIA
Vienna
STYRIA
CARINTHIA
CARNIOLA

H

FRANCE
Bordeaux

SPANISH NETHERLANDS
Rhine R.

FRANCHE COMTÉ
Geneva
SWITZER-LAND
VALTELLINE
Rhone R.
SAVOY
PIEDMONT
MILAN
Genoa
TYROL
Venice
VENETIAN REPUBLIC
Adriatic

40

PORTUGAL
Lisbon
Tagus R.
Burgos
Ebro R.
Madrid
SPAIN
Valencia
Guadalquivir R.
Seville
Granada
Barcelona

Avignon (to the papacy)
Marseilles

BALEARIC IS.

CORSICA (to Genoa)

Florence
PAPAL STATES
Rome

NAPLES
Naples

SARDINIA

35

Mediterranean

ALGIERS (Tributary to Ottoman Empire)

TUNIS

Palermo
SICILY

MALTA

G.

5 0 5 10 15

116

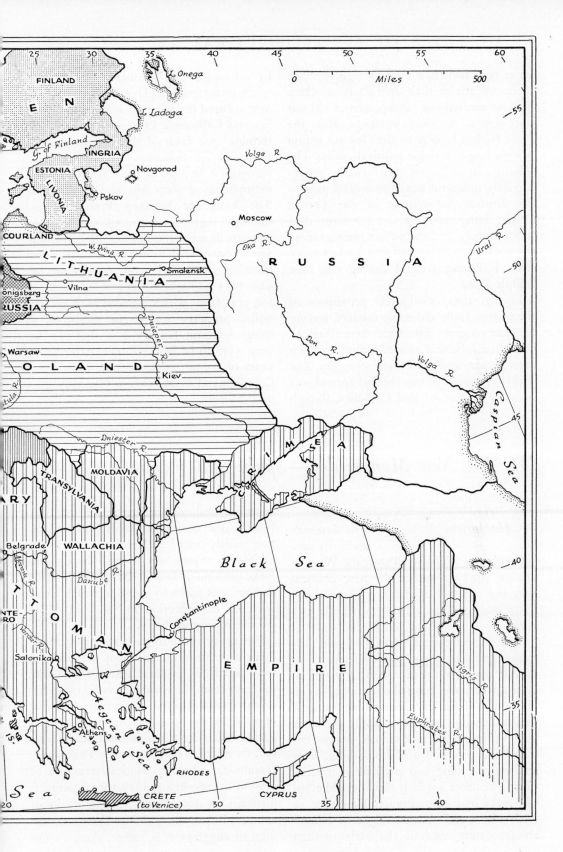

states now had their own foreign services, their own armies, their own finances—three obvious earmarks of "independence" in our state-system—is clear evidence that the Holy Roman Empire of the German nation was no longer a viable political entity. The Westphalia settlement also formally recognized the independence of two small states— the United Netherlands of the Dutch, already independent in fact for more than half a century, and the Swiss Confederation, the nucleus of which had first broken away from Habsburg control during the later Middle Ages.

Finally, the ecclesiastical provisions of the treaties really did settle matters, leaving German religious differences henceforth to take their relatively peaceful modern form of missionary and educational struggles. The Thirty Years' War was the last formal war between Protestants and Catholics, though by no means the last war in which their religious antagonism played a part. Calvinists now secured the same recognition as Catholics and Lutherans. Princes could still "determine" the faith of their territories, but the right of dissidents to emigrate was recognized. In most of Protestant Germany, multiplicity of sects was in fact accepted. The boundary between Protestant and Catholic regions recognized the Catholic gains made since the Catholic Reformation, and is today much as in 1648. On the vexed question of ecclesiastical reservation the year 1624 was taken as the *annus normalis,* the year from which ownership of ecclesiastical property was to be measured; as things were on January 1 of that year, so they were to be in the future. After thirty years of trying to exterminate each other, Catholics and Protestants in Germany gave up the effort.

IV: *The New Monarchies—Spain and France*

The *"Age of Absolutism"*

The sixteenth and early seventeenth centuries saw all over the West an uneven working out of the new political aims and methods of the Renaissance. The states that took part in the dynastic and religious wars we have just traced were all to a degree centralized states with paid professional armies and paid professional civilian bureaucrats. They had a central financial system with some control over taxation and the supply of money, a central legal system that made some attempt to apply the same kind of law to all individuals within the state, and a central authority—king, king and council, king and parliament, estates, Cortes, or other assembly—that could actually make new laws. Phrases like "Age of Absolutism" and "Divine Right of Kings" are frequently used of the early modern centuries, and not without reason. All over Europe, the control of central administration usually rested with a monarch who inherited his throne and claimed the right to make the kind of final decisions that modern democracies make by some sort of popular vote, or its reflection in the vote of an elected legislative body.

But everywhere in the sixteenth century there were strong survivals of old medieval local privileges, of local ways of life quite different from the standards set by the court or the capital. Indeed, an important school of modern European historians has urged against the older thesis of the absolute state the thesis of "corporatism." The social, economic, and even political structure of most of Europe before 1789, the corporatists maintain, is not along the neat chain of command that the political *theory* of absolutism suggests. It is, rather, along a complex series of adjustments among corporate bodies, law courts, provincial estates, town councils, guilds of merchants and of artisans, church bodies, a whole group-life surviving from the Middle Ages.

The early modern governments were clearly less "absolute," in at least one very significant sense of the term, than the government of a modern democracy like the United States. They could not possibly make *and enforce* the kind of regulation federal and state agencies nowadays can make and enforce—pure food and drugs acts, licensing the practice of medicine, setting standards of measure, even the kind of standardization of higher education we have achieved in the training of teachers, for instance, by accreditation and other controls. This last instance suggests that standardization, the efficient application of general rules to large areas and large groups, is in the United States partly a matter of voluntary control from *below*. Generally speaking, such collaboration from below was not attained in these first modern centuries. The standardization came from *above*, from a small group that had been won over to these new methods of governing, which did increase their power. It is this active attempt of a minority to achieve "streamlining" that justifies our use of terms like absolutism for these centuries.

Power and Limits
of Spanish Absolutism

Spain provides a clear-cut example of the difference between the concepts of absolutism with which this minority worked and the varied and often successfully recalcitrant groups on which this minority sought to impose its standardized rules. The reigns of the two hard-working Spanish monarchs, Charles V (technically, Charles I of Spain, 1516-1556) and Philip II (1556-1598), span almost the whole sixteenth century. Charles was rather a medieval survival than a modern king. He

did little to remodel the instruments of government he inherited from his grandparents, Ferdinand and Isabella (see Chapter II). Brought up in the Low Countries, Charles came to Spain a stranger, with a Flemish following that already had the modern northern European contempt for "backward" Spain, and showed it. His election to the imperial throne made him further suspect in Spain. In 1520, a group of Spanish cities, led by Toledo, rose up in the revolt of the *comuneros*. This, like most such uprisings, was compounded of many elements. The municipalities disliked the growth of central control; the aristocrats were restless in the face of the new monarchical dignity, no longer just like their own; the poor and the middling had class feelings and grievances. The *comuneros* were put down in 1521, but Charles had been frightened out of what reforming zeal he may have had, and did his best not to offend his Spanish subjects. His son, at least, was brought up to be a Spaniard first of all.

Philip II was much more willing and able to build a new-model centralized state in Spain. He did devise a system of consultative councils, topped by a council of state, and manned by great nobles; but these councils could do no more than advise. Philip made the final decisions, and the details were worked out by a series of private secretaries and local organs of government, not manned by nobles. Furthermore, Philip reduced the representative assemblies, the Cortes, to practical impotence, especially in Castile. Nobles and priests, because they did not pay direct taxes, no longer attended the sessions of the Cortes, and the delegates of the cities were left as a powerless rump. Above all, Philip had assured sources of income—his tax of a fifth of the precious cargoes from America, direct taxes from the constituent states of his realm, revenues from the royal estates and from the sale of offices and patents of nobility, revenues from the authorized sale, at royal profit, of dispensations allowed by the pope (permission to eat meat on Fridays and in Lent, and even something very close to the very indulgences that had raised Germany against the pope). Philip, like most monarchs of his time, had no need to worry over representative bodies with control of the purse. Yet he was always heavily in debt, and left his government almost bankrupt.

Even in this matter of revenue, where Philip's power at first sight looks so complete and unchecked, the actual limitations of the absolute monarch of early modern times are clear. Except by borrowing and self-exhausting expedients like the sale of offices, he could not notably increase his income. He could not summon any representative group together and get them to vote new monies. In the first place, the constituent parts of his realm, Castile, Aragon, Navarre, the Basque Provinces, the Italian lands, the Low Countries, the Americas, and the newest Spanish lands, named after the monarch himself, the Philippine Islands, had no common organs of consultation. Each had to be dealt with as a separate problem. For the most part the nobility and clergy were tax-exempt, at least from direct taxes, and could not be called upon for unusual financial sacrifices. Add to all this the difficulty of collection, the opportunities for graft, and the lack of a long accumulated administrative and financial experience, and one can see why Philip could not have introduced a more systematic general taxation.

Outside the financial sphere, the obstacles to really effective centralization were even more serious. The union of the crowns of Aragon and Castile, achieved by the marriage of Ferdinand and Isabella, had by no means made a unified Spain. To this day, regionalism—to call it by a mild name—is perhaps more acute in Spain than in any other large European state. In those days, some of the provinces did not even have extradition arrangements for the surrender of common criminals within the peninsula. Many of them could and did levy customs dues on goods from the others. The old northern regions, which had never been well conquered by the Moslems, preserved all sorts of *fueros* or privileges. Aragon still preserved the office of *justicia mayor*, a judge nominated, it is true, by the Crown, but for life, and entrusted with an authority something at least remotely like that of the United States Supreme Court.

What the Habsburgs might have accomplished in Spain had they been able to expend their full energies on the task of uniting and developing their lands can never be known. What they did do was exhaust the peninsula, and weaken the lands overseas, in their effort to secure hegemony over Europe and to subdue the Protestant heresy. This was indeed the great age of Spain, the age when both on land and on sea the Spanish were admired and envied as the best fighters, the age when Spain seemed destined to be mistress of both the Americas, the age when Spain seemed the richest of states, the age of Loyola and Cervantes, the golden age of Spanish religion, literature, and art. But it was a brief flowering, and Spanish greatness largely vanished in the seventeenth century.

The Spanish Economy   Spain is commonly considered to be a classic example of a great political unit that failed to maintain a sound economic underpinning for its greatness. The peninsula is mountainous, and its central tableland is subject to droughts, but its agricultural potentialities are greater, for example, than those of Italy, and it has mineral resources, notably in iron. Moreover, Spain was the first of the great European states to attain lands overseas, and a navy and merchant marine to integrate the great resources of the New World with an Old World base. Yet all this wealth slipped through Spain's fingers in a few generations. Certainly a major factor in this decline was the immense cost of the wars of Charles V and Philip II. The Low Countries, which had brought in a large revenue to Charles, were a pure drain on Philip's finances. The famous Spanish infantry had to be paid everywhere it went, and the money thus spent went out of Spain forever, with nothing in the long run to show for it. Philip took over from his father a heavy debt, which grew heavier through his long reign.

Now governmental expenditure on armed forces, though in itself unproductive, is not necessarily fatal to a national economy. If such expenditure stimulates even greater productivity within the nation and its dependencies, then the nation may bear it, and even grow in wealth, as did imperial Germany after 1870. But this was not true of sixteenth-century Spain. She drew from the New World vast amounts of silver and many articles—sugar, indigo, tobacco, cocoa, hides—which, sold abroad, realized money without which she could hardly have carried on her European wars at all. But it was not enough to pay for world dominion. The bullion passed through Spanish hands into those of bankers and merchants in other European countries, partly to pay for the Spanish armies and navies, partly to pay for the manufactured goods Spain had to send to the New World and use herself.

In accordance with an economic policy common to other colonial powers of the time, Spain forbade industrial production in her colonies and sought to supply them with manufactured goods. *But she could not, or did not, develop her own industrial production to take care of this need.* Her merchants had by royal decree a monopoly on trade with the Indies. But as the century wore on, they were more and more reduced to the role of mere middlemen, sending to the Indies goods increasingly imported from the rest of Europe—and paid for with the bullion of the Indies. The English, the Dutch, and other competitors smuggled goods into Spanish overseas territories on a large scale. To use a favorite modern term, Spain's governmental expenditures were not used to "prime the pump" for increased national productivity—or, more accurately, the pumps they primed were not Spanish pumps. By 1600, Spanish home industry was on the decline.

The free-trade economists of the nineteenth century offered a simple explanation for this failure of Spain to make good use of her economic opportunities—monopoly under government supervision. Sixteenth-century Spain was certainly moving toward that economic policy called mercantilism, which reached its fullest development in seventeenth-century France (see Chapter VI). Although Spain lacked the true mercantilist passion for building national wealth under government auspices, she used many mercantilist techniques, the endless regulation in general and the narrow channeling of colonial trade in particular. The Spanish system left little room for individual economic initiative. In Castile, a single institution, the famous *Casa de Contratación* (House of Trade), controlled every transaction with the Indies, and licensed every export and import. The amount of sheer paper work, in an age unblessed by typewriters and mimeographs, was enormous.

Yet bureaucratic methods and monopolies were not the sole source of difficulty. The whole direction of Spanish civilization turned Spanish creative energies into other channels than the industrial. Warfare, politics, religion, art, traditional farming, or simply living like an *hidalgo* (*hijo de algo,* "son of somebody," hence nobleman, gentleman) were respectable activities. What Americans broadly understand by "business" was, if not disgraceful, certainly not an activity on which society set a premium. Not that as a nation the Spanish were lazy; the lower classes especially had to work very hard. That epitome of so much we think of as Spanish, Don Quixote, was hardly a lazy man, but his activity was not exactly productive of material wealth. If we take into consideration the numerous holidays, the habit of the siesta, the large

numbers of beggars, soldiers, priests, monks, and *hidalgos,* as well as the lack of encouragement to new enterprises and techniques and the heavy hand of an inefficient bureaucracy—if we put all this together, it becomes clear that the total national effort was bound to be inadequate in competition with nations better organized for modern economic life.

The Spanish Style

Yet the Spanish supremacy, though short-lived, was real enough, and has helped make the world we live in. Half the Americas speak Spanish (or a rather similar tongue, Portuguese) and carry, however altered, a cultural inheritance from the Iberian Peniusula. French, Dutch, and English national unity and national spirit were hardened in resistance to Spanish aggression. The Spanish character, the Spanish "style," was set—some may say hardened—in this Golden Age, which has left to the West some magnificent paintings and one of the few really universal books, the *Don Quixote* of Cervantes (1547-1616). This Spanish style is not at all like those of France and Italy, so often tied with Spain as "Latin"—a term that is very misleading if used to contrast these nations with "Nordic" or "Germanic" nations. Perhaps the term is most misleading when it groups these lands and their peoples together as "sunny" or "gay." For the Spanish spirit is among the most serious, most darkly passionate, most unsmiling, in the West. It is a striving spirit, carrying to the extreme the chivalric "point of honor," the religious pain of living in this flesh, the desire for something more.

The Spanish spirit stands out in the painting illustrated on page 122. The artist was not a native Spaniard at all, but El Greco, "the Greek" (1541-1614). Born Domenico

El Greco, "Burial of the Count of Orgaz."

Theotokopouli on the island of Crete, trained both in the Byzantine tradition of the Aegean world and at the school of Titian in Venice, he settled at Toledo, the religious capital of Castile, when he was approaching the peak of his career. Despite his cosmopolitan background, El Greco belongs completely to the Spain of Philip II and the Counter-Reformation, not at all to the Renaissance.

The subject of the painting is a Spanish legend, the burial of the Count of Orgaz. This fourteenth-century Castilian nobleman had built a church at Toledo to honor Saint Augustine and Saint Stephen. When he died, the two saints miraculously appeared to bury his body. In the painting, the two saints (Augustine is the bearded one) gently lift the Count, and the aristocratic mourners gravely witness the miracle as an angel conveys the Count's soul to the Virgin, to Christ, Saint Peter, and the host of the blessed waiting above. The whole effect is heightened by El Greco's characteristic distortion of human figures, with their long, thin heads, their great eyes turned upward. The painting stretches toward heaven like the pinnacles of a Gothic cathedral; it is a most extraordinary effort to record the mystic's unrecordable experience.

The creations of Cervantes, in their very different way, carry the mark of the Spanish style. Spain is Don Quixote tilting with the windmills, aflame for the Dulcinea he has invented, quite mad. But it is also the knight's servant, Sancho Panza, conventional, earthy, unheroic, and sane enough, though his sanity protects him not at all from sharing his master's misadventures. Cervantes almost certainly meant no more than an amusing satire of popular tales of chivalry. But his story has got caught up in the web of symbolism we live by, and the Don and his reluctant follower are for us Spain forever racked between ambitious heroism and reluctant common sense.

The extreme of pride—pride of race, of faith, of nation—has seemed to the outside world the mark of Spain. Perhaps there is little to choose among the triumphant prides of nations in triumph. Yet as the "shot heard round the world" sounds very American, so the Cid, the legendary hero of the reconquest, is very Spanish in these verses as he goes off to his crusade:

> Por necesidad batallo
> Y una vez puesto en la silla
> Se va ensanchando Castilla
> Delante de mi caballo

[I fight by necessity: but once I am in the saddle, Castile goes widening out ahead of my horse.]

The French Monarchy North of the Pyrenees another of the new monarchies had emerged in the fifteenth century. Perhaps no province of France—not even Brittany with its Celtic language and autonomous traditions, not even Provence with its language of the troubadours, its ties with Italy, its long history as a separate unit—shows the intense awareness of its own separateness that is to be found in Aragon, Catalonia, or the Basque Provinces of Spain. Moreover, unlike Greece, Italy, and the Iberian Peninsula, France for the most part is not cut up by mountain ranges into relatively isolated regions; the mountain barriers are mostly on her borders. Even so, France was but imperfectly tied together under Francis I (1515-1547), contemporary of Charles V and Henry VIII. Provinces like Brittany, which had only recently come under the Valois crown, retained their own local representative bodies (estates), their own local courts (*parlements*), and many other privileges. The nobility held on to feudal memories and attitudes, though it had lost most of its old governmental functions to royal appointees. The national bureaucracy was most rudimentary, a patchwork that could hardly fit into a modern administrative chart, with its little boxes showing who consults with whom, who obeys whom in a chain of authority.

As we have seen, however, the kingdom of Francis I possessed strength enough to counter the threat of encirclement by Charles V. The King himself was not another Louis XI. Self-indulgence weakened his health and distracted him from the business of government; his extravagant court and, far more, his frequent wars nearly wrecked the finances of the state. Yet in many respects Francis was a good Renaissance despot, thoroughly at home in the age of Machiavelli. In adversity he had courage: witness his successful recovery after the disaster at Pavia in 1525. In diplomacy he was unscrupulous and flexible: witness his alliance with the Turks and with the German Protestants. Good-looking (at least until his health broke down), amorous, courtly, lavish, Francis comported himself as many people expect royalty to behave. He did things on the grand scale; it is reported that it took 18,000 horses and pack animals to move the King and his court on their frequent journeys. Francis built the famous chateaux of Chambord and Fontainebleau, two of the masterpieces of French Renaissance architecture. In Paris he remodeled the great palace of the Louvre and founded the Collège de France, second only to the University (the Sorbonne) as an educational center. He patronized men of letters and artists, among them Leonardo. Francis I, in short, had style.

Francis, however, was the last strong king of the House of Valois. After his death in 1547, his son Henry II and his grandsons, under the control of Catherine de' Medici, their mother, were barely able to maintain the prestige of the Crown. Possibly not even a greatly gifted ruler could have prevented the disorders of the second half of the sixteenth century, disorders that seriously crippled France in the international rivalries of the day. These are the years of the French religious wars, the crisis that almost undid the centralizing work of Louis XI and his successors.

The French Wars of Religion, 1562-1598

Obvious parallels exist between the French religious wars and the German Thirty Years' War. In both regions, important elements among the upper and middle classes welcomed the intellectual and spiritual concepts of Protestantism. In both regions, religious toleration at first found few supporters, and the result was endemic civil war. In both regions, the weakness of a land devoured by civil war involved it in the international strife between Catholic and Protestant and invited and secured foreign intervention. In both regions, exhaustion of the struggling parties brought with it in the end a perhaps reluctant official policy of religious toleration.

Yet the differences between the French and the German experience of wars of religion are striking and important. The French experience was briefer, and less crippling. Passions ran high, and the French wars laid one of the great blots on the historical record: the massacre of St. Bartholomew's Day (August 23-24, 1572). On that day, the Protestant leader Coligny was murdered in Paris and thousands of other Protestants in Paris and in the provinces were dragged from their beds and killed according to a prearranged plan. Yet armies were small, and the great masses of the French people went on living not too badly. By the end of the sixteenth century, in spite of the recent chaos, France was on the threshold of its own era of preponderance.

In France, Protestantism scarcely touched the great peasant masses. The Huguenots, as the French Protestants came to be known, were strong among the nobility and among the new classes of capitalists and artisans. The religious map of France also showed a territorial as well as a class division, an exception to the rule that in Europe the North tends to be Protestant and the South Catholic. The northernmost sections of France, up against the Low Countries, though affected by Lutheranism at first, remained ardently Catholic, as did Brittany, most of Normandy, and the region of Paris. By the latter sixteenth century the Protestants were strongest in south-central and southwest France. Even in these regions, however, the employer class was more likely to be Protestant, the workers to be Catholic. The French nobility took up with Protestantism in part for political reasons; the old tradition of local feudal independence among the nobles encouraged resistance to the centralized monarchy and its agents.

The Valois kings remained firm, though hardly pious, Catholics. Francis I had extended the royal gains made at papal expense in the Pragmatic Sanction of Bourges of 1438 (see Chapter II). In the Concordat of Bologna, 1516, the pope allowed the king

Francis I of France.

a very great increase in control over the Gallican Church, including the important right of choosing bishops and abbots. The German princes in revolt had everything to gain in a worldly way by confiscation of Catholic Church property and by the establishment of an Erastian Lutheran Church. But the French kings after 1516 had everything to lose by a Protestant movement that would strengthen their restive nobility and that in its Calvinist form was the very opposite of Erastian, was indeed often anti-monarchical.

The most striking development to come out of the French religious wars was the establishment of the French Crown and its bureaucrats as a mediating power between the extreme Catholics and the Protestants. At the outbreak of the wars in 1562, the Queen-Mother, Catherine de' Medici, firmly opposed the growing Protestant party, if only because the great nobles who headed that party seemed to threaten the Crown itself. As the wars went on, however, the Huguenots, in spite of St. Bartholomew's Day and defeats in the field, remained strong. The Catholic nobles organized a threatening league headed by the powerful Guise family, and both sides took to negotiating with foreigners for help, the Catholics with Spain and the Protestants with England. Thus the French rulers found themselves pushed into opposition to *both* groups.

The Victory
of Henry of Navarre

The wars culminated in the "War of the Three Henries" (1585-1589)—named for Henry III, the actual King of France and the last of the grandsons of Francis I; Henry, Duke of Guise, head of the Catholic League; and Henry of Navarre, the Protestant cousin and heir-apparent of the childless king. The mere threat that a Protestant, Henry of Navarre, might succeed to the throne pushed the Catholic League to the extreme of proposing a deliberate violation of the rules of succession by making an uncle of Henry of Navarre, the Catholic Cardinal of Bourbon, king. But in an established monarchy rules of succession are in fact what we call "constitutional" laws and have behind them the full force of public opinion. Moderate French public opinion, already disturbed by the extremes of both Catholics and Protestants, now turned against the Catholic League.

Paris, however, was a strongly Catholic city, and a popular insurrection there, the "Day of the Barricades" (May 12, 1588), frightened Henry III out of the city, which triumphantly acclaimed Guise. Henry III took the weak man's way out, and connived at—indeed almost certainly planned—the assassination of the two great men of the Catholic League, Henry of Guise and his brother Louis. Infuriated, the League rose in full revolt, and King Henry was forced to take refuge in the camp of his Protestant cousin, Henry of Navarre, where he in turn was assassinated by a monk.

Henry of Navarre was now by law King Henry IV (1589-1610), first of the House of Bourbon. The Catholics set up the aged Cardinal of Bourbon as "King Charles X," but in the decisive battle of Ivry in March, 1590, Henry won a great victory, and laid siege to Paris. Long negotiations now followed, and Henry was persuaded that if he would abjure his own Protestant faith he could rally the moderate Catholics and secure at least tolerated status for the Protestants. He turned Catholic in 1593, and Paris was surrendered, giving rise to the probably apocryphal but very apt tale that he had remarked, "Paris is well worth a Mass." With the Edict of Nantes in 1598, the French religious wars were ended, but full religious freedom was not achieved. The Huguenots were allowed the exercise of their religion in certain areas, and their great nobles were permitted it in their own households; but notably at Paris and its environs, and in episcopal and archiepiscopal cities, the Huguenots were forbidden public worship. Real trouble for the future lay in the provision that gave Huguenots special political privileges in certain fortified towns. In the same year, 1598, the Treaty of Vervins with Spain put an end to Spanish intervention, and restored to the French Crown all Spanish conquests in France.

The Politiques

Henry of Navarre was a gifted leader, a realist rather than a cynic—in spite of his remark about Paris being worth a Mass—and, as we shall see in Chapter VI, the restorer of the French monarchy. He was fortunate in coming on the scene after the passions of civil war were nearing exhaustion; he could hardly have succeeded in his work of pacification had France not been ready for it. The intellectual preparation for the Edict of Nantes and the revived French monarchy had been in large part the work of a group of men known by the untranslatable French term, *politiques*. The greatest of them, Jean Bodin, who died in 1596, has been rather unfairly labeled a proponent of absolute monarchy. He did indeed hold that the sole possibility of order in a divided France lay in obedience to a king above petty civil strife. But he was far from preaching that the king must be obeyed no matter what he did. He was rather a moderate who believed in acceptance of the limitations imposed by history and tradition on any practical program of politics. The *politiques* were convinced that under the supremacy of the French state Frenchmen could be allowed to practice different forms of the Christian religion.

Neither the wars of Francis I against the Habsburgs nor the religious wars of the later sixteenth century prevented the slow growth of French material prosperity and the flourishing of French culture. For French arts and letters, the sixteenth century is a somewhat delayed Renaissance, the century of the great chateaux and of Rabelais. The most striking original contributions made by the Frenchmen of the 1500's were those of the political and religious thinkers, *politiques* like Bodin and Protestants like Calvin.

V: The New Monarchies—England

Henry VIII, 1509-1547

In England, the first Tudor, Henry VII, had already established the new monarchy on a firm footing (see Chapter II). He left his son, Henry VIII, a full treasury and a well-ordered kingdom. That Henry VIII did not run through his heritage and leave an exhausted treasury was not because he lacked the will to spend lavishly. Henry, unlike his father, loved display, and all the trappings of Renaissance monarchy. His formal conference "at the summit" (to use a modern term) with Francis I near Calais in 1520 has gone down in tradition as the "Field of the Cloth of Gold."

Henry did not, however, seriously weaken England's finances, and for many reasons. Basically, we must make a distinction between the finances of a government and the economy of a whole society. We may sometimes, as on the eve of the great French Revolution of 1789, find a poor, even bankrupt, government in a reasonably prosperous society; we may even, as in eighteenth-century Prussia, find a prosperous, well-run government in a society relatively poor. Tudor England had the good fortune to enjoy *both* solvent government finances and a prosperous society. No doubt the great enclosures of land for sheep-farming and other factors helped create a new poor, but the middle classes and the new upper classes continued on the whole to thrive. Moreover, this national productivity was not unduly expended in foreign wars, the really major cause of disastrous financial difficulties of government. Good democrats have often accused European royalty of ruinous expenditures on palaces, retinues, pensions, mistresses, and high living of all sorts; yet the fact seems to be that such expenditures were but a very small part of the total outlay of society. Henry's wives—he had six —his court, his royal progresses, did not by any means beggar his country; the wars of Charles V and Philip II did beggar Spain.

Henry VIII made war in a gingerly manner, never really risking big English armies on the Continent, and contenting himself with playing a rather cautious game of balance of power. He made full use of the opportunities afforded him by the English Reformation to add to royal revenues by confiscation of monastic property, and, even

Henry VIII, by Holbein.

more important, by rewarding his loyal followers with lands so confiscated. Henry thus followed in the footsteps of his father in helping create a new upper class, which was soon actually a titled or noble class. In these critical years of English development, the new class was, in contrast to France, on the whole loyal to the Crown and yet, in contrast to some of the German states, by no means subservient to the Crown, by no means a mere titled bureaucracy. Henry continued the administrative policies of his father, strengthening his central administration and maintaining adequate supervision over the justices of the peace, independent land-owning gentlemen, not salaried agents of the Crown, and the keystone of English local government.

Tudor Parliaments   Most important of all, Henry was able to get what he wanted from his Parliaments, including statutes that separated the English Church from Rome, and grants for his wars and conferences. Henry's Parliaments were very far from being elected legislatures based on wide suffrage. The Tudor House of Lords had a safe majority of men—titled nobles and, after 1534, bishops of the Anglican Church—who were in fact of Tudor creation or allegiance. The House of Commons was composed of the knights of the shire, chosen by the freeholders of the shires, and of the burgesses, representatives of incorporated towns or boroughs (not by any means *all* towns). In most boroughs, a very narrow electorate chose these members of Parliament. Since the majority of the people of the shires were agricultural workers or tenants, rather than freeholders of land, the county franchise, too, was limited. In fact, the knights of the shire were chosen from among, and largely by, the squires and the lesser country gentlemen, a social class known by the very English term of "gentry." In brief, royal favor and royal patronage, as well as the patronage of the great lords, could pretty well mold the shape of a House of Commons.

Still, even the Tudor Parliaments are nearer a modern legislative assembly than the parallel assemblies, or estates, of the Continent. The great point of difference lies in the composition of the House of Commons, which had emerged from the Middle Ages not as a body representing an urban bourgeosie but as a composite of the rural landed gentry and the bourgeoisie of the towns, meeting in one body. On the Continent, the assemblies corresponding to the English Parliament were *estates* (*Stände* in German, *états* in French). They usually sat in three distinct houses—one representing the clergy, another all the nobles, great and small, and a third the lay commoners. Some countries, as for instance Sweden, had four estates—clergy, nobles, townsmen, and peasants. In England, however, the nobility were a small group, the eldest sons who had actually inherited the title. Younger sons, even of earls and dukes, had no title of nobility and, unless they were ennobled by the Crown, had nothing to do with the House of Lords. They fell back into the class of gentry, which was represented in the Commons. On the Continent, by contrast, all legitimate descendants of nobles were themselves generally noble, members of a definite class, not quite a caste, for commoners on the rise could marry into it, buy into it, and win royal approval of ennoblement at any time in modern history. It must be repeated that this "social mobility" is clear throughout western history, even though it does reach a peak in modern America.

Finally, in England Parliament came out of the Middle Ages with the power to make laws or statutes, including money laws. These laws did indeed require royal consent. But at the end of the fifteenth century Parliament had already obtained much more than the merely advisory powers which were all that the French Estates-General, for instance, really had.

Purely in terms of constitutional structure, then, the Tudor Parliaments could have quarreled as violently with the Crown as did the Stuart Parliaments in the next century (see Chapter VI). Although the Tudor monarchs had their difficulties with Parliament, on the whole they got what they wanted out of Parliament without serious constitutional crises. This was particularly true of Henry VIII and Elizabeth I. The monarchs succeeded in part, as we have noted, because their Parliaments, if not precisely packed, were generally recruited from men favorable to the Crown, to which they owed so much. But they also succeeded because they were skillful rulers, willing to use their prestige and gifts of persuasion to win the consent of Parliament, careful to observe the constitutional and human decencies. Moreover, both Henry and Elizabeth were good hearty persons, sure of themselves and their dignity, immensely popular with all classes of their subjects. Both were fortunate enough to be able to incorporate in their persons strong national feelings of patriotic resistance to the hated foreign foes, Rome and Spain.

The course of Tudor domestic history did not run with perfect smoothness. Henry VII had faced two pretenders; Henry VIII met opposition to his religious policy. A Catholic minority, strong in the north, continued throughout the sixteenth century to oppose the Protestant majority, sometimes in arms, sometimes in intrigues. The death of Henry VIII in 1547 marked the beginning of a period of really extraordinary religious oscillation.

Religious Difficulties Henry was succeeded by his only son, the ten-year-old Edward VI. Led by his uncle, the Duke of Somerset, Edward's government pushed on into Protestant ways. The Six Articles (see p. 85), by which Henry had sought to preserve the essentials of Roman Catholic theology, worship, and even church organization, were repealed in 1547. The legal title of the statute commonly called the Six Articles had been "An Act for Abolishing Diversity in Opinion." The goal was still uniformity, and in the brief reign of Edward VI an effort was made to prescribe uniformity of religious worship through a prayer book and articles of faith duly imposed by Parliament. Cranmer, Archbishop of Canterbury, was a convinced Protestant, and had committed himself by marriage—as did Luther —to a clear, symbolic break with Roman Catholicism. Under his supervision, the patient bulk of the English people was pushed into Protestant worship.

Then, in 1553, the young king, Edward VI, always a frail boy, died. Protestant intriguers vainly attempted to secure the crown for a Protestant, Lady Jane Grey, a great-granddaughter of Henry VII and a quiet, scholarly young woman with no ambitions. But Edward VI, as the law of inheritance prescribed, was followed by his older sister Mary, daughter of the Catholic Catherine of Aragon whom Henry VIII had put aside. Mary had been brought up a Catholic, and at once began to restore the old ways. Of course there was a rebellion, which flared into the open when Mary announced a marriage treaty by which she was to wed Philip of Spain. Yet "Bloody" Mary prevailed against the rebels, and Lady Jane Grey was executed for a plot she had never really shared in. The Catholic Cardinal Pole was made Archbishop of Canterbury, under Rome, and Cranmer was burned at the stake. Catholic forms of worship came back to the parishes, but significantly the land settlement of Henry VIII remained undisturbed.

Mary, too, died after a short reign, in 1558. The last of Henry's children left was Elizabeth, daughter of Anne Boleyn. She had at her father's request been declared illegitimate by Parliament in 1536. Henry's last will, however, rehabilitated her, and she now succeeded as Elizabeth I (1558-1603). She had been brought up a Protestant, and once more the conventional English churchgoer was required to switch religion. This time the Anglican Church was firmly established; the prayer book and Thirty-Nine Articles of 1563 issued under Elizabeth (see Chapter III) have remained to this day the essential documents of the Anglican faith.

The Elizabethan settlement, moderate and permanent though it was, did not fully settle the religious problem. England still had a Catholic party. Spain, especially after the repudiation of Catholicism, was a serious enemy; it seemed hardly likely that the heavy expenses of a real war could be long avoided. Moreover, independent Scotland could always be counted on in those days to take the anti-English side. The new Queen of Scotland was Mary Stuart, granddaughter of Henry VIII's sister, Margaret, and therefore the heir to the English throne should Elizabeth I die without issue. Mary did not wait for Elizabeth's death, but on the ground that Elizabeth was in fact illegitimate, herself assumed the title of "Queen of England and Scotland."

Finally, the English Catholics presented by no means the most serious of Elizabeth's religious difficulties; Protestant groups not satisfied with the conservatism of the Thirty-Nine Articles were coming to the fore. These people are called "Puritans," since they wished to "purify" the Anglican Church of what they considered papist survivals in belief, ritual, and church government. Actually, the Puritans themselves ranged from moderates to radicals. The moderates would be content with a simpler ritual but would retain bishops. The Presbyterians were Calvinists who would substitute councils (synods) of elders, or presbyters, for bishops, and would adopt the full Calvinist theology. The Brownists, named for their leader Browne, were the radical wing of Puritanism; they wanted to have each congregation an independent body.

Elizabeth the Queen Thus Elizabeth faced a decidedly grim prospect during the early years of her reign. The troubles of the reigns of Edward and Mary had undone some of the work of the two Henries; dissension seemed all around her. Yet she was to reign for nearly fifty years, and to give her name to one of the greatest times of flowering of English society and culture.

The personality of Elizabeth is hardly heart-warming. She was vain (or simply proud), not altogether proof against flattery, but too intelligent to be led astray by it in great matters. She was a good Renaissance realist (a better one than Machiavelli himself), somewhat too overpowering and impressive for a woman, but very effective in the pageantry and posing of public life. She was loved by her people if not by her intimates. She never married, a fact that has unleashed a good deal of not very sound

Elizabeth I.

medical and psychological explanation. But in the early years of her reign she played off foreign and domestic suitors one against another with excellent results for her foreign policy, in which she was always trying to avoid the expenses and dangers of war, trying to get something for nothing. One may believe that her spinsterhood settled on her at first as no more than a policy of state, and later as a convenient habit.

Under such able ministers as Burleigh and Walsingham, her government was put in excellent order. Thanks to skillful diplomacy, which made full use of the French and Dutch opposition to Spain, the showdown with Philip was postponed until 1588, when the kingdom was ready for it. Mary Queen of Scots proved no match at all for her gifted cousin, not merely because she was not a good politician, but even more because she had no sure Scottish base to work from. Mary was a Catholic, and Scotland under the leadership of John Knox was on its way to becoming one of the great centers of Calvinism. Mary managed everything wrong, including, and perhaps most important in a puritanical land, her love affairs. Her subjects revolted against her, and she was forced in 1568 to take refuge in England, where Elizabeth had her put in confinement. Mary alive was at the very least a constant temptation to all who wanted to overthrow Elizabeth. Letters, which Mary declared were forged, and over which historians still debate, involved her in what was certainly a very real conspiracy against Elizabeth, and she was tried, convicted, and executed in 1587.

The dramatic crisis of the reign was the war with Spain, resolved in the defeat of the great Spanish Armada in 1588. But Elizabeth's old age was not to be altogether quiet. In Ireland, the native masses were ruled by an Anglo-Irish landed class out of touch with the people. In 1542, the country had been made a kingdom, but by no means an independent one, since the crowns of England and Ireland were held by the same person. An earlier act, the Statute of Dro-gheda (Poynings's Act), in 1494 had put the Irish Parliament firmly under English control, and had made laws enacted in the English Parliament applicable to Ireland. The native Irish had remained firmly Catholic. The stage was set for the perennial Irish Problem, the long struggle for Irish national independence.

In 1597, the Irish rose under the leadership of Hugh O'Neill, Earl of Tyrone. The revolt had temporary success, but was put down bloodily in 1601 after the favorite of Elizabeth's old age, the Earl of Essex, had failed dismally to cope with it. Essex, too, involved himself in a plot against his sovereign, and was executed after its discovery and suppression. But the Elizabethan settlement of Ireland's troubles was no settlement, and we shall return to this running sore in Chapter VI.

The Elizabethan Age, then, was no age of quiet, but rather one of wars, rebellions, personal and party strife, and intense competition. None the less, it never reached the fatal depths of destruction of a Thirty Years' War, though for a while it had threatened to do so under "Bloody" Mary. There was a solid foundation under the state and society that produced the literature, music, architecture, science, and wealth and victories of the Elizabethan Age. That foundation was in part a good administrative system, itself based on a substantial degree of national unity, or, negatively, on the absence of the extreme local differences and tensions of the Continent. It was in part general economic prosperity, based on individual enterprise in many fields—enterprise often unscrupulous and, as far as raids on the commerce of foreigners like the Spaniards went, piratical. It was certainly something not simply material; it was a common sentiment that kept Englishmen together, and that traced for most of them limits beyond which they would not carry disagreement. Elizabeth herself played a large part in holding her subjects together;

her religious policy, for example, was directed at stretching the already broad principles and practices of the Church of England so that they would cover near-Catholicism and near-Congregationalism. But there was a limit to this stretching, and Elizabeth persecuted Catholics on the Right and Brownists on the Left.

The English Renaissance

The Age of Elizabeth I was a flowering of English culture symbolized for all of us by Shakespeare (1564-1616). Elizabeth's actual reign, from 1558 to 1603, by no means measures the Age accurately. Much of her father's reign belongs to the flowering, as do the first ten or fifteen years of the reign of her successor, James I, the first Stuart king.

This is the English Renaissance, tardiest of the great classical Renaissances. It has the range and variety we have found in other lands, and the same clear admiration for, the same dependence on, the old Greeks and Romans we have found elsewhere. It is hard to pick up a poem, an essay, a play, any piece of Elizabethan writing not purely religious, without coming very soon upon a classical allusion. Yet the English Renaissance did not imitate classical antiquity, so to speak, photographically. It holds on to much that could be grown only in the climate of the island. Tudor and early Stuart architecture is a clear case in point. The new palaces and manor houses are no longer much like the medieval castles; they are more open, more elegant. But they preserve all sorts of Gothic habits, mullioned windows, tracery and carving, traditional woodwork; they look English, not Italian or French.

Painting, sculpture, the plastic arts in all their range—music itself—are for England in these years at a high level. Elizabethan ladies and gentlemen cultivated all the muses, sang madrigals, played the lute, appreciated modern paintings, had their houses built in the modern style, dressed as did ladies and gentlemen in the center of European culture of this sort, Italy. Yet the commonplace is unavoidable: England is not a land of great original creation in music and the plastic arts. The greatness of Elizabethan England, when it is not in the deeds of Drake, Hawkins, Wolsey, Burleigh, the Tudors themselves, lies in the words of St. Thomas More, Shakespeare, Francis Bacon, Spenser, Ben Jonson, and many others who are part of the formal higher education of English-speaking people all over the world.

They are a hard group to generalize about. They are established "classics" and have suffered the popular admiration and neglect as well as the academic working-over that go with the status of classics in our modern culture. They belong to a culture now four hundred years past, and they wrote English before its structure and its word-order were tamed by the influence of French prose into their present straightforward simplicity. They are much easier to read about than to read. Finally, they have been targets for some debunking, but on the whole they have survived intact as classics. Shakespeare, notably, continues even outside the English-speaking world to be a kind of George Washington of letters, above reproach and a bit above reality.

These Elizabethans are overwhelmingly exuberant. They are exuberant even in refinement, full-blooded even in erudition. Above all, they are anxious to get in that something more, that transcending something that makes words more than words, and possibly more than sense. To a later generation, the tame, orderly admirers of measure and sense in the late seventeenth and eighteenth centuries, these Elizabethans were somewhat uncouth, undisciplined. To the nineteenth-century Romantics, they were brothers in romance, sharing the desire of the moth for the star. And indeed this exuberance, this love of the excessive,

is obvious in much Elizabethan writing, in the interminable, allusion-packed, allegory-mad stanzas of Spenser's *Faerie Queene*, in the piling up of quotations from the ancient Greeks and Romans, in Shakespeare's love of puns and all kinds of rhetorical devices, in the extraordinarily bloody nature of their tragedies—remember the end of *Hamlet*, which finds the stage littered with corpses.

There is, however, a balancing quality in the Elizabethans. They had a good carnal appreciation of this earth; they seemed even to have enjoyed their gloom when they left the world of the fleshly enjoyments for brief trips into transcendence. The absurd notion that Shakespeare's works were written by Bacon—a notion apparently based on the assumption that Shakespeare was not formally and academically well enough trained to write the plays, which is nonsense—has at least some meaning in terms of the spirit of the age. Francis Bacon, lawyer and humanist, philosopher of inductive science, and rather bad practitioner of experimental science, was at bottom a heaven-stormer, intent on solving the problems of the ages. Yet he was at the same time an earth-bound Tudor gentleman, quite capable of enjoying himself in this harsh world. Bacon and Shakespeare have at least this in common: they are hearty of mind and spirit, wide-ranging, bound by no narrow formulas of literary or philosophic taste, really willing to accept the world about them without drying up into conformity, willing to get beyond that world without indulging in complaint or rebellion.

However men may vary in their attempts to define the climate of Elizabethan opinion and the quality of its culture, there can be no doubt that the Elizabethans were good English patriots, lovers of their country in the first flush of its worldly success. Here is one of the most famous of quotations from Shakespeare, in itself an admirable sample of the English Renaissance, right down to the inevitable, and in this case rather flat, allusion to Greco-Roman mythology:

This royal throne of kings, this scepter'd isle,
This earth of majesty, this seat of Mars,
This other Eden, demi-paradise,
This fortress built by Nature for herself
Against infection and the hand of war,
This happy breed of men, this little world,
This precious stone set in the silver sea,

Which serves it in the office of a wall
Or as a moat defensive to a house,
Against the envy of less happier lands,
This blessed plot, this earth, this realm, this
England.*

———

* Richard II, Act II, Scene i.

Reading Suggestions on the Dynastic and Religious Wars

General Accounts

C. W. C. Oman, The Sixteenth Century (N.Y.: Dutton, 1936). Stresses political and military developments.

D. Ogg, Europe in the Seventeenth Century, 6th ed. (London: Black, 1948); and G. N. Clark, The Seventeenth Century, 2nd ed. (Oxford: Clarendon, 1947). Two very readable general histories, ranging in part well beyond the subject of this chapter.

C. J. Friedrich, The Age of the Baroque, 1610-1660 (N.Y.: Harper, 1952). This volume, in the "Rise of Modern Europe" series, is unusually firm and provocative. Emphasizes culture and political theory.

Special Studies: England

C. Read, The Tudors (N.Y.: Holt, 1936). A most readable introduction by a sound historian.

S. T. Bindoff, Tudor England (Harmondsworth, Middlesex: Penguin Books, 1952). A brief, popular account.

J. D. Mackie, The Earlier Tudors, 1485-1558 (Oxford: Clarendon, 1952); and J. B. Black, The Reign of Elizabeth, 1558-1603 (Oxford: Clarendon, 1936). These two volumes in the "Oxford History of England" are scholarly and comprehensive.

G. R. Elton, The Tudor Revolution in Government (Cambridge, England: Cambridge Univ. Press, 1953). An important study of the shift to the "new-model" bureaucratic state.

D. L. Keir, The Constitutional History of Modern Britain, 1485-1937, 4th ed. (London: Black, 1950). A good introduction to an important and difficult subject.

A. F. Pollard, Henry VIII, new ed. (N.Y.: Longmans, Green, 1951). An old and highly respected study.

J. E. Neale, Queen Elizabeth (N.Y.: Harcourt, Brace, 1934). Generally considered the best single volume on the famous queen. The author has also written several specialized works on aspects of political life under Elizabeth.

C. Read, Mr. Secretary Walsingham and the Policy of Queen Elizabeth (Cambridge: Harvard Univ. Press, 1925). A thorough study of a key figure in Tudor government.

A. L. Rowse, The Expansion of Elizabethan England (N.Y.: St. Martin's, 1955), and The England of Elizabeth: The Structure of Society (London: Macmillan, 1950). These complementary studies are the work of a "maverick" English scholar in rebellion against academic caution.

Special Studies: Primarily on Spain, Germany, and the Netherlands

R. B. Merriman, The Rise of the Spanish Empire in the Old World and the New (N.Y.: Macmillan, 1918-1934). Vols. III and IV of this detailed work deal with Charles V and Philip II.

R. Trevor Davies, The Golden Century of Spain (London: Macmillan, 1937). A standard shorter study of sixteenth-century Spain.

K. Brandi, The Emperor Charles V (London: Jonathan Cape, 1939). A very complete study of the man who first tried to secure something like control over the European state-system.

C. V. Wedgwood, The Thirty Years' War (London: Jonathan Cape, 1938). A full and generally well-balanced account.

S. R. Gardiner, The Thirty Years' War (N.Y.: Scribner's, 1874). A much older account, brief and good.

P. Geyl, The Revolt of the Netherlands, 1555-1609 (London: Williams and Norgate, 1945), and The Netherlands Divided, 1609-1648 (London: Williams and Norgate, 1936). Very good studies by a leading modern Dutch scholar.

C. V. Wedgwood, William the Silent (New Haven: Yale Univ. Press, 1945). An enthusiastic biography.

Special Studies: France

L. von Ranke, Civil Wars and Monarchy in France in the Sixteenth and Seventeenth Centuries (N.Y.: Harper, 1853). An old and famous work by one of the greatest nineteenth-century historians; may still be read with profit.

A. J. Grant, The Huguenots (London: Butterworth, 1934. Home University Library). A brief and reasonably dispassionate account.

J. E. Neale, *The Age of Catherine de' Medici* (London: Jonathan Cape, 1943). A solid study.

J. W. Thompson, *The Wars of Religion in France, 1559-1576* (Chicago: Univ. of Chicago Press, 1909). A detailed narrative.

Q. Hurst, *Henry of Navarre* (N.Y.: Appleton-Century-Crofts, 1938). A standard biography of King Henry IV of France.

Special Studies: Other Topics

G. Mattingly, *Renaissance Diplomacy* (Boston: Houghton Mifflin, 1955). Indispensable for the topic.

H. Nicholson, *The Evolution of Diplomatic Method* (N.Y.: Macmillan, 1954). A brief survey, which goes back to the Greeks, and is especially good on the techniques and spirit of early modern diplomacy.

G. H. Sabine, *A History of Political Theory*, rev. ed. (N.Y.: Holt, 1950). This admirably sane and lucid treatment has very useful sections covering topics dealt with in this chapter.

J. W. Allen, *Political Thought in the Sixteenth Century*, 3rd ed. (N.Y.: Barnes and Noble, 1951). A more detailed and difficult account of the subject.

F. L. Nussbaum, *A History of the Economic Institutions of Modern Europe* (N.Y.: Appleton-Century-Crofts, 1933). Incorporates the views of the important German economic historian, Sombart.

G. Renard and G. Weulersse, *Life and Work in Modern Europe* (*Fifteenth through Eighteenth Centuries*) (N.Y.: Knopf, 1926). Useful for the general economic background.

(*Note:* For other useful works on economics and political theory, consult the titles listed at the close of chapters II and III.)

C. W. C. Oman, *A History of the Art of War in the Sixteenth Century* (N.Y.: Dutton, 1937). A highly interesting study of an aspect of history often neglected.

J. F. C. Fuller, *A Military History of the Western World*, 3 vols. (N.Y.: Funk & Wagnalls, 1954-1956). By an informative and rather unorthodox general; Vols. I and II include material relating to this chapter.

L. Goldscheider, *El Greco* (London: Phaidon, 1954). An excellently illustrated book on the painter who expresses so well the Spanish "style."

Historical Fiction

Cervantes, *Don Quixote*, S. Putnam, trans., 2 vols. (N.Y.: Viking, 1949). Widely considered the best translation of this great classic.

H. J. C. von Grimmelshausen, *Simplicissimus* (N.Y.: Dutton, 1924). This novel of the Thirty Years' War, written in the seventeenth century, is an important document of social history. Good reading, despite its rather strange form.

W. Scott, *Kenilworth* (many editions). Elizabethan England is the scene of this novel by the famous Romantic writer of the early nineteenth century.

CHAPTER FIVE

The Expansion of Europe

Fifteenth Through Seventeenth Centuries

I: Introduction

Most historical geographies provide a series of maps showing what they commonly call the "known world" at certain periods—starting usually from the known world of Homer, little more than the eastern Mediterranean and its fringes. Next come the known worlds of Alexander the Great and the Romans, centered still on the Mediterranean, hazy or blank for much of interior Europe and Africa, with only the western fringes of Asia known, and with the Americas still unsuspected. Then from late medieval explorations through the great modern discoveries, the series goes on to the full fruition of geographical knowledge, which happened only yesterday. There is a revealing symbolism in that phrase "known world," for we really mean "known to interested members of Greco-Roman society and its Christian successor states of the West." The Chinese, too, had a "known world," which did not include ours until modern times.

Ancient and Modern
Expansion Contrasted

Men have always moved about on this planet. In the prehistoric ages of movement and migration, which include such daring feats as the Polynesian settlement of the Pacific islands, the movers kept no written records and no concrete ties with their place of origins. They were not organized states in expansion, but groups of individuals on the move, carrying no more than traditions, habits, and tools. The expansion of the West was a very different thing. From the very start in ancient Greece and Rome, records were kept, indeed maps were made, and the nucleus always remained in touch with its offshoots. Western society has expanded *as a society*, often as a group of states.

The western expansion, which began in the mid-fifteenth century, however, differed in important ways from the expansion that had carried the cultures of the ancient Near East as far as western and northern Europe. In the first place, this modern expansion was much faster and covered more ground. Although some secrets of the Arctic and the Antarctic, some details of the wilder interiors of the world, were not known until the twentieth century, it is broadly true that the whole world was revealed to Europeans within the two and a half or three centuries after 1450—within four long lifetimes. In the second place, this modern expansion was the first time our western society crossed oceans. Ancient and medieval navigation had clung to the narrow seas and the shorelines. The ancients had even commonly drawn up their boats on land to spend the night. Now westerners crossed Atlantic and Pacific, far from the protecting land. In the third place, this expansion carried westerners well outside the orbit of relations with Byzantines and Moslems, who were also successors to the cultures of the ancient Near East, into relations with a bewildering variety of races, creeds, and cultures, from naked savages to cultivated Chinese. Not since the Germanic peoples had been tamed and converted in the Dark Ages had westerners come into close contact with primitive peoples. Finally, and of very great importance, expanding Europe possessed a margin of superior strength in developed material resources that lasted in some respects up to our own time, a margin that enabled western society to do what no society had ever done before—extend its influence around the world.

An important element of that margin was the possession of firearms; yet firearms could be legally or illegally acquired by non-Europeans, and very soon were. The strength by which Europeans overcame the world was not quite so simple as the possession of firearms. It was a compound of technological and economic superiority and of superior political and social organization, which in turn permitted superior military organization. This superiority was not exercised from a common western center, but rather by half a dozen competing western nations, each anxious to cut the others' throats, and quite willing to arm and organize natives against its western competitors. Frenchmen in North America armed the savages against the English, and the English armed them against the French. Yet not even the Iroquois were able to maintain themselves against white society. French, English, Portuguese, Dutch, Spaniards, and later Germans and Americans all intrigued against one another in the Far East, and yet not until the mid-twentieth century did any Asiatic nation, and then only Japan, really compete successfully in war and politics with a western land. So great was western superiority that the rivalries of competing powers did not delay the process of expansion but probably stimulated and hastened it.

How far this physical superiority in the expansion of the West throughout the world was—and is—also a spiritual and moral superiority is a problem we in the West today cannot answer as firmly as did our fathers. But you will not understand the successful expansion of Europe if you do not realize that those who carried out the expansion, though moved often by greed, by love of adventure, by sheer despair over their lot at home, and by many other motives, were also moved by the conviction that they were doing God's work, the work of civilization, that they were carrying with them a better way of life. They were confident and energetic people, capable of great endurance and courage, and they have made over the face of the globe.

The Nature of Modern Expansion

Why did men living on the Atlantic coasts of Europe in the second half of the fifteenth century venture out on an ocean that ancient and medieval mariners had not seriously tried to penetrate? We cannot answer the question with finality. The great explorations were part of the Renaissance, part of a general stirring of European nations, of an era of adventure and the energetic pursuit of new things. So small a thing as the magnetic compass helped make ocean voyages possible. Without the compass, earlier mariners had been helpless, except when clear weather gave them sun or stars as guides. The actual origins of the compass are obscure, but we know that by the beginning of the fifteenth century it was familiar to European sailors, and was a normal part of navigation by the time of Columbus. Better instruments and better methods of determining a ship's position at sea were also fully in hand by the late fifteenth century. Shipbuilders were getting away from older types of traditional Mediterranean ships, building somewhat longer and narrower vessels that could stand the long swells of the ocean, deliberately trying to find the kind of ship that could be handled in these unknown waters. Technologically,

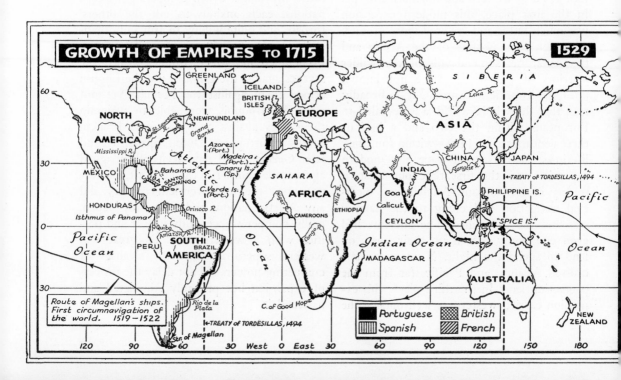

GROWTH OF EMPIRES TO 1715   1529

Route of Magellan's ships. First circumnavigation of the world. 1519–1522

Portuguese   British
Spanish   French

the way was ready for the great explorations.

Politically, the blocking or at least hindering of the usual trade routes in the Near East by the new and still unsettled Turkish power turned men's minds to the search for another way to India and China. Yet the Italians, especially the Venetians and Genoese, had installed themselves in the Near East and were making arrangements with the Turks in spite of difficulties. More important, actually, was the fact that Spain, Portugal, France, and England were all rising in political and economic activity, all on the way up that had been shown them by the Italians. Hindered in the Near East by Italians as well as by Turks, they eyed the unoccupied Atlantic.

Yet technology and the politics of the trade routes had to be taken advantage of by men, men in the state of mind that sent Columbus out across the unknown ocean—to see with his own eyes what was there, to test in experience a set of concepts. Columbus deliberately sought to prove his theory that because the earth is round—by 1492 a common concept among educated westerners—one can travel from Europe westward and reach Asia. No sensible person would maintain that even the first voyage of Columbus can be explained entirely in such purely intellectual terms; but neither can it be explained without such terms. One of the essential characteristics of the explorations and the subsequent expansion of Europe is that this was a movement guided in part by the new spirit of empirical science, the spirit that impelled men, if for instance they heard about the existence of unicorns, to go out and try to find some. Their medieval predecessors did not need to see a unicorn to believe in its existence. This new scientific spirit, however, did not immediately banish unicorns, mermaids, and sea serpents from men's minds, and has not yet done so now that the whole world has been thoroughly explored. Indeed, the first news of these strange worlds resulted in a whole new set of wonders, some real or merely exaggerated, some pure fantasy or myth, which the publishing of accounts of travel brought to all Europe.

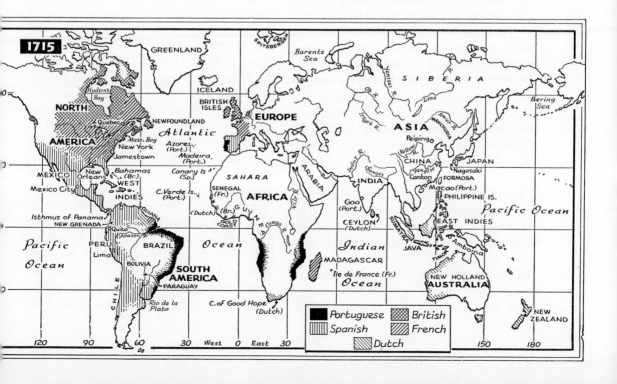

II: East by Sea to the Indies

*Prince Henry
and the Portuguese*　　The first of
the important
names in modern expansion is not that of a
bold explorer or *conquistador*, but that of
an organizing genius who directed the work
of others. Prince Henry of Portugal, known
as "the Navigator," lived from 1394 to 1460.
He was a deeply religious man, and he may
well have been moved above all by a desire
to convert the populations of India and the
Far East, whose existence had been known
to westerners since the thirteenth-century
travels of the Venetian Marco Polo. Indeed,
there was a widespread conviction in the
West that these distant peoples were in fact
already Christian, and needed only to be
brought in direct contact with the Roman
Catholic Church.

Prince Henry sent out frequent expeditions equipped with the best technical
means he and his colleagues could devise.
Gradually, these expeditions crept southward along the harsh desert coast of Africa
where the Sahara meets the Atlantic, until
in 1445 Cape Verde was doubled, and the
land began to grow greener and to trend
hopefully eastward. Whether Henry himself believed that Africa could be circum-
navigated is not absolutely certain, but according to ancient tradition the Phoenicians
had done it many centuries before the
Christian era, and Greco-Roman geographers had believed that Africa was surrounded by the ocean.

By 1472, after Henry's death, the Portuguese reached the end of the bulge of West
Africa at the Cameroons, and faced the
disheartening fact that the coast was once
more trending southward, not eastward.
But they kept on, stimulated by royal patronage, and in the next generation two
great explorers finished the job. In 1488,

Bartholomew Diaz, blown far south by a
great storm, turned northeast and found
that he had rounded the great cape we call
the Cape of Good Hope. He was followed
by Vasco da Gama, who set out in 1497
with four ships to reach India. He rounded
the Cape of Good Hope, thanks to the previous discoveries of Diaz, and worked northward along the east coast of Africa, coming
soon to an area of Arab trading where the
route to India was well known. Despite
Arab jealousy of the intruder, da Gama
secured a pilot and reached the Malabar
coast of India at Calicut ten months and
fourteen days out from Lisbon. The Portuguese now had an ocean route to the East.

On the next great voyage toward India,
the Portuguese made a lucky strike that was
to break the Spanish monopoly in South
America and to bring it about that one of
the great Latin-American states would be
Portuguese in language and culture. Pedro
Cabral, in 1500, started out to repeat da
Gama's voyage to India. But by now the
Portuguese were used to long voyages on
the open ocean, far from sight of land, and
they no longer needed to creep around the
coast of Africa. Cabral kept boldly southward from the bulge of Africa, and was apparently blown somewhat westward of his
course so that he made a landfall on the
bulge of the South American continent in
what is now Brazil. He at once detached a
ship and sent it home to announce his discovery. Now the voyages of Columbus were
of course well known to navigators by this
time, and some geographers think that in
fact Cabral set out deliberately to see what
he could find south of the route Columbus
had taken. Six years previously, in 1494,
Spain and Portugal had by the Treaty of
Tordesillas agreed to partition these new
lands along a north-south line three hun-

dred and seventy leagues (about a thousand miles) west of the Azores, so that Brazil came quite definitely into the Portuguese sphere.

The main Portuguese push, however, was toward India and the Far East. The explorer was succeeded by that other characteristic agent of European expansion, the trader. But the trader by no means worked alone. He was aided and protected by the power of the state, which, in accordance with mercantilist economic theory (see p. 181 ff.), aimed to set up for its nationals a monopoly of trade with the newly discovered lands. The great figure of early Portuguese imperialism is Alfonso de Albuquerque, governor of the Indies from 1509 to 1515, under whom the Portuguese set up a firm base in their capital at Goa in India, and from that base organized regular trade routes toward southeastern Asia and China. By 1557, the Portuguese had established a base at Macao in China near Canton, and they had begun trade with the Japanese. Portugal had assembled a colonial empire.

India

The India that Europeans thus reached around Africa had been marginally in touch with Europe for several thousand years. In the fourth century B.C., Alexander the Great had actually campaigned in northern India, and throughout the Middle Ages the Arabs had served as a link in trade, and, in at least vague general knowledge, as a cultural link between the West and India. But now a direct link was forged, never to be loosened. The link was not of course a form of union or assimilation, and especially in these early modern centuries, West and East hardly communicated at the higher levels of cultural interchange. Indeed, the Portuguese were contemptuous of the Indians. Among the Dutch, French, and English who followed the Portuguese to India, this attitude of contempt became set in the conventional idea

of white superiority. This feeling of European superiority among all the many agents of the West in India has probably been exaggerated both in our western literary tradition and in the minds of educated Indians quick to take offense. Still, this sense of superiority was there, perhaps most clearly reflected centuries later in Kipling's too famous

Oh, East is East and West is West, and never the twain shall meet,
Till Earth and Sky stand presently at God's great judgment seat. . . .*

Inescapably, this western superiority was a superiority on the battlefield. In the last analysis, and long after the initial European monopoly of firearms had ended, a European or European-trained and commanded native army or navy could always beat a native Asiatic army or navy. In India, at least, this European domination was greatly helped by the political and military disunity of the subcontinent. The Portuguese reached India at the time when in the north Moslem invaders were consolidating a foreign rule of the sort which, from the earliest Mesopotamian civilization, had periodically brought comparative order to these regions. This Mogul (Mongol) Empire in the north had little hold on regions of the south where the Europeans first got firm footholds. Local Indian rulers, whether they were Moslem or Hindu in faith, were in intense rivalry and were a ready prey to European promises of aid. All the European powers found it easy, not merely to get Indian princes on their side, but to raise and train on their own responsibility native armies to fight under Portuguese, French, Dutch or British flags.

Perhaps the lack of political and social integration in India is the basic reason why a few handfuls of Europeans were able to dominate the country until 1945. Indeed, the variety and range of Indian life are extraordinary. Some of the more isolated

---

* R. Kipling, *Ballad of East and West.*

parts of India in the Deccan or southern peninsula were inhabited by tribesmen of no higher level than many African tribesmen. Some, on the northern edges, were warrior tribesmen much like those of the highlands of Central Asia. In the great valleys of the Indus and the Ganges, and in the richer parts of the Deccan, there was a wealthy, populous society basically Hindu in culture, though when the Europeans arrived, it was dominated in many areas by Central Asiatic invaders of Moslem faith and culture. Hindu society itself was the result of an amalgamation between earlier native stocks and invaders from the north who certainly spoke a language closely related to Greek, Latin, and indeed our own, and who probably were white "Indo-Europeans" or "Aryans." The early history of India, however, is most confusing, and we cannot tell how many these invaders were, or just where they came from, though the invasion apparently had taken place between 2000 and 1200 B.C. It seems almost certain that their consciousness of differing from the natives is responsible for the characteristic Indian institution of *caste*.

According to the laws of caste, men and women were by the fact of birth settled for life in a closed group which pursued a given occupation and occupied a fixed position in society. When the Europeans reached India, there were apparently something over a thousand castes, including a group at the bottom without caste, the "untouchables." The ruling groups were of two main castes, the Brahmins or priests, and the Kshatriya or warriors. The great multiplicity of castes lay in the third group, the Vaisya or commonalty. In theory, marriage between members of different castes was forbidden, as was change of caste through social mobility. In fact, in the centuries since the invasion by the "Indo-Europeans" considerable human intermixture had undoubtedly occurred. Yet even today the upper classes in most of India are of a lighter color than the lower.

The most striking thing about Indian culture was the high place occupied by the priestly caste, the Brahmins. The Brahmin faith has strains of a most other-worldly belief in the evils of the life of the flesh and the attainment of salvation by a mystic transcendence of the flesh in ascetic denial. With this is a doctrine of the transmigration of souls, in which sinful life on earth is believed to lead to reincarnation in lower animal life, and virtuous life to lead, at least in some forms of Hindu belief, to ultimate freedom from flesh of any sort and reunion with the perfect, the ineffable. But official Brahminism became a series of rigid and complicated rituals, and the religion of the common people became, or rather retained from earlier times, an elaborate polytheism lush with gods and goddesses. Against all these corruptions there rose in the sixth century B.C. a great religious leader, Gautama Buddha, himself of noble stock. Buddhism is in origin one of the great higher religions of the world. It accepts the basic Brahminical concept of the badness of this world of the flesh, but it finds salvation, the *nirvana* of peaceful release from the chain of earthly birth and rebirth, in a life ascetic but not withdrawn, a life of charity and good works. The truly virtuous man, Buddha by his own example insisted, will not accept the *nirvana*, the reunion with a reality *not* of the senses which he might attain, but will stay on in this world to help his suffering fellow men.

Buddhism died out in the land of its birth, but it spread to China, Japan, and southeastern Asia, where it in turn became ritualistic, formalized, and without missionary reforming zeal. Furthermore, Buddhism divided into the Mahayana (Great Vehicle) in the north, and the Hinayana (Little Vehicle) in the south—that is, in Ceylon, Burma, Siam, and Cambodia. Great theological and organizational differences lie behind this split, not easily clarified to a westerner. Broadly, the Mahayana in theory emphasizes love of one's fellows as well as renunciation; the Hinayana emphasizes more the renunciation of this world by the elect, the chosen few.

The religious thought of India has left a residue of greater other-worldliness, of greater emphasis on a mystical subduing of the flesh, on a revulsion from struggle for wealth, satisfaction of the common human appetites, worldly place and power, than has Christianity or Islam. In the practice of Indian life even before the Europeans came to India, there was plenty of violence, plenty of greed, cruelty, and self-indulgence. Except as superstition and tabu and ritual, little of the higher religions of India had seeped down to the masses. To certain types of western minds, indeed, the educated classes of India have seemed to take refuge in other-worldly doctrines as a psychological defense against the worldly superiority of the West and the poverty and superstition of their own masses. But the fact remains that for three hundred years educated Indians have insisted that they feel differently about the universe and man's place in it than do we, that theirs is a higher spirituality—and there are westerners who believe these Indians are right.

China

China, too, resisted the West, and in many ways more successfully than did India. A very old civilization that goes back several millennia before Christ, and becomes reasonably historical about 1000 B.C., was established in the valleys of the Yangtze and the Yellow rivers. Indeed, the Yellow River valley produced, it is believed independently, one of the original civilizations. Like the other civilizations on the outskirts of the great nomadic reservoir of the Eurasian heartland, the Mesopotamian, the Indian, the European, it was subject to periodical incursions of the Eurasian tribesmen. It was against such incursions that the famous Great Wall of China was built in the third century B.C. On the whole, how-

ever, the Chinese protected their basic institutions against the nomads, whom they absorbed after a few generations. At just about the time when the first Europeans were setting up permanent trade relations with China, the last of these "barbarian" conquests took place. Early in the seventeenth century, Mongolian tribes established a state of their own in eastern Manchuria, to the north of China proper. In 1644, they seized the Chinese capital of Peking (today Peiping) and established the Manchu dynasty that lasted until 1911. But the Manchus, like other outsiders before them, left Chinese institutions almost untouched.

Chinese history is by no means the uneventful record of a "frozen" and unchanging society that some westerners have thought. It is filled with the rise and fall of dynasties, with wars and plagues and famines, with the gradual spread of Chinese culture southward and eastward, to the region of Canton, to Korea, to Japan. It has periods of effective governmental centralization, and periods of "feudal" disintegration. Its art and techniques were subject to periods of flourishing and decay. But there were many elements of continuity. First of all, at the base of Chinese social life was a community organization in the villages, held together by very strong family ties, a cult of ancestor worship, and hard work guided by traditional agricultural techniques. Second, at the top of this society was an emperor, Son of Heaven, the "natural" ruler of a great state. The Chinese were conditioned to at least formal imperial unity in somewhat the same way early medieval westerners were conditioned to the unity of Roman Catholic Christendom. Third, the business of running this vast empire was entrusted to one of the most remarkable ruling classes history has ever recorded, the *mandarins*, a bureaucracy of intellectuals, or at any rate of men who could pass literary and philosophical examinations in classics, examinations that required a rigorously trained memory. This class proved not very resilient in the face of the challenge of new ideas from Europe. But it had served the state for many centuries, and its existence is one of the reasons for the extraordinary stability of Chinese society.

Just as in India, there were in China an immense population at the very margin of existence, and a small upper class that enjoyed gracious living of a kind not available to the medieval western upper classes. The Chinese millions had their superstitions, their demons, their other-world. The earlier periods of Chinese cultural flowering show traces of mystic beliefs among the educated, traces of the eternal other-worldliness of the human spirit. Still, everyone who has known the Chinese, even the casual traveler who makes some effort to appreciate what is going on about him, finds in the Chinese people a lack of mysticism, other-worldliness, "tender-mindedness." Or, in positive terms, he finds a sense of worldly realism, an ac-

"A Sage under a Pine Tree," by Ma Yüan, 1190-1224 (Sung Dynasty).

ceptance of the universe as it appears to common sense, or at least to the "tough-minded," a concern with human relations, with politeness, decorum, and the arts of living.

It has been commonly said that China never had a religion, in the sense that Buddhism, Christianity, and Islam are religions with a firm doctrine of salvation in an order of existence quite different from that of our daily lives on earth. The conventional Confucianism of the upper classes is indeed a code of manners and morals, not a sacramental religion, not a religion in which the faithful undergo the miracle of sharing in something ineffable. Confucius, a sage who flourished early in the fifth century B.C., was no mystic, no prophet, but a moralist who taught an ethical system of temperance, decorum, obedience to the wisdom of the wise and the good. However, this lack of commitment to an other-worldly religion has hitherto by no means made the Chinese more receptive to western ideas. At least until our own times, China has resisted westernization more effectively than has any other great culture.

The Portuguese Empire The empire that the Portuguese founded in Asia and Africa was a trading empire, not an empire of settlement. They established along the coasts of Africa, India, and China a series of posts, or "factories," over which they hoisted the Portuguese flag as a sign that they had annexed these bits of territory to the Portuguese Crown. From these posts they traded with the natives. As all the European colonial powers did later, they offered relatively cheap and relatively mass-produced articles —guns, knives, gadgets of all sorts, cheap cloth, and a great deal else. In return, they got gold and silver (when they could), spices, still essential for meats in those days without refrigeration, silks and other luxuries, and, finally, raw materials such as

cotton and slaves, and, in the New World, tobacco and sugar.

Two guiding principles of this trade were accepted by almost all contemporaries, whether in the mother country or in the colonies, as simply facts of life. First, in this trade the mother country was the determining element, and would naturally produce goods and services while the colony produced raw materials. Second, foreigners, nationals of other European lands, were excluded from this trade; they could not deal directly with the colony or take part in the commerce between mother country and colony. The Portuguese, in sum, followed a policy of mercantilism.

Armed forces were essential to the establishment and maintenance of this colonial system. Relatively small land forces proved sufficient both to keep the natives under control and to ward off rival European powers from the trading posts. A large and efficient navy was, however, necessary, for the easiest way to raid a rival's trade was to wait until its fruits were neatly concentrated in the hold of a merchant vessel, and then take it at sea as a prize. Such deeds are known as piracy, a very common activity in these early modern centuries. Sometimes, especially in the eighteenth century, these pirates became in fact outlaws, men of no nation, willing to rob nationals of any country. In these earlier centuries, they were often openly an unofficial adjunct of a given navy, operating only against enemies or neutrals, never against their own nationals. A navy was, then, essential to protect the sea routes of a colonial power. The Portuguese fleet was not only a merchant fleet; under the command of governors like Albuquerque, it was a great military fleet that brushed aside Arab opposition and for a few decades ruled the oceans of the Old World.

The Portuguese made no serious attempt to settle large numbers of their own people either in the hot coast lands of Africa or in the already densely populated lands of

India and the Far East. Nor, save in the single respect we are about to encounter, did they attempt to make over these natives into pseudo-Portuguese. There were of course useful places at the top for Portuguese in the colonial services, both civilian and military; many of the natives were enlisted as common soldiers in the armed forces or used as domestic help and in subordinate posts such as clerks. These natives inevitably picked up, however imperfectly, the language and culture of the colonial power. But neither among the primitive Negro tribes of Africa nor among the Indian and Chinese masses did this process of Europeanization go very fast or far.

Nor did the Portuguese attempt to rule directly, to alter the political, social, or economic structure of native life. They left the old ruling chiefs and the old ruling classes pretty much as they had found them. In the total lives of these millions, the imported European wares played extremely little part in these early days. The native upper classes monopolized most of these wares, and Europe could not yet flood non-European markets with cheap manufactured goods made by power-driven machinery. Nothing western touched these masses of natives in the sixteenth century, nothing tempted them away from their millennial ways of life, in anything like the degree our twentieth-century West attracts and tempts the East.

There is one exception. The Portuguese, and even their relatively secular-minded rival nations in eastern Asiatic regions, the English, Dutch, and French, did attempt to Christianize the natives. From the very first, much sincerity, devotion, and hard work went into the Christian missionary movement. The earliest missionaries no doubt underestimated the difficulties they were to encounter. Many of them were in a sense partly converted themselves; that is, they came to be very fond of their charges, and

convinced that they were in fact almost Christians already. Some of the Jesuits in China, the first European intellectuals to live in this very civilized country, seriously believed that with just a bit more effort the full reconciliation between Christianity and Confucianism could be achieved.

From the start, difficulties arose between the missionaries, anxious to protect their charges, and the traders and colonial officials, driven by their very place in the system to try to exploit the natives. And there were from the start lazy and otherwise inadequate missionaries. Finances were always a serious problem, with so many tens of millions to convert and to tend, and with so few men, so little money, to do the work. Certainly, measured in statistical terms, the Christianizing of India and the Far East did not make a serious impression on the masses. Nor in Africa did these first missionaries do more than secure the superficial adherence of the natives. Certainly, however, Christianity has been part of the whole influence of the West on the East, not to be measured in terms of actual Christian church memberships in the East.

The Portuguese, though first in the field in the East, very soon had to yield to newer rivals—French, Dutch, English. A trading empire depends on naval protection and on an enterprising trading community at home, and in both these critical matters the Portuguese were unable to keep up the pace they had set. Like the Spaniards, they suffered from an inadequate, or at any rate inadequately run, home industry; their banking, their business methods, their initiative—if not their scruples—were not up to competition with the aggressive expanding powers of northwest Europe. After the sixteenth century, they ceased to add to their empire and their wealth, and took a decidedly secondary place in international politics; but they have kept lands in Asia and Africa into our own day.

III: West by Sea to the Indies

Columbus   In the earliest days of concerted effort to explore the oceans, the Spanish government had been too busy disposing of the last Moslem state in the peninsula, Granada, and uniting the disparate parts of Spain to patronize scientific exploration as the Portuguese had done. But individual Spanish traders were active, and Spain was growing in prosperity. As long ago as the end of the fourteenth century and the beginning of the fifteenth, Portuguese mariners had found the three groups of Atlantic islands, Azores, Madeira, and Canaries, well out in the stormy ocean, but still essentially European rather than American. By papal decree, the Canaries were assigned to the Crown of Castile, the others to Portugal. Once the marriage of Ferdinand and Isabella had united Aragon and Castile, the Spanish government wanted to catch up with the Portuguese. So it commissioned Columbus.

Columbus (1451-1506) was an Italian, born in Genoa. He was essentially self-educated, but, at least in navigation and geography, had educated himself very well. His central conception, that it would be possible to reach the Far East—"the Indies" —by sailing westward from Spain, was certainly not uniquely his. That the earth is a globe was a notion entertained by ancient Greek geographers, and revived with the renaissance of the classics. Toscanelli at Florence in 1474, Behaim at Nuremberg in the very year of Columbus' voyage, published maps that showed the earth as a globe —but without the Americas, and with the combined Atlantic and Pacific much narrower than they are in fact. To act on this notion by deliberately sailing west on the Atlantic had become with the growth of oceanic navigation a clear possibility. But it was still a strikingly novel idea—an idea that was not acceptable to conservative minds. It took a persistent, innovating personality to get support for such an expedition.

Columbus met with many rebuffs, but finally, with the support of the wealthy Spanish trading family of Pinzon, was able to get the help of Queen Isabella. Indeed, with the sole aim of reaching the Indies he might not have been able to set out. But, as his commission shows, he was also charged to discover and secure for the Spanish Crown new islands and territories, a mission that probably reflects the importance of ancient and medieval legends about Atlantis, St. Brendan's isle, and other lands beyond the Azores. Even if he did not reach the Indies, there seemed a chance that he would reach something new.

He reached a New World. Setting out from Palos near Cadiz on August 3, 1492, in three ships so small that they could all be propped up comfortably on the deck of a modern airplane carrier, he made a landfall on a Bahaman island on October 12 of the same year, and eventually went on to discover the large islands we know as Cuba and Santo Domingo. On a second voyage, in 1493, he went out with seventeen ships and some fifteen hundred colonists, explored further in the Caribbean, and laid the foundations of the Spanish Empire in America. On his third voyage in 1498-1500, he reached the mouth of the Orinoco in South America but encountered difficulties among his colonists, and was sent home in irons by the royal governor Bobadilla, who took over the administration of the Indies for the Crown. He was released on his return to Spain, and in 1502-1504 made a fourth and final voyage, in which he reached the mainland at Honduras. He died in comparative obscurity at Valladolid in Spain in 1506, totally unaware that he had reached, not Asia, but a new continent.

That continent was, by a freak of history, not destined to bear his name, though it is now liberally sprinkled with other place-names in his honor. News of Columbus' voyages soon spread by word of mouth in Europe. But printing was still in its infancy; there were no newspapers or geographical institutes; the international learned class—the humanists—were more interested in Greek manuscripts than in strange lands; and, from early Portuguese days on, governments had done their best to keep their discoveries as secret as possible. The most effective spreading of the word in print about the New World was done by another Italian in the Spanish service, Amerigo Vespucci, who wrote copiously about his explorations in the immediate footsteps of Columbus. Scholars still dispute whether or not Vespucci really made all the discoveries, from the southeastern United States to the tip of South America, that he claimed to have made. But his letters came to the attention of a German theoretical geographer, Martin Waldseemüller, who in 1507 published a map blocking out a land mass in the southern part of the New World which he labeled, from the latinized form of Vespucci's first name, America. The map was read and copied, and though Waldseemüller in a new map of 1513 removed it in favor of a noncommittal "Terra Incognita" (unknown land), he had successfully christened two new continents.

Later Explorers   From now on, the roster of discovery grows rapidly. Ponce de León reached Florida in 1512, and Balboa in 1513 crossed the Isthmus of Panama and saw a limitless ocean, on the other side of which the Indies did indeed lie, for it was the Pacific. Many other Spaniards and Portuguese in these first two decades of the six-

teenth century explored in detail the coasts of what was to be Latin America. It was now quite clear that an immense land mass lay athwart the westward route from Europe to Asia, and that even the narrow isthmus of Panama was an obstacle not readily to be overcome by a canal. Maritime exploration was therefore turned to the problem of getting around the Americas by sea and into the Pacific. North America proved an obstacle indeed, for none of the great estuaries—Chesapeake, Delaware, Hudson—promising though they looked to the first explorers, did more than dent the great continent, the breadth of which was totally unknown. The St. Lawrence looked even better, for to its first French explorers it seemed like the sought-for strait. But even the St. Lawrence gave out, and the rapids near Montreal, which showed it was only another river after all, received the ironic name of Lachine (China) Rapids, for this was not the way to China. Not until the mid-nineteenth century was the "Northwest Passage" discovered by the Englishman Sir John Franklin, who died in the Arctic wastes before he could return to civilization.

The "Southwest Passage" was found only a generation after Columbus, in the course of an expedition that is the most extraordinary of all the great voyages of discovery. Ferdinand Magellan, a Portuguese in the Spanish service, set out in 1519 with a royal commission bidding him to find a way westward to the Spice Islands of Asia. Skirting the coast of South America, he found and guided his ships through the difficult fogbound passage that bears his name, the Straits of Magellan, reached the Pacific, and crossed it in a voyage of incredible hardship. Scurvy alone, a disease we now know to be caused by lack of vitamin C, and a standard risk in those early days, meant that he and his men had to surmount torturing illness. After he had reached the islands now known as the Philippines, Magellan was killed in a skirmish with the natives. One of his captains, however, kept on along the known route by the Indian Ocean and the coast of Africa. On September 8, 1522, the "Victoria" and her crew of eighteen men— out of five ships and 243 men that had sailed in 1519—landed in Spain. For the first time, men had sailed around the world, and had proved empirically that the world is round.

What these explorations cost in terms of human suffering, what courage and resolution were needed to carry them through, is very hard for our easy-traveling generation to imagine. Here, from the bare report the sailor Pigafetta gives of Magellan's expedition, is a firsthand account of one of the crises:

Wednesday, the twenty-eighth of November, 1520, we came forth out of the said strait, and entered into the Pacific sea, where we remained three months and twenty days without taking in provisions or other refreshments, and we only ate old biscuit reduced to powder, and full of grubs, and stinking from the dirt which the rats had made on it when eating the good biscuit, and we drank water that was yellow and stinking. We also ate the ox hides which were under the main-yard, so that the yard should not break the rigging: they were very hard on account of the sun, rain, and wind, and we left them for four or five days in the sea, and then we put them a little on the embers, and so ate them; also the sawdust of wood, and rats which cost half-a-crown each, moreover enough of them were not to be got. Besides the above-named evils, this misfortune which I will mention was the worst, it was that the upper and lower gums of most of our men grew so much that they could not eat, and in this way so many suffered, that nineteen died, and the other giant, and an Indian from the county of Verzin. Besides those who died, twenty-five or thirty fell ill of divers sicknesses, both in the arms and legs, and other places, in such manner that very few remained healthy.*

Such accounts could be multiplied for every part of the newly discovered world and for every nation taking part in the expansion of the West.

* Lord Stanley of Alderly, *The First Voyage Round the World by Magellan*, translated from the accounts of Pigafetta, and other contemporary writers (London, 1874), 64-65.

The Foundation of the Spanish Empire

As a by-product of Magellan's voyage, the Spaniards who had sent him out got a foothold in the Far East, which they had reached by sailing west. As we have seen, by the Treaty of Tordesillas in 1494 Spain and Portugal had divided the world—the world open to trade and empire —along a line that cut through the Atlantic in such a way that Brazil became Portuguese. This same line, extended round the world, cut the Pacific so that some of the islands Magellan discovered came into the Spanish half. Spain conveniently treated the Philippines as if they also came in the Spanish half of the globe, though they are just outside it, and colonized them from Mexico.

Up to now, we have concerned ourselves mostly with maritime exploration and the founding of coastal trading stations. The Spaniards in the New World, however, very soon explored by land, and acquired thousands of square miles of territory. To the explorer by sea there succeeded the *conquistador*, half explorer, half soldier and administrator, and all adventurer. Of the *conquistadores* two, Hernando Cortés and Francisco Pizarro, have come down in history with a special aura of tough romance. With a handful of men they conquered the only two civilized regions of the New World: the Aztec empire of Mexico, conquered by Cortés in 1519-21, and the Inca empire of Peru, conquered by Pizarro in 1531-33. The narrative of these conquests, whether in the classic nineteenth-century histories of the American Prescott or in the narratives of actual participants, remains among the most fascinating if not among the most edifying chapters of western history. A book of this scope cannot possibly do justice to the drama of the conquerors of Mexico and Peru, nor to the many other Spaniards who in search of glory, salvation, gold, and excitement toiled up and down these strange new lands—Quesada in New Granada (later Colombia), Coronado, de

Lisbon. Departure of an exploration trip to America (by De Bry).

Soto, and Cabeza de Vaca in the southwest of what became the United States, Mendoza in the La Plata (the lands around the River Plate), Valdivia in Chile, Alvarado in Guatemala, and many others. These are the men who opened up the New World for Spain, as our own North American pioneers from Captain John Smith to Lewis and Clark and Kit Carson opened up the New World for the English-speaking peoples.

Unlike the great cultures of the Middle and Far East, the pre-Columbian cultures of the Americas went down pretty completely before the Europeans. It is certainly true that from Mexico to Bolivia and Paraguay there survive millions of men and women of Indian stock, true that for a full understanding of the Latin-American republics one needs to know something about the traditions and the folkways of many tribes and peoples. That Mexican artists and intellectuals have in our day proudly held up their Indian heritage against the Yankees, and against their own Europeanized nineteenth-century rulers, is important for us to know. But the structure of the Aztec or the Inca empire has simply not survived. The sun-god in whose name the Inca ruled, the bloody Aztec god of war, Huitzilopochtli, are no longer a part of the lives of men, as Confucius and Buddha are. In themselves, however, these cultures are fascinating examples of the variety of human life on this earth. And the fact that they existed at all, as organized, large territorial states, and that they made high achievements in the arts and the sciences, is further evidence against naive western notions of racial superiority.

The First
True Colonial Empire

Well before the end of the sixteenth century, the work of the *conquistadores* had been done, and in Latin America the first of the true colonial empires of Europe—in contrast to the trading empires in Africa and Asia—had been founded. Nowhere, save in the region of the La Plata and in central Chile, were the natives eliminated and replaced by a population almost entirely of European stock. Over vast reaches of Mexico and Central and South America, a crust of Spanish or Portuguese formed at the top of society, and made Spanish or Portuguese the language of culture; a class of mixed blood, the *mestizos*, was gradually formed from the union, formal or informal, of Europeans and natives; and in many regions the native Indians continued to maintain their stock and their old ways of life almost untouched. Finally, wherever as in the Caribbean the Indians were exterminated under the pressure of civilization, or as in Brazil they proved inadequate as a labor force, the importation of Negro slaves from Africa added another ingredient to the racial mixture.

Moreover, geography and the circumstances of settlement by separate groups of adventurers in each region combined to create a number of separate units of settlement tied together only by their dependence on the Crown, and destined to become the independent nation-states of Latin America today. Geography alone was perhaps a fatal obstacle to any subsequent union of the colonies, such as was achieved by the English colonies that became the United States of America. Between such apparently close neighbors as the Argentine and Chile, for instance, lay the great chain of the Andes, crossed only with great difficulty by high mountain passes. Between the colonies of the La Plata and the colonies of Peru and New Granada lay the Andes and the vast tropical rain-forests of the Amazon Basin, still essentially unconquered today. The highlands of Mexico and Central America are as much invitations to local independence as were the mountains of Hellas to the ancient Greeks, and to this day the Isthmus of Panama remains almost impassable the long way, across the canal. Cuba and the other Caribbean islands have the natural independence of islands. And even had the coastal fringes of Brazil not been settled by Portuguese, men of a different language from the Spaniards, these regions have no easy land connections with the rest of Latin America. Geography alone would have made Brazil independent.

The Spanish used the centralized administrative institutions that were now the rule among the new monarchies of Europe. At the top of the hierarchy were two viceroyalties, that of Peru with its capital at Lima and that of New Spain with its capital at Mexico City. From Lima the viceroy ruled for the Crown over the Spanish part of South America, save for Venezuela. From Mexico City the viceroy ruled over the mainland north of Panama, the West Indies, Venezuela, and the Philippines. Each capital had an *audiencia*, a powerful body operating both as a court of law and as an advisory council, and there were *audiencias* in such major centers as Guatemala, New Granada (modern Colombia), Quito, and the Philippines.

The Balance Sheet of Latin-American Empire

This was certainly a centralized, paternalistic system of government, which has rightly enough been contrasted with the "salutary neglect" in which the North American colonies were generally left by the home government until the crisis that led to the American Revolution. But it was not—given the vast areas and the varied peoples under its control, it could not be—as rigid in practice as it was in theory. The rudiments of popular consultation of the Spanish colonists existed in the *cabildos abiertos* or assemblies of citizens. Moreover, as time went on the bureaucracy itself came to be filled largely with colonials, men who had never been in the home country, and who developed a sense of local patriotism and independence. Madrid and Seville were simply too far away to enforce all their decisions. Notably in the matter of trade, it proved impossible to maintain the rigid monopolies of mercantilistic theory, which sought to confine trade wholly to the mother country, and to prohibit, or severely limit, domestic industry in the colonies. Local officials connived at a smuggling trade with the English, Dutch, French, and North

Americans which in the eighteenth century reached large proportions.

The hand of Spain was heaviest in the initial period of exploitation, when the rich and easily mined deposits of the precious metals in Mexico and Peru were skimmed off for the benefit both of the Spanish Crown, which always got its *quinto*, or fifth, and of the *conquistadores* and their successors, Spaniards all. This gold and silver did the natives no good, but in the long run it did no good to Spain, since it went to finance a vain bid for European supremacy. By the seventeenth century, the Latin-American colonial economy and society had settled down in a rough equilibrium. It was not a progressive economy, but neither was it a hopelessly backward one. Colonial wares —sugar, tobacco, chocolate, cotton, hides, and much else—flowed out of Latin America in exchange for manufactured goods and for services. Creoles (American-born of pure European stock) and mestizos were the chief beneficiaries of this trade. The Indians remained at the bottom of the social pyramid.

Certainly the two great Indian civilizations, the Mexican and the Peruvian, were wiped out by the Spaniards. Certainly all over Latin America the natives fell to the bottom of a caste system based on color, a system never quite as rigid as it became in North America, but still a system that damaged the native's pride and self-respect. Yet Spanish imperial policy toward the natives was in aim by no means ungenerous, and even in execution holds up well in the long and harsh record of contacts between whites and non-whites all over the globe. Especially in the Caribbean, but to a degree everywhere, the whites tried to use native labor. The first result was disastrous for the natives; new diseases, to which the natives had no immunity, decimated their ranks. Here, as with the gold and silver, some ironic spirit of history seems to have taken revenge on the whites: though the

question of the origin of syphilis is still disputed, many historians of medicine believe that it was brought from the West Indies, where it was mild, to western civilization, where it has been deadly. The attempt to regiment native labor in a plantation system, or to put it on a semi-manorial forced-labor system, known as the *encomienda*, proved almost as disastrous. Negro slavery was an inevitable result. Finally, the colonial whites tended toward the aggressive, the insensitive, the hard-boiled; by and large, the gentle souls stayed at home.

Yet, against all these forces making for harshness and cruelty, there were counteracting forces. The natives were regarded as wards of the Crown, and their actual enslavement was prohibited by the New Laws of 1542. The central Spanish government passed a good many laws to protect the Indians, and though these were often flouted in the colonies—a phenomenon not unknown in the English colonies—they put a limit to wholesale exploitation of the natives. Their cause was championed by men of great distinction, and notably by Bartholomew de Las Casas (1474-1566), "Father of the Indians," Bishop of Chiapas in Mexico. The kind of man he is is clear even in these brief passages from his *Short Report on the Indies* (1542):

God has created all these numberless people [Indians] to be quite the simplest, without malice or duplicity, most obedient, most faithful to their natural Lords, and to the Christians, whom they serve; the most humble, most patient, most peaceful, and calm, without strife nor tumults; not wrangling, nor querulous, as free from uproar, hate and desire of revenge, as any in the world.

• • •

Their food is so poor, that it would seem that of the Holy Fathers in the desert was not scantier nor less pleasing. Their way of dressing is usually to go naked, covering the private parts; and at most they cover themselves with a cotton cover, which would be about equal to one and a half or two ells square of cloth. Their beds are of matting, and they mostly sleep in certain things like hanging nets, called in the language of Hispaniola *hamacas* [hammocks].*

Unlike the Asian and African masses, the Indians were formally converted to Christianity. Church and State in the Spanish and Portuguese colonies in the New World worked hand in hand, undisturbed for generations by the troubles roused in Europe by the Protestant Reformation and the rise of a secular anti-Christian movement. The Jesuits in Paraguay set up among the Guarani Indians a remarkable society, a benevolent despotism, a utopia of good order, good habits, and eternal childhood for the Guarani. On the northern fringes of the Spanish world, where it was to meet the Anglo-Saxons, a long line of missions in California held the frontier. Everywhere save in wildest Amazonia and other untamed areas the Christianity of the Roman Catholic Church brought to the natives something of the western tradition, made them in some sense

* Francis Augustus MacNutt, *Bartholomew De Las Casas* (New York, 1909), 314-315.

part of this strange new society of the white men.

In the main, the Portuguese settlements in Brazil have a character much like those of the Spaniards elsewhere in Latin America. The Portuguese, perhaps because of the proximity of Brazil to European waters, had more serious trouble with rival nations than the Spanish did. Indeed, the existence of those fragments of imperial hopes, French, British, and Dutch Guiana just north of Brazil on today's map, is a witness to the fact that the northern maritime nations made a serious effort to settle in what became Brazil. The race mixture in Brazil came also in colonial times to be somewhat different from that in most Spanish colonies, except Cuba. A large number of Negroes were imported into tropical Brazil, and, because the white males drew no sexual color line, were thoroughly mixed with the rest of the population. But in its mercantilist economics, its close tie with the home country, its close union of Church and State, Brazil resembled the Spanish colonies.

IV: The Latecomers — France, Holland, England

Early French and English Activity

Spain and Portugal enjoyed a generation's head start in exploration and in founding empires of trade, and a whole century in founding empires of settlement. Without this head start, which they owed in part to their position as heirs of the Mediterranean trade, Spain and Portugal could scarcely have made the great mark in the world that they have made. For the northern Atlantic states soon made up for their late start. As early as 1497 the Cabots, father and son, Italians in the English service, saw something of the North American coast, and gave the English their

exploration-based claims. Another Italian, Verrazano, and the Frenchman Cartier gave France a claim based on exploration, claims reinforced by the early seventeenth-century detailed explorations of Champlain. Dutch claims began with the voyages of Henry Hudson, an Englishman who entered their service in 1609.

The English did not immediately follow up the work of the Cabots. Instead, they put their energies in the mid-sixteenth century into the profitable business of breaking into the Spanish trading monopoly. John Hawkins, in 1562, started the English slave trade, and his nephew, Francis Drake, penetrated to the Pacific, reached California, which he claimed for England under the name of New Albion, and returned to England by the Pacific and Indian oceans, completing the first English circumnavigation of the globe. By the end of the century, the great fishing grounds off northeastern North America had become an important prize, and under Sir Humphrey Gilbert in 1583 the English staked out a claim to Newfoundland which gave them and their later colonists a firm place in these valuable fisheries.

The Thirteen Colonies: Settlement

In 1584, Sir Walter Raleigh attempted to found a settlement on Roanoke Island in a land the English named, from their Virgin Queen Elizabeth, Virginia. Neither this, nor a colony sent out in 1587, managed to survive. But early in the next century the English got two permanent footholds, at Jamestown in Virginia, 1607, and at Plymouth in New England, 1620. Both were to become colonies of settlement, regions in which the sparse native population was exterminated and replaced by men and women of British stock. But in their inception both were nearer the pattern of trading posts set by the Spanish and Portuguese. Both were established by chartered trading companies with headquarters in England; both, and especially the Virginian, cherished at first high hopes that they would find, as the Spaniards had, great stores of precious metals. Both were disappointed in these hopes, and managed to survive the first terrible years of hardship by the skin of their teeth. Tobacco, first cultivated in 1612, and the almost legendary Captain John Smith, explorer and man of resourcefulness, saved the Virginia colony, and furs, notably beaver, codfish, and Calvinist toughness saved Plymouth. Both gradually built up an agricultural economy, supplemented by trade with the mother country and interloping trade with the West Indies. Neither received more than a few tens of thousands of immigrants from abroad. Yet both these and the later colonies expanded by natural increase in a country of abundant land for the taking. The thirteen colonies of 1776 were a substantial series of settlements with almost three million inhabitants.

Before these English colonies were completed, one important and one very minor foreign group had to be pushed out. The Dutch, after their successful resistance to Spain (see Chapter IV), had come into the competition for commerce and empire. They had founded a trading colony at New Amsterdam at the mouth of the Hudson, and had begun to push into the fur trade. This made them rivals of both the French and the English. They lacked an adequate home base to be a great power, however, and in a war with England in the 1660's they lost New Amsterdam, which was annexed by the English in 1664 and became New York. The Dutch, though very few in numbers, were destined to supply some important families to the future United States, as names like Stuyvesant, Schuyler, and Roosevelt suggest.

The Swedes, too, were now making a bid for greatness, and in 1638 they founded Fort Christiana on the Delaware. But New Sweden was never a serious competitor, and in 1655 Fort Christiana was taken over by the Dutch, who in turn were ousted by the English. Pennsylvania, chartered to the wealthy English Quaker, William Penn, in 1681, filled the vacuum left by the expulsion of the Swedes and the Dutch from the Delaware, and was to be the keystone colony before it became the keystone state.

By the early eighteenth century, the English settlements formed a continuous string from Maine to Georgia. Each of the thirteen was founded separately. None had quite identical charters. Perhaps American tradition exaggerates the differences between the southern and the northern group. Massachusetts was not settled by demo-

An Indian village near Roanoke Island in what is now North Carolina.

155

cratic plain people, "Roundheads," nor was Virginia settled by great English landowners, gentlemen or "Cavaliers." Both colonies —and all the others—were settled by a varied human lot, which covered most of the range of social and economic status in the mother country, save for the very top. Dukes did not emigrate. But the poorest could and did, as indentured servants or as impressed seamen who deserted ship. The middling men came, and everywhere, even in New England, a solid sprinkling of the well-to-do.

Still, it is true that New England was for the most part settled by Calvinist Independents (Congregationalists), already committed to wide local self-government and to a distrust of a landowning aristocracy; and it is true that the southern colonies, especially Virginia, were settled for the most part by Anglicans used to the existence of frank social distinctions and to large landholdings. In Virginia, the Church of England became the established church; in Massachusetts, the Puritan Congregationalists, nonconformists in the homeland, almost automatically became conformists in their new home, and set up their own variety of state church. Geography, climate, and a complex of social and economic factors, drove the South to plantation monoculture of tobacco, rice, indigo, or cotton even in colonial days, and drove New England and the Middle Colonies to small farming by independent farmer-owners and to small-scale industry and commerce. Some historians hold that the natural environment, and not any original difference of social structure and beliefs, accounts for the diverging growths of North and South and their eventual armed conflict.

The Thirteen Colonies: Institutions

To us who are their heirs, it has seemed that these English colonists brought with them the religious freedom, the government by discussion, and the democratic society of which we are so proud. So they did, though they brought the seeds, the potentialities, rather than the fully developed institutions. These colonists came from an England where the concept of freedom of religion was only beginning to emerge from the long struggles of the sects. It was quite natural for the Virginians and the New Englanders to set up state churches. Yet, just as in contemporary England, these immigrants represented too many conflicting religious groups to enforce anything like the religious uniformity that prevailed to the south among the Spanish colonists and to the north among the French. Even in New England, "heresy" appeared from the start, with Baptists, Quakers, and even Anglicans, who seeped into New Hampshire and eventually even into Boston. Moreover, some of the colonies were founded by groups which from the first practiced religious freedom and separated Church and State. In Maryland, founded in part to give refuge to the most distrusted of groups at home, the Catholics; in Pennsylvania, founded by Quakers who believed firmly in the separation of Church and State; in Rhode Island, founded by Roger Williams and others unwilling to conform to the orthodoxy of Massachusetts Bay—in all these colonies there was something like the complete religious freedom that was later embodied in the Constitution of the United States, and, as the eighteenth century came on, the characteristic modern freedom not to belong to any formal religious organization.

The seeds of democracy, too, existed, although the early settlers, not only in Virginia but even in the North, accepted class distinctions more readily than we now do. No formal colonial nobility ever arose, and the early tendency to develop a privileged gentry or squirearchy in the coastal regions was balanced by the equalitarianism of the frontier and the career open to talents in the towns. Government by discussion was firmly planted in the colonies from the start. All of them, even the so-called proprietary colonies like Pennsylvania, which were granted to a "proprietor," had some kind of colonial legislative body.

Here we come to the critical point of difference between the English and the Spanish and French governments in the New World. The Spanish and French governments were already centralized bureaucratic monarchies; their representative assemblies were no more than consultative and had no power over taxation. Royal governors in Latin America and in New France could really run their provinces, leaning on men they appointed and recalled, and raising funds by their own authority. England was indeed a monarchy, but a parliamentary monarchy, torn by two revolutions in the seventeenth century. Though the Crown was represented in most colonies by a royal governor, the English government had no such bureaucracy as the Spanish and French had. Royal governors in the English colonies had hardly even a clerical staff and met with great difficulty in raising money from their legislative assemblies. The history of the colonies is full of bickerings between governors and assemblies, in which the governor, with little local support, and with but sporadic backing from the home government, was often stalemated. Moreover, in the local units of government—towns in New England, counties in the rest of the colonies—there was the same participation of the people, the same absence of an authoritative bureaucracy. Finally, the settlers brought with them the common law of England, with its trial by jury, and its absence of bureaucratic administrative law.

In sum, not only the opportunities of an almost empty land—the frontier—but also English traditions and ideas and the weakness of the central government were major factors in the growth of American democracy. Frenchmen and Spaniards did not bring to their colonies what the English brought to theirs.

New France   To the north, in the region about the Bay of Fundy and in the St. Lawrence Basin, the French built on the work of Cartier and Champlain. New France was to be for a century and a half a serious threat to the English North American colonies. The St. Lawrence and the Great Lakes gave the French easy access to the heart of the continent, in marked contrast to the Appalachians which stood between the English and the Mississippi. The French were also impelled westward by the fact that the fur trade was by all odds their major economic interest, and furs are goods of very great value and comparatively little bulk, easily carried in canoes and small boats. Moreover, led by the Jesuits, the Catholic French gave proof of a far greater missionary zeal than did the Protestant English. The priest, as well as the *coureur des bois* (trapper), led the push westward. Finally, the French in North America were guided in their expansion by a conscious imperial policy directed from the France of the Bourbon monarchs, *la grande nation* at the height of its prestige and power.

The result was that not the English but the French explored the interior of the continent. By 1712 they had built up a line of settlements—or rather, isolated trading posts, with miles of empty space between, thinly populated by Indians—which completely encircled the English colonies on the Atlantic coast. The story of these French explorers, missionaries, and traders, admirably told by the American historian Francis Parkman, is one of the most fascinating pages of history. The names of many of them—La Salle, Père Marquette, Joliet, Frontenac, Cadillac, Iberville—are a part of our American heritage. From Quebec, one line of outposts led westward, and from Mobile and New Orleans, in a colony founded at the beginning of the eighteenth century and named after Louis XIV, Louisiana, lines led northward up the Mississippi to join with those from Canada and Illinois.

Yet, impressive though this French imperial thrust looks on the map, it was far too lightly held to be equal to the task of pushing the English into the sea. It was a trading empire with military ambitions, and save in Quebec it never became a true colony of settlement. And even there it never grew in the critical eighteenth century beyond a few thousand inhabitants. Frenchmen simply did not come over in sufficient numbers, and those who did come spread themselves out over vast distances as traders and simple adventurers. Frenchmen who might have come, the Huguenots who might have settled down as did the Yankee Puritans, were excluded by a royal policy bent on maintaining the Catholic faith in New France.

The Indies, West and East

The northwestern European maritime powers intruded upon the pioneer Spanish and Portuguese both in the New World and in the Old. The French, Dutch, and English all sought to gain footholds in South America, but had to settle for the unimportant Guianas. They broke up thoroughly the Spanish hold on the Caribbean, however, and ultimately made that sea of many islands a kaleidoscope of colonial jurisdiction and a center of constant naval wars and piracy. These West Indian islands, though today for the most part a seriously depressed area, were in early modern times one of the great prizes of imperialism. Here the cheap Negro slave labor that had replaced the exterminated Caribs raised for their masters on the plantations the great staple tropical crops, tobacco, fruits, coffee, and, most basic of all, cane sugar, which had as yet no rival in beet sugar.

The French, Dutch, and English also began to raid the trading empires the Iberian powers had set up in the Old World. They also raided each other, both in times of official peace and in wartime. By 1715, the bases of their trading and colonial empires had been firmly laid in Asia and Africa.

India proved in these early modern centuries to be the richest prize, and the most ardently fought for. The Mogul Empire (see above, p. 141) was not strong enough in southern India to keep the Europeans out, but it did prove strong enough to confine them on the whole to the coastal fringes. Gradually, in the course of the seventeenth century both the French and the English established themselves in India on the heels of decaying Portuguese power and wealth. The English defeated a Portuguese fleet in 1612, and immediately thereafter got trading rights at Surat on the western coast. Although the able and active Mogul emperor, Aurangzeb, tried to revoke their rights in 1685, he soon found their naval and mercantile power too much to withstand. In 1690, the English founded in Bengal in eastern India the city they were to make famous, Calcutta. Meanwhile, the French had got footholds on the south coast near Madras, at a place called Pondichéry, and soon had established other stations. By the beginning of the eighteenth century, the stage was set in India as in North America for the decisive struggle for overseas empire between France and Britain.

Both countries operated in India, as they had initially in North America, by means of chartered trading companies, the English East India Company and the French *Compagnie des Indes Orientales*. The companies traded, and in trading were backed up by their governments when it was clear that bits of land around the trading posts had to be held, and that the whole relation with India could not be a purely commercial one. Gradually, both countries became involved in support of their companies in Indian politics and wars. But neither country made an effort to found a New England or a New France in the East.

The Dutch, too, entered vigorously into the competition. Their own East India Company, founded in 1602, succeeded in the next few decades in pushing the Portuguese out of Ceylon. But the great Dutch effort rather bypassed India to concentrate on southeastern Asia, and especially the East Indies. Here again they pushed the Portuguese out, save for part of the island of Timor; they also discouraged English interlopers. In spite of their rapid political decline as a great power in the eighteenth century, they got so firm a hold in Java and Sumatra that their empire in the Netherlands East Indies was to last until our own day.

Africa

All three of the northern maritime powers needed to use the same basic ocean route around Africa that the Portuguese had pioneered in the fifteenth century. All three got African posts. The Dutch put themselves in a good strategic situation by occupying the southern tip of Africa, the Cape of Good Hope, in 1652. The Cape was for them essentially a fitting station for their ships on the long voyage to Indonesia and the Far East, but it was

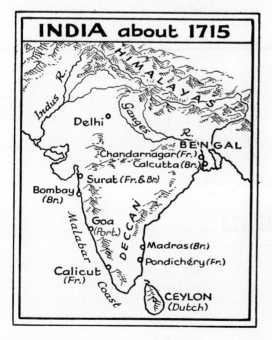

empty except for primitive tribes, and its climate was suitable for Europeans. Though immigration was never heavy, a colony of settlement did grow up, the nucleus of the Afrikaners of South Africa today. Here, notably, the French Huguenots were welcomed. In West Africa, the Dutch took from the Portuguese some posts on the Gold and Guinea coasts, and got a share of the increasingly lucrative slave trade.

The French also worked down the African coast, which was not held in the blocks of territory seen on the map today, but in separate posts which gave ample room for interlopers. In 1626, the French were in Senegal in West Africa. In the Indian Ocean they were on the island of Madagascar, formally annexed by Louis XIV in 1686, and in 1715 they took the island of Mauritius from the Dutch, rechristening it the Isle de France. The British broke into the competition by securing a foothold at the mouth of the Gambia River in West Africa (1662), later followed by other acquisitions at French and Dutch expense. Thus a map of Africa and adjacent waters in the eighteenth century shows a series of coastal stations controlled by the various European imperial powers. But the interior remained untouched, save by the slavers and native traders, and was to all intents and purposes unexplored. Only in the nineteenth century was the "Dark Continent" opened up to European expansion.

The Far East

China, long established as a great empire, was better able to withstand European pressure for territory. Somehow, even in the decay of their imperial power, the Portuguese were able to cling to Macao, and the Dutch, on their heels as always, obtained a station on Formosa in 1624. The Jesuits, bringing with them European instruments and learning that interested the Chinese, were able in the seventeenth century to get tolerated posi-

Jesuit missionary in China, about 1660.

tions in China, but they made little real headway against rooted Chinese ways of life. Indeed, the Chinese, convinced that their own land was the "Middle Kingdom" —that is, *central* in a spiritual and cultural sense—of the whole world, regarded the Europeans as ignorant barbarians who should be paying them tribute. They kept open only the slender privileged trade from Canton and Macao. This trade was indeed enough to keep Chinese and Europeans in firm contact, but the real opening of China was not yet.

In Japan, the European penetration started much as in China. In the sixteenth century the Portuguese, and in 1609 the Dutch, won trading footholds; in 1549, the great Jesuit missionary, St. Francis Xavier, had begun work with the Japanese. General trade with the Europeans was carried on from Nagasaki. But the Japanese reacted even more strongly than did the Chinese. Though Christianity did not make wholesale conversions, it did make considerable headway. The Tokugawa family, the feudal military rulers of Japan from 1600 to 1868, feared Christianity not only as a threat to national traditions but also as a threat to their own rule, because of the opportunities it might give European powers to intervene in Japanese politics and intrigue with the enemies of the Tokugawa. The Tokugawa therefore decided to close their land entirely to foreign dangers. In the early seventeenth century, they suppressed Christianity by force and literally sealed off Japan. Foreigners were refused entry, and Japanese were refused exit. Even the building of large ships capable of sailing the ocean was forbidden. The Dutch, strictly supervised, were allowed to cling to an island in Nagasaki harbor, where after 1715 they were limited to two ships a year. Not until the American Perry came to Japan in 1853 was this amazing self-blockade really broken and Japan thrown open to the world.

V: The Beginnings of One World

The expansion of Europe in these early modern centuries was not restricted to the Atlantic maritime powers. Although our own American tradition naturally centers on the Columbuses, the Magellans, the Captain John Smiths, general history must find a place for the extraordinary Russian exploration and conquest of

Siberia. This conquest we shall treat in Chapter VII. It offers all sorts of parallels with European expansion in the New World, from the chronological (the Russians crossed the Urals from Europe into Asia in 1483) to the political, for the expanding Muscovite state of Russia was a "new" monarchy, newer in some ways than the Spain of Charles V and Philip II or the England of Elizabeth I.

By 1715, the expansion of Europe was beginning to affect almost every part of the globe. European explorers, missionaries, traders, proconsuls of empire, had spread out in all directions. Even Arctic exploration, stimulated by the hope of finding a Northwest or a Northeast Passage that would shorten the route to the Far East, had already gone a long way by the beginning of the eighteenth century. Henry Hudson had found not only the Hudson River but also Hudson's Bay in the far north. In the late seventeenth century, English adventurers and investors formed an enterprise that still flourishes in Canada today—the Hudson's Bay Company, originally set up for fur trading along the great bay to the northwest of the French settlement in Quebec. In the late sixteenth century, the Dutch under Barents had penetrated far into the European Arctic, had discovered Spitsbergen, and had ranged across the sea named after their leader, the Barents Sea. Finally, the Russians under government patronage explored most of the long Arctic coasts of their empire early in the eighteenth century.

The Black Side of the Record

The record of expansion contains pages as grim as any in history. The African slave trade, begun by the Portuguese and entered by other peoples for its financial gains, is a series of horrors, from the rounding up of the slaves by native chieftains in Africa through their transportation across the Atlantic to their sale in the Indies. What strikes a modern most of all is the matter-of-fact acceptance of this trade, as if the Negroes were literally so much livestock. The Dutch slave trader *St. Jan* (note the irony of the saint's name) started off for Curaçao in the West Indies in 1659. Her log records every day or so deaths of slaves aboard, in parallel columns for Men, Women, Children, until between June 30 and October 29 there have died 59 men, 47 women, and 4 children. But there are still 95 slaves aboard when disaster strikes, thus simply and unmovingly recorded:

Nov. 1. Lost our ship on the Reef of Rocus, and all hands immediately took to the boat, as there was no prospect of saving the slaves, for we must abandon the ship in consequence of the heavy surf.
4. Arrived with the boat at the island of Cuaraçao; the Hon'ble Governor Beck ordered two sloops to take the slaves off the wreck, one of which sloops with eighty four slaves on board was captured by a privateer.*

And here is the Hon'ble Governor Beck's report to his Board of Directors in Holland:

What causes us most grief here is, that your honors have thereby lost such a fine lot of negroes and such a fast sailing bark which has been our right arm here.
Although I have strained every nerve to overtake the robbers of the negroes and bark, as stated in my last, yet have I not been as successful as I wished. . . .
I have witnessed with pleasure your honors' diligence in providing us here from time to time with negroes. That will be the only bait to allure hither the Spanish nation, as well from the Main as from other parts, to carry on trade of any importance. But the more subtly and quietly the trade to and on this island can be carried on, the better will it be for this place and yours.†

Americans need hardly be reminded of the fact that we virtually exterminated the native Red Indian population east of the Mississippi, and that if they massacred us

* *Documents Illustrative of the History of the Slave Trade to America*, Elizabeth Donnan, ed. (Washington, D. C., 1930), I, 143.
† *Ibid.*, 150, 151.

when they could, we replied in kind often enough, and with superior means. There were, of course, exceptions to this bloody rule. In New England, missionaries like John Eliot did set up little bands of "praying Indians," and in Pennsylvania, the record of the relations between the Quakers and the Indians was excellent. The white man's diseases, which in those days could hardly have been controlled, and the white man's alcoholic drinks, which were surely quite as hard to control, did more to exterminate the red men than did fire and sword.

The expansion of Europe, then, was a harsh and bloody business. But the modern reader must be reminded that what is usually called humanitarianism is on the whole modern, a movement that hardly attains wide social importance until the eighteenth century. No doubt Christianity brought a strain of gentleness into the West; no doubt many good Christians lived up to the high moral standards of loving-kindness set by Christianity. Still, it is a fact that in medieval and in Renaissance times life was frankly violent, and death and suffering were accepted as part of man's lot on this earth. Moreover, even those who were shocked at the suffering white men inflicted on those of another color could in perfect honesty tell themselves that God willed that the heathen should perish. Captain Underhill, after recording the massacre of the Pequots by the whites in New England, goes on in a tone which shows that unlike Governor Beck his conscience was troubled, but also that he had no real feeling of guilt:

Great and doleful was the bloody sight to the view of young soldiers that never had been in war, to see so many souls lie gasping on the ground, so thick, in some places, that you could hardly pass along. It may be demanded, Why should you be so furious? (as some have said). Should not Christians have more mercy and compassion? But I would refer you to David's war. When a people is grown to such a height of blood, and sin against God and man, and all confederates in the action, there he hath no respect to persons, but harrows them, and saws them, and puts them to the sword, and the most terriblest death that may be. Sometimes the Scripture declareth women and children must perish with their parents. Sometimes the case alters; but we will not dispute it now. We had sufficient light from the word of God for our proceedings.*

The Economic Record Seen in terms of economics, the expansion of Europe in early modern times was by no means the pure "exploitation" and "plundering" it sometimes appears to be in the rhetoric of anti-imperialists. There was robbery, just as there was murder or enslavement. There was, in dealing with the natives, even more giving of slight or nominal value in exchange for land and goods of great value. Just as all Americans are familiar with the slogan, "The only good Indian is a dead Indian," so they are familiar with a dozen variants of how little the Indians sold the island of Manhattan for. Finally, the almost universally applied mercantilist policy kept money and manufacturing in the hands of the home country. It relegated the colonies to the production of raw materials, a role not as well rewarded, generally speaking, as other economic roles, and one that tended to keep even colonies of settlement in a relatively primitive and certainly economically dependent condition.

Still, with all these limitations granted, the expansion of Europe was in economic terms an expansion of the total wealth produced here on earth. Although Europeans certainly took the lion's share in these early days, the expansion added to the goods available to non-Europeans. Although few Europeans settled in India or in Africa, their wares, and especially their weapons, began gradually the process of Europeanizing, or westernizing, the rest of the world. By the eighteenth century this process was only beginning, and in particular few of the

---

* *History of the Pequot War*, C. Orr, ed. (Cleveland, 1897), 81.

improvements in public health and sanitation that Europeans were to bring to the East had yet come about; nor had any greater public order come to India and Africa. But over the whole world, in the New World especially, there were signs of the Europeanization, or "modernization," to come.

Effects of Expansion on the West

The West has in its turn been greatly affected by its relations with other peoples. The list of items that have come into western life since Marco Polo and Columbus is long. It includes foodstuffs above all; utensils and gadgets, pipes for smoking, hammocks and pyjamas; styles of architecture and painting, bungalows and Japanese prints; and much else. Some of the novelties caught on more quickly than others. Tobacco, brought into Spain in the mid-sixteenth century as a soothing drug, had established itself by the seventeenth century as essential to the peace of mind of many European males. Potatoes, on the other hand, though their calory content is high and though they are cheaper to grow than the staple breadstuffs, did not immediately catch on in Europe. In France, where they are now a necessity of life, potatoes had to be popularized in a regular campaign which took generations to be effective. Tomatoes, the "love-apples" of our great-grandfathers, were long believed to be poisonous and were cultivated only for their looks.

Among westerners, knowledge of non-European beliefs and institutions eventually penetrated to the level of popular culture, where it is marked by a host of words—powwow, kowtow, tabu, totem, for instance. At the highest level of cultural interchange, that of religion and ethical ideas, however, the West took little from the new worlds opened after Columbus. The first impression of westerners, not only when they met the relatively primitive cultures of the New World, but even when they met the old cultures of the East, was that they had nothing to learn from them. Once the process of interchange had gone far enough, some individuals were impressed with the mysticism and other-worldliness of Hindu philosophy and religion, and with the high but quite this-worldly ethics of Chinese Confucianism. Others came to admire the dignity and simplicity of the lives of many primitive peoples. But for the most part what struck the Europeans—when they bothered at all to think about anything more than money-making and empire-building—was the poverty, dirt, and superstition they found among the masses in India and China, the low material standards of primitive peoples everywhere, the heathenness of the heathens.

Yet certainly exposure to these very different cultures acted as a stimulus in the West and broadened our horizons. The mere accumulation of so much new information gave the western mind something new to occupy itself with. Perhaps the first effect was no more than to increase the fund of the marvelous, the incredible. The early accounts of the New World are full of giants and pygmies, El Dorados where the streets are paved with gold, fountains of eternal youth, wonderful plants and animals. All this was a great stimulus to the literary and artistic imagination. From the island of Shakespeare's *Tempest* to the Xanadu of Coleridge's *Kubla Khan* you will find in our own literature the clear mark of all these new worlds.

But science, too, was stimulated. A dip into any of the early collections of voyages, say the famous and easily available voyages edited in English by Richard Hakluyt in 1582, gives an impression more of the realistic sense and careful observation of these travelers than of their credulity and exaggerations. Here is modern geography already well on the way to maturity, and here too is the foundation of the modern social sciences of anthropology, comparative government, even of economics. Here, as well as in the work of a Bacon or a Galileo, you will find the origins of that important modern western contribution to the culture of our world, natural science. A good example is the following attempt to report on the puzzling Hindu institution of caste. It is from the travels of Pietro della Valle, an early seventeenth-century Italian:

The whole Gentile-people of *India* is divided into many sects or parties of men, known and distinguisht by descent or pedigree, as the Tribes of the Jews sometimes were; yet they inhabit the Country promiscuously mingled together, in every City and Land several Races one with another. 'Tis reckon'd that they are in all eighty four; some say more, making a more exact and subtle division. Every one of these hath a particular name, and also a special office and Employment in the Commonwealth, from which none of the descendants of that Race ever swerve; they never rise nor fall, nor change condition: whence some are Husbandmen, others Mechanicks, as Taylers, Shoemakers and the like; others Factors or Merchants, such as they whom we call *Banians*, but they in their Language more correctly *Vania;* others, Souldiers, as the *Ragiaputi;* . . .

so many Races which they reckon are reduc'd to four principal, which, if I mistake not, are the Brachmans, the Souldiers, the Merchants and the Artificers; from whom by more minute subdivision all the rest are deriv'd, in such number as in the whole people there are various professions of men. In the substantial points of Religion all agree together; all believe the Transmigration of Souls, which according to their merits and demerits (as they think) are sent by God into other bodies, either of Animals more or less clean, and of more or less painful life, or else of men more or less noble and handsome, and more or less pure of Race, wherein they place not a little of their vain superstition; accounting all other Nations and Religions besides themselves unclean, and some more than others, according as they more or less differ from their Customs.*

A distinguished contemporary American historian, Professor Walter P. Webb, has found in the opening up of new lands to western society—and especially the vast, almost empty reaches of the New World— the main reason for the whole bursting out of western energies in the modern world.

* *The Travels of Pietro della Valle in India*, Edward Grey, ed. (London, 1892), I, 78-79.

A fifteenth-century European's fantastic conception of people in unknown lands.

This bonanza or windfall, he maintains, was the real force behind the growth of modern capitalism, the industrial revolution, the expansion of the West to make the beginnings of One World. But was the opening up of lands overseas—or overland as in Siberia—the basic "cause" of the great material progress the West has made in the last five centuries?

Here it must be noted again that the attempt to find a *single, one-way* causative factor in the great movements of history is a dangerous one. The great opportunities for expansion that the discoveries of the explorers gave to Europeans were certainly a factor in the rapid growth of productivity, population, and technical skills that characterizes the modern world. The great and easily acquired supplies of gold and silver from the New World were in the late sixteenth century a specific and useful "pump-priming" that furthered the growth of modern capitalism in northwest Europe. But the "frontier theory" of modern western capitalist society is no more to be taken as a sole explanation than, say, the Marxist theory of economic determinism or the Weber theory of the spirit of Protestant ethics. Most obviously, the roots of the discoveries themselves, like the roots of Protestantism and modern science, lie deep in the Middle Ages. Before the new worlds could be available to Europeans at all, trade, navigation, government organization—all had to arrive at the point where Henry the Navigator, Columbus, da Gama, and the others could proceed methodically to the discoveries and conquests that after all had been there for the Greeks, the Phoenicians, or the Vikings to make, had they been able.

The One World of 1700

By the beginning of the eighteenth century, there were still blank spots on the map of the world, especially in the interior of Africa and in the Pacific Northwest. Yet, in spite of this and in spite of the insignificance of the impression made by Europe on China and Japan, it was already clear that only one system of international politics existed in the world. From now on, all general wars tended to be world wars. They were fought, if only by privateers, on all the Seven Seas, and, if only by savages and frontiersmen, on all the continents. Sooner or later, any considerable transfer of territory anywhere, any great accession of strength or wealth anywhere, had its effect on the precarious international equilibrium that we call the balance of power. From the eighteenth century on, there was One World.

This was certainly not One World of the spirit. There was no common authority of any kind that could reach all men. There were pockets of isolated peoples. And the masses of the world, even at its center in Europe, were ignorant enough of what really went on in the hearts and heads of men elsewhere. But already western goods penetrated almost everywhere, led by firearms, but followed by a great many other commodities, not all of them "cheap and nasty." Already an educated minority was growing up all over the world from professional geographers to journalists, diplomatists, and men of business, who had to deal with what are now for the first time quite literally the affairs of the whole world and its peoples.

Reading Suggestions on the Expansion of Europe

General Accounts

P. Sykes, *A History of Exploration from the Earliest Times to the Present* (London: Routledge, 1934). A comprehensive treatment of the subject.

C. R. Beazley, *The Dawn of Modern Geography*, 3 vols. (London: John Murray, 1897-1906). An authoritative account; stops in 1420 but useful for the background of this chapter.

J. H. Parry, *Europe and a Wider World, 1415-1715* (London: Hutchinson's University Library, 1949). A good, up-to-date general study.

C. E. Nowell, *The Great Discoveries* (Ithaca: Cornell Univ. Press, 1954). A handy introductory manual.

J. H. Rose and others, eds., *The Cambridge History of the British Empire*, Vol. I (Cambridge, England: Cambridge Univ. Press, 1929). A convenient account of development up to 1783.

H. I. Priestley, *France Overseas through the Old Regime* (N.Y.: Appleton-Century-Crofts, 1939). A rather pedestrian study, but the best available in English.

Special Studies:
Primarily on Explorers and Navigators

E. Prestage, *The Portuguese Pioneers* (London: Black, 1933). Stresses the early Portuguese work.

E. Sanceau, *Henry the Navigator* (N.Y.: Norton, 1947). A good biography of the Portuguese sponsor of exploration.

S. E. Morison, *Admiral of the Ocean Sea*, 2 vols. (Boston: Little, Brown, 1942). The best book on Columbus; Professor Morison retraced Columbus' route as part of his preparation for writing.

H. H. Hart, *Sea Road to the Indies* (N.Y.: Macmillan, 1950). Deals with Da Gama and other Portuguese explorers.

C. McK. Parr, *So Noble a Captain* (N.Y.: Crowell, 1953). A very scholarly treatment of Magellan and his circumnavigation.

J. B. Brebner, *The Explorers of North America, 1492-1806* (N.Y.: Macmillan, 1933). A good account.

E. Heawood, *History of Geographical Discovery in the Seventeenth and Eighteenth Centuries* (Cambridge, England: Cambridge Univ. Press, 1912). Best work on the opening of the Pacific.

Special Studies:
Primarily on Asia and the East

The Cambridge History of India, 5 vols. (N.Y.: Macmillan, 1922-1937). A fully detailed account.

R. Grousset, *The Civilizations of the East*, 4 vols. (N.Y.: Knopf, 1931-34). Vol. III (China) is particularly good on Chinese culture. The other volumes deal with the Near and Middle East, India, and Japan.

K. S. Latourette, *The Development of China*, new ed. (Boston: Houghton Mifflin, 1956). Probably the best single introductory volume on the subject.

G. Sansom, *Japan: A Short Cultural History* (N.Y.: Appleton-Century-Crofts, 1943). Perceptive book by a distinguished British expert on the subject.

G. Sansom, *The Western World and Japan* (N.Y.: Knopf, 1950). A brilliant analysis, not only of the subject announced, but also of the whole problem of relations between East and West.

B. H. M. Vlekke, *Nusantara: A History of the East Indian Archipelago* (Cambridge: Harvard Univ. Press, 1943). Good introduction to the study of an important but often neglected area.

A. Hyma, *The Dutch in the Far East* (Ann Arbor: Wahr, 1942). Emphasizes social and economic developments.

Special Studies:
Primarily on the Americas

W. H. Prescott, *The Conquest of Mexico* and *The Conquest of Peru* (many editions). Two classic accounts, written a century ago, by a famous American historian.

C. H. Haring, *The Spanish Empire in America* (N.Y.: Oxford Univ. Press, 1947). The best general study of the subject.

S. E. Morison, ed., *The Parkman Reader* (Boston: Little, Brown, 1955). A convenient selection from the celebrated multi-volumed *France and England in North America* by Francis Parkman.

G. M. Wrong, *The Rise and Fall of New France*, 2 vols. (N.Y.: Macmillan, 1928). Sound study by a Canadian.

A. P. Newton, *The European Nations in the West Indies, 1493-1688* (London: Black, 1933). The best account.

S. E. Morison and H. S. Commager, *The Growth of the American Republic*, 4th ed. (N.Y.: Oxford Univ. Press, 1950). Vol. I of this excellent textbook summarizes the development of the thirteen English colonies.

Historical Fiction

N. Shute, pseud., *An Old Captivity* (N.Y.: Morrow, 1940). On the Viking explorer, Leif Ericson

L. Wallace, *The Fair God* (Boston: Osgood, 1873). A real thriller, unduly forgotten, on the Aztecs of Mexico; by the author of *Ben-Hur*.

S. Shellabarger, *Captain from Castile* (Boston: Little, Brown, 1945). On Cortés and the conquest of Mexico. The "cloak and bosom" school of historical fiction, but based on sound scholarship.

C. S. Forester, *To the Indies* (N.Y.: Bantam Books). An excellent novel on Columbus.

R. Sabatini, *The Sea Hawk* (Boston: Houghton Mifflin, 1923). A good melodramatic novel of adventures on the sea in the late sixteenth century.

C. Kingsley, *Westward Ho!* (many editions). Rather juvenile in tone, but gives a good picture of the excitement of English exploration.

W. Cather, *Shadows on the Rock* (N.Y.: Knopf, 1931). Sensitive re-creation of life in New France by a distinguished modern American novelist.

CHAPTER SIX

Divine-Right

Monarchy

—and Revolution

I: *International Politics—France as Aggressor*

By the mid-seventeenth century it was clear that neither the Spanish nor the Austrian Habsburgs were going to break down the European state-system and set up a new form of that haunting old institution, the Roman Empire. Yet for several generations, and in spite of Spain's reputation as a decaying power, men still feared a possible Spanish aggression. The actual aggressor in the great wars of the later seventeenth and early eighteenth centuries was France, who was the real victor in the Thirty Years' War. Well recovered from the wounds of her own religious wars, prospering economically and politically, with a young and ambitious king, Louis XIV (1643-1715), on the throne, France was ready for expansion.

As always in attempts to describe what the aggressor wanted, there is some exaggeration in attributing to Louis designs for "world conquest." Neither he nor his ministers can possibly have envisaged an organized world-state in which everyone was a subject of Louis XIV. Yet in North America, in India, in Holland, on the Rhine, in dozens of other places, the agents of Louis were hard at work trying to increase their master's power. Other peoples believed that France was threatening something they held dear—life, property, independence, self-respect. Under this threat, most of the European states finally united against the French aggressor, and beat him.

Before Louis XIV: Henry IV and Sully

Other kings in other days, like Louis XI of France and Henry VII of England, had accomplished the restoration of law and order. But only Henry of Navarre (Henry IV, 1589-1610) made the restorer a genuinely popular hero. Witty, dashing, with a pronounced taste for pretty women and bawdy stories, he was the most human king the French had had for a long time, and the best-liked monarch in their whole history. His court casually included his wife, his mistresses, and his children, legitimate and otherwise. He made jokes about his financial difficulties. And, most of all, he convinced his subjects that he was really concerned for their welfare. Among ordinary Frenchmen, Henry IV is still remembered as the king who remarked that every peasant should have a chicken in his pot on Sunday.

Henry's economic experts reclaimed marshes for farm land, encouraged the luxury crafts in Paris, and planted thousands of mulberry trees to foster the culture and manufacture of silk. His chief adviser, Sully (1560-1641), extended canals and launched a program of building roads and bridges that eventually won France the reputation of maintaining the best highways in Europe. Faced with a heavy deficit when he first took office, Sully systematically lowered it until he brought government income and expenditure into balance. From the economic standpoint, the France of Henry IV and Sully offers a preview of the ambitious policy pursued by the France of Louis XIV and Colbert in the name of mercantilism.

In 1610, when a Catholic madman assassinated Henry IV in the prime of his career, the new king, Louis XIII (1610-1643), was only nine years old. The succession of a child presents grave difficulties in a monarchy where the king really rules; in France, the reins of government went slack during the minority of Louis XIII. The queen-mother, Marie de' Medici, attempted to rule but showed little of her famous family's political skill. Her Italian favorites and French nobles, Catholic and Huguenot both, carried on a hectic competition which threatened to undo all that Henry IV had accomplished. In the course of these troubles, the French representative body, the Estates-General, met at Blois in 1614 for what was destined to be its last meeting until 1789 on the eve of the great French Revolution. Finally, Louis XIII came of age and, though incapable himself of asserting a strong rule, in 1624 picked a minister who could.

Before Louis XIV: Richelieu and Mazarin

The minister was Cardinal Richelieu (1585-1642), Bishop of Luçon, a sincere but certainly not an ardent Catholic, and also efficient and ambitious, a born administrator. As the virtual ruler of France for the next eighteen years, Richelieu proved to be a good Machiavellian and a good *politique*. He subordinated religion and every nonpolitical consideration to *raison d'état* (literally, reason of state), a phrase that he coined himself.

Raison d'état determined Richelieu's policy toward the Huguenots. The Edict of Nantes had given them certain political privileges, notably the right to govern some hundred fortified towns located mostly in the southwestern quarter of France. To Richelieu these Protestant towns formed a state within the state, a block to his program of strong centralization; they were to him a hundred centers of potential rebellion that should be brought under control. Alarmed, the Huguenots did in fact rebel. It took the royal forces fourteen months to besiege and take their chief stronghold, the port of La Rochelle, which finally fell in 1628. Richelieu thereupon canceled the political clauses of the Edict of Nantes but left its religious provisions intact.

The siege of La Rochelle lasted fourteen months, because France scarcely possessed a navy worth the name. In the next ten years, Richelieu created a fleet of thirty-eight warships for the Atlantic and a dozen galleys, manned by slaves (an exception to the rule that white men were never enslaved), for the Mediterranean. Meanwhile, he skillfully guided France through the Thirty Years' War, his eye always on the greatness of France, husbanding French resources carefully, committing them only when concrete gains for France seemed possible. Richelieu was one of the great practitioners of realistic power politics in international relations.

Raison d'état, indeed, motivated all his policies. He lived in elaborate style, accompanied on his travels by his private choir and corps of musicians, not just because he was fond of music but because he believed such a retinue befitted the chief minister of a great and splendid kingdom. In 1635, he founded the *Académie*, the famous French Academy, to compile a dictionary of the French language and to set the standards and style of the national culture. He tried to curb the factious nobles, though with only middling success, by ordering the destruction of some of their chateaux and forbidding the favorite aristocratic indulgence of private duels. More significant was his transfer of effective supervision over the local administration from the nobles to the more reliable *intendants*. These royal officials had existed earlier but had only minor functions; now they received greatly increased powers, particularly in the vital work of apportioning and collecting taxes.

Richelieu himself had picked and schooled his successor, the Italian-born Mazarin (1602-1661). Mazarin, too, was a cardinal and a past master of *raison d'état*. He, too, was careless about the finances of the French state and, unlike Richelieu, amassed an immense personal fortune during his public career. Soon after taking over, Mazarin faced the emergency of a long minority and regency. When the thirteenth royal Louis died in 1643, the fourteenth was a boy of four and a half. The feudal nobles resented being excluded from the regency by a foreigner; the judges and other high officials, who had invested heavily in government securities, particularly disliked Mazarin's casual way of borrowing money to meet war expenses and then letting the interest payments on government borrowings fall into arrears. The discontent boiled over in the uprising of the Fronde, 1648-1653, named for the slingshot used by Parisian children to hurl mud at passers-by.

The narrative history of the Fronde is a complicated set of plots, interspersed with some very mild battles and Mazarin's repeated flights from the country. Its upshot was to confirm Mazarin in his power, and to pave the way for the personal rule of Louis XIV. The youthful king got a bad fright when the *frondeurs* actually broke into the room where he was feigning sleep, and he resolved to hold firmly to the reins of state. The Fronde failed at bottom because it had no real roots in the country, not even in the rising middle classes. It was a struggle for power between Mazarin and his new bureaucracy, and two privileged groups, the old nobles and the newer official nobles of the law courts. Each of the noble groups distrusted the other, and in the long run Mazarin successfully applied the old Roman adage: Divide and rule.

The Successes of Louis XIV

Richelieu and Mazarin had seldom gone beyond the point of maintaining French power and prestige; they attemped little actual French expansion in Italy or in Germany and the Low Countries. Louis XIV, however, definitely did attempt to add to French territories. His main effort was no longer, as had been that of the Valois kings, toward Italy, but northeast toward Germany and Holland. He sought also to secure Spain, if not quite as a direct annexation, at least as a French satellite with a French ruler. Finally, French commitments overseas in North America and in Asia drove him to attempt, against English and Dutch rivals, the establishment of a great French empire outside Europe.

The first actual war of Louis XIV was a minor affair, but it showed how he was going to move. When he married the daughter of Philip IV of Spain, his bride had renounced her rights of inheritance. Now

Louis XIV, by Rigaud.

Louis claimed that, since her dowry had never been paid, her renunciation was invalid. His lawyers dug up an old family rule, the *right of devolution*, which Louis claimed gave his wife lands in what is now Belgium. In the ensuing "War of Devolution" with Spain, the great French general, Turenne, won various victories, but Louis was feeling his way and did not press them. A compromise peace at Aix-la-Chapelle in 1668 settled little and left the Dutch quite rightfully alarmed for the independence they had won from Spain.

In 1672, Louis began his war on the Dutch, against whom he eventually secured a fair number of allies, notably England, bought off in 1670, Sweden, and some of the German states. The Dutch, however, resisted stoutly under their strong leader, William III of Orange, a descendant of William the Silent. Even without William, Europe would probably have responded to the threat of French domination by an anti-French alliance. As it was, Spain, the Holy Roman Empire, and a still not very important German state, Brandenburg-Prussia, joined against France and her allies. The anti-French coalition was not very effective, and French diplomacy separated the allies at the treaties of Nijmegen (Nimwegen) in 1678-79. Holland was left intact at the cost of promising neutrality; Spain yielded to France the Franche Comté (County of Burgundy) and some towns in the Spanish Netherlands; Prussia, which had won a crucial battle against Sweden at Fehrbellin in 1675, was obliged by French pressure to give the Swedes back their Baltic German lands.

The power and prestige of France were now at their peak. Louis' place in Europe rested by no means solely on his armed forces. He was well served by a diplomatic corps trained in the niceties of *raison d'état*. Above all, he enjoyed to an unusual degree the position of leader and exemplar of culture and taste. Rulers all over Europe, and in particular the host of princes and prince-

lets in the Germanies, aped the standards of Louis' court at Versailles. French manners, French language, French clothes, French dishes, French art, were all the fashion. The prestige of France was not diminished by those who hated while they envied her; France was hardly loved, but she was admired and imitated. All in all, France in 1680 enjoyed assets Spain had never enjoyed. She was now *la grande nation*, adding to material power the very great power of cultural prestige.

The Failures of Louis XIV

Yet in the last three decades of Louis' reign most of these assets were dissipated, especially the concrete ones of wealth and efficient organization. Not content with the prestige he had won in his first two wars, Louis embroiled himself with most of the western world in what looked to that world like an effort to destroy the independence of Holland and most of western Germany, and to bring the great Iberian Peninsula under a French ruler. The third of his wars, the War of the League of Augsburg, broke out in 1688 basically over the continued French nibbling at bits of territory in western Germany. Louis' assertion of a dynastic claim to most of the lands of the German Elector Palatine was the last straw. The league against him was largely put together by his old foe, William of Orange, who after 1688 shared the throne of England with his wife Mary. Thenceforth, England was thoroughly committed to take sides against Louis. The great sea victory of the English over the French at Cape La Hogue in 1692 showed that England, not France, was to be mistress of the seas. But on land the honors were more nearly even. William was beaten in battle in the Low Countries time and again, but he was never decisively crushed. In Ireland, French attempts to intervene on behalf of the deposed English king, James II, were foiled at the battle of the Boyne in 1690.

Louis was growing old, and perhaps for the moment he had had enough. The Peace of Ryswick, concluded in 1697, was one of those comparatively rare peaces without victory, a general agreement to keep things as they were. It lasted barely four years, for in 1701 Louis, after much personal soul-searching, took a step that led to the great world war over the Spanish succession. His brother-in-law, the Habsburg king of Spain, Charles II, died in 1700 without a direct heir. For several years the diplomatists of Europe had been striving to arrange by general consent a succession that would avoid putting on the Spanish throne either a French Bourbon or an Austrian Habsburg. They had agreed on a Bavarian prince; but he had died in 1699, and the whole question was reopened. New plans were made, partitioning the Spanish inheritance between Habsburgs and Bourbons. But Charles II of Spain made a new will, giving his lands intact to Philip of Anjou, the grandson of Louis XIV, and then died. Louis could not withstand the temptation. He accepted on behalf of Philip, despite the fact that he had signed the treaty of partition. The threat to the balance of power was neatly summarized in the remark a gloating Frenchman is supposed to have made, "There are no longer any Pyrenees" (the great mountain chain that separates France and Spain). England, Holland, the Empire, and many German states formed the Grand Alliance to preserve the Pyrenees.

In the bloody war that followed, the French were gradually worn down in defeat. Their North American possession of Acadia (Nova Scotia) was taken by the English. In four great European battles, Blenheim (1704), Ramillies (1706), Oudenarde (1708), and Malplaquet (1709), the French were beaten by the Allies under two great generals, the English John Churchill, Duke of Marlborough, ancestor of Winston Churchill, and the Savoyard Prince Eugene. But the French were not annihilated. The last of the great Allied victories, Malplaquet, had cost the Allies 20,000 casualties, and somehow, by scraping the bottom of the barrel for men and money, the French managed even after Malplaquet to keep armies in the field.

Moreover, the Grand Alliance was weakening. The English, now following their famous policy of keeping any single continental power from attaining too strong a position, were almost as anxious to prevent the union of the Austrian and Spanish inheritances under a Habsburg as to prevent the union of the French and the Spanish inheritance under a Bourbon. At home, they faced a possible disputed succession to the throne, and some of the mercantile classes were sick of a war that was injuring trade, and that seemed unlikely to bring any compensating gains. In 1710, the Tory party, inclined toward peace, won a parliamentary majority and began negotiations that culminated in a series of treaties at Utrecht in 1713.

The Utrecht Settlement Utrecht was a typical balance-of-power peace. France was contained but by no means humiliated. She lost to England Newfoundland, Nova Scotia, and the Hudson's Bay territories, but she preserved Quebec and Louisiana, as well as her Caribbean islands. Louis gained in a sense what he had gone to war over, for Philip of Anjou was formally recognized as King Philip V of Spain and secured the Spanish lands overseas. The French and Spanish crowns were not, however, ever to be held by the same person; so the Allies, too, had won a point. Furthermore, England took from Spain the Mediterranean island of Minorca, which she handed back later in the century, and the great Rock of Gibraltar guarding the Atlantic entrance to the Mediterranean. The English also gained by what is called the Asiento the right to supply Negro slaves to the Spanish colonies, a right

EUROPE IN 1715

- ⊠ Brandenburg–Prussia
- ⫿ Austrian Habsburg Lands
- ⋰ Swedish possessions
- ⫽ Venetian possessions
- ⫿ Ottoman Empire
- ∿ Boundary of the Holy Roman Empire
- ✕ Battle sites

NORWAY

Oslo

Stockholm

SCOTLAND

North Sea

DENMARK

Copenhagen

Baltic

Edinburgh
Berwick

SWEDISH POMERANIA

ULSTER

Hamburg

Limerick

IRELAND

Boyne

Drogheda
Dublin

ENGLAND

Bremen

UNITED NETHERLANDS

Utrecht

Ryswick

Nimwegen

BRANDENBURG

Berlin

THE

SAXONY

EMPIRE

SILES

Fehrbellin

WEST-PHALIA

KINGDOM OF GREAT BRITAIN

London

Dover

Oudenarde

AUSTRIAN NETHERLANDS

Ramillies

Aachen

Prague

BOHEMIA

MORAVIA

Tor Bay
C. La Hogue

Seine R.

Mal-plaquet

Verdun

Metz

Toul

Rhine R.

LORRAINE

Rastadt

Blenheim

Augsburg

AUSTRIA

Vienna

STYRIA

Paris
Versailles

ALSACE

Stras-bourg

BAVARIA

Nantes

Orleans
Blois

Loire R.

FRANCHE COMTÉ

SWITZER-LAND

CARINTHIA

HU

Atlantic

Ocean

FRANCE

Geneva

Rhone R.

SAVOY

MILAN

TYROL

CARNIOLA

VENETIAN

Venice

REPUBLIC

Adriatic

Bordeaux

Burgos

Ebro R.

Avignon
(to the papacy)

Marseilles

Genoa

Florence

Adige R.

PAPAL STATES

Ragu

PORTUGAL

Madrid

Tagus R.

CORSICA
(to Genoa)

Rome

NAPLES

Lisbon

SPAIN

Valencia

Guadalquivir R.

Seville

Granada

Barcelona

BALEARIC IS.

MINORCA
(Br.)

SARDINIA
(to Austria, 1714;
to Savoy, 1720)

Naples

Gibraltar
(Br.)

Mediterranean

Palermo

SICILY

(to Savoy, 1
to Austria.

ALGERIA

TUNIS

MALTA

G.

Miles

0   500

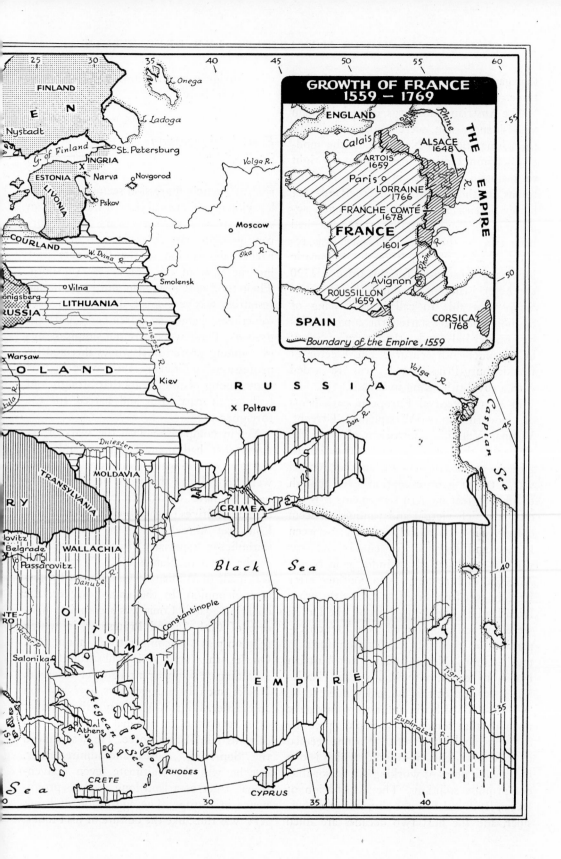

FINLAND

L. Onega

Nystadt

L. Ladoga

G. of Finland

St. Petersburg

INGRIA

ESTONIA   x   Narva   o Novgorod

LIVONIA   Pskov

Volga R.

o Moscow

COURLAND

W. Dvina R.

Oka R.

önigsberg   o Vilna   Smolensk

RUSSIA   LITHUANIA

Dnieper R.

Warsaw

OLAND   Kiev   R U S S I A

Volga R.

x Poltava

Don R.

Caspian Sea

Dniester R.

TRANSYLVANIA   MOLDAVIA

CRIMEA

RY

ovitz   WALLACHIA   Black   Sea

Belgrade

Passarovitz   Danube R.

NTE-   Constantinople

RO   O T T O M A N

Vardar R.

Salonika   E M P I R E

Tigris R.

Aegean Sea

Athens   Euphrates R.

RHODES

CRETE

Sea   CYPRUS

GROWTH OF FRANCE 1559 – 1769

ENGLAND

Rhine R.

Calais   THE

ALSACE
1648

ARTOIS
1659

Paris o   LORRAINE
1766

FRANCHE COMTÉ
1678

FRANCE

EMPIRE

1601

Rhône R.

Avignon

SPAIN   ROUSSILLON
1659

CORSICA
1768

— Boundary of the Empire, 1559

that gave them a chance also at interloping trade.

The Austrian Habsburgs, denied the main Spanish succession, were compensated with the former Spanish Netherlands, the modern Belgium. Holland was granted the right to maintain garrisons in certain fortified towns in these Austrian Netherlands for better defense against possible French aggression. Savoy, an Italian state that had been true to the Grand Alliance, was rewarded with Sicily; though diplomatic jockeying substituted for this prize in 1720 the lesser island of Sardinia, the Duke of Savoy was able to call himself King of Sardinia and thus started the long process that united Italy under the crown of Savoy in the nineteenth century. The Elector of Brandenburg-Prussia, too, was rewarded with a royal title, King in Prussia.

In all the general European settlements of modern times—Westphalia, Utrecht, Vienna, Versailles—historians discern the elements, the imperfections, that led to subsequent unsettlement and another general war. Utrecht is no exception, even though of all the great modern settlements it is the one in which victors and vanquished seem closest. First of all, the rivalry between France and England for empire overseas was not at all settled. In India, as in North America, each nation was to continue after Utrecht as before the effort to oust the other from land and trade. In Europe, the Dutch were not really protected from French expansion by the right to garrison forts in the Austrian Netherlands. The Austrian Habsburg leader, now the Emperor Charles VI, never forgot that he had wanted to be "Charles III" of Spain and never quite gave up hope that somehow he could upset the decisions made at Utrecht. No one seemed to have quite what he wanted, which is one of the difficulties of working out reasonable, compromise solutions. The distribution of Italian lands satisfied nobody, Italian or outsider, and the next two decades are filled with intrigues, negotiations, and very mild wars over Italy.

French Aggression in Review

In retrospect, this first period of French aggression seems one of the less violent and critical tests of the European state-system. True, these wars caused horrors enough, especially in the deliberate French devastation of the Palatinate during the War of the League of Augsburg. Their total cost in human and in economic resources was very great. The French were sometimes hated as foreigners and aggressors. These wars were not simply struggles among professional armies directed by professional politicians; they were in part wars among peoples, wars that brought out feelings of patriotism and hatred for the foreigner.

Yet in comparison with the wars of religion that had preceded them, and with the wars of nationalism and revolution that were to follow, the wars of Louis XIV seem to have lacked the all-out qualities of human drives toward both good and evil. Louis set himself up as a champion of Catholicism, especially after the revocation of the Edict of Nantes in 1685, and much was made of William of Orange as a Protestant champion. In the end, however, the coalition against Louis was a complete mixture of Catholic and Protestant, in which religion played a comparatively minor role. On the other hand, no lay substitute for the crusading religious spirit had yet emerged. Unlike such later aggressors as Napoleon and Hitler, Louis XIV was not the product of a revolution, a national awakening, an obvious stimulating force. He was indeed the "Sun King," a great and admired ruler, but he was the legitimate, even conventional, ruler of a land long used to prominence in Europe. The aggression of Louis XIV was thus, like the culture of his France, a moderate, measured, "classical" aggression. It lacked the heaven-storming fervor of aggressions born of revolution, aggressions that are really crusades, efforts to remake the world in the image of some exalted ideal, "totalitarian" aggressions.

II: The France of Louis XIV

Divine-Right Monarchy The admired and imitated French state of Louis XIV can stand in many ways as the best example of divine-right monarchy, the absolute monarchy of early modern times. We have for the France of Louis' prime one of those convenient but certainly oversimplified tags that history furnishes so abundantly. Perhaps Louis never actually said *"L'État, c'est moi"* (I am the State), but the phrase has stuck, and it is certainly not altogether misleading as an attempt to summarize a state of mind and an ideal. In theory, Louis was for his subjects the earthly representative of God on earth—or at least, in France. He held this position by the divinely ordained workings of the principle of primogeniture; he was not elected by his subjects, nor did he acquire his throne by force of arms. He was born to a position God had planned for the legitimate male heir of the tenth-century Hugues Capet. As God's agent, his word was final, for to challenge it would be to challenge the whole structure of God's universe. Disobedience was both a political and a religious offense.

Now though Louis has been dead less than three centuries, the ideas and sentiments centered on this divine-right monarchy are so utterly alien to contemporary Americans that it takes an effort of the historical imagination not to dismiss them as nonsense. There they were, however, clearly enough believed by many sensible men of the day. Two clues may help us understand why they were held so widely and so firmly. The first clue is the survival of the characteristic medieval view that right decisions in government are not arrived at by experiment and discussion, but by "finding" the authoritative answer provided for in God's scheme of things (see Chapter I). In the days of Louis XIV men still believed that God through his chosen agents directly managed the state. Men were indeed beginning to question this idea, but the full force of their questioning was not to come for another generation or two on the continent of Europe.

A second clue lies in the deliberate effort by the makers of the new French monarchy to cope with specific problems. Their central problem we have already noted: How to bring men together into those larger political units necessitated by the course of technological and economic growth, the overseas discoveries, and the pressure of a slow but steady increase of population. How to make men who were used to thinking, feeling, and behaving as Normans, Bretons, Flemings, Alsatians, Burgundians, Provençaux, Gascons, Basques—even just as villagers or members of a medieval "corporative" society (see Chapter IV)—think, feel, and behave as *Frenchmen*. The makers of the new French monarchy could not rely on a common language, for only a minority spoke standard French; the fifteen or twenty millions who had somehow to get along together as Frenchmen spoke several dozen mutually incomprehensible languages or dialects. And of course they could not rely on a common educational system, a common press, common participation in political life; all that lay in the future. They could, and did, attempt to set up at least a symbol of common Frenchness, a King of France who was king for Celtic-speaking Bretons as for Catalan-speaking southerners. That king collected taxes, raised armies, touched in a hundred ways the lives of ordinary men who had to feel somehow that the king had a right to do all this, had to feel that he was indeed doing this *for* them, rather than *to* them. A king who was, if not like the old Roman emperors a god himself, at least the agent of God, was the kind of king they could understand and accept.

Divine-right monarchy, with its corollary of obedience on the part of subjects, is thus one phase of the growth of the modern centralized nation-state. It was an institution that appealed to very old theological ideas, such as the Biblical admonition to obey the powers that be, "for the powers that be are ordained of God." But it was an institution that was also inspired by the newer ideas of binding men together in a productive, efficient state. In practice, naturally, the institution did not correspond to theory. Louis XIV was not the French state, and his rule was not absolute in any full, logical sense of that word. He simply did not have the physical means for controlling in detail what his subjects did. Such control is actually much more completely possible under modern techniques of communication, propaganda, and administration than it ever was in days of "absolute" monarchy.

The early modern monarchy in France and throughout the West was subject to many limitations besides those set by the physical possibilities of supervision. Medieval survivals made for diversities of many sorts, in language, laws, customs, even in weights and measures. All stood in the way of the uniformity, the administrative neatness and exactness, that are essential to the smooth working of a chain of command. Important groups still clung to medieval privileges—that is, to rights, immunities, a status, which they felt did not depend on the king's will, which were, certainly in the minds of those

who enjoyed them, legal limitations on the power of the king. Many of these groups were corporations—municipal boards, judicial boards, economic groups such as guilds—which usually possessed written charters and traditional privileges very difficult for the government to override. Two of these groups, the old nobility and the clergy, deserve special mention.

The Nobility

In all the important countries the feudal nobility maintained themselves into early modern times. The degree to which they were integrated into the new machinery of state was of crucial importance in the development of modern Europe. In Habsburg Spain, as indeed in the Habsburg lands of Central Europe, the old nobility generally accepted the new strength of the Crown, but maintained much of their privilege and all their old pride of status. In Prussia, they were most successfully integrated in the new order, becoming on the whole faithful servants of the Crown, but with a social status that set them clearly above mere bourgeois bureaucrats (see Chapter VIII). In England, as we shall shortly see, the nobility achieved a unique compromise with the Crown. In France, they were in effect shoved aside by the Crown and deprived for the most part of major political functions, but they were allowed to retain social and economic privileges and important roles as officers in the king's army.

This process of reducing the old French nobility to political powerlessness had begun during the fifteenth century, and had been hastened by the religious and civil wars of the sixteenth century. An important part of the nobility, perhaps nearly half, had espoused the Protestant cause, in large part from sheer opposition to the Catholic Crown. The victory of Henry IV, purchased by his conversion to Catholicism, was a defeat for the nobility. The process was completed by the increasing use under Richelieu and Louis XIV of commoners in the task of running the government, from the great ministers of state, through the *intendants,* down to local administrators and judges. These commoners were usually elevated to a status technically noble, a status that came to be hereditary, but they were known by a special term, the *noblesse de la robe* (from the robes or gowns worn by judges and other officials). This official bureaucratic nobility did not, however, have at first the social prestige of the old nobility of the sword, the *noblesse de l'épée.* The old nobles felt a contemptuous envy toward the newcomers of the gown; they knew they were shelved, and one of them, the Duc d'Antin, wrote pathetically shortly after Louis's death:

Kings who will reign in the future will recall that Louis XIV, one of the greatest kings on earth, would never employ persons of quality in any kind of government business; and that M. the Regent, a very enlightened prince, had begun by putting them at the head of all such business, and had been obliged to take them altogether out of the government after three years. What will they, what should they, conclude? *That men of this class are not suited to government affairs, that they are good only to be killed off in war.**

The Clergy

In medieval times, the clergy had been a separate order, backed by the supranational power and prestige of the papacy, and possessing privileges not wholly in the control of the Crown. In the new centralized France, however, the Crown had fostered a national Gallican Church which was indeed Catholic but also under good control by the monarchy. Under Louis, this Gallican union of throne and altar reached a high point, and the greatest of his bishops, Bossuet (1627-1704), wrote firmly in sup-

---

* Italics are ours. Duc d'Antin, *Mémoires,* quoted in P. E. Lémontey, *Histoire de la Régence et de la Minorité de Louis XV* (Paris, 1832), I, 194-195. Our translation.

port of royal absolutism. Yet even under Louis XIV the French clergy continued to possess important corporate privileges. They were not subject to royal taxation; they contributed of their own free will a gift of money which they voted in their own assembly.

Moreover, Louis was by no means wholly master of the religious beliefs and practices of his subjects. Whereas Richelieu had attacked only the political privileges of the Huguenots, Louis attacked their fundamental right of toleration and finally abolished it. Pressed by the clergy, he revoked the Edict of Nantes in 1685. After the revocation, fifty thousand Huguenot families fled abroad, notably to Prussia, Holland, Belgium, England, and the new colonial lands of British North America. The practical skills and intellectual gifts of these early "refugees" greatly strengthened the lands that received them. Some Huguenots also remained in France, where they continued to worship underground in spite of persecution.

The Royal Administration

Louis did not quite succeed in building up an administrative machine wholly under royal control. It was not for want of application that he fell short. When he began his personal rule in 1661, he was only twenty-two years old but had already impressed a seasoned observer of the court with his earnestness:

As the single desire for glory and to fulfill all the duties of a great king occupied his whole heart, by applying himself to toil he began to like it; and the eagerness he had to learn all the things that were necessary to him soon made him full of that knowledge. His great good sense and his good intentions now made visible in him the rudiments of general knowledge which had been hidden from all who did not see him in private; for he suddenly appeared like a politician in affairs of the State, a theologian in those of the Church,

The Palace of Versailles.

precise in matters of finance, speaking with justice, taking always the right side in council, sensitive to the interests of private persons, but an enemy to intrigue and flattery, and stern towards the grandees of his kingdom whom he suspected of a desire to govern him.

He was agreeable personally, civil and easy of access to every one; but with a lofty and serious air which impressed the public with respect and awe . . . , though he was familiar and gay with ladies.*

Louis continued to be "familiar and gay" with the ladies until finally, after the death of his Spanish queen, he settled down to a proper middle-aged marriage with Madame de Maintenon, a devout Catholic who had been the governess of his illegitimate children. Meanwhile, he had provided himself a setting worthy of the Sun King by building a few miles outside Paris the celebrated Palace of Versailles, which was more than a third of a mile long and housed a court of ten thousand.

At Versailles, Louis met regularly with his ministers, who headed departments essentially like those of any modern state— War, Finance, Foreign Policy, Interior. The

---

* *Memoirs of Madame de Motteville*, K. P. Wormeley, trans. (Boston, 1902), III, 243.

ministers were responsible directly to him, and not to any legislative body. The Estates-General never met during his lifetime. From the top, a reasonably clear chain of command proceeded down through the *intendants*, who were now the heads of *généralités* (big administrative units roughly corresponding to the older provinces), thence through smaller units to the town or village. Even the indefatigable Louis, however, could do no more than exercise general supervision over the affairs of his large and complex kingdom. And he probably could not have achieved even partial success without the invention of printing. For the familiar printed forms to be filled out were already in existence. And they are still there, duly filled out and filed in their hundreds of thousands in the local archives of France.

In practice, naturally, the royal administration was full of difficulties and contradictions. There were many superimposed and often conflicting jurisdictions, survivals of feudalism and the medieval struggle to control feudalism. The officials of Louis XIV, by the very fact of being nobles of the gown, possessed a privileged status which they could hand down to their heirs. They, too, tended to form a corporation, tended even as individuals to be more their own masters in their own bailiwicks than the theory of royal absolutism would allow. The key provincial administrators, the *intendants*, may seem to have been no more than agents of the Crown. Yet anyone who pursues in local history the detailed records of what the *intendants* actually did sees that many of them exercised considerable initiative and were by no means rubber-stamp officials. Nor was the old administrative device of moving the *intendants* about from one *généralité* to another sufficient to overcome this centrifugal tendency.

Still another set of institutions gave trouble. These were the *parlements*, the supreme courts of appeal in the various provinces, of which one, the Parlement of Paris, enjoyed special prestige and power from its place at the capital and from the size of its territorial jurisdiction, almost half of the kingdom. The judges who staffed the courts headed the nobility of the gown, owned their offices, and were not removable at the will of the king. In addition to the usual work of a court of appeals, the *parlements* claimed through their function of registering royal edicts something very close to what in American usage is called the right of judicial review. That is, they claimed to be able to refuse to register an edict if they thought it "unconstitutional," not in accord with the law of the land. The claim, of course, negated theoretical royal absolutism.

Actually, Louis got around the difficulty in his own lifetime. The Parlement of Paris had already lost a round in its struggle with the royal power by entering the lists against Mazarin in the Fronde. Now Louis successfully utilized another old institution, the *lit de justice* (literally, "bed of justice"), in which he summoned the Parlement of Paris before him in a formal session and ordered the justices to register a royal edict. In this way, for instance, he enforced measures against Jansenism, a Puritanical form of

Catholicism, which was strong among the judges. But the *parlements*, too, were to plague his eighteenth-century successors.

Mercantilism in Theory Just as divine-right monarchy was not peculiarly French, so the mercantilism identified with the France of Louis XIV was common to many other western states in the early modern period (see above, Chapter IV). But, like divine-right rule, mercantilism flourished most characteristically under the Sun King. Its most famous exponent was one of Louis' greatest ministers, Colbert (1619-1683).

Mercantilism comprised a set of economic aims and practices, particularly in the field of relations between government and business. It met severe criticism from the proponents of the free-trade or laissez-faire economic theory that supplanted it. Therefore it has often come down to us in the caricature its opponents chose to make of it for polemical purposes. The central doctrine of mercantilism, according to this caricature, is that hard money, gold and silver, is the basic wealth, that a given state should aim to acquire as much hard money as possible, and that therefore it should aim always at a "favorable balance of trade." It encourages exports to bring in money from abroad and discourages imports to prevent money from being paid out; it puts high protective tariffs against imports, and perhaps even places bounties on exports. In this simple form, the doctrine can readily be made absurd. A country that took in huge amounts of gold and silver would thereby simply increase prices within its borders, for gold and silver are merely media of exchange. No one can eat the precious metals or even find much practical use for them.

But mercantilism was much more than an oversimple and perhaps mistaken theory of international trade. It was part and parcel of the early modern effort to construct strong, efficient, political units. The mercantilists quite frankly aimed to make a given nation as self-sustaining as possible, as independent as possible of the need to import from other nations, which were its rivals and its potential enemies. As a policy, it is not entirely remote from us today; indeed, there are those who maintain that the policy of most twentieth-century nations is "neo-mercantilism."

Within a given nation, the mercantilists held that national production should provide the necessities of life for a hard-working population, and the necessities of power for a nation able to fight and win wars. These ends and the means for achieving them, they believed, demanded planning and control from above. They did not think that the old traditional ways of manor and guild, the old standard of the "just price," brought out the energies and abilities needed in an expanding economy. They were all for sweeping away these remnants of medieval controls. But they did not believe, as the free-trade economists after them were to believe, that all that was necessary was to destroy these controls and leave individual businessmen free to do whatever they thought would enrich them most as individuals. Instead, the mercantilists would channel the national economic effort by government subsidies, by grants of monopolies, by direct production in government-run industries, by encouraging scientific and technological research, and of course by protective tariffs.

At this point we come back to a phase of the expansion of Europe. Already in the seventeenth century many foodstuffs and raw materials were more easily available overseas than in Europe. The colonies could supply necessities that could not be so well produced at home, but that thanks to the existence of the colonies need not be imported from a rival. Thus the mercantilist viewed France overseas as a special part of France, a part that should be run from the homeland by a strong government, as indeed the homeland itself should be managed.

Since the homeland produced industrial goods and the colonies produced raw materials, the two were mutually supplementary, and free trade between the two would give each partner what it needed. This mercantilistic attitude toward colonies was held not only by absolutist France and Spain, but by the more limited governments of England and Holland.

Mercantilism in Practice: Colbert

The great practitioner of mercantilism, Colbert, never quite attained the supremacy reached by Richelieu and Mazarin; he was the collaborator, never the master, of Louis XIV. Other great ministers, Louvois for military affairs especially, stood in the way of his supremacy. Yet Colbert was influential in all matters affecting the French economy, most interested in foreign trade and in the colonies, and therefore in the merchant marine and in the navy. His hand was in everything, in invention, in technological education, in attracting enterprising foreigners to settle in France, in designing and building ships, in founding and encouraging industries. The eight big volumes of his Letters, Instructions, and Memorials, published in the nineteenth century, gave an admirable general view of the activities of this first great modern exponent of the controlled economy.

Whether the great prosperity France achieved in the first thirty years of Louis' reign came about because of, or in spite of, the mercantilist policies of Colbert is a question difficult to answer. The convinced adherent of laissez-faire doctrines will argue that France would have done even better had her businessmen been left alone. But this was not the seventeenth-century way, not even in England and Holland. Under the mercantilist regime, France did attain an undoubted leadership in European industry and commerce. That lead she lost, in part because the last two wars of Louis XIV were ruinously expensive, in part because from the eighteenth century on France's rival, England, took to the new methods of power machinery and concentrated on large-scale production of inexpensive goods. France remained largely true to the policies set by Colbert—relatively small-scale production of a variety of goods, often luxuries, and predominantly consumers' goods. But the difference between French and English industry was not so much a difference of economic theory as a difference of natural resources—coal, iron, and water power were more easily exploited in England than in France—and, even more, a difference in the focus of national energies. At bottom, France in early modern times, like Spain before her, spent an undue proportion of her national product in the ultimately unfruitful effort to achieve the political domination of Europe by force of arms.

III: England in Revolution

The Constitutional Tradition

To the men of the seventeenth century, France seemed the home of a stable government and society, and England seemed the land of violence and change. Within the century, to the scandal of continental Europeans living under divine-right monarchies, the English cut one king's head off and drove another into exile. It is hard for us today, to whom the English seem the most orderly of people, to realize that they were once regarded as politically disorderly, as hard to govern. Yet they ushered in with considerable turmoil an important modification of the new-model state, a modification that was to make its way with greater or less success, and greater or less deviation from the English original, all through western civilization by the end of the nineteenth century.

This modification should not yet in the seventeenth century be given the name of "democracy"; it is more safely called representative or parliamentary government. To the extent that such government used to the full the new methods of professional administration developed in the fifteenth and sixteenth centuries, it may be considered just as "absolute" as any divine-right monarchy. But representative government has grown in the West under historical conditions that have provided a check on the potential absolutism it shares with divine-right monarchy. This check is the concept of a "constitution," a set of rules, written or traditional, not to be altered by the ordinary processes of government. These rules are in the modern western tradition felt to be limitations on the authority even of a government elected by the majority of the people, a guarantee to the individuals and to groups that they may do certain things even though men in governmental posts of authority do not want them to. Without these rules and habits of constitutionalism, or "civil rights," the machinery of parliamentary government could be as ruthlessly absolute as the machinery of Soviet Russian government.

English-speaking people throughout the world have come to believe that England has always had a representative and constitutional government; or, put negatively, that England never went through the stage of divine-right absolute monarchy most of the continental states went through. This belief is partly correct. But it would be better stated as follows: England in the fifteenth and sixteenth centuries began, as did the continental states, to develop a new-model centralized monarchy; but the development in the seventeenth century was checked and modified by the continued growth of representative institutions at both the local and the national level. In France, for instance, cardinals and kings were able to raise money and govern without the Estates-General. In England, Parliament met in 1629 and quarreled violently with King Charles I. For eleven long years, until 1640, Charles too governed without calling Parliament. But in 1640 he felt obliged to call Parliament and, though he dismissed it at once when it proved recalcitrant, he had to call another in that same year. This was the famous Long Parliament, which sat—with changes of personnel and with interruptions —for twenty years, and which made the revolution that ended the threat of absolute monarchy in England. If we understand why Charles, unlike his French counterpart, was obliged to call Parliament, we have gone a long way toward understanding why England had a head start in modern representative government.

One very basic reason goes back to later medieval history. As we have already seen, the English Parliament diverged in one important detail of organization from continental parliaments. The House of Commons represented two different social groups not brought together in one house on the Continent, the aristocratic "knights of the shire" and the largely middle-class "burgesses" of the towns and cities. The strength of the Commons lay in the practical working together of both groups, which intermarried quite freely and, in spite of some economic and social tensions, tended to form a single ruling class with membership open to talented and energetic men from the lower classes.

The Middle Ages left another important heritage—the persistence in local government of magistrates who were not directly dependent on the Crown. We must not exaggerate: England, too, had its bureaucrats, its clerks and officials in the royal pay. But whereas in France and in other continental countries the new bureaucracy tended to take over almost all governmental business, especially financial and judicial affairs, in England the gentry and the higher nobility continued to do important local work. The Elizabethan Poor Law of 1601 put the care of the needy not under any national ministry but squarely on the smallest local units, the parishes, where decisions lay ultimately with the amateur, unpaid justices of the peace, recruited from the gentry. In short, the privileged classes were not, as in France, shelved, thrust aside by paid agents of the central government; nor did they, as in Prussia, become themselves mere agents of the Crown. Instead, they preserved a firm base in local government and an equally firm base in the House of Commons. When Charles I tried to govern without the consent of these privileged classes, when he tried to raise from them and their dependents money to run a bureaucratic government without these privileged amateurs, they had a solid institutional basis from which to resist.

The Role of the Crown

But they had to struggle. They had to fight a civil war. No matter how much emphasis the historian may put on the social and institutional side, he cannot ignore what looks like the sheer accident of human personality. The Tudors from Henry VII to Elizabeth I, with some faltering under Edward VI and Mary, had been strong personalities and had been firmly— quite as firmly as any Valois or Habsburg— convinced that they were called to absolute monarchy. They had slowly built up a very strong personal rule, handling their Parliaments skillfully, giving in occasionally in detail, but holding the reins firmly. Henry VIII and his daughter Elizabeth both commanded the kind of devotion from their subjects that can be built in time into formidable personal rule; they could hold the emotional loyalty of the English.

Their successors could not. Elizabeth I was childless, and in 1603 she was succeeded by the son of her old rival and cousin, Mary Queen of Scots. James Stuart, already King of Scotland as James VI, became James I of England (1603-1625), thus bringing the two countries, still legally separate, under the same personal rule. James was a pedant by temperament, very sure of himself, and above all sure that he was as much a divine-right monarch as his French cousins. He was a Scot—that is, a foreigner—and as such an object of distrust to his English subjects. He lacked entirely the Tudor heartiness and tact, the gift of winning people to him.

His son, Charles I (1625-1649), under whom the divine-right monarchy came to an end, was by no means as unattractive a monarch and, partly because of his martyrdom, has had his ardent partisans among historians. But if he had many of the graces of a monarch, it is still true that Charles I was no man to continue the work of the Tudors. He was quite as sure as his father had been that God had called him to rule England, and he could never make the happy compromises the Tudors made.

Issues between Crown and Parliament

The fundamental fact about the actual break between the first two Stuarts and their parliamentary opponents is that *both* were in a sense revolutionaries. Both were seeking to bend the line of English constitutional growth away from the Tudor compromise of a strong Crown working with and through a late medieval Parliament based on the alliance of gentry and commercial classes. James and Charles were seeking to bend the line toward divine-right monarchy of the continental type; the parliamentarians were seeking to bend it toward something quite as new in England and in the world, the establishment of a legislative body possessing the final authority in the making *and carrying out* of law and policy.

Behind this struggle lay the fact that the business of state was gradually growing in scope and therefore in money cost. Foreign relations, for instance, which had been most rudimentary in the Middle Ages, had by the end of the sixteenth century begun to take on modern forms, with a central foreign office, ambassadors, clerks, and the like, all needing money and personnel. The money required by Stuarts—and indeed by Bourbons, Habsburgs, and the rest of the continental monarchs—did not simply go for high living by royalty and the support of parasitic nobles. It went to run a government that was beginning to take over the many functions of the new-model state. Basically, James I and Charles I failed to get the money they needed because those from whom they sought it, the ruling classes, succeeded in placing the raising and spending of it in their own hands through parliamentary supremacy. The Parliament that won that supremacy was in fact a committee —a big one, but still a committee—of the ruling classes. It was not a democratic legislature.

One final fact in the background of this struggle between Crown and Parliament: religion played a major part in welding both sides into cohesive fighting groups. The struggle for power in England was in part a struggle to impose a uniform worship on Englishmen. The royalist cause was identified with High Church Anglicanism, that is, with an episcopalian church government and a liturgy and theology fundamentally Catholic, though not recognizing the authority of Rome. The parliamentary cause, at first supported by many moderate Low Church Anglicans, also attracted a strong Puritan or Calvinist element. Later, it came under the control of the Presbyterians and then of the extreme Puritans, the Independents or Congregationalists.

The term "Puritanism" in seventeenth-century English history is a confusing one, and must remain so to those who demand simple, clear-cut definitions. For it was used as a blanket term to cover a wide variety of religious experience, from that of moderate Anglicans to that of the radical splinter sects of the 1640's and 1650's. Its core went back to Zwingli and Calvin, to the repudiation of Catholic sacramental religion and the rejection of music and the adornment of the church. It placed a positive emphasis on sermons, on simplicity in church and out, and on "purifying" the tie between the worshiper and his God of Catholic "superstitions" and "corruptions."

The Reign of James I
(1603-1625)

In the troubled reign of James I, we may distinguish three major threads of the struggle in which his son was to go under—money, foreign policy, and religion. In all three issues, the Crown and its opposition each tried to bend the line of constitutional development in its own direction. In raising money, James sought to make the most of revenues which he did not need to ask Parliament to grant. Parliament sought to make the most of its own control over the purse strings by insisting on the principle that any new revenue-raising had to be approved by Parliament. On the whole, James got along, though he levied some taxes without parliamentary grant. One of these, on the somewhat insignificant commodity of imported dried currants, was refused by an importer named Bate. Bate's case was decided in favor of the Crown by the Court of Exchequer, and the decision attracted much attention because the judges held the King's powers in general to be absolute. Then a royal "benevolence"—a euphemism for a direct imposition on an individual—was resisted by a certain St. John, and his appeal was sustained by the Chief Justice, Sir Edward Coke, James then summarily dismissed Coke from office and thereby once again focused the attention of his subjects on his broad use of the royal prerogative.

Foreign affairs had certainly been regarded by the Tudors as strictly a matter of royal prerogative. The delicate problem of marriage for Elizabeth I, for instance, had indeed concerned her Parliaments and the public. But Parliament made no attempt to dictate a marriage, and Elizabeth was most careful not to offend her subjects in her own tentative negotiations. On the other hand, when James I openly sought a princess of hated Spain as a wife for his son Charles, his subjects did more than grumble. The Commons in 1621 made public petition against the Spanish marriage. When James rebuked them for what he considered meddling, the House drew up the Great Protestation, the first of the great documents of the English Revolution, in which they used what they claimed were the *historic* liberties, franchises, privileges, and jurisdictions of Parliament to assert what was in fact a *new* claim for parliamentary control of foreign affairs. James responded by dissolving Parliament and imprisoning four of its leaders. The Spanish marriage fell through, but the betrothal of Charles in 1624 to a French princess, also a Catholic, was hardly more popular with the English people.

In religion, the policy of Elizabeth I had been broad and moderate. Though she persecuted both extremes of Catholics and Puritans, she allowed much variety of actual practice within the Anglican Church. James neatly summed up his religious policy in the phrase, "No bishop, no king"—which meant that he believed the enforcement of the bishops' monarchical power in religion was essential to the maintenance of his own monarchical power. James at once tightened up on nonconformity. He called a conference at Hampton Court in 1604, at which he presided in person and used the full force of his pedantic scholarship against the Puritans. The conference dissolved with no real meeting of minds, and royal policy continued to favor the High Church, anti-Puritan party. In spite of James' failure to achieve anything like religious agreement among his subjects, his reign is a landmark in the history of Christianity among English-speaking peoples. In 1611, after seven years' labor, a committee of forty-seven ministers authorized by him achieved the English translation of the Bible that is still used among all the astounding variety of Protestant sects in the English-speaking world. The King James Version remains a masterpiece of Elizabethan prose, perhaps the most remarkable literary achievement a committee has ever made.

The Troubles of Charles I

Under Charles I, all his father's difficulties came to a head very quickly. England had been maneuvered into war against Catholic Spain, always a popular kind of war among Englishmen of the time. Though English forces were small, any war costs money; Charles found Parliament most reluctant to grant him funds, even though the members hated Spain. Meanwhile, in spite of his French queen, Charles got involved in a war against France. This he financed in part by a forced loan from his wealthier subjects, and by quartering his troops in private houses at the householders' expense. Consequently, Parliament in 1628 passed the Petition of Right, in which some of the most basic rules of modern constitutional government are first explicitly stated: No taxation without the consent of Parliament; no billeting of soldiers in private houses; no martial law in time of peace; no one to be imprisoned except on a specific charge and subject to the protection of regular legal procedure. Note that all the principles set forth in this Stuart Magna Carta are limitations on the Crown.

Charles, to get money in new subsidies from Parliament, consented to the Petition of Right. But he also collected duties not authorized by Parliament. Parliament protested by resolutions, not only against his unauthorized taxes but also against his High Church policy. The King now veered from conciliation to firmness; he dissolved Parliament in 1629 and then had Sir John Eliot, mover of the resolutions, and eight other members arrested. Eliot died in prison in the Tower of London, the first martyr on the parliamentary side.

For the next eleven years (1629-1640), Charles governed without a Parliament. He squeezed every penny he could get out of the customary royal revenues, never quite breaking with precedent by imposing a wholly new tax, but stretching precedent beyond what his opponents thought reasonable. Ship money illustrates how Charles worked. It had been levied by the Crown before, but only on coastal towns for naval expenditures in wartime; Charles now imposed ship money on inland areas, and in peacetime. A very rich gentleman named

King Charles I, by Van Dyck.

John Hampden from inland Buckingham-shire refused to pay it. In 1637, he lost his case in court by a narrow margin, but he directed public attention to the new expedient.

In religious matters, Charles was under the sympathetic guidance of a very High Church archbishop of Canterbury, William Laud, who systematically enforced Anglican conformity and deprived even moderate Puritans of their pulpits. In civil matters, Charles made use of an opportunist conservative, Thomas Wentworth, Earl of Strafford, who had deserted the parliamentary side.

England was seething with repressed political and religious passions underneath the outward calm of these years of personal rule. Yet England was certainly prosperous, at least as prosperous as she had been under Tudor rule. The total weight of the taxation that offended so many Englishmen was, as far as one can tell from the imperfect statistics of early modern times, less than on the Continent. The Englishmen who resisted the Crown by taking arms against it were clearly not downtrodden, poverty-stricken people revolting from despair, but hopeful, self-assertive people out to get the things they wanted—power, wealth, their own form of religious worship, their own newly conceived *rights*.

The Road to Civil War, 1638-1642

The English revolution actually began in Scotland. If Charles I had not had to contend with his fellow Scots, he could perhaps have weathered his financial difficulties for a long time. But in Scotland Laud's attempt to enforce the English High Church ritual and organization came up against the three-generations-old Scots Presbyterianism. In 1638, a Solemn League and Covenant banded the Presbyterians of the Scottish Kirk to resist Charles by force if

need be. Charles marched north against the Scots but concluded a temporizing pacification in 1639. Even this mild campaign had been too much for the treasury, and Charles, facing an empty treasury, called an English Parliament in 1640. This Short Parliament, firmly denying any money until the piled-up grievances of nearly forty years were settled, was dissolved at once. Then the Scots went to war again, and Charles, defeated in a skirmish, bought them off by promising them £850 a day until peace was made. Since he could not raise £850 a day, he had to call another Parliament, which became the famous Long Parliament of the revolution.

Holding the unpaid Scots army as a club over Charles' head, the Long Parliament put through a great series of reforms that struck at the royal power. It abolished ship money and other disputed taxes. It disbanded the unpopular royal administrative courts, like the Star Chamber (see Chapter II), which had become symbols of Stuart absolutism. The Star Chamber, operating as it did without the safeguards for the accused afforded by common law courts, had most certainly been used by the Stuarts in ways contrary to English traditions. Up to now, Parliament had been called and dismissed at the pleasure of the Crown; the Triennial Act of 1640 made obligatory the summoning of future Parliaments every three years, even if the Crown did not wish to do so. Parliament also attacked the royal favorites, whom Charles reluctantly abandoned. Archbishop Laud was removed, and Strafford, having been declared guilty of treason, was executed in May, 1641.

Meanwhile, Strafford's unfeeling policy toward the Irish had borne fruit in a terrible rebellion that resulted in the massacre of thousands of Protestants in northern Ireland. Parliament, unwilling to trust Charles with an army to put down this rebellion, drew up in 1641 the Grand Remonstrance summarizing all its complaints. Charles now made a final attempt to repeat the tactics that had worked in 1629. Early in 1642, he ordered the arrest of five of his leading opponents in the House of Commons, including Hampden of the ship-money case. The five took refuge in the privileged political sanctuary of the City of London, where the king could not reach them. Charles I left for the north and in the summer of 1642 rallied an army at Nottingham; Parliament simply took over the central government. The Civil War had begun.

Signs were already evident during these first years of political jockeying that strong groups in England and in Parliament wanted something more than a return to the Tudor balance between Crown and Parliament, and between religious conservatives and religious radicals. In politics, the Nineteen Propositions that Parliament submitted to the King in June, 1642, and that he of course rejected, would have firmly established parliamentary supremacy and left Charles a rather weak "constitutional" monarch much like the present English queen. In religion, the Root and Branch Bill, introduced in 1641 but not enacted, would have radically reformed the whole Church of England, destroying the bishops and all that the Catholic traditions stood for "root and branch." The moderates in politics and religion were plainly going to have trouble defending their middle-of-the-road policies among the extremists of a nation split by civil war.

The Civil War, 1642-1649

England split along lines partly territorial, partly social and economic. The royalist strength lay largely in the north and west, relatively less urban and less prosperous than other parts and largely controlled by country gentlemen loyal to throne and altar. Parliamentary strength lay largely in the south and east, especially in the great city of London and in East Anglia, where even the gentry were firm Puritans (see map on p. 116). The Scots were always in the offing, distrustful of an English Parliament but quite as distrustful of a king who had sought to foist episcopacy on their Kirk.

In the field, the struggle was at first indecisive. The royalists, or "cavaliers," recruited from gentlemen used to riding, had at first the important advantage of superior cavalry. What swung the balance to the side of Parliament was the development under a Puritan gentleman named Oliver Cromwell (1599-1658) of a special force, recruited from ardent Puritans of the eastern counties, and gradually forged under strict discipline into the famous "Ironsides." At Marston Moor in 1644, Cromwell won a crucial battle. The parliamentary army, now reorganized into the "New Model Army," staffed by radicals in religion and politics, stood as "Roundheads" (from their short-cropped hair) against the cavaliers. At the battle of Naseby in 1645, the New Model was completely victorious over the King, and Charles in desperation took refuge with the Scots army, who turned him over to the English Parliament in return for £400,-000 back pay.

Now there arose a situation that was to be repeated, with variations for time and place, in the French Revolution in 1792 and the Russian Revolution in 1917. The group of moderates who had begun the revolution and who still controlled the Long Parliament were confronted by the much more radical group who controlled the New Model Army. In religion, the moderates, seeking to retain some ecclesiastical discipline and formality, were Presbyterians or Low Church Anglicans; in politics, they were constitutional monarchists. The radicals, who were opposed to disciplined churches, were Independents or Congregationalists, and they already so distrusted Charles that they were able at least to contemplate that extraordinary possibility, an

England under a republican form of government. The situation was complicated by the Scots, firmly Presbyterian and hostile to the radical Roundheads, whom they regarded as religious anarchists.

The years after 1645 are filled with difficult negotiations, during which Charles stalled for time to gain Scots help. In 1648, Cromwell beat the invading and now royalist Scots at Preston, and his army seized the King. Parliament, with the moderates still in control, now refused to do what the army wanted, to dethrone Charles. The Roundhead leaders then ordered Colonel Pride to exclude by force from the Commons ninety-six Presbyterian members. This the Colonel did in December, 1648, in true military fashion, with no pretense of legality. After "Pride's Purge" only some sixty radicals remained of the more than five hundred members originally composing the Long Parliament; they were known henceforth as the Rump Parliament. The Rump brought Charles to trial before a special high court of trustworthy radicals, who condemned him to death. On January 30, 1649, Charles I was beheaded.

Cromwell and the Interregnum, 1649-1660

England was now a republic, under the government known as the Commonwealth. But the radicals did not dare call a free election, which would almost certainly have gone against them. From the start, the Commonwealth was in fact the dictatorship of a radical minority come to power through the tight organization of the New Model Army. From the start, too, Cromwell was the dominating personality of the new government. He was, in a sense, an unwilling dictator. In religion an earnest and sincere Independent, but no fanatic, a patriotic Englishman, strong-minded, stubborn, but no pathological luster after power, by no means unwilling to compromise, he

was nevertheless a prisoner of his position.

Cromwell faced a divided England, where the majority were no doubt royalist at heart and certainly sick of the fighting, the confiscations, the endless changes of the last decade. He faced a hostile Scotland and an even more hostile Ireland. The disorders in England had encouraged the Catholic Irish to rebel once more against the Protestant English "garrison." Finally, Cromwell faced a war with Holland, brought on largely by the Navigation Act of 1651, a typically mercantilist measure. By forbidding the importation of goods into England and the colonies except in English ships or in ships of the country producing the imported goods, the Navigation Act deliberately struck at the Dutch carrying trade.

By 1654, Cromwell had mastered these foes. He himself went to Ireland and suppressed the rebellion with bloodshed that is still not forgotten. In the so-called "Cromwellian Settlement," he dispossessed native Irish landholders in favor of Protestants; he achieved order in Ireland, but not peace. Charles II, eldest son of the martyred Charles I, landed in Scotland, accepted the Covenant—that is, guaranteed the Presbyterian faith as the established Scottish Kirk—and led a Scots army once more against the English. Once more the English army proved unbeatable, and at the battle of Worcester in September, 1651, the hope of the Stuarts went down for the time. Charles took refuge on the Continent, after a romantic escape in disguise. The Dutch War was almost wholly a naval one, and ended victoriously for the English in 1652. Cromwell also waged an aggressive war against Spain, from whom the English acquired the rich Caribbean sugar island of Jamaica. Even in this time of troubles, the British Empire kept on growing.

Cromwell, however, could not master the Rump Parliament, which brushed aside his suggestions for an increase of its membership and a reform of its procedures. In April, 1653, he forced its dissolution by appearing in Parliament with a body of soldiers. In December, 1653, Cromwell took the decisive step of setting himself up as Lord Protector of the Commonwealth of England, Scotland, and Ireland, with a written constitution—the only one England has ever had—known as the Instrument of Government. Under this constitution an elected Parliament of 460 members was provided for. It was in fact chosen by Puritan sympathizers, for no royalist dared vote. Even so, the Lord Protector had constant troubles with his Parliaments, and in 1656 yielded to pressure and accepted some modifications to his dictatorship. Oliver Cromwell died in 1658, and was succeeded as Lord Protector by his son Richard. But Richard Cromwell was a nonentity, and the army soon seized control. By now some army leaders saw in the restoration of the Stuarts the best hope of putting an end to the chronic political turbulence. To insure the legality of the move, General Monk, commander of the Protectorate's forces in Scotland, summoned back the Rump and readmitted the living members excluded by Pride's Purge. This partially reconstituted Long Parliament enacted the formalities of restoration, and in 1660 Charles Stuart came back from exile to reign as Charles II.

The Revolution in Review

It is no doubt misleading to say that there was a Reign of Terror in the English Revolution. Much of the bloodshed was the respectable bloodshed of formal battle between organized armies, not the revolutionary bloodshed of guillotine, lynching, and judicial murder. Still, Charles I was beheaded; Strafford, Laud, and others suffered the death penalty; royalists had their properties confiscated. Above all, the Puritans at the height of their rule in the early 1650's attempted to enforce on the whole population the difficult, austere life of the Puritan ideal. This enforcement took the

familiar form of "blue laws," of prohibitions on horse-racing, gambling, cock-fighting, bear-baiting, dancing on the green, fancy dress, on a whole host of ordinary phases of daily living.

This English Reign of Terror and Virtue, coming too early for modern techniques of propaganda and control over the masses, was in fact very different from the absolutism, say, of the communist minority in the Russian Revolution. Many an Anglican clergyman, though officially "plundered"— that is, deprived of his living—kept up his worship in private houses; many a cock fight went on in secluded spots. Nevertheless, the strict code was there, with earnest persons to enforce it, and with implacable enemies to oppose it. The famous remark of the historian Macaulay—that the Puritans prohibited bear-baiting, not because it gave pain to the bear, but because it gave pleasure to the spectators—is a sample of the deep hostility that still survives in England toward the reign of the Puritan "Saints." So too is the popular doggerel of the time:

> To Banbury came I, O profane one,
> Where I saw a Puritane-one,
> Hanging of his cat on Monday
> For killing of a mouse on Sunday.*

Many Englishmen have seemed rather ashamed of their great revolution, preferring to call it the "Civil War" or the "Great Rebellion," and recalling instead as their "Glorious Revolution" the decorous movement of 1688-89, to which we shall come in a moment. Yet the events of 1640-1660 are of major importance, not only in the history of England, but in the history of the West. Here for the first time the absolute monarchy was firmly challenged, and a constitutional and representative government was set up, based on a legislature backed by politically active private citizens. Though the Stuarts were restored, no English king ever again could hope to rule without a Parliament or restore the Court of Star

* Richard Brathwaite, *Barnabee's Journal* (London, 1774), Pt. I.

Chamber or take ship money, benevolences, and other controversial taxes. Parliament thenceforward retained that critical weapon of limited monarchy, ultimate control of the public purse by periodic grants of taxes.

Moreover, minority groups had gone much further, and in their extraordinary fermentations had foreshadowed much modern social thought and action. One such group, the Levellers, though they never attained power, won considerable sympathy from the revolutionary army. They put forward a program later carried by emigrants to the American colonies. The Levellers anticipated much of what we now call political democracy—universal suffrage, regularly summoned Parliaments, progressive taxation, separation of Church and State, protection of the individual against arbitrary arrest, and the like. There are even hints of the "socialistic" drive toward economic equality, though in those days it was tied up closely with Biblical ideas. The Diggers, for example, were a small sect that preached the sharing of earthly goods in a kind of communism. They actually dug up public lands in Surrey near London and began planting vegetables. They were driven off, but not before they had got their ideas into circulation. The Fifth Monarchy men, the Millennarians, and a dozen other radical sects preached the Second Coming and the achievement of some kind of utopia on earth.

Still more important, there emerged from these English struggles, even more clearly than from the religious wars on the Continent, the conception of religious toleration. The Independents, while they were in opposition, stood firmly on the right of religious groups to worship God as they wished. Though in their brief tenure of power they showed a willingness to persecute, they were never firmly enough in the saddle to make of England another Geneva or Boston. Moreover, many of the Puritans sincerely believed that compulsion should not be exercised to secure conformity.

At least one of the sects held to the idea and practice of religious toleration as a positive good. The Quakers, led by George Fox (1624-1691), were Puritans of the Puritans. They themselves eschewed all worldly show, finding even buttons ostentatious, the names of days and months indecently pagan, the polite form "you" in the singular a piece of social hypocrisy and legal oaths or oathtaking most impious. Hence they met for worship not on the day of the pagan sun-god, but on First Day; they addressed any man as "thee" or "thou"; and they took so seriously the basic Protestant doctrine of the priesthood of the believer that they did entirely without a formal ordained ministry. In the Religious Society of Friends, as they are properly known, any worshiper who felt the spirit move might testify in what in other sects would be a sermon. But Quakers felt too deeply the impossibility of forcing the inner light in any man, were too sure that conversion is the work of God alone, to try to *make* men Quakers. They would abstain entirely from force, particularly from that shocking kind of force we call war, and would go their own Christian way in peace, in the hope that in God's good time men would freely come to God's way.

Still another of our basic freedoms owes much to this English experience. Freedom of speech was a fundamental tenet of the Puritans, though again at the height of their power they by no means lived up to it. The pamphlet literature of the early years of the great turmoil is a lively manifestation of free speech in practice. And it received a classic statement in the *Areopagitica* of the poet, John Milton, who was the secretary of the Commonwealth.

The Restoration, 1660-1688

The Restoration of 1660 kept Parliament essentially supreme, but attempted to undo some of the work of the

Revolution. Episcopacy was restored in England and Ireland, though not as a state church in Scotland. Against the "dissenters," as Protestants who would not accept the Church of England were then termed, the so-called Clarendon Code set up all sorts of civil liabilities and obstructions. For instance, by the Five-Mile Act all Protestant ministers who refused to subscribe to Anglican orthodoxy were forbidden to come within five miles of any town where they had previously preached. Yet the dissenters continued to dissent without heroic sufferings. In characteristically English fashion, the Test Act of 1672, which prescribed communion according to the Church of England on all officeholders, local as well as national, was simply got around in various ways, though it was not actually repealed until 1828. One way was "occasional conformity," by which a dissenter of not too strict conscience might worship as a Congregationalist, say, all year, but might once or twice take Anglican communion. Another, developed in the eighteenth century, was to permit dissenters to hold office, and then pass annually a bill of indemnity legalizing their illegal acts. Dissenters remained numerous, especially among the artisans and middle-class merchants, and as time went on they grew powerful, so that the "nonconformist conscience" was a major factor in English public life.

The Restoration was also a revulsion against Puritan ways. The reign of Charles II (1660-1685) is a period of moral looseness, of gay court life, of the Restoration drama with its indecent wit (the Puritans in power had closed the theaters), of the public pursuit of pleasure, at least among the upper classes. But the new Stuarts had not acquired political wisdom. Charles II dissipated some of the fund of good will with which he started by following a foreign policy that seemed to patriotic Englishmen too subservient to the wicked French King Louis XIV. The cynic is tempted to point out that, if Charles's al-

liance with Louis in 1670 was most un-English, it did result in the final extinction of any Dutch threat to English seapower. And it sealed a very important English acquisition, that of New Amsterdam, now New York, first taken in the Anglo-Dutch War of 1664-1667.

What really undid the later Stuarts and revealed their political ineptitude was the Catholic problem. Charles II had come under Catholic influence through his French mother and very possibly embraced the Roman religion before he died in 1685. Since he left no legitimate children, the crown passed to his brother, James II (1685-1688), who was already a declared Catholic. In the hope of enlisting the support of the dissenters for the toleration of Catholics, James II issued in 1687 a "Declaration of Indulgence," granting freedom of worship to *all* denominations, Protestant dissenters as well as Catholics, in England and Scotland. This was in the abstract an admirable step toward full religious liberty.

But to the great majority of Englishmen, Catholicism still seemed what it had seemed in the time of Elizabeth I, the great menace to the English nation. Actually, by the end of the seventeenth century the few remaining Catholics in England were glad to be left in something like the status of the dissenters and were no real danger to a country overwhelmingly Protestant. But they were an unappeased majority in Ireland, and it was always possible to stir Englishmen to an irrational pitch by an appeal to their fear and hatred of Catholicism.

The political situation, moreover, was much like that under Charles I; the Crown wanted one thing, Parliament wanted another. Although James II made no attempt to dissolve Parliament or to arrest members, he simply went over Parliament's head by issuing decrees, like the "Declaration of Indulgence" granting full religious toleration, in accordance with what he called the "power of dispensation." Early in his reign, he had made a piddling rebellion by the

Duke of Monmouth, a bastard son of Charles II, the excuse for two ominous policies. First, his judges organized the "bloody assizes" which punished suspected rebel sympathizers with a severity out of all proportion to the extent of the rebellion. Second, he created a standing army of 30,000 men, part of whom he stationed near London in what appeared an attempt to intimidate the capital. To contemporaries it looked as though James were plotting to force both Catholicism and divine-right monarchy on an unwilling England. The result was the "Glorious Revolution."

The Glorious Revolution of 1688-1689   The actual revolution was in fact a *coup d'état* engineered at first by a group of James' parliamentary opponents who called themselves *Whigs*, in contrast to the *Tories* who tended to support at least the more moderate measures of the later Stuart monarchs. The Whigs were the direct heirs of the moderates of the Long Parliament, and they represented an alliance of the great lords and the prosperous London merchants. James II married twice. By his first marriage he had two daughters, both Protestant—Mary, who had married William of Orange, the great Dutch opponent of Louis XIV, and Anne. Then in 1688 a son was born to James and his second wife, who was Catholic, thus apparently making the passage of the crown to a Catholic heir inevitable. The Whig leaders responded with a great barrage of propaganda, including a "whispering campaign." It was rumored that the Queen had not even been pregnant, but that a new-born babe had been smuggled into her chamber in a warming pan, so that there might be a Catholic heir. Then the Whigs and some Tories negotiated with William of Orange, the son-in-law of James. William could hardly turn down a proposition that would give him the solid assets of English power in his struggle with Louis XIV. He accepted the offer of the English crown, which he was to share with his wife, the couple reigning as William III (1689-1702) and Mary II (1689-1694). On November 5, 1688, William landed at Tor Bay on the Devon coast with some 14,000 soldiers. When James heard the news, he tried to rally support, but everywhere the great lords and even the normally conservative country gentlemen were on the side of the Protestant hero. James fled from London to France in December, 1688, giving William an almost bloodless victory.

Early in 1689 Parliament formally offered the crown to William on terms that were soon enacted into law as the Bill of Rights. This famous document, summing up the constitutional practices the Parliament had been working for since the Petition of Right in 1628, is in fact almost a succinct form of written constitution. It lays down the essential principles of parliamentary supremacy—control of the purse, prohibition of dispensation power to the Crown, regular and frequent meetings of Parliament. Three major steps were necessary after 1689 to convert the British Constitution into a parliamentary democracy in which the Crown has purely symbolic functions as the focus of patriotic loyalty. These were, first, the concentration of executive direction in the hands of a committee of the majority of a given Parliament, that is, the Cabinet headed by a Prime Minister, the work of the eighteenth and early nineteenth centuries; second, the establishment of universal suffrage and payment of members of the Commons, the work of the nineteenth century, completed in the twentieth; and third, the abolition of the power of the House of Lords to veto legislation passed by the Commons, the work of the early twentieth century. Thus we can see that full democracy was still a long way off in 1689. William III and Mary certainly did not think of themselves as purely ornamental monarchs, without power over policy. They were indeed real rulers.

Childless, they were succeeded by Mary's younger sister Anne (1702-1714). Anne and her nonentity of a husband strove hard to leave an heir to the throne, but all their many children, perhaps merely because of the inadequacies of medical science of the day, were still-born or died in childhood. The exiled Catholic Stuarts, however, did better. The little boy born to James II in 1688, and brought up at the court of St. Germain near Paris, grew up to be known as the "Old Pretender." But in 1701 Parliament passed the Act of Settlement, which settled the crown, in default of heirs to Anne, the heir-apparent to the sick William III, not on the Catholic pretender but on the Protestant Sophia of Hanover or her issue. The line to her went back to her grandfather, James I. On Anne's death in 1714, the crown therefore passed to Sophia's son, George, first king of the House of Hanover. It need hardly be pointed out that in so regulating the succession Parliament had clearly established the fact that it, and not the divinely ordained succession of the eldest male in direct descent, made the King of England.

One more act of Queen Anne's reign helped settle for good an old problem. This was the formal union of the kingdoms of England and Scotland under the name of Great Britain in 1707. Scotland was to send sixteen peers to the Lords and forty-five members to the Commons of the Parliament of the United Kingdom. One flag, the Union Jack, with the superimposed crosses of St. George for England and St. Andrew for Scotland, was henceforth to be the national flag of Great Britain. The union, most necessary to insure the carrying out of the Hanoverian succession in both kingdoms, met with some opposition in both. But on the whole it went through with surprising ease, so great was Protestant fear of a possible return of the Catholic Stuarts. And, in spite of occasional sentimental outbreaks of Scottish nationalism even as late as our own day, the union has worked very well. With the whole of England and the colonies open to Scots businessmen, the nation famed for its thrifty and canny citizens achieved a prosperity it had never known before.

The Glorious Revolution did not, however, settle one other perennial problem—Ireland. The Catholic Irish rose in support of the exiled James II and were put down at the battle of the Boyne in 1690. William then attempted to apply moderation in his dealings with Ireland, but the Protestant "garrison" there soon forced him to return to the severe spirit of Cromwellian policy. Although Catholic worship was not actually forbidden, all sorts of galling restrictions were imposed on the Catholic Irish, including the prohibition of Catholic schools. Moreover, economic persecution was added to the religious, as Irish trade came under stringent mercantilist regulation. This was the Ireland whose misery inspired a great writer, Jonathan Swift, to make his bitter "modest proposal" that the impoverished Irish solve their economic problems by selling their babies as articles of food.

IV: *The Century of Genius*

In the seventeenth century the cultural, as well as the political, hegemony of Europe passed from Italy and Spain to France. Especially in literature, the France of Racine, Molière, Boileau, Bossuet, and a host of others set the imprint of a style on the West. Yet the men who achieved the abiding effect of the seventeenth century on our culture were truly international in origin and outlook, and were rather philosophers and scientists than men of letters. When the twentieth-century philosopher,

Alfred Whitehead, christened the 1600's the "century of genius," he was thinking above all of men like Galileo, Harvey, Newton, and Descartes.

Inductive Science

The Renaissance had certainly prepared the way for modern science, first by its successful attack on the abstract and deductive late medieval philosophy, and second by its emphasis on this world, on the life of the senses (see Chapter II). But the seventeenth century made the great advances that established the natural sciences as part of our common heritage. The Englishman Francis Bacon (1561-1626) bore a major part in the rise of modern science. Though he himself experimented in a somewhat random and unproductive fashion, he was the tireless proponent of one of the essentials of scientific achievement—observation of phenomena, the patient accumulation of data. If you observe enough facts, he seems to say, they will somehow make sense of themselves in a process called "induction," which he contrasts with the medieval "deduction" he was attacking:

> There are and can be only two ways of searching into and discovering truth. The one [deduction] flies from the senses and particulars to the most general axioms, and from these principles, the truth of which it takes for settled and immovable, proceeds to judgment and to the discovery of middle axioms. And this way is now in fashion. The other [induction] derives axioms from the senses and particulars, rising by a gradual and unbroken ascent, so that it arrives at the most general axioms last of all. This is the true way, but as yet untried.*

Both deduction and induction are essential in science, but Bacon's emphasis on induction was a necessary corrective in his time and helped to set modern science on its way.

Progress along that way was facilitated by the invention of new instruments, by the establishment of scientific societies, and by the advance of mathematics. Both the great

* Bacon, *The Great Instauration.*

figures of the "century of genius" and scores of unknown or now forgotten individuals contributed to the new instruments that permitted more exact measurements and more detailed observations. For instance, Dutch glassmakers probably first put two lenses together and discovered that they could thus obtain a greater magnification. By 1610, the Italian Galileo was using the new device in the form of a telescope to observe the heavens, and by about 1680 the Dutchman Van Leeuwenhoek was using it in the form of a microscope to discover tiny creatures—protozoa—hitherto unknown. Working from a discovery made by Galileo, another Italian, Torricelli, invented the barometer.

Two important organizations promoting scientific investigation were the English Royal Society for Improving Natural Knowledge, founded in 1662, and the French *Académie des Sciences*, founded in 1666. The one, in characteristic English fashion, was a private undertaking; the other, sponsored by Colbert for the greater glory of Louis XIV and the mercantilistic state, was a government enterprise. Both financed experiments and both published scientific articles in their "house organs," the *Philosophical Transactions* and the *Journal des Sçavans* (savants). Scoffers sometimes mocked their activities; Charles II, for example, roared with laughter at the news that the Royal Society was weighing the air. But ultimately the scientific societies exerted a strong affirmative influence, at least on the community of learned men. It would be hard even today to improve on the Royal Society's statement of purpose, in which it promised "to examine all systems, theories, principles, hypotheses, elements, histories and experiments" and "to question and canvass all opinions, adopting nor adhering to none, till by mature debate and clear arguments, chiefly such as are deduced from legitimate experiments, the truth of such experiments be demonstrated invincibly."

Meanwhile mathematics took a great leap forward. In 1585, Stevin, a Fleming, published *The Decimal, Teaching with Unheard-of Ease How to Perform All Calculations Necessary among Men by Whole Numbers without Fractions*. A generation later, Napier, a Scot, offered *The Marvelous Rule of Logarithms* (1616), which provided the principle of the slide rule and a wonderful short cut in the laborious processes of multiplying, dividing, and taking square root. Next, the Frenchman Descartes worked out analytical geometry, which brings geometry and algebra together, as in the plotting of an algebraic equation on a graph. The mathematical achievements of the century culminated in the perfection of a method of dealing with variables and probabilities. Pascal had made a beginning with his studies of games of chance, and Dutch insurance actuaries had devised tables to show the life expectancy of their clients. Then Newton and the German Leibniz, apparently quite independently of one another, invented the calculus. The detailed description of the new invention must be left to the experts, but its practical value is indicated by the fact that without the calculus, and indeed without Cartesian (from Descartes) geometry, Newton could never have made the calculations supporting his revolutionary hypotheses in astronomy and physics.

The Englishman Isaac Newton (1642-1727), building on the work of earlier astronomers, especially Copernicus, Kepler, and Galileo, made the great theoretical generalization that is now, of course in simplified form, part of every schoolboy's picture of the astronomical universe. This is the law of gravitation. The sun, the planets, and their satellites are, according to this theory, held in their orbits by the force of mutual attraction. Newton stated the formula that this force is proportional to the product of the masses of two bodies attracted one to the other, and inversely proportional to the square of the distance between them.

The law of gravitation is a part of physics as well as of astronomy. Physics too came of age in the seventeenth century, and like astronomy is capped by the work of Newton. Here too Galileo is of importance, though recent research has shown that a devoted follower may have invented the story of how by dropping balls of different weights from the Leaning Tower of Pisa he disproved Aristotle's theory that objects fall with velocities proportional to their weight. Galileo's studies of projectiles, pendulums, and falling and rolling bodies helped to establish modern ideas of acceleration. Newton, building on Galileo's work, formulated the three classic Laws of Motion:

1. That a body will continue in a state of rest, or of uniform motion in a straight line, until compelled to change its state by some force impressed upon it;
2. That every change of motion is proportional to the force that makes the change;
3. That to every action there is always an equal reaction.

Meanwhile, the mechanical views of the physicists were invading the science of life itself, biology. In 1628, Harvey, the physician of Charles I, published his demonstration that the human heart is in fact a pump, and that the human blood is driven by the heart along a system of circulation. And in 1679 the Italian Borelli showed that the human arm is a lever, and that the muscles do mechanical "work."

The Implications of Scientific Progress

All these investigations in the various sciences tended to undermine the older Aristotelian concept of something "perfect." Instead of perfect circles, Keplerian and Newtonian astronomy posited ellipses. Instead of bodies moving in straightforward fashion of themselves, Newton's laws of motion pictured bodies responding only to forces impressed upon them. All these investigations, in short, suggested a new major scientific generalization, a law or uniformity that simplified and explained, that co-ordinated many separate laws into one general law summing up millions of man-hours of investigation. The new law was not final and unalterable, and would almost certainly be modified, given time and further investigation. But still it would be a *relatively* permanent resting place, a plateau. Galileo almost made this achievement, and a dozen other major figures made essential contributions to the big generalization. It was Newton, however, who drew everything together into that grand mechanical conception that has been called the "Newtonian world-machine."

The Newtonian world-machine and, indeed, the whole of the new science had very important theological and philosophical implications. Natural science, strictly speaking, does not deal with the great problems of theology and philosophy. It does not give men *ends*, purposes, but rather *means*, and the theories it provides are always *explanations*, not *justifications*. Yet, historically speaking, the rise of modern science has been associated with a very definite world-view and system of values, for which the best name is *rationalism*. This is a wide term. It is perhaps possible to be at the same time a rationalist and a believer in a supernatural God. Again, however, historically, the balance of the influence of rationalism in the West has been to banish God entirely, or at any rate reduce him to a First Cause that started this Newtonian world-machine going, but does not—indeed cannot—interfere with its working.

For the rationalist takes as his model the neatly integrated mathematical universe that the scientists had worked out. He will not start with the revealed truths of Christianity, as the Schoolmen had done, but will question all formulations until he has something to start with as clear and as certain as the axioms of Euclidean geometry. Here is how the most influential of

these philosophers, the Frenchman Descartes (1596-1650), began to put himself straight:

I thought . . . that I ought to reject as downright false all opinions which I could imagine to be in the least degree open to doubt—my purpose being to discover whether, after so doing, there might not remain, as still calling for belief, something entirely indubitable. Thus, on the ground that our senses sometimes deceive us, I was prepared to propose that no existing thing is such as the senses make us image [*sic*] it to be; and because in respect even of the very simplest geometrical questions some men err in reasoning . . . , I therefore rejected as false (recognising myself to be no less fallible than others) all the reasonings I had previously accepted as demonstrations; and, finally, when I considered that all the thoughts we have when awake can come to us in sleep (none of the latter being then true), I resolved to feign that all the things which had entered my mind were no more true than the illusions of my dreams. But I immediately became aware that while I was thus disposed to think that all was false, it was absolutely necessary that I who thus thought should be somewhat; and noting that this truth *I think, therefore I am*, was so steadfast and so assured that the suppositions of the sceptics, to whatever extreme they might all be carried, could not avail to shake it, I concluded that I might without scruple accept it as being the first principle of the philosophy I was seeking.[*]

From this start, Descartes arrived finally at God—but a God who in his mathematical orderliness, in his remoteness from this confusing world, must seem most unreal to any believer in a personal God.

Scientist and rationalist helped greatly to establish in the minds of educated men throughout the West two complementary concepts that were to give the Enlightenment of the eighteenth century a pattern of action toward social change, a pattern still of driving force in our world. These were first, the concept of a regular "natural" order underlying the apparent irregularity and confusion of the universe as it

---

[*] *Discourse on Method*, Pt. IV, in *Descartes' Philosophical Writings*, N. K. Smith, ed. (London, 1952), 140-141.

appears to unreflecting man in his daily experience; and second, the concept of a human faculty, best called "reason," buried and obscured in most men by their faulty traditional upbringing, but capable of being brought into effective play by a good—that is, rational—upbringing. Both these concepts can be found in some form in our western tradition at least as far back as the Greeks. What gives them novelty and force at the end of the seventeenth century is their being welded into the doctrine of progress—the belief that all human beings can attain here on earth a state of happiness, of perfection, hitherto in the West thought to be possible only for Christians in a state of grace, and for them only in a heaven after death.

Two literary movements of the end of the seventeenth century are neatly symptomatic of the coming Enlightenment—the quarrel of the "ancients" and the "moderns" in France, the "battle of the books" in England. In both these literary disputes the issue was fundamentally the same. Can any "modern" write or paint or do anything better than the Greeks and Romans? Or, in terms of our own day, can we *progress* beyond those giants of old, beyond their Golden Age? It is significant that most Americans today would unhesitatingly answer that we *have* progressed far beyond the ancients. And it is significant of the turn the eighteenth century was to take that the educated public of the day generally considered the "moderns" to have won this battle of the books.

The Classical Spirit

Art and letters as well as science and philosophy had a part in setting the pattern of the Enlightenment. The characteristic style of the seventeenth century, which flowered in the France of Louis XIV, is often known as *l'esprit classique*. The classical spirit leans toward measure, toward discipline, toward conformity with "those rules of old discover'd, not deviz'd," toward a dignified eloquence, toward an aristocratic refinement and avoidance of the undignified that could forbid so vulgar an object as a handkerchief to the heroine in tears—that could in fact rather dislike even the tears. There seems something paradoxical in maintaining that devotees of the classical tradition could have aided in setting up attitudes that undermined the veneration paid those classics of classics, the Greeks and Romans. The paradox is heightened by the fact that the writers and artists of the Age of Louis XIV were generally pillars of the established order, supporters of authority and tradition.

The paradox, however, diminishes when you realize that the best writers of the age found in their classical models not a confirmation of existing standards but a better, simpler set of standards that the eighteenth century could later easily express in terms of nature and reason. Boileau (1636-1711), the chief literary critic of the day, who set the rules for writing poetry, issued the pronouncement, "Que toujours le bon sens s'accorde avec le rhyme" (Always have good sense agree with the rhyme). The great French dramatists, in particular, were trying to find in the infinite variety of men and manners something universal, something typical of all men and all times. Molière (1622-1673) makes the main characters of his satirical comedies not only individuals but also social types—the miser in *L'Avare*, the hypocrite in *Tartuffe*, the boastful and ignorant newly rich man in *Le Bourgeois Gentilhomme*. Corneille (1606-1684) and Racine (1639-1699) followed the classical canons of tragedy. They took subjects from mythology and wrote in the rhymed couplets of Alexandrine verse. To observe the rigid rules governing time, place, and action—the "unities" derived from Aristotle's *Poetics*—they pruned the dramatic action of irrelevance and restricted it to one place and a time-span of twenty-four hours. But within this rigid form Corneille and Racine created moving portraits of human beings seeking exalted ideals of honor or crushed by overwhelming emotions. The French tragedies of the seventeenth century may be ranked next to the Greek tragedies of antiquity, not so much because of their classical form, but rather because of their psychological insight and emotional power.

Even in its broadest sense, the term "classical spirit" does not do justice to the full range of seventeenth-century literature. La Rochefoucauld (1613-1680) mastered an epigrammatic prose of classic simplicity but used it for devastatingly cynical maxims far removed from the lofty ethical decencies of the classics:

We all have enough strength to bear the misfortunes of others. . . . We generally give praise only in order to gain it for ourselves. . . . Virtue in woman is often the result of love of reputation and ease. . . . We always find something not displeasing in the misfortunes of our greatest friends.*

With the seventeenth century the business of printing, as distinguished from the art of printing, began to take on some of the attributes of bigness. The number of people who could read increased all through the West, though most strikingly in northwestern Europe. From now on, there is a printed literature in all the main languages of the West, and a full history of ideas in the West would not neglect any of them. Yet seen in broad outline, German literature, though in bulk sufficient to occupy plenty of modern scholars, had not attained greatness or wide influence, and Spanish and Italian literature had passed their Renaissance peaks. The seventeenth was, as we have seen, the great century of French literary flowering. As yet, English remained a tongue peripheral to European culture, and English literature—even Shakespeare, and most certainly the Milton of *Paradise Lost* —was not generally known abroad. England by her political example, by her great

contributions to natural science, and at the end of the century by her political and philosophical writers, Locke above all, had indeed entered fully into the current of the common culture of the West. But the most important work of the two great English scientists Newton and Harvey, as well as the most important theorizing of Francis Bacon, was first published in Latin.

Yet to all of us to whom English is a mother-tongue the seventeenth century produced one of the great classics, Milton. We have already noted his famous defense of freedom of the press, the *Areopagitica*. *Paradise Lost* is the only epic written in English in the grand style that still finds readers—and it does find them, not all of them compelled by the formalities of higher education. Milton must be tagged a Christian humanist; both terms are important. His classical erudition is to a twentieth-century American staggering, and he needs copious footnoting. He was an active worker on the Puritan side in the Great Revolution, and has left many incidental prose writings, all of which seem now in style extremely difficult.

For to the historian of culture the major fact of English writing in the seventeenth century is not Milton, classic though he is, nor the brilliant, witty, and indecent comedies of the Restoration stage, but the simplification, the clarification, the modernization of English prose style that was achieved in the last half of the century. At the level of high formal culture, and perhaps above all under the influence of the poet Dryden (1631-1700), English began to model itself on French, on its straightforward word-order, on its comparative brevity, and on its polish, neatness, and clarity. But also at a level addressed to the common man, and exemplified in the prose of John Bunyan (1628-1688) of *The Pilgrim's Progress* and later, in that of Daniel Defoe (c.1660-1731) of *Robinson Crusoe*, English began to simplify itself. Even a modern American can read a piece of English prose picked at

---

* *The Maxims of La Rochefoucauld*, F. G. Stevens, trans. (London, 1939), 9, 49, 65, 173.

random from writings of 1700 and not feel he is reading something strange; this would hardly be true of a random choice from a mere fifty years earlier, which would seem almost another language.

The Arts

The term "classical spirit" hardly expresses the full achievement of seventeenth-century art. The France of Louis XIV did indeed produce neoclassical monuments like the balanced and columned *exterior* of Versailles or of the wings of the Louvre in Paris. But the *interior* of Versailles has acres of ceiling painted with smirking cherubs. This lavish embellishment is one aspect of Baroque, the foremost artistic style of the century.

Baroque added a profusion of detail and fantastic and theatrical effects to the basic geometrical patterns of Renaissance design. Sir Christopher Wren used a moderate Baroque style, still somewhat under classical restraints, for St. Paul's Cathedral in London, the only major church building ever designed and completed by a single architect. The dramatic qualities of Baroque are evident at Rome in the vast open spaces and eye-catching colonnades of St. Peter's Square, and at Versailles in the Hall of Mirrors, the majestic Staircase of the Ambassadors, and the elaborate gardens, lagoons, and fountains. Baroque at its most fantastic produced the *baldachino*, the twisting bronze canopy rising to a height of eight stories above the altar of St. Peter's. Though not Gothic in origin, the Baroque style yet achieved a kind of translation of Gothic decorative richness into classical terms. Some of its most interesting monuments are Mexican churches.

In painting, the late sixteenth-century master, El Greco, had achieved a thoroughly Baroque effect in his distorted and mystical canvases (see Chapter IV). Velasquez (1599-1660), the outstanding Spanish painter of the seventeenth century, how-

ever, followed the secular and realistic aspects of the Renaissance tradition. A court painter, he did forty portraits of the Habsburg king, Philip IV, and in some of his best work he produced what one critic has called "optical," as opposed to "photographic," realism. Velasquez depicts what the eye sees at a glance, rather than what is actually there.

In the Low Countries, the chief centers of northern European painting, artists planted themselves thoroughly in the workaday world of business, farming, taverns, and even almshouses. The Fleming Rubens (1577-1640) not only received commissions from French and English royalty but also made a fortune from his art and established a studio with two hundred students, a veritable factory of painting. The rosy, fleshy nudes for which Rubens is famous have the exuberance of Baroque, and he himself worked on the grand scale, contributing, it has been estimated, at least in part to more than two thousand pictures. Most of the Flemish and Dutch masters of the seventeenth century, however, seem rather apart from Baroque theatricality and still further apart from the "classical spirit." They were quite willing to paint handkerchiefs and even less dignified objects, and by their quiet realism they made the commonplace uncommonly lovely. In the hands of the greatest Dutch painter, Rembrandt (1606-1669), the commonplace—the municipal Night Watch, the Syndics of the Cloth Hall, even the Anatomy Lesson of Dr. Tulp—receives a transcendental glow that already deserves to be called "romantic."

In music, the term Baroque conveys much of the accomplishment of the seventeenth century. Here Italy took the lead, following in the paths laid out by the musicians of the Renaissance (see Chapter II). In Rome, Frescobaldi (1583-1644) released the dramatic potentialities of that most Baroque instrument, the organ, and attracted thousands to his recitals at St. Peter's. In Venice, Monteverdi (1567-1643), contending that

The Baldachino, St. Peter's, Rome.

"speech should be the master of music, not its servant," backed his contention in practice by writing the first important operas. This Baroque compound of music and the theater gained immediate popularity. Venice soon had no fewer than sixteen opera houses, which were already establishing the tradition of slighting the chorus and orchestra to pay for the "stars." The star system reached its height at Naples, the operatic capital of the later 1600's. There conservatories (orginally institutions for conserving orphans) stressed voice training; composers provided operatic vehicles that were little more than loose collections of arias; and the crowning touch of unreality came with the Neapolitan custom of having the male roles sung by women and the female by *castrati*—that is, eunuchs, permanent boy sopranos.

Rubens, "Rape of the Daughters of Leucippus by Castor and Pollux."

Rembrandt, "The Night Watch."

Seventeenth-century opera at its best rose above the level of stilted artificiality. Purcell (1658-1695), the organist of Westminster Abbey and virtually the only significant native composer of opera in English musical history, produced a masterpiece for the unpromising occasion of graduation at a girls' school. This was the beautiful and moving *Dido and Aeneas*. In France, Louis XIV realized the potentiality of opera for enhancing the resplendence of the Sun King, and from Italy imported Lully (1632-1687), musician, dancer, speculator, and politician extraordinary, who vied with Molière for the post of "cultural director" at court. Lully's operatic exercises on mythological themes are for the most part now forgotten, but the overtures and dances that he wrote for them live on as a prelude to the great eighteenth-century achievement in instrumental music.

Seventeenth-Century Culture in Review

The "century of genius," then, produced a rich and complex culture, at once scientific, classical, Baroque, and much else besides. It is the complexity that must now be underscored once more. In religion, for example, the seventeenth century was not simply a preparation for the toleration and the diluted "natural religion" of the eighteenth-century Age of Prose and Reason. Against the practical toleration resulting in England from the Glorious Revolution must be set the savage persecutions still prevailing in Ireland and Louis XIV's revocation of the Edict of Nantes. Remember, too, the variety of religious sects that flourished in revolutionary England, the heaven-stormers, the Quakers, whose otherworldly beliefs were to prove so disconcertingly compatible with material success in this world, the Independents, and all the others. In France, along with a conventional Gallican like Bossuet, there flourished the Quietists and the Jansenists, groups who went well beyond orthodoxy into mystical beliefs that conformists were already damning with one of the Enlightenment's favorite words of reproach—"enthusiasm." In Germany, the spiritual descendants of the Anabaptists were laying the foundation of that evangelical appeal to human emotions which in the very midst of the Age of Prose and Reason was to flourish in German Pietism and English Methodism, and which, through immigration, was to play so large a part in the early religious history of our own country.

The contrasts presented by the seventeenth century, this fecund "century of genius," come out in one of its great men, the Frenchman Pascal (1623-1662). As mathematician and physicist, Pascal has an important place in the history of science. His barometric experiment, carried out by Périer, measuring the height of a column of mercury at the foot and again at the summit of Mt. Puy-de-Dôme, in which he showed that the height of the mercury varied with the pressure of the air, gave the final blow to the old notion that "nature abhors a vacuum." For, as Pascal put it, she ought to abhor the vacuum as much at the foot as at the summit of a mountain. But Pascal was also a profoundly religious man, troubled in an age when men seemed in the name of reason to be deserting religion. As a Jansenist, he wrote an ardent tract against what he felt to be the easy morals of the Jesuits, and he left behind a great unfinished work on religion which we know as the *Pensées* (thoughts). Here he could write:

Man is but a being filled with error. This error is natural, and, without grace, ineffaceable. Nothing shows him the truth: everything deceives him. These two principles of truth, reason and the senses, besides lacking sincerity, reciprocally deceive each other. The senses deceive reason by false appearances; and just as they cheat reason they are cheated by her in turn: she has her revenge. Passions of the soul trouble the senses, and give them false impressions. They emulously lie and deceive each other.*

These are hardly the words of a rationalist. Nor is one of his best-known aphorisms: "Cleopatra's nose: if it had been shorter, the whole face of the earth would have been changed." The "century of genius" was no mere prelude to the Enlightenment, but an age in which men were "voyaging on strange seas of thought."

---

* Pascal, *Thoughts, Letters, and Opuscules*, O. W. Wright, trans. (Boston, 1882), 192.

Reading Suggestions on Divine-Right Monarchy and Revolution

General Accounts

D. Ogg, *Europe in the Seventeenth Century*, 6th ed. (London: Black, 1952); and G. N. Clark, *The Seventeenth Century*, 2nd ed. (Oxford: Clarendon, 1947). Two very readable general accounts. Clark's is perhaps the more useful, since it is organized by topics and centers on developments in France.

C. J. Friedrich, *The Age of the Baroque, 1610-1660* (N.Y.: Harper, 1952); F. L. Nussbaum, *The Triumph of Science and Reason, 1660-1685* (N.Y.: Harper, 1953); and J. B. Wolf, *The Emergence of the Great Powers, 1685-1715* (N.Y.: Harper, 1951). These three volumes in the "Rise of Modern Europe" series provide a treatment of the seventeenth century fully abreast of modern scholarship. Each contains an exhaustive bibliography.

Special Studies:
Primarily Economic and Military

E. F. Heckscher, *Mercantilism*, 2 vols., rev. ed. (N.Y.: Macmillan, 1955). A famous work, the subject of much scholarly controversy; indispensable for an examination of the topic.

H. Heaton, *Economic History of Europe*, rev. ed. (N.Y.: Harper, 1948); and S. B. Clough and C. W. Cole, *Economic History of Europe*, 3rd ed. (Boston: Heath, 1952). Two good general economic histories.

C. Petrie, *Earlier Diplomatic History, 1492-1713* (N.Y.: Macmillan, 1949). A useful manual on international affairs.

A. Vagts, *A History of Militarism* (N.Y.: Norton, 1937); E. M. Earle, ed., *Makers of Modern Strategy* (Princeton: Princeton Univ. Press, 1943); J. F. C. Fuller, *Military History of the Western World* (N.Y.: Funk & Wagnalls, 1954-1956). Three general books on military history containing useful material on seventeenth-century developments.

A. T. Mahan, *The Influence of Sea Power on History, 1660-1783* (Boston: Little, Brown, 1890). A most celebrated book, but no longer a very reliable guide to the subject.

E. Barker, *The Development of Public Services in Western Europe, 1660-1930* (N.Y.: Oxford Univ. Press, 1944). Attempts to treat an important topic usually totally neglected.

Special Studies: France

L. von Ranke, *Civil Wars and Monarchy in France* (N.Y.: Harper, 1853). This great old classic continues to be worth reading for the seventeenth century.

A. Guérard, *The Life and Death of an Ideal*, new ed. (N.Y.: Braziller, 1956). Perhaps the best single volume in English on the Age of Louis XIV; most suggestive, and does full justice to the cultural side.

C. V. Wedgwood, *Richelieu and the French Monarchy* (N.Y.: Macmillan, 1950), and M. P. Ashley, *Louis XIV and the Greatness of France* (N.Y.: Macmillan, 1947). Two good brief accounts in the "Teach Yourself History Library."

L. B. Packard, *The Age of Louis XIV* (N.Y.: Holt, 1929. A Berkshire Study). Very short and very good.

W. H. Lewis, *The Splendid Century* (N.Y.: Sloane, 1954). A well-written account with emphasis on French society.

J. E. King, *Science and Rationalism in the Government of Louis XIV* (Baltimore: Johns Hopkins Univ. Press, 1949). A significant monograph.

P. R. Doolin, *The Fronde* (Cambridge: Harvard Univ. Press, 1935). Interesting not only for the topic dealt with but for the thesis that the so-called absolute monarchy in France was really not so absolute.

C. W. Cole, *Colbert and a Century of French Mercantilism* (N.Y.: Columbia Univ. Press, 1939). A solid, detailed study.

Special Studies: England

L. von Ranke, *A History of England*, 6 vols. (Oxford: Clarendon, 1875). Another classic account by the great German historian.

S. R. Gardiner, *History of England, 1603-1642*, 10 vols.; *History of the Great Civil War, 1642-1649*, 4 vols.; and *History of the Commonwealth and Protectorate, 1649-1656* (N.Y.: Longmans, Green, 1904-1913). A really major work of detailed history.

G. Davies, *The Early Stuarts, 1603-1660*, and G. N. Clark, *The Later Stuarts, 1660-1714*, new eds. (Oxford: Clarendon, 1949). These two volumes in the "Oxford History of England" provide a briefer scholarly account.

C. H. Firth, *Oliver Cromwell and the Rule of the Puritans in England* (N.Y.: Putnam's, 1900). Often considered the best of the very many books on Cromwell.

C. V. Wedgwood, *The King's Peace, 1637-1641* (N.Y.: Macmillan, 1955). The first volume of a detailed study of the Great Rebellion by the best contemporary specialist.

G. Davies, *The Restoration of Charles II, 1658-1660* (San Marino, Calif.: Huntington Library, 1955). An authoritative monograph completing the work of Gardiner and Firth.

A. Bryant, *King Charles II* (N.Y.: Longmans, Green, 1931). An unusually sympathetic account.

F. C. Turner, *James II* (N.Y.: Macmillan, 1948). A balanced treatment of a highly controversial figure.

G. M. Trevelyan, *The English Revolution, 1688-1689* (London: Butterworth, 1938. The Home University Library). A very good study by a historian who has written several famous works on the Stuart period.

D. L. Keir, *The Constitutional History of Modern Britain, 1485-1937*, 4th ed. (London: Black, 1950). A good introduction.

J. R. Tanner, *English Constitutional Conflicts of the Seventeenth Century* (Cambridge, England: Cambridge Univ. Press, 1928). A full and scholarly account.

C. Brinton, *The Anatomy of Revolution*, rev. ed. (N.Y.: Knopf, 1957. A Vintage Book). Generalizations based on England's 17th-century revolution, France's 18th-century one, and Russia's 20th-century one.

W. Notestein, *The English People on the Eve of Colonization, 1603-1630* (N.Y.: Harper, 1954). An admirable piece of social and intellectual history.

G. P. Gooch, *English Democratic Ideas in the Seventeenth Century*, H. J. Laski, ed. (Cambridge, England: Cambridge Univ. Press, 1927). Essential for understanding the scope of the English revolution.

E. Bernstein, *Cromwell and Communism: Socialism and Democracy in the Great English Revolution* (London: Allen and Unwin, 1930). The second part of the title of this significant study is the more accurate.

Everybody's Pepys, O. F. Morshead, ed. (N.Y.: Harcourt, Brace, 1926). A useful abridgment of the famous diary kept during the 1660's; a fascinating document of social history.

Special Studies: The Century of Genius

C. Brinton, *Ideas and Men* (Englewood Cliffs, N.J.: Prentice-Hall, 1950); and J. H. Randall, Jr., *Making of the Modern Mind*, rev. ed. (Boston: Houghton Mifflin, 1940). Two general books on intellectual history with useful sections on the seventeenth century.

P. Smith, *A History of Modern Culture*, Vol. I (N.Y.: Holt, 1930). A mine of information on topics often passed over in general histories.

B. Willey, *The Seventeenth Century Background* (N.Y.: Anchor Books). Reprint of a modern classic; essays on Descartes, Hobbes, Milton, and other major figures in the intellectual and religious life of the century.

P. Hazard, *The European Mind, 1680-1715* (London: Hollis and Carter, 1953). A significant re-evaluation of the intellectual history of the period.

A. N. Whitehead, *Science and the Modern World* (N.Y.: Mentor Books). A major essay by a great philosopher and mathematician; not easy reading.

Charles Singer and others, eds., *A History of Technology* (N.Y.: Oxford Univ. Press, 1955-). The third volume of this magnificently designed work, will cover this period. The authoritative work of our time on the subject.

A. Wolf, *A History of Science, Technology, and Philosophy in the Sixteenth and Seventeenth Centuries*, rev. ed. (London: Allen and Unwin, 1950). A standard, detailed account. See also the works by H. Butterfield and A. H. Hall cited for Chapter II.

M. F. Bukofzer, *Music in the Baroque Era* (N.Y.: Norton, 1947); and H. Leichtentritt, *Music, History, and Ideas* (Cambridge: Harvard Univ. Press, 1938). Both are useful introductions to the development of music in the period; see also the works of

P. Láng and C. Gray cited in the reading suggestions for Chapter II.

Historical Fiction

A. Dumas, *The Three Musketeers, Twenty Years After, The Vicomte de Bragelonne* (many editions). The famous "D'Artagnan" trilogy, set in seventeenth-century France; properly swashbuckling, yet based on sound research.

T. Gautier, *Captain Fracasse* (N.Y.: Bigelow, Smith, 1910). A good picaresque tale, based on conscientious research; set in the France of Louis XIII.

A. Manzoni, *The Betrothed*, A. Colquhoun, trans. (N.Y.: Dutton, 1951). Milan about 1630; a famous Italian novel.

N. Hawthorne, *The Scarlet Letter* (many editions). The best introduction to the Puritan spirit through fiction.

R. Graves, *Wife to Mr. Milton* (N.Y.: Creative Age, 1944). A good novel, though not very kind to Milton.

W. M. Thackeray, *Henry Esmond* (many editions). A famous novel, set in England about 1700.

CHAPTER SEVEN

The Eastern Outposts

I: *The Heirs of Other Traditions*

The nation-states of western Europe all emerged from the debris of the Roman Empire in the West, the Latin or Germanic linguistic tradition, and the uniting bond of the Roman Catholic Church. They resembled each other more closely than any of them resembled either Russia or the Ottoman Empire, successor-states to the East Roman or Byzantine Empire with its center at Constantinople (Byzantium or, as the Turks called it, Istanbul), which had dominated the eastern Mediterranean world for eleven hundred years, between the fourth and the fifteenth centuries.

Although almost none of its vast territories, stretching thousands of miles from eastern Europe to the Pacific, had ever actually belonged to the Byzantine Empire, Russian government, religion, and culture derived largely from Byzantium. As for the Ottoman

Empire, it embraced not only most of the Balkan peninsula and other parts of eastern and southeastern Europe but also Anatolia (Asia Minor) and the Arab world, including Egypt, Syria, and North Africa. Moslem in religion and non-European in language, at first glance it appears entirely alien and strange to the European world. Yet in fact it occupied the territory and to a surprising degree inherited both the population and the institutions of Byzantium. Russia and the Ottoman Empire were the heirs of a different tradition: Byzantium was eastern not western, Greek not Latin, Orthodox not Catholic, yet both Roman and Christian, as was the West. With the Turks, moreover, we encounter a non-Christian people, adherents to the faith of Islam. Both these eastern powers played a fundamental role in the centuries we are now considering. Before we can understand their behavior, we must take a quick look at the traditions to which they had fallen heir.

The Byzantine emperor had ruled as a true autocrat: divinely ordained, the reflection here on earth of the single God in heaven, complete master of his subjects, who were called by a term meaning slaves. He lived in a "sacred palace," apart and mysterious, emerging to participate in a virtually constant round of formal ceremonies, regulated by a rigid code of etiquette. Not only did he promulgate the imperial law codes governing his subjects' behavior, but, "equal to the Apostles," he presided over the councils of the church, and pronounced on matters of doctrine. Very seldom was he challenged by the Patriarchs, who—unlike the Popes—usually were content to remain the head of a church that was rather a department of state. The Byzantines always maintained that theirs was the supreme state among all those on the inhabited globe. Often their might suited well with their pretensions: they won splendid victories, conducted skillful diplomacy, grew immensely rich, created a superb and opulent art, studied Greek classics, and kept them

alive during all the centuries when the West knew no Greek, and exerted a powerful attraction upon the barbarians of eastern Europe (many of whom were Slavs), who looked upon the great city of Byzantium with an understandable mixture of admiration and envy.

First the Bulgarians, and then the Russians, and eventually the Serbs accepted Christianity not from Rome (as did the Czechs and Poles and Croatians among their fellow-Slavs), but from Constantinople. Thus, the Russians inherited the tradition of ecclesiastical subordination to the state, and the immense emphasis on ritual, mystery, and magic in religion which was also characteristic of Byzantine Christianity. The quarrels between the churches of Rome and Constantinople, which culminated in a split (or schism) between the Roman Church and the Church of Byzantium in 1054, were therefore passed on by the Byzantines to their Russian pupils. Russians suspected and even hated Rome, and were thus cut off by their Byzantine heritage from most of the intellectual achievement of the West during the Middle Ages. Moreover, the Roman Church required the use of Latin in the ritual, which gave a linguistic unity to its services wherever they might be conducted, and ensured the education of its priests. But the Byzantine Church did not require Greek; it permitted the use of the native tongue for the church services, and thus shut the Russian clergy away from education, and initiated a certain cultural lag in Russian life, later to be reinforced by other factors.

Though the medieval Russian state, centering on the city of Kiev, fell before the Tartars in the early thirteenth century, many of the characteristic features of later Russian society had already appeared. The next two centuries under Tartar domination accentuated the lag behind western Europe. In the fifteenth century, after the defeat of the Tartars, the newly emerging state of Moscow reverted to the Byzantine heritage when it created its own new institutions.

The Ottoman Turks By that time, Byzantium itself had fallen, to the Ottoman Turks or Osmanlis (so-called after Osman, their first historic ruler), a tribe originally of central Asian origin, whose leaders began in the thirteenth century to move westward in the Anatolian plateau, and establish themselves in its northwest corner, immediately opposite Constantinople. In this region, the Greek population, discontented with harsh and ineffectual Byzantine rule, turned to the Osmanlis. The Osmanlis were Moslems, adherents of the religion of Islam (submission), founded in the nomadic society of Arabia in the seventh century by the Prophet Mohammed. Influenced by Judaism and Christianity, Mohammed wrote down the revelations that he believed came to him from the One God of the Jews and Christians. These were collected after his death in the Koran. Firmly monotheist, and believing that the trinitarian worship of the Christians was polytheism and therefore idolatry, he required his followers to pray five times daily facing Mecca, acknowledging God and Mohammed as his prophet, to fast one month in the year between sunrise and sunset, to give

Mohammed. In this miniature the Angel Gabriel appears to him in a vision, saying "Thou art the Prophet of God."

alms to the poor, and if possible to make a pilgrimage to Mecca. He believed in an afterlife, in which true Moslems were rewarded with fleshly delights. By the time of Mohammed's death in 632, he had converted only part of the population of Arabia itself, but the Moslem Arabs soon erupted from the peninsula, and carried their new faith by conquest into Syria and Persia, Egypt, North Africa, and Spain. From Persia it spread eastward into Central Asia, home of the nomadic Turkish tribes.

Everywhere Islam brought the Arabic language as the language of the faith, but in Persia it encountered the traditions of an ancient civilization closely linked with the Greco-Roman world. Thus subsequent generations of Moslems were deeply indebted both to Persia and to classical antiquity. The early caliphs, rulers of Islam, the representatives of Mohammed on earth, were absolute autocrats like the Byzantine emperors. In theory, Moslems believed that all the world that was not yet theirs they must some day conquer. Though in theory they gave a conquered infidel the choice between conversion to Islam and death, in practice they ruled peacefully over millions of Christians, who paid a special tax, and suffered other minor disabilities. When the Moslems declared a holy war, however, they often adhered to the letter of the harsh law.

The Mihrimah Mosque, Istanbul, built in the sixteenth century by a daughter of Suleiman the Magnificent.

Though Moslems, the Osmanlis were in the thirteenth and fourteenth centuries apparently not fanatical, and learned from the Greek population the arts of settled agricultural life. By the 1330's the nomad Osmanlis, rulers of northwest Anatolia, had settled down as farmers, and many of them had intermarried with the native Greeks. Too late, the Byzantine authorities realized the danger. Civil wars between rival claimants to the Byzantine throne gave the Turks new opportunities, as they were invited across the Straits to help one of the contestants. In 1356 they established a European capital at Adrianople; Constantinople itself became an island surrounded by Turkish territory.

The Byzantine Empire survived down to 1453, but only because the Turks decided to conquer the Balkan region first. Destroying independent Bulgarian and Serbian states, defeating the armies sent out by western Europe against them (1396), overcoming in the end the temporary setback administered to them in 1402 by the savage Tartar Timur (Tamerlane), the Osmanlis

moved to their inevitable triumph. After one of the most dramatic and vigorous sieges in history, they took Constantinople on May 29, 1453. The last Byzantine emperor perished bravely in the fight. The collapse of an empire that had ruled at the Straits for 1100 years shocked and alarmed the Christian world.

One of the chief reasons for Turkish success was the mutual hatred between Greek Orthodox eastern Christians and Roman Catholic western Christians. The westerners felt that the Greeks were treacherous schismatics. Too preoccupied with their own concerns to send more than token forces to help the Byzantines, they demanded that the Greeks accept papal supremacy, and thus re-unite the churches. For their part, the Greeks keenly remembered the outrages committed against them in the thirteenth century by the western crusaders who had occupied Constantinople for almost sixty years. Many Greeks openly preferred Turkish conquest to the acceptance of assistance from the West. Thus, though the Byzantine emperor had acknowledged papal supremacy at the Council of Ferrara-Florence in 1439, and the churches had been re-united officially, the act did not command the support of the Byzantine population, and it gravely shocked the Russian Orthodox Church.

The "end" of the Byzantine Empire proved in fact to be more of an appearance than a reality. By 1453, the Osmanlis had become a largely European people. The sultan, deeply impressed by the prestige of the empire he had overthrown, and ruling from its capital, imitated many of its institutions. He vanished into a newly built palace, much like the "sacred palace" of his Byzantine predecessors. In all probability the Turks took over, at least in part, the late Byzantine system of military land-holdings and rendering of military service. Eventually, they granted to western trading powers the same valuable trading privileges and extra-territorial rights that the Byzantines had for several centuries been in the habit of granting to the mercantile cities of Italy.

Most important, perhaps, the Moslem Osmanlis placed the religious life of their Orthodox subjects in the control of the Greek Patriarch of Constantinople. This meant that he had not only religious authority but that ecclesiastical taxation and ecclesiastical courts emptied the pockets and controlled the destinies of the Orthodox, who paid the Turkish government a special tax in lieu of military service, but were, except in disputes with Moslems, members of a different community, or *millet*. Byzantine ways of life continued strong throughout the Christian population of the Ottoman Empire, whether Greek or Slavic.

II: Muscovite Russia: From the Tartar Defeat to 1682

During the two centuries between the collapse of the Kievan Russian state and the rise of Moscow, Russia lay divided and subject to a variety of governmental and social systems. In the west, along the borders of Poland and Lithuania, a kind of feudalism reigned unchecked. In the north, the town commonwealth of Novgorod built up a prosperous mercantile existence on Baltic trade with the Germans, and explored and exploited a large, sparsely settled territory to the north and northeast. But neither rampant feudalism nor urban commercial oligarchy was to triumph. Moscow, southeast of Novgorod, northeast of the old capital of Kiev, emerged as the center of the revived Russian state.

The western feudal regions had fallen too greatly under the influence of the alien Roman Catholic Poles to act as the center of a new Russia. Novgorod suffered from severe internal social conflicts and wide economic discrepancies between rich and poor, while the sterile soil in the neighborhood rendered it dependent upon the Moscow region for its grain. The Moscow region triumphed as the result not only of its competitors' liabilities but of its own assets. Moscow itself, little more than a group of huts in the forest wilderness, none the less lay near the watershed from which the Russian rivers flow north into the Baltic or south into the Black Sea. In Russia, the rivers always provided the routes for trade. Thus, when the Tartar grip relaxed, and commerce could resume, Moscow could take advantage of its geographical situation.

Moreover, the princes of Moscow proved extraordinarily able. First to arrive on the ground in the emigration from the south-

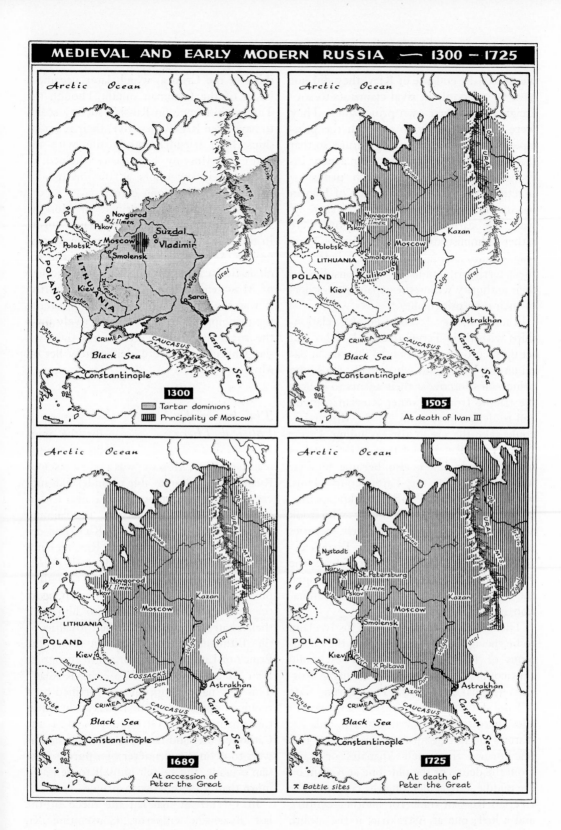

MEDIEVAL AND EARLY MODERN RUSSIA — 1300-1725

1300

Arctic Ocean

Novgorod
L.Ilmen
Pskov
Polotsk
Moscow
Suzdal
Vladimir
Smolensk
LITHUANIA
Kievan
POLAND
Sarai
URAL MTS.
CRIMEA
CAUCASUS
Black Sea
Constantinople
Caspian Sea

Tartar dominions
Principality of Moscow

1505

Arctic Ocean

Novgorod
L.Ilmen
Pskov
Polotsk
Moscow
Smolensk
Kazan
LITHUANIA
POLAND
Kulikovo
Kiev
Astrakhan
URAL MTS.
CRIMEA
CAUCASUS
Black Sea
Constantinople
Caspian Sea

At death of Ivan III

1689

Arctic Ocean

Novgorod
L.Ilmen
Pskov
Moscow
Kazan
LITHUANIA
POLAND
Kiev
COSSACKS
Astrakhan
URAL MTS.
CRIMEA
CAUCASUS
Black Sea
Constantinople
Caspian Sea

At accession of
Peter the Great

1725

Arctic Ocean

Nystadt
Narva
St.Petersburg
L.Ilmen
Pskov
Moscow
Kazan
Smolensk
POLAND
Kiev
X Poltava
Azov
Astrakhan
URAL MTS.
CRIMEA
CAUCASUS
Black Sea
Constantinople
Caspian Sea

At death of
Peter the Great

X Battle sites

west after the collapse of Kiev, they did not have to worry about rival claimants to sovereignty over their own principality. They were able very early to establish the principle of seniority and primogeniture, so that the royal domain did not suffer a new division with the death of each prince—a practice that had proved the ruin of Kievan Russia. Though they fought their share of wars, the early princes of Moscow were rather administrators than soldiers. They married into rich families, steadily increased their territorial holdings, and consolidated their authority within the expanding borders of their own principality.

In addition, they developed useful relationships with their Tartar overlords, who had set up their own capital far to the east, at Sarai on the Volga, and who usually chose the princes of Moscow as their agents to collect the tribute from the other Russian princes, and to deliver it to Sarai. So the Muscovites could take the credit for excluding Tartar agents from Russia, and thus attract settlers to their lands. They also became familiar with conditions at the Tartar court. Thus, when the moment of Tartar weakness came, it was the princes of Moscow who took advantage of it, winning the first victories in 1378 and 1380. Though the Tartars exacted a fierce vengeance for the defeats, the very turn of the tide must have encouraged the Russians to realize that Tartar domination need not last forever.

The Muscovite princes could justly claim to be the agents of liberation and the champions of Russian resurgence. They could thus command the newly crystallizing Russian national sentiment. The Tartar state at Sarai did not disintegrate for several decades thereafter, and even when it did, the Tartars did not disappear from Russian life, but formed three new khanates or states from the debris of the old: one at Kazan, on the middle Volga, blocking the course of the river to Russian trade for another century and a half; one at Astrakhan at the mouth of the Volga on the Caspian Sea; and a third in the Crimea, which later became a vassal of the Ottoman sultan. Though the Tartars' influence on Russian society seems to have been largely negative, their relationships, both friendly and hostile, with the house of Moscow had clearly helped to launch their successors as the masters of Russia upon their long career.

Most important, the princes of Moscow secured the support of the Russian Church. In the early fourteenth century the Metropolitan Archbishop made Moscow the ecclesiastical capital of Russia. When the line of Muscovite princes faltered temporarily, it was the Metropolitan who administered the principality loyally and effectively until the royal house recovered. Thus the Russian Church, as it were, deliberately bet on Moscow.

The Imperial Political Theory

By the middle of the fifteenth century, Moscow was a self-conscious Russian national state able to undertake successful wars against both the Polish-Lithuanian state and the Tartars. Proclaiming himself heir to the princes of Kiev, and determined to regain the ancient Russian lands lost to the Poles and Tartars, Ivan III (1462-1505) made a national appeal, though a purely dynastic one. Many nobles living in the western lands came over to him with their estates and renounced their loyalties to the Lithuanian-Polish state. In 1492, the Prince of Lithuania was forced to recognize Ivan III as sovereign of "all the Russias." This new national appeal was fortified by a religious appeal as well, for Ivan acted as the champion of Orthodoxy against the Catholic Poles and the Moslem Tartars. His wars took on the character of a purely Russian crusade. But he felt himself to be much more than a mere Russian prince.

In 1472, Ivan married the niece of the last Byzantine emperor, Constantine XI. Ivan adopted the Byzantine title of autocrat, used the Byzantine double eagle as his seal, and began to behave as a Byzantine emperor. He occasionally used the title tsar (Caesar). He no longer consulted his nobles, but reached decisions in solitude. Italian architects built him an enormous palace, the Kremlin, a building set apart, like the one at Byzantium. When the Holy Roman emperor in the 1480's decided to make an alliance with Ivan III, Ivan responded:

By God's grace we have been lords in our land since the beginning of time, since the days of our earliest ancestors. God has elevated us to the same position which they held, and we beg him to grant it to us and our children. We have never desired and do not now desire confirmation of this from any other source.[*]

Here is the claim to unlimited power derived from God that the Byzantine emperor had been accustomed to make.

By the time of Ivan III's grandson, Tsar Ivan IV, the Terrible (1533-1584), we find the theory re-stated in even more emphatic terms. One of Ivan's trusted nobles, Prince Kurbsky, fled from Russia, perhaps in part because he had suffered a military defeat and feared punishment, but also because he felt increasingly uneasy over Ivan's autocratic behavior. From abroad, Kurbsky wrote to Ivan denouncing him for his failure to maintain the traditional privilege of the great nobles (boyars) to be consulted about important questions of policy. The Tsar replied that he was entirely free to bestow favors or to inflict punishment upon his slaves as he chose. To Ivan, all Russian boyars were simply the slaves of the autocrat. In an equally famous exchange of letters with Queen Elizabeth I of England, Ivan the Terrible expressed his contempt for her willingness to be influenced by her subjects.

No doubt, part of the explanation for the rapid growth in Russia of autocratic theory and practice lies in the fact that the Russians lived in a constant state of war or preparation for war. A national emergency thus prolonged for centuries led naturally to a national dictatorship. Yet even more significant is the fact that in Muscovite territory feudalism had not, as it had, for example, in England, produced a united class of self-conscious nobles who would fight the rising monarchy for what they believed to be their traditional privileges. Kurbsky seems to have been an isolated voice, raised from outside Ivan's dominions. Inside, the nobles did not unite against the pretensions of the autocrat. Instead, they split into various factions, with which the Tsar could deal separately. Quite probably, the example of the Tartar Khans, who ruled despotically, and with whom the Muscovites had been in intimate relationship for so long, helped furnish a model and a precedent.

But most important of all, perhaps, was the ideology supplied by the Church and taken over largely from Byzantium. In the West, the Church itself was a part of feudal society, and jealous of its prerogatives. In Russia, as we have seen, it became the ally of the monarchy, and something like a department of state. Russian churchmen knew all about Rome's claim to world empire, and the age-long claim of Constantinople to be "new Rome," and therefore the successor of the old. Now that Constantinople had itself been conquered, Russian churchmen blamed the Byzantine defeat upon the emperors' concessions to the hated "heretical" papacy, and elaborated a famous new political theory that Moscow was the successor to the two former world capitals:

The Church of Old Rome fell because of its heresy; the gates of the Second Rome, Constantinople, have been hewn down by the axes of the infidel Turks; but the Church of Moscow, the Church of the new Rome, shines brighter than the Sun in the whole Universe. . . . Two Romes have fallen, but the Third stands fast; a fourth there cannot be.[*]

---

[*] F. Adelung, Kritisch-literarische Übersicht der Reisenden in Russland (St. Petersburg and Leipzig, 1846), I, 153. Our translation.

---

[*] Quoted by A. J. Toynbee, in Civilization on Trial (New York, 1948), 171

Russian churchmen also provided the imperial family with an imaginary ancestry going back to the Roman Emperor Augustus, and told the tale that the tsars had inherited certain insignia and regalia not only from the Byzantines but even from the Babylonians. At imperial coronations, the tsars were crowned with a cap and clothed in a jacket that were actually of Byzantine manufacture. This practice continued right down to the coronation of the last tsar in 1894. Thus the Church supplied the State with justification for its behavior. Imperial absolutism became one of the two chief features of Russian life. By the early sixteenth century the theory was complete, and the practice perfected. Behind both lay the Byzantine tradition.

Nobles and Serfs

Between the accession of Ivan III in 1462 and the accession of Peter the Great in 1689, the autocracy succeeded in overcoming the opposition of the old nobility. This was done in part by virtually creating a new class of military-service gentry who owed everything to the tsar. Their estates (*pomestie*), at first granted only for life in exchange for service, eventually became hereditary. The estates (*vochina*) of the old nobility, which had always been hereditary but for which they had owed no service, gradually became service-estates. Thus, by the end of the period, the two types of noble and the two types of estate had by a gradual process become almost identical. The hereditary nobles often owed service. The military-service nobles often had hereditary land. During the eighteenth century this process was to be completed, and state service was to become universal. A central bureau in Moscow kept a census of the "service" men and of their obligations in time of war.

This tremendously important social process was accompanied by the growth of serfdom. In a fashion familiar in earlier times in the West and in Byzantium, economic factors and political unrest had forced more and more peasants to seek out large landowners for dependence. The peasants would accept contracts that required rent in produce and service on the landlord's own land. They would accept a money loan that had to be repaid over a period of years with interest or in the form of extra services. By the early seventeenth century it had become customary that the peasant could not leave his plot until he had paid off his debt. Since the debt was often too big for him to repay, he could in practice never leave.

The process was enormously speeded up when the tsars gave estates to the new military-service gentry. An estate was not much good unless there was farm labor to work it. In a period of bitter agrarian and political crisis such as the sixteenth and seventeenth centuries, it became advisable for the government to help the service gentry to keep their farmers where they were. Also, since the peasants paid most of the taxes, it was easier for the government to collect its own revenues if the taxpayers stayed put. Gradually, it was made harder and harder for a tenant to leave his landlord, until by 1649 the avenues of escape were closed, and the serf was fixed to the soil. The landlord administered justice and had police rights on the estate. He collected the serfs' taxes. He himself could sell, exchange, or give away his serfs. And the serf status became hereditary; children of serfs were enrolled on the estate's census books as serfs like their fathers.

The Russian serfs were not emancipated until 1861. Together with the absolute autocracy, the institution of serfdom is the most characteristic feature of Russian society. It affected every Russian, whether landowner, serf, or neither, for all the centuries it existed. In a very real sense, the consequences of Russian serfdom are still with us today, posing a great problem not only for the rulers of the Soviet Union but for all the world that has to deal with

Russia. Russian serfdom became a fixed custom far later in time than did western European serfdom. And it was widely extended during the eighteenth century, at a moment when the serfs in western Europe had long been on their way to complete liberation. This is another illustration of the fact that Russia went through many of the same processes as the West, but with greater intensity and at a later time.

The Reign of Ivan the Terrible

Most of the disorders that distinguish Russian history in the sixteenth and seventeenth centuries have their origin in the long reign of Ivan IV, the Terrible (1533-1584). Pathologically unbalanced, Ivan succeeded to the throne as a small child. He experienced helplessly the indignities inflicted on him by the various rival groups of boyars who were maneuvering and intriguing for power. Devoted to the rites of the Church, and fancying himself as a theologian, Ivan was none the less horribly cruel. He had perhaps as many as seven wives; he murdered his own son in a fit of lunatic rage. Soviet historians have tried to turn him into a hero by explaining that his wrath was directed against the selfish nobles who were conspiring to take over Russia. But, though the nobles were selfish enough, the danger of their intrigues was surely hugely exaggerated by the Tsar.

When Ivan finally was strong enough, in 1547, to assume the crown and throw off the tutelage of the boyars, he embarked upon a period (1547-1560) usually regarded as one of sound government and institutional reform. He regulated the rapacity of the imperial administrators in the provinces, who had oppressed the population. Several localities obtained the right to elect their own officials, both judicial and financial; yet, in the absence of any real sense of local initiative, we may question the effectiveness of the changes. Ivan also convoked

the first *zemski sobor* (land assembly), a consultative body consisting of nobles, clerics, and representatives from the towns, to assist with the imperial business, particularly with important questions of war and peace. Though comparable in its social composition to the various assemblies of the medieval western European world, the *zemski sobor* under Ivan seems to have met only once, and can in no sense be regarded as a parliamentary body.

When Ivan fell ill in 1553, the boyars refused to take an oath of allegiance to his son. This action apparently reawakened all his savagery, and upon his recovery he broke with his former moderate advisers, withdrew from Moscow, denounced the boyars and clergy, and soon afterward created a fantastic new institution: the *oprichnina*, or "separate realm." This was to belong to him personally, while the rest of Russia, called the *zemshchina*, continued to be administered as before. But the men whom Ivan now appointed to run the *oprichnina* (called *oprichniks*) were urged on to punish those who were prominent in the *zemshchina*. The *oprichniks*, grimly dressed in black and riding black horses, bore on their saddle-bows a dog's head (for vigilance) and a broom (symbolizing a clean sweep). They were the forerunners of the grim secret police forces that have long characterized Russian society. They waged a fierce, relentless war on the boyars, confiscating their estates, exiling them, killing them off. The Tsar, as was said, had divided his realm in two, and had set one part of it warring on the other. And in the diary of one *oprichnik* we find this revealing entry: "Today I did no harm to anyone: I was resting." The *oprichniks* took over the old estates of the men whom they were destroying. By the time of Ivan's death, many of the *oprichniks* themselves had been murdered at his orders, and Russian administration had degenerated to a state approximating chaos. Yet Ivan was able to extend Russian authority far to the east against the Kazan and Astrakhan

Tartars, thus for the first time opening the whole Volga waterway to Russian commerce, and facilitating expansion further east, into Siberia.

The Time of Troubles

Though the territory was wide and the imperial rule absolute, ignorance, illiteracy, and inefficiency weakened the structure of Russian society. The few foreign observers who knew the Russia of Ivan could foresee chaos ahead. And the Tsar himself had his own dire forebodings: "The body is exhausted, the spirit is ailing, the spiritual and physical wounds multiply, and there is no doctor to cure me,"* he wrote in his last will. Though the old nobility had been dealt a series of blows, the new gentry had as yet no sense of corporate entity, and therefore was not firmly in control of the machinery. Ivan's son and heir, Fedor (1584-1598), was an imbecile, and with his death in 1598 the Moscow dynasty, descended from the rulers of the former Kievan state, died out. The cliques of rival nobles intrigued for power. Fedor's brother-in-law, Boris Godunov, emerged as the dominant figure in the state. During Fedor's reign he had managed to build up his own position of strength. When Fedor died, Boris summoned a *zemski sobor*, which duly elected him to be the new Tsar. One of his unsuccessful rivals for the throne was a certain Fedor Romanov, who, like Boris, came from the middle ranks of the nobility. After his election, Boris forced Romanov to become a monk, under the name of Filaret.

Though Boris Godunov was probably a man of talent, he could not overcome his handicaps: Ivan's legacy of disorder, the intrigues of the nobility, and the famine and plague that began in 1601. To the tens of thousands of peasants who had already fled from serfdom and the thousands of persons displaced from the cities and towns by the inequitable privileges accorded to the wealthier merchants, there were now added incalculable numbers of hungry refugees. Bands of brigands roamed the countryside, and when in 1603 a pretender arose under the protection of the King of Poland and declared that he was a son of Ivan the Terrible —who had in fact died long before—he was able to capture the support of many of the discontented. Russia was launched on the decade known as the Time of Troubles (1603-1613).

Boris Godunov died in 1605, and the Pretender, whoever he may really have been, ruled briefly as Tsar. But his Polish and Catholic leanings and the ambitions of the nobles led to an overturn within less than a year; he was murdered, and was succeeded as Tsar by a certain Shuisky, a representative of the ancient aristocracy against which Ivan the Terrible had waged such implacable warfare. But Shuisky could not hold on to power; new pretenders arose; the mobs of peasants and brigands were rallied once again; civil war continued, as the Poles seized the opportunity to take advantage of Russian weakness. The Swedes also intervened. Shuisky fell in 1610, and was succeeded by no one tsar but by a small group of boyars, who planned that the heir to the Polish throne would become Tsar of Russia.

Polish forces took over in Moscow, and it soon appeared that the King of Poland himself intended not to turn over the power to his son but to reign in Russia himself. It was this specter of a foreign and Catholic domination that aroused the national sentiments of the Russians. In answer to a summons from the Patriarch, there assembled a kind of national militia, drawn largely from the prosperous free farmers of the middle Volga region, organized by a butcher named Kuzma Minin, and led by a nobleman named Dmitri Pozharsky. These two are the national heroes of the Time of Troubles. Under their command the militia won the

---

* Quoted by M. T. Florinsky, *Russia, A History and an Interpretation* (New York, 1953), I, 208.

support of other rebellious elements, and drove the Poles from Moscow in 1613.

The Role of the Zemski Sobor

A *zemski sobor* more widely representative than any previous one now was summoned to Moscow, where it elected as Tsar Michael Romanov, son of Filaret, and who was only sixteen years old. From the election of Michael in 1613 to the Russian Revolution of 1917, the Romanov dynasty held the throne. Michael succeeded with no limitations placed upon his power by the *zemski sobor* or by any other body; he was that curious anomaly, an elected autocrat. For this reason the Time of Troubles has been called a turning-point in Russian history "at which history refused to turn." Yet amid the chaos left by the decade of civil war and foreign intervention, in the absence of any corporate body—baronage, townsmen, or clergy—with a program for limiting the power of the Tsar, we can hardly be surprised that the autocracy continued in Russia quite unimpaired. The great boyars were weakened by the discreditable role many of them had played during the civil war. But the service gentry, coming into their own, imitated their noble predecessors. The rebellious serfs had to go back to their serfdom, which indeed became more onerous and difficult to escape than ever before.

For the first ten years of the reign of Michael Romanov, the *zemski sobor* stayed in continual session. Since it had picked the new Tsar in the midst of crisis, it had indeed performed a constitutional function. It even included some representatives of the free peasantry. It assisted the uncertain new dynasty to get under way by endorsing the policies of the Tsar and his advisers, and thus lending them the semblance of popular support. One might have supposed that this would be the beginning of a new kind of partnership, and that, as had sometimes happened in the West, representatives of the various social classes would gain more and more political self-confidence and power, and might even transform the *zemski sobor* from a consultative to some sort of legislative assembly, a parliament.

But this was not to be. After 1623, for the remainder of the reign of Michael (down to 1645), and during the reign of his son and successor Tsar Alexis (1645-1676), the summons to the *zemski sobor* became more and more infrequent. It was still consulted on questions of the declaration of war or the making of peace, the approval of new taxation, and the sanctioning of important new legislation. It endorsed the accession of Alexis in 1645, and in 1649 confirmed the issuance of a new law code, summarizing and putting in order past statutes. After 1653 Alexis did not summon it again, nor did his son and successor, Fedor (1676-1682). Its last meetings were in 1682.

No law abolished the *zemski sobor*. None had created it. The dynasty was simply entrenched and no longer needed it. Tsardom, autocratic tsardom, was taken for granted. No tsar need consult with any of his subjects unless he felt the need to do so. No subject had the right to insist on being consulted, though all subjects had the duty to give advice when asked for it. As the Romanovs became entrenched, they no longer felt the need to consult anybody's wishes except their own and those of their court favorites.

Individually, the early Romanovs were neither distinguished nor talented. The central government consisted of a number of bureaus or ministries or departments (*prikazy*), often with ill-defined or overlapping areas of competence. Provincial governors continued to milk the long-suffering population, and local efforts at self-government were in practice limited to the choice of officials obliged to collect and hand over taxes to the central authorities. Opposition to the system there certainly was, but it came not from articulate or literate citizens leveling criticism or offering suggestions for improvement. It came from below, from the oppressed and hungry peasantry. And it expressed itself in the only form of action the serf knew: large-scale or small-scale revolt, the burning of the manor house, the slaughter of the landlord or the tax-collector, the ill-directed march about in the vast flat countryside. Such affairs were a matter of yearly occurrence, the largest and most famous being that of Stenka Razin (1676), the "Russian Robin Hood." Such Russian uprisings were almost never directed against the tsar but against the landlords and officials, of whose misdeeds the tsar was supposed not to know. Often indeed the peasant leaders would arouse their followers *in the name* of the tsar. Sometimes, as during the Time of Troubles, the leaders pretended to be tsars in order to obtain more followers.

The Role of the Church

During the sixteenth and seventeenth centuries the Church remained the partner of the autocracy. The tsar controlled the election of the Metropolitan of Moscow, and after 1589 that of the newly proclaimed Patriarch of Moscow, a rank to which the Metropolitan was elevated. In the seventeenth century, there were two striking instances when a patriarch actually shared power with the tsar. In 1619, the father of Tsar Michael Romanov, Filaret, became patriarch and was granted the additional title of "great sovereign." He assisted his son in all the affairs of state, and indeed dominated Russia. In the next generation, Tsar Alexis appointed a cleric named Nikon to the patriarchal throne, and made him "great sovereign" too. Nikon proved so arrogant that he aroused protests from clergy as well as laity. He also argued that the authority of the Patriarch in spiritual affairs exceeded that of the tsar, while in temporal matters the two were equal: a claim like that of the more powerful popes, but one that had almost never been advanced in Byzantium or in Russia. In 1666, a church council deposed Nikon, who died a mere monk. These two experiments with two-man government were never repeated. They are the exceptions that prove the rule in Russia: the Church depends upon the State.

As in the Byzantine Empire, so in Russia, monasteries became immensely rich. By 1500, it is estimated that they owned more than one-third of the land available for cultivation. Opposition to monastic worldliness arose within the Church itself, and one might have supposed that the government would have supported this movement. But those who favored monastic poverty also wished to enforce the non-interference of the State in monastic affairs. To preserve their right to control the monasteries in other respects, the government of the tsar was obliged to oppose this reforming movement with respect to monastic property.

The Church, almost alone, inspired the literature and art of the Muscovite period. History was written by monks, in the form of chronicles. Travel literature took the form of accounts of pilgrimages to the Holy Land, although we have one secular travel book, a report by a Novgorod merchant who went to India on business. A handbook of etiquette and domestic economy, called Household Management, advises its readers how to run a home and how to behave in company, revealing a conservative, well-ordered, and smug society. Theological tracts attack the Catholics, and also the Protestants, whose doctrines were known in the western regions. Almost all of this literature was written in Old Church Slavonic, the language of the liturgy and not the language of everyday speech. Though stately and impressive, Old Church Slavonic was not an appropriate vehicle for new ideas. There was no secular learning, no science, no flowering of vernacular literature, no lively debates on the philosophical level in the field of theology. In painting,

Russian ikon, showing St. Nicholas, who became the legendary Santa Claus.

the ikon, inherited from Byzantium, did flourish mightily, and various local schools produced works of great beauty and character.

The Expansion of Russia

The sixteenth and seventeenth centuries saw a tremendous physical expansion of the Russian domain. Russian pioneers, in search of furs to sell and new land to settle, led the way, and the government followed. Frontiersmen in Russia were known as Cossacks, or Kazakhs, a Tartar word meaning "free adventurer." The Cossacks were racially no different from the mass of Russians, but they lived on the frontiers and organized themselves for self-defense against the Tartars as our American pioneers did against the Indians. Two Cossack republics, one on the Dnieper, the other on the Don, lived in a kind of primitive democracy relatively independent of Moscow; other Cossack groups formed in the Volga, in the Urals, and elsewhere; they fought Tartars and Turks quite at their own free will. Cossacks could usually be counted upon to help the leader of any peasant uprising, and did so during the Time of Troubles.

Also the Cossacks were deeply involved in the advancement of the Russian frontiers both in Europe and in Asia. On the west, of course, Russia faced the Poland that had inherited former Russian lands, which they were determined to keep.

But Poland was already moving inexorably toward decline and downfall. Its monarchy, instead of being hereditary, was elective. Each time the throne fell vacant, the diet, or assembly, of the nobility, would choose a successor, usually the man who had given the biggest bribes. Once elected, the kings were quite powerless, since they had already agreed to transfer royal prerogatives to the diet, which cherished its famous institution of the *liberum veto*: any one of its members, by opposing any proposal, could effectively block it. All the minority of one had to do was to shout "I do not wish it!" and then gallop off before his colleagues could catch up with him and make him change his mind. The diet was not a parliament in the western sense of the term, but an assembly of men each of whom thought of himself as a power unto himself, more like the Security Council of the United Nations. Thus unanimity was necessary for all decisions. Loosely knit, the Polish national state had no regular army or diplomatic corps. Its nobility had no concept of service to the Crown or indeed any sense of loyalty except to their own social class. They helped destroy a once-flourishing urban middle class by persecuting Jewish shopkeepers and foreign merchants. On their estates, the fate of their serfs was harsher if possible than in Russia.

By the 1650's, the Russo-Polish conflict was concentrated in the Ukrainian lands, where Pole and Russian competed for the assistance of the Cossacks. Here bitterness had been exacerbated by the Jesuit effort to convert the Orthodox peasants. In 1595, after a group of Orthodox clergy had accepted papal supremacy in the Union of Brest, the Catholics declared that all those who remained outside the Union must be persecuted. The Polish authorities also interfered with the traditional liberties of the Dnieper Cossacks, and in 1648 the Cossack leader Khmelnitsky revolted against the Poles, inviting Tsar Alexis to assist him in 1651. By 1654, the *zemski sobor* had approved the Tsar's acceptance of a protectorate over the Ukrainian lands, and a long war with Poland ensued, during which the Cossacks changed sides repeatedly, maneuvering desperately to preserve their independence. In 1667, by the Treaty of Andrussovo, the Russians obtained all the lands on the east bank of the Dnieper, as well as the privilege of occupying Kiev, on the west bank, for two years. They never left it.

THE EASTERN OUTPOSTS ~ 223

The Cossacks, however, continued unruly, and in the next phase of the struggle, the Turks, as suzerains over the Crimean Tartars, whose territories bordered on the Ukraine, took an active part in the fighting, which involved Poland and Russia once more. The general European anxiety over the Turkish menace (see below, p. 243) eventually brought the Poles reluctantly to grant Russia by a new treaty of eternal peace (1686) all the lands yielded at Andrussovo, plus Kiev. The continued decline of Poland meant that Sweden, guardian of the Baltic shore, would emerge as the chief rival on the west.

To the south and southeast, in the direction of the Black Sea and the Caucasus, Russia had to move more slowly. Not only did the Crimean Tartars block the path, but behind the Tartars loomed the figure of their overlord, the Ottoman sultan, whom the tsars could not yet challenge. Thus the Russian claim to be the successor to Byzantium in the Orthodox world was a spiritual and ideological claim only. Indeed, when a group of Cossacks seized the key Tartar seaport of Azov at the mouth of the Don, and offered it to Michael Romanov as a gift if he would only come and help hold on to it, the cautious tsar not only refused the offer, but wrote an apologetic letter to the sultan explaining that he had had no part in the aggression.

The most dramatic advance of Russia during this era came to the eastward, across the Urals, and the vast spaces of Siberia, all the way to the Pacific Ocean. This movement has often been likened to the American expansion from the Atlantic seaboard to the Pacific. Compared with the Russian advance to the Pacific, the American westward movement was relatively slow, however: the Russians covered some 5,000 miles in about forty years; we took longer to go a shorter distance. But the Russian advance left vast areas "behind the lines" unsettled and unabsorbed at each stage, whereas our own more gradual movement tended to consolidate each stage rather more than the Russians did.

Then too, the American pioneer faced formidable geographic barriers of mountain and desert, whereas the Russian had easier going on the enormous Siberian flatlands, where the river basins—the Ob, the Yenisei, the Lena, and their tributaries—facilitated rapid progress. For the Americans too, the native inhabitants—the American Indian—often posed serious military and political problems, whereas the Siberian tribesmen, widely scattered across the area, seem on the whole to have helped the Russians rather than opposing them. Though enormous in extent, Siberia continued to be very sparsely inhabited.

It was the victories of Ivan the Terrible over the Kazan Tartars that led to the first major advances in the sixteenth century. Private enterprise led the way: the Stroganov family obtained huge concessions in the Ural area, where they made great fortunes in the fur trade, and discovered and began to exploit the first iron mines known in Russia. The Stroganovs hired bands of Cossack explorers, who led the movement. The government followed at some distance behind with administrators and tax-collectors, soldiers and priests, as each new area was opened up. At a suitable point on a river basin, the spearhead of the advance party would build a wooden palisade and begin to collect furs from the surrounding countryside. Almost before the defenses of each new position had been consolidated, the restless advance guard would have moved some hundreds of miles further eastward to repeat the process. The Daniel Boone of the Siberian adventure was surely the famous Cossack leader Yermak, whose exploits in his own lifetime took on legendary proportions.

Tobolsk, the first major Siberian center founded by the Russians, remained a major seat of administration; but Irkutsk and finally Okhotsk were reached by the 1640's. A Siberian *prikaz* in Moscow had nominal responsibility for the government of the huge area, but decisions had to be made on the spot because of the communications problem, although the Russians got an efficient postal service working quite early. Thus the Siberians always tended to have the independence traditionally associated with men of the "wide open spaces," and reinforced by the Cossack and outlaw traditions from which many of them sprang. Because Okhotsk and its neighborhood along the Pacific were intensely cold, and the ocean frozen for a good many months in the year, the Russians were soon looking enviously southward toward the valley of the Amur, which flowed into the Pacific at a point where the harbors were open all year round.

Explorations in this area brought the Russians into contact with the Chinese, whose lands they were now casually invading. But the Chinese government of the period did not care very much about these regions, which, from its own point of view, were far-northerly outposts. In 1689, the Chinese signed a treaty with Moscow, the first they had concluded with any European state. This treaty stabilized the frontier, demilitarized the Amur, and kept the Russians out of Manchuria, the home territory of the ruling Chinese dynasty. It also provided the two powers with a buffer region of Mongolian-inhabited territory, which acknowledged Chinese overlordship. Incidentally, it also recognized the Russian advances to the north. With almost incredible speed, the Russians had acquired an empire whose riches are even today by no means fully exploited. Russia's future as an Asian power with a vital interest in Pacific affairs was established at just about the time the English took New Amsterdam from the Dutch.

Russia and the West   During these two centuries foreigners and foreign ideas gradually penetrated Russia, a process warmly welcomed by some Russians, deeply deplored by others, and viewed in a mingled light by still others, who prized western technical advancement but feared western influence on Russian society. This ambivalent attitude toward westerners and western ideas became characteristic of later Russians: they loved what the West could give, but they often feared and even hated the giver.

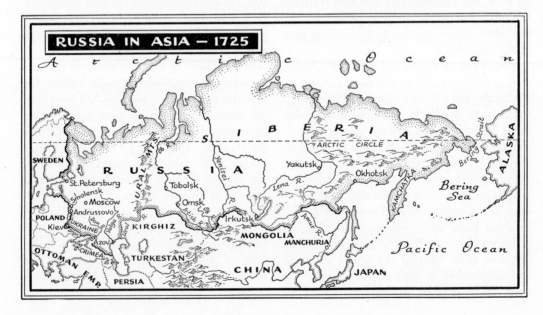

(Left) Italian artisans working on the Uspensky Cathedral in the Kremlin.
(Right) Religious ceremonies in front of the completed cathedral.

The first foreigners to come to Russia in any significant numbers were the Italians, who helped build the Kremlin at the end of the fifteenth century. But the Italians were not encouraged to teach the Russians their knowledge, and they failed to influence even the court of Ivan III in any significant way. The English, who arrived in the mid-sixteenth century as traders to the White Sea (they had been looking for an Arctic route to China), were welcomed by Ivan the Terrible. He gave them valuable privileges, and encouraged them to trade their woolen cloth for Russian naval supplies, which helped build the great Elizabethan fleets. The English were the first to teach Russians western industrial techniques. They got along well with the Russians and supplied a large number of officers to the Tsar's armies, mostly Scotsmen. At one moment during the Time of Troubles, there was even a plan to make King James I Tsar of Russia; and in fact James was quite receptive to the idea. Toward the middle of the seventeenth century, the Dutch were able to displace the English as the most important foreign group engaged in commerce and manufacturing, and set up their own glass, paper, and textile plants in Russia.

After the accession of Michael Romanov in 1613, the foreign quarter of Moscow, always called the "German suburb," grew rapidly. Foreign technicians of all sorts—textile-weavers, bronze-founders, clockmakers—received enormous salaries from the state. Foreign merchants sold their goods, much to the distaste of the native Russians, who begged the tsars to prevent the foreigners from stealing the bread out of their mouths. Foreign physicians and druggists became fashionable, though always suspected of being wizards by the superstitious common people. By the end of the seventeenth century, western influence is apparent in the life of the court. The first play in Russia was performed in 1672—a solemn Biblical drama about Esther. A few nobles began to buy books and form libraries, and to learn Latin and French and German. Some of them were eating salad and taking snuff, and shyly beginning to try their skills at the social arts. A few Russians went abroad to travel, and, of these few, all who could refused to go back.

The people, meanwhile, distrusted the foreigners, looted their houses when they dared, and jeered at them in the street. As one intelligent writer of the seventeenth century put it:

> Acceptance of foreigners is a plague. They live by the sweat and tears of the Russians. The foreigners are like bear-keepers who put rings in our noses and lead us around. They are Gods, we fools, they dwell with us as lords. Our Kings are their servants.

The most dramatic outbreak of anti-foreign feeling took place, as might have been expected, in the field of religion. Highly educated clerics from the western lands (the Ukraine) and Greek scholars recommended to Patriarch Nikon that the Holy Books be revised and corrected in certain places where the texts were not sound. Resentment against this reform took shape as a great schism in the Russian Church itself. Given the deep Russian regard for the externals of the faith, we must not be surprised at the horror that was aroused when the Russians were told that for centuries they had been spelling the name of Jesus incorrectly and had been crossing themselves with the wrong number of fingers. As at Byzantium, the religious protest reflected a deepseated hatred of change, particularly change proposed by foreigners. Declaring that the end of the world was at hand (since Moscow, the third Rome, had now itself become heretical), about 20,000 of the schismatics shut themselves up in their huts and burned themselves alive. When the world did not end, those schismatics who survived, always known as the "Old Believers," settled down and became sober, solid Russian citizens, many of them merchants and well-to-do peasants. Some later governments persecuted them, most did not; but the Russian Church was weakened as a result of the schism.

III: *The Era of Peter the Great (1682-1725)*

At the death of Fedor Romanov in 1682, Russia was still a backward eastern European country, with few diplomatic links with the West, and very little knowledge of the outside world. All contemporaries—and this includes Russians as well as foreigners—report on the brutality, the widespread immorality, the drunkenness, illiteracy, and filth prevalent among all classes of society. There was little education, even for the clergy, most of whom could not read, and who set no shining example to their flock by their mode of life. It is perhaps little wonder that students familiar with conditions in the Russia of the period before the advent of Peter the Great have saluted him as the great revolutionary who altered the face of his country, in considerable measure in terms of influences coming from the West. Yet the changes he made were neither so numerous nor so drastic as his admirers have often claimed. Moreover, the foundations for most of them were already present in the society he inherited. Finally, Russia would no doubt eventually have become a power of international importance even without Peter, although it would have taken longer. Even if we accept all these dilutions of the usual estimate of his contribution, however, the fact remains that Peter was an awe-inspiring—and terror-inspiring—figure.

Sophia: The Forerunner (1682-1689)

When Fedor died childless, he left a fifteen-year-old brother, Ivan, who was partly blind and almost an idiot, and several sisters, including the ugly but capable Sophia, all children of Alexis Romanov by his first wife. There was also a ten-year-old half-brother, son of Alexis by his second wife. This was Peter, as bright and vigorous as Ivan was debilitated. In this situation, there quickly developed a major court feud between the partisans of the family of the first wife, and those of the family of the second, Peter's mother, Natalia Naryshkina, who was still very much alive. At first, a *zemski sobor*, led by the Patriarch, elected Peter as Tsar; but Sophia, as leader of the opposing faction, succeeded in winning the support of the *streltsy*, or musketeers, a special branch of the military, many of whom were Old Believers. Undisciplined, and angry with their officers, some of whom had indeed been cheating them, the *streltsy* were a menace to orderly government.

Sophia and her supporters lured them on into making an attack on the Kremlin. The youthful Peter saw the infuriated troops murdering some of his mother's family and racing through the palace in pursuit of the rest, stabbing the furniture with swords and spears. For good measure, they killed a good many of the nobles living in Moscow, and pillaged the archives of the *prikaz* where the records of serfdom were kept. But, though their movement obviously had some social content, it was primarily a successful effort by Sophia to gain power. Sophia now became regent for both her brother Ivan and her half-brother Peter, who were hailed as joint Tsars.

But before her power was stabilized, she had to deal with her own instruments, the ungovernable *streltsy*, who terrorized the capital until threatened with open war by the regular army. Once the *streltsy* were calmed, Sophia moved to punish the Old Believers and any of the revolting serfs that could be captured. The first woman to govern Russia since Kievan times, Sophia was bound in any case to face severe opposition. Two campaigns against the Tartars in the Crimea were failures (1687, 1689). Nor could Sophia manage to get even her supporters to allow her to proclaim herself autocrat. And the maturing Peter, though out of favor and away from court, posed a threat to her position; in the end, the *streltsy* let her down. Sophia was shut up in a convent and Peter and Ivan ruled together in theory until Ivan's death in 1696, although in practice Ivan never counted for anything.

Peter the Great: A Character Sketch

The young Peter was almost seven feet tall, and extremely lively. Highly intelligent, he had learned to read and write (but never to spell) from a drunken tutor who was the only academic instructor the troubled times afforded. Even in his early years, Peter was fascinated by war and military games. He set up a play-regiment, staffed it with a good many full-grown men, enlisted as a common soldier in its ranks (promoting himself from time to time), ordered all sorts of equipment for it from the Moscow arsenals, and drilled it in war games with unflagging vigor, himself firing off cannon or pounding on a drum with equal enjoyment. He discovered a broken-down boat in a barn, and unraveled the mysteries of rigging and sail with the help of Dutch sailors settled in the foreigners' suburb. Sailing remained one of his keenest passions. Though he married at the age of sixteen, Peter neglected his wife, and preferred working on his military maneuvers (which grew ever more realistic and dangerous), sailing his boats, and relaxing with his peculiar circle of cronies.

This rowdy lot smoked huge quantities of tobacco (which horrified the conservative Muscovites, who believed that smoking was specifically forbidden by the Biblical text which says that what cometh out of the mouth defileth a man), and they regularly got themselves completely drunk. When thoroughly lit up, they would engage in carefully planned obscene parodies of church services, or play elaborate and highly dangerous practical jokes on the unoffending citizenry, roaring about Moscow in winter late at night on sleighs and treating the sleeping populace to shrieking serenades. Masquerades and parties lasted for days; staid Moscow ladies, accustomed to almost harem-like seclusion, were commanded to put on low-necked evening dresses in the western style, and dance and engage in social chit-chat. They were literally forced to guzzle with the Tsar and his friends: if a lady refused, Peter simply held her nose, and poured the wine down her throat. Peter spent enormous sums of state revenue on this sort of party, and richly endowed his boon companion Lefort, a young Swiss soldier of fortune who completely charmed the Tsar. He was the only man who could ever drink glass for glass with Peter, and legend says also that they alone escaped hangovers after their big evenings. Lefort became Field Marshal, Grand Admiral and "chief diplomat."

The almost frantic energy that Peter devoted to pleasure reflected only part of his appetite for new experience. Just as he served in the ranks of his own play-regiment and sailed his boats himself, so he eagerly learned any new technique that came to his attention. To his playing on the drum and trumpet he added at various times carpentry, shoe-making, cooking, clock-making, ivory-carving, etching, and—worst of all—dentistry. Once he had acquired a set of dentist's tools, nobody was safe, since Peter did not care at all whether the intended victim had a toothache or not. Whenever he felt the need to practice, he practiced—and those were the days before anesthetics. Preferring to wear shabby work clothes, driving his own horses, neglecting

formal obligations and paying little attention to court and church ceremony, Peter in his own person was a shock to the Muscovites, and not in the least in keeping with their idea of a proper tsar.

After Lefort died in 1700, Peter's favorite was a certain Menshikov, a man of low birth, who received high office in all the Russian services, the title of Prince, and a huge fortune. Unfortunately, like many of the public servants of the period, he was an unscrupulous grafter: as one of the Tsar's men, a Serb, remarked, "we all steal." Peter wrote to Menshikov as "my brother," and though he came to distrust him he never demoted or ruined him as he did many other favorites.

Even in his youth, Peter ignored his first wife, and later (1699) had her shut up in a convent and made a nun. Still later, he took on as mistress a girl from the Baltic region, who had already passed through the hands of Menshikov and others, and after some years of liaison with her, during which she gave birth to two of Peter's children, he finally married her in 1712. This was the Empress Catherine, a simple, hearty, affectionate woman, long devoted to her difficult husband, and able to control him as no other human being ever could. But again, one can understand the horrified reaction of the old-fashioned Russian noble.

The Western Trip

Anxious to try his hand at war, Peter led a campaign against Azov in 1695, but failed. Summoning his service men to build ships—an art they knew little about—he literally drafted them to work as artisans under Dutch direction at Voronezh on the Don. By 1696 he had a fleet of riverboats on the Don, sailed them downriver, and defeated the Turks at Azov. Since Europe was at the moment engaged in a furious campaign against the Turks (see below, p. 243), this rather surprising contribution from the Russians aroused much interest and curiosity. The project of forming a league against the Turks with the states of western Europe now gave Peter the pretext for a trip outside Russia, the first undertaken by a Russian sovereign since the Kievan period.

The symbolism of the huge Russian Tsar in all his vigor and crudity leaving his antiquated and stagnant country and emerging into the air of western Europe has always attracted students of the period. What interested Peter was western "know-how," especially naval know-how; he planned to go to Holland, England, and Venice, where the best ships (in his opinion) were made, find out how they were made, and bring the knowledge back to Russia for the advancement of Russian aims.

From the celebrated western trip many well-known pictures emerge: Peter laboring as a common hand on the docks in Holland; Peter and his suite, drunk and dirty, wrecking the handsome house and garden of the English diarist, John Evelyn, near London: "There is a house full of people," wrote Evelyn's harassed servant, "and that right nasty." Less well known perhaps are the spectacles of Peter dancing with a German princess, mistaking her whalebone corsets for her ribs, and commenting loudly that German girls have devilish hard bones; Peter receiving an honorary degree at Oxford; Peter deep in conversation (Dutch) with William Penn about the Quaker faith; Peter gobbling his food without benefit of knife or fork, or asleep with a dozen or so of his followers on the floor of a tiny room in a London inn with no windows open.

Though ostensibly traveling incognito as Peter Mikhailov, a noncommissioned officer in a Russian regiment, Peter's efforts to conceal who he was were a farce from the beginning. After all, there were no other authoritarian seven-footers in the party. He hired several hundred technicians to work in Russia, raised money when he needed it by selling to an English peer the monopoly of tobacco sales in Russia, and visited every sort of factory or museum or printing press he could find. He made, as we can easily imagine, an unforgettable impression.

Before Peter could get to Venice, the western trip was interrupted by news that the *streltsy* had revolted again (1698). Peter rushed home, and personally participated in the punishment of the alleged ringleaders and plotters. Peter and Menshikov and others rather enjoyed chopping off the heads of the victims. Though many innocent men surely suffered torture and death, Peter had broken the *streltsy* as a power in Russian domestic life.

From the West, Peter had returned more determined than ever to modernize his country and his countrymen. The very day of his return he summoned the court jester, and with his assistance went about with a great pair of shears, stopping his courtiers and clipping off their beards. Though this may seem a trivial joke, in fact it was an action full of symbolism. The tradition of the Orthodox Church held that God is bearded. If God has a beard, and if man was made in the image of God, man must also have a beard. Deprived of his beard, man is no longer made in God's image, and is a natural candidate for damnation. This was the way the Muscovite nobles and churchmen felt. But Peter now decreed that Russian nobles must shave, or else pay a substantial tax for the privilege of wearing their beards. Bronze beard-tokens worn around the neck certified that the tax had been properly paid; without such a token a bearded man ran the risk of being clipped on sight. A western traveler reports a conversation with an old man whose beard had been shorn off: the poor Russian had kept the beard-hair and was planning to have it buried in his coffin with him, so that he might prove to St. Nicholas that he had not committed sacrilege of his own free will.

Presently, Peter issued an edict commanding that all boyars, members of the gentry class, and the city population generally must abandon traditional Russian dress, which in-

The equestrian statue of Peter the Great, by Falconet, in Leningrad.

in 1698, he discovered that, instead of being eager to join him in a full-scale crusade against the Turks, the Austrians and their allies were anxious to end the Turkish war. Irritated by the Peace of Karlovitz of 1699, which he felt to be a betrayal of Russia (see below, p. 243), Peter none the less made a separate peace of his own with the Sultan in 1700. By this time, his plans for new aggression were already formed.

The victim was to be Sweden, at the hands of whose officials Peter fancied he had received a slight in the Baltic port of Riga on his way west in 1697. Peter's allies, already signed up in 1699, were to be Denmark and Poland, the latter under its elected king, Augustus the Strong, who was also Elector of Saxony and who had quickly become an intimate of Peter after their first meeting in 1698. The real engineer of the alliance and moving spirit of the war against Sweden, however, was a nobleman named Patkul from the Baltic shore, deeply resentful of measures taken by the Swedes against the feudal proprietors of that area. Energetically, Patkul went from interview to interview, holding out to Augustus and Peter the glittering prospect that after they had defeated Sweden they might divide her Baltic territories. In 1697, the Swedish throne had descended to a youth of fifteen, King Charles XII, whom Peter, Augustus, and Patkul hoped they might easily overcome. They did not appreciate Charles' fanatical love and affinity for fighting. They might have reconsidered had they seen him strengthening his sword-arm by beheading at a single stroke apiece whole flocks of sheep driven down his palace corridors in single file until the whole place swam in blood. The fact was, however, that Peter the Great characteristically rushed into war with Sweden unprepared.

Charles knocked Denmark out of the war before Russia even got in. He then frustrated Augustus' effort to take Riga, and completely defeated a vastly larger Russian force at Narva (1700), capturing the entire

cluded long robes with flowing sleeves and tall bonnets, and adopt western-style costume. The continued manufacture of the old-fashioned clothes was made illegal, and Peter added point to his decree by taking up his shears again, and cutting off the sleeves of all the people he met wearing the forbidden cloaks. The enactments on the beards and on dress, themselves perhaps not very important, were regarded by the victims as an assault on precious customs and a forcible introduction of hated foreign ways.

Peter's Wars

War was Peter's greatest interest. We can understand his policies at home only after we realize how closely related they were to the virtually constant warfare of his reign, and to the ever-mounting need for money for fighting. We have already seen him victorious over the Turks at Azov in 1696. On his way back to Russia

supply of modern cannon of which Peter was so proud. Instead of taking advantage of Peter's helplessness, however, and marching into Russia, Charles detoured into Poland, where he spent seven years chasing Augustus about, sponsoring his own King of Poland, a noble named Stanislas Leszczynski, and eventually forcing Augustus to sign an agreement to abandon the crown of Poland to Leszczynski, and to give up the Russian alliance. Charles then seized and executed Patkul.

During this interim, Peter had been busy rebuilding the shattered Russian armies, and had conquered from the Swedes the two Baltic provinces nearest to Russia, Ingria and Livonia. In the first he founded in 1703 a new city, St. Petersburg, soon to be the new capital of Russia, and from the beginning the apple of Peter's eye. Now, in late 1707, after a year of campaigning against Russia, Charles made the mistake of sweeping far to the south and east into the Ukraine in an effort to join forces with the Cossacks, whose leader Mazepa was an ally. Drawn deeply into Russia during the severe winter of 1708-1709, Charles' exhausted Swedish forces were finally defeated by the Russians in the decisive battle of Poltava (June 27, 1709). Charles managed to flee safely westward across the Dniester River and onto Turkish territory. The victory was complete, but the war continued.

Peter was able to reinstate Augustus as King of Poland, but he was not able to force the Turks to surrender to him the refugee King of Sweden. Charles indeed had embarked on a series of anti-Russian intrigues designed to bring about a war between Turkey and Peter, and thus to enable him to avenge his defeat. So Peter in some dismay found himself embroiled in war against the Turks (1710-1711). Now for the first time in history the Russians made an appeal to the Balkan Christian subjects of the Turks on the ground of their common Orthodox faith. Bearing banners modeled on those of Constantine, first Emperor of

Byzantium, and promising liberation from the Moslems, the Russian forces entered Turkish territory by crossing the river Pruth westward into the Danubian province of Moldavia (now a part of Rumania). Here the Turkish armies trapped Peter and forced him to surrender (1711). His position was desperate; he later said that the Turks could have extracted anything they wanted from him except the promise to give up St. Petersburg.

Indeed, the Turks could have dragged Peter off in captivity to Istanbul had they wanted. But they proved unexpectedly lenient. They required the surrender of Azov, the creation of an unfortified "no-man's land" between Russian and Ottoman territory, and the promise that Charles XII might pass unmolested through Peter's dominions on his way home to Sweden. It is little wonder that Charles was furious with the Turks for not taking full advantage of Peter's discomfiture. Tirelessly, Charles worked to bring about still another Russo-Turkish war. He came very close to success, but eventually the Turks tired of their firebrand visitor and expelled him by force. Their own peace with Russia was secure, and Charles went sadly home (1714).

Still the Great Northern War, as the Russo-Swedish struggle has come to be known, dragged on for seven more years of diplomatic intrigue and military and naval action, involving the Prussians (see below, p. 263), and gravely affecting the interests of all the western European powers. As Russian forces seized Finland, inflicted naval defeats on the Swedes in the Baltic, and occupied islands only a few miles from the Swedish coast, the Swedish empire was obviously dissolving, and the Russians were taking its place. To the last years of the Great Northern War (1714-1721) belong a whole series of matrimonial and other alliances and projects between Russia and the petty German courts, bringing the Russians deep into Central Europe, and embroiling them in a variety of questions in which Russia really had no national interest. Peter the Great even hoped to marry one of his daughters to Louis XV of France. From a remote and little-known state somewhere behind Poland, Russia had emerged as a major military power with enough might to affect the destiny of European states. The death of Charles XII in 1718 cleared the way for peace negotiations long contemplated and even begun. But it took a Russian landing in Sweden proper (1719) to force a decision.

At Nystadt (1721), Russia received all the former possessions of Sweden along the eastern shore of the Baltic, and part of Karelia. Peter returned Finland to Sweden and agreed to pay a substantial sum for the territories acquired. These Baltic territories were Peter's famous "window on the west," putting Russia into immediate contact with Europe, and ending the curious situation by which all seaborne traffic to Russia had had to sail around the northern edge of Europe and into the White Sea. When Peter declared himself "Emperor" in 1721, he was hardly claiming an unreasonable title, and the European powers recognized it in due course. Except for a brief adventurous campaign against the Persians (1722-1723), Peter fought no more wars. He ruled for thirty-five years, and only during the very last year was Russia at peace.

The Machinery of Government

Constant warfare requires constant supplies of men and money. The enlistment of volunteers, including serfs who for a short period were allowed to obtain their freedom in this way, provided cannon-fodder but not seasoned troops. So Peter's government developed a crude form of draft system according to which a given number of households had to supply a given number of recruits. More men died of disease, hunger, and cold than at the hands of the enemy, and anyone who thought he

could get away with it deserted. But the very length of the war meant that survivors served as a tough nucleus for a regular army.

Though Peter himself built a Baltic fleet at the first possible opportunity, Russian naval tradition failed to strike deep roots. From 800 ships at the moment of his death (mostly very small, of course), the fleet declined to fewer than twenty a decade later. And there was no merchant marine whatever. The apprehensions of the English and the Dutch that Russian emergence on the Baltic would automatically mean the creation of a new maritime nation proved unfounded.

To staff the military forces and the administration, Peter rigorously enforced the rule by which all landowners owed service to the state. He eventually decreed "civil death" for those who failed to register; this put them outside the protection of the law, and anyone could attack or kill them without fear of the consequences. Universal state service became compulsory for life. At the age of fifteen, every male child of the service class was assigned to his future post, in the army, in the civil service, or at court. Peter often forced the gentry to do jobs they considered beneath them; he did not care whether they were interested in their work or even very much whether they had been trained for it. He filled their ranks with newcomers and outsiders, who obtained grants of land, rank, and title. And he required that when a member of this class died he must leave his estate intact to one of his sons, not necessarily the eldest, so that it would not be divided anew in every generation. Thus the class of service nobility—which now substantially included the survivors of the nobility of ancient birth, the old boyars—was brought into a position of complete dependence upon the tsar. Some of the gentry tried to avoid service by pretending to be halfwitted; Peter in answer decreed that those whose mental state did not permit of service could neither marry nor inherit estates from their parents.

The system threw open the possibility of a splendid career to men with talent. A person without estates or rank who reached a certain level in any of the branches of the service (for example, major in the army) automatically received lands and a title of nobility. Of course the nobility of ancient birth viewed this as a cheapening of their position, and hated to see the new recruits come into their own social order. But under Peter there was little they could do about it.

To raise cash, Peter tried a variety of measures. He debased the currency; he taxed virtually everything—sales, rents, real estate, tanneries, baths, and beehives—and appointed special officials called "revenue-finders" to think up new levies. Tolls were collected on all forms of transportation. The government held a monopoly over a bewildering variety of important products, including salt and oil, coffins and caviar. The basic Russian tax on each individual household was not producing enough revenue, partly because the number of households had declined as a result of war and misery, and partly because households were combining in order to evade payment. Peter's government therefore substituted a head tax on every male—the "soul tax," as the Russians called it—making it useless for individuals to conceal themselves in households. This innovation required a new census, and the census produced a most important, and unintended, social result: the census-takers now classified as serfs a large number of floaters on the edge between freedom and serfdom, who thus found themselves and their children eternally labeled as unfree. At the cost of human misery, Peter's government managed in its later years to balance the budget.

In the administration, various new *prikazy* were first set up to centralize the handling of funds received from various sources. A system of army districts adopted for reasons of military efficiency led to the creation of the first Russian provinces: at first eight, then nine, then twelve—embracing all Russia. Each province had its own governor; and many of the functions previously carried on inefficiently by the central government were thus decentralized. With the Tsar often away from the capital, and many of the former *prikazy* abolished, decentralization had gone so far that Russia seemed at times to have little central government at all. But when Peter set out for the Pruth campaign in 1711, he created a nine-man "governing Senate," designed to exercise power in his absence. It too played a large part in the central preoccupation of the state, the collection of funds.

In the years beginning with 1712, Peter copied the Swedish system of central ministries to supersede the old *prikazy*. They were called "colleges," because they were administered not by a single minister but by a board of directors or *collegium*. There were nine of these colleges: foreign affairs, army, navy, commerce, mines and manufactures, justice, income, expenditure, and control. Each had a board of eleven directors, and decision was by majority vote of the board. Corruption now became more difficult, because the conduct of any one member of a college could be checked by all his colleagues. On the other hand, the lengthy deliberations of so many directors often delayed final policy decisions.

The total picture of Peter's efforts to increase the efficiency of government is one of mixed success at best. Attempts to model Russian local government on Swedish practice broke down because of the enormous difference between the two countries in literacy, size, tradition, and attitude toward civic responsibility. Corruption continued unchecked in high places. Savage punishments were inflicted on some of those who were caught, while others, like Menshikov, were apparently immune. And yet the cumbrous machinery that Peter gradually established, hit or miss, to meet the immediate needs of his wars, was superior to any that Russia had previously known.

More Innovations   Ever since 1703, Peter had been building a great city in the swamps he had seized from the Swedes. Thousands of men died in the effort to drain the marshes and create a seaport, a capital, and a town worthy of its imperial resident. Whenever he could spare the time, Peter would watch the progress of the work. Remote from the rest of Russia, St. Petersburg was a frightfully expensive place to live, because all food and building materials had to be transported great distances. But Peter moved the Senate there in 1714, made it the new capital, and literally commanded all the members of the nobility to build new houses there and make it their home. Palaces sprang up at the Tsar's command, but the nobles hated the place and complained bitterly about abandoning their beloved Moscow for this uncomfortable and costly town. Floods poured through the streets; Peter roared with laughter at the sight of people's furniture and household effects floating away. Wolves prowled through the broad new boulevards, and devoured a lady in front of Prince Menshikov's own house one fine day in June. Inconvenient, though splendidly constructed, St. Petersburg became the symbol of Peter's war against his own gentry.

Peter also determined to disarm all possible future threats to his power from the Church. Remembering the efforts of Nikon in the time of his father Alexis, and knowing full well how bitterly the clergy loathed the new regime he himself was trying to impose, he simply failed to appoint a successor when the Patriarch of Moscow died in 1700. Eventually, in 1721, he extended the collegiate system of administration to the Church itself. He put it under an agency first called the "spiritual college," and later the Holy Directing Synod, headed by a Procurator who was a layman. Thus the Church became more than ever a department of state. Peter's own statement of this purpose is remarkably frank:

From the collegiate government of the church there is not so much danger to the country of disturbances and troubles as may be produced by one spiritual ruler. For the common people do not understand the difference between the spiritual power and that of the autocrat; but, dazzled by the splendor and glory of the highest pastor, they think that he is a second sovereign of like power with the autocrat or with even more, and that the spiritual power is that of another and better realm. If then there should be any difference of opinion between the Patriarch and the Tsar, it might easily happen that the people, perhaps misled by designing persons, should take the part of the Patriarch, in the mistaken belief that they were fighting for God's cause.[*]

The educational advances of the period reflected Peter's technological and military interests. Naval, military, and artillery academies were established to educate future officers and also many civil servants. A high school, founded with state support by a Lutheran clergyman from the Baltic region in 1705, soon failed for lack of students. When the government tried to institute compulsory elementary education in the provinces by requiring the establishment of two schools in each province (1714), emphasis was put upon on mathematics and navigation, and the attempt was a failure. Part of the difficulty came from the government's inexperience and unwillingness to begin with primary education. This was left to the church schools, which were few and on the whole not very competent. Parental reluctance to see their children "wasting their time" in school reflected the absence of an educational tradition in Russia. At the highest level, as elsewhere, foreigners had to be summoned to provide Russia with scholars.

An Academy of Sciences founded just before Peter's death began with seventeen imported fellows, and eight students, also all imported. But probably the mere presence in the new capital of these exotic academies helped to stimulate the native intellectual developments that would charac-

[*] Quoted by E. Schuyler, *Peter the Great* (New York, 1884), II, 389.

terize the next generation. Such tokens as the first Russian newspaper (1703) and the printing of occasional textbooks also augured well for the future.

Peter of course continued the practice, begun long before him, of importing foreign technicians and artisans to practice their crafts and teach them to Russians. Peter quite understood the mercantilist ideas of the age. Offering great inducements, such as freedom from taxation and from government service, and all sorts of tariff protection, the Russians sought to develop manufacturing. Native Russian merchants entered the game as well. Though sometimes employing a substantial number of laborers, industrial enterprise in Russia, chiefly textiles and iron, continued to be backward. The labor force was recruited among unwilling and badly treated serfs and criminals. The factory-owning merchants were permitted to own and buy and sell serfs (otherwise a privilege restricted to the gentry) provided the serfs were attached to the plant in question, and provided they were always bought or sold as a body together with the factory itself. This was "possessional" industrial serfdom, hardly a system likely to provide much incentive to do good work. Russian produce continued inferior to comparable goods manufactured abroad. In the commercial field, Peter's heavy protective tariffs discriminated against foreign goods, encouraging smuggling and false registration of foreign agents as Russian nationals. The effort to make Russia a manufacturing nation exporting its own produce was a failure. But we must note that Peter's conquests in the Baltic did give Russia the great port of Riga, and that he successfully bent every effort to make St. Petersburg into a great trading center.

The Total Estimate

The records of Peter's secret police are full of the bitter complaints his agents heard as they moved about among the population listening for subversive remarks. The wives and children of the peasantry found themselves deserted by the men of the family, snatched away to fight on distant battlefields or to labor in the swamps to build a city nobody wanted. Serfs found their number increasing with the imposition of the new soul-tax and the multiplication of land-grants to service men. The tax burden was back-breaking. Service men found themselves in a kind of bondage of their own, condemned to work for the Tsar during the whole of their lives and seldom able to visit their estates. Nobles of ancient birth found themselves treated no differently from the upstarts who were flooding into their class from below. Churchmen of the conservative school were more and more convinced that Peter was the anti-Christ himself, as they beheld the number of foreigners in high places multiply ever more rapidly, and saw the many innovations imported into the government and social life from the hated West. Rumors circulated that this was not the true Tsar at all, but a changeling somehow substituted for the real Peter by the foreigners during the trip abroad, and sent back to persecute Russians and ruin Russia.

Among the lower orders of society resistance took the usual form: peasant uprisings, punished with fantastic brutality. The usual allies of the peasant rebels, the Cossacks, suffered sharp curtailment of their traditional independence and mass executions. Among the upper orders, the leaders of the noble and clerical opposition focused their hopes on Peter's son by his first wife, the young heir to the throne, Alexis, who, they hoped, would stop the expensive and (they felt) needless foreign wars, and move back to Moscow and comfortable Russian conservatism.

Alexis, an alcoholic, was afraid of his father, and was early estranged from him. Though not stable enough to lead a true conspiracy against Peter, he fanned the hopes of the opposition by letting them know he shared their views. Eventually he caused a scandal by fleeing abroad and asking asylum from his brother-in-law, the Austrian Emperor Charles VI. Promising him fair treatment and forgiveness, Peter lured Alexis back to Russia and made him the show-piece of one of those horrible Russian investigations of nonexistent plots. Many were tortured, killed, and exiled; and in the end Alexis himself was tortured to death in his father's presence.

In the early nineteenth century, when the first self-conscious group of Russian intellectuals came to develop a keen interest in the past history of their country, they made a central figure of Peter. He had, they felt, intensified western influences on Russian society, and had thus turned his back on Russia's peculiarly Slavic character and her Byzantine heritage. One group hailed these actions as necessary and inevitable in putting Russia on her proper course. Its opponents damned Peter for having forced an unnatural development upon his country, and for having warped its social and political life by imposing an alien pattern and interfering with the proper Russian ways of life. But both his friends and his enemies among these later intellectuals believed, as

most scholars have since argued, that what he did was drastic and revolutionary.

Yet we can see that Peter simply intensified the chief characteristics of Russian society. He made a strong autocracy even stronger, a universal service law for service men even more stringent, a serf more of a serf. His trip abroad, his fondness for foreign ways, his worship of advanced technology, his mercantilism, his wars, all had their precedents in the period of his forerunners. The Church, which he attacked, had already been weakened by the schism of the Old Believers, itself the result of western influences. Where Peter was radical was in the field of everyday manners and behavior: the attack on the beards, the dress, the calendar (he adopted the western dating from the birth of Christ and abandoned the traditional dating from a hypothetical year of the creation), his hatred of ceremony and fondness for manual labor, these things were indeed new. So too were the vigor and passion with which he acted. They were decisive in winning a revolutionary reputation for a monarch who in the major aspects of his reign was carrying out policies long since established.

IV: *The Ottoman Successor-State, 1453-1699*

The Osmanlis' far-distant past in Central Asia may well have given them their fondness and capacity for war and their rigid adherence to custom, as it did their native Turkish language. From the Persians and the Byzantines, they seem to have derived the exaltation of the ruler, the tolerance of religious groups outside the state religion, and the practice of encouraging such groups to form independent communities inside the state. Persian was always the literary language and the source of Turkish literature, both in form and in content. From Islam, the Turks took the sacred

law and their approach to legal problems, the Arabic alphabet in which they wrote their Turkish tongue, and the Arabic vocabulary of religious, philosophical, and other abstract terms. All the well-springs of their inheritance—Asian, Persian-Byzantine, and Moslem—tended to make them an exceptionally conservative people.

A Slave System

The most unusual feature of Ottoman society was the advancement of slaves to the highest positions within the state. This practice was not original with the Ottoman Turks, but their slave system of government reached a height never approached by any other important state. Except for the sultan himself, all the high officials of government, and of the sultan's household, as well as all the officers of the army and large bodies of picked troops, were slaves, almost always the children of Christians. They were picked in their early youth for their promising appearance and were especially educated for the sultan's service. As slaves, they owed all advancement to the sultan, and could be instantly removed from office and punished by death at any moment in their careers.

Since the sultan was entitled to one-fifth of all prisoners of war, he selected many of his slaves from that source. Sometimes they were bought, or were given as presents to the sultan. But perhaps a third or more were obtained through the regular levying of the "tribute of children" in the Balkan Christian provinces of the Ottoman Empire. Every four years until the early seventeenth century, specially trained officers, each with a quota of places to fill, visited the Balkan villages and selected and took away the strongest and ablest-appearing Slavic or Albanian youths, usually between fourteen and eighteen years of age. This practice has always aroused the natural horror of Christians. Yet two considerations make it less dreadful than it would seem at first. Since a married boy was ineligible, marriage was always an escape. Then too, unlimited opportunity for advancement within the system was open to the boys chosen. In poverty-stricken and remote Balkan villages, it is likely that being chosen was sometimes regarded as a positive privilege. We know of actual cases in which Moslem families paid Christian parents to take their sons and pass them off as Christian in the hope that they would be selected.

Once taken, all these youths were converted to Islam. Some resisted conversion, or had certain reservations; occasionally one of them escaped. But most of them seem to have become good Moslems or to have been indifferent to religious matters. The Turks felt conversion to be absolutely essential before the youths were given "federal employment." The system thus fulfilled the missionary zeal of Islam, and provided administrators and soldiers for the state. In theory, no born Moslem could ever be recruited into the system, since the law said that no born Moslem could be a slave. This limited the choice to born Christians, and in theory meant that no child of a member of the system would be eligible to enter it himself. The sons of members would often be given grants of land (fiefs), obliged to render military service, and thus transferred out of the system.

This ruling class of slaves was carefully educated. Of the seven or eight thousand chosen annually, all received systematic physical and military training. About one-tenth received higher education, and the very cream of the crop became pages in the sultan's own household and attended his palace school, where they were taught languages, Moslem and Turkish law, ethics and theology, horsemanship and military service. They were given an allowance, which was increased every year, and were carefully watched to see how their talents were developing. All left school at the age of twenty-five, and the graduates of the picked schools were then given jobs in the administration; the rest became *spahis* or cavalry forces. There was always plenty of room for advancement, since many were killed in war, and at the top levels many were demoted, dismissed, or executed for inefficiency or disloyalty. A typical career is that of one sixteenth-century Slav who graduated from the page corps as a gatekeeper, advanced to chief taster to the sultan, moved into the cavalry and became a general, was promoted to equerry, assigned to command the janissaries, sent to Europe and then to Egypt as provincial governor, and then passed through the three grades of vizier, finishing his career as grand vizier, the very top office of the state.

At the lower level, the less intelligent slaves were often farmed out for agricultural work in Asia Minor on some estate, and then drafted into the so-called janissary troops (from the Turkish words *yeni cheri*, "new forces"). Their training emphasized physical endurance, and they served not only in the army but as shipyard workers, palace gardeners, and the like. At the height of Turkish military successes, these measures produced formidable armies, sometimes amounting to more than a quarter of a million men on the march. Fearless in battle, they were the terror of all opponents. An ambassador from the Habsburgs who spent eight years in Constantinople in the 1500's compares their endurance favorably with that of European troops. The Turks, he says,

. . . take out a few spoonfuls of flour and put them into water, adding some butter, and seasoning the mess with salt and spices; these ingredients are boiled and a large bowl of gruel is thus obtained. Of this they eat once or twice a day. . . . In this way they are able to support themselves from their own supplies for a month or if necessary longer. Some fill a bladder with beef, dried, and reduced to powder which forms a highly nutritious food and expands greatly in the cooking. . . . Sometimes too they have recourse to horseflesh; dead horses are of course plentiful in their great hosts. . . . From this you will see that it is the patience, self-denial, and thrift of the Turkish soldier that enable him to face the most trying circumstances and come safely out of the dangers that surround him. What a contrast to our men! Christian soldiers on a campaign refuse to put up with their ordinary food and call for thrushes, and other such like dainty dishes. If these are not supplied, they grow mutinous and work their own ruin; and if they are supplied, they are ruined just the same. . . . It makes me shudder to think what the result of a struggle between such different systems can be. . . . On their side is the vast wealth of their empire, unimpaired resources, experience and practice in arms, a veteran soldiery, an uninterrupted series of victories,

readiness to endure hardships, union, order, discipline, thrift, and watchfulness. On ours are found an empty exchequer, luxurious habits, exhausted resources, broken spirits, a raw and insubordinate soldiery, and greedy generals; there is no regard for discipline, license runs riot, the men indulge in drunkenness and debauchery, and worst of all, the enemy is accustomed to victory, we, to defeat. Can we doubt what the result must be? *

The sultan's harem was a part of the slave institution, since all the women in it were slaves, together with all their household staffs and entertainers. The sultan's consorts, as slaves, gave birth to the heir to the empire, so that each new sultan was always by birth half-slave. Every official, who was himself a slave, had a slave-family of his own in miniature, and often received as a wife one of the members of the sultan's harem who had not been chosen as a consort. In Ottoman society there was no color line, and slavery carried no social taint. Rather, it was regarded as an accident of fortune. Relations between masters and slaves were often friendly, and masters often set their slaves free as a reward for service. The sultan picked his favorite, not necessarily his eldest, son to succeed him, and there was a law that the heir to the throne must kill all his brothers and half-brothers upon his accession. Every son of a sultan knew all the time he was growing up that he either must obtain the throne himself or be killed by whichever of his brothers or half-brothers did obtain it. In 1595, for instance, Mohammed III killed no fewer than nineteen brothers and half-brothers when he came to the throne.

The "Four Pillars" of Administration

Turkish writers thought of the state as a tent resting on four pillars. The first was the viziers, varying in num-

---

* O. G. Busbecq, *Turkish Letters*, C. T. Forster and F. H. B. Daniell, trans. (London, 1881), I, 220-221.

ber, to whom the sultan actually delegated many powers. The viziers presided over the council of state, kept the great seal, and could sometimes make decisions on policy. The council of state had no legislative power, all of which was vested in the sultan, but it did debate administrative or judicial questions. The second pillar was the financial officers, organized to collect revenues throughout the provinces. These revenues included the poll tax on the Christians, a tenth of all produce, and many of the old Byzantine taxes on commerce, as well as special levies of all kinds, including money realized by confiscating the fortunes of disgraced officials. The third pillar was the chancery, a secretariat that affixed the sultan's signature to documents, and prepared, recorded, and transmitted them, whether they were statutes, diplomas, certificates of title, or appointments.

The fourth pillar, unlike the other three, was not a department of state manned by slaves born as Christians. It was the judges, who were all born Moslems, and thus part of the only non-slave portion of the Ottoman governing system. Islam itself had responsibility for all legal matters and for education. One-third of state lands were set aside as religious property. Each tract had its own purpose: the support of mosques, of charitable or educational institutions, and even of inns or public baths. Income from such property supported the entire class of *ulema*, learned men who were connected with Islam as an institution.

Among the *ulema* were the *muftis*, or jurists, who answered questions that arose in the course of lawsuits, and that were submitted to them by the judges. It was their function to apply the sacred law of Islam, and they usually gave short replies, without explanation. These replies settled the case. Thus they were a powerful class, and the *mufti* in Istanbul, whom the sultan himself consulted, was known as the *Sheikh-ul-Islam*, the ancient or elder of Islam, and outranked everybody but the grand vizier.

Since he could speak the final word on the sacred law, he may even be said to have exercised a kind of check on the absolute power of the sultan himself. He alone could proclaim the beginning of war, or denounce the sultan for transgression of the sacred law, and summon his subjects to depose him. The opinions of the *muftis* were collected as a body of interpretative law, lying between the changeless, age-old sacred law of Islam and the current enactments of the sultans. The general acceptance by all Moslems of the supremacy of the sacred law and the hostility of the *muftis* to change were two of the factors that accounted for the failure of the Ottoman system to develop with the times. There are no "reformations" in Turkish history until the twentieth century.

The fourth pillar of the tent, the judges, were all members of the *ulema*. They were assigned to the various regions of the empire. The chief justices for Europe and Asia were the two most important. These two were members of the council of state, the only two members who were born Moslems and non-slaves. Thus the council was the only place where the two chief Ottoman institutions were combined: the ruling institution of the sultan's slave-family that ran military affairs and civil affairs except for questions of law and justice, and the Moslem institution that ran religious, legal, and educational affairs. Of course, the sultan himself at the very top of the tent was the supreme head of both institutions.

Weaknesses of the Ottoman System

This remarkable system had inherent weaknesses, some of which leap instantly to the eye. First, the effectiveness of the entire structure depended upon the character of the sultan himself. The harem upbringing and the ruthless family antagonisms to which each sultan was exposed did not tend to produce sultans who could act as wise and mature statesmen. Rather, they produced weaklings, drunkards, debauchees, and men of little experience or political understanding. Harem intrigue played a great role in the state.

Second, efficient operation of the administration depended upon maintaining the slave-system by excluding the born Moslem sons of the members of the slave ruling class from participation, and upon recruiting only new slaves to do the work. But as a matter of actual practice this rigid exclusion broke down early, and born Moslems, often the sons of slaves high in the system who were attracted by the possibilities of gain and power, were admitted. These Moslems obviously could not be regarded as slaves, and the chief restraints and fears that kept the machine running thus disappeared. Incompetent sultans and insubordinate soldiers together sped the decay of the state. Turbulent janissaries frequently deposed the sultan, and chose his successor from the ruling house.

Third, the whole concept of fixed, immutable, sacred law helped produce a society without flexibility and unable to adjust to change. This was especially true of the increasingly important change brought about by the impact of the West on the Ottoman Empire. This inflexibility did not begin to be seriously felt until the eighteenth century, but it then became of critical importance.

Fourth, in a society where religion was the only test of nationality, all Orthodox Christians were automatically regarded as Greeks, and lived under the control of the Patriarch. In the nineteenth century this situation was to prove a serious weakness, since it alienated many Slavs and Rumanians who might otherwise have been loyal subjects. Moreover, the disabilities placed on Christians made it difficult for their talents to be used or their loyalties to be relied upon unless they were converted to Islam and became members of the slave-system.

Ottoman Expansion to 1566

With this as a background, let us briefly examine the actual fortunes of the Ottoman state after its conquest of Constantinople in 1453. By the end of the 1460's, most of the Balkan Peninsula had been consolidated under Turkish rule. Thus the core of the new Ottoman state was Asia Minor and the Balkans, the same core around which the Byzantine Empire had been built. From this core before the death of Mohammed II in 1481, the Turks expanded across the Danube into modern Rumania, seized the Genoese outposts in the Crimea, and made this southern Russian region a vassal state under its Tartar rulers. They also fought against the Venetians, and even landed forces in Italy. The limits of their expansion were marked by the great Hungarian-held fortress of Belgrade, key to a further advance into Central Europe, and the island fortress of Rhodes in the Mediterranean, stronghold of an order of knights dating back to the Crusades, and key to a further naval advance westward.

Sultan Selim (1512-1520) nearly doubled the territories of the empire, but almost exclusively in Asia and Africa. In 1517, he annexed Egypt, and inherited the duty of protecting Mecca and Medina. He also assumed the title of caliph, with the sacred insignia of office. At one moment in his reign, Selim contemplated a general massacre of all his Christian subjects, and was barely dissuaded from carrying it out. This episode vividly illustrates the precariousness of Christian life under the Turks. It also demonstrates that the character of the Ottoman state was substantially altered by the acquisition of so much territory. It was now no longer necessary to appease the Christians by generous treatment, because the overwhelming majority of the population was Moslem. Moreover, most of the newly acquired Moslems were Arabs, who were far more fanatical than the Ottoman Turks had hitherto been.

The advance into Europe was resumed in the reign of the next sultan, the greatest of them all: Suleiman the Magnificent (1522-1566), a contemporary of the western Emperor Charles V and of Francis I of France and Henry VIII of England. The Ottoman Empire now became deeply involved in western European affairs. It participated in the dynastic wars between the imperial house of Habsburg and the French Valois, and affected the course of the Protestant Reformation in Germany by the threat of military invasion from the southeast. The newly consolidated national monarchies of the West had begun to outclass the old European enemies of the Turks, the Venetians and the Hungarians. Charles V had inherited Spain and now had to face the naval attacks of the Ottoman fleets. His younger brother, Ferdinand, as ruler of the Austrian and later the Hungarian territories, bore the brunt of the Turkish attacks on land. Cheering the Turks on were the French. Even though their king was called "the eldest son of the Church," their wars against the Catholic Habsburgs came first.

In 1521, Suleiman took Belgrade, and in 1522 Rhodes, thus removing the two chief obstacles to westward advance. In 1526, at Mohács in Hungary, he defeated the Christian armies, and the Turks entered Buda, the Hungarian capital on the middle Danube. In September, 1529, Suleiman besieged Vienna itself, posing a grave threat to Christendom. But the Turkish lines of communication were greatly overextended, and Suleiman had to abandon the siege after two weeks. Finally, in 1533, Ferdinand recognized Suleiman as overlord of Hungary. In the years that followed, Suleiman made good his claim to actual control over the south-central portion of Hungary, and added other lands north and east of the Danube. In North Africa he acquired Algeria, which remained the center of Ottoman power in the western Mediterranean until the nineteenth century. In Asia he defeated the Persians, annexed modern Iraq, including Baghdad, and secured an outlet on the Persian Gulf. He even fought naval wars against the Portuguese in the Persian Gulf and the Indian Ocean.

In 1536, a formal treaty was concluded between France and the Ottoman Empire, the first of the famous "capitulations." It permitted the French to buy and sell throughout the Turkish dominions on the same basis as any Turk. They were allowed resident consuls with civil and criminal jurisdiction over Frenchmen in Turkey. In Turkish territory, the French were to enjoy complete religious liberty, and were also granted a protectorate over the Holy Places in Palestine, the old aim of the Crusades. This was a great advance in prestige for the Roman Catholic Church. The Orthodox Church never accepted this settlement, however, and it underlay the Crimean War in the nineteenth century (see below, Chapter XV). These "capitulations" gave the French a better position in the Ottoman Empire than that of any other European power and thus contributed immensely to the wealth and prestige of France. And their provisions parallel earlier Byzantine trade treaties with Venice and Genoa, beginning at the end of the eleventh century. In this respect, as in so many others, the Ottoman sultans were behaving as the successors of the Byzantine emperors.

Ottoman Decline, 1566-1699

After Suleiman, despite occasional periods of success, the Ottoman system deteriorated. The Ottoman capture of Cyprus in 1571 led to the formation of a western league against the Turks, headed by the pope, an enterprise as near to a crusade as the sixteenth century could produce. In 1571, the league won the great naval battle of Lepanto, off the Greek coast. It destroyed the Ottoman fleet but failed to follow up the victory, permitting the Turks to recover.

By the end of the century the sale of government offices had become a regular practice and the repeated rebellions of janissaries were jeopardizing the sultan's position. In 1606, a peace was signed that put an end to one of the perennial wars against the Habsburgs. Previously, all treaties with western states had been cast in the form of a truce granted as a divine favor from the sultan to a lesser potentate, and had been accompanied by a provision that the other party would pay tribute as part of the settlement. This time the Turks had to negotiate as equals. They gave the Habsburg emperor his proper title, and were unable to demand tribute.

Indeed, had it not been for the convulsion of the Thirty Years' War, which preoccupied the states of western Europe, the Ottoman Empire might have suffered even more severely in the first half of the seventeenth century than it did. As it was, internal anarchy rent the state; troops rioted

and several sultans were deposed within a few years; the Persians recaptured Baghdad; and rebellion raged in the provinces. In 1622, the British ambassador wrote to his government:

The Empire has become, like an old body, crazed through many vices. All the territory of the Sultan is dispeopled for want of justice, or rather by reason of violent oppression: so much so that in his best parts of Greece and Anatolia a man may ride three, four, and sometimes six days, and not find a village to feed him and his horse. The revenue is so lessened that there is not wherewithal to pay the soldiers and maintain the court.*

Here we are already encountering what nineteenth-century statesmen two hundred years later were still calling the "sick man of Europe."

Yet a firm sultan, Murad IV (1623-1640), temporarily restored order, though only

* Quoted by E. S. Creasey, *History of the Ottoman Turks* (London, 1854), I, 392-393.

GROWTH & DECLINE of OTTOMAN EMPIRE, 1300-1725

Ottoman Empire: ■ 1300 ▨ by 1451 ▧ by 1481 ☐ by 1683
— Boundary of Ottoman Empire, 1725 × Battle sites

through the most brutal means. Despite a temporary retrogression after his death, what looked like a real revival began with the accession to power of a distinguished family of viziers, the Köprülüs. The first Köprülü ruthlessly executed 36,000 people in a five-year period (1656-1661), hanged the Greek patriarch for predicting in a private letter that Christianity would defeat Islam, rebuilt the army and navy, and suppressed revolt. As a result, he succeeded in leaving the grand vizierate to his son in 1661. Between 1661 and 1676, the second Köprülü led the Ottoman navies to a triumph in Crete, which they took from Venice. They temporarily won large areas of the Ukraine from the Russians and Poles, only to lose them again in 1681. In 1683, the Turks again penetrated the heart of Europe, and again besieged Vienna, with all Europe anxiously awaiting the outcome. For the second time in two centuries, the Turkish wave was broken, and now Europe began a great counter-offensive against the Turks. Although the Köprülüs had galvanized the warlike Ottoman armies into a last successful effort, they could not touch the real evils of the Ottoman system.

Now the Habsburgs drove the Turks out of Hungary, and the Venetians seized the Greek Peloponnesus. The Turks needed peace. In 1699, after an international congress at Karlovitz on the Danube, most of the gains of the European counter-offensive were recognized. The great territorial losses suffered by the Turks, the strengthening of the Habsburgs to the east, and the appearance of Russia as an important enemy of the Turks all stamp this settlement as a landmark. The western European powers could henceforth stop worrying about the Ottoman menace, which had preoccupied them ever since the fourteenth century, and which had replaced the Crusades as a great cause for which Christendom could occasionally be united. From now on, the importance of Turkey is no longer its military potential, but its diplomatic position as a power in decline over whose possible disintegration and division the states of Europe might squabble and negotiate. With Karlovitz, what we call the "eastern question" may be said to have begun.

The Subject Peoples

The Christian peoples of the Ottoman Empire, though all subject to the disabilities of Christians in Moslem states, did not experience a uniform fate during the long centuries of foreign domination. In Constantinople, for example, the Greeks came to enjoy a special status. Their patriarch, with his jurisdiction over all the Orthodox Christians of the empire, had his residence there, and around his court men of wealth and desire for influence congregated and intrigued. Endowed with a talent for sailing and for commerce, individual Greeks began to emerge as wealthy magnates as early as the sixteenth century, doing business for the sultan and enjoying various lucrative monopolies. By the time of the Habsburg counter-offensive after 1683, the Turkish authorities had come to realize that they must also have trained diplomats. In the last quarter of the seventeenth century, Greeks began to hold the post of chief assistant to the Grand Admiral of the Turkish fleet, and also the post of "chief interpreter," which amounted in fact to that of Secretary of State for Foreign Affairs. At Karlovitz itself in 1699 the chief Ottoman representative was Dr. Alexander Mavrogordato, a Greek from the island of Chios, a brilliant physician and a skillful diplomat. When the conference was on the point of breaking down because the diplomats could not decide who should enter the conference chamber first and who should sit above whom at the conference table, Dr. Mavrogordato rescued the whole meeting by proposing a round pavilion with a door for each delegate, and a round table with chair for each. Each entered at his own door at the same moment; nobody sat above anybody else.

After the battle of the Pruth (1711), the Sultan also appointed Greeks to rule over the Danubian principalities of Moldavia and Wallachia. But the peoples of the principalities (the Rumanians) lived in wretched ignorance and squalor, oppressed first by their native princes and then by the Greek rulers, both subject to the sultan. The lot of the Slavic subjects in the Balkans, the Serbs and Bulgarians, was not much better. The Serbs did preserve a certain independence in their own villages, dealing with the Ottoman authorities through elected head-men, and developing a tradition of sturdy rural life without an aristocracy. They were deeply devoted to their native church, which had been revived independent of the Greeks in 1557, and they suffered severely when they assisted the Habsburgs against the Ottoman Empire. Many thousands of Serbs emigrated into Habsburg territory in southern Hungary to escape persecution. Here they had their own patriarchate, and served as a source of inspiration and enlightenment for their brothers who still lived under the Turks. Closest to Constantinople and most thoroughly subjugated, the Bulgarians probably had the hardest lot of all. Yet in each of these peoples lay the seeds of a keen consciousness of national identity, needing only the discovery of their own past to take root and grow into a tangled jungle of national ambitions.

Reading Suggestions on the Eastern Outposts

Byzantium and Islam

A. A. Vasiliev, *History of the Byzantine Empire, 324-1453* (Madison: Univ. of Wisconsin Press, 1952). The standard comprehensive work in English.

E. Pears, *The Destruction of the Greek Empire and the Story of the Capture of Constantinople by the Turks* (London: Longmans, Green, 1903). A solid work on the last days of the Byzantine Empire.

A. Grabar, *Byzantine Painting* (N.Y.: Skira, 1953). Superb reproductions of mosaics and frescoes; a good introduction to the Byzantine "style."

H. A. R. Gibb, *Mohammedanism: An Historical Survey* (N.Y.: New American Library, 1955. A Mentor Book). A useful essay by the greatest western authority on the subject in our day.

P. K. Hitti, *History of the Arabs from the Earliest Times to the Present*, 6th ed. (N.Y.: St. Martin's, 1956). A full-length treatment, useful for reference.

A. Atiyah, *The Arabs* (Harmondsworth, Middlesex: Penguin Books, 1955). A readable popular introduction, though inaccurate in some details.

G. Ostrogorsky, *The History of the Byzantine State* (Oxford: Blackwell, 1956). A first rate general study.

Russia

V. O. Kluchevsky, *A History of Russia*, 5 vols. (London: Dent, 1911-1931). The greatest single work on Russian history, unfortunately translated poorly.

M. Florinsky, *Russia: A History and an Interpretation*, Vol. I (N.Y.: Macmillan, 1953). A good textbook, very solid and accurate.

E. Schuyler, *Peter the Great*, 2 vols. (N.Y.: Scribner's, 1884). An old but excellent work by an American diplomat and scholar.

B. H. Sumner, *Peter the Great and the Emergence of Russia* (N.Y.: Macmillan, 1951. Teach Yourself History Library). A very good introductory manual.

B. H. Sumner, *Peter the Great and the Ottoman Empire* (Oxford: Blackwell, 1949). A scholarly short monograph on Russo-Turkish relations.

D. Merejkowski, *Peter and Alexis* (N.Y.: Putnam's, 1905). A most interesting novel, dramatizing the conflict between the great Tsar and his son, who opposed Peter's westernizing policies.

The Ottoman Empire

E. S. Creasy, *History of the Ottoman Turks*, 2 vols. (London, 1854-1856). Despite its age, still a good general account; based on a ten-volume German work.

P. Wittek, *The Rise of the Ottoman Empire* (London: Royal Asiatic Society, 1938). A suggestive essay on the elements that helped to advance the Ottoman state.

A. H. Lybyer, *The Government of the Ottoman Empire in the Time of Suleiman the Magnificent*

(Cambridge: Harvard Univ. Press, 1913). A fundamental work on the institutions of the empire.

B. Miller, *Beyond the Sublime Porte* (New Haven: Yale Univ. Press, 1931), and *The Palace School of Mohammed the Conqueror* (Cambridge: Harvard Univ. Press, 1941). Studies of the Ottoman imperial palace and the Ottoman educational system, respectively.

Kritovulos, *History of Mehmed the Conqueror*, C. T. Riggs, trans. (Princeton: Princeton Univ. Press, 1954). The life of Emperor Mohammed II written by a Greek.

D. M. Vaughan, *Europe and the Turk: A Pattern of Alliances, 1350-1700* (Liverpool: Univ. of Liverpool Press, 1954). A compact and interesting study.

The Life and Letters of Ogier Ghiselin de Busbecq, C. T. Forster and F. H. Blackburne Daniell, eds., 2 vols. (London: C. K. Paul, 1881). Perceptive and amusing reports of a Habsburg ambassador to Suleiman the Magnificent.

J. C. Hurewitz, ed., *Diplomacy in the Near and Middle East: A Documentary Record, 1535-1914* (Princeton: Van Nostrand, 1956). A most helpful compilation.

H. A. Gibbons, *The Foundation of the Ottoman Empire* (N.Y.: Century, 1916). A useful work, the first to emphasize the importance of the European contribution to the Ottoman amalgam.

CHAPTER EIGHT

The Eighteenth Century:

The International Balance

I: Introduction: The Prospect in 1715

Long years of peace and quiet appeared to be in prospect for Europe in 1715. In the Baltic, as we have seen, the Great Northern War was nearing a settlement, to be reached in 1721. In the West, the Peace of Utrecht, signed in 1713, had restored the balance of power and had ended Louis XIV's attempt to extend French dominance. The death of the Sun King himself in 1715 gave fresh promise of international stability, for the crown of France passed to his great-grandson, Louis XV, a boy of five. A long regency was necessary, and a long regency meant that France would probably be too preoccupied with internal problems to play the aggressor. In many western states, moreover, government debts had mounted alarmingly. The great conflicts of Louis XIV had exhausted his own nation and had brought even his victorious opponents to the edge of bankruptcy.

In 1715 the forms of government in

Europe ranged from absolute monarchy, as in France and Russia, to the constitutional monarchy of Britain and the republics of the Swiss and the Dutch. The differences among these forms are important, but they should not conceal the fact that all governments in those days represented the interests of the privileged few. We shall see that almost every European state showed some of the characteristics of oligarchy. Historians use the term "Old Régime" to describe the oligarchical institutions of western Europe, particularly France; it was the Old Régime of the eighteenth century in contrast to the "new" régime issuing from the French Revolution of 1789.

In some respects, the Old Régime marked a radical change from the still older régime of the Middle Ages. Medieval Christian ideals had receded before the "classical spirit" of the seventeenth century (see above, Chapter VI); they would recede still further under the impact of the great eighteenth-century cultural and intellectual movement termed the Enlightenment. In western Europe, the great majority of peasants had long ago cast off the bonds of serfdom, and the bourgeoisie had partly overcome the medieval prejudice against commoners. And yet the Old Régime was often still close to the Middle Ages. Most Europeans of the eighteenth century lived in farming villages and retained their traditional parochial outlook; only a few had a real sense of nationalism, a sense of belonging to a larger entity transcending the local or provincial unit. The Old Régime had its social foundations firmly based on the medieval division of society into the first estate of the clergy, the second estate of the nobility, and the third estate of everybody else. Peasants, merchants, craftsmen, and other members of the third estate had improved their lot since the Middle Ages, but most of them still remained within the great majority of the underprivileged. Only the wealthier bourgeois families enjoyed a voice in politics. Europe had always been in the main agrarian, parochial, and oligarchical; in 1715, it seemed likely to remain so forever.

The Old Régime, however, did not last forever. Its apparent stability was deceptive, and by the middle of the eighteenth century its foundations were beginning to crumble under the pressure of revolutionary economic changes. At the same time, the leaders of the Enlightenment were voicing the demands for reform that culminated in the great French Revolution of 1789. The international balance established at Utrecht likewise proved unstable. The defeat of Louis XIV had not ended the world-wide rivalry of France and Britain, which again provoked a war in 1740. Meantime, Russia was moving from semi-isolation to take an active and often an aggressive part in international affairs, and the once obscure German state of Prussia was emerging as a first-rate military power, intent on expansion.

II: *The Economic Revolutions in the West*

Three great sets of economic changes—in commerce, in agriculture, and in industry—helped to undermine the Old Régime and to alter the European balance. These were in fact economic revolutions, slower and less dramatic than political revolutions, but in the long run every bit as revolutionary in their effects upon human history. All three, of course, continued after the close of the eighteenth century, and we shall return to examine them again in the nineteenth century (see Chapter XIII). Between 1715 and 1789 the commercial revolution was the most mature of the three. It extended to almost every European country, and it profoundly influenced war, politics, and society. In comparison, the agricultural and industrial revolutions were still in their infancy; yet they were lusty infants, already providing farms and workshops with new techniques.

The Commercial Revolution

The basic institutions of the commercial revolution had developed before 1715. Banking and insurance houses dated back to the Renaissance and beyond, and chartered trading companies dated back to the sixteenth century. Mercantilism, the philosophy underlying the policies of government toward commerce, had matured in the Spain of Philip II and the France of Louis XIV and Colbert. The steady growth of trade in the eighteenth century, however, quickened the pace of the commercial revolution. The record-breaking volume of trade, for example, increased the demand for insurance on ships and cargoes. The insurance brokers of eighteenth-century London, like many other businessmen, often gathered in coffee houses to discuss business, news, and politics. Specialists in marine insurance gravitated to Edward Lloyd's coffee house in Lombard Street and continued to meet there after Lloyd himself died in 1713. Thus was born Lloyd's of London. The name stuck, even after the firm moved from the coffee house to more dignified quarters in 1774. Lloyd's developed the standard form of policy for marine insurance and published *Lloyd's List*, the first detailed and accurate shipping newspaper.

Meantime, other aids to commerce were appearing. The improvement of charts and the installation of lighthouses and buoys made navigation safer. At sea, captains learned to determine their geographical position by using two new instruments, the sextant and the chronometer. The sextant, an elaboration of the telescope, showed the altitude of the sun at noon and thus indicated the ship's latitude. Whereas ordinary clocks behaved erratically because of the motion of the ship, the chronometer ran very accurately. It was kept on Greenwich Mean Time (the time at the meridian running through Greenwich near London). The two new instruments made it possible to calculate the ship's longitude, which represented the difference between Greenwich Mean Time and the local time aboard ship, calculated at noon with the sextant.

On land, the improvements in communication and transport came much more slowly than they did at sea. Except for the good highways of France, European roads were scarcely better than paths or trails. The shipment of goods overland remained slow, unsafe, and expensive until after 1750, when the construction of turnpikes and canals gradually eased the situation. The pioneer English canal, built in 1759-1761 by the Duke of Bridgewater, cut in half the cost of moving coal from the mines on his estate to the new factory town of Manchester. This was the beginning of the revolution in transport, which culminated after 1800 in the hard-surfaced highway and the railroad.

Businessmen also faced the handicaps resulting from restrictive guild regulations and from the inconvenience and profusion of local weights, measures, coins, and tolls. Sweden, for example, used copper for coins of all denominations, including a monstrosity weighing 43 pounds. Baden, one of the smaller German states, had 112 separate measures for length, 65 for dry goods, 123 for liquids, and 163 for cereals, not to mention 80 different pound weights. Even in France, where Louis XIV had expected all things to be uniform and centralized, all sorts of local taxes and other obstacles to internal trade persisted.

Economic reformers attacked most of these anachronisms before 1789, but they won only an occasional victory, notably in standardizing and simplifying money. The success or failure of a state in its battle against guild restrictions and local taxes was an important matter, directly affecting its prosperity. In England, which had long been a unified national state, economic localism was dying, and trade thrived. In disunited Germany, on the other hand, commerce languished; presumably few merchants had the patience to master the weights and measures of Baden.

The survival of local vested interests showed the limitations upon the power of the mercantilist state. Mercantilism meant that trade should be regulated on the national, rather than the local, level. But no eighteenth-century government, not even the English, possessed the staff of officials needed to make national regulation effective; states had to rely heavily on private companies and individuals to execute most of their policies. Thus the English East India Company exercised not only a trading monopoly in its colonial preserve but also virtual sovereign powers. Inventors worked on their own, not in government laboratories, although occasionally, under the pressure of business groups, the state offered prizes on matters of critical importance. The English Parliament promised £20,000 for the invention of a reliable "sea-going" clock; even so, the inventor of the chronometer had to wait twenty-five years to collect his prize money.

The Mississippi and South Sea Bubbles

This contrast between private enterprise and governmental sluggishness is best illustrated by two speculative booms of the early eighteenth century—the "Mississippi Bubble" in France and the "South Sea Bubble" in England. In 1715, hardly a state in Europe could manage the large debts that had piled up during the recent wars. Yet every state had to find some way of meeting at least a part of the large annual interest on its bonds and other debts, or else go bankrupt. The governments of France and England chose the way of experiment. They shifted responsibility for the management of state debts to joint-stock companies, which they rewarded with trading concessions. The commerce of the companies, it was hoped, would prove so lucrative that their profits would easily cover the interest charges on government bonds.

John Law (1671-1729) presided over the experiment in France. He was a Scottish mathematical wizard who studied monetary problems and banking methods, especially in Amsterdam, then the commercial capital of Europe. Law was a mercantilist, but with a difference. He agreed with the doctrine that the strength of a state depended upon the quantity of money it possessed. But, he asserted, the limited supply of silver and gold made it difficult to increase the amount of specie circulating in any country and therefore difficult to promote business. Paper money, Law concluded, was the solution—paper money backed by a nation's wealth in land and in trade. The quantity of paper money in circulation could easily be raised or lowered in accordance with the needs of business. Trading companies would prosper as never before, the whole country would prosper, and, in the midst of the general prosperity, government debts would be paid off.

On the death of Louis XIV, Law secured an opportunity to try his "system." His gambling crony, the Duke of Orléans, now Regent of France (1715-1723), permitted him to set up a central bank in Paris. The value of French money had been sinking steadily because the government debased the coinage. Law's bank, following the practice of the Bank of Amsterdam, issued paper notes of stable value; business activity was at once stimulated. Next, Law set up the Mississippi Company, which received a monopoly of commerce with the Louisiana colony and soon absorbed the other French colonial trading companies.

Law's system now reached to almost every corner of the French economy, and Law himself, appointed controller-general, became the economic dictator of the kingdom. His company took over the government debt, agreeing to accept government bonds in partial payment for shares of Mississippi stock. Many bondholders responded enthusiastically to Law's offer, for the bonds had depreciated to 20 per cent or less of their face value. Law, however, had to sell additional shares of Mississippi stock in order to obtain sufficient working capital for his company. To attract cash purchasers, he painted the company's prospects in brightest colors; in short, Law deliberately promoted a boom in Mississippi stock. Investors, large and small, caught the fever of speculation, and by the close of 1719 Mississippi stock was selling at forty times its par value.

The Mississippi Bubble soon burst, for Law's paper money could not stand the strain. As the price of Mississippi shares rose higher and higher, cautious investors became convinced that the boom could not last and decided to cash in. They sold their shares, received payment in banknotes, then took the notes to Law's bank and demanded their redemption in specie. The bank exhausted its reserves of gold and silver and suspended specie payments in February, 1720. Law was forced to relinquish the post of controller-general in May, 1720; he fled France shortly thereafter.

The Mississippi Bubble had international repercussions, for within a few weeks of Law's resignation the South Sea Bubble burst in London. It might have been expected that management of the English government's debt would devolve upon the Bank of England. Founded in 1694 as a private institution (it was fully nationalized only after World War II), the Bank of England issued banknotes and performed other valuable services in the last wars against Louis XIV. The debt, however, was taken over not by the Bank but by the new South Sea Company, which paid the government the exorbitant sum of more than seven and a half million pounds. The resources of the South Sea Company were slim; they consisted largely of the right to exploit the trading concessions that Britain obtained under the Asiento agreement at the end of the War of the Spanish Succession. These privileges were limited to furnishing Spain's American colonies with 4800 slaves annually and to sending one ship a year to Panama for general trade.

The South Sea Company, like the Mississippi, invited government creditors to transfer their bonds into company stock. To push up the price of the stock and thus attract fresh capital, its directors encouraged purchasers to buy stock with a down payment of only 10 per cent in cash, and spread false reports of forthcoming sailings by the company's ships on voyages of unparalleled promise. South Sea shares, with a par value of £100, sold for £129 in January of 1720, and for £1050 in June. Dozens of other promoters sprang into action, advertising schemes for wheels of perpetual motion, for making salt water fresh, "for carrying on an undertaking of great advantage, but nobody to know what it is." The gullibility of the investing public was remarkable, but it was not inexhaustible. South Sea shares slipped to £150 in September, 1720. Parliament now ordered an investigation of the company and, to protect the company's creditors, seized the estates of the South Sea directors.

The two bubbles produced some unfortunate results. The collapse of the Mississippi scheme ruined Law, whose talents, if used more discreetly, might have arrested the financial paralysis of the French government. In England, the South Sea fiasco long impeded the development of new stock companies, which were henceforth required to buy costly charters. It tarnished the reputations of many in high places. The mistresses of George I and the King himself had been "let in on the ground floor" and had endorsed the venture too enthusiastically. More than a hundred members of Parliament had borrowed money from the company in order to buy its shares on the installment plan.

The bubbles, however, were not unmitigated misfortunes. They were the growing pains of the European economy, of states groping for solutions to new and baffling financial problems. As Voltaire later declared, Law's "imaginary system gave birth to a real commerce," and France became more prosperous. The Mississippi Company, reorganized after 1720, consistently made a handsome profit. In England, the South Sea Bubble scarcely affected the strongest institutions. The East India Company went right on paying an annual dividend of 5 to 10 per cent. The Bank of England, no longer competing with the South Sea Company for government favors, became more than ever the financial mainstay of the realm. In the political shake-up following the Bubble, the Whig statesman, Robert Walpole (see p. 255), came to power with a program of honoring the debt as a *national* debt. This was a novel concept and a great step forward in fiscal morality in an age when most states still treated their debts as the monarch's personal obligation, to be recognized or repudiated as he saw fit.

The Agricultural Revolution

The agricultural revolution, the second of the great changes transforming the economy of the modern world, has centered on technological improvements that enable fewer farmers to produce more crops. The application of scientific discoveries to agriculture is actually an old story, as old as the irrigation ditches of ancient Mesopotamia and the improved plows and horse-collars of the Middle Ages. What was new and revolutionary in the eighteenth century was the tempo: for the first time the advance in farming techniques began to move at a rapid rate. The leaders of the movement were the "improving landlords" of England, notably Jethro Tull, Viscount Townshend, Robert Bakewell, and Arthur Young.

Jethro Tull (1674-1741) studied the painstaking methods used in French truck-gardens and vineyards, where farmers obtained a heavy yield from small plots by planting seeds individually and by carefully hoeing the soil around each plant and vine. Tull adapted French methods to the much larger grain fields of England. Instead of scattering seed broadcast, he planted it deeply in regular rows with a horse-drawn "drilling" machine, and he cultivated his crops with a horse-drawn hoe.

Viscount Townshend (1674-1738) used his Norfolk estate to experiment with two valuable new crops brought in from Holland—turnips and clover. By storing sufficient turnips to feed all the livestock until the arrival of the spring pasturing season, Townshend avoided the customary slaughter of stock at the onset of winter. Clover, by fixing nitrogen in the soil, increased the fertility of the land and curtailed the wasteful practice of letting fields lie fallow every third year. "Turnip" Townshend's four-year rotation—planting the same field to turnips, barley, clover, and wheat, in successive years—soon became the standard procedure on many English estates.

Robert Bakewell (1725-1795) applied scientific principles to raising livestock. Before Bakewell's time, most farm animals were gaunt and tough creatures. Bakewell inbred selected strains of sheep, doubled the average weight of his stock, and marketed lamb and mutton of really appetizing quality. Although a critic complained that Bakewell's meat was "too expensive to buy and too fat to eat," his methods were widely copied.

Arthur Young (1741-1820) became the great publicist of the new agriculture.

Gifted with a rare capacity for traveling, observing, and reporting, he began to make systematic trips through the farming districts of the British Isles and the Continent. In one five-year period, during the late 1760's and early '70's, he produced more than a dozen volumes on agrarian practices and economic problems. Campaigning for the innovations of Tull and Townshend, Young put his arguments so persuasively and entertainingly that he soon gained an international reputation.

Essentially, the agricultural revolution was an important stage in the evolution from the largely self-sufficient medieval manor to the modern capitalist farm producing specialized crops for the market. The techniques recommended by the improving landlords of the eighteenth century were capitalistic, since they required a large investment of money. They also required large plots of land unencumbered by such traditional practices as the utilization of fields in common by many individuals and the subdivision of fields into long, narrow strips ill-suited to the new agriculture. The improving landlords therefore demanded that the common fields be enclosed, fenced off as the private land of an individual proprietor. England had already experienced a great enclosure movement in Tudor days, when enclosures had extended privately owned sheep pastures (see above, p. 38). The new movement was directed chiefly at increasing the land available for planting and growing crops. It reached its peak in the last decades of the eighteenth century and the first decades of the nineteenth, when Parliament passed hundreds of separate enclosure acts affecting several million acres. Rural England was assuming its modern aspect of large fields fenced by hedgerows.

From the standpoint of social welfare, enclosures brought unhappy results. The development of large capitalistic estates ruined many small farmers, who could not afford to install fences, buy tools, and become improving landlords. And enclosures forced some of them to seek work in the towns. From the standpoint of agrarian productivity, however, enclosures marked a great step forward. They promoted the creation of large farms well suited to the application of drill-planting, horse-hoeing, and crop rotation. Britain, in consequence, as yet experienced no difficulty in feeding her growing population.

The Beginnings of the Industrial Revolution

By increasing farm output yet releasing part of the labor force for jobs off the farm, the agricultural revolution was assisting the industrial revolution. Industry required, further, raw materials for its factories, markets for its manufactures, and capital to finance the building of factories and to equip them with machines. The raw materials and the markets were supplied in part by the colonies overseas, and the capital in part by merchants. Thus the commercial revolution, too, assisted the industrial revolution.

Some of the elements that made for industrial change had first appeared at the close of the Middle Ages. To take an example from textiles, the making of yarn and cloth had long been organized according to the "domestic system," in which spinners or weavers worked at home on simple wheels or looms. Many spinners and weavers, however, did not buy their own raw materials or market their finished products; rather, they worked as wage-laborers for a capitalist, an entrepreneur who furnished the raw materials and sold the finished yarn and cloth. In some commodities, moreover, there was not a domestic system at all but a primitive factory system, in which the workmen were assembled in a large workshop. Such "factories," which of course still made goods by hand labor rather than machines, were particularly common in enterprises utilizing expensive materials or requiring close supervision for some other reason, from the making of luxury cloth with gold and silver threads to cannon foundries.

The industrial revolution supplanted the domestic system and transformed the factory system. Machines superseded simple hand tools, and water or steam replaced human muscles and animal energy as the source of power. Because the power-driven machines were often big, complicated, and costly, large factories were needed to house them. By 1789, these revolutionary changes had affected only a few industries; but those involved were key industries—mining, metallurgy, munitions, and textiles.

Coal-mining was becoming a big business in the eighteenth century. The increased demand for coal resulted partly from the needs of iron smelters, which had long used charcoal to make iron from the raw ore. In England, where almost all the great forests had been cut down, the price of charcoal rose so high by 1750 that the output of English smelters was declining rapidly. Ordinary coal could not replace charcoal as smelter fuel because the chemicals in coal made the iron too brittle. Here necessity mothered invention. The Darby family of Coalbrookdale in Shropshire discovered how to remove the chemical impurities from coal by converting it into coke through an oven process. Since coke was almost pure carbon, it produced iron of high quality.

In England, the Darbys and other private firms were the pioneers in metallurgy. On the Continent, governments took the lead—a significant exception to the general rule about the inability of the state to

Metal-planing and metal-cutting factory in the eighteenth century, as illustrated in the Encyclopédie *(see p. 277).*

solve economic problems. Warfare required weapons and munitions in unprecedented quantities; France and Prussia met the demand by setting up state-financed and state-operated foundries and arms factories.

The revolution in textiles was focused on the cheaper production of cotton cloth. The "flying shuttle," a technical device first applied to the hand loom in England (1733), enabled a single weaver to do work that had previously required the services of two. The looms equipped with the flying shuttle soon used up the supply of hand-spun thread. Then, in 1764, James Hargreaves devised his "spinning jenny," a series of spinning wheels geared together which made eight threads simultaneously. Soon the jenny was adapted to water power, and its output was increased to a hundred or more threads at once. Moreover, in the 1760's the Scotsman, James Watt, introduced the steam engine, which would eventually free industry from dependence on unreliable water power.

The full sweep of industrial development, however, could not come until the canal and the railroad provided cheap transport of heavy freight. The shortage of capital and the paucity of skilled labor also retarded the advance of industry. A Swedish inventor of the early 1700's designed excellent machines for cutting wheels and files but could not raise the money to put them into operation. And in Britain the difficulty of making precisely fitting parts for Watt's engine held back its production. The eighteenth century had taken many of the initial steps in the industrial revolution; it remained for the nineteenth century to apply them on a truly revolutionary scale.

III: *The Western Powers*

The Assets of Britain   Britain's leadership in the economic revolutions was making her the wealthiest nation in the world. The City, the square mile comprising the City of London proper and including the chief business houses, recovered quickly from the South Sea Bubble and was soon challenging Amsterdam's position as the international capital of trade and finance. In the course of the eighteenth century, British merchants outdistanced their old trading rivals, the Dutch, and gradually took the lead over their new competitors, the French. Judged by the three touchstones of mercantilism—commerce, colonies, and sea power—Britain was the strongest state in Europe.

The British colonial empire, however, was not a mercantilist undertaking in the full sense. Supervision of the colonies rested with a government department, the Board of Trade, which followed an easygoing policy contrasting with the rigid mercantilistic controls exerted by other imperial powers over their possessions. This was the famous policy of "salutary neglect." In the long run, as the American Revolution was to show, "salutary neglect" did not satisfy the colonists, but in the short run it worked reasonably well, and the British Empire surpassed all others in prosperity and self-reliance.

The Royal Navy surpassed all others by virtue of its superior officer corps and its greater size. Future captains went to sea at the age of sixteen, or even younger, and passed through a long course of practical training before receiving commissions. The ships they commanded in the wars of the mid-eighteenth century were inferior in design to those of Britain's enemies, France and Spain; but there were more of them. Britain had a 2 to 1 advantage over France in number of warships, a 6 to 1 lead in merchant ships, and a 10 to 1 lead in total number of experienced seamen, merchant and naval. Service on His Majesty's ships two hundred years ago was not exactly pleasant. The food doled out to the sailors was monotonous, wormy, and unhealthful. Captains frequently ordered the punishments of flogging and of keel-hauling, in which the offender was dragged along the barnacle-encrusted keel from bow to stern. These, however, were the common afflictions of all sailors in the eighteenth century; they did not put the British navy at a comparative disadvantage.

The army, on the other hand, constituted Britain's chief liability. Its officers were reputed to be the poorest in Europe, and its soldiers were in part mediocre mercenaries from the German state of Hesse-Cassel, the Hessians of the American Revolutionary War. A large army would have been both expensive and, since the British Isles were relatively safe from invasion, unnecessary. Moreover, the British feared a standing army as an instrument of potential absolutism, for they remembered the use that Cromwell and James II had made of this weapon (see above, Chapter VI).

The Glorious Revolution, which had done so much to confirm distrust of the army, had also confirmed Britain's unique and greatest asset—the supremacy of Parliament over the king. Parliament had replaced James II with William and Mary; when Anne, the last Stuart monarch, died in 1714, Parliament had already arranged for the succession of the House of Hanover. Under the first two Hanoverians, the cabinet, which was the instrument for the everyday assertion of parliamentary supremacy, underwent a rapid development. George I (1714-1727) and George II (1727-1760) did not abdicate all their royal powers. They took a direct interest in the South Sea Bubble and other financial matters; they sometimes intervened personally in the conduct of diplomacy and war.

The first two Georges chose their cabinet ministers from the Whig party, not because Parliament forced them to, but because it suited their convenience, and, even more, because they really had no choice. They thoroughly distrusted the other party, the Tories, some of whom were involved in futile Jacobite plots to restore to the English throne the descendants of James II (Jacobite from Jacobus, Latin for James). The Whigs, in contrast, had engineered the Glorious Revolution and had arranged the Hanoverian succession; they now controlled the House of Commons. For two decades after the collapse of the South Sea Bubble, from 1721 to 1742, Robert Walpole, who led the Whigs in the Commons, headed the cabinet. Although the title was not yet official, he was in fact prime minister. And in 1733, when he forced the resignation of some ministers who opposed his plan for a drastic reduction of customs duties, he took a major step toward establishing the important principle of cabinet unanimity on a critical issue.

Thus, by the death of George II in 1760, it was *customary* for the king to select his ministers from the majority party in the House of Commons, but it was not yet *obligatory*. The next Hanoverian king, George III, tried vainly to change the custom (see Chapter X). The formative years of the English cabinet preceding 1760 had already shaped the great instrument that would eventually assure the control of the executive branch by Parliament and thus by the people who elected the members of Commons.

The Whig party that ruled England under the first two Georges was a coalition of landed gentry and "funded" gentry, of landowning nobles and squires and of businessmen from London and other towns. In the Whig party the political leaders of town and country renewed an alliance that had first appeared in the later Middle Ages when the knights of the shire had joined the burgesses to form the House of Commons. In the Whig Parliaments the country gentlemen predominated by sheer numbers. Family ties, common political aims, and a common reverence for property bound together the senior and junior partners of the Whig party. To consolidate the gains of the Glorious Revolution, the Whigs opposed Jacobite schemes and supported the unprepossessing Hanoverians. To protect their lands and other investments, they passed legislation making death the penalty for stealing livestock, for cutting down cherry trees, and for other relatively minor violations of the sanctity of property.

Robert Walpole himself exemplified the fusion of landed and funded elements in the party. He inherited his manners and his tastes from his father, a country squire. He fixed the English politician's tradition of the long country weekend in order to indulge his passion for hunting; he drank heavily and habitually told bawdy stories at mixed dinner parties. Like many Whig squires, Walpole married into the aristocracy of trade; his wife was the daughter of a well-to-do timber merchant and former Lord Mayor of London. As prime minister, Walpole, the country gentleman, promoted the interests of the City. His basic policy coincided with the City's program: financial stability through the gradual retirement of the national debt, political stability through the cabinet system and the new Hanoverian dynasty.

Democracy scarcely existed in Walpole's England. In the professions, a social minority, the "gentlemen," alone could hope to become army and navy officers, lawyers, clergymen, and physicians. In politics, though the aristocracy of commerce gained admission to the Whig oligarchy, the millions of ordinary people were excluded. The landed gentry alone supplied the justices of the peace, who ran the local courts, fixed wage scales, superintended the relief of the poor, provided for the maintenance of bridges and highways, and were in general the despots of the English countryside. Fanatic defenders of the propertied

classes, the justices of the peace represented the most unattractive side of oligarchy. The saying that "You may as well be hanged for [stealing] a sheep as a lamb" is a bitter reminder of their standards of justice.

In the main, only gentlemen had the right to vote for members of Parliament. The small number of voters in many constituencies encouraged corruption, particularly in the "rotten" or "pocket" boroughs, boroughs with such a tiny electorate that control of their vote reposed in the pocket of some wealthy lord. Politicians bribed the voters outright or else promised them places on the government payroll. An immensely rich Whig, the Duke of Newcastle, controlled the outcome of elections in four counties and in seven pocket boroughs. Families with influential connections often obtained an immense amount of government patronage, as one tombstone records:

> Here rest all that was mortal of Mrs. Elizabeth Bate,
> Relict of the Reverend Richard Bate,
> A woman of unaffected piety
>   And exemplary virtue.
> She was honourably descended
> And by means of her Alliance to
> The illustrious family of Stanhope
> She had the merit to obtain
> for her husband and children
> Twelve separate employments
> In Church and State.
> She died June 9, 1751, in the 75th year of her age.*

In Britain, as on the Continent, the ruling classes governed the voteless masses. But there was an all-important difference between the island kingdom and the continental countries. The British ruling classes, selfish and narrow-minded though they often were, had at their best a sense of *noblesse oblige*, of public spirit and civic-mindedness. Within the aristocracy of land and trade there were fewer social barriers than on the Continent, and the doors were usually open to energetic newcomers from

* Quoted by G. M. Trevelyan, *England under Queen Anne* (New York, 1930-1934), III, 317.

the lower classes. The English gentry as a whole were responsive to the need for economic changes and, eventually, for political and social reforms as well. The British parliamentary system, for all its oligarchy and corruption, provided the most enlightened government in eighteenth-century Europe.

The Liabilities of France

Where Britain was strong, France was weak. The France of Louis XV (1715-1774) suffered from the rigidity of its colonial system, the inferiority of its navy, and the very mediocre abilities of most of its statesmen. The Ministry of the Navy, which ruled the overseas empire, regarded these possessions as so many warships permanently at anchor. It refused to sanction any steps toward self-government and applied the same detailed regulations to colonies as different as the sugar islands of the West Indies and the wilderness of Canada. Under this regime, the mother country prospered and the colonies languished. French foreign trade increased severalfold during the eighteenth century; commercial activity doubled in Nantes, Bordeaux, and other ports. Refineries grew up to process the raw sugar imported from the plantations of Guadeloupe and Martinique. Overseas, however, the plethora of regulations stifled the initiative of the colonists. The French imperial system lacked the elasticity and the energy to meet the test of war successfully.

The French navy needed greater resources and better leadership. Its warships, though admirably designed, were inadequate in number. Since Dutch and British vessels carried much of France's commerce, the French merchant marine was too small to supplement the fleet. French naval officers, though rigorously trained in the classroom, lacked the experience gained by British captains in a lifetime at sea. In the best (or worst) manner of the Old Régime, aristocratic officers thwarted the rise of officers from the middle class. In fairness, it must be added that French rulers neglected the navy in order to concentrate on the army. France was above all a land power, and its vulnerable northeastern frontier, lying across the Flemish plain, invited invasion. Except in size, however, the army of Louis XV scarcely lived up to the great traditions of Louis XIV. The troops were poorly trained. The military organization was top-heavy with superfluous officers; there was one officer to fifteen men in the French army, compared with one to thirty-five in the more efficient Prussian army. Aristocratic officers despised their bourgeois colleagues, and many of them regarded a commission simply as a way of increasing their wealth.

Both the navy and the army underwent important reforms after the defeats suffered by France in the Seven Years' War (see p. 270). The number of warships was increased, and the officer corps of the army was cleared of much dead wood. These improvements accounted in part for the excellent showing made by France in the American Revolutionary War and in the military campaigns resulting from her own revolution. They came too late, however, to save the vanishing prestige of the Old Régime.

The Old Régime was weakest at its very head, the monarchy itself. Successful divine-right monarchy required a perpetual series of able kings, ably assisted by men like Colbert and Richelieu. There were no "sun kings" in France after the death of Louis XIV, and few ministers of the caliber of their illustrious predecessors. The Duke of Orléans, the Regent from 1715 to 1723, was a gambler, drunkard, and pervert. He did, however, attempt two important administrative experiments. He allowed John Law to try out his "system," and, in place of Louis XIV's method of ruling through individual bourgeois ministers, he set up councils staffed largely by men from distinguished noble families. Although the first experiment, as we have seen, produced some beneficial results, the second failed so completely that the Regent abandoned it after a three-year trial. It was impossible to reform the French government by restoring the nobles to their old feudal role of counselors. The French second estate had outlived its usefulness. The Regency proved that the nobles were unable to govern, the mid-century wars that they were unable to lead French armies to victory.

Soon after the regency of Orléans, power passed to a statesman, Cardinal Fleury, the tutor of Louis XV and the chief minister from 1726 until his death in 1743 in his ninetieth year. Without attempting basic reforms, the aged Cardinal, in the words of Voltaire, "treated the state as a powerful and robust body which could cure itself." Fleury did not remedy the chronic and deep-seated injustice and inefficiency of French fiscal methods. But he did stabilize the coinage, and he put the farming of taxes on a more businesslike basis by allowing the tax-farmers the comparatively modest profit of 7½ per cent. To make loans more readily available, he established state pawnshops in the chief cities of France. The success of Fleury's policies greatly impressed Lady Mary Montagu, the wife of an English diplomat, who wrote in 1739:

France is so much improved, it is not . . . the same country we passed through twenty years ago. Everything I see speaks in praise of Cardinal Fleury; the roads are all mended. . . . The French are more changed than their roads; instead of pale, yellow faces, wrapped up in blankets, as we saw them, the villages are filled with fresh-coloured lusty peasants, in good cloth and clean linen. It is incredible the air of plenty and content that is over the whole country.*

The air of "plenty and content" remained after Louis XV began his personal rule in 1743, but the administrative stability achieved by Fleury soon vanished. Intelligent but timid and debauched, Louis XV

* *Letters*, Everyman ed. (New York, 1906), 271-272.

did not have the interest or the patience to supervise the details of government. He appointed and dismissed ministers on a personal whim or at the bidding of his mistresses and favorites. Key ministers, like the controller-general or the foreign secretary, remained in office but two or three years on the average. Each change in personnel meant a shift in policy, and Louis aggravated the instability by conspiring against his own appointees. France had both an official foreign policy and the "King's Secret," conducted by royal agents who continually countered the regular diplomats. Louis XV allowed the reins of government to go slack, yet refused to give them over to firmer hands.

Nevertheless, in spite of all this, France remained a great power. French tastes, French thought, and the French language retained their international pre-eminence. The misgovernment and the other weaknesses of the Old Régime were relative rather than absolute. They did not alter the fact that France was still the most populous country in Europe and possessed almost inexhaustible reserves of strength. Her army, though enfeebled, was the largest in the world, and her navy was the second largest. The French led the world in overseas trade until the British forged ahead of them in the last quarter of the eighteenth century.

The Other
Western States

Spain was the only other state in western Europe with a claim to great-power status. Weakness had ended the major international roles that Sweden and Holland had played during the seventeenth century. The campaigns of Charles XII had killed off the flower of Swedish manhood; for half a century after his death in 1718 two factions, derisively nicknamed "Hats" and "Caps," nearly wrecked the government. The Dutch, exhausted by the wars against Louis XIV, were losing their commercial leadership. Spain, by contrast, suffered little damage in the war over the succession to her throne. The loss of Belgium and parts of Italy in 1713 reduced the unwieldy Spanish domains to more manageable size. The new Bourbon kings were a marked improvement over the last Spanish Habsburgs. Philip V (1700-1746), the first of the Spanish Bourbons, infused fresh life into the country's fossilized institutions by importing French advisers schooled in the system of Louis XIV. Philip and his advisers cut down the excessive formalities of Spanish administration and reduced the powers of the noble-dominated councils that had been the real locus of authority in seventeenth-century Spain. They improved the tax system, encouraged textiles and other new industries, built up the navy, and forti-

fied strategic points in the Spanish empire in America.

The new dispensation, however, did not strike at the root causes of Spanish decline. The greed of governors and the restrictions of mercantilism still checked the progress of the colonies. The mother country remained impoverished, burdened with reactionary noble and clerical castes, and hampered by inadequate resources. Philip V was dominated by his strong-willed second wife, Elizabeth Farnese. Since Philip's son by his first marriage would inherit Spain, a single ambition possessed Elizabeth: to provide thrones for *her* two sons, the issue of Philip's second marriage. Elizabeth's persistent attempts to secure the succession of Italian states for them repeatedly threatened the peace of Europe.

IV: *Italy and Germany*

In 1715, both Italy and Germany were still a political patchwork of states, large, small, and minute; they were, in the old phrase, mere "geographical expressions." By 1715 the Italian states had lost most of the political and economic power they had enjoyed during the Renaissance. It is not hard to see why. The opening of new worlds overseas and the rise of Spain, England, and the other Atlantic powers naturally diminished the importance of the Mediterranean. In the Mediterranean itself, the Ottoman Turks and their satellites in North Africa long menaced Italian shipping and trade. Moreover, beginning with the French invasion of 1494, Italy was threatened with direct conquest by the rising new powers.

The Spanish Habsburgs made the conquest. For almost two centuries before 1715, Spain ruled Milan, Naples, and Sicily directly and dominated the rest of the peninsula. Then, in the readjustment of the

European balance in 1713, the Italians exchanged one foreign master for another. The Austrian Habsburgs took over the Italian possessions and the Italian hegemony of their Spanish cousins. On the completion of the postwar readjustment in 1720, the political map of the peninsula (see pp. 174-175) shows Austria established in Lombardy. Flanking Lombardy are the two decaying commercial republics of Venice and Genoa, and the small but rising state of Piedmont-Savoy (technically the Kingdom of Sardinia after its acquisition of that Mediterranean island in 1720). Farther down the peninsula come the Grand Duchy of Tuscany (formerly the Republic of Florence), the Papal States, and the Austrian Two Sicilies—that is, Naples and the island of Sicily.

Yet, Italy must not be written off as a negligible quantity in eighteenth-century Europe. Venice still produced great painters, and Naples was the schoolmaster of European musicians. Lombardy, Tuscany, and Naples not only contributed to the economic and intellectual advances of the century but also experienced some of the practical reforms stemming from the new spirit of reason. Above all, Italy continued to be a stake in balance-of-power politics. In the 1730's, for example, as the by-product of a crisis over Poland (see below, p. 264), the elder son of Elizabeth Farnese secured the Two Sicilies, and the Austrians obtained in compensation the succession of Tuscany. In 1768, Genoa ceded the island of Corsica to France. Defenseless Italy was the natural victim of ambitious dynasts and empire-builders.

In Germany, the Peace of Westphalia in 1648 had added to the sovereign rights of the individual states and had reduced almost to zero the authority of their nominal overlord, the Holy Roman Emperor. Germany suffered severely from the blighting effects of the Thirty Years' War and the campaigns of Louis XIV. But Germany, unlike Italy, was not defenseless: it contained two considerable powers, Austria and Prussia.

The Habsburg Domains The Austrian Habsburgs won a series of military and diplomatic victories in the two decades before 1715. They were pressing their *Drang nach Osten* (the German phrase for "Push to the East") against the Ottoman Empire (see p. 243), and in the Utrecht settlement they obtained Belgium and parts of Italy. Yet these acquisitions were removed from the central bloc of Habsburg lands in Austria, Hungary, Bohemia, and Silesia. The Emperor Charles VI (1711-1740) scarcely made a beginning at consolidating his rule over this disjointed empire. He spent much of his reign persuading his own noble subjects to ratify the Pragmatic Sanction, a constitutional agreement whereby, in the absence of sons, his daughter Maria Theresa would succeed him

in all his territories. The empire thus carefully preserved was a dynastic creation, an assemblage of lands largely devoid of common interests or real unity. The Austrian, Bohemian, and Hungarian nobles preserved most of their medieval prerogatives and, by controlling local estates and diets, controlled the grant of taxes and the appointment of officials. Finance and the army were the chief practical weaknesses of the Habsburg regime. In 1740, when Charles VI died, the pay of the civil service and the army was more than two years in arrears. Small wonder that the army itself fell short of its paper strength of 100,000 men and was ill prepared for the great test of strength with Prussia that came in 1740.

The Rise of Prussia Whereas Austria enjoyed the appearances rather than the realities of great-power status, Prussia possessed few of the appearances but a great many of the realities. In 1715, Prussia looked to be little more than just another German state. Its territories were scattered across North Germany from the Rhine on the west to the Vistula and beyond on the east. These lands had meager natural resources and carried on relatively little trade. With less than three million inhabitants, Prussia ranked only twelfth among the European states in population. Even her capital city, Berlin, located on the unimportant River Spree, had scarcely any of the obvious geographical advantages enjoyed by Rome, Constantinople, Paris, London, and the other great capitals. Prussian greatness came in large measure from the energetic policies of very able Hohenzollern rulers, beginning with the seventeenth-century Great Elector.

The Hohenzollern house had been established since the fifteenth century as Electors of Brandenburg, which lay between the Elbe and Oder rivers. A Hohenzollern had been the last Master of the Teutonic Knights, a crusading order, partly religious and wholly military and imperialistic in character, which had pushed the Germanic frontier beyond the Vistula to a land called Prussia at the southeast corner of the Baltic Sea. In 1618, when this Prussian area fell to Brandenburg, it was separated from the center of Hohenzollern power by lands belonging to Poland. In western Germany, the Hohenzollerns acquired parcels of land in the lower Rhine Valley early in the seventeenth century. Thus, when Frederick William, the Great Elector (1640-1688), succeeded to the Hohenzollern inheritance as the Thirty Years' War was drawing to a close, his lands consisted of a nucleus in Brandenburg with separate outlying regions to east and west. With extraordinary persistence, the rulers of Brandenburg-Prussia for the next two hundred years devoted themselves to the task of making a solid block of territory out of these scattered bits.

The Great Elector directed his foreign policy toward the expulsion of the Swedes from the Pomeranian territories, between Brandenburg and the Baltic, which they had acquired in 1648. Hence his alliance with the French against the Swedes in the 1670's during the Dutch War of Louis XIV, and hence his bitter disappointment that, despite his victory over the Swedes at Fehrbellin in 1675, Prussia got nothing when peace was made in 1679. Under the Great Elector's son, the mediocre Frederick I (1688-1713), Prussia played but a minor part in the great wars that humbled Louis XIV, and she got but minor territorial gains at Utrecht. The Hohenzollerns did, however, secure a useful gain in prestige. In 1701, as the price for entering the Grand Alliance against Louis XIV, Frederick assumed the title, "King in Prussia," and his new status was confirmed at Utrecht. Though technically Frederick was king only in Prussia proper,

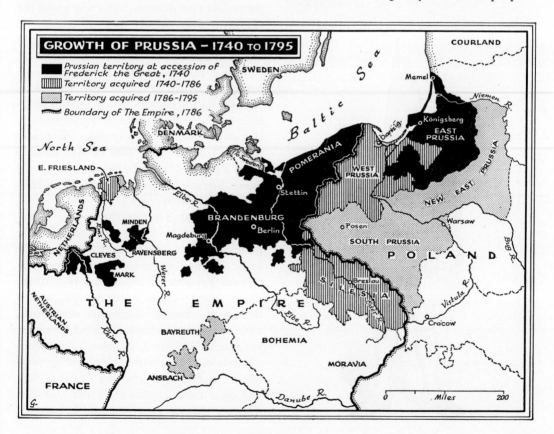

which lay outside the boundaries of the Holy Roman Empire, even a partial royal title conferred new dignity on the dynasty.

The Great Elector himself had thoroughly prepared the ground for his successors' assumption of royal responsibilities. He had found his lands largely ruined by the Thirty Years' War, the farms wasted, the population cut in half, the army reduced to a disorderly rabble of a few thousand men. He repaired the damage systematically. He encouraged the immigration of Polish Jews and other refugees from religious persecution, notably 20,000 French Huguenots to whom he gave partial exemption from taxation. The Great Elector built a small but efficient standing army that enabled Prussia to command large foreign subsidies for participating in the coalitions against Louis XIV.

One of the giant soldiers of Frederick William I of Prussia.

Finally, and most important, the Great Elector's administrative policies set the Hohenzollern pattern of centralized absolutism. He began to curb the independence of the *Junkers*, as the landed gentry of the eastern Hohenzollern lands were called. He confirmed their power over the serfs on their own estates, but he pared down the authority of the Junker-controlled provincial diets and made Berlin the real political capital of the Prussian state. He gradually gathered in his own hands the crucial power of levying taxes, which he collected through his own appointees, the nucleus of the famous Prussian civil service. The money thus secured went to the army, officered largely by *Junkers*, who could hardly have a career except in the royal service. The Great Elector was aided by a Lutheran state church that taught the virtues of obedience and discipline.

The Great Elector's son, Frederick I, like many German princes, was a victim of the continent-wide mania for imitating the splendors of Louis XIV. Frederick thought that a suggestion of marital infidelity enhanced sovereign majesty, and so, though happily married, he maintained an official mistress with whom he took decorous afternoon promenades. In futile attempts to copy the other luxuries of Versailles, he nearly bankrupted his state. But he did become King Frederick I, and he and his talented queen attracted artists and intellectuals to the Hohenzollern court.

The second Hohenzollern king, Frederick William I (1713-1740), resumed the policies of the Great Elector. Frederick the Great summed up the change in an epigram: "Under Frederick I Berlin was the Athens of the north; under Frederick William it became the Sparta." Economy, absolutism, and the army preoccupied this Spartan king. Frederick William I dismissed the supernumeraries of the court and reduced government expenses to a fraction of what they had been. He reiterated the order *"Ein Plus Machen"* (show a surplus) and bequeathed a full treasury to his son. But his frugality did not extend to projects that he thought really worth while. He financed the immigration of 12,000 South German Protestants who opened up new farmlands in East Prussia.

To increase centralization, Frederick William I set up a small board of experts to administer his provinces and the departments of his government. This had the explicit and resounding title of *Generaloberfinanzkriegsunddomänendirektorium* (General Superior Finance War and Domain Directory—General Directory, for short). The King insisted on hard work and punctuality. He treated the counselors of the General Directory as he treated lesser officials, paying them meanly and belaboring them with his cane for slovenly performance of their duties.

Frederick William I doubled the size of the standing army, but he maintained the laboring force of his underpopulated state by furloughing troops for nine months a year to work on farms. To secure guns and uniforms, he established state factories. The army also prompted his sole extravagance— a regiment of tall grenadiers, all six feet or over, who wore special caps more than a foot high to increase the impression of size. In recruiting his beloved "giants," the king threw economy to the winds, paying exorbitant prices and even trading royal musicians and prize stallions for especially tall specimens. Frederick William husbanded his army much too carefully to undertake

a really adventurous foreign policy. He engaged in but a single significant military campaign—against Sweden in the last stages of the Great Northern War—and then only after much persuasion by Peter the Great. At the close of the war, Frederick William obtained from Sweden part of Pomerania and also the important Baltic port of Stettin, thereby partially fulfilling the Great Elector's old aim of liquidating the Swedish possessions in Germany.

Eighteenth-century observers rightly called the Prussia of Frederick William an "armed camp" and berated its army for being a "gigantic penal institution" in which minor infractions of regulations entailed the death penalty. The King himself, obsessed with military matters, showed scant concern for culture; he despised everything French, and neglected the education of his subjects. With typical parsimony and shortsightedness, he refused to raise the inadequate fees of judges and lawyers, so that corruption and lethargy obstructed the course of justice in Prussia. Yet this regime worked and, in terms of power, worked extremely well. The Junkers, for all their feudal outlook, were intensely loyal to the Hohenzollerns and made some of the best army officers of the century. The army itself, though smaller than those of France, Russia, and Austria, was the best drilled and the most rigidly disciplined in Europe. When Frederick William I died in 1740, the Prussian David was ready to fight the Austrian Goliath.

V: War and Diplomacy, 1715-1763

In the very year of Frederick William's death, his son and successor, Frederick II (1740-1786), the famous Frederick the Great, attacked Austria. Here was one of the great issues at stake in the wars

and diplomacy of the eighteenth century— the expansionist designs of Prussia. The chief victims of Hohenzollern expansion were Austria, Sweden, and Poland. A second major issue was the expansion of Russia westward and southward, already pursued so energetically by Peter the Great. Throughout the eighteenth century Peter's successors on the Russian throne tried, with more or less success, to enlarge Russia's windows on the world (see Chapter IX). The chief victims of this Romanov expansion were Sweden, Poland, and Turkey. The third great international issue of the century was the colonial and commercial rivalry between Britain and the Bourbon monarchies of France and Spain.

All manner of secondary issues also entered into the play of international relations in the eighteenth century. The old competition between France and Austria, going back to the Habsburg-Valois wars of the 1500's, remained very lively. The family ambitions of Elizabeth Farnese added a new disturbing element and threatened the Austrian hegemony in Italy. And the Austrian Habsburgs themselves still pursued the aim of driving the Turk from the Danube and extending their own domains southeast to the Black Sea. In the Austro-Turkish War of 1716-1718, the Habsburg Emperor Charles VI scored a major success and by the Treaty of Passarowitz in 1718 recovered the piece of Hungary remaining under Turkish rule and secured parts of present-day Rumania and Yugoslavia. A second Turkish War, 1735-1739, however, revealed the infirmity of the Austrian army. Austria and Russia were allied in this war but soon fell to quarreling over the division of the prospective spoils. In the end there was almost nothing to divide, and Charles VI was obliged to hand back the Ottoman lands annexed in 1718. In the negotiations leading to the Austro-Turkish settlement of 1739, the Ottoman Empire received powerful support from France—an example of the way in which the French traditionally used the Turkish alliance to curb the expansion of the Habsburgs.

Meantime, in the early 1730's, another crisis had developed in eastern Europe and ranged Bourbon and Habsburg on opposing sides. This concerned the crown of Poland. In the early stages of the Great Northern War, Charles XII of Sweden had unseated the Saxon King of Poland, Augustus the Strong, and had placed on the throne a Polish nobleman, Stanislas Leszczynski. Thanks to the support of Peter the Great, Augustus had soon recovered his throne. Stanislas, however, had by no means completed his historical role, for he eventually gave his daughter, Marie, in marriage to Louis XV of France. When Augustus the Strong died in 1733, French diplomats engineered the election of Stanislas to succeed him. But both Austria and Russia disliked the prospect of a French puppet on the Polish throne, and Russia sent 30,000 troops into Poland and convoked a rump session of the diet which elected a rival king, Augustus III, son of Augustus the Strong. The stage was set for the War of the Polish Succession, 1733-1735—Stanislas, France, and Spain *versus* Augustus III, Russia, and Austria.

French and Austrian armies fired away at each other for a while in the Rhine Valley and in northern Italy, hundreds of miles from Poland; then the diplomats worked out a compromise settlement. To the satisfaction of Austria and Russia, Augustus III secured the Polish throne. From the French standpoint, Stanislas Leszczynski was well compensated for his loss. He became the Duke of Lorraine, a principality on the northeastern border of France, with the provision that when he died Lorraine would go to his daughter, Marie, and thence to the French crown. France would thus move one step closer toward filling out her "natural" frontiers. To be sure, Lorraine already had a duke, Francis, husband of the Habsburg heiress, Maria Theresa; the awkwardness was neatly resolved by transferring Francis to the Italian Grand Duchy of Tuscany, where the old line of rulers conveniently died out in 1737. Finally, as a by-product of the settlement, Elizabeth Farnese of Spain capped twenty years of maternal perseverance by procuring the Kingdom of Naples for "Baby Carlos," her elder and now grown-up son.

Early Eighteenth-Century Diplomacy in Review

The War of the Polish Succession may well seem futile and trivial, much ado about a kingship possessing no real power. And the postwar settlement, which affected chiefly Italy and Lorraine, may seem to be a striking case of diplomatic irrelevance. Yet the whole Polish crisis is a most instructive example of the workings of dynastic politics and of the constant shifts in the balance of power. Certainly no great national issues were at stake, except for the rather nebulous ones of French, Russian, and Austrian prestige. The statesmen regarded thrones as the pawns of diplomacy, to be assigned without reference to the wishes of the populations involved. None of them contemplated canvassing Neapolitan sentiment on Carlos or conducting a referendum to see whether the Poles preferred Stanislas or Augustus. None of them gave a thought to the welfare of Poland, which came out of the crisis weaker than ever.

The complicated arrangements of the 1730's preserved the balance of power by giving something to almost everybody involved. Although the diplomats could not prevent a little war over Poland, they did keep it from becoming a big one. Indeed, throughout the period from 1713 to 1739 the force of diplomacy operated to avoid or at least to localize wars. Britain and France took the lead in the campaign to keep any one power from upsetting the international apple-cart. For example, the British dispatched a squadron to the Baltic during the last part of the Great Northern War so that Tsar Peter's gains would not be too great. To prevent the dismemberment of European Turkey, Britain intervened in the negotiations between Turkey and Austria at Passarowitz in 1718, and the French revived their Ottoman alliance in the 1730's.

The informal diplomatic partnership of Britain and France did not last very long, for it ran afoul of their growing competition for commerce and empire. Neither Walpole nor Fleury could prevent the world-wide war between Britain and France that broke out in 1739 and 1740 and that lasted, with many intervals of peace, until the final defeat of Napoleon in 1815. This "Second Hundred Years' War" had already begun back in the days of Louis XIV. The peace of 1713 had not fully settled the rivalry between Britain and France (and France's Bourbon partner, Spain). Thus the war of 1739 was as much the renewal of an old struggle as the onset of a new one.

The specific issue behind the crisis of 1739 was the comparatively minor question of British chagrin at the disappointing results of the Asiento privilege, which gave Britain little more than a token share in the trade of the Spanish American colonies. What British captains could not get legitimately they got by smuggling. Spain retaliated by establishing a coast-guard patrol in American waters to ward off smugglers. British merchants complained bitterly of the rough treatment handed out by the Spanish guards, and in 1738 they exhibited to Parliament Captain Jenkins, who claimed that Spanish brutality had cost him an ear. Jenkins duly produced his severed ear, preserved in salt and cotton batting. Asked to state his reaction on losing the ear, he replied, "I commended my soul to God and my cause to my country." But Walpole could restrain neither the anti-Spanish fever sweeping the country to which Jenkins had commended his cause, nor the bellicose faction of "Boy Patriots" that had arisen within Walpole's own Whig party. In October, 1739, to the joyful pealing of church bells, Britain began the War of Jenkins' Ear against Spain. "They are ringing their bells now," Walpole observed tartly. "They will be wringing their hands soon." As if to vindicate his prophecy, the British fleet promptly made a mess of the opening campaign in the Caribbean, and France showed every sign of coming to Spain's assistance. Dynastic ties had already brought the two Bourbon monarchies into alliance; now French economic interests were at stake, for France supplied the bulk of the wares which cheaper British contraband was driving out of the Spanish colonial market.

The War of the Austrian Succession, 1740-1748

In 1740, a chain of events occurred that soon bound the colonial war to a great continental conflict over the Austrian succession. On the death of the Emperor Charles VI in 1740, the Habsburg domains fell to his daughter,

Maria Theresa. Expecting to outwit Maria Theresa because she was young, politically inexperienced, and a woman, the German princes chose to ignore the Pragmatic Sanction guaranteeing her succession. They looked forward to yet another victory in their contest against Habsburg domination; the Elector of Bavaria, for one, hoped to become Holy Roman Emperor. The first to strike, however, was Frederick the Great, who had just inherited the Prussian throne. In December, 1740, Frederick suddenly invaded Silesia, a Habsburg province in the upper Oder Valley to the southeast of Brandenburg.

In the ensuing War of the Austrian Succession, England and Austria were ranged against France, Spain, Prussia, and some lesser German states. Frederick won an emphatic victory in the campaigns on the Continent. The Prussian army astounded Europe

The Battle of Culloden, showing the rigid battle formations used in the eighteenth century.

by its long night marches, sudden flank attacks, and other tactics of surprise quite different from the usual deliberate warfare of sieges. Frederick, however, antagonized his allies by repeatedly deserting them to make secret peace arrangements with Austria. The Anglo-Austrian alliance worked no better than the Franco-Prussian one. Many Englishmen felt that George II was betraying their true interests overseas by entangling them in German politics and the defense of Hanover. Nevertheless, the British nation still preferred the Hanoverians to the Stuarts. In 1745, "Bonnie Prince Charlie," the grandson of the deposed James II, secured French backing and landed in Britain. He won significant recruits only among the chronically discontented Scottish highlanders, and in 1746 he was defeated at Culloden in northern Scotland. Jacobitism, never a very important political threat, was dead.

Outside Europe, the fighting of the 1740's was quite indecisive. The New England colonists took Louisburg, the French naval base on Cape Breton Island commanding the approach to the St. Lawrence. On the other side of the world, the French took the port of Madras from the English East India Company. On the seas, the British fleet did not win a real victory until 1747, and by then British merchant ships had suffered numerous attacks from French privateering expeditions.

The peace settlement ending the War of the Austrian Succession faithfully reflected the outcome of the actual fighting. Overseas, the Treaty of Aix-la-Chapelle (1748) restored both Louisburg and Madras to their former owners. In Central Europe, the war made Prussia a first-rate power by confirming her acquisition of Silesia. The new province brought not only a large increase in the Prussian population but also an important textile industry and large deposits of coal and iron. Maria Theresa got scant compensation for the loss of Silesia. Although her husband, Francis, won rec-ognition as Holy Roman Emperor, she had to surrender Parma and some other territorial crumbs in northern Italy to Philip, the second son of Elizabeth Farnese.

The Uneasy Peace, 1748-1756

The peace made in 1748 lasted only eight years. Then another and greater conflict, the Seven Years' War of 1756-1763, broke out, caused partly by old issues left unsettled at Aix-la-Chapelle and partly by new grievances arising from the War of the Austrian Succession. The world struggle between Britain and the Bourbons, in which the old war had been an indecisive preliminary engagement, kept right on in the undeclared warfare waged during the years of nominal peace after 1748. In Asia, the English and French East India companies fought each other once removed, so to speak, by taking sides in the rivalries of native princes in southern India. By 1751, the energetic French administrator, Dupleix, had won the initial round of this indirect fight. Then the English, led by the equally energetic Clive, seized the initiative, and in 1754 Dupleix was called back home by the directors of the French company, who were unwilling to back his aggressive policy. In North America, English colonists from the Atlantic seaboard had already staked out claims to the rich wilderness between the Appalachians and the Mississippi. But the French, equally intent on appropriating the area, stole a march on them and established a string of forts in western Pennsylvania from Presqu'Isle (later Erie) south to Fort Duquesne (later Pittsburgh). In 1754, a force of Virginians under the youthful George Washington tried unsuccessfully to dislodge the French from their strategic position at Fort Duquesne.

Colonists and mother country did not always see eye to eye on matters of basic policy. French recall of Dupleix is one example of such divergence. Another example is provided by the curious situation prevailing in the West Indies, then regarded as the greatest prizes of empire because they produced most of the world's sugar. New England traders could obtain sugar and its by-products (molasses and rum) more cheaply from the French plantations of Santo Domingo (Haiti), Guadeloupe, and Martinique than from Jamaica and other British sugar islands. French sugar made New England rum; New England rum besotted African Negroes; and, to complete this notorious "triangle trade," the sale of African slaves to French planters lined Yankee pockets—all in open violation of the mercantilist regulations that theoretically governed both the French and British empires.

In Europe, the dramatic shift of alliances called the Diplomatic Revolution immediately preceded the outbreak of the Seven Years' War. In the new war the fundamental conflicts were the same as in the old —Britain versus France, Prussia versus Austria—but the powers reversed their alliances. Britain, which had joined Austria *against* Prussia in the 1740's, now paired off *with* Frederick the Great. And France, which had sided *with* Frederick before, now not only stood *against* him but also joined with her hereditary enemy, Habsburg Austria. The Diplomatic Revolution expressed the resentment of the powers at the disloyal behavior of their old partners. The French had bitter memories of Frederick's repeated desertions and secret peace arrangements. Britain deplored Austrian reluctance to defend English continental interests, which included maintaining the territorial integrity of Hanover and excluding the French from the Austrian Netherlands. Austria, in turn, regarded Hanover and Belgium as peripheral to her main concern, the recovery of Silesia.

In 1755, the British almost unwittingly touched off the Diplomatic Revolution. In order to enlist a second power in the task of preserving the status quo in Hanover, they concluded a subsidy treaty with Russia. The Anglo-Russian treaty alarmed Frederick the Great, for he feared an eventual conflict with Russia for control of the Baltic and Poland. In January, 1756, the Prussian king concluded an alliance with Britain which detached her from Russia. The alliance between England and Prussia isolated France and gave the Austrian chancellor, Kaunitz, exactly the opportunity he had been waiting for. What Austria needed in order to avenge herself on Frederick and to regain Silesia was an ally with a large army; what Austria needed was the alliance of France, not Britain. Using the Anglo-Prussian alliance as an argument, Kaunitz convinced Louis XV and his mistress, Madame de Pompadour, to drop the traditional Bourbon-Habsburg feud in favor of a working partnership. The last act of the Diplomatic Revolution occurred when Russia joined the Franco-Austrian alliance. Russia had taken a minor part in the War of the Austrian Succession as an ally of England. In the new war the Russian Empress Elizabeth (1741-1762), entered as the full partner of Austria and France. Elizabeth hated Frederick the Great and feared his aggression all the more now that he had deprived her of her English ally.

The Seven Years' War, 1756-1763

The great coalition against Prussia was still in the process of formation when the war itself began. In May, 1756, Britain and France made official the state of hostilities already existing between them in North America. Three months later, Frederick the Great opened the war season in Europe by taking the offensive against the coalition menacing him. Once more the powers were engaged in a war that was really two separate wars—one continental, the other naval and colonial.

In the European campaigns of the Seven Years' War, both Frederick the Great and the Hohenzollern system faced a most formidable test. Prussia confronted the forces of Austria, France, and Russia, whose combined population was more than fifteen times larger than her own. She had almost no allies except for the British, who supplied financial subsidies but little actual military assistance. The traditions established by the Great Elector and developed by Frederick William I and Frederick the Great enabled the nation to survive. The King himself set a commanding example. In 1757, he wrote to one of his French friends:

I am assaulted from every side. Domestic trials, secret afflictions, public misfortunes, approaching calamities—such is my daily bread. But do not imagine I am weakening. If everything collapses I should calmly bury myself beneath the ruins. In these disastrous times one must fortify oneself with iron resolutions and a heart of brass. It is a time for stoicism: the disciples of Epicurus would find nothing to say. . . .*

Frederick's "iron resolution" and "heart of brass" led him to adopt any expedient, fair or unfair, to gain his ends. To fill up the depleted ranks of his army, he ruthlessly violated international law by impressing soldiers from Prussia's smaller neighbors, Mecklenburg and Saxony. Since British subsidies covered only a fraction of his war expenses, he seized Saxon, Polish, and Russian coins. Then he melted them down, kept for Prussian use a large part of their precious metallic content, recast them with baser metals, and returned them to circulation.

A final factor, perhaps the most important one of all, in saving Prussia was the inadequacy of the coalition arrayed against her. Most fortunately for Frederick, his enemies were never capable of exploiting their military successes to deliver a knock-out blow. Russia's generals were timid, and those of France and Austria were sometimes downright incompetent. Morever, the French, the strongest of the allies, had to fight a two-front war, in Europe and overseas, and

did not possess the financial resources to do justice to both. The grand alliance created by Kaunitz suffered from the frictions that always beset wartime coalitions; indeed, his coalition did not last out the war. When Elizabeth of Russia died in January, 1762, she was succeeded by Tsar Peter III, a passionate admirer of Frederick the Great, who at once deserted Elizabeth's allies and placed Russia's forces at Frederick's disposal; no wonder the grateful Prussian king called him "a divine ruler to whom I ought to erect altars!" Although Peter III occupied the Russian throne for only a few months, his brief rule marked a decisive turning in the Seven Years' War. In 1763 Prussia won her war, and Austria agreed to the Peace of Hubertusburg confirming the Hohenzollern retention of Silesia.

Meanwhile, Frederick's British partner was gaining a smashing victory abroad. Actually, Britain made a very lame start in the Seven Years' War, suffering setbacks on almost every front during the first year and a half of the fighting. At sea, the British lost the important Mediterranean base of Minorca in the Balearic Islands, a disaster to which the home government contributed by sending (too late) reinforcements (too few) under Admiral Byng (a poor choice). Byng was unfairly saddled with the whole blame and was executed—"in order to encourage the others," Voltaire observed ironically. In North America, the British lost the outpost of Oswego on Lake Ontario and fumbled an attack on Louisburg, the key to French Canada. The most dramatic of Britain's misfortunes occurred in India. In June, 1756, the Nawab of Bengal, a native ally of the French, crowded 146 British prisoners into one small room with only two windows. The result was the atrocious "Black Hole" of Calcutta, thus described by an officer of the English East India Company:

It was the hottest season of the year, and the night uncommonly sultry. . . . The excessive pressure of their bodies against one an-

---

* Quoted in G. P. Gooch, *Frederick the Great* (London, 1947), 41.

other, and the intolerable heat which prevailed as soon as the door was shut, convinced the prisoners that it was impossible to live through the night in this horrible confinement; and violent attempts were immediately made to force the door, but without effect, for it opened inward.

At two o'clock not more than fifty remained alive. But even this number were too many to partake of the saving air, the contest for which and for life continued until the morn. . . .

An officer, sent by the nawab, came . . . with an order to open the prison. The dead were so thronged, and the survivors had so little strength remaining, that they were employed near half an hour in removing the bodies which lay against the door before they could clear a passage to go out one at a time; when of one hundred and forty-six who went in no more than twenty-three came out alive, —the ghastliest forms that were ever seen alive.*

William Pitt turned the tide in favor of Britain. The "Great Commoner" (so named because of his long and able service in the House of Commons) was the most famous representative of the Whig oligarchy. In Parliament he sat for Old Sarum, a notorious "rotten" borough. In the late 1730's he had led the Whig rebels against Walpole's pacifistic policy, the "Boy Patriots" who forced Britain into the War of Jenkins' Ear. Now Pitt's great war ministry (1757-1761) organized victory from defeat. It ended the shilly-shallying policies of the cabinets that had held office since Walpole's downfall in 1742. Budget deficits rose higher and higher, but Pitt used his personal and business connections with the City to assist the successful placement of government loans. He gave the Anglo-Prussian alliance meaning by sending Frederick substantial subsidies and placing English forces in Hanover under an able Prussian commander in place of the bungling Duke of Cumberland, a son of George II. Everywhere Pitt replaced blundering generals and admirals; everywhere

he transformed the character of the naval and colonial war by his energetic measures.

Britain's overwhelming command of the seas enabled her to continue trading abroad at a prosperous pace, while French overseas trade rapidly sank to one-sixth of its pre-war rate. And it prevented the French colonies abroad from receiving even the modest amount of money and meager reinforcements available for them at home. Cut off from significant aid and faced by generally superior British forces, the French outposts of empire fell in quick succession. In Africa, Britain's capture of the chief French slaving station ruined the slavers of Nantes in the mother country. In India, Clive and others avenged the "Black Hole" by punishing the Nawab of Bengal and capturing the key French posts. In the West Indies, the French lost all their sugar islands, except for Santo Domingo. In North America, the 65,000 French, poorly supplied and poorly led, were helpless against the million British colonists, fully supported by their mother country. Fort Duquesne was taken at last, and very appropriately renamed after Pitt, and the British went on to other triumphs in the war that the colonists called "French and Indian." In Canada, the English General Wolfe took Louisburg (1758) and in the next year, 1759, lost his life but won immortal fame in a great victory on the Plains of Abraham outside Quebec. When the remaining French stronghold, Montreal, fell in 1760, the doom of France's American empire was sealed.

This rain of victories made the British public exultant, and they expected sweeping gains in the postwar settlement. Their exultation was soon dampened and their expectation disappointed. Pitt had won the war, but he did not make the peace: the accession of the obstinate and ambitious George III in 1760 led to the royal dismissal of the Prime Minister. In the Peace of Paris, 1763, ending hostilities between Britain and France, the successors of Pitt allowed France to retain stations in India and on

* R. Orme, *A History of the Transactions of the British Nation in Indostan* (London, 1778), II, sec. 1, 74 ff.

NORTH AMERICA AND
THE CARIBBEAN, 1763

SITUATION AFTER THE SEVEN YEARS' WAR

Hudson's
Bay

HUDSON'S BAY

COMPANY

NEWFOUNDLAND

ST.PIERRE
MIQUELON
(Fr.)

Quebec
Louisburg

Montreal
NOVA SCOTIA

Presque Isle

Boston

Ft.Duquesne
New York
Philadelphia

Atlantic
Ocean

BERMUDA
(Br.)

Charleston

LOUISIANA

Mississippi R.

W.FLORIDA
New
Orleans
(Sp.)

BAHAMAS
(Br.)

Gulf of Mexico

SANTO DOMINGO

CUBA

JAMAICA

HONDURAS

(French)

Caribbean   Sea

GUADELOUPE
MARTINIQUE

LESSER
ANTILLES

SPAIN

THE 13 COLONIES

FLORIDA

Territory

SOUTH
AMERICA

BRITISH TERRITORY:
  Held before 1763
  Acquired from France
  Acquired from Spain
  Proclamation Line of 1763

G.

the African slave coast. Above all, they permitted the French to recover their islands in the West Indies. The restoration of the old order in the Caribbean was a great relief to British planters, whose markets had been flooded by sugar from the captured French island of Guadaloupe during the war. But to outraged patriots it seemed as though Britain had let the grand prize slip through her fingers.

Though France retained her Caribbean empire, she lost all her possessions on the mainland of North America. Britain secured both Canada and the vast disputed territories between the Appalachians and the Mississippi. Moreover, she also obtained Florida from Spain, which had committed the folly of joining France in 1762 when the war was already lost. And, though the French retained a few trading posts in India, they were not allowed to fortify them or to continue their old policy of manipulating the politics and rivalries of native states. For Britain the Seven Years' War marked the beginning of a virtually complete ascendancy in India; for France it marked the end of an era of empire-building.

VI: Conclusion: The International Balance in Review

The peace settlements of Hubertusburg and Paris ended the greatest international crisis between the death of Louis XIV and the outbreak of the French Revolution. New crises were to arise soon after 1763, as the next chapters will show in detail —in 1768, a Russo-Turkish war; in 1772, the first partition of Poland; in 1775, the American War of Independence. The new crises in the East did not fundamentally alter the international balance; they accentuated shifts that had long been under way. And American independence, though it was the first step in the emergence of a great power,

did not produce immediate world-shaking results. Britain lost the thirteen colonies, but otherwise maintained the maritime and imperial supremacy won in 1763.

The international balance established in 1763, then, remained largely unchanged down to 1789. In the incessant struggle for power during the eighteenth century the victorious states were the strongest states— Britain, Prussia, and Russia. The states that were less fit—France, Spain, Austria, Turkey—survived, though they sometimes suffered serious losses. The weakest units, Poland and Italy—as a Spanish diplomat observed early in the century—were being "pared and sliced up like so many Dutch cheeses."

The Duke of Choiseul, the foreign minister of Louis XV during the Seven Years' War, remarked that the "true balance of power resides in commerce." Choiseul's remark held a large measure of truth, but not the whole truth. The world struggle between Britain and the Bourbon empires did much to justify the mercantilist view that conceived of international relations in terms of incessant competition and strife. According to the mercantilist doctrine of the fixed amount of trade, a state could enlarge its share of the existing supply only if it reduced the shares held by rival states, either through war or, in time of peace, through smuggling and retaliatory legislation. All this was borne out by the War of Jenkins' Ear and by British success, and French failure, in maintaining overseas trade during the course of the Seven Years' War.

In the warfare of the eighteenth century, it is evident, economic motives and economic resources often played a more decisive role than they had played in the past. Yet the modern concept of economic warfare was only beginning to take shape. In the 1740's London brokers supplied both insurance and information on naval movements to enemy shipowners. Moreover, economic factors did not fully explain all the changes in the international balance during the century. The stakes involved in the conquests of Peter the Great, or in the aggressions of Frederick, or in the strife over Poland and Italy, were not commercial. The stakes were the aggrandizement of Romanovs, Hohenzollerns, and Habsburgs, and of the nobles and Junkers supporting these dynasties. The stakes were on occasion as relatively trivial as the determination of Elizabeth Farnese to get royal, or at least ducal, thrones for Carlos and Philip.

Efficient utilization of Prussian economic resources played its part in the victories of Frederick the Great. But his success depended still more on qualities that had little to do with economics—his own brilliant and ruthless leadership, the discipline of the society that he headed. Even Britain, the best argument to support Choiseul's contention, owed much of her success to her social and political system, which allowed Pitt to come forward, the right man at the right time. War, in sum, mirrors not only the economy but the many other institutions of the society that wages it.

For all its wars, the eighteenth century was a period of comparative calm between the age of religious strife that had preceded it and the storms of liberalism and nationalism that were to be loosed upon the world by the French Revolution. The prospect in 1715, the prospect of long years of peace and quiet, had not, after all, been wholly deceptive. The Seven Years' War of the eighteenth century, for example, did not begin to equal in destructive force the Thirty Years' War of the seventeenth. Much more was involved here than the relative shortness of the Seven Years' War. Few of the combatants now had the feeling of fighting for a great cause, like Catholicism or Protestantism or national independence. The fighting itself was conducted in a more orderly fashion than it had been a hundred years before; soldiers were better disciplined, and armies were better supplied; troops lived off the land less often and no longer constituted such a menace to the lives and property of civilians. Even warfare indicated that this was the century of order and reason, the Age of the Enlightenment.

Reading Suggestions on the International Balance

General Accounts

The following three volumes in the "Rise of Modern Europe" series (N.Y.: Harper) provide a good detailed analysis of eighteenth-century Europe and very full bibliographies: P. Roberts, *The Quest for Security, 1715-1740;* W. L. Dorn, *Competition for Empire, 1740-1763;* L. Gershoy, *From Despotism to Revolution, 1763-1789.*

A. Sorel, *Europe under the Old Regime* (Los Angeles: Ritchie, 1947). Translation of the first volume of a major French work on diplomatic history; a classic survey of the international balance in the eighteenth century.

C. A. Petrie, *Diplomatic History, 1713-1933* (London: Hollis and Carter, 1946). A useful introductory manual.

Note: The economic histories by Heaton and by Clough and Cole, and the military history by Fuller, already suggested for earlier chapters, are very useful for the eighteenth century. So, too, is the great work on mercantilism by Heckscher (see Chapter VI). For general works on the rivalries of the powers outside Europe, see the reading suggestions for Chapter V.

Special Studies

W. E. H. Lecky, *A History of England in the Eighteenth Century,* 8 vols. (London: Longmans, Green, 1883-1890). A famous and detailed old account.

B. Williams, *The Whig Supremacy, 1714-1760* (Oxford: Clarendon, 1939). A competent modern survey.

C. G. Robertson, *Chatham and the British Empire* (N.Y.: Macmillan, 1948. Teach Yourself History Library); and J. H. Plumb, *Chatham* (N.Y.: Macmillan, 1953). Brief accounts of the elder Pitt, addressed to the general reader.

J. H. Plumb, *The First Four Georges* (N.Y.: Macmillan, 1957). A most readable and authoritative account.

J. H. Plumb, *Sir Robert Walpole: The Making of a Statesman* (Boston: Houghton Mifflin, 1956). The first volume of what promises to be the definitive work on Walpole.

H. Dodwell, *Dupleix and Clive* (London: Methuen, 1920). A balanced treatment of the imperial antagonists in India.

L. Kronenberger, *Kings and Desperate Men* (N.Y.: Knopf, 1942). An entertaining chronicle of eighteenth-century England; good on social and literary developments.

A. M. Wilson, *French Foreign Policy during the Administration of Cardinal Fleury, 1726-1743* (Cambridge: Harvard Univ. Press, 1936). A sound monograph, and one of the few good books in English on the France of Louis XV.

G. P. Gooch, *Louis XV* (London: Longmans, Green, 1956); and N. Mitford, *Madame de Pompadour* (London: Hamish, Hamilton, 1954). Recent but rather old-fashioned books on these celebrated personages.

S. B. Fay, *The Rise of Brandenburg-Prussia to 1786* (N.Y.: Holt, 1937. A Berkshire Study). An admirable little volume, packed with information.

R. R. Ergang, *The Potsdam Führer* (N.Y.: Columbia Univ. Press, 1941). A splendid book on Frederick William I, both lively and detached.

A. Goodwin, ed., *The European Nobility in the Eighteenth Century* (London: Black, 1953). Very suggestive surveys.

J. A. Marriott, *The Eastern Question: An Historical Study in European Diplomacy,* 4th ed. (Oxford: Clarendon, 1940). A standard survey.

Sources and Historical Fiction

A. Young, *Tours in England and Wales* (London: London School of Economics and Political Science, 1932). One of many sets of "tours" by this perceptive and readable observer.

Lady Mary W. Montagu, *Letters* (N.Y.: Dutton, 1906. Everyman ed.). By perhaps the best of the many excellent letter-writers of the century; particularly valuable for first-hand impressions of the Ottoman Empire.

J. C. Hurewitz, ed., *Diplomacy in the Near and Middle East: A Documentary Record* (Princeton: Van Nostrand, 1956).

H. Fielding, *Tom Jones* (many editions). The greatest of eighteenth-century English social novels.

T. G. Smollett, *The Adventures of Roderick Random* (N.Y.: Oxford Univ. Press, 1952. World's Classics). A novel that provides a good contemporary account of life in His Majesty's Navy.

CHAPTER NINE

The Eighteenth Century:

The Enlightenment

I: *Basic Principles and Traits*

Reason, natural law, progress—these were the key words in the vocabulary of the eighteenth century, the Age of the Enlightenment. This was the age when many believed that human reason could free men from the errors and misfortunes of the past and lead them to perpetual peace, utopian government, and a perfect society. *Reason* would discover the *natural laws* regulating existence, thereby insuring the *progress* of the human race.

The prophets of this optimistic creed were known by the French name of *philosophes*, though few of them were philosophers in the strict sense. The *philosophes* were publicists, economists, political scientists, and social reformers. They derived their basic principles from their great predecessors of the seventeenth century; their belief in the powers of human reason came partly from John Locke, their faith in natural law from Sir Isaac Newton.

The Inheritance from Locke and Newton   John Locke (1632-1704) wrote a celebrated defense of England's Glorious Revolution, the *Two Treatises of Government* (1690). Men are, he contended, "by nature all free, equal, and independent"; they submit to government not because they acknowledge any divine right on the part of the monarch but because they find it convenient to do so. In effect, Locke continued, they make a compact or contract to be governed, a contract that they may break by revolutionary action if the monarch does not live up to his obligations, as James II had not lived up to his. To strengthen his case against absolute monarchy, Locke outlined a new psychology. Defenders of political and religious absolutism contended that divine-right monarchy was an inevitable human inheritance, that the inclination to submit to absolute authority was present in men's minds when they were born. In the *Essay concerning Human Understanding* (1690), Locke denied the existence of innate ideas:

Let us then suppose the mind to be . . . white paper, void of all characters, without any ideas. How comes it to be furnished? . . . To this I answer, in one word, from EXPERIENCE. . . . Our observation employed either about *external sensible objects, or about the internal operations of our minds perceived and reflected on by ourselves, is that which supplies our understandings with all the materials of thinking.* These two are the fountains of knowledge, from whence all the ideas we have, or can naturally have, do spring.*

In other words, the two "fountains of knowledge" were environment rather than heredity, and reason rather than faith. Locke's matter-of-fact outlook and his empiricism (reliance on experience) place him among the rationalists. He believed that human reason, though unable to account for everything in the universe, explains all that men need to know. "The candle that is

Essay (New York, 1947), Bk. II, Ch. I.

set up in us," he wrote, "shines bright enough for all our purposes."

Locke pointed the way to a critical examination of the Old Régime. The *philosophes* read and admired both his political writings and his *Essay concerning Human Understanding.* They applied his test of common sense to existing social and economic institutions and found them complex and absurd. Locke's psychology suggested that teachers could make human institutions over by remolding the thinking of the rising generation. In this enterprise the *philosophes* were attracted by the concept of the Newtonian "world-machine."

Indeed, the *philosophes* seized on Newton's scientific discoveries as revelations of ultimate truth. Those who could follow Newton's mathematical calculations read him in the original Latin or in translation; those who could not, turned to *Newtonianism for Ladies* or one of the other popularizations of the *Principia.* In the principle of gravitation, Newton had disclosed the natural force that held the universe together; he made the universe make sense. The eighteenth century believed that other Newtons would find comparable laws governing and explaining all phases of human activity. The *philosophes* pictured themselves as the Newtons of statecraft, justice, and economics who would reduce the most intricate institutions to formulas as neat as Sir Isaac's own mathematical laws and principles.

The world and everything in it, the *philosophes* concluded, resembled a giant machine. Hitherto, men had hampered its operations because they did not understand the machinery. Once they grasped the basic laws by which it ran, they would at last permit the "world-machine" to function smoothly and beneficently. The optimism of the age was summed up in a book aptly entitled *The Progress of the Human Mind* (1794), written by the *philosophe* Condorcet when he was in hiding during the French revolutionary Reign of Terror (see Chapter X). Condorcet asked:

If men can predict, with almost complete assurance, the phenomena whose laws are known to them . . . , why should it be regarded as a vain enterprise to chart, with some degree of probability, the course of the future destiny of mankind by studying the results of human history? Since the only basis of belief in the natural sciences is the idea that the general laws, known or unknown, regulating the phenomena of the universe are regular and constant, why should this principle be any less true for the development of the intellectual and moral faculties of man than for the other operations of nature? *

"Nature has placed no bounds on the perfecting of the human faculties," Condorcet concluded, "and the progress of this perfectibility is limited only by the duration of the globe on which nature has placed us." †

Eighteenth-century Science

The technological and scientific advances of the eighteenth century further strengthened the faith in natural law and progress. The *philosophes* hailed both the practical achievements in industry and agriculture and the rapidly expanding frontiers of the pure sciences. Biology and chemistry were now starting to acquire a modern look. Linnaeus (1707-1778), a Swede, demonstrated the natural laws of family relationships in biology. He took every known plant and animal, classified it by species, then bracketed several species together in a genus—and so on up the hierarchy of classification from genus through order to class. Thus arose a practice that biologists still follow in assigning every specimen two Latin names, that of its genus and that of its species.

The modern science of chemical analysis began with Black and Lavoisier. Joseph Black (1728-1799), a Scottish professor, exploded the old theory that air was composed of a single element. He proved the existence

of several air-like substances or gases. Lavoisier (1743-1794), a French chemist and physicist, continued Black's study of gases, invented the name "oxygen," and demonstrated that water was made up of oxygen and hydrogen. He asserted that all substances were composed of a relatively few basic chemical elements, of which he identified twenty-three.

Meanwhile, astronomy and physics were consolidating the great advances they had made in the seventeenth century. Laplace (1749-1827), the "Newton of France," rounded out the great Isaac's investigation of celestial mechanics and explained the movement of the solar system in a series of mathematical formulas and theorems. The versatile American, Benjamin Franklin (1706-1790), showed that electricity and lightning were really the same thing. By flying a kite during a thunderstorm at Philadelphia, Franklin obtained an electrical charge in a key attached to the kite-string. This experiment aroused a lively interest across the Atlantic, and was repeated at Versailles for the instruction of the French royal family.

Indeed, almost everybody who was anybody attempted experiments. Voltaire made chemistry his hobby; Montesquieu studied physics; and a noble French lady reportedly kept a corpse in her carriage, so that she might employ her travels profitably in dissection and the study of anatomy. Almost every state in Europe had its *philosophes* and its royal society or learned society to promote the progress of knowledge. Scientists and *philosophes* paid scant attention to national frontiers. Even when their countries were at war, they often kept on visiting and corresponding—a striking example of the eighteenth century's disposition toward "business as usual."

French Leadership

With roots reaching back into seventeenth-century England and with branches extending to Scotland, Germany,

---

* Condorcet, *Esquisse d'un Tableau Historique des Progrès de l'Esprit Humain* (Paris, n.d.), 203. Our translation.
  † *Ibid.,* 5.

Italy, Spain, and the New World, the Enlightenment fully exhibited the cosmopolitan qualities of its century. Yet many, though by no means all, of the *philosophes* were French, and French leadership set an indelible stamp upon the whole Enlightenment. The Age of Reason marked the high point of French cultural hegemony, and it was a great American *philosophe*, Thomas Jefferson, who maintained that every man had two homelands, "his own and France." The French language endowed the Enlightenment with its medium of communication; the *salons* of Paris set the style of enlightened writing; the great *Encyclopédie*, edited and published in France, provided the vehicle for enlightened thought.

By the eighteenth century, French was the accepted international language. Louis XIV had raised it to supremacy in diplomacy; Racine and the other great seventeenth-century writers had made it preeminent in literature. There was much justice in the claim that "a dangerous work written in French is a declaration of war on the whole of Europe." Almost everywhere, and as far as distant Russia, rulers, aristocrats, and intellectuals preferred French to their native tongues. Frederick the Great seldom deigned to use German. In 1783, it was the Academy of Berlin that conducted a competition for the best reply to the question, "What has made the French language universal?" The prize-winning essay furnished the answer in a single sentence: "Precise, popular, and reasonable, it is no longer just French; it is the language of humanity."

The Parisian *salons* taught writers precision, reasonableness, and the popular touch. The *salon* was the reception room of a large private home where guests assembled for a long afternoon or evening of conversation under the guidance of the hostess, usually a wealthy woman from the nobility or the upper bourgeoisie. Although the *salons* were sometimes snobbish and superficial, they often practiced a kind of democracy. They afforded young *philosophes* the opportunity to receive a hearing—and to obtain a square meal; they welcomed and, if the need arose, protected, new men and new ideas. Their pressure affected the outcome of elections to the French Academy, which they helped to bring under the control of the *philosophes* in the 1760's.

The great organ of the *philosophes* was the *Encyclopédie*, which published the first of its many volumes in 1751. Its roster of 160 contributors amounted to a Who's Who of the Enlightenment; it included Voltaire, Montesquieu, Rousseau, Condorcet, Quesnay, and Turgot. For years the editor-in-chief, Denis Diderot (1713-1784), put in a fourteen-hour working day, every hour devoted to his crusade for reason and progress. Diderot and his associates had no intention of issuing a neutral compendium of factual information. As Diderot explained in the article on the word "encyclopedia," they aimed to assemble knowledge

. . . in order that the labors of past centuries should not prove useless for succeeding centuries; that our descendants, by becoming better informed, will at the same time *become happier and more virtuous*. . . .*

The purpose of the *Encyclopédie* was didactic: to expose the vices of the existing order, especially its religious superstition and intolerance, and to instruct the public in the virtues of natural law and in the wonders of science.

In the face of formidable opposition, the *Encyclopédie* accomplished its purpose. The Church condemned its materialism and its highly critical and skeptical articles on religious issues. Louis XV tried to keep it from being printed and circulated. The publishers, without consulting Diderot, reduced some of the controversial articles to a meaningless hash by ordering the printers to cut out all passages likely to cause offense. The indignation of Diderot, the ridicule leveled by the *philosophes* at their detractors, the intense curiosity of the subscribers to the

---

* (Our italics. Our translation.)

Encyclopédie, and the help extended to the editors by Choiseul, the foreign minister, and by Madame de Pompadour, herself an "enlightened" spirit—all frustrated the censors and facilitated the completion of publication.

II: *The Reform Program of the* Philosophes

*Laissez-Faire
Economics*   The articles written for the *Encyclopédie* by François Quesnay (1694-1774) announced the economic program of the Enlightenment. The versatile Quesnay, biologist, surgeon, and personal physician to Louis XV and Madame de Pompadour, headed a group of thinkers and publicists who adopted the name of Physiocrats, believers in the rule of nature. The new title revealed the basic outlook of the school. The Physiocrats felt with absolute certainty that they would, as Quesnay claimed, discover natural economic laws "susceptible of a demonstration as severe and incontestable as those of geometry and algebra."

"The sovereign and the nation should never lose sight of the fact that the land is the only source of wealth, and that agriculture increases wealth." * Thus Quesnay introduced the new Physiocratic concept of natural wealth and consigned almost the whole of mercantilism to limbo. He belittled the significance of money: "The riches which men need for their livelihood do not consist of money; they are rather the goods necessary both for life and for the annual production of these goods." Mercantilist states, Quesnay argued, made goods more expensive by levying tariffs and other indirect taxes, whereas they should have collected only a single, direct tax on the net income from land. "*Laissez faire, laissez passer*," the Physiocrats urged—live and let live, let nature take its course. They repudiated the controlled economy of mercantilism and enunciated the "classical" or "liberal" doctrine of the free economy. The state ought not interrupt the free play of natural economic forces. Most of all, it ought not to interfere with private property, so necessary for the production of agricultural wealth.

The classic formulation of laissez-faire was made by the Scotsman, Adam Smith (1723-1790), in his famous *Inquiry into the Nature and Causes of the Wealth of Nations* (1776). Adam Smith carried to vigorous completion the Physiocrats' attack on the theoretical structure of mercantilism. It was wrong to restrict imports by tariffs for the protection of home industries:

It is the maxim of every prudent master of a family never to attempt to make at home what it will cost him more to make than to buy. The tailor does not attempt to make his own shoes, but buys them of the shoemaker. The shoemaker does not attempt to make his own clothes, but employs a tailor. . . .

What is prudence in the conduct of every private family, can scarce be folly in that of a great kingdom. If a foreign country can supply us with a commodity cheaper than we ourselves can make it, better buy it of them with some part of the produce of our industry. . . .*

Like the Physiocrats, Adam Smith attributed the wealth of nations to the production of goods; but, as befitted a citizen of Britain, the leading commercial and industrial state of the day, he took a less agrarian view of the matter. For Adam

---

* Quesnay, "Maximes Générales du Gouvernement Economique d'Un Royaume Agricole," in E. Daire, ed., *Physiocrates* (Paris, 1846), I, 82. Our translation.

* *Wealth of Nations*, Bk. IV, Ch. 2.

Smith, production depended less on the *soil* (the Physiocratic view) than on the *labor* of farmers, craftsmen, and mill-hands. Finally, in the most famous sentence of *The Wealth of Nations*, Adam Smith reduced government to the status of a passive policeman:

According to the system of natural liberty, the sovereign has only three duties to attend to; . . . first, the duty of protecting the society from the violence and invasion of other independent societies; secondly, the duty of protecting, as far as possible, every member of the society from the injustice and oppression of every other member of it, or the duty of establishing an exact administration of justice; and thirdly, the duty of erecting and maintaining certain public works and certain public institutions, which it can never be for the interest of any individual, or small number of individuals, to erect and maintain.*

The mercantilists had exalted the state over the individual and had declared a ceaseless trade warfare among nations. Adam Smith and the Physiocrats, reversing the emphasis, proclaimed both the economic liberty of the individual and free trade among nations to be natural laws. This laissez-faire program of the Enlightenment marked a revolutionary change in economic thought and foreshadowed the individualism of the industrial revolution in the nineteenth century (see Chapter XIII). It did not, however, revolutionize the economic policies of the great powers. Mercantilism retained much vitality, as we shall shortly see; Turgot, for instance, the chief practical exponent of Physiocratic doctrine, tried vainly to emancipate French agriculture and French business during his brief tenure as chief minister in the 1770's (see Chapter X). The Physiocrats forgot what so many *philosophes* forgot. They overlooked the difficulty of adjusting the complexities of politics and the realities of human nature to the simple and reasonable dictates of natural law.

---

* *Ibid.*, Bk. IV, Ch. 9.

Justice

The attitude of letting nature take its course, so evident in laissez-faire economics, also determined the outlook of the Enlightenment on questions of justice. The *philosophes* believed that man-made legislation prevented the application of the natural laws of justice. They were horrified by the cumbersome judicial procedures of the Old Régime and by its unjust and antiquated statutes. New law-givers were needed to humanize and simplify the legal codes, and a new science was needed to make the punishment of crime both humane and effective.

The new science, which anticipated much of modern sociology, was promoted by Cesare Beccaria (1738-1794), an Italian *philosophe* and the author of the *Essay on Crimes and Punishments* (1764). Beccaria formulated three natural laws of justice. First, punishments should aim to

. . . prevent the criminal from doing further injury to society, and to prevent others from committing the like offence. Such punishments, therefore, . . . ought to be chosen, as will make the strongest and most lasting impressions on the minds of others, with the least torment to the body of the criminal.*

Second, justice should act speedily

. . . because the smaller the interval of time between the punishment and the crime, the stronger and more lasting will be the association of the two ideas of *Crime* and *Punishment.* †

And last:

Crimes are more effectively prevented by the *certainty* than by the *severity* of the punishment. . . . The certainty of a small punishment will make a stronger impression than the fear of one more severe. . . .**

Beccaria attacked both torture and capital punishment because they diverged so sharply from these natural laws. Torture, he claimed, falsely assumed that "pain

---

* *Essay on Crimes and Punishments*, Ch. 12.
† *Ibid.*, Ch. 19.
** *Ibid.*, Ch. 27.

should be the test of truth, as if truth resided in the muscles and fibres of a wretch in torture." Jail sentences, not execution, should be imposed as punishments. Beccaria asserted, however, that punishment alone was not enough. The best method of preventing crime was to "let liberty be attended with knowledge," to "perfect the system of education."

Education

In education, too, the Old Régime failed to pass the tests of reason and natural law. The *philosophes* deplored both the widespread ecclesiastical control of schools and universities and the heavy emphasis placed upon theology, Greek and Latin, and ancient history. They called this version of the humanities "savage" and demanded more consideration of science, modern languages, and modern history.

Jean-Jacques Rousseau (1712-1778) proposed the most drastic reform of education. Rousseau was a rebel. He rebelled against the strict and disciplined society of his birthplace, Calvinist Geneva. He rebelled against the intensive bookish studies he had been forced to pursue as a young boy, and against the polite conventions he later encountered in the Paris *salons*. The result of Rousseau's rebellion was *Emile* (1762), half treatise and half romance, a long and fervent plea for progressive education.

Emile had two heroes—Emile, the student, and Rousseau himself, the teacher. The training that Rousseau prescribed for his pupil departed in every particular from eighteenth-century practice:

Life is the trade I would teach him. When he leaves me, I grant you, he will be neither a magistrate, a soldier, nor a priest; he will be a man.*

Rousseau followed a policy of laissez-faire toward his pupil. He did not argue with

_____
* *Emile*, Everyman ed. (New York, 1911), 9.

Emile, or discipline him, or force him to learn reading at any early age. Emile observed the world of nature from first-hand experience, not in books. He learned geography by finding his own way in the woods, and agriculture by working in the fields. And when in his teens he was finally taught to read, his first assignment was Defoe's *Robinson Crusoe*, "the best treatise on an education according to nature."

Rousseau's educational program had many faults. It was impractical, for it assumed that every child should have the undivided attention of a tutor twenty-four hours a day; and it fostered the total and apparently permanent dependence of pupil upon teacher. When Emile married and became a father, he implored his tutor to remain at his post: "I need you more than ever now that I am taking up the duties of manhood." And yet *Emile* was a most important book, if not a great one. Rousseau returned to some of the great ideas of the past—to the Renaissance concept of the universal man and to the ancient Greek ideal of the sound mind in the sound body. Pestalozzi (1746-1827), a Swiss educator and humanitarian, adapted the theoretical program of *Emile* to the practical requirements of the classroom and set a powerful example by teaching geography, drawing, and other useful novelties in his experimental school. Still more influential was the reaction of Pestalozzi against the barracks tradition of drilling lessons into the student through a combination of endless repetition and bodily punishment. Pupils of the twentieth century may thank the educational reformers of the eighteenth for having discovered the natural law that children should be treated as children, not as miniature adults.

Attitudes toward Religion

The attacks on clerical teaching methods formed part of a vigorous and growing body of criticism aimed at the role of the clergy in the Old Régime. "*Ecrasez l'infâme!*" shouted the *philosophes* —crush the infamous thing, stamp out religious fanaticism. They particularly assailed the Jesuit Order, the symbol and instrument of militant, intolerant Catholicism. Their campaign won the support of Catholic monarchs, and in 1773 Pope Clement XIV dissolved the Society of Jesus.

The attack of the *philosophes* on intolerance was part of the general religious attitude called *deism* (from the Latin *deus*, god). Deist doctrines arose in seventeenth-century England, the England of the Civil Wars and Newtonian science, where the deists sought settlement of religious strife by the use of reason rather than by resort to arms. All men, they asserted, could agree on a few broad religious principles. Since the Newtonian world-machine implied the existence of a mechanic, the deists accepted God as the creator of the universe and as the ultimate judge of human conduct. But they denied, or at least doubted, that God answered prayer or extended grace. For the deists, the role of God lay in the dim past and the distant future, not the immediate present.

Voltaire (1694-1778) was the chief exponent of deism in France and the coiner of the anticlerical watchword, "*Ecrasez l'infâme!*" Voltaire, indeed, was a one-man Enlightenment, who devoted his prodigious energy and talent to the propagation of new ideas. Plays, tales, epic poems, histories, essays, and letters poured from his pen. Clear, witty, and often bitingly satirical, they were immensely popular, not least when they had to be printed outside France or under an assumed name in order to evade the censorship. Voltaire made Frenchmen aware of Newton, Locke, and Shakespeare. He set a new style in history-writing by discussing economics and culture as well as the usual politics and wars, thus foreshadowing the "new history" and the "surveys of civilization" of the twentieth century.

Voltaire experienced intolerance at first hand. As a young man he spent a year in the gloomy Paris prison, the Bastille, and three years of exile in England because he had criticized the French government and

Thirteen glimpses of Voltaire (from drawings by Hubert).

had offended a member of the privileged nobility. The relative religious and political freedom of Britain made an immense impression on the refugee:

If there were just one religion in England, despotism would threaten; if there were two religions, they would cut each other's throats; but there are thirty religions, and they live together peacefully and happily.*

Back in France, Voltaire carried on a lifelong crusade for toleration. In 1762, a Protestant merchant, Jean Calas, was accused of having murdered his son to prevent his conversion to Catholicism. Calas died in agony, his body broken on the wheel. Voltaire discovered that the accusation against Calas was based solely on rumor, and that the court condemning him had acted under the pressure of a fanatical Catholic mob. Voltaire campaigned for three years until the original verdict was reversed, and the name of Calas was cleared.

The existence of evil—of injustices like that which broke Calas—confronted the Age of Reason with a major problem. Few of the *philosophes* accepted the traditional Christian teaching that evil arose from original sin, from the fall of Adam and Eve. If God were purely benevolent, they asked, why then had he created a world in which evil so often prevailed? Could a perfect God produce an imperfect creation? Alexander Pope, Voltaire's great English contemporary, answered that this was the best of all possible worlds:

All Nature is but Art, unknown to thee;
All chance, direction which thou canst not
    see;
All discord, harmony not understood;
All partial evil, universal good:
And, spite of Pride, in erring Reason's spite,
One truth is clear, *Whatever is, is right.*

But Voltaire, in his most famous story, *Candide*, ridiculed the optimists and commented with bitter sarcasm on the disasters that abounded in the best of all possible worlds.

A real disaster inspired the writing of *Candide*—the great earthquake and tidal wave that engulfed the city of Lisbon on November 1, 1755, and killed upwards of 15,000 people.

Deism enabled Voltaire to effect a kind of reconciliation between a perfect God and the imperfect world. As a deist, Voltaire believed that God was indeed the Creator:

When I see a watch . . . , I conclude that an intelligent being arranged the springs of this mechanism so that the hand should tell the time. Similarly, when I see the springs of the human body, I conclude that an intelligent being has arranged these organs to be kept and nourished in the womb for nine months; that the eyes have been given for seeing, the hands for grasping, etc.*

But, Voltaire concluded, there was no way to determine whether or not God would attempt to perfect his creation. On one point Voltaire had no doubts: he never questioned the social usefulness of religion. "Man," he stated, "has always needed a brake." For the masses of people almost any religion, no matter how primitive, was better than atheism.

Baron d'Holbach (1723-1789), however, the most outspoken atheist of the Enlightenment, contended that men did not need the brake of religion; simple self-interest would suffice to make them behave morally. For Holbach, organized religions were sinister institutions that thwarted the benevolent operations of reason and natural law, and God was merely a "phantom of the imagination," whose existence was denied by the evils and imperfections of the world that he had supposedly created. A wealthy man, Holbach extended the hospitality of his *salon* to all comers, including Jesuit refugees from anticlerical persecution. His tolerance impressed his contemporaries more than his atheism did, and most of the *philosophes* continued to prefer deism, that halfway house between belief and disbelief.

---

* *Lettres Philosophiques*, Letter No. 6. Our translation.

* *Le Traité de Métaphysique*, Ch. II. Our translation.

Political Thought: Montesquieu

"In politics as in religion toleration is a necessity," decreed Voltaire. To him, therefore, tolerant Britain seemed utopia, and he paid the British constitution the most flattering compliment at the command of his age when he claimed that it "might have been invented by Locke, Newton, or Archimedes." Montesquieu (1689-1755), a French lawyer and *philosophe*, set out to analyze the political virtues of Britain. In his major work, *The Spirit of the Laws* (1748), Montesquieu sought to define the principles underlying both the British constitution and governments in general. He began with the very sensible premise that no one system of government suited all countries. Laws, he wrote,

... should be in relation to the climate of each country, to the quality of its soil, to its situation and extent, to the principal occupation of the natives, whether husbandmen, huntsmen, or shepherds: they should have relation to the degree of liberty which the constitution will bear; to the religion of the inhabitants, to their inclinations, riches, numbers, commerce, manners, and customs.*

Montesquieu cautioned against supposing that old customs and traditions could simply be legislated out of existence, and he cited the telling example of Peter the Great's failure to establish western ways in Russia by decree.

In spelling out the influence of heredity and environment upon forms of government, Montesquieu concluded that republics were best suited to the small and barren countries, limited monarchies to the middle-sized and more prosperous, and despotisms to vast empires. Britain, being middle-sized and prosperous, was quite properly a monarchy limited by aristocracy. The hereditary nobility sat in the House of Lords; a kind of nobility of talent, the elected representatives, composed the Commons.

_____
* *The Spirit of the Laws*, Thomas Nugent, trans. (New York, 1949), Bk. I, Ch. 3.

All this was admirable in Montesquieu's view, for he pronounced the mass of people "extremely unfit" for government. If only France had let her aristocrats retain their old political functions, she would never have sunk to her present low state.

Montesquieu found another key to the political superiority of Britain in the famous concept of checks and balances. In Parliament, Lords and Commons checked each other. In the government as a whole, the balance was maintained by means of *the separation of powers:*

When the legislative and executive powers are united in the same person, or in the same body of magistrates, there can be no liberty; because apprehensions may arise, lest the same monarch or senate should enact tyrannical laws, to execute them in a tyrannical manner. Again, there is no liberty, if the judiciary power be not separated from the legislative and executive. Were it joined with the legislative the life and liberty of the subject would be exposed to arbitrary control; for the judge would be then the legislator. Were it joined to the executive power, the judge might behave with violence and oppression.*

Montesquieu, however, failed to see that the British constitution was moving, not toward the separation of powers, but toward their concentration in the House of Commons; the cabinet was becoming the instrument for the assertion of legislative supremacy over the executive. In fairness, it must be added that these developments were far from obvious in 1748 when *The Spirit of the Laws* appeared.

Montesquieu likewise ran into trouble when he tried to derive specific corollaries from his general theorem about the influence of climate and geography on human institutions. Autocracy and Catholicism, he asserted, flourish in the Mediterranean states because they are endowed with a warm climate and rich natural resources. Moderate government and Protestantism, conversely, are at home in the colder and harsher environment of northern Europe. The facts

_____
* *The Spirit of the Laws*, Bk. XXI, Ch. 6.

did not always confirm this rule about North and South. Freedom-loving Protestant Britain and Holland behaved in good northern fashion; but if Montesquieu were correct, Prussia—barren, northern, Protestant Prussia—should have been a citadel of liberty, not the stronghold of Hohenzollern absolutism. By jumping to conclusions from insufficient evidence, Montesquieu committed a fault common in the Enlightenment. But he avoided another fault common to the age. He had too firm a grasp on political realities to assume that governments either were or should be the same everywhere. Later political thinkers made good use of the comparative methods introduced by *The Spirit of the Laws* and refined Montesquieu's judgments on the interrelationship of geography, religion, and politics.

Political Thought: Rousseau

From the standpoint of contributions to American history, as we shall see, Montesquieu and Locke are the most important political thinkers of the Enlightenment. From the European standpoint, the most important is Jean-Jacques Rousseau, whose ideals inspired the radicals of the French Revolution. Rousseau started with a sweeping generalization very typical of the Enlightenment. Whereas nature dignifies man, he contended, civilization corrupts him; man would be corrupted less if civilized institutions followed nature more closely. This was the theme that ran through many of Rousseau's principal writings. In *Emile*, he placed it at the heart of his program for educational reform; in the *Discourse on the Moral Effects of the Arts and Sciences* (1750), he used it to win a competition set by the Academy of Dijon. The Academy asked: Has the restoration of the arts and sciences had a purifying effect upon morals? Certainly not, the prize-winner answered; it has nearly ruined them.

In a second discourse, *On the Origin of the Inequality of Mankind* (1755), Rousseau blamed the vices of civilization on private property:

The first man who, having enclosed a piece of ground, bethought himself of saying, 'This is mine,' and found people simple enough to believe him, was the real founder of civil society. From how many crimes, wars, and murders, from how many horrors and misfortunes might not any one have saved mankind, by pulling up the stakes, or filling up the ditch, and crying to his fellows: 'Beware of listening to this imposter; you are undone if you once forget that the fruits of the earth belong to us all, and the earth itself to nobody.' *

Men accepted laws and governors in order to protect their property:

. . . They had too many disputes among themselves to do without arbitrators, and too much ambition and avarice to go long without masters. All ran headlong to their chains, in hopes of securing their liberty; for they had just wit enough to perceive the advantages of political institutions, without experience enough to enable them to foresee their danger. †

Government was evil, Rousseau concluded, but a necessary evil. "What, then, is to be done? Must societies be totally abolished? . . . Must we return again to the forest to live among bears?" No, civilized men could not return to a remote and primitive existence, could "no longer subsist on plants or acorns, or live without laws and magistrates." **

In his major political work, *The Social Contract* (1762), Rousseau strove to reconcile the liberty of the individual and the institution of government through a new version of the contract theory of government. Earlier theories of contract had hinged on the agreement between the people to be governed, on the one hand, and a single governor or small group of gov-

---

* "Discourse on the Origin of Inequality," in *The Social Contract and Discourses,* Everyman ed. (New York, 1913), 192.

† *Ibid.,* 205.

** *Ibid.,* 228.

ernors on the other. Earlier theories postulated a political contract; Rousseau's contract was indeed social. A whole society agreed to be ruled by its *general will:*

> Each of us puts his person and all his power in common under the supreme direction of the general will, and, in our corporate capacity, we receive each member as an indivisible part of the whole.*

"Each individual," Rousseau continued, "may have a particular will contrary or dissimilar to the general will which he has as a citizen." If the individual insisted on putting self-interest above community interest, he should be obliged to observe the general will. "This means nothing less than that he will be forced to be free." † Thus, the general will was ethical as well as political in nature, for it represented what was best for the whole community, what the community *ought* to do.

Formulating the general will, Rousseau believed, was the business of everybody. The power of legislation, he contended, could never be properly transferred from the people to an institution like the British Parliament:

> The deputies of the people . . . are not and cannot be its representatives; they are merely its stewards, and can carry through no definitive acts. Every law the people has not ratified in person is null and void—is, in fact, not a law. The people of England regards itself as free; but it is grossly mistaken; it is free only during the election of members of Parliament. As soon as they are elected, slavery overtakes it, and it is nothing.**

Executing the general will, however, could legitimately be the business of a smaller group. Like Montesquieu, Rousseau believed that the number of governors should vary inversely with the size and resources of the state—monarchy for the wealthy, aristocracy for the state "of middling size and wealth," and democracy for the small

and poor. Rousseau doubted, however, that any state was ready for that most complete form of democracy in which the many actually execute the laws. "Were there a people of gods, their government would be democratic. So perfect a government is not for men." *

Rousseau was quite aware that *The Social Contract* was not a manual of practical politics; when he made suggestions for the reform of the Polish government, his proposals were moderate, indeed rather conservative, in character. The great influence of Rousseau, however, has come chiefly from *The Social Contract;* it has not been exerted on behalf of moderation and conservatism. Almost every radical political doctrine in the past two centuries has owed something to Rousseau. Patriots and nationalists hail him as an early prophet of the creed that nations do—and should—differ. Throughout his writings he referred to "the dear love of country," and *The Social Contract* concluded with a plea for the establishment of a "civil religion." The moral code of early Christianity might be retained, Rousseau allowed, but the State should no longer have to compete with the Church for the allegiance of citizens.

Many have found in Rousseau a man who exalted the national welfare over particular individual wills, who indeed worshiped the State. Collectivists find justification in his attacks on the evils of private property and in his insistence that "the fruits of the earth belong to us all." Dictators have used the doctrine of the general will to sanction the methods of the police state. Without bothering about the niceties of ascertaining the general will, the dictator simply assumes that he has a special knowledge of it, as in the case of Hitler's celebrated "intuition." In forcing his subjects to obey his dictates, he is "forcing them to be free," in accordance with the precept of Rousseau.

But Rousseau was also the prophet of

---

* *The Social Contract,* Everyman ed. (New York, 1913), 13.
† *Ibid.,* 15.
** *Ibid.,* 78.

* *The Social Contract,* 56.

democracy and individualism. The authoritarian interpretation overlooks both his personal career of rebellion against the Old Régime and the strong idealistic tone of his writings. "Were there a people of gods, their government would be democratic." This declaration has inspired the democratic disciples of Rousseau from the French Revolution on down to the present. The people are not gods? Then they must be trained in godliness. Rousseau himself suggested how this might come about. *Emile* showed how education, if made suitably progressive, would help, and *The Social Contract* implied that men might one day become so virtuous that they would always follow the general will naturally, would no longer need to be "forced to be free."

Enlightened Despotism   Many *philosophes*, however, sought a short cut to utopia, a political method that was more practicable than that of Rousseau or Montesquieu and that could operate within the framework of existing monarchical institutions. They found the answer in enlightened despotism. The Physiocrats, the chief proponents of enlightened despotism, had little sympathy with the concern of Montesquieu and Rousseau for the precise status of the legislative power. In the Physiocratic view, God was the legislator, nature preserved the divine legislation, and the sole duty of government lay in administering these natural laws. Democracy and aristocracy alike had the fatal weakness of delegating administrative authority to individuals whose passing selfish aims clashed with the permanent welfare of the nation. By contrast, the Physiocrats explained, the personal interests of hereditary monarchs coincided with national interests through their "co-ownership" of the territories under their rule. Because kings were best situated to work for the true national interest, they should be despots, not in any sinister sense but on the model of the benevolent strong men of the past, like the greatest of the Renaissance Italian despots. The enlightened despot would unearth the natural laws decreed by God and clear away the accumulation of artificial, man-made law that was choking progress.

This program of enlightened despotism won an immediate, enthusiastic response from European monarchs. And no wonder: it afforded them the chance to pose as the champions of reason and progress while pressing their age-old fight to make royal authority more absolute. In the late eighteenth century self-styled "enlightened despots" occupied many European thrones—in Prussia, Frederick the Great; in Austria, Joseph II; in Russia, Catherine the Great; in Spain, Charles III; in Sweden, Gustavus III; and still others. Their lands were proving-grounds not only for the theory of enlightened despotism but also for the whole reform program of the Enlightenment.

III: *The Enlightened Despots*

Prussia:
Frederick the Great   Of all the monarchs of eighteenth-century Europe, Frederick II, the Great, of Prussia (1740-1786), appeared best attuned to the Enlightenment. As a youth, he rebelled against the drill-sergeant methods of his father, Frederick William I. He delighted in music, and played the flute, which he took with him everywhere, even on military campaigns. An attentive reader of the *philosophes*, he exchanged letters with them and brought Voltaire to live as his pensioner in his palace at Potsdam near

Berlin. He wrote a pamphlet, *Anti-Machiavel*, denouncing the immorality of *The Prince*. And he himself laid down the fundamental requirements for an enlightened despot:

> Princes, sovereigns, kings are not clothed with supreme authority to plunge with impunity into debauchery and luxury. . . . [The prince] should often remind himself that he is a man just as the least of his subjects. If he is the first judge, the first general, the first financier, the first minister of the nation, . . . it is in order to fulfill the duties which these titles impose upon him. He is only the first servant of the state, obliged to act with fairness, wisdom, and unselfishness, as if at every instant he would have to render an account of his administration to his citizens.*

Frederick was indeed "the first servant of the state," toiling long and hard at his desk or on the battlefield. But did he also act with "fairness, wisdom, and unselfishness"? Despite his *Anti-Machiavel*, Frederick conducted foreign and military affairs in true Machiavellian style; his invasion of Silesia would have aroused the envy of Caesar Borgia. At home, closeted in his Potsdam palace where he conducted the business of state by correspondence, he drove his subordinates like slaves. Viewed as a general, a diplomat, and the master mechanic of Prussian administration, Frederick the Great was efficient and successful, but he was scarcely enlightened. His claim to be an enlightened despot must rise or fall on the record of his social and economic reforms.

No Physiocrat could have done more than Frederick to improve Prussian agriculture. From England he imported clover, crop rotation, and the iron plow, which turned up the soil more effectively than the old wooden share. He drained the swamps of the lower Oder Valley, opened up farms in Silesia and elsewhere, and brought in 300,000 immigrants to populate the new lands. After the ravages of the Seven Years' War, he gave the peasants tools, stock, and seed to repair their ruined farms. He nursed along the admirable German tradition of scientific forestry, then in its infancy.

Yet Frederick was hostile to the doctrine of laissez-faire and cut imports to the bone in order to save money for support of the army. His mercantilism stimulated the growth of Prussian industry, particularly the textiles and metals needed by the army. But it also placed a staggering burden of taxation on his subjects and produced several economic absurdities. For instance, Frederick tried to make Prussia grow its own tobacco, for which the climate was not suited. And, since the German taste for coffee required a large outlay of money abroad, he laid a heavy duty on imported coffee beans, and even established a special corps of French "coffee-smellers" to trap smugglers.

The religious and social policies of Frederick the Great likewise combined the Age of Reason at its most reasonable with the Old Régime at its least enlightened. A deist, Frederick prided himself on religious tolerance. He invited Jesuits to seek refuge in Prussia and protected the minority of Catholics in his predominantly Protestant kingdom, urging them to build their church steeples as high as they liked. Yet the same Frederick consistently practiced anti-Semitism. He levied special heavy taxes on his Jewish subjects and tried to exclude them from the professions and from the civil service. Jews, he alleged, were "useless to the state."

Frederick the Great rendered Prussians a great service by his judicial reforms. He reduced the use of torture; he put an end to the curious custom of taking appeals from the ordinary courts to university faculties and instituted a regular system of appellate courts. He mitigated the venal practice of bribing judges by insisting that "tips" received from litigants be placed in

---

* "Essai sur les Formes de Gouvernement et sur les Devoirs des Souverains." *Oeuvres Posthumes* (Berlin. 1788), VI, 64, 83-84. Our translation

a common pool from which each judge should draw only his fair share. Yet the same Frederick did nothing to loosen the ties of serfdom that still bound much of the Prussian peasantry. When he gave the peasants material assistance and urged them to learn the "three r's," his aims were severely utilitarian. Peasants were to learn nothing beyond the rudiments of reading and writing; otherwise, they might become discontented with their station in life. Regarding the middle class, too, with disdain, Frederick respected only the landed nobility and gentry. And even the favored Junkers did not escape Frederick's penny-pinching. Although he appointed only Junkers as army officers, he discouraged them from marriage because every officer's wife represented a potential widow to whom the state would owe a pension.

Frederick seemed constitutionally incapable of getting along with other people. Voltaire, the great French champion of toleration, could not tolerate the strain of daily association with Frederick. When the King requested Voltaire to edit his indifferent French poetry, Voltaire made a cutting remark about washing the dirty linen of royalty; Frederick retorted by comparing his guest to an orange, to be sucked dry and thrown away. The two men eventually renewed their friendship through the less demanding medium of correspondence. Frederick despised and neglected his wife. His subjects sighed with relief at the news of his death, and his will directed that he be buried beside his pet dogs. "Such," remarked a French observer, "is the last mark of contempt which he thought proper to cast upon mankind." This judgment is too harsh. Actually, Frederick embodied two often conflicting political philosophies—the humane principles of the Enlightenment and the severe traditions of the Hohenzollerns. He was an enlightened despot only so far as the precepts of the Age of Reason could be reconciled to the realities of Hohenzollern kingship.

Austria: Maria Theresa and Joseph II

Frederick's decisive victory in the War of the Austrian Succession laid bare the basic weaknesses of the Habsburgs' dynastic empire. The Empress Maria Theresa (1740-1780) at once saw the need for starting reforms and often took as her model the institutions of her hated but successful Hohenzollern rival. She increased taxes, especially on the nobility, strengthened the central government at the expense of local aristocratic assemblies, and obliged the non-German provinces to accept the hegemony of the German officials and the German language of Vienna. Maria Theresa employed both force and charm to get her way. The nobles of Hungary momentarily forgot their anti-German tradition when the beautiful and spirited empress, her infant son in her arms, personally appealed to their chivalry in the crisis of the War of the Austrian Succession.

The Empress was the first housewife of the realm as well as the first servant of the state. She was the mother of sixteen children, and she adored and respected Francis, her grasping, fickle husband. Maria Theresa, however, was a devout Catholic and fundamentally out of sympathy with the Age of Reason. "Lady Prayerful," as Catherine the Great called her, banned the works of Rousreau and Voltaire and even forbade the circulation of the Catholic *Index*, lest that list of forbidden books pique the curiosity of her subjects.

The true Habsburg representative of enlightened despotism was Joseph II, the eldest son of Maria Theresa, named by her to be emperor and co-regent on the death of Francis in 1765. Frederick the Great wrote Voltaire an estimate of the new emperor:

Born in a bigoted court, he has cast off its superstition; raised in magnificence, he has assumed simple manners; nourished on incense, he is modest; burning with a thirst for glory, he sacrifices his ambition to the filial duty which he executes scrupulously; and, having had only pedantic teachers, he still has enough taste to read Voltaire and to appreciate his merits.*

Frederick exaggerated only a little. Earnest and industrious in the highest degree, Joseph promised to make "philosophy the legislator of my empire." Maria Theresa thwarted Joseph until her death in 1780; for fifteen years, mother and son clashed, particularly over Joseph's anticlericalism. As a loving son Joseph mourned the passing of Maria Theresa, but as a *philosophe* he welcomed the release from her tutelage. The impatient emperor, now the sole ruler of Austria, plunged into activity; during his ten-year reign (1780-1790), eleven thousand laws and six thousand decrees issued from Vienna.

Joseph at once reversed his mother's religious policy. Calvinist, Lutheran, and Orthodox gained full toleration for the first time in the history of Catholic Austria. And, with a generosity unparalleled in Habsburg annals, the Emperor took measures to end the ghetto existence of the Jews. He exempted Jews from paying special taxes and from wearing the yellow patch as a badge of inferiority. Joseph brought the Catholic Church under strict state control, making himself rather than the pope the arbiter of church activities in Austria. He encouraged what he considered socially useful in Catholicism and dealt ruthlessly with what he judged superfluous and harmful. Thus he established hundreds of new churches and at the same time made religious holidays less frequent. He called monks "the most dangerous and useless subjects in every state," and promised to convert "the monk of mere show into a useful citizen." He cut in half the number of monks and nuns and, of 2100 monasteries and nunneries, he suppressed 700, chiefly those run by the contemplative orders. Houses actively engaged in educational or charitable work were generally spared. The government sold or

leased the lands of the suppressed establishments, applying the revenue to the support of the hospitals that were beginning to earn Vienna its reputation as a great medical center.

Unlike Frederick the Great, Joseph really believed in social equality and popular education. His government provided the teachers and textbooks for primary schools. More than a quarter of the school-age children in Austria actually attended school—the best record of any country in late eighteenth-century Europe. Everyone in Vienna, high and low, was invited to visit the Prater, the great public park of the capital, the entrance to which bore the inscription, "A place of pleasure for all men, prepared for them by their friend." The new Austrian legal code followed the recommendations of Beccaria in abolishing capital punishment and most tortures and in prescribing equality before the law. Aristocratic offenders, like commoners, were sentenced to stand in the pillory and to sweep the streets of Vienna. Joseph's peasant policy marked the climax of his equalitarianism. He freed the serfs, abolished most of their obligations to the manorial lords, and deprived the latter of their traditional right of administering justice to the peasantry.

Joseph's economic policies incorporated both the new doctrines of the Physiocrats and the old practices of mercantilism. He levied high tariffs on imports, yet experimented with the collection of a single tax on land as recommended by Quesnay. In politics, however, Joseph adhered to his mother's Germanizing program. He customarily spoke German, patronized German writers, and made the French playhouse in Vienna a German-language theater. He rode roughshod over the autonomous rights of Bohemia, Belgium, and Hungary.

Joseph's reforms aroused increasing opposition. The devout peasants, almost oblivious of his well-meaning attempts to improve their social and economic status, keenly resented his meddling with old re-

* "Correspondance avec les Souverains," *Oeuvres Complètes de Voltaire* (Paris, 1828), LXXIV, 37. Our translation.

Emperor Joseph II of Austria, working a plow.

ligious customs. The nobility clamored against his equalitarian legislation; in the case of the single-tax experiment, their opposition was so violent that he had to revoke the decree a month after it was issued. Hungary and Belgium rose in open rebellion against his centralizing efforts and forced him to confirm their autonomous liberties. In foreign policy, too, the ambitious—and in this instance unenlightened—plans of Joseph II miscarried. By participating in the Turkish war of the late 1780's (see below, p. 304), Austria gained only a narrow strip of Balkan territory. Meantime, Joseph twice attempted to annex lands belonging to the important South German state of Bavaria, where the death of the ruling family opened another of those succession quarrels so common in the eighteenth century. On both occasions, Joseph was thwarted by Frederick the Great, who was determined to check any advance of Habsburg power in Germany.

Joseph II worked himself to death, as one of his friends observed, by "governing too much and reigning too little." The Emperor defended his habit of interfering personally in the details of government:

What else can I do in this country devoid of mind, without soul, without zeal, without heart in the work? I am killing myself because I cannot rouse up those whom I want to make work; but I hope I shall not die until I have so wound up the machine that others cannot put it out of order, even if they try to do so.[*]

Joseph never got the machine properly wound up; he could not implant in the Austrian bureaucracy the almost inhuman Prussian discipline that was needed to serve his purposes. Joseph II died unshaken in the conviction that he had pursued the proper course, yet believing that he had accomplished nothing. In the judgment of posterity, however, Joseph appears as the most truly enlightened despot. In ten years he attempted more than Frederick attempted in almost half a century. Though some of his major reforms, like the abolition of serfdom, were repealed soon after his death, others survived him, helping to transform the Habsburg lands into a more modern centralized state.

Sweden and Spain   Among the lesser enlightened despots, Gustavus III of Sweden and Charles III of Spain ranked high. Gustavus III (1771-1792), the nephew of Frederick the Great, was the most theatrical monarch of the century. While he distracted Swedish

---

[*] Quoted in Prince de Ligne, *His Memoirs, Letters, and Miscellaneous Papers* (Boston, 1902), II, 132.

party leaders at the opera one evening, his soldiers staged a *coup* that enabled him to revive the royal authority and to dissolve the powerful factions of Hats and Caps (see above, p. 258). Gustavus announced in ringing speeches his devotion to the Age of Reason. In economics and religion, his enlightenment outdistanced that of his uncle in Prussia, for he removed obstacles to both domestic and foreign trade and extended toleration to Jews as well as to the non-Lutheran Christian sects. Success, however, turned the head of Gustavus III. As he became more and more arbitrary, the nobles determined to recover their old power; in 1792, he was assassinated at a masquerade in Stockholm, and oligarchy resumed its feeble course in Sweden.

Charles III (1759-1788), Elizabeth Farnese's "Baby Carlos," inherited the Spanish crown on the death of his half-brother. He was a remarkably homely monarch, but he had already been seasoned in the struggle against feudal and clerical conservatism by a long and successful apprenticeship as King of Naples. In Spain, Charles III energetically renewed the progressive policies begun by his father, Philip V (see Chapter VIII). Though a pious Catholic, he objected strongly to the political activities of the Church and even expelled the Jesuits from the native country of their founder, Loyola. He consolidated the authority of the Crown and reduced that of the aristocracy. He curbed the privileges of the great sheep-ranchers, whose almost unlimited grazing rights blighted Spanish agriculture. To enliven the torpid Spanish economy, he undertook irrigation projects, reclaimed waste lands, and established new roads, canals, banks, and textile mills. The results were as-

tonishing: Spain's foreign commerce increased fivefold during the reign of Charles III. His successors, however, abandoned his forward-looking policies, and Spain soon slipped back into her old and unenlightened ways.

The Limitations of Enlightened Despotism

The problem of succession, in fact, sapped the whole structure of enlightened despotism. So long as monarchs came to the throne by the accident of their birth, there was nothing to prevent the unenlightened mediocrity from succeeding the enlightened despot. This happened in Spain, in Sweden, and in Prussia, where the great Frederick was followed by his nephew, Frederick William II (1786-1797), who was little more than a nincompoop. The principal exception occurred in Austria, where the enlightened Leopold II (1790-1792), fresh from an effective apprenticeship in Tuscany, salvaged some of the reforms of his brother, Joseph II.

Even the least of the enlightened despots improved a few of the bad features of the Old Régime. But not even the best of them struck a happy balance between enlightenment and despotism. Joseph II was too doctrinaire, too inflexible in his determination to apply the full reform program of the Age of Reason. Frederick, on the other hand, obsessed with the desire to strengthen the Crown, helped to entrench the power of elements often hostile to the whole Enlightenment. And in Russia, the century after the death of Peter the Great provided another striking illustration of the limitations of enlightened despotism.

IV: Russia, 1725-1825

The Fate of the
Autocracy, 1725-1762

When Peter the Great died, he left a tangled family situation in which nobody could truly decide who was his legitimate successor. Over the course of the next thirty-seven years, the throne changed hands seven times. The succession zigzagged back and forth across the family tree of the Romanovs: first to Peter's widow, who ruled as Empress Catherine I (1725-1727); then to Peter's young grandson, son of the murdered Alexis (see above, Chapter VII), who became Peter II (1727-1730); then to Peter's niece, who reigned for a wretched decade as Empress Anne (1730-1740); then to Anne's great-nephew, Ivan VI, who was only eight weeks old when he began his one-year reign (1740-1741); then to Peter's own daughter by Catherine I, the Empress Elizabeth (1741-1762); then to Elizabeth's nephew, Peter III, who reigned only for six months in 1762; and finally to Peter III's brilliant young widow, who became Catherine II, the Great, and dominated Russia as Peter I himself had done (1762-1796). More important than the individuals who governed Russia between the death of Peter the Great and the accession of Catherine the Great were the social forces contending for power, and the social processes at work in an autocracy suddenly deprived of its autocrat and for so long unable to produce a new one. At every stage in the series of palace overturns, the guards' regiments founded by Peter exercised a decisive influence. The service nobility, no longer restrained by the tsar, now entered into its era of dominance.

On the death of Peter the Great, his immediate circle, particularly Menshikov (see Chapter VII), had every reason to fear the passage of the throne to the nine-year-old Peter, son of Alexis, and possible heir to the loyalties of the old nobility who had hated Peter the Great. Menshikov therefore strongly supported his one-time mistress, the Empress Catherine I, and succeeded in rallying to her side members of the guards who had come to like her while on campaigns. Catherine herself took little interest in affairs of state, and in practice Menshikov ran Russia during the two years of her reign. He tried to make himself secure by appointing a six-man "Supreme Privy Council" at the top of the administration, and to perpetuate his power he even planned to marry his daughter to the young heir, the future Peter II. On the death of Catherine I in 1727, he took the eleven-year-old boy into his house, where he proceeded to make him an alcoholic, like his father.

But Menshikov's arrogance had alienated even his followers. By 1728, the old boyars, led by the families of Dolgoruky and Galitsyn, had captured the throne, and Menshikov was exiled. Two Dolgoruky princes put themselves on the Supreme Privy Council, and the young Peter was engaged to a member of their family. The ascendancy of boyar families marked the return to supreme influence of a group that had been losing power ever since the days of Ivan the Terrible. Their plans were brought into crisis by the sudden death of Peter II on the very day scheduled for his coronation (January 19, 1730).

Their program can be studied in the set of conditions they now drew up for submission to the new candidate for the throne, Anne, the widow of the Duke of Courland. Summoning her from her petty Baltic principality, the Dolgoruky and Galitsyns demanded that before she take the throne, she sign the "Articles" they had prepared. By their terms, she undertook never to marry or name an heir, and to continue the Supreme Privy Council, which by now had eight members, including four Dolgoruky and two Galitsyns. She further swore not to make peace or war, levy taxes, confer ranks in the army above that of colonel, or spend state funds without the specific consent of the Council. Moreover, the Councillors claimed for themselves supervision over the guards' regiments. This insistence on limiting the power of the new Empress reflected the outraged feelings of the old boyars, who had long been claiming the right to be consulted on all matters of state. The entire program was the most explicit constitutional destruction of all that Peter the Great had striven for. Anne signed the "Articles." Had she kept to their provisions, Russia would have embarked on an era of boyar oligarchy, concentrated in families of ancient birth.

But the military-service nobility looked with horror at the prospect of taking orders indefinitely from the small group of old boyars. And the service gentry had the power, in the guards' regiments. What they wanted was an autocrat who would loosen the bonds that Peter the Great had forged for them. And so, when one of the Supreme Privy Councillors, the clever German Ostermann, convinced Anne that she need not abide by the Articles, the gentry in its armed might supported him. Anne simply tore up the Articles, and the attempt to create an oligarchy of the two great families failed. It was the gentry who now had the real power in Russia.

Once in power, Anne allowed her lover, the German adventurer Biren, and a flock of Germans to obtain the most influential positions in the state. The secret police, briefly abolished after the death of Peter the Great, was now revived, and many thousands suffered torture, exile, and death at its hands. When Anne died, the German favorites fell out among themselves. Ostermann, a man of real ability, together with an excellent soldier, Marshal Münnich,

brought about Biren's downfall and exile; then Ostermann forced Münnich out. Meanwhile, the tsar was the infant Ivan VI, whose mother, a German princess, acted as regent, and was so lazy that she lounged in her bedroom without the energy even to put on her clothes. Foreign intrigue produced the next shift in the imperial title. The French were deeply anxious to terminate the power of Ostermann, who had been instrumental in cementing an alliance between Russia and France's traditional enemy, Austria. The intrigues of a clever and able French ambassador played on the patriotic feelings of the guardsmen, disgusted with the behavior of the Germans at court. In 1741 a guards' *coup* brought to the throne a true daughter of Peter the Great, Elizabeth. The infant Ivan VI vanished into a prison cell with his indolent mother.

Elizabeth inherited her father's lust for life but not his brains or interest in affairs of state. A succession of lovers had kept her busy all her life, and her habits did not change when she came to the throne. Though owning thousands of splendid dresses, she lived rather sluttishly in grubby palaces and enjoyed most of all a rousing peasant banquet with plenty to drink and lots of rustic music. Important state papers languished for days because the Empress could not be bothered to read them, much less sign them. Though she proclaimed her intention of restoring her father's methods of rule, she had no clear conception of what these had been. In an autocracy the autocrat has to take an interest in the affairs of state and assume responsibility for them; this Elizabeth did not do, and Russia drifted.

Soon after her accession, Elizabeth proclaimed her nephew, the half-mad Peter, heir to the throne. In 1745 he married a clever little German princess, the future Catherine II. Peter III, as he became after his succession in January, 1762, has had a bad "press"; he surely was not unusually intelligent, but was hardly the utter lunatic portrayed in the memoirs of his celebrated wife, who loathed him. The chief trouble with Peter seems to have been his great admiration for Prussia and his dislike of Russia. His effort to introduce rigid discipline on the Prussian model into the Russian army and his hatred for the influential guards' regiments cost him the friends he needed most. He could have played his war-games with his toy soldiers, held court-martials on rats whom he convicted of gnawing cardboard fortresses, and swilled his favorite English beer with impunity, and he would not have been any worse than many another tsar. But to drill the guards in the Prussian manner was unforgivable. So a new palace revolution took place, and Peter was eventually murdered by one of Catherine's lovers. The Empress' own role in this overturn is still obscure.

Nobles and Serfs, 1730-1762

A deeply dissatisfied social group that had the power to make and unmake autocrats naturally had a program for the redress of its own grievances. Once the gentry had enabled Anne to tear up the Articles in 1730, it at once began strenuous efforts to realize the program and thus to emancipate itself from the servitude riveted upon it by Peter. Anne repealed the law requiring the noble to leave his estate intact to one of his sons. She founded a military school for noblemen's sons, graduation from which entitled one to a commission; no longer did young gentlemen have to start their careers in the ranks, as under Peter. Anne shortened the term of service from life to twenty-five years, and exempted one son of every family with at least two sons, so that there would be one member of each generation able to look after the estate.

Simultaneously came a deepening of the authority of the nobles over the serfs. The proprietors became the government's agents for the collection of the poll tax. Serfs could no longer obtain their freedom by enlisting

in the army and could not engage in trade or purchase land without written permission from their masters. Masters could deport their serfs to Siberia, and might punish them physically in any way they wished. Moreover, under Elizabeth, a series of laws restricted the right to own serfs to those who were already nobles. Thus the class that had been open to new recruits under Peter was closed by his daughter.

In 1762, finally, Peter III decreed that the nobles no longer need serve at all unless they wished to do so; except in the midst of a war, they might resign any time they chose. It was little wonder that some of the nobles proposed to erect a solid gold statue of Peter III. To understand the revolutionary nature of this liberation of the nobles from a duty to serve, we must remember that they had historically obtained their lands and serfs only on condition that they would serve. Now they kept their lands and serfs but had no obligations. Yet the service that had been hated when it was compulsory became fashionable now that it was optional; there was really little else for a Russian noble to do except serve the state. In contemplating all this, a great Russian historian remarked that the logic of history would have properly required that all serfs be liberated the day after the nobles were released from their duty to serve. But nothing could have been further from the thoughts of Peter III or of any other Russian leader.

In these middle decades of the eighteenth century, successive waves of foreign influence affected the Russian nobility. It was not only the influx of foreigners that brought in western habits; it was also the involvement of Russia in the European wars of the period, and the increased travel abroad by Russians. Especially under Elizabeth, when the hated Germans disappeared from court, the way was clear for the French to exert their influence. With the French language came the literature, and many a Russian noble bought French books by the yard for his library because it was the thing to do. The champagne business boomed as never before (the Russians liked the sweet kind that most Frenchmen despised). French styles of dress were slavishly copied by both men and women. Francomania took its extreme form among those Russians who were ashamed of being Russian and who would not fall in love with a young girl who spoke no French. Indeed, the noble and the peasant no longer spoke the same language. This deep rift between the Frenchified nobles and the Russian people was to prove of critical importance for later Russian history.

Catherine the Great, 1762-1796

With the advent of Catherine II after the murder of her husband, Peter III, we come to the most arresting personality to occupy the Russian throne since the death of Peter. Brought up in a petty German court, she found herself translated to St. Petersburg as a mere girl, living with a husband she detested, and forced to pick her way through the intrigues that flourished around the Empress Elizabeth. She managed to steer clear of trouble only by using her keen wits. Catherine fancied herself as an intellectual; she wrote plays, edited a satirical journal, and steeped herself in the literature of the Enlightenment. Both before and after ascending the throne she maintained a goodly supply of lovers, several of whom had important roles in affairs of state.

Catherine had a truly twentieth-century feeling for the importance of public relations, and cared deeply that leading spirits in the West should think well of her and of the state of Russia under her rule. Hence her voluminous correspondence with westerners. She invited Diderot to take up in Russia the task of editing the *Encyclopédie;* then she bought his library, but he kept his books, and received a pension—very favorable publicity for Russia and the Russian

Empress. Diderot himself visited Russia in 1773; though he came back entranced with Catherine, who, he said, had the soul of Brutus and the charms of Cleopatra, the visit was not entirely a success: Catherine complained that in the excitement of conversation the learned *philosophe* pinched her legs until they were black and blue. Voltaire, though he judiciously stayed away from Russia, accepted Catherine's bounty, and in return poured out the praises that she yearned for:

. . . All eyes must now be turned toward the north star. Your Imperial Majesty has discovered a road to glory hitherto unknown to all other sovereigns. . . . You have truly become the benefactress of Europe and you have acquired more subjects by the greatness of your soul than others have conquered by force of arms.[*]

Catherine would perhaps have liked to reform conditions in Russia; there was something of the enlightened despot about her "style." But as a woman and a foreigner and a usurper, owing the throne to a conspiracy, she could not act upon her principles. Depending as she did upon the good will of the nobility, she could not lay a finger on the institution of serfdom. Indeed, she had to reward her supporters with vast grants of state land, inhabited by hundreds of thousands of state peasants, who once could not be sold but who now became privately owned serfs who could be sold. Even in theory, Catherine felt, Russia was so large that the only possible form of government was an autocracy. As an autocrat she was as arbitrary as any of her predecessors.

Once firmly established on the throne, however, Catherine decided to convoke a commission to codify the laws of Russia, a task that had not been accomplished since 1649. Catherine herself, with the help of advisers, spent three years composing the *Instruction* to the delegates, a long, rather

---

[*] Letter of June 21, 1776, in *Documents of Catherine the Great*, W. F. Reddaway ed. (Cambridge, England, 1936), 10. Translation ours.

windy document, full of abstract argument drawn from Montesquieu's *Spirit of the Laws* and Beccaria's *Crimes and Punishments* but altered to conform with the Empress' own beliefs. Here one can discern no intention to meddle with the fundamental institutions of Russia, but some concern for eliminating the worst abuses inherent in the institutions. The 564 delegates to the commission were elected by organs of the central government and by every social class in Russia except the serf peasants. Each delegate—noble, townsman, crown peasant, Cossack—was charged to bring with him a collection of written documents from his neighbors presenting their grievances and demands for change.

Many of these survive and teach us a great deal about the state of public opinion in Catherine's Russia. Nobody seems to have been dissatisfied with the autocracy; at least we find no requests that it modify its power or consult its subjects. People did seek more rights and duties for local government, and wanted their own obligations more clearly defined. Each class of representatives was eager to extend the rights of that class: the free peasants wanted to own serfs; the townsmen wanted to own serfs and be the only class allowed to engage in trade; the nobles wanted to engage in trade, and to have their exclusive right to own serfs confirmed. After 203 sessions lasting over a year and a half, devoted to inconclusive and sometimes heated debate, Catherine put an end to the labors of the commission in 1768. It had not codified the laws, but from Catherine's own point of view it had been a success; she knew that most of her subjects supported her as absolute autocrat. It is important to remember that the commission, with all its imperfections, was the last effort by the tsardom to consult the Russian people as a whole for 138 years—until revolution summoned the first Duma (parliament) into existence in 1906 (see Chapter XV).

Catherine turned the spadework of the legislative commission to good advantage in her later reforms, which resulted from the great rebellion of the Cossacks under the leadership of Pugachev, 1773-1775. Pugachev roused the frontiersmen to revolt against Catherine's cancelation of their special privileges. Pretending to be Tsar Peter III, and promising liberty and land to the serfs who joined his forces, Pugachev swept over a wide area of southeastern Russia and finally marched toward Moscow. Like the disturbances of the seventeenth century, Pugachev's revolt revealed the existence of bitter discontent in Russia, a discontent directed not at the supreme autocrat but at the landlords and local officials.

The ramshackle structure of provincial administration almost collapsed under the strain of Pugachev's rebellion. Orders filtered down slowly to local officials, and the soldiers defending the government moved almost as slowly. When the rebels were finally suppressed, and Pugachev was traveling northward in an iron cage before being drawn and quartered, Catherine took action. Her reorganization of local government (1775) created fifty provinces where there had been twenty before. She thus replaced a small number of unwieldy units with a larger number of small provinces, each containing roughly 300,000 to 400,000 inhabitants. The reform of 1775 gave the nobles the lion's share of provincial offices but subjected them to the close direction of the central government, which had its own administrative, financial, and legal representatives in each province.

In the charter of 1785 the nobles received exemption from military service and taxation and secured absolute mastery over the fate of their serfs and their estates. A charter to the towns in the same year (1785) disclosed Catherine's sympathy with the tiny but growing middle class. It established the principle of municipal self-government, but the principle remained a dead letter because of the rigorous class distinctions maintained in the backward urban centers of

*Catherine the Great, by
Giovani Battiste Lampi.*

Russia. For the serfs, needless to say, there was no charter. Indeed, besides adding almost a million to their number by the gifts of state lands to private persons, Catherine increased still further the power of the proprietors. Long accustomed to selling the serfs without their land, the landlords now received the right to make such sales legally. Serf families were broken up, violent punishments and even torture employed (one notorious lady tortured seventy-five of her own serfs to death; but she was imprisoned for it), serfs were gambled away at cards, given as presents, and mortgaged for loans. All serf-owners were not cruel any more than all slave-owners in our own slave states, but both institutions tended to degrade both master and man. As in the American south, there was a distinction in Russia between field hands and household servants: great landowners often had hundreds of the latter, some of whom were formed into orchestras, gave dramatic performances, tutored the sons of the family, or acted as household poets and scientists.

The contrast between the climate of the Enlightenment which surrounded the court and the actual conditions in Russia was keenly felt by sensitive men. Foremost among them was a young noble, Alexander Radishchev, educated abroad and widely traveled. In his *Journey from St. Petersburg to Moscow* Radishchev included vivid and horrifying vignettes of serfdom and the abuses of the administration. Moreover, Radishchev's poetry praised Cromwell, the regicide. It is possible that the author's truly western culture might have enabled him to get away with this in the early days of Catherine's reign. But by 1790 the French Revolution was under way, and Catherine had begun to hate the French and "their abominable bonfire" as much as she had formerly loved them. Proposing to burn the dangerous books of the Enlightenment, which had produced the tragedy of revolution, she could hardly overlook the subversive character of Radishchev's book. Off he went into exile in Siberia. Similarly, the humanitarian freemason, Nicholas Novikov, manager of the newly active Moscow University Press, editor of newspapers, and sponsor of campaigns to raise money and food for famine-stricken peasants, also found himself jailed on flimsy charges. Though Novikov had done nothing against the régime, it could not tolerate the continuance of any enterprise it did not dominate. The two enlightened intellectuals and humanitarians, Radishchev and Novikov, not only serve as an illustration of the contrast between Catherine's professed principles and her actual conduct but also provide the first real example of thoroughly westernized individual Russians.

Paul (1796–1801)

Catherine's son Paul (who may or may not have been the son of Catherine's husband Peter III) succeeded his mother in 1796 as a man of forty-two. All his life his mother had deeply distrusted him, fearing that there might be a conspiracy to oust her and install Paul, ostensibly at least a legitimate Romanov. The best-educated Russian royal personage to date, active and eager to serve the state, Paul found himself given no duties, kept in the dark about the secrets of state, and even deprived of his two eldest children, Alexander and Constantine, whom Catherine insisted on educating herself. Paul liked military life, and admired Prussian methods, but all he could do was drill a small garrison on his country estate and dress them in Prussian uniform.

Consequently, when Paul finally did succeed to the throne, he appeared to be motivated chiefly by a wish to undo his mother's work and act in every possible way contrary to the precedents she had set. He exiled some of his mother's favorites, and released many of her prisoners, including Radishchev and Novikov. Paul believed in legality and system, and hoped to install a great deal more of both in Russia. He tried to restore more power and order to the central government by putting the colleges (see above, p. 233) under single ministers in place of the former boards of directors.

Paul's behavior, however, was spasmodic and eccentric. He forbade the importation of all sheet-music into Russia because he feared that all music would be as revolutionary as the *Marseillaise*. He imposed a strict curfew on the capital. He issued a manifesto limiting to three the number of days per week a serf might be required to work on his master's land, but it is not clear whether this was a binding law or only a recommendation. In any case, he continued to give away state lands, and transformed some half a million state peasants into privately owned chattels. What was probably fatal to Paul was his policy of toughness toward the nobility. A noble, he is said to have remarked, is the man I am talking to at the moment, and he ceases to be a noble when I stop talking to him. This definition could hardly be expected to appeal to the privileged masters of Russia. Paul exacted compulsory service again, and in the provinces he curtailed the powers of the nobility. Nobles found themselves forced to meet the bills for public buildings, paying new taxes on their lands, and subjected to corporal punishments for crimes. Paul, like Peter III, wanted to Prussianize the army, and especially to inculcate in the officers a sense of responsibility for the men. In the guards' regiments such programs were detested, and a conspiracy of guardsmen ended in 1801 with Paul's murder and Alexander's succession. The forces behind the *coup* were the same as those that had engineered so many shifts of power during the preceding century. The precise degree to which Alexander was informed of the *coup* in advance is sometimes debated, but he knew at least that the conspirators intended to force his father's abdication.

Alexander 1 (1801-1825)

In Alexander I there came to the throne an emperor whom historians usually call "enigmatic." Educated by a liberal Swiss tutor, he absorbed so much of the new eighteenth-century doctrines that he actually blossomed out with a red-white-and-blue ribbon, the colors of revolutionary France, on hearing of the fall of the Bastille to the Paris mob. Nothing could have been more unexpected of the eventual heir to the Russian throne. Yet the application of liberal principles in Russia would involve a direct challenge to all the most powerful forces in society. So, although Alexander would occasionally say to his intimates that some day he would grant Russia a constitution and himself retire to a castle on the banks of the Rhine, in fact this was little but romantic twaddle. Tall and handsome, utterly devastating to the ladies, charming and cultivated, Alexander liked to please everybody; he vacillated, compromised, and in the end accomplished very little. Moreover, he loved power dearly, and always shied away from proposals to limit it.

The quarter-century of his reign was twice interrupted by major wars against Napoleon, in 1805-1807, and in 1812-1815 (see Chapter XI). In the first period of relative peace, 1801-1805, Alexander gathered round him a small group of youthful intimates, which he called the "unofficial committee." One of the members, Stroganov, had been an active member of the Jacobin Club in Paris during the revolution; two others greatly admired the English system of government. Meeting regularly after dinner over coffee and brandy, the unofficial committee had as its self-appointed task the preparation of a constitution for Russia, after due study of all known constitutions. But the records of its deliberations reveal that its discussions were little more than the unsystematic talk of pleasant, well-born young men who had dined well. A decree sponsored by the committee did abolish the system of colleges, and created eight new ministries to take their places; but this in fact had already been almost accomplished by Paul. When the committee stopped meeting in 1803, it had done nothing with regard to serfdom. But the Tsar himself in these years passed two laws, whose very mildness shows how little he intended to disturb existing institutions. One of them forbade the public advertisement of sales of serfs without land, but the law was easily circumvented. The other created a new category of "free farmers," serfs who had been freed by their masters, and prescribed that if a proprietor freed an entire village of serfs he must confer their land upon them at the same time. This left the initiative for liberation entirely in the hands of the proprietor, and as matters turned out fewer than 40,000 among all the millions of serfs in Russia actually received their freedom.

In the second period of peace, 1807-1811, Alexander had as his chief mentor a remarkable figure, Michael Speransky, son of a Russian priest, intelligent, well-educated, and conscientious. Utilizing Montesquieu's principle of the separation of powers, Speransky drafted for Alexander a constitutional project that would have made Russia a constitutional monarchy. A series of elected assemblies, beginning at the lowest level of administrative subdivision and continuing on up through district and province, would culminate at the top in a great national assembly, the duma. A similar pyramid of courts was sketched, while a new set of executive institutions was also planned. The duma would have to approve any law promulgated by the Tsar and would have been a real Russian parliament. It is true that Speransky was conservative, and that the franchise as he proposed it would have enormously favored the nobility, while the serfs of course would not have participated in government. It is also true that Speransky did not include emancipation of the serfs in his proposal. None the less, the plan was decidedly advanced. Speransky was realistic, and knew that not everything could be accomplished at once. Indeed, as it turned out, Alexander balked at executing the plan that he himself had commissioned Speransky to draw up.

This is one of the most critical moments in all Russian history. Why did Speransky fail? He instituted a reform of the civil service, requiring examinations and a system of promotion by merit, which disturbed many of the almost illiterate and thoroughly incompetent men in high office. He even proposed that the nobility pay an income tax, a measure not likely to make its proposer popular. Friends and intimates of the Tsar spread slander about Speransky. But at bottom Alexander himself was at fault and unwilling to act on his own alleged beliefs. Speransky's scheme was shelved, except for two elements that in no way diminished the power of the Tsar. A Council of State, which could advise the Tsar, was created, but he was not obliged to take its advice. Since he appointed and dismissed all members, the effect was simply to increase imperial efficiency, not to limit imperial authority. Further administrative efficiency was obtained through the reorganization of the ministries, whose duties were set out clearly for the first time, eliminating overlapping.

During the second war against Napoleon (1812-1815) Alexander fell under the influence of a Baltic Baroness named Madame de Krüdener, a mystical lady now repenting an ill-spent youth. She convinced the Tsar that he was a "man from the North" designed by destiny to overthrow Napoleon and institute a new order. At the Russian court an atmosphere of pious mysticism, deeply conservative, replaced the earlier flashes of liberal views. Although the leading spirits of the new religiosity were all nominally Orthodox, its character was rather Protestant. It was based upon assiduous reading of the Bible, and it also included a mixture of elements from Masonry, Pietism (see below, p. 306), and the more eccentric Russian sects. It aimed at the union of all Christendom in one new faith and thus aroused the fear and opposition of many Orthodox clerics. Its real importance, however, lay in its impact on Alexander, who was now convinced that as the bearer of a sacred mission all he needed to do was follow the promptings of his inmost feelings.

During the last decade of Alexander's reign, 1815-1825, the most important figure at court was Count Arakcheev, a competent but brutal officer, who once bit off the ear of one of his men as a punishment. The chief innovation of the decade, accomplished under Arakcheev's direction, was the hated system of "military colonies," the drafting of the population of whole districts to serve in the regiments quartered there. When not drilling or fighting, the soldiers were to work their farms, and their entire lives were subject to the whims of their officers. Far from being a kind of model community, the individual military colony was a wretched sort of concentration camp. By the end of Alexander's reign almost 400,000 soldiers were living in these dreaded places.

Though Alexander gave Russia no important reforms, he did act on liberal principles outside Russia, in Poland and in Finland. By the Vienna settlement of 1815 (see below, Chapter XI), Alexander as King of Poland could give the Poles any form of government he chose. In fact, he gave the Poles an advanced constitution, with their own army, their own Polish officialdom, and the free use of their own language. He allowed the Finns, after their annexation by Russia in 1809, to preserve their own law codes and the system of local government introduced during the long preceding Swedish rule. But the "liberal Tsar" was liberal only outside his Russian dominions.

Russian Foreign Policy, 1725-1796

The motives of Russian foreign policy in the century between the death of Peter the Great and that of Alexander I were still the ancient ones of expansion against Sweden, Poland, and Turkey. But as a new member of the European power constellation, Russia found that pursuit of these old aims was now involving her in affairs that had primary significance for western Europe. The diplomatic pattern was set early in the period, when Ostermann concluded an alliance with the Habsburg Empire in 1726. This was to be a cornerstone of Russian foreign policy. Yet, especially in their joint undertakings against the Turks, the Russians and Austrians found, as early as the 1730's, that they had conflicting ambitions in southeast Europe. This early conflict of interests was a cloud, still no larger than a man's hand, but destined to swell into the colossal thunderhead that exploded in the World War of 1914-1918. To the eighteenth century also belong the first regular Russian diplomatic service, the first Russian participation in the international game of espionage and intrigue,

and the first real Russian foreign ministers: Ostermann and his Russian successor Bestuzhev-Ryumin, men of enormous personal influence on the course of Russian foreign relations.

In the War of the Polish Succession (see above, p. 264) Russian forces took part in alliance with Austria in support of Augustus III and helped to force the abdication of Stanislas Leszczynski. Immediately, the Russians and Austrians became allies in a new war against the Turks, 1735-1739 (see also p. 264). Though Marshal Münnich successfully invaded the Crimea, Russian gains at the Treaty of Belgrade in 1739 were limited to Azov. The Austrians failed to cooperate satisfactorily in an invasion of the Danubian principalities and made it clear that they did not relish a Russian advance into the principalities and thus to the Habsburg frontiers.

The War of the Austrian Succession, opening in 1740, found the Russians pre-

RUSSIAN EXPANSION in EUROPE, 1725-1825

Acquired between 1730-1740
Acquired by Elizabeth 1741-1762
Acquired by Catherine 1762-1796
Acquired by Alexander I. 1801-1825

occupied with the dynastic problem at home. We have already seen how the French ambassador worked to assist the elevation of Elizabeth to the throne, and in this way to bring about the downfall of the pro-Austrian Ostermann. But, since Bestuzhev-Ryumin continued Ostermann's policies, French hopes were largely disappointed. Prussian (and therefore anti-Austrian) influence manifested itself with the appearance of Peter III as heir, and with the choice of the future Catherine II as his bride. Thus, during the War of the Austrian Succession, there was a good deal of rival jockeying for Russian assistance. Eventually, the advance of Frederick the Great along the Baltic shore alarmed the Russians, and so, as the war ended, a Russian corps was leisurely pushing westward, intending to join the fighting in the Rhineland.

Russian anti-Prussian sentiment crystallized during the interval of peace before the outbreak of the Seven Years' War. Bestuzhev labored mightily to obtain an alliance with England, which he managed in 1755, the Russians accepting a large subsidy in exchange for a promise to keep troops in readiness against the Prussians. But the Diplomatic Revolution of 1756 (see Chapter VIII), making Prussia and England allies, negated this arrangement. The Russians thus remained loyal to Austria and fought the Prussians in the Seven Years' War. Once more Russian forces marched west, so slowly that there was suspicion of treason and the commander was removed. In 1758 the invasion of East Prussia began; and eventually in 1760 Russian forces entered Berlin. Elizabeth's death and the succession of the pro-Prussian Peter III led the Russians to change sides and join the Prussians briefly against the Austrians and French. Catherine, on her succession, withdrew the Russian forces, but did not again attack the Prussians. Thus Russia found herself excluded from the peace conferences of 1763.

In foreign policy, Catherine the Great was as vigorous and unscrupulous as she was at home. She stuck strictly to business, concentrating on the traditional Russian anti-Polish and anti-Turkish aims. In 1763, only a year after she became Empress, the throne of Poland fell vacant, and Catherine secured the election of her protégé and former lover, a pro-Russian Pole, Stanislas Poniatowski. Frederick the Great joined with Catherine in a campaign to win rights for the persecuted Lutheran and Orthodox minorities in Catholic Poland. One party of Polish nobles, their national pride offended at foreign intervention, resisted, and secured the aid of France and Austria. These powers adopted the stratagem of pressing Turkey into war with Russia to distract Catherine from Poland.

In the first Russo-Turkish War (1768-1774), Catherine's forces won a series of victories. A Russian Baltic fleet, sent all the way around Europe and into the Mediterranean through the Straits of Gibraltar, destroyed the Turkish fleet in the Aegean (1770), largely owing to the superior seamanship of a few English officers who were advising the otherwise inefficient Russians. But the Russians failed to follow up their initial advantage by storming the Straits and attacking Istanbul, and operations shifted to the Crimea and the Danubian principalities. While the Russians and Turks were discussing peace terms, Frederick the Great had concluded that Russia had been too successful against the Turks, and would surely seize most of Poland for herself unless he acted quickly.

So Frederick took the leading part in arranging the first partition of Poland (1772). Poland lost to Russia, Prussia, and Austria almost one-third of her territory and one-half of her population in this act of international highway robbery. Frederick's share of the loot—the lands immediately to the west of East Prussia—was the smallest but the most startegic: it included the region that had previously separated Brandenburg from East Prussia. Maria Theresa, the Empress of Austria, abandoned her Turkish

PARTITIONS OF POLAND, 1772·1793·1795

	1772	1793	1795
To Prussia			
To Russia			
To Austria			

0   Miles   200

and Polish allies to participate in the grab. She did seem somewhat reluctant, but, as Frederick the Great observed caustically, "She wept, but she kept on taking." Russia received a substantial area of what is now known as Belorussia, or White Russia.

Two years later, the Russians imposed upon the Turks a most humiliating peace treaty, at Kutchuk Kainardji (1774). Catherine annexed much of the formerly Turkish stretch of Black Sea coast, and two places in the Crimea; the rest of the Crimea was separated from the Ottoman Empire as an independent Tartar state. She also obtained something the Russians had long coveted: freedom of navigation on the

Black Sea and the right of passage through the Bosphorus and the Dardanelles. A vaguely worded clause gave her various rights to protect the Christian subjects of the sultan. This last provision gave the Russians a convenient excuse for intervening in Turkish affairs later on.

Indeed, now Catherine began to dream of expelling the Turks from Europe, and reviving the Byzantine Empire at Istanbul under Russian protection and domination. She saw to it that her younger grandson was christened Constantine to prepare him for this splendid inheritance, and imported Greek-speaking nurses to train him in the language. She also proposed to set up a

303

kingdom of Dacia (the Roman name for the area) in the Danubian principalities to be ruled by her lover and general, Potemkin. By way of preparation, in 1783, Catherine annexed the supposedly independent Tartar state of the Crimea, where she built a naval base at Sebastopol. To achieve these grandiose designs, Catherine had to have the consent of Austria, and invited Joseph II on a famous tour by river-boat of the newly developed and annexed territories of the Russian southwest. It was on this tour that the Austrian Emperor was allegedly shown the famous "Potemkin villages," mere cardboard façades facing the river to look like settlements but with nothing behind them; like so many other good stories, this one is untrue. At Sebastopol, however, signs pointed across the Black Sea, saying, "This way to Byzantium." In a second Russo-Turkish war (1787-1791), Catherine's allies, the Austrians, once again provided feeble assistance and made a separate peace. Again, a conflict of interests over the European lands of the Sultan precipitated Austro-Russian disagreement. In the end, Catherine had to abandon the Greek project, as her scheme was called, and content herself with annexing the remaining Turkish lands along the northern coast of the Black Sea and securing recognition of Russian sovereignty over the Crimea.

Before her death, Catherine completed her work by participating in two more partitions of Poland. The second partition came as the result of a Polish constitutional movement, supported by the Prussians in opposition to Russian interest. Once Catherine's hands were free of her Turkish war, she intervened on the pretext of defending the established order in Poland and fighting the virus of revolution. In 1793, both she and the Prussians took large new slices of Polish territories, the Austrians not participating. An attempted Polish revolution against the reduction of their state to a wretched little remnant dominated by foreigners was followed by the third and final partition of 1795, by which Poland disappeared from the map. This time Austria joined the other two powers and obtained Cracow; Prussia got Warsaw, and Russia secured Lithuania and other Baltic and east Polish lands.

But the spectacular successes of Catherine meant the embodiment in Russia of millions of human beings—Poles, Lithuanians, Belorussians—who loathed the Russians, and left a legacy of trouble. It also meant that Russia had destroyed useful buffers in the shape of the Polish and Tartar states, and now had common frontiers with her potential enemies, Prussia and Austria. The last two partitions of Poland had been made possible by the preoccupation of the western powers with their war against revolutionary France; the story of Russian foreign policy after Catherine forms part of the larger story of this great war (see Chapter XI).

V: The Culture of the Enlightenment

Catherine the Great usually appears on a list of the enlightened despots, and Peter the Great and Tsar Alexander I might well be added at the start and the end of the list, respectively. Yet Russian history in the eighteenth century furnishes one more illustration of the failure of the Enlightenment to achieve happy political results. The trouble did not lie entirely with the practitioners of the new political creed, however thin their veneer of enlightenment might be. The political theory of the Age of Reason itself was at fault. The *philosophes* cheerfully expected men to see reason when it was pointed out to them, to abandon the habits of centuries and revise their behavior in accordance with natural law. But men would not always see reason; as Joseph II discovered to his sorrow, they *would* cling perversely to irrational customs and unnatural traditions. The rationalism of the Enlightenment tended to omit the complexities of human nature from its calculation.

Responsibility for this major shortcoming lay partly with the "classical spirit" of the seventeenth century, inherited by the Enlightenment of the eighteenth. The writers of the Age of Louis XIV had found in their classical models, not a confirmation of existing standards, but a better, simpler set of standards that the eighteenth-century *philosophes* easily adapted to the concept of "nature's simple plan." The great writers do indeed achieve the miracle of giving life to these abstractions. But the lesser ones make only bloodless types, and encourage in their hearers and readers—the men and women who finally do work out social change—the belief that these easy mental images are somehow more real, and certainly more desirable, than the bewildering complexity of their concrete experiences. Like the "classical spirit," the spirit of natural science went too far when it was applied uncritically to problems of human relations. It gave men the illusion that what was going on in their minds would shortly go on in reality.

A minor *philosophe*, the Abbé Mably, got at this central problem by putting it in the form of a question: "Is society, then, a branch of physics?" Most of the *philosophes* and their followers believed that it was. They applied to the unpredictable activities of man the mathematical methods used in the physical sciences. The Physiocrats, for example, tried to reduce the complexities of human economic activities to a few simple agricultural laws. Like the stars in their courses, human beings were thought to fit neatly into the Newtonian world-machine.

Philosophy

A few eighteenth-century minds disagreed. David Hume (1711-1776), a brilliant Scottish philosopher, doubted the wisdom of assuming that society was a branch of physics, indeed doubted everything. His skeptical mind insisted on submitting principles to the test of factual observation. The errors and illusions of the *philosophes*, he said, resulted from their failure to do this. They deduced untested conclusions from two great abstract principles—faith in natural law, belief in reason.

Hume made short work of the *philosophes'* appeals to nature. The laws of justice, he argued, were not the absolute and inflexible "Laws of Nature and Nature's God":

. . . Suppose a society to fall into such want of all common necessaries, that the utmost frugality and industry cannot preserve the greater number from perishing, and the whole from extreme misery; it will readily, I believe, be admitted, that the strict laws of justice are suspended, in such a pressing emergence, and give place to the stronger motives of necessity and self-preservation. Is it any crime, after a shipwreck, to seize whatever means or instrument of safety one can lay hold of, without regard to former limitations of property?[*]

Nor could human conduct be analyzed "in the same manner that we discover by reason the truths of geometry or algebra."

It appears evident that the ultimate ends of human actions can never, in any case, be accounted for by *reason*, but recommend themselves entirely to the sentiments and affections of mankind, without any dependance on the intellectual faculties. Ask a man *why he uses exercise:* he will answer, *because he desires to keep his health.* If you then enquire, *why he desires health,* he will readily reply, *because sickness is painful.* If you push your enquiries farther, and desire a reason *why he hates pain,* it is impossible he can ever give any. . . .[†]

David Hume was among the first and most profound critics of the Age of Reason.

---

[*] *An Enquiry concerning the Principles of Morals,* L. A. Selby-Bigge, ed. (Oxford, 1902), 186.
[†] *Ibid.,* 293.

The Romantics of the next generation would repeat his warnings against reason and his pleas on behalf of the "sentiments and affections of mankind" (see Chapter XI). In his own day, Rousseau and Kant were also worried by rather similar problems. Rousseau both represented the Enlightenment and foreshadowed the revolt against it. No *philosophe* defended natural law more ardently, yet no Romantic argued more convincingly in support of emotion and faith. "Too often does reason deceive us," Rousseau wrote in *Emile*. "We have only too good a right to doubt her; but conscience never deceives us; she is the true guide of man;... he who obeys his conscience is following nature and he need not fear that he will go astray." *

Immanuel Kant (1724-1804), who taught philosophy at the University of Königsberg in Prussia, raised Rousseau's argument to the level of metaphysics. Kant believed in a higher reality reaching ultimately to God. He called the eternal verities of the higher world "noumena," in contrast to the phenomena of the material world. Knowledge of the noumenal realm, Kant believed, reached men through reason—reason, however, not as the Enlightenment used the term, not as common sense, but as intuition, almost as mysticism. The highest expression of the Kantian reason was the "categorical imperative." This was the moral law within, the conscience implanted in man by God. It was the inescapable realization welling up in the individual that, when confronted with an ethical choice, he must choose the good and avoid the evil. Kant's redefinition of reason and his rehabilitation of conscience marked a high point in the intellectual reaction against the dominant rationalism of the Enlightenment. The popular reaction took the very different form of the evangelical revival, which began with the German Pietists of the eighteenth century.

The Evangelical Revival

The Pietists were the spiritual descendants of the sixteenth-century Anabaptists. Deploring alike the growing Lutheran concern with the formal aspects of religion and the deists' emphasis on natural law, the Pietists asserted that religion came from the heart, not the head. The God of the Pietists was more than the remote inventor of a world. The chief leader of Pietism was a German nobleman, Count Zinzendorf (1700-1760), founder of the Moravian Brethren, who set up a model community based on Christian principles. Moravian emigrants to America planted a colony at Bethlehem, Pennsylvania, founding the "Pennsylvania Dutch" traditions of thrift, hard work, and strict living. In England, meanwhile, the example of Zinzendorf and other Pietists inspired John Wesley.

Ordained a priest of the Church of England, John Wesley (1703-1791) at first stressed the ritualistic aspects of religion. But the failure of his two-year ministry to the backward colony of Georgia (1736-1737) convinced him of the weakness of religious formalism. Disillusioned, Wesley felt his own faith evaporating: "I went to America, to convert the Indians: but Oh! who shall convert me! Who, what is he that will deliver me from this evil heart of unbelief?" * Pietism converted Wesley. Following the teachings of the Moravian Brethren, whom he met in England and America, he found faith through emotional conviction.

For more than fifty years, Wesley labored tirelessly to share his discovery, traveling throughout the British Isles, and preaching in churches, in the fields, at the pitheads of coal mines, and even in jails. Angry crowds came to scoff but remained to pray. When Wesley died in 1791, his movement had already attracted more than a hundred

---

* *Emile*, Everyman ed. (New York, 1911), 249-250.

* John Wesley, *Journal*, Everyman ed. (New York, 1907), I, 74.

thousand adherents. They were called Methodists, because of their methodical devotion to piety and to plain dressing and plain living. Though Wesley always considered himself a good Anglican, the Methodists eventually set up a separate organization—their nonconformist "Chapel" in contrast to the established Church of England. The new sect won its following almost entirely among the lower and middle classes, from people who sought the religious excitement and consolation that were denied them by deism and by the formalism of the Church of England.

In the practical realm, too, Methodism clashed with enlightened rationalism. Where the *philosophes* advised public reform, the Methodists favored private charity. And where the *philosophes* recommended attacking the *causes* of social evils, the Methodists accepted these evils as part of God's inscrutable plan and sought to mitigate their *symptoms*. They began agitation against drunkenness, the trade in slaves, and the barbarous treatment suffered by prisoners, the insane, and the sick. John Wesley established schools for coal-miners' children and opened dispensaries for the slum-dwellers of London and Bristol. The Methodists had in full measure the Puritan conscience of the nonconformists.

Literature

The middle-class public so strongly attracted to Methodism welcomed the novels of the English writer, Samuel Richardson (1689-1761). A printer by trade, he turned to writing late in life and produced three gigantic novels in the form of letters by the chief characters. In *Clarissa Harlowe* (1748), the best of them, Richardson devoted 2400 pages of small print to the distresses of Clarissa, whose lover was a scoundrel, and whose relatives were a greedy pack, scheming to secure her considerable property. Drugged and betrayed, Clarissa soon lost almost everything, but to the end she preserved the capacity to pour out her distresses on paper. If anyone missed the point of *Clarissa Harlowe*, he had only to turn to Richardson's preface:

What will be found to be more particularly aimed at in the following work is—to warn the inconsiderate and thoughtless of one sex, against the base arts and designs of specious contrivers of the other—to caution parents against the undue exercise of their natural authority over their children in the great article of marriage—to warn against preferring a man of pleasure to a man of probity upon that dangerous but too-commonly-received notion, *that a reformed rake makes the best husband* —but above all, to investigate the highest and most important doctrines not only of morality, but of christianity, by showing them thrown into action in the conduct of the *worthy* characters; while the *unworthy*, who set these doctrines at defiance, are condignly, and, as may be said, consequentially punished.

Modern readers are likely to find *Clarissa Harlowe* tedious and sentimental. But the eighteenth century was entranced. *Clarissa* was read aloud at family gatherings, the story runs, and whenever some new distress overwhelmed her, the members of the family retired to their separate rooms for a good solitary cry. In spite of sentimental exaggerations, Richardson's vivid descriptions of the struggles of passion and conscience carried emotional and psychological conviction.

The novel as a literary form really came into its own during the eighteenth century, particularly in England. By no means all the masters of English fiction were sentimentalists. In *Roderick Random* (1748), Tobias Smollett gave an authentic report on life in the navy, with all its cruelty and misery. Henry Fielding introduced a strong leaven of satire and burlesqued the absurdities of Richardson. In his masterpiece, *Tom Jones* (1749), Fielding covered the whole English social scene and depicted both the hard-riding country squires and the low characters of the city slums. Richardson gave the English novel emotional and moral earnestness; Smollett and Fielding added a vigorous realism.

The Enlightenment was an age of prose. With a few exceptions, notably Alexander Pope (1688-1744), it produced no poets of great consequence. The literary monuments of the age were the great English novels, the tales and all the varied writings of Voltaire, the letters and essays of the *philosophes*, and, finally, Gibbon's *History of the Decline and Fall of the Roman Empire* (1788). Edward Gibbon used history for a sustained Voltairean attack on Christian fanaticism; he also perfected a Ciceronian prose style which, by its balance and elegance, expressed very well the "style" of the Age of Reason.

Art

The classicism of the Enlightenment strongly affected its art. Gibbon's great history, the researches of scholars and archaeologists, and the discovery in 1748 of the well-preserved ruins of ancient Roman Pompeii, buried under lava from Vesuvius, kept the interest in classical antiquity at a high pitch. To the Enlightenment, the balance and symmetry of Greek and Roman temples represented, in effect, the "natural laws" of building. Architects retreated somewhat from the theatrical extravagance of the Baroque style and adapted classical models with great skill and variety. They produced the elegance of the London town house, the monumental magnificence of the buildings flanking the Place de la Concorde in Paris, and the pastoral charm of George Washington's house at Mount Vernon. Lisbon, rebuilt after a disastrous earthquake, was a model of efficient and handsome town-planning. The fashion for "colonial" and "Georgian" styles in the twentieth century testifies to the lasting influence of neoclassical architecture.

Painting, too, came under the influence of neoclassicism. The artistic tsar of Georgian England was Sir Joshua Reynolds (1723-1792), the first president of the Royal Academy. Beauty, he told the academy, rested "on the uniform, eternal, and immutable laws of nature," which could be "investigated by reason, and known by study." Sir Joshua and his contemporaries, though preaching a coldly reasoned aesthetic, applied warmth and vitality to the actual portraits that they painted of wealthy English aristocrats, This was the age of Reynolds, Lawrence, Gainsborough, Romney, and many others—the golden age of English portraiture.

And it was also the age of William Hogarth (1697-1764), who cast aside the academic restraints of neoclassicism to do in art what Fielding did in the novel. Instead of catering to a few wealthy patrons, Hogarth sought a mass market for the engravings that he turned out in thousands of copies. Instead of seeking proportion and harmony, as Reynolds advised, he sketched with brutal frankness the vices of London. *Marriage à la Mode*, *The Rake's Progress*, *The Harlot's Progress*, *Beer Street*, and *Gin Lane* were his satires and sermons on a particularly licentious and drunken society.

The realism of Hogarth was far from being the only exception to the prevailing neoclassicism. The fashions for the oriental, the natural, and the Gothic, which were to be so important in the Romanticism of the early nineteenth century, were already beginning to catch on. The taste for the exotic produced Chinese wallpaper, the "Chinese" furniture of Thomas Chippendale, and the familiar Chinese pattern of "willow-ware" plates. Gardens were bestrewn with pagodas and minarets, and gardeners abandoned the tortured shrubs of Louis XIV's geometrical landscaping for the wild English garden. The wilder and more natural the effect, the better it was liked. Even the dominance of neoclassical architecture was threatened. At Strawberry Hill near London, Horace Walpole, the son of the great Robert, concocted a curious Gothic house that had an abundance of Gothic "gloomth"—battlements in the medieval style, and "lean windows fattened with rich saints in painted glass."

The Great Musicians

The crowning glory of eighteenth-century culture was its music. The first half of the century was the age of Bach and Handel, and the second half was the age of Haydn and Mozart. Johann Sebastian Bach (1685-1750) brought to perfection the Baroque techniques of seventeenth-century composers. He mastered the difficult art of the fugue, an intricate version of the round in which each voice begins the theme in turn while the other voices simultaneously repeat and elaborate it. He resolved a complicated problem in musical mathe-matics by creating a six-part fugue for his *Musical Offering*, based on a theme by Frederick the Great and offered to the Prussian monarch. Bach also composed a wealth of material for the organ, the most Baroque and the most religious of instruments. Sacred themes inspired many of his cantatas, the Mass in B minor, and the two gigantic choral settings of the Passion of Christ according to St. John and to St. Matthew. The religious music of Bach, dramatic and deeply felt, was a world apart from the anticlerical temper of the Enlightenment.

George Frederick Handel (1685-1759) had a stormy international career. Born in Germany, Handel studied in Italy, then spent most of his adult years in England trying desperately to run an opera company. The intrigues, the clashes of temperament,

"Shortly after Marriage," (one of the Marriage à la Mode series), *by Hogarth.*

and the fiscal headaches inevitable in artistic enterprise nearly ruined him. Yet Handel wrote more than forty operas, including *Xerxes*, famous for "Handel's Largo." He took epic themes from the Bible and used them for *The Messiah* and other vigorous oratorios directed at a mass audience and arranged for large choruses. These massive performances differed greatly from the original oratorios of seventeenth-century Italy, small-scale works written for the tiny prayer chapels called oratories.

Although Bach and Handel composed many instrumental suites and concertos, it was not until the second half of the century that orchestral music really came to the fore. New instruments then appeared, headed by the piano, which greatly extended the limited range of the older keyboard instrument, the harpsichord. New forms also appeared, the sonata and the symphony, developed largely by Joseph Haydn (1732-1809). Haydn wrote more than fifty piano pieces in the form of the sonata, in which two contrasting themes are stated in turn, developed, interwoven, repeated, and finally resolved in a *coda* (the Italian for "tail"). Haydn then applied the sonata to the orchestra, grafting it on the Italian operatic overture, thus enlarging it into the first movement of the symphony.

The operatic landmark of the early century was John Gay's *Beggar's Opera* (1728). This tuneful work, "popular" in the highest sense of the term, caricatured English society and politics in Hogarthian vein. Christoph Gluck (1714-1787) revolutionized the technique of the tragic opera. "I have striven," he said,

to restrict music to its true office of serving poetry by means of expression and by following the situations of the story, without interrupting the action or stifling it with a useless superfluity of ornaments. . . . I did not wish to arrest an actor in the greatest heat of dialogue . . . to hold him up in the middle of a word on a vowel favorable to his voice, nor to make display of the agility of his fine voice in some long-drawn passage, nor to wait while the orchestra gives him time to recover his breath for a cadenza.*

Gluck executed this declaration of operatic independence. His operas were well-constructed dramas in music, not casual vehicles for the display of the vocal pyrotechnics so long favored in Italian opera. Gluck adhered to the old custom of taking heroes and heroines from classical mythology, but he invested shadowy figures like Orpheus, Eurydice, and Iphigenia with new vitality.

Opera, symphony, and chamber works all reached a climax in Wolfgang Amadeus Mozart (1756-1791). As a boy, Mozart was cruelly exploited by his father, who carted "Wolfgangerl" all over Europe to show off his virtuosity on the harpsichord and his amazing talent for composition. Overworked throughout his life, and in his later years overburdened with debts, Mozart died a pauper at the age of thirty-five. Yet his youthful talent ripened steadily into mature genius, and his facility and versatility grew ever more prodigious. He tossed off the sprightly overture to *The Marriage of Figaro* in the course of an evening. In two months during the summer of 1788, he produced the three great symphonies familiar to concert audiences as No. 39 (E flat major), No. 40 (G minor), and No. 41 ("The Jupiter"). Mozart's orchestral works also included a long list of concertos, with the solo parts sometimes for piano or violin and sometimes, just to show that it could be done, for bassoon or French horn. In chamber music, Mozart experimented with almost every possible combination of instruments.

Three of Mozart's great operas were in the comic Italian vein of *opera buffa*. In *Così Fan Tutte* ("Thus Do All Women") he combined amorous farce with enchanting melodic duets. Still more enchanting music graces *The Marriage of Figaro*, based on a famous satire of the Old Régime, in which

---

* Preface to *Alcestis*, as translated by Eric Blom and quoted in Curt Sachs, *Our Musical Heritage* (New York, 1948), 287.

Figaro the valet outwits and outsings his noble employers. Tragic overtones appear in *Don Giovanni*, depicting the emotional havoc wrought by Don Juan on earth before his eventual punishment in hell. Mozart composed with equal skill mournful and romantic arias for the Don's victims, elegantly seductive ballads for the Don himself, and a ribald catalog of the Don's conquests for his valet ("A thousand and three in Spain alone"). The instruments in the pit dotted the "i's" and crossed the "t's" of the plot—scurrying violins to accompany characters dashing about the stage, portentous trombones to announce the entrance of the Devil. In his last opera, *The Magic Flute*, Mozart abandoned the usual Italian libretto and tried to create a consciously German work. The music, as always, was lovely, but only the vaguest political significance emerged from the confused and fantastic libretto, which apparently sought to vindicate the enlightened ideas of Joseph II and to decry the conservatism of Maria Theresa.

The Magic Flute was a rare exception to the generally cosmopolitan character of eighteenth-century music. The great composers with the German names had very little national feeling. Almost all of them felt equally at home in Vienna, Prague, Milan, Paris, and London, and they gratefully accepted patrons in whatever country they found them. The fortunate Haydn moved from the princely estate of the Hungarian Ezterhazys to score an equal success with the paying public of the London concert-halls. Italian music was never totally eclipsed, nor was German dominance complete. Bach patterned his concertos on Italian models, Haydn borrowed Italian operatic overtures for his symphonies, and every operatic composer of the century profited from the labors of his Italian predecessors.

The great composers also had the human touch so often lacking in the Age of Reason. They borrowed freely from folk-tunes and ballads, the popular music of their day, and were rewarded by having their themes whistled in the streets. Mozart's operas, Haydn's symphonies, and the great choral works of Bach and Handel have never lost this popular appeal. They have always retained the capacity to appeal to the listener's emotions. In this sense, music probably came closest to resolving harmoniously the great conflict in eighteenth-century civilization, the conflict between reason and emotion, between the abstractions of the Enlightenment and the realities of human existence.

In other realms, however, as the century drew toward its close, the lines were drawn for the vigorous prosecution of the conflict. In thought, the ideas of Kant and Hume were challenging the rationalism of the *philosophes*. Romantic artists and Romantic writers were preparing to hurl defiance at the defenders of classicism. And in politics, as the century ended, the European powers sought to check the French Revolution, the greatest effort to realize on earth the Enlightenment's dream of reason, natural law, and progress, "the heavenly city of the eighteenth-century philosophers."

Reading Suggestions on the Enlightenment

General Accounts

W. L. Dorn, *Competition for Empire, 1740-1763* (N.Y.: Harper, 1940); and L. Gershoy, *From Despotism to Revolution, 1763-1789* (N.Y.: Harper, 1944). The first of these two volumes, in the "Rise of Modern Europe" series, provides a useful analysis of the Enlightenment, and the second offers a full treatment of the enlightened despots.

G. Bruun, *The Enlightened Despots* (N.Y.: Holt, 1929. A Berkshire Study). A first-rate brief account.

Special Studies: The Enlightenment

G. R. Havens, *The Age of Ideas: From Reaction to Revolution in Eighteenth-Century France* (N.Y.:

Holt, 1955). A very useful volume, fully abreast of modern research.

P. Smith, *The History of Modern Culture*, Vol. II (N.Y.: Holt, 1934). Notable for painstaking amassing of relevant details.

E. Cassirer, *The Philosophy of the Enlightenment* (Boston: Beacon). An important study of the great principles of 18th-century thought.

P. Hazard, *European Thought in the Eighteenth Century* (London: Hollis & Carter, 1954). A significant re-evaluation of the Enlightenment.

K. Martin, *The Rise of French Liberal Thought*, J. P. Mayer, ed. (N.Y.: New York Univ. Press, 1954). A revised edition of a brilliant and opinionated work.

C. Becker, *The Heavenly City of the Eighteenth-Century Philosophers* (New Haven: Yale Univ. Press, 1932). A charming and influential essay, stressing the continuities between the medieval Age of Faith and the enlightened Age of Reason.

J. B. Bury, *The Idea of Progress: An Inquiry into Its Origins and Growth* (N.Y.: Dover, 1955). Inexpensive reprint of a famous old work on the most important idea of the Enlightenment.

J. Morley, *Diderot and the Encyclopaedists*, rev. ed. (London: Macmillan, 1923). An old but perceptive account by a noted Victorian Liberal. Morley also wrote useful studies of Voltaire and Rousseau.

N. Torrey, *The Spirit of Voltaire* (N.Y.: Columbia Univ. Press, 1938). A thoughtful estimate by a modern scholar.

A. Cobban, *Rousseau and the Modern State* (London: Allen & Unwin, 1934). A good introduction to the implications of Rousseau's thought.

J. S. Schapiro, *Condorcet and the Rise of Liberalism* (N.Y.: Harcourt, Brace, 1934). A useful study.

R. R. Palmer, *Catholics and Unbelievers in Eighteenth-Century France* (Princeton: Princeton Univ. Press, 1939). An excellent monograph.

M. F. Bukofzer, *Music in the Baroque Era* (N.Y.: Norton, 1947). An informative work on the period down to 1750. See also the general musical histories by Láng and Gray cited for Chapter II

F. Fosca, *The Eighteenth Century: From Watteau to Tiepolo* (N.Y.: Skira, 1953). A superbly illustrated work on painting.

Special Studies: The Enlightened Despots

G. P. Gooch, *Frederick the Great, the Ruler, the Writer, the Man* (N.Y.: Knopf, 1947); and

F. J. P. Veale, *Frederick the Great* (London: Hamish, Hamilton, 1935). Two modern and reasonably balanced evaluations of the great Hohenzollern.

C. L. Morris, *Maria Theresa, The Last Conservative* (N.Y.: Knopf, 1937); and S. K. Padover, *The Revolutionary Emperor, Joseph II* (N.Y.: Ballou, 1934). Informative treatments, warmly sympathetic to their respective subjects.

M. I. Florinsky, *Russia: A History and an Interpretation*, 2 vols. (N.Y.: Macmillan, 1953). A full and reliable textbook account.

G. Scott Thomson, *Catherine the Great and the Expansion of Russia* (N.Y.: Macmillan, 1950. Teach Yourself History Library). A sound brief introduction. Of the many biographies of Catherine, perhaps the best is still the old K. Walizewski, *The Romance of an Empress* (N.Y.: Appleton, 1894).

Sources

C. Brinton, ed., *The Portable Age of Reason Reader* (N.Y.: Viking, 1956). A good cross section of the writings of the century on many subjects.

Introduction to Contemporary Civilization in the West, Vol. I, 2nd ed. (N.Y.: Columbia Univ. Press, 1954). This source book includes much longer excerpts from the *Philosophes'* writings than are generally found in such collections.

B. R. Redman, ed., *The Portable Voltaire* (N.Y.: Viking, 1949). A good selection from Voltaire's work, prefaced by an informative introduction.

Montesquieu, *The Spirit of the Laws*, F. Neumann, ed. (N.Y.: Hafner, 1949). A well-edited edition of a rambling classic.

Rousseau, *The Social Contract and Discourses* (N.Y.: Dutton, 1913), and *Emile* (N.Y.: Dutton, 1955. Everyman ed.) Convenient editions of Jean-Jacques' important writings.

F. de La Fontainerie, ed., *French Liberalism and Education in the Eighteenth Century* (N.Y.: McGraw-Hill, 1932). Translations of proposals by educational reformers.

Beccaria, *Essay on Crimes and Punishments* (Stanford, Calif.: Academic Reprints, 1953). One of the very best introductions to the writing and thinking of the *philosophes;* short and pungent.

A. Smith, *Selections from "The Wealth of Nations"* (Chicago: Regnery). A convenient abridgement of this famous and lengthy work.

S. Richardson, *Clarissa* (N.Y.: Modern Library, 1950). Shortened version of the celebrated novel.

CHAPTER TEN

Revolution

in America

and France

I: George III and the American Revolution

George III
George III,
King of
Great Britain from 1760 to 1820, was the
first Hanoverian born and bred in England.
He proposed to reassert some of the
royal prerogatives that had lapsed under the
first two Georges. He attempted a policy
that may, with some exaggeration, be
termed a dilute form of enlightened despotism. Now the actual enlightenment of
"Farmer George" did not go much beyond
writing articles on turnips for Arthur
Young's *Annals of Agriculture*. He was no
full-fledged despot, but he did try to wrest
control of the House of Commons from the
long-dominant Whig oligarchy and retain
it by the Whig devices of patronage and
bribery. He endeavored to beat the Whigs
at their own parliamentary game.

Virtuous as a person, devoted as a family
man, George as a monarch was stubborn,
short-sighted, and in the long run unsuccess-

ful. It was easy for him at first to exploit the factional strife among the Whigs, maneuver Pitt out of office in 1761, and make his friend and tutor, Lord Bute, the head of the cabinet. Bute and the King, however, found it hard to justify their failure to deprive France of the sugar-rich West Indies in the Peace of Paris (see Chapter VIII). The Commons ratified the treaty, but George dismissed Bute in 1763 in order to appease the critics of British diplomacy at home.

The harshest criticism came from John Wilkes, a member of the House of Commons, who dubbed the Peace of Paris "the peace of God, for it passeth all understanding." Wilkes' bitter attack on the treaty in his paper, the *North Briton*, infuriated the King. Bowing to the royal anger, the Commons ordered the offending issue of the *North Briton* to be burnt. Wilkes, who first fled to France, later ran for Parliament three separate times, and three times the Commons, under royal pressure, threw out his election. When Wilkes finally took his seat again in 1774, he was a popular hero, and riots had occurred in defense of "Wilkes and Liberty." A wise king would have trimmed his sails, but George III did not relax his determination to manage both Parliament and cabinet. After seven years of short-lived, unstable ministries (1763-1770), George finally cast Lord North in Bute's old role. During North's ministry (1770-1782), the new policy of royal intervention first stiffened, then wavered, and at length collapsed entirely in the face of disaster. At home, the King unwittingly prepared the way for the increase of parliamentary authority; abroad, he lost the thirteen North American colonies.

Background of the Revolution

The breach between colonies and mother country first became serious at the close of the Seven Years' War when Britain began to retreat from the old policy of "salutary neglect" and to interfere more directly and more frequently in matters affecting the colonies. But, by 1763, the colonies had acquired the habit of regulating their own affairs, though the acts of their assemblies remained subject to the veto of royally appointed governors or of the King himself. The vast territories in Canada and west of the Alleghenies acquired in 1763 brought Britain added opportunities for profitable exploitation and added responsibilities for government and defense. In 1763, an uprising of the Indians under Pontiac threatened frontier posts in the area of the Ohio Valley and the Great Lakes. In the absence of effective concerted action by colonial militias, British regulars were brought in to crush Pontiac. The continuing threat from the Indians prompted the royal proclamation of October, 1763, forbidding "all our loving subjects" to settle west of a line running along the summit of the Alleghenies. To His Majesty's "loving subjects" in the colonies, however, the proclamation seemed deliberately designed to exclude them from the riches of the West.

The colonists resented still more keenly the attempt by Parliament to raise more revenue in North America. The British government had very strong arguments for increasing colonial taxes. The national debt had almost doubled during the Seven Years' War; the colonies' reluctance to recruit soldiers and raise taxes themselves had increased the cost of the war to British taxpayers; now the mother country faced continued expense in protecting the frontier. Surely the Americans would admit the reasonableness of the case for higher taxes.

That, however, was precisely what the Americans did *not* admit. The first of the new revenue measures, the Sugar Act of 1764, alarmed the merchants of the eastern seaboard because the customs officers actually undertook to collect duties on molasses, sugar, and other imports. Here was a departure from the comfortable laxity of salutary neglect. And here was a threat to the colonial economy, for the import duties had to be paid out of the colonies' meager supply of metal coin. The second revenue measure, the Stamp Act of 1765, imposed a duty on a wide variety of items, including legal and commercial papers, liquor licenses, playing cards, dice, newspapers, calendars, and academic degrees. These duties, too, drained the supply of specie, which was now so low that some merchants faced bankruptcy.

The revenue measures touched off a major controversy. Indignant merchants in the New World boycotted all imports rather than pay the duties, and in October, 1765, delegates from nine of the thirteen colonies met in New York City as the "Stamp Act Congress." The Congress complained that the new duties had "a manifest tendency to subvert the rights and liberties of the colonists." The Congress resolved:

That His Majesty's liege subjects in these colonies are entitled to all the inherent rights and liberties of his natural born subjects within the kingdom of Great Britain.

That it is inseparably essential to the freedom of a people, and the undoubted right of Englishmen, that no taxes be imposed on them but with their own consent, given personally or by their own representatives.

That the people of these colonies are not, and from their local circumstances cannot be, represented in the House of Commons in Great Britain.

That the only representatives of these colonies are persons chosen therein by themselves, and that no taxes ever have been, or can be constitutionally imposed on them, but by their respective legislatures.*

The Stamp Act Congress thus enunciated the celebrated principle of no taxation without representation. Britain surrendered on the practical issue, but did not yield on the principle. The appeals of London merchants, near ruin because of the American boycott against British goods, brought the repeal of the Stamp Act in 1765. Nevertheless, in the next year Parliament passed the Declara-

* *Documents of American History*, H. S. Commager, ed. (New York, 1940), 58.

An English commentary on the Boston Tea Party and the tarring and feathering of a royal tax collector, who is forced to drink under a liberty tree.

tory Act asserting that the King and Parliament could indeed make laws affecting the colonies.

For the next decade, Britain adhered firmly to the principles of the Declaratory Act, and colonial radicals just as firmly repeated their opposition to taxation without representation. Parliament again tried to raise revenue, this time by the Townshend duties (1767) on colonial imports of tea, paper, paint, and lead. Again the merchants of Philadelphia, New York, and Boston organized boycotts. In 1770, Lord North's cabinet withdrew the Townshend duties except for the three-penny tariff on a pound of tea, retained as a symbol of parliamentary authority over the colonies. Three years later, the English East India Company, reduced almost to bankruptcy by its own corrupt officials, took a calculated risk and attempted the sale of its surplus tea in North America. It hoped to overcome American opposition to the hated duty by making the retail price of East India tea, duty included, far cheaper than that of Dutch tea smuggled by the colonists. The result was the Boston Tea Party. On December 16, 1773, to the cheers of spectators lining the waterfront, a group of Bostonians, who had a large financial stake in smuggled tea, disguised themselves as redskins, boarded three East India ships, and dumped into the harbor tea chests worth thousands of pounds.

Britain answered defiance with coercion, and the colonists met coercion with resistance. The Quebec Act (1774), incorporating the lands beyond the Alleghenies into Canada, bolted the door to the westward expansion of colonial frontiers. The "Intolerable Acts" (1774) closed the port of Boston to trade and suspended elections in Massachusetts. At Lexington and Concord in April, 1775, the "embattled farmers" of Massachusetts fired the opening shots of the War of Independence. At Philadelphia on July 4, 1776, the delegates to the Continental Congress formally declared the American colonies independent of Great Britain.

Implications
of the Revolution

For the mother country, the American Revolution implied more than the secession of thirteen colonies. It involved Britain in a minor world war that jeopardized her dominance abroad and weakened the power and prestige of King George III at home. The most crucial battle in North America came early in the war—Burgoyne's surrender of his British forces at Saratoga in 1777. Burgoyne had been marching south from Montreal with the aim of driving a wedge between New England and the other rebellious colonies. Not only did he fail completely, but his surrender convinced the French that support of the

American colonists would give them an excellent chance to renew their world-wide struggle with Britain and avenge the humiliation of 1763. Entering the war in 1778, France soon gained the alliance of Spain and eventually secured the help, or at least the friendly neutrality, of most other European states. The intervention of the French prepared the way for the victory of George Washington's forces and the final British surrender at Yorktown in 1781. Meantime, the British lost 3,000 merchant vessels before the Royal Navy finally rallied. In the peace signed at Paris in 1783, Britain, of course, recognized the independence of her former colonies. To Spain she handed back Florida, which she had taken in 1763, and the strategic Mediterranean island of Minorca. But she kept Gibraltar, which the Spanish had also hoped to recover, and she ceded only minor territories to France.

During the early years of the war, the British public had generally been inclined to agree with Dr. Samuel Johnson that the Americans were "a race of convicts" and "ought to be thankful for anything we allow them short of hanging." But the temper of opinion changed as the strength of American resistance became evident, as instances of British mismanagement piled up, and as most of Europe rallied to the rebellious colonies. By 1780, George III and his policy were so unpopular that the House of Commons passed a resolution declaring that "the influence of the crown has increased, is increasing, and ought to be diminished."

The influence of the Crown *was* diminished. In 1782, Lord North, who had been imploring the King to accept his resignation for three years, finally stepped down. In the next year, the post of prime minister fell to William Pitt the Younger, son of the heroic Pitt of the Seven Years' War. The new minister, though only twenty-five years old, was already a seasoned parliamentarian and was to head the cabinet for the next eighteen years. With the advent of Pitt, control of British politics shifted away from the King and back to the professional politicians. George III briefly contemplated abdication and then gradually resigned himself to the rather colorless role of constitutional monarch. The British flirtation (it was really no more than that) with enlightened despotism had come to an end.

In the rebelling colonies public opinion was far from unanimous in support of the Revolution. Many colonists, including southern planters and well-to-do Pennsylvania Quakers, either backed the mother country or took a neutral position in the struggle. New York supplied more recruits to George III than to George Washington. Some of these "Loyalists" or "Tories" were to flee to Canada when independence became a fact. It has been estimated that perhaps only one-third of the colonists actively backed the Revolution. The revolutionary minority came in part from social groups who had the habit of questioning established authority—the pioneers living on the frontier, and the numerous Presbyterians, Congregationalists, and members of other strong-minded Protestant sects. Like adolescents everywhere, the colonists resented parental tutelage yet appealed to family precedent. They claimed that they were only following the example set by Englishmen in 1688 and defended by John Locke.

The ideas of Locke and Newton were as well known and as much respected in North America as they were in Europe. They underlay the Declaration of Independence:

When in the Course of human events, it becomes necessary for one people to dissolve the political bands which have connected them with another, and to assume among the Powers of the earth, the separate and equal station to which the Laws of Nature and Nature's God entitle them, a decent respect to the opinions of mankind requires that they should declare the causes which impel them to the separation.

After this opening paragraph, the Declaration applied to the colonies Locke's theory of contract and his justification of revolution:

We hold these truths to be self-evident, that all men are created equal, that they are endowed by their Creator with certain unalienable Rights, that among these are Life, Liberty and the pursuit of Happiness. That to secure these rights, Governments are instituted among Men, deriving their just power from the consent of the governed. That whenever any Form of Government becomes destructive of these ends, it is the Right of the People to alter or to abolish it, and to institute new Government. . . .

The Declaration of Independence revealed the debt of the American Revolution to the English prophets of the Enlightenment. The Constitution of the new republic was to show its indebtedness to the French *philosophes*, particularly Montesquieu. The delegates to the Constitutional Convention at Philadelphia in 1787 borrowed from *The Spirit of the Laws* the idea of separating the executive, legislative, and judicial powers. The president's check on the Congress through his veto power, the congressional check on the executive and judiciary through impeachment and the right of confirming appointments, and the check imposed on each house of Congress by the requirement that both houses consent to legislation—these familiar balancing devices were derived in part from Montesquieu. The recurrent tensions between President and Congress thus originated in the American adaptation of an eighteenth-century French misreading of British constitutional practice. The "Founding Fathers" also copied from the constitutions of the thirteen original states and from English precedents. The first ten amendments to the Constitution (1791), guaranteeing freedom of religion, freedom of the press, and other basic liberties, were largely taken from the English Bill of Rights of 1689.

The Constitution abounded in compromises. It attempted a balance between states' rights and the central power of the federal government, and between the democratic principle of a directly elected House of Representatives and the aristocratic principle of an indirectly elected and conservative Senate. It was a compromise designed to win support from both rich and poor and from both the aristocratic opponents and the democratic supporters of the recent revolution. Like any compromise, it did not at first please all parties, but it worked well enough to make the new American republic a going concern. The "Founding Fathers" of the United States of America had succeeded perhaps better than any other statesmen of the century in adjusting the ideals of the *philosophes* to the realities of practical politics.

II: *The Causes of the French Revolution*

In France, as in the thirteen North American colonies, a financial crisis produced a revolution. There was not only a parallel but also a direct connection between the revolution of 1776 and that of 1789. French participation in the War of American Independence increased an already excessive governmental debt by more than 1,500,000,000 *livres* (the *livre* then was worth approximately the value of a United States dollar after World War II). Further, the example of America fired the imagination of discontented Frenchmen. To them Benjamin Franklin, the immensely popular American envoy to France, was the very embodiment of the Enlightenment, and the new republic overseas promised to become the utopia of the *philosophes*. At most, however, the American precedent only speeded up developments in France. The basic factors causing the upheaval of 1789 were almost fully matured in 1776. And, just as the reasons for revolution were more deeply rooted and more complicated in France than in America, so the Revolution itself was to be more violent and more sweeping.

The *immediate* cause of the great French Revolution of 1789 was financial. A rapidly mounting deficit drove the monarchy steadily toward bankruptcy. King Louis XVI vainly tried one expedient after another and finally summoned the Estates General, the central representative assembly that had last met 175 years earlier. Once assembled, the deputies of the nation initiated the reforms that were to destroy the Old Régime in France.

The *basic* causes of the French Revolution reached deep into the society and economy of France and into the country's political and intellectual history. Behind the financial crisis of the 1780's lay decades of fiscal mismanagement going back at least to the reign of Louis XIV. The nobles and clergy, jealously guarding the remnants of their privileges, refused to pay a fair share of the tax burden. Resentment against inequitable taxation and inefficient government built up among the unprivileged—the peasantry, the workers, and, above all, the bourgeoisie. The ideas of the *philosophes* translated bourgeois resentment into a program of active reform.

The Monarchy

France, the home of the Enlightenment, was never ruled by an enlightened despot until the advent of Napoleon. King Louis XV had refused to take decisive steps to remedy the abuses of the Old Régime. What Louis XV would not do, his grandson and successor could not do. Louis XVI (1774-1792), unlike his grandfather, was earnest and pious, but he had a slow mind and was both irresolute and stubborn. Louis labored under the additional handicap of a politically unfortunate marriage. Marie Antoinette, his wife, was frivolous and ignorant; worse still, she was a Habsburg, the daughter of Maria Theresa, a constant reminder to French patriots of the Franco-Austrian alliance that had led so quickly to the humiliations of the Seven Years' War.

For want of a bold mechanic, the machinery of centralized royal absolutism was gradually falling apart. The fact that it functioned at all could be credited to a relatively few capable administrators, notably the *intendants* who ran so much of provincial France. The best of the *intendants*, like the Physiocrat Turgot at Limoges, provided a welcome touch of enlightened despotism, but they could do little to stay the slow disintegration of the central government.

The whole legal and judicial system required reform. The law needed to be modernized and codified to end the overlapping of the two legal systems—Roman and feudal—that prevailed in France. The courts needed a thorough overhaul to make them swift, fair, and inexpensive. Many judges and lawyers purchased or inherited their offices and regarded them not as a public trust but as a means to private enrichment. Louis XV had permitted his ministers to attack the Parlement of Paris, the stronghold of these vested interests and the highest court in France. One of the last acts of his reign had been the cancellation of its privileges; one of the first moves taken by Louis XVI was the restoration of its full authority. Many Frenchmen regarded the Parlement of Paris as a symbol of constitutionalism against the absolute monarchy, but it was also a formidable obstacle in the way of social and economic reform.

The First and Second Estates

Like the monarchy itself, the social and economic foundations of the Old Régime were beginning to crumble and slip by the middle of the eighteenth century.

The first estate, the clergy, occupied a position of conspicuous importance in France. Though amounting to less than one per cent of the total population, the clergy possessed extensive and lucrative lands and performed many functions that are normally undertaken by the state today. The Church kept records of vital statistics, dispensed relief to the poor, and ran the educational system, such as it was. The Gallican Church, however, was a house divided. The lower clergy came almost entirely from the third estate; humble, poorly paid, and generally hardworking, the priests resented the wealth and the arrogance of their ecclesiastical superiors. The bishops and abbots maintained the outlook of the noble class into which they had been born. Although some of them took their duties seriously, others regarded church office as a means of securing a comfortable income. Dozens of prelates turned the administration of their bishoprics or monasteries over to subordinates, pocketed the revenue for themselves, and took up residence in Paris or Versailles.

The wealth and the lax discipline of the Church invited criticism. Well-to-do peasants and townspeople coveted the rich ecclesiastical estates. Taxpayers grumbled at the tithes levied by the Church, at the Church's exemption from taxation, and at the meager size of the "free gift" voted by the clergy to the government in lieu of taxes. The peasants on the whole remained moderately faithful Catholics and regarded the village priest, if not the bishop, with esteem and affection. The bourgeois, however, more and more accepted the anticlerical views of the *philosophes*. They interpreted Voltaire's plea to "crush the infamous thing" as a mandate to strip the Church of wealth and power.

Like the clergy, the nobles of the Old Régime, the second estate, enjoyed privilege, wealth—and unpopularity. Although forming less than 2 per cent of the population, they held about 25 per cent of the land. They had virtual exemption from taxation; they monopolized army commissions and appointments to high ecclesiastical office. The French aristocracy, however, comprised not a single social unit but a series of differing groups. At the top were the hereditary nobles, a few of them descended from royalty or from feudal lords of the Middle Ages, but more from families ennobled within the past two or three centuries. These "nobles of the sword" tended to view their countrymen, including the lesser nobility, as vulgar upstarts. In spite of their failure during the regency of Orléans (see Chapter VIII), they dreamed of the day when they might rule France again, as the feudal nobles had ruled in the Middle Ages. Clustered at Versailles, they neglected their duties as the first landlords of the realm.

Below the nobility of the sword came the "nobility of the robe," including the robed justices of the Paris Parlement and other high courts and a host of other officials. The nobles of the robe, or their ancestors, had originally secured aristocratic status by buying their offices. But, since these dignities were then handed down from father to son, the mercenary origins of their status had become obscured with the passage of time. By the late eighteenth century there was often little practical distinction between the gentry of the robe and their brethren of the sword; intermarriage of the two groups was common. As a group, the nobles of the robe were richer than the nobles of the sword and almost everywhere, except at Versailles itself, they exerted more power and influence by virtue of their firm hold on key governmental positions. The ablest and most tenacious defenders of special privilege in the dying years of the Old Régime were the rich judges of Parlement, not the elegant but ineffectual courtiers of Versailles.

Many noblemen, however, possessed little wealth, power, or glamor. They belonged to the lowest category of French aristocracy —the hobereaux, the "little falcons" or "sparrow-hawks." They vegetated on their country estates, since they could afford neither the purchase of a government office nor the expensive pleasures of the court. In the effort to conserve at least a part of their traditional status, almost all the hobereaux insisted on the meticulous collection of the surviving feudal and manorial dues from the peasantry. Their exhumation of old documents to justify levies sometimes long forgotten earned them the abiding hatred of the peasants and prepared the way for the document-burning of the Revolution.

Not every noble was a snobbish courtier or a selfish defender of the status quo. A few hobereaux calmly drifted down the social ladder to become simple farmers. Some nobles of the robe, attracted by the opportunities for wealth, took part in business enterprises. Even the loftiest noble families produced enlightened spirits, future supporters of revolution.

The Third Estate

In 1789, the third estate included more than 95 per cent of all Frenchmen. The great majority of these commoners were peasants. In some respects, the status of the peasantry was more favorable in France than it was anywhere else in Europe. Serfdom, which was still so prevalent in central and eastern Europe, had disappeared almost entirely except in a few areas. While enclosures were gradually pushing small farmers off the land in England, small peasant holdings existed by the millions in France. Three out of every four adult peasants, it is estimated, held some land.

Nevertheless, Arthur Young, the observant English economist, noted many signs of rural misery in a tour of France in the late 1780's. In the southwest, for example:

Pass Payrac, and meet many beggars, which we had not done before. All the country, girls and women, are without shoes or stockings; and the ploughmen at their work have neither sabots nor feet to their stockings. This is a poverty, that strikes at the root of national prosperity. . . . It reminded me of the misery of Ireland.*

Although the degree of agrarian distress varied greatly from province to province, the total picture was far from bright. The trouble came chiefly from three factors—backward methods of farming, the shortage of land, and overpopulation. The efficient techniques of the agricultural revolution made little headway in France before 1789. Vast areas were not cultivated at all or lay fallow every second or third year in accordance with medieval practice. The crowded and constantly increasing rural population simply could not find full employment or a decent livelihood. Primitive farming required large tracts of land, but the property-holding three-quarters of the French peasantry controlled less than one-third of the land. The average holding was so small that even a propertied peasant might face starvation in poor crop years. The peasant who owned no land turned to begging and sometimes to theft.

Rising prices and heavy taxes also oppressed the peasants. The upward trend of prices in France throughout the eighteenth century brought prosperity to many towns, but to the backward rural economy it meant the new hardship of inflation. The price of farm products rose less swiftly than that of the goods which the farmers had to buy. To the Church the peasants paid the tithe, and to the nobility they paid the obsolete dues that the impecunious hobereaux were pressing for. To the state they owed a land tax, an income tax, a poll tax, and a variety of other duties, of which the most widely detested was the gabelle, the obligatory purchase of salt from government agents, usually at an exorbitant price.

France had a long history of agrarian unrest, going back to the jacquerie, a savage peasant uprising during the Hundred Years'

War. By 1789 there had been no new uprisings, but unemployment and poverty had created a revolutionary temper among the peasants. They did not want a change in the form of government; they ignored the reform program of the Enlightenment. But they most emphatically wanted more land, if need be at the expense of the clergy and the nobility. They wanted an end to manorial dues, and, finally, they wanted relief from a system of taxation that bore hardest upon those who could least afford to pay.

The other members of the third estate, the urban workers and the bourgeois, had little reason to cherish the Old Régime. "Labor," in our modern sense of a large, self-conscious body of factory workers, hardly existed in pre-revolutionary France. Yet almost every sizable town had its wage-earners, employed chiefly in small businesses or workshops. These urban laborers felt with particular sharpness the pinch of rising prices. They were not, however, to take the commanding role in the Revolution itself; geographically scattered, lacking in class cohesiveness, they were ready to follow the lead of the bourgeoisie.

The bourgeoisie included Frenchmen of very divergent resources and interests—rich merchants and bankers in the cities, storekeepers and lawyers in country villages and towns, doctors and other professional men, and thousands upon thousands of craftsmen running their own little businesses. Implacable hostility to the privileged estates and warm receptiveness to the propaganda of the philosophes cemented this sprawling middle class into a political force. The bourgeois suffered fewer hardships than the peasants and workers did, but they resented the abuses of the Old Régime even more keenly. Though they paid a smaller proportion of their incomes in taxes, they violently denounced the unequal assessments. While profiting by the rise in prices, the wealthier and more enterprising businessmen complained of guild regulations and other obsolete restrictions on free commer-

* Travels in France, C. Maxwell, ed. (Cambridge, England, 1929), 23-24.

cial activity. They found it galling to be snubbed by the nobility, treated as second-class subjects by the monarchy, and excluded from the better posts in government, Church, and army.

In sum, the men of the middle class fully realized their own growing economic importance, and they wanted social and political rights to match. Because they were wealthier, better educated, and more articulate than the peasants and wage-earners, they took the preponderant part in formulating the grievances of the entire third estate. These grievances were compiled in statements called *cahiers* and submitted to the Estates General in 1789.

The *cahier* of the third estate of the Longuyon district in Lorraine provides a good sample of the bourgeois reform program.* Sizable portions of this *cahier* dealt exclusively with local problems, like the destruction of the district's woods to supply fuel for iron-smelters. Other portions, however, showed a sharp awareness of the great issues of the day. The *cahier* pronounced the freedom of the press the "surest means of maintaining the freedom of the nation." It deplored the harshness of the criminal laws; they should conform to "the customs and the character of the French nation, the kindest people in the universe." It recommended "a social contract or act between the sovereign and his people," to safeguard "the personal freedom of all citizens" and "prevent the recurrence of those disastrous events which at present oppress the king and the nation." There followed a spirited assertion of the sanctity of private property; a rebuke to Rousseau's economic principles thus accompanied the appeal to his political philosophy. The third estate of Longuyon, however, believed in a large measure of equality. It proposed that "all Frenchmen should have the right and the hope of secur-

ing any State office, of whatever grade, and all military and ecclesiastical dignities." Existing taxes should be swept away, to be replaced by levies on "all property without distinction as to owners, and on all persons without distinction of order and rank."

The Financial Crisis The chronic financial difficulties of the French monarchy strengthened the hand of the middle-class reformers. The government debt, already large at the accession of Louis XVI, tripled between 1774 and 1789; about half the increase resulted from French participation in the American War of Independence. In 1789, the debt stood at 4,500,000,000 *livres*. The budget for 1788, the only one computed for the Old Régime, made alarming reading:*

	(In *livres*)
Estimated Expenses	
For debt service	318,000,000
For the court	35,000,000
For other purposes	276,000,000
Total	629,000,000
Estimated Revenues	503,000,000
Estimated Deficit	126,000,000

Note here the very high proportion of revenues consumed by interest payments on the debt.

Louis XVI, in his feeble way, tried to cope with the growing emergency. On coming to the throne in 1774, he named as chief minister Turgot, a leading Physiocrat with a brilliant record as *intendant* of Limoges. Turgot temporarily reduced the deficit by imposing strict economies, particularly on the expenditures of the court. To increase prosperity and to propitiate the third estate, he curtailed the ancient guild monopolies, lifted restrictions on the internal shipments of grain, and replaced the *corvée*, the work on highways demanded of peasants, with a tax affecting nobles and commoners alike. At this the vested interests rebelled and,

---

* The full text of this *cahier* is printed in B. F. Hyslop, *A Guide to the General Cahiers of 1789* (New York, 1936), 318-326. The quotations that follow are in our translation.

* Based on the figures in G. Lefebvre, *The Coming of the French Revolution* (Princeton, 1947), 21-22.

seconded by Marie Antoinette, secured Turgot's dismissal in 1776. The ousted minister admonished Louis XVI: "Remember, sire, that it was weakness which brought the head of Charles I to the block."

Louis ignored Turgot's warning. The government continued to raise new loans— 653,000,000 *livres* between 1783 and 1786 alone. Then in 1786 the bankers refused to make new advances. The French government was caught between the irresistible force of the third estate's demands for tax relief and the immovable object of the other estates' refusal to yield their fiscal exemptions. Calonne, the finance minister in 1786, proposed to meet the crisis by reviving Turgot's reforms. In the hope of persuading the first two estates to consent to heavier taxation, he convoked the Assembly of Notables, the chief aristocratic and ecclesiastical dignitaries of the kingdom. But the Notables declined to be persuaded.

Louis XVI dissolved the Notables and dismissed Calonne. Then, with unaccustomed firmness, he decided to levy a uniform tax on all landed property. The clergy replied by reducing their "free gift" for 1788 to one-sixth of what it had previously been. The Parlement of Paris declared the new tax law illegal and asserted that only the nation as a whole assembled in the Estates General could institute so sweeping an innovation. The King retreated and in the summer of 1788 announced that the Estates General would meet the following spring.

The Estates General   Louis XVI thus revived a half-forgotten institution which had represented the nation, after a fashion, but which scarcely seemed likely to enact drastic social and economic reforms. The three estates, despite their immense variation in size, had customarily received equal representation and equal voting power, so that the two privileged orders could outvote the commoners. The Estates General of 1789, however, met under unique circumstances.

Its election and subsequent meeting took place during an economic crisis that heightened the chronic social and financial tensions. In 1786, a trade treaty between France and Britain lowered French tariffs on British manufactures and allowed cheaper British textiles and metals to invade the French market. By 1789, thousands of French craftsmen were out of work. Nor was this all; hail and drought ruined the harvest of 1788, and the winter of 1788-89 was so bitter that the Seine froze over at Paris, blocking shipments of grain by water. In the spring of 1789, the price of grain rose to double the normal, and in some localities to quadruple.

France had survived depressions, bad weather, and poor harvests many times in the past without experiencing revolution. This time, however, the added economic hardships were in effect the last straw. Starving peasants begged, borrowed, and stole, poaching on the hunting preserves of the great lords and attacking their game wardens. The turbulence in Paris boiled over in a riot (April, 1789), witnessed by Thomas Jefferson, then the American minister to France:

... The Fauxbourg St. Antoine is a quarter of the city inhabited entirely by the class of day-laborers and journeymen in every line. A rumor was spread among them that a great paper manufacturer ... had proposed ... that their wages should be lowered to 15 sous a day [three-quarters of a *livre*]. ... They flew to his house in vast numbers, destroyed everything in it, and in his magazines and work shops, without secreting however a pin's worth to themselves, and were continuing this work of devastation when the regular troops were called in. Admonitions being disregarded, they were of necessity fired on, and a regular action ensued, in which about 100 of them were killed, before the rest would disperse.*

---

* *Autobiography of Thomas Jefferson,* P. L. Ford, ed. (New York, 1914), 133-134.

These disturbances impressed a sense of urgency on the deputies to the Estates General.

The methods followed in electing the deputies aided the champions of reform. Contrary to precedent, and against the violent opposition of the Parlements, the third estate secured double representation, thus gaining as many seats as the clergy and the nobility combined. In each district of France, moreover, the third estate chose its deputy not by secret ballot but in a public meeting. Since this procedure greatly favored bourgeois orators over inarticulate farmers or workers, middle-class lawyers won control of the commoners' deputation. Finally, the radicals of the third estate found a few sympathizers in the second estate and many more in the deputation of the first estate, where the discontented lower clergy had a large delegation:

THE ESTATES GENERAL, 1789

Estate	No. of Deputies
First:	
Higher Clergy	94
Lower Clergy	More than 200
Second	270
Third	578

A majority of the deputies were prepared to make drastic changes in the Old Régime.

But would they succeed in doing so? In all past meetings of the Estates General each estate, or order, had deliberated separately, with the consent of two estates and of the Crown required for the passage of a measure. In 1789, the King and the privileged orders favored retaining this "vote by order." The third estate, on the contrary, demanded "vote by head," with the deputies from all the orders forming a single unit. Pamphleteers invoked Rousseau's concept of the general will. "What is the third estate?" wrote Abbé Siéyès in an influential broadside of the same name. "Nothing." And what should it be? "Everything."

. . . If votes are taken by order, five million citizens will not be able to decide anything for the general interest, because it will not please a couple of hundred thousand privileged individuals. The will of a single individual will veto and destroy the will of more than a hundred people.*

This crucial question of procedure came to a head soon after the Estates General convened on May 5, 1789, at Versailles. Siéyès and Mirabeau, a renegade nobleman, led the campaign for vote by head. On June 17, the third estate cut the Gordian knot of procedure by accepting Siéyès' invitation to proclaim itself the "National Assembly." It completed its revolutionary repudiation of the Old Régime by inviting the deputies of other estates to join its sessions.

A majority of the clerical deputies, chiefly parish priests, accepted; the nobility refused. The King barred the commoners from their meeting place, whereupon they assembled at an indoor tennis court on June 20 and solemnly swore never to disband until they had given France a constitution. To the "Tennis-Court Oath" Louis replied by commanding each estate to resume its separate deliberations. The third estate and some deputies of the first disobeyed. Louis, vacillating as ever, now gave in and on June 27 directed the noble and clerical deputies to join the National Assembly. The nation, through its representatives, had successfully challenged the King and the vested interests. The Estates General was dead, and in its place sat the National Assembly, pledged to reform the society and the constitution of France. The revolution was under way.

---

* Emmanuel Siéyès, *Qu'est-ce Que le Tiers Etat?*, E. Champion, ed. (Paris, 1888), 82. Our translation.

III: The Dissolution of the French Monarchy

Popular Uprisings
(July-October, 1789)

The National Assembly had barely settled down to work when a new wave of rioting swept over France, undermining further the position of the King. The economic depression grew more severe during the summer of 1789. Unemployment increased, and bread threatened to be scarce and expensive at least until completion of the new harvest in the autumn. Meanwhile, the commoners feared that the King and the privileged orders might attempt a counter-revolution. Large concentrations of troops appeared in the Paris area early in July—to preserve order and protect the National Assembly, the King asserted. But the Parisians suspected that Louis was planning the forcible dissolution of the Assembly. Suspicion deepened into conviction after Louis dismissed Necker, the popular financier who had been serving as the chief royal adviser.

The reaction to Necker's dismissal was immediate and revolutionary. On July 12 and 13, the men who had elected the Paris deputies of the third estate formed a new municipal government and a new militia, both loyal to the National Assembly. Paris was forging the weapons that made it the leader of the Revolution. Mobs were roaming the streets, demanding cheaper bread,

The Bastille, July 14, 1789.

parading busts of Necker draped in mourning, and breaking into government buildings to obtain arms. On July 14, the armed mob stormed the Bastille, a fortress in the eastern part of the city, and massacred its garrison.

The fall of the Bastille had little practical significance, but its symbolic value was immense. The gloomy pile frowned like a monstrous sentry over a restless working-class quarter of Paris. Its capture and subsequent demolition symbolized the loosening of the shackles of the Old Régime. Further, the public imagined the Bastille to be crowded with innocent victims of royal tyranny. Actually, there were only seven prisoners to be liberated at the time of its capture—five criminals (mostly forgers) and two mental cases. But the anticlimactic facts have never destroyed the legend. The Fourteenth of July has remained the great national holiday of Frenchmen.

Rioting spread over much of France late in July, as the provincial population responded to the news from Paris or acted on its own. In town after town, mobs attacked the local counterpart of the Bastille. The countryside experienced the "Great Fear," one of the most extraordinary attacks of mass delusion on record. From village to village word spread that "brigands" were coming, aristocratic hirelings who would destroy crops and villages and force the National Assembly to preserve the status quo. There were in fact no brigands, only an occasional starving farmhand trying to steal food. But the peasants in many districts went berserk, clutching hoes and pitchforks, anything resembling a weapon. When the brigands did not materialize, they attacked chateaux and broke into any building that might house a hoard of grain or the hated documents justifying collection of manorial dues. The wiser nobles voluntarily gave the peasants what they wanted; the others saw their barns and archives burnt. The Great Fear, beginning as a psychological aberration, ended in an uprising of the peasantry against its traditional oppressors.

By the end of July, 1789, four distinct sets of revolutionary events had taken place in France: (1) the constitutional revolution of June, resulting in the creation of the National Assembly; (2) the Paris revolution and the taking of the Bastille; (3) the comparable outbreaks in provincial cities and towns; and (4) the Great Fear. Each of the four drove another nail into the coffin of the Old Régime. The transformation of the Estates General into the National Assembly and the creation of new local governments destroyed the political superiority of the first two estates. The Great Fear began the destruction of the social and economic privileges of the clergy and nobility. Everywhere, legally constituted officials were turned out, taxes went unpaid, and valuable records were destroyed.

The "October Days," the last crisis of a momentous year, demonstrated anew the impotence of Louis XVI and the power of his aroused subjects. As the autumn of 1789 drew on, Parisians still queued for bread and still looked suspiciously at the royal troops stationed in the neighborhood of their city. Rumors of the Queen's behavior further incensed them. Marie Antoinette made a dramatic appearance at a banquet of royal officers, clutching the Dauphin in her arms. And, on hearing that the people had no bread, she was said to have remarked callously: "Let them eat cake." This story was false, but it echoed and re-echoed in the lively new Paris papers that delighted in denouncing the "Austrian bitch." On October 5, 1789, an array of determined Paris housewives marched the dozen miles from Paris to Versailles in the rain. They disrupted the National Assembly and succeeded in extracting a kiss from a baffled Louis XVI. This bizarre demonstration had very significant consequences. On October 6, the women marched back to Paris, escorting "the baker, the baker's wife, and the baker's son"—in other words, the royal family, who took up residence in the Tuileries

Palace. More important, the National Assembly, too, moved to Paris. The most revolutionary place in France had captured both the symbol of the Old Régime and the herald of the new.

The National Assembly (1789-1791)

The outlines of the new regime were already starting to take shape before the October Days. The Great Fear prompted the National Assembly to abolish in law what the peasants were destroying in fact. On the evening of August 4, 1789, the Viscount de Noailles, a liberal nobleman, addressed the deputies:

> The kingdom at this moment hangs between the alternative of the destruction of society, and that of a government which will be the admiration and the examplar of Europe.
> How is this government to be established? By public tranquillity. . . . And to secure this necessary tranquillity, I propose:
> (1) . . . That taxation will be paid by all the individuals of the kingdom, in proportion to their revenues;
> (2) That all public expenses will in the future be borne equally by all.*

The deputies voted the proposals of Noailles. In addition, the clergy gave up its tithes, and the liberal minority of the second estate surrendered the nobility's game preserves, manorial dues, and other medieval rights. The assembly made it a clean sweep by abolishing serfdom, forbidding the sale of justice or of judicial office, and decreeing that "all citizens, without distinction of birth, can be admitted to all ecclesiastical, civil, and military posts and dignities." When the memorable session inaugurated by Noailles' speech ended at two o'clock on the morning of August 5, the Old Régime was dead.

Three weeks later, on August 26, 1789, the National Assembly formulated the Declaration of the Rights of Man. "Men are born free and equal in rights," it asserted (Art. 1). "These rights are liberty, property, security and resistance to oppression" (Art. 2). Property it called "an inviolable and sacred right" (Art. 17), and liberty "the exercise of the natural rights of each man" within the limits "determined by law" (Art. 4). "Law," the Declaration stated, "is the expression of the general will. All citizens have the right to take part, in person or by their representatives, in its formation" (Art. 6). "Any society in which the guarantee of rights is not assured or the separation of powers not determined has no constitution" (Art. 16).*

The Declaration of the Rights of Man mirrored the political and economic attitudes of the middle class. It insisted on the sacredness of property. It committed the French to the creed of constitutional liberalism already affirmed by the English in 1688-89 and by the Americans in 1776, and it incorporated the key phrases of the *philosophes:* natural rights, general will, and separation of powers. The National Assembly made a resounding statement of the ideals of the Enlightenment. Yet, as the subsequent history of the Revolution soon demonstrated, the Assembly found no magic formula by which to translate these ideals into practice.

The economic legislation of the National Assembly provided a case in point. Belief in the theory of the equal taxation of all Frenchmen did not solve urgent practical problems of finance. The new and just land tax imposed by the deputies simply could not be collected. Tax-collectors had vanished in the general liquidation of the Old Régime, and naive peasants thought that they owed nothing to a government turned revolutionary. Once again, the French state borrowed until its credit was exhausted, and then, in desperation, the National Assembly ordered the confiscation of church

---

* *Archives Parlementaires*, Series 1, VIII, 343. Our translation.

* All passages from the Declaration are as translated in the Appendix to G. Lefebvre, *The Coming of the French Revolution* (Princeton, 1947).

lands (November, 1789). "The wealth of the clergy is at the disposition of the nation," it declared, explaining that ecclesiastical lands fell outside the bounds of "inviolable" property as defined in the Declaration of the Rights of Man because they belonged to an institution and not to private individuals.

The government thus acquired an asset worth at least 2,000,000,000 *livres*. On the basis of this collateral it issued *assignats*, paper notes used to pay the government's debts. The *assignats* had adequate security behind them and temporarily eased the financial crisis. Unfortunately, the Revolution repeated the mistake of John Law (see Chapter VIII): it did not know when to stop. As the state sold parcels of confiscated land—that is, as it reduced the collateral securing its paper money—it should have destroyed *assignats* to the same amount. The temptation not to reduce the number of *assignats* proved too great to resist. Inflation resulted: the *assignats*, progressively losing their solid backing, depreciated until in 1795 they were worth less than 5 per cent of their face value.

This economic experiment resulted in the redistribution of some of the best farmland in France. Many peasants enlarged their holdings by buying former ecclesiastical property. But the bourgeoisie also invested heavily in these lands, while the poor and landless peasants gained nothing, since they did not have the money to buy. Following the doctrine of laissez-faire, the National Assembly abolished the guilds and the irksome internal tariffs and tolls. And, deeming the few primitive organizations of labor unnatural restraints on economic freedom, it abolished them too. In June, 1791, following an outbreak of strikes, it passed the Le Chapelier Law banning both strikes and labor unions.

Since the suppression of tithes and the seizure of ecclesiastical property deprived the Church of its revenue, the National Assembly agreed to finance ecclesiastical sal-

aries. The new arrangement virtually nationalized the Gallican Church and made it subject to constant government regulation. The Assembly's decision to suppress monasteries and convents caused little difficulty; many of these establishments were already far gone in decay. But an uproar arose over the legislation altering the status of the secular hierarchy.

The Civil Constitution of the Clergy (June, 1790) redrew the ecclesiastical map of France. It reduced the number of bishoprics by more than one-third, making the remaining dioceses correspond to the new civil administrative units known as departments (see below). It transformed bishops and priests into civil officials, paid by the state and elected by the population of the diocese or parish; both Catholics and non-Catholics (the latter usually a small minority) could vote in these elections. A new bishop was required to take an oath of loyalty to the state, and the Civil Constitution stipulated that he might not apply to the Pope for confirmation, though he might write to him as the "Visible Head of the Universal Church."

These provisions stripped the "Visible Head of the Universal Church" of effective authority over the Gallican clergy and ran counter to the whole tradition of the Roman Church as an independent ecclesiastical monarchy. Naturally the Pope denounced the Civil Constitution. The National Assembly then required that every member of the French clergy take a special oath supporting the Civil Constitution, but only seven bishops and fewer than half of the priests complied. The National Assembly thus opened a breach between the Revolution and a large segment of the population. Good Catholics, from Louis XVI down to humble peasants, rallied to the non-juring clergy, those who refused the special oath. The Civil Constitution of the Clergy, supplying an issue for rebellion and civil war, was the first great blunder of the Revolution.

The Constitution of 1791

The major undertaking of the National Assembly was its effort to put limited monarchy on a permanent footing, culminating in the Constitution of 1791. The Assembly devised a neat and orderly system of local government to replace the bewildering complex of provincial units that had accumulated under the Old Régime. It divided the territory of France into eighty-three departments of approximately equal size. The departments were subdivided into *arrondissements* or districts, and the districts into communes—that is, municipalities. The commune-district-department arrangement resembled, on a reduced scale, the American pattern of town-county-state. In the communes and departments, elected councils and officials enjoyed considerable rights of self-government. The administration of the new France, on paper anyhow, was to be far more decentralized than that of the Old Régime.

Separation of powers was the guiding principle in the reconstruction of the central government. The Constitution of 1791 established an independent hierarchy of courts staffed by elected judges. It vested legislative authority in a single elected chamber. Although the king still headed the executive branch, his actions now required approval by his ministers. But he was given the power of veto, a suspensive veto that could block legislation for four years. Louis XVI, no longer the absolute "King of France," acquired the new constitutional title, "King of the French."

The new constitution subscribed to many principles issuing straight from the Enlightenment. It promised to give France a new law code, and it declared marriage a civil contract, not a sacrament. The state took over the old ecclesiastical functions of keeping records of vital statistics and providing charity and education. Indeed, the Constitution promised a system of free public education. In foreign policy revolutionary France would be more virtuous and less aggressive than autocratic France:

> The French nation renounces the undertaking of any war with a view of making conquests, and it will never use its forces against the liberty of any people.[*]

The Constitution of 1791 went a long way toward instituting popular government, but it stopped well short of full democracy. Restricting the political equality promised by the Declaration of the Rights of Man, it divided Frenchmen into two classes of citizens, "active" and "passive." It limited the right of voting to "active" citizens, who paid annually in taxes an amount equal to at least three days' wages for labor in the locality. The "passive" citizens, numbering about one-third of the male population, enjoyed the full protection of the law but did not receive the franchise. Moreover, the new legislature was chosen by a process of indirect election. Ordinary "active" citizens did not vote for their deputies but for a series of electors, who were required to be men of substantial wealth, and who ultimately elected the deputies. The French middle class evidently assumed that a certain minimum of worldly goods was necessary for political wisdom.

The decentralized and limited monarchy established by the Constitution of 1791 was doomed to fail. It was too radical to suit the King and most of the aristocracy, and not radical enough for the goodly number of bourgeois who were veering toward republicanism. The majority in the National Assembly supporting the Constitution suffered the fate commonly experienced by the politically moderate in a revolution: they were squeezed out by the extremists. Despite their moderate intentions, they were driven to enact some drastic legislation, notably the Civil Constitution of the Clergy, which weakened their own position.

The radical republicans were the Jaco-

[*] J. H. Stewart, *A Documentary Survey of the French Revolution* (New York, 1951), 260.

bins, so named because they belonged to the "Society of the Friends of the Constitution," which maintained its Paris headquarters in a former Jacobin monastery. The Jacobins accepted the Constitution of 1791 only as a stopgap until they might end the monarchy and set up a republic based on universal suffrage. They used all the techniques of a political pressure group. They planted rabble-rousing articles in the popular press and manipulated the crowds of noisy and volatile spectators at the sessions of the National Assembly. Their network of political clubs extended throughout the provinces, providing the only nation-wide party organization in France. Almost everywhere, Jacobins captured control of the new department and commune councils. In local elections, as in the elections to the Estates General, an able and determined minority prevailed over a largely illiterate and politically inexperienced majority.

The defenders of the Old Régime played into the hands of the Jacobins. From the summer of 1789 on, alarmed nobles and prelates fled France in a steady stream, leaving behind more rich estates to be confiscated and giving Jacobin orators and editors a splendid opportunity to denounce them as rats leaving a supposedly sinking ship. Many of these aristocratic *émigrés* gathered in the German Rhineland to intrigue for Austrian and Russian support of a counter-revolution. The King's grave misgivings about the Civil Constitution of the Clergy prompted his disastrous attempt to join the *émigrés* on the Franco-German frontier. In June, 1791, disguised as a valet and governess, Louis and Marie Antoinette left the Tuileries. But a local official along the route recognized the royal profile from the portrait on the *assignats*. The alarm was sent ahead, and at Varennes in northeastern France a detachment of troops forced the royal party to return to Paris. After the abortive flight to Varennes, the revolutionaries viewed Louis XVI as a potential traitor and kept him closely guarded in the Tuil-

eries. The experiment in constitutional monarchy began under most unfavorable auspices.

The Legislative Assembly, Oct. 1791- Sept. 1792

On October 1, 1791, the first and the only legislative assembly elected under the new constitution commenced its deliberations. No one faction commanded a numerical majority in the new assembly:

POLITICAL COMPLEXION OF THE
LEGISLATIVE ASSEMBLY, 1791

	Approximate No. of Seats
Right (Constitutional Monarchists)	265
Center (Plain)	345
Left (Jacobins, Girondins)	130

(Here, as is still the practice in most continental European assemblies, the Right sat to the right of the presiding officer as he faced the assembly, the Left to his left, and the Center in between.)

The balance of political power rested with the irresolute deputies of the Center, who were neither strong defenders of the Constitution nor yet convinced republicans. Since they occupied the lowest seats in the assembly hall, they received the derogatory nickname of the Plain or Marsh. The capable politicians of the Left soon captured the votes of the Plain, to demonstrate anew the power of a determined minority.

Leadership of this minority came from a small contingent of Jacobins known as Girondins because they clustered around the deputies from Bordeaux, in the Gironde department. The Girondins specialized in patriotic oratory. They pictured revolutionary France as the intended victim of a great reactionary conspiracy, engineered by the *émigrés*, aided at home by the non-juring clergy and the royal family, and abetted abroad by a league of monarchs under Leopold II, the Austrian emperor. But Louis XVI, despite the flight to Varennes, was no traitor, and Leopold II cautiously limited his aid to the *émigrés*. The sudden death of Leopold in March, 1792, and the accession of his inexperienced and less cautious son, Francis II, at once increased the Austrian threat. At the same time, belligerent Girondins secured control of French diplomacy. On April 20, 1792, the Legislative Assembly declared war on Austria. In the eyes of Frenchmen the war was defensive, not the sort of aggression that the nation had forsworn in the fine phrases of its constitution.

The war went badly for France at the outset. Prussia soon joined Austria, and on July 25, 1792, the Prussian commander, the Duke of Brunswick, issued a manifesto drafted by an *émigré*. The manifesto was a threat: "If the Tuileries is attacked, by deed or word, if the slightest outrage or violence is perpetrated against the royal family, and if immediate measures are not taken for their safety, maintenance and liberty"—then Paris would witness "a model vengeance, never to be forgotten," and the persons responsible for the disorders would be handed over to the "tortures which they have richly deserved." * The Duke of Brunswick's manifesto did not frighten the French, as it was intended to do. On the contrary, it stiffened the already firm determination of republicans to do away with the monarchy. All through the early summer of 1792 the Jacobins of Paris had been plotting an insurrection. They won the sup-

* *Le Moniteur Universel*, August 3, 1792. Our translation.

port of a formidable following—patriotic army recruits, provincial radicals who had come to the capital to celebrate the third anniversary of the Bastille's taking, Paris workingmen angered by the depreciated value of the *assignats* and by a new food shortage. One by one, the forty-eight *sections* or wards into which the city was divided came under the political control of the Jacobins.

The process came to a climax on the night of August 9-10, 1792, when the leaders of the *sections* ousted the regularly constituted authorities of the Paris municipal administration and installed a new and illegal Jacobin commune. The municipal revolution in Paris at once produced decisive results. On the morning of August 10, the forces of the new commune attacked the Tuileries and massacred the King's Swiss guards. Though Louis XVI and the royal family found temporary safety with the Legislative Assembly, the uprising of August 10 sealed the doom of the monarchy. It demoralized the Assembly, thereafter little more than the errand boy of the illegal Paris commune. With most of the deputies of the Right and the Plain absent, the Assembly voted to suspend the King from office, to imprison the royal family, and to order the election of a constitutional convention. Until this new representative body should meet, a temporary Jacobin committee was to run the government. The birth of the First French Republic was at hand.

IV: *The First French Republic*

The weeks between August 10 and the meeting of the Convention on September 21 were weeks of crisis and tension. The value of the *assignats* depreciated by 40 per cent during August alone. Rabble-rousing Jacobins continually excited the populace of Paris, already stirred by the economic difficulties and by the capture of the Tuileries. Excitement mounted still higher when the news arrived that Prussian troops had invaded northeastern France. In the emergency, Danton, the Jacobin minister of justice, won immortality by urging that the way to beat the enemy was to show "*de l'audace, encore de l'audace, toujours de l'audace*"—boldness, more boldness, always boldness.

In Paris, audacity took the form of the "September massacres," lynchings of supposed traitors and enemy agents. For five days, beginning on September 2, bloodthirsty mobs directed by Jacobin agents moved from prison to prison. At each stop they tried prisoners before impromptu courts and then executed them. The number of victims exceeded one thousand and included ordinary criminals as well as aristocrats and non-juring priests who were often quite innocent of the treason charged against them. The crowning horror was the mutilation of the Princesse de Lamballe, the Queen's maid of honor. The mob paraded her severed head on a pike before the window of the royal prison so that Marie Antoinette might see "how the people take vengeance on their tyrants."

Soon a rather minor French victory—it was called the "miracle" of Valmy (September 20, 1792)—turned the Duke of Brunswick and the Prussians back from the road to Paris; more solid French successes followed later in 1792. Then the tide turned again, washing away the conquests of the autumn. By the summer of 1793 half-defeated France faced a hostile coalition including almost every major power in Europe. No wonder an atmosphere of perpetual emergency surrounded the Convention.

Gironde and Mountain In theory, the election of the National Convention (August-September, 1792) marked the beginning of true political democracy in France. Both "active" and "passive" citizens were invited to the polls. In practice, however, only 10 per cent of the potential electorate of 7,000,000 actually voted. The others abstained or were turned away from the polls by the watchdogs of the Jacobin clubs, ever on the alert against "counter-revolutionaries." The result was a landslide for the republicans:

POLITICAL COMPLEXION OF THE
CONVENTION, SEPTEMBER, 1792

Approximate No. of Deputies

The Right (Gironde)	165
The Center (Plain)	435
The Left (Mountain)	150

The radicalism of the Convention was underlined by the Jacobin antecedents of both its Right and its Left. Many ties in common existed between the Gironde and the Mountain (so named because these left-wing deputies sat high up in the meeting hall). Both factions came from the middle class, both were steeped in the ideas of the *philosophes*, and both united to declare France a republic (September 21, 1792).

Bitter hostility and rivalry, however, soon arose between the Gironde and the Mountain. The Girondin deputies represented provincial interests. As one of them told the Convention:

I fear the despotism of Paris. . . . I do not want a Paris guided by intriguers to become to the French Empire what Rome was to the Roman Empire. Paris must be reduced to its proper one-eighty-third of influence, like the other departments.*

As firm adherents of laissez-faire, the Girondins favored a breathing spell in revolutionary legislation. Their political program was outlined in the draft constitution completed early in 1793 by one of their most distinguished deputies, Condorcet, the prophet of progress (see Chapter IX). Condorcet's draft proposed a large measure of decentralization—"federalism" was the revolutionary term. The legislature and the executive would be independent of each other; as further checks and balances, election results would be determined by proportional representation, projected laws would be submitted to a popular referendum, and voters would have the right to recall unworthy elected officials.

* Lasource, September 25, 1792. *Archives Parlementaires*, Series 1, LII, 130. Our translation

Execution of Louis XVI, January 21, 1793.

The leaders of the Mountain, in contrast, favored an all-powerful central government over federalism. Instead of Girondin laissez-faire, they demanded state intervention in economic affairs to appease their urban supporters. The most powerful leader of the Mountain proved to be Maximilien Robespierre (1758-1794), whose speeches were lay sermons couched in the solemn language of a new revelation. He put his creed most forcefully in a discourse delivered in February, 1794:

What is the goal toward which we are striving? The peaceful enjoyment of liberty and equality: the rule of that eternal justice whose laws have been engraved . . . upon the hearts of men, even upon the heart of the slave who ignores them and of the tyrant who denies them.

We desire an order of things . . . where our country assures the welfare of each individual and where each individual enjoys with pride the prosperity and the glory of our country; where the souls of all grow through the constant expression of republican sentiments; where the arts are the ornament of the free-dom which in turn ennobles them; and where commerce is the source of public wealth, not just of the monstrous opulence of a few houses.*

Like Rousseau, Robespierre had faith in the natural goodness of humanity, in "the laws of justice engraved upon the hearts of men." He was sure that he knew the general will, and that the general will demanded a Republic of Virtue. If Frenchmen would not be free and virtuous voluntarily, then he would force them to be free and cram virtue down their throats.

Robespierre and the Republic of Virtue triumphed. The Girondins met a significant defeat when, after one hundred hours of continuous voting, starting on January 15, 1793, the Convention declared "Citizen Louis Capet" guilty of treason and by a narrow margin sentenced him to the guillotine without delay. Louis XVI died bravely on January 21, 1793. Although the majority

* *Le Moniteur Universel*, February 7, 1794. Our translation.

333

of the French population disapproved of the King's execution, the majority did not control the Convention. There some of the Girondin deputies had asserted that Louis did not deserve to die. They took a courageous stand in defense of the humanitarian principles of the Enlightenment, but they also exposed themselves to the charge of being "counter-revolutionaries."

The march of events soon destroyed the Girondins. In February, 1793, the Convention rejected the constitutional draft drawn up by the political expert of the Gironde, Condorcet. In March, the army under Dumouriez, a Girondin general, suffered a series of defeats in the Low Countries, and in April Dumouriez deserted to the enemy. Meanwhile, in February, 1793, the Convention declared war on Britain, Spain, and Holland, and France faced a formidable number of enemies. The leaders of the Mountain pressed for the expulsion of Girondins from the Jacobin clubs. Finally, on June 2, 1793, the Jacobin *sections* of Paris invaded the Convention and forced it to arrest twenty-nine Girondin deputies, who were soon consigned to the guillotine. The Reign of Terror had begun.

The Reign of Terror (June, 1793 – July, 1794)

How was it that the advocates of democracy now imposed a ruthless dictatorship upon France? Here is Robespierre's explanation:

. . . To establish and consolidate democracy, to achieve the peaceful rule of constitutional laws, we must first finish the war of liberty against tyranny. . . . We must annihilate the enemies of the republic at home and abroad, or else we shall perish. . . .

If virtue is the mainstay of a democratic government in time of peace, then in time of revolution a democratic government must rely on *virtue* and *terror*. . . . Terror is nothing but justice, swift, severe and inflexible; it is an emanation of virtue. . . . It has been said that

terror is the mainstay of a despotic government. . . . The government of the revolution is the despotism of liberty against tyranny.*

The Convention duly voted a democratic constitution, drawn up by the Mountain, granting universal manhood suffrage, and giving supreme power, unhampered by Girondin checks and balances, to a single legislative chamber. When the instrument was submitted to a referendum, less than 2,000,000 of the 7,000,000 qualified Frenchmen voted, and the ballots cast went almost unanimously for ratification. The Convention then postponed indefinitely the operation of this Constitution of 1793, which always remained a dead letter.

The real government of the Terror centered on a twelve-man Committee of Public Safety, composed of Robespierre and other stalwarts from the Mountain. Though nominally responsible to the Convention, the Committee of Public Safety enjoyed a large measure of independent authority and acted as a kind of war cabinet. A second group of deputies, the Committee of General Security, supervised police activities and turned suspected enemies of the Republic over to the new Revolutionary Tribunal, whose sixteen judges and sixty jurors were divided into several courts to speed the work of repression. At the local level, the Mountain scrapped much of the self-government inaugurated under the Constitution of 1791. Local Jacobin clubs purged department and commune administrations of political unreliables, while special local courts supplemented the grim labors of the Revolutionary Tribunal. To make sure that provincial France toed the line, the Mountain sent out trusted members of the Convention as its agents, the "deputies on mission." From the standpoint of administration, the Terror marked both an anticipation of twentieth-century dictatorship and a return to the age-old French princi-

---

* *Le Moniteur Universel*, February 7, 1794. Our translation.

ple of centralization. The deputies on mission were the successors of the *intendants* of Richelieu, and indeed of the imperial agents whom Charlemagne had sent to oversee his provinces a thousand years before the Terror.

The Record of the Terror

The "swift, severe, and inflexible justice" promised by Robespierre took the lives of 20,000 Frenchmen. Although the Terror claimed such social outcasts as criminals and prostitutes, its

Sketch of Marie Antoinette on her way to the guillotine, by David.

main purpose was military and political— to clear France of suspected traitors, including Marie Antoinette, and to purge the Jacobins of dissidents. It fell with the greatest relative severity on the clergy, the aristocracy, and the Girondins. Many of its victims came from the Vendée, a strongly Catholic and royalist area in western France

which had revolted against the Republic's attempts to recruit soldiers. The record of the Terror was bloody indeed, at least by eighteenth-century standards. And by any standard the Terror perpetrated some grisly deeds. In the *noyades* (drownings) at Nantes, more than 2,000 suspects were set adrift on the River Loire to perish in leaky boats.

The wartime hysteria that helped to account for the excesses of the Terror also inspired a remarkably practical kind of patriotism. On August 23, 1793, the Convention issued a decree epitomizing the democratic nationalism of the Jacobins:

> From this moment, until the time when the enemy shall have been driven from the territory of the Republic, all Frenchmen are permanently requisitioned for the service of the armies.
>
> Young men will go into combat, married men will manufacture arms and transport supplies; women will make tents and uniforms and will serve in the hospitals; children will make old linen into bandages; old men will be carried into the public squares to arouse the courage of the soldiers, excite hatred for kings and inspire the unity of the Republic.*

The army drafted all bachelors and widowers from eighteen to twenty-five. Hundreds of open-air forges were installed in Paris to manufacture weapons. Since the war prevented the importation of the saltpeter needed for gunpowder, the government sponsored a great campaign to scrape patches of saltpeter from cellars and stables.

By the close of 1793, the forces of the Republic had driven foreign troops off French soil. Credit for this new shift in the tide of battle did not rest solely with the Jacobins. The military successes of the Republic reflected in part the improvements made in the army during the dying years of the Old Régime; they resulted still more from the weaknesses of the coalition aligned against France (see below, p. 342). Yet they could scarcely have been achieved without

---

* *Le Moniteur Universel*, August 24, 1793. Our translation.

the new democratic spirit that allowed men of the third estate to become officers and that made the French army the most determined and the most enterprising in Europe.

Total mobilization demanded an approximate, if not total, equality of economic sacrifice. To exorcise the twin devils of inflation and food shortage, the Terror issued the *"maximum"* legislation, placing ceilings on prices and wages. Wages were pegged at a point 50 per cent over the 1790 wage-rate; prices at 33 per cent above the 1790 price level. The government rationed scarce commodities, forbade the use of white flour, and directed all patriots to eat *pain d'égalité* —"equality bread," a loaf utilizing almost the whole of the wheat. Finally, early in 1794, the Convention passed the "Laws of Ventôse," named for a month in the revolutionary calendar. These laws authorized seizure of the remaining properties of the *émigrés* and other opponents of the Republic and recommended their distribution to landless Frenchmen.

Socialist historians have often found in the *maximum* and the Laws of Ventôse evidence that the Terror was moving from political to social democracy, that the Republic of Virtue was indeed beginning the socialist revolution. The *maximum*, however, resembled nothing so much as the economic controls employed in the nonsocialist United States during World War II, right down to the provision permitting wages to rise proportionately more than prices. Though the *maximum* temporarily checked the depreciation of the *assignats*, black markets flourished during the Terror; even the government patronized them.

Although the redistribution of property foreseen by the Laws of Ventôse did anticipate socialism, the provision was never enforced. Furthermore, the Convention was assured that the Mountain did not intend a general assault on private property:

The revolution leads us to recognize the principle that he who has shown himself the enemy of his country cannot own property. The properties of patriots are sacred, but the goods of conspirators are there for the unfortunate.*

To the thorough-going socialist not even the properties of patriots are sacred. The middle-class leaders of the Terror were not genuine socialists; only the emergencies of the Revolution forced them to abandon laissez-faire. They had to make food cheaper for townspeople—whence the *maximum*; and they had to promise men some hope of future well-being—whence the Laws of Ventôse.

The Terror presented its most revolutionary aspect in its drastic social and cultural reforms. "In our land," Robespierre announced, "we desire to substitute all the virtues and all the miracles of the Republic for all the vices and all the nonsense of monarchy." When Robespierre said "all," he meant "all"— clothing, the arts, amusements, the calendar, religion. The Republic of Virtue could tolerate nothing that smacked of the Old Régime. Even the traditional forms of address, "Monsieur" and "Madame," gave way to the newly orthodox "Citoyen" (citizen) and "Citoyenne" (citizeness).

Ever since 1789, revolutionaries had discarded elaborate gowns and knee-breeches (culottes) as symbols of idleness and privilege. With the solitary exception of Robespierre, good republican men were *sans-culottes* (literally, without knee-breeches), attired in the long, baggy trousers of the humble peasant or workman. Women affected simple, high-waisted dresses, copied from the costumes of the ancient Romans. Rome became the model for behavior—the virtuous Rome of the Republic, of course, before Caesar had paved the way for the sordid Empire. "The arts," said Robespierre, "are the ornament of the freedom which in turn ennobles them." Playwrights, authors, and editors who failed to ornament freedom

---

* Saint-Just, February 26, 1794, in *Le Moniteur Universel*, February 27, 1794. Our translation.

properly, experienced censorship or even the guillotine. The Jacobins reduced the many lively newspapers of the early revolution to a few dull semi-official organs.

The sweeping reform of the calendar (October, 1793) was a high point in Jacobin meddling. September 22, 1792, the first day of the Republic, was designated as the initial day of Year I. Roman numerals were used for the years, and the traditional mythological names of the months were abandoned for more "natural" ones:

THE MONTHS OF THE REVOLUTIONARY CALENDAR

Fall: Vendémiaire (Grape-Harvest)
            Brumaire (Misty)
            Frimaire (Frosty)

Winter: Nivôse (Snowy)
            Pluviôse (Rainy)
            Ventôse (Windy)

Spring: Germinal (Seed)
            Floréal (Flowering)
            Prairial (Meadow)

Summer: Messidor (Wheat-Harvest)
            Thermidor (Heat)
            Fructidor (Ripening)

Each month had thirty days, divided into three weeks of ten days, with every tenth day set aside for rest. The five days left over at the end of the year became special holidays dedicated to Genius, Labor, Noble Actions, Awards, and Opinion. The new calendar, for all its sanctimonious touches, was a worthy product of the Enlightenment. Yet it naturally antagonized workmen, who disliked laboring nine days out of ten, instead of six out of seven. It never really took root, and Napoleon scrapped it a decade later.

The Convention had much better luck with another reform close to the spirit of the Age of Reason—the metric system. A special committee, including Condorcet, Laplace, Lavoisier, and other distinguished intellectuals, devised new weights and measures based on the decimal system rather than on confused and illogical custom. In August, 1793, a decree made the meter the standard unit of length, and supplementary legislation in 1795 established the liter as the measure of volume and the gram as the unit of weight. The Anglo-Saxon countries have been the chief nations to cling to older and less rational weights and measures.

By and large, however, the force of tradition proved too strong for the Terror. Nowhere was this more evident than in the attempts to legislate a new religion. Many churches of the old religion were forcibly closed and turned into barracks or administrative offices, and their medieval stained glass and sculpture were often destroyed. Robespierre, however, believed that the Republic of Virtue should acknowledge an ultimate author and judge of morality. The Convention therefore decreed (May, 1794) that "the French people recognize the existence of the Supreme Being and the immortality of the soul." At the festival of the Supreme Being, June 8, 1794, Robespierre set fire to three figures representing Vice, Folly, and Atheism. From the embers the statue of Wisdom emerged, but smudged with smoke because of a mechanical slip-up. The audience laughed. The deistic concept of the Supreme Being was too remote and the mechanics of the new worship too artificial to appeal to the religious emotions of Frenchmen.

The Thermidorean Reaction

Indeed, the whole Republic of Virtue was too abstract in ideals, and too violent in practice, to retain popular support; it demanded superhuman devotion to duty and inhuman indifference to bloodshed. During the first half of 1794, Robespierre pressed the Terror relentlessly; even the members of the Committees of Public Safety and General Security began to feel that they might be the next victims. Soon Robespierre lost his backing in the Convention. Shouts of "Down with the tyrant!" drowned out his attempts to address the deputies on the ninth of Thermidor, Year II (July 27, 1794). The Convention ordered Robespierre's arrest, and on the next day the great fanatic went to the guillotine.

The leaders of the Thermidorean Reaction, many of them former Jacobins, soon dismantled the machinery of the Terror. They disbanded the Revolutionary Tribunal, recalled the deputies on mission, and deprived the Committees of Public Safety and General Security of their independent authority. They closed the Paris Jacobin Club and invited the surviving Girondin deputies to resume their old seats in the Convention. They took the first step toward the restoration of Catholicism by permitting priests to celebrate Mass, though under state supervision and without state financial support. The press and the theater recovered their freedom. Pleasure-seekers again flocked to Paris, liberated from the somberness of the Republic of Virtue. France was resuming a normal existence.

Normality, however, exacted its price. In southern and western France a counter-revolutionary "White Terror," equaling the great Terror in fury, took the lives of many, not only supporters of the Mountain but also purchasers of former church and noble lands. The men of Thermidor precipitated the most acute inflation of the whole revolution by canceling the economic legislation of the Terror. No longer checked by the *maximum*, the prices of some foods rose to a hundred times the level of 1790, and the *assignats* sank so low in value that businessmen refused to accept them. Impoverished Parisians staged several demonstrations against the Thermidoreans in the course of 1795. Sometimes the rioters voiced their support of the discredited Mountain and sometimes they let themselves be used by royalist agents; but always they clamored for bread and lower prices.

The Thermidorean Reaction concluded with the passage of the Constitution of 1795, the last great act of the Convention. The men of Thermidor wanted both to retain the Republic and to assure the dominance of the propertied classes. The Constitution of 1795 therefore denied the vote to the poorest quarter of the nation and required that candidates for public office possess a considerable amount of property. It established a two-house legislature: a lower Council of Five Hundred, and an upper Council of Elders, both to be elected piecemeal after the American practice of renewing one-third of the Senate every two years. The Council of Five Hundred nominated, and the Elders chose, five directors who headed the executive. Otherwise the Directory was almost totally independent of the legislative councils.

The Constitution of 1795 marked the third great effort of the Revolution to provide France with an enduring government. It followed in part the American precedent of 1787, in part the French precedent of 1791, and, most of all, the precepts of Montesquieu. It embodied the separation of powers and deferred to the aristocracy of wealth, though not to that of birth. By abandoning the political democracy of the still-born Constitution of 1793 and by reverting to the restricted suffrage of 1791, it demonstrated that the most radical phase of the Revolution had passed.

The new regime of the Directory dealt harshly with the recurrent plots of royalists or Jacobin extremists. It suppressed with ease the "Conspiracy of the Equals" (1796-97), engineered by Gracchus Babeuf, the one undoubted socialist of the Revolution. Yet, in spite of these successes, political instability plagued the Directory. The directors and the legislative councils clashed repeatedly, each side seeking to turn the political balance in its own favor, and each, in consequence, violating the Constitution. The councils sacked directors before their terms were finished; the directors refused to seat duly elected councilors in the legislature.

The Directory made a vigorous attack on economic problems. It levied high protective tariffs, both as a measure of war against England and as a concession to French businessmen. Again responding to business pressure, it destroyed the plates used to print the now almost worthless *assignats* and in 1797 withdrew paper money from circulation. The return to hard money required stringent governmental economies. The Directory instituted these economies, and it eased the crushing burden of the national debt by simply repudiating two-thirds of it. In short, the Directory brought at least a semblance of order out of the chronic financial chaos. But it did not bring peace, and therein lay its downfall. The continuing war dominated all the other activities of the Directory; soon all French factions were maneuvering for the political support of the army. The result was the *coup d'état* of Brumaire in 1799 and the dictatorship of a general, Napoleon Bonaparte.

Reading Suggestions on the American and French Revolutions

George III and the American Revolution—Secondary Accounts

L. H. Gipson, *The Coming of the Revolution, 1763-1775*, and J. R. Alden, *The American Revolution, 1775-1783*, both in the "New American Nation" series (N.Y.: Harper, 1954). Full and up-to-date accounts.

C. Becker, *The Declaration of Independence* (N.Y.: Knopf, 1948). A most instructive monograph, particularly valuable for tracing the European roots of the Declaration.

M. Beloff, *Thomas Jefferson and American Democracy* (N.Y.: Macmillan, 1949. Teach Yourself History Library). A good introduction to one of the most versatile and engaging of the Founding Fathers.

L. B. Namier, *The Structure of Politics at the Accession of George III*, 2 vols. (London: Macmillan, 1929); and *England in the Age of the American Revolution* (London: Macmillan, 1930). Detailed studies of the English political situation in the 1760's. For further suggestions on eighteenth-century English history, see the reading list for Chapter VIII.

George III and the American Revolution—Sources

B. Dobrée, ed., *The Letters of King George III* (London: Cassell, 1935). A very readable collection, giving much of the flavor of late eighteenth-century English politics.

M. Beloff, ed., *The Debate on the American Revolution, 1761-1783* (London: Kaye, 1949). A useful compilation from British speeches and writings for and against the American revolutionaries.

M. Beloff, ed., *The Federalist* (N.Y.: Macmillan, 1948). The famous papers written by Madison, Hamilton, and John Jay in defense of the American constitution.

H. S. Commager, ed., *Documents of American History*, 5th ed. (N.Y.: Appleton-Century-Crofts, 1949). A handy collection.

The French Revolution— Secondary Accounts

L. Gershoy, *The French Revolution and Napoleon* (N.Y.: Appleton-Century-Crofts, 1933). A first-rate textbook.

C. Brinton, *A Decade of Revolution, 1789-1799* (N.Y.: Harper, 1934). A volume in the important "Rise of Modern Europe" series; emphasizes contrasting interpretations of the revolution.

H. A. Taine, *The Ancient Régime* (N.Y.: Holt, 1876), and *The French Revolution* (N.Y.: Holt, 1878-1887). The classic detailed account from the conservative point of view.

F. V. A. Aulard, *The French Revolution: A Political History* (N.Y.: Scribner's, 1910). The classic detailed account from the middle-of-the-road republican point of view.

A. Mathiez, *The French Revolution* (N.Y.: Knopf, 1928), and *After Robespierre: The Thermidorean Reaction* (N.Y.: Knopf, 1931). The classic detailed account from the left-wing point of view, much influenced by economic determinism.

A. de Tocqueville, *The Old Régime and the Revolution* (N.Y.: Anchor Books). Inexpensive edition of a celebrated century-old account.

G. Lefebvre, *The Coming of the French Revolution* (N.Y.: Knopf, 1957. A Vintage book). A superlative short study of the causes and early course of the revolution by an outstanding French expert.

G. Salvemini, *The French Revolution, 1788-1792* (N.Y.: Holt, 1954). A detailed and perceptive account by a distinguished Italian scholar.

C. Brinton, *The Jacobins* (N.Y.: Macmillan, 1930). An instructive analysis of the leading revolutionary faction.

R. R. Palmer, *Twelve Who Ruled* (Princeton: Princeton Univ. Press, 1941). Good brief studies of the members of the Committee of Public Safety.

H. Belloc, *Robespierre* (N.Y.: Putnam's, 1927), and *Danton* (N.Y.: Putnam's, 1928). Sound biographies.

G. Bruun, *Saint-Just: Apostle of the Terror* (Boston: Houghton Mifflin, 1932). Excellent brief biography.

J. M. Thompson, *Robespierre and the French Revolution* (N.Y.: Macmillan, 1953. Teach Yourself History Library), and *Leaders of the French Revolution* (Oxford: Blackwell, 1948). Useful introductions by a British expert.

The French Revolution— Sources and Historical Fiction

J. H. Stewart, *A Documentary Survey of the French Revolution* (N.Y.: Macmillan, 1951). An ably edited collection of constitutional texts and other source materials.

A. Young, *Travels in France*, C. Maxwell, ed. (Cambridge, England: Cambridge Univ. Press, 1929). Shrewd and lively reports by the English agricultural expert who traveled in France on the eve of the revolution and during its early days.

E. L. Higgins, *The French Revolution as Told by Contemporaries* (Boston: Houghton Mifflin, 1938). A handy compendium of eye-witness reports.

Anatole France, *The Gods Are Athirst* (N.Y.: Roy, 1953). Far and away the best fictional treatment; has the additional virtue of brevity.

Victor Hugo, *'93* (Boston: Page). The clash of revolutionary and counter-revolutionary forces dramatized by the great French Romantic writer.

C. Dickens, *A Tale of Two Cities* (many editions). A famous and colorful novel.

CHAPTER ELEVEN

Napoleon

I: *The Rise of Napoleon*

Edmund Burke, the British political philosopher, foresaw very early the whole long process that culminated in Napoleon's dominance of France and Europe. In 1790, Burke warned the French —and his own countrymen—in his *Reflections on the Revolution in France*:

Everything depends on the army in such a government as yours; for you have industriously destroyed all the opinions, . . . all the instincts which support government. Therefore the moment any difference arises between your National Assembly and any part of the nation, you must have recourse to force. Nothing else is left to you. . . .

It is besides to be considered, whether an assembly like yours . . . is fit for promoting the discipline and obedience of an army. It is known, that armies have hitherto yielded a very precarious and uncertain obedience to any senate, or popular authority. . . . The officers must totally lose the characteristic disposition of military men, if they see with perfect submission and due admiration, the dominion of pleaders; especially when they find that they have a new court to pay to an endless succession of those pleaders. . . . In the weakness of one kind of authority, and in the fluctuation of all, the officers of an army will remain for some time mutinous and full of faction, until some popular general who understands the art of conciliating the soldiery, and who possesses the true spirit of command, shall draw the eyes of all men upon himself. Armies will obey him on his personal account. There is no other way of securing military obedience in this state of things. But the moment in which that event shall happen, the person who really commands the army is your master; the master . . . of your king, the master of your assembly, the master of your whole republic.*

In 1790, Burke was a solitary prophet; no one else outside France paid much heed to the French army. Sovereigns and statesmen who deplored the Revolution believed that the very intensity of domestic problems made France incapable of a vigorous foreign policy. Catherine the Great predicted as late as 1792 that ten thousand soldiers would be sufficient to conquer France. *Philosophes* and liberals hailed the peaceful promise of the Revolution. The capture of the Bastille delighted Charles James Fox, a leading English Whig: "How much the greatest event it is that ever happened in the world! and how much the best!"

The First Coalition (1792-1795)

The war that broke out in the spring of 1792 soon destroyed the illusions of French military weakness and French liberal purity. The war was to last continuously, save for a few intervals of peace, down to the final defeat of Napoleon. It deserves to be called the World War of 1792-1815, for almost all the European powers eventually participated in it and the fighting itself ranged far beyond Europe.

---

* Everyman ed. (New York, 1910), 217, 215-216.

By the time the war was a year old Austria and Prussia, the charter members of the First Coalition against France, had been joined by Holland, Spain, and, most significantly, Great Britain. Both ideological and strategic factors brought Britain into the conflict early in 1793. She regarded the attack on the Tuileries, the September massacres, and the execution of Louis XVI as outrages against human decency and the institution of monarchy. And the French invasion of the Austrian Netherlands in the fall of 1792 raised the unpleasant prospect that this Belgian "cockpit of Europe" would fall under French control. The early campaigns of the war were indecisive. Late in 1792, the French followed up their success at Valmy by the invasion of Belgium, only to lose ground again in 1793 after the defeat and desertion of Dumouriez (see above, p. 334). Then in 1794 the French definitely gained the advantage, and by 1795 French troops had occupied Belgium, Holland, and Germany west of the Rhine.

One reason for French success we have already seen—the Convention's energetic mobilization of national resources. Another reason, equally important yet easy to overlook, was the weakness of the First Coalition. The partners in the coalition had no first-rate commander, nor did they achieve effective coordination of their efforts. The Duke of Brunswick's failure to take Paris in 1792 resulted as much from his own deficient generalship as from the "miracle" of Valmy. Moreover, the partitions of Poland in 1793 and 1795 greatly assisted the French. The Polish question kept Catherine the Great from supplying the mere 10,000 troops that she deemed sufficient to crush France; the pick of the Prussian army was diverted to occupation duty in newly annexed Polish provinces. By 1795, furthermore, things had come to such a pass that the Prussians did not dare attack the French for fear of being assaulted from the rear by their nominal Austrian ally!

Prussia was the first member of the coalition to make peace. In the Treaty of Basel (1795) she ceded to France the scattered Prussian holdings west of the Rhine on the understanding that she might seek compensation elsewhere in Germany. Spain and Holland likewise deserted the coalition in 1795. Thus France at last secured her "natural frontiers." Besides Belgium and the Rhineland she had also annexed Savoy and Nice, thereby extending her southeastern border to the crest of the Alps. These conquests, however, belied the ideals of the Revolution. In declaring war on Austria in 1792 France had sworn to uphold the promise of the Constitution of 1791: that she would never undertake a war of conquest. This was to be "not a war of nation against nation, but the righteous defense of a free people against the unjust aggression of a king." But the conquering armies of the First Republic brought closer the day when nation would fight nation—when the European nations would invoke "the righteous defense of a free people against the unjust aggression" not of a king, but of revolutionary France.

Napoleon's
Early Career

At the close of 1795, only Britain and Austria remained officially at war with France. The Directory picked Austria as the first target and assigned Napoleon Bonaparte to lead the attack against the Habsburg forces in northern Italy. The youthful commander was at once a *philosophe*, a revolutionary, an inspired general, and a ruthlessly ambitious adventurer. He was born in Corsica in 1769, shortly after the time when France acquired that Mediterranean island from the decadent Republic of Genoa. Napoleon retained throughout his life the strong family loyalty characteristic of Corsican society. From his hands the members of the Bonaparte clan were to receive all the spoils of conquest, even thrones.

As a youth, Napoleon attended military school in France. Largely cut off from his fellow students because he was a "foreigner," he devoted himself to his studies and read widely, especially in Rousseau. When the Revolution broke out, Napoleon helped to overthrow the Old Régime in Corsica but soon went back to France to resume his military career. The young army officer defended the Convention, but more from expediency than from political conviction. He commanded the artillery when the forces of the Jacobin Convention recaptured the rebellious Mediterranean seaport of Toulon in December, 1793. In October, 1795, he delivered the famous "whiff of grapeshot" that saved the Thermidorean Convention from a rising of discontented Parisians. He married Josephine de Beauharnais, a widow six years his senior and an intimate of the ruling clique of the Directory. Josephine's connections and Napoleon's own demonstrated talent as an artillery officer gained him the Italian command in 1796.

In the space of a year, Napoleon cleared the Austrians out of Italy and made them sue for peace. In this famous campaign he showed his remarkable ability to strike quickly and surprise the enemy before they could consolidate their defenses. He also demonstrated his flair for what would now be called propaganda and public relations. Witness the proclamation that he issued on April 26, 1796:

Soldiers! In two weeks you have won six victories; you have made 15,000 prisoners; you have killed or wounded more than 10,000 men.

Deprived of everything, you have accomplished everything. You have won battles without cannon, negotiated rivers without bridges, made forced marches without shoes, encamped without brandy, and often without bread. Only the phalanxes of the Republic, only the soldiers of Liberty, would have been capable of suffering the things that you have suffered.

You all burn to carry the glory of the French people; to humiliate the proud kings who dared to contemplate shackling us; to go back to your villages, to say proudly: 'I was of the conquering army of Italy!'

Friends, I promise you that conquest; but there is a condition you must swear to fulfill: to respect the people whom you are delivering; to repress horrible pillaging.

Peoples of Italy, the French army comes to break your chains; greet it with confidence; your property, religion and customs will be respected.*

Here was Napoleon's characteristic policy of promising all things to all men. He encouraged the nationalism of underpaid and underfed French soldiers and whetted their appetite for booty. Yet he appealed also to the nationalism of the Italians, promising them liberation from Austria and guaranteeing the orderly conduct of the French army. He did not, of course, publicize the money that he seized from Italian governments and the art treasures that he took from Italian galleries and shipped back to France.

In the Treaty of Campoformio (1797) terminating the Italian campaign, Austria acknowledged the loss of Belgium and Lombardy and recognized the two puppet states that Napoleon set up in northwestern Italy, the Ligurian Republic of Genoa and the Cisalpine Republic of Lombardy. In return, the Habsburgs received the Italian possessions of the Venetian Republic and a secret French assurance that, despite the specific promise made at Basel in 1795, Prussia would not be permitted to compensate for her losses in the Rhineland by lands elsewhere in Germany.

Napoleon now turned to Britain. He decided not to attack her directly, but rather to hit at her indirectly through Egypt, then a dependency of Turkey. This would-be Alexander the Great, seeking new worlds to conquer, talked grandly of digging a canal at Suez, giving French merchants the monopoly of a new short trade-route to India, and exacting belated retribution from Britain for Clive's victory in the Seven Years' War. Since Napoleon

* Abridged from *Le Moniteur Universel*, May 17, 1796. Our translation.

shared the passion of the Enlightenment for science and antiquity, he invited archaeologists and other experts to accompany his army and thereby helped to found the study known as Egyptology. One of his experts, Champollion, deciphered the Rosetta Stone, the first key to the translation of ancient Egyptian hieroglyphics.

From the military standpoint, however, the campaign failed totally. Having eluded the British Mediterranean fleet commanded by Nelson, Napoleon landed in Egypt in July, 1798, and quickly routed the Mamelukes, the ruling oligarchy. Then on August 1, 1798, Nelson discovered the French fleet anchored at Abukir Bay along the Egyptian coast and destroyed it. Nelson's victory deprived the French of supplies, of reinforcements, and even of news from home. After a year of futile campaigning in the Near East, Napoleon suddenly left Egypt in August, 1799, and returned to France. The soldiers whom he thus deserted were not so fortunate; they remained in Egypt until 1801, when arrangements were completed for their withdrawal.

Brumaire   Apparently quite unmoved by his failure in Egypt, Napoleon found the situation back in France ripe for a decisive political stroke. During his absence Jacobinism had experienced a significant revival; several hundred members of the legislative councils belonged to the old Jacobin Club, now resurrected as the "Society of the Friends of Liberty and Equality." Abroad, the Directory had established four new satellite republics with classical names—the Roman, the Parthenopean in Naples, the Batavian in Holland, and the Helvetian in Switzerland. But this new success of French imperialism provoked a renewal of war on the Continent. The Habsburgs resented the extension of French influence over their former Italian preserve, and Paul I of Russia feared that

Napoleon would harm Russian Mediterranean interests. The eccentric Tsar was head of the Knights of Malta, a Catholic order of knighthood dating back to the time of the Crusades. Since Napoleon had expelled the Knights from their headquarters on the island of Malta, Paul joined with Austria and Britain in forming the Second Coalition (December, 1798). In the ensuing campaigns, Russian troops fought in Italy and Switzerland in alliance with the Austrians, in Holland in alliance with the English, and even off the western shores of Greece in the Ionian islands. The Russian General Suvorov, who defeated the French repeatedly, became the hero of western Europe. By August, 1799, the French had been expelled from Italy, and their puppet republics—Cisalpine, Roman, and Parthenopean—had been dismantled.

Thus, patriotic Frenchmen were ready to welcome any military hero, and conservative Frenchmen were ready to welcome a champion of order against the new Jacobin threat. Napoleon got a rousing reception on his return from Egypt. Soon he was engaged in a plot to overthrow the Directory, with the complicity of two of the five directors, Roger-Ducos and Siéyès, the champion of the third estate. On November 9 and 10, 1799 (18 and 19 Brumaire by the revolutionary calendar) the plot was executed. First, Napoleon forced the resignation of the three directors not in the plot; next, to win over the consent of the two legislative councils, he hinted at the danger of a Jacobin conspiracy. He gained the approval of the Elders, but in the Council of Five Hundred he ranted incoherently and fainted. His brother, Lucien, the presiding officer of the Council, saved the situation until a detachment of troops had expelled a majority of the Five Hundred. This almost comic *coup d'état* of Brumaire ended the Directory. The preparation of a new constitution was entrusted to the victorious triumvirate of Roger-Ducos, Siéyès, and Napoleon, of whom only Napoleon really counted. It all happened just as Edmund Burke had predicted:

> In the weakness of authority, . . . some popular general shall draw the eyes of all men upon himself. Armies will obey him on his personal account. . . . The person who really commands the army is your master.

II: *Napoleon and France*

Napoleonic Government

The constitution drawn up after Brumaire was based on the autocratic maxim, "Confidence from below, authority from above." It erected a very strong executive, somewhat disguised by terminology borrowed from the ancient Roman Republic and by other republican window-dressing. Three consuls shared the executive authority—or rather, Napoleon as First Consul took the lion's share, leaving his two colleagues only nominal power. Four separate bodies had a hand in legislation: (1) the Council of State proposed laws; (2) the Tribunate debated them but did not vote; (3) the Legislative Corps voted them but did not debate; (4) the Senate had the right to veto legislation. The members of all four bodies were either appointed by the First Consul or elected indirectly by a process so complex that Bonaparte had ample opportunity to manipulate candidates. The core of this system was the Council of State, staffed by Bonaparte's hand-picked choices, which served both as a sort of cabinet and as the highest administrative court in the land.

The three remaining bodies were intended merely to go through the motions of enacting whatever the First Consul decreed. Even so, the debates of the Tribunate sometimes got in his way, and he finally abolished it in 1807.

Napoleon soon cast off the other restrictions imposed on his own authority by the constitution. In 1802, he persuaded the legislators to drop the original ten-year limitation on his term of office and make him First Consul for life, with the power to designate his successor and amend the constitution at will. In 1804, he took the next logical move and declared himself hereditary Emperor of the French. A magnificent coronation took place at Notre Dame in Paris on December 2. The Pope consecrated the Emperor, but Napoleon placed the crown on his own head.

Each time Napoleon revised the Constitution in a non-republican direction he made the republican gesture of submitting the change to the electorate. Each time, the results of the plebiscite were overwhelmingly favorable: in 1799-1800, the vote was 3,011,-107 for Napoleon and the Consulate, and

Napoleon, sketched at the theater.

1,562 against; in 1802, is was 3,568,885 for Napoleon and the life Consulate, and 8,374 against; in 1804, it was 3,572,329 for Napoleon and the Empire, and 2,579 against. Although the announced results were perhaps rigged a little, the vast majority of Frenchmen undoubtedly supported Napoleon. His military triumphs appealed to their growing nationalism, and his policy of stability at home insured them against further revolutionary changes. Confidence did indeed seem to increase from below as authority increased from above.

If by any chance confidence failed to materialize below, Napoleon had the authority to deal with the recalcitrant. He wiped out the local self-government remaining from the early days of the Revolution. In place of locally elected officials he substituted those appointed by himself— prefects in departments, sub-prefects in *arrondissements*, mayors in communes—and all were instructed to enforce compliance with the Emperor's dictates. Napoleon, far more than the Jacobins, made France a highly centralized police state.

Men of every political background staffed the imperial administration. Napoleon cared little whether his subordinates were returned *émigrés* or ex-Jacobins, so long as they had ability. Besides, their varied antecedents reinforced the impression that narrow factionalism was dead and that the Empire rested on a broad political base. Napoleon paid officials well and offered the additional bait of high titles. With the establishment of the Empire he created dukes by the dozen and counts and barons by the hundred. He rewarded outstanding generals with the rank of Marshal and lesser civilian officials with the Legion of Honor.

Law and Justice

Napoleon revived some of the aristocratic glamour of the Old Régime, but not its glaring inequalities. His series of law codes, the celebrated *Code Napoléon* (1804-1810), declared all men equal before the law without regard to their rank and wealth. It extended to all the right to follow the occupation, and embrace the religion, of their choosing. It gave France the single coherent system of law which the *philosophes* had demanded and which the revolutionary governments had been too busy to formulate.

The *Code Napoléon* did not, however, embody the full judicial reform program of the Enlightenment; it incorporated from the old Roman law some practices that strengthened the absolutism of the Empire. In trial procedure, it permitted some use of torture; it favored the interests of the state over the rights of the individual. Though Napoleon confirmed the revolutionary legislation permitting divorce by mutual consent, and though he himself divorced Josephine, he generally preserved the legal superiority of the man of the family. The code canceled revolutionary legislation protecting the interests of wives, minors, and illegitimate children. Napoleon appointed judges himself and empowered the prefects to select jurors. Now confirming the principles of 1789, and now betraying them, Napoleonic law and justice offered a fair summary of the fate of the Revolution under the Empire.

A similar ambiguity clouded Napoleon's attitude toward civil liberties. He practiced religious toleration of a sort and welcomed former political heretics into his administration. But Napoleonic generosity stemmed always from expediency, never from any fundamental belief in liberty. If he failed to get his way by conciliation, then he used force. In the western departments, where royalist uprisings had become chronic since the revolt in the Vendée, he massacred the rebels who declined his offer of amnesty in 1800. In 1804, he kidnapped the Duke of Enghien from the neutral German state of Baden because the Duke was believed to be the choice of monarchist conspirators for the throne of France. Though Napoleon immediately discovered the Duke's innocence, he had him executed none the less.

Even more damaging to Napoleon's reputation in democratic eyes was his repression of the freedom of speech. In July, 1801, for instance, he directed his librarian to read all the newspapers carefully and

. . . make an abstract of everything they contain likely to affect the public point of view, especially with regard to religion, philosophy, and political opinion. He will send me this abstract between 5 and 6 o'clock every day.

Once every ten days he will send me an analysis of all the books or pamphlets which have appeared . . . , calling attention to any passages that might bear on moral questions, or interest me in a political or moral connexion.

He will take pains to procure copies of all the plays which are produced, and to analyse them for me, with observations of the same character as those above mentioned. This analysis must be made, at latest, within 48 hours of the production of the plays.*

And so on through "bills, posters, advertisements, institutes, literary meetings, sermons and fashionable trials." No segment of public opinion escaped Napoleon's manipulation. He reduced by five-sixths the number of Paris newspapers and pestered theater managers with suggestions for improving the patriotic tone of plays. When he wanted to arouse French opinion, he simply started a press campaign, as in this instance from 1807:

A great hue and cry is to be raised against the persecutions experienced by the Catholics of Ireland at the hands of the Anglican Church. . . . Bishops will be approached so that prayers will be offered entreating an end to the persecutions of the Anglican Church against the Irish Catholics. But the administration must move very delicately and make use of the newspapers without their realizing what the government is driving at. . . . And the term 'Anglican Church' must always be used in place of 'Protestants,' for we have Protestants in France, but no Anglican Church.†

* Quoted in J. M. Thompson, *Napoleon Self-Revealed* (Boston, 1934), 81.
† *Lettres Inédites de Napoléon* (Paris, 1897), I, 93-94. Our translation

Religion

Political considerations colored all Napoleon's decisions on religion. "I do not see in religion the mystery of the incarnation," he said, "but the mystery of the social order. It attaches to heaven an idea of equality which prevents the rich man from being massacred by the poor." * Since French Catholics loathed the anticlericalism of the Revolution, Napoleon reasoned that he had everything to gain by working out a reconciliation with Rome.

The Concordat that was negotiated in 1801 by Napoleon and Pope Pius VII accomplished the reconciliation. The French state agreed to pay clerical salaries and to suppress the popular election of bishops and priests. The bishops were to be nominated by the government, and then consecrated by the pope; the priests were to be appointed by the bishops. At this point Napoleon's concessions stopped. By declaring that Catholicism was only the faith of the "majority of Frenchmen," rather than the state religion, the Concordat implicitly admitted the toleration of Protestants and Jews. Furthermore, it granted to the French government vague but extensive powers to regulate church activities. The Concordat of 1801 was a resounding confirmation of the principles of 1789, for it canceled only the most extreme provisions of the Civil Constitution of the Clergy. Pius VII accepted such important measures of the Revolution as the abolition of the tithe and the confiscation of ecclesiastical lands. And, by granting Napoleon regulatory powers over the Gallican Church, he permitted that church to become in effect the ward of the French state.

So far as France was concerned, the Concordat worked reasonably well. It conciliated large numbers of Catholics, and was to remain in force until 1905. The Concordat, however, did not bring complete peace between France and the Vatican, for Napoleon insisted that the Pope should render to Caesar the things that were Caesar's. When Pius VII objected to Napoleon's making a French satellite of the Papal States, the new Caesar lectured him on the proper division of authority between the spiritual and temporal powers. Pius VII passed the last years of the Napoleonic regime as Bonaparte's prisoner, first in northern Italy and then in France.

Education

The Revolution and Napoleon cost the Church its monopoly over education. The Constitution of 1791 had promised France a system of state schools. The Convention, while doing little to apply this principle to primary education, did set up institutions for specialized training, like the famous Paris engineering school, the *Ecole Polytechnique*. In each department it established a "central school" to provide secondary education of high quality at relatively low cost. Napoleon abolished these flourishing central schools in 1802 and replaced them with a smaller number of *lycées* open only to the relatively few pupils who could afford the tuition or who received state scholarships. The change had a political motive. The *lycée* students wore uniforms and marched to military drums, and the curriculum, too, served the ends of patriotic indoctrination. To provide for the general supervision of the school system Napoleon founded in 1808 a governmental body with the misleading name of the "University," which controlled the institutions ordinarily called universities.

Napoleon, then, scarcely had the modern democratic belief that schools should provide free and, politically speaking, reasonably neutral training. He neglected primary schooling almost completely. Yet, building on the revolutionary base, he did advance the construction of the modern secular French school system. The educa-

---

* Quoted in H. A. L. Fisher, *Napoleon* (New York, 1913), Appendix I.

tional competition of Church and State, so often a bitter issue in modern French life, dates back to the Revolution and Napoleon.

Economics

Political aims likewise determined the economic program of an emperor determined to promote national unity. The French peasants wanted to be left alone to enjoy the new freedom acquired in 1789; Napoleon did not disturb them, except to raise army recruits. The middle class wanted a balanced national budget and the end of revolutionary experiments with paper currency and a controlled economy. Napoleon continued the sound money of the Directory and, unlike the Directory, balanced the budget, thanks to the immense plunder that he gained in war. He greatly improved the efficiency and probity of tax-collectors and established the semi-official Bank of France (1800) to act as the government's financial agent. He strengthened the curbs placed on labor by the Le Chapelier Law of 1791 (see above, p. 328) and obliged every workman to carry a written record listing his jobs and his general reputation. Rich war con-tracts and subsidies kept employment and profits high. As the war went on and on, however, Napoleon found it particularly difficult to appease the peasantry and the bourgeoisie. Despite the levies on conquered countries, he had to draft soldiers from the peasantry and increase the already unpopular taxes on salt, liquor, and tobacco.

In summary, the domestic policies of Napoleon I had something in common with the methods of all the celebrated one-man rulers. Like Caesar in Rome, Napoleon rendered lip-service to the Republic while subverting republican institutions; he used prefects to impose centralized authority as Louis XIV had used *intendants;* and, like modern dictators, he had only contempt for free speech. Yet Napoleon was also a genuine enlightened despot. His law code and some of his educational reforms would have delighted the *philosophes.* He ended civil strife without sacrificing the redistribution of land and the equality before the law gained in 1789 and after. Abandoning some revolutionary innovations, modifying others, and completing still others, Napoleon regimented the Revolution, but he did not wholly destroy it.

III: Napoleon and Europe

To many Frenchmen, Napoleon was the brilliant Man of Destiny; to most Europeans, on the other hand, Napoleon was the sinister Man on Horseback, the enemy of national independence, the foreigner who imposed French control and French reforms. As French conquests accumulated, and as nominally free countries became French puppets, Europe grew to hate the insatiable imperialism of Napoleon. Napoleonic France succeeded in building up a vast empire, but only at the cost of arousing the implacable enmity of the other European nations.

The War (1800-1807)

Napoleon had barely launched the Consulate when he took to the field again. The Second Coalition, which had reached the peak of its success in August, 1799, was now falling to pieces. The hot-headed Tsar Paul I had soon decided that his allies were more dangerous than his enemies and created a league of Russia, Sweden, Prussia, and Denmark against Britain. Indeed, Paul now planned to defeat the English, to partition Turkey, and to conquer India, all in alliance with Napoleon. But these fantastic plans were still on paper when

Paul was murdered in 1801 and succeeded by Alexander I. Meanwhile, in 1800, Napoleon attacked the Austrians in Italy and forced them to sue for peace. The Treaty of Lunéville (1801) extended the gains that Napoleon had secured from Austria four years before at Campoformio. This time Austria had to agree that the German states which had lost territory to France west of the Rhine should be compensated to the east of the Rhine, and that France should have a voice in allotting these compensations. The Lunéville treaty gave Napoleon the right to superintend the reshaping of Germany.

After Lunéville, as after Campoformio, Britain alone remained at war with France. British taxpayers, however, wanted relief from the heavy burden of war taxes; British merchants longed to resume trading with continental markets partially closed to them since 1793. Though Britain had been unable to check Napoleon's expansion in Europe, she had very nearly won the colonial and naval war by 1801. She had captured former Dutch and Spanish colonies, and Nelson's fleet had expelled the French from Egypt and Malta. The British cabinet was confident that it held a strong bargaining position and could obtain favorable terms from Napoleon. But in the Peace of Amiens (1802) the British promised to surrender almost all their colonial conquests and got nothing in return. The French refused either to reopen the Continent to British exports or to relinquish Belgium, which remained, in Napoleon's phrase, "a loaded pistol aimed at the heart of Britain."

The one-sided Peace of Amiens provided only a brief truce in the world-wide struggle of Britain and France. Napoleon had no intention of giving up the struggle permanently until he had destroyed British commercial and colonial supremacy and in effect had reversed the direction of the Second Hundred Years' War. Meanwhile, he was alarming Austria and Prussia by using the right granted by Lunéville to revise the map of Germany. In 1803, more than a hundred German states were abolished, chiefly city-states and small ecclesiastical principalities. The chief beneficiaries of this territorial readjustment were the south German states of Bavaria, Württemberg, and Baden, which Napoleon clearly intended to make a "third" Germany dominated by France, as opposed to the "first" and "second" Germanies, dominated by Austria and Prussia, respectively.

He aroused Britain by new tariff restrictions (1803) and by a grandiose project for an American colonial empire centering on the island of Haiti (Santo Domingo) and on the vast Louisiana territory that Spain had handed back to France in 1801. In Haiti, however, the continued local resistance and a virulent outbreak of yellow fever took a fearful toll of the French troops and forced Napoleon to abandon the American project. In 1803, therefore, he sold the whole of Louisiana to the United States for $11,000,000.

By now, Britain and France were again at war. From 1803 through 1805, Napoleon actively prepared to invade England. He assembled more than a hundred thousand troops and a thousand landing barges on the French side of the Straits of Dover. In 1805, he sent Admiral Villeneuve and the French fleet to the West Indies to lure the British fleet away from Europe. Then Villeneuve was to return post-haste to convoy the French invasion force across the Channel while Nelson was still vainly combing the Caribbean. Villeneuve failed to give Nelson the slip; back in European waters, he put in at a friendly Spanish port instead of heading directly for the Channel as Napoleon had ordered. Nelson engaged the combined French and Spanish fleets off Cape Trafalgar at the southwest corner of Spain (October, 1805). He lost his own life but not before he had destroyed half of his adversaries' ships without sacrificing a single one of his own. Trafalgar gave the British undisputed control of the seas for the balance of the war and killed French hopes of a successful cross-Channel invasion.

By the time of Trafalgar, Austria and Russia had joined with Britain in the Third Coalition. Bonaparte routed his continental opponents in the most dazzling campaign of his career. At Ulm, on the upper Danube (October, 1805), he captured 30,000 Austrians who had moved westward without waiting for their Russian allies. He met the main Russian force and the balance of the Austrian army near the Moravian village of Austerlitz. The ensuing battle (December 2, 1805) fittingly celebrated the first anniversary of Napoleon's coronation as emperor. Bringing up reinforcements secretly and with great speed, Napoleon completely surprised his opponents. Within the month he forced the Habsburg emperor, Francis II,

to sign the humiliating Treaty of Pressburg, giving the Austrian Tyrol to Bavaria and Venetia to the Napoleonic puppet kingdom of Italy.

A still harsher fate awaited the Prussians, brought back into the war for the first time since 1795 by Napoleon's repeated interventions in German affairs. The Prussian army, however, had not kept up with the military improvements introduced since the campaigns of Frederick the Great. In October, 1806, the French pulverized the main Prussian contingents in the twin battles of Jena and Auerstädt, and occupied Berlin. Napoleon decided to postpone a final settlement with Prussia until he had beaten his only remaining continental opponent. Russia went down at Friedland (June, 1807).

Napoleon's great string of victories against

"The Battle of Trafalgar." Painting by Turner.

UNITED KINGDOM
OF GREAT BRITAIN
AND IRELAND

North Sea

K. OF DENMARK & NORWAY

SWED

IRELAND

SCOTLAND

Atlantic Ocean

WALES ENGLAND

London

NETHERLANDS

Oldenburg

Hamburg

Antwerp

K. of WESTPHALIA

Berlin

Waterloo ✕
Amiens

CONFEDERATION

Auerstädt ✕
Jena ✕
✕ Leipzig

Meuse R.
Rhine R.

Varennes

OF THE

Prague

Longuyon

RHINE

Austerli

Paris
Versailles

Valmy

LORRAINE

Luneville

Strasbourg

Nantes

Loire R.

FRANCE

Ulm
Danube R.

ALSACE

Basel

Press
Vienna

BAVARIA

Girmide R.

Bordeaux

Limoges

Lyons

SWITZ.

S. TYROL

Campo-
formio

ILLYRIAN PRO

Payrac

Rhone R.

PIED-
MONT

Milan

Venice

Adriatic

Marengo ✕

OF ITALY

Nice

Genoa

PORTUGAL

Ebro R.

Madrid

Tagus R.

SPAIN

Guadalquivir R.

TUSCANY

CORSICA

ELBA

PAPAL
STATES

Rome

K. OF
NAPL

BALEARIC IS.

Naples

SARDINIA

Mediterranean

C. Trafalgar ✕

SICILY

MALTA
(Br.)

NAPOLEONIC EUROPE, 1812

Empire of France
States under French control
Allied with France
✕ Battle sites

0   Miles   500

55 20 15 10 5 0 10 15

50

45

40

35

5 10 15

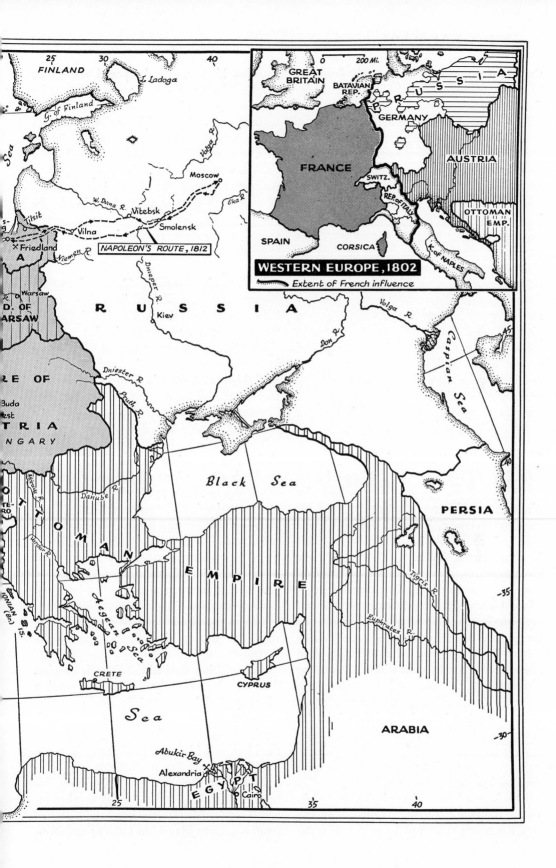

FINLAND

G. of Finland

L. Ladoga

Moscow

W. Dvina R. Vitebsk

Volga R.

Oka R.

Tilsit

Vilna

Smolensk

Friedland

Niemen R.

NAPOLEON'S ROUTE, 1812

Warsaw

D. OF
ARSAW

R   U   S   S   I   A

Dnieper R.

Kiev

Don R.

Volga R.

E OF

Dniester R.

Buda
est

Pruth R.

Caspian Sea

RIA

NGARY

Black   Sea

PERSIA

O T T O M A N

Danube R.

Maritza R.

TE-
RO

Vardar R.

Aegean Sea

E M P I R E

Tigris R.

Euphrates R.

–35

ONIAN (Br.)
IS.

CRETE

CYPRUS

Sea

ARABIA

–30

Abukir Bay

Alexandria

EGYPT

Cairo

25   35   40

Inset:

GREAT
BRITAIN

BATAVIAN
REP.

0   200 Mi.

P R U S S I A

GERMANY

RUSSIA

FRANCE

SWITZ.

AUSTRIA

REP. OF ITALY

OTTOMAN
EMP.

SPAIN

CORSICA

K. OF NAPLES

WESTERN EUROPE, 1802

Extent of French influence

the Third Coalition resulted partly from the blunders of his enemies. The miscalculations of Austrian, Prussian, and Russian generals contributed to French successes at Austerlitz and at Jena. Further, the French army was the most seasoned force in Europe, its soldiers of every rank were well trained, and its officers were promoted because of ability rather than because of seniority or influence. Bonaparte seldom risked an engagement unless his forces were the numerical equal of the enemy's; then he staked everything on a dramatic surprise, as at Austerlitz. Yet even this almost invincible French army had defects. The pay was low and irregular, the medical services were a disgrace, and the supplies were so badly managed that French soldiers usually had to live off the land. Eventually, these shortcomings were to weaken French striking power; in 1807, however, they did not prevent the ascendancy of Napoleon in Europe.

The Empire at Its Height (1807-1812)

Napoleon reached the pinnacle of his career when he met his Russian adversary, Tsar Alexander I, on a raft anchored in the Niemen River at Tilsit in East Prussia. There, in July, 1807, the two emperors drew up a treaty dividing Europe between them. Alexander acknowledged France's hegemony over central and western Europe and secured in return the recognition of eastern Europe as the Russian sphere. Napoleon pledged Russia a share in the spoils if the Ottoman Empire should be dismembered. He demanded no territory from the defeated Tsar, only a commitment to cease trade with Britain and to join the war against her. The Tilsit settlement, however, made Alexander bitterly unpopular at home, where Russian propaganda had been denouncing Napoleon as anti-Christ.

Prussia was the chief victim at Tilsit. While the two emperors negotiated on the raft, Frederick William III (1797-1840), the Prussian king, nervously paced the banks of the Niemen. He had good cause to be nervous, for Tilsit cost him almost half his territory. Prussia's Polish provinces formed a new puppet state, the Grand Duchy of Warsaw, which Napoleon assigned to a French ally, the King of Saxony. Prussian territory west of the Elbe River went to Napoleon to dispose of as he wished. To complete the humiliation, Napoleon stationed occupation troops in Prussia and fixed the maximum size of its army at 42,-000 men.

Under this latter-day Caesar almost all Europe could be divided into three parts. First came the French Empire, including France proper and the territories annexed since 1789. Second were the satellites, ruled in many cases by relatives of Napoleon. And third came Austria, Prussia, and Russia, forced by defeat to become the allies of France. Only Britain, Sweden, and Turkey remained outside the Napoleonic system.

The frontiers of the French Empire at their most extensive enclosed Belgium and Holland; the sections of Germany west of the Rhine and along the North Sea; the Italian territories of Piedmont, Genoa, Tuscany, and Rome; and finally, physically detached from the rest, the "Illyrian Provinces," stretching along the Dalmatian coast of the Adriatic, taken from Austria in 1809, and named after a province of the old Roman Empire. These annexations were usually subdivided into departments and ruled by prefects, just like the home departments of France.

The satellites flanked the French Empire. The Kingdom of Italy, an enlarged version of the Cisalpine Republic, included the northern and central Italian lands not directly annexed by France. Napoleon was the king, and his stepson, Eugene de Beauharnais, was viceroy. In southern Italy, Napoleon gave the crown of Naples to his brother Joseph and then to his brother-in-law, Joachim Murat. Brother Joseph moved from Naples to Madrid in 1808 when Napoleon deposed the Spanish Bourbons in order to force the unwilling Spaniards to remain in the war against Britain.

In Central Europe, Napoleon energetically pursued his project of a "third" Germany. He decreed a further reduction in the number of German states and in 1806 finally dissolved that useless museum piece, the Holy Roman Empire. In its place he created the Confederation of the Rhine, which included almost every German state except Austria and Prussia. At the heart of this confederation Napoleon carved out for his brother Jerome the Kingdom of Westphalia, which incorporated the Prussian holdings west of the Elbe seized at Tilsit. Switzerland and the Grand Duchy of Warsaw completed the roster of French satellites.

Napoleon longed to give dignity and permanence to his creations. It was not enough that his brothers and his in-laws should sit on thrones; he himself must found a dynasty, must have the heir so far denied him in fifteen years of childless marriage. He divorced Josephine, therefore, and in 1810 married Marie-Louise, the daughter of the Habsburg Francis II. In due time, Marie-Louise bore a son, whom his father grandiloquently called "The King of Rome."

"Napoleon II," however, was never to rule in Rome or anywhere else. Throughout the satellites Bonaparte curbed the power of the Church, abolished serfdom, built roads, and introduced the new French law codes. Everywhere, however, he exacted a heavy toll of tribute and subjection. In the Kingdom of Italy, for instance, he doubled the tax rate previously levied by the Austrians; half the revenues of the kingdom went to defray the expenses of the French army and the French government. Napoleon flooded his relatives with instructions on the government of their domains and brought them abruptly to heel whenever they showed signs of putting local interests above those of France. When Louis Bonaparte in Holland dared to disobey the imperial orders, his brother delivered a crushing rebuke:

In ascending the throne of Holland, Your Majesty has forgotten that he is French and has stretched all the springs of his reason and tormented his conscience in order to persuade himself that he is Dutch. Dutchmen inclining toward France have been ignored and persecuted; those serving England have been promoted. . . . I have experienced the sorrow of seeing the name of France exposed to shame in a Holland ruled by a prince of my blood.*

* *Lettres Inédites de Napoléon* (Paris, 1897), I, 382-383. Our translation.

Gillray, "Tiddy-Dolly, the great French Gingerbread-Baker, drawing out a new Batch of Kings—his Man, Hopping-Talley, mixing up the Dough"—a British comment on Napoleon's imperialism.

Louis' boldness cost him his throne; his Dutch kingdom was annexed to France in 1810.

The Continental System

Nowhere was Napoleon's imperialism more evident than in his attempt to regulate the economy of the whole Continent. The Continental System had a double aim: to build up the export trade of France and to cripple that of Britain. The collapse of Napoleon's cross-Channel invasion plans led him to expand the earlier tariff measures against Britain into a great campaign to bankrupt the nation of shopkeepers. The defeat of the Third Coalition gave him the opportunity to experiment with economic warfare on a continental scale and to carry to extremes the warlike implications of mercantilism.

The Berlin Decree, issued by Napoleon in November, 1806, forbade all trade with the British Isles and all commerce in British merchandise. Britain replied by requiring that neutral vessels wishing to trade with France put in first at a British port and pay duties. This regulation enabled Britain to share in the profits of neutral shipping to France. Napoleon retaliated with the Milan Decree (December, 1807), ordering the seizure of all neutral ships that complied with the new British policy. The neutrals, in effect, were damned if they did and damned if they didn't.

Napoleon's vassals and allies had to support the Continental System or suffer the consequences. Of all the "un-French" activities countenanced by Louis Bonaparte in Holland, the worst, in Napoleon's view, was his toleration of Dutch smuggling of English contraband. The Emperor likewise expected the satellites to contribute to French industrial prosperity. When the Italians objected to the regulation of their silk exports, Napoleon lectured his viceroy, Eugene, on the facts of economic life:

All the raw silk from the Kingdom of Italy goes to England. . . . It is therefore quite natural that I should wish to divert it from this route to the advantage of my French manufacturers; otherwise my silk factories, one of the chief supports of French commerce, would suffer substantial losses. . . . My principle is *France first*. . . .

It is no use for Italy to make plans that leave French prosperity out of account; she must face the fact that the interests of the two countries hang together.*

The gigantic attempt to make "France first" failed almost totally. Only a few French industries benefited from the Continental System; the cessation of sugar imports from the West Indies, for example, promoted the cultivation of native sugar beets. But the decline of overseas trade greatly depressed Bordeaux and other French Atlantic ports. The increasing difficulty and expense of procuring raw materials like cotton caused widespread unemployment and produced a rash of bankruptcies. The new French markets on the Continent did not compensate for the loss of older markets overseas; the value of French exports declined by more than one-third between 1805 and 1813.

The Continental System did not ruin Britain, although it did confront the British with a severe economic crisis. Markets abroad for British exports were uncertain; food imports were reduced; and, while prices rose sharply, wages lagged behind. Both farm workers, already pinched by the enclosure movement (see Chapter VIII), and factory workers suffered acutely. Yet, fortified by her leadership in the economic revolutions and by the overwhelming superiority of her navy and merchant marine, Britain rode out the storm. Every tract of land at all capable of growing food was brought under the plow, and today one can see barren heights on Dartmoor that were last cultivated during the Napoleonic Wars. Exporters not only developed lucra-

---

* Quoted in Thompson, *Napoleon Self-Revealed*, 274-275.

tive new markets in the Americas, the Ottoman Empire, and Asia but also continued to supply some of their old customers on the Continent. They smuggled their goods in neutral ships and with spurious "Made in France" labels. Napoleon lacked the vast naval force to apprehend smugglers at sea, and he lacked the large staff of incorruptible customs inspectors to control contraband in the ports. The best he could do was to confess his failure by confiscating and re-selling contraband *after* it had already been sold.

The Continental System antagonized both the neutral powers and Napoleon's allies. French seizure of American vessels in European ports under the terms of the Milan Decree put a dangerous strain on Franco-American relations. But British restrictions likewise bore heavily on the Americans. British impressment of American seamen on the pretext that they were deserters from the Royal Navy, together with the designs of American expansionists on Canada, produced the indecisive Anglo-American War of 1812, which actually lasted until 1814.

The Downfall of Napoleon

In Europe, the political and military consequences of the Continental System formed a decisive and disastrous chapter in Napoleonic history. The chapter opened in 1807, when the Emperor declined to tolerate Portugal's economic ties with Britain. To impose the Continental System on Portugal, he suggested that France and Spain partition the country. The Spanish rulers agreed, not suspecting that Napoleon planned to use the Portuguese expedition as an excuse for French military occupation of Spain itself. In 1808 he lured the Spanish royal family away from Madrid and made his brother Joseph King of Spain. But every measure taken by Napoleon—the removal of the incompetent Bourbons, the installation of a foreign monarch, the attempted enforcement of the Continental System, and, not least, the suppression of the Inquisition and the curtailment of noble and clerical privileges—violated Spanish tradition and offended Spanish nationalism. The irreconcilable Spaniards began fighting Napoleon in 1808.

This Peninsular War, named after the Iberian Peninsula, swiftly grew from a minor irritation to a deadly cancer on the body of the Napoleonic Empire. The Spaniards employed ambushes, poisoned wells, and other guerrilla devices. The expedition that Britain sent to assist them was ably commanded by Sir Arthur Wellesley (later the Duke of Wellington), generously supplied from home, and firmly based on Britain's unshakable command of the seas. Napoleon poured more than 300,000 troops into the Peninsular campaign, but his opponents quickly gained the upper hand in 1812, when he detached part of his Spanish forces for the invasion of Russia. In 1813, King Joseph left Madrid forever, and Wellington, having liberated Spain, crossed into southern France.

Napoleonic imperialism also aroused a national spirit among the traditionally disunited Germans. Men of letters launched a campaign against the traditional influence of the French language and French culture. Johann Grimm and his brother Wilhelm contributed not only their very popular—and very German—*Fairy Tales* (1812) but also philological researches designed to prove the innate superiority of the German language. The philosopher Fichte delivered at Berlin the highly patriotic *Addresses to the German Nation* (1807-08), claiming that German was the *Ursprache*, the fountainhead of language. And the Germans themselves, Fichte continued, were the *Urvolk*, the oldest and greatest of nations, the true Chosen People.

Napoleon began to feel the impact of German nationalism when Austria re-entered the war in 1809. For the first time in its history, the Habsburg monarchy attempted a total mobilization comparable to that decreed by the French Convention in 1793. In spite of the new spirit, however, the Austrians lost the campaign and for the fourth time in a dozen years submitted to a peace dictated by Napoleon. The Treaty of Schönbrunn (1809) stripped them of the Illyrian Provinces and assigned their Polish territory of Galicia to the Grand Duchy of Warsaw. Francis II gave his daughter to Napoleon in marriage, and his defeated land became the unwilling ally of France. Leadership in the German revival passed to Prussia.

The shock of Jena and Tilsit jarred Prussia out of the lethargy that had overtaken her since the death of Frederick the Great in 1786. The new University of Berlin, founded in 1810, attracted Fichte and other prophets of German nationalism. Able generals and statesmen came to power. General Scharnhorst headed a group of officers who improved the efficiency of the army, abolished its inhuman discipline, and made all social classes liable to military service, even the previously exempted educated and well-to-do. The top limit of 42,000 soldiers imposed upon Prussia by Napoleon was evaded by the simple device of assigning recruits to the reserve after a fairly brief period of intensive training and then inducting another group of recruits. The social and administrative reorganization of the Prussian state was inspired by the energetic Stein, an enlightened aristocrat. Stein conciliated the middle class by granting towns and cities some self-government. To improve the status of the peasantry, he promoted the great edict of October, 1807, at long last abolishing serfdom in Prussia. The edict, however, did not break up the large Junker estates or provide land for the liberated serfs; nor did it terminate the feudal rights of justice exercised by the Junker over his peasants. Stein and the others eliminated only the worst abuses of the Old Régime and left authority where it had traditionally

rested—with the king, the army, and the Junkers. The Hohenzollern state was not so much reformed as restored to the tradition of Frederick William I and Frederick the Great.

The event that finally allowed an aroused German nationalism to turn its full force against Napoleon was the French debacle in Russia. French actions after 1807 soon convinced Tsar Alexander that Napoleon was not keeping the Tilsit bargain and was in fact intruding on Russia's sphere in eastern Europe. When Alexander and Napoleon met again at the German town of Erfurt in 1808, they could reach no agreement, though they concealed their differences by a show of great intimacy. French acquisition of the Illyrian provinces from Austria in 1809 raised the unpleasant prospect of French domination over the Balkans, and the simultaneous transfer of Galicia from Austria to the Grand Duchy of Warsaw suggested that this Napoleonic vassal might next seek to absorb the Polish territories of Russia. Meanwhile, Napoleon's insistent efforts to make Russia enforce the Continental System increasingly incensed Alexander. French annexations in northwest Germany completed the discomfiture of the Tsar, for they wiped out the state of Oldenburg, where his uncle was the reigning duke. All these factors caused an open break between the Tsar and the Emperor, and the famous invasion of Russia by the French in 1812.

For the invasion Napoleon assembled the *Grande Armée* of nearly 500,000 men. A large proportion of the Grand Army, however, were not Frenchmen but unwilling conscripts in the service of a foreign master. The supply system broke down almost immediately, and the Russian scorched-earth policy made it very hard for the soldiers to live off the land. As the Grand Army marched eastward, one of Napoleon's aides reported:

There were no inhabitants to be found, no prisoners to be taken, not a single straggler to be picked up. We were in the heart of inhabited Russia and yet we were like a vessel without a compass in the midst of a vast ocean, knowing nothing of what was happening around us.*

Napoleon marched all the way to Moscow without ever managing to strike a knockout blow. He remained in the burning city for five weeks (September-October, 1812) in the vain hope of bringing Tsar Alexander to terms. But Russian obduracy and the shortage of supplies forced him to begin a retreat that became a nightmare. Ill-fed and inadequately clothed and sheltered, the retreating soldiers suffered horribly from Russian attacks on stragglers, and from the deadly onslaughts of "General Winter." Less than a quarter of the Grand Army survived the retreat from Moscow; the rest had been taken prisoner or had died of wounds, starvation, disease, or the cold.

The Russian leaders had feared that Napoleon would liberate the serfs and turn them against their masters. Nevertheless, the peasants, despite the ill-treatment to which they had been subject for so long, formed guerrilla bands, harassed Napoleon's forces, and in every way proved that their patriotic sentiments outweighed their class grievances. Kutuzov, the victorious Russian commander, now wanted to allow Russia's allies to prosecute the war. But Alexander insisted on pursuing the French, and sent Russian armies westward beyond the Russian frontiers on the track of Napoleon's forces.

The British had been the first to resist Napoleon successfully, at Trafalgar and on the economic battlefields of the Continental System. Then had come Spanish resistance, then Russian. Now in 1813 almost every nation in Europe joined the final coalition against the French. Napoleon raised a new army, but he could not replace so easily the equipment squandered in Russia. In October, 1813, he lost the "Battle of the Nations," fought at Leipzig in Saxony, and by April, 1814, the forces of the coalition occupied Paris. The Emperor abdicated, to begin an honorable exile as ruler of the minute island of Elba not far from the Italian coast.

The statesmen of the victorious coalition gathered in the Congress of Vienna to draw up the terms of peace (see below, pp. 369-374). The Bourbons returned to France in

---

* A. A. L. de Caulaincourt, *With Napoleon in Russia* (New York, 1935), 62.

"And they are like wild-cats." Etching by Goya from his series on the disasters of the Peninsular War.

the person of Louis XVIII, a younger brother of Louis XVI. Realizing that he could not revive the Old Régime intact, the new king issued the Charter of 1814 establishing a constitutional monarchy. The returned *émigrés*, however, showed no such good sense. They unleashed a new "White Terror" against the Revolution and all its works. Then, on March 1, 1815, Bonaparte pulled his last surprise: he landed on the Mediterranean coast of France.

For a hundred days, from March 20, 1815, when Napoleon re-entered Paris, the French Empire was reborn. Once again the Emperor rallied the French people, this time by promising a truly liberal regime. He never had time, however, to show the sincerity of his promise, for on June 18, 1815, the British under Wellington and the Prussians under Blücher delivered the final blow at Waterloo, near Brussels. Again Napoleon went into exile, to the remote British island of St. Helena in the South Atlantic. There, in 1821, he died of cancer.

The Legacy of the Revolution and Napoleon

Bonapartism, however, did not die in 1815 or in 1821. A Napoleonic legend arose, glossing over the faults of its hero, depicting him as the paladin of liberalism and patriotism, and paving the way for the advent of another Napoleon in 1848 (see Chapter XIV). This legend, with its overtones of hero-worship and belligerent nationalism, was one element in the legacy bequeathed by revolutionary and Napoleonic France. A second, and still more powerful, element was the great revolutionary motto—*Liberté, Egalité, Fraternité*. The motto lived on, to inspire later generations of Jacobins in France and elsewhere. And behind the motto was the fact that the French enjoyed a larger measure of liberty, equality, and fraternity in 1815 than they had ever known before 1789.

True, the Mountain's deputies on mission and Napoleon's censors and prefects gave new force to the old traditions of absolutism and centralization. But the middle class had won its freedom from obsolete restraints, and Protestants, Jews, and free-thinkers had gained toleration both in France and in French-dominated countries. The revolutionary and Napoleonic regimes established the principle of equal liability to taxation. They provided a greater degree of economic opportunity for large numbers of the third estate by breaking up the large landholdings of the clergy and nobility and by removing obstacles to the activity of businessmen, big and little. The *Code Napoléon* buried beyond all hope of exhumation the worst legal and social inequalities of the Old Régime.

The Revolution and Napoleon promoted fraternity in the legal sense by making all Frenchmen equal in the eyes of the law. They advanced fraternity in a broader sense by encouraging nationalism, the feeling of belonging to the great corporate body of Frenchmen who were superior to all other nations. French nationalism had existed long before 1789; but it remained for the Convention to formulate a new hyper-nationalistic creed in its decree of August 23, 1793, providing for the total mobilization of the French nation. The Napoleonic Empire then demonstrated how easily nationalism on an unprecedented scale could lead to imperialism of unprecedented magnitude. Alexis de Tocqueville, the great French student of democracy, wrote a hundred years ago:

The French Revolution was . . . a political revolution, which in its operation and its aspect resembled a religious one. It had every peculiar and characteristic feature of a religious movement; it not only spread to foreign countries, but it was carried thither by preaching and by propaganda.

It roused passions such as the most violent political revolutions had never before excited. . . . This gave to it that aspect of a religious revolution which so terrified its contemporaries, or rather . . . it became a kind of new religion in itself—a religion, imperfect it is true, without a God, without a worship, without a future life, but which nevertheless, like Islam, poured forth its soldiers, its apostles, and its martyrs over the face of the earth.*

Its early adherents were fanatics—Robespierre and the Jacobins. Its later exponents —the men of Thermidor and Brumaire—

* A. de Tocqueville, *The State of Society in France Before the Revolution of 1789*, 3rd ed. (London, 1888), 9-11.

modified the creed in the interests of practicality and moderation. Even in the hands of Napoleon, however, the Revolution remained a kind of religion, demanding observance of political orthodoxy and punishing heretics, as Napoleon punished King Louis Bonaparte of Holland, by the political equivalent of excommunication. And after 1815, as we shall see in the next chapter, the French Revolution continued to pour forth "its soldiers, its apostles, and its martyrs."

IV: *The Romantic Protest*

By the time of Waterloo, however, Europe was reacting strongly not only against Napoleon but also against the French Revolution, which had made Napoleon possible, and against the Enlightenment, which had made the Revolution possible. The reaction against the Enlightenment took the form of the Romantic movement. Romantic writers and artists protested against the omnipotent reason of the eighteenth century and on behalf of faith, emotion, tradition, and the other values that the Age of Reason had spurned. The Romantic protest against reason reached its full force in the early decades of the nineteenth century—the Romantic decades of 1800 to 1830 or 1840. But, as we have already seen, the movement of protest had been gathering strength during the latter part of the eighteenth century. Wesley and the Pietists challenged the deism of the *philosophes;* Rousseau proclaimed conscience, not reason, the "true guide of man"; Hume appealed to the "sentiments and affections" of men, not to their reason. Then in 1790 Edmund Burke, the great political philosopher of Romanticism, neatly turned against the *philosophes* their favorite appeal to the simple mathematical laws of Newtonian science. Natural rights, he explained,

. . . entering into common life, like rays of light which pierce into a dense medium, are, by the laws of nature, refracted from their straight line. Indeed in the gross and complicated mass of human passions and concerns, the primitive rights of men undergo such a variety of refractions and reflections, that it becomes absurd to talk of them as if they continued in the simplicity of their original direction. The nature of man is intricate; the objects of society are of the greatest possible complexity. . . .*

Literature: The Revolt against Reason

The Romantic protest may be followed most readily in literature. In the 1770's, the German literary world experienced a movement called *Sturm und Drang* ("Storm and Stress") after a play by an obscure dramatist. The hero of the play, totally incapable of settling down, flees Europe to fight in the American Revolution:

Have been everything. Became a day-labourer to be something. Lived on the Alps, pastured goats, lay day and night under the boundless vault of the heavens, cooled by the winds, burning with an inner fire. Nowhere

* *Reflections on the Revolution in France*, Everyman ed. (New York, 1910), 59.

rest, nowhere repose. See, thus I am glutted by impulse and power, and work it out of me. I am going to take part in this campaign as a volunteer; there I can expand my soul, and if they do me the favour to shoot me down,—all the better.*

The restlessness and self-pity of the *Sturm und Drang* were particularly evident in the *Sorrows of Young Werther*, an immensely popular and lugubrious short novel by the youthful Goethe.

Goethe himself (1749-1832), whose long and productive career extended right through the Romantic era, was in some respects a good eighteenth-century *philosophe*. He was interested in natural science and settled happily at the enlightened court of a small German state at Weimar. Yet Romantic values lie at the very heart of his greatest work—many would say the greatest work in the German language—*Faust*. Begun when Goethe was in his twenties, and finished only when he was eighty, this long poetic drama was less a play in the conventional sense than a philosophical commentary on the main currents of European thought. According to the traditional legend, the aged Faust, weary of book learning and pining for eternal youth, sold his soul to the Devil, received back the enjoyment of his youth for an allotted time, and then, terror-stricken, went to the everlasting fires. Goethe transformed the legend. Faust does indeed find intellectual pursuits disillusioning and profitless:

> . . . Grey is all theory,
> The golden tree of life is green! †

Faust makes his infernal compact, but is ultimately saved through his realization that he must sacrifice selfish concerns to the welfare of others. A drama of man's sinning, striving, and redemption, Goethe's *Faust* has been called "the last great poem of the Middle Ages." This return to the Middle Ages is a striking feature of the whole Romantic movement, as we shall see presently.

All over Europe, by the early 1800's, Romantic writers had caught the mood of the *Sturm und Drang* and were rebelling against the "classical spirit." They praised the color and the vigor of the Bible and Shakespeare, and made impassioned demands for a new literary renaissance. In England, the Romantic protest was sounded in *Lyrical Ballads* (1798), by Wordsworth and Coleridge. There were other great English Romantic poets—Byron, Shelley, Keats—but Wordsworth (1770-1850) and Coleridge (1772-1834) pressed farthest in their reaction against classicism and rationalism. To *Lyrical Ballads* Coleridge contributed *The Rime of the Ancient Mariner*, a supernatural tale of the curse afflicting a sailor who slays an albatross. Still more famous are the lines beginning another poem by Coleridge:

> In Xanadu did Kubla Khan
>   A stately pleasure dome decree;
> Where Alph, the sacred river ran,
> Through caverns measureless to man
>   Down to a sunless sea.

The world of the "sunless sea" and "caverns measureless to man" is far indeed from the optimistic universe of the *philosophes*.

Wordsworth was less concerned than Coleridge with the exotic and the supernatural, but he, too, rejected the Enlightenment. At times he was anti-intellectual:

> Up! up! my Friend, and quit your books;
> Or surely you'll grow double:
> Up! up! my Friend, and clear your looks;
> Why all this toil and trouble?
>
> .   .   .
>
> Come forth into the light of things,
> Let Nature be your teacher.
>
> She has a world of ready wealth,
> Our minds and hearts to bless—
> Spontaneous wisdom breathed by health,
> Truth breathed by cheerfulness.
>
> One impulse from a vernal wood
> May teach you more of man,

---

* Klinger, *Sturm und Drang*, quoted in Kuno Francke, *A History of German Literature as Determined by Social Forces*, 4th ed. (New York, 1931), 309.

† *Faust*, Everyman ed. (New York, 1925), 61.

Of moral evil and of good,
Than all the sages can.

Sweet is the lore which Nature brings;
Our meddling intellect
Mis-shapes the beauteous forms of things:—
We murder to dissect.

Enough of Science and of Art;
Close up those barren leaves;
Come forth, and bring with you a heart
That watches and receives.*

To find Wordsworth at his best, one should read the long autobiographical poem, *The Prelude*. Here is a brief passage from it that suggests his essential attitude toward the mystery of existence:

Dust as we are, the immortal spirit grows
Like harmony in music; there is a dark
Inscrutable workmanship that reconciles
Discordant elements, makes them cling
        together
In one society.†

In place of the light shed by Newton's laws Wordsworth found "a dark inscrutable workmanship," and in place of the *philosophes'* belief in the perfectibility of man through mortal reason he put his faith in the "immortal spirit" of the individual.

Literature: The Return to the Past

It may seem a very long leap indeed from the un-Newtonian universe of Wordsworth to the Romantics' enthusiasm for the Middle Ages in general and for the earlier history of their own nations in particular. And yet nationalism at bottom is an irrational, almost mystical, force that in effect "reconciles discordant elements, makes them cling together in one society." The heightened sense of nationalism evident almost everywhere in Europe by 1815 was in part a matter of simple political self-preservation. In the crisis of the Napoleonic wars the Spaniards naturally became more aware of their Spanish heritage, the Germans of their Germanic one, and so on. Actually, however, the Romantic return to the past, though intensified by the French Revolution and Napoleon, had begun before 1789 as part of the general retreat from the Enlightenment. The *philosophes* hated the Middle Ages, especially the medieval preoccupation with religion. Naturally the forerunners of the Romantic movement tended to cherish what the *philosophes* so detested.

The German writer, Herder (1744-1803) advanced a theory of cultural nationalism. Each separate nation, he argued, like any individual organism, had its own distinct personality, its *Volksgeist* or "folk spirit," and its own pattern of growth. The surest measure of a nation's growth was its literature—poetry in the nation's youth, prose in its maturity. Stimulated by Herder, students of medieval German literature collected popular ballads, and the Grimms compiled their *Fairy Tales*. By putting a new value on the German literature of the past, Herder helped to free the German literature of his own day from its bondage to French culture. Herder, however, was no narrow nationalist; he asserted that the cultivated man should know cultures other than his own. Some German Romantics, however, stirred by the patriotic revival after Jena and Tilsit, carried national enthusiasm to an extreme that Herder would have deplored. Thus Fichte and the Grimms claimed pre-eminence for the German language, and the mere fact of being German appeared to be a cardinal virtue.

Many nations experienced a notable revival of their older literature during the Romantic epoch. In Britain, Sir Walter Scott (1771-1832) assisted in collecting the vigorous folk ballads of the Middle Ages and went on to write more than thirty widely popular historical novels, of which *Ivanhoe*, set in the days of Richard Lionheart and the Crusades, is a good sample. France had Victor Hugo and his great novel

---

* *The Tables Turned*, from *Lyrical Ballads*, lines 1-4, 15-32.
† *The Prelude*, Bk. I, lines 340-344.

of the fifteenth century, *Notre Dame de Paris* (1831). And Russia had her great poet, Pushkin (1799-1837), who deserted the archaic Slavonic language of the Orthodox Church to write the first classic works in the national vernacular. He introduced local color from Russian history and from the newly acquired provinces in the Crimea and the Caucasus, and he celebrated his own exotic grandfather, Hannibal, the African Negro slave of Peter the Great.

Music

Musicians, too, sought out the popular ballads and tales of the national past. To achieve color and drama, composers of operas and songs turned frequently to Shakespeare's plays, Scott's novels, and the poems of Goethe and Pushkin. In short, literature and music often followed parallel paths of development during the Romantic era. But the parallel was never complete. Romantic musicians scarcely revolted against their great eighteenth-century predecessors in the sense that Romantic poets were revolting against the *philosophes*. Rather, Romantic music evolved peacefully out of the older classical school.

The composer who played the commanding part in this evolution was Beethoven (1770-1827), a Fleming by ancestry and a Viennese by adoption. Whereas Coleridge had said that the Romantic artist might be careless in matters of diction and meter, Beethoven showed a classical concern for the forms and techniques that were the musical counterparts of diction and meter. Yet he also reshaped the great tradition that he inherited from Bach, Haydn, and Mozart. For example, where Mozart and Haydn had used the courtly minuet for the third movement in a symphony, Beethoven introduced the more plebeian and rollicking *scherzo*. Where earlier composers had indicated the tempo with a simple *allegro* (fast) or *andante* (slow), Beethoven added such Romantic designations as *appassionato*

and "Strife between Head and Heart." His compositions sometimes suggest vigorous conflicts and emotions: witness the dramatic opening notes of the famous Fifth Symphony, often compared to the rappings of fate. In good Romantic fashion, Beethoven drew inspiration from nature, as in the "Pastoral Symphony," with its musical thunderstorm and peaceful forest, complete with bird songs.

After Beethoven, orchestral works took on increasingly heroic dimensions. The pioneer was the Frenchman Berlioz (1803-1869), one of the first composers to utilize the full complement of instruments, especially winds and percussion, that constitute the modern orchestra. His experiments with the theatrical possibilities of the orchestra culminated in one of the great landmarks in musical history, the aptly titled "Fantastic Symphony" (1830).

Music for the human voice reflected both the increased enthusiasm for instruments, particularly the newly perfected piano, and the general Romantic nostalgia for the past. In composing songs and arias, Romantic musicians devoted as much skill to the accompaniment as to the voice part itself. Franz Schubert (1797-1826), Beethoven's Viennese contemporary, made a fine art of blending voice and piano in more than six hundred exquisite *Lieder* (songs), seventy of them musical settings of poems by Goethe. Meantime, Von Weber (1786-1826) was striving to create a truly German opera. He took an old legend as the libretto for *Der Freischütz* ("The Freeshooter," 1820), which ran the good Romantic gamut of an enchanted forest, a magic bullet, and an innocent maiden outwitting the Devil. For the choruses and marches of *Der Freischütz* he employed many folk-like melodies. Weber was by no means the only serious composer to utilize national folk tunes. The Russian Glinka (1804-1857) cast aside the Italian influences that had previously dominated the secular music of his country. He based his opera,

Romantic painting. Constable, "Dedham Mill," 1820.

Russlan and Ludmilla (1842), on a poem by Pushkin and embellished it with dances and choruses derived from the native music of Russia's Asiatic provinces.

The Arts

In the fine arts, the forces of Romanticism gained no such triumph as they won in literature and music. The virtual dictator of European painting during the first two decades of the nineteenth century was the French neoclassicist, David (1748-1825). The official painter of the French Jacobins, David depicted dramatic contemporary events like the Tennis-Court Oath. He generally used traditional techniques: in the "Tennis-Court Oath," for example, he first drew the deputies naked, as if they were ancient athletes, and later painted in their clothes.

More direct and powerful—and much closer to the Romantic temper—were the works of the great Spanish painter, Goya (1746-1828). No one could have any illusions about Spanish royalty after looking at Goya's revealing portraits of the enlightened Charles III and his worthless successors. After viewing Goya's etchings on the Peninsular War, no one could doubt the horrors of warfare (see illustration on p. 359). Goya is said to have made the sketches for these etchings in the very blood of the executed Spanish patriots whose agonies he was portraying. The outraged patriotism and frightening immediacy of Goya, however, attracted few imitators.

The two men responsible for establishing a Romantic school of painting were Constable and Delacroix. The lovely paintings of the English landscape by Constable (1776-1837) made nature artistically respectable once more. Delacroix (1799-

Gothic revival in architecture. The Houses of Parliament, London.

1863), a Frenchman, insisted that color and light mattered more than classical purity of line; young painters, therefore, should study the flamboyant canvases of Rubens, whom David had excommunicated from the ranks of orthodox artists. The purpose of art was "not to imitate nature but to strike the imagination." Delacroix proceeded to strike the imagination of his contemporaries by painting "The Massacre of Scio" (1824), a bloody episode in the Greek War of Independence (see Chapter XII). Today the picture seems more conventional and less moving than Goya's etchings of the Peninsular War. At the time, however, it was denounced as "barbarous, drunken, delirious"—the "massacre of painting." French painters were now divided into opposing schools: the Romantic followers of Dela-croix, and the still powerful disciples of David.

In early nineteenth-century architecture, the contrasting schools were the neoclassical and the neo-Gothic. As the century opened, the vogue for Roman buildings introduced by the French Revolution reached its height in Napoleon's *Arc de Triomphe* and in the monumental Paris Church of the Madeleine, actually copied from a Roman temple, the *Maison Carrée* ("square house") at Nîmes. In Britain, neoclassical architecture still flourished, but it met competition from the Gothic revival, stimulated partly by the wealth of medieval architectural lore in Scott's novels and partly by the revival of religion. British architects applied the Gothic manner to every kind of building after 1820, not only to churches, but also to railway stations, elaborate villas, and modest cottages. While the high vaulting, arched windows, and general "gloomth" of Gothic were singularly inappropriate to residential construction, the Gothic revival was not an unmitigated artistic calamity. It fostered the preservation and restoration of medieval masterpieces half ruined by centuries of neglect. The British Houses of Parliament demonstrated a century ago—and college buildings sometimes demonstrate today—that a skilled architect could adapt the old style to new demands successfully and tastefully. The Gothic revival, finally, was a really spectacular victory of Romantic longing over the practical outlook that dominated so much of nineteenth-century life.

Religion and Philosophy

Neo-Gothic architecture was one sign of the religious revival that accompanied the Romantic protest. Another sign was the pope's re-establishment in 1814 of the Jesuit order, whose suppression had been one of the great victories of the Enlightenment. Most of the Romantics were horrified by the religious skepticism of the *philosophes;* an outspoken atheist like Shelley was an isolated exception to the general rule. In Germany, Catholicism gained many converts among Romantic writers, and in England Wordsworth and Coleridge vigorously defended the established Church. Coleridge declared:

. . . that the scheme of Christianity, as taught in the liturgy and homilies of our Church, though not discoverable by human reason, is yet in accordance with it; that link follows link by necessary consequence; that Religion passes out of the ken of Reason only where the eye of Reason has reached its own horizon; and that Faith is then but its continuation. . . .*

This declaration reads almost as though it were a restatement of Kant's moral philos-

ophy; and indeed Coleridge had studied the writings of Kant and his disciples.

The greatest of Kant's disciples, and the most characteristically Romantic philosopher, was Hegel (1770-1831), a professor at the University of Berlin. Like his master, Hegel attacked the tendency of the Enlightenment to see in human nature and human history only what first met the eye. The history of mankind, properly understood, was the history of human efforts to will good, and this in turn was the unfolding of God's plan for the world. Good, he stated,

. . . is God. God governs the world; the actual working of his government—the carrying out of his plan—is the History of the World.*

For Hegel, history was a *dialectical* process, that is, a series of conflicts. The two elements in the conflict were the *thesis*, the established order of life, and the *antithesis*, the challenge to the old order. Out of the struggle of thesis and antithesis emerged the *synthesis*, no mere compromise between the two but a new and better way, another step forward in man's slow progression toward the best of all possible worlds. The synthesis, in turn, broke down; a new thesis and antithesis became locked in conflict; the dialectic produced another synthesis— and so on. Men who helped to perfect a new synthesis were, in Hegel's judgment, "heroes" and "world-historical individuals" who "had an insight into the requirements of the time" and who knew "what was ripe for development."

This dialectical philosophy of history was the most original and influential element in Hegel's thought, the antecedent of the dialectical materialism of Karl Marx (see Chapter XIII). It is difficult for citizens of a twentieth-century democracy to appreciate that Hegel was once even more famous as a liberal idealist. His emphasis on duty, his choice of Alexander the Great, Caesar, and

---

* *Biographia Literaria*, Everyman ed., 334.

* *The Philosophy of History*, J. Sibree, trans (New York, 1944). 36.

Napoleon as "world-historical" heroes, his assertion that the state "existed for its own sake"—all this suggests a direct link between Hegel and authoritarianism. In fairness, however, it should be pointed out that Hegel himself seems to have foreseen the final political synthesis not in a brutal police state but in a liberalized Prussian monarchy.

Thus Hegel, too, believed in the perfectibility of man, though he suggested that the process would be more laborious than a *philosophe* like Condorcet had ever imagined. The Romantics by no means disowned all the favorite beliefs of the Enlightenment. Not only a modified doctrine of progress but also eighteenth-century cosmopolitanism lived on in the Romantic era. Homer, Cervantes, Shakespeare, and Scott all won wide and appreciative audiences in many countries. The very greatest figures of the age, Beethoven and Goethe, deserve to be called citizens of the world. On balance, however, the disparities between Romanticism and the Enlightenment clearly outnumber the similarities. By the early 1800's the Newtonian world-machine, the concept of the universe so favored by the *philosophes*, was fading out of sight. In its place stood the neo-Gothic world of religious mystery, the Hegelian world of dialectic, and the Wordsworthian world of impulses from the vernal wood.

V: The Conservative Outlook and the Vienna Settlement

Romanticism, by its stress on the variety of individuals, ultimately enriched the doctrines of liberalism, and by its emphasis on the values of the nation it strengthened the force of nationalism. The immediate political impact of Romanticism, however, was neither liberal nor national but conservative and counter-revolutionary. Of the English Romantics, for example, only Byron and Shelley adhered to the radical political views of the Enlightenment. Wordsworth and Coleridge soon lost their youthful enthusiasm for the French Revolution and adopted a conservative political philosophy.

The new conservative political outlook owed much to the writings of Edmund Burke (1729-1797). Burke could not stomach the simple and optimistic view of human nature taken by the *philosophes*, as we have already seen: "The nature of man is intricate; the objects of society are of the greatest possible complexity." Burke, therefore, revered the institutions that had grown up over the long course of human history. He did not, however, believe that these institutions were petrified; they had developed gradually in the past, they would develop gradually in the future. Political change was possible but difficult, Burke concluded. Reforms had to be introduced so that "the useful parts of the old establishment" might be preserved; they had to be managed slowly and "with circumspection and caution"—in a word, conservatively.

Burke approved of the American Revolution; in his view, it was not so much a revolution as a reaffirmation of the glorious tradition of 1688. The same reasoning drove Burke to violent condemnation in his *Reflections on the Revolution in France* (1790). The men of 1789 destroyed everything, good, bad, and indifferent, thereby imperiling the social contract itself. "Society is indeed a contract," Burke stated, but he did not mean what Rousseau had meant:

The state ought not to be considered as nothing better than a partnership agreement in a trade of pepper and coffee, calico or tobacco, or some such other low concern, to be taken up for a little temporary interest, and to be dissolved by the fancy of the parties. It is to be looked on with other reverence; because it is not a partnership in things subservient only to the gross animal existence of a temporary and perishable nature. It is a partnership in all science; a partnership in all art; a partnership in every virtue, and in all perfection. As the ends of such a partnership cannot be obtained in many generations, it becomes a partnership not only between those who are living, but between those who are living, those who are dead, and those who are to be born.*

The Congress of Vienna

The force of tradition bore heavily upon the politics of Europe in 1815, for this was the end of the Age of Napoleon and the beginning of the Age of Metternich—Prince Clement Wenceslas Lothair Népomucène Metternich (1773-1859), Austrian foreign minister from 1809 to 1848, and the chief figure in European diplomacy during most of his long career. An aristocrat through and through, Metternich shared Burke's reverence for the past:

Man cannot make a constitution properly speaking: that is made only by time. . . . Let people write as much as they like—and the less will always be the better—and yet you will have nothing in your hand but a sheet of paper. England alone has a Constitution, of which the Magna Carta is but a subordinate element. The English Constitution is the work of centuries. . . . Social order ever progresses in this way; it cannot be otherwise, since it is the law of nature.†

Moreover, Metternich was convinced that the Austrian Empire was particularly susceptible to injury by the liberal and nationalistic energies released by the Enlightenment and the Revolution. Tradition was the cement that held together the differing parts of the Habsburg realm.

In 1814 and 1815, Metternich was host to the Congress of Vienna, which approached

the great task of rebuilding Europe with truly conservative deliberateness. For the larger part of a year, the diplomats indulged to the full in balls and banquets, concerts and hunting parties. "Congress dances," remarked an observer, "but it does not march." Actually, the brilliant social life served the very businesslike purpose of distracting the lesser fry while the important diplomats settled things in small, private conferences.

Four men made most of the major decisions at Vienna—Metternich, Castlereagh, Talleyrand, and Tsar Alexander I. Viscount Castlereagh, the British foreign minister, shared the conservative outlook of Metternich. He was less concerned with punishing the French for their past sins than with preventing the appearance of new Robespierres and Bonapartes. Castlereagh announced that he went to Vienna "not to collect trophies, but to bring the world back to peaceful habits." Talleyrand, the foreign minister of Louis XVIII of France, scored at Vienna the greatest success of his long career. Originally a money-minded bishop of the Old Régime, he had in succession rallied to the Revolution in 1789, supported the Civil Constitution of the Clergy (one of the very few bishops to do so), served as Napoleon's foreign minister, and intrigued against the Emperor during the years after Tilsit. Now he was serving the restored Bourbon king, and in his old age he was later to take an important part in the Revolution of 1830 (see below, p. 385). This supremely adaptable diplomat soon maneuvered himself into the inner circle at Vienna, and the representatives of the victorious powers accepted the emissary of defeated France as their equal. Talleyrand was particularly adept in exploiting his nuisance value—acting as the spokesman of lesser diplomats who resented being shoved aside, and making the most of the differences that inevitably appeared among the victors.

To these differences Alexander I contributed greatly. Metternich actually called

---

* *Reflections*, Everyman ed., 93.
† *Memoirs of Prince Metternich, 1815-1829*, Prince Richard Metternich, ed. (New York, 1881), III, 366.

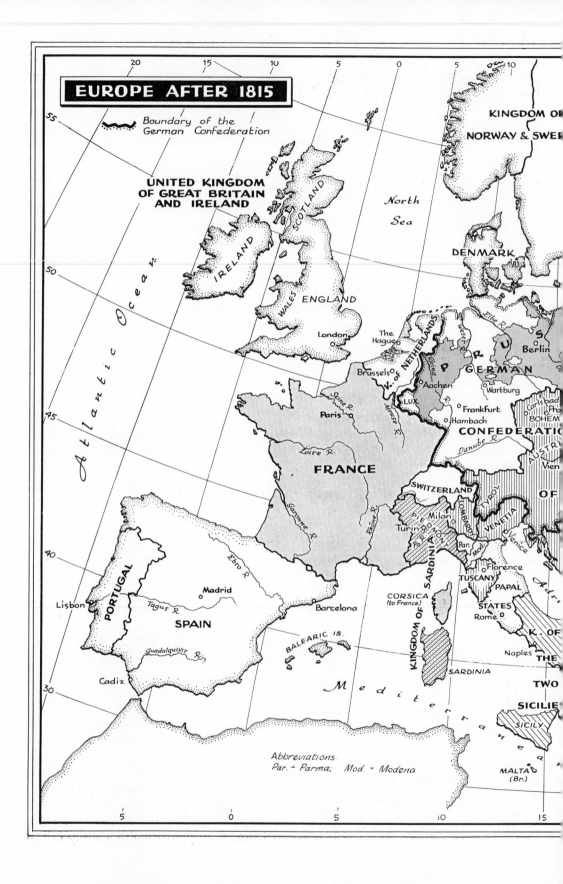

EUROPE AFTER 1815

〰 Boundary of the German Confederation

KINGDOM OF NORWAY & SWE

UNITED KINGDOM OF GREAT BRITAIN AND IRELAND

SCOTLAND

IRELAND

WALES

ENGLAND

London

North Sea

DENMARK

Atlantic Ocean

The Hague
Brussels
K. of NETHERLANDS
LUX
Aachen

Elbe R.
Weser R.
Rhine R.
PRUS
Berlin
GERMAN
Wartburg
Frankfurt
Carlsbad
BOHEM
Hambach
CONFEDERATI
Danube R.

Paris
Seine R.
Meuse R.
Loire R.

FRANCE
Garonne R.
Rhône R.

SWITZERLAND
TYROL
LOMBARDY
VENETIA
Venice
AUSTR
Vien

OF

Milan
Turin
PIEDMONT
Po R.
Par.
Mod.
Florence
TUSCANY
PAPAL
STATES
Rome
K. OF
THE

PORTUGAL
Lisbon
Ebro R.
Madrid
Tagus R.
SPAIN
Guadalquivir R.
Cadiz
Barcelona
BALEARIC IS.

CORSICA
(to France)

KINGDOM OF SARDINIA

SARDINIA

Naples

Mediterranean

TWO
SICILIE
SICILY

MALTA
(Br.)

Abbreviations.
Par. = Parma; Mod. = Modena

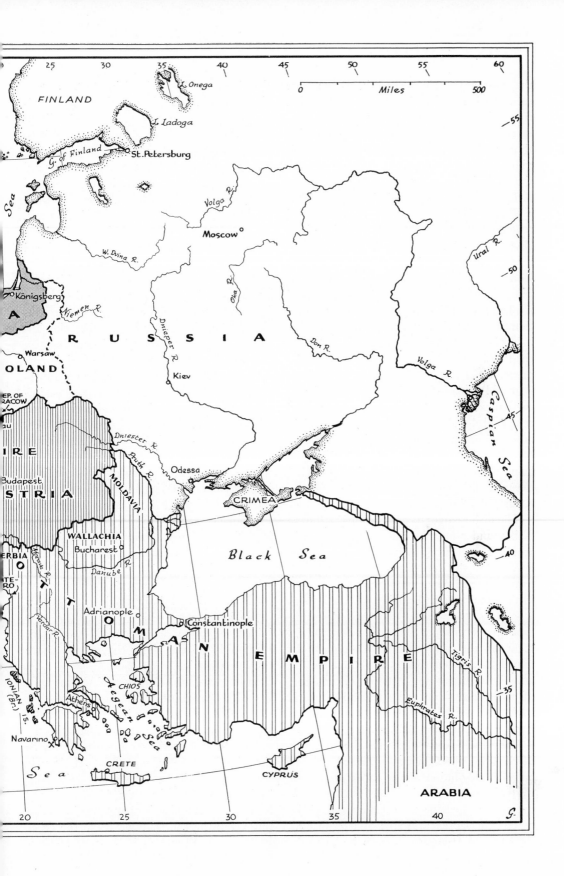

FINLAND

L. Onega

L. Ladoga

G. of Finland

St.Petersburg

Sea

Königsberg

Volga R.

Moscow

W. Dvina R.

Niemen R.

A

R U S S I A

Ural R.

-55

-50

Warsaw

POLAND

EP. OF RACOW

au

RE

STRIA

Budapest

Dniester R.

Dnieper R.

Kiev

Oka R.

Don R.

Volga R.

Caspian Sea

-45

MOLDAVIA

Odessa

Pruth R.

CRIMEA

ERBIA

WALLACHIA

Bucharest

Danube R.

Morava R.

O

Black Sea

-40

ITERO-RO

T

T

O

M

Vardar R.

Adrianople

A

N

Constantinople

E

M

P

I

R

E

Tigris R.

Euphrates R.

-35

IONIAN (Br.) Is.

Athens

CHIOS

Aegean Sea

Navarino

Sea

CRETE

CYPRUS

ARABIA

25   30   35   40   45   50   55   60

0   Miles   500

20   25   30   35   40

G-the Tsar a Jacobin, although, as we have seen in Chapter IX, Alexander's reputation for enlightenment was only partially deserved. By 1814 the Tsar had acquired a thoroughly Romantic enthusiasm for religion. For hours on end, he prayed and read the Bible in the company of Baroness von Krüdener, and under her influence prepared a "Holy Alliance" whereby all states would regenerate their policies by following literally the teachings of Christ. In the first months at Vienna it was not Alexander's Romantic scheme of a Holy Alliance but rather his Polish policy that nearly disrupted the Congress. He proposed a partial restoration of pre-partition Poland, with himself as its monarch. Austria and Prussia would lose the Polish lands they had grabbed late in the preceding century. Alexander won the support of Prussia by backing her demands for the annexation of Saxony, whose king had remained loyal to Napoleon. Metternich, however, did not want Austria's traditional Prussian rival to make such a substantial gain. Moreover, both Metternich and Castlereagh disliked the prospect of a large, Russian-dominated Poland.

The dispute over Saxony and Poland gave Talleyrand a magnificent chance to fish in troubled waters. Thus it was that in January, 1815, the representative of defeated France joined Metternich and Castlereagh in threatening both Prussia and Russia with war unless they moderated their demands. The threat produced an immediate settlement of the controversy. Alexander obtained Poland but agreed to reduce its size and allow Prussia and Austria to keep part of their loot from the partitions. Prussia took about half of Saxony; the King of Saxony retained the balance.

Once the Saxon-Polish question was out of the way, the Congress achieved a fairly amicable resolution of the other important dynastic and territorial questions. According to the doctrine that Talleyrand christened "the sacred principle of legitimacy," thrones and frontiers were to be re-established as they had existed in 1789. In practice, however, legitimacy was ignored almost as often as it was enforced. The diplomats at Vienna were statesmen enough to realize that they could not undo all the changes worked by the Revolution and Napoleon. Hence, although they restored Bourbon dynasties to the thrones of France, Spain, and Naples in the name of legitimacy, they did not attempt to revive all the hundreds of German states that had vanished since 1789.

In Germany, the Congress provided for thirty-nine states, loosely grouped together in a confederation. The German Confederation came close to reincarnating the impotent Holy Roman Empire; its chief organ, the diet, was to be a council of diplomats from sovereign states rather than a representative national assembly. The most important members of the confederation were, of course, Prussia and Austria, for the German-speaking provinces of the Habsburgs were considered an integral part of Germany. Prussia and Austria both obtained important new territories at Vienna. Prussia, in addition to her Saxon annexation, expanded the old scattered Hohenzollern lands in western Germany into the imposing new Rhine Province. Austria lost Belgium, which was incorporated into the Kingdom of the Netherlands. But she recovered the old Habsburg territory of Lombardy in Italy, to which Venetia was now joined, and she also secured Napoleon's Illyrian Provinces along the eastern shore of the Adriatic.

In Italy, too, the Congress of Vienna confirmed the tradition of political disunity. It restored the Bourbon Kingdom of Naples in the south and the Papal States in the center. In the northwest it gave Genoa to the Kingdom of Piedmont-Sardinia. Austria was in a position to dominate Italy both by her possession of Lombardy-Venetia and by the close family ties between the Habsburgs and the ruling dynasties in the other Italian states. Elsewhere in Europe, the Congress of Vienna restored and somewhat enlarged the independent Republic of Switzerland. It transferred Norway from the rule of Denmark to that of Sweden; Sweden, in turn, handed Finland over to Russia. Great Britain received Malta, controlling the "waist" of the Mediterranean, and, outside Europe, the former Dutch colonies of Ceylon and the Cape of Good Hope.

The Quarantine of France

France at first was given her boundaries of 1792, which included the minor territorial acquisitions made during the early days of the Revolution. Then came Napoleon's escape from Elba and the Hundred Days. The final settlement reached after Waterloo assigned France the frontiers of 1790, substantially those of the Old Régime. In addition, the French were to return Napoleon's art plunder to its rightful owners, to pay the victorious allies an indemnity of 700,000,000 francs (approximately $140,000,000), and to finance an army of occupation on their soil for not more than five years.

The Vienna diplomats did not so much punish France as take measures to quarantine any possible new French aggression. Castlereagh conceived the policy of strengthening France's neighbors so that they would be able to restrain the troublemaker in the future. Thus to the north the French faced the Belgians and the Dutch combined in the single Kingdom of the Netherlands. On the northeast they encountered the Rhine Province of Prussia, and on the east the expanded states of Switzerland and Piedmont. The Quadruple Alliance, signed in November, 1815, constituted the second great measure of quarantine. The four allies —Britain, Prussia, Austria, and Russia— agreed to use force, if necessary, to preserve the Vienna settlement. At Castlereagh's insistence, the allies further decided on periodic conferences to consider the measures

"most salutary for the repose and prosperity of Nations, and the maintenance of the Peace of Europe." The Quadruple Alliance was to be both a watchdog against France and an experiment in government by international conference, a modest first step along the road leading to the League of Nations and United Nations of the twentieth century.

Public opinion, especially in the English-speaking countries, unfortunately confused the Quadruple Alliance with Alexander's Holy Alliance scheme and identified the Holy Alliance with the blackest reaction. The Holy Alliance, signed in September, 1815, was actually a fairly harmless document dedicated to the proposition that "the policy of the powers . . . ought to be guided by the sublime truths taught by the eternal religion of God our Saviour." Although most of the major European rulers signed the Holy Alliance, only Tsar Alexander seems to have taken it seriously. Castlereagh called it "a piece of sublime mysticism and nonsense," and the Pope, refusing an invitation to join, remarked that the Vatican could very well dispense with interpretations of Christian doctrine by the laity.

Together with Westphalia (1648), Utrecht (1713), and Versailles (1919), the Vienna settlement of 1814-15 marked one of those rare attempts at the massive political reconstruction of Europe. Of the four, Vienna in many respects succeeded best. There was to be no major European war until the Crimean conflict of the 1850's, and none embroiling the whole of Europe until 1914. Most of the leading diplomats at Vienna could have said with Castlereagh that they acted "to bring the world back to peaceful habits." Seldom have victors treated the defeated aggressor more generously. Castlereagh, above all, deserves credit for his project of pacifying international disputes through conferences of the Quadruple Alliance.

In operation, however, the Quadruple Alliance never fulfilled the noble aims of Castlereagh. Within five years of the Congress of Vienna, revolution broke out again in Europe, causing serious dissension within the Quadruple Alliance. And for these outbreaks the Congress of Vienna was itself partly responsible, because it attempted to stifle liberal and national aspirations. In the long run, however, these aspirations could not be denied, and the persistence of revolution forms the main thread through the political history of the Continental European states in the first half of the nineteenth century.

Reading Suggestions on Napoleon

The Napoleonic Era—Secondary Accounts

G. Bruun, *Europe and the French Imperium, 1799-1814* (N.Y.: Harper, 1938). Another indispensable volume in the "Rise of Modern Europe" series; Napoleon viewed as an enlightened despot.

A. Guérard, *Napoleon I* (N.Y.: Knopf, 1956), and H. A. L. Fisher, *Napoleon* (N.Y.: Oxford Univ. Press, 1945. Home University Library). Good short biographies.

F. M. Kircheisen, *Napoleon* (N.Y.: Harcourt, Brace, 1932). Perhaps the best of the more detailed biographies.

F. M. H. Markham, *Napoleon and the Awakening of Europe* (N.Y.: Macmillan, 1954. Teach Yourself History Library). A popular introduction.

E. Heckscher, *The Continental System: An Economic Interpretation* (Oxford: Clarendon, 1922). An important monograph.

J. Seeley, *The Life and Times of Stein: Germany and Prussia in the Napoleonic Age* (Boston: Roberts, 1879). An old detailed treatment, still worth reading.

W. C. Langsam, *The Napoleonic Wars and German Nationalism in Austria* (N.Y.: Columbia Univ. Press, 1930). An informative monograph.

H. A. L. Fisher, *Studies in Napoleonic Statesmanship: Germany* (Oxford: Clarendon, 1903). A detailed and balanced evaluation of the impact of French reforms on German satellites.

P. Geyl, *Napoleon, For and Against* (New Haven: Yale Univ. Press, 1949). A most interesting collection of judgments passed on Napoleon in later epochs.

C. K. Webster, *The Congress of Vienna, 1814-1815* (London: Bell, 1934). A very sound account.

C. Brinton, *The Lives of Talleyrand* (N.Y.: Norton, 1936). Spirited defense of the great French opportunist.

The Napoleonic Era— Sources and Historical Fiction

R. M. Johnston, ed., *The Corsican* (Boston: Houghton Mifflin, 1910). Napoleon's biography compiled from his own words.

Napoleon I, *Letters*, J. M. Thompson ed. (N.Y.: Dutton, 1954. Everyman ed.). A splendid and most revealing collection.

L. Tolstoy, *War and Peace* (many editions). The justly famous novel of great length about the Russian campaign.

A. A. L. de Caulaincort, *With Napoleon in Russia* (N.Y.: Morrow, 1955). Vivid eye-witness account by one of Bonaparte's chief aides.

The Retreat from Reason and Revolution—Secondary Accounts

A. N. Whitehead, *Science and the Modern World* (N.Y.: New American Library. A Mentor Book). Includes a significant reappraisal of the Romantic protest.

G. Brandes, *Main Currents in Nineteenth-Century Literature* (London: Heinemann, 1901-1905). An important detailed account.

C. Brinton, *Political Ideas of the English Romanticists* (London: Oxford Univ. Press, 1926). A useful study.

I. Babbitt, *Rousseau and Romanticism* (N.Y.: Meridian Books). Reprint of a notable hostile essay.

G. Boas, *French Philosophies of the Romantic Period* (Baltimore: Johns Hopkins Univ. Press, 1934). A perceptive study.

K. Francke, *A History of German Literature as Determined by Social Forces* (N.Y.: Holt, 1907). A lively general treatment, fully meeting the requirements of its title.

E. L. Woodward, *Three Studies in European Conservatism* (London: Constable, 1929). Includes a thoughtful essay on Metternich.

P. Viereck, *Conservatism Revisited* (N.Y.: Scribner's, 1949). Metternich sympathetically re-evaluated by a modern liberal conservative.

M. Raynal, *The Nineteenth Century: Goya to Gauguin* (N.Y.: Skira, 1951). A superbly illustrated introduction to nineteenth-century painting.

K. Clark, *The Gothic Revival* (London: Constable, 1950). An instructive and entertaining commentary on the neo-Gothic mode in English architecture.

A. Einstein, *Music in the Romantic Era* (N.Y.: Norton, 1947). A suggestive survey.

The Retreat from Reason and Revolution— Sources and Historical Fiction

E. Burke, *Reflections on the Revolution in France* (many editions). The famous rhetorical denunciation of the Enlightenment and its works.

A. Cobban, ed., *The Debate on the French Revolution, 1789-1800* (London: Kaye, 1950). Useful selections summarizing contrasting English reactions to the Jacobinism across the Channel.

The best approach to the Romantic movement is through the writings of its great men. The following are particularly recommended (almost all are available in several editions): the Waverley novels of Sir Walter Scott; the two great novels by Victor Hugo, *Notre Dame* and *Les Misérables; The Red and the Black* (*The Scarlet and Black*, in some translations), the masterly novel by Stendhal; and the poems of Wordsworth and Coleridge.

CHAPTER TWELVE

Revolution and Counter-Revolution

1815-1850

I: Introduction: The Persistence of Revolution

The history of the western world during the half-century or so after Napoleon's downfall is crammed with major events. In the period between 1815 and 1870 the industrial revolution came of age, modern doctrines of socialism were born, and Darwin initiated a great revolution in science. In politics, during the same period, Great Britain, France, and the United States took important steps toward democracy, and Italy and Germany at last achieved their national unification. All these developments, though they were well under way by the middle years of the nineteenth century, reached a climax in the 1860's and 1870's. Detailed treatment of them will, therefore, be postponed to later chapters—the impact of industrialism to Chapter XIII; the growth of the Atlantic democracies to Chapter XIV; the unification of Italy and Germany to Chapters XIV and XV; and the Darwinian revolution to Chapter XVI. In this chapter we shall survey the political history of continental Europe during the generation immediately following 1815.

On the Continent, the post-Napoleonic age was an age of revolution. Despite the ascendancy of conservative forces in 1815, revolutionary outbreaks occurred in the 1820's, in 1830, and in 1848. None of these revolutions was as formidable as the great upheaval of 1789; few of them fully attained their goals; many were suppressed by still powerful counter-revolutionary forces. But all of them disturbed the status quo to some degree and played a part in the destruction of the European balance established by the peacemakers at Vienna in 1814-15.

The leaders of these early nineteenth-century revolutions despised as useless and regressive the traditions so revered by conservatives. Opposing the counter-revolutionary alliance of Throne and Altar, they stood for Liberty, Equality, and Fraternity. Liberty and Equality continued to mean demands for the expansion of the individual's political power through the widening of civil rights, the institution of representative assemblies, and the granting of constitutions—limited monarchies for the majority of states, and republics for the most advanced, like France. Liberty and Equality continued to mean the abolition of feudal and clerical privileges in society and, with few exceptions, laissez-faire in economics. For these aspects of the revolutionary program the proper label is that vague but indispensable term—*liberalism*. Almost every leader of revolution proclaimed himself a liberal, although, as we shall soon see, the kind of liberalism actually practiced by revolutionaries varied from the narrow to the sweeping.

The third word of the great revolutionary motto came to have a more precise meaning. Fraternity, now greatly intensified by the Romantic cult of the nation and the national past, continued to evolve into the formidable doctrine of nationalism. The nationalists of the post-1815 generation dreamed of a world in which each nation would be free of domination by any other, and all nations would live together harmoniously. In terms of practical politics, this signified movements toward national unity and national independence. It meant growing pressure for the unification of Germany and Italy. And it meant demands for national freedom by peoples living under the control of a foreign power—by Belgians against their Dutch rulers, by Poles against Russians, by Greeks and Serbs against Turks, and by Italians, Hungarians, and Czechs against the Austrian Habsburg government in Vienna, to mention only the most striking examples.

II: The Revolutions of the 1820's

The Iberian States and Naples

The first revolutionary outbreaks after 1815 took place in Spain, Portugal, and the Kingdom of the Two Sicilies. In all three states the return to legitimacy restored the Old Régime at its least enlightened. The great majority of the population responded to the restoration calmly, even enthusiastically. The aristocracy were delighted to recover their ancient privileges; the poor and ignorant peasants welcomed the return of familiar traditions. But a small minority, drawn chiefly from the middle class, the intellectuals, and the army, dissented. In Spain and Italy, they greatly regretted the abrogation of the *Code Napoléon*, and of the anti-feudal and anticlerical legislation introduced by the French. In all three states the discontent of the liberal minority produced the revolutionary movement of 1820.

The trouble began in Spain. During the war against Napoleon, representatives from Cadiz and other commercial towns had framed the Constitution of 1812. This document, providing for universal suffrage and a severely limited monarchy, was very liberal—too liberal, indeed, to be entirely workable in a country like Spain, with her deeply rooted feudal and clerical traditions. The Bourbon King Ferdinand VII, who resumed the Spanish crown in 1814, soon suspended the constitution, restored the social inequalities of the Old Régime, and re-established the twin instruments of Spanish clericalism, the Jesuits and the Inquisition. Finally, Ferdinand determined to recapture the rebellious Spanish colonies in the New World.

The colonial independence movement was caused directly by the refusal of the colonial populations either to recognize Napoleon's brother Joseph as their king or to accept the closer ties between colonies and mother country proposed by patriots in Spain. Behind the Spanish-American independence movement lay several other factors: the powerful examples of the American and French revolutions; the sympathetic interest of Great Britain, always anxious to release lucrative markets from Spanish mercantilist restrictions; and the accumulated resentment of colonial peoples at the centuries of indifferent rule by Spanish governors. The colonial rebels won their initial success at Buenos Aires in 1810, and their movement then spread rapidly to Spain's other American possessions. Ferdinand threatened to crush the rebels by force; to transport troops he augmented the small Spanish fleet with three leaky hulks purchased from Russia. At the end of 1819, this motley new armada, carrying 20,000 men, was about to sail from Cadiz. It never sailed, for on January 1, 1820, a mutiny broke out at Cadiz led by the liberal Colonel Riego. Uprisings soon followed in Madrid, in Barcelona, and in other Spanish cities. The revolutionaries sang "Riego's Hymn," with the refrain "Swallow it, you dog" (the "it" referred to the Constitution of 1812). Ferdinand surrendered before the force of the revolutionaries.

The liberal minorities in Portugal and Naples soon followed the Spanish lead. An army faction seized control of the Portuguese government in 1820, abolished the Inquisition, and set up a constitution on the Spanish model of 1812. In Naples, the revolution was the work of the *Carbonari* (charcoal-burners), a secret society with a vaguely liberal program and a membership of more than 50,000. King Ferdinand I of the Two Sicilies, who was the uncle of the Spanish Ferdinand VII, gave in at the first sign of opposition in 1820 and accepted a constitution of the Spanish type.

The strength of the revolutionary movement of 1820 ebbed as quickly as it had risen. The Spanish Constitution of 1812 did not work in states where the population had next to no experience in the difficult art of self-government. The reforms introduced precipitately by the inept liberal leaders in Spain and Naples soon alienated the bulk of the population at home and alarmed the conservative leaders of the great powers. Only in Portugal did the revolutionary ré-

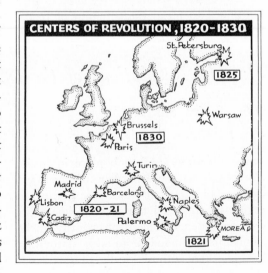

CENTERS OF REVOLUTION, 1820-1830

gime survive for long, and there it inaugurated a long period of confusion and instability. The great Portuguese colony of Brazil profited by the confusion to declare itself independent of the mother country (1822).

The revolutions of 1820 tested both the stability of the Vienna settlement and the solidarity of the Quadruple Alliance of Britain, Prussia, Austria, and Russia. Legitimacy was again restored in Spain and Italy, but the process of restoration split the Quadruple Alliance in two. Britain increasingly moved toward a policy of non-intervention in the domestic affairs of other states; her three continental allies increasingly favored armed intervention to suppress revolution. The split became evident at the conference of the Quadruple Alliance meeting at Troppau in Silesia late in 1820. Castlereagh, the British foreign minister, knowing that the Neapolitan revolution threatened the Habsburg hegemony in Italy, was willing that Austria should intervene in Naples, but without the backing of the Alliance. The Alliance, Castlereagh declared, was never designed "for the superintendence of the internal affairs of other states." Metternich, on the other hand, was determined to secure a blanket commitment from the alliance. In spite of the protests of Britain, the Troppau Protocol (November, 1820) was signed by Austria, Prussia, and Russia. It declared that

States which have undergone a change of Government, due to revolution, the results of which threaten other states, *ipso facto* cease to be members of the European Alliance, and remain excluded from it until their situation gives guarantees for legal order and stability. If, owing to such alterations, immediate danger threatens other states, the Powers bind themselves, by peaceful means, or if need be by arms, to bring back the guilty state into the bosom of the Great Alliance.*

Under the terms of the Troppau Protocol, an Austrian army duly toppled the revolu-

* Quoted in W. A. Phillips, *The Confederation of Europe* (New York, 1920), 208-209.

tionary government of Naples in 1821, and in 1823 a French army crossed the Pyrenees and restored the absolute authority of Ferdinand VII.

The French intervention in Spain provoked the strong opposition of Great Britain and ended the Quadruple Alliance. Canning, who had succeeded Castlereagh as British Foreign Minister in 1822, suspected that the continental powers might now aid Spain to recover her former American colonies. So also did the United States, which had recognized the independence of the Latin-American republics. But America also feared both a possible Russian move southward from Alaska along the Pacific coast and an attempt by Britain to extend her sphere of control in the Caribbean. Therefore, when Canning proposed a joint Anglo-American statement to ward off any European interference in Latin America, the government of President Monroe refused the invitation.

In a message to the American Congress in December, 1823, however, President Monroe included the statement that is known to history as the Monroe Doctrine. Here are its key passages:

In the wars of the European powers, in matters relating to themselves, we have never taken any part, nor does it comport with our policy to do so. It is only when our rights are invaded, or seriously menaced, that we resent injuries or make preparation for our defence. With the movements in this hemisphere, we are, of necessity, more immediately connected, and by causes which must be obvious to all enlightened and impartial observers. The political system of the allied powers is essentially different, in this respect, from that of America. . . . We owe it, therefore, to candor, and to the amicable relations existing between the United States and those powers, to declare, that we should consider any attempt on their part to extend their system to any portion of this hemisphere, as dangerous to our peace and safety. With the existing colonies or dependencies of any European power, we have not interfered, and shall not interfere. But with the governments who have declared their independence, and maintained it, and whose independence we have, on great consideration, and on just principles, acknowledged, we could not view any interposition for the purpose of oppressing them, or controlling, in any other manner, their destiny, by an European power, in any other light than as the manifestation of an unfriendly disposition towards the United States.

This famous document marked an important assertion of policy on the part of the youthful American republic, but it had little immediate international significance. The European powers were not fully committed to the project of restoring Spain's American empire. And, so far as they were deterred from that venture, they were deterred less by the Monroe Doctrine than by the opposition of Canning and the potential opposition of the British fleet.

The Greek War of Independence, 1821-1829

The British fleet was soon to take an important part in the Greeks' bid for national independence. The Greek revolt was part of the general movement of the Balkan nations for emancipation from their Turkish overlords. During the last quarter of the eighteenth century, the Christian peoples of the Balkan peninsula began to awaken to their national identities, to cherish their national past, and especially to put a high value on their native languages. The first Balkan outbreak against the Turkish authorities came in Serbia in 1804; it was led by a well-to-do pig-raiser named Karageorge. From the first, the Serb nationalists knew they would need outside help; some turned to Russia, others to Austria, setting a pattern that was to become standard. Napoleon's venture in the Illyrian Provinces (see above, p. 380) stimulated the south Slavic desire for independence. Although Karageorge's effort came to an end in 1813 with his own defection, his rival, Milosh Obrenovich, succeeded by 1830, with Russian support, in becoming prince

of an autonomous principality of Serbia. He still paid tribute to the sultan, and a Turkish garrison remained in his capital. Independence had not been won, but great strides toward it had been made.

Meantime, the Greeks had launched their revolution. Leadership of their movement came from the group known as the "Island" Greeks—merchants from the islands and ports of the Aegean Sea who dominated the commerce of the Near East and had established flourishing business outposts at Vienna, Marseilles, London, and Russia's Black Sea port of Odessa. The "Island" Greeks revived not only the old Greek trading tradition but also some of the old Greek zeal for self-government. From their home islands and from their merchant colonies abroad they poured forth a stream of patriotic exhortation. Greek nationalism sponsored a campaign to purge the modern Greek language of its Turkish and Slavic words and to return it to the classical tongue of the Age of Pericles. In the political realm, a secret society was formed in Odessa by expatriate Greeks, headed by Ypsilanti, a Greek aristocrat who was a general in the Russian army, and patterned after the Carbonari of Italy and the Freemasons.

In 1821, Ypsilanti led a Greek expedition into the Rumanian areas of the Ottoman Empire but failed in his aim to stir up a major revolt. The conspirators were more successful in Greece proper, where they fomented a revolt among the peasants of the Morea, the southern peninsula of Greece. The ensuing war for independence was a ferocious conflict: the Morean peasants slaughtered every Turk they could lay their hands on; the Ottoman government retaliated by killing or selling into slavery thirty thousand Greeks from the prosperous Aegean island of Chios (Scio), an atrocity that inspired Delacroix's famous painting. In the work of repression the Ottoman emperor enlisted the aid of his powerful Egyptian vassal, Mehemet Ali. By 1827, it ap-

Romantic painting. Delacroix, "The Massacre at Scio," 1824.

peared likely that the punitive expedition organized by Mehemet Ali would recapture the last rebel strongholds. Then Britain, France, and Russia intervened to save the Greek independence movement at its darkest hour.

The three-power action resulted from the combined pressures of public opinion and strategic interests. In Britain and France, and also in Germany and the United States, the Philhellenic (pro-Greek) movement had won legions of supporters. "We are all Greeks," Shelley declared in 1821:

> Our laws, our literature, our religion, our arts, have their roots in Greece. But for Greece, Rome . . . would have spread no illumination with her arms, and we might still have been savages and idolators.*

Philhellenic committees sent supplies and money and demanded that civilized governments intervene openly. Intervention hinged on the action of Russia, for Greek patriots had formed their secret society at Odessa, on Russian soil and with Russian backing. For a time, Metternich was able to restrain Russia; ultimately, Russia rallied openly to the Greek cause. The British and French governments now feared to let Russia act alone lest she gain mastery over the whole Near East. A three-power intervention seemed the only course that would both rescue the Greeks and check the Russians.

Neither aim was fully achieved. In October, 1827, Russian, British, and French squadrons sank the Turkish and Egyptian vessels anchored at Navarino in western Greece and thereby destroyed the chief Ottoman base. The subsequent Treaty of Adrianople, 1829, allowed Russia to annex outright only a little Turkish territory. But it did arrange that the Ottoman Danubian provinces of Moldavia and Wallachia, the core of present-day Rumania, should become a virtual Russian protectorate. After considerable wrangling, the European pow-

ers accorded formal recognition to an independent Greek state of very modest size, which left many Greeks still within the Ottoman Empire. Neither nationalism nor liberalism had won a complete victory in the Greek war. Greek patriots now schemed for the day when they might enlarge the boundaries of their new kingdom. And Greek politicians were to threaten its stability and disillusion Philhellenists abroad by continuing the endless feuds that had divided them even in their desperate struggle for independence.

The Decembrist Revolt in Russia

Russia, who did so much to determine the outcome of revolutions elsewhere, herself felt the revolutionary wave, but with diminished force. A brief uprising took place in December, 1825, and in January, 1826, on the death of Tsar Alexander I. Its leaders, the "Decembrists," vainly attempted to apply and extend the program of liberal reforms which the Tsar himself had barely begun. As we have already seen in Chapter IX, the last period of the reign of Alexander I thoroughly disappointed Russian liberals. While superstition and reaction continued to color the Tsar's policies at home, liberal ideas continued to penetrate his country. As in other European countries, secret societies flourished in Russia after 1815. The introduction of Freemasonry during the eighteenth century, and the secret ritual connected with many of the lodges, had given jaded Russian nobles something of a thrill and had also enabled them to meet on equal terms with men from other ranks of society. Masonry played a role in arousing humanitarian urges and social conscience; it also afforded a cover of secrecy under which subversive ideas might be incubated. Moreover, the contrast between the relatively enlightened West and backward Russia made a sharp impression on officers who had served in the cam-

---

* Preface to *Hellas*.

paigns against Napoleon. One of the future Decembrist leaders reported:

From France we returned to Russia by sea. The First Division of the Guard landed at Oranienbaum and listened to the *Te Deum*. . . . During the prayer the police were mercilessly beating the people who attempted to draw nearer to the lined-up troops. . . . Finally the Emperor appeared, accompanied by the Guard, on a fine sorrel horse, with an unsheathed sword, which he was ready to lower before the Empress. But at that very moment, almost under his horse, a peasant crossed the street. The Emperor spurred his horse and rushed with the unsheathed sword toward the running peasant. The police attacked him with their clubs. We did not believe our own eyes and turned away, ashamed for our beloved Tsar.[*]

High-ranking officers at St. Petersburg secretly formed the Northern Society, which aimed to make Russia a limited, decentralized monarchy, with the various provinces enjoying rights somewhat like those of the states in the American republic. The serfs would receive their freedom but no land, and the whole series of reforms would be achieved by peaceful means. A second secret organization, the Southern Society, acquired a more radical character. Its leader was Colonel Pestel, and its membership included many relatively impoverished officers. On every main issue the program of the Southern Society went beyond that of the Petersburg group. It advocated a highly centralized republic, the granting of land to liberated serfs, and the use of violence—specifically, assassination of the Tsar—to gain its ends. Pestel himself, a Jacobin by temperament and an admirer of Napoleon, planned to install a dictatorship as an interim government between the overthrow of the tsardom and the advent of the

republic. In the interim period secret police would operate on behalf of the dictatorship.

Both the Northern Society and the Southern Society tried to profit by the political confusion following the death of Alexander I. Since Alexander left no son, the crown would normally have passed to his younger brother, Constantine, his viceroy in Poland. Constantine, however, had relinquished his rights to a still younger brother, Nicholas, but in a document so secret that Nicholas never saw it. When Alexander died, therefore, Constantine declared that Nicholas was the legal tsar, and Nicholas declared that Constantine was. While the two brothers were clarifying their status, the Northern Society summoned the Petersburg garrison to revolt against Nicholas. Throughout the day of December 26, 1825, the rebels stood their ground in Russia's capital city until Nicholas finally subdued them. Two weeks later, the Southern Society launched a movement that was doomed from the start because its leader, Pestel, had already been arrested.

The Decembrist revolt, for all its ineffectiveness, was an important episode. It thoroughly alarmed Tsar Nicholas I (1825-1855), who now resolved to follow a severely autocratic policy. Although he dismissed the highly unpopular Arakcheev and put an end to the military colonies, he also had five of the Decembrists executed and exiled more than a hundred others to Siberia, where many of them contributed to the advance of local government and education. The Decembrists were the first in the long line of modern Russia's political martyrs, and the program of Pestel's Southern Society may now be seen as a kind of early blueprint for the revolutionary dictatorship that came to Russia in the Bolshevik uprising of 1917.

[*] Quoted in Anatole G. Mazour, *The First Russian Revolution* (Berkeley, Calif., 1937), 55.

III: The Revolutions of 1830

France:
The July Revolution   The next revolutionary
wave—that of 1830—originated in the traditional center of unrest, France. King Louis
XVIII (1814-1824) had given the Bourbon
restoration in France a fairly promising beginning. From the first, he followed a
middle-of-the-road policy, exemplified by
the Charter that he granted in 1814. The
preamble of the Charter asserted the royal
prerogative: "The authority in France resides in the person of the king." But the
document then proceeded to establish a constitutional monarchy. The legislature was
to be composed of a Chamber of Peers appointed by the king, and a Chamber of
Deputies elected on a very restricted suffrage that allowed fewer than 100,000 of
France's thirty millions the right to vote.
"In the King alone is vested the executive
power," the Charter stated, but in practice
Louis followed the custom of limited monarchies by appointing ministers who were
backed by a majority of the legislature.
The Charter confirmed many of the decisive changes instituted in France since 1789.
It guaranteed religious toleration, equality
before the law, and equal eligibility to civil
and military office; it likewise accepted the
revolutionary property settlement and the
Code Napoléon.

The Charter, however, greatly irritated
the ultra-royalist faction, drawn from the
noble and clerical *émigrés*, who had returned to France after their revolutionary
exile. These "Ultras," grouped around the
King's brother, the Count of Artois, were
determined to recover both the privileges
and the property they had lost during the
Revolution. Louis XVIII held the Ultras at
bay for five years. When the election of
1815 gave them control of the Chamber of
Deputies, he dismissed the Chamber and
held a new election, which returned a less
fanatical majority. He chose moderate ministers who worked to pay off the indemnity
to the victorious allies and, in general, to
put French finances in good order. Then,
however, France suffered an attack of anti-
revolutionary fear, aroused by the revolutions in Spain and Italy and by the assassination of the Duke of Berri, the King's
nephew, early in 1820. The Ultras obliged
Louis XVIII to appoint a reactionary ministry, which sent French troops to aid Ferdinand VII in Spain.

The tempo of the reaction quickened
when Louis XVIII died and the Ultra
leader, Artois, became King Charles X
(1824-1830). Charles actually attempted to
turn back the clock and become a divine-
right monarch. He allowed the Church
greater influence by encouraging the activities of the Jesuits, who were still legally
banned from France, and by appointing
clerics as principals and administrators in
the state school system. The *émigrés*, in
compensation for their lost property, were
granted state annuities; to finance the annuities, the interest on government bonds
was lowered from 5 to 3 per cent. The in-
demnification of the *émigrés* could be defended as a sensible political move that
lifted the last threat of confiscation from
those who had acquired property during
the Revolution. But the reduction of interest
on government obligations infuriated many
influential Parisian bourgeois and other
bondholders.

Opposition to Charles X grew rapidly,
aided to no small extent by two young historians who were to play an important part
in French politics. Adolphe Thiers (1797-
1877) published a popular and sympathetic
History of the French Revolution and

edited a liberal Paris newspaper. François Guizot (1787-1874) wrote a *History of Civilization*, an enthusiastic account of the rise of those wealthy bourgeois who so detested the Ultras. Guizot also headed a nation-wide organization, *"Aide-toi, le ciel t'aidera!"* ("The Lord helps those who help themselves"), which urged Frenchmen to defend their legal rights against the encroachments of Charles X.

In 1829, Charles X increased the political tension by appointing as his chief minister Polignac, an Ultra of Ultras. Polignac hoped to bolster the waning prestige of his monarch by scoring a resounding diplomatic victory. He therefore attacked the Dey of Algiers, a largely independent vassal of the Ottoman emperor, and notorious for his collusion with the hated Barbary Pirates. The capture of Algiers (June, 1830) laid the foundation of the French empire in North Africa. Meanwhile, the liberal opposition in the Chamber of Deputies had pronounced Polignac's ministry unconstitutional because it had never received the approval of the legislature. In the hope of securing a more tractable chamber, Charles X staged a new election in May, 1830, but the opposition won. On July 25, 1830, without securing the legislature's approval, Charles and Polignac issued ordinances muzzling the press, dissolving the newly elected Chamber, ordering a fresh election, and introducing new voting qualifications that would have disfranchised the bourgeois voters who were the mainstay of the opposition. The King and his chief minister believed that public opinion, mollified by the recent victory at Algiers, would accept these July Ordinances calmly. They miscalculated utterly.

Aroused by the protests of Thiers and other liberal journalists, the workers and students of Paris staged a riot. They threw up barricades and on July 28 captured the Paris City Hall. There they proclaimed their intention of making France a democratic republic with the Marquis de Lafa-

yette, that aged symbol of revolution, as its president. The moderately liberal leaders of the Chamber of Deputies, on the other hand, wanted a safe and sane constitutional monarchy. Headed by Thiers, the wealthy banker Laffitte, and the perennial king-maker Talleyrand, the moderates won handily. They had the money, they had the brains, and they had the perfect candidate for the throne—Louis Philippe, the Duke of Orléans.

Louis Philippe's father had participated in the revolutionary disturbances of 1789 and had won the nickname of "Philip Equality." Louis Philippe himself had fought in the revolutionary army at Valmy in 1792 but had emigrated in 1793 before the worst excesses of the Terror. He had no use for the pomp of royalty; he dressed and acted like the sober and well-to-do businessman he was. At the close of July, 1830, the astute Louis Philippe persuaded the gullible Lafayette of his admiration for republicanism. Having won the support of the titular republican leader by this deception, the moderate deputies named Louis Philippe king in place of Charles X, who abdicated and fled to England. Though they substituted the tricolor of the Revolution for the white flag of the Bourbons, they kept most of the central provisions of the Charter of 1814. The suffrage, though enlarged, was still so restricted that only slightly more than 200,000 Frenchmen had the right to vote. Thus the almost bloodless July Revolution left France a long way from democracy; the July Monarchy, as the new regime was termed, made a very narrow interpretation of the ideals of the great revolution.

Belgium

Within a month of the July uprising in Paris, a nationalistic and liberal revolution began in Belgium. The union of Belgium and Holland, decreed by the peacemakers of 1815, did not work out very well. King William I of the Netherlands made Dutch the official language throughout his realm and refused to grant special privileges to the Catholic Church in Belgium. He denied the pleas of Belgians for larger representation in the legislature, where the Belgian provinces, though they had almost twice the population of the Dutch, received only half the seats. A common loyalty to the Catholic Church and a common concern for local rights and customs formed the foundation of Belgian nationalism. They welded together two different linguistic groups, the Flemish in the provinces north of Brussels and the French-speaking Walloons of the southern provinces.

The revolution broke out in Brussels on August 25, 1830, at a performance of a Romantic opera which depicted a revolt in Naples. Headed by students, inspired by the example of Paris—and perhaps incited by French agents—the audience rioted against Dutch rule. By the end of September, Dutch rule was collapsing almost everywhere in Belgium. The insurgents recruited their fighters chiefly from the industrial workers, many of whom were the victims of low pay and frequent unemployment. The Belgian workers, however, like the Parisian workers, lacked good leadership and a concrete political program. The better-organized middle-class liberals soon captured control of the revolutionary movement and predominated in the national Belgian congress that convened in November, 1830.

This congress proclaimed Belgium independent and made it a constitutional monarchy. The new constitution provided for real local self-government, put rigorous limits on the king's authority, and subordinated the executive to the legislature. Although it did not establish universal suffrage, the financial qualifications for voting were markedly lower in Belgium than they were in Britain or France, and the electorate was proportionately larger. The con-

gress first chose as king the Duke of Nemours, a son of Louis Philippe. Britain protested violently, for this would have brought Belgium within the orbit of France. The congress then picked Leopold of Saxe-Coburg, a German princeling, and the widowed son-in-law of George IV of Britain. Leopold was admirably fitted for the exacting role of a constitutional monarch in a brand-new kingdom. He had already shown his political shrewdness by refusing the shaky new throne of Greece; he now demonstrated it by marrying a daughter of Louis Philippe, thus mitigating French disappointment over the aborted candidacy of the Duke of Nemours.

The Belgian revolution made the first permanent breach in the Vienna settlement. Although it aroused little enthusiasm among the great powers, representatives of Britain, France, Prussia, Austria, and Russia guaranteed both the independence and the neutrality of Belgium. King William, stubborn as the proverbial Dutchman, tried to retake Belgium by force in 1831-32. A French army and a British fleet successfully defended the Belgians, and negotiations finally resulted in Dutch recognition of Belgium's new status in 1839.

Poland

Revolution did not always succeed in 1830; the case of Poland contrasted tragically with that of Belgium. In 1815, the Kingdom of Poland possessed the most liberal constitution on the Continent; twenty years later, it had become a mere colony of the Russian Empire. The constitution given to the Poles by Tsar Alexander I preserved the *Code Napoléon* and endowed the diet with limited legislative power. A hundred thousand Poles received the franchise, more than the total number of voters in the France of Louis XVIII, which had a population ten times greater. In practice, however, difficulties arose. Many of the men chosen for official posts in Poland were not acceptable to the Poles; indeed, one may doubt that any government imposed by Russia would have pleased them. Censorship, unrest, and police intervention soon developed during the last years of Alexander I.

The advent of the highly conservative Nicholas I in 1825 increased political friction, although the new tsar at first observed the Polish constitution. Meantime, Romantic doctrines of nationalism made many converts at the Universities of Warsaw and Vilna (in Lithuania). Polish nationalists demanded the transfer from Russia to Poland of provinces that had belonged to the pre-partition Polish state—Lithuania, White Russia, and the Ukraine. Secret societies on the *Carbonari* model arose in these provinces and in the Kingdom of Poland.

The secret society of army cadets in Warsaw launched a revolution in November, 1830. The rebels were doomed from the start. They split into the two hostile camps of "Whites" and "Reds," the former representing the highly conservative aristocrats, the latter the somewhat less conservative gentry. Neither "Whites" nor "Reds" gained the support of the peasants, whom both factions had long oppressed. The misery of the Poles increased with a terrible epidemic of cholera, the first outbreak of that dreadful Asiatic scourge in Europe. Russian forces, at first taken off guard, were masters of the situation by 1833. Nicholas I then scrapped the constitution, imposed a regime of permanent martial law, and closed the Universities of Warsaw and Vilna, the chief centers of Polish nationalist propaganda. To escape the vengeance of Nicholas, Polish intellectuals fled the country by the tens of thousands.

Italy and Germany

The liberals and nationalists of Italy and Germany likewise suffered defeat in the early 1830's. Italian insurgents briefly controlled the little duchies of Parma and Modena and a sizable part of the Papal States. Again, as in 1821, Metternich sent troops to restore legitimacy in Italy. Metternich did not require soldiers to preserve legitimacy in Germany; whenever a crisis arose, the Diet of the German Confederation obediently followed the Austrian lead. Royal absolutism, Old-Régime style, still dominated German politics. In Prussia, King Frederick William III (1797-1840) had promised to grant a constitution but never made good on his pledge. Mildly liberal constitutions, on the order of the French Charter of 1814, appeared only in Weimar and a few south German states where French influence remained considerable.

Liberalism and nationalism did not as yet stir the great mass of the German people, sleeping peacefully at their sovereigns' feet, as the poet Heine aptly remarked. Political agitation came almost entirely from the small minority of intellectuals—journalists, Romantic writers, university professors, and students. After 1815, German university students formed a new organization, the *Burschenschaft* ("Students' Union"). In October, 1817, to celebrate the three-hundredth anniversary of Luther's Ninety-Five Theses, the *Burschenschaft* burned a Prussian officer's corset and various other symbols of reaction. In March, 1819, a demented theological student, perhaps influenced by *Burschenschaft* extremists, assassinated Kotzebue, a reactionary writer and a Russian agent. Metternich, already alarmed by the student prank of 1817, now got the Diet of the German Confederation to approve the Carlsbad Decrees (September, 1819), which stiffened press censorship, dissolved the *Burschenschaft*, and curtailed academic freedom.

Despite the Carlsbad Decrees, political ferment continued in Germany. In 1830 and the years following, a few rulers in northern Germany, notably in Saxony and Hanover, were forced to grant their subjects a constitution. Excited by these minor successes, twenty-five thousand revolutionary sympathizers gathered at Hambach near the Rhine in May, 1832, to toast Lafayette and demand the union of the German states under a republic. Effective action for unification, however, was another matter. In 1833, the revolutionaries made an extremely feeble effort to seize Frankfurt, the seat of the Diet and capital of the German Confederation, and then relapsed into inactivity.

The Lessons of 1830   The European revolutionary movement of 1830 emphasized two great facts of political life. First, it widened the split between the West and the East. Britain and France were committed to support mild liberalism both at home and in neighboring Belgium. On the other hand, Russia, Austria, and Prussia were more firmly committed than ever to the counter-revolutionary principles of the Troppau Protocol. In 1833, Nicholas I, Metternich, and Frederick William III formally pledged their joint assistance to any sovereign threatened by revolution.

Second, revolution succeeded in 1830 only in France and Belgium, only where it enlisted the support of a large segment of the population. It failed in every country where the revolutionaries represented only a fraction of the people. In Poland, the great bulk of the peasantry viewed both "Whites" and "Reds" as oppressors. The Italian revolutionaries still relied on their Romantic *Carbonari* tradition. In Germany, revolution was a matter of student outbursts, toasts to Lafayette, and other gestures by a small minority. Liberal and nationalist intellectuals needed to make their doctrines penetrate to the grass roots of society, or at least to the lower levels of the middle class. They needed to develop able political leaders and to mature well-laid plans for political reform. These were the tasks they undertook after 1830; their success was to be tested in the most formidable and widespread political uprising in nineteenth-century Europe—the Revolutions of 1848.

IV: The Revolutions of 1848

Common Denominators   In surveying a complex international phenomenon like the revolutions of 1848, it is essential to keep in mind the common elements that underlay the uprisings. One such common denominator was nationalism, which prompted German and Italian attempts to gain political unification and also inspired the subject peoples of the Habsburg Empire to seek political and cultural autonomy. The Romantic movement had stimulated a nationalistic renaissance among most peoples in central and eastern Europe. For the national minorities within the Habsburg Empire, as for the Christian nationalities within the Ottoman Empire, the new nationalism tended to be focused on language. The Czech language, for example, was on the verge of extinction in the later eighteenth century; the population of Bohemia increasingly used the German language of their Austrian rulers. By 1848, however, a Czech linguistic and literary revival was in full swing. Patriotic histories of Bohemia and collections of Czech folk-poetry kindled a lively interest in the national past and fostered dreams of a Pan-Slavic awakening in which the Czechs would lead their brother Slavs. Some nationalists in 1848 preached with Mazzini, the democratic Italian patriot, that each nation's "special mission" fulfilled the "general mission of humanity." Others, however, advanced a more aggressive program that stressed the conflicts, rather than the harmonies, among nations.

Liberalism, the second common denominator of the revolutions, also encompassed a wide range of programs. In central and eastern Europe, where the Old Régime largely survived, liberals demanded constitutions to limit absolute monarchy and to liquidate the last vestiges of feudal rights and manorial dues. In France, where constitutional monarchy had already been

CENTERS OF REVOLUTION, 1848-1849

Berlin
Frankfurt
Prague
Paris
1848-49
Vienna
Budapest
Milan
Turin
Venice
Florence
Rome
Naples

achieved, many liberals sought to replace the constitutional monarchy of Louis Philippe with a democratic republic. French liberalism, in fact, shaded into socialism. The Paris radicals of 1848 demanded the guarantee of the right to work and other measures that still seem rather socialistic today, more than a century later.

Finally, in the Europe of 1848, as in the France of 1789, an economic crisis helped to catalyze discontent into revolution. A disastrous blight ruined the Irish potato crop in 1845 and soon spread to the Continent. The grain harvest of 1846 failed in western Europe, resulting in a sharp rise of the price of bread and in bread riots and

actual starvation. The agrarian crisis was accompanied by a severe industrial depression in western Europe. The railroad-building boom of the early 1840's had collapsed by 1847, and produced a crop of business failures. Consequently, the increase in the number of unemployed people coincided with the rise of food prices, thereby intensifying social misery.

France

The economic crisis hit France with particular severity. Railroad construction almost ceased, throwing more than half a million laborers out of work; coal mines and iron foundries, in turn, laid men off. Widespread unemployment increased discontent among French workers already embittered by their low wages and by the still lower esteem in which they were held by the government of Louis Philippe. The July Monarchy encouraged the rapid expansion of industry and trade. But the government largely ignored the social misery that accompanied the new prosperity. In its eighteen years of existence, it took only two steps for the welfare of the industrial working class: an extension of the primary school system in 1833, and a laxly enforced law in 1841 limiting the labor of children. There was a great deal of truth in the famous judgment passed by De Tocqueville, an acute political observer— that "Government in those days resembled an industrial company whose every operation is undertaken for the profits which the stockholders may gain thereby."

The 200,000 landowners, investors, and businessmen who had the right to vote formed the "stockholders" of the July Monarchy. "Get rich!" was the reply made by Guizot, a leading politician, to those who demanded extension of the suffrage. Anyone who wanted to vote could do so, provided he first made himself rich enough to meet the stiff property qualifications for the ballot. The government banned labor organizations and punished rioters after workmen rose during the early 1830's to demand a republic and increased wages. It imposed a censorship when the press caricatured the pear-shaped head and the familiar umbrella of the businessman-king.

The opposition, though stifled in the 1830's, revived rapidly during the 1840's. It was not a united opposition—a fact that goes far to explain the hectic course of the revolution it set off. Heading one group was Adolphe Thiers, a principal architect of the July Monarchy, who was shelved by Louis Philippe in 1840 in favor of Guizot, the chief minister from then until 1848. Thiers continued to support the principle of constitutional monarchy; the chief difference between him and Guizot was the fact that he was out of office while Guizot was in. The disappointed republicans of 1830 formed a second opposition group. The third, and smallest, group took in various socialists, who were to gain recruits from the economic depression of the late 1840's. Potentially more formidable than any of these, but as yet representing only a vague, unorganized sentiment, were the Bonapartists. The return of the Emperor's ashes from St. Helena to Paris in 1840 revived the legend of a glorious and warlike Napoleon, so different from the inglorious, peace-loving Louis Philippe.

In the summer of 1847, constitutional monarchists of the Thiers faction joined with republicans to stage a series of political banquets throughout France calling for reform and for the resignation of Guizot. This campaign appeared comparatively harmless until a particularly large banquet was announced for February 22, 1848, to be held in a radical quarter of Paris. When the Guizot ministry forbade the Paris banquet, the Parisians substituted a large demonstration. On February 23, Louis Philippe dismissed Guizot and prepared to summon Thiers to the ministry. His concessions came too late. Supported by the Parisian working class, by students, and by the

more radical republican leaders, the demonstration of February 22 turned into a riot on the 23rd. More than fifty of the rioters that attacked the residence of Guizot were killed or wounded. It has never been decided who fired the first shots, but the casualties of February 23rd at once intensified the revolutionary atmosphere. On the next day, Louis Philippe abdicated.

As in July, 1830, so in February, 1848, working-class radicals and bourgeois moderates competed to fill the political vacuum created by the King's abdication. The radicals demanded a republic that would institute the social and economic changes summed up in the formula, the right to work. Thoroughly revolutionary in spirit, these radicals still lacked the organization to prosecute revolution successfully; their new leaders were only somewhat less gullible than Lafayette had been in 1830. The middle-class moderates were ready to grant universal suffrage but were determined to protect the rights of property and to keep social and economic concessions to a minimum.

The moderates secured the direction of the provisional government formed on February 24. As a sop to the aroused Parisians, they promised to guarantee the right to work and authorized the establishment in Paris of National Workshops, apparently inspired by the socialist, Louis Blanc (1811-1882). Louis Blanc had long advocated "social workshops," which the workers themselves would own and run with the financial assistance of the state. The National Workshops of 1848, however, were simply a relief project organized along semi-military lines, and enrolling more than 100,000 unemployed from Paris and the provinces. About 10,000 of the recruits received two francs (40 cents) a day for working on municipal improvements; the rest received a dole of one franc a day.

The moderates commanding the provisional government gained new strength as a result of the election of April, 1848—the first election in European history in which almost the entire adult male population of a country exercised the right to vote. Eight million Frenchmen went to the polls to select members of the National Assembly that was to draw up a new constitution. The conservative peasants, who still made up the bulk of the French population, approved the fall of the July Monarchy but dreaded anything resembling an attack on private property. Of the almost 900 deputies elected, therefore, only a hundred or so sympathized with the Paris radicals.

The latter, however, refused to accept the decision of the country. On May 15, a noisy mob invaded the meeting hall of the National Assembly in Paris and proposed the dissolution of the Assembly and the formation of a new provisional government at the Paris City Hall. The moderates, now thoroughly alarmed, decided that the National Workshops threatened law and order because they concentrated so many economically desperate men in Paris. The Assembly therefore dissolved the Workshops and gave the recruits the alternative of enlistment in the army or accepting work in the provinces. The workers of Paris re-sisted. From June 23 to June 26, 1848, the working-class districts of the capital rose in insurrection until they were finally subdued by the troops brought in by General Cavaignac, the energetic Minister of War.

These "June Days" were a landmark in modern history, the first large-scale outbreak of genuine class warfare, with both sides demonstrating a very strong class feeling. The specter of social revolution, for the moment a grim reality, terrified the propertied classes throughout France and throughout Europe. The spirit of panic accounted for the severe repression of the insurgents: nearly 1,500 were killed during the fighting; others were subsequently deported; all socialist clubs and newspapers were padlocked. France became a virtual military dictatorship under General Cavaignac.

The fears of the moderates were evident in the formal constitution of the Second French Republic which the National Assembly completed in November, 1848. The Assembly declared property inviolable and rejected a motion to list the right to work among the fundamental rights of French citizens. In other respects, however, the constitution was a daring venture in politi-

Daumier, "The Uprising," 1848.

cal democracy. It assigned legislative power to a single chamber, which was to be elected by universal male suffrage every three years. It gave executive authority to a President, to be chosen by popular election every four years. The French Constitution of November, 1848, thus inaugurated a regime based partly on Montesquieu's doctrine of the separation of powers and on the American type of presidential government. Yet France was ill prepared to undertake political democracy. The military rule exercised by Cavaignac while the Assembly was drafting the constitution was one ominous sign. Another was the outcome of the presidential election in December, 1848. Fewer than half a million votes were polled by the three genuinely republican candidates; a million and a half were cast for General Cavaignac; some five and a half million votes and the Presidency of the Republic went to Louis Napoleon Bonaparte, the nephew of the great Napoleon. President Bonaparte was to subvert the constitution in 1851 and then to proclaim himself Emperor Napoleon III (see Chapter XIV). The French Revolution of 1848, like that of 1789, had produced a republic that ended in a Napoleonic empire.

Italy

In 1849, President Bonaparte sent French troops to Rome to defend the Pope against Italian radicals. By then the Italian revolutions were waning fast. The Italian revolutionary movement was ambitious, but weak and divided. It attempted to cast off the Austrian hegemony with only the slender military resources of the separate Italian states. Piedmont rejected the offer of assistance from revolutionary France in 1848 with the proud statement, *Italia farà da sè*—Italy will do it alone.

Throughout the 1840's three schools of liberalism, none of them commanding really wide popular support, competed for leadership. Two of them were only very moderately liberal and agreed that political power in emancipated Italy should be limited to the nobility and the bourgeoisie. But they disagreed on the issue of leadership for united Italy. One group of moderates, centered in the north, favored the single leadership of Piedmont. The other group of moderates called themselves the "Neo-Guelfs" because, like the Guelf political faction of the Middle Ages, they expected the Pope to free Italy from the control of a German emperor. The Neo-Guelf leader, the priest Gioberti (1801-1852), declared that the fate of Italy depended on "the union of Rome and Turin" (the Piedmontese capital). The Pope would head, and the army of Piedmont would defend, a federation of Italian states, each with its cautiously liberal constitution.

The third group of liberals, "Young Italy," asserted that Italy should be unified as a single state, which should be a democratic republic. The founder of "Young Italy" was Mazzini (1805-1872), the great democratic idealist of modern Italian history. Here is a statement of Mazzini's political credo:

We believe, therefore, in the Holy Alliance of the Peoples as being the vastest formula of association possible in our epoch;—in the *liberty* and *equality* of the peoples, without which no true association can exist;—in *nationality*, which is the *conscience* of the peoples, and which, by assigning to them their part in the work of association, . . . constitutes their mission upon earth, that is to say, their *individuality*, without which neither liberty nor equality are possible;—in the sacred *Fatherland*, cradle of nationality; altar and workshop of the individuals of which each nation is composed.[*]

A good European as well as an ardent Italian nationalist, Mazzini inspired the formation of Young Germany, Young Poland, and other similar movements, all joined together in a federation called "Young Europe."

Revolution struck first (January, 1848)

---
[*] "Faith and the Future," in *Life and Writings of Joseph Mazzini* (London, 1905), III, 129.

in the Kingdom of the Two Sicilies, where the King was obliged to grant a moderately liberal constitution along the lines of the French Charter of 1814. During the next two months, King Charles Albert of Piedmont, the Grand Duke of Tuscany, and Pope Pius IX (1846-1878)—whose mild reforms aroused great liberal expectations—all followed suit. The news of the revolution in Vienna (see below, p. 396) provoked a successful insurrection in Milan, the capital of Austrian Lombardy (March 18-22). At the same time, Venice, the capital of the other Austrian province, proclaimed itself the independent Republic of St. Mark. The swift collapse of Habsburg rule in Lombardy-Venetia inspired a national crusade against the Austrians. Charles Albert of Piedmont assumed command; Naples, Tuscany, and the Pope sent soldiers. For the moment, it seemed likely that both nationalism and liberalism would win in Italy.

But only for the moment. During the spring and early summer of 1848, Piedmont annexed Lombardy-Venetia and the two small North Italian duchies of Parma and Modena. The other Italian states, jealous of their particularist traditions, commenced to fear the imperialism of Piedmont more than they desired the unification of Italy. On April 29, 1848, Pope Pius IX announced that his "equal affection" for all peoples obliged him to adopt a neutral position in the war with Austria and to recall his soldiers. Moreover, Pius was alarmed by the increasingly radical political temper of the Roman population and by the threats of German bishops to create an anti-pope. The Neo-Guelf cause had received a fatal blow. In May, 1848, the King of Naples withdrew his contingents from the war, and the Austrians, taking the offensive, crushed the forces of Charles Albert at Custozza (July, 1848). *Italia farà da se* was an empty boast; Italy had not been able to do it alone.

A few months later, the revolutionary movement got a brief second wind. Roman radicals, dissatisfied with the mildly liberal constitution of March, rose up in November, 1848. After Pius IX had fled to Neapolitan territory, they transformed the Papal States into the democratic Roman Republic, headed by Mazzini himself. In March, 1849, radicals in Piedmont forced a reluctant Charles Albert to renew the war with Austria, but at the battle of Novara (March 22) Austria again overwhelmed Piedmont. In August, 1849, the Austrians put an end to the Republic of St. Mark after a prolonged siege and bombardment of Venice. Meanwhile, besieged by French troops, Mazzini's Roman Republic had surrendered (July, 1849).

Again subdivided into many sovereign states, again dominated by the Habsburgs, Italy returned almost completely to its pre-revolutionary status. The only bright spot in the picture was the emergence of Piedmont as the natural leader of Italian nationalism and liberalism. Despite the defeats at Custozza and Novara, despite the loss of the territories momentarily annexed in 1848, Piedmont enjoyed the prestige of having twice defied the hated Austrians.

Germany

The course of the German revolutions in 1848 roughly paralleled that of the Italian. In Germany, too, liberalism and nationalism won initial victories and then collapsed in the face of internal dissension and Austrian resistance. The failure in Germany was the more surprising—and ominous—since the revolutionary movement had begun to recruit support among peasants who wished to abolish the relics of manorialism and among laborers who were discontented by the industrial revolution. Liberal and nationalist agitation, however, centered in the well-to-do bourgeoisie and in the professional classes, especially university professors, who enjoyed more influence and respect in Germany than anywhere else in Europe. Except for a few republicans and socialists, the German liberals were moderates. They wanted constitutional monarchy in the various German states, an end to the repressive hegemony of Metternich, and the strengthening of the German Confederation.

The hero of German liberals was King Frederick William IV of Prussia (1840-1861). Attractive and cultivated, the Prussian king was also infatuated with divine-right concepts of kingship. He promised much but delivered little. He promised to carry out his father's unhonored pledge to give Prussia a constitution and a representative assembly. But the diet that he convoked at last in 1847 was neither popularly elected nor allowed the initiative in legislation.

Not this royal knight-errant, but rather the *Zollverein* (customs union) constituted Prussia's most solid contribution to German unification before 1848. In 1818, Prussia had abolished internal tariffs within its scattered territories and had applied a uniform tariff schedule to imports. This reasonable innovation so stimulated commerce that by 1844 almost all the German states, except for Austria, had joined the customs union. The *Zollverein* liberated Germany from the oppressive burden of local tolls and taxes and cleared the way for her phenomenal economic development later in the century. It suggested that the state which had achieved the economic unification of the Germans might naturally take the initiative in political unification.

Political unification seemed almost a certainty in 1848. Stimulated by the example of Paris, the revolutionaries scored their first successes in the western German states at the end of February, 1848. From there, the demands for constitutions, civil liberties, and a strengthened German Confederation spread rapidly. By mid-March, demonstrators were throwing up barricades in Berlin. Frederick William IV accepted some of the liberals' demands and appealed for calm among "ye inhabitants of my true and beautiful Berlin." His appeal came too late. Before it could be fully publicized, rioting broke out with redoubled violence, and more than two hundred rioters, chiefly workingmen, were killed. The mob broke into the royal palace and forced the King to go through a grotesque ceremony of saluting the corpses of the victims. Overwrought by the humiliation to himself and by the death of his subjects, Frederick William accepted all the demands of liberals and nationalists. He summoned a constitutional convention for Prussia, declared Prussia "merged in Germany," and proclaimed himself "King of the free regenerated German nation."

Drastic reform of the German Confederation now began. In May, 1848, a great constitutional convention held its first session at Frankfurt, the capital of the Confederation. Its members, popularly elected throughout Germany, represented the flower of the German intelligentsia: 18 doctors, 33 clergymen, 49 university professors, 57 schoolteachers, 223 lawyers and judges —but only one dirt farmer, and not a single laboring man.

The Frankfurt Assembly had to decide the geographical limits of Germany. The Confederation included Austria proper but excluded most of the non-German Habsburg territories. Neither did it include the eastern provinces of Prussia, notably those acquired in the partitions of Poland. The Austrian issue divided the assembly into two camps: the "Big Germans" who favored, and the "Little Germans" who opposed, the inclusion of Austria and Bohemia in the projected German state. Austrian opposition to a "Big Germany" insured the Assembly's adoption of the "Little Germany" proposal. On the question of Prussian Poland, the Frankfurt Assembly voted by a large majority to include some Prussian areas in which the Poles formed the majority of the population. The arguments advanced against the Poles in the assembly debates revealed German nationalism at its most superheated. One orator declared that the minority of Germans had a natural right to rule the Poles, who had "less cultural content":

It is high time for us . . . to wake to a wholesome national egotism, to say the word right out for once, which in every question places the welfare and honour of the fatherland uppermost. . . . Our right is none other than the right of the stronger, the right of conquest.*

In contrast, the national constitution promulgated by the Frankfurt Assembly in March, 1849, was a decidedly liberal document, a combination of principles drawn from the American federal system and British parliamentary practice. The individual states were to surrender many of their powers to the German federal government. The federal legislature would consist of a lower house, elected by universal male suffrage, and an upper house, chosen by the governments and the legislatures of the constituent states. Ministers responsible to the legislature would form the federal executive; over all would preside a constitutional monarch, the German emperor. The Assembly elected the King of Prussia to be emperor, but Frederick William, ignoring his fine promises of March, 1848, and alarmed by Austrian opposition, rejected the offer. He called the Frankfurt Constitution a "bastard" product. Since the major candidate for the imperial office had balked, the Frankfurt Assembly soon came to an end. It had never secured recognition from foreign governments, had never raised a penny in taxes, had never exerted real sovereignty over Germany. It had demonstrated that the national unity of Germany could not be achieved through moral suasion.

German liberalism, too, suffered a major defeat. After the initial shock of the revolutions, the German princes either revoked or abridged the constitutions that they had granted in 1848. In Prussia, Frederick William and his conservative advisers repeatedly doctored the work of the constitutional convention summoned in 1848. The end product, the Constitution of 1850, made Prussia relatively safe for autocracy and aristocracy down to World War I (for details, see Chapter XV).

The Habsburg Domains

The fate of German and Italian nationalism in 1848 rested partly with the outcome of the revolutions in the Habsburg Empire. If these revolutions had immobilized the Habsburg government for a long period, then Italian and German unification might have been realized. But Austria, though buffeted by wave after wave of revolution, rode out the storm. The success of the counter-revolution in the Habsburg Empire assured its victory in Italy and Germany.

The nature and the outcome of the Habsburg revolutions depended in turn on the complex structure of nationalities within the Austrian Empire:

NATIONALITIES UNDER HABSBURG RULE, 1848

Nationality	Percentage of Total Population
German	23
Magyar (Hungarian)	14
Czech and Slovak	19
South (Yugo-) Slav	
Slovene	4
Croat	4
Serb	5
Pole	7
Ruthenian (Little Russian)	8
Rumanian	8
Italian	8

These national groups were not always neatly segregated geographically, each in its own compartment. For instance, in the Hungarian part of the Empire the Magyars dominated but fell slightly short of a numerical majority. Hungary contained important minorities of Slovaks, Rumanians, Croats, Serbs, and Germans.

Nationalism developed particular force not only among Italians and Czechs but also

---

* Quoted in J. G. Legge, *Rhyme and Revolution in Germany* (London, 1918), 397.

among Magyars and Croats. Magyar nationalism won its first victory in 1844, when it secured the substitution of the Hungarian language for the traditional Latin as the official language of the Hungarian sections of the Empire. Now Hungary was largely a rural country, still dominated by nobles and country squires who controlled its political life by their monopoly of seats in the county assemblies and the central diet. One school of Magyar nationalists aimed at the gradual modernization of Hungary's culture and economy along English lines. The more extreme nationalists, however, whose spokesman was the spellbinding orator, Louis Kossuth (1802-1894), regarded the linguistic reform of 1844 as but the first in a revolutionary series of projects cutting the ties with the Vienna government. Magyar nationalists bitterly opposed the satisfaction of the growing national aspirations of their Slavic subjects, like the Croats whose national awakening had begun when their homeland was exposed to French revolutionary influences as the Illyrian Provinces of Napoleon's empire.

The antagonism between Croats and Magyars revealed an all-important fact about the nationalistic movements within the Habsburg Empire. Some nationality groups—Italians, Magyars, Czechs, Poles—resented the German-dominated government in Vienna. Others, notably the Croats and Rumanians, were not so much anti-German as anti-Hungarian. Here was a situation where the central government might apply to advantage the policy of "divide and conquer," pitting the anti-Magyar elements against the anti-German Magyars, and conquering both. This was substantially what happened in 1848.

Liberalism also played a significant part in the Habsburg revolutions. Austria proper was the center of liberal discontent. The expanding middle class desired guarantees of civil liberties, a voice in government, and the lifting of the mercantilist restrictions that hampered business activity. In Vienna,

as in Paris and Berlin, the workers went further and demanded radical democratic reforms. From 1815 to 1848, the Habsburg government virtually ignored the grumblings and protests that arose in almost every quarter of the Empire. If Prince Metternich had had his way, he would probably have made some concessions to liberal and nationalist aspirations. But Metternich, though he enjoyed a nearly free hand in foreign affairs, did not have his way in domestic policy. He was blocked by the emperors—the bureaucratic Francis I (1792-1835) and the feeble-minded, epileptic Ferdinand I (1835-1848)—and by the vested interests of the aristocrats.

The news of the February revolution in Paris shook the Empire to its foundations. Four separate revolutions broke out almost simultaneously in March, 1848—in Italy (as we have just seen), in Hungary, in Vienna itself, and in Bohemia. In Hungary, Kossuth and his ardent Magyar supporters forced Emperor Ferdinand to accept the "March Laws," which gave Hungary political autonomy within the Empire. The March Laws instituted parliamentary government and substituted an elected legislature for the feudal Hungarian diet. They abolished serfdom and ended the immunity of nobles and gentry from taxation. But the new constitution rode roughshod over the rights of non-Magyars in Hungary by making use of the Hungarian language a requirement for election as a deputy to the legislature.

Aroused by the Hungarian revolt, the workers and university students of Vienna rose on March 12. On the next day, Prince Metternich resigned from the post he had held for thirty-nine years and fled to Britain disguised as an English gentleman. Although the imperial government repeatedly promised reforms, rioting continued in Vienna, and by May the political atmosphere was so charged that Emperor Ferdinand and his family left the capital. Pending the meeting of a constituent assembly in July, the effective government in Vienna was entrusted to a revolutionary council.

Meanwhile, in Prague, the Bohemian capital, Czech nationalists were demanding rights similar to those granted the Magyars in the March Laws. Discontent mounted with the news that the "Big German" faction at Frankfurt was contemplating the inclusion of Bohemia in a German federation. In June, 1848, the Czechs organized a Pan-Slav Congress to promote the solidarity of Slavic peoples against "Big German" encroachments. The Pan-Slav Congress set off demonstrations, in the course of which Princess Windischgrätz, the wife of the commander of the Austrian garrison at Prague, was accidentally killed (June 12, 1848). Five days later, Prince Windisch-

Metternich.

grätz, after bombarding Prague, dispersed the Czech revolutionaries and established a military dictatorship in Bohemia. The counter-revolution was beginning.

A month later (July), the Austrian army in Italy defeated Piedmont at Custozza. In September, 1848, the Vienna Constituent Assembly, which represented all the provinces of the Empire except the Italian and Hungarian, passed a great reform measure that actually strengthened the counter-revolution. It emancipated the peasantry from their last remaining servile obligations, notably the requirement to work for their landlords. The peasants, the great core of the Habsburg population, had secured their main ambition; they therefore tended to withdraw their support from further revolutionary activities.

The time was ripe for the policy of "divide and conquer." In the Hungarian provinces, the Germans, Slovaks, Rumanians, Serbs, and Croats, all outraged by the discrimination against them in the March Laws, had risen up against the Magyars. In September, 1848, the imperial government authorized Jellachich, the governor of Croatia, to invade central Hungary. While the hard-fighting Magyars still held off the forces of Jellachich, the radicals of Vienna revolted again, proclaiming their support of the Magyars and declaring Austria a democratic republic. The armies of Jellachich and Windischgrätz crushed the Vienna revolution (October 31, 1848) and executed the radical leaders.

The counter-revolution was hitting its full stride. In November, 1848, the energetic and unscrupulous Prince Felix Schwarzenberg (1800-1852), the brother-in-law of Windischgrätz, became chief minister of the Habsburg government. Schwarzenberg engineered the abdication of the incapable Ferdinand I in December and the accession of Ferdinand's eighteen-year-old nephew, the Emperor Francis Joseph (1848-1916). Schwarzenberg declared that the promises made by the old emperor could not legally bind his successor and therefore shelved the constitutional projects of the Austrian Constituent Assembly. Schwarzenberg's reassertion of the dominance of Vienna infuriated the Magyars. In April, 1849, the parliament of Hungary declared the country an independent republic and named Kossuth its chief executive. Russia now providentially offered Austria military assistance, for Tsar Nicholas I feared that the revolutionary contagion might spread to Russian Poland unless it was checked. Schwarzenberg accepted the Tsar's offer, and in August, 1849, Russian troops helped to subjugate the Hungarian republic.

The Lessons of 1848   By 1850, almost all the constitutional governments established in 1848 were being destroyed. In France President Bonaparte, in Prussia Frederick William IV, and in Austria and Italy Prince Schwarzenberg guided the triumphant course of the absolutist revival. Kossuth, Mazzini, and other revolutionaries went into exile. In the early months of 1848, enthusiastic liberals had hailed the arrival of the "peoples' springtime." It had been a false spring.

Mazzini himself undertook to explain why counter-revolution had cut short the peoples' springtime. In 1850, he wrote from London:

Why, then, has *reaction* triumphed?
Yes: the cause is in ourselves; in our want of organisation; . . . in our ceaseless distrust, in our miserable little vanities, in our absolute want of that spirit of discipline which alone can achieve great results; in the scattering and dispersing of our forces in a multitude of small centres and sects, powerful to dissolve, impotent to found. . . . It is in the narrow spirit of *Nationalism* substituted for the spirit of Nationality; in the stupid presumption on the part of each people that they are capable of solving the political, social, and economical problem alone; in their forgetfulness of the great truths that the cause of the peoples is one; that the cause of the Fatherland must lean upon Humanity. . . . The language of narrow nationalism held at Frankfort destroyed the German Revolution; as the fatal idea of aggrandisement of the House of Savoy [Piedmont] destroyed the Italian Revolution.*

The revolutionaries of 1848 had not fully learned the lessons of 1830. They relied too heavily on spontaneous mass uprisings and expended too much energy on factional arguments. The strength of their movement was sapped by the disputes between working-class radicals and bourgeois moderates, between the followers of Gioberti and those of Mazzini, between "Big" and "Little" Germans, and between Magyars and Slavs.

"The narrow spirit of nationalism" deplored by Mazzini was by no means dispelled after 1848. It was to haunt the Habsburg Empire for the rest of its days and eventually to destroy it. The failure of the liberals to unify Italy and Germany in 1848 transferred the leadership of the nationalist movements from the amateur revolutionaries to the professional politicians of Piedmont and Prussia. In the case of Italy, the transfer augured well, for Piedmont, alone among the Italian states, retained the moderately liberal constitution it had secured in 1848. In the case of Germany, however, the anti-liberal Bismarck was to achieve through "blood and iron" what the Frankfurt Assembly had not accomplished by peaceful means.

Equally prophetic was the class warfare of the June Days in Paris. New demands for drastic social and economic reform were arising alongside the older demands for political liberties and constitutions. Europe was beginning to feel the challenge of the forces released by industrialism. The year 1848 saw not only revolutions but also the first publication of *The Communist Manifesto* by Marx and Engels.

---

* Preface to "Faith and the Future," written fifteen years after the essay. *Life and Writings of Joseph Mazzini* (London, 1905), III, 76-77.

Reading Suggestions on Revolution and Counter-Revolution

Note: Some of the titles suggested for Chapter XI will also be of use for the topics covered in this chapter.

General Accounts

F. B. Artz, *Reaction and Revolution, 1814-1832* (N.Y.: Harper, 1950). This volume in the "Rise of Modern Europe" series presents a detailed survey of almost all aspects of European history during the period indicated.

A. J. May, *The Age of Metternich, 1814-1848* (N.Y.: Holt, 1933. A Berkshire Study). A useful brief introductory account.

L. C. B. Seaman, *From Vienna to Versailles* (N.Y.: Coward-McCann, 1956). A brilliant, provocative, and sometimes provoking essay of interpretation by a young English scholar; not a beginner's survey.

P. Robertson, *Revolutions of 1848: A Social History* (Princeton: Princeton Univ. Press, 1952). Detailed, colorful, and well balanced survey of the main revolutionary movements.

Special Studies

R. Postgate, *Story of a Year: 1848* (N.Y.: Oxford Univ. Press, 1956). A lively and well-illustrated chronicle, confined to the events of a single year.

L. B. Namier, *1848: The Revolution of the Intellectuals* (London: British Academy, 1947). An important essay, castigating some of the "liberals" of 1848 for their illiberal attitudes.

J. Lucas-Dubreton, *The Restoration and the July Monarchy* (N.Y.: Putnam's, 1929). Perhaps the most useful detailed history of France available in English for the period prior to 1848; written from the conservative point of view.

D. C. McKay, *The National Workshops* (Cambridge: Harvard Univ. Press, 1933). Useful monograph on an important aspect of the French revolution of 1848.

H. Treitschke, *History of Germany in the Nineteenth Century*, 7 vols. (N.Y.: McBride, Nast, 1915-1919). Well-written and strongly Prussian and nationalistic in tone.

A. J. P. Taylor, *The Course of German History* (N.Y.: Coward-McCann, 1946). A lively essay on the period since 1815; unsympathetic to German nationalism.

B. King, *A History of Italian Unity, 1814-1871*, 2 vols., rev. ed. (London: Nisbet, 1924). An old and rather pedestrian account, but still highly useful.

A. J. Whyte, *The Evolution of Modern Italy* (Oxford: Blackwell, 1944). A good introductory account.

A. J. P. Taylor, *The Habsburg Monarchy, 1809-1918*, 2nd ed. (London: Hamish Hamilton, 1948). A spirited brief treatment.

A. G. Mazour, *The First Russian Revolution, 1825* (Berkeley: Univ. of California Press, 1937). Excellent monograph on the Decembrist movement.

C. W. Crawley, *The Question of Greek Independence* (Cambridge, England: Cambridge Univ. Press, 1930). Instructive monograph on the Greek war of independence.

D. Perkins, *The Monroe Doctrine, 1823-1826* (Cambridge: Harvard Univ. Press, 1927). Authoritative monograph on the genesis of the famous doctrine.

Sources

I. Silone, ed., *The Living Thoughts of Mazzini* (N.Y.: Longmans, Green, 1939). Useful selections from the prolific writings of the great Italian democratic nationalist.

J. C. Legge, *Rhyme and Revolution in Germany: A Study in German History, Life, Literature, and Character, 1813-1850* (London: Constable, 1918). Fully lives up to its title; contains many lively quotations from personages of the epoch.

CHAPTER THIRTEEN

The Impact

of the Economic

Revolutions

I: The Industrial Revolution

On May 1, 1851, in London, Queen Victoria opened the "Great Exhibition of the Works of Industry of All Nations." The first of many "world's fairs," this international exposition displayed the latest mechanical marvels in a setting that was itself a marvel of engineering—the Crystal Palace, a structure of iron and glass stretching like a mammoth greenhouse for more than a third of a mile in Hyde Park.

The London exhibition, of course, marked neither the beginning nor the end of industrialism. Machines and factories had already begun to change the face of Britain in the late eighteenth century (see Chapter VIII), and in the century since 1851 they have altered profoundly not only Britain and other western nations but also many other countries on the globe.

In the mid-nineteenth century it was

plain that revolutionary changes in technology and business organization were bringing revolutionary consequences for society and politics. Industrialism bound nations closer together by stimulating international exchange and by lowering the barriers of distance through improved transport and communication. Yet it heightened international tensions by fortifying nationalism with economic ambition and by inspiring a bloodless war for markets and raw materials. Businessmen demanded national policies that would foster economic development, and they sought the political rights that would give them a voice in determining those policies. The industrial revolution raised standards of living and enabled increasing numbers of men to enjoy the decencies and comforts of existence. It also aggravated problems of unemployment, low wages, and bad living and working conditions. Industrial workers clamored for the right to work, to organize, to strike, and to vote.

The rise of industry and labor promoted divergent schools of social and political thought. One school believed in the kind of liberalism preached by the exponents of laissez-faire and practiced by the July Monarchy in France. What was good for business was necessarily good for labor, too. If a worker wanted economic security and political status, he should win them through his own efforts, by becoming rich enough to obtain them. Another school of liberals, however, believed that the state should occasionally assist the workers. These moderate reformers satisfied some workingmen, but others turned to the more drastic but still peaceful changes of the type recommended by Louis Blanc and his fellow advocates of Utopian socialism. Still others accepted revolutionary socialism, the violent and inevitable class war predicted by Marx and Engels.

In short, many of the great economic and political issues that are still very much with us today came to the fore a century ago or

earlier. Industrialism created a new labor problem and intensified the older farm problem. It sharpened the differences between the champions of relatively free international trade and the economic nationalists who demanded protective tariffs. It divided liberals into the opponents and the defenders of the benevolent or welfare state. It created a radical wing of the working class, soon to be split between the rival schools of Utopian and Marxian socialism. It altered the course of human history even more radically than did a great political upheaval like the French Revolution of 1789. The force that produced these momentous changes fully deserves to be recognized by history as the Industrial Revolution.

The background of the industrial revolution stretches far into the western past. The factors that prepared Europe and America for industrialism included, obviously, the capitalism of the Renaissance and the colonialism and mercantilism of the sixteenth and later centuries. Less obviously, they also included the political, religious, scientific, and intellectual forces that shaped the early modern world. The rise of the competitive state system, the Protestant stress on hard work, the brushing aside of tradition by the scientists of the seventeenth century and by the *philosophes* of the eighteenth—all played their part in creating a society and culture ready for sweeping economic changes. Although the ultimate causes of the industrial revolution involved a wide range of human institutions, its immediate causes were largely economic. Four interlocking developments, beginning in the eighteenth century, directly produced the industrial revolution of the nineteenth: (1) the increasing application of power-driven machinery to the processes of production; (2) the more efficient production of coal, iron, and steel; (3) the building of railroads and other swift methods of transport and communication; and (4) the expansion of banking and credit facilities.

The Machine   A hundred years ago, cotton was the king of mechanized industries. Beginning with the spinning jenny in the 1760's, the use of machinery gradually spread to many phases of cotton manufacturing. In 1793, the American Eli Whitney devised the cotton "gin," an engine that separated the fibers of the raw cotton from the seeds and enabled a single slave to do what had previously required the hand labor of fifty slaves. Meanwhile, British inventors perfected a power-driven loom for weaving cotton thread into cloth. By 1851, the British census listed more than half a million workers employed in cotton manufacturing alone.

Advances in mechanical engineering made this rapid expansion possible. British engineers studied the precision techniques used by watchmakers. They devised a lathe that turned screws of almost perfect regularity, and they developed machines for sawing, boring, and turning the pulley blocks used by British vessels in the Napoleonic Wars. Eli Whitney, meantime, was undertaking important experiments at his arms factory in Connecticut. He explained that he planned to "make the same parts of different guns, as the locks, for example, as much like each other as the successive impressions of a copper-plate engraving." In other words, Whitney was discovering the concept of standardized parts, one of the basic principles of our assembly-line methods today.

Many American and British manufacturers, however, ignored the revolutionary implications of Whitney's experiments. The tempo of mechanization, though quicken-

Industrial marvels on display at the Great Exhibition, London, 1851.

ing, was held back by the survival of handicraft techniques; it was dependent on the appearance of new inventions. For example, the mechanization of the woolen and clothing industries did not come until the 1850's, when Britain produced a machine for wool-combing and the American, Isaac Singer, popularized the sewing-machine.

Coal and Iron

Coal ranked with cotton as an industry that pioneered in the solution of technical problems. Steam engines pumped water from the mines; ventilating shafts and power fans supplied them with fresh air; and safety lamps gave miners protection against dangerous underground gases. The coal output of Britain, then the world's leading producer, rose steadily from about 16,000,000 tons in 1816, to 30,000,000 in 1836, and 65,000,000 in 1856.

The increased consumption of coal resulted chiefly from the steady expansion of the iron industry, which used large quantities of coal to make the coke needed in smelting. The efficiency of smelting advanced rapidly after the development of the blast furnace (1828), in which fans provided a blast of hot air to intensify the action of the hot coke on the iron. Thanks to the blast furnace, Britain produced iron strong enough for use in bridges and in factory buildings. Yet the best grade of iron lacked the tremendous strength of steel, which is iron purified of all but a minute fraction of carbon through a process of prolonged, intensive heating. Steel for industrial purposes could be made in the early 1800's, but only by ruinously expensive

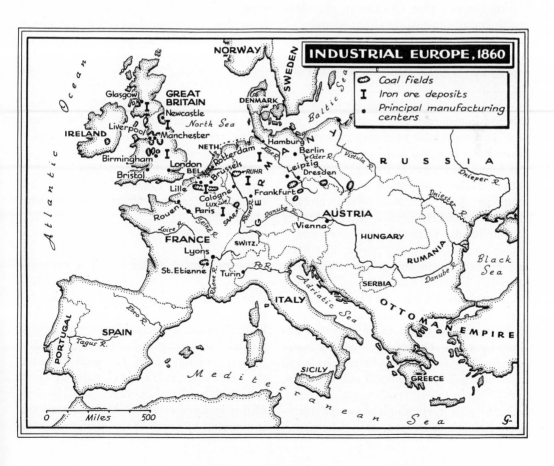

INDUSTRIAL EUROPE, 1860

Coal fields
I Iron ore deposits
• Principal manufacturing centers

methods. Then in 1856 Bessemer, an Englishman of French extraction, invented the converter, which accelerated the removal of impurities by shooting jets of compressed air into the molten metal. A decade later, Siemens, a German living in England, devised the "open-hearth" process, which utilized scrap as well as new iron, and which handled larger amounts of metal at one time than the converter could. The inventions of Bessemer and Siemens lowered the cost of making steel so substantially that the world output increased tenfold between 1865 and 1880.

Transport and Communication

A great consumer of iron and steel was the railroad, which marked the culmination of the revolution in transport. During the first three decades of the nineteenth century, many hundreds of miles of canal were dug in Europe and in North America. Highway construction was improved by the Scot, Macadam, who devised the durable road-surfacing material of broken stones that still bears his name. Canals and improved roads, however, did not provide a means for overland shipment of heavy items like coal and iron. The answer was found, of course, in the railroad. In the 1820's, methods of rolling rails and constructing solid roadbeds were already known; only mechanization remained to be accomplished. Then George Stephenson and others put the steam engine on wheels and created the locomotive. In 1830, Stephenson's "Rocket" demonstrated its power by running twelve miles in fifty-three minutes on the new Liverpool and Manchester Railway, the first line to be operated entirely by steam. The railroad building boom was soon in full swing: Britain had 500 miles of track in 1838, 6,600 miles in 1850, and 15,500 in 1870.

Steam also revolutionized water transport. Fulton's steamboat, the "Clermont," made a successful trip on the Hudson River in 1807, and soon steamers plied the inland waterways of the United States and Europe. Ocean-going steamships, by contrast, long proved uneconomical to operate because of the inefficiency of the marine engine. Only passengers and mails went by steamship; most freight was still handled in sailing ships, like the beautiful and efficient American clippers. Finally, in the 1860's, the development of better marine engines and the substitution of the screw propeller for the cumbersome paddle wheel forecast the eventual doom of the commercial sailing vessel. All these improvements in transportation by sea and by land greatly aided industry by facilitating shipments of raw materials and finished products and by opening almost the whole world as a potential market.

Meanwhile, communications were also experiencing radical improvements. A mild beginning was made in 1840, when Great Britain inaugurated the penny post: to send a letter from London to Edinburgh, for instance, now cost only a penny, less than one-tenth of the old rate. More dramatic was the utilization of electricity for ultra-swift communication. An impressive series of "firsts" started with the first telegraph message, from Baltimore to Washington in 1844. Then came the first submarine cable, under the English Channel in 1851; the first transatlantic cable, 1866; and the first telephone, 1876.

Banking and Capital

The exploitation of all these new inventions and discoveries required a constant flow of fresh capital. Here the older commercial community supported the young industrial community. Tobacco merchants of Glasgow provided the funds that made their city the foremost industrial center of Scotland, and tea merchants in London and Bristol financed the ironmasters of South Wales. Bankers played such an important role that Disraeli, the British politician, listed the Barings of London and the international house of Rothschild among the great powers of Europe. In the early nineteenth century each of the five Rothschild brothers, sons of a German Jewish banker, established himself in an important economic center—London, Paris, Frankfurt, Naples, and Vienna. The Rothschilds prospered because, in an age of frequent speculation, they avoided investment in unduly risky undertakings, and because they facilitated investment by residents of one state in the projects of other states. The Paris Rothschild, for instance, negotiated the investment of British capital in the construction of French railroads during the 1840's.

Banks further assisted economic expansion by promoting the use of checks and banknotes in place of specie. During the Napoleonic War the shortage of coins forced some British mill-owners to pay their workers in goods; the British government empowered local banks to issue paper notes supplementing the meager supply of coins. But, whenever financial crises occurred—and they came frequently before 1850—dozens of local banks failed, and their notes became valueless. Parliament therefore encouraged the absorption of small shaky banks by the larger and solider institutions, and in 1844 it gave the Bank of England a virtual monopoly of the issuing of banknotes, thus providing a very reliable paper currency. It also applied, first to railroads and then to other companies, the principle of limited liability, indicated by the familiar "Ltd." after the names of British firms. In the early industrial revolution the shareholders in most British companies had unlimited liability: they might find their personal fortunes appropriated to satisfy the creditors of an unsuccessful company. The practice of limiting each shareholder's liability to the value of his shares encouraged wider public investment by diminishing the risk.

The Timetable of Industrialization

Fiscal legislation was only one factor among many accounting for the industrial leadership of Britain in the nineteenth century. She possessed large and easily available deposits of coal and iron; the geographical compactness of the British Isles made shipments from mine to smelter and from mill to seaport short and cheap. Britain had a large reservoir of potential factory labor in the marginal farmers, driven off the land by the enclosure movement, and the Irish, emigrating from their poverty-ridden and overcrowded island. The commercial and naval leadership gained by Britain in the eighteenth century and fortified by the Napoleonic Wars paved the way for her industrial leadership. It facilitated the search for raw materials and markets, and the profits from overseas trade and the empire swelled the capital available for investment in industry. And the construction of great docks along the lower Thames during the Napoleonic Wars entrenched London in its position as the greatest economic center in Europe.

The tangible signs of Britain's economic predominance were evident on every hand about 1850—in the teeming London docks, in the thriving financial houses of the City, in the exhibits at the Crystal Palace, in the mushrooming industrial cities of the Midlands and the North of England, and in other quarters of the globe as well. British capital and thousands of skilled British workers participated in the construction of French railroads. American trains ran on rails rolled in British mills. Cotton goods made in Lancashire clothed a sizable part of the world's population.

Yet Britain did not monopolize inventive skill. France, for example, devised the chlorine process of bleaching cloth and the Jacquard loom for weaving intricate patterns. Germany led the world in agricultural chemistry and in the utilization of the valuable by-products of coal. And from the

United States came Eli Whitney, Morse and the telegraph, Singer and the sewing-machine, and Cyrus McCormick, whose reaper (1831) was the first of many agricultural machines developed in America.

The timetable of industrialization depended on much besides inventions; factories required raw materials, large amounts of capital and skilled labor, and a favorable political climate. The presence of all these elements made Britain the workshop of the world in the nineteenth century. But when other countries, notably the United States and Germany, began to enjoy a favorable combination of industrial requisites, Britain lost the advantage of her head start. Although the textiles of New England had been flourishing since the early 1800's, the exploitation of rich agricultural resources dominated the American economy until the time of the Civil War. Germany's industrialization awaited the stimulus provided by the successful completion of political unification in 1871. During the last third of the nineteenth century, both America and Germany began to hit their stride indus-trially; by 1900, they were formidable rivals of Great Britain.

Since 1900, the industrial revolution has marched steadily on, ever intensifying and ever widening. Oil and electricity have ended the dominance of coal; aluminum and the alloys have challenged that of steel; rayon and other synthetic fibers have partly displaced cotton and wool; automobiles, trucks, and airplanes have partly superseded the railroad. Industry has indeed revolutionized our world and our lives. It has created great corporations, which are virtually powers in their own right; it has made possible the newspaper, the radio, and other media of mass communication; it has devised assembly-line methods of mass production applicable to many fields of human endeavor. The full nature and the full consequences of the industrial revolution, especially since 1900, will become more evident in later chapters of this book. In this chapter, we shall stress the economic and social consequences of industrialism in the nineteenth century.

II: Economic and Social Consequences of Industrialization

The Agricultural Revolution

Improvements in industry brought improvements in farming, thus accelerating the agricultural revolution that had begun in the eighteenth century (see Chapter VIII). Factory-made implements like the reaper and the steel plow improved the cultivation of old farmlands and sped the opening of new lands, like the North American prairie. The mechanical cream-separator raised the dairy industry to a big business. Railroads and steamships sped the transport of produce from farm to market. The processes of canning, refrigeration, and freezing, all first applied on a wide scale during the last third of the nineteenth century, permitted the almost indefinite preservation of many perishable commodities. Farmers found steadily expanding markets by producing the raw materials consumed by the mills of industry and the food required by teeming new factory towns. International trade in farm products increased rapidly during the second half of the nineteenth century. Imported flour, chiefly from Canada, accounted for one-quarter of the bread consumed in Britain during the 1850's and for one-half in the 1870's. Denmark and the Netherlands increasingly furnished the British table with bacon, butter, eggs, and cheese; Australia supplied its mutton and Argentina its beef.

Germany now partly assumed Britain's old role as the pioneer of scientific agriculture. German experimenters, shortly after 1800, extracted sugar from beets in commercially important quantities, thus ending Europe's dependence on the cane sugar of the West Indies. In the 1840's the German chemist, Liebig, published a series of influential works on the agricultural applications of organic chemistry. Plant growth, Liebig argued, depended on three basic elements—nitrogen, potassium, and phosphorus. But the production of crops and fodder leached these elements from the soil; formerly fertile lands might go the way of "the once prolific soil of Virginia, now in many parts no longer able to grow its former staple productions—wheat and tobacco." Liebig's gloomy predictions did not generally come true, for his teachings promoted the wide use of fertilizers—guano from the nesting islands of sea-birds off the west coast of South America, nitrate from Chile, and potash from European mines.

Farming progressed and prospered in the nineteenth century as never before. Yet the agricultural revolution exacted a price, sometimes a very high price. Faced with the competition of beet sugar, the sugar-cane islands of the West Indies went into a prolonged depression. In the most industrialized countries the social and political importance of agricultural interests began to decline. Farming was no longer the principal occupation of Englishmen in the nineteenth century, and land was no longer the almost universal yardstick of wealth and political power. The manufacturers and merchants of Britain scored a decisive victory over the landed gentry in the campaign to repeal the Corn Laws, the tariffs on the importation of the wheat and other cereals which the English term collectively "corn." The powerful Anti-Corn Law League protested that the tariffs "artificially enhance the price of food in this country," and "prevent the exchange of the products of . . . industry for the food of other countries." Free trade was the remedy prescribed by the Anti-Corn Law League, and free trade came when Parliament repealed the Corn Laws in 1846. The decisive factor was the disastrous attack of black rot that ruined the Irish potato crop two years running and made the importation of cheap grain imperative to prevent the worsening of an already disastrous famine in Ireland (see also below, p. 442). Industrial Britain thus abandoned the attempt to be self-sustaining in food.

Changes in Population As a matter of fact, the population of the British Isles was growing so rapidly that self-sufficiency was virtually impossible. The number of inhabitants in England and Wales more than tripled during the course of the nineteenth century, from about 9,000,000 in 1800 to 32,500,000 in 1900. Yet in some predominantly agricultural countries the rate of increase almost matched that of industrial Britain. For example, the Russian population, then in the great majority rural, rose from about 36,000,000 in 1800 to about 100,000,000 in 1900.

The most important social change flowing from the industrial revolution was not the increase in the population but the alteration in its structure and balance. Wherever mills, mines, and factories were opened, towns and cities appeared. The growth of an urban population caused a rise in the numbers and influence of the two social classes that form the backbone of an industrial society. These are the businessmen and the workingmen. Industrialists, bankers, managers, and promoters of every sort joined the already established capitalists to form the modern middle class or bourgeoisie. Millhands, railwaymen, miners, clerks, and a host of other recruits swelled the ranks of wage-earning laborers.

The impact of capital and labor upon

London slums. Woodcut after Doré.

the other miseries of industrial labor have produced some of the most sordid pages of modern history, but they do not tell the whole story. The slums of the ugly new factory towns a hundred years ago were often horrible indeed, yet they sometimes represented a positive improvement over the rural slums in which the grandparents of the mill-hands had lived. Too often, country cottages concealed behind their picturesque exteriors a contaminated water supply, a total lack of sanitary facilities, and an appalling incidence of infant mortality and tuberculosis. In the cities, infant mortality dropped because of improvements in medicine and sanitation. Adults lived longer because they had better hospital facilities, ate a more balanced and nourishing diet—when they could afford it—and observed a higher standard of personal cleanliness.

The Aspirations of the Middle Class

Both the businessmen and the workingmen nourished grievances—and aspirations. A revealing view of middle-class complaints and hopes is given in a famous parable published by the French Utopian socialist, Saint-Simon, in 1819. Saint-Simon supposed that France suddenly lost fifty of her best mechanical engineers, architects, doctors, bankers—and so on through a long list comprising the three thousand leading men in business, science, and the arts. These men, Saint-Simon stated, are "the most useful to their country"; "the nation would become a lifeless corpse as soon as it lost them."

Let us pass on to another assumption. Suppose that France preserves all the men of genius that she possesses in the sciences, fine arts and professions, but has the misfortune to lose in the same day Monsieur the King's brother [and many other members of the royal family]. Suppose that France loses at the same time all the great officers of the royal household, all the ministers (with or without portfolio), all the councillors of state, all the chief magis-

the life of industrial nations was becoming increasingly evident by the middle of the nineteenth century. Some of the signs pointed to steady material progress—the wonders of the Crystal Palace, or the conquest of space by the railroad, the steamship, and the telegraph. Other signs, however, portended serious dislocation and violent change. The repeal of the Corn Laws buried an old agrarian way of life in Britain. The industrial depression of the late 1840's suggested an alarming pattern for economic slumps. By throwing hundreds of thousands out of work it aggravated social discontent, and in Paris, where its effects were intensified by the political events of the Revolution of 1848, it led to the class warfare of the "June Days" (see Chapter XII).

Now it is essential for the student of history to fix his attention on both the peaceful and the disruptive social effects of the industrial revolution. Unemployment and

trates, marshals, cardinals, archbishops, bishops, vicars-general, judges, and, in addition, ten thousand of the richest proprietors who live in the style of nobles.

This mischance would certainly distress the French, because they are kind-hearted, and could not see with indifference the sudden disappearance of such a large number of their compatriots. But this loss of thirty-thousand individuals, considered to be the most important in the State, would only grieve them for purely sentimental reasons and would result in no political evil for the State.

These suppositions underline the most important fact of present politics: . . . that our social organization is seriously defective. . . .

The scientists, artists, and artisans, the only men whose work is of positive utility to society, and cost it practically nothing, are kept down by the princes and other rulers who are simply more or less incapable bureaucrats. Those who control honours and other national awards owe, in general, the supremacy they enjoy, to the accident of birth, to flattery, intrigue and other dubious methods. . . .

These suppositions show that society is a world which is upside down.*

To the men of the middle class, society indeed seemed upside down. In the Britain of the 1820's the new industrialists had small opportunity to mold national policy. Booming industrial cities like Manchester and Birmingham sent not a single representative to the House of Commons. A high proportion of businessmen belonged not to the Church of England but to non-Anglican Protestant chapels; nonconformists, as these dissenters were now termed, still suffered discrimination when it came to holding public office or sending their sons to Oxford or Cambridge. Even in France, despite the gains made in 1789, the bourgeois enjoyed as yet only the second-class citizenship sketched by Saint-Simon.

The middle classes very soon won the place in the sun which they felt they deserved. In Britain, the gradual process of reform gave them substantially all they wanted. The high spot, higher even than

* Saint-Simon, *Selected Writings*, F. M. H. Markham, ed. (New York, 1952), 72-74.

the repeal of the Corn Laws, was the Reform Bill of 1832, which extended the suffrage to the middle class (for details, see Chapter XIV). In France, as we have already seen, the bourgeois had their revolution in 1830 and got their citizen-king. In Belgium, the revolution of 1830 marked a very great advance in the power of the middle class. Elsewhere the movements of 1830 and 1848 had less favorable results, yet even at their most disappointing they represented a step forward in the political evolution of the middle class.

The Grievances of the Working Class

The grievances of workingmen were more numerous than those of their masters, and they were more difficult to satisfy. The right of laborers to vote and their right to organize and carry on union activities may serve as examples. In Britain, substantial numbers of workers first secured the vote in 1867, a generation after the enfranchisement of the wealthier middle class. In France, universal male suffrage was tried for a brief period starting in 1848; it became permanent only with the establishment of the Third Republic after 1870. During most of the nineteenth century, labor unions and strikes were regarded as improper restraints on the free operation of natural economic laws. Hence the specific ban on such combinations, as they were termed, imposed by the British Combination Acts at the close of the eighteenth century.

Continental governments imposed similar restrictions. It took labor a long time to win legal recognition of union activities— until 1890 in Germany, for instance, 1867 in Austria, and 1872 in the Netherlands. In France, the July Monarchy repressed strikes with great brutality; unions gained legal status only in 1884. In Britain, Parliament modified the Combination Acts early, in the 1820's, but did not repeal them until 1876.

Labor's drive for political and legal rights, however, was only a side issue during the early days of the industrial revolution. Workmen faced more immediate problems: they had to find jobs and to make ends meet on inadequate wages. The modern western world has always experienced the business cycle, with its alternations of full employment and unemployment. The industrial revolution intensified the cycle. Boom periods became more hectic and more prosperous, and general depressions, like that of the late 1840's, became more frequent and more severe. Factories at first made little attempt to provide a fairly steady level of employment in both boom times and slack times. When a batch of orders came in, machines and men were worked to capacity until the orders were filled. Then the factory simply shut down to await the next flurry of orders.

A century and more ago labor sometimes got such low wages that only a single man could maintain himself on his earnings. The French or British textile worker who was a family man might have to put both his children and his wife to work as a matter of sheer economic necessity. Humanitarian tradition probably exaggerates the extent to which industry exploited and degraded women and children, probably tends to view the exceptional instance of extreme hardship as the average situation. Nevertheless, exploitation and degradation unquestionably did occur. Just as one lynching is a shocking thing, so it is a shocking thing to encounter one example of the kind here recorded in the testimony of a factory worker, Samuel Coulson, before a British parliamentary committee in 1831-32:

At what time in the morning, in the brisk time, did those girls go to the mills?
In the brisk time, for about six weeks, they have gone at 3 o'clock in the morning, and ended at 10, or nearly half-past, at night.

What intervals were allowed for rest or refreshment during those nineteen hours of labour?

Breakfast a quarter of an hour, and dinner half an hour, and drinking a quarter of an hour.

Was any of that time taken up in cleaning the machinery?
They generally had to do what they call dry down; sometimes this took the whole of the time at breakfast or drinking, and they were to get their dinner or breakfast as they could; if not, it was brought home.

Had you not great difficulty in awakening your children to this excessive labour?
Yes, in the early time we had them to take up asleep and shake them when we got them on the floor to dress them, before we could get them off to their work; but not so in the common hours.

What was the length of time they could be in bed during those long hours?
It was near 11 o'clock before we could get them into bed after getting a little victuals, and then at morning my mistress used to stop up all night, for fear that we could not get them ready for the time. . . .

So that they had not above four hours' sleep at this time?
No, they had not.

For how long together was it?
About six weeks it held; it was only done when the throng was very much on; it was not often that.

The common hours of labour were from 6 in the morning till half-past eight at night?
Yes.

With the same intervals for food?
Yes, just the same.

Were the children excessively fatigued by this labour?
Many times; we have cried often when we have given them the little victualling we had to give them; we had to shake them, and they have fallen to sleep with the victuals in their mouths many a time.

Did this excessive term of labour occasion much cruelty also?
Yes, with being so very much fatigued the strap was very frequently used.

· · · ·

What was the wages in the short hours?
Three shillings a week each.

When they wrought those very long hours
what did they get?
Three shillings and sevenpence halfpenny.

For all that additional labour they had only
sevenpence halfpenny a week additional?
No more.*

Excessively long hours, low pay, and sub-human working conditions were the most general grievances of early industrial workers. Many plants tolerated conditions hazardous to their employees. Few had safety devices to guard dangerous machinery, and cotton mills maintained both the heat and the humidity at an uncomfortably high level because threads broke less often in a hot, damp atmosphere. Many workers could not afford decent housing, and if they could afford it, they could not always find it. Some of the new factory towns were reasonably well planned, with wide streets and space for yards and parks. Some even had a copious supply of good water and arrangements for disposing of sewage. But in rapidly growing London the Thames soon became an open sewer so foul that riverside dwellers were reluctant to open their windows. Fantastic numbers of human

*Bland, Brown, and Tawney, *English Economic History: Select Documents* (London, 1915), 510-513.

beings were jammed into the overcrowded slums of Lille in France and of Liverpool and Manchester in England.

When a man sweated all day in a dirty, overheated factory, when he returned to cold, damp lodgings with no bathing facilities, when he ate chiefly bread and potatoes—his health was bound to suffer. Lord Shaftesbury, an English reformer of the 1840's, predicted that, unless conditions were improved, Lancashire would soon become "a province of pigmies." The industrial nations also threatened to remain nations of semi-literates. Until they finally made provisions for free public schools, during the last third of the nineteenth century, educational facilities were grossly inadequate. In England, as often as not, only the Sunday school gave the millhand's child a chance to learn his abc's. The millhand himself, if he had great ambition and fortitude, might attend one of the adult schools known as "mechanics' institutes." No wonder that in the 1840's one-third of the men and one-half of the women married in England could not sign their names on the marriage register and simply made their mark. And no wonder that Disraeli, the Tory reformer, wrote of Britain as "two nations" —the rich and the poor.

Industrial landscape. Steel works at Pittsburgh, 1876.

III: The Responses of Liberalism

Faced with the widening cleavage between rich and poor, nineteenth-century liberals at first held to the hands-off doctrine of laissez-faire.

Suffering and evil are nature's admonitions; they cannot be got rid of; and the impatient attempts of benevolence to banish them from the world by legislation . . . have always been productive of more evil than good.*

Such was the argument advanced by liberals in the British Parliament against the first piece of legislation proposed to safeguard public health. Human interference with the processes of nature would only make things worse; nature would have to take her course.

The Classical Economists

The thinkers who advanced these ideas in the early nineteenth century are known to history as the classical economists; to their enemies they were the architects of the "dismal science." The most famous of them were two Englishmen, Thomas Malthus (1766-1834) and David Ricardo (1772-1823). "Dismal science" is hardly too strong a term for the theories of Malthus. Though educated for the ministry, Malthus became perhaps the very first professional economist in history. In 1798, he published the famous *Essay on the Principles of Population*, a dramatic warning that the human species would always breed itself into starvation.

In the *Essay*, Malthus formulated a series of natural laws:

The power of population is indefinitely greater than the power in earth to produce subsistence for man.
Population, when unchecked, increases in a

geometrical ratio. Subsistence only increases in an arithmetical ratio. . . . Through the animal and vegetable kingdoms, nature has scattered the seeds of life abroad with the most profuse and liberal hands. She has been comparatively sparing in the room and the nourishment necessary to rear them. . . . Necessity, that imperious, all-pervading law of nature, restrains them within the prescribed bounds. Among plants and animals its effects are waste of seed, sickness, and premature death. Among mankind, misery and vice.*

Misery and vice would spread, Malthus believed, because the unchecked increase in human numbers would lower the demand for labor and therefore lower the wages of labor.

When the wages of labour are hardly sufficient to maintain two children, a man marries and has five or six. He of course finds himself miserably distressed. He accuses the insufficiency of the price of labour to maintain a family. . . . He accuses the partial and unjust institutions of society, which have awarded him an inadequate share of the produce of the earth. He accuses perhaps the dispensations of Providence, which have assigned to him a place in society so beset with unavoidable distress and dependence. In searching for objects of accusation, he never adverts to the quarter from which his misfortunes originate. The last person that he would think of accusing is himself, on whom in fact the whole of the blame lies. . . .†

The reduction of the human birth rate was the only hope that this prophet of gloom held out to suffering humanity. It was to be achieved by "moral restraint," specifically by late marriage and by "chastity till that period arrives."

Ricardo, too, was a prophet of gloom. He attributed economic activity to three main forces: there was rent, paid to the owners of great natural resources like farmland and

* *Essay on the Principles of Population*, Bk. I, Ch. 1.
† *Ibid.*, Bk. IV, Ch. 3.

* *The Economist*, May 13, 1848.

mines; there was profit, accruing to the enterprising individuals who exploited these resources; and there were wages, paid to the workers who performed the actual labor of exploitation. Of the three, rent was in the long run the most important. Farms and mines would become depleted and exhausted, but their produce would continue in great demand. Rent, accordingly, would consume an ever larger share of the "economic pie," leaving smaller and smaller portions for profit-making capitalists and wage-earning workers.

Ricardo tempered his pessimistic forecasts with many qualifications and reservations. He did not, for instance, believe that the size of the economic pie was altogether fixed, in other words, that the total wealth of mankind was irrevocably "frozen." Still, he did sketch a picture of eventual stagnation, of man as the exploiter, the depleter, the wastrel. Adam Smith had cheerfully predicted an increasing division of labor, accompanied by steadily rising wages. Ricardo, in contrast, brought labor and wages under the Malthusian formula:

Labour, like all other things which are purchased and sold . . . , has its natural and its market price. The natural price of labour is that price which is necessary to enable the labourers, one with another, to subsist and to perpetuate their race, without either increase or diminution.

. . .

The market price of labour is the price which is really paid for it, from the natural operation of the proportion of the supply to the demand; labour is dear when it is scarce, and cheap when it is plentiful. . . . It is when the market price of labour exceeds its natural price, that the condition of the labourer is flourishing and happy. . . . When, however, by the encouragement which high wages give to the increase of population, the number of labourers is increased, wages again fall to their natural price, and indeed . . . sometimes fall below it.*

___
* On the Principles of Political Economy, Ch. V, in The Works and Correspondence of David Ricardo, P. Sraffa, ed. (Cambridge, England, 1951), I, 93-94.

Ricardo's disciples hardened this principle into the "Iron Law of Wages," which bound workmen to an everlasting cycle of high wages and large families, followed by an increase in the labor supply, a corresponding increase in the competition for jobs, and an inevitable slump in wages. In the long run, the worker was doomed to an endless economic treadmill. Ricardo himself, however, regarded the cycle not as an "iron law" but simply as a probability. Unforeseen factors might in the future modify its course and might even permit a gradual improvement of the worker's lot.

It is easy to see why Malthus and Ricardo were regarded as great exponents of laissez-faire. It is more difficult for the twentieth-century observer to understand why they were also ranked among liberals. Yet the classical economists were indeed liberals in a sense; like the eighteenth-century philosophes, they did not doubt that natural laws were superior to man-made laws. What distinguished the classical economists from their predecessors of the Enlightenment was, of course, their pessimism. Adherents of the "dismal science" no longer viewed nature as the creation of the beneficent God of the deists; she was at best a neutral force and at worst a sinister one. Man himself—wasteful, careless, improvident—seemed once more afflicted with a kind of original sin. The classical economists put a new stress on the realities of the human predicament and supplied a needed corrective to the naive optimism of the philosophes.

Yet the classical economists, too, had their naive faith. They viewed the economy as a world-machine governed by a few simple, almost unalterable laws– Malthusian laws of population, Ricardian laws of rent and wages. The history of the last century has demonstrated the inadequacy of their view. Malthus did not foresee that scientific advances would make the output of agriculture expand at a positively geometrical ratio. He did not foresee that the perils of increasing birth rates would sometimes be averted by the use of contraceptives, first popularized during the nineteenth century, or by recourse to emigration. Many millions of people moved from crowded Europe to lightly populated America during the nineteenth century. Moreover, the size of the economic pie expanded far beyond the expectations of Ricardo, and so did the portions alotted to rent, to profit, and to wages.

The classical economists did not take sufficient account of the immense changes being worked by the agricultural and industrial revolutions. Nevertheless, the laissez-faire liberalism that they championed won particular approval from the new industrial magnates. The captains of industry were perhaps disturbed by Ricardo's prediction that profits would inevitably shrink; but they could take immense comfort from the theory that "suffering and evil" were "nature's admonitions." It was consoling to the rich to be told, in effect, that the poor deserved to be poor because they had indulged their appetites to excess. In the world of laissez-faire economics whatever was, was right, or at any rate ordained by nature. To the working class, however, the vaunted freedom of laissez-faire often meant freedom to be undernourished, ill-housed, and alternately overworked and unemployed. Understandably, the poor did not like to hear that they deserved to be poor. They sometimes felt that whatever was, was wrong and needed to be remedied, if necessary by interference with supposedly sacred natural laws.

To sum up: in the face of positive social evils, the classical economists offered only the essentially negative policy of laissez-faire. They were often very earnest men, honestly convinced that letting nature take her course was the only thing to do. Yet they were open to the accusation of acting without heart and without conscience, and of advancing economic theories that were only rationalizations of their economic interests. It is not surprising that, as a practi-

cal social and political philosophy, strict laissez-faire liberalism today is almost extinct.

Utilitarianism: Bentham The retreat from laissez-faire originated with a man who was himself the friend and patron of the classical economists—Jeremy Bentham (1748-1832). Bentham behaved precisely as popular opinion expects an eccentric philosopher to behave. He amazed his guests by trotting and bobbing about the garden before dinner, or, as he put it, performing his "anteprandial circumgyrations." In death, he directed that his body be mummified and kept at the University College of London, which he had helped to found. In life, he projected dozens of schemes for the improvement of the human race, among them a model prison and reformatory which he called the "Panopticon," because guards stationed in a central block could survey the activities of all the inmates. He coined new words by the dozen, too, some of them happily forgotten but others valuable contributions to the language, like "minimize," "codify," and "international."

Bentham submitted all human institutions and principles to the great test of utility, and denounced those which failed to measure up. The French revolutionaries' Declaration of the Rights of Man moved him to a characteristic outburst: "*Natural rights* is simple nonsense: natural and imprescriptible rights, rhetorical nonsense,—nonsense upon stilts." It was nonsense because Bentham did not believe that natural laws determined morality:

Nature has placed mankind under the governance of two sovereign masters, *pain* and *pleasure*. It is for them alone to point out what we ought to do. . . . They govern us in all we can do, in all we say, in all we think: every effort we can make to throw off our subjection, will serve but to demonstrate and confirm it. In words a man may pretend to abjure their empire: but in reality he will remain subject to it all the while. The *principle of utility* recognizes this subjection, and assumes it for the foundation of that system, the object of which is to rear the fabric of felicity by the hands of reason and of law.

. . .

The interest of the community is one of the most general expressions that can occur in the phraseology of morals: no wonder that the meaning of it is often lost. When it has a meaning, it is this. The community is a fictitious *body*, composed of the individual persons who are considered as constituting as it were its *members*. The interest of the community then is, what?—the sum of the interests of the several members who compose it.

It is in vain to talk of the interest of the community without understanding what is the interest of the individual. A thing is said to promote the interest, or to be *for* the interest of an individual, when it tends to add to the sum total of his pleasures: or, what comes to the same thing, to diminish the sum total of his pains.*

Bentham listed a dozen or so simple pleasures and pains—the pleasures of the senses and the corresponding pains, the pleasure of wealth and the pain of privation, the pleasure of skill and the pain of awkwardness, and so on. Each category was subdivided, the pleasures of the senses, for instance, into those of taste, intoxication, smelling, touch, hearing, seeing, sex, health, and novelty. And each pleasure or pain could be evaluated according to its intensity, its duration, its certainty or uncertainty, its propinquity or remoteness, its fecundity, and its purity. This "felicific calculus," as Bentham termed it, was a good example of the eighteenth century's attempts to measure the immeasurable and to apply the exact methods of natural science to the subtleties of human behavior.

Nevertheless, Bentham was no doctrinaire *philosophe*. He dismissed the eighteenth-century theory of political contracts as a mere fiction. Ordinarily, he believed, governments could best safeguard the security

---

* *An Introduction to the Principles of Morals and Legislation*, Wilfrid Harrison, ed. (New York, 1948), Ch. I, 125-127.

of their subjects by following a hands-off policy. In social and economic matters, they should generally act as "passive policemen." Hence the close and sympathetic relationship between Bentham and the classical economists. Yet Bentham realized that the state might have to become a more active policeman when the pursuit of self-interest by some individuals worked against the best interest of other individuals. If the pains endured by the many exceeded the pleasures enjoyed by the few, then the state would have to step in and do something about it. In such a situation Bentham believed the state to be, in a word of his own devising, "omnicompetent," fit to undertake anything for the general welfare. Twentieth-century theories of the welfare state owe a good deal to this aspect of Bentham's utilitarianism.

By the time of his death, Bentham was gaining an international reputation. He had advised reformers in Portugal, Russia, Greece, and Egypt, and his writings were to exert a broad influence, particularly in France, Spain, and the Spanish-American republics. As late as 1920, his "Panopticon" provided the plan for an American prison (in Joliet, Illinois). His most important disciples, however, were English. The next chapter will show how a group of them, the Philosophic Radicals, pressed for reforms by parliamentary legislation. Here we shall see how his most important English follower, Mill, broadened and deepened utilitarianism into a doctrine of democratic liberalism.

Democratic Liberalism: Mill

John Stuart Mill (1806-1873) grew up in an atmosphere dense with the teachings of utilitarianism and classical economics. From his father, who worked closely with Bentham and was a good friend of Ricardo, he received an education almost without parallel for intensity and speed. He began the study of Greek at three, was writing history at twelve, and at sixteen organized an active "Utilitarian Society." At the age of twenty the overworked youth suffered a nervous breakdown; as Mill relates in his *Autobiography*, he had become "a mere reasoning machine." So Mill turned to music and to the poetry of Wordsworth and Coleridge; presently he fell in love with Mrs. Taylor, a woman of warm personality, to whom he assigned the major credit for his later writings. The two maintained a close but Platonic friendship for twenty years until the death of Mr. Taylor at length enabled them to marry. Mill's personal history is important, for it goes far to explain why he endowed the liberal creed with the qualities which it so markedly lacked in the hands of the classical economists. He gave it new warmth and compassion.

Mill's humane liberalism stands forth most clearly in his essay *On Liberty* (1859) and his *Autobiography* (1873). But it is evident, too, in his more technical works, notably *The Principles of Political Economy*. He first published this enormously successful textbook in 1848 and later revised it several times, each revision departing more and more from the "dismal science" of Ricardo and Malthus. Even the first edition of the *Principles* rejected the gloomy implications of the "iron law" of wages:

By what means, then, is poverty to be contended against? How is the evil of low wages to be remedied? If the expedients usually recommended for the purpose are not adapted to it, can no others be thought of? Is the problem incapable of solution? Can political economy do nothing, but only object to everything, and demonstrate that nothing can be done?*

Of course something could be done, and Mill proceeded to outline schemes for curbing overpopulation by promoting emigration to the colonies and by "elevating the

---

* J. S. Mill, *Principles of Political Economy*, Bk. II, Ch. xiii (Boston, 1848).

habits of the labouring people through education."

This one example is typical of the way in which Mill's quest for positive remedies led him to modify the laissez-faire attitude so long associated with liberalism. Although he did not accept the socialistic solution of abolishing private property, he sympathized with the French "National Workshops" of 1848 and with some of the moderate socialistic projects that we shall examine later in this chapter. He asserted that the workers should be allowed to organize trade unions, form co-operatives, obtain higher wages, and even receive a share of profits. These changes could best be secured by private enterprise, Mill believed, and not by public intervention. But he also believed that there were some matters so pressing that the state would have to step in. He read the reports of parliamentary investigating committees, and he was shocked by their accounts of human exploitation and degradation. So he recommended legislation to protect child laborers and to improve intolerable living and working conditions.

Where Bentham had accepted universal suffrage and universal education only as ultimate goals for the distant future, Mill made them immediate objectives. All men, he believed, should have the right to vote; all should be prepared for it by receiving a basic minimum of schooling, if need be at state expense. Moreover, women should have the same rights—for Mill was a pioneer in the movement for feminine emancipation. He also proposed the introduction of proportional representation in the House of Commons, so that political minorities might be sure of a voice and might not be overwhelmed by the tyranny of the majority.

The scheme of proportional representation and the fears that actuated it are particularly characteristic of Mill. He made protection of the individual's rights the basis of his famous essay *On Liberty*:

A government cannot have too much of the kind of activity which does not impede, but aids and stimulates, individual exertion and development. The mischief begins when, instead of calling forth the activity and powers of individuals and bodies, it substitutes its own activity for theirs; when, instead of informing, advising, and, upon occasion, denouncing, it makes them work in fetters, or bids them stand aside and does their work instead of them. The worth of a State, in the long run, is the worth of the individuals composing it; . . . a State which dwarfs its men, in order that they may be more docile instruments in its hands even for beneficial purposes—will find that with small men no great thing can really be accomplished. . . .*

* *Utilitarianism, Liberty, and Representative Government*, Everyman ed. (New York, 1910), 169-170.

Mill, then, did not so much reject, as modify and broaden, the liberalism of the classical economists. Probably he had a more tender conscience than did Adam Smith or Ricardo or even Bentham; certainly he lived at a later time, when the vices of industrialism were plainer. At any rate, he found the exceptions to the rule of laissez-faire more numerous and more urgent than his predecessors had ever imagined them to be. Liberalism, as we understand the term today, is the legacy not of the "dismal scientists" but of Mill and of the enlightened politicians who have made the western nations more democratic over the past century.

IV: *The Socialist Response—the Utopians*

In his later years, Mill referred to himself as a "socialist." By his standard, however, most of us are at least passive socialists today. Universal suffrage for men and for women, universal free education, the curbing of laissez-faire in the interests of the general welfare, the use of the taxing power to limit the accumulation of masses of private property—all these major reforms foreseen by Mill are widely accepted policies in the twentieth-century democracies. But they are not authentically socialistic. The authentic socialist does not stop, as Mill did, with changes in the *distribution* of wealth; he goes on to propose a radical change in arrangements for the *production* of goods. The means of production are to be transferred from the control of individuals to the control of the community as a whole.

Socialism—like fascism, liberalism, democracy—is one of those key words in the vocabulary of politics so heavily loaded with moral connotations that they are bound to be controversial. Everyone uses the word, yet mostly to indicate emphatic approval or disapproval of a given policy. The

historian, however, attempts to use the word neutrally, for purposes of description and not of passing judgment. Historically, then, socialism denotes any political or economic philosophy that advocates the vesting of production in the hands of society and not those of private individuals. In practice, it usually means that the state, acting as the trustee of the community, owns major industries like coal, railroads, and steel. Socialism in its most complete form involves public ownership of almost all the instruments of production right down to the land itself with its farms and its mineral deposits.

Today we tend to term this complete form "communism"; a century ago, however, the terms "socialism" and "communism" were used almost interchangeably. A hundred years of history have gone into making the distinction now usually drawn between the two. The distinction is not simply one between incomplete and more complete versions of the same thing. Both present-day "socialists" and "communists" promote the collectivization of property. But today the socialists believe this should be achieved gradually and peacefully through normal political procedures and with at least some compensation for private owners. The communists believe that it should be achieved swiftly and violently, by revolution and outright seizure. Though the ends have their similarities, the means are worlds apart. This highly significant difference reflects the development of two divergent schools of socialist thought in the nineteenth century, the Utopian and the Marxian.

The Utopian socialists were essentially good sons of the Enlightenment. If only men would apply their reason to solving the problems of an industrial economy, if only they would wipe out man-made inequalities by letting the great natural law of brotherhood operate freely—then utopia would be within their grasp, and social and economic progress would come about almost automatically. This is the common belief linking together the four chief Utopians of the early nineteenth century—Saint-Simon, Fourier, Robert Owen, and Louis Blanc.

Saint-Simon and Fourier

Saint-Simon (1760-1825), despite his personal reverses in business, never lost the enthusiasm for businessmen that we have already seen in his parable of the old and the new leaders of France. Saint-Simon would have given supreme political power to the great leaders of industry, science, and art. But he reminded them: "Christianity commands you to use all your powers to increase as rapidly as possible the social welfare of the poor!" * Saint-Simon had all the Enlightenment's respect for science, yet he proclaimed the one science transcending all others to be the application of the Golden Rule. Reform should come peacefully, through "organiza-

tion," and it should affect particularly the idlers, the rich drones of existing society. "Organization" was Saint-Simon's favorite word, but he seldom attempted to spell out precisely what he meant by it.

By contrast, his compatriot and contemporary, Fourier (1772-1837), evolved an elaborate socialist plan, carried down to the last detail. Fourier was shocked when he found that in Paris a single apple cost a sum that would have bought a hundred apples in the countryside. Clearly, he concluded, something was amiss in a society and economy that permitted such fantastic divergences. He compared the historical importance of his apple with that of Newton, and honestly believed himself to be the Newton of the social sciences. Just as Newton had found the force holding the heavenly bodies in a state of mutual attraction, so Fourier proclaimed his own discovery of the force holding the individuals of human society in a state of mutual attraction.

According to Fourier, human beings are moved by *l'attraction passionnelle:* they are attracted one to another by their passions. He drew up a list of passions, rather like the list of pleasures in Bentham's "felicific calculus"—sex, companionship, food, luxury, variety, and so on. It seemed obvious to Fourier that existing society frustrated the satisfaction of these instincts. Society, therefore, needed remodeling, needed to be rearranged into units that he called *phalanges,* "phalanxes." Some 1800 volunteers would compose each phalanx; they would form a kind of community company, agreeing to split its profits three ways —five-twelfths to those who did the work, four-twelfths to those who undertook the management, and three-twelfths to those who supplied the capital.

Fourier's phalanx, with its relatively generous rewards to managers and capitalists, fell short of complete equality. However, it gave labor the largest share of the profits, and it foreshadowed many other features of socialist planning. Adult workers

---

* Saint-Simon, *Selected Writings*, F. M. H. Markham, ed. (New York, 1952), 116.

who did the most dangerous or unpleasant tasks would receive the highest remuneration. The inhabitants of the phalanx were to live in one large building, a sort of apartment hotel, which would provide the maximum opportunity for the satisfaction of man's sociable instincts, and would also make the routine of daily living more efficient by substituting one central kitchen for hundreds of separate ones. The sordid features of housekeeping could be left to the children, who (according to Fourier) loved dirt anyhow and could form special squads to dispose of garbage and refuse.

From start to finish, the phalanx bore witness to Fourier's reaction against the monotony of the ordinary worker's existence. Places of work would be made as pleasant as possible by frequent, colorful redecoration. Members of the phalanx would change their jobs eight times a day because "enthusiasm cannot be sustained for more than an hour and a half or two hours in the performance of one particular operation." They would work from four or five in the morning to eight or nine at night, needing only five hours of sleep, since the delightful variety of work would not tire them and the days would not be long enough to permit them to taste all the pleasures of existence.

Hopefully expecting some millionaire to finance his phalanxes, Fourier announced that he would be in his office every day at noon. For ten years he kept his daily office hour; naturally, no rich philanthropist ever appeared. Yet Fourier cannot be dismissed as a mere ineffectual crackpot. He undoubtedly had many wild notions and carried the principle of uninhibited human association to the extreme of advocating sexual promiscuity, thereby identifying "free love" and Utopian socialism in the popular mind. But he also made substantial contributions to socialist theory and to social psychology. Some of his recommendations, like higher pay for dangerous jobs and devices for relieving the tedium of work, have become common practice in the world of modern business.

Owen

One of the greatest Utopians was a self-made British businessman, Robert Owen (1772-1858). When he was still in his twenties, Owen took over the large cotton mills at New Lanark in Scotland, a day's ride from Glasgow. Although the former owner of the mills had been accounted benevolent by the standards of the day, conditions there shook Owen to the core. A large part of the working force consisted of children who had been recruited from charitable institutions in Edinburgh when they were between six and eight years old. These youngsters did get a little schooling after hours, but Owen found many of them "dwarfs in body and mind." Adult laborers at New Lanark fared little better.

Owen set out to show that he could increase his profits and increase the welfare of his laborers at the same time. He soon made New Lanark over into a model industrial village. For the adults he provided better working conditions, a ten-and-a-half-hour day, higher pay, and cleaner and roomier housing. He restrained the traditional Scottish Saturday night drunk by closing down the worst resorts, making good liquor available at cheap prices, and punishing offenders who made themselves a public nuisance. Toward children he took no such brutish attitude as that of Fourier. He raised the minimum age of employment to ten, hoping ultimately to put it at twelve, and he gave his child laborers time for some real schooling. Owen's educational practices were very much in the manner of Rousseau; advanced bookish subjects were avoided, while crafts, nature study, and other "practical" subjects received much attention.

Owen inherited much of the optimism of the *philosophes;* he also inherited some of

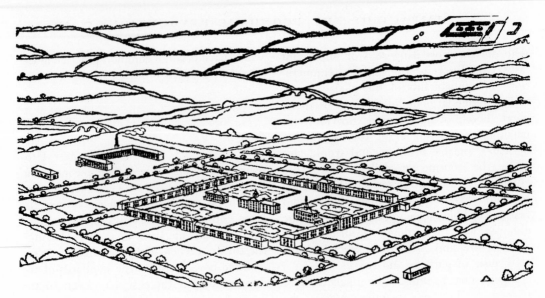

Sketch of an "Agricultural and Manufacturing Village of Unity and Mutual Co-operation," projected by the British Utopian socialist, Robert Owen, 1817.

their failures and disappointments. Despite his own success as a philanthropic capitalist, few businessmen followed his example. Disappointed but not disheartened, Owen drew up plans for an idealized version of New Lanark, very much like Fourier's phalanx. He called his utopia a "parallelogram," for the buildings were to be arranged in that geometrical pattern. It was to be a voluntary organization, relatively small in size, neatly balanced between farming and industry, decidedly advanced in Owen's recommendation for the partial abandonment of conventional ties of marriage and the family. In the 1820's, Owen financed an abortive effort to set up a parallelogram at New Harmony, Indiana. The failure of this venture did not dampen his enthusiasm. He spent the rest of his career publishing and supporting projects for social reform. He advocated the association of all labor in one big union—an experiment that failed; and he sought to reduce the expenditures of workingmen by promoting the formation of consumers' co-operatives—an experiment that succeeded. Throughout, he offended many of his contemporaries by his advocacy of sexual freedom and by his Voltairean attacks on established religion.

The Early Utopians Appraised

Both Owen and Fourier attracted a fair number of followers not only in their native lands but also in the United States, where various religious sects were already launching ventures in communal living. The American Fourierists included many intellectuals, among them the crusading editor, Horace Greeley, and the poet, John Greenleaf Whittier. They sponsored more than thirty attempts to set up phalanxes; two of the most celebrated were Brook Farm, near Boston, and Phalanx, in New Jersey. America also witnessed more than half a dozen Owenite experiments in addition to New Harmony. Like New Harmony itself, however, most of these utopias did not prosper very long; and the few that got firmly established soon returned to conventional ways of individual profit-taking and family life.

Owen and Fourier relied on private initiative to build from their blueprints the model communities that they so hopefully expected to become widely copied examples for the reconstruction of society. Saint-Simon, too, believed in the power of example, but with his stress on "organization" he presumably meant to give government a larger role. The early followers of Saint-Simon in France developed the strain of social Christianity in the master's teaching and formed a fantastic religious cult. Later, some of the Saint-Simonians did achieve notable feats of practical "organization"; De Lesseps, for one, promoted the digging of the Suez Canal. But it remained for another student of Saint-Simon, Louis Blanc, to recommend "organization" on a large scale by the state.

Implacable critic of the bourgeois policies of the July Monarchy, Louis Blanc (1813-1882) devised the scheme that helped to produce the controversial workshops of the Paris revolution in 1848. He first outlined his plan in a pamphlet, *The Organization of Labor* (1839). "What proletarians need," he wrote, "is the instruments of labor; it is the function of government to supply these. If we were to define our conception of the state, our answer would be, that the state is the banker of the poor." * The government would finance and supervise the purchase of productive equipment and the formation of "social workshops." Naturally, it was to be a democratic government, and it would withdraw its support and supervision once the workshops were on their feet. As the workshops gradually spread throughout France, socialistic enterprise would replace private enterprise, profits as such would vanish, and labor would be the only class in society. Much of Louis Blanc's socialism is typically Utopian; he, too, relies on the workers' voluntary participation to perfect arrangements for communal living. The real novelty of his plan lies in the role, however brief, assigned to the state. With Blanc, socialism is beginning to move away from the realm of private philanthropy and into the realm of politics.

------

* "L'Organisation du Travail," in *The French Revolution of 1848*, J. A. R. Marriott, ed. (Oxford, 1913), I, 14. Our translation.

V: *The Socialist Response—Marx*

With Karl Marx (1818-1883), who came from the Prussian Rhineland, socialism assumed its most extreme form—revolutionary communism. Where the early socialists had anticipated a gradual and peaceful evolution toward utopia, Marx forecast a sudden and violent proletarian revolution, by which the workers would capture governments and make them the instruments for securing proletarian welfare. Of all the socialists, Marx was the most dogmatic and the most cocksure. He was sure that he alone knew the answers and that the future of mankind would develop inevitably according to the pattern which he found in human history. His supreme self-confidence and his truculence and intolerance have earned him the label of the "Red Prussian."

Basic Principles   Marx found three laws in the pattern of history. First, *economic determinism*: he believed that economic conditions largely determined all other human institutions—society and government, religion and art. Second, the *class struggle*: he believed that history was a dialectical process, a series of conflicts between antagonistic economic groups. The antagonists were the "haves" and the "have-nots"—in Marxian terms, the propertied bourgeois and the propertyless proletarians, who, possessing nothing but their working skills, had nothing to fall back on in bad times and were thus at the mercy of their masters. Third, the *inevitability of communism*: he believed that the class struggle was bound to produce one final upheaval that would raise the victorious proletariat over the prostrate bourgeoisie in eternal triumph.

The Marxian philosophy of history derived from many older schools of thought. Marx himself was born and died in the nineteenth century; yet he belonged in spirit partly to the eighteenth. He early acquired the kind of faith in natural law that had characterized the *philosophes;* in his case it was faith in the natural laws of economic determinism and the class struggle. From this followed the boast of Marx and his disciples that their socialism alone was "scientific," as opposed to the dreamy and unrealistic doctrines of the Utopians.

The philosophy of Hegel (see Chapter XI) provided the intellectual scaffolding for Marxism. Although Hegel had died in 1831, his influence permeated the University of Berlin during the time that Marx was a student there (1836-1841). Marx translated the Hegelian dialectic into the language of the class struggle. He made the thesis the bourgeoisie, and the antithesis the proletariat; the synthesis was to be a classless utopia issuing from the communist revolution. In his later years, Marx explained his relation to Hegel:

My dialectic method is not only different from the Hegelian but is its direct opposite. To Hegel, the life-process of the human brain, . . . which, under the name of 'the Idea,' he even transforms into an independent subject, is the demiurgos of the real world, and the real world is only the external, phenomenal form of 'the Idea.' With me, on the contrary, the ideal is nothing else than the material world reflected by the human mind, and translated into forms of thought.*

But Marx also declared:

The mystification which dialectic suffers in Hegel's hands, by no means prevents him from being the first to present its general form of working in a comprehensive and conscious manner. *With him it is standing on its head. It must be turned right again,* if you would

discover the rational kernel within the mystical shell.*

By the time Marx was thirty, he had completed the outlines of his theory of scientific, revolutionary socialism. He had also become a permanent exile from his native Germany. On leaving the University of Berlin, he worked for a newspaper at Cologne in the Prussian Rhineland, then moved to Paris in 1843 after his atheistic articles had aroused the authorities against him. Exiled again, because the government of Louis Philippe feared his anti-bourgeois propaganda, he went to Brussels in 1845. Wherever he happened to be, he read widely in the economists of the past and talked long and hard with the socialists and other radicals of his own generation.

Everything Marx read and everyone he met strengthened his conviction that the capitalistic order was unjust, rotten, doomed to fall. From Adam Smith's labor theory of value he concluded that only the worker should receive the profits from the sale of a commodity, since the value of the commodity should be determined by the labor of the man who produced it. The "iron law of wages," however, confirmed Marx's belief that capitalism would never permit the worker to receive this just reward. And from reading other economists and observing the depression of the late 1840's, he concluded that economic crises were bound to occur again and again under a system that allowed labor to consume too little and capital to produce too much.

Meanwhile, Marx began his long friendship and collaboration with Friedrich Engels (1820-1895). In many ways, the two men made a striking contrast. Marx was poor and quarrelsome, a man of few friends; except for his devotion to his wife and children, he was utterly preoccupied by his economic studies. Engels, on the other hand, was the son of a well-to-do German manufacturer and represented the family textile

---

* Preface to the second edition of *Capital*, Modern Library ed. (New York, n.d), 25.

* *Ibid.* Italics ours.

business in Liverpool and Manchester. He loved sports, women, and high living in general. But he also hated the iniquities of industrialism and, when he met Marx, had already written a bitter study, *The Condition of the Working Class in England*. Both Engels and Marx took an interest in the Communist League, a small international organization of radical workingmen. In 1847, the London office of the Communist League requested them to draw up a program. Engels wrote the first draft, which Marx revised, and the result, published in January, 1848, was *The Manifesto of the Communist Party*.

The Communist Manifesto

Today, more than a century after its original publication, the *Manifesto* remains the classic statement of Marxian socialism. It opens with the dramatic announcement that "A spectre is haunting Europe—the spectre of Communism." It closes with a supremely confident appeal:

Let the ruling classes tremble at a Communist revolution. The proletarians have nothing to lose but their chains. They have a world to win.
Workingmen of all countries, unite!

In the few dozen pages of the *Manifesto*, Marx and Engels rapidly block in the main outlines of their theory. "The history of all hitherto existing society," they affirm, "is the history of class struggle." Changing economic conditions determine that the struggle should develop successively between "freeman and slave, patrician and plebeian, lord and serf, guild-master and journeyman." The guild system gave way first to manufacture by large numbers of small capitalists, and then to "the giant, modern industry."

Modern industry will inevitably destroy bourgeois society. It creates a mounting economic pressure by producing more goods than it can sell; it creates a mounting

social pressure by narrowing the circle of capitalists to fewer and fewer individuals and by forcing more and more people down to the propertyless status of proletarians. These pressures increase to the point where a revolutionary explosion occurs, a massive assault on private property. Landed property will be abolished outright; other forms of property are to be liquidated more gradually through the imposition of severe income taxes and the denial of the right of inheritance. Eventually, social classes and tensions will vanish, and "we shall have an association in which the free development of each is the condition for the free development of all."

"The free development of each is the condition for the free development of all" —the *Manifesto* provides only this vague description of the society that would exist after the revolution. Since Marx defined political authority as "the organized power of one class for oppressing another," he apparently expected the state to disappear once it had created a classless regime. He also apparently assumed that the great dialectical process of history, having achieved in the classless society its final synthesis, would then cease to operate in its traditional form. But, readers of the *Manifesto* may inquire, is it possible for the process to be so transformed? Would not the dialectic continue forever creating economic and political theses and antitheses? Will not the state always be with us? To these questions Marx offered no satisfactory answer beyond the implication that somehow the liquidation of bourgeois capitalism would radically alter the course of human history and bring the human race close to perfection.

Certainly Marx oversimplified the complexities of human nature by neglecting the non-material interests and motives of men. The history of the century since the publication of the *Communist Manifesto* has demonstrated that neither proletarians nor bourgeois have proved to be the simple economic stereotypes of Marx. Labor has often behaved in scandalously un-Marxian fashion by assuming a markedly bourgeois outlook and mentality. And capitalism has put its own house in better order by eliminating the worst injustices of the factory system. No more than Malthus did Marx foresee the notable rise in the standard of living that would take place between the mid-nineteenth and mid-twentieth centuries.

Marx never made a greater mistake than when he failed to observe the growing strength of nationalism. The *Manifesto* confidently expected the class struggle to transcend national boundaries. In social and economic warfare, nation would not be pitted against nation, nor state against state; the proletariat everywhere would fight the bourgeoisie. "Workingmen have no country" and "national differences and antagonisms are vanishing gradually from day to day." In Marx's own lifetime, however, national differences and antagonisms were increasing rapidly from day to day. Within a few months of the publication of the *Manifesto*, the revolutions of 1848 were revealing the antagonism between Italians and Austrians, Austrians and Hungarians, Hungarians and Slavs, Slavs and Germans. The *Communist Manifesto* thus revealed the greatest blind spots of Marxian socialism. The communist movement in its subsequent history has often shown a comparable failure to appreciate the significance of nationalism and has made a comparable attempt to squeeze human nature into the rigid mold of economic determinism.

Just as the *Manifesto* foreshadowed some of the weaknesses of international communism, so also it anticipated its strengths. First, it anticipated the remarkable character of communist propaganda. It supplied those effective catch-phrases that have become the mark of the communist movement —the constant sneering at bourgeois morality, bourgeois law, bourgeois property, and the dramatic references to the "spectre haunting Europe" and to the proletarians who "have nothing to lose but their chains." Second, the *Manifesto* anticipated the emphasis later to be placed on the party's role in forging the proletarian revolution. The communists, Marx declared in 1848, were a spearhead, "the most advanced section of the working class parties of every country." In matters of theory, "they have over the great mass of the proletariat the advantage of clearly understanding the line of march, the conditions, and the ultimate general results of the proletarian movement."

Third, the *Manifesto* anticipated the equally great role to be played by the state in the revolution. Among the policies recommended by Marx were "centralization of credit *in the hands of the state*," and "extension of factories and instruments of production *owned by the state*." * The *Manifesto* thus faintly foreshadowed the totalitarian state of the Soviet Union. And, finally, it clearly established the line dividing communism from the other forms of socialism. Marx's dogmatism, his philosophy of history, and his belief in the necessity for a "total" revolution made his brand of socialism a thing apart. Like a religious prophet granted a full revelation of the universe and its meaning, Marx expected his gospel to supplant all others. He scorned and pitied the Utopian socialists. They were about as futile, he wrote, as "organizers of charity, members of societies for the prevention of cruelty to animals, temperance fanatics, hole-and-corner reformers of every kind."

The Later Career of Marx

Age neither mellowed Marx nor greatly altered his views. From 1849 until his death in 1883, he lived in London. There, partly because of his own financial mismanagement, the Marx family experienced at first hand the misery of a

* Italics ours.

proletarian existence in the slums of Soho; poverty and near-starvation caused the death of three of the Marx children. Eventually, Marx obtained a modest income from the generosity of Engels and from his own writings.

Throughout the 1850's Marx contributed a weekly article on British politics or international affairs to Horace Greeley's radical paper, *The New York Tribune.* He produced a series of pamphlets, of which the most famous was *The Eighteenth Brumaire of Louis Napoleon,* a study of the fall of the short-lived Second French Republic. Meantime, he spent his days in the British Museum, reading the reports of parliamentary investigating committees and piling up evidence of the conditions of miners and factory hands. Thus Marx accumulated the material for his full-dress economic study, *Das Kapital.* The first volume of this massive analysis of capitalism appeared in 1867; further volumes, pieced together from his voluminous notes, were published after his death.

In *Das Kapital,* Marx elaborated, but did not substantially revise, the doctrines of the *Communist Manifesto.* For example, he spelled out his labor theory of value. According to Marx, the worker created the total value of the commodity that he produced yet received in the form of wages only a part of the price for which the item was sold; the difference between the sale price and the worker's wages constituted *surplus value.* This celebrated Marxian concept of surplus value represented something actually created by labor but appropriated by capital as profit.

Das Kapital goes on to relate surplus value to the ultimate doom of capitalism. It is the nature of capitalism, Marx insists, to diminish its own profits by replacing human labor with machines and thus gradually choking off the source of surplus value. Hence will come the mounting crises of overproduction and underconsumption predicted by the *Manifesto.* In a famous passage toward the close of Volume I of *Das Kapital,* Marx compared capitalism to an integument, a skin or shell, increasingly stretched and strained from within. One day these internal pressures would prove irresistible:

This integument is burst asunder. The knell of capitalist private property sounds. The expropriators are expropriated.*

In 1864, three years before the first volume of *Das Kapital* was published, Marx joined in the formation of the First International Workingmen's Association. This was an ambitious attempt to organize workers of every country and of every variety of radical belief. But the First International resembled a loose federation rather than a coherent political party. It soon began to disintegrate, and it expired in 1876. Increasing persecution by hostile governments helped to bring on its end; but so, too, did the internal quarrels that repeatedly engaged both its leaders and the rank and file of its members. Marx himself set the example by his intolerance of disagreement and his utter incapacity for practical politics.

In 1889, the Second International was organized; it lasted down to the time of World War I and the Bolshevik revolution in Russia. The Second International was more coherently organized and more political in character than the First International had been. It represented the Marxian socialist parties which, as we shall see in later chapters, were becoming important forces in the political life of the major countries of continental Europe. Among its leaders were men more adept than Marx himself at the political game. Yet the old spirit of factionalism continued to weaken the International. Some of its leaders tenaciously defended laws handed down by the master and forbade any co-operation between socialists and the "bourgeois" political parties; these were the "orthodox" communists. Other leaders of the Second International, how-

---

* *Capital,* Modern Library ed., 837.

ever, were from the orthodox standpoint "heretics." They, too, called themselves disciples of Marx; yet they revised his doctrines in the direction of moderation and of harmonization with the views of the Utopians. These "revisionists" believed in cooperation between classes rather than in a struggle to the death, and they trusted that human decency and intelligence, working through the machinery of democratic government, could avert the horrors of class war.

VI: *Other Responses*

Socialism, both Marxian and Utopian, and liberalism, both bourgeois and democratic, were the most important responses to the economic and social problems of the nineteenth century. But they were not the only responses. Nationalists revived the old economic philosophy of mercantilism, not only advocating tariffs to protect the economy at home but also demanding empires abroad to provide new markets for surplus products, new fields for the investment of surplus capital, and new settlements for surplus citizens. Analysis of this neo-mercantilism may be postponed to later chapters. Here we shall deal with other sets of responses—anarchism, and the reform program known as "Christian socialism" or "Christian democracy."

The Anarchists

An anarchist believes that the best government is no government at all. Most of the recipes for socialism contained at least a dash of anarchism. The Utopians, by and large, mistrusted governments, and Marx anticipated that his longed-for revolution would eventually produce a classless society where, in the famous phrase, "the state would wither away." For a few of Marx's contemporaries, however, it was not enough that the state should wither at some distant time; this instrument of oppression should be annihilated here and now. The means to this end was terrorism, especially assassination of heads of state.

The anarchistic terrorists provided the stereotype of the bearded, wild-eyed, bomb-carrying radical. Half a century and more ago, their assassinations took an impressive toll—the French President Carnot in 1894, King Humbert of Italy in 1900, and the American President McKinley in 1901. Otherwise terrorism accomplished little directly except to drive the governments that it hated to more vigorous measures of defense and retaliation. Yet, negative and destructive though it was, the doctrine did leave its mark on the proletarian movement.

A famous exponent of anarchism was the Russian Bakunin (1814-1876), who helped to shape the revolutionary movement in his native country (see Chapter XV) and, by his participation in the First International, won the attention of workers from many countries. Bakunin apparently wanted to replace the state with a loose confederation of autonomous units that would both end the injustices of private property and assure individuals complete freedom. The millennium was to be achieved through an international rebellion set off by small groups of anarchist conspirators.

Bakunin contributed to the formation of the program known as *anarcho-syndicalism*. "Anarcho" connotes its distrust of political action; "syndicalism" comes from the French *syndicat*, an economic grouping, particularly a trade union. The anarcho-syndicalists disbelieved in political parties, even Marxist ones; they believed in direct action by the workers. Direct action was to culminate in a spontaneous general strike that would free labor from the capitalistic yoke. Meantime, workers could rehearse for the great day by forming unions and by engaging in acts of anti-capitalist sabotage. These theories found their most forceful expression in a book called *Reflections on Violence* published early in our own century by the French exponent of anarcho-syndicalism, Georges Sorel.

Proudhon

The writer most frequently cited by the anarcho-syndicalists was the French publicist, Proudhon (1809-1865). "What is property?" Proudhon asked in a famous pamphlet of 1840; "property is theft." Karl Marx praised him for his "scientific" socialism, but within a few years Marx's praise had turned to contempt. A second pamphlet by Proudhon, *The Philosophy of Poverty*, elicited a Marxian rebuttal tartly entitled *The Poverty of Philosophy*. Part of the trouble was that Proudhon did not automatically accept the rightness of Marx's own views on the best way to improve the social and economic order.

Moreover, the property that Proudhon called "theft" was not all property but unearned income, the revenues that men gained from investing their wealth rather than from the sweat of their brows. Of all the forms of unearned income, the worst, in Proudhon's view, was the "leprosy of interest"; and the most diabolical of capitalist villains was the money-lender. Under existing conditions only those who were already rich could afford to borrow, but in the utopia envisaged by Proudhon all men would be able to secure credit. Instead of private banks and the Bank of France, there would be only a "People's Bank," lending to all without interest and issuing notes that would soon replace ordinary money. The credit provided by the People's Bank would enable each man to become a producer on his own.

Thus, where Marx foresaw a revolution in ownership of the means of production, Proudhon foresaw a "revolution of credit," a revolution in financing production. Where Marx proposed to have the proletariat liquidate the bourgeoisie, Proudhon proposed to raise the proletarians to the level of the bourgeois by making every worker an owner. Proudhon's utopia was not collectivized or socialized; it was a weakly organized association of middle-class individualists. Because Proudhon dreaded restraints upon the individual, he opposed the social workshops of Louis Blanc and the phalanxes of Fourier; they were too restrictive. He projected, instead, a society founded upon "mutualism." Economically, mutualism would take the form of associations of producers, rather like the producers' cooperatives sometimes found in agriculture today. Politically, it would take the form of a loose federation of these associations, which would replace the sovereign, centralized state.

Proudhon's doctrines exerted a strong appeal in a country like France, with its devotion to individualism. France had tens of thousands of small businessmen on the lower fringes of the middle class, often on the edge of being pushed down into the proletariat, often denied financial credit by the bankers whom Proudhon attacked so bitterly. "Mutualism" and "federalism," furthermore, were part of the revolutionary tradition, inherited from the Girondins (see Chapter X). Proudhon naturally fed the anarchist strain in anarcho-syndicalism. Yet much of his teaching contradicted the syndicalist strain. Not only did he dislike trade unions as unnatural restrictions on individual liberty; he deplored all activities suggesting class strife, including the very strikes so beloved by the syndicalists. At times Proudhon, despite his anarchism, seemed to favor the methods of the police state. His hatred of bankers made him an anti-Semite, because of the number of Jews engaged in finance. It is difficult to decide whether Proudhon should be assigned a place at the extreme Left of the political spectrum, or at its extreme Right.

The Christian Socialists

By contrast, the Christian socialists occupy a position close to the political Center. Historically, the Christian socialists were a small group of English reformers, drawn from the clergy of the established Church and active in the mid-nineteenth century. Their church, they believed, needed to put theological problems to one side and direct its efforts to the remedying of social abuses. One of their best known leaders was Charles Kingsley (1819-1875), who wrote earnest social novels and a stream of pamphlets against the wickedness of laissez-faire. Kingsley delivered telling blows at one of the unhealthiest of industries, tailoring. His didactic novel, *Alton Locke*, and his bitter tract, *Cheap Clothes and Nasty*, both published in 1850, exposed the "show-shops" and "slop-shops" which forced tailors and seamstresses to labor hard and long for meager pay, often in appallingly crowded and unsanitary surroundings.

Kingsley proposed the following remedies for these sweatshops:

First—this can be done. That no man who calls himself a Christian—no man who calls himself a man—shall ever disgrace himself by dealing at any show-shop or slop-shop. It is easy enough to know them. The ticketed garments, the impudent puffs, the trumpery decorations, proclaim them. . . . Let no man enter them—they are the temples of Moloch—their thresholds are rank with human blood.

. . .

But let, secondly, a dozen, or fifty, or a hundred journeymen say to one another: 'It is competition that is ruining us, and competition is division, disunion, every man to himself, every man against his brother. The remedy must be in association, co-operation, self-sacrifice for the sake of one another. . . . Why should we not work and live together in our own workshops, or our own homes, for our own profit?'

. . .

And, again, let one man, or half-a-dozen men arise who believe that the world is not the devil's world at all but God's: that the multitude of the people is not, as Malthusians aver, the ruin, but as Solomon believed, 'the strength of the ruler.' . . . Let a few men who have money, and believe that, arise to play the man.

Let them help and foster the growth of association by all means. Let them advise the honourable tailors, while it is time, to save themselves from being degraded into slop-sellers by admitting their journeymen to a share in the profits. . . . Let them, as soon as an association is formed, provide for them a properly ventilated workshop, and let it out to the associate tailors at a low fair rent. I believe that they will not lose by it—because it is right. God will take care of their money. The world, it comes out now, is so well ordered by Him, that model lodging-houses, public baths, washhouses, insurance offices, all pay a reasonable profit to those who invest money in them—perhaps associate workshops may do the same. . . .

But above all, so soon as these men are found working together for common profit, in the spirit of mutual self-sacrifice, let every gentleman and every Christian . . . make it a point of honour and conscience to deal with the associated workmen, and get others to do the like. *It is by securing custom, far more than by gifts or loans of money, that we can help the operatives.*[*]

These passages summarize the positive doctrine of the Christian socialists, which is notable for its attack on materialism and its stress on brotherly love as against un-brotherly strife, on association and co-operation as against exploitation and competition. It is notable also for its optimism: if men would only act as Christians, they might solve their social problems. Indeed the Christian socialists were more Christian than socialistic; they relied more on private philanthropy than on state intervention. Kingsley himself set an example for concrete im-

---

[*] C. Kingsley, "Cheap Clothes and Nasty," in *Alton Locke*, Eversley ed. (London, 1893), I, 103-107.

provement when he helped to launch the Working Men's College in London and promoted other activities of the type that organizations like the YMCA have made familiar.

The Catholic Response

Catholics, too, reacted against the evils of industrialism. Essentially, their program resembled that of the Anglican Christian socialists, but they called it by the more accurate name of "Christian democracy" or "social Christianity." Christian democracy formed a central part of the Catholic response to the problems of the modern world. As we shall see in later chapters, these problems bore heavily upon the Church. Anticlerical legislation threatened its position in France, Germany, Italy, and elsewhere. The Papal States and then Rome herself, after more than a thousand years of papal rule, passed to the control of the newly unified Kingdom of Italy. Science, nationalism, and the materialistic doctrines issuing from the industrial revolution were all competing for the loyalties of men. In Catholic countries the working classes especially were drifting away from the Church.

The Church first tried to take refuge in the past. Pope Pius IX (1846-1878) issued in 1864 the *Syllabus of Errors*, which condemned many social theories and institutions that were not consecrated by centuries of tradition. Socially minded Catholics were disturbed by the apparent hostility of the Pope to trade unions and democracy and by his statement that it was an error to suppose that he "can and ought to reconcile and harmonize himself with progress, liberalism, and modern civilization."

The Catholic Church, however, has not endured all these centuries by turning its back on progress, liberalism, and modernity. Pius IX was followed in the See of Peter by Leo XIII (1878-1903), who fully recognized the rapid changes being worked by science and technology. As a papal nuncio, Leo had witnessed them at first hand in the industrial regions of Belgium, France, and Germany. He knew that Catholicism was flourishing in the supposedly hostile climate of the democratic United States. Leo XIII came to terms with the modern world in a series of famous documents, the most celebrated of which was the encyclical letter, *Rerum Novarum* ("concerning new things," 1891).

In *Rerum Novarum*, Leo XIII exposed the defects of capitalism with as much vigor as any socialist. Then he attacked with equal vigor the socialistic view of property and the socialistic doctrine of class war. He pronounced it a "great mistake" to believe

. . . that class is naturally hostile to class, and that the wealthy and the workingmen are intended by nature to live in mutual conflict. . . . Each needs the other: Capital cannot do without Labor, nor Labor without Capital. . . . Perpetual conflict necessarily produces confusion and simple barbarity.*

Leo therefore urged the economic man to act as a Christian man of good will:

Religion teaches the laboring man . . . to carry out honestly and fairly all equitable agreements freely entered into; never to injure the property, nor to outrage the person, of an employer; never to resort to violence . . . nor to engage in riot or disorder; and to have nothing to do with men of evil principles, who work upon the people with artful promises, and excite foolish hopes which usually end in useless regrets, followed by insolvency. Religion teaches the wealthy owner and the employer that their work-people are not to be accounted their bondsmen; that in every man they must respect his dignity and worth as a man and as a Christian; that labor is not a thing to be ashamed of, if we lend ear to right reason and to Christian philosophy, but is an honorable calling, enabling a man to sustain his life in a way upright and creditable; and that it is shameful and inhuman to treat men like chattels to make money by, or to look upon them merely as so much muscle or physical power.†

---

* *The Great Encyclical Letters of Pope Leo XIII* (New York, 1903), 218.
† *Ibid.*, 219.

The state must always remain subordinate to the interests of the individuals who compose it. But this did not mean that government should adopt an attitude of laissez-faire. On the contrary, Leo repeatedly claimed that the state should indeed take measures for the general welfare. On behalf of capital, it should discourage agitators and protect property from violence. On behalf of labor, it should work to remove "the causes which lead to conflict between employer and employed." For example, it should curb exploitation by regulating child labor, limiting the hours of work, and insisting that Sundays be free for religious activity and for rest. Leo also believed that the workers must help themselves, and *Rerum Novarum* concluded with a fervent appeal for the formation of Catholic trade unions.

These Catholic unions exist today, but they are only a minority in the realm of organized labor. Neither the Christian democracy of Leo nor the Christian socialism of the Anglican reformers has achieved all that the founders hoped. Probably neither has greatly curtailed the appeal of Marxism. Yet both movements have attracted an important following and have made a real contribution to what may be termed the development of a social conscience on the part of the western democracies. There is a larger element of Christian socialism than most Americans would suspect in the British Labor party. And the Christian democrats have played an important role in the politics of many continental European states, especially since World War II. At the very least, the Anglican and Catholic reformers enriched the liberal response to the problems of industrialism and broadened the liberal appeal.

Reading Suggestions on the Economic Revolutions

General Accounts

W. Bowden, M. Karpovich, A. P. Usher, *An Economic History of Europe Since 1750* (N.Y.: American Book, 1937); S. B. Clough and C. W. Cole, *Economic History of Europe*, rev. ed. (Boston: Heath, 1946); and H. Heaton, *Economic History of Europe*, rev. ed. (N.Y.: Harper, 1948). Three useful general economic histories.

J. Clapham, *An Economic History of Modern Britain*, 3 vols., 2nd ed. (Cambridge, England: The University Press, 1930-1938). A major scholarly work on the homeland of the economic revolutions.

L. Mumford, *Technics and Civilization* (N.Y.: Harcourt, Brace, 1934). A sweeping survey, often very stimulating, of technology and its impact.

T. S. Ashton, *The Industrial Revolution, 1760-1830* (N.Y.: Oxford Univ. Press, 1948. Home University Library). A clear and sound introductory account, centered on Britain.

Special Studies

P. Mantoux, *The Industrial Revolution in the 18th Century*, rev. ed. (N.Y.: Harcourt, Brace, 1929). A standard survey of the beginnings of industrialism.

J. L. and B. Hammond, *The Bleak Age*, rev. ed. (Harmondsworth, Middlesex: Penguin Books, 1947). An exposé, aimed at the general reader, of the social results of industrialism, which the authors view with unrelieved horror. The Hammonds have written other detailed volumes in the same vein.

M. C. Buer, *Health, Wealth, and Population in the Early Days of the Industrial Revolution* (London: Routledge, 1926). Takes a decidedly more cheerful view of the social results of industrialism than do the Hammonds.

C. Brinton, *English Political Thought in the Nineteenth Century*, new ed. (Cambridge: Harvard Univ. Press, 1949). Includes essays on Bentham, Owen, Mill, and Kingsley.

J. S. Schapiro, *Liberalism and the Challenge of Fascism: Social Forces in England and France, 1815-1870* (N.Y.: McGraw-Hill, 1949). Suggestive essays on major thinkers, better balanced when dealing with liberalism than when dealing with the "challenge of fascism."

E. Halévy, *The Growth of Philosophic Radicalism* (Boston: Beacon). The standard study of Bentham and Utilitarianism.

H. W. Laidler, *Social-Economic Movements: An Historical and Comparative Survey of Socialism, Communism, Coöperation, Utopianism* (N.Y.:

Crowell, 1949). A handy survey of the subjects listed.

E. Wilson, *To the Finland Station* (Garden City, N.Y.: Anchor Books, 1953). A sympathetic yet balanced survey of socialism, Utopian and Marxian.

F. E. Manuel, *The New World of Henri St.-Simon* (Cambridge: Harvard Univ. Press, 1956). An important book about a man whose influence is still felt, especially among technologists.

F. Podmore, *Robert Owen, A Biography* (N.Y.: Appleton, 1924). One of many useful studies of Owen.

I. Berlin, *Karl Marx: His Life and Environment*, 2nd ed. (N.Y.: Oxford Univ. Press, 1948. Home University Library). A short and extremely good biography.

L. Schwarzchild, *The Red Prussian: The Life and Legend of Karl Marx* (N.Y.: Scribner's, 1947). A hostile interpretation.

R. Fülöp-Miller, *Leo XIII and Our Times* (N.Y.: Longmans, Green, 1937). A very sympathetic study.

Sources

A. E. Bland, P. A. Brown, R. H. Tawney, eds., *English Economic History: Select Documents* (London: Bell, 1915). A convenient collection of important source materials, like the reports of parliamentary investigations, that are often hard to locate.

J. S. Mill, *Autobiography* (N.Y.: Columbia Univ. Press, 1944), and *Utilitarianism, Liberty, and Representative Government* (N.Y.: Dutton, 1910. Everyman ed.). Essential writings by the most important nineteenth-century English liberal thinker.

C. H. de Saint-Simon, *Selected Writings*, F. M. H. Markham, ed. (N.Y.: Macmillan, 1952). A use-ful compilation from the works of the early French Utopian.

The Life of Robert Owen, by Himself (N.Y.: Knopf, 1920).

E. Burns, ed., *A Handbook of Marxism* (N.Y.: Random House, 1935). Most useful selections from the writings of Marx and his followers.

The Great Encyclical Letters of Pope Leo XIII (N.Y.: Benziger, 1903). Essential reading for an understanding of modern Catholic social philosophy.

Historical Fiction

C. Dickens, *Hard Times* (N.Y.: Dutton, 1907. Everyman ed.). Short and relatively little known, this is one of Dickens' best social novels; excellent descriptions of "Coketown" and of middle-class attitudes.

E. Gaskell, *North and South* (N.Y.: Dutton, 1914. Everyman ed.) and *Mary Barton* (N.Y.: Dutton, 1912. Everyman ed.). Two very sound social novels set in mid-nineteenth-century England.

B. Disraeli (Lord Beaconsfield), *Sybil* (Harmondsworth, Middlesex: Penguin Books). An important fictional presentation of the "two nations," rich and poor, by a leading politician and reformer of Victorian Britain.

C. Kingsley, *Alton Locke* (N.Y.: Harper, 1850). Not a very good novel, but a useful delineation of Kingsley's Christian program for social reform.

E. Zola, *Germinal* (many editions). The best French novel on industrial problems; markedly more realistic and less sentimental than its English counterparts.

E. Bellamy, *Looking Backward, 2000-1887* (N.Y.: Modern Library, 1951). An interesting American adaptation of Utopian socialist views.

CHAPTER FOURTEEN

The Western Democracies in the Nineteenth Century

We shall now trace the background history of the major self-governing western states: Great Britain, France, Italy, and the United States. These are now all democracies; and though they have all had their moments—sometimes years—of lapsing from democratic standards, they are all, as the world goes, "old" democracies.

The smaller nations of western and northern Europe—the Netherlands, Belgium, Switzerland, the Scandinavian countries—

are also part of the North Atlantic community. All these smaller states have worked out their own national variants of liberalism and democracy. In particular, the Scandinavian countries, with their homogeneous populations, their common Lutheran religion, their common traditions, and their very high rate of literacy, have sometimes surpassed the larger states in making democracy function effectively. Visitors to Copenhagen or Stockholm are impressed not only by their tidiness but also by the absence of slums and other signs of poverty. And the co-operatives of Denmark and Sweden have received much praise as the "middle way" between socialism and uncontrolled individualism.

These smaller states have also helped to maintain the balance of international politics and to shape European opinion, a role for which they are particularly well suited by their relative detachment from ambitious nationalist aspirations. In many fields their citizens have contributed proportionately more heavily to our modern western culture than their numbers would suggest. To cite only a few examples: Switzerland supplied the great historian of the Renaissance, Burckhardt, and Belgium the poet and playwright, Maeterlinck. From Finland came the composer Sibelius; from Norway, Ibsen and his modern social dramas; from Holland, the physicist Lorentz, winner of the Nobel Prize in 1902; and from Sweden, Nobel himself, the munitions king who endowed the Nobel prizes for peaceful achievement.

We must, however, turn to the states that fate, or history, has assigned the major roles in our story. Of these in the nineteenth century, Britain was unquestionably the first, the leading power.

I: Britain, 1815-1914

The Process of Reform In the years immediately after Waterloo, Britain went through a typical postwar economic crisis. Unsold goods accumulated, and the working classes experienced widespread unemployment and suffering. Although trade unions were forbidden by the Combination Acts, the workers none the less asserted themselves in strikes and in popular agitation that helped prepare the way for the parliamentary Reform Bill of 1832. But by the 1820's economic conditions had improved, and Britain had embarked on the first stage of those political reforms that were to make of her a democratic state.

Into this process, of course, there went economic and social drives, and the Britain of our mid-twentieth century was to be not only a very complete political democracy but also in part an economic and a social democracy. But the process of reform focused always on concrete political action. It is a process of which the British are very proud, for it was achieved without revolution and almost without violence or indeed any serious civil disturbance. The fruits of discussion, education, and propaganda were consolidated in a specific "reform bill," followed by another stage of preparatory work and another reform bill.

Parliamentary Reform The process is most clearly marked in the great milestones of parliamentary reform that transformed the government of Britain from an oligarchy into a democracy. Britain emerged from the Napoleonic Wars with its executive, a cabinet of ministers presided over by a prime minister, wholly under the control of Parliament. The Crown was now, as the nineteenth-century political writer Bagehot was to put it, largely "decorative." On that decorative post, held for most of the century (1837-1901) by Queen Victoria, who has given her name to an age and a culture, were centered the patriotic emotions of loyal British subjects. Victoria never thought of herself as a mere figurehead; she was a determined, sensible, emotional, conventional, and intellectually unsophisticated Victorian lady.

Real power lay in the legislative branch, in the early nineteenth century by no means directly representative of the masses. The

House of Lords, which for all save money bills had equal power with the lower house, was composed of the small, privileged class of peers. The House of Commons, its members unpaid, was recruited wholly from the gentry, the professional classes, and very successful businessmen, and was chosen by less than one-sixth of the adult male population. We cannot go into the details of the suffrage qualifications and the electoral districts ("parliamentary constituencies") of the unreformed Parliaments; they were varied, the result of the piling up of concrete acts since the Middle Ages, a sort of crazy quilt of social classes and geographical distribution. The fact is that in 1815 both the working classes in town and country and the run of prosperous but not spectacularly successful middle-class people were excluded from the franchise. Moreover, the largely rural South, once the most populous area of the kingdom, now had more representatives than it deserved, including a large contingent from the "rotten boroughs." The teeming new industrial centers of the North, such as Manchester, Liverpool, Sheffield, were grossly under-represented.

Projects to begin modernizing the structure of representation came close to being adopted in the late eighteenth century. But the wars with Revolutionary and Napoleonic France made reform impossible; in wartime and in the immediate postwar years, even moderate reformers were denounced as Jacobins. In 1819, a nervous Tory government permitted the soldiery to break up a large and peaceful mass meeting assembled at St. Peter's Field near Manchester to hear speeches on parliamentary reform. This "Peterloo" massacre resulted in several deaths, the wounding of hundreds, and the temporary curtailment of free speech and the free press. Suppression, however, was not the British way, and soon after Peterloo the great campaign of agitation was resumed which produced the parliamentary reform of 1832.

In this campaign the middle class did not hesitate to appeal to the lower classes for aid by using freely the language of popular rights, and even of universal suffrage. Many popular leaders talked as if the Reform Bill would bring political democracy to England at once. Yet much of the preparation for reform was actually the work, not of liberal agitators, but of conservatives. Guided by enlightened individuals such as Canning and Robert Peel, the Tory governments of the 1820's lifted the various restrictions on civil rights imposed during the war period and the postwar crisis. They partially repealed the Combination Acts against trade unions; reformed the antiquated criminal code, so that, for example, the theft of a sheep no longer carried with it in theory a death penalty; and began the reduction in protective tariffs that was to lead to free trade. The seventeenth-century Test Act, which, though not observed, legally excluded nonconformists from public life, was repealed. So, under the name of "Catholic emancipation," were the laws that really did exclude Catholics from public life. In international politics, Canning lined Britain up as a "liberal" power against the conservative monarchies of central and eastern Europe (see Chapter XII).

The Reform Bill itself was enacted under the leadership of the Whig Lord Grey, backed by a full apparatus of agitation and pressure groups. Tory opponents of parliamentary reform were won over—even the very Tory Duke of Wellington was converted at the last moment—until only the Tory House of Lords blocked the measure. At this climax, Lord Grey persuaded King William IV (1830-1837) to threaten the creation by royal prerogative of enough new Whig peers to put the reform through the Lords. This threat, combined with the real danger of popular violence, put the bill through on June 4, 1832.

This First Reform Bill did not bring political democracy to England. It did diminish the great irregularities of electoral districts, wiping out more than fifty rotten boroughs and giving seats in the Commons to more than forty hitherto unrepresented industrial towns. The franchise was made more uniform; the number of voters was increased by about 50 per cent so that virtually all the middle class got the vote. The bill by no means enfranchised the working classes; it actually excluded some working-class voters in a few boroughs that had had wide popular franchises.

From the new ground of the partly reformed Parliament, the agitation for a still wider suffrage went on. The middle class had won its gains, not in the name of its own admission to an oligarchy, but in the name of the right of all competent men to have the vote. With the gradual spread of literacy to the lower classes, with their gradual political awakening, the middle classes could not find very good arguments for refusing to extend the franchise; moreover, a good many of the British middle classes sincerely believed in a gradual widening of the franchise.

The Second Reform Bill came in 1867 in no such dramatic series of crises as those which had won over Wellington and William IV in 1832; the bill was indeed, by one of the ironies of history, put through by that Tory party that traditionally stood for resistance to the widening of the suffrage. But the three decades after 1832 had produced a ground swell of agitation for more parliamentary reform, a ground swell with many cross-currents from downright radical republicanism to a resigned belief that democracy was irresistibly the wave of the future. Disraeli (1804-1881), the Tory leader in the Commons, almost certainly thought that if one party did not put through reform the other one would. With a politician's sense of reality, he decided his party might as well get the credit, and therefore, as he himself once put it, "caught the Whigs bathing and walked away with their clothes." Disraeli also thought that the newly enfranchised urban working class, hostile to their middle-class employers, would vote for the Tories, who were country gentlemen, good responsible caretakers of the lower classes, not exploiters like the middle-class businessmen. Astute though he was, Disraeli's guess was not in the immediate instance correct. The first election after the reform saw the voters turn the Tories out of office in 1868.

The Second Reform Bill by no means introduced full manhood suffrage. Like the first, it was a piecemeal change that brought the electoral districts into more uniformity and equality, but left them still divided into boroughs and shires as in the Middle Ages. It about doubled the number of voters in Britain by giving the vote to householders —that is, settled men owning or paying rent on their dwellings—in the boroughs. But the Reform Bill of 1867 did not give the vote to men without the "stake" of property —that is, men who did not own a piece of real estate or even a bank account, men who were therefore felt by many upper-class Victorians to be irresponsible, willing to vote away other people's property. It did, however, give the vote to several millions of wage-earners without other sources of income.

The next reforms in the series were, more logically, put through by the Liberal party, the former Whigs under the leadership of Gladstone (1809-1898). Even these reforms of 1884 and 1885 did not introduce universal manhood suffrage or a neat democratic uniformity. They still tinkered with medieval forms, which were now pretty completely modernized. Lodgers and a few "floaters" (people whose specific "home" was hard to define in settled Victorian terms), and women were still without the vote; districts were not quite equalized; a few thousand voters with business property in one district and a home in another could vote twice; and graduates of Oxford and Cambridge could vote a second time for special university members. Still, by 1885 Britain was clearly a political democracy, in which the majority of the people, through their representatives in the House of Commons, were politically "sovereign." Perhaps not quite, for the hereditary House of Lords had still a veto power over legislation that did not specifically appropriate money. This last limitation was in fact removed in 1911, in a kind of codicil to the reforms of the nineteenth century, when the Parliament Act of that year left the Lords with no more than a delaying or suspensive veto.

The Two-Party System: Liberals and Conservatives

We have outlined above the legislative landmarks in the nineteenth-century democratization of the British constitution. Now the dynamics of that process are certainly in part explicable in terms of the "class struggle." Broadly speaking, over the century the "have nots"—perhaps better, the "have littles"—gained a voice in the politics of Britain they did not have in 1815. But the central human institution of the dynamics, the *party*, clearly does not present a neat alignment of the "have littles" against the "have much." That should be clear even from the very summary account of the reform bills we have given. The Disraeli who took the "leap in the dark" of 1867 was a conservative, not a radical leader, and he hoped that the newly enfranchised workingmen would vote conservative, not radical. He was wrong in 1868, but in the longer run not wholly wrong, for after his death his party was returned to power triumphantly under the even wider franchise of 1885 for a ten-year tenure of power, 1895-1905. Some British poor and middling men obviously voted for the party of their "betters."

The fact is that the British party system was not clearly based on an opposition between a possessing class and a non-possessing class. The eighteenth-century oligarchic factions of Whigs and Tories were trans-formed in the course of the nineteenth century into the modern mass parties of Liberals and Conservatives, both organized on a national basis, with local committees at the bottom, and making full use of party machinery for getting out the vote. The Whigs, in broadening into the Liberals, sought an electoral base ranging from the old great families, still represented in the early and middle part of the century by men like Grey and Palmerston, to the little and big businessmen, the nonconformists, the radical white-collar men. The Tories, in broadening into Conservatives, sought a base, first under Peel and then under Disraeli, from the country gentlemen, army and navy officers, and Anglican clergymen to the agricultural laborers, the small towns-people, and even some of the urban white-collar and working classes. Both parties frankly appealed to the "people"; and the Conservatives, with their "Primrose League" in memory of Disraeli's favorite flower, their appeal to love of Queen and country, their record of social legislation against the worst evils of the new factory system, did at least as good a job in building a party machine as did the Liberals. In the Victorian heyday, the librettist Gilbert was quite justified in having his guardsman sing in the operetta "Iolanthe":

> That every boy and every gal
>   That's born into the world alive
> Is either a little Liberal
>   Or else a little Conservative.

The Two-Party System: An Explanation

The two-party system is almost wholly confined to the English-speaking lands, to Britain, the United States, and the British Commonwealth countries. On the Continent, not only in France, Italy, and pre-Hitler Germany, but also in the little democracies of Scandinavia, Switzerland, Holland, and Belgium, the multi-party system has prevailed, and governments are generally coalitions of parties with separate organizations. English-speaking opinion probably exaggerates the defects and dangers of multi-party democracy. At least under good economic conditions and in the absence of great danger from war, even the politically divided Third French Republic was a going concern. But it is clear that a two-party democracy does have distinct advantages in the way of stability and continuity of policy, if only because a given group can enjoy a longer, more assured tenure of power. The historian must attempt somehow to explain why the English-speaking peoples have developed this unique institution. He must seek somewhat different explanations for Britain and for the United States, for though both have two-party systems, their total political situations and traditions are far from alike.

In terms of political psychology, the two-party system means that the millions of individual voters who make up each party are in greater agreement than disagreement over what the party stands for; or at least that when they vote for a candidate they feel he stands more for what they want than for what they don't want. Each voter makes some kind of compromise *within himself*, takes something less in practice than he would ideally like. This sort of compromise the French voter of the 1880's for instance did not need to make, at any rate not to anything like the same degree as the British voter. The Frenchman could choose, from among a dozen or more platforms and candidates, the one tailored closest to his desires.

We must still ask why Englishmen made these compromises, why they agreed more than they disagreed. The answer must be sought in the long working out of British history. One part of it lies in the relative security of the islands from external foes, in the long years in which British political habits of moderation and compromise could mature without the constant pressure of foreign wars. The immediate crisis of war may indeed promote a temporary unity in a threatened nation, like the France of 1792-1794. But long, steady exposure to war danger—and all continental states were so exposed—seems in fact to encourage party divisions in the threatened country, seems to promote psychological tendencies to seek final and extreme solutions.

This same relative isolation of Britain also contributed to the relatively mild form that the universal western struggle between feudalism and the new-model centralized state took there. In France, and on the Continent generally, the new model triumphed only in the seventeenth century, and in the form of divine-right monarchy. Continental states in the nineteenth century had only just gone through—or were still going through—the popular revolutionary modification of absolutism, and were still torn by major class antagonisms between a noble privileged class, backed usually by orthodox religion, and a middle class. In England, as we have seen in earlier chapters, that struggle had taken place a full century and a half earlier and had never been quite as bitter as on the Continent. It had left England in charge of a ruling class that was itself the product of a compromise between the old landed gentry and the new commercial classes, a ruling class that could develop within itself habits of moderation and compromise. The deep abyss the French Revolution had dug between nineteenth-century royalists and republicans and between "clericals" and "anticlericals" on the Continent did not exist in nineteenth-century England.

Thus, even more important than the fact that the Liberals and Conservatives each held together as parties whose members could sink differences in a common party action is the fact that both parties had a wide area of mutual agreement above and beyond party. To put it quite baldly, there wasn't much difference between the Conservatives and the Liberals. When one went out of power and the other came in, the ship of state tacked a bit, but it did not change direction. The Conservative Disraeli and the Liberal Gladstone were perhaps not quite shadowboxing in their heated parliamentary exchanges, but they clearly were not fighting to kill, nor perhaps even for the knockout.

To sum up, government by discussion, Her Majesty's Government and Her Majesty's Opposition equally loyal to established ways, under the shelter of the English Channel and the British navy, in a prosperous land without deep-seated class antagonisms or insuperable class barriers and rigidities—all this had developed in the British people habits of compromise, of law-abidingness, a sort of political sportsmanship. And these habits survive even in the mid-twentieth century, when Victorian geographical security has gone with the airplane and Victorian prosperity has gone with the rise of competing industrial nations.

Reforms
of the Utilitarians

The Reform Bill of 1832 was followed by a series of major reforms that helped make over, not merely British political life, but British economic and social life as well. The inspiration of these reforms came in large part from a small but influential middle-class group, the "Philosophic Radicals" or Utilitarians (see Chapter XIII). These disciples of Bentham and of the Enlightenment believed that men are, if once educated, impelled by rational self-interest and thus automatically do what is best for all their fellows. Under the influence of the Philosophic Radicals, English local government and the English legal system were made simpler, and were cleansed of some of the impediments to efficient government action left by the long accumulation of traditional stopgaps. Legal procedures, for instance, which had been so complicated that the Chancery Court was many years

behind its backlog of cases, were gradually speeded up. In local government, though many old offices remained, the essential work was done by an elective council and by elective officers with supervisory powers over the professional civil servants—including now for the first time professional "policemen." Indeed, London policemen are still called "Bobbies," after Robert Peel's innovation of the late 1820's.

The middle-class radicals, however, believed firmly that that government governs best which governs least, and they sought rather to expedite that minimum of government than to add to its tasks. They believed in education, but not in compulsory public education; private initiative would in their opinion do well what the government would do poorly and tyrannically. Large-scale government reform of British popular education had therefore to wait until 1870. Meanwhile, the private initiative preached by the Utilitarians sponsored mechanics' institutes and other means of adult education. It also sponsored all sorts of private schools, and universities in London, Manchester, and some other British cities. These universities, resembling in many ways our American urban universities, first broke into the centuries-old monopoly of Oxford and Cambridge. Although these "provincial" or "red-brick" universities have today attained great practical and intellectual distinction, they are still socially by no means the equals of Oxford and Cambridge.

The typical Utilitarian reform, the one that stirred up public opinion most thoroughly, was the New Poor Law of 1834. This bill codified, centralized, and made more coherent a complicated system of public relief that had originated in the Elizabethan Poor Law of 1601 and earlier Tudor legislation. But it did more: it shifted the base of this relief. The old methods of poor relief, "outdoor relief," had gradually come to permit supplementary payments from the parishes to able-bodied poor working on low wages, supplements for children, and in general by no means generous but still easy-going "doles" direct to families in their homes. The new system would have none of this laxness, this encouragement of men in what the Utilitarian, in spite of his belief in human rationality, rather feared was their "natural" laziness. Poor Law Unions united parishes for greater efficiency, and supplied in the workhouses the "indoor relief" by which able-bodied paupers were made as uncomfortable as decency would allow. This discomfort would, it was held, then encourage them to try to become self-supporting outside. The New Poor Law offended humanitarians in the upper classes, and was a hard blow to democrats who had backed the First Reform Bill in the hope of improving conditions of the working classes. Nevertheless, from the point of view of middle-class business interests, it had the decided merit of making poor relief both more efficient and more economical.

Free Trade

Greatest of these Utilitarian reforms in its long-run consequences was the repeal of the Corn Laws in 1846, after a long campaign headed by the Anti-Corn-Law League. This effective pressure group worked, as did the American Anti-Saloon League much later, on both political parties. The movement against tariffs on grains was led by Richard Cobden, an agitator so respectable, so high-minded, so Victorian, that he no longer seems much like an agitator. What the Free Traders wanted, and ultimately got, was a political economy in which food and other raw materials were imported from abroad without tariffs, and manufactures were exported to pay for the imports. In the long run—in another century—the difficulty for Britain would lie in the fact that other parts of the world too would become industrial workshops. In the short run, in the early nineteenth century, the difficulty was that protective tariffs in

favor of English agriculture made importation of the cheapest possible foodstuffs from abroad impossible. To this difficulty the English industrialists addressed themselves in the campaign against the Corn Laws. Their victory was achieved in 1846 by the conversion of the Conservative leader Peel to their cause, and by the alliance of Peelites and Liberals that put the bill through. Britain was now a free-trade nation, the only major free-trade nation in a world that never quite lost its mercantilist preconceptions and habits.

The Improvement of Labor

Still another series of reforms helped make the prosperous England of Gladstone and Disraeli. These were the Factory Acts, begun in 1802 and 1819 with bills sponsored by Peel's father. Addicts of the economic interpretation of history hold that middle-class people put through reforms like those of the Poor Law and the repeal of the Corn Laws, but that the landed gentry and upper-class intellectuals, jealous of the new city wealth and outraged by the ugliness of the new industrial towns, put through reforms like those of the Factory Acts regulating hours of labor, sanitation, and the labor of women and children. It is true that many leaders of the movement to use the power of the state to regulate some part of economic life were not themselves businessmen or industrialists. They were either members of the old Tory ruling class or intellectuals, like Coleridge, Disraeli, Carlyle, Ruskin, and Matthew Arnold, who preached against the horrors of working-class life in prosperous Victorian England. And it is true that the formal philosophy of the British business class was laissez-faire. But the practice was a different matter: none of the Factory Acts and similar reforms of the nineteenth century could really have gone through Parliament successfully without some support from both political parties. Moreover, neither landed gentry nor industrialists and businessmen were mutually exclusive "classes" in a neat Marxist sense. Rather, they were thoroughly mingled in education, marriage, and even in economic interests, since the gentry invested in stocks and bonds and the industrialists invested in landed estates. The elder Peel, father of the Factory Acts, was a self-made industrialist.

The Factory Acts followed a sequence not unlike the sequence of acts that reformed the suffrage. The first acts were very modest indeed; they underlined the frightful conditions they were designed to remedy. That of 1819, for instance, applied only to the cotton industry, forbade night work for children, and limited day work to twelve hours. Even so, it provided for no really effective inspection, and was violated with impunity by many employers. The Act of 1833, forbidding child labor entirely below the age of nine, and restricting it to nine hours for those below thirteen, and twelve for those below eighteen, marked an important stage by setting up salaried inspectors to enforce the law.

By the end of the nineteenth century, there was on the books a whole code of labor legislation, regulating hours of labor for everyone, giving special protection to women and children, and including provisions that made the employer responsible for workmen's compensation in industrial accidents. Then in 1911 came the great National Insurance Act, which provided through combined payments from the state, from employers and from employees, compulsory health and unemployment insurance. The "welfare state" was firmly established in Britain well before the Labor party had come to power.

Education

The same story of piecemeal but cumulative reform holds true in education. The commonly held Victorian idea that education is not properly a function of the state postponed a general education act until 1870. The issue was complicated by the wrangling of Anglicans and nonconformists, for many existing schools were controlled by a society that made instruction in the doctrines of the Church of England compulsory. But even before 1870 a government committee had been supplementing local education boards by making grants from the national treasury (in 1860 these grants reached nearly a million pounds), by providing an inspection service, and by helping to organize teacher training. School attendance, however, was not compulsory, and the average age for leaving school was eleven years. After workingmen got the vote in 1867, worried Tories—and Liberals—began to urge the slogan, "Educate your masters." The bill of 1870, put through under Gladstone's Minister of Education, William Forster, did not quite set up compulsory national education at the elementary level. It did permit the local boards to compel attendance, and it did extend national aid and supervision. The religious difficulty was solved by the provision that religious instruction in tax-supported schools should be nonsectarian and not required of the pupils. Church schools were allowed public aid, a feature that continued on into our own time.

Still, the basis for widespread compulsory education was firmly laid, and by the end of the century illiteracy in Britain had pretty generally been eliminated. Beginnings were made in publicly supported schools at the secondary level, though the British "public school," which in American terms is a "private school," continued until our own day to maintain a privileged position in the British social system. In comparison with the public school systems in Germany, France, and the United States, British education on the eve of World War I was administratively complex and full of anomalies. On the whole, though, it got the job done, and the general level of popular education in the British Isles was at least as high as in the other liberal democracies.

Chartism

Only one of the major reform movements of the nineteenth century seems to have failed completely. This was Chartism, which played a major role in the political excitements of the 1830's and 1840's, and greatly alarmed the conservative classes. The Chartists were the closest (but still not very close) English equivalent of the radical parties which on the Continent carried on the Jacobin tradition of the French Revolution, mingled with the elements of nascent socialism. The Chartists had a formal program drawn up in a "People's Charter," calling for universal manhood suffrage, the secret ballot, abolition of property requirements for members of Parliament, payment of members, equal electoral districts, and annually elected Parliaments. Their strength lay in the new urban industrial proletariat, and especially in the more active and radical members of the proletariat, men who clearly believed that if they got the political democracy they wanted the masses would vote themselves, if not full socialism, at least a considerable degree of leveling of incomes, probably by graduated income taxes. Their leaders were often doctrinaire radicals prone to quarreling among themselves over ideas, and unsparing of bourgeois sensibilities in such matters as religion. They frightened the majority of Englishmen, who felt that the Chartists wanted to lead England in the same paths that had led the French to the Reign of Terror. The movement petered out in a monster petition to Parliament which was never even considered, and in the rising prosperity of the 1850's and 1860's it was effectively stifled. Yet of the original Chartist program all but the demand for annual Parliaments, which soon seemed pointless even to radicals, was achieved by the outbreak of war in 1914.

Foreign Policy

Nowhere does the basic unity that underlies the party strife of nineteenth-century Britain come out more clearly than in foreign relations. The strife is real enough on hundreds of concrete matters of detail; but so is the unity in the broad lines of British policy. Almost all Englishmen (an unavoidable term, which has to include Scottish, Welsh, and Ulstermen) were agreed on the fundamental position of Britain: maintain the European state-system in balance, preferably by diplomatic rather than military action, but seek no new territories in Europe; police the seas with the British navy; open world markets to British goods; maintain—and in Africa extend—the vast network of the British Empire, made up of self-governing, English-speaking lands and colonial "possessions" in lands inhabited by the darker-skinned peoples. It is certainly true that the Liberals verbally and emotionally sided in Europe with the liberal nationalist movements, that they sympathized with the struggling Italians, Greeks, and Poles, and that they disliked the old Metternichian powers, especially Russia. It is even true that a Liberal —or better, a belated Whig—foreign minister like Palmerston in mid-century pursued an active policy of near-intervention in behalf of oppressed nationalities, and that British benevolence was a factor in the attainment of Italian unity.

Yet the only European war in which Britain became involved between 1815 and 1914 was the Crimean War of 1854-56, in which France and England went to war as allies against Russia to protect Turkey and their own Near Eastern interests from Russian aggression (see Chapter XV). This was a somewhat blundering war on both sides. But it at least checked Russian advance for a time and made the ultimate disposition of the Balkan regions of the decaying Turkish Empire a matter of European concern. It was, in fact, a typical balance-of-power war in which Britain played its traditional role of taking arms against a major power that seemed about to add unduly to its lands or its "spheres of influence."

Imperial Policy   On imperial policy it seems at first glance as though British public opinion really was deeply divided. Disraeli and Gladstone were never so gladiatorially fierce as when the Conservative defended the greatness of the Empire and the Liberal attacked imperialism at home and abroad as un-Christian and unprofitable. And it would be absurd to maintain that in action there was no real difference between the two. Disraeli, on the one side, triumphantly made his royal mistress, Queen Victoria, even more than royal as Empress of India (1876), and bought up the financially embarrassed Khedive of Egypt's shares in the French-built Suez Canal, thus initiating the British control of Egypt. On the other side, Gladstone withdrew British troops from Afghanistan, neglected the British General Gordon surrounded by rebels in the Sudan, and conceded independence to the Boer Republics in South Africa. Yet Gladstone kept British armies on the northwest frontier of India. It was under his administration in 1882 that the British actually bombarded Alexandria and monopolized control of Egypt. Gladstone did send troops to rescue Gordon, though they arrived too late, and even in South Africa the Boer Republics were freed only under the "suzerainty" of Britain. In short, Gladstone regretted and no doubt even neglected the Empire; but he kept it (for details, see Chapter XVII).

The Irish Problem   Much nearer home, a nationality problem grew more acute as the nineteenth century came to a close, and did draw something more than a verbal line between Conservatives and Liberals. This was the Irish problem, a problem that had

beset the English in one form or another, now acute and now mild, ever since the Norman-English conquest of Ireland in the twelfth century. The English, and the Scots who came to settle in the North of Ireland province of Ulster in the sixteenth and seventeenth centuries, had remained as a privileged landowning group in the midst of a subject population of native Irish peasants. As the nineteenth century opened, the English attempted to solve the problem by a formal union of the two kingdoms, with Irish members admitted to the British Parliament, in which they were of course a minority. In the prevailing temper of nineteenth-century Britain, it was quite impossible to deny the Irish natives all political rights; and indeed, beginning with the Catholic Emancipation Act of 1829, the various suffrage reforms we have outlined above were extended to Ireland. The Irish, led by Daniel O'Connell, the "Great Emancipator," organized politically to press for reforms and, eventually, for home rule of the kind the dominions were gradually achieving. They sought not only for political home rule, but also for land reforms, and for disestablishment of the Anglican Church in Ireland—that is, abolition of a state church supported by taxes levied on both members and non-members of the church.

Irish hatred for the English was fanned by the disastrous potato famine of the 1840's, when blight ruined a crop essential to the Irish food supply. Although the beginnings of modern transportation by railway and steamship existed, the British government was not organized for prompt and efficient relief measures, nor was the kind of international organization for such relief afforded nowadays by the Red Cross yet in existence. The result was a medieval famine in the heart of modern western civilization, in which tens of thousands died of starvation, and other tens of thousands were forced to migrate, mostly to the United States. The immigrants added to British difficulties, for they carried their rancors with them, and formed pressure groups, like the Fenian Brotherhood organized in New York in 1858 to raise funds to aid Irish resistance and to make trouble generally for the British wherever they could.

British governments made piecemeal reforms. The Anglican Church in Ireland was disestablished in 1869 and in the next year an Irish Land Act began a series of agrarian reforms that were designed to protect the tenant from "rack-renting"—the extraction by the landlord, often an absentee member of the British "garrison," of as high a rent as the tenants, forced by overpopulation into intense competition, could pay. The reforms were neither far-reaching nor rapid enough to satisfy the Irish. Moreover, the emotional strength of Irish nationalism grew with the spread of elementary education and the usual literary and cultural forms of national self-consciousness. The Irish question was not just a matter of land, or of religion, but also of a peculiarly intense form of underdog awareness of cultural differences and of nationality. Then in the 1870's a brilliant Irish leader arose, Charles Parnell, himself a Protestant descendant of the "garrison," but a firm Irish patriot. Under the leadership of Parnell in the British Parliament, the Irish nationalists were welded into a firm, well-disciplined party which, though it held less than a hundred seats, could often swing the balance between Liberals and Conservatives.

The critical step came when in 1885 Gladstone was converted to Home Rule, and introduced his first Home Rule Bill. This bill provided for a separate Irish parliament with some restrictions on its sovereignty, and of course under the Crown. Gladstone's decision split his own Liberal party in something like the way Peel's conversion to Free Trade had split the Conservatives in 1846. A group led by Joseph Chamberlain, who had begun political life as the reform leader of the great city of Birmingham, seceded under the name of "Liberal Unionists." In effect, they joined the Conservative party, which was often known in the next few decades, so great were the passions aroused in Great Britain by this proposed cutting loose of Ireland, simply as the "Unionist" party. Gladstone lost the election brought on by the split, and Home Rule was dropped for the moment.

Agitation continued in Ireland. It became more bitter when Parnell, involved in a divorce scandal, was dropped by the virtuous Gladstone and by some of his own Irish followers. In 1892, however, Gladstone won a close election on the Irish issue—or, rather, he obtained enough English seats to get a Second Home Rule Bill through the Commons with the aid of eighty-one Irish nationalists. The bill was defeated, however, in the Conservative House of Lords, and was dropped once more. The Conservatives, when they came in for their ten-year reign in 1895, sought to "kill Home Rule by kindness," carrying several land reform bills that furthered the process of making Ireland a land of small peasant proprietors.

But Ireland was now beyond the reach of kindness, and Irish problems were no longer—if they ever had been—largely economic and administrative. Irish nationalism was now a full cult, nourished by a remarkable literary revival in English and in Gaelic. Irish men and women everywhere—including definitely the Irish-Americans—were keyed to a pitch of emotional excitement. They would be satisfied with nothing less than an independent Irish nation.

The Liberals, back in power after 1905, found they needed the votes of the Irish nationalists to carry through their proposal for ending the veto power of the Lords. After some soul-searching, the Liberals struck the bargain: Home Rule in return for the Parliament Act. They introduced in 1912 a Home Rule Bill which—the Parliament Act in 1911 having destroyed the veto power of the Lords—was placed on the books as a law. It never went into force, however, for as Home Rule seemed about to become a fact the predominantly Protestant North of Ireland, the province of Ulster, bitterly opposed to separation from Great Britain, was organized to resist by force of arms. The Home Rule Bill as passed carried the rider that it was not to go into effect until the Ulster question was settled. The outbreak of war in 1914 made such a settlement out of the question, and the stage was set for the Irish Revolution of our own day (see p. 709).

The Threat to Free Trade

As Great Britain approached the twentieth century, then, new problems arose to disturb the underlying serenity and assurance of the Victorian Age. The Boer and Irish troubles, the rising international tensions that were to lead to World War I (see Chapter XVIII), and the difficulties of adjusting the new distribution of national income made necessary by the rise of the "welfare state," confronted the British people all at once. Though here as always in history we must avoid the temptation to seek a single underlying cause, there was undoubtedly one major factor at work. The long lead Britain had gained in the industrial revolution was being lost as other nations acquired the technical skills of large-scale production. Germany, the Low Countries, the United States, and in a measure all the West, were competing on the world market.

Under such conditions, it was natural that some Britishers should come to doubt the wisdom of the Free Trade policies that had won the day in 1846. For the Germans and others were not only underselling the British abroad; they were actually invading the British home market. Why not protect that market by a tariff system? Few Britishers were foolish enough to believe that the home islands, already by the 1880's too densely populated to feed themselves and constitute a self-sufficient economy, could surround themselves with a simple tariff wall. But the Empire was world-wide, with abundant resources, with thousands of square miles of agricultural lands. Within it the classical mercantilist interchange of manufactures for raw materials could still provide a balanced economic system. Britain could still be, if not the workshop of the world, at least the workshop of a quarter of the world, the British Commonwealth and Empire.

The same Joseph Chamberlain who led the secession from the Liberals on the question of Home Rule for Ireland also led a secession on an issue of much more fundamental importance. He became a protectionist. He gave special importance to the establishment of a system of imperial preference through which the whole complex of lands under the Crown would be knit together in a tariff union. The Conservatives, never wholly reconciled to Free Trade, welcomed the recruits, and the new Unionist party made protection a major plank in its program. Liberal opposition, however, was still much too strong, and there was opposition even in Conservative ranks. Chamberlain, reversing the aims but imitating the methods of Cobden and the Anti-Corn Law League of the 1840's, organized a Tariff Reform League. In 1903, he introduced a sweeping measure that would have restored moderate duties on foodstuffs and raw materials (largely to give a basis for negotiating with the dominions, which already had tariff systems of their own) and on foreign manufactured goods. But the Conservative leader, Balfour, did not dare go so far, and Chamberlain resigned with his bill unpassed. The new Liberal government after 1905 continued the policy of Free Trade. The rift Chamberlain had made in the Liberal party was, however, never really repaired. Its right wing was driven to Toryism; its left wing to the Labor party.

The Welfare State   The Liberals were, however, committed to another policy not as consciously planned to enable Britain to compete directly with her industrial rivals, but quite as contrary to the classical philosophy of laissez-faire as was protectionism. This was the welfare state—social security through compulsory insurance managed by the state, and in part financed by the state, minimum-wage laws, progressive taxation on incomes and inheritances, compulsory public education, public works and services of all kinds. The dramatic point in the working out of the program was the "People's Budget" of 1909, introduced by a new figure on the political stage, the Liberal Chancellor of the Exchequer, Lloyd George (1863-1944). This budget, which frankly proposed to tax the rich to finance the new welfare measures, and also the rising naval costs brought on by the armament race with Germany (see Chapter XVIII), was clearly no ordinary tax measure. It was a means of altering the social and economic structure of Britain. Its opponents rightly called it "not a budget, but a revolution." It passed the Commons, but was thrown out by the Lords, even though it was a "money bill." The Liberals went to the country, and after an exciting election in which the Liberals gained but two seats, they were able to put through the Parliament Act of 1911, which took away from the Lords all power to alter a money bill, and left them with no more than a three-year delaying power over all other legislation. The Liberal program of social legislation was saved. It was saved under conditions strongly reminiscent of 1832, for the new king, George V (1910-1936), had promised Prime Minister Asquith that if necessary he would create enough new peerages—which might have meant several hundred—to put the Parliament Act through the House of Lords. As in 1832, the threat was enough, and the Peers yielded.

But was it a *Liberal* program? The dissenting Liberals who had followed Joseph Chamberlain out of the party in the 1880's thought not, and it was normal enough for Chamberlain's two sons, Austen and Neville, who played an important part in twentieth-century politics, to think of themselves as Conservatives. For what happened in the generation after 1880 was a major change in the political orientation of British parties. The Liberals, who had believed that that government governs best which governs least, and least expensively, had come to believe that the state must interfere in economic life to help the underdog, had come to adopt Lloyd George's plan for redistributing the national wealth by social insurance financed by taxation of the rich and well-to-do. And the Conservatives, who in the mid-nineteenth century had stood for factory acts and at least mild forms of the welfare state, were now in large part committed to a laissez-faire program against government "intervention" astonishingly like that of the Liberals of 1850.

The Labor Party   One factor in this change had been the growth of the British Labor party, which originated in a number of groups formed in the late nineteenth century. Labor, though never perfectly unified (and always troubled by cleavages between its left and right wing and between its "intellectuals," like the Fabians Bernard Shaw, H. G. Wells, the Webbs, and the rank-and-file trades-unionists), had developed by 1905 into a party able to command fifty-three seats in the Commons. It wanted the welfare state, and indeed some Laborites wanted a socialist state in which at least the major industries were nationalized. Part of the motivation for the Liberal program of social legislation was a desire to forestall Labor. Just as in 1867 the Tories had "walked away with the Whigs' clothes" and had given the workingman the vote, so in 1911 the Liberals stole Labor's clothes and gave the workingman social security. But these tactics worked no better in the twentieth century than in the nineteenth, and the workingmen on the whole stuck by the Labor party, leaving the Liberals to die on the branch.

Not all the motivation of the Liberals in these early years of the twentieth century was, however, mere fear of Labor. In part, their conversion from laissez-faire to social security was a positive one, a sincere belief that the logic of their democratic assumptions must drive them to raise the general standard of living in Britain by state action. Something broadly analogous

was happening throughout the democratic West—in France, in the smaller democracies, and, a few decades later, in the United States. An important part of the bourgeoisie in all these countries swung over, not to doctrinaire socialism, but to programs of social legislation put through by the usual machinery of change under a wide democratic suffrage. The English Chartists back in the early nineteenth century had had the apparently naive belief that universal suffrage would pave the way to greater economic equality. In the long run, events were to prove that the Chartists were far from being entirely wrong.

II: France—Second Empire and Third Republic

The Coup d'Etat of 1851

One hundred years ago France seemed to many English-speaking critics, as she seems to many today, a rather uncertain member of the community of nations ruled by the democratic decencies—that is, government by discussion, peaceful alternation of "ins" and "outs" through the working of the party system, and the usual freedoms of the "rights of man." The democratic revolution, so optimistically begun in 1848 (see Chapter XII), had by 1852 brought still another Bonaparte to the throne of France in Napoleon III, nephew of the first Napoleon. As President of the Second Republic, Prince Louis Napoleon had soon quarreled with the National Assembly, which refused to amend the Constitution of 1848 to allow him a second term of office. Fearful of radicals and socialists, the Assembly also whittled down the universal male suffrage of 1848 and thus enabled the Prince-President to pose as the champion of persecuted popular democracy.

The coup d'état of December 2, 1851, artfully timed for the sacred Bonapartist day

of Napoleon's first coronation (December 2, 1804) and the greatest Napoleonic victory, the battle of Austerlitz (December 2, 1805), was a stereotyped affair. Controlling the army, Louis Napoleon and his fellow conspirators found it easy to purge the Assembly and make way for a popular vote on a new constitution. Even the expected street fighting on the barricades of Paris, which broke out on December 3, proved to be no wholesale bloodletting. It left victims enough as martyrs, however, and, politically more important, it enabled the President to pose as the champion of order against a largely imaginary socialist plot. Napoleon quickly got himself approved by a plebiscite, which by 7,500,000 votes to 640,000 gave him the right to draw up a new constitution.

The plebiscite was accompanied by skillful propaganda, but it was not crudely a work of force. Though many opponents of Napoleon simply did not vote, it seems that at least a very substantial majority of Frenchmen over twenty-one really were willing to try another dictator. There were many reasons why men voted "yes." Almost all were weary of the struggles of the last three years. Many were frightened by the specter of socialism, now for the first time under that name a definite factor in western politics. For nearly three decades the full force of fashionable French literature had been at work making the Napoleonic legend, and identifying the name of Napoleon with the "pooled self-esteem" of French patriotism. Many a man voted "yes" not to Louis Napoleon, but to the music of the "Marseillaise," the cannon of Austerlitz, to all the glories of France.

The Second Empire, 1852-1870: Domestic Developments

The new constitution set up a lightly veiled dictatorship very much like that of Napoleon I. The "chief of state" (he became formally "emperor" on the sacred date, December 2, in 1852) had full authority; he was responsible only to the nation. He governed through ministers, judges, and a whole bureaucracy, in the appointment of which he had the final voice. The popularly elected assembly, the *Corps Législatif*, was filled with "official" candidates sent up by influence of the efficient appointed officials in the provinces. It had no power to initiate or amend legislation; it had only a veto, which in the first few years it rarely used. Yet Napoleon III insisted that he was no mere tool of the possessing classes, no conservative, but an agent of real reform, an emperor of the masses, a kind of continental equivalent of the "Tory democrat" that Disraeli in England was claiming to be. This claim indeed has been made by almost all our recent dictators, from Stalin to the Peróns; they all claim to be *real* democrats, real protectors of ordinary men who in the classical western democracies, they insist, are actually victims of capitalist exploitation. Napoleon III has sometimes been seen as the first of these modern dictators, as a "proto-fascist"; and the careful student of his career can learn much that throws light on our own problems today.

Certainly by comparison with later social legislation in Germany, Britain, or Scandinavia, Napoleon's concrete achievements in direct benefit of the workers were slight. He did carry through a great program of public works, notably in Paris, where his prefect Haussmann cut through the medieval mazes of streets those broad straight avenues which all the world knows so well, and which, incidentally, can be easily swept by gunfire and make street fighting that much more difficult. And he did help with housing and encourage workers' mutual aid societies. But the legal code of labor in France in 1860 was less "modern" than that of England. The standard of living of French labor in the growing cities was well behind that of Britain, and behind that of Germany and the smaller democracies. French labor did indeed benefit from the general prosperity that came to France in the 1850's as it came to Great Britain, but the gains in wages were at least counterbalanced by rising prices.

It was the bourgeoisie that made most out of the Second Empire. Napoleon's government encouraged improvement in banking facilities, helped the great growth of French railways by state guaranties, and in general furthered the rise of industry in the two decades after 1850. That rise was, especially in large-scale heavy industries, definitely inferior to that of the British and to the already growing basic German industry. But it was in absolute terms a very real rise. Paris grew into a major metropolitan area, and centers like Lyons and Rouen in textiles, Clermont-Ferrand and St. Etienne in metallurgy, and many other cities came to have genuine industrial economies, with all the problems of slums, trade unions, and other signs of modernity. Yet there remained then as under later French governments an adhesion to older methods of doing business, to small firms often under family control, to luxury trades in which handicraft skills remained important in spite of the machine, to a kind of conservatism which meant that in quantitative terms of actual production France fell behind the industrial West. In the '60's she lost her Continental leadership in iron and steel production to the new Germany, and was subsequently far outdistanced by the burgeoning economy of the United States. Her growth in population, too, fell well behind that of the others. At the end of the nineteenth century, she was not much more than 50 per cent more populous than at the beginning—and this with almost no emigration. Britain, in spite of a large emigration, had about tripled her population, and Germany, too, was growing rapidly. Even Italy, with slender natural resources and less industry than France, was growing in population faster than France, and was to outstrip her in our own times.

The Second Empire: Foreign Policy

Yet the France of the Second Empire was still a very great power, and the extent of her comparative decline was by no means clear to contemporaries. Although the French gained little from the Crimean War, they did at least have the satisfaction of playing host to the postwar congress at Paris in 1856. And the Paris Exposition of 1855, a counterpart of the famous London exhibition of 1851, was a great success that showed Napoleon III at the height of his power. He had pledged himself to use that power for peace, but he allowed himself, partly through a romantic interest in "oppressed nationalities," partly from age-old motives of prestige, to become involved in a war against Austria for the liberation of Italy. French armies won victories in this war of 1859; characteristically, in these modern times of "publicity," the names of the battles of Magenta and Solferino were taken up into dressmaking, cookery, and urban real estate. But in 1860

the Italians took things into their own hands and set about organizing the whole peninsula, including papal Rome, into an Italian kingdom. Napoleon depended too much on Catholic support at home to be able to permit the extinction of papal power; moreover, the too great success of his plans was threatening the European balance of power. He therefore temporized, permitting the union of most of Italy under the house of Savoy, but protecting the Pope's temporal power with a French garrison in Rome, leaving Venetia still in Austrian hands, and taking Nice and the French-speaking part of Alpine Savoy away from Piedmont as a reward for his services. He thus managed to offend most Italians, as well as most of his own Catholic supporters at home.

To make matters worse, in 1861 Napoleon began a wild adventure in Mexico, supporting with French arms and men an expedition to put the Austrian prince Maximilian on an imperial throne. The Europeanized Mexican upper classes were in part willing to support this venture, for like most Latin Americans of the nineteenth century, their cultural ideal was France. But from the start the Mexican people resented the foreign intruder, and Maximilian had to rely heavily on French support to penetrate to Mexico City, where he was proclaimed Emperor in June, 1863. The United States, engaged in the Civil War, could do nothing at the time against what Americans regarded as an infraction of the Monroe Doctrine. But after peace had been restored in the United States, the American government protested strongly. The rival of Maximilian, the republican leader Juarez, had no difficulty in defeating the Mexican supporters of Maximilian, once Napoleon under American pressure had abandoned them. The unfortunate Maximilian fell before a firing squad in 1867. This unsuccessful venture was the last attempt made by a European power to install a new government in any of the Americas in defiance of the Monroe Doctrine.

The "Liberal Empire" Napoleon had come to power, as we have seen, on a platform of national unity against the extreme demands of the social revolutionists of 1848. But in spite of the plebiscite, it became more and more clear that if France had a national unity, it was not of the monolithic, totalitarian sort, but a unity that had to be worked out in the open competition of modern western political life—with parties, parliamentary debate, newspapers, in short, with government by discussion. Napoleon could not in fact be a symbolic head of state, above the struggle, nor even a final umpire. He could not be a republican, though much of France was republican; he could not be a legitimate monarchist, though much of France, and particularly the conservative France which held authoritarian views, was loyal to the legitimacy of the Bourbons, or the somewhat dubious legitimacy of the Orléanists. He could not even be a good devout Catholic, in spite of the orthodoxy of his wife, the Empress Eugénie, for his Bonapartist background was heavily tinged with the anticlericalism of the eighteenth century, and his bungling of the Italian problem had deeply offended clericals. He could only head an "official" party, relying on the manipulative skills of his bureaucrats to work the cumbersome machinery of a parliamentary system designed, like that of Napoleon I, as a disguise for dictatorship.

As the pressure of genuine party differences rose, in reflection of genuine moral, social and economic group interests, Napoleon slowly abandoned the measures of repression he had begun with, and sought to establish himself in something like the position of a constitutional monarch. An act of 1860 gave the Legislative Assembly power to discuss freely a reply to the address from the throne, and throughout the 1860's these powers were extended in the name of the "Liberal Empire." Gradually, political life in France took on a pattern of parliamentary government, with a Right, Left, and Center. As a result of the general election of 1869, the government was faced with a strong legal opposition, thirty of whom were declared republicans. On July 12, 1869, Napoleon capitulated, and granted the Legislative Assembly the right to propose laws, and to criticize and vote the budget. Partial ministerial responsibility seemed just around the corner as Napoleon entrusted the government to the head of the moderates, Emile Ollivier. A plebiscite in May, 1870, overwhelmingly ratified these changes.

It is at least possible that the Second Empire might thus have been converted into a constitutional monarchy. The changes had indeed been wrung from the Emperor by popular agitation, not merely political but also economic in the form of strikes. It is quite as possible that the radical republican ground swell would have gone on to submerge the Empire in any case. But the disastrous defeats of the French armies in the Franco-Prussian War into which Napoleon was maneuvered by the skill of Bismarck (see Chapter XV) put an end to the experiment of the Liberal Empire. On September 4, 1870, after the humiliating capitulation of Sedan, a Parisian mob forced a rump Legislative Assembly to decree the fall of the Empire, and at the classic center of French republicanism, the Paris City Hall, the Republic was proclaimed.

The Birth of the Third Republic The new Republic was too good a child of 1792 to give up the war against the national enemy. A government of national defense tried to continue the struggle, but the miracle of Valmy (see Chapter X) was not to be repeated. In October, General Bazaine surrendered a large French force at Metz, and the disorganized elements of other French armies were helpless before the powerful German forces. An exhausted nation, sick of the war, chose in February a National Assembly that met at Bordeaux and sued for peace. The special circumstances of that election, however, placed on the new Republic an additional handicap. For meanwhile Paris, besieged by the Germans, had resisted desperately until starvation forced its surrender in January, 1871. Even under pressure of the siege, Parisian radicals tried to seize power and revive the old Paris Commune, or city government, of 1792. These radicals could not stomach the capitulation that the rest of the country seemed to be preparing. In the elections to the National Assembly, their intransigence helped to turn the provincial voters toward conservative candidates pledged to make peace—and to restore, not the Republic, but the old monarchy.

This new Assembly, on March 1, 1871, voted to accept a peace ceding Alsace and a substantial part of Lorraine to Germany and paying an indemnity of five billion francs (about $1,000,000,000). Then the Paris National Guard, which had not been disarmed by the Germans, went over to the radicals, and the Paris Commune was set up. Marxist legend has consecrated the Commune of 1871 as the first major social-ist government. The Communards were in fact rather Jacobins, radical anticlericals and highly patriotic republicans who wanted a society of small independent shopkeepers and artisans, not the abolition of private property. In any case, they had no chance in the besieged city to introduce sweeping social reforms. But they alarmed the rest of France, and their refusal to accept the peace was a challenge the National Assembly had to meet. To the horrors of the first siege by the Germans were added the horrors of a new siege by the government of the National Assembly, which gathered its troops at Versailles and in the "Bloody Week" of May 21-28 advanced through the barricades to clear the city.

The Third French Republic was thus born in foreign and in civil war, and began with a heritage of unresolved cleavages. Indeed, it was not at all clear in 1871 that there was a Third Republic at all. More than half the members of the new National Assembly were monarchists, anxious to undo the formal declaration of a republic made in Paris right after Sedan. But now we encounter one of those concrete events that are the despair of those who seek the clue to history in vast impersonal forces beyond the play of human personality. About half

The Paris Commune, 1871. Destruction of the Vendôme column commemorating Napoleon I.

the monarchist deputies were pledged to the elder "legitimate" Bourbon line represented by the Count of Chambord, grandson of Charles X, and the other half to the younger Orléanist line that had come to the throne in 1830, represented by the Count of Paris, grandson of Louis Philippe. Chambord might have become in fact what he was to his supporters, King Henry V, had he been willing to make the slightest concession to Orléanist sentiments and accept the revolutionary blue, white, and red tricolor flag that Louis Philippe had himself accepted as the flag of France. But he insisted on the white flag and gold lilies of Bourbon, which for millions of Frenchmen meant complete repudiation of all that had happened since 1789. Chambord did not, of course, act just for a white flag and against a tricolor one; but behind these symbols lay real motives tied up with all French history. He meant to be king, not just a Victorian symbol; but no one could be that sort of king in France any longer.

In the resulting stalemate, the republican minority was able to maintain itself, and slowly gather strength. Thiers, the elder statesman of the Orléanist monarchy, who had been a leader in the opposition to Napoleon III, was recognized as "President of the Republic" and carried through the final settlement with Germany. He was succeeded in 1873 by Marshal MacMahon, a soldier and a monarchist, who was elected to hold the government together while the monarchist majority made peace between Bourbons and Orléanists. That peace was never made, as Chambord continued to insist on the white flag, and in 1875 a series of constitutional measures formally established the Third Republic.

The Constitution of 1875

These laws, known collectively as the Constitution of 1875, provided for a president elected by an absolute majority of Senate and Chamber of Deputies sitting together as a National Assembly, the usual ministers, and a bicameral legislature elected by universal manhood suffrage. The Senate was chosen by indirect election, the Chamber of Deputies by direct election; all legislation had to pass both houses, though only the lower could initiate finance bills. The critical point was that of the responsibility of the ministers. Had the president been able to dismiss them, a new Napoleon III might easily have arisen to destroy the Republic. MacMahon attempted to exercise this power when on May 16, 1877, he dismissed the anticlerical premier, Jules Simon, and got the conservative Duke of Broglie to form a cabinet. But the Chamber was now really republican and voted "no confidence" in Broglie by a big majority. MacMahon was thus forced to dissolve the Chamber and call for a new national election—which he could do constitutionally. In the new elections the republicans, though losing some seats, still retained a good majority in the Chamber, and could now force the president to name a republican premier. Disgruntled, MacMahon resigned in 1879 and was succeeded by a conservative republican, Jules Grévy. This crisis of the *seize mai* (May 16) set a precedent for the Third Republic: no president thereafter dared to dissolve the Chamber, and the presidency became a ceremonial office, made fun of in the press and on the stage. But at any rate, nine years after its establishment in name, the Third Republic had at last become a fact.

It was in form a kind of republican transposition of constitutional monarchy, with an ornamental president instead of an ornamental king. The real executive, as in England, was the ministry, in effect a committee responsible to the legislature—indeed to the Chamber of Deputies, which soon became the focus of political action, leaving the Senate little more than a dignified republican refuge for elder statesmen. The Chamber, reflecting the political habits of the country, was composed not of two, but of a dozen or more parties, so that any ministry had to be supported by a coalition subject to constant shifting in the play of personalities and principles. The result was a marked instability of ministries. The "life expectancy" of a ministry under the Third Republic was hardly a year.

Yet such a figure is misleading. A French ministry under the Third Republic—and indeed under the present Fourth Republic—does not usually resign and give way to a totally different ministry with totally different policies. Instead, its personnel is shifted a bit, a compromise or so is made with certain parliamentary groups, and the new ministry carries on much as did the old. For instance, Briand, the great champion of collective security (after the war of 1914-1918), headed ten different cabinets at various times between 1909 and 1926; Delcassé, the architect of France's entente with England, served as foreign minister continuously through several cabinets and seven years (1898-1905). And in our own day two individuals from the same party, Schuman and Bidault, alternated in the foreign ministry through a dozen cabinets of the Fourth Republic. Moreover, the day-to-day task of governing is carried on by a civil service, by experts in the law courts and in the educational system as well as in the executive department. This permanent personnel, subject only to broad policy control from above, preserves a basic continuity in French political action.

The system is highly democratic, for it can work only by means of constant and subtle compromises. These, the essence of democratic government, are made in France —and in most of the democratic world outside the English-speaking countries—by the several parties in the legislature *after* an election. In the English-speaking countries, these compromises are made *before* an election, *within* each of the two major parties. Probably the English-speaking method both conceals antagonisms and encourages the

habit of willing compromise more effectively than does the continental method. But neither method will work if the underlying antagonisms are really intense, beyond compromise. For example, the American two-party system obviously failed to avert the Civil War, had indeed begun in the 1850's to break down into a plural-party system.

Boulanger and Panama Bitter antagonisms did indeed threaten the Third French Republic between 1879 and 1914, but they did not destroy it. For one thing, the Republic's opponents on the Right and on the Left could never get together. On the Right, although the royalists eventually patched up their quarrels between Bourbon and Orléanist, and although they had some support in literary circles, they could not recover the strength they had dissipated in the 1870's. Nor could the Bonapartists make serious gains in public opinion, though they survived as a political group into the twentieth century. The Catholics, though they feared the anticlerical orientation of many republicans, were after the accession of Pope Leo XIII in 1878 encouraged to develop their way of life by frank acceptance of the freedom of worship that the Constitution of the Republic offered them. The out-and-out Rightist enemies of the Republic were forced to do violence to their own conservative and legitimist principles and to seek some new man who would win over the floating discontent always present in a modern industrial state and set up a dictatorship.

In the 1880's, they hoped that they had found such a man in General Boulanger, an ambitious soldier who had as minister of war catered to French desire for revenge on Germany. But the Boulangist movement was founded on a man of straw. The General cut an impressive figure in public appearances, and in by-elections to fill vacancies in the Chamber he showed he could command a popular following. But from the point of view of conservatives he had compromising origins and radical friends, and, as it became clear that Boulanger in power might rush the country into war, his following threatened to desert him. In January, 1889, he swept a by-election in Paris, but his nerve failed when he was faced with the need to resort to the classic technique of the *coup d'état*. Instead of seizing power by force of arms, he sought refuge with his mistress. The government now took courage and threatened to try him for treason; Boulanger fled to Brussels and committed suicide on the grave of his beloved in 1891. The Republic had surmounted its first great crisis.

Boulanger's cause had gained strength from a scandal in republican ranks. Daniel Wilson, President Grévy's son-in-law, was implicated in the selling of posts in the Legion of Honor. The opposition press made out that the government was riddled with graft. More fuel went on the fire in the early 1890's, when there burst into publicity one of those crises of corruption, graft, and racketeering that seem endemic in modern western societies. This was the Panama scandal which was brought on by the failure of De Lesseps' attempt to duplicate in Panama his success in building the Suez Canal. It involved accusations of criminal corruption against ministers, deputies, financiers, and an unfortunate Jewish banker, Reinach, who either committed suicide or was murdered just before his trial. And indeed, as in the somewhat comparable Crédit Mobilier scandal in the United States in 1873, it was established that ministers and deputies had accepted financial reward for backing the shaky Panama company. Bad as it was, the Panama scandal was to pale before the Dreyfus affair. For with this famous affair a force that was to trouble the Western world for decades to come first really attained dramatic intensity. This was anti-Semitism.

The Dreyfus Case   Dreyfus, a Jew and a captain in the French army, was the almost accidental victim of an espionage intrigue and of the anti-Semitism then prevalent in France, especially in military and Catholic circles. Accused of selling military secrets to the Germans, he was railroaded into trial as a scapegoat and was convicted of treason in 1894. Colonel Picquart, an intelligence officer, became convinced that the document on which Dreyfus had been convicted was a forgery, and that the real traitor was a disreputable adventurer of Hungarian blood but of French birth, Major Esterhazy. Picquart was quietly shipped off to Africa by his superiors, who wished to let sleeping dogs lie. But the Dreyfus family, by independent investigation, arrived at the conclusion that Esterhazy was the traitor, and sought to reopen the case. Esterhazy was tried and acquitted, but the affair was now too public for such silencing. In 1898, the famous novelist Zola brought matters to a crisis by publishing his open letter, "*J'Accuse.*" Zola accused the military leaders, one by one, of sacrificing an innocent man deliberately in order to save the reputation of the army.

France was now divided into Dreyfusards and Anti-Dreyfusards; the former defended in Dreyfus the Republic, the latter attacked it. All the far Left, which had hitherto held aloof from the affair as just one more example of the rottenness of the bourgeois state, now rallied to the Third Republic. Dreyfus was brought back from his prison on Devil's Island in French Guiana, and was retried in the midst of a frenzied campaign in the press and on the platform. The military court, faced with new evidence brought out by the suicide of Colonel Henry, the real forger of the most incriminating of the original documents used to convict Dreyfus, again found Dreyfus guilty of treason, but with the almost incredible qualification—in a treason case—of "extenuating circumstances." This attempt at face-saving saved nothing. Dreyfus was pardoned by the President of the Republic in 1899, and in 1906, after the tensions had abated, he was acquitted and restored to the army with the rank of major.

The Dreyfus affair presents a remarkably well-documented case study in social psychology. The simple juridical issue—was this man guilty or not guilty of treason—never wholly disappeared in the mass hysteria. Many Frenchmen who did not like Dreyfus or Jews or who did revere the Church, Army, and the whole apparatus of the Right, none the less sought to make up their minds solely on the basis of the facts. Yet many on both sides worked themselves up to a point where the question of Dreyfus' guilt was wholly submerged in this great confronting of the "two Frances"—the France of the Republic, heir to the great revolution and the principles of 1789, on the one hand, and, on the other, the France of the monarchy, of Throne and Altar, which had never really reconciled itself to the great revolution. For the ordinary person, the open admission of forgery by Colonel Henry and his subsequent suicide were enough; he now thought Dreyfus innocent. But for the violent Anti-Dreyfusard, Henry's act made him a hero and a martyr; he had died for his country! A paper was circulated in Paris asking for a memorial to Henry:

Colonel Henry's Devotion to his Country.
Public subscription for a monument to be raised to him.
When an officer is reduced to committing a pretended forgery in order to restore peace to his country and rid it of a traitor, that soldier is to be mourned.
If he pays for his attempt with his life, he is a martyr.
If he voluntarily takes his life,
HE IS A HERO.[*]

These were months of real mass hysteria, in which both sides were swayed by emotions far too strong for reason to control.

---

[*] F. C. Conybeare, *The Dreyfus Case* (London, 1898), 298.

The Republic after Dreyfus

With the victory of the Dreyfusards, the Republic moved to the Left and punished the Church for its support of the army and the Anti-Dreyfusards. The triumphant republicans in a series of measures between 1901 and 1905 destroyed the Concordat of 1801 between Napoleon I and the Pope which had established the Roman Catholic Church in a privileged position in the French state (see Chapter XI). The Catholic teaching orders were forced to dissolve, and some 12,000 Catholic schools, which had been formidable rivals of the state school system, had to close down. The state was no longer to pay the clergy, and private corporations organized by the faithful were to take over the expenses of worship and the ownership and maintenance of the churches. The Catholics refused to accept this settlement, and the churches remained technically government property.

But, though the separation had been carried out amid great bitterness, though the debates had revived the ferocious language of the 1790's, there was no recourse to the violence of the past. Catholicism was not proscribed, and somehow or other worship continued in churches that were not the full legal property of the faithful. Catholic education was indeed severely hindered, but there was no formal persecution. The separation did not really alter the fundamental social position of the Church in France. The upper classes, and the peasantry of the north and west, remained loyal Catholics; many of the townspeople, and the countryfolk in the southwest and center especially, remained what they had become over the last few centuries, indifferent Catholics or outright and determined secularists.

The indifferent Catholics and the anti-clericals formed the backbone of the central supporting party of the Republic, the Radical Socialists, who were not socialists at all but petty bourgeois, French Jeffersonians. Indeed, the French Republic of the early twentieth century was a typically bourgeois state. It made certain concessions to demands from the workers for social security and better living conditions, but not nearly so many as the British constitutional monarchy was then making, nor indeed so many as the only partly constitutional German monarchy had made already. Trade unions in France were legal, but they had hard sledding against the reluctance of French workers to pay dues and accept union discipline. Moreover, good democrats, like Clemenceau and Briand, had no scruples about using force against strikers.

France remained fundamentally in the twentieth century what she had been since 1789, a land of small farm-owning peasants, very conservative in their farming methods, and of relatively small family-controlled industries, very conservative in their business methods. There were some elements of big industry by the early 1900's, and French steel production at that time was actually growing faster than that of Britain, Germany, and the United States. None the less, great industry was not typical of the French economic scene, which was backward in comparison with the achievements of the industrial giants just mentioned, but at the same time well balanced by old-fashioned standards of the nearly self-sufficient national economy.

The Third Republic had weathered the storms of domestic differences at bottom because, though some Frenchmen disliked it intensely, and though many Frenchmen felt toward it that distrust of the "government" not unknown in the American de-mocracy, most Frenchmen felt it somehow to be the embodiment of *la patrie*, the fatherland. Differences did arise among them, notably on questions of imperial policy. The great expansion of French power in Africa, Indo-China, and Oceania which made the world empire of France second only to Britain's was the work of a determined minority (see Chapter XVII). Many Frenchmen viewed their colonies with antagonism or apathy.

France since 1870 had often seemed dangerously divided on matters of domestic and imperial concern; yet on foreign policy the Third Republic was essentially united. Disagreement on the big question of foreign policy concerned details of timing, not ultimate aims. France wanted revenge for 1870; France wanted Alsace-Lorraine back. In the complex workings of international politics from 1870 to 1914, the foreign ministries of the Third Republic, shifting though their personnel was through the workings of the multi-party system, none the less brought France to a position of strength in which revenge on Germany became possible. Democracies are sometimes held to be at a disadvantage in the conduct of foreign relations in comparison with states under strong monarchic or dictatorial control. Yet in 1871, indeed as late as 1890, democratic France was isolated, and imperial Germany was the center of a marvelous system of alliances; in 1914, democratic France was firmly allied with a powerful Britain and a Russia powerful at least for the moment, and imperial Germany, save for a weak Austro-Hungarian ally, was essentially isolated.

III: *Italy, 1848-1914*

Italian national unity, which seemed after the events of 1848-49 (see Chapter XII) as far away as ever, was triumphantly achieved between 1859 and 1870. The Kingdom of Italy that began to emerge after 1860 had a constitution very much like that of the Third French Republic, with an ornamental king instead of an ornamental president. The ministry was responsible to a lower house which in practice developed a multi-party system rather like that of France. At first, a property qualification severely limited the suffrage; after 1881, this qualification was low enough—a direct tax of 19 lire, or about $4.00—so that the electorate numbered over 2,000,000. What amounted to full universal manhood suffrage was not, however, introduced until 1912.

Cavour and the Completion of Unification

The architect of Italian unification was Cavour (1810-1861), who became the chief minister of Piedmont in 1852. Though of aristocratic origin himself, and trained for the highly conservative career of an army officer, Cavour enthusiastically supported the economic revolutions and the aspirations of the business classes. He visited France and England as a young man and was deeply influenced by their economic accomplishments and by their eco-

nomic and political ideas and institutions. Back in Piedmont, he applied the newest agricultural methods to his family estates and promoted the introduction of steamboats, railroads, industries, and banks in order to prepare Piedmont for leadership in unified Italy. Cavour was a good, moderate, mid-nineteenth-century liberal.

But Cavour was also a superlatively adept practitioner of the realistic diplomacy often called *Realpolitik*. As the chief minister of Piedmont, he set about cultivating French and English support, bringing Piedmont into the Crimean War on their side against Russia. He got no immediate award, for England was unwilling to take steps that would offend Austria. But, though bitterly disappointed, he put a good face on his defeat, and finally persuaded Napoleon III that the Austrian hold in northern Italy was an anachronism, a flying in the face of the principle of nationality. In 1859, France and Piedmont went to war with Austria, and won bloody victories at Magenta and Solferino in June. Sympathetic nationalist risings broke out in Tuscany and the Papal States. But the threat of Prussian help to Austria alarmed Napoleon, who held a conference with the Emperor of Austria, Francis Joseph, at Villafranca (July, 1859) and arranged a compromise by which Lombardy was to go to Piedmont but Venetia to remain Austrian, and the rest of the peninsula to remain divided. Cavour resigned in bitter protest.

He had, however, already won. A wave of popular agitation in the smaller states of northern and central Italy brought almost bloodless revolutions, and plebiscites demanding annexation to Piedmont. Cavour came back into office to accept the annexations, and to take advantage of the promising situation developing in the Papal States and the South. For in May, 1860, a most successful expedition had set out for Naples and Sicily under the command of a radical, indeed republican, nationalist agitator, Garibaldi. Cavour deeply distrusted Garibaldi's

radicalism, which he feared might make Italy a republic and might so alarm the powers that they would intervene to undo Cavour's own annexationist achievements. For these reasons, Cavour sought first to prevent the departure of Garibaldi's expedition, and then, after this had proved impossible, to control its progress and exploit its success in the interests of his own policy. Garibaldi and his thousand "redshirts" had relatively little trouble in overcoming the feeble opposition of the Bourbon Francis II in Sicily. Recruits swarmed to his flag. Popular opinion throughout the West, even in cautious England, was overwhelmingly on the side of this romantic adventurer. Garibaldi, who had announced his loyalty to the King of Piedmont, Victor Emmanuel, now crossed the Straits of Messina with the approval of the British minister, Lord Palmerston, and continued his victorious march on the mainland. Cavour, alarmed lest Garibaldi bring on a crisis with Napoleon by taking Rome, sent Piedmontese troops into the Papal States. They disposed of the papal forces easily, and occupied all save the area about Rome itself. King Victor Emmanuel soon joined forces with Garibaldi near Naples and assured the triumph of Cavour's policy. Meanwhile, in plebiscites, Naples and Sicily voted for union with the North.

The upshot of all these rapidly unrolling events was the proclamation of the Kingdom of Italy with Victor Emmanuel of Savoy at its head, and with Florence as its capital, in March, 1861. Cavour died in June, but what had seemed impossible only two short years ago at Villafranca had now been realized. Rome, under French occupation, and Venetia, still held by Austria, kept the new kingdom from the territorial completion the patriots wanted. Garibaldi made an attempt in 1862 to take Rome in a filibustering expedition, but the troops of the new kingdom were too much for him. He was beaten and captured, but soon amnestied. He returned to make still another attempt on Rome in 1867 after the French had with-

Meeting of Garibaldi (left) and King Victor Emmanuel (right).

drawn, but was defeated by French troops who now once more returned to occupy the city.

Venetia and Rome soon came easily into the kingdom in the play of international politics, and cost Italy little in bloodshed. Venetia came as a reward for Italy's siding with Prussia in the brief war of 1866 that saw Prussia defeat Austria; Rome came when the war of 1870 with Prussia forced Napoleon III to withdraw from papal territory (see Chapter XV). On October 2, 1870, Rome was annexed to the Kingdom of Italy and became its capital. All the peninsula, save for Trieste and Trent in the North, was now under one rule. These two small bits of *Italia Irredenta* (Italy unredeemed) were of no small importance, for Italian patriots remained unreconciled to Austrian possession of them, and went to war against Austria and her German ally in 1915 largely to obtain them.

Assets and Liabilities of United Italy

The new kingdom started out with the asset of favorable public opinion throughout the non-Catholic segments of the western world. Italian national unity seemed a natural and desirable thing, and it had been achieved without very much bloodshed, with a mixture of Garibaldian romance and Cavourian realism. Within the kingdom the enthusiasm that had brought the *Risorgimento* (resurrection) to fruition was now in the service of united Italy. Italians were a frugal, hard-working people, and in the north they made promising beginnings in the new industry of the machine age.

Yet striking liabilities impeded the new Italy. The Italians had, like the French, a division between Catholics and anticlericals—better, anti-Catholics—difficult for a modern American to understand. Still, the division was perhaps less sharp than in France; there were in Italy more middle-of-the-roaders in practice. On the other hand, ardent Italian Catholics were embittered by the circumstances of the final drive for union, the annexation of the Papal States without the Pope's consent, the "Roman question." Italy lacked coal and iron; in terms of modern economic competition, she was a "have-not" country, a shocking discovery that the Italians made in the years following unification. Much of mountainous central Italy and all southern Italy were really marginal to nineteenth-century western civilization, with a poverty-stricken, illiterate peasantry rooted in age-old local ways utterly different from those of modern urban life, and with a small feudalistic aristocracy to whom a man like Cavour was really quite incomprehensible. Neapolitans and Sicilians resented the new political preponderance of North Italians in the unified kingdom, much as American Southerners resented Yankee "carpetbaggers" after the Civil War. If one spoke of the "two Italies," the division would be that between the already somewhat industrialized North, especially the thoroughly "modern" Po Valley, and the rural, impoverished South, still "medieval."

Moreover, at least half of Italy lacked experience in self-government. It had no tradition of government by discussion, of law-abidingness, of comfortable middle-class compromise. Italy was not indeed the land of mixed stereotypes—sunny gaiety, dark passions, music, and *banditti*—which northern Europeans and Americans believed it to be. It was a land of deep-seated class antagonisms, regional variations, fervent localism, a whole inheritance from the past which made democratic government very difficult.

The Roman question became a chronic rather than a critical one. The Pope, who refused to accept the legality of the new kingdom, simply stayed in the Vatican Palace as a "prisoner." The Vatican remained the center of the world-wide organization of the Roman Catholic Church, and in no important sense was the Pope impeded in the exercise of his powers over the faithful throughout the world. Within Italy, the Church forbade Catholics to participate in politics and urged a Catholic boycott of the new state. Gradually, in fact, Catholics did take an increasing part in politics, but the Roman question itself remained unsettled until 1929, when Mussolini and Pope Pius XI agreed to set up the Vatican City as a sovereign state of 108 acres.

The new kingdom made appreciable economic progress. Railroads, built and managed by the state, were pushed rapidly into the backward South, a brand-new merchant marine brought the new Italian flag into the seven seas, and an army and navy gave it standing as a power. Even the national finances seemed for a time under conservative leadership to be sound. In the political

field, the 1880's brought a letdown, the growth of parliamentary corruption, the beginning of a long era of unashamed political opportunism. Meantime, the industrial proletariat was small, labor inadequately organized, and the socialists were both too small and too rent by divisions to constitute a dynamic instrument of opposition and reform.

Moreover, Italy was now launching itself on a career of imperial aspiration which seems a good example of the desire to keep up with the Joneses. Since France—the envied "Latin" sister—and Britain had empires, since a great power had to have an empire, and since Italy, or rather the guiding groups in Italy, wanted to be a great power, some way of territorial expansion had to be found. The conventional economic explanations of the imperialist drive hardly make sense for the Italy of the 1880's and 1890's, a nation with no important exportable capital, with no need for colonial markets, and with plenty of domestic difficulties. True, Italy had a rapidly expanding population that found relatively few economic opportunities at home, especially in the South. But, since other countries had such a head start in empire-building, what was left open to Italian seizure was very little indeed. And even these leftovers were not suitable for colonial settlement by Europeans. They were the poorer parts of Africa, hardly worth the difficulty of exploitation.

Even so, the effort to take Ethiopia (then called Abyssinia) drained the resources of the government, and was halted by the disastrous military defeat inflicted by the Abyssinians on the Italian expeditionary force at Adowa in 1896. The general depression of the 1890's, a bank scandal, and the Adowa failure cast a shadow on the last years of the century. Grave bread riots broke out in Milan in May, 1898, the *"fatti di Maggio"* (deeds of May), and in 1900 King Humbert was assassinated by an anarchist. The accession of a new king,

Victor Emmanuel III, who was believed to have liberal leanings, gave new heart to many, and the years just before the outbreak of World War I were on the whole years of comparative quiet and prosperity, of partial reconciliation with the Church, and of the final establishment of universal suffrage. Giolitti, the political leader from 1901 to 1914, though as corrupt a manipulator of the electorate as his predecessors, was also an intelligent moderate who did much to end social tensions and to promote the growth of western-style political parties. Parliamentary democracy seemed at last to be sending down solid roots. And in the years 1890-1914 the vast emigration to North and South America—the number of emigrants exceeded half a million in the peak year of 1913—almost canceled out the serious economic difficulties attendant on the high Italian birth rate and lack of new industrial employment.

Yet the men who ran Italy could never quite content themselves with a position, say like that of a Mediterranean Sweden, quite outside the competition for empire and quite outside the "great powers." Italy was not a great power, but her leaders, and their millions of followers, wanted very much to make her one. Pushed out of Abyssinia, and forced by the increasing tensions of international politics to yield to the French in Tunisia, Italy finally got from the other great powers a free hand in poverty-stricken and parched Tripoli, a fragment of the old Turkish Empire in North Africa now known as Libya. In 1911, she went to war with Turkey over Tripoli, thus stimulating the cycle of Balkan wars that were to ripen into World War I.

IV: *The United States*

World War I was also to mark the full participation in the international balance of another relative newcomer to the family of nations, the United States. The simplest and in many ways the most important fact of her brief national history is that in a little over a century the United States secured in terms of actual power a position like that of the great states that have filled these pages for many chapters—Austria, France, England, and the rest. The United States came to be a "great power," despite words and even sentiments that placed her outside international competition, in "isolation." Two simple sets of statistics point up this fact. In 1790, the United States comprised 892,000 square miles, and in 1910 3,754,000 square miles; even more important, the population of the United States was 3,929,000 in 1790, and 91,972,000 in 1910. The 1910 population was greater than that of either of the most powerful European states, Germany and Great Britain, indeed second only to that of Russia. And, still more important, American industrial and agricultural capacities were already greater than those of any other single country.

The Federal Union   The land that had become so powerful in a brief century was in the late eighteenth century almost empty beyond the Alleghenies, save for a few Indians of Stone Age culture; yet millions of square miles were as suited to intensive human use as any in Europe. Most interested observers knew this at the end of the American Revolution, and they expected the central parts of the North American continent to fill up with white men eventually. But most of them, including Americans like Jefferson, did not believe that the process would be as rapid as it in fact was. Moreover, all but the most sanguine felt that the developed and fully peopled continent could not possibly come under one political rule. They felt that it must be divided—as indeed the South American continent came to be—into a number of independent nations on essentially the European model. Indeed, the most pessimistic or merely hostile observers did not believe that the thirteen Atlantic seaboard colonies gathered together to fight the British could possibly maintain their own union. Here is a sample prediction:

As to the future grandeur of America, and its being a rising empire under one head, whether republican or monarchical, it is one of the idlest and most visionary notions that ever was conceived even by writers of romance. The mutual antipathies and clashing interests of the Americans, their difference of governments, habitudes, and manners, indicate that they will have no centre of union and no common interest. They never can be united into one compact empire under any species of government whatever; a disunited people till the

end of time, suspicious and distrustful of each other, they will be divided and subdivided into little commonwealths or principalities, according to natural boundaries, by great bays of the sea, and by vast rivers, lakes, and ridges of mountains.*

Yet hold together the former colonies did. Though the union was often sorely tested, once in the greatest war Americans have fought, it is a central fact of history that the United States did not go the way of the Latin American states. Why the United States held together cannot be explained by any single factor. Geography was certainly kinder to her than to the Latin Americans, for the Appalachians were no real barrier at all; the Rockies were not the barrier the Andes are; and the Mississippi Valley, unlike that of the Amazon, was a help rather than a hindrance to settlement and communications. The rail-

---

* Josiah Tucker, Dean of Gloucester, quoted in John Fiske, *The Critical Period of American History, 1783-1789* (Boston, 1888), 57-58.

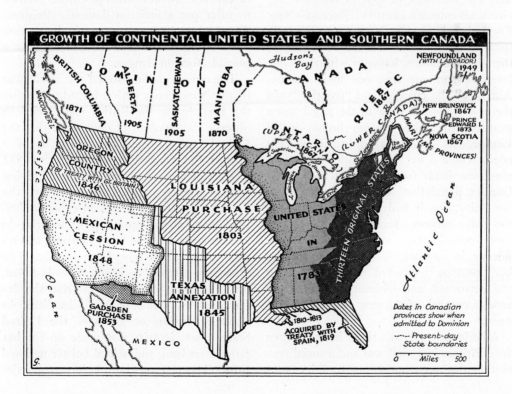

GROWTH OF CONTINENTAL UNITED STATES AND SOUTHERN CANADA

road and the telegraph arrived just in time to enable goods and ideas to move fast and far enough to hold Americans together. The communications and transportation network already developed by 1860 enabled the North to count on the West in the decisive struggle of the Civil War. The sheer size of the new republic after the decisive acquisition of the Mississippi-Missouri Valley by purchase from Napoleon in 1803 seemed historically compatible with a loosely held empire of many tongues and peoples, like those of ancient Persia or Rome, but not with a unified nation-state. The achievements of modern technology in effect reduced sheer size to manageable proportions. After the first transcontinental railway was completed in 1869, Californians could get to the federal capital more quickly than New Yorkers could in 1800.

Yet it will not do to emphasize purely material factors in the holding together of the United States. The resistance to Britain had helped forge a genuine national patriotism. The colonists, in spite of contrasts between seventeenth-century "Puritan" New England and "Cavalier" tidewater South, in spite of Dutch and German elements in the middle colonies, brought with them one language and one law, one basic culture. Almost all the colonies had "frontiers"—in the new American sense of the word, not a guarded line with custom houses as in Europe, but free areas on their western edges where a lively population was winning new lands from the wilderness. This frontier population was a powerful force for unity, for it had little attachment to the older centers of colonial (now state) group-consciousness, and it had great confidence in its own "manifest destiny" to keep pushing westward with the blessing and patronage, and without more than the remote control, of the new federal government.

Americans gained their independence from Britain in a civil war and a social revolution that were rather mild affairs compared, say, with the French Reign of Terror. And, after the more committed Loyalists had left for Canada or Britain, Americans took up national life without any seriously alienated minorities. They achieved at the Philadelphia convention of 1787 and in the campaign for adoption during the next two years a federal constitution that set up a central government with the essential attributes of all governments—the ability to tax individuals (not just to obtain monies as contributions from constituent states), to control armed forces, and to maintain a monopoly of foreign relations. The new constitution, in short, set up a sovereign federal state, not a mere league of sovereign states. On the whole, this result was achieved under conservative groups anxious to preserve their economic and social privileges, afraid that democracy in separate, quasi-independent states would go too far. But this conservative conclusion to the American Revolution gave the infant federal state a safer start. Finally, the threat that British control of Canada seemed to offer put a limit on domestic divisions. The United States grew up in its earliest years aware of the need for union against a possible foreign danger.

The new republic entered the world war of the Napoleonic period in 1812. Neither the French nor the British really tried to observe the freedom of commerce that the United States claimed as the right of a neutral, but the British, who were by 1812 masters of the sea, seemed to be infringing neutral rights more seriously than the French. Moreover, American expansionists, the "war hawks," saw a possible prize in Canada to be wrested from England, and no such prize to be got from France. The American attempt to invade Canada failed, not only from ineptness, but from the determined resistance of the Canadians. In isolated combats on the seas, the United States won victories that made up for her failures on land, and helped bolster national pride. The war on the whole was a stale-

Ruins at Charleston, South Carolina, at the close of the Civil War.

mate, in which the United States experienced no important gains or losses.

Civil War and Reconstruction

The great test of the new republic has been called the "Civil War" by the Northerners and the "War between the States" by the Southerners. War broke out in 1861 after long years of sectional strife within the union between North and South. The Civil War was really an abortive nationalist revolution, the attempt of the Confederate states to set up a separate sovereign nation. The South was predominantly agricultural, with a society based on plantation slavery and on a single major crop, cotton, much of which was exported abroad. The North was increasingly industrial, with a society based on free labor and on independent farm owners.

To the conflict of economic interest was added, as almost always in human affairs, a conflict of ideals, of ways of life. That conflict was not as deep-seated, as irreconcilable, as it seemed to be to the generation that went to war in 1861—or the South, like Ireland or Poland, would presumably have tried again to free itself. But the fires of conflict were fanned especially by the question of slavery, which seemed immoral to many in the North and which seemed the order of nature to many in the South. They were fanned also by writers and preachers on both sides, the Northerners thinking of themselves as heirs of the Puritans, the Southerners as heirs of the Cavaliers. With the secession of South Carolina and its sister states, antagonism reached the point of open war.

In retrospect, the victory of the North has an air of inevitability, especially since by 1861 the middle and upper Mississippi Valley was bound firmly to the North by economic and cultural ties. In population—especially since the South could not, did not dare, use the Negroes as soldiers—and in industrial resources above all, the North was greatly superior. Yet, aided by a very able corps of officers, by the advantages in morale that accrue to determined underdogs, and by the disastrous early overconfidence of the North, the South won initial victories that gave its cause great momentum. But the North thwarted the efforts of Confederate diplomats to secure British intervention and was able to improvise a naval force that gradually established a blockade shutting off the South from importation of necessary war materials. In the long run, Northern strength in men and materials wore the Southern armies down.

The striking thing about the Civil War

is not that the North won it finally in the field, but that the South accepted the verdict of battle as final, that the Union in which Americans today have grown up should be so firm and final. The "Road to Reunion" after 1865 was indeed no easy one, and in the first years of the Reconstruction period after the war it appeared to many an almost impossible one. With the assassination of Lincoln by the fanatical Booth in 1865, the one great moderate who might have lessened the vengefulness of the Northern radicals was lost. The South was occupied by Northern soldiers, the illiterate Negroes were enfranchised, and Northern "carpetbaggers" and Southern "scalawags"—and many sincere idealists who believed they could bring liberty and equality to a "misguided" South—combined to bring what seemed a reign of terror to old Confederates.

Yet even in these early days the Civil War did not end, as such wars have often ended, in wholesale reprisals, executions, and exile. Northerners had sung during the war, "We'll hang Jeff Davis to a sour apple tree"; but after the war Jefferson Davis, President of the Confederacy, was not hanged on a sour apple tree or anywhere else. He was imprisoned for two years, and then lived quietly for another thirty, of course writing a book to justify his career. The fate of Davis measures the miracle of reunion. The soldiers of the South returned, often to devastated homes and lost fortunes, but they returned home under amnesty. Gradually the crusading fervor of the North wore off, and the Southerners, reinforced by new men, some of them immigrant Northerners, took over control in their states. Slavery, abolished by Lincoln's proclamation in 1863, was never restored, but the Negroes were in effect disenfranchised, "white supremacy" was restored, and the race question in the New South took on forms familiar to us today.

And it was a "New South," which is one of the basic reasons why the region has come to accept the Civil War as ended, with due sentimental compensations in wistful feeling for the past. Slowly in the late nineteenth century, more rapidly in the twentieth, it has built up its own industries, taken steps to free itself from cotton monoculture and to integrate its economy and its society with the rest of the country. The South remained throughout this period a relatively backward area, with its own special problems of poverty, illiteracy, and race difficulties, but it was not an alien land, not an oppressed nationality eager to revolt.

The end of Reconstruction, usually assigned to the year 1876, left the Democratic party in control of what came to be called the "solid South." This was a natural development, for it was the Republican party that had guided the North during the war, and that had tried to carry through Reconstruction. This fact has worked to strengthen the American two-party system, since with so solid a block secure for the Democrats, the Republicans have been forced either to make compromises among themselves to preserve their own party unity, or to lose power; and the Northern Democrats have been forced to make compromises with their Southern wing. The fact that the presidency, the great prize of political action, could be obtained only by securing a majority of the Electoral College meant also that a careful balancing of regional interests had to be maintained; a minority party could get nowhere in American politics.

This is not, of course, the whole explanation for the fact that the United States, like Britain, has long maintained a two-party system. It is striking that the two-party system has endured so firmly in both countries despite the great differences between the American political machinery of checks and balances among executive, legislative, and judiciary and the British political machinery centered in an omnipotent Parliament. It is tempting to see in both an underlying habit of political compromise with common roots in a long past of government by discussion.

Economic and Social Development

In 1865, the American economy was in many senses still "colonial" —that is, it produced foods and other raw materials to be exchanged abroad for manufactured goods and, in financial terms, it was dependent on foreign money markets (chiefly London). By 1914, the United States had been transformed into a great industrial nation, with its agriculture already to a high degree mechanized, and with financial resources so great that after World War I New York was to take over in part the place of London as a world financial center. This transformation could not have taken place, certainly not at the rate it did, without the existence of abundant manpower, of great and still almost untouched natural resources, and of the traditions of individual initiative and freedom of enterprise—which in part were certainly a product of the "frontier." Europe played a significant role in American economic growth by furnishing investment capital and, above all, by sending forth a steady flow of emigrants.

This great expansion in national wealth was achieved in a climate of opinion that supported overwhelmingly the view that the federal government should not interfere directly with business enterprise beyond maintaining public order, enforcing contracts, exercising some control over the actual coinage of money—and maintaining a protective tariff. Nor, of course, were the state and local governments to go beyond such appropriate limits. This view we have already met in the classical economists who followed Adam Smith in Britain and in some of the continental states. It is a view that in the West has generally accompanied the first stages of the industrial revolution. But this revolution came relatively late to the United States, and for this if for no other reason a belief in free enterprise, in a minimum of government interference in economic activities, maintained itself more firmly in the twentieth century there than in the other parts of the western world.

This belief was reinforced by the Fourteenth Amendment to the Constitution, passed in 1866 and aimed to protect the freed Negroes in the South from state action to deprive them of civil rights. The Amendment contained the famous "due process" clause: "nor shall any state deprive any person of life, liberty, or property without due process of law." In the great era of free enterprise that followed the Civil War, the Supreme Court of the United States interpreted the celebrated clause to mean that state governments should not deprive businessmen—including corporations as "persons"—of property by regulating wages, prices, conditions of labor, and the like.

Immigration since the 1890's had brought in millions of aliens from eastern and southern Europe, men and women ignorant of American ways, and readily exploited by unscrupulous or merely conventional employers. These immigrants were hard to organize in labor unions; moreover, they and their children, uprooted, scorned though they might be, readily absorbed the American belief that no man is a proletarian by nature. Yet even at the height of this "Gilded Age" or "Age of the Robber Barons" there was a movement toward the welfare state. Apparently there never was a time when laissez-faire was a universally accepted principle (expect for the tariff), and wistful businessmen who look back to the nineteenth century in America as free from the curse of government interference are simply inventing a myth.

Much the same forces that had produced the Factory Acts in Britain gradually brought to the United States minimum-wage acts, limitation of child labor and women's labor, sanitary regulation, control of hours of labor, and workman's compensation. Characteristically, and in spite of the Fourteenth Amendment, these measures were taken at the state rather than at the national level, and they varied greatly in the different states. The state of Wisconsin early established a reputation for advanced social legislation, but many of the older northeastern states played an important part in the movement. By the early twentieth century, public opinion was ready for increased participation of the national government in the regulation of economic life.

Theodore Roosevelt, a Republican, president from 1901 to 1909, promised to give labor a "square deal" and to proceed vigorously with "trust-busting," attacks on the great trusts or combinations that had come to monopolize important sectors of the American economy. Although Theodore Roosevelt did not always fulfill his promises, his administration did assail the trusts in railroads and tobacco and did press the federal regulation of great corporations. A federal prosecution of the Standard Oil Company begun in 1906 resulted in 1911 in a Supreme Court decision dissolving the great holding company. Some of the separated parts familiar today, such as Esso (Standard of New Jersey), Socony-Vacuum (Standard of New York), and Calso (Standard of California), are in fact "bigger" than was the dissolved parent company of John D. Rockefeller. Yet the work of the radicals of 1900, particularly the "muckrakers" who wrote exposés of questionable business practices for popular magazines, was clearly not in vain. American "big business" is in the 1950's bigger than it was in the days of Theodore Roosevelt. But, to put the matter nicely and in good terms, it is aware of its responsibilities to the public—or, to put it not so nicely, it is afraid of what might happen to it if it followed the advice of one of the great nineteenth-century "robber barons," Cornelius Vanderbilt, "The public be damned!" In short, big business in the

United States is ultimately, as in democratic theory it must be, under the control of public opinion. This is a "realistic," not an "idealistic" statement: American public opinion is not at bottom hostile to the existence of wealthy individuals, but it does resent excessive exploitation by big corporations.

During the first administration of Woodrow Wilson (1913-1917), a Democrat, the process of regulation gained momentum. The Federal Reserve Act of 1913, for example, gave federal officials more control over banking, credit, and currency. Approval of such measures was not, of course, unanimous, since Americans differ loudly and widely about almost everything from metaphysics to sports. But, save for the Civil War, they have usually been willing in the end to differ no more than vocally, to accept varieties of belief and action where they appeared harmless or avoidable, to conform to the law with no more than occasional violence. To outsiders, and to many native critics, American life in the decades between the Civil War and 1917 often seemed one great brawl, a more-than-Darwinian struggle for wealth and power. Yet this apparently anarchistic society achieved extraordinary material things—bridges, dams, railroads, great cities—which required the co-operation of millions of men and women disciplined to a common task. This paradox of the co-existence in the United States of "rugged individualism" and social cohesion still disturbs many commentators on the American scene.

In spite of the more than usual dose of distrust of "government" common in western—perhaps in human—tradition, government has in the United States come to play a larger and larger part in the lives of all. Although this is true of local and state governments too, it holds more especially of the federal government. The gradually increasing importance of the federal government, and the gradually decreasing initiative of state governments, are as objectively clear in the period 1789-1917 as is the material growth of the United States in population and wealth.

The Myth of Isolation

Quite as objectively clear, though still the subject of infinite debate among Americans, is the emergence of the United States as a great international power. The United States was never literally "isolated." From the very beginning, she had a Department of State and the proper apparatus of ministers, consuls, and, later, ambassadors. She was involved in the world war of the Napoleonic era, and by the Monroe Doctrine of the 1820's she took the firm position that European powers were not to extend their existing territories in the Western Hemisphere. This was no mere negation, but an active extension of American claims to a far wider sphere of influence than the continental United States. Although Americans took no part in the complex balance-of-power politics in Europe, they showed an increasing concern with a balance of power in the Far East, where they had long traded. After the brief war of 1898 with Spain, a war that broke out in Cuba, always a close concern of the United States, Americans found themselves directly involved with the newly annexed territories of the Philippine Islands, Hawaii, Puerto Rico—in short, with an American empire.

Theodore Roosevelt, who owed his rapid political rise partly to his military leadership of the "Rough Riders" in the Spanish War, was a vigorous imperialist. He pressed the building of the Panama Canal, upheld the Far Eastern interests of the United States, and advocated a larger navy. This new "navalism," which also had assertive spokesmen in Britain and Germany, derived many of its doctrines from the writings of an American officer, Captain Alfred T. Mahan. Mahan's book, *The Influence of Sea Power upon History* (1890), and his later works assigned navies a place of pre-eminent importance in determining power status and found an influential audience both at home and abroad.

Furthermore, over these many decades of expanding wealth and trade, the United States had come to take full part in international commercial relations. In these relations she had, save when the federal government was blockading the Confederacy, stood out firmly for rights to trade even though there was a war on somewhere, stood out for the "rights of neutrals." This fact alone would probably have brought the United States into the world war of 1914-1918, as it had brought her eventually into the world war of 1792-1815. But in 1917 America was, as she had not been in 1812, a great and active participant in the world state-system.

Reading Suggestions on the Western Democracies

Britain

E. Halévy, *A History of the English People in the Nineteenth Century*, 2nd rev. ed., 5 vols. (N.Y.: P. Smith, 1949-1951). The classic detailed study; does not cover the entire period.

E. L. Woodward, *The Age of Reform* (Oxford: Clarendon, 1938); and R. C. K. Ensor, *England, 1870-1914* (Oxford: Clarendon, 1936). Two full and very useful volumes in the *Oxford History of England*.

D. Thomson, *England in the Nineteenth Century* (Harmondsworth, Middlesex: Penguin Books, 1950). An excellent short account.

P. Magnus, *Gladstone: A Biography* (N.Y.: Dutton, 1955). A sound study of the great Victorian Liberal. *Note:* See also titles cited for Chapter XIII.

France

A. Guérard, *Reflections on the Napoleonic Legend* (N.Y.: Scribner's, 1924). Interesting study of the magnetic attraction exerted by Bonaparte after his death.

F. A. Simpson, *The Rise of Louis Napoleon*, 3rd ed. (London: Longmans, Green, 1950), and *Louis Napoleon and the Recovery of France*, 3rd ed.

(London: Longmans, Green, 1951). The most detailed study in English; goes only to 1856.

J. M. Thompson, *Louis Napoleon and the Second Empire* (Oxford: Blackwell, 1954). A useful synthesis, based on detailed scholarly works.

A. Guérard, *Napoleon III* (Cambridge: Harvard Univ. Press, 1943). A spirited attempt to picture the emperor in the attractive role of "Caesarean democrat."

D. W. Brogan, *France under the Republic* (N.Y.: Harper, 1940). A witty, perceptive, but allusive history of the Third Republic.

D. Thomson, *Democracy in France: The Third and Fourth Republics*, 2nd ed. (London: Oxford Univ. Press, 1952). A brilliant essay of interpretation; assumes basic factual knowledge on the part of the reader.

R. Soltau, *French Political Thought in the Nineteenth Century* (New Haven: Yale Univ. Press, 1931). A good survey, though perhaps unfair to the conservative thinkers.

G. Chapman, *The Dreyfus Case: A Re-assessment* (N.Y.: Viking, 1956). The most searching treatment of the "Affair" available in English; neglects the historical results of the case.

G. Bruun, *Clemenceau* (Cambridge: Harvard Univ. Press, 1943). A first-rate brief biography of the redoubtable politician of the Third Republic.

S. B. Clough, *France: A History of National Economics, 1789-1939* (N.Y.: Scribner's, 1939). A valuable treatment of topics often hard to find information on; the notes are most helpful.

Italy

A. J. B. Whyte, *The Making of Modern Italy* (Oxford: Blackwell, 1944). One of the very few good accounts in English.

B. King, *A History of Italian Unity*, 2 vols., rev. ed. (London: Nisbet, 1924). An old account, but still informative.

D. Mack Smith, *Garibaldi* (N.Y.: Knopf, 1956). Brief and up-to-date; the best account available in English.

D. Mack Smith, *Cavour and Garibaldi, 1860: A Study in Political Conflict* (Cambridge, England: Cambridge Univ. Press, 1954). Important monograph; essential reading for a full understanding of the two men.

A. J. B. Whyte, *The Political Life and Letters of Cavour, 1848-1861* (London: Oxford Univ. Press, 1930). Useful introduction.

B. Croce, *A History of Italy, 1871-1915* (Oxford: Clarendon, 1929). By a distinguished philosopher of history; thoughtful, but controversial because of its severe judgments on Italian parliamentary leaders.

The United States

R. B. Morris, ed., *Encyclopaedia of American History* (N.Y.: Harper, 1953). A standard reference work.

S. E. Morison and H. S. Commager, *The Growth of the American Republic*, 4th ed., 2 vols. (N.Y.: Oxford Univ. Press, 1950-1951). One of the very best textbooks.

C. A. and M. A. Beard, *The Rise of American Civilization* (N.Y.: Macmillan, 1936). A famous popular account, written from the standpoint of the economic interpretation of history.

O. Handlin, *Chance or Destiny: Turning Points in American History* (Boston: Little, Brown, 1955). Most readable general essay by a distinguished scholar.

L. Hartz, *The Liberal Tradition in America: An Interpretation of American Political Thought since the Revolution* (N.Y.: Harcourt, Brace, 1955). Provocative survey that has stirred up considerable controversy.

R. Hofstadter, *The American Political Tradition* (N.Y.: Knopf. A Vintage Book); and C. Rossiter, *Conservatism in America* (N.Y.: Knopf, 1955). Complementary studies, emphasizing the liberal and conservative strands respectively.

R. Hofstadter, W. Miller, D. Aaron, *The United States: The History of a Republic* (Englewood Cliffs, N.J.: Prentice-Hall, 1957). A readable account, well illustrated.

Historical Fiction

B. Disraeli, *Coningsby* (N.Y.: Dutton, 1911. Everyman ed.). Significant for its statement of the enlightened Conservative political position.

A. Trollope, *The Prime Minister* (London: Oxford Univ. Press, 1951. World's Classics ed.). Probably the best novel on Victorian politics.

E. Zola, *The Downfall* ("La Débacle") (N.Y.: Appleton, 1902). Good novel of the French defeat in 1870; by the famous naturalistic writer.

R. Martin du Gard, *Jean Barois* (N.Y.: Viking, 1949). Sound novel about the crisis of the French conscience over the Dreyfus affair.

W. D. Howells, *The Rise of Silas Lapham* (many editions). One of the best fictional introductions to American middle-class life in the late nineteenth century.

U. Sinclair, *The Jungle* (N.Y.: Viking, 1946). A famous exposé of the bad conditions in the meatpacking industry of Chicago about 1900.

MacK. Kantor, *Andersonville* (N.Y.: Signet, 1957). Grim and realistic novel of the American Civil War based on detailed research; considered by many critics the best single work of fiction on the subject.

M. Mitchell, *Gone with the Wind* (N.Y.: Macmillan, 1936). Important for its faithful reflection of widely held Southern attitudes toward the War between the States.

CHAPTER FIFTEEN

Central and Eastern Europe

To the Outbreak of World War I

In this chapter, we shall deal with Germany (1850-1914), the Habsburg Monarchy (1850-1914), and Russia (1825-1914). These three empires were partners in crime in the partitions of Poland of the late eighteenth century, and firm allies in the Metternich system of European balance after 1815. After 1850, they passed through periods of mutual affection and hatred. In 1914 all went to war, with Germany and Austria-Hungary as allies against Russia. Internally they had much in common, al-though each followed its own peculiar development. In contrast with the countries of western Europe, these were the lands of autocratic monarchy and relatively powerless parliaments, although parliaments were more significant in Germany and Austria-Hungary than in Russia, where the Duma appeared on the scene very late (1906), and then played a decreasingly important role. In 1914, all three were "empires," a title that only the tottering Ottoman state also claimed in Europe.

469

I: Germany, 1850-1914

In 1914, the militarist and nationalist German Empire was a powerful, unified industrial state with a highly educated, obedient, and competent population. By supporting the Balkan policies of its ally, Austria-Hungary, it helped to plunge the entire world into the first of the twentieth century's wars of mass slaughter. Germany had emerged as a great continental power only after 1850, although for more than 1400 years millions of Germans had been living in the heart of Europe under a variety of political regimes. The militarism, the authoritarianism, the whole social and cultural tone of the Germany of 1914 were determined by the fact that it was the Kingdom of Prussia that had achieved German unification. Characteristic Prussian attitudes had overcome other German ways of looking at society, and had imposed themselves on non-Prussians. The Prussian triumph was complete by 1871.

Between 1850 and 1871, and especially after 1862, Prussia moved with ever-accelerating speed from triumph to triumph. Doubters and protesters were silenced or dazzled by the glitter of each new achievement; moral objections were generally regarded as unpatriotic. Bismarck, who directed policy, spoke of respect for legality and decency as "humanitarian twaddle" and proclaimed an era when "blood and iron" alone would decide. The ends seemed so desirable and were being gained so rapidly that even stern moralists could tell themselves that this time they need not examine the means. They shook their heads and voted the government new subsidies.

The creation of imperial Germany was above all the work of Otto von Bismarck (1815-1898). Brilliant, unscrupulous, ruthless, a genius at maneuver and at concealing his real intentions, Bismarck was often bewilderingly inconsistent in his policies. Sometimes he pursued two apparently contradictory policies at the same time, until the moment came when he had to make a final decision on which policy to follow. His intense loyalty to the Prussian Crown, however, did not falter during his long years in office, although after his dismissal by William II in 1890 he felt that his work was being undone and he often tried to embarrass the Emperor and his own successors in the government. He could not endure criticism of himself. He loathed liberals, Catholics, and socialists at different periods, and despised his intellectual inferiors even when they belonged to his own class, the Prussian landed nobility: the Junkers. Whatever his policy of the moment, force lay at its roots. Influential before 1862, he towered over Prussia from 1862 to 1871, and over the German Empire thereafter until 1890. Yet his efforts could not have succeeded had they not met with general approval from the German people, who had hungered for unity since before 1848.

Prussia and the German Confederation, 1850-1859

The first major question facing the statesmen of Central Europe after the Revolutions of 1848 was whether Prussia or Austria would dominate the German Confederation. Indeed, in a broader sense, this was a question of what form the Confederation would now take. A creation of the Congress of Vienna (see Chapter XI), it had been temporarily shaken and

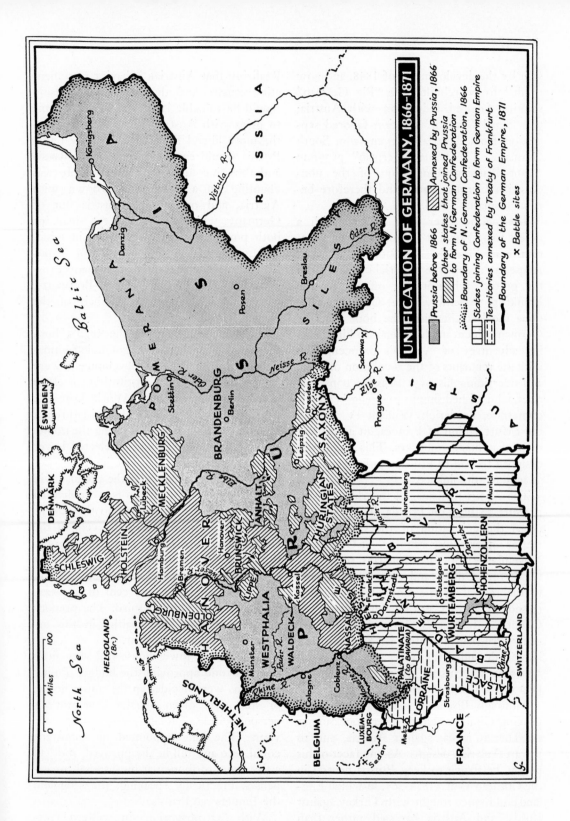

UNIFICATION OF GERMANY, 1866–1871

Prussia before 1866
Annexed by Prussia, 1866
Other states that joined Prussia to form N. German Confederation
Boundary of N. German Confederation, 1866
States joining Confederation to form German Empire
Territories annexed by Treaty of Frankfurt
Boundary of the German Empire, 1871
x Battle sites

split by the developments of 1848, and now needed to be rebuilt. The "Big German" solution favored federation with Austria; the "Small German" solution favored separation from Austria or even from South Germany. The "Small German" program meant Prussian domination of the non-Austrian German states, and therefore became Bismarck's goal.

The period after 1848 opened with a defeat for a Prussian "Small German" solution. King Frederick William IV, who had refused to accept the imperial crown "from the gutter" when it was offered by the Frankfurt Assembly (see Chapter XII), none the less cherished the hope that the German princes might offer it to him. Taking advantage of Austria's preoccupation with the remnants of the revolution of 1848, and overriding his own Prussian conservatives, who wished simply to strengthen their own state, Frederick William IV formed the Erfurt Union of Princes, an agreement to pool military resources. This union was designed to lead to Prussian political as well as military dominance.

The Austrians managed to bring Russian pressure to bear on Prussia. The Tsar opposed the unification of the Germans no matter under whose auspices. At Olmütz, in November, 1850, the Prussians renounced the Erfurt Union, and reluctantly agreed to the revival of the Confederation. This episode is known as the "humiliation" of Olmütz, a term that shows how bitterly many Prussians resented it. Yet Bismarck himself defended the treaty, and as a result was sent as Prussian representative to the Diet of the Confederation.

Although Bismarck made a speech approving Olmütz, he took every occasion at the Diet to work against Austria, and to thwart Austrian designs. As one facet of his policy, he strove to keep Prussia neutral in the Crimean War (1854-56), in which England and France fought with Turkey against Russia, and Austria harassed rather than helped the Russians (see below, p. 483).

Realizing that Austrian behavior was alienating Russia, and that Russian friendship would be valuable later when Prussia came to grips with Austria, Bismarck frustrated the more liberal Prussians who hoped that Prussia would enter the war against Russia and thus line up with the West. He was counting on a military showdown with Austria, and on pushing Austria out of Germany, which he felt was too small for both powers. With this purpose in mind, he also wooed the French Emperor Napoleon III, despite the horror that many Prussians felt over dealings with a Bonaparte, whom they regarded as the heir of the French Revolution.

Simultaneously, during the 1850's, both the constitutional and the economic foundations of future Prussian development were laid. The Prussian Constitution of 1850 lasted down to the end of World War I. It provided for a bicameral legislature: a hereditary upper house including the nobles and royal appointees, and an elected lower house. But the method of electing this lower house made it certain that the popular will would be frustrated. Electors were divided into three classes, according to the size of the taxes they paid. The 4 per cent of the electorate who paid high taxes selected one-third of the representatives. The 14 per cent of middle taxpayers selected another third, and the remaining 82 per cent of low taxpayers selected the last third. The preponderant power of the wealthy in this arrangement is only too clear.

Even so, the lower house had very little to do beyond approving the budget. Policy questions were decided in the upper house, or still more often by the king and his personal circle of military and political advisers. The king appointed his ministers, could veto any bill he disapproved, and had a fixed sum of money at his disposal for expenses. Practically speaking, the king and the Junkers ran Prussia.

With her possessions in western Germany, including the Ruhr, Prussia had the richest coal deposits in Europe. She now began to build the iron and steel industry without which her future political and military triumphs would have been impossible. Alone among the continental nations, the Prussians turned over the planning of their new railway system to the army general staff, which laid out the lines with an eye to rapid and efficient mobilization and transportation of troops in time of war.

Bismarck Comes to Power

Indeed military concerns led directly to the beginning of Bismarck's undisputed domination of Prussian policies. The regent William, who became King William I in 1861, succeeding Frederick William IV, was above all a soldier. His minister of war, Roon, a friend of Bismarck's, easily persuaded the King that an army reorganization was necessary. He wanted to increase the number of conscripts called in each year from 40,000 to 63,000, and to lengthen the term of their service from two to three years. Behind Roon's military projects lay a political motive: to keep the army as conservative as possible, and to make it as big as possible, so that it might serve as counterweight to any liberal or revolutionary tendencies in the state. A prolonged political crisis arose over these aims in 1861 and 1862, when the Prussian parliament refused to vote the budget. At the very height of the crisis, Roon summoned Bismarck back to Berlin, and the King, convinced that here was a man who did not care about parliaments, appointed Bismarck prime minister of Prussia and minister of foreign affairs.

On the fallacious principle that there was a "gap" in the constitution that permitted the government to collect taxes even when the budget had not been approved by parliament, Bismarck now collected and spent revenue quite illegally. Again and again he dissolved the parliament, called new elections, faced another hostile house, and then

Bismarck.

repeated the process. Yet after four years (1862-1866) of this unconstitutional behavior he got away with everything in the end, because of the glittering successes he scored in foreign policy.

Since Bismarck intended to overthrow the German Confederation as it was then constituted, he opposed Austrian efforts to reform it. Austria wished to create an assembly of delegates chosen by the parliaments of the member states, in addition to those named by the princes, and a directorate of six monarchs. Bismarck prevented William I from attending a congress of princes called by Austria to discuss these proposals, and thus wrecked the congress (1863). In 1863, he kept Austria out of the *Zollverein*, the German Customs Union (see above, p. 394), and consolidated his good relations with Russia during the Polish revolt (see below, p. 505) by concluding the Alvensleben convention, which allowed the Russians to pursue fleeing Poles onto Prussian territory and capture them there. Thus Bismarck wooed the Russians a second time, as he had during the Crimean War.

The Schleswig-Holstein Question, 1863-1865

When the King of Denmark died in late 1863, the celebrated Schleswig-Holstein question gave Bismarck further opportunities. The Prime Minister of England once remarked that only three men had ever understood this complex problem, and that one was dead and one insane, while he himself, the third, had forgotten all about it. In brief, the duchies of Schleswig and Holstein at the southern base of the Danish peninsula had been ruled by the King of Denmark, but not as part of Denmark. A fifteenth-century guarantee assured the duchies that they could never be separated from each other. Yet Holstein to the south was a member of the German Confederation; Schleswig to the north was not. Holstein was mostly German in population; Schleswig was mixed German and Danish. In 1852, Prussia had agreed in an international conference on an heir who would succeed both to the Danish throne and to the duchies. At the same time, Prussia had joined the other powers in recommending that Denmark and the duchies should be united by a constitution. But, when the constitutional union of Denmark and the duchies was attempted, the duchies resisted, and the Danes tried to incorporate Schleswig. German patriots objected. The Prussians and Austrians wanted the duchies to have special representation inside the Danish parliament, and insisted that Schleswig should *not* be incorporated into Denmark. None the less, the King of Denmark in 1863 followed a policy that supported annexation.

Into this situation Bismarck now moved to win the duchies for Prussia. He wanted both the prestige that Prussia would gain and the valuable commercial port of Kiel in Holstein. First he maneuvered Prussia and Austria together into a victorious war against Denmark (1864), although Austria had no real interest in the duchies. Then he quarreled with the Austrians over the administration of the duchies. At the Convention of Gastein, 1865, it was decided that Prussia was to administer Schleswig and that Austria was to administer Holstein. But this arrangement provided only a temporary halt in Bismarck's drive against Austria.

War with Austria, 1866

Bismarck kept nagging Vienna about Austrian behavior in Holstein. He tried and failed to tempt France into an alliance. But he did succeed in lining up the Italians, who secretly obliged themselves to go to war on the side of Prussia if Prussia fought Austria within three months. This was contrary to the constitution of the German Confederation, which forbade members to ally themselves with a foreign power against other members. So distressed was William I at this illegality that he lied flatly when the Austrian Emperor asked him if such a treaty existed. Finally, Bismarck suddenly proposed that the German Confederation be reformed, and that an all-German parliament be elected by universal suffrage, which everybody knew he hated.

Bismarck probably advanced this proposal for universal suffrage in order to make it appear that his quarrel with Austria rested on a less sordid ground than the mere Schleswig-Holstein question. Yet the proposal also reflected his calculation that enfranchisement of all Germans would weaken the Progressive party, heir to the liberalism of 1848, and would produce many conservative and royalist votes from the peasantry. He had seen how Napoleon III had risen to imperial power in France on the strength of universal suffrage. And he had been influenced by conversations with Ferdinand Lassalle, a German socialist, who argued that universal suffrage would weaken the middle classes. Bismarck had hoped that the Austrians might try to throw his plan out, but the other members of the Confederation asked Prussia to propose a full plan of reform. Austria now laid the Schleswig-Holstein question before the Diet of the Confederation. Bismarck ordered Prussian troops into Holstein, and declared that the Diet's vote for federal action against Prussia for violating federal (Holstein) territory was unconstitutional. He had succeeded in provoking war with Austria. It was an all-German civil war, since Bavaria, Wurtemberg, Saxony, and Hanover (the four other German kingdoms) and most of the lesser German states sided with Austria.

The war lasted seven weeks, and was virtually decided in less than three. The Austrians had to commit a substantial part of their forces against Italy. Skillfully using their railway network, the telegraph, and superior armaments, the Prussians quickly invaded Bohemia, and defeated the Austrians at Königgrätz (Sadowa). This battle has been referred to as a Gettysburg won by the secessionist Prussians. As the rapid German civil war continued, the Prussians defeated the Bavarians and entered Frankfurt, seat of the German Confederation. The states of Hanover, Hesse-Cassel, and Nassau were all annexed to Prussia and their dynasties were expelled. Schleswig-Holstein and the free city of Frankfurt were also taken over.

Bismarck successfully opposed the generals, and even his king, who wished to punish Austria severely. Except for the cession of Venetia to Italy, Austria suffered no territorial losses as a result of the Peace of Prague (1866), but she did pay a small indemnity. Most important from Bismarck's point of view, Austria had to withdraw forever from the German Confederation, which now ceased to exist. Germany north of the Main River was to join a new North German Confederation to be organized by Prussia. However, it was stipulated that the German states south of the Main were to be free to form an independent union of their own. But Bismarck had previously concluded secret treaties of alliance with the most important South German states— Bavaria, Wurtemberg, and Baden—who promised to put their armies at the disposal of the King of Prussia in case of war. So the proposed South German union could never come into existence. Bismarck thus broke the Peace of Prague before it had been concluded, a real piece of diplomatic skill. Bismarck's gentle treatment of Austria was not just a matter of generosity. He was convinced that Prussia would need Austrian help in the future. Now that he had expelled Austria from Germany, imposed a "Small German" solution, and elevated Prussia to the position of dominance, he had scored his point.

Now Bismarck was free to turn to the Prussian parliament, with which he had been feuding for four years. He asked for an "indemnity," that is, a certification that all the revenue he had illegally collected and illegally spent, ever since the parliament had refused to pass the budget in 1861, had in fact been legally collected and legally spent. The deputies were so dazzled by the feats of arms against Denmark and Austria, and by the enormous new acquisitions of power and territory, that they voted the indemnity, and awarded Bismarck personally a cash gift of roughly $300,000. The indemnity marked an important defeat for parliamentary government.

The North German Confederation

An assembly elected by universal manhood suffrage now debated and adopted a constitution for the new North German Confederation, of which the Prussian king was president. The draft that Bismarck submitted is eloquent testimony to his determination to "kill parliamentarism through parliament." The future parliament (*Reichstag*) was to have no power over the budget, and the ministers were not to be responsible to it. Instead, a Federal Council (*Bundesrat*), consisting of delegates from the member states and voting according to instructions from their sovereigns, would reach all key policy decisions in secret, and would have veto power over any enactment of the Reichstag. A chancellor would preside over the Bundesrat but would not have to explain or defend its decisions before the Reichstag. Since Prussia now had not only its own votes in the Bundesrat, but those of the newly annexed states, Bismarck's plan in effect made it possible for the king of Prussia to run Germany.

This plan was only slightly modified so that the future chancellor would have to sign every act undertaken by the king of Prussia as president of the Confederation. But the executive was in no way made "responsible" to the Reichstag. Bismarck's plan also specified that, beginning five years later in 1872, the size of the army would be fixed by law, and that the Reichstag would have a vote on the budget. However, Bismarck, who became chancellor, saw to it that the debate on the military budget did not take place every year, but that sums were appropriated for long periods in advance. The constitution did little more than sanction Prussian military domination over Germany.

Showdown with France

During the next four years, the power of the new Prussian-dominated German state began to make itself felt. Increasing uneasiness reigned in Europe. As long as Bismarck needed the benevolent neutrality of Napoleon III, he had hinted that he might not object if Napoleon took Belgium. Now the gullible Napoleon found that Bismarck no longer remembered the matter. Hoping to be compensated for his assistance in making peace between Prussia and Austria, Napoleon III made unscrupulous attempts to acquire Luxemburg by purchase from the King of Holland. Again he was frustrated by Bismarck. Suddenly confronted with the new Germany, many members of the French public and press hoped to get "revenge for Sadowa," and became strongly anti-German. The German press responded in kind. Napoleon III strove to create an alliance with Austria and Italy in order to thwart further Prussian expansion. But the Austrians shied away from a true commitment, and the Italians were unable to reach an agreement with the French because of the Roman question (see above, pp. 457-458).

When the Spaniards ousted their queen in 1868, one of the eventual candidates for the throne was a prince of a Catholic branch of the Hohenzollern family, whom Bismarck secretly backed by discreetly bribing influential Spaniards. Because of family dynastic practice, it was necessary to secure the consent of the reluctant King William I of Prussia, and this Bismarck finally extracted without hinting that war with France might result. Napoleon, also deep in Spanish intrigue, feared that a Hohenzollern on the Spanish throne would expose France to a two-front attack. French diplomatic pressure was exerted directly on King William, and the Hohenzollern candidate withdrew. At this moment, Bismarck seemed to be defeated.

But the French, overstimulated by their success, now demanded that William publicly endorse the withdrawal of the candidacy and promise never to allow it to be renewed. William, who was at Ems, courteously refused, and sent a telegram to Bismarck describing his interchange with the French ambassador. Bismarck then abridged this famous Ems telegram and released it to the press and all the European chanceries. He made it seem that William had thoroughly snubbed the French ambassador, and that the ambassador had been "provocative" to the King. Public opinion in Germany was now inflamed, and Bismarck set out to bait the French still further by unleashing a violent campaign against them in the German press and boasting of his prowess in editing the Ems despatch. The French reacted as Bismarck had hoped: they declared war on July 19, 1870.

Within six weeks the Germans had advanced into France, bottled up one French army inside the fortress of Metz, defeated another at Sedan, and captured Napoleon III himself. The protracted siege of Paris followed, ending in surrender early in 1871. A new French government had to sign the Treaty of Frankfurt. Bismarck forced the French to pay a billion-dollar indemnity, to cede the rich province of Alsace and some two-fifths of Lorraine (which the German military wanted as a defense against possible future French attack), and to support German occupying forces until the indemnity had been paid.

The German Empire

Even before this peace had been imposed, King William of Prussia was proclaimed Emperor of Germany in the great Hall of Mirrors in Louis XIV's palace at Versailles. Bismarck had to make a few unimportant concessions to the rulers of the South German states to secure their entry into the new empire, but he never had to consult the Reichstag, which simply hastened to send its own deputation begging the King to accept the crown. The proclamation took place in a ceremony of princes and soldiers. When a constitution for the new empire was adopted, it was simply an extension of the constitution of the North German Confederation of 1867.

As Chancellor of the German Empire from 1871 to 1890, Bismarck became the leading statesman in all Europe. He felt that Germany had no further need for territory or for war. As a nineteenth-century realist with no dream of world-empire, he felt that his limited goals had been attained. As diplomat, he henceforth worked for the preservation of Germany's gains against threats from abroad, especially the threat that haunted him most: foreign coalition against Germany. As politician, he worked for the preservation of the Prussian system against all opposing currents.

Bismarck's chancellorship falls naturally into two periods: (1) a period of free trade, co-operation with the Liberals, and opposition to the Catholics (1871-1878); and (2) a period of protective tariffs, co-operation with the Catholics, and opposition to the socialists (1878-1890).

Domestic Developments, 1871-1878

At home, a multitude of economic and legal questions arose as a result of the creation of the new empire. Working with the moderate Liberal party in the Reichstag, Bismarck put through a common coinage and a central bank, co-ordinated and unified the railroads and postal systems, and regularized the legal and judicial systems. In 1871, the Reichstag voted to maintain 1 per cent of the population under arms for three years. In 1874, Bismarck, simply by threatening to resign, forced the Reichstag to fix the size of the army at 401,000 for a seven-year period, until 1881. In 1880, a year before the period expired, he forced an increase to 427,000 for another seven years, to 1888. The privileged position of the army made a military career ever more attractive, and served as a constant spur to German militarism.

But the great drama of the 1870's in Germany was furnished by Bismarck's attack on the Roman Catholic Church, the *Kulturkampf* ("battle for civilization"). The "Syllabus of Errors," published by the Vatican in 1864 (see Chapter XIII), denounced the toleration of other religions, secular education, and state participation in church affairs. Then in 1870 the first general council of the Church to meet since the Council of Trent in the Reformation period adopted the dogma of papal infallibility. This dogma asserted that the judgments of the pope on faith and morals were infallible. To many non-Catholics this seemed to say that no state could count on the absolute loyalty of its Catholic citizens.

In Germany, the Catholics were a large minority of the population. They had formed a political party, the Center, that quickly became the second strongest party in the Empire. The Center defended papal infallibility and wished to restore the pope's temporal power, which had been ended by the unification of Italy. The Center not only had many sympathizers in the Catholic Polish provinces of Germany but also sponsored a labor movement of its own, which seemed to pose a social threat. Catholic peasant and workman, priest and nobleman, all opposed the Protestant urban middle class and the Prussian military predominance in the state. Bismarck identified his clerical opponents with France and Austria, the two nations he had defeated in making the new Germany.

In collaboration with the Liberals, Bismarck put through laws expelling the Jesuits from Germany, forbidding the clergy to criticize the government, and closing the schools of religious orders. In Prussia, civil marriage was now required, appropriations for the Catholic Church were stopped, and priests were forced to study at secular universities. The Pope declared these laws null and void, and summoned all good Catholics to disobey them. Catholic services stopped in towns and villages, and many Catholics were deprived of their sacraments.

Bismarck never appreciated that the Church thrives on persecution. By declaring that he would not "go to Canossa," he summoned up for Protestant Germans the picture of the medieval German Emperor Henry IV humbling himself before the Pope in 1077. But Bismarck in the end had to go to Canossa, and repealed in the eighties most of the anti-Catholic measures he had passed in the seventies. By then he needed the support of the Center party against his former allies the Liberals, whose demands for power he found exorbitant, and against the growing menace of the Social Democrats. Moreover, the Protestant church itself and many of the conservative Prussian nobility had grown alarmed over the excesses of the anti-Catholic campaign.

Domestic Developments, 1878-1890

Indeed, in 1877 and 1878 Bismarck had begun a gradual shift in policy, dictated in the first place by the need for more revenue. The Empire got its money in part from indirect taxes imposed by the Reichstag on tobacco, alcohol, sugar, and the like. The rest came from the individual states, which controlled all direct taxation and made contributions to the imperial budget. As military costs mounted, the government's income became insufficient, and Bismarck did not want to increase the Empire's dependence on the states by repeatedly asking them to increase their contributions. He wanted the Reichstag to vote higher indirect taxes, but its Liberal members naturally suspected that if they acceded he might do to them what he had formerly done to the Prussian parliament. They suspected that he might govern without them if a dispute arose, and depend on the money he would collect from the higher taxes they had granted him. Therefore they wanted some sort of guarantee before they untied Bismarck's hands.

Basically, German tariff policy had been one of free trade, with little protection for German goods. But after a financial panic in 1873, the iron and textile industries put pressure on Bismarck to shift to a policy of protection that would help them compete with England. Moreover, an agricultural crisis led conservatives to abandon their previous support of free trade, and to demand protection against cheap grain from eastern Europe. In 1879, Bismarck put through a general protective tariff on all imports, a move on which his former allies, the Liberals, were split.

In order to avoid granting the constitutional guarantees demanded by the Liberals, Bismarck gradually abandoned the *Kulturkampf*. The Catholic Center favored his protectionist policy; moreover, the lessening of the clerical threat in France and the conclusion of a firm German alliance with Austria in 1879 (see Chapter XVIII) removed the foreign causes for the attack on the Church. Bismarck therefore secured the support of the Center as well as that of the conservatives. Thus he was able to avoid making concessions to the Reichstag, and thus he launched Germany on an era of protection. The protectionist policy spurred still further the rapid and efficient growth of industry, especially heavy industry. Politically, the conservative Protestant agrarian forces now grew stronger, and gained many urban votes. But Bismarck never entirely trusted the Center, and strove successfully to remodel the Liberals into a stanchly conservative industrialist group.

While he was easing the *Kulturkampf* and swinging to protection in 1878-1879, Bismarck also began to proceed against the Social Democratic party. The Marxists Liebknecht and Bebel had founded this small party in 1869; in 1875, they enlarged it, much to Marx's own disgust, by accepting the followers of Lassalle, an apostle of non-violence. The German Social Democrats were not nearly so revolutionary as their own Marxist phraseology suggested, and had no doubt inherited some of Lassalle's willingness to make a deal with the

existing regime. They did not threaten the state, as Bismarck pretended to think, but they had many supporters among intellectuals and former liberals, and a substantial trade-union following. They polled half a million votes in 1877, about 10 per cent of the total electorate. These revisionist Social Democrats were prepared to concentrate their efforts on improving working conditions rather than on revolution. But Bismarck always needed an enemy against whom he could unify his supporters; besides, he had been deeply impressed by the Paris Commune (see Chapter XIV), and believed that something similar might occur in Germany.

Using as a pretext two attempts by alleged Social Democrats to assassinate William I, Bismarck called a general election in 1878 and rammed through the Reichstag a bill making the Social Democratic party illegal, forbidding its meetings, and suppressing its newspapers. Individual socialists could even be expelled from their domiciles by the police. Abandoning their alleged principles, the Liberals supported this law, but they would not allow Bismarck to make it a permanent statute. He had to apply to the Reichstag for its renewal every two or three years; it was renewed each time, until just before Bismarck's own downfall in 1890. Interestingly enough, Social Democrats were still allowed to run for the Reichstag, and their votes increased during the years when they were suffering legal disabilities.

But Bismarck felt that "a remedy cannot be sought merely in repression of Socialist excesses—there must be simultaneously a positive advancement of the welfare of the working classes." As a result, all during the 1880's, the government put forward a series of bills in favor of the workers: in 1882 compulsory insurance against illness, and in 1884 against accidents. The sickness insurance funds were raised by contributions from both workers and employers; the accident insurance funds were contributed altogether by the employers. In 1889, old-age and invalidism insurance followed, with employers and employees contributing equally, and with an additional subsidy from the state. The German system of social security as developed initially under Bismarck did not reduce the Social Democratic vote, but it did provide much that the worker desired.

William II

Bismarck's faithful William I died at the age of ninety in 1888, and his son, Frederick III, already mortally ill, ruled for only about three months. The next emperor was Frederick's son, William II, a young man of twenty-nine whose ad-

"Dropping the Pilot." Punch comments on William II's dismissal of Bismarck, 1890.

vent his father had greatly feared because of his immaturity, impulsiveness, and conceit. The entire Bismarckian system had been built to support an autocratic King of Prussia as Emperor of the Germans. William I allowed Bismarck to act for him, but William II was determined to act for himself. This determination underlay the subsequent controversy between him and Bismarck.

On his accession, William loudly proclaimed his sympathy with the working-man. When the anti-socialist law came up for renewal, the Emperor supported a modified version that would have taken away the power of the police to expel Social Democrats from their residences. Bismarck opposed the measure, hoping that the Social Democrats would indulge in excesses which would give him the excuse to suppress them by armed force. As a result, there was no anti-socialist law after 1890. Other differences arose between the Chancellor and the Emperor over relations with Russia and over procedure in reaching policy decisions. Finally, in March, 1890, William commanded Bismarck to resign.

Although four chancellors succeeded him during the years before the outbreak of war in 1914, none of them can be compared with Bismarck in ability and influence. The years 1890-1914 are truly the years of William II. Energetic but unsteady, pompous and menacing but without the intention or the courage to back up his threats, emotional and vacillating, William was ill-suited to govern any country, much less the militaristic, highly industrialized, imperial Germany with its social tensions and its lack of political balance.

Domestic Tensions, 1890-1914

Party structure reflected the strains in German society. The Liberals, a party of big business, usually had little strength in the Reichstag, although many industrialists were on intimate terms with the Emperor personally. The great landowners banded together in protest against a reduction in agricultural duties which was included in a series of trade treaties concluded between Germany and other continental European countries between 1892 and 1894. In 1894, they organized the Agrarian League, which spearheaded all conservative measures and became enormously powerful in German politics. In 1902, they forced a return to protection.

The electoral strength of the Social Democrats increased during William's reign from 1,500,000 to 4,250,000, and embraced one-third of the voting population by 1914. Freed from interference by the removal of the anti-socialist law, they organized trade unions, circulated newspapers, and successfully brought pressure on the regime for more social legislation. The party had no immediate plan for a revolution, although its radical wing expected, especially after the Russian revolution of 1905 (see below, p. 507), that a revolution would come. The moderate or "revisionist" wing, which expected no open conflict between capital and labor, felt that by allying with the middle class to attain a majority in the Reichstag the Social Democrats might eventually overthrow the militarist regime. This the radical wing scornfully dismissed as mere temporizing.

As the Social Democrats became more powerful, the government allied itself more closely with the Catholic Center. Between 1895 and 1906, and again between 1909 and 1914, a coalition of conservatives and the Center formed the majority group in the Reichstag. The coalition did not wish to see any increase in the powers of parliament. Yet left-wingers within the Center party occasionally called for a liberalization of the system and for tactical purposes would even ally with the Social Democrats.

Meanwhile, issues of military, colonial, and foreign policy began to complicate the internal politics of Germany. The size of the army rose from 479,000 in 1892 to 870,000 in 1913. And for the first time Germany sought a big navy after Admiral Tirpitz became minister of the navy in 1897. The Emperor issued a series of warlike and grandiose statements hailing Germany's "future on the waters," and he and Tirpitz planned a high-seas fleet to supersede the naval forces that had been designed for coastal defense and for the defense of commerce. The navy boom was at least partly intended to supply a market for the expanding steel industry. A Navy League, ostensibly a private organization but constantly hand in glove with the regime, spread propaganda on behalf of the new fleet. The first rather modest naval law of 1898 provided for a navy that was doubled by the second law of 1900.

But the army and navy were only the most obvious weapons of world power. Bismarck's saturated country seemed saturated no longer. The Colonial Society thrived as Germany seized lands in the Far East and in Africa (see Chapter XVII), despite the drain on the budget (for the colonies were never profitable), and despite scandal after scandal (for the Germans were often brutal colonial administrators). "Pan-Germans" planned the great Berlin-Baghdad railway to the Near East and cried shrilly for more and more adventure and conquest.

William's naval and colonial policies embittered Germany's relations with Great Britain. In 1896, the Emperor himself sent the Boer President Kruger a telegram congratulating him on his having repelled the Jameson Raid (see below, p. 553), and hinting that Germany would have been willing to intervene on the side of the Boers against Britain. Again in 1908, he gave an interview to a London newspaper, the *Daily Telegraph,* in which, with monumental indiscretion, he protested his friendship for Britain, yet at the same time declared that the English had been ungrateful to him in not acknowledging that his own military plans, sent to them in secrecy, had enabled them to win the Boer War. Of course there was nothing in his claim.

The *Daily Telegraph* affair aroused a storm of protest against William in Germany itself, and the Emperor had to apologize and promise to do better in the future. This episode illustrates the dangerous instability of the man who was all-powerful in a mighty military state. Moreover, it also reveals the general uneasiness that underlay the apparently smooth and prosperous surface of William's Germany. The protest against the anachronistic system under which Germans lived and labored, and against the external bombast and internal insecurity of the regime, was expressed in the enormous vote which the Social Democrats won in 1912.

II: *The Habsburg Monarchy, 1850-1914*

The extraordinary empire of the Habsburgs has been called ramshackle, heterogeneous, and anachronistic. And much scorn has been poured upon it for its incompetence, its smugness, its stupidity, and its failure to keep up with modern times. No doubt these charges are largely justified. But in recent years voices have been raised mourning the Empire's disappearance, and regretfully echoing a nineteenth-century Czech patriot's celebrated remark that if the Empire did not exist it would be necessary to invent it. These expressions of longing come not only from reactionaries, monarchists, and clericals lamenting a past hopelessly beyond recovery. They can be heard from the lips of old men in Tito's Yugoslavia and in the "people's republics" of Rumania, Poland, and Hungary. These old men remember with longing a regime which they felt in their youth to be oppressive and unfair. Perhaps these sentiments are not so much praise for the Habsburgs as blame for the communists who now rule much of the former Habsburg territory, and for the extreme nationalist or fascist regimes that preceded the communist triumph. In any case, it is depressing to reflect that the problem of the national hatreds and rivalries that haunted and finally destroyed the Habsburgs is with us still in modified form today, and that this same problem still causes suffering and threatens war.

During the entire period from 1850 to 1914, the Emperor Francis Joseph sat on the Habsburg throne. Simple in his personal life and immensely conscientious, he worked hard at his desk, reading and signing state papers for hours every day. But he was without fire or imagination, uninterested in books dealing with current problems, or even in newspapers, devoted to the rigid court etiquette prescribed for Habsburgs, inflexibly old-fashioned and conservative, and selfish in the old Habsburg way, always ready to dismiss a minister of whose further usefulness he was not convinced. He was intensely pious. He loved to hunt. His mere longevity inspired loyalty, but it must be admitted that he was a dull fellow, in every sense of the term. Except for Prince Schwarzenberg between 1849 and 1852, Francis Joseph never had a prime minister. He was his own prime minister, and had to make decisions on policy himself. His decisions usually came too late, and conceded too little. His responsibility for the course of events in this period is large.

Political Experiments, 1850-1867

The period of Habsburg history from 1850 to 1914 may be divided into unequal portions, with the dividing line coming in 1867 when the Empire became the dual monarchy of Austria-Hungary. Before 1867, there was a decade of reaction which ended in 1859 with the war against Piedmont and France (see Chapter XIV); then came eight years of political experimentation from 1859 to 1867, punctuated by the war of 1866 with Prussia. The ten years following the repression of the revolutionary movements of 1848-1849 are usually called the "Bach period," from the name of a repressive minister of the interior. All parts of the Empire were now for the first time unified and directly ruled from Vienna by German-speaking officials.

In 1855, the state signed a concordat with the Catholic Church giving clerics a greater influence in education and in other fields than they had enjoyed since the reforms of Joseph II. Because the repressive domestic policies of the Bach system required expensive armies and policemen, the state went into debt. Instead of investing in railroads and industry, Austria spent its money on enforcing the Bach system. These expenditures left it at a disadvantage compared with Prussia. Then, during the Crimean War, instead of repaying Tsar Nicholas I for Russia's aid in subduing the Hungarian revolution, Austria "astonished the world by her ingratitude." Not only did Francis Joseph fail to assist the Russians, he actually kept them in fear of an attack by occupying the Danubian principalities (modern Rumania). In 1857, Austria experienced a severe financial crisis partly as a result of this long mobilization.

The defeat of 1859 at the hands of the French and Italians, and the loss of Lombardy brought about the end of the Bach system. War continued to threaten, and the nationalities inside the Empire, es-

pecially the Magyars, could not be kept in a state of smoldering discontent which would render their troops unreliable. Several solutions were now tried in an effort to create a structure that would withstand the domestic and foreign strains, but which would not jeopardize the Emperor's position. Francis Joseph made no effort to consult the people. Instead, he listened first to the nobles, who favored a loose federalism, and then to the bureaucrats, who favored a tight centralism.

First, a constitutional change in 1860, the "October Diploma," set up a central legislature to which the aristocratic provincial assemblies throughout the Empire were to send delegates, and which would deal with economic and military questions. All other problems were to be left to the provinces. This, however, did not satisfy the most important non-German province in the Empire—Hungary. Except for the great magnates, the Magyars were still discontented and continued to press the

Emperor Francis Joseph.

demands for autonomy that they had made in 1848. But Francis Joseph, who hated the thought of abandoning the uniformity of the Bach system even though he was ready to soften its rigor, opposed the Magyar wishes for special treatment. He was leaning on the aristocracy in the hope that they could hold off liberalism.

On the other hand, the German liberals and bureaucrats of Austria felt that the October Diploma went too far and gave the Magyars too much. To them it seemed that the Empire was being dismembered on behalf of the nobility, who dominated the provincial assemblies. The "February Patent" of 1861 was actually a new constitution in line with their views. It proclaimed a more centralized scheme. The imperial legislature took over most of the powers the October Diploma had reserved for the provincial assemblies or diets.

Great landowners, town chambers of commerce, townsmen, and peasants formed the four classes of electors to these provincial diets, and there were tax qualifications for all members of the last two classes. As in the Prussian constitution of 1850, the class or "curial" system was highly discriminatory, and worked to disfranchise the peasants. Moreover, in regions like Bohemia, where the town population was heavily German and the countryside population heavily Czech, it worked to benefit the rich and the Germans. Yet it continued until 1907, favoring the Germans and hurting the Czechs.

Naturally, the Magyars objected to this second solution even more than to the first, and flatly refused to participate. To the applause of the Germans in Vienna, including the liberals, Hungary was returned to authoritarian rule. Czechs and Poles also eventually withdrew from the central parliament and left only a German rump. Disturbed, the Emperor suspended the February Patent; he began to negotiate with the Magyars, who were represented by the intelligent and moderate

Francis Deák, but the negotiations were interrupted by the war with Prussia in 1866. The Austrian defeat at Sadowa, the expulsion of Austria from Germany, and the loss of Venetia seemed to threaten the entire Habsburg system. Francis Joseph resumed negotiations with the Magyars, with the help of the great Magyar noble, Andrássy, and of Beust, who had become Austrian foreign minister. In 1867, a formula was found which was to govern and preserve the Habsburg domains down to the World War of 1914-1918.

The Dual Monarchy, 1867

This was the famous *Ausgleich*, or "compromise," which created the "dual monarchy" of Austria-Hungary. The Hungarian constitution of 1848 was restored, and the entire Empire was reorganized on a strict partnership basis. Austria and Hungary were united in the person of the emperor, who was always to be a Catholic legitimate Habsburg, and who was to be crowned King of Hungary in a special ceremony in Budapest. For foreign policy, military affairs, and finance, the two states had common ministers appointed by the emperor. A customs union subject to renewal every ten years also united them. Every ten years the quota of common expenditure to be borne by each partner was to be settled. A unique body, the "delegations," made up of sixty members from the Austrian and sixty members from the Hungarian parliament, meeting alternately in Vienna and in Budapest, was to decide on the common budget. After the budget had been approved, it had to be ratified by the full parliaments of both countries, and signed by the emperor-king. The delegations also had supervisory authority over the three joint ministers, and might summon them to give an account of their activities. Every ten years, when the quota of expenses and the customs union needed joint consideration, a new crisis arose.

Otherwise, Hungary and Austria were separate states. As King of Hungary, Francis Joseph appointed cabinet ministers, professors, bishops, civil servants, and other officials. He was obliged at least once a year to summon the Hungarian legislature, which had an upper house of hereditary peers and a lower house elected by an elaborate system with more than fifty types of voters. However, qualifications regarding economic status and nationality made the Hungarian lower house entirely undemocratic; the voters never totaled more than 6 per cent of the population. For its part, Austria retained the parliament and the seventeen provincial assemblies provided by the February Patent of 1861. According to the new Austrian constitution of 1867, the authority of the emperor somewhat resembled that of other constitutional monarchs, with the fundamental exception that he could legislate by himself when parliament was not in session. Since he could dissolve parliament at will, he enjoyed a very large discretion.

The dual structure of Austria-Hungary was unique in Europe, and indeed in history. Because of it, many domestic developments in the two parts of the monarchy may be considered quite separately. Yet one overwhelmingly important and complicated problem remained common to both halves of the monarchy: the problem of the national minorities that had not received their autonomy. Some of these minorities (Czechs, Poles, Ruthenes) were largely in Austria; others (Slovaks, Rumanians) were largely in Hungary; the rest (Croats, Serbs, Slovenes, all of them south Slavs) were in both states. These nationalities were at different stages of development and of national self-consciousness. Some of them were subject to pressures from fellow-nationals living in states outside the dual monarchy.

The Austrian constitution of 1867 provided that all nationalities enjoy equal rights, and guaranteed that each might use its own language in education, administration, and public life. Even the Hungarians in 1868 abandoned on paper the fierce Magyar chauvinism of Kossuth and the superpatriots of 1848 (see above, p. 396), and put on the statute books a law that allowed the minorities to conduct local government in their own language, to hold the chief posts in their counties, and to have their own schools. But in practice, neither the Austrian nor the Hungarian statute was respected. The nationalities suffered varying degrees of discrimination and even persecution. Since the nationality problem was common to Austria and to Hungary, and since it brought down the entire dual monarchy in the end, we must examine it in some detail.

The Czechs

After 1867, the highly nationalistic Czechs felt that they were entitled to an *Ausgleich* on the model which the Magyars had obtained. They talked of the lands of the Crown of St. Wenceslaus (who died in 929), by which they meant the provinces of Bohemia, Moravia, and Austrian Silesia, as possessing rights comparable to those that the Magyars had successfully claimed for the lands of the Crown of St. Stephen (997-1038). Not only was this argument historically unsound, but the Czechs never had the power or the opportunity that the Magyars had to bring pressure on the Austrians. Czech deputies boycotted the Austrian parliament in the hope that Francis Joseph would consent to become King of Bohemia in Prague as he had become King of Hungary in Budapest.

In 1871, the Emperor did indeed offer to be crowned as King of Bohemia. The Bohemian diet, from which all the Germans had withdrawn in a fury, drew up proposals that would have produced a triple instead of a dual monarchy, with arrangements quite parallel to those enjoyed by the Magyars. The rage of Austrian and Bohemian Germans, the opposition of Magyar politicians, and a Slavic uprising in southern Austria forced Francis Joseph to change his mind. He discharged the ministers who had sponsored the advances to the Czechs, and the episode came to an end. Deeply disappointed, the Czech nationalist leaders returned to passive resistance.

By 1879, when the Czech deputies returned to the Vienna parliament, they were divided into "old Czechs" and "young Czechs." The moderate "old Czechs" sought autonomy, but under aristocratic and clerical auspices; the more impetuous and radical "young Czechs" held democratic and liberal views and favored a pro-French and pro-Russian foreign policy. Against German opposition, the Czechs secured cultural and political gains, including a statute that required all government officials and judges in Czech lands to render decisions and conduct trials in the language of the petitioner. This meant that many German civil servants would have to learn Czech; most Czech civil servants knew German already. The natural result was an increase of Czechs in the civil service, and the development of an experienced body of Czech officials.

During the 1880's, fierce Czech-German strife broke out in Bohemia, and for a time the angry Germans boycotted the Bohemian diet. In 1890, the Vienna ministry and the "old Czechs" temporarily reached a compromise on an administrative division of Bohemia along national Czech and German lines. But the militant "young Czechs" swept the next elections and, when the administrative partition bill was presented, simply rioted on the floor of their diet. The government's answer was repression: Prague was placed under a state of siege.

The siege was not lifted until 1897, when a new ministry in Vienna needed the support of Czech votes. The language enactments were broadened to require that all civil servants in Czech lands after 1901 be bilingual. These new concessions to the Czechs produced German filibusterings, rowdyism, duels, press blasts, throwing of inkwells, and blowing of whistles in parliament. Government in Vienna became bedlam, and the ministry resigned. Martial law was clamped down on Prague once more, and Czech extremists began to make pro-Russian and Pan-Slav gestures, even calling for a general Slav showdown with the Germans. Alarmed German extremists called Prague the "western Moscow." All compromise plans failed and at the turn of the twentieth century the moderates on both sides of the Czech question were disappearing in the waves of noise and hatred emanating from German and Czech extremists. No parliament could stay in session, and the Austrian government had to be conducted by imperial decree.

Under the stress of prolonged agitation, and influenced by the apparent triumph of constitutionalism in Russia (see below, p. 509), Francis Joseph finally decided to reform the franchise. In 1907, the "curial" system came to an end. All male citizens of the Austrian lands were now enfranchised and could vote for deputies of their own nationality. Of the 516 deputies in the new parliament, 233 would be German and 107 Czech, a figure almost proportional to the census figures.

Yet in 1913 the Bohemian diet was dissolved by a *coup*, and in 1914 Czech deputies in the Austrian parliament refused to allow national business to proceed. Thus war began with both parliament and the Bohemian diet dissolved, and with the Emperor and ministers ruling by themselves. Perhaps chief among the many causes for this general parliamentary breakdown was the failure to give the Czech provinces the self-government they had vainly sought since 1867. Most Czechs did not wish to cut loose from the Empire and establish a separate state of their own. Amounting to about 23 per cent of the Austrian population, the Czechs formed a hard core of discontent.

Yet, political considerations apart, the Czechs had prospered in the Empire. From the economic and cultural points of view, they were by far the most advanced of the Slavic peoples in either part of the dual monarchy. By 1900, the famous Skoda armament works had become the largest in the Empire and the rival of Krupps in Germany. Porcelain and glassware, lace and beer, sugar and the tourist trade, made the Czech middle class rich and Czech craftsmen famous. Laboring conditions were bad, however, and the Czech Social Democrats were weakened by their refusal to work with their German opposite numbers.

Czech nationalism was fostered by an active Czech-language press, by patriotic societies, by Czech schools, and by the famous *sokols* ("hawks"), a physical-training society with strong nationalist leanings.

NATIONALITIES IN CENTRAL AND EASTERN EUROPE

About 1914

Political boundaries, 1914
Boundary between Austria and Hungary
Abbreviations:
Ger.-Germans; Mag.-Magyars;
Gr.-Greeks; A.-Armenians;
Swed.-Swedes
(Many scattered national minorities are not shown)

At the ancient Prague University learned Czech scholars taught, of whom Thomas Masaryk, married to an American, became the most famous. Professor of philosophy and student of Slavic culture, but a lover of the West, Masaryk deeply influenced generations of students, and upheld democratic ideals in politics. Historians studied the heroic past of the Czechs, and poets, novelists, and musicians glorified it for the popular audience. Deprived of their national autonomy and exposed to German bias though the Czechs were, they can hardly be regarded as a persecuted minority. They had their language and their freedom to develop under Austrian domination.

Poles and Ruthenians   Of all the minorities in Austria, the Poles were the most satisfied. Most of them lived in Galicia, where they formed the landlord class and generally oppressed their peasants, especially the backward Ruthenians (Ukrainians). Although the Galician Poles, like the Czechs, asked for provincial self-government on the Magyar model, and although, like the Czechs, they were denied this request, they did enjoy privileges that made them the only contented Poles in Europe. They had their own schools, and Polish was the language of administration and the courts. The Poles enjoyed favorable financial arrangements, and after 1871 there was a special ministry for Galicia in Vienna.

The contrast between this generous treatment and the brutality suffered by the Poles living in Prussian and Russian Poland led Poles everywhere to look to Austrian Galicia as the center of national life and culture. Polish refugees from tyranny elsewhere took refuge in the cities of Cracow and Lemberg. Here were splendid Polish universities, noble families living grandly as they always had in Poland, and political opportunities to serve the Crown in the provincial administration. The universities trained generations of Poles who were available later for service in independent Poland. Only the Ruthenians and the Jews suffered discrimination and hardship.

The Poles eliminated Ruthenians from the Galician diet and long kept them from the imperial parliament. The Ruthenians themselves were divided into an older pro-Russian generation, and a younger generation of Ukrainian nationalists, often fanatical, who hated Poles and Russians alike and who hoped for their own autonomous status within the monarchy. Under the new suffrage laws of 1907, 27 Ruthenians were returned to parliament in Vienna. All 27 inveighed against the Poles, and 22 of them inveighed against the other five, who were pro-Russian. In 1908, a Ukrainian assassinated the Polish governor of Galicia after a horrible instance of Polish police brutality. Thus the large Polish minority, about 18 per cent of the Austrian population, lived in contentment and loyalty, persecuting their Ruthenian tenants. Since they hated Russia, Pan-Slavism never tempted them as it did the Czechs; they were not even very much interested in a future independent Poland.

Other Minorities in Austria   The other minorities in Austria, the Italians and south Slavs, were far less numerous. Less than 3 per cent of the population was Italian in 1910; about 4½ per cent was Slovene; and less than 3 per cent was Serb and Croat. The Italians of the south Tyrol and Istria, where their center was the seaport of Trieste, were far more important than their numbers warranted, however, because of the existence of the Kingdom of Italy across the monarchy's frontier. Almost all of them wanted to belong to Italy, and Italy regarded their lands as *Italia Irredenta*. Of all the Austrian minorities, the Italian steadily proved itself the most anxious to get out of the Habsburg Monarchy altogether.

Among the south Slavs in Austria proper, the Slovenes were the most contented. Scattered in six provinces, and often living at odds with their German or Italian neighbors, they usually made only local demands, like that for lecture courses in Slovene at Graz University. The Croats in Austria (mostly in Dalmatia) were fewer and less disaffected than those in Hungary, and the Serbs in Austria were far fewer and less disaffected than the Serbs in Hungary and in the separate province of Bosnia. Yet both Serbs and Croats in Austria were divided into groups that preferred autonomy within the Empire and groups that hoped one day to join an independent south Slav state (Yugoslavia).

Minorities in Hungary   In Hungary, minority problems were even more acute. Magyar behavior toward other national groups grew increasingly outrageous as moderate counsels vanished in the face of shortsighted demagoguery. The Slovaks, the Rumanians, and the Serbs and Croats living in Hungary proper were the worst victims of a deliberate policy of Magyarization, but even the Croatians of Croatia, whose province had its own constitutional special status, suffered. The Magyar aim was actually to destroy the national identity of the minorities and to transform them into Magyars. The weapon they used was language.

It is perhaps difficult to understand the passionate attachment felt by the backward peasant peoples of southeastern Europe for their own languages. Yet, deprived of economic opportunity and sometimes of complete religious freedom, these peoples in the nineteenth century found in the languages they talked a living proof of national identity. The Magyars too,

who made up only 55 per cent of the population of their own country exclusive of Croatia, had a fanatical devotion to their own language, an Asian tongue quite unrelated to the German, Slavic, or Rumanian languages of the minorities. They tried to force it upon the subject peoples, particularly in education. All state-supported schools had to give instruction in Magyar; the state postal, telegraph, and railroad services used only Magyar.

The Slovaks, numbering about 11 per cent of the population of Hungary, were perhaps the most Magyarized. Poor peasants for the most part, the more ambitious of them often became Magyars simply by adopting the Magyar language as their own. As time passed, a few Slovaks came to feel a sense of unity with the closely related but far more advanced Czechs across the border in Austria. The pro-Czechs among the Slovaks were usually liberals and Protestants. Catholic and conservative Slovaks toward the end of the century found their leader in a priest, Father Hlinka, who wanted Slovak autonomy. After Czechoslovakia had been formed in 1918, the Hlinka movement continued to be anti-Czech, and became pro-Hitler in the 1930's.

The Rumanians, who lived in Transylvania, amounted in 1910 to 16½ per cent of the population of Hungary, and possessed a majority in Transylvania itself. For centuries they had been downtrodden by the Magyars, and had had to fight to achieve recognition of their Orthodox religion. Indeed, largely in the hope of receiving better treatment, many of them had become "Uniates," accepting the supremacy of Rome but preserving their own liturgy. Despite laws designed to eliminate the use of the Rumanian language, and a great deal of petty persecution, the Rumanians stoutly resisted assimilation. For redress of grievances, many looked to Vienna, which before the *Ausgleich* had often been a source of assistance against the Magyars, but which was now committed to give the Magyars a free hand. These Rumanians hoped that Transylvania might again be made autonomous, as it had once been in the past. They pressed for the enforcement of the liberal Hungarian nationalities law of 1868. They wanted their language and their church to have equal standing with other languages and other churches.

But when in 1892 the Rumanians petitioned Vienna on these points, their petition was returned unopened and unread. When they circulated the petition abroad, their leaders were tried and jailed. It was little wonder that many Transylvanian Rumanians ceased to look west to Vienna for help that never came and began to look south and east across the Carpathians to Rumania, where their fellow-nationals had a kingdom of their own and a strong wish to annex Transylvania.

Under Magyar rule, some Serbs and Croats lived in Hungary proper and others in Croatia. In 1910, those in Hungary totaled about 600,000, of whom two-thirds were Serbs. Living in a compact mass in the southern and western frontier regions, these were the inhabitants of the old Habsburg "military frontier" against the Turks. They were transferred to Magyar rule in 1869, and they resented it. The Serbs especially disliked Hungarian administration, and looked to the independent kingdom of Serbia to the south. But a far greater menace to Hungarian unity was provided by Croatia proper.

Croatia

The Croats, though connected since the eleventh century with the Crown of Hungary, had become strongly nationalistic under the impact of the Napoleonic occupation, and had fought on the side of the monarchy against the Magyar revolutionaries of 1848. None the less, Francis Joseph, as part of the *Ausgleich* settlement, handed them back to the Magyars. Croatian nationalists were deeply disappointed. Led by the Roman Catholic Bishop Strossmayer, a man of deep intelligence, high culture, and liberal views, they had hoped for an autonomous Croatia and Dalmatia inside the Empire, which would serve as a nucleus to attract all the other southern Slavs. But instead, the Magyar moderates, led by Deák, worked out in 1868 an *Ausgleich* of their own between Hungary and Croatia.

All military and economic affairs were to be handled in Budapest by a special cabinet minister for Croatian affairs. Representatives from the Croatian parliament at the Croatian capital of Zagreb would sit in Budapest whenever Croatian affairs were under discussion. Croatian delegates would be part of the Hungarian "delegation" of the dual monarchy. The Croatian language could be spoken by Croat representatives at the sessions of any body they attended, and the language of command in the Croatian territorial army would be Croatian. The Croats would control their own educational system, their church, their courts and police, but all taxes would be voted by Budapest and collected by agents of Budapest. Although the Croats were far better off than any national minority in Hungary, this "compromise" did not satisfy them.

The "Party of the Right," the ancestor of Croat extremism in our own day, wanted a completely autonomous Croatia, and scorned as inferior the Serbs and other non-Catholic south Slavs, whom Strossmayer had hoped to attract. Further problems were created in Catholic Croatia by the existence of a Serb Orthodox minority (more than a quarter of the population), which spoke the same language as the Croats, and which was racially indistinguishable from them. But the Orthodox minority worshiped in different churches, and was therefore subject to religious discrimination.

For twenty years at the close of the nineteenth century the Hungarian-appointed governor cleverly fostered this Serb-Croat antagonism by using the Serbs for local offices. He received the support only of those Croats who had become Magyar-speaking, usually great landowners or government officials. By 1903, Serbs and Croats were beginning to cooperate against Hungarian rule, and to spread pro-Slav propaganda in Dalmatia. In 1905, Croats asked Vienna for Dalmatia and for electoral reforms, but professed that they wanted to observe faithfully the arrangement of 1868 with Hungary. Serbians endorsed these Croatian demands, though some Serbs hoped for union with independent Serbia, and some Croats still hoped for complete independence.

The hopes of the moderates were dashed by the fearfully unpopular Railways Servants Act (1907), which forced all railroad workers to speak Magyar. Croats began to boycott Hungarian-made goods; the Croatian diet refused to collaborate with the new governor, who ruled in arbitrary fashion. In 1909, he arrested fifty-odd Croats and Serbs and charged them with plotting to unite Croatia and Bosnia with Serbia. The evidence was ridiculously inadequate, and the defendants, though condemned, obtained a reversal of the sentences on appeal to a higher court. But these Zagreb trials gave the Slavic press a splendid opportunity to denounce the policy of the dual monarchy.

In the same year, 1909, a celebrated Austrian historian, Friedjung, charged in the Vienna press that the Croatian and Serbian politicians in Croatia were plotting with Serbians in Serbia. Friedjung was eventually forced to admit that his documentary sources, which in all probability had been fed to him by the Vienna foreign office, were forgeries. The Zagreb trials and the Friedjung case, coming only five years before the assassination of Francis Ferdinand by a Bosnian Serb and the outbreak of war, demonstrate the incompetence of the dual monarchy in dealing with its own loyal south Slav inhabitants.

Bosnia-Herzegovina

We must complete our examination of the national minorities in the dual monarchy with a brief discussion of the region of Bosnia-Herzegovina, which had a special status. In the 1870's, these two provinces had been part of the Ottoman Empire for about four centuries. Although entirely south Slav from the ethnic point of view, the population included in 1879 about half a million Moslems, half a million members of the Orthodox Church, and perhaps 150,000 Catholics, as well as a few Jews. Under Turkish rule, those who accepted Islam enjoyed economic advantages. By the nineteenth century, most of the Orthodox Christian population consisted of peasants working on the estates of Moslem landlords and looking across the frontiers to Serbia in hope of liberation. Some of the Catholics were educated in Strossmayer's seminary, and leaned toward eventual absorption in his south-Slav state, but almost nobody wanted to join the Habsburg Monarchy as it was then constituted.

The Herzegovinian uprising of 1875 precipitated first a general Balkan Slavic attack on the Turks, and then a Russo-Turkish War (see below, p. 505). Before Russia went to war against the Turks, the Austrian and Russian foreign ministers reached an agreement on the future status of the two provinces. But they later disagreed on what the agreement had been. At the Congress of Berlin in 1878, the Austrians obtained the right to occupy the provinces, but not to annex them.

From 1878 to 1908, the forces of the monarchy occupied Bosnia and Herzegovina, which at first furiously resisted the entry of the Habsburg troops, and forced them to fight a little war to establish themselves. The sovereignty of the Turkish sultan was recognized throughout this period, but in fact the provinces were ruled from Vienna, though not as part of either Austria or Hungary. Instead, they were put under the common Austro-Hungarian minister of finance.

The discontent of the Orthodox Serbs of Bosnia was fanned by propaganda from Serbia itself. Patriotic Serbs considered that the first logical step toward creating a greater Serbia would be to incorporate these provinces inside their own frontiers, and they resented the decision of the Congress of Berlin that had allowed Habsburg occupation. However, so long as the occupation was not turned into annexation, the Serbs preserved the hope that the provinces might some day become theirs, and meanwhile flooded them with agents and plotters. The Moslems, though favored by the Habsburg authorities, never reconciled themselves to the ending of Turkish rule, and the Catholics hoped to join Croatia.

Thus these provinces perpetually threatened to create an explosion. The more intelligent observers in Vienna pressed for some sort of an all-south-Slav solution, not unlike that of Strossmayer. This would have put Dalmatia, Croatia, and Bosnia-Herzegovina together into a south-Slav kingdom under Francis Joseph, with the same status as Hungary—a triple rather than a dual monarchy. The advocates of this solution, known as "trialists," met the fiercest kind of hatred from the Magyars.

However, the Young Turk Revolution of 1908 caused the adventurous Austrian foreign minister Aehrenthal to fear that the status of the provinces might be changed. Fortified by a previous secret agreement with Russia, Aehrenthal simply annexed the two provinces in October, 1908, and announced that they would be given a diet of their own. This move precipitated a major European crisis (see Chapter XVIII), which threatened world war, but eventually subsided, leaving the Serbs bitterly resentful. Serbian ambition to acquire the provinces now seemed permanently checked. The humiliation of Serbia, the disappointment of Russia, the solidarity of Germany with Austria-Hungary as revealed by the crisis, helped set the stage for the catastrophe of 1914. The discontent of the population of Bosnia, when added to the discontent of the Czechs and Italians in Austria, and of the Slovaks, Rumanians, Croats, and other south Slavs in Hungary, goes far to account for the wartime weakness and postwar disintegration of the dual monarchy.

Yet the minority question, critical though it was, does not provide the entire answer. We must now briefly consider the Austrian-German and Hungarian majorities, both in their separate development and in their critical relationship to each other. Only then can we see that even the two ruling groups were subject to divisive forces that crippled them individually and together.

Austrian Society and Politics, 1867-1914

From the earliest days of the *Ausgleich*, the Austrian liberals fought the clerical conservatives. They legalized civil marriages, secularized all but religious instruction, canceled the concordat of 1855 after the proclamation of papal infallibility in 1870, and taxed church property (1873). These measures were the Austrian counterpart of the German *Kulturkampf*, but they were much milder, since Austria was 90 per cent Catholic and did not share the Protestant Prussian suspicion of the Vatican. The liberals were discredited by the financial crash of 1873, during which it was revealed that some of them had accepted bribes in return for voting in favor of charters for shady and unstable new companies. From this period dates the earliest political anti-Semitism in Austria, since some Jewish liberals were involved in the scandals and served as convenient scapegoats. Economic advance during the early years of the monarchy had brought the usual increase in the working class, which after the crash turned toward socialism in both its Marxist and its milder forms.

The Austrian aristocrats, who often owned great estates which they ruled almost like independent potentates, were on the whole frivolous in their tastes, and took little interest in the problems of the nineteenth and twentieth centuries. They squandered their incomes on high living and gambling. Yet they supplied almost all the political leadership that the nation got. The large size of their estates was one fundamental reason for the small size of the average peasant holding, and made it necessary even for landowning peasants to try to obtain part-time employment on a noble's property. The peasants' standard of living and level of literacy were extremely low, yet the influence of the clergy kept them subservient to their masters, loyal to the dynasty, and almost contented with their lot.

The middle class of town-dwellers and men of business, so familiar in western Europe, came later and was smaller in number in Austria. The wealthier tried to imitate the aristocracy's mode of life and to buy their way into the charmed circle. Others joined the professions, which they found overcrowded and badly paid. The unemployment of the intellectual is an extremely dangerous matter politically.

Among the bourgeoisie there were many Jews. Numbering 5 per cent of the total population of Austria, the Jews (except for very few) could not be aristocrats, peasants, members of the clergy, bureaucrats, or army officers. So they were forced to enter trade, the professions, and the arts, where they often prospered and distinguished themselves. What we mean when we refer loosely to pre-war "Viennese" life, with its charm and gaiety, its cultivation, its music, its cafés, its high reputation in medicine and science, was the life of a society very largely Jewish or part-Jewish. Conversion, intermarriage, and assimilation were not uncommon among the upper-middle-class Jews.

Anti-Semitism, fanned by the continued migration of poorer Jews from regions of eastern Europe where oppression had rendered them squalid and uncouth, was general among the non-Jews of Austria. But we must distinguish between the social anti-Semitism of most aristocrats, which was often simply a form of snobbery, and the serious political anti-Semitism of the lower middle classes, often the unsuccessful competitors of the Jews in the world of small shop-keeping. Partly out of religious prejudice, partly out of distaste for the liberal politics usually preferred by the middle-class Jews, the clericals inveighed against them. One response among the Jews to the swelling chorus of anti-Semitism was Zionism (sponsorship of a Jewish state in Palestine), which originated in the dual monarchy.

The stresses inherent in this social structure, aggravated by the problems of the national minorities, produced two important new political movements among the Germans of Austria: Pan-Germanism and Christian Socialism. In the early 1880's, even moderate Austrian Germans wanted to hand over the Slavic lands of Austria to the Hungarians, and then, stripped to the German core, to unite economically with Germany. The Pan-Germans were more radical and more violent. They opposed the Habsburg dynasty. They opposed the Catholic Church, and led a noisy movement called "Away from Rome" (Los von Rom). They demanded that Austria become Protestant and unite politically with Germany. They were furiously anti-Slav and anti-Semitic. They adored Bismarck and Wotan, but Bismarck did not encourage them. The pan-Germans never managed to become more than an extreme vocal minority.

The Christian Socialists, on the other hand, became the most important Austrian political party. Strongly Catholic and loyal to the Habsburgs, they appealed at the same time to the peasant and the small businessman by favoring social legislation and by opposing big business. They too were violently anti-Semitic. At first skeptical of the value of Christian Socialism, the clergy later made the movement its own, and especially in the country prevailed on the people to vote for its candidates. The most famous single Christian Socialist was the perennial Mayor of Vienna after 1895, Karl Lueger, the idol of the lower middle classes of the capital. For years he sponsored public ownership of city utilities, parks, playgrounds, free milk for school children, and other welfare services. Lueger always catered to his followers' hatred of Jews, Marxian socialists, and Magyars. Hitler, who saw Lueger's funeral procession in 1910, hailed him in *Mein Kampf* as the greatest statesman of his times. It is impossible to understand the doctrines of German Nazism in this century without understanding the social and racial structure of the Habsburg Monarchy in which Hitler grew up, and especially the doctrines and the appeal of Pan-Germanism and Christian Socialism.

To the Pan-Germans and the Christian Socialists, the Austrian Social Democrats, founded in 1888, responded with a Marxist program calling for government ownership of the means of production and for political action organized by class rather than by nationality. But the Austrian Social Democrats were not revolutionaries, and set as their goals such political and social gains as universal suffrage, secular education, welfare legislation, and the eight-hour day. They were usually led by intellectuals, many of them Jewish, but they were followed by an ever-increasing number of workers.

On the nationality question, Social Democratic leaders strongly urged a reform in the direction of democratic federalism. Each nationality should have control of its own affairs in its own territory; in mixed territories, minorities should be protected; and a central parliament should decide matters of common interest. Cultural autonomy for the nationalities of a multi-national state was by no means an impractical or doctrinaire Marxist idea. Its practicality was later attested by the Soviet Russians, faced as they were with a similar problem and much influenced by the thinking of Austrian Social Democrats on the question. The program of the Social Democrat, Karl Renner, who lived to be chancellor of the Austrian Republic when it was founded in 1919 and again when it was re-created in 1945, might have averted the necessity for the foundation of any republic at all. A believer in the dual monarchy, Renner advocated treating the nationalities as if they were churches, and allowing each citizen to belong to whatever one he chose. Each of these "national associations" would have its own schools, and disagreements among them would be settled by a high court of arbitration. Who is to say that if these reasonable views had been adopted, the monarchy might not have been preserved?

Hungarian Society and Politics, 1867-1914

In Hungary, the social structure was somewhat different. The great landed gentry, owning half of Hungary in estates of hundreds of thousands of acres apiece, were a small class numerically. Loyal to the dynasty, sometimes kind to their tenants, and socially contemptuous of all beneath them, they were often intelligent and discriminating, yet more often just as frivolous and empty-headed as their

Austrian counterparts. But Hungary had a much larger class of country gentlemen, the squirearchy, whose holdings were far smaller and whose social position was lower, but whose political influence as a group was even greater. After the emancipation of the serfs in 1848, and during later periods of uncertain agricultural conditions, many members of the gentry became civil servants or entered the professions. The peasantry suffered from small holdings, insufficient education, primitive methods of farming, and a low standard of living.

The Magyars were countryfolk, and the towns for centuries had been centers for Germans and Jews. But during the nineteenth century, the towns became steadily more Magyar, as members of the gentry and peasantry moved into them. The Jewish population grew enormously during the same period, mostly by immigration from the north and east. In Hungary, many Jews were converted and assimilated and became strongly Magyar in sentiment and behavior. When they grew rich enough, they bought land and titles, and became gentry. But here too they were greatly disliked, especially among the poorer city population, and in the countryside, where they were associated with money-lending and tavern-keeping, two professions that kept the peasant in their debt. Yet though anti-Semitism existed in Hungary, it never gained as many followers or became as important a political movement as in Austria.

At the bottom of the social pyramid was a small class (never more than 20 per cent of the population) of industrial workers in the cities, mostly in the textile and flour-milling industries. Wages were low, and living and working conditions were abominable, like those in Russia rather than those in the West. Yet more and more welfare measures were passed toward the end of the century. Because of its feebleness and lack of self-consciousness, this class could not be organized into an effective socialist party.

Although the Catholic Church was immensely powerful and rich in Hungary as in Austria, Catholicism was the faith only of about 60 instead of 90 per cent of the population. Some Hungarian magnate families and many of the gentry had never returned to Catholicism after the Reformation. They remained Calvinists. Several hundred thousand Germans, chiefly in Transylvania, were Lutheran. And in Transylvania also there were Magyar Unitarians. Clericalism could never become in Hungary the dominant force it was in Austria.

Thus, because of its differing social and religious structure, Hungary could not produce strong parties like the Austrian Social Democrats and Christian Socialists. Austria had a relatively liberal franchise before 1907 and universal manhood suffrage thereafter. Hungary, in contrast, never really changed its law of 1874, by which only about 6 per cent of the population could vote. Moreover, Magyars of all shades were pretty well united in their determination to subjugate the national minorities in Hungary. Internal political or social issues, therefore, did little to determine Hungarian political alignments. The only real issue, and the chief source of Magyar political differences, was the question of Hungary's position in the dual monarchy.

Hungarian opponents of the *Ausgleich* were in the early days organized into two groups. The Kossuthists favored complete independence; a slightly more moderate party called the "Tigers" wished to improve the position of Hungary inside the monarchy by securing for the Hungarians control over their own army, diplomatic service, and finances, and by limiting the tie with Austria to the person of the monarch. When the great Deák passed from public life, one of the Tigers, Coloman Tisza, abandoned his opposition to the *Ausgleich*, joined the pro-*Ausgleich* Deákists, and came to power in 1875, to govern as prime minister for the next fifteen years. Thereafter, this merger of the

Tigers and Deákists dominated Hungary except for the period from 1905 to 1910, and stayed in power largely by electoral manipulation. Called the Liberals, this group resisted any reform of the franchise and agrarian conditions, or of the treatment of the minorities. Kossuthists maintained their opposition to the *Ausgleich*.

In 1902, the provision that Hungary's contribution to the common army should be increased proportionally with the increase in population led the Kossuthists and other nationalists to demand once more that the Magyar language be used to command Hungarian troops, and that they be allowed to carry the Hungarian flag. When the ministry refused to make these demands its own, the Kossuthists began to filibuster, and effectively paralyzed the Hungarian parliament. Since the Emperor refused to yield to pressure, the crisis between Magyar separatists and the government grew ever more acute. Coloman Tisza's son, Stephen, became premier in 1903, and worked through the increasing storm to preserve the *Ausgleich*. When he tried to limit debate in order to permit the accomplishment of official business, his opponents wrecked the parliament chamber. He called an election in 1905, but he was defeated by an opposition coalition including the Kossuthists, who now won a majority. When Francis Joseph refused to meet the demands of the new majority and appointed a loyal general as premier, the Kossuthists screamed military dictatorship, and urged patriots not to pay taxes or perform military service.

Actually, the entire struggle between the partisans of dualism and those of independence moved only the ruling caste of Magyars, and bore no relation to the sentiments and needs of the larger part of the population. To mitigate the struggle, Francis Joseph had only to threaten to decree universal suffrage for Hungary, as he intended to do in Austria. This would open the gates to the discontented minorities, and would encourage social and economic change. Under this threat, the opposition coalition eventually yielded (1906) and voted the necessary economic and military laws. They obtained the right to revise the franchise themselves, a task they had every interest in putting off.

In 1910, the younger Tisza, who had refurbished the Liberal party and now called it the Party of National Work, won a victory in the elections by the time-honored methods of corruption and intimidation. Worried about war with Russia and convinced that Austria and Germany were necessary allies for Hungary, Tisza dropped the separatists' demands, which had been convulsing the country for more than a decade. Hungary got no bank, no separate army, and no substantial franchise reform. Kossuthists had to be removed by force from parliament, and gag-rule had to be imposed. Tisza was kept busy fighting sabre duels with the Kossuthist leaders. In this atmosphere, Hungary received the news that the heir to the throne had been assassinated.

III: Russia, 1825-1914

The third and largest of the great eastern European empires, Russia, took far longer, as was its way, to catch up with the political and social developments elsewhere in Europe. Thus there was no parliament in Russia until after the revolution of 1905, and even then the tsardom was able to weaken and eventually to dominate the new representative body. Serfdom did not disappear until 1861, and agrarian problems were in some ways intensified by the liberation of the peasants. Each time reform came, in the 1860's and in 1905-1906, it came as a direct result of military defeat abroad, which rendered reform absolutely essential. Thus the reforms of Alexander II (1855-1881) were inspired by Russia's defeat in the Crimean War (1854-56), and the revolution of 1905 was made possible by Russia's failure in the Russo-Japanese War (1904-1905). During most of the nineteenth and early twentieth centuries, even after the reforms, the Russian tsars claimed for themselves the same autocratic rights that Peter the Great and his Muscovite predecessors had exercised. Thus the Russian people experienced long periods of reaction: the entire reign of Nicholas I (1825-1855), and a protracted period from 1866 through 1904, including the last fifteen years of Alexander II's reign (1866-1881), the whole of Alexander III's (1881-1894), and the first ten years of Nicholas II's (1894-1917), the last of the tsars.

The failure to adjust willingly to the currents of the times and the attempt to preserve autocratic rule produced unparalleled discontent in Russia. Disillusioned and angry intellectuals in the 1830's and 1840's gave way to proponents of social change in the 1850's and early 1860's, and then to determined revolutionaries and terrorists in the late 1860's and the years that followed. Although Marxist literature was known early in Russia, and Marxist political groupings existed after 1896, the Marxists were by no means either the most numerous or the most effective of Russian revolutionaries. Native non-Marxist revolutionary parties long performed the killings and other acts of violence that convulsed the regime and won the support of large groups of Russians. It was only Lenin's transformation of the Marxist doctrines and his adaptation of Marx to the Russian scene that made it possible for his Bolsheviks to emerge as an important threat. And it was only Lenin's supreme tactical skill and boldness

that enabled him to bring his Bolsheviks, still a minority, to power during the revolution of 1917, a movement that was itself made possible by Russian losses in still another war. There was nothing inevitable about the triumph of the Bolsheviks (see Chapter XIX).

Amid the official attempts to preserve sixteenth-century patterns, Russia experienced the impact of nineteenth- and twentieth-century industrialization. New resources were developed, thousands of miles of railroads were built, and factories sprang up, engaged in both heavy and light industry. A new laboring class thronged the cities, as elsewhere in Europe, but it lived and worked under conditions far worse than those in almost any other country. The native Russian revolutionaries looked to the peasants, in traditional Russian fashion, to provide them with their base, and they considered peasant problems paramount. The Marxists, on the other hand, true to the teachings of their master, recruited their following among this new proletariat, and focused their attention on its problems. But they deliberately relied for their tightly organized leadership almost exclusively on a little body of intellectuals and theorists.

Despite censorship and an atmosphere of repression, Russia experienced during the nineteenth century an amazing literary flowering. Poets, novelists, and playwrights produced works that rank with the greatest of all time. Like a sudden blossoming of orchids on an iceberg, the Russian literary renaissance cannot easily be explained. The literary talents of the Russian people had long lain dormant, and now awoke in an expression of unparalleled vigor and beauty.

Nicholas I
(1825-1855)

Coming to the throne amid the disorders of the Decembrist Revolution (see above, Chapter XII), Nicholas I

(1825-1855) remarked sardonically that this was a *nice* beginning for his reign. Deeply curious about the motives of the noble revolutionaries, the Tsar himself personally presided over the investigation into their movement and prescribed their punishment. He used their confessions as a source of information on the state of Russian opinion. Nicholas I has been more resoundingly damned by liberals, both Russian and foreign, than has any other tsar. They have portrayed him as a kind of scarecrow of an autocrat. Reactionary and autocratic though he was, literal-minded and devoted to military pursuits, he was perhaps not such an inflexible tyrant as he has been made out.

Nicholas I worked hard at the business of the state, and firmly believed that the imperial word was sacred. Although he despised all constitutions, he honored the liberal constitution which his elder brother Alexander had granted to the Poles (see above, p. 386) until the Poles themselves revolted. He believed that his own autocratic power had been ordained by God; the autocrat could not, even if he wished, limit his own authority. Naturally such a man loathed the thought of revolution anywhere, and was perfectly prepared to cooperate abroad with the Metternich system. At home, he was prepared to make changes and improvements, but not to touch the fundamental institution of the autocracy. Though he was uneasy over the dangers inherent in serfdom, he was afraid to reform it in any serious way, because he feared that concessions would stimulate revolution among the peasants. Nicholas leaned heavily on the nobility as a class, referring to its members as his "benevolent police-chiefs."

So personal was Nicholas' rule that his own chancery or secretariat became the most important organ of Russian government. He enlarged it by creating several sections, including a notorious "third section" for political police activity, which spread rapidly and kept Russian political life under surveillance. This enormous expansion of the Tsar's own secretariat did not result in the abolition of any of the older organs of government. Consequently, bureaucratic confusion became very great, paper work was multiplied, and much injustice was done through sheer incompetence. Although the Russian laws were collected for the first time since 1649 under the direction of Speransky (see above, Chapter IX), the collection was not a true codification or modernization.

In the field of education, Nicholas favored the improvement of technical schools, but was deeply worried about the possibility that subversive foreign ideas might penetrate into the universities. After the Revolutions of 1848 in Europe, his reactionary minister of education, Uvarov, abolished the study of philosophy in the University of St. Petersburg, because, as he said, the usefulness of the subject had not been proved, and it might do harm. Uvarov formulated Nicholas' policies under the three heads of Autocracy, Orthodoxy, and Nationality: the unlimited power of the monarch, the sanctity of the Russian Church, and the adoption of policies in accordance with the "Russian national character." The result was a police-state, complete with censorship and terror, yet not nearly so efficient as a twentieth-century despotism.

We have already seen Nicholas putting down the Polish revolution of 1830 and intervening in 1849 to restore Hungary to the Habsburgs (see Chapter XII). He believed in dynastic friendships, and counted on the alliance with Prussia and Austria without realizing that conflicting national interests were more important than friendships between monarchs. Thus he failed to see that Prussia would combat his own efforts to thwart the unification of Germany, and that Austria's interests conflicted with his own in southeastern Europe. It was partly Nicholas' failure to see the weaknesses of his own system of alliances that led him into the disastrous Crimean War.

The Crimean War

Like other Russian leaders before him, Nicholas confidently expected the collapse of the Ottoman Empire. Russia wished to protect the Orthodox subjects of the sultan, and also had important economic interests at stake. The great Russian wheat-producing areas in the south were being developed in earnest, and Odessa on the Black Sea had become a great commercial port for the grain trade. Nicholas hoped to establish a Russian sphere of influence in the Balkans, and even to take possession of Istanbul itself. We have already witnessed his intervention in the Greek War of the 1820's (see Chapter XII). When the governor of Egypt, Mehemet Ali, revolted against the Ottoman Sultan in 1832 and threatened Istanbul, Nicholas landed a Russian army and got credit for saving the sultan's capital.

In 1833, the Turks paid the bill for these services by signing the Treaty of Unkiar Skelessi with Russia. Nicholas took the Ottoman Empire under his protection, and the Turks agreed to close the Straits (the Bosporus and Dardanelles) to the warships of any nation. Alarmed at the preponderance that the treaty gave to Russia in an area of the world vital to British imperial and commercial interests, British diplomacy turned its efforts to undoing it. The next time Mehemet Ali revolted, in 1839, the British were able to put him down with their fleet before he came within distance of a Russian land force. In 1841, all the other important powers joined Russia in guaranteeing the integrity of Turkey, thus putting an end to the exclusive position obtained by Russia at Unkiar Skelessi.

During the next twelve years (1841-1853), Nicholas tried to reach an agreement with Britain on what should be done with Ottoman territory if Turkey collapsed. The British did not believe that such collapse was imminent, and they hoped to prevent Russia from doing anything to hasten it. The two parties misunderstood each other. By 1853, the Tsar mistakenly felt that Britain was not opposed to Russian domination of Turkey, and Britain mistakenly believed that the Tsar would not act in Turkey without consulting her.

Then a dispute arose over whether the Roman Catholics, backed by Napoleon III, or the Orthodox clergy, backed by the Tsar, should have the right to perform certain functions in the Christian "Holy Places" in Palestine, which was still part of the Ottoman dominions. This trivial dispute was the immediate cause of the Crimean War (1853-1856). But the underlying cause was the Tsar's wish to re-establish the exclusive Russian position in the Treaty of Unkiar Skelessi, and the British unwillingness to permit him to do so. Nicholas coupled a demand for this exclusive position with the demand that the Turks settle the dispute over the Holy Places amicably. The latter demand was possible; the former was not. When Nicholas occupied the Danubian principalities to enforce his demands, the situation became even tenser. And so, after many months of elaborate diplomatic negotiations in which all the powers strove to work out a suitable formula to avoid war, the drift toward war proved too strong to be checked.

Famous as the occasion of the charge of the Light Brigade, and of Florence Nightingale's pioneer efforts to save the lives of sick and wounded soldiers, the Crimean War consisted mostly of the siege of the great Russian naval base at Sebastopol in the Crimea. Military operations on both sides were inefficiently conducted, but eventually the Russians were compelled to surrender. In the Peace of Paris of 1856, Russia was forbidden to fortify the Black Sea coast or to maintain a fleet there. This made it impossible for the Russians to defend their own shores or to conduct their shipping in security. It now became the paramount object of Russian foreign policy to alter the Black Sea clauses of the treaty. Not only had Russia lost the war, but Prussia had not helped her, and Austria had been positively hostile (see above, p. 472). Nicholas did not live to see the total failure of his policy. He died during the war, and was succeeded by his son Alexander II (1855-1881).

Alexander II and Reform

By this time a very substantial segment of Russian public opinion favored reforms, in reaction to the long period of repression at home and failure abroad. Moreover, the economic developments of the early nineteenth century had rendered the system of serfdom less and less profitable. In the south, where land was fertile and crops were produced for sale as well as for use, the serf tilled his master's land usually three days a week, but sometimes more. In the north, where the land was less fertile and could not produce a surplus, the serfs often had a special arrangement with their masters called "quit-rent." This meant that the serf paid the master annually in cash instead of in work, and usually had to labor at home as a craftsman or go to a nearby town and work as a factory hand or small shopkeeper to raise the money. It is probable that about a quarter of the serfs of all Russia paid quit-rent by 1855. Neither in the south nor in the north was serfdom efficient in agriculture. As industries grew, it became clearer and clearer to factory owners who experimented with both serf and free labor that serf labor was not productive. Yet free labor was scarce, and the growing population needed to be fed. Many estates were mortgaged to state credit institutions, because of inefficient management and the extravagance of the landlords. Serfdom had become uneconomic.

But this fact was not widely realized among Russian landowners, who knew only that something had gone wrong somewhere. They wished to keep things as they were, and they did not as a class feel that emancipation was the answer. Yet the serfs showed increasing unrest, and cases of revolt rose in number. Abolitionist sentiment had now spread widely among intellectuals. Conscious of the unrest, Alexander II, though almost as conservative as his father, determined to embark on reforms, preferring, as he put it, that the abolition of serfdom come from above rather than from below. An emancipation law was

Ceremony during emancipation of Russian serfs

eventually formulated and proclaimed early in 1861.

A general statute declared that the serfs were now free, laid down the principles of the new administrative organization of the peasantry, and prescribed the rules for the purchase of land. A whole series of local statutes governed the particular procedure to be followed in the different provinces. Without going into details of the widely varying local practices, we may say that all peasants, crown and private, were freed, and that each peasant household received its homestead and a certain amount of land, usually the amount the peasant family had cultivated for its own use in the past. The land usually became the property of the village commune, which had the power to redistribute it periodically among the households. The government bought the land from the proprietors, but the peasants had to redeem it by payments extending over a period of 49 years. The proprietor retained only the portion of his estate that had been farmed for his own purposes.

This statute, liberating more than 40 million human beings, has been called the greatest single legislative act in history. There can be no doubt that it acted as an immense moral stimulus to peasant self-respect. Yet there were grave difficulties. The peasant had to accept the allotment, and since his household became collectively responsible for the taxes and redemption payments, his mobility was not greatly increased. The commune took the place of the proprietor, and differing local conditions caused great difficulty in administering the law. Moreover, the peasants in general got too little land, and had to pay too much for it. They did not get important forest and pasture lands. The settlement, however, was on the whole surprisingly liberal, despite the problems it failed to solve and despite the agrarian crises that developed in part as a result of its inadequacies.

The end of the landlords' rights of justice and police on their estates made it necessary to reform the entire local administration. By statute, in 1864, provincial and district assemblies, or *zemstvos,* were created. Chosen by an elaborate electoral system that divided the voters into categories by class, the assemblies none the less gave substantial representation to the peasants. The assemblies dealt with local finances, education, medical care, scientific agriculture, maintenance of the roads, and similar economic and social questions. Starting from scratch in many cases, the *zemstvos* made great advances in the founding of primary schools and the improvement of public health. They brought together peasant and proprietor to work out local problems. They served as schools of citizenship for all classes, and led tens of thousands of Russians to hope that this progressive step would be crowned by the creation of a central parliament, or *duma.* Despite the pressure that such men tried to bring on the government, the duma was not granted, partly because after the first attempt on the life of the Tsar in 1866 the regime swung away from reform and toward reaction.

But before this happened, other advances had been made. The populations of the cities were given municipal assemblies, with duties much like those of the *zemstvos* in the countryside. The Russian judicial system and legal procedure, which were riddled with inequities, were reformed. For the first time, juries were introduced, cases were argued publicly and orally, all classes were made equal before the law, and the system of courts was completely overhauled. Censorship was relaxed, new schools were encouraged, the universities were freed from the restraints that Nicholas had imposed on them, and the antiquated and often brutal system of military service was modernized and rendered less severe.

Yet, despite all these remarkable advances accomplished in a relatively few years, Alexander II became the target for revolutionaries in 1866, and terrorist activity continued throughout the seventies until the assassins finally killed the Tsar in 1881. It is impossible to understand these developments without taking a brief look at Russian intellectual life under Nicholas and Alexander.

Russian Intellectual Life

Early in Nicholas' reign, Russian professors and students, influenced by German philosophers, were devoting themselves to passionate discussions on art, philosophy, and religion. Many intellectuals outside the universities followed suit. These were the first groups known as the "intelligentsia," a peculiarly Russian class. By the 1830's, they were beginning to discuss Russia's place in the world, and especially its true historical relationship to the West and the proper course for it to follow in the future. Out of their debates there arose two important opposing schools of thought: the "Westerners" and the "Slavophiles" (friends of the Slavs).

The Westerners stated their case in a famous document called the "Philosophical Letter," published in 1836, though written earlier. Its author, Chaadaev, lamented the damaging effect of Byzantine Christianity and the Tartar invasions upon Russian development, and declared that Russia had made no contribution to the world. He hailed Peter the Great's efforts at westernizing Russia as a step in the right direction. He regarded the Roman Church as the source of much that was fruitful in the West of which Russia had been deprived. Nicholas I had Chaadaev certified as insane, and commanded that he be put under house arrest with a physician visiting him every day. Yet, despite scorn and censorship, the Westerners could not be silenced. They continued to declare that Russia was a society fundamentally like the West, but that history had delayed its full development. Russia should now catch up.

In response, the opponents of the Westerners, the Slavophiles, vigorously argued that Russia had its own national spirit, like the *Volksgeist* that Herder (see Chapter XI) had discovered in the Germans. Russia was, they maintained, essentially different from the West. The Orthodox religion of the Slavs was not legalistic, rationalistic, and narrow like the Roman Catholicism of the West, but substantial, emotional, and broad. The Slavophiles violently attacked Peter the Great for embarking Russia on a false course. The West ought not to be imitated but opposed. The Russian upper classes should turn away from their Europeanized manners, and look for inspiration to the simple Russian peasant who lived in the truly Russian institution of the village commune. Western Europe was urban and bourgeois; Russia was rural and agrarian. Western Europe was materialistic; Russia was deeply spiritual. Like the Westerners, the Slavophiles attached fundamental importance to the national religion, and made it the center of their arguments; but they praised where the Westerners damned. The Westerners' views had democratic and constitutional political implications; the Slavophiles' views had anti-constitutional and anti-democratic implications.

It is very important, however, to realize that this does not mean that the Slavophiles embraced the "nationality" doctrine of Nicholas I, or that they approved of his regime. These were not the chauvinist nationalists who appeared later. They opposed the tyranny and the bureaucratic machine of Nicholas I as bitterly as did the Westerners. But they wanted a patriarchal, benevolent monarchy of the kind they fancied had existed before Peter the Great, instead of a constitutional regime on the western pattern. Instead of a central parliament, they looked back with longing to the feudal Muscovite assembly, the *zemski sobor*, and to other institutions of the tsardom before Peter. Extremists among them went about the streets dressed in the old boyars' robes that Peter had made illegal. Many intellectuals shifted back and forth between the hotly debating camps, and few ever adopted in full the ideas of either side.

Alexander Herzen (1812-1870), for example, began his intellectual career as a Westerner and a devotee of French culture. The illegitimate son of a nobleman brought up in his father's house, he was charming, engaging, and highly intelligent. Like most Russians, he was not a good interpreter of western society, however, and was deeply fascinated with the thought that its structure might be rotten and doomed. The failure of the Paris revolution of 1848, which he saw as an eye-witness, convinced him that this was true, and he now became a revolutionary socialist. At the same time, he became convinced that the Westerners' thesis must be wrong: how could Russia in a short time pass through the stages of development which the West had taken centuries to experience but which Russia had missed? So Herzen became a Slavophile. As a revolutionary, he preached the destruction of existing institutions, and as a Slavophile he looked to Russia, with its peculiar institution of the peasant commune, the *mir*, to provide an inspiration for all Europe. Herzen became an influential publicist and issued a Russian-language paper in London which was widely read by Russian intellectuals. His memoirs provide perhaps the best picture preserved to us of the intellectual ferment of the age of Nicholas.

Michael Bakunin (1814-1876) reached roughly the same conclusions as Herzen at roughly the same time. But he was a practical anarchist tactician who loved violence, not a peaceful man of letters (see also Chapter XIII). He enjoyed participating in revolutions, and had a long career in and out of jail in most of the countries of Europe. He looked forward to a great revolution spreading perhaps from Prague to Moscow and thence to the rest of Europe, followed by a tight dictatorship; beyond this he was entirely vague about the future. Atheism was a fundamental part of his program —not a casual part, as it always was to the Marxists. In his long career, Bakunin was to exert from abroad a considerable influence on Russian radicals.

Nihilism, Populism, Terrorism

In the 1860's, and especially after the emancipation in Russia, the Russian "intelligentsia," like intellectuals elsewhere in Europe, reacted against the romanticism of their predecessors. Suspecting idealism, religion, and metaphysics, they turned now to a narrowly utilitarian view of art and society. As one of these young men said, a pair of shoes to him was worth more than all the madonnas of a great Renaissance painter. All art must have a social purpose, and the bonds holding the individual tightly to society must be smashed. Away with parental authority, with the marriage tie, with the tyranny of custom. For these people the name "nihilist" (a man who believes in nothing) quickly became fashionable. The portrait of a nihilist was drawn by the great novelist Turgenev in Bazarov, the hero of his novel *Fathers and Sons*. Rude and scornful, obstinate and arrogant, Bazarov was actually accepted as a model by intellectual leaders of youth in revolt against established ways of behavior. Yet nihilism as such was not a political movement. The nihilists enjoyed shocking their parents by calling for an end to the old moral system, advocating, for instance, the extermination of everybody in Russia over the age of 25.

In the 1860's, many of these young Russian intellectuals went to Switzerland, where the proper Swiss bourgeoisie were scandalized at the men with their hair cut long and the girls with their hair cut short, at their loud voices and insolent behavior.

The standard cartoonist's picture of a Russian revolutionary dates from the first startled glimpse which the Swiss had of the nihilists, who at the time had not even begun to be interested in political revolution. Bakunin influenced many of them during their stay in Switzerland, and urged them to go back to Russia and preach an immediate revolution to the peasants.

Also present in Switzerland were two other important Russian revolutionary thinkers: Lavrov and Tkachev. Lavrov (1823-1900) taught his followers that as intellectuals they owed a great debt to the Russian peasant, whose labor for many generations had enabled their ancestors to enjoy leisure and had made their own education possible. More gradual in his approach and more realistic in his estimates of the Russian peasant than Bakunin, Lavrov advised the nihilist students first to complete their education and then to return to Russia and go among the peasants, educating them and spreading among them propaganda for an eventual, not an immediate, revolution of the masses. On the other hand, Tkachev (1844-1886) taught that no revolution could ever be expected from the peasant masses, but that it would have to come from a tightly controlled small revolutionary elite, a little knot of conspirators who would seize power. Though not very influential at the time, Tkachev was important in Lenin's later thinking.

Under the impact of these teachers, especially Bakunin and Lavrov, Russian nihilism turned to a new kind of movement, which is called "populism." Young men and women, swept by idealistic fervor, decided to return to Russia and live among the peasants. When a government decree in 1872 actually summoned them back, they found that a parallel movement had already begun at home. About three thousand young people now took posts as teachers, innkeepers, or store-managers in the villages. Some tried to spread revolutionary ideas, others simply to render social service. Their romantic views of the peasantry were soon dispelled. The young populists did not know how to dress like peasants or how to talk to peasants. Suspicious of their talk, the peasants often betrayed them. The populists became conspicuous, and were easily traced by the police, who arrested them in droves. Two famous mass trials were held in the 1870's, at which the general public for the first time learned about the populist movement. After the trials, the populists who remained at large decided that they needed a determined revolutionary organization. With the formation of the "Land and Liberty" society in 1876, the childhood of the Russian revolutionary movement was over.

The revolutionaries had been stimulated by Alexander II's grant of reforms. So great had the discontent become that it is doubtful whether any Russian government could have proceeded fast enough to suit the radicals, who had come to believe in violent overturn of the regime and were not satisfied with piecemeal and gradual reform. Stemming from John Stuart Mill and from western Utopian socialists like Fourier and Robert Owen (see Chapter XIII), Russian socialism was not yet greatly influenced by Marx. In some ways it was almost Slavophile, not urban but rural, not evolutionary but revolutionary, not a mass political party but a conspiracy. Its members lived underground and developed a conspiratorial psychology. They proposed to overthrow a bourgeois society before one ever got started. The movement became more and more radical, and in 1879 those who believed in the use of terror as a weapon separated from the others and founded the group called the *People's Will*; the anti-terrorists called themselves the *Black Partition*.

The members of the People's Will now went on a hunt for Tsar Alexander II himself. They shot at him and missed. They mined the track on which his train was traveling, and blew up the wrong train. They put dynamite under the dining room of the palace, and exploded it. But the Tsar was late for dinner that night, and eleven servants were killed instead. They rented a cheese shop on one of the streets along which he drove, and tunneled under it. Finally they killed him (March, 1881) with a crude hand-made grenade, which blew up the assassin too. The supreme irony was that Alexander II had that day signed a document designed to summon a consultative assembly, which everybody expected to lead to further constitutional reform. His successor, the reactionary Alexander III (1881-1894) refused to confirm the document, and Russia was left to stagnate in a renewed repression. The terrorists were rounded up and punished, and their organization was smashed. Despite their occasional high-flown claims to enormous popular support, they had never numbered more than a mere handful of people, and their movement had been a failure.

Foreign Policy under Alexander II

In foreign policy, Alexander II made an uneven record. In Europe, the Russians successfully repressed the Polish uprising of 1863. They seized the opportunity provided by the Franco-Prussian War of 1870, and simply tore up the Black Sea provisions of the Treaty of Paris, declaring unilaterally that they would no longer be bound by them. This was an illegal act, to which the powers later reluctantly gave their assent. It was another illustration of the immorality in international affairs that Bismarck had made fashionable.

In 1877, the Russians went to war against Turkey on behalf of the rebellious Balkan Christians of Bosnia-Herzegovina and Bulgaria. By the peace of San Stefano, dictated early in 1878 to the defeated Turks, Russia obtained, contrary to her previous agreements, a large independent Bulgarian state, which Russian policy-makers hoped to turn into a useful Balkan satellite. But the powers at the Congress of Berlin later in the same year reversed the judgment of San Stefano. They permitted only about one-third of the planned Bulgaria to come into existence as an autonomous state, while another third obtained autonomy separately, and the rest went back to Turkey. Russian public opinion resented the powers' depriving Russia of the gains scored in the Russo-Turkish War. Bitterness ran particularly high among those who hoped to unite all Slavs in a kind of federation, the Pan-Slavs (not to be confused with the Slavophiles).

Meanwhile, in Asia, encroachments begun under Nicholas I against the Chinese territory in the Amur River valley were regularized by treaty in 1860. Russian settlements in the "maritime province" on the Pacific Ocean continued to flourish. In Central Asia, a series of campaigns conquered the Turkish khanates, and added much productive land to the crown. Here, however, the advance toward the northwest frontier of India brought Russia into a region of great interest to Britain, and fanned hostile public opinion in Britain.

The Reaction, 1881-1904

The reign of Alexander III and the first ten years of the reign of his son, Nicholas II, formed a quarter-century of consistent policies (1881-1904). Both tsars loathed liberalism as expressed in the earlier reforms, and were determined that there would never be any more of it. Yet a peasant bank set up under Alexander III made the redemption payments easier for the peasants to pay. And a few pieces of labor legislation enacted under the influence of Bismarck's example made working conditions a bit more tolerable—for example, hours were shortened for women workers. Offsetting these measures were the establishment of a special bank that extended credit to the impoverished nobility, the re-institution of rigorous censorship, and the institution in the countryside of so-called "rural leaders" or "land captains" in place of the elected justices of the peace of Alexander II. Election procedure for the *zemstvos* and for the city assemblies was made far less democratic. Now there began a vigorous persecution of the minority nationalities, a policy called "Russification," and quite in line with the "nationality" of Nicholas I's formula. The Finns, Poles, Ukrainians, Armenians, and Jews all suffered discrimination, varying from loss of their own institutions, which the Finns had enjoyed, to outright government-sponsored massacres in the case of the Jews. On his accession, Nicholas II referred to all hopes for a change as "senseless dreams."

These years were notable also for the steady growth of the Russian railroad network, largely built and owned by the state. The Donets coal basin was exploited for the first time; the Baku oil fields came into production; steel and cotton output soared. In 1892, there came to the Ministry of Finance a self-made railroad man, Witte, who for the next twelve years was personally responsible for the ever-mounting economic progress. Witte began the Trans-Siberian railroad, put Russia on the gold standard, attracted much foreign capital, especially French, for investment, and balanced the budget, in part through government monopoly of the sale of vodka. The railroad network doubled in length between 1894 and 1904, and the need for rails stimulated the steel industry. Correspondingly, the number of urban workers multiplied, and strikes called in protest against wretched working conditions mounted in number. In 1897, the working day was fixed by the state at eleven hours for adults, and other provisions were adopted to improve and regularize conditions. These, however, were difficult to enforce.

Under the circumstances, many of the young generation of revolutionaries now turned to Marxist "scientific" socialism, preaching the class struggle and predicting the inevitable downfall of capitalism. A small clandestine group of "intelligentsia," formed in 1894-1895 at St. Petersburg, proposed to overthrow the regime, working with all opponents of the class system. The members of the group included Lenin, a vigorous young intellectual of upper-middle-class origin, whose brother had been executed for an attempt on the life of Alexander III. In 1898, this group and others formed the Social Democratic party, which in 1900 began to publish its own newspaper. Within party ranks, grave dissension sprang up over the question of organization. Should the party operate under a strongly centralized directorate, or should each local group of Social Democrats be free to agitate for its own ends? In the tradition of Bakunin and Tkachev, Lenin insisted on the tightly knit little group of directors at the center. At the party congress of Brussels and London in 1903, the majority voted with him. Lenin's faction thereafter was called by the name Bolshevik, meaning majority, as against the Menshevik (minority) group, which favored a loose democratic organization for the party. Both groups remained Social Democrats, or SDs, as they were often called.

Meanwhile, the non-Marxist revolutionaries, who were the direct heirs of the People's Will tradition, also organized a political party. They were the Social Revolutionaries, or SRs, with their own clandestine newspaper. Where the SDs as Marxists were interested almost exclusively in the urban workers, the SRs as populists were interested in the peasantry. Their chief aim was to redistribute the land, but they continued in their terrorist ways. They assassinated several cabinet ministers, using as their slogan the cry, *We don't want reforms, we want reform.*

A third political grouping was that of

the moderates and liberals, not SD or SR in orientation, but mostly veterans of the *zemstvos* and intellectuals indignant over the government's policies of repression who favored only such measures as compulsory free private education and agrarian reform. The regime stupidly made no distinction between these men and the die-hard terrorists or the rabid Marxists. Thus the moderates also gradually organized and had their own clandestine paper favoring a constitution and a national parliament for Russia. In 1905, they took the name Constitutional Democrats, and were thereafter usually referred to as Kadets, from the Russian initials KD. Faced by this political activity among its radical and moderate opponents, the government only tightened the reins, and by 1904 had adopted the view that a short victorious war was all that would be necessary to unite the country.

The Russo-Japanese War

Trans-Siberian railway construction made it desirable for the Russians to obtain a right of way across Chinese territory in Manchuria. They took the initiative in preventing Japan from establishing herself on the Chinese mainland after her defeat of China in 1895, and then required the Chinese in exchange to allow the building of the new railroad. In 1897, they seized Port Arthur, the very port they had earlier kept out of Japanese hands. Further friction with the Japanese took place in Korea, where both powers had interests. Then, after the Boxer Rebellion of 1900 in China (see Chapter XXI), the Russians kept their troops in Manchuria after the other nations had withdrawn theirs. Although the Russians promised to withdraw their forces by stages, they failed to do so, largely because Russian foreign policy fell into the hands of shady adventurers, some of whom had a lumber concession in

Korea and wanted war with Japan. After it became apparent that the war party had got control in Russia, the Japanese without warning attacked units of the Russian fleet anchored at Port Arthur in February, 1904. The Russo-Japanese War had begun.

Far from their bases and taken by surprise, the Russians none the less stabilized a front on land. But their fleet, which had steamed all the way around Europe and across the Indian Ocean into the Pacific, was decisively defeated by the Japanese in the battle of Tsushima (May 27-29, 1905). To the Russian people, the war was a mysterious, distant political adventure of which they wanted no part. Many intellectuals opposed it, and the SRs and SDs openly hoped for a Russian defeat, which they expected would shake the government's position. Alarmed at the growing unrest at home, the Russian government was persuaded by President Theodore Roosevelt to accept his mediation, which the Japanese also actively wished.

Witte, the go-getting businessman who had opposed the war from the first, was sent to Portsmouth, New Hampshire, and secured excellent terms for Russia. By the Treaty of Portsmouth (1905), Russia recognized the Japanese protectorate over Korea, ceded Port Arthur and the northern half of Sakhalin Island, together with fishing rights in the North Pacific, and promised to evacuate Manchuria. Russian prestige as a Far Eastern power was not deeply wounded or permanently impaired by the defeat or by the treaty. Yet the effect of the defeat in Asia was to transfer Russian attention back to Europe, where a world crisis had already begun to gather.

The Revolution of 1905

The most important immediate result of the Russo-Japanese War was its impact on Russian domestic developments. While it was still going on,

Plehve, the reactionary minister of the interior, was assassinated by an SR bomb in July, 1904. His successor was a moderate. The *zemstvo* liberals, the future Kadets, were encouraged, and held banquets throughout Russia to adopt a series of resolutions for presentation to a kind of national congress of *zemstvo* representatives. Although the congress was not allowed to meet publicly, its program—a constitution, basic civil liberties, class and minority equality, and extension of *zemstvo* responsibilities—became widely known and approved. The Tsar temporized, issued so vague a statement that all hope for change was dimmed, and took measures to limit free discussion.

Ironically, it was a police agent of the government itself who struck the fatal spark. He had been planted in the Petersburg factories to combat SD efforts to organize the workers and to substitute his own union. He organized a parade of workers to demonstrate peacefully and to peti-

tion the Tsar directly for an eight-hour day, a national assembly, civil liberties, the right to strike, and a number of other moderate demands. When the workers tried to deliver the petition, Nicholas left town and ordered the troops to fire on the peaceful demonstrators, some of whom were carrying his portrait to demonstrate their loyalty. About a thousand workers were killed on "Red Sunday" (January 22, 1905). This massacre made revolutionaries out of the urban workers. Strikes multiplied, the moderate opposition joined with the radical opposition, and university students and professors demanded the same reforms as wild-eyed bomb-hurlers.

Amid mounting excitement, the government at first seemed to favor the calling of a *zemski sobor*, consultative, not legislative, in the old Russian pattern rather than the western parliamentary one, but still a national assembly of sorts. But then even this project was whittled away, as the timid, vacillating, and unintelligent Nich-

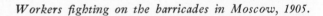

Workers fighting on the barricades in Moscow, 1905.

olas II listened to his reactionary advisers. Under the impact of delays and disappointments, demonstrations and outbreaks occurred during the summer of 1905. In October, the printers struck. No newspapers appeared, and the printers, with SD aid, formed the first "soviet" or workers' council. When the railroad workers joined the strike, communications were cut off between Moscow and Petersburg. Soviets now multiplied. Of the one formed in St. Petersburg, Lenin declared that it was "not a workers' parliament, nor an organization of proletarian autonomy, but a combat organization pursuing definite ends."

This reflects the Bolsheviks' view of the soviet as an instrument for the pursuit of their program of armed revolt, for the establishment of a provisional government, for the proclamation of a democratic republic, and for the summoning of a constituent assembly. This program, put forth by the most "extreme" of the revolutionaries of 1905, differed relatively little from the program of the most moderate liberals, who would, however, have kept the monarchy, and striven to obtain their ends by persuasion and pressure rather than by violence. At the time, and for years to come, the Bolsheviks, like other Marxists, accepted the view that it was necessary for Russia to pass through a stage of bourgeois democracy before the time for the proletarian revolution could come. They were therefore eager to help along the bourgeois revolution.

Nicholas was faced, as Witte told him, with the alternatives of imposing a military dictatorship and putting down the opposition by force, or of summoning a truly legislative assembly with veto-power over the laws. The Tsar finally chose the latter course, and in October, 1905, issued a manifesto that promised full civil liberties at once, and a legislative assembly or *duma* to be elected by universal suffrage. In effect, this famous October Manifesto put an end to the autocracy, since the duma was to be superior to the tsar in legislation.

Yet the issuance of the October Manifesto did not meet with universal approval or even end the revolution at once. On the Right, a government-sponsored party called the "Union of the Russian people" demonstrated against the manifesto, proclaimed its undying loyalty to the autocrat, and organized its own storm troops, or "Black Hundreds," which killed more than 3,000 Jews in the first week after the issuance of the manifesto. The armies returned from the Far East, and proved to be still loyal to the government. Thus the soviets of 1905, unlike those of 1917 (see Chapter XIX), included only workers, and no soldiers. On the Left, the dissatisfied Bolsheviks and SRs made several attempts to launch their violent revolution, but failed, and the government was able to arrest their leaders and eventually to put them down after several days of street fighting in Moscow in December, 1905. In the Center, one group of liberals, pleased with the manifesto, urged that it be used as a rallying point for a moderate program. These were the Octobrists, so called after the month in which the manifesto had been issued. The other groups, the Kadets, wished to continue to agitate by legal means for further immediate reforms. But the real fires of revolution had burned out by the opening of the year 1906.

The Dumas, 1906-1914

Suffrage for the Duma was universal, but voters chose an electoral college which then selected the 412 deputies. Although SRs and SDs boycotted the elections out of discontent over the indirect election system, many of their number were elected. The Kadets were the strongest single party. Quite against the expectation of the government, the peasants' vote was not conservative, but highly liberal. But even before the first Duma had met,

Witte was able to reduce its powers. He secured a large French loan, which made the government financially independent of the Duma, and issued a set of "fundamental laws," which the Duma was not to be competent to alter. The Crown was to continue to control war and foreign policy; the minister of finance was to control loans and currency. The tsar's council of state was transformed by adding members from the clergy, nobility, the *zemstvos*, the universities, and chambers of commerce. It became a kind of upper house, which had equal legislative rights with the Duma, and could therefore submit a rival budget, for example, which the government could then adopt in preference to that of the Duma. Finally, the tsar could dissolve the Duma at will, provided he set a date for new elections. When it was not in session he could legislate by himself, although his enactments had later to be approved by the Duma.

The first Duma, the "Duma of Popular Indignation," met between May and July, 1906. It addressed a list of grievances to the Tsar, asking for a radical land reform that would give the peasants all state and church land, and part of the land still in private hands. The government flatly refused to accept this attack on property, and after some parliamentary skirmishing the Duma was dissolved. The Kadet membership, maintaining incorrectly that the dissolution was unconstitutional, crossed the frontier into Finland, and there issued a manifesto urging the Russian people not to pay taxes or report for military service unless the Duma was recalled. Its authors were soon tried and declared ineligible for office; so future Dumas were deprived of the services of this capable Kadet group of moderates.

With the dissolution of the first Duma there came to power as chief minister the highly intelligent and conservative Peter Stolypin, who stayed in office until 1911, when he was assassinated. Together with

Witte, he was the leading statesman of the last period of tsarist Russia. Stolypin put through a series of agricultural laws which enabled the peasants to free themselves from the commune. A peasant wishing to detach his property could demand that he be given a single tract, which meant that the scattered strips assigned to other families would also be consolidated so that each would obtain a single plot. This program Stolypin called the "wager on the strong and sober"; he was encouraging the initiative and enterprise of individual Russian peasants who had the will to operate on their own as successful small farmers. His program accomplished much of what he hoped for. It is estimated that about a quarter of the peasant households of European Russia (almost 9,000,000) emancipated themselves from the communes during the years between 1906 and 1917. Only war and revolution kept the process from going still further. Lenin and others who hoped for revolution were deeply suspicious and afraid of Stolypin's agrarian reforms. They rightly feared that the peasant grievances would be removed, and understood that no revolution in Russia could in the end succeed without the peasants.

Simultaneously with his agrarian program, Stolypin carried on unremitting war against terrorists and other revolutionaries. He showed no hesitation in acting in the most unconstitutional fashion when it suited him. He did everything he could to interfere with the elections to the second Duma, but the SRs and SDs were well represented, and the Duma itself (March-June, 1907) would not work with the government. It was dissolved because it refused to suspend the parliamentary immunity of the SD deputies, whom Stolypin wanted to arrest.

After the dissolution of the second Duma, the government quite illegally altered the election laws, cutting the number of delegates from the peasants and national minorities, and increasing the number from the gentry. By this means the government got a majority, and the third Duma (1907-1912) and the fourth (1912-1917) lived out their constitutional lives of five years apiece. Unrepresentative and limited in their powers though they were, they were still national assemblies. In their sessions the left-wingers could be heard, and could question ministers like any other members. The Dumas improved the conditions of peasant and worker. Their commissions, working with individual ministers, proved extremely useful in increasing the efficiency of government departments. The period of the third Duma, however, was also notable for the continuation of "Russification," and the Finns in particular lost their remaining rights (1910).

Under the fourth Duma, the government, with Stolypin dead, tended more toward reaction. The Leftists organized busily for another revolution, working in unions, cooperatives, evening classes for workmen, and a whole network of other labor organizations. A vast web of police spies challenged them at every turn. Meanwhile, the imperial family drifted into a very dangerous situation, as the fanatically religious and autocratically minded empress fell more and more under the sway of a half-mad, wholly evil, dirty, ignorant, and power-hungry monk from Siberia. This man, Rasputin, had the mysterious ability, possibly hypnotic, to stop the bleeding of the young heir to the throne, who suffered from hemophilia. Since the Empress had enormous influence on her beloved husband, Nicholas II, Rasputin became in a real sense the ruler of Russia, much to the horror of a great many loyal supporters of the imperial house, and greatly to the detriment of the rational conduct of affairs in an enormous twentieth-century state. At the moment when the World War began, Russia was in the throes of a major crisis precipitated by the government's perenially reactionary policies, the scandal of Rasputin's persistent influence, and the indignation of the loyal Duma.

IV: Conclusion

Parliamentary government was, as we have seen, a comparative stranger to the three eastern European empires. The King of Prussia, with Bismarck's help, used his extraordinary military system to conquer and unify Germany. He imposed on all non-Austrian Germans the Prussian system of autocracy almost undiluted by a weak and subservient parliament, and backed by the army and the Junkers. The Habsburg emperor, though faced after 1907 with an Austrian parliament elected by universal suffrage, in 1914 still made virtually all policy decisions by himself. The Hungarian parliament was never genuinely representative, and the emperor successfully used universal suffrage as a threat to quell Magyar separation. The tsars, forced at last by defeat in wars to grant a modified constitution in 1905, were still able to hamstring their own central legislative body, and to wield a preponderant personal influence in politics.

In all three countries, none the less, for the first time in their history, modern political parties during this period coalesced around principles. As in the West, the governments collaborated with parties or coalitions of parties, but always faced an opposition. What a party stood for was determined largely by the peculiar circumstances of the country that gave it birth. Yet certain parallels reached across national boundaries. Although no group in Russia can be compared with the German Catholic Center, the Austrian Christian Socialists do resemble it in many ways. No group in either Germany or Austria is comparable with the Russian populists (Social Revolutionaries). Yet German Liberals, Austrian Liberals, and Russian Kadets or Octobrists can perhaps be roughly equated. So can the Pan-Germans with the Pan-Slavs. The Social Democrats were Marxist in all three countries, but increasingly less revolutionary in Germany and Austria-Hungary, and increasingly more so in Russia.

All three countries during this period experienced an economic boom and an occasional depression; the industrial revolution struck them late, but with terrific impact. By the turn of the twentieth century, Germany had made such advances that its steel production surpassed that of England, and was second in the world only to that of the United States. Though far behind Germany both in resources and in technology, Austria-Hungary too was becoming rapidly industrialized. In Russia, transport and industry boomed.

Yet in all three countries, the landed nobility continued to exercise political influence quite out of proportion to their numbers. Everywhere the existence of a new and underprivileged class of urban workers stimulated intellectual leaders to form Marxist political groups, to preach the class struggle, and, except in Russia, to strive for immediate improvements in conditions rather than for the violent overthrow of the regime. Last of all the European countries, Russia emancipated her serfs in 1861, and began a new era of agrarian experiment and unrest. In Germany, protection was the great agrarian issue after the late 1870's. In Austria-Hungary, the peasants suffered with docility.

All three countries had minority problems of varying seriousness. Germany persecuted the Poles and, after 1871 and less severely, she persecuted the Alsatians and Lorrainers. More and more, Russia persecuted the Finns, Poles, Ukrainians, and Armenians. In Austria-Hungary alone, however, the minority problem proved fatal. German anti-Slav sentiment in Austria, and Magyar mistreatment of all non-Magyars in Hungary, alienated potentially loyal subjects, and finally helped explode the state from inside. In all three countries the Jews created a special problem and suffered different degrees of discrimination and persecution.

In Germany, a combination of circumstances led first to an assault by the government on the Catholic Church and then to an alliance between the government and the Catholic political party. In the Habsburg Monarchy, a milder anticlericalism had its day, but the Church retained its hold on the population and continued to exercise enormous political influence. In Russia, the Orthodox Church as usual played almost no role in the cultural development of the people. But one group of influential intellectuals attacked it as the source of Russia's troubles, while another group hailed the Church as the true source of Russia's strength and the fountainhead of all national virtue.

So it was that the main currents of the time flowed with uneven force over the Germans, Austrians, and Russians. Nationalism, materialism, militarism, imperialism, clericalism, constitutionalism, landlordism, and socialism were all experienced to a varying degree by all the countries. What determined each country's answer to social pressure, however, was its own peculiar past and its own peculiar character.

Reading Suggestions on Central and Eastern Europe

General Accounts

R. C. Binkley, *Realism and Nationalism, 1852-1871* (N.Y.: Harper, 1935). Though this volume, in the "Rise of Modern Europe" series, develops a somewhat implausible thesis about the possibilities of "federative polity," it provides an often illuminating discussion of the period indicated.

C. J. H. Hayes, *A Generation of Materialism, 1871-1900* (N.Y.: Harper, 1941). Another volume in the "Rise of Modern Europe" series, this does some penetrating probing beneath the surface of an apparently successful era, particularly in Germany.

A. J. P. Taylor, *The Struggle for Mastery in Europe, 1848-1918* (Oxford: Clarendon, 1954). A crisp survey of diplomatic history.

Special Studies: Germany

R. Flenley, *Modern German History* (N.Y.: Dutton, 1953), and K. S. Pinson, *Modern Germany, Its History and Civilization* (N.Y.: Macmillan, 1954). Two textbooks, of which Pinson's is the longer and Flenley's perhaps the more useful.

F. Darmstaedter, *Bismarck and the Creation of the Second Reich* (London: Methuen, 1948). A valuable study.

E. Eyck, *Bismarck and the German Empire* (London: Allen & Unwin, 1950). Translation and condensation of a large standard work in German.

A. J. P. Taylor, *Bismarck: The Man and the Statesman* (N.Y.: Knopf, 1955). A provocative and often hostile re-evaluation of the famous Prussian.

F. Meinecke, *The German Catastrophe* (Cambridge: Harvard Univ. Press, 1950). A useful antidote to Taylor, by a very great German historian.

T. Veblen, *Imperial Germany and the Industrial Revolution*, new ed. (N.Y.: Viking, 1954). An old, brilliant, and still very important analysis by a great American sociologist.

J. H. Clapham, *The Economic Development of France and Germany, 1815-1914*, 3rd ed. (Cambridge, Eng.: The University Press, 1928). An old but still instructive introduction to the subject.

Special Studies: The Habsburg Monarchy

A. J. May, *The Hapsburg Monarchy, 1867-1914* (Cambridge: Harvard Univ. Press, 1951). Concise general account.

A. J. P. Taylor, *The Habsburg Monarchy, 1809-1918*, 2nd ed. (London: Hamish Hamilton, 1948). A spirited brief treatment.

R. A. Kann, *The Multinational Empire*, 2 vols. (N.Y.: Columbia Univ. Press, 1950). A monograph, arranged nationality by nationality, and discussing national sentiments and the government's efforts to deal with them.

O. Jászi, *The Dissolution of the Habsburg Monarchy* (Chicago: Univ. of Chicago Press, 1929). From a rare point of view, that of the liberal Magyar.

R. W. Seton-Watson, *German, Slav, and Magyar* (London: Williams and Norgate, 1916). By the greatest British authority on southeast Europe, the author of many other valuable studies of the area.

E. Wiskemann, *Czechs and Germans* (London: Oxford Univ. Press, 1938). A good case history of national antagonisms.

Special Studies: Russia

H. Seton-Watson, *The Decline of Imperial Russia, 1855-1914* (N.Y.: Praeger, 1952). The only sound work in English covering virtually all the period dealt with in this chapter.

G. T. Robinson, *Rural Russia under the Old Régime*, 2nd ed. (N.Y.: Macmillan, 1949). A splendid monograph on the peasant question.

R. Hare, *Pioneers of Russian Social Thought* (N.Y.: Oxford Univ. Press, 1951). Chapters, varying in value, on the chief non-Marxist thinkers of nineteenth-century Russia.

N. V. Riasanovsky, *Russia and the West in the Teaching of the Slavophiles* (Cambridge: Harvard Univ. Press, 1953). A useful study of one side of the chief intellectual controversy of the period.

D. Footman, *Red Prelude* (New Haven: Yale Univ. Press, 1945). A good biography of Zhelyabov, *narodnik* and terrorist.

B. Pares, *The Fall of the Russian Monarchy* (London: Cape, 1939). An excellent study of the period between 1905 and 1917; by an authority who was frequently on the spot.

A. Herzen, *My Past and Thoughts*, 6 vols. (London: Chatto & Windus, 1924-1927). The classic picture of nineteenth-century Russia, by its most distinguished rebel.

S. Witte, *Memoirs* (N.Y.: Doubleday, 1921). The somewhat apologetic memoirs of the man who did most to industrialize imperial Russia.

B. D. Wolfe, *Three Who Made a Revolution* (Boston: Beacon, 1955). A fine triple study of Lenin, Trotsky, and Stalin; with emphasis on the period before 1914.

A. Lobanov-Rostovsky, *Russia and Asia*, rev. ed. (Ann Arbor, Mich.: Wahr, 1951). A useful introductory survey.

B. H. Sumner, *Russia and the Balkans, 1870-1880* (Oxford: Clarendon, 1937). A monograph including a helpful discussion of Panslavism.

Historical Fiction

T. Mann, *Buddenbrooks* (N.Y.: Pocket Books). Inexpensive reprint of a long novel about a family in imperial Germany.

G. Hauptmann, *The Weavers, Hannele, The Beaver Coat* (N.Y.: Rinehart, 1951). Three plays that convey some of the flavor of nineteenth-century Germany.

R. Musil, *The Man without Qualities* (N.Y.: Coward-McCann, 1953). A novel steeped in the atmosphere of pre-1914 Vienna.

M. Jókai, *Eyes Like the Sea* (N.Y.: Putnam's, 1901). Fictionalized autobiography of a romantic Hungarian novelist, the author of many novels that give insights into Magyar nationalism.

I. Turgenev, *Fathers and Sons* (sometimes called *Fathers and Children*—many editions) and *Smoke* (N.Y.: Dutton, 1949. Everyman ed.). Superb contemporary realistic fiction reflecting Russian intellectual and political life.

F. Dostoevsky, *The Brothers Karamazov* (several editions), and *Crime and Punishment* (several editions). Famous novels depicting the turbulent life of Russian intellectuals in the mid-nineteenth century; more romantic in tone than Turgenev's works.

The Portable Chekhov (N.Y.: Viking, 1947). A selection from the short stories and plays of this skillful portraitist of the upper classes in tsarist Russia.

L. Tolstoy, *Anna Karenina* (several editions). A celebrated novel set in late nineteenth-century Petersburg and the countryside.

CHAPTER SIXTEEN

The Intellectual

Revolution

The sources for the intellectual history of the nineteenth century—the great books and the ephemeral books, the articles, stories, advertisements, sermons, paintings, sculptures, all the accumulated symbols of culture—have been preserved in bewildering quantity. The late century seems, in our present retrospect, to have presented samples of almost all varieties of human thought and feeling, of all western "styles."

A detailed catalogue of these varieties would be dull and confusing. Here we shall center on one main theme—the qualifications, emendations, even repudiations, made by the late nineteenth century in the western heritage of the Enlightenment, that heritage of optimistic faith in simple, static, reformist "reason" and a simple "natural law" ruling men and matter. The most striking of these emendations was made by Darwin.

I: Darwinism

The Origin of Species

In 1859 there was published in London a volume on natural history that began with the true scientist's caution:

When on board H.M.S. "Beagle," as naturalist, I was much struck with certain facts in the distribution of the organic beings inhabiting South America, and in the geological relations of the present to the past inhabitants of that continent. These facts, as will be seen in the latter chapters of this volume, seemed to throw some light on the origin of species— that mystery of mysteries, as it has been called by one of our greatest philosophers. On my return home, it occurred to me, in 1837, that something might perhaps be made out on this question by patiently accumulating and reflecting on all sorts of facts which could possibly have any bearing on it. After five years' work I allowed myself to speculate on the subject, and drew up some short notes; these I enlarged in 1844 into a sketch of the conclusions, which then seemed to me probable: from that period to the present day I have steadily pursued the same object.*

Darwin's *On the Origin of Species by Means of Natural Selection*, thus modestly and cautiously introduced to the public, is one of the books that mark a revolution in intellectual history. Like all important revolutions, the Darwinian was no bolt from the blue. Into Darwin's work had gone long years of preparation, not merely those of Darwin's own life, but those of his predecessors and colleagues in the scientific study of what was then called natural history and is now called biology. The set of facts before him was the long record of the hundreds of thousands of years of organic life on earth. Already well established by geologists like Sir Charles Lyell and by paleontologists, this record told of

* Charles Darwin, *The Origin of Species*, Introduction.

the rise, development, sometimes of the disappearance, of thousands of different forms of plant and animal organisms, or *species*. It contradicted an important part of the commonly accepted theory men of the West had about the past of organic life. The Bible in the Book of Genesis described all forms of life as begun in the space of a single week by a Creator about 6,000 years ago. And this same religious account furthermore stated explicitly that all existing men and animals were descended from single pairs of each species preserved in Noah's ark during a great universal flood that took place some time after the Creation.

Now Darwin was by no means the first to find a discrepancy between the historical and scientific record and the accepted Biblical explanation. The men of the Enlightenment had felt compelled by the facts of the record to give up the Biblical explanation. Some of them had gone so far as to conceive the record as a very long evolutionary process in which no God, at least no personal, Christian God, had a hand, but only the impersonal forces of Nature or the deist's "watchmaker God" (see Chapter IX). But they had arrived at no satisfactory explanation of how Nature or the watchmaker God had done the job; they had no theory of how organisms had evolved. This Darwin gave the world.

Darwin's Theories

One of his clues he found in the work of the economist Malthus (see Chapter XIII). In his *Essay on Population*, Malthus had pointed out that organisms—including man—tended to multiply to a point where there simply was not food enough for them all. In the intense competition for food, some of these organisms did not get enough, and died. This was the germ of the conception Darwin phrased as the *struggle for existence*. He next asked himself what determined that certain individuals would survive and that others would die. Obviously the surviving ones got more food, better shelter, better living conditions of all sorts. If they were all identical organisms, the only explanation—apart from the intervention of a supernatural being—would have to be mere chance. But it was clear from observation that individual organisms of a given species are not identical. Their variations appear even at birth. Thus in a single litter of pigs there may be sturdy, aggressive piglets and a runt. The runt, even if a sentimental farmer tries to protect it, is likely to get shoved aside in suckling by his sturdier brothers, and starve. In the wild state, in free competition, the runt is almost certain to die. In the struggle for existence, the runt is proved unfit.

Here is the second of Darwin's key phrases, the *survival of the fittest*. The organism best endowed in its variations to get food and shelter lives to procreate young that will tend to inherit these favorable variations. The variations are slight indeed, but over generation after generation they are cumulative; finally an organism so different from the long-distant ancestor is produced that we can speak of a new species. This new species has *evolved*. It has evolved by the working of *natural selection*. Man as a plant and animal breeder has long made use of this process, and has hastened and indeed guided it for his own purposes by *artificial selection*, by breeding only the best strains. But man has been doing this with domesticated plants and animals for but a tiny period of geological time, and with but few species. Over the aeons, natural selection has been the working force; and for man himself, natural selection alone has been at work, since man has yet to breed his own kind as he breeds his domestic plants and animals.

Darwin held that the variations in individuals of the same species at birth are accidental, and that they are generally transmitted through inheritance. He did not—and this is a very important point—believe that the evidence showed that variations produced in an individual organism in the course of its life could be transmitted to its offspring. Thus, Darwinism denies the inheritance of "acquired characteristics." Obviously, a man with an amputated leg will not produce one-legged children. Experimenters have docked the tails of generations of laboratory rats, but the rats are still born with long tails.

Today, nearly a century after the publication of the *Origin of Species*, Darwin's work as a biologist is still accepted in most of its larger outlines. Later work, however, has found that variations of importance in the evolutionary process are probably not so much the numerous tiny ones Darwin emphasized, but rather bigger and much rarer ones now known as "mutations." Darwin believed that what he called "sexual selection"—that is, the ability of the fittest individual to attract and mate with fittest individuals of the opposite sex and thus produce the fittest offspring—was a very important factor in natural selection. Although sexual selection is by no means wholly discarded by geneticists today, many of them do not accept Darwin's version of it. The actual mechanism of heredity we know much better than Darwin did, thanks to the work of an Austrian monk, Gregor Mendel, in the late nineteenth century.

The Effect on Theology

The *Origin of Species* stirred up a most heated theological controversy. It added fuel to a fire kindled earlier by historical and linguistic scholarship with its tendency to apply the same standards to the Bible that the scholar would apply to Homer, or to the old Norse and Germanic epics. Fundamentalists, both Protestant and Catholic, simply stuck by Genesis and damned Darwin and all his work. But the Catholic Church and many Protestant bodies eventually took at least a neutral attitude toward Darwinism, which they viewed as a biological hypothesis neither necessarily correct nor necessarily incorrect. The great majority of Christians tacitly or openly accepted sufficient modification of Genesis to accommodate themselves to the scientist's time-scale, and adjusted the classic theological arguments from first cause, design, and the like to a God who worked his will in accordance with organic evolution; and they accepted the assimilation of the Biblical account, at least in part, with other fallible histories. In short, they were willing to grant that the *men* who wrote the Bible were not infallible. Moreover, it was quite clear to reflective men that nothing Darwin or any other scientist or scholar could produce would give ultimate answers to the kind of problem set by the existence of God. It was quite clear to them that since God's eye is now on the sparrow, it must once have been on the dinosaur. Christians can be Darwinians: millions of them are.

The Effect on Social and Economic Attitudes

The theological conflict had pretty well run its course by the beginning of the twentieth century. More important in the long run was the use men made of some of Darwin's basic concepts—or at least, of his more smoothly coined phrases—in debates on matters moral, economic, and political. The blanket term, "Social Darwinism," which covers all these transfers of ideas from biology to the social sciences and human relations, takes in a very wide range of persons and ideas. Darwin himself was a biologist, not a "Social Darwinist."

The central idea that social and political thinkers took over from Darwin was that of competition. It was of course already central in their thinking, but Darwin buttressed it with the prestige of the natural sciences. The majority of these late nineteenth-century thinkers interpreted the human struggle as a struggle for the means of livelihood. There is, they were sure, among men a human "struggle for life." The variations that counted here were the variations that brought success in economic competition—the variations that produced inventors, business organizers, even perhaps the political, artistic, and professional leaders. Darwin's work in natural history came to confirm the economist's doctrine of laissez-faire and the nineteenth-century liberal's doctrine of individual freedom.

Formal economics did not indeed make much use of, or have much need for, Darwin. The classical economists had already brought the arguments for laissez-faire to their height. On the whole, for the rest of the century, the economists were to temper somewhat the rigor of the doctrine of competition among individuals. But the average successful middle-class person in the West took Darwin to heart. Here was scientific confirmation of the middle-class notions that the universe was designed to reward hard work, thrift, intelligence, and self-help and to punish laziness, waste, stupidity, and reliance on charity. Above all, the middle-class person of the time took Darwin to confirm the notion that the poor were poor because they were unfit, badly designed for living. The work of Darwin confirmed the complementary notion that attempts by private charity or by state action to take from the rich and moderately well-to-do and give to the poor were useless and quite contrary to nature, shocking efforts to reverse the course of evolution. If a man cannot earn enough to feed himself, it was argued, he had better die; lowlier organisms too incompetent to feed themselves certainly die off, to the greater good of the species. Herbert Spencer (1820-1903), an ardent British evolutionist, summed it up neatly:

Of man, as of all inferior creatures, the law by conformity to which the species is preserved, is that among adults the individuals best adapted to the conditions of their existence shall prosper most, and the individuals least adapted to the conditions of their existence shall prosper least. . . . Pervading all Nature we may see at work a stern discipline which is often a little cruel that it may be very kind. . . . The ultimate result of shielding men from folly is to fill the world with fools.*

Spencer himself, if it came to that, could not have stood by while the unemployed and their families starved to death. He had an almost maniacal hatred of the state, of local government as well as national; he held out even against compulsory sewage in cities. But even Spencer could not transfer to the struggle for existence among human beings the fine ruthless freedom of the jungle, of what Tennyson called "Nature red in tooth and claw." He was against all forms of government provision for what we now call "social security." But what government may not do the ethically sound individual will do as charity. The rich and well-to-do will take care of the poor voluntarily—not enough to spoil them, not enough to frustrate the designs of evolution by letting them prosper and propagate their kind, but enough to prevent their starving or freezing to death.

In his *Principles of Ethics*, Spencer discovers that the softer emotions promoted by Christianity and the other higher religions—kindness, dislike of cruelty, love—were also in accord with the intentions of the laws of the universe as summed up in evolution. Mutual extermination might be the law for tigers, but not for human beings. Indeed, Spencer and many other Social Darwinists held that altruistic moral senti-

* Herbert Spencer, *Principles of Ethics* (London, 1879-1893), section 257; *Social Statics* (London, 1851), p. 149; *Autobiography* (London, 1904), II, 5.

ments that impel us toward charity are the highest achievement of the evolutionary process, and that a society with many altruists is thereby shown to be the fittest for survival.

Eugenics

The Social Darwinists were, then, faced with this primary difficulty. Darwin seemed to have shown that the unmitigated struggle for life within a given species, and among rival species, was the law of the universe; but human history, and human feelings, showed that men could not in practice look on with indifference while their fellow men starved to death. One way out of the dilemma was that of Spencer, a sort of humanized and mitigated struggle in which the incompetent were shelved but not destroyed. Many who held this view accompanied it with a faith in what came to be called eugenics. For them the question was not so much the elimination of the unfit but the deliberate encouragement of the production of the fit. Darwin had begun his *Origin of Species* with a consideration of the extraordinary success men had had with artificial selection in the breeding of plants and animals. Why not do the same thing with human beings? Since, according to strict Darwinian theory, acquired characteristics were not transmitted by heredity, no amount of manipulation of the social environment, no amount of wise planning of institutions, would alter human beings. Therefore, the only way to secure permanent improvement of the race was by deliberate mating of the fit with the fit.

The eugenicists, however, ran at once against the fact that man, though he domesticates plants and animals, is still himself a "wild" animal. The individual human being in choosing a mate is no doubt influenced by a great variety of motives, which the social scientist still understands only imperfectly. But no master human breeder, not even an understandable master principle or idea, decides who shall mate with whom. So far, the eugenicists have had little success with the positive side of their program. On the negative side, they have urged that the obviously unfit, the idiots, the feeble-minded, the insane, be prevented, even if necessary by compulsory sterilization, from having children. Some few American states have passed laws for such compulsory sterilization, but only a tiny handful of human beings, not enough to affect in the slightest the course of human physical evolution, have undergone this treatment. Moreover, the eugenicists have aroused the opposition of many Christians, who believe that it is wrong to tamper with God's human creations.

"Racism"

By far the commonest way out of the dilemma facing the Social Darwinists lay in the obvious notion that it is not so much among individual human beings that the struggle for existence really goes on, as it is among human beings organized in groups, as tribes, "races," territorial states. The struggle that counts is not the struggle, say, among individual Englishmen to survive, but the struggle between the entity England—or Great Britain—and its rivals. The struggle for existence among men is now lifted from the biology of the individual to the politics of the group. And for the nineteenth century the group had to be the nation-state, perhaps kindred nation-states that could be organized for the struggle as one bloc of states, such as the "Nordic" or the "Latin," or perhaps at the very widest the Caucasian or white peoples in competition with the colored peoples, yellow, brown, or black. This struggle had an ultimate form: war. The group that defeated another group in war had thereby shown itself to be fitter than the beaten group, and it had a right—indeed in evolutionary terms a duty—to

eliminate the beaten group, seize its lands, and people them with its own fitter human beings. The English imperialist Cecil Rhodes held that a world wholly and exclusively peopled with Anglo-Saxons would be the best possible world.

The idea of a Chosen People was of course not a new one in Darwin's time. But there is no doubt that Darwin's work, however little he may have meant it to be, was a most important element in the special forms that competition among organized states took in the latter half of the nineteenth century, and right on to our own day. Darwinism came too late to do more than prop up the philosophy of laissez-faire in economics. But Darwinism came at just the right time to intensify the struggle among organized human groups in international politics.

The particular groups or states that were to benefit as the elect of evolution in this special political sense varied with the aims, sympathies, and actual citizenship of the individual who was seeking to promote an ultimate evolutionary victory. Britain, Germany, the United States, the Latins, the Slavs, the Nordics, the whites, even indeed the Christians, were all defended as the true elect of evolution. Most of the writers who preached this kind of political evolution proceeded from the assumption that at bottom the men of a given group had certain physical traits in common, traits that gave them their superiority, and that could not possibly be transmitted to men of another group. Most of these writers, in short, were "racists" who believed that in fact *homo sapiens* had already evolved into what were really separate species. A black skin, for instance, was for them a sign of innate inferiority. The blacks would simply have to go the way of the dinosaurs, into extinction. Evolution had spoken.

There were indeed all sorts of half-way stations proposed by these writers. Few of them quite dared to preach what has in our own day been christened *genocide*—that is, the actual wholesale murder of "inferior" and beaten "races." We had to wait for Hitler for this. Most of them, though perhaps they held that in the long run the inferior peoples would in fact die out, were willing to see the inferiors duly subjected to the superiors, to have the less fit peoples serve as hewers of wood and drawers of water for their masters. Indeed, some Social Darwinists applied their theories to a new form of caste organization, which came to be known as "élitism." For them, the distinction between superior and inferior was not always one of race or even of existing state organizations, but one that applied to a cross section of the whole human race. The fit were not limited to any one race, but they were still marked out by the rigid hand of biological inheritance. They were the master group, the élite, the "supermen"; and they should everywhere band together against the dull average men. The German, Friedrich Nietzsche (1844-1900), who gave currency to the phrase "superman," was a subtle and difficult thinker, who disliked Darwin as a grubbing Englishman. Still Nietzsche's influence among the half-educated who admired him in the late nineteenth and early twentieth centuries was to further racist and élitist causes.

Theories of the evolution-guided superiority of certain groups were not limited to Europe. In the United States, the innate, unchangeable superiority of whites to blacks was an article of faith among many whites in the North and almost universally in the South. This faith was greatly bolstered by Darwinian anthropologists and biologists. The notion that the degree of blondness, and other readily visible traits, such as long-headedness and tallness, measured suitableness for citizenship in a great democracy helped dictate the American immigration act of 1924, which encouraged immigrants from northwestern Europe, and very seriously discouraged those from southern and eastern Europe. The American, Madison Grant, in his *The Passing of the Great Race*, published in 1916, asserted that the Nordics—the tall, long-headed, light-haired peoples of northern Europe— were "a race of soldiers, sailors, adventurers and explorers, but above all, of rulers, organizers and aristocrats." Grant continued:

Before leaving this interesting subject of the correlation of spiritual and moral traits with physical characters we may note that these influences are so deeply rooted in everyday consciousness that the modern novelist or playwright does not fail to make his hero a tall, blond, honest and somewhat stupid youth and his villain a small, dark and exceptionally intelligent individual of warped moral character. So in Celtic legend as in the Græco-Roman and mediæval romances, prince and princess are always fair, a fact rather indicating that the mass of the people were brunet at the time when the legends were taking shape. In fact, 'fair' is a synonym for beauty. Most ancient tapestries show a blond earl on horseback and a dark haired churl holding the bridle.

. . .

In depicting the crucifixion no artist hesitates to make the two thieves brunet in contrast to the blond Saviour. This is something more than a convention, as such quasi-authentic traditions as we have of our Lord strongly suggest his Nordic, possibly Greek, physical and moral attributes.[*]

The title of Madison Grant's book, however, betrays an anxiety that is never far from the surface even in the most confident of these Social Darwinists. Grant feared that his "great race," gifted summit of evolution though it was, was paradoxically not going to survive. The lower races were breeding faster; democratic equalitarianism was lopping off the best and encouraging the worst. Somehow evolution was going wrong. Degeneration, not progress, was the mark of the times. Like those other "scientific" determinists, the Marxists, the Social Darwinists believed that men of good will had to set to work with pen and tongue to help along the predetermined process and keep it on the right track.

---

[*] Madison Grant, *The Passing of the Great Race*, 4th rev. ed. (New York, 1921), 229-230.

A New Historical Determinism

Darwinian science no more than Newtonian science really answered the great questions about good and evil, about the ends of human life, that men have been asking and answering ever since we have had historical records. Darwinian science, and indeed the physics, chemistry, and other sciences that flourished in the nineteenth century, recast for many the whole frame of reference in which these questions were asked. Do not mistake. Traditional Christianity, as well as many other supernatural faiths, survived Darwin as they had survived Newton. Many men continued to believe that a God, or gods, not bound by the laws men discovered in laboratory experiments and in other systematic observations, guided their steps and gave meaning to their lives in this world and in the other world after death. But with the spread of popular education, especially in the West, great numbers came to believe that no such God or gods existed, that the material universe of science and common sense went on its regular ways in accordance with laws or uniformities which men might eventually understand completely, and which they were already beginning to understand quite well. And in its turn, this materialist view of the universe had repercussions on all but the most determined and fundamentalist of the supernatural faiths; at the very least, they pared down the scope of divine action, cribbing and confining it.

Darwin's work and that of many other scientists, in combination with the work of historians and philosophers and men of letters, worked a major change in the way men looked at their universe. It is an undue simplification to say that the Newtonian universe was static, the Darwinian dynamic, but the generalization is a good rough working approximation. The eighteenth-century Enlightenment was certainly feeling its way far more than its later Romantic critics admitted toward a view of the universe as developing, progressing, evolving. But, as one can see from the work of so typical a *philosophe* as Condorcet, the eighteenth century had no good explanation of the way change came about. This explanation Darwin provided for natural history, and the Romantic historians and their fellow workers in other fields provided it for human history.

Today we are still in the climate of opinion set for us in the late nineteenth century. We still believe, to a greater or less degree, in what has been labeled "historicism"—that is, in the doctrine that the course of history in the widest sense shows a regular, if bewildering, unfolding that has "determined" everything now existing and that will determine everything in the future. The wildest believer in this doctrine had to admit that since he could not in fact understand the whole process in the past, he could not wholly understand the present or wholly predict the future. Still, the clue lay in the past, out of which the present has developed as the oak has developed from the acorn.

The Christian and Hebraic calendar made the earth 6,000 years old, but the Darwinian calendar envisaged millions of years for organic life alone. It might seem, therefore, that historicism, especially when reinforced by the emphasis Darwin put on the immense reaches of time, would confirm conservative opposition to rapid change, or at least encourage in men a certain resignation in the face of the slow-moving process of evolution on this earth. And so it did for some men. Darwin's grandson, Sir Charles Galton Darwin, published in 1953 a book entitled *The Next Million Years*. He concluded that, since it is now held that it takes about a million years for a species to evolve, it will be a million years before evolution produces a creature any better than man; and that therefore for the next million years we shall have a history much like that of the last few thousand, with wars, revolutions, pestilence, the rise and fall of thousands of Egypts, Romes, Britains, and Americas.

But historicism in the nineteenth and twentieth centuries has had for others a quite different consequence. It has served to convince impatient and hopeful men that they had really mastered the secrets of the universe, that they understood as misguided predecessors had not just where the forces of history were leading. They could, then, help the process instead of hindering it, perhaps even hasten it! Marxism is the classic example of this faith in historical determinism, but nationalism, racism, and a host of others all drew nourishment from it. The extraordinary speeding-up of technological improvements lent strength to this view that moral and political improvement could also be speeded up. The doctrine of Evolution, then, though logically you can argue that it should have lessened the force of utopian faiths, did in fact increase them. People thought of the sureness of evolution and forgot its slowness.

II: Literature and the Arts

The Victorian Age It is risky to generalize about the literature and the art of the later nineteenth century. But these years do largely deserve to be called the "Victorian Age." This age has not the neatness of style we can find in ancient Athens or Renaissance Italy or Elizabethan England. We can evoke a Victorian drawing room, where Maud or Mélanie in ringlets and crinolines, surrounded by whatnots, bric-a-brac, plush hangings, and Landseer engravings, reads Tennyson, Longfellow, or Heine, or plays Liszt on the pianoforte. But so much went on outside that drawing room!—not only in the lives of peasants, workers, and businessmen, but even in art and letters. Maud or Mélanie might indeed have been reading Dickens or Balzac, but these writers hardly fitted the drawing room. Nor would Thoreau and Melville, Zola and Dostoevski. It is quite certain that the girls would not have been reading Marx.

For the safest thing we can say about the formal culture of the second half of the nineteenth century is that it had wide variety, that indeed it was very *eclectic*. We may also add that a great deal of this formal culture was now, more clearly than ever before in western history, produced and cultivated by men and women in conscious revolt against the tastes of the politically and economically dominant class of their time—that is, the middle class. Unless Maud and Mélanie were very advanced young women indeed, they did not like much of what a hundred years later we single out as important in Victorian art and literature. If they were ordinary middle-class young women, they read sentimental novels now forgotten save by the social historian, and they lived in a culture to which the derogatory overtones that the word "Victorian" still often has apply well enough.

Their fathers and brothers, indeed, were often so concerned with industry and trade that they had no time for literature and the arts, which they tended to leave to their womenfolk. Or if they did have wider concerns, these concerns were rather with political and social problems, with the material betterment of their class, and—to be fair—with that of the working class too. But most of these middle-class men felt that the most that could be done for the workers was to raise their standard of living slowly under existing capitalist laissez-faire. They held that Church and State should join to restrain by law and by religion of an essentially puritanical cast the lack of self-restraint these middle-class men found too characteristic of their inferiors. For with these Victorians laissez-faire was a strictly economic matter; in morals they believed firmly that organized institutions should interfere to restrain the populace from the drunkenness, idleness, and loose living they were supposedly inclined to. Libertarians in economics, the educated, middle-class Victorians were most certainly authoritarians in morals.

The Realistic Novel

In literature, the later nineteenth century was a great period for the novel. Here the accepted label for the novel of the time is "realism," in contrast with the Romanticism of the earlier part of the century. Yet as one usually finds in examining these sharp contrasts between the cultural attitudes of succeeding generations in the modern West, the realists are quite obviously children of the Romanticists. The Romantic of 1830, fleeing this ugly world for an idealized Middle Ages, when knighthood was in flower and there were no sooty factories, or writing of the idyllic Indian tribes of America, can indeed look very different from the realist of 1860, analyzing with fascination and disgust the men and women of the mill towns, the slums of the great cities, the unidyllic countryside of peasant labor. Yet in the sense of close attention to authentic detail, of effort to picture men and women as they really were, there is much realism even in the work of a Romantic novelist like Victor Hugo. Certainly no sharp break occurred about 1850.

The Englishman Dickens (1812-1870) and the Frenchman Balzac (1799-1850) were both writing in the period we label "Romantic." Both revel in exaggerations, both pour themselves out freely in undisciplined torrents of words, both achieve an effect of unreal intensity—Romantic traits, surely. Yet both are thoroughly immersed in the world of their time, both are in many ways realists. On the other hand, the leading French realist of the later nineteenth century, Flaubert (1821-1880), wrote one of his novels, *Salammbô*, about an ancient and, in spite of his great efforts at historical accuracy, not very real Carthage. And in his masterpiece, *Madame Bovary*, which analyzes the romantic longings of a small-town doctor's wife, Flaubert betrays a most ambivalent feeling toward his heroine. Indeed, he once said, "*I am Madame Bovary*." Flaubert hated the bourgeois world he wrote about quite as much as did the escapist writers of an earlier generation.

Nevertheless, there remains a difference between the writing of the second half of the century and that of the first. The realists did abandon the Romantic pursuit of the ideal and the remote and chose subjects close to their own lives. They did generally avoid tempestuous extremes and concentrate on the quieter ordinary folk. They did pay great attention to choosing the right word, the word that should stand exactly for the experience, the emotion depicted, and not rouse all sorts of irrelevant overtones. We may take as good realists the Englishman Trollope and the Russian Turgenev. Trollope (1815-1882) wrote dozens of novels about Victorian clergymen and politicians and country gentlemen, carefully observing the English decencies, never raising his voice or his style, but imparting understanding, sympathy, and a suitable, modest irony. Turgenev (1818-1883) wrote about his fellows with classic restraint, skirting delicately the depths of the Slavic soul. Or we may take William Dean Howells (1837-1920), who in the *Rise of Silas Lapham* and other novels sought to apply realism to the American scene.

The Naturalistic Novel: Zola

Howells seemed to later critics a representative of what they called the "genteel tradition." They accused him of omitting the more unpleasant facts of life, of softening the crudities of the new industrial civilization. For as the twentieth century drew near the realists were confronted with a rebel generation that found them not "realistic" enough. This school rose first in France, where they took for themselves the name of "naturalists." Their leader, Emile Zola (1840-1902), shows clearly the influence of the scientific revolution inspired by the work of Darwin. For Zola was not content with the realist's aim to reflect the life around him with simple accuracy; he sought to arrive at laws of human development, much as the biologist seeks for laws of organic development.

The novel was to Zola an instrument of scientific generalization. He would do for society, for men in their relations with other men, what Darwin had done for natural history. He would show what men are like, of course, but he would also show how they came to be what they are, and even what they were going to be. He called his great series of novels about a family under the Second Empire, the Rougon-Macquart, the "natural history" of a family. In a famous manifesto he championed the "experimental novel":

... The experimental novel is a consequence of the scientific evolution of the century; it continues and completes physiology, which itself leans for support on chemistry and medicine; it substitutes for the study of the abstract and the metaphysical man the study of the natural man, governed by physical and chemical laws, and modified by the influences of his surroundings; it is in one word the literature of our scientific age, as the classical and romantic literature corresponded to a scholastic and theological age.*

Zola's work points up one of the tendencies not only of the late nineteenth-century novel, in those days the spearhead of literature, but of other forms of literature as well. The literature of the time, and to a great

* Zola, *The Experimental Novel*, Belle M. Sherman, trans. (New York, 1893), 23.

extent of the twentieth century too, is overwhelmingly a literature of discontent, of protest against things-as-they-are. Now it is quite true that from the ancient Greek philosophers and the Hebrew prophets on, great thinkers have held that their times were peculiarly out of joint. They had to protest against the abuses of their age, had to stir their fellows into bettering their ways. But there are certainly periods when the intellectuals are *relatively* conformist, *relatively* well disposed to the existing government and society—the Elizabethan Age, and the Age of Louis XIV, for example. And there are ages when the intellectuals, even though they are bitterly against things-as-they-are, write with hope and confidence of what is to come—as in the eighteenth-century Enlightenment. We have already noted that the Romantic movement has its pessimistic side. With the second half of the nineteenth century there sets in a strain of pessimism—at least among many leading writers—that has continued to this day. It is by no means the only strain in modern western literature, and it is by no means a strain of unrelieved pessimism. Writers on the Left, notably the socialists, are obliged by their creed to hold that somehow mankind will win through to a better society.

The Literature of Pessimism and Protest

The pessimists reacted against the eighteenth-century doctrine of the natural goodness of man. Certainly "nature" and "natural" as they figure in the work of a Zola carry very different connotations from these words as the eighteenth, and even the early nineteenth, centuries used them. Nature by the late nineteenth century apparently made men greedy, selfish, combative, not very bright, and extremely addicted to a variety of irregular sexual relations which brought out to the full their other bad traits. Sometimes, as with the English novelist Thomas Hardy (1840-

1928), this pessimism is built up from a series of incidents in private lives into a grand cosmic irony not without its consoling side. But for the most part these writers are concerned directly with the cruelties, stupidities, the downright insanities of ordinary people.

In France, De Maupassant (1850-1893), a master of the short story, wrote sparely and simply, after the manner of his master Flaubert, about the tragedies and comedies of ordinary life; but the tragedies, or at least the ironies, prevail. In Russia, Chekhov (1860-1904), a medical man by training, used the prose drama and the short story to show how life harasses us all. Ibsen (1828-1906) in Norway, Brieux (1858-1932) in France, and George Bernard Shaw (1856-1950) in England all helped to develop the characteristically late-nineteenth-century form of the drama, the "problem play." The problem was sometimes one of wide moral and political concern, as in Ibsen's *Enemy of the People* or Shaw's *Man and Superman*, but it was very often concerned mainly with the stupid tangles of men's private, and in particular their sex, lives. Ibsen shocked his contemporaries in his *Doll's House* by having his heroine rebel against the "doll-house" atmosphere that her husband had created for her. His *Ghosts* scandalized his contemporaries by bringing to the stage the problem of syphilis.

The problem play, the problem novel, the problem short story spread through all the literatures of the West. They spread with the usual speed to the United States, where by the end of the nineteenth century the "genteel tradition" was already scorned by the bright young men, and the novelists Stephen Crane (1871-1900) and Theodore Dreiser (1871-1945) were bringing out the harsh realities of war, business, and love. It took a while for the extremes of "naturalism" to gain the United States, and it was not until our own day, and then of all places in the South of magnolia and roses, that William Faulkner and Erskine Caldwell,

and their many followers really plumbed the depths behind the Anglo-Saxon four-letter words they used so freely.

Most of this realistic or naturalistic writing, even when it is by no means of Marxist inspiration, is hostile to the middle classes. The bourgeois is no longer just the Philistine the Romantic disliked, the puritanical conformist, the stuffy enemy of sweetness and light. He is still that, but he is also the rapacious titan of industry, the jingoistic nationalist, authoritarian browbeater of his children, the tasteless addict of "conspicuous consumption" (a phrase of the American economist, Thorstein Veblen), the hypocritical practitioner of a "double standard" of sexual morality, and worse. Flaubert, who began so much, may be said to have begun this with his unfinished *Bouvard et Pécuchet*, in which he makes his two bourgeois "heroes" run the gamut of human futility, failing ludicrously in their effort to educate themselves. In England, Samuel Butler (1835-1902) in *The Way of All Flesh* set the pattern, since followed freely, for the novel in which the writer-son blames all on the tyrannical male parent. Shaw found a great simple phrase to sum up what was wrong—"middle class morality." Ibsen's *Enemy of the People* is ironically named; the real enemy of the people is the people themselves, not the misunderstood leader who would bring them better things.

Even where the writers are not embittered, even where their main concern is to balance good and evil as, one suspects, they are balanced in life, the middle class does not often come out well. English novelists like H. G. Wells, Galsworthy, and Arnold Bennett, French novelists like Anatole France, Spanish novelists like Pio Baroja, and most writers of tsarist Russia find something wrong with the middle classes. An epitome, a bit more kindly than usual in Europe, of this attack on the middle classes is afforded by an American, who wrote in the 1920's, chronologically rather later than the period with which we are here concerned, but quite in its "style." Sinclair Lewis' *Main Street* and *Babbitt* are realistic rather than naturalistic novels, and George Babbitt is almost a hero without ironic quotation marks. Still, Babbitt came to sum up for thousands of American intellectuals what was wrong with a naive materialistic civilization. The novels of Sinclair Lewis sold by the hundred thousands, so that it is clear that "George Babbitt" himself in real life must have relished, or at least read, these satires on his way of life. Indeed, since many of the writers we have been dealing with were able to sell their works in a mass market, one is forced to conclude that a good portion of the middle classes in the West were in revolt against their own shortcomings.

Not all that was written between 1850 and the outbreak of war in 1914 was a literature of scorn or protest. The daughters of the Maud or Mélanie with whom we began could about 1900 read the standard conventional fare, historical novels, novels of escape, novels of true love. They could even find in writers like Kipling men who, if not exactly convinced that this was the best of possible worlds, were at least convinced that the English middle classes were the best of the lot. They could, in short, read for pleasure and edification, and go on with the serious business of life.

Poetry

Few writers tried to make poetry "naturalistic" in Zola's sense. Nor, on the other hand, was the late nineteenth century a period in which the epic or the grand philosophical poem, like Wordsworth's *Prelude*, flourished. Poets did attempt the drama in verse, but these dramas remained poetry to be read in the study, not plays for the boards. Tennyson, who can stand very well for the more conventional Victorian poets, tried the epic in his *Idyls of the King*, based on the legends about King Arthur's court, and he tried the philosophical poem,

such as *In Memoriam*, and several "closet" dramas. But he perhaps succeeded best in his shorter lyrics.

In England Tennyson, in America Longfellow and his New England colleagues, in France Victor Hugo, wrote the staple poetry the late nineteenth century liked and read a great deal. These poets deserve the tag, "household words." In form, their work differs little from the norms set by the earlier Romantic movement, and their subjects are love, death, nature, patriotism, faith, doubt, and longing, the eternal lyric repertory. And they sometimes came down into the arena to deal with politics, as in Whittier's anti-slavery poems, and in James Russell Lowell's "Biglow Papers," poems in Yankee dialect on the crisis of the Civil War. The spiritual crisis brought on by loss of Christian faith in a scientific age is evident in many poems of Matthew Arnold and Arthur Hugh Clough, as well as Tennyson. Even the horrors of the industrial revolution are apparent in Thomas Hood's "Song of the Shirt":

With fingers weary and worn,
  With eyelids heavy and red,
A woman sat in unwomanly rags,
  Plying her needle and thread—
    Stitch! stitch! stitch!
In poverty, hunger, and dirt,
  And still with the voice of dolorous pitch
She sang the 'Song of the Shirt!'

Work! work! work!
While the cock is crowing aloof!
  And work—work—work,
Till the stars shine through the roof!
It's O! to be a slave
  Along with the barbarous Turk,
Where woman has never a soul to save,
  If this is Christian work!*

Yet in these same years poetry went far along the road that brought it to our times, when the serious poet usually writes difficult, private, experimental verse for a handful of initiates. Poetry for the Romanticist was indeed the reflection of his own

---

* Thomas Hood, *Poetical Works*, Epes Sargent, ed. (Boston, 1855), 145.

inner world, but he hoped it would not prove by any means a private world. He wanted to be read, perhaps even by the Philistines, as indeed he was. In the second half of the nineteenth century, the French Parnassians deliberately sought the seclusion of perfect form, of polished verse fit for but few, of "art for art's sake." Still later, with Symbolists like Mallarmé, they went on to very difficult verse indeed, in which the meaning had to be wrung with effort from symbols nested one within another, in which the harmonies, like those of modern music, are by no means at once apparent to the untrained listener. Significantly, when twentieth-century poets went back for precedents to their literary "fathers" or teachers, they did not go to Tennyson, Hugo, Longfellow, or Kipling, but to late Victorian poets hardly known to their contemporaries, like the English Gerard Manley Hopkins and the American Emily Dickinson. Here is a passage from Hopkins:

> Across my foundering deck shone
> A beacon, an eternal beam. | Flesh fade, and mortal trash
> Fall to the residuary worm; | world's wildfire, leave but ash:

> In a flash, at a trumpet crash,
> I am all at once what Christ is, | since he was what I am, and
> This Jack, joke, poor potsherd, | patch, matchwood, immortal diamond,
> Is immortal diamond.*

Painting

In Victorian literature, then, there was a popular and conventional, but not vulgar, level of writing represented by men like Hugo and Tennyson. In painting, there was a similar level, represented by artists whose work now fills many galleries—the Fontainebleau school in France; Watts, Burne-Jones, and Rossetti in England; George Inness, and later Winslow Homer and John Singer Sargent in the United States; and many, many others throughout the West. The *avant garde*, the advanced innovators in art, the rebels, gave the paintings of these men the derogatory label "academic." Actually, the academic painters were technically very skillful, for they had the advantage of the long tradition of western painting since the Renaissance.

---

* Gerard Manley Hopkins, *Poems*, 3rd ed. (New York, 1948), 112.

An impressionist painting by Claude Monet ("La Grenouillière").

They could mirror man and nature faithfully, more faithfully than the camera. They were perhaps realists, but they were not naturalists in Zola's sense. They rather avoided the shambles of the industrial revolution, and to their *avant garde* opponents they seemed too much concerned with the pretty in nature and with the aristocratic or striking in portraiture.

The first great innovators in later nineteenth-century painting were the French impressionists. This school once had to content itself with separate salons, for the academics would have none of it. But it is now safely enshrined as "classic." The impressionists, too, show one of the cross-fertilizations between science and art, but in a rather subtler way than does the naturalist movement in fiction. One of the things science does is to show us that the "real" world is not what the hasty eye finds, that things are not what they seem. The impressionists were not content with the camera eye of the academics. Light, they learned from the physicists, was not a simple thing, but a complex that the eye puts together from the prismatic reflections of nature. So they proposed to break up light into its constituent colors and then allow the viewer's eye to reassemble them. They painted landscapes for the most part, and they built up their trees and flowers and buildings and skies from thousands of little dabs of color, so that the result, when seen from a few feet away, is hardly more than a formless mesh of color, but seen from an adequate distance does indeed take the form of a landscape, a landscape flooded in light.

The great master of the impressionist school, Claude Monet (1840-1926) was a prolific painter, whose work is well represented in public museums. Monet repeatedly painted the same subjects, notably Rouen Cathedral and the lily pond in his own garden, to show how they varied in appearance at different times of day and under changing conditions of light. Light interested many other painters, like Turner in England, who specialized in marine pictures (see illustration on p. 351), and the Anglicized American, Whistler, who did misty scenes in London and, incidentally, was very ashamed of the fact that he had been born in Lowell, Massachusetts.

Realism of a less technically experimental kind, realism more like that of the novel, is

Edouard Manet, "The Death of Maximilian."

A landscape by Cézanne (near Aix-en-Provence, with Mont Sainte Victoire in background).

to be found in a nineteenth-century school of painting represented by the Frenchman Edouard Manet (1832-1883). This realism is in part one of subject. One of Manet's masterpieces is the execution of Emperor Maximilian of Mexico, the unhappy victim of the imperial ambitions of Napoleon III, and he has left many portraits of ordinary people. But it is also a realism of sharp, sometimes almost harsh color, of simple but effective drawing. Some of the best work of the middle of the century was done in drawing and engraving, where new methods of reproduction made prints available to all. Here again the French are at their best, severe moralists in the Voltairean tradition, as in the caricatures of Daumier (see illustration on p. 391) and Forain.

Toward the end of the century the *avant garde* turned to another technique, somewhat more difficult than impressionism to describe. The great figure here is another Frenchman, Cézanne (1839-1906). This painter, too, wanted to go beyond the smooth techniques of the academics, but he found impressionism too fuzzy, too obsessed with light. The impressionists had to him lost the sense of shape, lost the three di-mensions of the real world—at least, of the "real" world of human binocular vision. He proposed to put them back, not with the classic, flowing perspective inherited by the academics from the Italians, but with blocks, chunks of color blended into a result that is after all realistic. From Cézanne there stemmed in a sense much of twentieth-century painting. Cubism, which is the exaggeration of Cézanne's insistence on hard three-dimensionality, is most obviously in his debt, but so too are Abstractionism and even Surrealism. Cézanne's work and that of two of his contemporaries, the Dutchman Van Gogh and the Frenchman Gauguin, were once thought wild, private, and unprofitably experimental. But they are now popular in museums and in countless inexpensive reproductions. Neither the artist nor the sociologist understands this process, by which the once outrageous innovation becomes an established classic, well enough to be sure whether a given contemporary work will or will not survive. Indeed, the purchase of contemporary art for private or public collections remains one of the most speculative of human ventures: the odds are heavily against the investor.

The Other Arts

The nineteenth century was not a great period for sculpture. An age that had mastered the industrial arts so well produced monumental statues aplenty. The most famous for Americans is the Statue of Liberty in New York harbor, the work of the French sculptor Bartholdi, a gift from the Third French Republic to the American Republic. But the statues of statesmen and warriors that adorn public places everywhere in the West are so conventionally realistic that we hardly accept them as human beings. Sculpture in the large at least would appear to be an aristocratic art, designed for the palace and the formal garden. Its nineteenth-century civic use seems at its best—or least bad—in Paris, in the decoration of the great Arc de Triomphe, a delayed memorial to the Grand Army of Napoleon I, and in the new Opera and many other buildings. Toward the end of the century, Frenchmen like Rodin and Maillol began a break with the formal statuary of their time, simplifying and strengthening the contours of their men and women, treating their subjects with less academic convention and more power (see illustration at right). It should be noted that inexpensive, small-scale copies of the great sculpture of antiquity and the Renaissance now became common, and many a Victorian drawing room in Europe and in Europe overseas boasted a plaster Venus or a bronze Mercury. Museums, too, could all afford large plaster casts. Some direct acquaintance with the great artistic achievements of the past was now available to a very wide public.

Indeed the nineteenth century knew almost too much of the past of the arts and was too eclectic and derivative in its tastes. Certainly this eclecticism weighed heavily on the architect. Somewhere on earth in these years someone built something in almost every style that had ever been used. Men built Chinese pagodas, Egyptian pyramids, Greek temples, and, especially in America, Gothic universities. In the United States buildings were typed for style: banks, those solid institutions, went back to Greece and Rome, at least for their fronts; churches and universities relied on Gothic; public buildings went in for the Renaissance, duly modified by the reigning taste in the Paris Ecole des Beaux-Arts (School of Fine Arts); private citizens went in for anything that pleased them for their own houses, modified by the traditions of their region. Individual architects worked on a historic style that they adapted in their own way. Thus the American Richardson revived the Romanesque, the early medieval predecessor of Gothic, with its round arches and its solidarity, achieving certainly a style of his own, which can be seen in Trinity Church in Boston—and in many railroad stations on the Boston and Albany.

Two broad styles may be found in the confusion of nineteenth-century architecture. One style, for public buildings, was basically Renaissance, with pediments, bal-

Maillol, "La Méditerrané."

conies, sometimes with domes, and with friezes and other decorations. This style varied somewhat from nation to nation. French public buildings, under the influence of the Beaux-Arts, looked at least vaguely like a chateau in Touraine; German buildings kept a touch of the huddled Middle Ages; and British buildings, much imitated in Boston and New York, were simpler, more in the manner of Palladio. The other style, for private homes, was represented in Europe by the "villa," and in America by the residence, often a "mansion," that the successful businessman built for himself on Elm Sreet. In the United States this style was at its most flaunting in the mansions of the 1870's, the "era of General Grant." These were big houses, for families were large, domestic servants were plentiful and cheap, and building costs were relatively low. They ran to high ceilings, for the bourgeois wanted nothing to remind him of the low rooms of his peasant past. Today they look too tall for their width, and their lines seem much too broken by little towers, porches, scrollwork, all sorts of decorative devices. But they had the latest comforts, if they were in a town large enough—gas light, bath and water closet, and central heating, though western Europeans came rather slowly to this last innovation.

In architecture, as in sculpture, true innovation began toward the end of the century. In structural steel, men now had a way of emancipating themselves from the limitations that had so taxed the Gothic builders; they could now go almost as high as they pleased. They began to do so in the United States, where the first "skyscraper," the Home Insurance Building in Chicago, was put up in 1885. Although some later skyscrapers ended up in Gothic towers, abundantly decorated, the general tendency imposed by the materials was toward simplicity of line. This taste for simplicity began to spread, and with the twentieth century the way was open for modern "func-

tional" architecture. Structural steel should remind us that some of the most satisfying work of the late nineteenth century was not primarily meant for beauty, but very often achieved it. The great bridges of the time, for example, the Firth of Forth Bridge in Scotland, and Brooklyn Bridge, are still handsome as well as impressive and useful.

In the minor arts of furniture, household decoration, and clothing, the Victorian Age seems to us now most characteristic and most ugly. Although it is hard to believe that men will ever collect "antiques" of the 1870's as they now collect the work of earlier periods, horsehair sofas and marble-topped tables are nowadays coming into the trade in antiques. So, we return to the Victorian drawing room with which we began. It was an incredibly heavy and incredibly dark room, for the height of the windows was canceled by the dark carpets, upholstery, and hangings, and by the mahogany or walnut furniture. And it was cluttered with what were known as *objets d'art*. Our taste in interior decoration today is different from that of the Victorians in part because in our society domestic labor is scarce and expensive; the mere job of dusting the bric-a-brac of a nineteenth-century house would be too much for the modern housewife.

Music

One great art remains to be discussed—music. The place of leadership that France has occupied for most of nineteenth-century art goes in music clearly to Germany. From Richard Wagner through Brahms to Richard Strauss the great names of music are to an extraordinary degree German. Theirs was indeed no monopoly. The Russians with Moussorgsky, Rimsky-Korsakov, Tschaikovsky, and their colleagues wrote music that is now part of our inheritance. Verdi and other Italians wrote operas a little too conventional for the highbrow, but still played all over the world. And toward the end of the century Frenchmen like Claude Debussy began the shift from Wagnerian grandiloquence to the subtleties and understatements of modern harmony. Still, the most representative composer of the later nineteenth century clearly remains Wagner (1813-1883).

Wagner set out to make the opera the supreme manifestation of the drama. He gave up the routine recitative—the relatively undramatic passages "explaining" the action— interlarded with arias in which the singer or singers dropped what action there had been and advanced boldly to the front of the stage to launch into song. He sought rather to combine music and action in a realistic and dramatic whole. His characteristic device was the *Leitmotiv*, a definite and recognizable melodic theme associated with a given character or symbolizing an element in the drama. These themes he wove together for both voices and orchestra into a continuous flow of music. He chose epic subjects: the four operas of the *Ring of the Nibelungen*, in which he drew on the Teu-

Daumier caricature. How the public feels after listening to the music of the future by Wagner.

tonic myths, by no means without thought for Teutonic greatness; *Parsifal*, on the theme of the Holy Grail; *Tristan and Isolde*, a drama of fated love and death taken from the Arthurian legends. Wagner's operas call for robust voices, which in turn call for barrel-chested tenors and huge sopranos ill-suited to concepts of romantic love or indeed of heroism. In our time Wagner's popularity has suffered because of his Victorian heaviness, his inordinate lengths, and the great noise he makes. Nietzsche once wrote aptly that Wagner's music *sweats*.

In concert music, the Wagnerian desire to marry music to the rest of life shows itself in the vogue of program music, that is, music that suggests something definite— birdcalls, thunderstorms, a battle, death and transfiguration. The tone poem, of which Richard Strauss (1864-1949) was master, takes a theme and develops it orchestrally without regard for the classic form of the symphony. Strauss wrote tone poems on Don Quixote, on Nietzsche's *Zarathustra*, even, in his "Domestic Symphony," on the cares and humors of family life. But the older forms of "absolute" music, the symphony and the various kinds of chamber music, survived the vogue for programs. Light music flourished, in the tuneful operettas of Offenbach, like *La Belle Hélène*, based on the legend of Helen of Troy, in the waltzes of Johann Strauss and Waldteufel, and for Anglo-Saxons in the satirical operas of Gilbert and Sullivan.

The Arts in Review   To sum up, the literature and the art of the late nineteenth century had all sorts of cross-currents, which were set in motion by the differences between countries, as we have seen, and also by the differences between social classes. There was a popular culture, an art of the simple age-old story and of the picture that tells a similar story. This popular art was perhaps more sentimental, more hopeful of human happiness, and less satirical and earthly than the popular art of an earlier period like the Middle Ages. There was also a more formal culture, or in American terms, a high-brow culture, which on the whole deserved to be called "realistic" and "materialistic," though it was not devoid of Romantic attempts to flee this harsh world for a better one. Formal art and literature were above all eclectic, borrowing freely from the past, and therefore they are very hard to pin down in terms of "style."

Perhaps we may call this culture "middle class," for much of it deals with bourgeois lives, and reflects the seriousness, the devotion to hard work, the concern with earning a living, the conventional morality, the puritanical streak we associate with the middle classes. But it also produced an art and literature of protest against things-as-they-are, which ranged from the gentle satire of a Trollope to the great disgust of a Nietzsche, through all the moral and political shades of Marxism, socialism, the Single Tax, free love, the rights of women, a revived Christianity, attempts to import Buddhism, or Islam, or other oriental faiths, and a refurbished eighteenth-century rationalism. Its span can be neatly summarized in two utopian tales, both very popular in their time, with quite opposite ideas of the perfect life. In *Looking Backward* (1888), by the American Edward Bellamy, the machine has made life perfect for all; Bellamy vaguely anticipates radio, for his hero can push a button in his room and hear sweet music. In *News from Nowhere* (1891), by the Englishman William Morris, men have broken up all their horrid machines, and have gone back to what Morris considered the real comforts of the Middle Ages, that best of all periods.

III: *Philosophy*

Idealism and Realism   The art and literature of the later nineteenth century furnish samples of almost the full range of human attitudes toward the world. The formal philosophy and the less formal view of life taken by ordinary educated people varied quite as widely, and we can find as many different schools in metaphysics and ethics as we can find in literature and art. The philosophical school of idealism was born in its modern form in the Germany of Kant and Hegel (see Chapters IX, XI). In the later nineteenth century it continued to thrive in the land of its birth; it made converts in the Oxford School of T. H. Green, Bradley, and Bosanquet, and in the American philosopher, Josiah Royce; and it even penetrated into the Latin countries. The philosophical opposite of idealism, now christened "realism," was at least as widespread. Modern realism, though as a philosophy it attempted to answer questions the scientist does not try to answer *insofar as he is a scientist*, had its roots in the same soil as modern science and the scientific rationalism of the eighteenth-century *philosophes*.

The American philosopher, William James (1842-1910), found two terms to sum up this polar antithesis of idealism and realism that runs through western philosophical tradition. Men are, wrote James, by disposition either "tender-minded" or "tough-minded." They are either toughmindedly convinced that the world of sense-experience is the *real* world or tendermindedly convinced that the world of sense-experience is somehow an illusion, or at any rate an imperfect, changing, and therefore unreal copy or reflection of the *real* world which is in our minds imperfectly—and perfectly in God's mind.

One might conclude that, since the later nineteenth century was a period of great material progress, deeply concerned with this world of the senses, then on the whole the "tough-minded" would prevail over the "tender-minded." Yet this was by no means true in formal philosophy, where the tender-minded were quite numerous and articulate. Perhaps the ordinary unreflective man leans toward the tough-minded side, if only because common sense urges upon him the presence of the world of sense-experience, the world of matter. But there are no reliable statistics on this point, and to the extent that Christianity forms an inescapable underpinning for the world-view of western men, not even common sense can altogether dispose of the world of the tender-minded, of concepts like "soul," "spirit," and "other world."

Certain common denominators, however, underlay the formal thought of the later nineteenth century. Here, too, Darwinism left its mark. The thought of the period had a historical and evolutionary cast that not even the tender-minded could avoid. The idealist, following Hegel, believed that above the whirl and change of this world of the senses there was an unchanging, perfect world of the Absolute. But he also believed that this imperfect world was being slowly drawn toward that other world, developing by ways he could only incompletely understand, but developing, growing, evolving. On the other hand, the nineteenth-century realist no longer held that his reason could give him a neat mathematical formula for the good life; he too thought that everything grows, that even what is made according to human plans must take account of nature's mysterious ways of growth.

The Cult of the Will

A second and related note in the thought of the period is an emphasis on will, often capitalized into Will, on doing, on the life-force that makes the "struggle for existence." The word appears everywhere, even as a title—Schopenhauer's *World as Will and Idea*, Nietzsche's *Will to Power*, William James' *Will to Believe*. It appears but slightly disguised in the French philosopher Henri Bergson's "creative evolution" and "élan vital" and in Bernard Shaw's "life-force." It lies behind the use of the word "myth" by the French anarcho-syndicalist, Georges Sorel, and the German Hans Vaihinger's phrase, the "philosophy of the as-if." For both these latter thinkers, the great ideas, the great abstractions of Right and Wrong, are not mere attempts of the mind to understand the world; indeed they are quite false if taken as analytically descriptive of this world. But they are, rather, the guides our desires, our wills, set up for our action. They are fictions, myths, "as-if," but all the more *real* for being such. The Italian idealist philosopher Croce summarized: true knowing is doing, making.

The pragmatism of William James, somewhat unfairly described by its critics as the philosophy that nothing succeeds like success, is clearly one of these philosophies of the will. To James, himself "tough-minded," reality is no Absolute as in the idealist tradition; indeed, reality is nothing fixed and certain. Reality is what works for us human beings; truth is what we want to believe. James thought he had saved himself from the obvious danger of this line of thought—that is, making reality and truth purely subjective, purely a matter of the individual's judgment—by granting that not everything we want is practical, that not all our desires "work." If my will to believe tells me I can make a broad jump of three hundred feet, experience, the "pragmatic" test, will prove that I cannot. But to many of James' critics, he had by no means saved himself from subjectivism. Pragmatism remained to these critics a doctrine dangerously erosive of traditional values, leading either to an exaltation of mere vulgar success, or to a silly belief in believing for the sake of believing.

The Revolt against Reason

The cult of the will brings us to a major current in the broad stream of later nineteenth-century thought, to the center of nineteenth-century repudiation of the thought of the eighteenth, a repudiation never universal, and more evident among the creative writers, artists, intellectuals, than among ordinary educated men and women. This was an intensification of the revolt against reason already initiated by the Romantics earlier in the century; it may be called "anti-intellectualism," "irrationalism," or, more exactly, "anti-rationalism." Even this last term is somewhat misleading, for it stresses negation, whereas the attitude it describes is also an affirmation. There seems, however, to be no better term for the attitude than anti-rationalism.

One further caution. This anti-rationalism is one of the "roots" of contemporary totalitarianism, and especially of fascist and Nazi totalitarianism (see Chapter XX). But it is by no means a simple synonym for totalitarianism. It is a much broader and more inclusive term. It is quite possible to have been influenced by anti-rational currents and remain a good, if not altogether orthodox, democrat and individualist. It is quite possible to be a Marxist totalitarian and reject a great deal, especially in its psychological core, of modern anti-rationalism. Indeed, the Marxist is in an important sense a naive rationalist: get the economy to work perfectly, he says, and men will behave themselves perfectly.

The basic position of anti-rationalism, and one for which it is heavily indebted to the Romantic movement, is a rejection of the eighteenth-century Enlightenment's belief that the ordinary human being is naturally reasonable. To the extent that it rejects the Enlightenment, anti-rationalism is indeed a negation, as the "anti" implies. But it has its positive side—the belief that if men can accept and understand their true, complex nature, their irrationality, and their dependence on forces beyond their immediate control, they can win their way to a richer life than the rationalists ever planned for them.

The Chastened Rationalists

Broadly speaking, there are two kinds of anti-rationalism, which shade into one another: the moderate and the extreme. Moderate anti-rationalism at bottom is trying to salvage as much as possible of the eighteenth-century belief in human rationality. Such on the whole is the attitude of modern psychology from Freud and William James on. This psychology seeks to aid human reason by pointing out the difficulties under which it must work. Reason, these thinkers maintain, is limited by men's instincts or "drives," by their biological inheritance of animality, so much emphasized by the evolutionists, and by their sociological inheritance of custom and tradition, so much emphasized by historians and by the school of Edmund Burke (see Chapter XI).

To use a metaphor from John Locke, moderate anti-rationalists regard human reason as a flickering candle, not as the great white universal light it appeared to be to *philosophes* like Condorcet. *But they do not wish to extinguish this candle.* On the contrary, they wish to keep it alive, to nurse it along into greater and greater brightness. This process, in keeping again with the views of the evolutionist, they regard as inevitably long and slow, likely to be hindered rather than helped by ambitious plans to hasten it. These moderate thinkers were not so much anti-rationalists as they were disillusioned or chastened rationalists.

The Extreme Anti-rationalists

By contrast, the second kind of anti-rationalism would actually put out the candle of human reason. For the extreme anti-rationalists reason is not just feeble; it is bad. It is for them, so to speak, a mistake evolution has made, a wrong turning, from which the human race must somehow retrace its steps to a sounder life of instinct, emotion, and faith. Thomas Hardy, the English novelist, put the position clearly in the remark, "Thought is a disease of the flesh." There was a strong dose of this extreme anti-rationalism in the Nazi movement. Hitler himself distrusted reason as a degenerate French invention. Good Germans, he hoped, would come to think with their blood, with their German folk inheritance. This is the attitude reflected in the cry of a Spanish falangist general in 1936:

"Down with intelligence and long live death!" Extreme anti-rationalism may also be found at the bottom of some of the wilder movements in modern art, which want to do away with all the rules of grammar or harmony or perspective, and write or compose music or paint from the heart—or the guts—without regard for "meaningless forms."

The position of these extremists is strongly rooted in the Romantic movement, with its emphasis on the heart as against the head, on fresh instinct as against stale logic, on "the desire of the moth for the star," on always wanting more, more, more. (See Chapter XII).

IV: Psychology

The historian of modern thought finds it convenient to group together many of the manifestations of the attitude toward life of a given period under the natural science that enjoyed nearly universal prestige at the time. This is the science that finds its way through the channels of popularization to the drawing room, the lecture platform, the press, and the schools.

A sequence of the radiation of the sciences into general thought may be observed in the smooth coins of conversation and journalism of a given age. The novels, newspapers, and letters of the eighteenth century referred constantly to Newton, to universal attraction and repulsion, to the world-machine. In the early nineteenth century the Frenchman Fourier set up what he called *l'attraction passionnelle*—a sort of political and social gravity, and asserted, "I am the Newton of social science" (see Chapter XIII). Similarly, as we have just seen, the Social Darwinists of the late nineteenth century were all talking about the "struggle for existence" and the "survival of the fittest." And of course in the twen-

tieth century phrases like "reflex," "sublimation," "inferiority complex," "Oedipus complex," and many others have gone from the laboratory of the psychologist and the couch of the psychoanalyst into common speech. A more detailed account of anti-rationalism, in both its moderate and extreme forms, may therefore begin with the science of psychology to which both owe so much.

Pavlov

From the Russian psychologist, Pavlov, whose basic work was done toward the end of the nineteenth and the beginning of the twentieth century, we get the now familiar term "conditioned reflex." Pavlov's dogs are as famous as any laboratory animals have ever been. After being repeatedly fed at a certain signal, such as a bell, his dogs came to water at the mouth in anticipation of food at a mere signal. The natural—that is the untrained—response of watering at the mouth would ordinarily come only when the dog had actual food before him; Pavlov got the same response artificially by a signal that certainly did not smell or look like food to the dog. The upshot was clear evidence that training or conditioning could produce automatic responses in the animal that were essentially similar to the kind of automatic responses the animal is born with.

Pavlov's experiments had important implications for the social scientist. They confirmed eighteenth-century notions about the power of environment, of training and education, in the sense that environment can be manipulated to give organisms new responses. But—and this is a bitter blow to eighteenth-century optimism—they suggested that once such training has taken hold, the organism has, so to speak, incorporated the results almost as if they had been the product of heredity, not environment, and further change becomes very difficult, in some instances impossible. Pavlov, after having trained some of his dogs, tried mixing his signals, frustrating and confusing the dogs by withholding food at the signal that had always produced food for them. He succeeded in producing symptoms of a kind close to what in human beings would be neurosis.

Now the cautious social scientist does not, of course, take over Pavlov's conditioned reflexes and apply them uncritically to all human behavior. He does not assume, for instance, that the Vermonter voting the straight Republican ticket is behaving quite like the dog watering at the mouth as an accustomed bell is rung. Even in Vermont, voting Republican is not quite a conditioned reflex. But the cautious social scientist will hold that concepts like that of the conditioned reflexes do throw light on a great deal of habit-determined human conduct. For the anti-rationalist, Pavlov's work was further demonstration that a very great deal of our behavior is not determined, or even greatly influenced, by what goes on in the cerebral cortex, the part of our brain that "thinks."

Freud

Anti-rationalism also derived much from another great psychologist, Sigmund Freud (1856-1939). Freud was a physician, trained in Vienna in the medical tradition of the late nineteenth century. His interest was early drawn to mental illness, where he soon found cases in which patients exhibited symptoms of very real organic disturbances, but for which no obvious organic causes could be found. Under analysis, as Freud's therapeutic treatment came to be called, the patient, relaxed on a couch, is urged to pour out what he can remember of his earliest childhood, or indeed infancy. After many such treatments, the analyst can hope to find what is disturbing the patient, and by making him aware of what that is, can hope to cure him.

Had Freud merely contended himself with this kind of therapy, few of us would have heard of him. But from all this clinical experience he worked out a system of psychology that has had a very great influence, not only on psychiatry and psychology, but

Sigmund Freud.

on some of our basic conceptions of human relations. Freud starts with the concept of a set of "drives" with which each person is born. These drives, which arise in the unconscious, are expressions of the *id*. Freud never tried to locate the id physiologically; he used the term, which in Latin means "this [thing]," to avoid the moralistic overtones in words like "desires." These drives try to get satisfaction and pleasure, to express themselves in action. The infant, notably, is "uninhibited"; that is, his drives well up into action from the id without restraint from his conscious mind. But by no means without restraint from his parents or nurse—and there's the difficulty. The infant finds himself frustrated. As he grows, as his mind is formed, he comes to be conscious of the fact that some of the things he wants to do are objectionable to those closest to him, and on whom he is so dependent. He himself therefore begins to repress these drives from his id.

With his dawning consciousness of the world outside himself, he has in fact developed another part of his psyche, which Freud at first called the "censor," and later divided into two phases which he called the "ego" and the "superego." The *ego* is the individual's private censor, his awareness that in accordance with what Freudians call the "reality principle" certain drives from his id simply cannot succeed. The *superego* in a way is what common language calls "conscience"; it is the individual's response as part of a social system in which certain actions are proper and certain actions improper.

There is no doubt a simplification, but perhaps not a misleading one, if the matter is put this way: the ego is servant of the id, rejecting, modifying, or permitting its drives in accordance with what the ego judges is so, the "reality principle," the "facts"; the superego too is the servant of the id, or better, guardian, often a tyrannical guardian, acting in accordance with what the superego judges ought to be the "right," the

proper thing to do. Or, more simply, the ego deals with nature, including human nature; the superego deals with culture, which can only be human culture. Both ego and superego act to curb, restrain, "suppress" the individual.

Now these drives of the id, and indeed in most of its phases the dictates of the superego, are for Freud a sort of great reservoir of which the individual is not normally aware; that is, they are part of his "unconscious." (Pavlov's conditioned reflexes are of course also unconscious.) In a mentally healthy individual, enough of the drives of the id succeed so that he feels contented. But even the healthiest of individuals has of course had to repress a great deal of his drives from the id. This successful repression the Freudians account for in part at least by a process they call "sublimation." That is, they think that the healthy individual somehow finds for a drive suppressed by ego or superego, or by both working together, a new and socially approved outlet or expression. Thus a drive toward sex relations not approved in one's circle might be sublimated into the writing of poetry or music, or even into athletics.

With the neurotic person, however, Freud held that drives, having been suppressed, driven back down into the unconscious, find no suitable other outlet or sublimation, and continue, so to speak, festering in the id, trying to find some outlet. They find all sorts of outlets of an abnormal sort, symptoms of illness in great variety. They display themselves in all sorts of neuroses and phobias, which have in common a failure to conform to the "reality principle." The neurotic individual is "maladjusted." And if the failure to meet the reality principle is really complete, the individual is insane, "psychotic," and lives in an utterly unreal private world of his own.

Freud, especially in his earlier years, did indeed hold that the id is wholly, or almost wholly, sexual in nature. One of his favorite early terms for the *contents* of the id, so to speak, is *libido,* from the Latin for desire, with strong overtones of "lust." He claimed to have found evidences of sexuality even in the behavior of infants. Now our western society frowns on these earlier manifestations of sexuality. Mothers in Freud's day, for instance, would try hard to prevent the child's sucking its thumb, in Freudian terms an obvious, and harmless, form of eroticism. Other forms of infantile sexuality meet with even stronger disapproval. The infant and later the child are therefore obliged to repress their sexuality. In the neurotic person, Freud believed, this repression is the main source of his difficulties. As an adult, he finds it impossible to achieve normal sex relations, and "regresses" to earlier stages of eroticism. Since "irregular" manifestations of sexuality are very strongly condemned by our society, the individual driven to them by his unconscious either suppresses them, or if he indulges in them, feels a great sense of guilt. Either way, according to Freud, he may end as a neurotic.

Freud's therapy rested on the belief that if the individual neurotic could come to understand why he behaved as he did he could make a proper adjustment and lead a normal life. But here Freud parted company with the rationalist tradition of the eighteenth century. He held that there was no use preaching at the individual, reasoning simply with him, telling him the error of his ways, pointing out what was unreasonable in his behavior. Reason could not get directly at the unconscious, where the source of his trouble lay. Only by the long slow process of psychoanalysis, in which the individual day after day sought in memories of his earliest childhood for concrete details, could the listening analyst pick from this stream of consciousness the significant details that pointed to the hidden repression, the "blocking" that came out in neurotic behavior. Freud gave special importance to the dreams of the patient, which he must patiently describe to the

analyst; for in dreams, Freud thought, the unconscious wells up out of control, or but partly controlled, by the ego. Once the patient, however, got beneath the surface of his conscious life, and became aware of what had gone wrong with his hitherto unconscious life, he might then cure himself.

The Implications of Freudianism

What is important for us in the wider implications of Freud's work, his part in the broad current of anti-rationalism, is first this concept of the very great role of the unconscious drives, that is, the unthinking, the non-rational, in our lives. Ordinary reflective thinking is for the Freudian a very small part of our existence. We are back at the metaphor of reason as a flickering candle, or to use another well-worn metaphor, of reason as simply the small part of the iceberg that shows above the water, while submerged down below is the great mass of the unconscious. Much even of our conscious thinking is, according to the Freudian, what psychologists call "rationalization," thinking dictated, not by an awareness of the reality principle, but by the desires of our id. One can get a good measure of the difference between eighteenth-century rationalism and Freudian psychology by contrasting the older belief in the innocence and natural goodness of the child, Wordsworth's "mighty prophet, seer blest," with the Freudian view of the child as a bundle of unsocial or antisocial drives, as in fact a little untamed savage.

But second, and most important, note that the Freudians do not wish to blow out the candle of human reason. They are moderate, not extreme, anti-rationalists; they are chastened rationalists. Their whole therapy is based on the concept, which has Christian as well as eighteenth-century roots, that "ye shall know the truth, and the truth shall make you free." Only, for the Freudian, truth is not easily found, not distillable into a few simple rules of conduct which all men, being reasonable and good, can use as guides to individual and collective happiness. It is on the contrary very hard to establish, and can be reached only by a long and precarious struggle. Many will not reach it, and will have to put up with all sorts of maladjustments and frustrations. The Freudian is at bottom a pessimist in that he does not believe in the perfectibility of man. But he is also something of an idealist; he believes in the struggle to make human life better here on earth, even if it cannot be made perfect.

V: Political and Social Thought

Many psychologists who rejected Freud's system as a whole nevertheless agreed with him on the great part played in human motivation by instinct, impulse, drives, urges, by something non-rational if not irrational. Their anti-rationalism came over in many ways into political and social thought. Here the distinction between moderate and extreme anti-rationalists is most important.

Many of the extreme anti-rationalists turned violently against democracy, which seemed to them to rest on an altogether false estimate of what human beings were really like. The democrat believes at bottom that the ordinary man can be freed from the weight of erroneous traditions, habits, and prejudices. Once he has the real facts before him, he can attain by free discussion among his fellows a series of decisions that will be incorporated in acts and institutions under which all men can live happily. But if you hold that most, or even many, men are by nature incapable of fair, dispassionate thinking and discussion, if you hold that the load of tradition, habit, and prejudice cannot by any system of education be lifted from them, if in short you hold that men are by nature irrational, you will at least have to revise drastically your notions of democracy, or reject them.

The extreme anti-rationalist rejected the notions of democracy. The German philosopher Nietzsche, who did most of his work in the 1880's, will do as a sample of such political thinkers in this period. Nietzsche wrote mostly in short aphoristic passages, which are hard to systematize and are often quite contradictory. But the central line of his thinking led to the concept of a new aristocracy, to the "superman" (in German, *Uebermensch*). Nietzsche's followers, who were numerous thoughout the West in the two decades before 1914, insisted that he meant a new *spiritual* aristocracy. The supermen would be above the petty materialism and national patriotism of the middle classes. Nietzsche's opponents, who were also many, held that he was just another preacher of Nordic superiority, that his supermen were, as he put it in one of his famous passages, "the blond beasts" who had so often terrorized Europe. Certainly some of his German followers took him at his word, and held that he meant the real live Germans to be his supermen.

At any rate, Nietzsche was clearly an enemy of democracy, which he held to be second only to its child, socialism, as a society in which the weak unjustly and unnaturally ruled the strong. Here are some of his aphorisms, from which the reader can judge for himself:

Democracy represents the disbelief in all great men and in all élite societies: everybody is everybody else's equal. 'At bottom we are all herd and mob.'

I am opposed to Socialism because it dreams

ingenuously of 'goodness, truth, beauty, and equal rights' (anarchy pursues the same ideal, but in a more brutal fashion).

I am opposed to parliamentary government and the power of the press, because they are the means whereby cattle become masters.*

Clearly Nietzsche hoped that the herd, the slaves, the masses would, in spite of their crass materialism, somehow recognize the true masters, the new enlightened despots.

Pareto

The Italian sociologist Pareto (1848-1923) well displays the mixed attitude of many late nineteenth-century anti-rationalists toward democracy. He is in some sense a disillusioned liberal, trying to fight his way out of disillusion, but unwilling to accept any simple élitist formula like Nietzsche's superman or the fascist "leader-principle," and even more unwilling to go back to medieval concepts of an ordered Christian society.

Pareto in his *The Mind and Society* is concerned chiefly with the problem of separating out in human actions the rational from the non-rational. What interests Pareto is the kind of action that is expressed in words, ritual, symbolism of some kind. Buying wool socks for cold weather is one such action. If they are bought deliberately to get good socks at a price the buyer can afford, this is rational action in accord with the doer's interests; it is the kind of action the economist studies statistically. If, however, they are bought without regard for price by a sentimental lover of England who buys imported English socks in order to do his bit to help England, then clearly something else, something the economist has to disregard in his price statistics, has come into play. This something else is the substance of Pareto's study.

Pareto distinguishes part of such social action as *derivations*, which are close to what most of us know as rationalizations. These

* Friedrich Nietzsche, *The Will to Power*, A. M. Ludovici, trans. (London, 1910), II, 206.

are the explanations and accompanying ritualist acts associated with our religion, our patriotism, our feelings for groups of all kinds. Prayer, for instance, is for Pareto a derivation; he was, like so many of this period, a materialist, at bottom hostile to Christianity, though he approved of it as a means of social concord. It is irrational, or non-rational, to pray for rain, because we know as meteorologists that rain has purely material causes quite beyond the reach of prayer. These derivations are indeed a factor in human social life, but they do not really move men to social action.

What does move men in society, and keeps them together in society, says Pareto, are the *residues*. These are expressions of relatively permanent, abiding sentiments in men, expressions that usually have to be separated from the part that is actually a derivation, which may change greatly and even quickly. Pagan Greek sailors sacrificed to Poseidon, god of the sea, before setting out on a voyage; Christian Greek sailors a few centuries later prayed, lighted candles, and made vows to the Virgin Mary just before sailing. The *derivations* are the explanations of what Poseidon and the Virgin respectively do. They vary. The believer in the Virgin thinks his pagan predecessor was dead wrong. The *residues* are the needs to secure divine aid and comfort in a difficult undertaking, and to perform certain ritual acts that give the performer assurance of such aid and comfort. The residues are nearly the same for our two sets of sailors. Both the pagans and the Christians have the same social and psychological needs and satisfy them in much the same ways, though with very different explanations of what they are doing.

Two of the major classes of residues Pareto distinguishes stand out, and help form his philosophy of history. These are first the residues of *persistent aggregates*, the sentiments that mark men who like regular ways, solid discipline, tradition and habit, men like the Spartans, the Prussians.

or any rigorously disciplined military class. Second, there are the residues of the *instinct for combinations*, the sentiments that mark men who like novelty and adventure, who invent new ways of doing things, who like to cut loose from the old and the tried, men not easily shocked, men who hate discipline, men like most intellectuals—and many entrepreneurs. In societies of many individual members, men influenced largely by one or the other of these major residues tend to predominate, and to characterize that society. Like most philosophers of history, Pareto is far from clear on just how a conservative society where the residues of persistent aggregates predominate changes into another kind of society. But he does have this conception of a pendulum swing, even a struggle of thesis and antithesis.

The nineteenth century in the West was in Pareto's mind a society in which the residues of instinct of combinations played perhaps the greatest role of which they are capable in a human society. The nineteenth century was a century of competition among individuals full of new ideas, inventions, enterprises, convinced that the old ways were bad, that novelty was the great thing to strive for at the expense of everything else. It was a society notably out of equilibrium. It had to turn toward the other kind of residues, toward the persistent aggregates, toward a society with more security and less competition, more discipline and less freedom, more uniformity and less variety. It had to go the way we seem to be going in the twentieth century.

Pareto's final general conception is that of an equilibrium in a society. It is an equilibrium constantly disturbed, at least in western society, but constantly renewed by a sort of natural healing force not to be supplanted by any social physician or planner. Pareto does not entirely rule out the possibility that human beings by taking thought may in little ways here and there change social arrangements in such a way that what they plan turns out to be a reality.

But the overwhelming emphasis of his work is that change in human conduct as a whole must be distinguished from change in human ideas and ideals. Since man is what he is, and, in our western culture, since the residue of instinct of combinations is so widespread, there is bound to be change in many fields of human interest. Fashion and all its commercial dependents can almost be said to be change for change's sake. But for Pareto there was also a level of human conduct where change is very slow indeed, almost as slow as the kind of change the geologist and the evolutionist study.

This level of human conduct where change is very slow indeed is the level of the residues. At most, Pareto held, the skilled political leader can manipulate the derivations in such a way that some residues are made relatively inactive, and others are activated. He cannot possibly produce new residues or destroy old ones. The wise leader according to Pareto will read Francis Bacon's famous aphorism, "Nature is not to be commanded save by obeying her," as "*Human* nature is not to be commanded save by obeying it"—or at least by taking it into account. You must not expect human beings to be consistently unselfish, sensible, devoted to the common good, kindly, wise. Above all, you must not expect that any institution, any law, any constitution, any treaty or pact, will make them so. But Pareto goes a bit beyond this position. Planning, except for limited and always very concrete ends, is dangerous. Not only is it very likely that a big, ambitious, legislated change will not achieve the results the planners planned; it is likely to produce unpredictable and perhaps unfortunate results. Until we know more of social science, Pareto holds, the best thing to do is to trust to what the upstart intellectual arrogantly condemns as the irrational side of human nature. We must believe that the ingrained habits of the human race are, even by evolutionary standards, more useful to survival than the impertinent logic of the reformers.

Political Thought in Review

Pareto is trying to be a chastened rationalist, and in spite of the use fascists have made of his work, deserves to be so classified. He is essentially a nineteenth-century liberal who felt uncomfortable in a world in which the great wars of our own time were clearly brewing, a world in which the Victorian decencies were slowly dissolving. But many thinkers whose sympathies with the democratic system of values were clearer than Pareto's were none the less influenced by the anti-rationalist's doubts about the natural goodness and reasonableness of ordinary human beings. John Stuart Mill in the mid-nineteenth century had worried over the "tyranny of the majority" (see Chapter XIII). Walter Bagehot, a good English liberal much influenced by Darwin, pointed out in his *Physics and Politics* (1872) how strong was the accumulated force of habit and tradition, which he called the "cake of custom," how hard it was to persuade men to rational action. By the end of the century, liberals throughout the West were facing the problem of revising their attitudes toward life to conform with the new emphasis on the tough network of habit, custom, and prejudice.

Already by 1914 the broad lines of the social attitudes of our own time were being laid out. One line goes toward some kind of revolutionary élitism, toward the seizure of power by a minority that believes itself to have the formula whereby the gifted few can put order into a society threatened with chaos because of attempts to make decisions by counting heads, no matter what is inside them. The variety of these specific formulas is, however, very great, for the late nineteenth century was in its political and ethical ideas at least as eclectic as it was in architecture. Some make race the mark of the élite, and go so far as to preach world rule for their chosen race. Others make class the mark of the élite, and seek to achieve the "dictatorship of the proletariat." Indeed, as Marxian socialism developed in Lenin's hands the élitist implications, which were never very much hidden in the work of that truculent and impatient hater of human beings as they are, Karl Marx, come out openly as the doctrine that the enlightened minority must seize power and rule dictatorially for a while, at least. Others dream of a brand-new élite, such as Nietzsche's supermen, to be created by a kind of new religion. Others look to eugenics to make possible the breeding of such a new élite—though it must be confessed that in spite of their appeal to natural science, these are among the most impractical of the lot.

A second line goes toward a more flexible form of élitism, one that tries to conserve as much as possible of democratic values. On the whole, English Fabianism and continental revisionist socialism deserve this classification. The leaders of these movements want no violent overturns, no seizure of power. They believe in gradualness, even in the basic democratic counting of heads. But there is in all of them a strong touch of doubt as to the political capacity of the ordinary man. They are not for the extension of New England town-meeting democracy to the millions of the modern state. They hope they can persuade the millions to elect legislators who will listen to the wise planners who have studied the social sciences, who can devise the wise new institutions that will make human life so much better. Above all, the planners themselves will by no means disdain what the anti-rationalists have taught them about the irrationality of ordinary men; they will make full use for good ends of what they can learn from the "practical" politician, the advertising man, the skilled professional manipulator of human beings; they will be Machiavellians, but Machiavellians on the side of the angels.

A third line seeks to preserve and protect what they consider a good, or at any rate an existing, élite from democratic drives toward equality, especially in the form of state intervention in economic and social life to promote security for all. This is substantially the line followed by men like Pareto, by the American sociologist William Graham Sumner, by the English philosopher Herbert Spencer, and by many others throughout the West. They are not unfairly labeled conservatives, for they seek to preserve in its broad lines an established order. But they are not simply routine, unphilosophical conservatives who opposed any changes at all. They have a definite philosophy, strongly influenced by the spirit of the times, by the anti-rationalism we have here outlined. Their basic position is a distrust of the instrument of thought applied unsparingly to human society, and in this they go back to Burke and indeed to philosophical conservatives throughout the western tradition.

But they are clearly children of their age, above all in their concrete fears of "socialism." Most of them believe in progress, and most of them prize material plenty, peace, industrial society. They hold, however, that on the whole the existing middle classes, the existing leaders of a business world, the existing—or rather, the recently existing—network of Victorian habits and morals, are the best insurance that progress will continue. Above all, they fear planners and planning, at least in political positions. They distrust the state. At bottom, they are good Darwinians, who believe that the evolutionary process depends on the struggle for life among competing individuals fettered as little as possible by planned human attempts to "rig" the struggle. They believe that social evolution cannot be hastened, and that attempts to hasten it, no matter how well meant, will in fact retard it by limiting actual human variation and initiative. They are by no means altogether without sympathizers among us today, but it must be admitted that theirs has not, so far, been the "wave of the future." The Herbert Spencer who thought compulsory sewage disposal in cities was an interference with the "right" of the individual to conduct his own private struggle against typhoid fever would be even more uncomfortable in the midtwentieth century than he was in the late nineteenth.

Reading Suggestions on the Intellectual Revolution

General Accounts

C. Brinton, *Ideas and Men* (Englewood Cliffs, N.J.: Prentice-Hall, 1950). The later chapters of this general survey of intellectual history are also available in an inexpensive reprint: *The Shaping of the Modern Mind* (N.Y.: New American Library, 1953. A Mentor Book).

R. C. Binkley, *Realism and Nationalism, 1852-1871* (N.Y.: Harper, 1935), and C. J. H. Hayes, *A Generation of Materialism, 1871-1900* (N.Y.: Harper, 1941). These two volumes provide fairly full coverage of the topics treated in this chapter.

Special Studies: Darwinism

C. Darwin, *On the Origin of Species by Natural Selection* (N.Y.: Modern Library, 1936), and *Journal of Researches into the Geology and Natural History of the Various Countries Visited during the Voyage of H.M.S. Beagle round the World* (N.Y.: Dutton, 1908. Everyman ed.). Respectively, Darwin's classic exposition, and his often fascinating report on the *Beagle* expedition that provided some of the evidence for his theories.

J. Barzun, *Darwin, Marx, Wagner* (Boston: Little, Brown, 1941). An interesting study; finds common denominators in men usually catalogued as quite different.

H. Spencer, *The Man versus the State*, A. J. Nock, ed. (Caldwell, Idaho: Caxton, 1940). A representative work by a whole-hearted Social Darwinist.

Sumner Today, M. R. Davie, ed. (New Haven: Yale Univ. Press, 1940). Selected essays by William Graham Sumner, the most famous American Social Darwinist.

W. Bagehot, *Physics and Politics* (Boston: Beacon, 1956). An early and suggestive adaptation of Darwinism to the political realm; very good reading, unlike the work of some other Social Darwinists.

R. Hofstadter, *Social Darwinism in American Thought* (Boston: Beacon, 1955). Interesting study of the ultimate impact of Darwin's theories.

Special Studies: Literature and the Arts

G. M. Young, *Victorian England: Portrait of an Age* (Garden City, N.Y.: Doubleday, 1954. An Anchor Book). A brilliant evocation.

E. Wilson, *Axel's Castle, A Study in the Imaginative Literature of 1870-1930* (N.Y.: Scribner's, 1931). A suggestive study.

G. Brandes, *Main Currents in Nineteenth-Century Literature*, 6 vols. (London: Heinemann, 1901-1905). A valuable detailed study.

R. E. Fry, *Characteristics of French Art* (London: Chatto & Windus, 1932). Includes brief but highly useful essays on major French painters of the nineteenth century.

M. Raynal, *The Nineteenth Century: Goya to Gauguin* (Geneva, Switzerland: Skira, 1951). A superbly illustrated volume on painting.

S. Giedion, *Mechanization Takes Command* (N.Y.: Oxford Univ. Press, 1948). Interesting account of the effects of industrialism on the arts.

P. H. Láng, *Music in Western Civilization* (N.Y.: Norton, 1941), and C. Gray, *History of Music*, 2nd ed. (N.Y.: Knopf, 1947). Two very different and helpful histories of music.

Special Studies: Psychology and Thought

B. P. Babkin, *Pavlov, A Biography* (Chicago: Univ. of Chicago Press, 1949). Good introduction to the work of the famous Russian psychologist; by one of his former students.

S. Freud, *An Outline of Psychoanalysis* (N.Y.: Norton, 1949). The great psychologist's last word on his craft.

E. Jones, *The Life and Work of Freud* (N.Y.: Basic Books, 1953). Widely considered the best book on Freud.

Five articles on psychology by Ernest Havemann in *Life Magazine*, January 7-February 4, 1957, form an admirable introduction to this important phase of modern intellectual history.

D. Riesman, *The Lonely Crowd* (Garden City, N.Y.: Doubleday, 1954. An Anchor Book). Temperate application of the findings of social psychology to the American scene.

H. Bergson, *The Two Sources of Morality and Religion* (Garden City, N.Y.: Doubleday, 1954. An Anchor Book). Characteristic work by an important critic of rationalism.

G. Sorel, *Reflections on Violence* (Glencoe, Ill.: Free Press, 1950). A significant and very readable application of the anti-rational view to social and political problems.

R. Humphrey, *Georges Sorel, Prophet without Honor* (Cambridge: Harvard Univ. Press, 1951). Good study of Sorel, with a valuable discussion of anti-intellectualism.

G. Wallas, *Human Nature in Politics* (London: Constable, 1908). A pioneer study of the non-rational elements in politics.

C. Brinton, *English Political Thought in the Nineteenth Century*, new ed. (Cambridge: Harvard Univ. Press, 1949), and E. Barker, *Political Thought in England, 1848-1914* (London: Butterworth, 1930. Home University Library). Two useful studies.

D. C. Somervell, *English Thought in the Nineteenth Century* (London: Methuen, 1929). Valuable work; emphasizes formal thought.

The Philosophy of Nietzsche (N.Y.: Modern Library, 1937). A convenient collection, including *Thus Spake Zarathustra* and other representative works of the controversial German philosopher.

C. Brinton, *Nietzsche* (Cambridge: Harvard Univ. Press, 1941), and G. A. Morgan, Jr., *What Nietzsche Means* (Cambridge: Harvard Univ. Press, 1941). Two very different interpretations.

G. C. Homans and C. P. Curtis, Jr., *An Introduction to Pareto* (N.Y.: Knopf, 1934). The handiest approach to a difficult thinker.

Novels and Dramas

G. Flaubert, *Madame Bovary* (many editions). The classic novel of French realism.

E. Zola, *Germinal* (many editions) and *L'Assommoir* (translated under several titles). Two characteristic novels by the great French exponent of naturalism.

S. Butler, *The Way of All Flesh* (many editions). A good example of gloomy naturalism in the novel, English-style.

S. Lewis, *Babbitt* (N.Y.: Harcourt, Brace, 1949), and *Main Street* (N.Y.: Harcourt, Brace, 1950). Novels that are important documents of American social history in the early twentieth century.

E. Bellamy, *Looking Backward, 2000-1887* (N.Y.: Modern Library, 1951); H. G. Wells, *A Modern Utopia* (N.Y.: Scribner's, 1905); and W. Morris, *News from Nowhere* (N.Y.: Longmans, Green, 1901). Three contrasting visions of Utopia in the light of science and industrialism.

H. Ibsen, *Ghosts, An Enemy of the People, A Doll's House, The Master Builder* (N.Y.: Modern Library, no date). Four pioneering dramas by a master of late nineteenth-century realism.

E. Brieux, *Damaged Goods*, preface by G. B. Shaw (London: Fifield, 1914). The famous play about venereal disease.

G. B. Shaw, *Man and Superman* (Harmondsworth, Middlesex: Penguin Books), and *Back to Methuselah* (N.Y.: Oxford Univ. Press, 1947. World's Classics). Two of Shaw's many plays that discuss aspects of the modern intellectual revolution.

CHAPTER SEVENTEEN

Nineteenth-Century Imperialism

I: *The Movement in General*

In the *Oxford English Dictionary*, which tries to find the earliest possible example of a definition, the editors can go no further back than 1881 for "imperialism: the principle of the spirit of empire; advocacy of what are held to be imperial interests." The word is new; what it stands for is very old indeed.

Imperialism, New and Old

We must not let the term "imperialism" make us lose our sense of proportion. We must not assume, as many modern publicists have, that the movement was something altogether new, unprecedented, and especially virtuous or especially wicked. Yet there were some important new elements in the imperialism of western peoples in the nineteenth century, as the very form of the word suggests. An "ism" is a belief, a set of principles that men hold consciously as a guide to living. In early modern times groups of Europeans went abroad for all sorts of motives, which were seldom neatly correlated into a public policy and seldom debated very widely among the people. Nineteenth-century imperialism, by contrast, was in almost every country a major part of political life, with goals, methods, and advocates known to all who were concerned with politics. And since by 1900 almost all of western and central Europe, the United States, and indeed all the outposts of European culture enjoyed high literacy and widespread public discussion, imperialism took its place with liberalism, conservatism, nationalism, socialism, and a host of other "isms" as a subject of universal debate.

A second obvious novelty had become clear by the outbreak of World War I in 1914. The process of western imperial expansion had gone territorially about as far as the geography of the planet earth permits. Through a long catalogue of imperial forms, ranging from outright annexation to "spheres of influence," almost all the globe had come under western control or western influence. All that was left at the beginning of the twentieth century was the bleak and uninhabited continent around the South Pole, which the leading nations were engaged in exploring and dividing.

The Economic Aspect

Carefully defined, this third point—the economic aspect—may be said to distinguish nineteenth-century imperialism from early forms of imperialism. No doubt the economic motive runs through all forms of territorial expansion from prehistoric times to the present. It is clear in the earliest days of Spanish and Portuguese expansion in the quest for gold, silver, and profits. But, as the nineteenth century wore on, imperialist nations were responding to economic pressures in a new form. English liberals hostile to imperialism, like J. T. Hobson, whose *Imperialism* was published in 1902, differentiated this form from older ones a bit too sharply. They made it into an over-simple and unique explanation that did violence to the complex of motives behind the movement. The differentiation was put even more sharply for the Marxists by Rosa Luxemburg and. with due variations, by Lenin himself, notably in his *Imperialism as the Latest Stage of Capitalism* (1917).

According to these economic critics of imperialism, capitalists and industrialists in the older countries began to discover in the nineteenth century that they were unable to market at home all they could produce. But, being capitalists, they could not bring themselves to solve their difficulties by paying *less* in interest, dividends, and other payments to their own kind of people, the upper classes, and paying *more* in wages, pensions, bonuses, and the like to their workmen. Instead of sharing the wealth and creating at home the mass purchasing power and the mass market they needed, they preferred to turn to the non-western world, to markets abroad, to the exploitation of dependent peoples. This attempt to bolster the capitalist system meant competition among the great western industrial powers for land and peoples to exploit. Lenin stressed the need to use the finance-capital that was rapidly accumulating, rather than the need for markets. The great bankers, according to Lenin, drove the willing politicians into the search for dependencies, a search that marked what he termed the inevitable "last stage of capitalism."

No one who has studied this great nineteenth-century expansion questions that economic pressures were among the motivations of the men who carried it out. Quite impeccably anti-Marxist Americans some-times hold that capitalism in the United States has been saved by its higher wages and mass market, and that in Europe capi-talism is in shakier condition because Euro-pean businessmen have been reluctant to give their workingmen a greater portion of the total product of industry, and because European nation-states "protected" by tariffs are not big enough to provide mass markets. Furthermore, as we have already seen, leading industrial powers in both America and Europe were experiencing an increasing demand for higher tariffs by the late 1800's. In the United States and Ger-many, and even in free-trading Britain, in-dustrialists wanted protection against for-eign competitors. This was an era of neo-mercantilism, reviving and "streamlining" the older mercantilist doctrines of Colbert and others. Colonies as well as tariffs en-tered into the strategy of the neo-mercantil-ists, as they had done in the case of the old.

In sum, there is something in the Hob-son-Luxemburg-Lenin argument. But by no means everything. The great outpouring of western energies into the rest of the world in the century between the Napoleonic Wars and the War of 1914, like such great bursts of energy as the Renaissance, cannot be explained by any such one-way causa-tion as the economic interpretation sets up. Into this outpouring there went all the pooled self-esteem of nationalist feeling, the desire of rulers and of the majority of the politically conscious among the ruled to "keep up with the Joneses"—that is, to have an empire because the British, or the French, or the Portuguese, had one. There went the cumulative pressures of military and naval rivalries, of "geopolitics," as the earlier rivalries among nation-states widened into a global scale. There went the heady theories of philosophers of progress, the magic of evolution by competition among peoples, in which the fittest were obviously destined to rule over the less fit. There went the honest conviction that the West had the mission of bringing to less fortunate peoples the great moral gift of civilization. This conviction was often blind to facts at home as well as abroad, often singularly obtuse in its attitudes toward natives and toward competing westerners. But it was at its best in many missionaries, Christian and secular —a warm, humane desire to make life better for all on this earth.

The Powers Involved

The year 1870 is a con-venient dividing line between the more active age of imperialism that was to come and the less active age that had preceded. The period from 1815 to 1870 saw a partial decline in imperial fortunes, as most of Spain's American colonies gained their in-dependence, and as Britain took the first steps leading to the virtual independence of Canada (see below, p. 575). In this same period, however, the French established themselves in Algeria, and the British ex-tended their rule in India. The dividing line of 1870 does not mark a sharp break in the history of imperialism, but rather the ac-celeration of a movement that had never ceased.

The successful competitors in nineteenth-century imperialism, those who brought new lands under their flags, were Great Britain, which already in 1815 had a great empire, France, Germany, Italy, and the United States. Even little Belgium, itself a "new" nation in 1830, acquired a tremen-dous piece of tropical Africa, the Congo, 900,000 square miles in area in comparison to the homeland's 11,775 square miles. Russia did not expand overseas, and indeed parted with her vast but thinly inhabited possession in North America when the tsar-ist government sold Alaska to the United States in 1867. But she began the effective settlement of the great areas east of the Urals, and began to push into the border-lands of the Middle and Far East, toward

SOUTH AMERICA, 1914

///// Disputed areas, 1914 (Boundaries through these areas as defined by 1942)

⊙ Capital cities

Dates here show when territories were acquired by powers concerned

GUIANAS
(Br.) (Dutch) (Fr.)
1781 1667 1626
1803

LATIN AMERICA 1828
After the Wars for Independence

Area shown in map of Caribbean America

U.S. OF MEXICO

REPUBLIC OF HAITI

UNITED PROVINCES OF CENTRAL AMERICA

GREAT COLOMBIA

GUIANAS

PERU

EMPIRE OF BRAZIL

BOLIVIA

PARAGUAY

CHILE

URUGUAY

ARGENTINE CONFEDERATION

0   Miles   2,000

0   Miles   800

Persia, India, and China. One of the old empires, that of Holland, on the whole marked time. Another, that of Portugal, lost Brazil, which became independent in 1822; but the Portuguese pushed far inland from their old colonies on the African coasts. The remnants of the Spanish empire were practically wiped off the map when the Spanish-American War of 1898 brought the loss of the rich islands of Cuba and the Philippines.

In the process of expansion, the expanding nations inevitably rubbed up against one another in all sorts of competition, from the merely economic to actual shooting war. Almost every great international conflict of the nineteenth century, save for the mid-century duels between Prussia and Austria and between Prussia and France, had a direct concern in imperialist rivalries outside Europe. And even the wars for the unification of Germany and Italy were by no means without overtones of reference to the great scramble for overseas lands. Imperial competition is a complicated story, then, woven into the whole fabric of international relations in the nineteenth century. We shall note briefly the major areas of inter-European rivalries and then summarize the growth of the major empires over the century.

The Areas Involved

The Monroe Doctrine (see Chapter XII), toward which European nations were increasingly respectful as the strength of the United States increased, helped to keep both American continents free from further actual annexation by outside powers. So, too, did the British navy. Toward the fateful year of 1914, the competition between Britain and Germany for markets and for fields of investment in South America grew intense, and was one of the many factors that brought these powers to war. Since no state was strong enough to take from Britain her older colonies, throughout the nineteenth century British problems in both colonies of settlement and colonies of exploitation were limited to the British system itself. However, although these were not international problems, Germany and Russia sometimes threatened to become involved in them during the last decades of the pre-war period. The Americas and the lands of the British Empire were then, on the whole, outside the scramble.

A major field of imperialist rivalry and penetration was the Near or Middle East, essentially the widespread lands under varying degrees of Turkish control, and Persia. In earlier chapters (XII and XV) we saw how the Balkans and the Straits became major issues in nineteenth-century diplomatic history. The whole "Eastern Question," as it is sometimes called, revolved around the problem of what was to be done with these old lands, which were peopled almost wholly by Moslems. They were backward lands by nineteenth-century western standards, mostly with poor rainfall and farm lands exhausted by centuries of primitive agriculture. They were poor also in natural resources (for their great wealth in petroleum was not really known or very important until the twentieth century). England, France, and Russia were in active competition over the Near East early in the nineteenth century, and they were later joined by Italy and Germany.

Africa was the scene of the most spectacular imperial rivalry. In 1815, except for the nominally Turkish lands of North Africa, the little Dutch settlement at the Cape of Good Hope (taken over by the British in 1815), and a string of Portuguese, Spanish, French, and British "factories" or trading posts along the old Portuguese exploration route that went back to the fifteenth century, Africa was untenanted by Europeans and, in the interior, almost unexplored. It was peopled by Negro races, long subjected to the horrors of the slave trade, and often living at the level of primitive tribesmen. The slave trade was pretty well abolished in many areas by mid-century, and exploration was pretty well under way. Then in the latter half of the century the great powers—Britain, France, and Germany—with Portugal, Italy, and Belgium tagging along, succeeded in blocking out in territorial units under their respective flags almost the whole of the continent. The only exceptions were the small Republic of Liberia, which had been set up by American anti-slavery groups as a land for emancipated American Negro slaves (though very few of them went there), and the mountainous and backward inland state of Abyssinia (now known as Ethiopia). And Abyssinia, coveted by Italy, had a very narrow escape. In 1896, the Abyssinians, under their Emperor Menelek and with French help, defeated an Italian army at Adowa and secured a respite in independence until the Italians tried again under Mussolini.

The Far East, too, was a major scene of imperialist rivalries. European powers strengthened their hold on older colonies and acquired new ones in Southeast Asia—the mainland areas of Burma, Indo-China, and Malaya, and the island groups between Australia and the mainland. But the ancient, thickly populated, highly civilized Chinese Empire was never subjected, as was Africa, to actual partition and direct annexation.

China was, however, not well enough organized politically or industrially to stand up against European penetration, and was by the end of the century subjected to a rough, *de facto* partitioning among Britain, France, Germany, and Russia. Each power, operating from certain treaty ports as centers, was able to exercise a degree of control—basically economic—over considerable areas. European rivalry, and the rising power of the United States, which was exercised in favor of the "Open Door" policy of permitting as much free trade in China as was possible and of preserving Chinese sovereignty, served to counterbalance Chinese weakness, and kept China on the list of independent nations.

Finally, Japan kept herself isolated from the rest of the world for two centuries, from the mid-seventeenth to the mid-nineteenth. This compact island empire was closed to foreigners during the period when the European powers slowly strengthened their small holds in China. Then in 1854 the American naval officer, Perry, got from Japan a treaty opening her ports to outside trade. By adopting some western ways, particularly economic ways, Japan was able not merely to preserve her real independence during the late nineteenth century but actually to begin her own imperial expansion on the mainland of Asia after winning a brief war with China in 1894-1895 (see p. 569 below).

II: *The British Empire*

We may now move on through the imperial record, country by country. Nineteenth-century Britain retained and, with the help of emigrants from the mother country, developed the great areas that were suitable to white colonization—Canada, Australia and New Zealand, and South Africa. This section focuses on Britain's imperial possessions in Africa and Asia. The development of self-government in Canada,

Australia, and New Zealand will come more appropriately at the close of this chapter, in our survey of the results of nineteenth-century imperialism.

South Africa

In 1815, Britain had just acquired from the Netherlands Cape Colony at the southern tip of Africa. Cape Colony was inhabited by a few Dutch and French Huguenot colonists and was suited, in spite of a relatively low rainfall, to European living. As Britishers moved in, the older colonists, known in their own Dutch vernacular as Boers, grew more and more discontented. The adoption of English as the sole official language, the abolition of slavery throughout the Empire in 1834, the attempts of the government at London to protect the native blacks, and other measures of Victorian liberalism went against the grain of the patriarchal Boers, who were fundamentalist Christians for whom slavery was ordained of God and for whom liberalism was the work of the devil. Between 1835 and 1837, some ten thousand Boers moved north overland in the "Great Trek," a heroic folk migration that bulks even larger in contemporary nationalist South African feeling than do the comparable sagas of covered-wagon days in American tradition. After some confused three-cornered fighting among Boers, British, and native Zulus, the Boers established two virtually independent South African states—the Transvaal and the Orange Free State. Well inland, on territory suitable for grazing but not for intensive agriculture, these thinly populated states lived on for a time hardly noticed by the outside world.

The British in South Africa noticed them, of course, and many of the British wished to add these lands to the Empire. They settled from the sea another British province to the east, along the Indian Ocean side, known as Natal. In the course of the century, Cape Colony and Natal, which together had a black population heavily outnumbering the British and remaining Boers combined, acquired the self-governing rights that British colonies of settlement in Canada, Australia, and New Zealand were also acquiring. British South African leaders for the most part wanted to bring the Boer Republics under the British flag. But as the London home government swung between Tory and Liberal domination, it also swung between a policy of imperialist expansion and the "Little Englander" policy of leaving the Trekkers alone. In 1852, by the Sand River Convention the British acknowledged the independence of Transvaal. But in 1877 they reversed themselves and annexed it as a step toward the federation of all South Africa under the British Crown. The Boers revolted in 1880 and the Liberal Gladstone, then in power, lived up to his principles by making at Pretoria in 1881 a treaty with the Boers which re-established Transvaal as independent, though under the "suzerainty" of Great Britain.

The British were already filtering up through the semi-desert country to the west of the Boer Republics when the discovery of gold and the development of the diamond industry in these republics undid Gladstone's work. The Transvaal was no longer just a poor and isolated grazing country; it offered a great source of wealth that tempted quite a different kind of settler. The region about Johannesburg, the famous Rand, filled up with adventurers of a dozen nations, all looking to Britain to protect them from the conservative Boers, to whom they were undesirable *Uitlanders* (outlanders, foreigners).

The Boer War and After

The inevitable conflict came to a head with the Jameson Raid of December 29, 1895—midsummer in South Africa. The British in South Africa were now under the leadership of Cecil Rhodes, prime minister of Cape Colony, a determined and articulate imperialist who had made a quick fortune consolidating the chaotic diamond industry. The raid itself, under a follower of Rhodes, Dr. Jameson, was an invasion of Transvaal from British territory to the west, and was planned to coincide with a rising of Uitlanders in Johannesburg. But the rising did not take place, and the President of Transvaal,

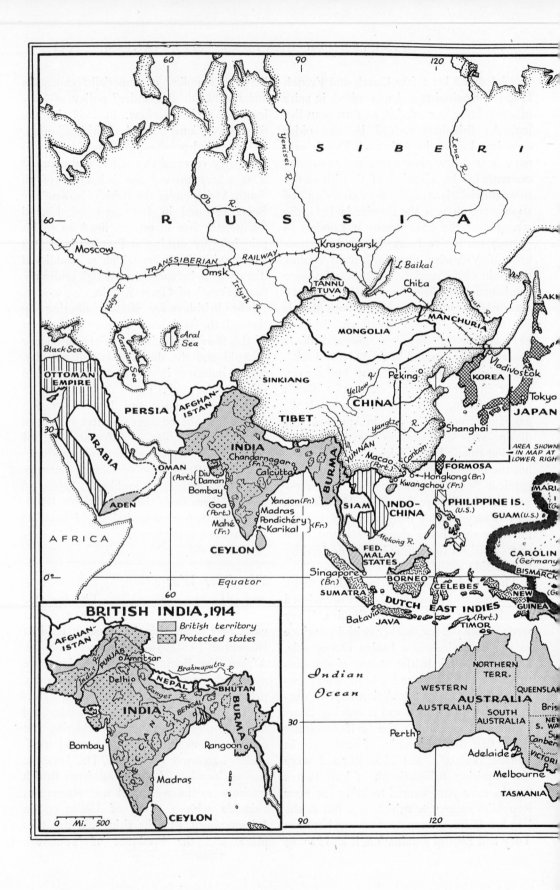

S I B E R I

Yenisei R.

Lena R.

R U S S I A

Ob R.

60 —

Moscow

TRANSSIBERIAN RAILWAY

Krasnoyarsk

Omsk

Irtysh R.

L. Baikal

Chita

Amur R.

TANNU TUVA

MONGOLIA

MANCHURIA

SAKH

Volga R.

Aral Sea

Black Sea

Caspian Sea

OTTOMAN EMPIRE

PERSIA

AFGHAN-ISTAN

SINKIANG

Yellow R.

Peking

KOREA

Vladivostok

Tokyo

30 —

ARABIA

TIBET

CHINA

yangtze R.

Shanghai

JAPAN

INDIA

Chandarnagar *(Fr.)*

Calcutta

YUNNAN

Macao *(Port.)*

Canton R.

AREA SHOWN IN MAP AT LOWER RIGHT

OMAN *(Port.)*

Diu
Daman

Bombay

BURMA

FORMOSA

Hongkong *(Br.)*

Kwangchou *(Fr.)*

MARI (G

ADEN

Goa *(Port.)*

Mahé *(Fr.)*

Yanaon *(Fr.)*
Madras
Pondichéry
Karikal } *(Fr.)*

SIAM

INDO-CHINA

PHILIPPINE IS. *(U.S.)*

GUAM *(U.S.)*

AFRICA

CEYLON

Mekong R.

FED. MALAY STATES

CAROLIN *(Germany*

BISMARCK

0° —

Equator

Singapore *(Br.)*

SUMATRA

BORNEO

CELEBES

NEW GUINEA

(Ge

Batavia

DUTCH EAST INDIES

JAVA

(Port.)

TIMOR

BRITISH INDIA, 1914

| | British territory |
| | Protected states |

AFGHAN-ISTAN

PUNJAB

Amritsar

Indus R.

Delhi

NEPAL

Brahmaputra R.

BHUTAN

Ganges R.

BENGAL

INDIA

BURMA

Bombay

Rangoon

Madras

CEYLON

0   Mi.   500

Indian Ocean

NORTHERN TERR.

WESTERN AUSTRALIA

QUEENSLAND

AUSTRALIA

SOUTH AUSTRALIA

Bris

NEW S. WA

30 —

Perth

Canber

Adelaide

VICTORI

Melbourne

TASMANIA

60

90

120

60

90

120

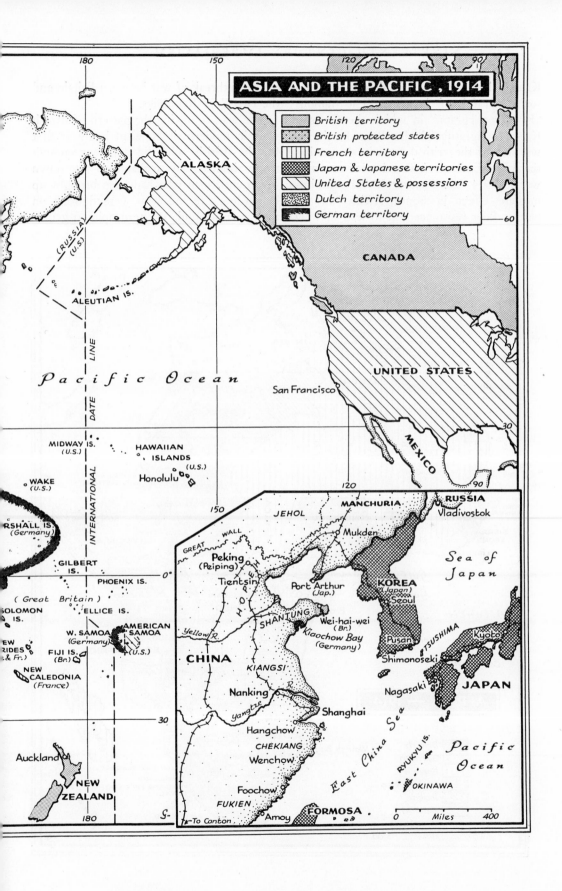

ASIA AND THE PACIFIC, 1914

British territory
British protected states
French territory
Japan & Japanese territories
United States & possessions
Dutch territory
German territory

ALASKA

CANADA

(RUSSIA)
(U.S.)

ALEUTIAN IS.

DATE LINE

Pacific Ocean

UNITED STATES

San Francisco

MEXICO

MIDWAY IS.
(U.S.)

HAWAIIAN
ISLANDS
(U.S.)

WAKE
(U.S.)

Honolulu

INTERNATIONAL

RSHALL IS.
(Germany)

GILBERT
IS.

PHOENIX IS.

(Great Britain)

SOLOMON
IS.

ELLICE IS.

EW
RIDES
(& Fr.)

W. SAMOA
(Germany)

AMERICAN
SAMOA
(U.S.)

FIJI IS.
(Br.)

NEW
CALEDONIA
(France)

Auckland

NEW
ZEALAND

JEHOL

MANCHURIA

RUSSIA

Vladivostok

GREAT WALL

Mukden

Sea of
Japan

Peking
(Peiping)

Tientsin

Port Arthur
(Jap.)

KOREA
(Japan)

Seoul

HOPEH

SHANTUNG

Wei-hai-wei
(Br.)

Pusan

TSUSHIMA

Kyoto

CHINA

Yellow R.

Kiaochow Bay
(Germany)

Shimonoseki

KIANGSI

Nanking

R.

Nagasaki

JAPAN

Yangtze

Shanghai

Hangchow

CHEKIANG

Wenchow

East China Sea

Pacific
Ocean

RYUKYU IS.

Foochow

OKINAWA

FUKIEN

To Canton

Amoy

FORMOSA

0   Miles   400

Kruger, had no trouble in defeating Jameson's handful of invaders. The famous "Kruger telegram," in which the German Kaiser congratulated the Boer President, was one of the critical steps in sharpening the Anglo-German rivalry that led to world war in 1914 (see Chapter XVIII). Its immediate effect in South Africa was to harden Boer resistance and to lead in 1899 to the outbreak of war between Britain and the two Boer Republics.

The war, following the pattern of British wars in modern times, went badly at first for the British, who did not have enough troops immediately available to put down determined men who had been brought up in outdoor life and who were fighting on their own ground. Western opinion gener-

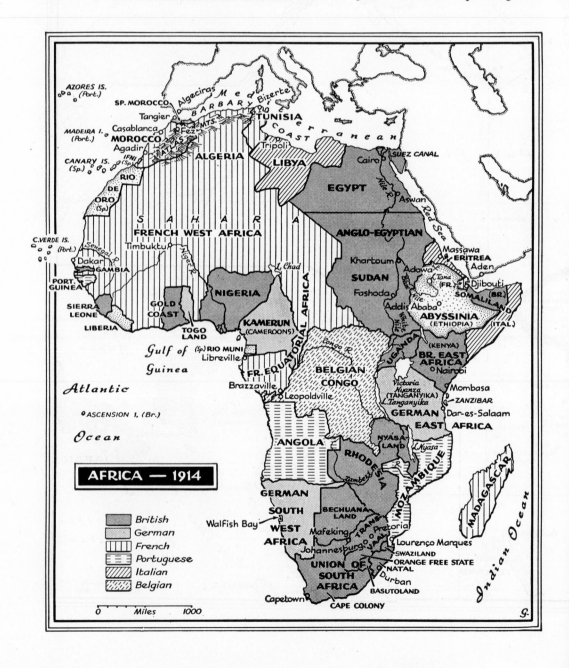

AFRICA — 1914

British
German
French
Portuguese
Italian
Belgian

0   Miles   1000

ally sided with the underdog Boers, and even in Britain many Liberals and Laborites strongly opposed the war. But in the long run the overwhelming strength of the British prevailed. By the middle of 1900 the British had won in the field, but they needed another eighteen months to subdue the desperate guerrilla bands into which Boer opposition dissolved. In 1902, by the Treaty of Vereeniging, the Boers accepted British rule, with the promise of ultimate self-government. This promise the British fulfilled speedily. In 1910 there came into being a Union of South Africa, uniting Cape Colony, Transvaal, Orange Free State, and Natal in a state in which the central government was stronger than the provinces. English and Afrikaans, as the South African Dutch dialect had come to be called, were set up as equally official languages.

On the eve of World War I, South Africa was among the self-governing British dominions. British and Boer seemed to be well on the way to composing their long quarrel, and to be ready to collaborate in setting up a new outpost of the West. But there were ominous signs even then. The Boers had by no means been Anglicized, and they were still fundamentally opposed to their partners in empire. And the two European elements together were in a minority of one to four as compared with the non-Europeans—the native blacks, the East Indians (who had come in numbers as immigrants, especially to Natal), and the "colored" peoples of mixed blood. The seeds of the current troubles in South Africa were clearly present even in the hopeful days immediately after the establishment of the Union.

Egypt

At the opposite end of Africa, Britain during the last half of the nineteenth century took over from the French the control of Egypt, nominally a vassal state of the crumbling Ottoman Empire. French influence there, already strong in the eighteenth century, was increased by Napoleon's expedition (see Chapter XI); indeed, a degree of French cultural influence persists among the Egyptian upper classes and intellectuals to this day. Under French supervision, a private company built between 1859 and 1869 the Suez Canal, which united the Mediterranean with the Red Sea and shortened the sea trip from Europe to India and the Far East by thousands of miles. The British had bitterly opposed the building of this canal under French patronage; but now that it was finished, the canal came to be considered an essential part of the "lifeline" of the British Empire.

Accordingly, the British took over Egypt and with it Suez. They carried out this action skillfully and slowly, threatening at crucial moments to use force, but not using it on any large scale. The decisive step in the process was the purchase by the British under Disraeli of 176,000 shares of stock in the Suez Canal Company. These shares had originally been assigned to the ruler of Egypt, the Khedive, as the price of his consent and co-operation in the canal

Disraeli purchases the Suez Canal shares held by the Khedive of Egypt.

THE LION'S SHARE.

project. The Khedive, a great and unwise spender, was heavily in debt to European financiers by 1875, and he sold his shares for a good price. The largest block of Suez stock was now in British hands.

By the eve of World War I, Britain exercised virtual sovereignty over Egypt. The Khedive and his government remained, and on paper Egypt was still a separate state. But a British Resident was always at hand to exercise firm control, especially over foreign relations. Under this British regime— the word "protectorate" is the usual term —much was done to modernize Egypt. The standard of living of the masses in Egypt was by no means raised to anything like that of the European masses. But the great dam at Aswan on the Nile, finished in 1902, was the first of a series of public works that added to the total productive power of the country, improved public health, lowered the mortality rate, and strengthened the numbers and prosperity of the middle class. Modernization also meant the beginnings of a wider literacy, of an educated middle class, and indeed of an intellectual class that earned its living by the written or spoken word. Most of these people responded by hating the British and by nursing a constantly growing nationalism—"Egypt for the Egyptians." We shall encounter this pattern again elsewhere.

The Rest of British Africa

In between South Africa and Egypt the British pieced out their African possessions throughout the century. At its end, they had the lion's share of the continent. They had only 4,000,000 square miles out of over 11,000,000, but they controlled 61,000,000 people out of not much over 100,000,000. A mere listing of these holdings would be a dull and unenlightening catalogue. They can be found, usually colored red, in any good atlas of the turn of the century and on a famous British post-age stamp of late Victorian times (see also map on p. 556). A good sample of these colonies is Nigeria, in which the great administrator Sir Frederick (later Lord) Lugard worked out the characteristic British method of colonial government in tropical Africa that was known as "indirect rule."

The colony and protectorate of Nigeria, centering around the great river Niger, was formally put together from earlier West African colonies in 1914. Northern Nigeria was ruled by Moslem emirs of the Fulani race whose culture was superior to that of the subject and exploited Negroes; southern Nigeria was inhabited by numerous heathen tribes that had long been harassed by slave raids. The British had first to subject the Fulani by force, a process that was completed late in the nineteenth century.

They then applied, as a French statesman put it, "with method but not with system," what came to be called indirect rule. Emirs and chieftains were confirmed in their separate rules, subject to the banning of internal warfare, the abolition of slavery, and similar measures imposed from above. A British Resident supervised the rule of the leading chiefs, with district Residents (later Commissioners) to supplement the work in the local subdivisions. But native law, native religion, and native traditions, in so far as they did not conflict violently with western standards, were carefully maintained. The British staff was never large; Lugard complained that in 1903 he had only one British administrator on the average for every 400,000 natives. But somehow the handful of imperial officials were able to ensure the peace. Slowly, much too slowly for impatient idealists, railroads, roads, improved agriculture, commerce, and education—the externals at least of western civilization—began to appear in Nigeria. Early in this century the first African Negro students began to appear in British universities. By mid-century, there was already a western-educated class in West Africa, using English as their chief language.

Other British Spheres   In the Americas, Britain maintained her colonial dependencies in the Caribbean, in Bermuda and the Bahamas, and, on the mainland, in British Honduras and British Guiana. Limited self-government of the seventeenth-century kind, which some of them had lost in the mid-nineteenth century, was only gradually granted them in the twentieth. These were all tropical or semitropical lands, with a relatively small planter class and with large Negro or mixed lower classes. These lands suffered gradual impoverishment as a result of certain economic developments, notably the great competition offered to the staple cane sugar of the region by the growth in temperate climates of the beet-sugar industry, together with an increase in population beyond the limited resources of the region. By 1914, the British West Indies had already become a "problem area."

In the Pacific and in Southeast Asia, Britain in the nineteenth century added some red dots on the map of her empire, and especially in Malaya she developed the great industries of rubber and tin that were to be major factors in her economy after World War I. She took an important part in the process of opening China to western trade by means of treaty-port concessions and spheres of influence. Indeed, Britain took one of the great steps in breaking down Chinese attempts to keep off the foreigner, for in 1841 she waged what has come to be called invidiously but not unjustly the "Opium War." This war was brought on by a Chinese attempt to control the opium trade in which British merchants had an important stake. By the Treaty of Nanking in 1842, Britian acquired Hong Kong and secured the opening of five ports, including Canton and Shanghai.

India:
Political Organization   In China, however, Britain was but one, though the most important, of the Great Powers scrambling

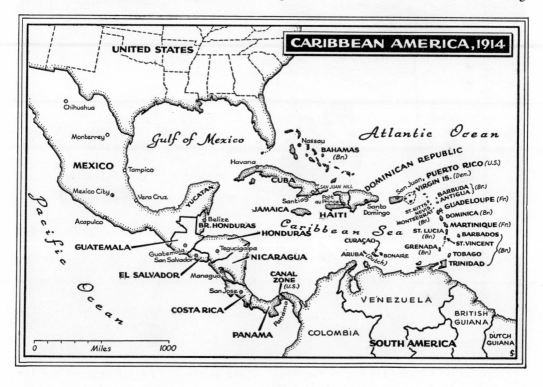

Chinese painting of the arrival of one of the first English steamers and her passengers at Canton, about 1840.

for empire in that densely peopled land. In India her victory over France in 1763, confirmed by her victory in 1815, left her in sole control over a subcontinent of Asia, for the remnants of French and Portuguese possessions there hardly counted. India was the richest of Britain's overseas possessions, the center and symbol of empire, as the imaginative Disraeli realized when in 1877 he had Queen Victoria proclaimed Empress of India.

In 1763, India was already a great and well-peopled land, but not, in the European sense, a single *nation*. It was a vast congeries of races and religions, ranging from the most cultivated and philosophic Brahmins to the most primitive tribesmen, still in the Stone Age. As the nineteenth century began, the two main methods of British control had already become clear. The richest and most densely populated regions, centering on the cities of Calcutta, Madras, Bombay, and the Punjab, were maintained under direct British control. The British government did not annex these lands directly; they were first administered as the property, so to speak, of the English East India Company, a chartered enterprise surviving from the great days of mercantilism in the seventeenth and eighteenth centuries. The company in its heyday, led by empire-makers like Clive and Warren Hastings, had taken on enormous territories, and made treaties like a sovereign power. Hastings was prosecuted for "high crimes and misdemeanors" in a famous trial of the late eighteenth century. But what he acquired the British kept.

In the nineteenth century the company was regarded by most economists and political thinkers as a shocking anomaly, and the India Office of the central government in London gradually took over the real control and administration of British India. The trading monopoly of the company had long since been undermined. In 1857, the company's native army of Sepoys rebelled. As usual in such major uprisings, the rebellion was brought on by a number of causes. But the basic cause was that the soldiers, Hindu, Moslem, and others, all had come to fear that British ways were being imposed on them to the destruction of their own ways. The Sepoy Rebellion was put down, but not before several massacres of Europeans had occurred, and not without a serious military effort by the British. The mutiny meant the end of the English East India Company. In 1858, the British Crown took over the company's lands and obligations, announcing that no further annexations were sought in India.

The rest of India—roughly a third of its area and a fourth or a fifth of its population—came to be known as the "feudal" or "native" states. These were left nominally under the rule of their own princes, who might be the fabulously rich Sultan of Hyderabad or Gaekwar of Baroda, or merely a kind of local chieftain. The "native" states were actually governed by a system of British Residents somewhat like the system we have just seen in Nigeria. The India Office never hesitated to interfere with the succession, or to disallow acts of princes, or even to assume direct rule for a time when it was thought necessary. The "native" states add many picturesque notes to a detailed history of India, but in the long run the distinction between direct and indirect rule in India did not mean very much in practice.

India: "The Meeting of East and West"

The years between 1763 and 1919 in India are a fascinating record of what Arnold Toynbee, the philosopher of history, calls "contacts between civilizations." Indeed, anyone who wants to understand the great contemporary problem of relations between the West and the rest of the world—to use clear terms, between white peoples and colored peoples—will do well to learn all he can of this great meeting of East and West in the subcontinent of India.

In material terms, many phases of the British rule in India are readily measurable. In 1864, the British *Statesman's Year Book* gave the population of India as about 136,-000,000, and in 1904 close to 300,000,000. Although the latter figure includes additional territories, in Burma and elsewhere, it is clear that nineteenth-century India saw a significant increase in total population. In 1901, nearly 15,000,000 males out of a total of 150,000,000 were literate in some language; one out of ten could read and write, a low rate of literacy by western standards, but already a high one by contemporary Asian standards. It is characteristic of Indian society that the comparable figures for women in the same census of 1901 show that only one out of one hundred and fifty could read and write.

Such statistics are plentiful, and what they show is an India on the eve of World War I with thousands of miles of railroads, telegraph lines, universities (teaching in English), hospitals, factories, and great and busy seaports. But, in proportion to the total population, India did not have these advantages to anything like the extent that even the poorest of European countries had them. Statistics show a native ruling class sometimes fantastically rich, and an immense peasant class for the most part living as their ancestors had lived, on the edge of starvation. A middle class was just beginning to form, and, like all the middle classes formed in non-European lands under European penetration, it had proportionately far more aspirants to genteel white-collar professional posts than to posts in commerce, engineering, and industry.

The total wealth of India certainly increased under British rule in this century and a half, and in 1914 it was spread more widely among the Indian populations, save for the most primitive areas, than it had been in 1763. Proportionately less and less wealth went directly from an "exploited" India to an "exploiting" Britain. The familiar Englishman of the seventeenth and eighteenth centuries, the "nabob" who made a fortune in India and retired with it to comfort, and perhaps to a peerage, in

Execution of mutineers after the Sepoy Rebellion in India, 1857.

England, almost ceased to exist as the nineteenth century wore on. Anglo-Indian economic relations took on more and more the form of trade between a developed industrial and financial society in Britain and a society geared to the production of raw materials in India. In this trade, native Indians took an increasing part if only as middlemen, and toward the end of the century native industries, notably textile manufacturing, financed for the most part with British capital, began to arise in India.

Throughout the century, of course, a large number of British—small in proportion to the total population, but numbering in the thousands—were basically supported by the Indian economy; they "lived off India." Some of them were private businessmen, but the greater number were military and civilian workers, the latter the celebrated Indian Civil Service who "ran" India. Yet natives were gradually working their way into positions of greater responsibility, into both private and public posts at the policy-making level.

Of the British ruling class in India one very important fact is now plain: it did not, like the English and Scots who went to Ireland in early modern times, really take root in India. Britain—one must be careful not to say "England," for the Scots played a conspicuous role in India as they did throughout the Empire—was always "Home," always the place where one hoped to end one's days. Though son not infrequently followed father in the Indian army or civil service, or even in business, these "Sahibs" as a whole never became fully adjusted to life in India. The spiritual climate was perhaps an even greater barrier than the physical climate. Here is a letter from an Englishwoman in Madras in 1837:

It is wonderful how little interested most of the English ladies seem by all the strange habits and ways of the natives. . . .
I asked one lady what she had seen of the country and the natives since she had been in India. 'Oh, nothing!' said she: 'thank goodness, I know nothing at all about them, nor I don't wish to: really I think the less one sees and knows of them the better!' *

The natives, too, often found the gap between East and West too great to be bridged. Another Englishwoman writes in 1913:

Coming home we saw a native cooking his dinner on a little charcoal fire, and as I passed he threw the contents of the pot away. Surprised, I asked why. 'Because,' I was told, 'your shadow fell on it and defiled it!' †

Yet the work of raising the economic basis of Indian life was in large part the work of the British. They were often overbearing, insensitive, white men at their worst in their dealings with the natives. But they were, more often than the doctrinaire liberal will admit, men devoted to the task of bettering the lot of their charges, men who made a real effort to understand them. Their work is reflected in the following passage from an "Address from the Inhabitants of Dhuboy to the English Collector" on the morning of his final departure:

. . . All castes who looked up to him obtained redress, without distinction and without price. When he took the poor by the hand he made him rich: under his protection the people were happy, and reposed on the bed of ease. When he superintended the garden, each gardener performed his duty; and all the trees in the garden flourished. So equal was his justice, that the tiger and the kid might drink at the same fountain; and often did he redeem the kid from the tiger's mouth. . . . In this country we have not known any government so upright as that of the English:—Alas! if our protector forsakes us we shall be disconsolate as a widow: we shall mourn the loss of a father and weep as for the death of a mother!—ALLA! in thy mercy continue him to us! **

* Hilton Brown, ed., *The Sahibs* (London, 1948), 225.
† *Ibid.*, 230.
** *Ibid.*, 223-224.

III: The Other Empires

The French:
North Africa

The British victory in the "Second Hundred Years' War," capped by their defeat of Napoleon in 1815, had stripped France of all but insignificant remnants of her former empire. Yet during the nineteenth century France succeeded in building up a new colonial empire second in area only to that of the British. France, despite her frequent revolutionary changes in government, maintained an imperialist policy that added between 1824 and 1914 close to three and a half million square miles to the lands under the tricolor flag, and some fifty million people, almost all non-European. The figures for area are indeed somewhat misleading, for a million and a half square miles are included in the Sahara Desert, which is almost uninhabited.

Little of this second French colonial empire was suitable for settlement by Europeans. The great exception was French North Africa, including Tunisia, Algeria, and Morocco. As the provinces of Africa and Mauretania, these lands were once flourishing parts of the Roman Empire; after France took them over, they reached a greater degree of material prosperity than they had enjoyed for nearly eighteen centuries. These lands, which have a typically Mediterranean climate, are inhabited chiefly by Berber and Arab peoples of Moslem faith. Though the total native population increased greatly under French rule, something over a million European colonists moved in. In majority French, but with sizable groups of Italians and Spaniards, these colonists took some land from the natives, though they added to the total arable acreage by initiating irrigation projects and other improvements. They remained, however, an alien group.

The French got a toe-hold in North Africa in 1824 through an expedition against the Algerian pirates, with whose Tripolitan counterparts, incidentally, the United States had fought in 1801. The French stayed on, increasing their control over Algeria and adding protectorates over Tunisia to the east in the 1880's and over Morocco to the west in the early twentieth century. Britain gave the French a free hand in Morocco as compensation for their exclusion from Egypt (see above, p. 557).

Especially in Algeria and Tunisia, the French promoted European settlement while trying not to antagonize the natives. They called their policy one of "assimilation," in contrast with the British policy of hands off and indirect rule. They hoped, they explained, to assimilate Africans into French civilization, making them ultimately into good children of the eighteenth-century Enlightenment, good citizens of the Republic founded on the principles of 1789. They hoped to create an empire of "100,000,000 Frenchmen," more than half of them overseas, and to draw on abundant native manpower to fill up the ranks of the Republic's armies.

In the military sense, the policy of assimilation worked out somewhat as the French had hoped; in the main, however, assimilation was difficult and only partially successful. The French, always desirous of spreading their culture, did indeed assimilate part of the native ruling classes. Under the Third Republic they made Algeria politically a part of France itself, organizing it into three departments and giving them representatives to the Chamber of Deputies, with a franchise open to the small group of Europeanized natives as well as to colonists. In Morocco, the French took a somewhat different tack. They sought, in part successfully, to open the country to French business and to the international tourist trade. Their urban center of Casablanca became a great modern city. And, without quite admitting the fact, they really abandoned assimilation for something close to the British policy of indirect rule. In 1912, the very able colonial administrator, Marshal Lyautey, began to organize turbulent Morocco, applying the "splash of oil" policy—that is, he pacified certain key centers by establishing firm working relations with the natives and then let pacification spread over the surface of Morocco like a splash of oil on water. The sultan and his feudal subordinates were maintained in Morocco, relatively free to carry on many of their age-old ways, but stripped of real power.

The French: Tropical Africa

In 1815, the British had left France her small posts in West Africa at the mouth of the Senegal River, together with the slight foothold France had obtained in the seventeenth century on the great Island of Madagascar off the East African coast. By 1914, the French had been very successful in the partition of Africa, perhaps at bottom because the British preferred French to German aggrandizement, especially after 1870. By 1914, at any rate, France numbered in Africa alone nearly as many inhabitants as in her home territories (about 39,000,000).

Except in North Africa, these people were almost all Negroes who were still essentially at the Stone Age level of material culture, and who were for the most part untouched by either Islam or Christianity. Except in certain coastal towns, where their administration and business were concentrated, the French had not by 1914 achieved very much toward assimilating or westernizing these vast districts. Most of their attempts to hasten the economic development of their African lands by organized joint-stock companies failed miserably.

It is quite possible that France spent more on these African colonies than she gained from them. Indeed, one of the stock arguments of nineteenth-century anti-imperialists was that colonies did not "pay" the mother country, and the French African colonies were one of their favorite exhibits. One economist—an Englishman, to be sure, and presumably unmoved by much that moves Frenchmen—concluded that in 1892 French gains from colonial trade were 16,000,000 francs, whereas net government expenditures for the colonies were 174,-000,000 francs. For 1915, he made an even more discouraging estimate.* Such figures, however, seem not to have discouraged any of the great powers in their imperialist efforts. Obviously the simplest form of the economic interpretation of history, the notion that political entities are moved by simple bookkeeping concepts of economic profit and loss, does not hold true for nineteenth-century imperialism.

Again, though French colonies in tropical Africa had by no means been modernized even in material conditions by 1914, everywhere a beginning had been made. Everywhere the tricolor went, there also went the beginnings of medicine and hygiene, modern methods of communication, industry, and agriculture, and formal education for at least a few natives. In justifying the policy of assimilation, the French claim for themselves, in contrast with the British, a lack of race prejudice, a willingness to accept the blacks as equals. This contrast is underlined by the English author whose figures we have just quoted:

Of course, it is true that the French also attempt to understand the native and in the main to give him freedom to produce as he pleases. The Frenchman actually tends much more to be a 'good fellow' with the natives

* Constant Southworth, *The French Colonial Venture* (London, 1931), 122.

than does the Briton, who is much more aloof. But this greater democracy does not seem to inspire a greater degree of confidence. Somehow, the Briton is more apt to succeed in instilling in the native confidence in the results of producing by the system that he recommends.*

Although there is some truth in the claim for greater French toleration, the deed is not quite up to the word. The French in Africa did not often marry Negroes; but intermarriage is in this real world an unreal test of racial equality. Negroes very rarely *commanded* white Frenchmen in military or civilian activity. Both at home and in Africa, on the other hand, once the Negroes seemed firmly under control, the French went a long way toward encouraging Negro art and folkways, in keeping with a policy very close to the ideal delineated by Lugard for Nigeria. The British, however, especially in the twentieth century, edged toward some kind of assimilation; African Negro undergraduates in British universities took on a lot more of Britishness than just their fine standard English accent. The contrast between British and French African policies was far from complete.

The French: Asia

In Asia, the French took over in the nineteenth century lands that came to be called French Indo-China. These lands included two rich rice-growing deltas (around Hanoi in the north and Saigon in the south), inhabited by peoples culturally and in part racially related to the Chinese. They also included Cambodia, culturally related to India, and the primitive mountain peoples of Laos. French experience here on the whole ran parallel to imperialist experience elsewhere in Southeast Asia, though the Anglo-Saxon fondness for nagging the French has tended to create the impression

* *Ibid.*, 193.

that the French did far worse in Indo-China than did the Dutch in Java or the British in Malaya. Slow but real material progress was made, though the basic problem of poverty among the masses remained unsolved. Native nationalist movements, nourished by educated natives with jobs of less dignity and authority than they believed should be theirs, rose in strength as the years went on. France also took part, from her base in Indo-China, in the struggle for control of China proper. The French sphere of influence was southern China, in particular the province of Yunnan adjoining Indo-China, and in 1898 the French got a lease on a port in Kwangchow Bay.

The Germans

We can be brief in listing the colonial acquisitions of the other powers. Germany and Italy came late to the imperial scramble, as they came late to national unity. Nevertheless, Germany was clearly a great power, and Italy aspired to be one; hence, both sought to acquire the token colonies, at least, that seemed necessary to that dignified status. Germany in 1914 had three really large pieces of tropical and subtropical Africa—the Kameruns (Cameroons), German Southwest Africa, and German East Africa—and the smaller Togoland, close to a million square miles in all. These were not rich or well-developed areas, and their total contribution to the German economy was almost negligible. The German achievement on the whole was not greatly different from that of other European powers in Africa; it was neither morally nor economically much better or much worse. In the Pacific, the Germans picked up some small islands, and a large, primitive territory on the island of New Guinea. Germany took part in the attempted partition of China; *her* ninety-nine-year lease was on Kiaochow Bay.

The German drive for colonies was quite self-conscious; it was well organized in a pressure group with all the fixings of modern propaganda. Bismarck himself, who cared little for the prestige of colonies, was obliged to give way and consent to African ventures. His successors went further, and William II helped Germany to enter one of the most confused and dangerous fields of imperialist expansion, the Near East. On the eve of World War I, the German "Berlin to Baghdad" push was well under way, and the Germans had supplanted the British as patrons of the Turks.

The Italians and Belgians

Italy, condemned to the role of weakest of the great powers, got very little, even out of the partition of Africa. Tunis, which she coveted, went instead to France. Italy's major imperial effort centered on the African lands at the southern end of the Red Sea, but after her defeat by the Abyssinians under Menelek in 1896 she had to content herself with a few thousand square miles of desert in Eritrea and Somaliland. Italian efforts to add to this inadequate empire by taking Tripoli from its nominal Turkish suzerains succeeded, but these same efforts led to the Italo-Turkish war of 1911, which was in a sense the real beginning of World War I (see Chapter XVIII). The Italians had so little to work with it is hard to assess their success or failure.

Little Belgium, largely through the enterprise of her King Leopold II (1865-1909), managed to acquire a large piece of equatorial Africa. This project began as the Congo Free State, with all sorts of noble ideals of co-operative European civilizing missions in Africa; but it ended up in 1908 as simply the Belgian Congo. Nineteenth-century scandal about forced labor and native exploitation in the Congo called Leopold's experiment to the attention of the world and provided liberal anti-imperialists with fresh arguments. But the Belgians, who have long since moderated Leopold's policies, still have the Congo.

The Americans

To the horror and indignation of many Americans, to the delight of others, the United States at the very end of the century joined the great powers and acquired overseas lands. In 1898, she waged a brief and successful war with Spain, for which the immediate cause was the still mysterious sinking of the American battleship *Maine* in the harbor of Havana, Cuba. The Spanish-American War left the United States in control of the remnants of the Spanish Empire in America (the Caribbean islands of Cuba and Puerto Rico) and the archipelago of the Philippines off the coast of Asia. Meantime, the United States also acquired Hawaii (1898) and part of the Samoan Islands in the Pacific (1899). Then in 1903 American support of a revolution in Panama, then a part of Colombia, assured the independence of a new republic and direct American control of the zone of the projected Panama Canal.

The Americans withdrew from Cuba, leaving her as an independent republic, though subject under the Platt Amendment of 1901 to what in foreign eyes has always seemed American "protection." The rest of her acquisitions the United States kept for the time, though in the Philippines she had to put down an armed rising by Filipinos who wanted immediate independence. American anti-imperialists attempted to upset the somewhat anomalous arrangement under which their government kept lands without strict authorization from the American Constitution. But a Supreme Court decision in the so-called "Insular Cases" (1901) held that territory might be subject to American jurisdiction without being incorporated constitutionally in the United States of America. Under this decision, Americans began the process of training the Filipinos for eventual independence. Meanwhile, the United States, too, had an empire, which on the maps was duly colored as an American possession.

The Japanese

One more empire was being formed during the decades before World War I, the only empire to be created by a people of non-European stock—the Japanese. Even during their isolation (see Chapter V), the Japanese had maintained an interest in western developments, particularly in technology, and had imported western books through the trading station that the Dutch were allowed to maintain at Nagasaki. More important, in 1853 the basic political and economic structure of Japan had long needed overhauling. An oligarchy of the feudal type ruled, but its ineffective government, its grasping tax-collection, and the economic misery resulting all made it widely unpopular. Discontent was growing, especially among two important social classes. One was the urban middle class of merchants and craftsmen. Although the industrial revolution had not yet reached Japan, the country already had populous cities, notably Tokyo (then called Yedo or Edo). The urban middle class, somewhat like the French bourgeoisie on the eve of 1789, wanted political rights to match their increasing economic power. The other discontented class may be compared roughly with the poorer gentry and lesser nobility of Europe under the Old Régime. These were the *samurai* or feudal re-

President Theodore Roosevelt and Panama.

tainers, a military caste now threatened with impoverishment and political eclipse. The *samurai* dreaded the growth of cities and the subsequent threat to the traditional domination of agriculture and the landlords; many of them also resented the fact that they were largely excluded from positions of power by the prevailing oligarchical regime. These social pressures, more than any outside western influence, forced the modernization of Japan.

Economically, the transformation proceeded rapidly. By 1914, much of Japan resembled an advanced western country. She, too, had railroads, fleets of merchant vessels, a large textile industry, big cities, and big business firms. The industrialization of Japan was the more remarkable in view of her meager supplies of many essential raw materials. But she had many important assets. As a glance at the map will show, her geographical position with respect to Asia is very like that of the British Isles with respect to Europe. Japan, too, found markets for her exports on the continent nearby and used the income to pay for imports. The ambitious Japanese middle class, supplemented by recruits from the *samurai*, furnished aggressive business leadership. A great reservoir of cheap labor existed in the peasantry, a large and submissive class. The peasants, who needed to find jobs away from the overcrowded farms, were inured to a very low standard of living, and were ready to work long and hard in factories for what seemed by western standards indecently low wages.

Politically, Japan appeared to undergo a major revolution in the late nineteenth century and to remodel her government along western lines. Actually, however, the change was by no means so great as it seemed. A revolution did indeed occur, beginning in 1868 when the old feudal oligarchy crumbled under the pressure of the discontented elements. Authority and prestige were restored to the position of emperor ("mikado"), a largely forgotten office whose incumbents had for years had no real power. In 1889, the emperor bestowed a constitution on his subjects, with a bicameral diet composed of a noble House of Peers and an elected House of Representatives.

The architects of these changes, however, were not democrats. They were aristocrats, ambitious young *samurai*, supported by allies from the business world and determined to make Japan over from above as they wished. The result was to substitute a new oligarchy for the old; a small group of aristocrats dominated the emperor and the state. The constitution of 1889, rather like that of the German Empire, provided only the outward appearances of liberal parliamentary government. The ministry was responsible not to the diet but to the emperor, and hence to the dominant ruling class. The diet itself was scarcely representative; the right to vote for members of its lower house was limited to a narrow electorate, including the middle class but excluding the peasants and industrial workers. As Sir George Sansom, a British expert on Japan, has observed, she had no trouble in accepting western "things," but a great deal in handling western "ideas."

Japan began her expansion by taking from China, after a brief war in 1894-1895, the island of Formosa, which she annexed, and the piece of Asiatic mainland closest to Japan, the peninsula of Korea, whose independence China was forced to recognize as a preliminary to eventual Japanese annexation. But Russia, too, had designs on Korea; the results of this rivalry were the Russo-Japanese War of 1904-1905 and a second great Japanese victory (see Chapter XV). Japan now secured unchallenged preponderance in Korea, which she annexed in 1910, special concessions in the Chinese province of Manchuria, and the cession by Russia of the southern half of the island of Sakhalin, to the north of the main Japanese islands. She had expanded in the classic European way.

By 1914, the Japanese empire was undergoing rapid economic development by emigrants from the home islands. But the harsh treatment of the subject peoples by their new masters was preparing the way for later troubles in the Far East. So, too, were the grandiose projects for taking over China formulated by Japan's rulers, whose heads had been turned by their spectacular string of easy successes.

IV: The Debate Over Imperialism

In the nineteenth century all the western countries, even monarchical states like Germany, had a wide range of free public opinion, and some kind of parliamentary government by discussion. The kind of expansion we call imperialism, therefore, had to be defended articulately, since it was attacked articulately. The defense and attack are both important parts of the intellectual history of our times, for the debate, under greatly changed conditions, still goes on in mid-twentieth century.

Pro: The Argument from Social Darwinism One central argument for the defense borrowed heavily from the Social Darwinists (see Chapter XVI). Europeans both in Europe and in their "colonies of settlement," so ran the argument, were able to beat non-Europeans in war. By this very fact they had shown that they were in terms of evolution and progress more fit to survive than were the non-Europeans. Eternal competition is the price of survival. White men, this argument insisted, are simply better specimens of *homo sapiens* than are colored men; Anglo-Saxons (or Germans, or Slavs, or Latins, depending on the writer's origins) are simply better specimens than other white men.

An imperialist like Cecil Rhodes, to judge from much that he wrote and said, very likely dreamed of a world which in the fullness of time and evolution would be peopled entirely by Anglo-Saxons. Their breed would actually be improved over their ancestors of 1900, after the inferior peoples had died out—or had been killed off. But these were very distant views indeed. The prospect of ruddy Kentish farmers actually established in freeholds along the Congo was too unrealistic at the end of the nineteenth century. Imperialistic doctrine generally held that throughout the tropical world, the superior white men would put order and prosperity into the lives of colored men, would as trustees of civilization give up the comforts of Europe to rule in discomfort in the hot countries. Some imperialists thought that this benevolent rule of white men in the tropics would last indefinitely, since in their opinion non-whites were totally unable to undertake tasks of leadership and to assume moral responsibility.

Pro: The Argument of Duty Other European imperialists, however, took the attitude that, though the non-whites could not run their own affairs then, they could ultimately learn to do so. For the present and for a good many years to come, whites would have to educate them on the spot; someday—the length of time judged necessary varied with the temperament of the judge —these non-whites would have matured sufficiently to take over responsibilities now confined to whites. These are not responsibilities of *ownership*, but rather responsibilities of *trusteeship*. Kipling put the case comfortably enough—for white men—in his famous poem:

Take up the White Man's Burden—
 Send forth the best ye breed—
Go bind your sons to exile
 To serve your captives' need;
To wait in heavy harness,
 On fluttered folk and wild—
Your new-caught, sullen peoples,
 Half-devil and half-child.*

This argument of trusteeship was by all odds the most popular defense of imperialism, particularly among Anglo-Saxon peoples.

Yet the historian, aware of the complexities of human nature, will be wary of the notion that the ethical arguments of the imperialists were insincere. Many a European both in and out of the colonies of exploitation really believed in the trusteeship theory, and really did his best to live up to it. The Christian missionary is a major factor in the nineteenty-century expansion of the West. Indeed, Kenneth Latourette's long and thorough history of the expansion of Christianity has a final volume entitled *The Great Century* for the nineteenth century. More formal converts to Christianity were made all over the world in this century, so often labeled the century of materialism, than ever before.

How thorough the conversion of the colored peoples was is a difficult problem. In areas of primitive culture, whole tribes nominally accepted Christianity but continued many of the immemorial ways of their heathen past. In India, China, and Japan, old civilized countries with deep-rooted religious faiths of their own, Christianity did not win over anything like a majority of the people. Nevertheless, the missions did succeed in the course of the

century in building up devoted native followers, of whom the most intelligent were often sent to Europe or the United States to complete their education.

Pro: The Defensive Argument

Finally, the imperialist philosophy of 1900 was by no means based on an unworried sense of white supremacy. Western civilization is one of the most worrying of all civilizations. Many publicists regarded imperialism as essentially defensive. The whites, outnumbered in a harsh world, had to organize themselves and hold the non-whites off. There was talk of the "yellow peril" and of white "race suicide." The writings and speeches of such apparently confident imperialists as Rhodes, Kipling, the German Emperor Wilhelm II, and Theodore Roosevelt sounded this curious note of fear and uncertainty. We are the best, but really we are a little too good for this world; we cannot breed fast enough.

One further aspect, or variation, of the defensive argument involved the importance of naval bases and coaling stations. Here the appetite tended to grow by eating: first, the French could argue that security of the homeland required control of North Africa, but presently the far-off holdings in Indo-China demanded a string of bases along which the navy could operate to protect the empire.

Con: Anti-Imperialist Arguments

Against imperialism, opponents marshaled a great many arguments. To the Social Darwinists the anti-imperialists replied by denying that the struggle for existence applied to human groups in the way it applied to plants and animals. It is precisely by sublimating the crude conflict of kill-or-be-killed into the higher rivalry for cultural excellence that

* "The White Man's Burden," from "The Five Nations," *Rudyard Kipling's Verse, 1885-1932* (London, 1933), 320.

human societies transcend the struggle for life. Each group, each race, has something to contribute to the total of civilization, and the deliberate destruction or suppression of any group lames and lessens the others, prevents the true working out of evolution—that is, cultural evolution—among human beings as contrasted with mere animals. The anti-imperialists also brought forward very prominently the economic argument we have already noted. They worked hard to show that in fact, especially in Africa, colonies did not "pay," that the imperialist appeal to self-interest in the homeland was a delusion, the dishonest work of propagandists for the privileged minority in the homeland and in the colonies who *did* profit personally from imperialist ventures.

From this point the anti-imperialists went on to maintain that support at home for colonial expansion rested therefore on the ordinary man's vicarious satisfactions from national achievements. The ordinary man liked to see his country figure in the world atlas as an imperial power. He liked to think of Britain's empire on which the sun never set; or, if he was a Frenchman, of the tangible evidence that France was still a great power, still carrying on her *mission civilisatrice;* or, if he was an Italian, that at last Italy too was a nation, and behaving as nations should. The anti-imperialists were on the whole not very successful in their attempts to use ridicule and irony against behavior that they found irrational. But their conviction that human action ought to be rational and devoted to the greatest good of the greatest number placed them firmly in the liberal tradition.

So strong was the anti-imperialists' belief that they were right—in spite of the growth of empires all about them—that in Britain the school of "Little Englanders,"

much influenced by laissez-faire economics, came to the comforting assurance that imperialism was impossible. The colonies, they held, must inevitably drop away from the mother country—to use their favorite stereotype—like ripe fruit from a tree. Why not then avoid getting into the futile process further by *not* taking any more of Africa or China? Why not hasten the inevitable by giving up the empire?

Not all the anti-imperialists were liberals or idealists. Indeed in France some of the most vehement were the extreme nationalists who wanted revenge on Prussia for the French defeat in the war of 1870. These *revanchards* were not sorry for the Negroes; they opposed French colonialism because it distracted French energies from what they thought was the sole proper national business—getting ready to beat the Germans.

What sank into the mind and feelings of the ordinary westerner as a result of the anti-imperialist arguments was an uneasy awareness that somehow the practice of imperial expansion did not square with the best avowed intentions of democracy. Particularly in the United States, the feeling grew that imperialism and colonialism were contrary to the ideas of liberty and equality, even if the imperialists honestly claimed to be following the "trusteeship" principle. America took over an empire in 1898, but not without vigorous protests from numerous groups of anti-imperialists, and not without specific promises from the government that it would "free" dependents the moment they were capable of self-rule. This opposition of Americans to colonialism, especially when practiced by themselves, is one of the important factors in the world situation of the mid-twentieth century, and we shall return to it in later chapters.

V: The Results of Imperialism

The Results in General

The broad general results of this long phase of European expansion down to 1914 may now be summarized. First and most obviously, in the nineteenth century almost the whole planet was affected by the process. The white man was almost everywhere by 1914, and white explorers not infrequently found that the tin can, that ubiquitous symbol of the West, had got there ahead of them. Second, the expansion of Europe was accompanied by a numerical expansion of the whole human race. Between 1800 and 1900 the population of the world just about doubled, from some 800,000,000 in 1800 to some 1,600,000,000 in 1900. European white stock did indeed account for the most spectacular part of the rise, but non-whites in Asia and elsewhere also increased. We do not sufficiently understand human population growth to say flatly that the expansion of Europe *caused* the growth of population among non-European peoples in the nineteenth century. But it did bring to many areas of the world some increase of law and order, some increase in material production and improvements in transportation and distribution, health and sanitation—factors that probably contribute to population growth. And, with such exceptions as the native Australian "Blackfellows" and some North American Indians, European expansion did not usually mean the physical extermination of non-European peoples.

Third, we may say with no reservations whatever that by 1914 it was quite clear that "natives" were beginning to reject the claims of white supremacy. Among the more civilized and long-established peoples in the Near East and Asia the educated classes were already developing a sense of nationalism. They took over from the West that particular form of group consciousness that is attached to a territorial political unit and that is shared, in principle at least, by all who live within the unit. This nationalism was a new thing outside Europe, and a very important one for us today, for it has gone on increasing and developing. In the early twentieth century, it was most evident in Japan and, to some extent, China, and in advanced "colonial" nations like Egypt and India.

This new phenomenon was not the same thing as simple hostility to whites, or to particular nations among the whites. It was an organized political faith—in short, modern "patriotism." Naturally, Egyptian, Indian, and Chinese patriots were first of all concerned with getting rid of their European imperial masters; their attitudes were those of oppressed nationalistic groups everywhere, even in Europe itself. They were touchy, addicted to nursing grievances imaginary as well as real, eager to seize on any national trait that could be glorified, admiring, hating, and envying their masters. Above all, they were organized on a new principle taken from the West, a principle that is ultimately perhaps more destructive of their own traditional cultures than anything else that has come to them from the West. This is the equalitarian and leveling, if not democratic, spirit inherent in the secular religion of nationalism. In theory at least nationality transcends the dividing lines of profession, social class, and even caste. The fellah, the Egyptian peasant whose ancestry reaches back through the centuries, could claim to be as good an Egyptian as the aristocratic pasha—indeed a better one, since he was uncorrupted by European culture. People began to talk and write of "Arab" nationalism.

Fourth, and in spite of the gloomy economic conclusions of anti-imperialists, there seems no doubt that over the century the homelands of Europe gained in total wealth from their expansion overseas. Indeed, raw materials from overseas were necessary to maintain the standard of living in thickly populated countries like Britain, Germany, Belgium, and the Netherlands. Theoretically, these raw materials could have come into European lands in free trade with free countries overseas; actually they came in part from imperial expansion.

Finally, imperialist rivalries, especially after 1870, exacerbated the normal rivalries among the European great powers, and were thus a major factor in the complex of causes that brought on general war in 1914. This is particularly true of the Anglo-German rivalry, which, unlike that of France and Germany or of Austria and Russia, had no long historical background. This Anglo-German rivalry was everywhere by 1900— among commercial travelers of both nations, trying to sell machinery in Peru; among missionaries trying to convert the heathen in Africa; among army officers, naval officers, editors, organizers, all seeking to make German influence more important than British somewhere or to keep British influence more important than German. The rivalry extended even to the academic world and to that world in the United States. There were those who regarded the Rhodes Scholarships for study at Oxford (1904) as a British attempt to counterbalance the great prestige that the German universities, and especially their degree of Ph.D., had acquired in America during the latter nineteenth century.

The Colonies of Settlement

Thus far our account of the nineteenth-century expansion of Europe has been limited largely to the "colonies of exploitation," the protectorates,

and the spheres of influence held by Europeans. No such account is at all complete, for the most striking thing about this expansion was that it involved an actual transplantation of Europeans to "colonies of settlement" on a scale incomparably greater than in the previous three centuries since Columbus.

The colonies of settlement were originally very thinly inhabited lands. Australia, indeed, was almost empty; and the whole native Indian population of America north of the Rio Grande was almost certainly in 1800 not over a million. The European settlers simply overwhelmed these primitive peoples. In Tasmania, a large island to the south of the Australian mainland, the natives were totally wiped out, and in Australia itself they were very nearly wiped out. In the United States the Red Indians were so far eliminated that many an American grew up in the nineteenth century without ever seeing a redman except in a Wild West show.

In most of Latin America, however, the native Indian stock, far from being wiped out, persisted; the upper class, politically and economically, was drawn from European "creole" stock; and a great many people of mixed European and Indian and Negro blood filled the lower social ranks. In the far south of the continent, in the Argentine, Uruguay, and Chile, conditions resembled more clearly those in the United States, and these twentieth-century nations are now almost wholly European in stock.

The expansion of Europe into the Americas was also an expansion of Africa. By 1850 the leading European powers had pretty generally got the slave trade under control; but the nucleus of Negroes brought in by the trade in the earlier centuries continued to grow. Despite handicaps of race barriers, strongest in the United States, the Negroes multiplied; by 1900, for example, there were some 9,000,000 of them in the United States.

Canada: Background of Revolt

Apart from the extraordinary growth of the United States, the most important phase of the nineteenth-century movement of Europeans overseas is the growth of what is now called the British Commonwealth of Nations, or, more correctly, simply the Commonwealth. Doubtless it is an oversimplification to claim that the British learned their lesson from the American Revolution, and that consequently in Canada, Australia, and South Africa they were wise enough to abandon the policies of George III and Lord North. But the formula is fundamentally sound. The first laboratory for this experiment in a new kind of "colonialism" was Canada (see map on p. 461).

The rebellious thirteen colonies of North America had wanted to add a fourteenth, and had tried hard to win Canada. But a complex of causes all contributed to leaving Canada in British hands at the peace in 1783. The French Canadians in Quebec distrusted the new Protestant power growing up to the south; the American rebels had grave difficulties keeping up an army to cope with the British in the United States itself; America's French ally did not wish the new country to be too strong. Later, as we have seen in Chapter XIV, the United States failed in the War of 1812 to reverse the verdict of 1783.

Upper Canada, which was mainly British in stock, and Lower Canada (Quebec), which was mainly French, and the Maritime Provinces of Nova Scotia, New Brunswick, and Prince Edward Island were at first quite separate British "colonies," as the American thirteen had once been. Each had an apparatus quite like the old American one—a royal governor appointed by the Crown, a council appointed by the governor, and an elected assembly based on a more or less popular franchise. But just as in the thirteen colonies during the preceding century, the arrangement bred conflicts between the assemblies and the royal government. In 1837, revolts broke out in both Lower and Upper Canada, with popular leaders like Mackenzie and Papineau arrayed against the governor and his followers, and with essentially the same kind of constitutional and financial grievances that the thirteen colonies had had sixty years before.

Canada: Durham and A New Status

The revolt of 1837 was a military fiasco, and it is probable that public opinion in both provinces was against the rebels; there was a fear that too close an imitation of the American Revolution would lead to absorption by the United States. But the British government was alarmed, and sent out as governor-in-chief of all the British North American provinces the Earl of Durham, a young lord of Whig antecedents and Utilitarian leanings. Durham, feeling that he was not properly supported from London, resigned after less than a year in Canada. But the famous report he made to the British Parliament on his return in 1839 became the cornerstone of the new British imperial structure of dominions, a constitutional document that Durham's admirers have sometimes ranked with Magna Carta.

The Durham Report proposed the union of Upper and Lower Canada and the establishment of responsible government—that is, a popularly elected legislature with ultimate authority—for both the union and each of the separate provinces. The report is still of great interest. Durham had all the average Englishman's insensitivity to things French, and it is an understatement to say that he never understood the Québecois of Lower Canada. But he was true to his principles—even these French Canadian Catholics must have their own responsible government. As he wrote:

The maintenance of an absolute form of government on any part of the North American Continent can never continue for any long time, without exciting a general feeling in the United States against a power of which the existence is secured by means so odious to the people; and as I rate the preservation of the present general sympathy of the United States with the policy of our Government in Lower Canada as a matter of the greatest importance, I should be sorry that the feeling should be changed for one which, if prevalent among the people, must extend over the surrounding Provinces. The influence of such an opinion would not only act very strongly on the entire French population, and keep up among them a sense of injury and a determination of resistance to the Government, but would lead to just as great discontent among the English. In their present angry state of feeling, they might tolerate, for a while, any arrangement that would give them a triumph over the French; but I have greatly misunderstood their character if they would long bear a Government in which they had no direct voice. Nor would their jealousy be obviated by the selection of a Council from the persons supposed to have their confidence. It is not easy to know who really possess that confidence; and I suspect that there would be no surer way of depriving a man of influence over them than by treating him as their representative without their consent. . . . *

The actual realization of Durham's recommendations was achieved with due British slowness. The first step, the Union Act of 1840 passed by the British Parliament, though it did unite Upper and Lower Canada, was at the very least unspecific on the critical point of responsibility—that is, on whether an administration defeated in the legislature had to resign or not. Nearly a decade later, under the governorship of Lord Elgin, the principle was quietly established in practice, never to be withdrawn. Nor was the next step unduly hurried. The British North America Act of 1867 achieved in principle the union of all the British provinces in North America, except Newfoundland, oldest of all, whose separatist tendencies were so strong it did not

* Sir Reginald Coupland, *The Durham Report* (Oxford, 1954), 155-156

join Canada until 1949. The act of 1867 set up the Dominion of Canada by the union of Ontario, Quebec, and the Maritime Provinces, with provision for the admission of territories in the west as provinces on something like the pattern for admission of the western states in the United States. There were still many survivals of the former "colonial" status of Canada, from the bestowal of titles, especially knighthood with its unrepublican and undemocratic "Sir," to the possibility of judicial appeal from Canadian courts to the Privy Council in Westminster. Above all, the relation of Canada to Britain in terms of international affairs, armed forces, right of secession, and much else was not yet spelled out, and was not to be spelled out formally until the Statute of Westminster in 1931 (see Chapters XXI and XXIII).

The Extension of Dominion Status

The individual provinces of Australia had common British origins and had relatively short lives as separate territorial units—the oldest, New South Wales, dates only from 1788. But, in spite of these facts, these provinces developed their local differences and separateness, symbolized by the fact that they used differing gauges for their railroads. They gained the essentials of self-government in the Australian Colonies Government Act of 1850, but federal union of New South Wales, Victoria, Queensland, and the others was not achieved until the Commonwealth of Australia was formed in 1901. The influence of the American example is clear in the constitution of the Commonwealth, which provides for a senate with equal membership for each of the six states, a house of representatives apportioned on the basis of population, and a supreme court with something close to the American power of judicial review. But in Australia as in the other British dominions, the parliamentary system of an executive (prime minister and cabinet) dismissible by vote of the legislative body was retained; the American "presidential" system was deliberately rejected.

Australia, like Canada, was essentially an empty country in 1800, and like Canada it filled gradually with immigrants, mostly from Britain. Perhaps the head start of the United States, with its great attraction for European immigration, slowed down the growth of these British dominions. But the process, though slow, was steady, and by 1914 all the dominions, including the quiet islands of New Zealand, traditionally most "English" of them all, were prosperous, democratic societies just settling down from the last of the pioneer stage. Their narrative history is most interesting, but we cannot go into it here, nor into the fascinating and illuminating subject—insufficiently pursued—of the likenesses and unlikenesses of the corporate personalities of these new countries and the United States, all offsprings of the "frontier."

The Commonwealth in Review

In the nineteenth century, Americans pushing west and Russians pushing east added millions of square miles to their respective lands as colonies of settlement. Although in both, and especially in America, this process of the "frontier" had important effects on their national character, it did not create great immediate problems concerning the "independence" of the settlers. The British, however, went thousands of miles overseas for their colonies of settlement. They found very soon that these colonies could not be treated as the long tradition since 1450 prescribed—that is, as mere outposts of the mother land with no political self-rule, held in strict mercantilist economic leading strings. Nor could they be, if only because of the separating seas, simply added as they filled up as a territorial continuation of the mother land, like Siberia or the American West. By 1914, the British at home and the citizens of their overseas colonies of settlement had worked out something new in political configurations, unprecedented in man's brief history.

Canada, Australia, New Zealand were indeed by 1914 wholly self-governing. They could and did even levy customs dues on imports from Britain. They had the beginnings of military forces of their own, and of course complete control of that clear attribute of "sovereignty"—their own internal police. Men were even beginning to speculate about whether they were not in possession of that other clear attribute of sovereignty—the right to conduct foreign relations, both diplomatic and military. For example, could Canada be at peace with a country with which Great Britain was at war?

The test came in 1914. All the dominions went to war against Germany and her allies. Even the dubiously loyal Union of South Africa went to war against the sender of the Kruger telegram; we are bound to record that the always land-hungry Boers had their eyes on the German colonies in Africa, and especially on the big empty colony of German Southwest Africa, right adjacent to the Union. The government of each dominion, however, went through the formal process of declaring war, just as "sovereign" countries do. Yet the relation between Canada, for instance, and Great Britain was something different from the relation between two such sovereign countries as the Argentine and Spain. The dominions had not quite set up wholly for themselves, or, to revert to the favorite cliché of the nineteenth-century Little Englander, they had not dropped off like ripe fruit. The nature of the tie between the dominions and Britain was not clear then, and it must be admitted it is not fully clear now. But it exists, and to it also we shall return in a chapter on imperialism in our own day.

Reading Suggestions on Nineteenth-Century Imperialism

General Accounts

W. L. Langer, *The Diplomacy of Imperialism, 1890-1902*, 2nd ed. (N.Y.: Knopf, 1951). A detailed study of a particularly hectic period of the imperial scramble; also includes a valuable discussion of the forces making for imperialism.

J. A. Hobson, *Imperialism, A Study* (London: Nisbet, 1902). Perhaps the most famous attack on imperialism.

V. I. Lenin, *Imperialism, The Highest Stage of Capitalism* (N.Y.: International Publishers, 1939). The classic expression of the communist interpretation of imperialism.

B. Kidd, *The Control of the Tropics* (N.Y.: Macmillan, 1898). A good example of the serious defenses of imperialism offered at the end of the nineteenth century.

J. A. Schumpeter, *Imperialism and Social Classes* (N.Y.: Noonday, 1955). A valuable essay on imperialism from the standpoint of the economist and sociologist.

E. M. Winslow, *The Pattern of Imperialism* (N.Y.: Columbia Univ. Press, 1948). A study of the forces, especially political, making for modern imperial expansion.

K. S. Latourette, *A History of the Expansion of Christianity*, 7 vols. (N.Y.: Harper, 1937-1945). Volumes 5 and 6 of this major work concern the expansion of Christianity into the non-European world, 1800-1914.

Special Studies: Africa

L. Woolf, *Empire and Commerce in Africa* (London: Allen & Unwin, 1919). A detailed and highly critical account from a left-wing point of view.

H. H. Johnston, *The Opening Up of Africa* (N.Y.: Holt, 1911. Home University Library). Sympathetic popular account by the author of many other works on Africa.

H. L. Hoskins, *European Imperialism in Africa* (N.Y.: Holt, 1930. A Berkshire Study). Handy introductory manual.

R. L. Buell, *The Native Problem in Africa* (N.Y.: Macmillan, 1928); and H. A. Wieschoff, *Colonial Policies in Africa* (Philadelphia: Univ. of Pennsylvania Press, 1944). Two solid and helpful studies.

C. W. de Kiewiet, *A History of South Africa, Social and Economic* (Oxford: Clarendon, 1941), and E. A. Walker, *A History of South Africa*, 2nd ed. (N.Y.: Longmans, Green, 1940). Two good studies of the area.

Basil Williams, *Cecil Rhodes* (London: Constable, 1921). Probably the best book on the famous empire-builder.

Basil Williams, *Botha, Smuts, and South Africa* (N.Y.: Macmillan, 1948. Teach Yourself History series). Introduction to the period following the Boer War.

F. D. Lugard, *The Dual Mandate in British Tropical Africa*, 3rd ed. (Edinburgh: Blackwood, 1926). Significant detailed account of British colonial policy in action.

H. R. Rudin, *Germans in the Cameroons, 1884-1914: A Case Study in Imperialism* (New Haven: Yale Univ. Press, 1938). Good study of the topic indicated.

L. de Lichtervelde, *Léopold of the Belgians* (N.Y.: Century, 1929), and L. Bauer, *Leopold the Unloved, King of the Belgians and of Wealth* (Boston: Little, Brown, 1935). Vindicating and attacking, respectively, the great exploiter of the Congo.

Special Studies: Asia

J. T. Pratt, *The Expansion of Europe into the Far East* (London: Sylvan Press, 1947). Excellent introduction to the subject.

D. E. Owen, *Imperialism and Nationalism in the Far East* (N.Y.: Holt, 1929. A Berkshire Study). Handy brief introductory manual.

K. S. Latourette, *The Development of China*, new ed. (Boston: Houghton Mifflin, 1956). A good survey.

A. C. Lyall, *The Rise and Expansion of British Dominion in India*, 5th ed. (London: Murray, 1914). Sympathetic account.

R. Coupland, *Britain and India, 1600-1941* (N.Y.: Longmans, Green, 1941). Very brief introduction by an authority on imperial questions.

G. Sansom, *The Western World and Japan, A Study in the Interaction of European and Asiatic Cultures* (N.Y.: Knopf, 1950), and *Japan, A Short Cultural History*, rev. ed. (N.Y.: Appleton-Century, 1943). Two indispensable works by a great authority on Japan.

E. O. Reischauer, *Japan, Past and Present* (N.Y.: Knopf, 1946). Helpful and reliable brief introduction.

B. H. Sumner, *Tsardom and Imperialism in the Far East and Middle East, 1880-1914* (London: British Academy, 1944). Good short account.

H. Brown, ed., *The Sahibs: The Life and Ways of the British in India as Recorded by Themselves*

(London: Hodge, 1948). An illuminating compilation.

Special Studies: The British Empire and Dominions

J. H. Rose and others, eds., *The Cambridge History of the British Empire*, 7 vols. (N.Y.: Macmillan, 1929-1940). This solid work, more useful for facts than for interpretation, has separate volumes on such major areas as India, Canada, and Australia and New Zealand.

P. Knaplund, *The British Empire, 1815-1939* (N.Y.: Harper, 1941). An authoritative and scholarly survey by an American specialist.

C. E. Carrington, *The British Overseas: Exploits of a Nation of Shopkeepers* (Cambridge, England: Cambridge Univ. Press, 1950). An advanced and detailed study from a British point of view.

D. G. Creighton, *Dominion of the North: A History of Canada* (Boston: Houghton Mifflin, 1944). A good account.

R. Coupland, ed., *The Durham Report* (Oxford: Clarendon, 1946). The famous document that in a sense marks the beginning of the development of the British Commonwealth.

Special Studies: Other Subjects

S. H. Roberts, *History of French Colonial Policy, 1870-1925*, 2 vols. (London: King, 1929). Detailed and substantial study.

D. W. Brogan, *France under the Republic* (N.Y.: Harper, 1939). Contains a brief and illuminating treatment of French imperialism.

M. E. Townsend, *The Rise and Fall of Germany's Colonial Empire, 1884-1918* (N.Y.: Macmillan, 1930). A useful account.

J. W. Pratt, *America's Colonial Experiment* (Englewood Cliffs, N.J.: Prentice-Hall, 1950). A valuable survey of the American empire.

D. Perkins, *Hands Off: A History of the Monroe Doctrine* (Boston: Little, Brown, 1941). A useful popular account by a leading specialist.

Historical Fiction

R. Kipling, *Kim* (many editions) and *Soldiers Three* (many editions). Famous works by the even more famous champion of imperialism.

N. Coward, *Cavalcade*, in *Play Parade* (Garden City, N.Y.: Garden City Publishing, 1933). A patriotic play and a sentimental tribute to old imperial glories.

S. Cloete, *The Turning Wheels* (Boston: Houghton Mifflin, 1937). A novel about nineteenth-century Boers.

O. Schreiner, *The Story of a South African Farm* (London: Benn, 1930). An older novel about South Africa.

A. Gide, *The Immoralist* (N.Y.: Knopf, A Vintage Book). A novel in which the European hero is thoroughly corrupted by North Africa.

E. M. Forster, *A Passage to India* (many editions). A celebrated and astringent novel about the British in India.

L. Hémon, *Maria Chapdelaine* (N.Y.: Macmillan, 1940). The best-known novel about rural French Canada.

H. H. Richardson, *The Fortunes of Richard Mahony* (N.Y.: Readers Club, 1941). A series of novels about modern Australia by an Australian.

H. Rider Haggard, *King Solomon's Mines* (N.Y.: Longmans, Green, 1926). A splendid example of the rousing novel of imperialist adventure.

CHAPTER EIGHTEEN

The First World War

I: Introduction

On June 28, 1914, the Habsburg Archduke Francis Ferdinand, heir to the throne of Austria-Hungary, and his wife were assassinated in the streets of Sarajevo, capital of the recently (1908) annexed provinces of Bosnia and Herzegovina, which had been occupied by Austria-Hungary since 1878 (see Chapter XV). The assassin, Princip, was a Serbian nationalist. Bosnia had long been coveted by the Serbs, and, as we have already seen, many of its Serb and Croat inhabitants longed for a more effective expression of their nationalist aspirations than they had achieved under Habsburg rule. The Austro-Hungarian government, alarmed by the ambitions of Serbian nationalists, took the occasion of the assassination to send a severe ultimatum to Serbia. The Serbian refusal to accept the ultimatum in its entirety led to an Austrian declaration of war on Serbia, on July 28. Within the week, the great states of Europe were engaged in a general war—the Central Powers (Austria-Hungary and Germany) against the Allies (Serbia, Russia, France, and Britain). Princip's revolver was eventually to kill some ten million men.

This was the first general war, the first war to involve most of the members of the world state-system, since the wars of the French Revolution and Napoleon a century earlier. There had indeed been wars enough, foreign and civil, in the century between. They were, however, wars between two parties, like the Franco-Prussian War of 1870, the bloody American war between North and South in 1861-1865, and a whole series of colonial wars against rebellious natives. Even the Crimean War of 1853, between Russia on the one hand and Great Britain, France, Turkey, and Piedmont on the other, was by great diplomatic effort kept from spreading out into a world war, and was confined to relatively minor fighting in the small peninsula of Crimea in the Black Sea.

The important thing to note is that in 1914 a great many people in Europe and America felt that this sort of general war was all but impossible. These people, predominantly liberal intellectuals, had been alarmed by the series of crises we shall shortly describe, crises that showed how close a general war might be. But they had followed hopefully the movements for international peace and co-operation—the Red Cross, the international labor movements, and the Hague conferences of 1899 and 1907, which, though they failed to achieve their avowed purpose of armaments limitation, did set up a tribunal for the arbitration of international disputes, the "world court."

World War I was long, bloody, and destructive. The shock of its outbreak, vastly increased by the strains of the war itself, and above all by the failure of the postwar peace settlement, brought on in the 1920's a most extraordinary discussion of the causes of the war. This discussion was by no means limited to professional historians. It was carried on in the press and on the platforms by all the agencies that touched public opinion. Most of it was designed to "revise" the verdict of the Versailles Treaty of 1919, in which the victorious Allies declared Germany and Austria-Hungary solely responsible for precipitating the war of 1914. The beaten Germans, penalized in the peace, had obvious reasons for trying to prove themselves innocent of war guilt. But important currents in public opinion in Great Britain, the United States, and even in France also flowed into this "revisionist" movement. So far did revisionism go in the 1920's that some American historians parceled out varying portions of the guilt among the victors and vanquished alike, with the confidence of schoolmasters handing out merits and demerits.

We cannot be so confident today. From our further perspective, the question of war guilt in 1914 fades out into a question of historical causation, and into the fact of historical tragedy. We can say with the English writer, George Meredith:

> In tragic life, God wot,
> No villain need be! Passions spin the plot.
> We are betrayed by what is false within.*

No one power or group of powers caused the war of 1914. Its causes lie deep in the history of the state-system of western civilization, and, more particularly, in its history since 1870. The dramatic date of the assassination of Francis Ferdinand, June 28, 1914, serves as a dividing line between the ultimate, or long-term, factors and the proximate, or short-term, factors.

---

* *Modern Love*, XLIII.

II: Causes of the War

The Shift in the Balance of Power

In the long term, an obvious factor that made war more likely was the unification of Germany and Italy. The creation of these two new major states in the 1860's and 1870's altered the always delicate balance of power in the European state-system. The efforts of statesmen during the next forty years to adjust the system and to take account of the two new powers and their claims proved ultimately unsuccessful. The older established powers were by no means willing to give up their own claims. We have seen that ever since the modern European—or, better, the western—state-system developed out of medieval fragmentation the separate units, the states, have tried to grow. They have tried to grow in wealth, in prestige, and, most of all, in territory. In the second half of the nineteenth century, with the principle of national sovereignty well established, with even the smaller states like Switzerland and Sweden generally accepted as not to be swallowed, there was little territory in Europe that could be easily disposed of for the purpose of making adjustments. Unification had closed Germany and Italy, which as recently as 1815 had been classic areas for "compensation." Only southeastern Europe, the Balkan lands of the obviously weakening Turkish Empire, remained in the late nineteenth century as possible pickings for ambitious powers. Even there, the growth of national feeling in states like Rumania, Serbia, Bulgaria, and Greece made sheer annexation difficult. Nevertheless, Russia and Austria-Hungary both had ambitions in the Balkans; behind them, aiming rather at domination of Turkey and the Near East, came Germany and Great Britain.

Meantime, influenced by their rivalries in Europe and abroad, the great powers were also choosing sides in a series of alliances and agreements. By the early years of the twentieth century two camps existed—the Triple Alliance of Germany, Austria-Hungary, and Italy, and the Triple Entente of France, Britain, and Russia. The system, as many people at the time saw clearly, had grown so tightly organized that there was almost no free play left, and with the wisdom of hindsight we can now see that after 1900 almost any crisis might have led to war. Sarajevo was the one that did.

This state of international politics was christened by an English liberal, Lowes Dickinson, "the international anarchy." It was, however, no chaos, but a highly organized rivalry, "anarchical" only in the sense that there was no higher authority to put a stop to the rivalry. In concrete instances, two or more powers wanted the same piece of land, as a territorial addition or as a sphere of influence. France and Great Britain both wanted Egypt; France and Germany both wanted Morocco; Russia and Austria-Hungary both wanted control over the Balkans; Russia and Japan both wanted Manchuria; and so on around the map. Compromises were made, lands and spheres of influence were shared, but in the long run there simply wasn't enough to go around.

In this scramble a rough distinction can be made between the "haves," or "saturated powers," and the "have-nots," the powers that had not done well in previous competition. Notable among the "have-nots" were Germany and Italy, which had not been united nations when the other great powers were expanding overseas, and which did not yet have in 1870 colonial empires. They had to take the leavings in Africa and Oceania. The "have-nots" were not always aggressors, nor were the "haves" always the defenders of the status quo. The latter, even powerful Britain, wanted some things that others wanted. Yet in these years Germany, newly united, with a rapidly growing population, with an efficient industrial economy, appears as the power with most to gain by disturbing the system radically. Germany appears, to use a morally neutral word, as the main "perturber." And Great Britain, as the old-established leader of the world, rich, powerful, and full of prestige, appears as the main defender of the world-system of states as embodied in international law, or, more cynically, as the defender of things-as-they-are.

The Role of Public Opinion

We have in this outline used the shorthand of names like "Great Britain" or "Germany." But these are mere symbols, as colored blobs on a map are symbols, for millions of human beings whose desires somehow do add up into the actions of states, did add up to the war of 1914. In no state were the millions all in agreement. There were Germans who wanted no bit of Africa or any other piece of land. There were Englishmen who, far from being content with Britain's place in the world, wanted more, wanted Britain to be for the whole round world what Rome had been for the Mediterranean world in the first centuries of the Christian Era, hoped eventually to kill off all but Englishmen (and perhaps Scotsmen) in a fine Darwinian struggle. There were everywhere in Europe at least a few absolute pacifists, men who were determined under any conditions to refuse to fight, men who once war broke out became "conscientious objectors." We must not think of the war and the events that led up to it as simply the work of a few men at the top in each nation, the professional soldiers, the villainous diplomats in frock coats and striped trousers. In all the countries, there was a spectrum that ran from the militarist to the pacifist, through all shades of opinion.

But the outbreak of the war saw in each belligerent nation a broad national public opinion in support of the government. In 1914 some men marched to war convinced that war was a beneficial thing. Here is the account of a young German on the last train out of Switzerland before the outbreak of war:

An elderly gentleman was sitting in our compartment. He began to talk to us at once, as if we were intimate acquaintances. On the back of his hotel bill he had added up the numerical strength of the European armies and balanced them against each other. He compared the two totals and assured my mother that the spiritual qualities of the German troops compensated for the numerical superiority of the Russians. For in this war spiritual qualities alone would decide the day, and Germany's spiritual qualities were the best in Europe. As a university professor he knew that our youth were ready for the fray, and full of ideals. At last the hour had come when our people could enter on its great world mission. He himself had been almost cast into despair by the crass materialism of the last few years —particularly in the lower classes; but at last life had regained an ideal significance. The great virtues of humanity, which had found their last refuge in Germany—fidelity, patriotism, readiness to die for an idea—these were triumphing now over the trading and shop-keeping spirit. This was the providential lightning flash that would clear the air. . . .*

German Aspirations

The Germans were led by their Kaiser, William II, who had come to the throne in 1888. The "revisionist" historians have been able to show that in the hectic five weeks after the assassination at Sarajevo the Kaiser, contrary to world opinion at the time, did not work

* Ernst Glaeser, *Class of 1902*, Willa and Edwin Muir, trans. (London, 1929), 171-172.

steadily for war, that indeed he tried to prevent war. But he cannot be even partially absolved for the long-term, for the ultimate, causes of the war. In the decisive years between 1888 and 1914 he was the posturing, aggressive leader of patriotic expansion, the "White Knight" leading his people to glory (see also Chapter XV). He was perhaps more of a figurehead, less of an actual maker of policy than the world took him to be, but still a willing and effective figurehead for expansionists.

German ambitions and German fears produced an intense hatred of Britain, a hatred mixed with envy and a sense of inferiority, a hatred that focused on the English upper classes, perfectly tailored, serene in effortless superiority, the favorite children of fortune. Many a German tourist, perhaps quite accidentally given an Italian hotel room inferior to that given a traveling Englishman, would come home burning with indignation at this personal evidence that Germany was being denied its place in the sun. In the German navy, in the years before the war, there was a simple toast in the officers' mess: *Der Tag* (The Day). Everyone knew that this was the day of the declaration of war between Germany and Britain. These feelings are all condensed in the famous "Hymn of Hate" of the German poet Ernst Lissauer:

We will never forego our hate,
Hate by water and hate by land,
Hate of the head and hate of the hand,
Hate of the hammer and hate of the Crown.
Hate of the seventy millions choking down.
We love as one, we hate as one,
We have one foe and one alone:
England!*

British Aspirations

Few Englishmen returned this hate; the English were still on top. Yet as the years wore on, the expensive race between Britain and Germany in naval armaments continued; in incident after incident German and British diplomats took opposite sides; and—this seemed especially important to the hard-headed—German wares of all sorts undersold British wares in Europe, in North and South America, and in Asia. Englishmen began to think that someone ought to teach these ill-mannered Germans a lesson. Moreover, they had begun to worry about their own position of

---

* Ernst Lissauer, "A Chant of Hate Against England," trans. by Barbara Henderson, in Burton E. Stevenson, comp., *The Home Book of Verse*, 3rd ed. (New York, 1918), II, 2549-2550.

Berlin crowds singing "Deutschland über Alles," 1914.

prosperity and leadership. In India, the greatest possession of the English, it was clear already that great concessions toward self-government would have to be made to the natives. Close at home the Irish question was in one of its most acute phases, with Ulster in arms against the proposed Home Rule. Englishmen were worried about their obsolescent industrial plant, their apparent inability to produce goods as cheaply and as efficiently as the Germans; they were self-critical about their failures as salesmen abroad, their stodgy self-satisfaction.

A great many Britishers thought of themselves as good liberals and good internationalists, anxious to preserve the peace and the decencies of international life. Many were radicals and Labor party men committed to pacifism. The coming of war in 1914 was to show how thoroughly almost all these men identified Great Britain and righteousness. As for the bulk of the conservatives, they were as nationalist as in any other great country. In Britain, their nationalism attached itself to the Empire, to the "White Man's Burden," to a whole set of symbols that the Germans found intolerable.

The Other Belligerents

In democratic France as in democratic England there was a wide spread of opinion on international politics. A numerous socialist Left was committed to pacifism and to the concept of a kind of international strike of workers at the threat of actual war. A more moderate group also opposed conventional patriotic aggressiveness toward the foreigner. Both among the men who conducted French foreign relations and among the general public, however, there remained right down to the eve of the Great War the embittered patriotism of the beaten. Frenchmen wanted *revanche*, revenge for the defeat of 1870.

They wanted Alsace-Lorraine back. For all these years, the statue representing Strasbourg among the cities of France in the Place de la Concorde in Paris was draped in black. With the warmest patriots, the organizers of patriotic societies, the editors of patriotic journals, this feeling for revenge was obsessive.

By the opening decade of the 1900's many observers thought that the new generation was losing its desire for revenge, that Frenchmen had at last decided to accept the verdict of 1870. But French diplomatists continued to preserve and strengthen the system of alliances against Germany, and in the excited weeks of July, 1914, it was clear that the French were ready for war.

In the other major belligerents, too, the ultimate decisions of governments won much popular support. Russians were filled with the "pooled self-esteem" of nationalism, were convinced that God and the right were on their side. Italians saw in war the chance to get *Italia Irredenta* (Trent, Trieste, and their surrounding lands) and still more territory from the Habsburg Monarchy. In the dual monarchy, as we have seen, the loyalty of subject nationalities could scarcely be counted on; but the dominant Germans of Austria and Magyars of Hungary welcomed the opportunity to put the troublesome Slavs in their place for good and all.

The Era of Bismarck, 1871-1890

The road to Sarajevo starts in 1871, at the Treaty of Frankfurt, where France was obliged to cede Alsace and Lorraine to the new German Empire. It was no straight road, but one of many twists and turnings, and few historians would now maintain that 1871 made 1914 inevitable. We cannot follow the road in detail, but we must map its main course.

For some twenty years Bismarck was its

chief engineer. In fairness to the Iron Chancellor, it must be said that during his last twenty years in office he sought peace, and indeed obtained it. Powerful elements in the new empire made it impossible for him to grant to France the same kind of generous peace he had given Austria in 1866. Yet Bismarck did try to salve the wound he knew France had suffered; he encouraged her to expand her empire in North Africa by the acquisition of Tunis in 1881, even though this offended the Italians, who also coveted Tunisia. But he feared a French attempt at revenge, and sought to isolate her diplomatically by building a series of alliances from which she was excluded. Germany, he insisted, was now a "saturated" power, and wanted nothing more in Europe; and in a famous phrase he insisted that all the Balkans were not worth "the bones of a single Pomeranian grenadier." Above all, he sought to keep on good terms with both Austria and Russia, and, what was much more difficult, to keep both these powers on good terms with each other. Since both wanted predominance in the Balkans, Bismarck's task was formidable.

As a result of the Turkish War of 1877-1878, the Russians succeeded briefly in setting up a greater Bulgaria as a kind of client state that brought Russian influence almost to the gates of Constantinople (see Chapter XV). Since both Britain and Austria-Hungary were unwilling to allow Russia this increase of power, Bismarck played host to a general European diplomatic congress at Berlin (1878), at which Russian gains were considerably pared down. Both Russia and Austria-Hungary were discontented over this compromise. Nevertheless, Bismarck soon laid the cornerstone of his diplomatic system by a defensive alliance with Austria-Hungary in 1879, an alliance that held right down to 1918. And he was able to make a secret treaty, the so-called League of the Three Emperors, which bound Germany, Russia, and Austria together. The three powers agreed to act together in dealings with Turkey, and to maintain friendly neutrality should any one of them be at war with a fourth power other than Turkey. Next, working skillfully on Italian annoyance over the French expansion in Tunis, Bismarck secured an alliance among Germany, Austria-Hungary, and Italy, directed chiefly against France. This was the famous Triple Alliance of 1882, often renewed, which on paper still existed in 1914.

On this series of tightropes Bismarck maintained a precarious balance through the 1880's. Chief in his mind was the danger that the Russians, always fearful of Austrian schemes in the Balkans, would desert him and ally themselves with France, still a great power and anxious to escape from the isolation that Bismarck had designed for her. In 1887, Russia did refuse to renew the League of the Three Emperors, but Bismarck was able to repair the breach for the moment by a secret Russo-German agreement known as the Re-insurance Treaty. The two promised each other neutrality in case either was involved in a war against a third power; but this neutrality was not to hold if Germany made an "aggressive" war against France or if Russia made an "aggressive" war against Austria. Since Russian nationalist agitation continued against both Austria and Germany, Bismarck in 1888 made public as a warning to Russia the terms of the Austro-German alliance, and allowed the main terms of the Triple Alliance to be known informally.

Formation of the Triple Entente, 1890-1907

Then in 1890 the young Emperor William II dismissed Bismarck. The Emperor's advisers, headed by Baron von Holstein, persuaded him not to renew the Re-insurance Treaty with Russia, in spite of Russian desire for such renewal.

Shortly afterward, what Bismarck had worked so hard to prevent came about. After lengthy negotiations, Russia and France in 1894 came together in an alliance that ended French isolation. It was formally a defensive alliance, in which each was to come to the aid of the other if Germany or Austria made "aggressive" war against either, and it was accompanied by the necessary military agreements between the two general staffs. Against the Triple Alliance there now stood, quite openly, a Dual Alliance of France and Russia. England as yet remained technically uninvolved.

The next great stage in the tightening network of alliances was to bring Great Britain in against the Central Powers. Britain had long kept her hands free on the Continent, refusing formal alliances. In the 1890's, her prime minister, Lord Salisbury, asserted that hers was a policy of "splendid isolation." But in the two decades after the accession of Kaiser William II

Britain was to commit herself to a formal alliance with Japan and to an "understanding" (in French, *entente*) with France and Russia. What chiefly drove Britain to these actions was the naval race with Germany and the rapid worsening of Anglo-German relations, a worsening even more evident perhaps at the level of public opinion than at the level of formal diplomacy.

A good concrete instance of this rising hostility is the Kruger telegram of 1896, in which the Kaiser congratulated President Kruger of the Boer Republic of Transvaal on the defeat of the Jameson raid (see p. 553). It may be that the Kaiser and his circle hoped at bottom that this gesture would be taken by the English government as a kind of polite and permissible diplomatic blackmail, an evidence of how great a nuisance the German government could be to the British if it were not on their side. But the British press took the telegram as an unbearable insult, and the Ger-

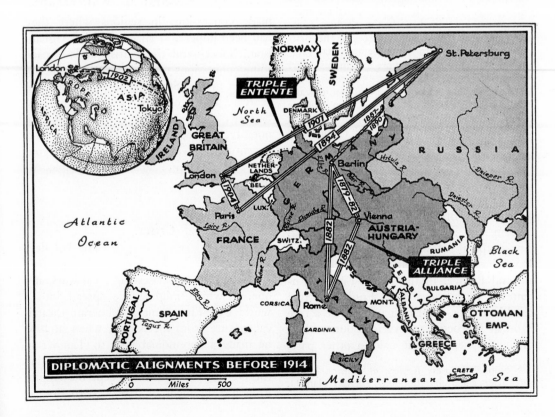

DIPLOMATIC ALIGNMENTS BEFORE 1914

man press replied angrily to British anger. Here is a sample from the dignified and conservative London *Saturday Review*, a passage that shows how clear the shape of things to come already was to the knowing:

It is not only the German Emperor that is in the dark as to the strength of Great Britain. The 'Times' published on Monday a letter from 'A German in England,' declaring that Germany hates England because she cannot win her alliance, and then proceeds, 'Europe is a camp, and if it came to fighting, England, with all her wealth and position, would rank as a second-class Power, because she has not the number of soldiers, nor sufficient armament for a great struggle.' And, therefore, we are told, 'with that growing hatred of England on the Continent a kind of contempt for her has grown.' But this 'German in England' contradicts himself. If England is only a second-class Power, why should Germany get so angry because she cannot secure her as an ally? Germany does not rage against Spain because Spain has not joined the Triple Alliance, nor does the Kaiser write insulting messages about the Portuguese. The truth is that German military pride, combined with the trading German's envy of British commerce and the British Empire, make him try to believe that England is a second-class Power; but in his heart he knows better. He knows that now, even more than at the end of the Napoleonic wars, England is the Arbiter of Europe. Her alliance would make the Triple Alliance invincible, and were her aid given to Russia and France, the German hegemony on the Continent would be doomed.[*]

It was fear of Russia rather than fear of Germany, however, that inspired Britain to make the first break with formal isolationism, the alliance with Japan in 1902. The outbreak of war between Russia and Japan hastened negotiations between Britain and France. In the Anglo-French Entente of 1904 France gave England a free hand in Egypt, England gave France a free hand in Morocco, and various outstanding difficulties between the two in other parts

of the world were ironed out. More important, the base was laid for general collaboration between the two in international affairs. Only six years previously, in 1898, there had been a grave flare-up of the traditional colonial rivalry between France and England when a French column was met by a British column at Fashoda, in the disputed Sudan territory of the upper Nile Valley. Fashoda caused quite as big an outbreak of fury in the French and the British press as the Kruger telegram only two years before had caused in the German and the British press. Yet Fashoda left wounds much less deep than the Kruger telegram; the contemporary press is not always a faithful guide to the climate of public opinion, let alone to that of professional diplomacy.

The final stage in aligning the two camps came in 1907 when Russia, chastened by her defeat at the hand of Japan and encouraged by the French, came to an agreement with Great Britain. Both countries made concessions in regions where they had been imperialist rivals—Persia, Afghanistan, Tibet—and the British at last made some concessions toward the Russian desire to open up the Straits. The agreement was scarcely based on any genuine sympathy between the two peoples, for the British, notably, had been Russophobic for well over a century. Nevertheless, it did round out the Triple Entente against the Triple Alliance.

A Decade of Crises, 1905-1914

The last decade before 1914 is a series of crises and local wars, any one of which might have spread into a world war. First came a deliberate theatrical gesture from the Kaiser, when in 1905 he made a ceremonial visit to Tangier in Morocco as a way of telling the world that the Germans would not accept the Anglo-French assignment of Morocco to France.

---

[*] "Notes," *Saturday Review of Politics, Literature, Science and Art* (London), LXXXI (Jan. 11, 1896), 27.

The net effect was to tighten the entente between France and Britain, for the British indicated clearly to the French that they would support them. Indeed at this time there began the informal military and naval conferences between the British and the French that the French, at least, believed "committed" the British to armed support if the Germans attacked. Although the French Foreign Minister, Delcassé, a partisan of firm policy toward the Germans, was forced out of office, even this partial victory did the Germans no good. French public opinion was infuriated by this intervention in their domestic politics. In the end, a general international conference at Algeciras in Spain (1906) backed up the French, who went ahead with their plans for a protectorate in Morocco. At Algeciras American diplomatic influence was used on the side of France; the United States, too, was beginning to emerge from its own variety of isolationism.

A decisive turn of the road toward Sarajevo came in 1908. Austria formally proclaimed the annexation of the old Turkish provinces of Bosnia-Herzegovina, which she had occupied since 1878. Austria's decisive act infuriated the Serbs, who wanted to add Bosnia to their state. It also infuriated the Russians, all the more since few Russians knew that their diplomat Izvolski had in fact made an informal agreement with the Austrian minister Aehrenthal in September, 1908, to accept the annexation of Bosnia-Herzegovina in return for Austrian support of an agreement permitting Russian warships to use the Straits. In the event, Austria did the annexing, but Russia did not get her use of the Straits. This wound to Russian pride was profound.

War now broke out on the edges of Europe. In 1911, the Italians sent troops to Tripoli, the poorest part of North Africa, but at least a part that had not yet been taken from the Turks by other Europeans. Then in 1912 war spread to the Balkans. Nationalist revolutionaries called the

"Young Turks" had risen successfully against the Sultan in 1908. The Young Turks wanted the modern industrial achievements of the West, they wanted its political apparatus of representative government, and they wanted above all to have Turks respected, admired, and feared as members of a thoroughly modern *nation*. Some of their intellectuals followed the nineteenth-century Romantic pattern back into the past, where they found, not the nomad Turks of history, but fine sturdy "Turanians" from the inspiring steppes of Central Asia. There was even a "Pan-Turanian" movement, strangest of the "Pan" movements, which sought to group Magyars, Turks, and the Turkish peoples of Central Asia, who were all only distantly related to each other, as children of a common destiny. No wonder the Habsburgs were alarmed! It began to look as if those who hoped to divide up Turkey had better hurry while the dividing was good. In the hurry, the world got swept into the War of 1914, the preliminary stages of which were the Balkan Wars.

In the first of these wars, in 1912, an alliance of Bulgaria, Serbia, and Greece beat the Turks, and started the process of dividing up most of European Turkey. But here Austria imposed an absolute veto on granting Serbia territories that would give her access to the Adriatic Sea. Meanwhile, the victors quarreled among themselves, and in the Second Balkan War, of 1913, the Greeks and Serbs, joined by the Rumanians and the all-but-beaten Turks, readily defeated the Bulgarians. Turkey got back some of her territory in Europe. But the Balkans were in a state of unusual uncertainty and bad blood when Francis Ferdinand was assassinated.

The Final Crisis, July–August, 1914

There are millions of words in print about the proximate causes of World War I and the six weeks between

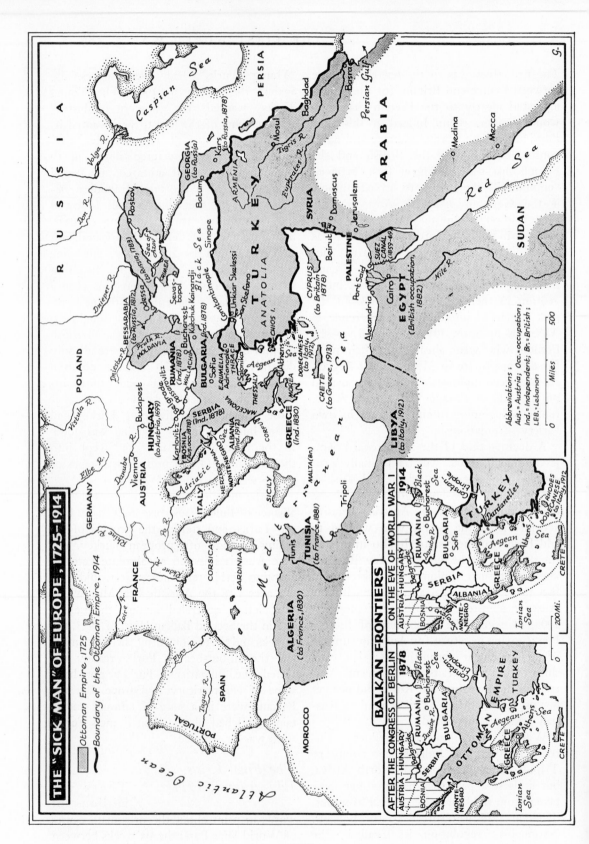

THE "SICK MAN" OF EUROPE, 1725–1914

Ottoman Empire, 1725
Boundary of the Ottoman Empire, 1914

BALKAN FRONTIERS

ON THE EVE OF WORLD WAR I
1914

AFTER THE CONGRESS OF BERLIN
1878

the assassination on June 28 and the general spread of war on August 4, when Britain came in against Germany. Thanks to the end of the rule of Hohenzollern, Habsburg, and Romanov houses as a result of the war, the secret archives were thrown open much sooner than would be normal. And in the pressure of debate over the question of war guilt in the 1920's, even the victorious countries, Britain, France, and the United States, opened their archives to a surprising extent. These are weeks for which documents, often telegrams, can be dated by the hour and minute. These are weeks in which messages are constantly crossing each other, confusing things hopelessly. These are weeks in which professional diplomatists and statesmen, egged on by an excited—and it must be said often *irresponsible*—press, nevertheless tried for the most part to master the crisis without recourse to war.

The diplomats and statesmen were drawn into war because almost all of them believed that they faced an alternative worse than war, a defeat or humiliation for their nation. Austria believed correctly, though positive proof was then lacking, that the Serbian government had some foreknowledge of the plot of the assassin Princip and should therefore have given her warning. For this reason, and also because she wished to check the Serb agitation that had long been unsettling the Yugoslav peoples living in the dual monarchy, Austria decided to make stiff demands on Serbia after the assassination of Francis Ferdinand. Before doing so, however, she consulted her German ally, who promised to support whatever policy Austria might adopt toward Serbia. This German response has became famous as a diplomatic "blank check," duly signed by Germany in advance with the precise amount to be filled in later by Austria.

Thus encouraged, the Austrian government, on July 23, sent Serbia an ultimatum to be answered within forty-eight hours.

The ultimatum made many separate demands, which added up to an insistence that Serbia and Serb propagandists keep their hands off Habsburg territories and populations, now and in the future. Most of the demands the Serbs accepted, at least in principle; but they refused to accept two of them, which would have permitted Austrian police or military men to take, on Serbian soil, an actual part in a Serbian investigation of Princip's plot. Probably Serbia had some assurance that Russia was willing to give her a kind of "blank check," and would assist her if the partial refusal of the ultimatum led to war. The Serbian reply, therefore, was a little less virtuously honest than it seemed to be to most of the world in July, 1914. Still, the Austrian ultimatum appears to have been couched in terms deliberately unacceptable to the Serbs, and the Serb reply seems to have been a base for more consideration than it got from the Austrians. Because the Serbs had not accepted the whole of the ultimatum, Austria declared war on July 28, after

Princip, immediately after the assassination at Sarajevo, June 28, 1914.

turning down as inconsistent with national honor a European conference proposed by the British foreign minister, Sir Edward Grey.

From now on, the German diplomatists, backed by William II and actually resisting the German military men, tried to hold back their Austrian ally. It is impossible to clear William from responsibility for the German "blank check," which had emboldened Austria and had perhaps been designed by Germany to do just that. Now, however, the Germans certainly tried to revoke the check and made a last effort to stop the spread of the war. Since Russia was beginning the full mobilization of her armies, the Kaiser, on July 29, told Tsar Nicholas II in a personal telegram of the German attempt to get the Austrians to compromise. Apparently this telegram served to get full Russian mobilization modified into partial mobilization and to get direct Austro-Russian talks resumed on July 30. For a brief moment it looked as if the crisis might be overcome.

But mobilization was not easy in Russia, a country of long distances, poor communications, and bureaucratic red tape, and the Russian military feared that their enemies would get the jump on them. At the last moment Russia made her mobilization general again. Germany at once insisted that all Russian mobilization cease, and, when it continued, ordered her own at 4:00 P.M. on July 31, and declared war on Russia at 7:00 P.M. the same day. France, meantime, had determined to stand by her Russian ally, now evidently about to be attacked, and had mobilized at 3:55 P.M. the same day. Germany declared war on France on August 3.

Britain was still wavering. Although her entente with France did not legally bind the two nations together, it had led, as we have just seen, to the very close co-ordination of defense plans by the French and British military and naval staffs. Perhaps,

then, Britain would have come into the war anyway. What made her entry certain was the German violation of the neutrality of Belgium, which both Britain and Prussia had joined with other powers to guarantee in 1839. The German military were determined to take decisive action in the West and to knock France out of the war before the Russians could get their slow-moving armies into action. Accordingly, German plans called for a sweep through a corner of Belgium to avoid the heavily fortified and hilly terrain in northeastern France. On August 2, the Germans had notified Belgium that they intended to march through her territory, though they promised to respect her territorial integrity in the peace to come.

Belgium rejected this demand, and appealed to the other guaranteeing powers. Sir Edward Grey, though opposed in the British cabinet by two pacifists, seized firmly on this ground of action, and on August 4 Britain declared war on Germany. The German chancellor, Bethmann-Hollweg, informed of this action, let slip the phrase that Britain had gone to war just for a "scrap of paper"—the treaty of 1839 that guaranteed Belgium against invasion. This unhappy phrase, seized upon by the press of the world, not only solidified British opinion in favor of the war but was responsible more than any other single factor for the charge of war guilt laid against Germany.

The Entry of Other Powers

By August 6, when Austria declared war on Russia, all the members of the Triple Alliance and the Triple Entente had come to blows, with the exception of Italy, who, however, had never really been a good ally of Austria because of the Irredentist issue. Italy, refusing to consider herself bound by the Triple Alliance, declared her neutrality. The Central Powers of Germany and Austria-Hungary, then, stood against the Allies—Russia, France, Britain, and Serbia. Japan came in on the side of the Allies late in August, and Turkey came in on the Austro-German side in November, 1914. After competing territorial offers from both Allies and Central Powers, a divided Italy finally joined the Allies in May, 1915.

As the war turned into a stalemate, in the winter of 1916-1917, the Germans made the desperate decision to try to get at Great Britain by the only way that seemed available. They would use their submarines to cut off the food and raw materials that came to the British Isles from overseas, and without which their peoples would have starved. This unrestricted submarine warfare meant sinking American ships that Americans held were quite legally bringing such supplies to England and France, in accord with international law. On April 6, 1917, the United States completed the roster of great powers involved in the conflict by declaring war on Germany.

Dissident Americans, then and since, have declared that the United States was enticed into the war by the wicked few—by sentimental lovers of England or France; by bankers who had lent money to the Allies and wanted to protect their investments; by silly idealists who agreed with President Wilson in wishing to "make the world safe for democracy"; and, of course, by scheming Allied diplomatists, corrupt Europeans who held a strange fascination over American "babes in the wood." Yet it is debatable that the United States would ever have entered the war had there been no unrestricted submarine warfare by the Germans. The Germans considered even food sent in American ships to England to be contraband of war, and they torpedoed American ships without warning. To avoid war, therefore, the United States would have had to forbid all American ships to

sail to any European port or perhaps any port outside the States from which goods might have been transshipped to the Allies. In short, we should have had to put an embargo on all American shipping to foreign ports, or else put up with German torpedoes. Neither course would seem to have been acceptable to a majority of Americans in 1917. Since many of the Latin-American states followed the lead of the United States, there were all told from 1914 through 1918 something over sixty separate declarations of war or severances of relations. It was indeed a world war.

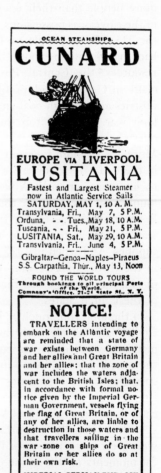

Two advertisements that appeared in New York City newspapers, 1915. The sinking of the British liner, Lusitania, by a German submarine (May, 1915) claimed more than one thousand lives, some of them American.

III: The Course of the War

Resources
of the Belligerents

As the opposing nations lined up in 1914, the Allies had an overwhelming superiority in total population and resources. Germany, Austria-Hungary, and Turkey had in their own continental lands not over 150,000,000 people; Britain, France, Russia, and Italy in their own continental lands had at least 125,000,000 more people than their enemies. Moreover, in their overseas possessions, which included the 315,000,000 people of India, the Allies had many millions more. As for material resources, the Central Powers had, especially in Germany, admirably organized industries and enough coal and iron to fight a long war. But here too the statistics were overwhelmingly in favor of the Allies. Moreover, though German submarines and, in the early days, surface raiders were able to interrupt seriously Allied lines of communication overseas, on the whole the Allies were still able to get from these overseas sources indispensable food and other supplies. And when in 1917 a beaten Russia, in the throes of a revolution, ceased to be of aid, the Allies gained the great resources of the United States.

In the long run, much as in the American Civil War, the side with the most men and materials wore down its enemies and won the war. But it was by no means the uneven struggle that the statistics of total population and material resources would indicate. Again as in the Civil War, the weaker side had initially important advantages, won great victories, seemed indeed at critical moments on the point of final victory. Not until the very last months before the armistice of November, 1918, could the Allies really feel confident of victory.

Geography gave Germany and Austria the advantages of being side by side, and of having interior lines of communication, which enabled them to make rapid transfers of troops from one threatened front to another. Though the Germans and Austrians did not always see eye to eye, they did speak the same language, and had for long been firmly allied; moreover, Germany was the predominant partner, and the ultimate decisions were made by her general staff. Most important of all, Germany in particular was more ready for war than were her enemies. She had an efficiently organized military machine and a good stock of munitions, her industry could be readily geared to war, her plans were complete, her people were united in support of the war, and they enjoyed the great psychological advantage of being on the offensive, of carrying the war to the enemy. Indeed, no important part of the war was ever fought on German soil; it ended, with important results for later history, with the German army still in being, with the soil of the German Fatherland still uninvaded.

By contrast, geography had separated the western Allies from Russia. German control of the Baltic and Turkish control of the Straits proved throughout the war a serious obstacle to communication between Russia and her allies, who had to take roundabout and difficult routes through Archangel in Arctic waters and even through Vladivostok on the Pacific at the end of the long, slow, single-track Trans-Siberian railway. For the Allies, transfer of troops between eastern and western fronts was militarily almost impossible, even had it been politically possible. It was not, however, politically possible, and here is one of the greatest weaknesses of the Allies.

Russia, Britain, and France had only recently come together, as friendly powers and not as close allies. Each of them was a strongly marked nationality, having many sources of conflict with the others. They had no long tradition of mutual co-operation, no common language. France and England were democracies, and though the peoples of both rallied firmly to the national cause in 1914, they were unused to the kind of firm, centralized, political and military control that is necessary in war. As for unified military planning and administration, it was never achieved between Russia and the western Allies. Even among Britain, France, and the United States on the Western Front, it was not achieved until the French General Foch was appointed commander-in-chief in 1918, and then only imperfectly.

Finally, of the three great Allied powers in 1914, only France was ready with a good big land force, and France, with only 39 millions of people as against Germany's 65 millions, was the weakest of the Allies in manpower. Britain was indeed prepared on the sea, and her navy was an invaluable asset; but it could not be of direct use against the German army. Russia had universal military service and an army great in numbers. But she had vast distances to overcome, an inadequate railway system, a relatively undeveloped heavy industry, an army whose morale had been shaken by the recent defeat at the hands of the Japanese, a people whose morale had been shaken by the recent abortive revolution, a military and a political organization riddled with inefficiency and corruption.

The Western Front: German Offensive

The Germans had a plan, the so-called Schlieffen plan, which they immediately put into execution. It called for a holding operation on the left, with a strong right wing that was to advance swiftly through Belgium, take Paris, and then fall on the rear of the French armies.

While this great enveloping movement in the west swiftly eliminated France, relatively weaker German forces, it was planned, would hold down the slow-moving Russians. With France beaten, the Germans could turn their full force against the Russians and beat them. Then there would be only the British left, and the future would take care of them.

The German plan almost succeeded. It failed for two reasons, to which a great number of separate tactical factors contributed. In the first place, the German chief of staff, Moltke, had seriously modified the Schlieffen plan by weakening the critical right wing, partly in order to send divisions to the east, which, ironically, arrived there too late to participate in the disastrous defeat of the Russians. By the time the German right wing neared Paris, it had too few divisions to take the capital and then roll up the French army to the eastward. In the second place, the French, with help from the Belgians and British, exploited the German weakness at the critical moment and stopped the drive short of its goals. The Germans lost the first great battle, known as the Battle of the Marne.

The German advance, which had been almost continuous since August 2, had been stopped. In the next few weeks the opposing forces engaged in what came to be called the "race for the Channel," with the Germans trying to outflank the Allies and get the Channel ports, thus shutting the short sea passage to future British reinforcements. They failed here, too, and throughout the war the ports of Calais and Boulogne, and indeed a small southwestern corner of Belgium, were to remain in Allied hands—a valuable military advantage.

By the autumn of 1914 the Western Front was thus stabilized. For over three hundred airline miles between the Channel and the Swiss border near Basel, hundreds of thousands of soldiers faced each other in

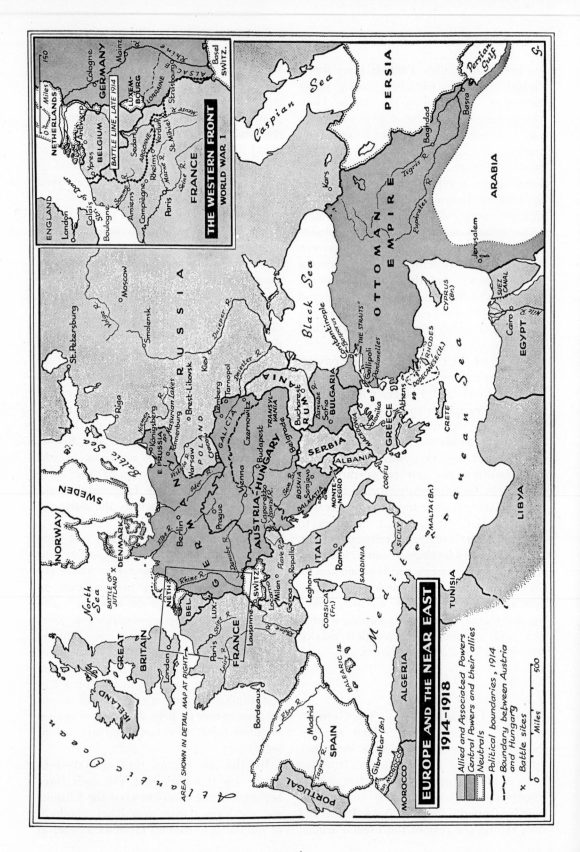

THE WESTERN FRONT
WORLD WAR I

EUROPE AND THE NEAR EAST
1914–1918

Allied and Associated Powers
Central Powers and their allies
Neutrals
Political boundaries, 1914
Boundary between Austria
  and Hungary
x   Battle sites

Miles
0   500

AREA SHOWN IN DETAIL MAP AT RIGHT

a continuous line that was full of bends called "salients." Both sides "dug in" and formed a series of rough fortifications. The central feature of these fortifications was a series of parallel trenches deep enough to conceal a man standing upright. As time went on, these trenches were greatly improved; they were supplied with parapets, machine-gun nests, and an elaborate network of approach trenches and strong points, until the whole front became one immense fortification. Thousands of local actions in the four years of trench warfare shifted the lines here and there, and a series of partial break-throughs occurred on both sides. But on the whole the lines held, and the actual fighting in the west was confined to an extraordinarily narrow, though very long, field.

On this Western Front the ultimate decision was reached; but there were many other fronts. Some of them were disparagingly called "the side-shows" by those who advocated concentrating in the west. Yet in perspective we can now see that they all played a part in determining the final result. Since, over the long pull, the Germans had fewer men and resources, the dispersal of energies that these "side-shows" called for, and the continuous need to bolster their Austrian and Turkish and Balkan allies, were major factors in their defeat. For the sake of clarity, we shall here take up these other fronts separately and briefly, but the reader must never forget that for the belligerents the war was a whole; its wide-flung theaters were mutually dependent, with each one influencing the others.

The Eastern Front The Eastern Front, where the Russians faced both the Germans and the Austrians, was no mere side-show. Millions of men were involved on both sides, and had the Russians not held out, as they did, until the end of 1917 the Allies in the west could never have withstood the rein-

forcements that the Germans and Austrians would have been able to send to France and Italy. The war in the east was more a war of movement than the war in the west. But even in the east there were long periods of stalemate, especially during the winters, periods when the opposing armies faced each other in long lines of improvised fortifications.

The Russians began well. Against the exposed Austrian salient of Galicia (Austria's share of the eighteenth-century partitions of Poland), the Russians threw in vast masses of men. They pushed the Austrians out of the oil-rich lands around Lemberg (later the Polish Lwów, now the Russian Lvov), and by the end of September, 1914, they had reached the northern ends of some of the passes leading into Hungary through the Carpathian Mountains. Against the Germans, who also had to defend in East Prussia a salient surrounded on the east and south by Russian territory, the Russians won the Battle of Gumbinnen, in August, 1914, and so alarmed the German general staff that the Germans felt obliged to reorganize their eastern command. General von Ludendorff, under the nominal command of his senior, Von Hindenburg, and aided by a brilliant junior, Von Hoffmann, turned successively against the two Russian armies, which were attempting a pincers movement. Late in August, at Tannenberg, the Germans decisively defeated a Russian army under Samsonov, who committed suicide. And early in September they won another decisive victory against the Russians at the Masurian lakes, thus clearing East Prussia of Russians.

The Germans' hard-pressed Austrian allies to the south were by now clamoring for help, and the Western Front was still demanding men. Hindenburg and his aides had to do their best with what they had. In a series of hard-fought battles in Poland they succeeded in relieving the pressure on the Austrians. The end of the year 1914 found the Austrians still hanging on in

Galicia, and found the Germans in a good position to push eastward from East Prussian and Polish bases. In two great joint offensives in May and July, 1915, the Central Powers won substantial successes; they inflicted severe losses on the Russians from which the Russians never really recovered. At the end of the year 1915 the battle line ran roughly from near Riga, deep in the Baltic provinces of Russia, to the eastern edge of Galicia at Tarnopol and Czernowitz.

In 1916, the Russians, with a new commander, General Brusilov, undertook a great new offensive against the Austrians in the south. The Russian need to bolster their failing morale would probably have made some action necessary, but the Russians were also being pressed by the Allies to do something to help the Italians, who were threatened by the Austrians in the region of Trent. It seems likely that the Brusilov offensive was begun too soon, without adequate preparation. It scored a striking success at first; in places, the Russians drove the Austrians back some eighty miles, and they took large numbers of prisoners. But once more the Germans came to the rescue; with fresh troops transferred from the west, they halted Brusilov before he had won a decisive success.

It was from the backwash of this defeat that the Russian Revolution, which began early in March, 1917, was born. In the moderate phase of that uprising, before the Bolshevik revolution of November, 1917, Brusilov undertook one last desperate offensive. But he was soon checked, and the way was open for the Bolsheviks to carry out their promise to make peace. By the end of 1917, Russia was out of the war. She was forced by the Central Powers to sign the extraordinarily punitive Peace of Brest-Litovsk (March, 1918), by which she lost her Polish territories, her Baltic provinces, the entire Ukraine, Finland, and some lands in the Caucasus. The Caucasian lands went to Turkey; most of the others came under the temporary domination of Austria and Germany.

The Italian Front

In April, 1915, Italy concluded with Britain, France and Russia the secret Treaty of London, which promised the Italians their long-sought-for Trent and Trieste, and other lands at Austrian and Turkish expense. In May, the Italians formally declared war on Austria-Hungary (they did not declare war on Germany until August, 1916), and a new front was added along the Austro-Italian frontier at the head of the Adriatic. Much of this front was too mountainous for effective action, and it was pretty much confined to some sixty miles along the Isonzo River. For two years there was a series of bloody but indecisive actions along this river that at least pinned down several hundred thousand Austrian troops. Then in the late autumn of 1917, with Russia already beaten, came the blow that very nearly knocked Italy out. Once again the Germans supplied the propulsive force. Ludendorff, now in supreme command, sent six German divisions to the Isonzo. The Germans and Austrians broke through at Caporetto, and sent the Italians into a retreat across the Venetian plains, a retreat that was really a rout. French and British reinforcements were hastily rushed across the Alps, but what did most to stop the Austro-Germans was probably the grave difficulty, under modern conditions of warfare, of supplying mass armies of infantry in rapid advance. The Italians were able to hold along the line of the Piave River, almost at the Po.

Balkan and Turkish Fronts

Serbia's part in the outbreak of the war had insured that there would be a Balkan front from the start.

The Austrians failed here also, and although in December, 1914, they did manage to take the Serbian capital, Belgrade, they were driven out again. Bulgaria, wooed by both sides, finally came in with the Central Powers in the autumn of 1915. The Germans sent troops and a general, von Mackensen, under whom the Serbs were finally beaten. The remnant of their armies was driven to take refuge on the island of Corfu in neutral Greece. To counter this blow in the Balkans, the Allies had already landed a few divisions in the Greek town of Saloniki, and had established a front in Macedonia. The Greeks themselves were divided into two groups. One was headed by King Constantine, who at bottom was sympathetic with the Central Powers, but who for the moment was seeking only to maintain Greek neutrality. The other was a pro-Ally group headed by the able old politician Venizelos. Although the Allies rode roughshod over formal notions of Greek neutrality, Venizelos did not get firmly into the saddle until June, 1917, when Allied pressure compelled King Constantine to abdicate in favor of his second son, Alexander.

Meanwhile Rumania, whom the Russians had been trying to lure into the war, finally yielded to promises of great territorial gains at the expense of Austria-Hungary and came in on the Allied side late in August, 1916, a most inopportune time. Stiffened by German help, the Austrians swept through Rumania and by January, 1917, held most of this oil-rich country. When the Russians made the separate Peace of Brest-Litovsk with the Germans in March, 1918, the Rumanians were obliged to make cessions of territory to Bulgaria, and to grant a lease of oil lands to Germany.

In spite of the formal accession of Greece, the Macedonian front remained in a stalemate until the summer of 1918, when, with American troops pouring rapidly into France, the Allied military leaders decided they could afford to build up their forces in Saloniki. The investment paid well, for under the leadership of the French general, Franchet d'Esperey, the Allied armies on this front were the first to break the enemy completely. The French, British, Serbs, and Greeks began a great advance on September 15, 1918, all along the line from the Adriatic to the Bulgarian frontier. They forced the Bulgarians to conclude an armistice on September 30, and by early November they had crossed the Danube in several places. The armistice in the west on November 11 found the tricolor of France, with the flags of many allies, well on its way to Vienna. This hark-back to Napoleon helped inspire in the French a somewhat unfounded confidence that they were once more the dominant nation on the continent of Europe.

The most interesting of the "sideshows" was one that had important repercussions in World War II. With the entry of Turkey into the war in November, 1914, and with the Western Front capable of being held against the Germans by the French alone, a group of British military and political leaders advanced the idea that British strength should be put into amphibious operations somewhere in the Aegean area. A steady drive could also be made overland toward Vienna and Berlin through territory where the Central Powers were not expecting an attack in force. The great exponent of this "Eastern Plan" was Winston Churchill, First Lord of the Admiralty. The British decided to try the plan. The point of attack chosen was the Dardanelles, the more westerly of the two straits that separate the Black Sea from the Aegean. The campaign is known as the "Gallipoli campaign" from the long narrow peninsula on the European side of the Straits which was one of the keys to the whole action. Here Allied victory would have had the additional advantage of opening communication with Russia via the Black Sea.

In March, 1915, the British and French fleets tried to force the Straits, but they abandoned the attempt somewhat prematurely when several ships struck mines. Later landings of British, Australian, New Zealand, and French troops at various points on both Asian and European shores of the Dardanelles were poorly co-ordinated and badly backed up. They met with fierce and effective resistance from the Turks—a junior officer named Mustafa Kemal greatly distinguishing himself—and in the end they had to be abandoned. Russia remained sealed in by the Straits all during the war. But Churchill continued to believe that the Dardanelles plan had failed, not because it was a bad plan, but because it had not been carried out with determination. And in the Second World War he was to revive, against American military opinion, something of his old plan, which became known as the plan to strike at the "soft underbelly" of the Axis.

The Near East
and the Colonies

A whole series of fronts throughout the world was involved in what we may call the colonial "clean-up," the subduing of the German overseas empire and of the outlying parts of the Turkish Empire. The Turks, trained and in part officered by German experts, often resisted effectively. In Mesopotamia, in April, 1916, they forced the surrender of the British general, Townshend, who had landed at Basra from India in 1915 and had marched up the Tigris-Euphrates Valley. But the Turks were never able to take the Suez Canal, nor to advance far into Russian Armenia. Moreover, the British were able to play on the Arabs' dislike for their Turkish suzerains. In a series of desert campaigns the romantic Colonel T. E. Lawrence, an Englishman who knew the Arabs intimately, played a leading part. By the end of 1917, the British held Bagdad and Jerusalem. In September, 1918, a great British offensive in Palestine was so successful that on Septem-

ber 30 the Turks concluded an armistice which took them out of the war.

These campaigns, fought in the lands that had been the cradles of western civilization, were of great importance in making the world we live in today. For from them came not only the independent Arab nations (Syria, Lebanon, Iraq, Jordan, Saudi Arabia, Egypt) but also the Jewish national state of Israel, to which these Arab states are so hostile. In November, 1917, in the Balfour Declaration, the British promised "the establishment in Palestine of a national home for the Jewish people." This promise bore fruit in the mandate of 1922 from the League of Nations, by which such a state was set up under British protection.

In the colonies the Germans, though cut off from the homeland by the British navy, fought well. In German East Africa they actually managed to hold out to the bitter end in a series of skillful campaigns, so that they still had forces in the field in East Africa on Armistice Day, 1918. But elsewhere they were fighting with inadequate bases and with inadequate forces, so that by the end of 1914 the British, Australians, South Africans, French, and Japanese had pretty well taken over the German overseas possessions.

The War at Sea

This brings us to a most important front—the war at sea. In the long pull, British sea power, reinforced by the French and later by the Italian and the American navies, once more proved decisive. The Allied command of the sea made it possible to draw on the resources of the rest of the world, and in particular to transfer with surprisingly few losses large numbers of British and American troops to the crucial Western Front. Quite as important, sea power enabled the Allies to shut Germany and her allies off from overseas resources. The Allied blockade slowly but surely constricted Germany, limiting not merely military supplies for her armies, but food supplies for her civilian population. At the end of 1918, Germans were suffering from malnutrition, an important factor in their willingness to surrender without fighting to the bitter end.

Yet the war at sea was not easy for the Allies. The submarine, which the Germans had invested in heavily, proved every bit as dangerous as British alarmists before the war had feared. When the Germans launched their unrestricted submarine warfare, they made dangerous inroads on the merchant ships that were essential to the very life of Britain. By the end of 1917, some 8,000,000 tons of shipping had been sunk by the Germans, most of it by submarines. And at one point in 1917 the British had barely enough food reserves to last a month. The submarine menace was eventually overcome by a series of measures co-ordinated between the Allies and the Americans—extensive use of the convoy system, attack on the submarines by depth bombs, constant anti-submarine patrols, and development of small, fast "subchasers." But we might wonder what would have happened in 1916-1917 (and again in 1942-1943) if the Germans had contented themselves with holding actions on land and had put all their productive fighting energies into the submarine. This they did not do in either war.

The navy of surface vessels that the Germans had built up since the 1890's—and that, as we have seen, was so important in the growth of Anglo-German hostility—never played a really decisive part in the war itself. German surface-raiders caused severe damage in the first year, but they were finally swept off the seas. Once, however, the main German fleet threw a very bad scare into the British. This was the famous Battle of Jutland, which has been re-fought over and over again by naval historians. Fought in the North Sea on May 31 and June 1, 1916, this running battle resulted in the sinking of twice as much Brit-

Aerial dogfight during World War I.

ish as German tonnage, and showed how good the German navy was. But the German admiral, Scheer, was forced to run into port before the British capital ships, for which he was no match. Although Jutland was a tactical victory for the Germans, the strategic victory remained with the British, for never again did the German surface navy seriously threaten British command of the sea in European waters. At the war's end the German high command attempted to get the fleet out in a heroic last stand. It was the German sailors' refusal to take the ships out—their mutiny, in fact—that gave a critical push to the German revolution which led to the Armistice of 1918.

The Western Front: Allied Victory

This war also saw the beginnings of air warfare. German lighter-than-air machines, the Zeppelins, raided London many times in 1916-1917, and both sides made airplane bombing raids on nearby towns. But the total damage was relatively light, and had no decisive effect on the final result. The airplane was of more importance in scouting, and especially in spotting for artillery; in spite of its short range in those days, it also proved useful as a means of locating submarines. The fighter plane was greatly improved during the war, and the base was laid for the development of the air forces we now know. Indeed, the airplane made greater strides in these four years of war than it had made since the Wrights first flew at Kitty Hawk in 1903.

Although the great new invention of the airplane did not itself alter traditional warfare, a new type of warfare was indeed developed, especially on the great Western Front, the warfare of the trenches. The machine gun, the repeating rifle, and fast-firing artillery, with the guidance of spotter planes, could pour in such deadly fire that it was almost impossible for either side to break through the opposing trench systems on a wide front. Both sides tried to break through in the two years after the Marne, and both sides suffered losses of a kind that had never been suffered before.

Two new weapons almost broke the deadlock. The first was poison gas, which was first used by the Germans in shells in October, 1914, with disappointing results. Then in April, 1915, the Germans used chlorine gas discharged from cylinders. The overwhelmed French broke in a line five miles wide, leaving the line completely undefended. But the Germans had not prepared to follow through, and the gap was closed once the gas had dispersed. Meanwhile the experts developed a simple countermeasure, the gas mask, which became part of the equipment of every soldier on both sides. The age-old balance of attack and defense was once again reestablished.

The second new weapon came much nearer to producing decisive success. This was the tank, a sort of armored land battleship for which plans had been made back in the Renaissance by the fertile Leonardo da Vinci. But Da Vinci's tank remained a mere

sketch for lack of propulsive power. In the second decade of the twentieth century, however, the internal-combustion engine was ready to do what horses could not do. The tank was a British invention that had been nursed along in its infancy by the always adventurous Winston Churchill. But the new weapon was used too soon, in inadequate numbers and before adequate mechanical tests had been made, in the British Somme offensive of 1916. Even so, nine tanks led or accompanied the infantry triumphantly through the German lines to the capture of Flers. Had the tanks been withheld for a few more months, and backed up with careful planning, they might have broken the German lines on a wide front. The Germans naturally took up the tank at once, and were soon producing their own.

The technique of attack in the west gradually developed over the years, and in the end broke the defensive stalemate. Long and careful artillery preparation, known as a "barrage," literally flattened out a section of the enemy defenses and the "no man's land" in front of them, and forced the enemy to retire to rear trenches. Then, accompanied or preceded by tanks, the infantry edged in while the artillery barrage was lifted and focused on the next enemy line. It was a slow and costly process, which did not work on a wide scale until 1918. Then the Germans, with the Russians out of the fight, made a last and almost successful effort to break through, trying to separate the British from the French. With the failure of the last German push in the summer, Foch ordered a general attack. French, British, and American armies had all broken the German lines by early autumn, and were just gaining freedom of action in the open country when the Germans surrendered. The Germans later maintained that they were not beaten decisively in the field. Most experts now think the Germans could not have stopped an Allied invasion in 1919.

Morale
on the Fighting
Fronts

The long narrow battle lines of the four-year trench war were the scene of a concentrated destruction hardly equaled in the war of 1939-1945; at some points in France the top soil was blown completely away by shellfire, producing a desert that is still visible today. The war, however, was not unique, unprecedented, or unlike all other wars, as many an excited publicist at the time declared. It produced military heroes and military scapegoats, great generals and generals who failed. As with the Confederacy in the American Civil War, the defeated Germans seem to have had the most-praised generals, the Ludendorffs, the Mackensens, the Hoffmanns. The old traditional chivalrous warfare, the warfare of athletic heroes, was continued, and even heightened in the air, where the "aces" of the highly individualistic duels between planes were the Rolands of a machine age. And in many of the fronts on land, and in the war at sea, the age-old melodrama of war lost none of its reality. Lawrence in Arabia was no disgrace to the tradition of Sir Walter Scott or even, in the eyes of good patriotic Englishmen, to the tradition of Homer.

Yet especially on the Western Front, this war seemed to many of its participants an unheroic nightmare of blood and filth. Sensitive young intellectuals, who in earlier times would never have had to fight, survived to write bitterly about their experiences—in war novels like *Under Fire*, by the Frenchman Barbusse, or *All Quiet on the Western Front* by the German Remarque, and in war poems like those of Siegfried Sassoon and Wilfred Owen. But this literature cannot be trusted fully as an accurate reflection of what the millions of common soldiers who were not intellectuals felt about the war. We know simply that they

French soldiers in the trenches near Verdun.

stood it for four years. But for most of them the dullness, the discomforts, and the brief terror of battle must have tested their patriotism and worn out their sense of adventure.

The Home Fronts   These soldiers and sailors were, for the most part, not professionals; they were civilians, "drafted," lifted from civilian families unused to the ways of the military. Behind the front, on the production lines, subject to the unheroic but harassing strains of rationing and all sorts of limitations in daily living, subject also to the constant prodding of war propaganda, the families too were part of this great "total war." They too stood it, though in France in 1917, after the bloody failure of a great offensive under General Nivelle, civilian and military discontent, fanned by politicians, came almost to the point of breaking French morale. And in Germany, the collapse that resulted in the armistice of November 11, 1918, though it obviously had many complex causes, looks like a general failure of morale, a psychological collapse under intolerable spiritual and material pressures.

For the Germans, still influenced by nineteenth-century ideas about the rights of the individual and laissez-faire economics, were slow to organize their society for total war. They failed notably to ensure the proper and equitable distribution of food supplies, so that as 1918 wore on whole sectors of the urban population began to suffer from malnutrition. Nor were finances and war production managed with that perfection of techniques that most of the world had already come to expect of the Germans. Rationing, strict control of production, price control, systematic use of the resources of conquered countries, these and many other measures were employed by the Germans, but not with the care, decisiveness, and long preparation that char-

acterized them in the conflict of 1939-1945.

All countries engaged in the war, the democratic western Allies as well as the autocratic Central Powers, sooner or later felt obliged to introduce drastic wartime economic planning, which anticipated in some sense the more collectivistic economy of today. Everywhere there was compulsory military service. Even in Britain, proud of its long devotion to the rights of the individual, the famous Defense of the Realm Act—known with wry affection as DORA—clamped down severely on the Englishman's sacred right to say and do what he liked, even if he did not seem to be giving aid and comfort to the enemy. In the United States, all sorts of men, including the famous "dollar-a-year men," business executives who were working for the government for the first time, flocked to Washington and helped build up an enormous new central government, which regulated the economy as it had never been regulated before. And of course all the belligerents engaged in the war of propaganda, or, as it came to be called in the next great war, in psychological warfare.

The Allies won the battle of the production lines, in which the United States played a major if not a decisive part. We have already noted that in material resources the Allies had a marked potential superiority over the Central Powers; this superiority they were eventually able to realize to the full. Had the Germans not given up when they did, and had the Allies staged the all-out offensive in the west they had planned for the spring of 1919, it seems certain that they would have overwhelmed the Germans. Allied production was slow in getting started. The French, in particular, were lamed by the loss in the first few weeks of the war of their most highly developed industrial regions in the north and northeast. The British even maintained for a few months in 1914 the delusive slogan, "Business as usual." There were mistakes, bottlenecks, and experiments like that of the tanks which failed at first because of undue haste. At the beginning the Allies were often at cross-purposes in production as well as in actual military strategy. And not even at the end were all the Allied resources pooled as effectively as they were to be in the Second World War. Nevertheless, by the end of 1917 the Allied military machine was adequately, indeed in some ways wastefully, supplied.

The Role of Propaganda

The Allies also won the most critical phase of the war of propaganda. They sought to convince the neutral world, especially the neutrals of western civilization, the United States, Latin America, and the Swiss, Dutch, Scandinavians, and Spanish, that the Allies were fighting for the right and the Central Powers for the wrong. It was not a complete victory, for important groups in all these countries remained "pro-German" to the end, and Spain on the whole was probably pro-German, or at least anti-French and anti-English. Still, it seems that a majority of the neutral West was early convinced that the cause of the Allies was just. This conviction was strengthened from the very start by the traditional liberalism of France and Britain in contrast with the traditional autocracy of the German and the Austrian empires, though the presence of the autocratic Russian Empire on the Allied side somewhat handicapped Allied propagandists. The conviction was greatly strengthened in the early days of the crisis of 1914 by the intransigence of the Austrians toward the Serbs, and in particular by the blundering phrase of Bethmann-Hollweg, that Britain had gone to war for a mere "scrap of paper."

The sense of Allied rightness was strengthened by early Allied propaganda, which was often one-sided and unfair. Notably, it accused the Germans of frightful atrocities in Belgium. The Germans did indeed impose rigorous military controls on conquered populations, but little in their record was worse than is usual, and perhaps inevitable, in all warfare. Allied propaganda also simplified and falsified the complex chain of causation that produced the war, making it appear that the Germans and the Austrians were wholly responsible for the outbreak of the war, that the predatory "Potsdam gang" had planned the whole thing from the beginning, and that Serbs, French, Russians, and British had been wholly innocent of deed or word that might have brought on the war. This propaganda backfired shortly after the war; revulsion against its unfairness had much to do with the widespread acceptance of the extreme revisionist thesis that on the whole Germany, in particular, had been quite guiltless of starting the war.

Political Repercussions

Except in Russia, the four years of war saw no major changes in political structure. The Central Empires retained until their collapse their incompletely responsible parliamentary governments, and the parliaments on the whole were reasonably submissive. And in spite of the inevitable strengthening of the executive in wartime, France, Britian, and the United States carried on their democratic institutions. In the United States the critical presidential election of 1916 came just before American entrance into the war, and resulted by a narrow margin in the return of the incumbent, Woodrow Wilson. In Britain and France the democratic process brought to power in the midst of wartime crisis two strong men—Lloyd George and Clemenceau—who carried through with great vigor the prosecution of the war, and who, though their fame was dimmed in the troubled years after the war, remain in historic memory as great national heroes.

In Britain the skillful but indecisive Liberal leader Asquith proved unable to master events, even though he widened his government into a coalition in May, 1915. In December of that year he was succeeded by another Liberal, Lloyd George, the architect of Britain's social insurance system (see Chapter XIV), who had also proven himself an admirable organizer of war production. Under Lloyd George the coalition really worked, and his position as war leader was to remain unchallenged. We shall meet him again at the peace negotiations, as we shall meet his French counterpart, Clemenceau. The "Tiger," as Clemenceau was known to his friends and enemies alike, came to power at the end of 1917, at a time when defeatism threatened both the military and the internal strength of France. Clemenceau took firm command of the war effort and disposed of the disaffected politicians with the decisiveness—and disregard for the peacetime "rights of man"—of an old Jacobin.

IV: The Peace

As in Westphalia in 1648, at Utrecht in 1713, and at Vienna in 1815, the warring powers gathered in a great meeting to make the peace settlement. This time they met at Paris—or, rather, in suburban Paris. They met at Versailles to settle with the Germans, at St. Germain to settle with the Austrians, at Neuilly to settle with the Bulgarians, at the Grand Trianon (in the park of Versailles) to settle with the Hungarians, and at Sèvres to settle with the Turks. But peace congresses almost never meet in a world that is really at peace. There are always aftermaths, local wars and disturbances, lesser diseases that follow the great bout of illness. The aftermaths of 1918-1919 were particularly numerous and acute, and conditioned the whole work of the peace congresses. To them we must turn briefly before we consider the actual settlements.

The Aftermath of World War

The sorest spot was Russia, now in the throes of civil war and foreign invasion. No sooner had the Germans been forced to withdraw from the regions they had gained at Brest-Litovsk (see above, p. 598) than the Allies sent detachments to various points along the rim of Russia—on the Black Sea, on the White Sea in the far north, and on the Pacific (for details see Chapter XIX). The Allies still hoped to restore in Russia, if not the monarchy, at least a moderate democratic republic. Their dread of final Bolshevik success (the term "Bolshevism" was then almost universally used, instead of communism) and of the possible spread of Bolshevism westward, added to the tensions at Versailles and confirmed the conservative position Clemenceau and Lloyd George were taking.

And Bolshevism was indeed spreading westward. The German revolution of November, 1918, had been carried out under socialist auspices. But all through the winter of 1918-1919 there were communist riots and uprisings, and in Bavaria in April a soviet republic was proclaimed. The government of the new republic of Germany put these communist uprisings down, but only by an appeal to the remnants of the old army and to officers thoroughly hostile to the new republic. In the break-up of the Austro-Hungarian monarchy in the autumn of 1918, the successor states—Czechoslova-kia, Austria, Hungary, Yugoslavia, Rumania —which had been formed in whole or in part out of the former Habsburg lands, were disturbed by all sorts of social and economic troubles. In Hungary, Bela Kun, who had worked with Lenin in Moscow, won power by means of a socialist-commu-nist coalition, and then elbowed out his socialist colleagues and set up a communist dictatorship. In August, a Rumanian army that had invaded Hungary forced Bela Kun to flee. Finally, all through the Germanies groups of ex-soldiers, the *Freikorps*, were roving about, stirring up trouble, and threatening the overthrow of the German Republic (for details, see Chapter XX).

In the Near East the Allies had even worse troubles to face. Greece, which had been so hard to drag into the war, was now in full cry against the Turks. Her national-ists had revived the old hope of a restored Byzantine Empire, with the Greeks once more in command of the Straits. Her ar-mies, not without Allied encouragement, landed at Smyrna in Asia Minor in the spring of 1919 and marched off in the track of Alexander the Great. The French and the British, to whom control over differ-ent parts of the former Turkish Empire had been assigned, began at once having trouble with their new Arab subjects—or wards. The Jews were already pressing for the es-tablishment of a national home in Palestine in accordance with the Balfour Declara-tion, and the Arabs were already opposing them.

In India the aftermath of war was bad in-deed. The universal epidemic of influenza in 1918 (which most public-health experts be-lieve killed more people than were killed in battle) had been especially disastrous in In-dia. Indians had fought well as professional soldiers during the war on the Allied side; educated Indians thought their country was ripe for much more self-rule. The disor-ders of 1918-1919 culminated in the Am-ritsar massacre of April, 1919, in which a British general, reverting to old-time methods, ordered his soldiers to fire on an unarmed crowd, killing or wounding some 1600 people. Amritsar shocked world opin-ion, added to the odium the Allies were al-ready acquiring among liberals everywhere, and knitted India more closely together in opposition to the British. In China the weakening of Russia had been taken by the Japanese as a signal to renew their ambi-tious plans in the north of China, and in-deed the American troops sent to Vladi-vostok in Siberia (see Chapter XIX) were there less to oppose the Bolsheviks than to oppose the Japanese.

So the world was in turmoil and disorder when the Allies, great, small, and middle-sized, assembled in Paris to make the peace. The problems that faced the peacemakers were world-wide, complex, and often in-soluble—insoluble in the sense that no deci-sion on a given problem, say the disposition of the Adriatic port of Fiume which was claimed by Italians and Yugoslavs, could possibly satisfy all the major groups con-cerned, to say nothing of the minorities. Yet the world hoped, and indeed expected, from the peacemakers more than it had in any previous crisis. Public opinion in the eighteenth and nineteenth centuries had built up a tremendous faith in the possibil-ity of a peaceful, just, and happy world. This war had been a war to "make the world safe for democracy," a "war to end war." It had produced in the American President Wilson a man who could phrase skillfully the hopes of men, and who as he journeyed to Paris after the Armistice appeared to be the heroic savior and hope of mankind.

These liberal dreams and expectations were, however, by no means the sole ten-ants of men's minds. All men were not Wil-sonians. There were, inevitably, the selfish, the disillusioned, the narrow, the jingoists, and the professionals who had made prom-ises to the Italians and the Rumanians, who had planned all sorts of compensations and adjustments. There were, more important, the plain ordinary men and women who wanted peace and security but who also wanted national glory and the punishment of the wicked Germans who, they believed, had put them through those four years of hell. There were, in short, thousands of conflicting hopes and fears, all of them embodied in living human flesh, not just the abstractions they must seem to be on the printed page.

The Fourteen Points

The more generous of these hopes were in 1918 clearly embodied in one man and in one text. Woodrow Wilson, on January 8, 1918, in an address to the American Congress, had announced the famous Fourteen Points, which were widely accepted by people in Allied and even in enemy countries as a platform for the peace to come, but were also widely misunderstood and subject to the most divergent interpretations. Here they are:

I. Open covenants of peace, openly arrived at, after which there shall be no private international understandings of any kind but diplomacy shall proceed always frankly and in the public view.

II. Absolute freedom of navigation upon the seas, outside territorial waters, alike in peace and in war, except as the seas may be closed in whole or in part by international action for the enforcement of international covenants.

III. The removal, so far as possible, of all economic barriers and the establishment of an equality of trade conditions among all the nations consenting to the peace and associating themselves for its maintenance.

IV. Adequate guarantees given and taken that national armaments will be reduced to the lowest point consistent with domestic safety.

V. A free, open-minded, and absolutely impartial adjustment of all colonial claims, based upon a strict observance of the principle that in determining all such questions of sovereignty the interests of the populations concerned must have equal weight with the equitable claims of the government whose title is to be determined.

VI. The evacuation of all Russian territory and such a settlement of all questions affecting Russia as will secure the best and freest co-operation of the other nations of the world in obtaining for her an unhampered and unembarrassed opportunity for the independent determination of her own political development and national policy and assure her of a sincere welcome into the society of free nations under institutions of her own choosing; and, more than a welcome, assistance also of every kind that she may need and may herself desire. The treatment accorded Russia by her sister nations in the months to come will be the acid test of their good will, of their comprehension of her needs as distinguished from their own interests, and of their intelligent and unselfish sympathy.

VII. Belgium, the whole world will agree, must be evacuated and restored, without any attempt to limit the sovereignty which she enjoys in common with all other free nations. No other single act will serve as this will serve to restore confidence among the nations in the laws which they have themselves set and determined for the government of their relations with one another. Without this healing act the whole structure and validity of international law is forever impaired.

VIII. All French territory should be freed and the invaded portions restored, and the wrong done to France by Prussia in 1871 in the matter of Alsace-Lorraine, which has unsettled the peace of the world for nearly fifty years, should be righted, in order that peace may once more be made secure in the interest of all.

IX. A readjustment of the frontiers of Italy should be effected along clearly recognizable lines of nationality.

X. The peoples of Austria-Hungary, whose place among the nations we wish to see safeguarded and assured, should be accorded the freest opportunity of autonomous development.

XI. Rumania, Serbia, and Montenegro should be evacuated; occupied territories restored; Serbia accorded free and secure access to the sea; and the relations of the several Balkan states to one another determined by friendly counsel along historically established lines of allegiance and nationality; and international guarantees of the political and economic independence and territorial integrity of the several Balkan states should be entered into.

XII. The Turkish portions of the present Ottoman Empire should be assured a secure sovereignty, but the other nationalities which are now under Turkish rule should be assured an undoubted security of life and an absolutely unmolested opportunity of autonomous development, and the Dardanelles should be permanently opened as a free passage to the ships and commerce of all nations under international guarantees.

XIII. An independent Polish state should be erected which should include the territories inhabited by indisputably Polish populations, which should be assured a free and secure access to the sea, and whose political and economic independence and territorial integrity should be guaranteed by international covenant.

XIV. A general association of nations must be formed under specific covenants for the purpose of affording mutual guarantees of political independence and territorial integrity to great and small states alike.*

The fourteenth point, the germ of the League of Nations, was especially dear to Wilson.

Just how great a part the Fourteen Points played in the final surrender of the Germans is a delicate and much disputed issue. On October 4, 1918, a German government was set up under the liberal Prince Max of Baden; this development provided a sort of antechamber to the real German revolution of a few weeks later. Prince Max's government did indeed announce its own acceptance of the Fourteen Points, and that of its Austrian ally, and began negotiations with Wilson, who stalled them off until the real revolution of early November. In November, events moved too fast for formal diplomacy, although on November 5 the Allies conceded the Fourteen Points as a basis for negotiation, with some reservations. But it is quite certain that German public opinion, and liberal opinion throughout the world, thought the Allies had promised a peace in accord with the Fourteen Points. The Peace Conference, such opinion held, would translate Wilson's ideals into concrete facts.

* Woodrow Wilson, *War and Peace: Presidential Messages, Addresses, and Public Papers,* R. S. Baker and W. E. Dodd. eds. (New York, 1927), I, 159-161.

Opposing Hopes and Promises

The hopes and promises that opposed and contradicted the Fourteen Points were not neatly embodied in a single document. We may classify them roughly in three categories: the previous diplomatic commitments made by the Allies; the immediate and widespread popular hopes fanned by Allied propaganda and confirmed at the last moment by some Allied statesmen; and—much more difficult to pin down—the long-established habits and traditions that had become part of the dominant policies and trends of each nation, big and little.

In the first category, the most difficult of the diplomatic commitments was the contradictory set of promises made to both Italy and Serbia by the original Entente, including Russia, about the disposal of Habsburg lands. And there were other commitments, especially in the Balkans, that were very difficult to sort out. In the second category were the promises, widely believed by the British and French peoples, that Germany would be made to suffer to the full for her war guilt. She would have to pay the whole cost of the war in reparations, her war criminals would be punished, she would be rendered incapable ever again of assuming the role of the aggressor. In some vague way, everything would shortly be much better for everybody.

Finally, in the third category were the deeply rooted drives of the various nations —French drives for revenge against Germany, for restoration of French hegemony in Europe, and, no doubt paradoxically but very humanly, for security, the Italian Irredentist drive, the British longing for a Victorian serenity and economic leadership well armored against German commercial competition, and the nationalist aspirations of the new states of Central Europe that had at last been released from long frustration. And by no means the least important was the old and firmly held American tradition that

Lloyd George, Clemenceau, and Wilson in Paris during the peace negotiations, 1919.

Americans call "isolationism," the desire to be free from European alliances and entanglements and to go their own pioneer way, the feeling that the war had somehow not "belonged" in our tradition, that it had been an episode with which we were finished. Many liberals of the time felt that all these drives were ignoble and backward-looking; but these drives were also "natural," embedded in habit and tradition. They were indeed the toughest of the forces that quickly put the Fourteen Points into the background at Versailles.

The Process of Peacemaking

The Peace Conference met formally on January 18, 1919. Nearly thirty nations involved in the war against the Central Powers sent delegates. Russia was not represented. The defeated nations took no part in the deliberations; they were simply notified of the final terms and asked to sign. The Germans, in particular, were given but the slightest chance to comment on or criticize the terms offered them. Very soon the German publicists coined a term for the treaty—"*Diktat*," the imposed, the dictated peace. The Germans' anger over this failure of the Allies to negotiate with their new and virtuous republic was to play a large part in the ultimate rise of Hitler.

Although a few western liberals were from the first disillusioned by the exclusion of the defeated nations from the Peace Conference, the conference did get off to a good start. Wilson's reception in Europe had been extremely enthusiastic. People everywhere were still rejoicing over the end of the nightmare. The Fourteen Points seemed already a realized peace; and for the future, the proposed association of nations, working together in the freedom of parliamentary discussion, would soon eliminate the costly burdens of armament. Wilson's hopeful phrases sounded in press and pulpit, and none more loudly than his "open covenants openly arrived at." To many a liberal these words meant that the peace would be made in a sort of big, idealized New England town meeting, in which the representatives of all the powers, big and little, would have their free say in public, in which decisions would ultimately be taken by majority vote, in which the caucus, the smoke-filled room, the backstairs intrigues would all be missing.

These liberals were almost at once disillusioned, for the conference soon fell into the familiar pattern of centuries. The small nations were excluded from the real negotiations; the business of the conference was carried on in private among the political chiefs of the victorious great powers—the Big Four of Wilson, Lloyd George, Clemenceau, and Orlando (it was really a Big Three, for Italy was not strong enough to impose her Orlando, who was a much less striking character than his colleagues). Decisions were made in the traditional way of diplomacy, with all the pressures, chi-canery, intrigues, compromises, and plain horse-trading that go on when leaders get together in private. Public opinion was consulted only indirectly, as each states-man sought to make sure that he had at least a majority of his own nation behind him.

The hopeful members of the general pub-lic were by no means the only ones who grew disillusioned as the Paris Conference went the way of the Vienna Congress a hundred years before. The professional dip-lomatists of the little and middle-sized powers had probably never really expected that they would be treated on equal terms, but the completeness of their exclusion from the real work of the conference an-noyed them, and angered their people back home. More important, all the major pow-ers had brought with them large staffs of experts, economists, political scientists, historians, career men in many fields. These bright young men were sure they knew better than their elders how to solve the problems of human relations, were confi-dent that they would do the real work and make the really important decisions. They drew up report after report, some of which went up through devious channels to Cle-menceau or Lloyd George or Wilson. But they did not make policy. The disillusion of the young experts was great and long-lived, and since many of them were quite articu-late they did much to discredit the work of the conference.

One of them, the English economist John Maynard Keynes, lived to influence his gov-ernment in the 1930's and '40's as he could not do in 1919. But he took immediate re-venge in a book called *The Economic Con-sequences of the Peace* (1919). To Keynes the peace was a "Carthaginian" peace, an attempt to destroy Germany as Rome had destroyed Carthage. But since Germany was an essential part of Europe, to attempt to destroy Germany by weakening her eco-nomically would inevitably harm all Eu-rope. Germany could not possibly pay the reparations the Allies were asking from her, the new states of Central Europe were al-ready erecting tariff barriers, and nothing had been done at Versailles to bind Europe together. Keynes' book at once became the bible of liberal opponents of the work of Versailles.

Wilson and his experts were gradually badgered into accepting harsher peace terms. The reparations bill against Ger-many was lengthened; Poland, Italy, and Ja-pan made claims to lands that clearly were not theirs; the victors more and more openly showed that they proposed to be-have as victors in war habitually have be-haved. Wilson gave way or compromised on a dozen points, and then chose to stand fast against the weakest of the Allies. He would not let the Italians have the Adriatic sea-port of Fiume, which had once been the sole seaport of Hungary. They might have neighboring Trieste and their coveted Trentino, where they could rule over Ger-man or Slavic-speaking minorities, indeed, in some areas, majorities; but Fiume they might not have. The Italian delegation left the conference in anger, but Wilson was im-movable. The fate of Fiume was not settled at the conference; only in 1924, by treaty with Yugoslavia, did the city go to Italy in return for Susak, a port right next door that served the Yugoslavs quite ade-quately.

But Wilson did get his new international organization, the cornerstone of his plans for a better world. The covenant of the League of Nations was an integral part of the Treaty of Versailles. The League was no true supranational state, but a kind of permanent consultative system composed of the victors and a few neutrals. The way was left open for the Germans and the Rus-sians to join the League, as they later did. But in 1919-1920 Wilson's League looked a lot like Metternich's and Castlereagh's old Congress system of 1815, by no means worth the sacrifices Wilson had made to ob-

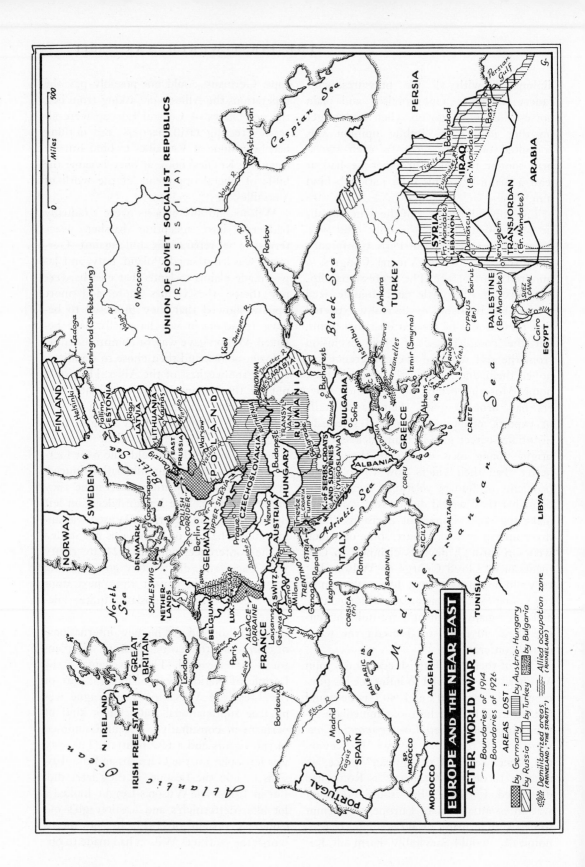

EUROPE AND THE NEAR EAST
AFTER WORLD WAR I

AREAS LOST:
by Germany ▦ by Russia ▦▦ by Austria-Hungary ▤ by Turkey ▨ by Bulgaria
Demilitarized areas (RHINELAND, "THE STRAITS") ▥ Allied occupation zone (RHINELAND)
— Boundaries of 1914
— Boundaries of 1926

tain it. The League had an assembly in which each member-state had one vote, and a council in which the five great powers (Britain, France, Italy, the United States, and Japan) had permanent seats, and to which four other member-states were chosen by the assembly for specific terms. A permanent secretariat, to be located at Geneva, was charged with administering the affairs of the League. In its working out, as we shall see (Chapter XXII), the League never fulfilled the hopes of the liberals. It did not achieve disarmament, nor did its machinery of peacemaking prove capable of preventing aggression. The great powers simply went on their usual ways, using the League only as their policy-makers—their heads of state rather than their diplomats —saw fit.

The Territorial
Settlement

Central to all the work in Paris was the problem of territorial changes. Here, peacemakers were confronted not merely, as at most peace conferences in our western society, with the claims of the victorious Allies but also with the claims of the new nations that had sprung up from the disintegrating Austrian, Russian, and Turkish empires. They had to try to satisfy the eternal land hunger of those who run nations, without violating too obviously another great Wilsonian principle, the "self-determination of peoples." This principle was hard indeed to apply in much of Central Europe, where peoples of different language and national self-consciousness were mixed together in an incredible mosaic of unassimilated minorities (see map on p. 487). The result was to multiply the number of "sovereign" nations in this world. Nationalism, which some hopeful people had thought was on the wane, was now fanned to intense new life in a dozen states.

France received Alsace-Lorraine back

from Germany. Clemenceau also hoped both to annex the small but coal-rich Saar Basin of Germany as compensation for French coal mines destroyed by the Germans during the war, and to detach from Germany the territory on the left (or west) bank of the Rhine, thereby strengthening French security and setting up a Rhineland republic that might become a French satellite. Both French hopes, opposed by Wilson and Lloyd George, went unrealized. The Saar was to be separated from Germany for fifteen years as an international ward supervised by the League of Nations. At the end of the fifteen-year period a plebiscite would determine its future status; meanwhile, its coal output was to go to France. The Rhineland remained part of the German Republic, though it was to be demilitarized and occupied for a time by Allied soldiers.

Belgium was given some small towns on her German border. Italy gained her Irredenta of Trent and Trieste, indeed in generous measure, for thousands of German and Slavic-speaking peoples were included within her new boundaries. Poland, erased from the map as an independent state in 1795, was now restored and given lands that she had had before the partitions of the eighteenth century and that contained important minorities of Germans and other non-Polish peoples. The old Habsburg Empire was entirely dismembered. The heart of its German-speaking area was constituted as the truncated Republic of Austria, which was forbidden to join itself to Germany, and the heart of its Magyar-speaking area became a diminished Kingdom of Hungary. The Czech-inhabited lands of Bohemia and Moravia were joined with Slovakia and the Ruthenian lands of the Carpatho-Ukraine further east in the brand-new "succession state" of Czechoslovakia. On the northwest, the Czechoslovak Republic extended to the mountain ranges separating Bohemia from Germany, but on the Czech side of this "natural" frontier there lived many Sudeten Germans. From the first, therefore, the new republic faced the problem of a large and discontented Sudeten minority.

Another "succession state" was Yugoslavia, officially the Kingdom of Serbs, Croats, and Slovenes, which, as its full name suggests, represented a great expansion of pre-war Serbia to include the south Slav territories of the Habsburgs. Rumania, too, profited by the break-up of the old dual monarchy by receiving the former Hungarian lands of Transylvania. Rewarded also with Bessarabia, a Russian province that the Bolsheviks could not defend, Rumania emerged with doubled territory. In the southern Balkan Peninsula, Greece received all of Thrace, at the expense of Turkey and Bulgaria.

Out of the former tsarist domains held at the end of the war by the Germans there were set up, in addition to Poland, the "Baltic republics" of Estonia, Latvia, and Lithuania. Once Europe had settled down, plebiscites were provided for to determine certain other territorial adjustments, notably whether certain parts of East Prussia and Silesia should go to Poland or remain German. The new Polish state had been granted access to the Baltic Sea through the so-called "Polish corridor," a narrow strip of land which had once been Polish, and which terminated in the almost wholly German city and port of Danzig. The Poles wanted Danzig, but the Allies compromised by setting up a Free City of Danzig and by giving the Poles free trade with the city. Even so, the Polish corridor now separated East Prussia from the rest of Germany, and Germans had to cross it in sealed trains.

Outside Europe, the Near East presented the most acute problems. By the Treaty of Sèvres the Turks were left in Europe with no more than Constantinople and a small strip of land around it, and in Asia with only their homeland of Anatolia. For the rest, the old, feudal, desert country of Arabia was recognized as independent and presently became known as Saudi Arabia, after its ruler, Ibn Saud. Mesopotamia and Palestine were given as mandates —a term we shall shortly explain—to Britain, while Syria and Lebanon were given as mandates to France. The Greeks were to hold Smyrna and nearby regions in Asia Minor for five years, and then submit to a plebiscite. But the Treaty of Sèvres never went into effect, though it was duly signed by the Sultan. In Anatolia a group of army officers led by Mustafa Kemal revolted against the government at Constantinople and galvanized the Turkish people into a new national life. The Turks drove the Greek army out of their country and set up a Turkish republic with its capital not at Constantinople but at Ankara in the heart of Anatolia. With this new government the Allies were finally obliged to conclude the Treaty of Lausanne in 1923. The new peace transferred the Smyrna area and eastern Thrace from Greek to Turkish control and was in general more advantageous to the Turks than the Treaty of Sèvres had been.

This treaty embodied in dramatic form a principle new in part in the West—the formal transfer of populations. True, peoples had been evicted by conquerors before; witness among other instances the eviction of the French Acadians from Nova Scotia by the British in the eighteenth century, or the settling of our Indians in Indian Territory. But here was an exchange: Greeks in Turkey were moved to Greece, Turks in Greece were moved to Turkey. No very significant discontented national minorities were left. Each government was to take care of the transferred populations, and though much hardship occurred, on the whole the plan worked.

The Mandates

For the rest of the world the old straightforward annexing of the overseas territories of defeated powers, as

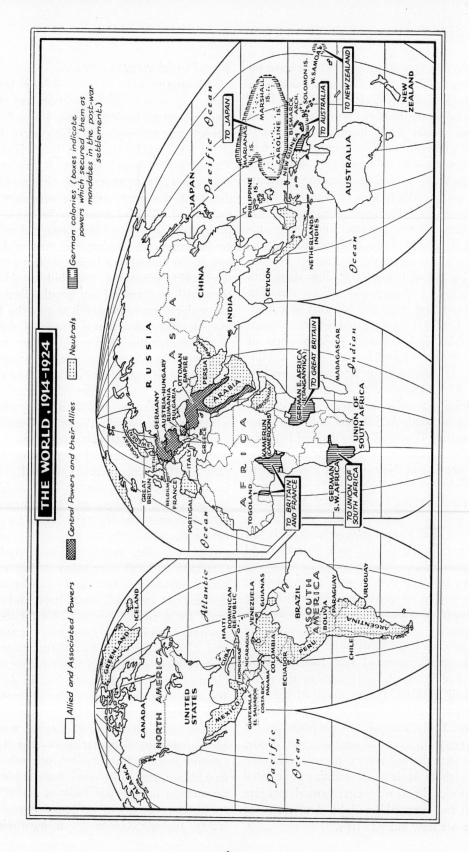

THE WORLD, 1914-1924

☐ Allied and Associated Powers
▨ Central Powers and their Allies
⬚ Neutrals
▥ German colonies (boxes indicate powers which secured them as mandates in the post-war settlement)

TO JAPAN
MARIANAS IS.
MARSHALL IS.
PHILIPPINE IS.
CAROLINE IS.
NEW GUINEA
BISMARCK ARCH.
SOLOMON IS.
W. SAMOA
TO NEW ZEALAND
TO AUSTRALIA
NEW ZEALAND
AUSTRALIA
NETHERLANDS INDIES

Pacific Ocean
Indian Ocean

JAPAN
CHINA
INDIA
CEYLON

RUSSIA
A S I A

GERMANY
AUSTRIA-HUNGARY
RUMANIA
BULGARIA
OTTOMAN EMPIRE
PERSIA
ARABIA

NORWAY
SWEDEN
GREAT BRITAIN
NETHERLANDS
BELGIUM
FRANCE
ITALY
GREECE
PORTUGAL

A F R I C A
TOGOLAND
KAMERUN (CAMEROONS)
ABYSSINIA
GERMAN E. AFRICA (TANGANYIKA)
TO GREAT BRITAIN
MADAGASCAR
UNION OF SOUTH AFRICA
GERMAN S.W. AFRICA
TO UNION OF SOUTH AFRICA
TO BRITAIN AND FRANCE

Atlantic Ocean
Pacific Ocean

GREENLAND
ICELAND
ALASKA
CANADA
NORTH AMERICA
UNITED STATES
MEXICO
CUBA
HAITI
DOMINICAN REPUBLIC
GUATEMALA
HONDURAS
EL SALVADOR
NICARAGUA
COSTA RICA
PANAMA
COLOMBIA
VENEZUELA
GUIANAS
ECUADOR
BRAZIL
PERU
BOLIVIA
PARAGUAY
SOUTH AMERICA
CHILE
ARGENTINA
URUGUAY

practiced in 1713, 1763, and 1815, seemed no longer possible in 1919. Liberal opinion both in Europe and in America had already been offended to the bursting point, and Wilson himself would never have permitted outright annexations. The consequence was the mandate system, whereby control over a given territory was assigned to a particular power by the League of Nations, which undertook periodic inspections to see that the terms of the mandate were being fulfilled. This system was designed by its proponents as a means of educating and improving colonial peoples, leading them into the ways of democratic self-government, and preparing them for eventual independence. Under it the former German overseas territories and the non-Turkish parts of the Ottoman Empire were now distributed. Of Germany's African possessions East Africa (now called Tanganyika) went to Britain; Southwest Africa went to the Union of South Africa; and both the Cameroons and Togoland were divided between Britain and France. In the Pacific, the German portion of New Guinea was given to Australia, western Samoa to New Zealand, and the Caroline, Marshall, and Mariana island groups to Japan. In the Near East, as we have seen, France thus secured Syria and Lebanon, while Britain took Palestine and Mesopotamia.

The mandate system may seem to have been a way of disguising annexation, the hypocritical tribute of reactionary vice to progressive virtue. And so to a man like Clemenceau it probably was. The Japanese quite openly annexed and fortified their new Pacific islands in defiance of the terms of their mandate. But to many of the men who put through the idea of mandates the system really was what it professed to be, a nursery for eventual nationhood. For the most part the mandatory powers did make some show at least of treating mandated territories in a way that would prepare them for eventual freedom. And many of them are now indeed "free."

The Punishment of Germany

After land transfers, the most important business of the Peace Conference was reparations, which were imposed on Austria, Hungary, Bulgaria, and Turkey as well as on Germany. It was, however, the German reparations that so long disturbed the peace and the economy of the world. The Germans were made to promise to pay for all the damage done to civilian property during the war, and to pay at the rate of five billion dollars a year until 1921, when the final bill would be presented to them. They would then be given thirty years in which to pay the full amount. The amount was left indefinite at Versailles, for the Allies could not agree on a figure. But the totals suggested were astronomical. It was clear from the first that the payments would ultimately have to be in goods—German goods in competition with the goods of the Allies. A Germany prosperous enough to pay reparations could not be the weak and divided nation that men like Clemenceau really wanted. Thus from the very start the "realists" at Versailles—Lloyd George and Clemenceau—cherished quite inconsistent hopes for the future.

The Versailles settlement also required Germany to hand over many of her merchant ships to the Allies and to make large deliveries of coal to France, Italy, and Belgium for a ten-year period. Furthermore, a whole miscellany of articles in the treaty was directed toward the disarmament of Germany on land, on sea, and in the air. The German army was to be limited in size to 100,000 men, and the western frontier zone, extending to a line 50 kilometers (about 30 miles) east of the Rhine, was to be completely "demilitarized"—that is, to contain neither fortifications nor soldiers. In addition, the Allies could have armies of occupation on the left bank of the Rhine for fifteen years, and perhaps longer. The treaty forbade Germany to have either submarines or military planes and severely limited the number and size of surface vessels in her navy.

Last, and by no means least important, Article 231 of the Treaty of Versailles obliged Germany to admit that the Central Powers bore sole responsibility for starting the war in 1914. Here is the article that was to cause so much history to be written:

The Allied and Associated Governments affirm, and Germany accepts, the responsibility of Germany and her allies for causing all the loss and damage to which the Allied and Associated Governments and their nationals have been subjected as a consequence of the war imposed upon them by the aggression of Germany and her allies.

The Settlement Evaluated

To the Germans, Versailles was of course a cruel and humiliating peace, the *Diktat*, the great national grievance on which Hitler was to play so skillfully. To liberals of the time and later, it seemed as it did to Keynes an unsound, revengeful peace, above all disastrous in its unrealistic reparations policy. In our present world of cold and hot wars, Versailles almost arouses nostalgia. It was at least a settlement, and one that in the best moments of the 1920's seemed a basis for slow improvement in international relations (see Chapter XXI).

The League it set up was potentially a means by which a new generation of international administrators might mitigate the old rivalries of nations. The reparations could be, and indeed were, scaled down to something more reasonable. The new succession states were based on a national consciousness that had been developing for at least a hundred years. Though the theorist might protest at the "Balkanization of Europe," the creation of more weak and discontented little states like those in the Balkans, the fact remains that it would

have been hard to deny national independence, or at least autonomy, to the Czechs, the Poles, the Baltic peoples, and the south Slavs. Germany, though she certainly was not treated generously, was at least not wiped off the map, as Poland had been in the eighteenth century. She was not even actually demoted to a second-rate position in the world. She remained, as she was shortly to prove, a first-rate power. In the long series of settlements under our modern western state-system, which goes back to the Italian wars of the fifteenth century, Versailles looks nowadays like neither the worst nor the best, but like a typical compromise peace.

It was, however, too much for the American people, who were not used to the harsh needs of international compromise. But it is an oversimplification to argue that this was solely a matter of American idealism turning away in disgust from a settlement that was all too spotted with unpleasant realities. The final American refusal to ratify the Treaty of Versailles, like all great collective decisions, was the result of many forces. Politics certainly played an important part, for the Republicans had won control of both the Senate and the House of Representatives in the congressional elections of November, 1918. The President of course was still Wilson, a Democrat, and Wilson made no concessions to the Republicans either by taking a bipartisan delegation of Democrats and Republicans to Paris with him or by accepting modifications in the treaty which would have satisfied some of his Republican opponents. The Senate thereupon refused to ratify the treaty.

It is, however, extremely unlikely that even a much more pliable and diplomatic American president than Wilson could have secured from the Senate ratification of another important treaty involved in the proposed settlement. This was the project of a defensive alliance among France, Britain, and the United States into which Wilson had been pushed as the penalty for refusing to accept French proposals for a separate Rhineland republic and for annexation of the Saar. With the United States out, Britain refused a mere dual alliance with France against a German attack. France, still seeking to bolster her security, patched up a series of alliances with the new nations to the east and south of Germany—Poland, and the "Little Entente" of Yugoslavia, Czechoslovakia, and Rumania.

The peace thus left France with an uneasy hegemony in Europe, a hegemony dependent on the continued disarmament and economic weakening of Germany, on the continued isolation of Russia, and on the uncertain support of her new allies. Moreover, France had been disastrously weakened by the human and material losses of the war, and her position of leadership, though it alarmed the British with their long memories of French rivalry in the past, was an unreal thing. In reality, Germany was the strongest nation in Europe, and the Great War had checked, but not halted, her attempt to dominate the Continent and indeed the world. The next German attempt was to draw both Britain and America back from the isolation into which they attempted to withdraw after the collapse of the system planned at Paris in 1919.

Reading Suggestions on the First World War

The Background: General Accounts

Q. Howe, *A World History of Our Own Times*, Vol. I (N.Y.: Simon & Schuster, 1949). Survey from 1900 to 1918 by a capable and opinionated publicist.

A. J. P. Taylor, *The Struggle for Mastery in Europe, 1848-1918* (Oxford: Clarendon, 1954). A crisp and suggestive survey.

S. B. Fay, *The Origins of the World War*, 2nd ed. (N.Y.: Macmillan, 1932). A fully documented account by an American scholar; somewhat sympathetic to Germany.

B. E. Schmitt, *The Coming of the War, 1914*, 2 vols. (N.Y.: Scribner's, 1930). Another well-documented scholarly account; somewhat sympathetic to Britain.

H. E. Barnes, *The Genesis of the World War: An Introduction to the Problem of War Guilt* (N.Y.: Knopf, 1926). An extreme statement of the "revisionist" position on war guilt.

M. von Montgelas, *The Case for the Central Powers, An Impeachment of the Versailles Verdict* (N.Y.: Knopf, 1925). Representative of the German "revisionist" school.

L. Albertini, *The Origins of the War of 1914*, 2 vols. (N.Y.: Oxford Univ. Press, 1952-1953). By an Italian scholar; stresses the role of Italy.

The Background: Special Studies

W. L. Langer, *European Alliances and Alignments, 1871-1890*, 2nd ed. (N.Y.: Knopf, 1950). A detailed scholarly survey, favorable to Bismarckian diplomacy.

W. L. Langer, *The Diplomacy of Imperialism, 1890-1902*, 2nd ed. (N.Y.: Knopf, 1951). Includes much material pertaining to the shifting alliances of the European powers.

L. C. B. Seaman, *From Vienna to Versailles* (N.Y.: Coward-McCann, 1956). Interesting essay in interpretation by a young British scholar.

E. M. Carroll, *French Public Opinion and Foreign Affairs, 1870-1914* (N.Y.: Century, 1931), and *Germany and the Great Powers, 1866-1914: A Study in Public Opinion and Foreign Policy* (Englewood Cliffs, N.J.: Prentice-Hall, 1938). Scholarly studies in a significant area of research.

R. J. S. Hoffman, *Great Britain and the German Trade Rivalry, 1875-1914* (Philadelphia: Univ. of Pennsylvania Press, 1933). A helpful monograph.

E. L. Woodward, *Great Britain and the German Navy* (Oxford: Clarendon, 1935); A. J. Marder, *The Anatomy of British Sea Power* (N.Y.: Knopf, 1940); and B. Brodie, *Sea Power in the Machine Age* (Princeton: Princeton Univ. Press, 1943). Three useful studies of the important question of naval power.

E. N. Anderson, *The First Moroccan Crisis, 1904-1906* (Chicago: Univ. of Chicago Press, 1930), and I. C. Barlow, *The Agadir Crisis* (Chapel Hill: Univ. of North Carolina Press, 1940). Two useful monographs on the issue of Morocco in pre-war diplomacy.

E. M. Earle, *Turkey, The Great Powers, and the Bagdad Railway* (N.Y.: Macmillan, 1923).

Scholarly account of another major issue of pre-war diplomacy.

A. F. Pribram, *Austrian Foreign Policy, 1908-1918* (London: Allen & Unwin, 1923). Balanced statement from the Austrian standpoint.

P. Renouvin, *The Immediate Origins of the War* (New Haven: Yale Univ. Press, 1928). Scholarly account from the French point of view.

G. P. Gooch and H. Temperley, eds., *British Documents on the Origins of the War, 1898-1914*, 12 vols. (London: His Majesty's Stationery Office, 1926-1938). Representative of the great collections of diplomatic documents published by the governments of the major belligerents after World War I.

Outbreak of the World War: German Documents Collected by Karl Kautsky (N.Y.: Oxford Univ. Press, 1924), and *German Diplomatic Documents, 1871-1914*, 4 vols. (London: Methuen, 1928-1931). English translations of some of the vast number of German diplomatic documents.

The Background of the War: American Policy

T. A. Bailey, *A Diplomatic History of the American People*, 4th ed. (N.Y.: Appleton-Century-Crofts, 1950), and S. F. Bemis, *A Diplomatic History of the United States*, 3rd ed. (N.Y.: Holt, 1950). Two standard surveys.

W. Millis, *The Road to War: America, 1914-1917* (Boston: Houghton Mifflin, 1935). Readable journalistic account, highly critical of Wilson's policy.

C. C. Tansill, *America Goes to War* (Boston: Little, Brown, 1938). Scholarly treatment, also critical of Wilson's policy.

C. Seymour, *American Diplomacy during the World War*, 2nd ed. (Baltimore: Johns Hopkins Univ. Press, 1942). Sympathetic toward Wilson's policy.

The War

W. S. Churchill, *The World Crisis*, 6 vols. (N.Y.: Scribner's, 1923-1931). Detailed survey by the famous British statesman.

C. R. M. Cruttwell, *History of the Great War* (Oxford: Clarendon, 1934). Perhaps the best one-volume history.

Note: There are many detailed military histories of World War I. The problems that arose on the home front have been the subject of a large number of special studies published under the auspices of the Carnegie Endowment for International Peace. Some idea of their scope may be had by consulting *Economic and Social History of the World War: Outline of Plan, European Series* (Washington, D.C.: Carnegie Endowment for International Peace, 1924). Another useful collection of special studies has been published by the Hoover Library of War, Revolution, and Peace at Stanford University.

The Peace

H. W. V. Temperley, *A History of the Peace Conference of Paris*, 6 vols. (London: Frowde, Hodder and Stoughton, 1920-1924). The standard detailed account; by a British scholar.

H. G. Nicolson, *Peacemaking, 1919* (London: Constable, 1933). A good shorter account; by a British expert on diplomacy.

P. Birdsall, *Versailles Twenty Years After* (N.Y.: Reynal & Hitchcock, 1941). Balanced reappraisal by an American scholar.

T. A. Bailey, *Wilson and the Peacemakers* (N.Y.: Macmillan, 1947). Sound study of America's role.

J. M. Keynes, *The Economic Consequences of the Peace* (N.Y.: Harcourt, Brace, 1920), and E. Mantoux, *The Carthaginian Peace; or, the Economic Consequences of Mr. Keynes* (N.Y.: Scribner's, 1952). Respectively, the most famous attack on the Versailles settlement and a thoughtful study of the results of that attack.

Historical Fiction

E. Childers, *The Riddle of the Sands* (London: Nelson, 1913), and H. H. Munro ("Saki"), *When William Came* (N.Y.: Lane, 1914). Two unusual novels, written before the outbreak of the war and predicting what it might be like. Childers' is a story of intrigue and adventure, and "Saki's" is a forecast of the German occupation of Britain.

J. Romains, *Verdun* (N.Y.: Knopf, 1939). Excellent and balanced novel about French troops on the western front, 1914-1916.

H. Barbusse, *Under Fire* (N.Y.: Dutton, 1917) and E. M. Remarque, *All Quiet on the Western Front* (N.Y.: Lion Books). Two famous novels, by a Frenchman and a German, respectively, reflect the horror aroused in intellectuals by trench warfare.

J. Dos Passos, *Three Soldiers* (N.Y.: Modern Library, 1941) and E. Hemingway, *A Farewell to Arms* (many editions). Two American novels about the war, indicative of the post-war disillusionment of the "lost generation."

e. e. cummings, *The Enormous Room* (N.Y.: Modern Library, 1941), and A. Zweig, *The Case of Sergeant Grischa* (N.Y.: Viking, 1928). Novels about prisoners of war and the eastern front, respectively.

C. S. Forester, *The General* (Boston: Little, Brown, 1947). Astringent novel about the "brass" in World War I.

J. Buchan, *Greenmantle* (London: Nelson, many eds.). A novel of espionage indicating that the war contained its ingredient of high adventure in addition to blood and guts.

What Price Glory? in M. Anderson and L. Stallings, *Three American Plays* (N.Y.: Harcourt, Brace, 1926). A famous play showing that the war had its rowdy side.

CHAPTER NINETEEN

Communist

Russia

1917-1941

I: *Introduction*

On June 22, 1941, Adolf Hitler's German armies poured over the frontier of his Russian ally and began a rapid advance toward Moscow, toward the major Russian industrial centers, and toward the most productive Russian agricultural centers. The Russia Hitler invaded was no longer the Russia into which Napoleon had sent the Grand Army a hundred and twenty-nine years before or the Russia whose millions of embattled soldiers had perished in the First World War against the Germany of William II and his Habsburg allies. It was no longer the Russia of the tsars. Since 1917 it had been the Russia of the Bolsheviks. Yet it was still Russia.

Along with the tsars, the nobility and the bourgeoisie had gone down to ruin after the Communist revolution of 1917, and the clergy as a class had suffered almost as much.

A small, tightly knit, conspiratorial group of fanatical Marxist revolutionaries had seized power and for the next twenty-four years had striven to make Russia over. Drawn mostly from the peculiarly Russian class of the intelligentsia, and declaring themselves to be the representatives of the industrial proletariat, the Bolsheviks had worked gigantic changes, especially in the years after 1928. Industry, proceeding under forced draft, had expanded enormously, and the proportion of the population employed in industry had risen to almost 50 per cent; the proportion engaged in agriculture had fallen correspondingly.

The peasant had been a victim of serfdom until 1861, had been subject to the initiative-destroying domination of the commune until 1906, and had then been encouraged by Stolypin to make himself a free farmer (see Chapter XV). Now, under the Bolsheviks, he found himself subjected to new and grievous pressure. Agriculture had been collectivized and the age-old longing of the peasant for private property in land had been ruthlessly suppressed.

These staggering social and economic changes had not been accomplished without internal friction. Inside the government, personal rivalries, plots, counterplots, fake plots, and charges of plots had produced repeated purges extending down through the ranks of the population. The choking conspiratorial atmosphere which the Bolshevik rulers had breathed during their long years of underground preparation for a seizure of power now enveloped the citadels of power. Personal rivalries for domination of the machinery of the state were cloaked beneath the Byzantine theological language of doctrinal controversy over fine points in the sacred writings of Marx and Lenin. Yet the controversies had immediate significance in the formulation and choice of government policies. The Communist party, the secret police, and the army had become the interlocking agencies which ran the state at the bidding of the dictator. The dictator himself, Stalin, had made his own career possible chiefly through the ruthless use of his position as Secretary of the Communist party.

The foreign policy of the Communist state had passed through a brief period in which ideological considerations had seemed occasionally to outweigh national interest in the old sense. It had then returned to the pursuit of traditional Russian ends, coupled with the objective of promoting eventual world-revolution. But in furthering Russian aims abroad the Bolshevik leaders were now in possession of an instrument more flexible than any the tsars had ever commanded. This was the Communist International, or Comintern, a federation of the Communist parties in the individual countries of the world. These parties could often be used as promoters of purely Russian ends rather than strictly Communist ends. With the shifting stresses and strains of international politics during the late 1920's and 1930's, the "line" of the Comintern shifted often and bewilderingly, but always in accordance with the aims of the Soviet foreign office. Usually the majority of communists elsewhere in the world fell meekly into position, and loudly proclaimed when necessary the opposite of what they had proclaimed the day before.

Yet the changes during the first twenty-four years of the Soviet period, vast though they were, could not conceal the continuities between the new Russian system and the old. The dictator of 1941, the revered leader of his people, for whom his followers made increasingly grandiose claims, was not unlike the tsar of 1917 in his assumption of autocratic power. The individual Russian of 1941, despite his sufferings under the new system, had remained deeply patriotic, ready to sacrifice himself for his country, even under a government he hated. The peasant of 1941 still yearned hopelessly for his land; the worker struggled for economic advancement and social security. Bureaucrats, managers, intellectuals, and artists, all in the service of the state, formed in 1941 a new élite which replaced but did not differ greatly from the old privileged class. A police force superior in efficiency to those of Ivan the Terrible, Peter the Great, and Nicholas I, but not different in kind, in 1941 exercised thought control over all citizens, and terrorized even prominent members of the system itself.

More and more, Stalinist communism had taken on the trappings of a religion, with its sacred books, its heresies, its places of pilgrimage, its doctrinal quarrels. Thus the old Russian orthodoxy had by 1941 not been replaced but rather modified. Russian nationalism, too, asserted itself ever more

insistently and crudely, until finally, in the war that Hitler began, the government encouraged the cult of traditional heroes of earlier times, and even glorified Ivan the Terrible himself, no longer a symbol of "feudal" domination but a symbol of the Russian national spirit. The early revolutionary departures from accepted standards in Russian marriage, family life, and education, had by 1941 all been abandoned in favor of a return to conventional bourgeois behavior. The first twenty-four years of Soviet domination, 1917-1941, are the subject of this chapter, which will trace in some detail the vast changes here summarized and will attempt to demonstrate the survival of the old Russia beneath the veneer of the new.

II: *The Revolution of 1917*

Ridden by domestic crisis though Russia was in 1914 (see Chapter XV), the country greeted the outbreak of World War I with demonstrations of national patriotism. The Duma supported the war, and did yeoman service in organizing Red Cross activities. The left-wing parties—the radical agrarian SRs (Social Revolutionaries) and the Marxist SDs (Social Democrats)—though they abstained from voting war credits, offered to assist the national defense. By 1917 more than 15,-000,000 Russians had been drafted into the armies. Losses in battle were staggering from the first; the Russians suffered more than 3,800,000 casualties during the first year of war. On the home front, criticism was aroused by the inadequate handling of the supply of munitions, and by mid-1915 the Center and Left groups in the Duma were urging moderate reforms, such as the end of discrimination against minority nationalities and an increase in the powers of the *zemstvos*, the local assemblies. The Em-

press Alexandra took the lead in opposing all such measures, and kept urging her weak husband, Tsar Nicholas II, to act more autocratically. When Nicholas took personal command of the armies in the field and prorogued the Duma (autumn, 1915), she became virtually supreme at home. The supremacy of the Empress meant also the supremacy of her favorite, the unscrupulous adventurer Rasputin.

With the Empress and Rasputin in control, a gang of shady adventurers, blackmailers, and profiteers bought and sold offices, speculated in military supplies, put in their own puppets as ministers, and created a series of shocking scandals. Confusion, strikes, and defeatism mounted at home during 1916, while the armies slowly bled to death at the front. Even the conservatives had begun to denounce Rasputin publicly, and in December, 1916, he was poisoned, shot several times, and ultimately drowned, all in one nightmare evening, by a group of conspirators closely related to the imperial family. Despite repeated warnings from moderates in the Duma that the government itself was preparing a revolution by its failure to create a responsible ministry and to clean up the mess, the Tsar remained apathetic. Relatives of the imperial family and members of the Duma began independently to plot for his abdication. In the early months of 1917 all conditions favored a revolution, but the revolutionaries were not prepared.

The March Revolution

On March 8, strikes and bread-riots broke out in the capital, and four days later Romanov rule, which had governed Russia since 1613, was doomed. Yet this revolution of March, 1917, has been well called leaderless, spontaneous, and anonymous. SRs and both Bolshevik and Menshevik factions of SDs (see above, p. 506) were genuinely surprised at what happened. Indeed, the Bolshevik leaders were either abroad in exile, or under arrest in Siberia. The determining factor in the overthrow of the Tsar was the disloyalty of the garrison of Petrograd (the new Russian name given to St. Petersburg during the war). Inefficiency had led to a food shortage in the capital, though actual starvation had not set in. When the Tsar ordered troops to fire on striking workers, only a few obeyed, and on March 12, in revulsion against the order, the troops joined the strikers, broke into the arsenals, and began to hunt the police, who quickly disappeared from the scene. The Duma lagged behind the revolting troops and workers in estimating the situation, and the Tsar lagged behind the Duma. By March 14, when the Tsar had finally decided to appoint a responsible ministry, it was too late; the cabinet had vanished. Troops ordered to put down the revolt simply melted away and joined the rebels.

A Soviet of workers and soldiers, modeled on the 1905 Soviet of workers (see above, p. 509), but now including soldiers as well, was formed by leftists released from prison by the enthusiastic mobs. The Soviet proceeded to organize a workers' militia, to create a food-supply commission, and to issue newspapers. Its fifteen-man executive committee became the policy-makers of the revolution. The Soviet located its headquarters across the hall from the Duma, which had not dissolved as ordered, but remained in session. The Marxists among the Soviet leaders still believed in the necessity of a preliminary bourgeois revolution, and did not yet regard the Soviet itself as an organ of power. They favored the creation of a provisional government, in which they would not participate, but to which they would offer limited support. They put themselves at the disposition of the Duma, and asked for its leadership. Thus the Duma, a limited assembly elected by a restricted franchise, was literally forced by the Soviet into the position of leading the revolution.

Negotiations between the Soviet and a Duma committee brought a provisional

Tsar Nicholas II and his family, 1917.

government into existence. Despite the widely differing social and economic aims of Soviet and Duma, both agreed to grant political liberties immediately and to summon a constituent assembly, which was to establish the future form of government by giving Russia a constitution. The provisional government was composed mainly of Kadets (Constitutional Democrats) and other moderates and was headed by the liberal Prince Lvov, chairman of the union of *zemstvos* and of the Red Cross. It included also one radical member of the Soviet, Alexander Kerensky, Minister of Justice, a clever labor lawyer and member of the Duma also, who accepted office despite the understanding that members of the Soviet would not do so.

After some abortive efforts to save the dynasty in the person of the Tsar's brother, Nicholas finally abdicated, and his brother refused the throne because of the popular hatred of the family. Under pressure from the Soviet, the provisional government arrested Nicholas II and the Empress on March 20. The Duma had thus accepted the mandate given it by the revolutionaries.

The Provisional Government

The provisional government is usually regarded as having been a total failure. Measured by the final results, such a view is perhaps justified. But the judgment of history must take into consideration the dreadful difficulties that faced the provisional government. These were not only immediate and specific, but general and underlying. Russian moderates had had no experience of authority. They were separated by a great cultural gulf from the lower classes. Their opportunity to rule now came to them in the midst of a fearful war, which they felt they had to pursue while reconstructing and democratizing the enormous and unwieldy Russian Empire.

Moreover, the Soviet possessed many of the instruments of power, yet refused to accept any responsibility. Workers and soldiers in the capital supported the Soviet, while in the provinces the new governors appointed by the provisional government had no weapon except persuasion to employ against the local peasant-elected soviets, which multiplied rapidly. Present-day critics of the provisional government often denounce its failure to suppress its revolutionary opponents, but they overlook the fact that the provisional government did not possess the tools of suppression. The Petrograd garrison, for instance, by agreement with the Soviet, could not be removed or disarmed. The support given by the Soviet to the provisional government has been compared to the kind of support that is given by a hangman's noose.

The two great specific issues facing the provisional government were agrarian discontent and the continuation of the war. The peasants wanted land, and they wanted it immediately. The provisional government, however, made up as it was of responsible liberals, believed in acting with deliberation and according to law. It could not countenance irregular or violent actions, and refused to sanction peasant seizure of land, despite increasing disorder in the countryside. Instead, it appointed a commission to collect material on which future agrarian legislation was to be based —an act totally inadequate to the emergency.

As to the war, the members of the government felt in honor bound to their allies not to make a separate peace. Moreover, most of them still unrealistically hoped that Russia might win, and gain the territories which the Allies had promised. But the Soviet subverted discipline in the armies at the front by issuing a "declaration of the rights of soldiers," which virtually put an end to the authority of officers over enlisted men. Although the Soviet made it as hard as possible for the government to pursue the war, it did not sponsor a separate peace. Even the Bolshevik members of the Soviet, who now began to return from exile, supported only Russian participation in general peace negotiations, which they hoped would begin immediately.

Lenin and Bolshevism

The most important of the returning Bolshevik exiles was Lenin. His real name was Vladimir Ilyich Ulianov. Son of a provincial official and intellectual, Lenin became a revolutionary in the late 1880's and, as we have already seen (p. 506), took a chief role in the early years of the SDs as the leader of the party's Bolshevik wing. He had returned to Russia from abroad for the Revolution of 1905, but he left Russia once more in 1908, and stayed abroad until 1917.

When the news of the March Revolution reached Lenin in Switzerland, he made desperate efforts to get back home. Finally, through the Swiss Social Democrats, he made contact with the German general staff, which felt that it would be a good investment to see that Lenin reached Russia, where he might disrupt the Russian war effort against Germany. Thus it was that the German military transported Lenin across Germany from Switzerland to the Baltic in the famous sealed railroad car. He arrived at the Finland Station in Petrograd on April 16, 1917, a little more than a month after the March Revolution.

Most Russian Social Democrats had long regarded a bourgeois parliamentary republic as a necessary preliminary to an eventual socialist revolution and socialist society. For this reason they were prepared to help in transforming Russia into a capitalist society, though not without grave doubts that the bourgeois capitalists might be as bad as the tsar and the landlords, or that the masses might be "deluded" into accepting the new system. They favored the

Lenin.

creation of a democratic republic, at the same time believing that complete political freedom was absolutely essential for their own future rise to power. Despite the Marxist emphasis upon the industrial laboring class as the only proper vehicle for revolution, Lenin early realized that in Russia, where the "proletariat" embraced only about 1 per cent of the population, the SDs must seek other allies. At the time of the Revolution of 1905 he began to preach the need for limited alliances for tactical purposes between the Bolsheviks and the SRs, who commanded the support of the peasantry. When the alliance had served its purpose, the SDs were to turn on their allies and destroy them. Then would come the socialist triumph.

Instead of a preliminary bourgeois democratic republic, Lenin called in 1905 and later for an immediate "revolutionary-democratic dictatorship of the proletariat and the peasantry," a concept that seems to us self-contradictory, and is surely vague. Lenin's view, however, was not adopted by most Bolsheviks. Together with the Mensheviks they continued to believe and urge that a bourgeois revolution and a parliamentary democracy were necessary first steps along the road to ultimate success.

Because Lenin did not trust the masses to make a revolution (by themselves, he felt, they were capable only of "trade-union consciousness"), he favored a dictatorship of the Bolshevik party over the working class. Because he did not trust the rank and file of Bolshevik party workers, he favored a dictatorship of a small élite over the Bolshevik party. And in the end, because he really trusted nobody's views but his own, he favored, though never explicitly, his own dictatorship over this élite. Another future Russian leader, the brilliant intellectual Leon Trotsky, warned early in the game that the concept of one-man dictatorship was implicit in Lenin's views.

Trotsky, for his part, voiced an opinion of his own, held by neither Mensheviks nor Bolsheviks. The bourgeoisie in Russia, he argued, was so weak that the working class could telescope the bourgeois and socialist revolutions into one continuous movement. After the proletariat had helped the bourgeoisie achieve its revolution, he felt that the workers could move immediately to power. They could nationalize industry and collectivize agriculture, and, although foreign intervention and civil war were doubtless to be expected, the Russian proletariat would soon be joined by the proletariats of other countries, which would make their own revolutions. Except for this last point, Trotsky's analysis proved to be an accurate forecast of the course of events.

Lenin had been deeply depressed by the failure of 1905, and by the threat posed by Stolypin's agrarian reforms. He almost despaired when the socialist parties of Europe went along with their governments in 1914 and supported the war. To him this meant the end of the second socialist International, for the Social Democrats had failed to recognize the war as the "bourgeois-imperialist" venture that it appeared to Lenin to be. He preached defeatism as the only possible view for a Russian SD to follow.

Lenin's greatest talent was not as an original thinker but as a skillful tactician. He often seemed able to judge with accuracy just what was politically possible in a given situation, and he was not afraid to gamble. Thus, even before he returned to Russia in April, 1917, he had assessed some of the difficulties facing the provisional government, and had determined that the masses could take over. Immediately upon his arrival, he hailed the world-wide revolution, proclaiming that the end of imperialism, "the last stage of capitalism," was at hand. Ignoring the positions previously taken by Bolsheviks and Mensheviks alike, he demanded now that all power immediately be given to the soviets. His speeches sounded to the SDs themselves like the ravings of a madman.

Almost nobody but Lenin felt that the loosely organized soviets could govern the country, or that the war would bring down the capitalist world in chaos. In April, 1917, Lenin called not only for the abandonment of the provisional government and the establishment of a republic of soviets but for the confiscation of estates, the nationalization of land, and the abolition of the army, of government officials, and of the police. These demands fitted the mood of the people far better than the cautious and well-meant efforts of the provisional government to bring about reform by legal means. Dogmatic, furiously impatient of compromise, entirely convinced that he alone had the truth, Lenin galvanized the Bolsheviks into a truly revolutionary group waiting only for the moment when they would be able to seize power.

The Coming of the November Revolution

The months from March to November, 1917, before the Bolsheviks came to power, can be divided into a period between March and July, during which revolution deepened, a feeble reaction from July to September, and a new quickening of the revolutionary current from September to the final uprising in November. In the first period, the government faced a crisis, because the Kadet ministers wished to maintain the Russian war aim of annexing the Straits, while the Soviet wanted a peace "without annexations or indemnities." Out of the crisis Kerensky, the war minister, emerged as the dominant leader. He failed to realize that it was no longer possible to restore the morale of the armies, which were dissolving under the impact of Bolshevik propaganda. A new offensive ordered on July 1 collapsed, as soldiers refused to obey orders, deserted their units, and rushed home to their native villages, eager to seize the land. Ukrainian separatism also plagued the officials of the government. The soviets became gradually more and more Bolshevik, as Lenin and Trotsky worked tirelessly at recruitment and organization. Although the June congress of soviets in Petrograd was less than 10 per cent Bolshevik in make-up, the Bolshevik slogans of peace, bread, and freedom won overwhelming support.

Yet an armed outbreak by troops, who had accepted the Bolshevik slogans, found the Petrograd Soviet unwilling and unable to assume power. While the mob roared outside, the Soviet voted to discuss the matter two weeks later and meanwhile to keep the provisional government in power. A regiment loyal to the Soviet protected it against the working class. The government declared that Lenin was a German agent, and, as his supporters wavered, raided the newspaper offices of *Pravda* ("Truth," the Bolshevik paper); Lenin had to go into hiding to avoid arrest. This episode of mid-July is what is known among Bolsheviks as "playing at insurrection." Though shots had been exchanged and overt action had been embarked upon, there had been no revolutionary follow-through. Power had not been seized, probably because Lenin felt that the Bolsheviks did not have enough support in the provinces.

Now Kerensky became premier. The government hardened its attitude toward the Ukrainians, but could not come to a popular decision on either land or peace. General Kornilov, chosen by Kerensky as the new commander-in-chief of the armies, quickly became the white hope of all conservative groups, and in August plotted a *coup*, intended to disperse the Soviet. His attitude toward the provisional government was uncertain, but, had he succeeded, he would probably have demanded a purge of its more radical elements. The plot, however, was a failure, because railroad and telegraph workers sabotaged Kornilov's movements, and because his troops simply would not obey him. The Bolsheviks, adopting the slogan "We will fight against Kornilov, but will not support Kerensky," threw themselves into preparations for the defense of Petrograd, which proved to be unnecessary. By September 14, Kornilov had been arrested, and the affair ended without bloodshed. The threat from the Right helped the Bolsheviks greatly, and sentiment in the Petrograd and Moscow soviets now for the first time became predominantly Bolshevik.

The Kornilov affair turned the army mutiny into a widespread revolt. Instances of violence multiplied. As peasants refused to pay rent, pastured their animals on the landlords' pasture land, and often burned the manor house and killed its owner, so the soldiers moved from disobedience to the murder of their officers. Orderly and legal reform had attracted nobody. The peasants could not be convinced that the nobility owned less than a quarter as much land

Machine guns in action against revolutionaries in Petrograd.

as the peasants, and that rash action only retarded progress. As disorder mounted in the countryside, the Bolsheviks tightened their hold over the soviets in the cities.

Lenin returned to Petrograd on October 20; soon thereafter the Bolsheviks got control over a Military Revolutionary Committee, originally chosen to help defend Petrograd against the advancing Germans, and now transformed, under the guidance of Trotsky, into a general staff for the revolution. Beginning on November 4, huge demonstrations and mass meetings were addressed by Trotsky, and on November 7 the insurrection broke out.

In Petrograd, the revolution had been well prepared and proceeded with little bloodshed. Kerensky escaped in a car of the American Embassy. The Military Revolutionary Committee, as an organ of the Petrograd Soviet, simply took over. The Bolsheviks called a second congress of soviets, and when the Mensheviks and right-wing SRs walked out, Trotsky called them the refuse that would be swept into the garbage can of history. Co-operating with the left-wing SRs and adopting their land program, Lenin abolished all property rights of landlords and transferred the land thus affected to local land committees and soviets of peasant deputies. Though Lenin did not in the least approve of the system of individual small holdings which this decree put into effect, he recognized the psychological advantage which the adoption of the SR program would gain him. He also urged an immediate peace without annexations or indemnities, and appealed to the workers of Germany, France, and England to support him in this demand. Finally, a new cabinet, called a Council of People's Commissars, was chosen, with Lenin as President, and Trotsky as Foreign Commissar.

As Commissar of Nationalities the Bolsheviks installed a younger man, a Georgian, named Joseph Stalin, who had been a successful organizer of bank robberies in the days when the party treasury was filled in this way, but whose role had otherwise been relatively obscure. Under Lenin's coaching, Stalin had also become the party authority on minority questions and had published a pamphlet on the subject in 1913.

Outside Petrograd, the revolution moved more slowly. In Moscow there was a week of street-fighting between Bolshevik Reds and Whites, as anti-Bolshevik forces were already known. Elsewhere, in factory towns, the procedure was usually fast, in nonindustrial centers usually slower. Most of Siberia and of Central Asia came over, but Tiflis, the capital of Georgia, went

Menshevik and passed resolutions calling for a constituent assembly and the continuation of the war. The reason for the rapid and smooth success of the Bolsheviks was that the provincial garrisons opposed the war and willingly allied themselves with the workers. Local Military Revolutionary Committees were created in most places and held elections for new local soviets. Naturally there was much confusion at first, but surprisingly little resistance to the consolidation of the authority of the new regime. Gradually the town of Rostov-on-Don, near the Sea of Azov, became the main center of resistance, as Kornilov and other generals, together with a number of the leading politicians of the Duma, made their way there.

This initial triumph of the revolution did not mean that the population of Russia had been converted to Bolshevism. By cleverly sensing the mood of the people, Lenin had opportunistically given the Bolsheviks a set of slogans around which the people could rally, although some of the slogans did not at all correspond with the true Bolshevik views. As we shall shortly see, the Russian people was in fact strongly anti-Bolshevik. But the Bolsheviks had triumphed, and the democratic hopes for freedom of the press and other freedoms were now doomed to disappointment.

Deprived of competent civil servants, the new regime worried along through an atmosphere of continued crisis. Late in November, 1917, an agreement was reached with the Left-Wing SRs, three of whom entered the government, and peace negotiations were begun with the Germans. The revolution proper was over. Lenin was in power.

The Constituent Assembly

It is of great interest to record that the Bolsheviks now permitted elections for a constituent assembly. Lenin had no use for this sort of democratically chosen parliament, which he considered "inferior" to the soviet. Yet, probably because he had so long taunted the provisional government with delaying the elections, he seems to have felt compelled to hold them. The Russians for the first and last time in their history had a completely free election, under universal suffrage. Lenin himself accepted as accurate figures showing that the Bolsheviks polled about one-quarter of the vote. The other socialist parties, chiefly the SRs, polled 62 per cent. As was to be expected, the Bolshevik vote was heaviest in the cities, especially Moscow and Petrograd, while the SR vote was largely rural.

Lenin allowed the constituent assembly to meet only once, on January 18, 1918. Lenin dissolved it the next day by decree, and sent guards with rifles to prevent its ever meeting again. The anti-Bolshevik majority was naturally deeply indignant at this pure act of force against the popular will, but there was no public outburst, and the delegates disbanded. In part, this was because the Bolsheviks had already taken action on the things that interested the people most—peace and land—and in part because of the lack of a democratic parliamentary tradition among the masses of the Russian people.

In spite of the many years of agitation by intellectuals and liberals for just such a popular assembly, Russia did not have the large middle class, the widespread literacy, the tradition of debate, and the respect for the rights of the individual which seem to be an essential part of constitutionalism. Yet it is surely extreme to decide that there was no chance for constitutional government in Russia in 1917-1918. Was the constituent assembly "an attempt to transplant an alien concept of government to a soil where it could never flourish"? Or was it "a noble experiment incorporating a sound principle but doomed by the crisis into which it was born"? The fact that

Lenin had the rifles to prevent the constituent assembly from fulfilling the function which the popular will had assigned to it does not answer the question either way.

III: *War Communism and NEP, 1917-1928*

The first period of Soviet history, which runs from the end of 1917 to the end of 1920, is usually called the period of "war communism," or "military communism." The term itself of course implies that the main features of the period were determined by military events. Civil war raged, and foreign powers intervened on Russian soil. But the term is also somewhat misleading. This was a period of militant as well as military communism, symbolized early in 1918 by the change of the party's name from Bolshevik to Communist. At the same time the capital was shifted from Petrograd, with its exposed location on the western fringe of Russia, to the greater security of Moscow, in the heart of the country.

Flushed with victory in Russia, the Bolsheviks firmly believed that world-revolution was about to begin, probably first in Germany, but surely spreading to Britain and even to the United States. This view led the Bolsheviks to hasten the construction of a socialist state in Russia, and to take a casual attitude toward their international affairs, since they expected that relations with capitalist states would be very temporary. Although the actions of the Russian government during this period were later described almost apologetically as emergency measures, this is only partly true. Many of the decisions that were taken in part under the spur of military pressure were also regarded as leading to a new society.

A supreme economic council directed the gradual nationalization of industry. Sugar and petroleum came first, and then in June, 1918, a large group including mines, metallurgy, and textiles was nationalized. By 1920, all enterprises employing more than ten workers (more than five, if motor power was used) had been taken over by the state. The state organized a system of barter, which replaced the free market. Internal trade was illegal; only the government food commissary could buy and sell; money disappeared as the state took over distribution as well as production. It appropriated the banks, repudiated the tsarist foreign debt, and in effect wiped out savings. Church and State were separated by decree, and judges were removed from office and replaced by appointees of the local soviets.

The government subjected the peasantry to ever more arbitrary and severe requisitioning. It mobilized the poorer peasants against those who were better off, called *kulaks* (from the word meaning "fist" and used to apply to usurers, as if to say "hard-fisted"). By calling for a union of the hungry against the well-fed, the regime deliberately, and not for the last time, sowed class hatred in the villages and stimulated civil war in the countryside. It should be remembered that by western European standards even a Russian *kulak* was often wretchedly poor. The decree forming the first secret police, the "Cheka" (from the initials of the words meaning "extraordinary commission"), was issued in December, 1917, only a few weeks after the revolution and long before any intervention from abroad. Terror became a weapon in the civil war.

Before the Communist government could function at all, peace was necessary, as the army had virtually ceased to exist. Negotia-

RUSSIA IN REVOLUTION, 1917-1921

TRANS-SIBERIAN RAILROAD

////// Russian territorial losses, Brest-Litovsk, 1918
——— Boundaries as of 1914

tions between the Russians and the Germans and Austro-Hungarians at Brest-Litovsk dragged on into 1918, the Russians hoping that revolution would break out in Germany, and the Germans demanding enormous territorial cessions, which they increased as the Russians delayed. Finally, on March 3, 1918, the Russians signed the Peace of Brest-Litovsk, which deprived them of the entire Ukraine, the Baltic provinces, Finland, and some Caucasian lands. It cost Russia one-third of its population, 80 per cent of its iron, and 90 per cent of its coal. Many communists resigned rather than accept the peace, and the Left SRs quit the government. The Germans overran the Ukraine and the Crimea, and installed a highly authoritarian landlord regime, against which the communists continued to agitate. The Whites, with German help, put down the Reds in Finland. It is, however, hard to see how the Bolsheviks could have avoided signing the Peace of Brest-Litovsk, despite its savagery.

Civil War

During the months following Brest-Litovsk, disorder in the countryside as a result of requisitioning and class warfare was swelled by the outbreak of open civil war. During the war a brigade had been formed inside Russia of Czechs resident in the country and of deserters from the Habsburg armies. When Russia withdrew from the war, it was decided to send the Czech brigade across Siberia by rail, and then by ship across the Pacific, through the Panama Canal, and across the Atlantic to France, to fight the Germans there. On the rail trip across Siberia, the Czechs got into a brawl with a trainload of Hungarian prisoners, and one of the Hungarians was killed. This obscure quarrel on a Siberian railway siding between members of the unfriendly races of the Habsburg Empire precipitated civil war in Russia. When the Soviet government tried to take reprisals against the Czechs, who numbered fewer than 35,000 men, the Czechs seized a number of the towns of western Siberia. The local soviets were unprepared, and the SRs were sympathetic to the Czechs. Local anti-Bolshevik armies came into being. It was under threat from one of them in July, 1918, that a local soviet decided to execute the Tsar and his entire family rather than lose possession of them. All were murdered.

By late June, 1918, the Allies had decided to intervene in Russia on behalf of the opponents of Bolshevism. The withdrawal of Russia from the war had been a heavy blow to them, and they hoped to re-create a second front against the Germans in the east. The idea of a capitalist "crusade" against Bolshevism, popularized by Soviet and pro-Soviet historians as the sole motive for the intervention, was in fact a far less impelling motive. Moreover, the Allies had been at war a long time, and their populations were war-weary. So it is perhaps not to be wondered at if they viewed with disfavor communist efforts to stimulate revolution in all the capitalist nations of the world.

Out at the eastern end of the Trans-Siberian Railroad in Vladivostok, the Czechs overthrew the local soviet in June, and by early August, 1918, British, French, Japanese, and American forces had landed. The assignment of the Americans was to occupy Vladivostok and to safeguard railroad communications in the rear of the Czechs. Of the Allies, only the Japanese had long-range territorial ambitions in the area. In effect, the Bolshevik regime had now been displaced in Siberia; the SRs disbanded the soviets and re-established the *zemstvos*, calling for "all power to the constituent assembly." There were three anti-Red governments of varying complexions in three different Siberian centers. Elsewhere, in August, 1918, a small British and American force landed at the White Sea port of Archangel. An SR assassin killed the chief of the Petrograd Cheka, and Lenin himself was wounded.

The regime now sped its military preparations. As Minister of War, Trotsky imposed conscription, and, by a mixture of cajolery and threats of reprisals against their families, secured the services of about 50,000 tsarist officers. The Red Army, which was Trotsky's creation, grew to over 3,000,000 strong by 1920. Its recapture of Kazan and Samara on the Volga in the autumn of 1918 temporarily turned the

tide in the crisis that seemed about to engulf the Soviet state.

The German collapse on the Western
Front permitted the Bolsheviks to repudiate the Treaty of Brest-Litovsk, and to
move back into parts of the Ukraine,
where they faced the opposition of a variety of local forces. Elsewhere, the opposition consisted of three main armies. General Denikin led an army of Whites,
which moved from Rostov-on-Don south
across the Caucasus and received French
and British aid. Admiral Kolchak's forces in
western Siberia overthrew the SR regime
in Omsk, and Kolchak became a virtual dictator. General Yudenich's army, including
many former members of the German
forces, operated in the Baltic region, and
threatened Petrograd from the west. Allied
unwillingness to negotiate with the Bolsheviks was heightened by the successful
Red *coup* of Bela Kun in Hungary (see
Chapter XX), which seemed to foreshadow
further spread of revolution.

In the spring of 1919, the Reds defeated
Kolchak, and by winter took Omsk. In
1920, the Admiral was arrested and executed. Though the Reds also reconquered
the Ukraine, mutinies in their own forces
prevented them from consolidating their
victories and from moving, as they had
hoped to do, across the Russian frontiers and
linking up with Bela Kun in Hungary. In the
summer of 1919, Denikin took Kiev and
struck north, advancing to within two
hundred and fifty miles of Moscow itself.
But his position was weakened by the repressive character of the regime he
brought with him and by his recognition of
Kolchak as his superior officer, together
with the poor discipline of his troops and
his own rivalry with one of his generals,
Baron Wrangel. Yudenich advanced to the
suburbs of Petrograd, but the Reds by the
end of 1919 were able to defeat the White
threat everywhere, though Wrangel retained an army in the Crimea.

Even after the defeat of the Whites,
the Reds in 1920 had to face a new war
with the Poles, who hoped to keep Russia
weak and to create an independent Ukraine.
After an initial retreat, the Red armies
nearly took Warsaw, from which they
were repelled only because the French
chief of staff, General Weygand, assisted
the Poles. The Reds, eager to finish off the
Whites, and persuaded that there was after
all no hope for the establishment of a communist regime in Poland, concluded peace
in October, 1920. The Poles obtained a
large area of territory in White Russia and
the western Ukraine. This area was not inhabited by Poles but had been controlled
by Poland down to the eighteenth-century
partitions. It lay far to the east of the
"Curzon line," the ethnic frontier earlier
proposed by the British foreign minister,
Lord Curzon. The Reds then turned on
Wrangel, who had erupted from the
Crimea and had established a moderate regime in the territory he occupied. He was
forced to evacuate, assisted by a French
fleet, in November, 1920. The White
movement had virtually come to an end.

Why the Counter-revolution Failed

Many factors
accounted for
the Whites' failure and the Reds' victory.
The Whites could not get together on any
political program beyond the mere overthrow of the Reds. They adopted a policy
of "nonanticipation," which meant that
some future constituent assembly would
settle the governmental structure of Russia.
Their numbers included everybody from
extreme tsarists to SRs, and they disagreed
so violently on the proper course for Russia
to follow that they could agree only to postpone discussion of these critical problems.

Moreover, their movement was located
on the geographical periphery of Russia—
in Siberia, in the Crimea, in the Ukraine, in
the Caucasus, and in the Baltic. But the
Whites never reached an understanding

with the non-Russian minorities who lived in these regions. Thus they ignored the highly developed separatist sentiments of the Ukrainians and others, to which the Bolsheviks were temporarily willing to cater.

Further, the Whites could not command the support of the peasantry. Instead of guaranteeing the results of the land division already carried out with Bolshevik sanction, the Whites often restored the landlords and undid the land division. During the war the peasantry on the whole grew sick of both sides. This attitude explains the appearance of anarchist bands, especially in the south. Then too, the Whites simply did not command as much military strength as the Reds, who outnumbered them in manpower and who had inherited much of the equipment manufactured for the tsarist armies. Holding the central position, the Reds had a unified and skillful command, which could use the railroad network to shift troops rapidly. The Whites, moving in from the periphery, were divided into at least four main groups, and were denied effective use of the railroads.

Finally, the intervention of the Allies on the side of the Whites was ineffectual and amateurish. It may even have harmed the White cause, since the Reds could pose as the national defenders of the country and could portray the Whites as the hirelings of foreigners. In the light of hindsight, it seems safe to say that either the Allies should have mounted a full-fledged military operation against the Reds, or, if this was impossible (as it probably was, in view of the condition of their own armies after the end of the First World War), they should have stayed out of Russia and allowed the civil war to burn itself out.

NEP ("The New Economic Policy")

Since 1914, Russia had been deeply involved in fighting and crises. By early 1921, with the end of the civil

war, famine was raging and sanitation had broken down. Family ties were disrupted, human beings were brutalized, and class hatreds were released on an unparalleled scale. Industry was producing at a level of about one-eighth of its pre-war output, and agricultural output had decreased by at least 30 per cent. Distribution approached a breakdown. The communist regime appeared to be facing its most serious trial of all: the loss of support in Russia.

A large-scale anarchist peasant revolt broke out in early 1921, and lasted until mid-1922. Lenin remarked that this revolt frightened him more than all the Whites' resistance. But the decisive factor in bringing about a change in policy was the mutiny at the Kronstadt naval base near Petrograd in March, 1921. Formerly a stronghold of Bolshevism, Kronstadt now produced a movement of rebellious anarchists who called for "soviets without communists" to be chosen by universal suffrage and secret ballot, for free speech and free assembly, for the liberation of political prisoners, and for the abolition of requisitioning. Except for the last item and for the phraseology of the first, the program was ironically similar to that of all liberals and socialists in tsarist Russia. The Kronstadt movement seems to have expressed the sentiments of most Russian workers and peasants. Had the government been conciliatory, there might have been no bloodshed; but Trotsky went to war against the rebels, and defeated them after a bloody fight.

This episode led directly to the adoption of the "New Economic Policy," always referred to by its initials as NEP. But the underlying reason for the shift was the need for reconstruction, which seemed attainable only if militant communism were at least temporarily abandoned. Lenin himself referred to "premature" attempts at socialization. It was also necessary to appease the peasants, and to ward off any further major uprisings. Finally, the expected world revolution had not come off, and the resources of capitalist states were badly needed to assist Russian reconstruction. Concessions to foreign capitalists were now possible; indeed, the adoption of NEP coincided with the conclusion of an Anglo-Russian trade treaty. Abroad, NEP was hailed as the beginning of a Russian "Thermidor," a return to normality like that following the end of the Terror in the French Revolution (see Chapter X).

Under NEP the government stopped requisitioning the whole of the peasant's crop above a minimum necessary for subsistence. The peasant had still to pay a very heavy tax in kind, but he was allowed to sell the remainder of his crop and keep the money. The peasant could sell his surplus to the state if he wished, but he could also choose to sell it to a private purchaser. Peasant agriculture became in essence capitalist once more, and the profit motive had reappeared. Lenin imitated Stolypin by guaranteeing the peasant permanency of tenure. The whole system tended to help the *kulak* grow richer, and to transform the poor peasant into a hired, landless laborer.

Elsewhere in the economy under NEP the state retained what Lenin called "the commanding heights"—heavy industry, banking, transportation, and foreign trade. In domestic trade and in light industry, however, private enterprise was once more permitted. This was the so-called "private capital sector" of the economy, in which workers could be paid according to their output, and factory managers could swap some of their products in return for raw materials.

Lenin himself described NEP as a partial return to capitalism, and urged the communists to become good businessmen. Yet NEP was never intended as more than a temporary expedient. Lenin believed that it would take a couple of decades before the Russian peasant could be convinced that co-operative agriculture would be the most efficient. He also argued that a temporary relaxation of government intervention would increase industrial production and give the Russians a useful lesson in entrepreneurship.

Economic recovery was indeed obtained. By 1926-1927, industrial production was back at pre-war levels, although agriculture had not kept pace. But NEP was bitterly disliked by leading communists, who were shocked at the reversal of all the doctrines they believed in. By 1924, private business accounted for 40 per cent of Russian domestic trade, but thereafter the figure fell off. Those who took advantage of the opportunities presented by the NEP were known as NEPmen. They were often persecuted in a petty way by hostile officials, who tried to limit their profits, tax them heavily, and drag them into court on charges of speculation. The *kulak* had essentially the same experience. Thus the government often seemed to be encouraging private enterprise for economic reasons and simultaneously to be discouraging it for political reasons.

Within the Communist party, one group favored the increase of the private sector of the economy and the extension of NEP, as a new road toward the socialist goal. These were the so-called "Right deviationists." Their opponents favored the ending of concessions, the liquidation of NEPmen and *kulaks*, and a return to Marxist principles at home and the fostering of world revolution abroad—in short, the pressing of the "socialist offensive." These were the "Left deviationists," who included Trotsky. In the Center stood men who attacked both deviations, the Right as an abandonment of communism, the Left as likely to lead to a disruption of the worker-peasant alliance.

The Struggle for Power: Stalin versus Trotsky

But the big question of NEP was not the only one to agitate the communist leaders in the early twenties.

Lenin suffered two strokes in 1922, and another in 1923, and finally died in January, 1924. During the last two years of his life he played an ever lessening role. Involved in the controversy over NEP and the other controversies was the question of the succession to Lenin. Thus an individual communist's answer to the question of how to organize industry, what role to give organized labor, and what relations to maintain with the capitalist world depended not only upon his estimate of the actual situation but also upon his guess as to what answer was likely to be politically advantageous. From this maneuvering the Secretary of the Communist party, Joseph Stalin, was to emerge victorious by 1928.

The years between 1922 and 1928, especially after Lenin's death, were years of a desperate struggle for power between Stalin and Trotsky. Lenin foresaw this struggle with great anxiety. He felt that Trotsky was abler, but feared that he was overconfident, and inclined to make decisions of his own. He felt that Stalin had concentrated enormous power in his hands, in his role as party secretary, and feared that he did not know how to use it. When he learned that Stalin had gone counter to his orders in smashing the Menshevik Republic of Georgia instead of reaching an accommodation with its leaders, he wrote angrily in his testament that Stalin was too rude, and that his fellows should remove him from his post as general secretary. At the moment of his death, Lenin had published a scathing attack on Stalin, had broken off relations with him, and was about to try to relegate him to the scrapheap. Trotsky's suggestion that Stalin poisoned Lenin is not based on any evidence, but it is clear that Lenin's death rescued Stalin's career, and that, far from being the chosen heir, as he later claimed, he did not enjoy Lenin's confidence at the end.

During these years Trotsky argued for a more highly trained managerial force in industry, and for economic planning as an instrument that the state could use to control and direct social change. He favored the mechanization of agriculture and the weakening of peasant individualism by encouraging rural co-operatives, with even a hint of the collective farms where groups of peasants, in theory, would own everything collectively, rather than individually. As Trotsky progressively lost power, he championed the right of individual communists to criticize the regime. He referred to the policies of Stalin and his other increasingly powerful enemies as "bureaucratic degeneration," and came to the conclusion that only through the outbreak of revolutions in other countries could the Russian socialist revolution be carried to its proper conclusion. Only if the industrial output and technical skills of the advanced western countries could be put at the disposal of communism could Russia hope to achieve its own socialist revolution. This is the famous theory that socialism cannot succeed within the boundaries of one country: either world revolution must break out, or Russian socialism is doomed to inevitable failure.

The opponents of Trotsky's "Left deviation" found their chief spokesman in Nikolai Bukharin. A man who never held such responsible administrative posts as Lenin or Trotsky or Stalin, and who had often shifted his position on major questions, Bukharin none the less took a consistent line during these years; as editor of *Pravda* he was extremely influential. A strong defender of NEP, Bukharin softened the rigorous Marxist doctrine of the class struggle by arguing that since the proletarian state controlled the commanding heights of big capital, and since big capital would win, socialism was sure of success. This view is not unlike the "gradualist" position taken by western European Social Democrats. Bukharin did not believe in an ambitious program of rapid industrialization; he favored co-operatives, but opposed collectives. In foreign affairs he was eager to co-operate abroad with non-communist groups who might be useful to Russia. Thus he sponsored Soviet collaboration with Chiang Kai-shek in China and with the German Social Democrats.

In his rise to power, Stalin used Bukharin's arguments to discredit Trotsky and to eliminate him. Then, partly because Bukharin's policies were failing, Stalin adopted many of Trotsky's policies, and eliminated Bukharin. Original Stalinist ideas, however, developed during this process. Stalin was not basically an intellectual or a theoretician; he was a party organization stalwart. He adopted theoretical positions partly because they seemed to him the ones most likely to work, and partly because he was charting his own course to supreme power. He came to favor rapid industrialization, and to understand that this meant an unprecedentedly heavy capital investment. At the end of 1927, he suddenly shifted from his previous position on the peasantry, and openly sponsored collectivization. This shift arose because of his concern that agricultural production was not keeping pace with industry. He declared that the balance could be redressed only if agriculture, like industry, was transformed into a series of large-scale unified enterprises.

In answer to Trotsky's argument that socialism in one country was impossible, Stalin maintained that an independent socialist state could exist. This view did not at all imply the abandonment of the goal of world revolution, as has often been thought. Stalin always maintained that the socialist state (Russia) should be the center of inspiration and assistance to communist movements everywhere; Russia would help them and they would help Russia. But, in his view, during the interim period before the communists had won elsewhere it was perfectly possible for Russia to exist as the only socialist state, and indeed to grow more socialist all the time. In international relations this doctrine of Stalin made it possible for the Soviet Union to pursue either a policy of "peaceful coexistence" with capitalist states, when that seemed most profitable, or a policy of militant support of communist revolution everywhere, when that seemed most profitable. Stalin's "socialism in one country" also struck a responsive chord in the rank and file of Russian communists, who were disappointed in the failure of revolutions elsewhere. It also meant that Russia, not the West, was to be the center of the new society. Stalin's doctrine reflected his own Russian nationalism rather than the more cosmopolitan and more western views of Trotsky.

The Struggle for Power: Stalin's Victory

Analysis of the rival theories competing for acceptance in Russia in the twenties helps explain the alternatives before the communist leadership. It does not explain how Stalin won. To understand this we must move from the realm of theory and political platforms to the realm of practice and political power. At the end of the civil war, Stalin was Commissar of Nationalities. In this post he dealt with the affairs of 65,000,000 of the 140,000,000 inhabitants of the new Russian Soviet Republic. He managed the destiny of the Asiatics, whom he, as one of them, understood. Their local Bolshevik leaders became his men; where they did not, as in his native Georgia, he ruthlessly crushed them. Though a Georgian, he identified himself with Russian nationalism in the interests of a centralized Bolshevik state.

It was Stalin who took charge of creating the new Asiatic "republics" which enjoyed the appearance of local self-government, programs of economic and educational improvement, and a chance to use their local languages and develop their own cultures. It was he who in 1922 proposed and guided the adoption of a new Union of Socialist Soviet Republics as a substitute for the existing federation of republics. In the U.S.S.R., Moscow would control war, foreign policy, trade, and transport, and would co-ordinate finance, economy, food, and labor. And on paper it would leave to the republics home affairs, justice, education, and agriculture. A Council of Nationalities, with an equal number of delegates from each ethnic group, would join the Supreme Soviet as a second chamber, thus forming the Central Executive Committee, which would appoint the Council of Peoples' Commissars—the Government. To this constitutional reform Stalin pointed as an achievement equal to Trotsky's military organizational work during the civil war.

Stalin was also Commissar of the Workers' and Peasants' Inspectorate. Here his duties were to eliminate inefficiency and corruption from every branch of the civil service, and to train a new corps of civil servants. His teams moved freely through all the offices of the government, observing and recommending changes, inspecting and criticizing. In creating this post Lenin had hoped to clean house, but the ignorance and the lack of tradition that rendered the tsarist and Bolshevik civil service incompetent and corrupt operated in Stalin's inspectorate as well. Indeed many tsarist civil servants entered the Bolshevik service in the 1920's. Although the Inspectorate could not do what it was established to do, it did perform another role. It gave Stalin control over the machinery of government. Lenin attacked Stalin's work in the Inspectorate just before he died, but by then it was too late.

Stalin was also a member of the Politbureau, the tight little group of party bosses elected by the Central Committee, which included only five men throughout the civil war. Here his job was day-to-day management of the party. He was the only permanent liaison officer between the Politbureau and the Orgbureau, which allocated party personnel to their various duties, in factory, office, or army unit. In addition to these posts, Stalin became general secretary of the party's Central Committee in 1922. Here he prepared the agenda for Politbureau meetings, supplied the documentation for points under debate, and passed the decisions down to the lower levels. He controlled party patronage—that is to say, all party appointments, promotions, and demotions. He saw to it that local trade unions, co-operatives, and army units were put under communist bosses responsible to him. He had files on the loyalty and achievement of all managers of industry and other party members. In 1921, a Central Control Commission, which could expel party members for unsatisfactory conduct, was created; Stalin, as liaison between this commission and the Central Committee, now virtually controlled the purges, which were designed to keep the party pure.

In a centralized one-party state, a man of Stalin's ambitions who held so many key positions had an enormous advantage in the struggle for power. Yet the state was so new, the positions were so much less conspicuous and so much more humdrum than the Ministry of War, for instance, held by Trotsky, and Stalin's manner was so generally conciliatory, that the likelihood of Stalin's success did not become evident until it was too late to stop him. Inside the Politbureau he formed a three-man team with two other prominent Bolshevik leaders, the demagogue, Zinoviev, and the expert on doctrine, Kamenev. Zinoviev was chairman of the Petrograd Soviet and boss of the Communist International; Kamenev was Lenin's deputy and president of the Moscow Soviet. All three were old Bolsheviks, in contrast to Trotsky, who had been a Menshevik and an independent.

The combination of Stalin, Zinoviev, and Kamenev proved unbeatable. The three put down all real and imagined plots against them by the use of the secret police. They resisted Trotsky's demands for "reform," which would have democratized the party to some degree and strengthened his position while weakening Stalin's. They initiated the cult of Lenin immediately before his death, and kept it burning fiercely thereafter, so that any suggestion for change coming from Trotsky seemed almost an act of impiety. They dispersed Trotsky's followers by sending them to posts abroad. They prevented the publication of Lenin's "testament," so that the rank and file of the party would not know about Lenin's doubts concerning Stalin. They publicized all Trotsky's earlier statements in opposition to Lenin, and did not hesitate to "revise" history in order to belittle Trotsky. They were confident, and rightly so, that Trotsky was too good a communist to rally around him such anti-Bolshevik groups as old Mensheviks, SRs, and NEPmen.

Early in 1925, Stalin and his allies were able to force the resignation of Trotsky as Minister of War. Soon thereafter the three-man team dissolved; Stalin moved into alliance with Bukharin and other right-wing members of the Politbureau, to which he began to appoint some of his own followers. Using all his accumulated power, he beat his former allies on all questions of policy, and in 1926 they moved into a new but powerless alliance with Trotsky. Stalin now (1926) deposed Zinoviev from the Politbureau, charging him with intriguing in the army. Trotsky was the next one to be expelled from the Politbureau, and Zinoviev was ousted as president of the Comintern.

In 1927, differences of opinion over Stalin's foreign policy in England and in China (see below, p. 652) led to public protests by the opposition. And these in turn led to the expulsion of the opposition from the party itself. Refusing to renounce his views, Trotsky was deported to Siberia, the first stage in a long exile that took him to Turkey, Norway, and Mexico, where he died in 1940 at the hands of an assassin armed with an ice-pick. The others recanted and obtained a new lease on life. Stalin's victory was virtually complete.

IV: Stalin's Supremacy: Internal Affairs, 1928-1941

The Communist party congress that expelled Trotsky in December, 1927, also brought NEP to an end and proclaimed that the new "socialist offensive" would begin in 1928. The thirteen years between 1928 and 1941 were to see almost incredible changes in the domestic life of Russia—collectivized agriculture, speedy industrialization, forced labor, the great purges and the extermination of all political opposition, the building of an authoritarian state apparatus, and a "retreat" to bourgeois standards in almost every department of social and intellectual life.

Collectivized
Agriculture
In 1928, the failure of the peasants to deliver to the cities as much grain as had been required seemed to underline the dangers inherent in the land divisions of 1917 and in the concessions of NEP. Farm productivity on the small individual holdings was not high enough to feed the city population. Food prices for the workers were high, yet the kulaks wanted further concessions. Grain was hoarded. Stalin had often inveighed against "fanning the class struggle in the countryside," and had denied the intention of collectivizing agriculture rapidly or on a mass scale. The government economic plan issued during 1928 set a figure of 20 per cent of Russian farms as the *maximum* to be collectivized by 1933. Yet during 1929, Stalin embarked on immediate full-scale collectivization, declared war on the kulaks, and virtually put an end to individual farming in Russia.

The government did not have the money

or the credit to import food. Further, no governmental machinery is adequate to force peasants to disgorge crops that they are hiding. Therefore, the government enlisted on its side the small peasants; in exchange for their assistance in locating and turning over the *kulaks'* crops, they would be promised a place on a collective farm, to be made up of the *kulaks'* land and equipped with their implements. Probably a good many of the subsistence farmers (about 20 per cent of the number of private farms, possibly 5,000,000 households) more or less welcomed this opportunity. Initial encouraging reports led Stalin to go full speed ahead. The *kulaks*, he declared in late 1929, were to be liquidated as a class. There were about 2,000,000 households of them, perhaps as many as 10,-000,000 people in all. They were now to be totally expropriated, and at the same time barred from the new collectives. Since no provision was made for them, this move turned collectivization into a nightmare.

Peasants now were machine-gunned into submission; *kulaks* were deported to forced labor camps or to desolate regions in Siberia. In desperate revolt against the command to join collectives, the peasants burned crops, broke plows, and killed their cattle rather than turn them over to the state. More than half the horses in all Russia, 45 per cent of the cattle, and two-thirds of the sheep and goats were slaughtered. Russian livestock has never since caught up with the losses it suffered because of the excesses of collectivization. Land lay uncultivated, and over the next few years famine took a toll of millions of lives. As early as March, 1930, Stalin showed that he was aware of the ghastly mistakes he had made. In a famous statement on "dizziness with success" he put the blame on local officials who had been too eager to rush through the program. By contradicting his own orders of a few months before he managed to escape some of the hatred that would otherwise have

been directed at him. As usual, many Russian peasants disliked the man they could see, the local official, and were willing to exculpate the "little father" in the capital.

Fifty per cent of Russian farms had been hastily thrown together into collectives during this frightful year. Only an additional 10 per cent were added during the next three years, so that by 1933 60 per cent in all had been collectivized. The number rose again later in the 1930's, until by 1939 more than 96 per cent of Russian farms were collectivized. In 1941, there were 250,000 collectives, 900,000,000 acres in extent, supporting 19,000,000 families.

The 1930's also brought a modification of the original rules governing collectives. Originally collectives had been of two main types: there was the *sovkhoz*, or soviet farm, not strictly a collective at all but a state-owned enterprise, operated by the government and worked by hired laborers who were government employees; and there was the *kolkhoz*, or collective farm proper. The *sovkhozes* were designed as centers of government research and development in agriculture, and were often very large in size. But they were mostly brought to an end by Stalin in the 1930's, when he ordered some forty million acres originally allotted to them to be distributed among the *kolkhozes*. As of 1941, the *sovkhozes* occupied no significant area of land.

The *kolkhoz* itself was also originally of two types: the commune, in which all the resources of the members without exception were owned together, and the *artel*, or co-operative, in which a certain amount of private property was permitted to the members. After Stalin's modifications of the system in the thirties, the *artel* became the overwhelmingly predominant form of collective farm. In an *artel* each family owns its homestead, some livestock, and minor implements; these can be left by will to the owner's descendants. But most of the work is done on the collectively operated land. Each collective has its own managing board, responsible to the government, which oversees the work of the peasants, who are organized in brigades, each under a brigadier. Like factory laborers paid on a "piece-work" basis, peasants are remunerated according to their output, which is measured by the artificial unit of the "labor day." One day's work in managing a farm may be, for example, assessed at three labor days, while one day's work weeding a vegetable patch may be assessed at only half a labor day.

Each *kolkhoz* must turn over to the government a fixed amount of produce at fixed rates, and the total of all these amounts is designed to guarantee the feeding of the urban population, especially workers in heavy industry and members of the Red Army. In addition, the *kolkhoz* pays further taxes to cover government expenses for local construction and education. Any surplus beyond what must be delivered to meet these obligations may be sold by the peasant directly to the consumer, without the participation of any middleman. Private resale is regarded as speculation and is subject to punishment. After 1934, the government obtained at least two-thirds of its revenue by the resale on the markets at a large profit of farm produce bought at low fixed prices from the *kolkhoz*. This government profit is known as the "turnover tax."

The government assists and controls the *kolkhoz* through the supply of mechanical equipment furnished by the machine tractor stations. The collectives cannot own their own tractors, but must rent them from the stations, paying in exchange a fee ranging up to perhaps 20 per cent of the crop. The stations are important centers for political surveillance, and include staff members who are agents of the regime. By the decision when and to whom to allot tractors and how many tractors to allot, administrators of the machine tractor stations can directly affect the success of a collective; their good will is therefore of the utmost importance to the management.

In general, the aim of collectivization was to reorganize farming so as to ensure food for the industrial labor force, which was being increased by recruitment from the farms themselves. Collectivization certainly increased the total food supplies at the disposal of the government and released farmers for work in industry. But it seems certain that the over-all rise in agricultural production was small, and that in many cases the yield per unit decreased.

Industrialization

Intimately related to the drive in agriculture was the drive in industry. Here, too, Stalin had viewed with scorn the grandiose plans of the "superindustrializers" and as late as 1927 had proposed an annual increase rate in industrial production of only 15 per cent. But just as he shifted to the frantic pace of collectivizing agriculture, so he first gradually, then suddenly, shifted to forced draft in industry also.

In 1928 began the era of the Five-Year Plans, each setting incredibly ambitious goals for production over the next five years. In 1929 and 1930, Stalin appropriated ever higher sums for capital investment, and in June, 1930, he declared that industrial production must rise by 50 per cent in the current year, a fantastic and impossible figure. Under the First Five-Year Plan, adopted in 1928, annual pig-iron production was scheduled to rise from 3,500,000 tons to 10,000,000 tons by 1932, but in that year Stalin demanded 17,000,000 tons instead. It was not forthcoming, of course, but Stalin's demand for it was symptomatic of the pace at which he was striving to transform Russia from an agricultural to an industrial country.

Part of the reason for this rapid pace lay precisely in the collectivization drive itself. Large-scale farming, to which Stalin was committing Russia, must be mechanized farming. Yet there were only 7,000 tractors in all Russia at the end of 1928. Stalin secured 30,000 more during 1929, but this was nowhere near a beginning. Industry had to produce millions of machines, and the gasoline to run them. Since the countryside had to be electrified, power stations were needed by the thousands. And literally millions and millions of peasants had to be taught how to handle machinery. But there was nobody to teach them, and no factories to produce the machinery. The output of raw materials was inadequate, and the plants to process them were not there.

Another part of the reason for the drive to industrialize lay in the tenets of Marxism itself. Russia had defied all Marx's predictions by staging a proletarian revolution in a country almost without a proletariat. Yet despite the communists' initial political successes, Stalin felt that "capitalism had a firmer basis than communism in Russia, so long as it remained a country of small peasants." The communists felt that the world proletariat expected them to industrialize Russia, but even more they were determined to create as a support for themselves the massive Russian proletariat which as yet did not exist. Further, Stalin was determined to make Russia as nearly self-sufficient as possible, in line with his theory of socialism in one country. Underlying this was a motive at least as intense as any dictated by Marxist doctrine—Russian nationalism.

The strength of this motive is revealed in a speech that Stalin made in 1931:

To slacken the pace means to lag behind, and those who lag behind are beaten. We do not want to be beaten. No, we don't want to. . . . Old Russia . . . was ceaselessly beaten for her backwardness. She was beaten by the Mongol Khans, she was beaten by Turkish Beys, she was beaten by Swedish feudal lords, she was beaten by Polish-Lithuanian gentry, she was beaten by Anglo-French capitalists, she was beaten by Japanese barons; she was beaten by all—for her backwardness. For military backwardness, for cultural backwardness, for political backwardness, for industrial backwardness, for agricultural backwardness. She was beaten because to beat her was profitable and went unpunished. . . . We are fifty or a hundred years behind the advanced countries. We must make good this lag in ten years. Either we do it or they crush us.*

Whatever one may think of this quotation as history (and it omits all Russia's *victorious* wars), it reveals that Russian national self-interest as interpreted by Stalin required the most rapid possible industrialization. And it is of interest that ten years afterward the Germans did attack, something Stalin could of course not have predicted so accurately, but something that he seems to have sensed.

Stalin seems also to have felt that he had only to keep a fierce pressure on the management of industry, and the desired commodities and finished goods would be forthcoming in the desired quantities. The goals of the First Five-Year Plan were not attained, although fulfillment was announced in 1932. Immediately, the second plan, prepared by the state planning commission, went into effect, and ran until 1937; the third was interrupted only by Hitler's invasion. Each time the emphasis was on the elements of heavy industry—steel, electric power, cement, coal, oil. Between 1928 and 1940 steel production was multiplied by four and one-half, electric power by eight, cement by more than two, coal by four, and oil by almost three. Similar developments took place in chemicals and in machine production. Railroad construction was greatly increased, and the volume of freight carried quadrupled with the production of new rolling stock.

By 1940, Russian output was approaching that of Germany, although Russian efficiency and the Russian standard of living were far lower. What the rest of Europe had done in about seventy-five years Russia

---

* Quoted in Isaac Deutscher, *Stalin* (New York, 1950), 328.

had done in about twelve. Enthusiasm was artificially whipped up by wide publicizing of the high output of individual workers called "Stakhanovites," after a coal miner who had set production records. "Stakhanovites" and "heroes of labor" were richly rewarded, and the others were urged to imitate them in "socialist competition."

All this was achieved at the expense of dreadful hardships, yet eyewitnesses report that many of the workers were as enthusiastic as if they had been soldiers in battle, as indeed in a sense they were. Valuable machinery was often damaged or destroyed by inexperienced workers right off the farm. The problems of repair, of replacement, of achieving balance between the output and consumption of raw materials, of housing workers in the new centers, of moving entire industries thousands of miles into the Ural region and Siberia, were unending and cost untold numbers of lives. An American eyewitness estimates that Russia's "battle of ferrous metallurgy alone involved more casualties than the battle of the Marne."

Administratively, the Russian economy is directly run by the state. The Gosplan, or state planning commission, draws up the Five-Year Plans, and supervises their fulfillment at the management level. The Gosbank, or state bank, regulates the investment of capital. An economic council is in charge of the work of various agencies, a partial listing of which will point up the immensity of its undertakings. Its major divisions are metallurgy and chemistry (iron and steel, nonferrous metals, chemicals, rubber, alcohol); defense (aviation, armaments, munitions, tanks, ships); machinery (heavy machines, medium machines, machine tools, electrical industry); fuel and power (coal, oil, electric power); agriculture and procurement; and consumer's goods (grain, meat and dairy products, fisheries, textiles, light industry). Under iron and steel, for example, there function the production trusts controlling their own mines as well as blast furnaces and rolling mills. These are the so-called "combinats," or great production complexes like that at

A new Soviet industrial center: Magnitogorsk in the Urals.

Magnitogorsk in the Urals. In each plant, as in each collective, the manager is responsible for producing the quota set for him within the maximum cost allowed him. He is consulted on production targets, and has considerable leeway in selecting his staff and allocating labor and raw materials. He is bound to render a rigid accounting to the government, which of course fixes the price he must pay for his raw materials.

The Social Impact

The social effects of the economic program have been dramatic. Urban population rose from about 18 per cent in 1926 to about 33 per cent in 1940. The number of cities with a population between 50,000 and 100,000 doubled, and the number of cities with a population exceeding 100,000 more than quadrupled. The largest cities, Moscow and Leningrad (the new name for Petersburg-Petrograd after the death of Lenin), almost doubled in size, and among smaller cities, to take just one example, Alma Ata in Siberia grew from 45,000 to 230,000 between 1928 and 1939. The entire social picture was radically altered.

The relative freedom to choose one's job which had characterized the NEP period naturally disappeared. Individual industrial enterprises signed labor contracts with the *kolkhozes* by which the *kolkhoz* was obliged to send a given number of farm workers to the factories, often against their will. Peasants who had resisted collectivization were simply drafted into labor camps. In the factories, the trade unions became simply another organ of the state. The chief role of the unions is to achieve maximum production and efficiency, to discourage absenteeism and poor work. Trade unions may not strike, or engage in conflict with management. All they can do is administer the social insurance laws, and seek improvements in workers' living conditions by negotiation.

Thus in the U.S.S.R. the old privileged classes of noble landlords, already weak at the time of the revolution, ceased to exist. The industrial, commercial, and financial bourgeoisie, which was just coming into its own at the time of the revolution, was destroyed after 1928, despite the temporary reprieve it had experienced under NEP. Most of the old intelligentsia, who had favored a revolution, could not in the end stomach Stalin's dictatorship, and many of them emigrated. Of the million and a half émigrés from Russia after the revolution, only a very small number (contrary to the general view in the West) were cousins of the Tsar. Those of the old intelligentsia who remained were forced into line with the new Soviet intelligentsia, which Stalin felt to be a very important class. All were compelled to accept the new Stalinist dogma and to drop their interest in the outside world. The new intelligentsia was expected to concentrate on technical advance, and on new administrative devices for speeding up the transformation of the country.

Although the effect of these social changes would presumably have been to level all ranks, Stalin set himself against the old Bolshevik principles of equality. The Marxist slogan, "From each according to his capacity, to each according to his needs," was shelved in favor of a new one, "From each according to his capacity, to each according to his work." Where Lenin had allowed none of the members of the government to earn more than a skilled laborer, Stalin set up a new system of incentives. A small minority of bureaucrats and skilled laborers, factory managers, and successful *kolkhoz* bosses earned vastly more than the great majority of unskilled laborers and peasants. Together with the writers, artists, musicians, and entertainers who were willing to lend their talents to the services of the regime, these men became a new élite, separated by a wide economic and social gulf from the toiling masses.

They had a vested interest in furthering a regime to which they owed everything, and without which they would be nothing.

One is told by Soviet propagandists that this is a temporary situation. The present society in the Soviet Union is described as "socialist," while "communism," not yet achieved, is regarded as the goal toward which the U.S.S.R. is still moving. Yet, just as the "withering away" of the state, which the Marxists predicted, was instead replaced under Stalin by the enormous swelling of state power and state machinery, so the equality predicted by the Marxists was replaced by a new caste system. The means of production are publicly owned in the Soviet Union, as the Marxists urged. But the power of the state, the birth of a new élite, the brutalization of millions of human beings, and the ruthless use of force after the revolution had been achieved were all the contributions of Stalin.

The Purge Trials

Stalin's program was not achieved without opposition. The crisis of 1931 and 1932, when industrial goals were not being met and the countryside was being swept by starvation, created discontent inside the regime as well as outside. A small number of officials circulated memoranda advocating Stalin's deposition as General Secretary, an act which the party had every right to perform. Stalin jailed them for conspiracy, and one leading Bolshevik committed suicide. It is widely believed that Stalin's own wife reproached him at this time with the ravages that the terror was working, and that she too committed suicide. Stalin's attack against those he believed to be his enemies took the form of the famous purges, which began in 1934 and continued at intervals until 1938.

These purges remain the most mysterious episode in Soviet history. They are often compared with the Jacobin Terror of the French Revolution, when the revolution "devoured its children." But, in contrast to the rapid appearance of the Terror in France, the purges did not begin for seventeen years after the Russian Revolution. Members of the opposition had been demoted, expelled from the party, and even exiled, as in the case of Trotsky; but nobody had been executed. There is an entirely credible story that the Bolshevik leaders had agreed among themselves early in their career never to start guillotining each other. Yet, when the terror began in Russia, it was even more drastic than it had been in France. Moreover, unlike Robespierre, Stalin managed to survive.

From exile, Trotsky continued to attack Stalin in a journal called *The Bulletin of the Opposition*. Clever as always, he scored telling points against Stalin, and his words were carefully read by Soviet officials. Yet the older generation of communists, though they may have hated Stalin, made no move against him. A younger group, however, seemingly more restless and convinced that Stalin had abandoned Lenin's program, found the model for conspiracy in the heroes of the terrorist movement who had assassinated Alexander II (see Chapter XV). They were apparently prepared to use terrorism against Stalin and his henchmen. Even within the Politbureau men loyal to Stalin grew restless at his ruthlessness, and urged him to relax the pressure; Sergei Kirov, boss of Leningrad, took the lead.

Stalin at times seemed to yield to this urging, as when he ordered more gentle treatment for rebellious *kulaks* in June, 1932, and limited the powers of the political police. But at other times he seemed to be taking the opposite course, as when he issued a decree making an entire family responsible for the treason of any of its members. On the whole, however, tension relaxed during 1932-1934. Kirov proclaimed a new era of lenience at a party conference, and former leaders of the opposition, including Bukharin, were appointed to help draft a new and liberal constitution.

Then on December 1, 1934, Kirov was assassinated by a young terrorist communist in Leningrad. Although the story that Stalin himself had plotted the assassination cannot be confirmed, it is clear that Stalin now determined to strike at the opposition. The assassin was executed. Accused of complicity, Zinoviev and Kamenev were jailed, and forced to admit that they had plotted to restore capitalism. Yet the drafting of the new "democratic" constitution went on. Stalin became ever more withdrawn, ever more autocratic, ever more resolved to destroy the old Bolsheviks, as Ivan the Terrible had destroyed the old nobility. After an interlude during 1935 and early 1936, during which Stalin said that "life had become more joyous," the purges proper began.

The official story was that Trotskyite agitation abroad was linked with the murder of Kirov, and the alleged plans for the murder of Stalin. A series of public political trials took place. In the first (1936), Zinoviev, Kamenev, and fourteen others admitted these charges and were executed. In the second (1937) seventeen other leading Bolsheviks declared that they had knowledge of a conspiracy between Trotsky and the German and Japanese intelligence service, by which Russian territory was to be transferred to Germany and Japan. All were executed. Then (June, 1937) came the secret liquidation of the top commanders in the Red Army, who were accused of conspiring with "an unfriendly foreign power" (Germany) with a view to sabotage. All were executed after an announcement that they had confessed. The last of the public trials took place in March, 1938, as twenty-one leading Bolsheviks, including Bukharin, confessed to similar charges and were executed.

But these public trials and the secret trial of the generals give only a faint idea of the extent of the purge. Every member of Lenin's Politbureau except Stalin and Trotsky was either killed or committed suicide to avoid execution. Two vice-commissars of foreign affairs and most of the ambassadors of the diplomatic corps, fifty of the seventy-one members of the Central Committee of the Communist party, almost all the military judges who had sat in judgment and had condemned the generals, two successive heads of the secret police, themselves the leaders in the previous purges, the prime ministers and chief officials of all the non-Russian Soviet Republics—all were killed or vanished. A list of those who disappeared reads like a "who's who" of high officialdom in state and party throughout the twenties and thirties. Literally thousands were executed or disappeared without a trace. The public trials probably included only those who were willing to confess, whether guilty or not. The rest were condemned privately.

Although it is clear that many of those who were executed opposed Stalin, the charges against them were certainly not true. Had they been true, the great conspiracy involving almost everybody but Stalin himself would surely have accomplished more than the assassination of Kirov. It is altogether unlikely that any of the top communists conspired with Hitler, little though they loved Stalin. Some who confessed may have felt so great a loyalty to the cause of communism, however perverted, that they sacrificed themselves for Stalin's soviet state. Some doubtless hoped to save their families, or even themselves, and a few leaders were spared the death penalty to encourage confessions from the others. Many may have hoped that the confessions were so ridiculous that nobody could believe them.

What Stalin apparently wanted was to destroy utterly all possibility of future conspiracies. So he trumped up charges against anybody who conceivably could become a member of a regime that might replace his own. One partial explanation of his action is that he felt sure that war with Germany was inevitable, and he did not trust anybody but himself to meet it. Despite the enormous upheaval of the purges, no breakdown took place in the state. New bureaucrats were found to take the places of the old. The new Stalin-trained officials, uncultivated but competent, boorish and without experience in the western world, now manned all top-level positions.

The Authoritarian State

In the midst of the purges, in 1936, Stalin proclaimed the new constitution, the "most democratic in the world." By its provisions nobody was disfranchised, as priests and members of the former nobility and bourgeoisie had previously been. Civil liberties were extended, but even on paper these have never been more than a sham, since the constitution provides that they can be modified in the "interest of the toilers." The fact that the U.S.S.R. is a one-party state prevents elections from being anything but an expression of unanimity. The right to nominate candidates for the Supreme Soviet belongs to Communist party organizations, trade unions, co-operatives, youth groups, and cultural societies; but all are completely dominated by the party. The party picks the candidates, and no more than one for each post is ever presented to the voters. The party controls the soviets, and the party hierarchy and government hierarchy overlap and interlock.

Every citizen is eligible for membership in the party on application to a local branch, which votes on his application after a year of trial. Communist children's organizations feed the youth groups, which in turn feed the party. The party is organized both territorially and functionally in pyramidal form, with organizations at the bottom level in factory, farm, and government office. These are grouped together by rural or urban local units, and these in turn by regional and territorial conferences and congresses. The party organizations elect the All-Union party congress, which selects the Central Committee of the party, and which is in theory the highest policy-making organ, though actually no party congress was held between 1939 and 1954. The Central Committee selects the Politbureau. At each level of the party pyramid there are organizations for agitation and propaganda, for organization and instruction, for military and political training. The party exercises full control over the government, which simply enacts formally what the party has decided upon. The Five-Year Plans, for example, were party programs that went into effect even before they were formally adopted by the government.

The highest organ of the government is the Supreme Soviet, made up of two houses —a Soviet of the Union, based on population, and a Soviet of Nationalities, elected according to national administrative divisions. In theory, the Supreme Soviet is elected for a term of four years. The Supreme Soviet itself does little; it appoints a presidium which issues the decrees and carries on the work of the Supreme Soviet between sessions. It also appoints the Council of Ministers (long called the Council of People's Commissars). This cabinet, rather than the Supreme Soviet or its presidium, enacts most of the legislation, and is thus the legislative as well as the executive organ of the Russian state. The chairmanship of the Council of People's Commissars, the chairmanship of the Politbureau, and the General Secretariat of the Communist party were all posts held by Stalin, who in addition served as Commissar of Defense, chief of the State Defense Council, which ran the country during wartime, and Generalissimo. Similar overlapping of party and government posts has been the regular practice.

In 1924, Stalin's constitutional reform had created the new Union of Soviet Socialist Republics, including the enormously large Russian Federative Republic, the Ukraine, White Russia, Georgia, Armenia, and Azerbaidjan, and three central Asiatic Soviet Socialist republics: Uzbekistan, Turkmenistan, and Tadjikistan. In 1936, Kazakh and Kirghiz republics were added, making a total of eleven. As a result of the annexations of the Baltic states and of Finnish and Rumanian territory in 1940, five more republics were created: Lithuania, Latvia, Estonia, Karelia, and Moldavia. These sixteen "Union" republics ranged in population from the Russian, with about 114,000,000 people, and including most of Siberia, through the Ukrainian, with more than 40,000,000, down to the Karelian, with about 800,000. This last was abolished in 1956, and its territory absorbed by the Russian Federative Republic, apparently to convince the Finns that they had no chance of regaining it. Within the Russian republic are sixteen "autonomous" republics, and numerous other subdivisions, all called "autonomous." The larger SSR's have similar subdivisions.

Each of the Union republics and autonomous republics has a government patterned exactly on that of the Soviet Union, except that the supreme soviet of each republic is unicameral and not bicameral, since it lacks a chamber of nationalities. Many complaints have been heard in recent years about the way in which "Great-Russian chauvinism" has permeated official policy toward the individual minority republics. Although this soviet descendant of tsarist Russification policy has always been a menace, it is widely believed that in the years before World War II, the chief objective was not to try to Russify the nationalities but to communize them. With this end in view, the party permitted and encouraged local nationalities to revive their culture, study their past traditions, and use their own language. Like every other cultural manifestation permitted in the U.S.S.R., these national cultural achievements were "managed." Not only was it impossible for anti-Soviet or anti-communist material to appear in print or in any of the plastic arts, but, as everywhere, all artistic effort was closely supervised and had to serve the regime positively.

Although the Stalin constitution specifically gives each republic the right to secede, this provision is pure window-dressing. The central government is overpoweringly stronger than the government of any one republic, which in any case is often not even made up of natives. Although each of the sixteen republics was in 1944 given its own foreign office by an amendment to the constitution, this amendment was never intended to give them autonomy in this critically important field. Actually, it seems simply to have been a device for securing representation of the Ukraine and White Russia in the United Nations. The representatives of these two republics to the United Nations have never been anything but extra Soviet delegates.

The Russian Thermidor?

The period between 1934 and 1941, notable for the purges and for the constitutional development of Stalin's one-party state, is also called by many shrewd observers of revolutions the true Russian "Thermidor," as distinct from NEP. The term "Thermidor" has come to mean a period in which a revolution has burnt itself out, and the prevailing mood shifts from messianic enthusiasm to one of desire for normality. In revolutionary France, the shift was signalized by the fall of Robespierre and the Jacobin regime and the advent of the Directory, a different government with different objectives, policies, and personnel, which was in turn succeeded by Napoleon's dictatorship. In the U.S.S.R. the striking fact was that Stalin stayed in office throughout: he was in effect the Russian Robespierre, Directory, and Napoleon all rolled into one. If we accept the parallel, the Russian Thermidor was a managed and manipulated Thermidor, involving no real liberalization of the regime or relaxation of controls. Yet perhaps the parallel is not entirely valid, since Stalin resembled Napoleon far more than he did the weak Directory.

In any case, the period of the late 1930's saw a wholesale retreat from many ideas of the revolution. Simultaneously with the purges and the new constitution, the bread ration was raised, the *kolkhoz* was reformed to permit the individual farmer to own his homestead, new medals and titles were awarded to leading workers in plants and to scientists, engineers, and military men. In the Red Army traditional tsarist distinctions between officers and men were restored, and marshals were named for the first time. Thus, without relaxing political control, Stalin introduced an element of relaxation into the daily life of the rank and file, at the very height of his Terror. The standard of living went up as the production of consumer's goods was encouraged, and as workers were invited to spend their earnings on little luxuries previously unavailable.

Simultaneously, the state rediscovered Russia's great past. The standard communist teaching had been that proletarians have no fatherland; the very name of Russia had almost been abandoned. Now, in contrast, officially controlled organs of opinion editorialized that one should love one's own country, and hailed the heroes of the tsarist era. Alexander Nevsky, who had defeated the Teutonic knights; Dmitri Donskoi, who had defeated the Tartars; Peter the Great; Kutuzov, who had defeated Napoleon; even Ivan the Terrible— all were praised to the skies. The reputations of the great literary figures of the nineteenth century underwent a similar rehabilitation. This retreat to Russian nationalism reached its climax during World War II, when the Marxist *Internationale* itself was dropped as the national anthem.

The old Bolsheviks had attacked the family as the backbone of the old order, had made marriage difficult and divorce easy, had drawn no distinction between legitimate and illegitimate children, and had encouraged promiscuity and abortions. Stalin's state now rehabilitated the sanctity of marriage, denounced the seducer, made divorces very hard to get, declared the family essential to the state, and encouraged children to obey their parents. Doubtless the shift came in part as a result of the falling birth rate and increasing juvenile delinquency, but it was none the less part of the abandonment of radicalism.

The early Bolsheviks had destroyed the old school system, abolished homework and examinations, and allowed children to administer the schools collectively with their teachers. Attendance fell off, the schools became revolutionary clubs of youngsters, and the training of teachers was neglected. The universities deteriorated, since anybody aged sixteen could enroll in them. Degrees were abolished, and technical training was stressed to the exclusion of other subjects. Under NEP, this chaotic situation was modified, and the basic problem of increasing literacy was seriously tackled. But the subjects of ordinary school curricula were replaced by the so-called "project" system, with heavy emphasis on labor problems and Marxist theory. The teachers had little to do except memorize texts, and quiz the children to test their mastery of them. The Communist party itself took over the universities, purged the faculties, and compelled the students to spend one week in three at work in factories—a system that helped neither the student nor the university, and cannot have increased industrial production by very much.

The "thermidorean reaction," as might have been expected, changed this system drastically. Training of teachers improved, their salaries were raised, and regular ranks in the civil service were established for them. The old pre-revolutionary system of admissions and degrees in the universities was restored, as was the pre-revolutionary school curriculum. Examinations and homework re-appeared; discipline was enforced on school children. The emphasis on political education was reduced, and co-education was abandoned. Fees for tuition were restored for secondary schools, the Russian counterpart of the American high school or the French *lycée*. These tuition fees made higher education difficult to obtain except for children of the new élite or unusually talented students who were able to win state scholarships. Literacy rose to about 90 per cent, if we may believe Soviet figures.

The educational reforms certainly made books, theaters, museums, and libraries available to many more Russians than ever before. Newspapers and periodicals multiplied, and the regime's respect for science and learning was genuine. But the regime's attitude was narrowly utilitarian and thoroughly intolerant. All cultural activities were measured by their positive contribution to the state. Education became indoctrination. Systems of ideas that might rival communism were not allowed to compete, since the government could always silence those who might be their spokesmen. In this respect the Soviet regime was even more authoritarian than that of a ruler like Tsar Nicholas I (see Chapter XV).

Under Nicholas I, censorship prevented the writer from saying certain things, but it did not positively prescribe what he must say. It was a negative, not a positive censorship, and it left a margin of personal freedom that permitted some of the greatest works of all literature to be written in Russia. The Soviet censorship, on the other hand, was positive, and required of all artists that they constantly praise the new system, and devote their talents to publicizing its merits. The party line extended into all cultural fields, even music, where talented composers had to apologize abjectly for failing to produce communist

symphonies, whatever they may be. The creative artist did not know from day to day whether his efforts would win him a Stalin prize or a sentence to a Siberian labor camp.

Neither did the scientist or scholar. Sciences like physics and genetics involve philosophical presuppositions. Soviet biologists, for example, have been punished for accepting standard western scientific principles that simply cast doubt on the possibility of creating a new biological race in one generation. The defenders of the "new Soviet man" stoutly proclaimed that it *is* possible. In the humanities even the students of word-roots and early linguistic development were victimized, and historians and social scientists steered a particularly perilous course.

The Russian Thermidor came last of all, and doubtless very reluctantly, to modify the traditional communist position on religion. Here militant atheism had been the policy of the early Bolsheviks. They jailed and sometimes executed bishops and priests; they sponsored an atheist society and a museum of anti-religious propaganda. Behind this attitude lay more than the standard Marxist feeling that religion was the opium of the masses; in Russia, the Orthodox Church had always been a pillar of tsarism, and had held back the intellectual advance of the country. Many years of attacks on religion, however, failed to eradicate Orthodoxy from among the people. When in 1937 Hitler built a Russian church in Berlin, and took every occasion to speak kindly of the Orthodox Church, Stalin moved in the religious field also. Declaring that Christianity had contributed to past Russian progress, the government called off its anti-religious propaganda and enlisted its own atheist society to rehabilitate the Church. Church-going became respectable once more, although members of the party were not encouraged to profess religion. As a result, when war came, the leading church dignitaries supported the regime enthusiastically, although Hitler won a number of Ukrainian clerics to his side. In 1943, Stalin received high churchmen; the government lowered taxes on church property, lifted the curfew for Easter, and appointed a new Patriarch, on whose subservience the regime could count.

Viewed together, the changes of the Thermidor period seem to have had a double purpose. They were designed in part to retain popular loyalty during a period when the party itself was being disrupted by the purges. But they were also designed in part to strengthen the country to meet an expected attack from Germany. However far the return to old and popular forms and ideas was carried, it was always the regime that took the lead. And never at any moment did Stalin relax his firm control over all departments of national life.

V: Soviet Foreign Policy, 1918-1941

Foreign Office and Comintern, 1918-1928 During the period of "war communism," the Bolsheviks had a chance to reflect upon their previously firm conviction that the world revolution was to be expected in the immediate future. The communist states in Bavaria and in Hungary proved to be short-lived (see Chapter XX); everywhere the moderates triumphed. As the civil war drew to a close, Lenin and his followers realized that to re-build a shattered Russia it would be necessary to deal with the capitalist world. In the Foreign Office they had two competent men: Chicherin, a learned aristocrat turned Bolshevik, and Litvinov, his shrewd and able chief assistant. These two and their staff now became diplomats in the service of the Soviet state, like diplomats in the service of other states.

But the idea of world revolution was of course not abandoned. Lenin in 1919 founded the Third International, known thereafter as the Comintern. It issued what amounted almost to a new Communist Manifesto, summoning communists all over the world to unite against the "bourgeois cannibals" of capitalism. Zinoviev was put in charge, and his chief assistants were also Russians. Labor, socialist, and anarchist parties in Bulgaria, Norway, Italy, and Spain began to adhere to the new organization, although many withdrew in disgust when it became clear that the Bolsheviks were establishing a dictatorship in Russia with secret police and an army. Yet the Comintern continued to operate side by side with the Foreign Office, and during the next few years often in seeming contradiction to it. This duality gave Russian foreign policy a unique aspect. The maintenance of the Comintern aroused suspicion abroad, and made capitalist states reluctant even to recognize the new Russia.

The Foreign Office concluded a trade treaty with England in 1921, at the beginning of the NEP period, which bound Russia not to stir up the peoples of the British Empire by any means, and re-opened trade between the two countries. Similar treaties were concluded between Russian and Poland, the Baltic States, Scandinavia, Germany, and Italy. A truce had been arranged between the communist and capitalist worlds. In 1922, the Russians were invited to an international economic conference at Genoa. The British and French were convinced that NEP meant a return to capitalism, and had worked out a scheme for investment in Russia as part of a program for the postwar economic reconstruction of Europe. Not only did the Russians reject this plan, but they signed with defeated

Germany the Treaty of Rapallo (April, 1922), which provided for the renunciation of all claims for reparations and implied a German willingness to recognize Bolshevik nationalizations. This recognition the other powers, especially France, were unwilling to grant because of the large amounts of capital they had invested in Russia before the revolution. Rapallo relieved Russian isolation, and brought German technical knowledge to the service of the Bolsheviks. They permitted the Germans to build and operate armament and aircraft factories on Russian soil in defiance of the Treaty of Versailles.

In 1923, at Lausanne, Russia lost a dispute with Britain over international regulation of the Straits, and further friction with Britain arose over Afghanistan. But Britain recognized the Soviet regime in 1924, despite Trotsky's description of the mild Laborite Ramsay MacDonald as a "Christian Menshevik" whose country was full of cockroaches—a comment that illustrates some of Russia's difficulty in getting along with the rest of the world. Later in the same year, 1924, the so-called "Zinoviev letter" was published in England. It purported to instruct the British Communist party in the techniques of revolution, and it may or may not have been genuine; but the "Zinoviev letter" influenced the British voters to return a Conservative government, which denounced the treaties with Russia. In 1927, a raid on the offices of a Russian firm doing business in London produced further evidence of communist agitation in England, and the government now broke relations with Russia altogether. The Anglo-Russian council of trade unions set up by the communists collapsed when the Russians criticized British moderation in the general strike of 1926. Meantime, the United States had no diplomatic relations with the Soviet regime, and did not recognize it until 1933.

During the years 1918-1927, the Comintern compiled a record of failure. First, the Russians failed to keep in line the leaders of the Italian Left in a conference at Leghorn in 1921, and thus contributed handsomely to the success of Mussolini in the next year. They failed in Bulgaria to collaborate with a liberal agrarian regime, and allowed the triumph of a fascist group in 1923. Most important, they failed in Germany, where a revolution actually threatened during 1923 as a result of French occupation of the Ruhr (for details of these events, see Chapters XX and XXI). After Lenin's death, the feud between Stalin and Trotsky was reflected in the Communist parties of other countries and cost the Comintern heavily.

The Russians failed in Poland, where they helped Pilsudski to dictatorial power in 1926, after which he turned against them. They failed in the Moslem and colonial world. But their greatest failure came in China (see also Chapter XXI), where in 1923 the Chinese nationalist revolutionary leader, Sun Yat-sen, agreed to take communist advice and received one of the Comintern's best men, Borodin. Borodin helped Sun re-organize his political party, the Kuomintang, and admitted communists to it, although this alienated the right-wing supporters of the national party. In March, 1926, Sun having died, Chiang Kai-shek, who later married a sister of Sun's wife, led a *coup* against the government, and began to arrest communists. It is often argued that, had Stalin at that moment broken with Chiang and proceeded to sponsor a Chinese communist revolution, he might well have won China. Indeed Trotsky analyzed the situation that way at the time. But Stalin in his own analysis went back to a theory that the Bolsheviks had not espoused since Lenin's return to Russia in April, 1917: the theory that a bourgeois revolution must precede a socialist revolution, and that all the communists could and should do in China was to help Chiang achieve this first revolution. The eventual result was a series of massacres of Chinese communists by Chiang, and a loss of prestige for Stalin and for Russia.

Indeed Stalin had apparently never really believed in the effectiveness of the Comintern as an instrument of world revolution. When he came to sole power, he could not abandon it, however, because of the criticism he would have aroused, and because he sought to dilute and eventually to eradicate the largely Trotskyite sentiments of communists in other countries. He therefore applied to the Comintern the same techniques he had used against the party at home, and established full control over it through use of the Russian delegation. This delegation was responsible to the Politbureau, and as the representative of the only successful revolutionary country it enjoyed great prestige. Successively, the Comintern was influenced to denounce the enemies of Stalin: Trotsky and the Left in 1924, Bukharin and the Right in 1928. Thereafter there was no divergence between the Comintern and the Foreign Office.

Stalin and the West, 1928-1939

Simultaneously with the adoption of the "new socialist offensive" at home, Stalin swung the Comintern leftward into a new period of militant revolutionary activity. The Social Democrats of western countries were denounced now as "social fascists" and as the most dangerous enemies of communism. The communists were going to bring about revolutions by themselves. Yet Stalin's personal belief in the possibility of revolution elsewhere seems to have been small. "One Soviet tractor is worth more than ten good foreign communists" is a remark quoted as typical of the views of Stalin's entourage in the days of the First Five-Year Plan; it reflects his real contempt for the rest of the world and his deep-rooted Russian nationalism.

This lack of real interest in the behavior of communists abroad and the failure to understand the true play of forces inside other countries led directly to the triumph of Hitler in Germany in 1933 (see Chapter XX). The communists in Germany, who had been instructed by the Comintern that the Social Democrats and not the Nazis were their worst enemies, fought the Nazis in the streets, but allied themselves with them in the Reichstag. They believed that a Nazi triumph would very soon be followed by a communist revolution. Thus even after Hitler came to power, the Russians renewed their nonaggression pact with Germany.

Yet the shock of realization that Hitler had meant precisely what he said about liquidating communists, and the fear that the U.S.S.R. itself might be in danger, soon led Stalin to modify Russian policy in the direction of collective security. After Hitler had refused to guarantee the Baltic states jointly with Stalin, Russia entered the League of Nations in September, 1934. The Soviet delegate, Litvinov, now became the most eloquent defender of universal disarmament and punishment for aggressors. Soon afterwards, the Russians began to negotiate for an "eastern Locarno" security pact to balance the agreement reached by the western European nations at Locarno in 1925 (see below, p. 681). Although no such structure could be created because of Polish and German hostility to the U.S.S.R., Russia did sign pacts with France and Czechoslovakia in 1935 providing for consultation, under the terms of the League, in the event of aggression, and for mutual aid, if the League certified that aggression had occurred. Soviet aid to Czechoslovakia, if the Czechs became victims of aggression, was to be delivered only if the French, who were bound to the Czechs by a long-standing alliance, honored their obligations first.

In view of the shift in soviet foreign policy, the Comintern also shifted its line.

In 1935 the recent deadly enemies, the Social Democrats and bourgeois liberals of the West, were to be warmly embraced as allies against the fascist menace. Communists were to take the lead in forming "popular fronts" against fascism, and might properly welcome anybody, no matter how conservative in other ways, who would stand together with them on this principle. Revolutionary propaganda and anti-capitalist agitation were to be soft-pedaled. The communists in all the countries of the world led the fight for the defense budgets that they had previously sabotaged. Inside the Soviet Union the adoption of the "popular front" strategy was probably not unrelated to the purges, since the "Right deviationists" were anxious to reach an accommodation with the fascist states, and the "Left deviationists" insisted on the steady pursuit of world revolution.

This was the period when popular front governments came to power in France and Spain, and when many young men and women in the West with bright hopes and little knowledge of the Soviet Union accepted the communists as their true brothers in arms against the menace of Hitler. However effective the "popular front" may have been as a tactic with western individuals, the purges inside Russia disillusioned western governments. A state that had to exterminate its top civil and military personnel for the crime of collaborating with the enemy did not make an attractive ally.

Russia and the western European bloc each assumed that the chief purpose of the other was to turn the full force of Hitler's forthcoming attack away from itself and in the opposite direction. That Hitler intended to attack, nobody could doubt. On September 12, 1936, in a speech at Nuremberg, he specifically declared once more that

if I had the Ural mountains with their incalculable store of treasures in raw materials, Si-

beria with its vast forests, and the Ukraine with its tremendous wheatfields, Germany under National Socialist leadership would swim in plenty.*

There was, then, much reason for the West to hope that the attack would be directed against the U.S.S.R.; this Stalin was determined to avert.

Soviet intervention in the Spanish Civil War (see below, Chapter XX) is an interesting demonstration of Stalin's real position. General Francisco Franco, who led an army revolt against the republican government of Spain in 1936, soon obtained aid from Mussolini and Hitler. The Russians, though reluctant to intervene in Spain at all because of their anxiety to prove their respectability to the western powers, realized that a failure to help the Spanish republic would cost them support all over the world. But their aid was too little and came too late, and consisted largely of police agents who devoted themselves to fighting Spanish anarchists and Trotskyites. The Russians hoped that the western powers would intervene also, feeling that if they did so they would be irrevocably committed to continue the fight against Hitler on other battlefields. But western neutrality in Spain helped convince Stalin that a western alliance could not be counted upon.

A still more important factor here was the western appeasement of Hitler, which reached its climax in the Munich agreement of Britain, France, Germany, and Italy in September, 1938. From the Russian point of view, the Munich cession of Czech lands to Hitler, and the French failure to support Czechoslovakia and thus make operative the Russo-Czech alliance, could have only one purpose—to drive Hitler east. Stalin was apparently ready to support the Czechs if the French did too; when they did not, he seems to have decided that he had better sound out Hitler for an under-

* A. Hitler, *My New Order*, R. de Sales, ed. (New York, 1941). 400.

After the Hitler-Stalin pact, August, 1939.

standing. Thus a truly operative alliance between Stalin and the West proved impossible between 1935 and 1939.

When the British and French realized that appeasement had failed to stop Hitler, they sought reluctantly for a firmer alliance with the U.S.S.R. From March to August, 1939, Stalin kept open both his negotiations with the West and his slowly ripening negotiations with the Germans, which at first seemed to be concerned only with a trade agreement. The British and French mission, when it finally arrived in Moscow, was not composed of sufficiently high-ranking men to inspire Russian confidence. Moreover, the western powers naturally refused to turn over to Stalin the territories that he wanted as a bulwark against Germany—Finland and the Baltic republics of Estonia, Latvia, and Lithuania.

The growing eagerness of the Germans to secure a nonaggression pact gave Stalin the opportunity he sought to divert the war from Russia. In May, 1939, Litvinov was dismissed as foreign minister because he was Jewish and could therefore not negotiate with Germans; he was replaced by Molotov. In the pact Molotov eventually reached with Hitler late in August, 1939, both powers undertook to remain neutral to-

ward each other in the event of war. A secret additional protocol provided for a division between Germany and Russia of Poland, which Hitler was about to attack. At worst, this put Russia's frontier farther west in the event of a subsequent German attack. The Russians lived up to the economic clauses of the agreement to the letter, although the Germans did not. The publication of the Hitler-Stalin pact necessitated an abrupt shift in the world communist line, which had remained stanchly "popular front." Now it was once more necessary for puzzled communists to denounce liberals and Social Democrats as enemies. They had to call the war that Hitler launched against Poland within a few days an "imperialist war," in which there was no difference between the two sides and in which communists should not get involved.

Stalin and the Second World War

Stalin overrated the military power of the Poles to resist Hitler, and thus miscalculated the course of the first weeks of war. Faced with the complete collapse of Poland, he marched into the eastern portion. Disturbed by the lull ("the phony war") on the western fronts, he probably feared that Hitler would turn against him at once. This might well have happened had Hitler been able to secure peace with France and England, as he strove to do. During the lull, in December, 1939, came Stalin's attack on Finland, which, unlike the Baltic states, had refused to grant him strategic bases. The attack on the Finns by Stalin aroused a storm of anti-Russian sentiment in the West. Both Britain and France supported the recruitment of armies of volunteers, and considered air raids against Russian targets in support of the Finns. The League of Nations expelled Russia. Despite severe setbacks to the Russian troops, the war was won by the spring of 1940 before the western allies were able to give the Finns effective aid.

And in the spring of 1940, Stalin's second major calculation went awry. Like many observers, he apparently expected France to hold out a long time and had believed that, even if Hitler eventually defeated

Stalin.

the French, Germany would be greatly weakened. Now instead came the lightning German operations in the west, and the war on the Continent was over. Only the British held out (see Chapter XXII). Preoccupied with the security of his western frontiers, Stalin simply seized the three Baltic republics and staged rigged plebiscites in which the Latvians, Estonians, and Lithuanians asked to be included in the Soviet Union. He demanded of Rumania in June, 1940, the province of Bessarabia, whose loss after World War I the U.S.S.R. had never recognized, and also northern Bukovina, which had formerly been Habsburg, not Russian, territory, but which had a large Ukrainian population and was strategically valuable. Parts of these territories were annexed to existing SSRs and parts were incorporated into the new Moldavian SSR. The Germans had expected Russian seizure of Bessarabia, but not of Bukovina; they permitted the seizure, however, telling the Rumanians that they could expect no help from Hitler. But that was as far as Hitler's co-operation with Stalin in eastern Europe went. The re-annexation of Bessarabia had given the U.S.S.R. the mouths of the Danube, controlling an important artery. The Russians seemed to be moving into southeast Europe, a region in which the Germans were not prepared to let them operate alone.

Only a few weeks after the Russian seizure of Rumanian territory, Hitler asserted his own southeastern interests by forcing the Rumanians to cede territory to Hungary (August, 1940) and then guaranteeing the new Rumanian frontiers, a guarantee that could apply only against the U.S.S.R. Soon afterwards, German troops appeared in Finland, "to reinforce the German armies in Norway," Hitler explained. And in the autumn of 1940 German troops entered Rumania proper, "to guard the Rumanian oil-fields against British sabotage." These maneuvers on his new frontiers deeply disquieted Stalin.

In October, 1940, Italy attacked Greece, and open war had spread to the Balkans. In November, when Molotov went to Berlin, Hitler tried to dazzle him with grandiose offers of an enormous future Soviet sphere of influence extending through Persia to the Persian Gulf and Indian Ocean, and including India, after the British Empire was destroyed. Each time this luscious bait was held out, Molotov tried to bring the discussion back to southeast Europe and Finland, and to establish Russia's sole rights in this sphere. This the Germans would not allow. After the failure of the conversations, Hitler ordered preparations for an attack on the U.S.S.R.

In the spring of 1941, the Germans had to rescue the Italians from the Greek campaign, which had bogged down in Albania. This rescue was preceded by the movement of German troops into Bulgaria, which the U.S.S.R. regarded as essential to its own defense. Then came an unsuccessful German effort to win Yugoslavia without war, and swift victorious German campaigns in Yugoslavia and Greece (March-May, 1941). Germany alone ruled supreme in the Balkan region, and, though the Yugoslav and Greek resistance had delayed the German timetable, Hitler was able to launch the invasion of the U.S.S.R. on June 22, 1941. Stalin must have known it was coming; indeed the western powers had warned him. But he seems to have hoped against hope to the end. A few weeks before it came, Stalin, proudly calling himself an Asiatic, had secured a neutrality pact with Japan, Hitler's ally. The Japanese, deeply engaged in China, and intending to go to war with the United States, wished as much as did the Russians for insurance against a war on two fronts.

VI: Conclusion

Karl Marx, who scorned and disliked Russia, would have been utterly dumfounded had he lived to see that backward agricultural land, almost without a proletariat, produce the only successful European communist revolution. Although much ink has been spilled in an effort to discover why a Marxist revolution took place in the country where, in theory, the conditions were least favorable, the problem is not really so difficult. Two possible general solutions suggest themselves: either Marx was wrong, or what happened in Russia was not a Marxist revolution at all. Or perhaps both these answers are partly right. It seems clear that Marx did not correctly estimate the revolutionary force latent in the Russian peasantry; since Marx died in 1883, he could not foresee the full inadequacy of the tsarist regime, the extent of tensions created by World War I, or the feebleness of the provisional government of 1917. But it also seems clear that to bring the Bolsheviks to power it took Lenin's appreciation of the importance of the peasantry, his grasp of the immediate situation, his willingness to risk everything, and his luck at being in the right place at the right time with the right weapons.

On the other hand, the revolution was not wholly Marxist. Once the Bolsheviks were in power, of course, it was inevitable that the succession of real situations they faced should modify their Marxist-Leninist theories. Thus civil war and foreign intervention brought chaos from which NEP provided a necessary respite. And in Stalin there came to power an amalgam of Marxist, Russian nationalist, and power-hungry politician such as nobody could have foreseen. Moved by a combination of motives, Stalin proceeded hastily and brutally to make over Russia in a decade. Although he fell short of his goal, his program had created an industrial state not totally unprepared for the blows that Hitler was to deal it. Slaves of the state though they were, collectivized by force, industrialized by force, purged, terrorized, and struggling by the million to exist in forced labor camps, the Russians in World War II succeeded, with much help from the United States, in defeating Hitler and his allies.

How much the loyalty of Russians to Stalin was due to the failure of the German invaders to treat them well, and how far Hitler with a different policy might have won their support are questions with which we cannot deal here. The Russians were facing a coalition of fascist states—Germany, Italy, Hungary, Rumania, and others grouped together in an alliance called "the Axis powers" (from the German-Italian "Axis"), a coalition pledged to the utter destruction of communism. It is to the history of these powers and of the fascist doctrine that they pursued that we now turn.

Reading Suggestions on Communist Russia

General Accounts

E. H. Carr, *A History of Soviet Russia*, 4 vols. (N.Y.: Macmillan, 1950-1954). The only attempt at a complete history of the Soviet Union, 1917-1924, from original sources; Carr is a somewhat uncritical admirer of Lenin, and his work must be used with care.

B. Moore, Jr., *Soviet Politics: The Dilemma of Power* (Cambridge: Harvard Univ. Press, 1950). An illuminating analysis of the relationship between communist ideology and Soviet practice.

R. N. Carew Hunt, *The Theory and Practice of Communism* (N.Y.: Macmillan, 1951). An excellent introduction to the subject.

M. Fainsod, *How Russia Is Ruled* (Cambridge: Harvard Univ. Press, 1953). An analysis of the Soviet system in 1953, firmly rooted in the historical background.

W. W. Rostow and others, *The Dynamics of Soviet Society* (N.Y.: New American Library, 1954). Attempt by a group of scholars to determine why the Russians behave as they do.

Special Studies

W. H. Chamberlin, *The Russian Revolution, 1917-1921*, 2 vols. (N.Y.: Macmillan, 1935). Still the standard work on the subject.

L. Trotsky, *The History of the Russian Revolution*, 3 vols. (N.Y.: Simon & Schuster, 1932). A brilliant and biased study by one of the leading participants.

B. D. Wolfe, *Three Who Made a Revolution* (Boston: Beacon, 1955). Excellent triple study of Lenin, Trotsky, and Stalin.

D. Shub, *Lenin* (N.Y.: Doubleday, 1948. Abridgment available as a Mentor Book). The best biography of Lenin in English.

I. Deutscher, *The Prophet Armed* (N.Y.: Oxford Univ. Press, 1954). A good biography of Trotsky, by a sympathetic hand.

I. Deutscher, *Stalin: A Political Biography* (N.Y.: Oxford Univ. Press, 1949). The most complete account in English.

J. Maynard, *Russia in Flux* (N.Y.: Macmillan, 1948). Enlightening though sometimes far-fetched attempts to show basic continuities between the old and new regime.

C. Brinton, *The Anatomy of Revolution* (N.Y.: Knopf, 1957. A Vintage Book). Comparison of the Russian revolution with the French revolution of 1789 and the English seventeenth-century revolution.

H. Schwartz, *Russia's Soviet Economy*, 2nd ed. (Englewood Cliffs, N.J.: Prentice-Hall, 1954). Good introduction to the subject.

N. Timasheff, *The Great Retreat* (N.Y.: Dutton, 1946). An account of the social changes in Russia during the Soviet period.

R. Pipes, *The Formation of the Soviet Union* (Cambridge: Harvard Univ. Press, 1954). Excellent monograph on the question of national minorities in Russia, 1917-1923.

J. W. Wheeler-Bennett, *Brest-Litovsk, The Forgotten Peace* (London: Macmillan, 1938). Excellent monograph.

L. Fischer. *The Soviets in World Affairs*, 2nd ed. (Princeton: Princeton Univ. Press, 1951). The only study of Soviet foreign policies up to 1929.

M. Beloff, *The Foreign Policy of Soviet Russia*, 2 vols. (N.Y.: Oxford Univ. Press, 1947, 1952). A solid study covering the years 1929-1941.

F. C. Barghoorn, *The Soviet Image of the United States* (N.Y.: Harcourt, Brace, 1950). How the

U.S.S.R. looks at the U.S.A.; by a former representative of the American Department of State.

E. Lyons, *Assignment in Utopia* (N.Y.: Harcourt, Brace, 1937). An American journalist records his disillusionment with Soviet communism.

R. H. Crossman, ed., *The God That Failed* (N.Y.: Bantam Books). Brief statements by Arthur Koestler, Stephen Spender, Ignazio Silone, and other intellectuals recording their disenchantment with communism.

V. A. Kravchenko, *I Chose Freedom* (N.Y.: Scribner's, 1946). The most celebrated of many works by ex-Soviet officials and citizens who preferred the West to the U.S.S.R.

Historical Fiction

A. Koestler, *Darkness at Noon* (N.Y.: New American Library). A famous novel, presenting in fictional form a keen analysis of the attitudes of the Old Bolsheviks whom Stalin purged.

V. Serge, *The Case of Comrade Tulayev* (N.Y.: Doubleday, 1950). Another excellent novel of the purges.

G. Blunden, *The Room on the Route* (Philadelphia: Lippincott, 1947). Perhaps the most vivid fictional portrayal of the impact of terror on the ordinary person.

A. Tolstoy, *Road to Calvary* (N.Y.: Knopf, 1946). Translation of a Stalin Prize Novel about the revolution and civil war.

The Rise

of Fascism

1918-1939

I: Introduction

In this chapter we shall deal with the rise of fascism in Europe in the period between the two great wars. By 1939, authoritarian governments of the Right were in firm control of· Italy, Germany, Spain, and all the countries of eastern and southeastern Europe except Russia. The process by which these regimes came to power differed widely from country to country, as did some of the external features of the regimes. At first glance, fascism is more complex and more difficult to understand than communism, a doctrine whose development can be traced from Marx through Lenin before its followers were able to put it, or something like it, into practice in Russia. Unlike communism, fascism has no such line of theoretical development. Its proponents often seem to have acted first and worried about doctrine later, devising theories to meet the needs of the moment.

Fascism has been called the revolution of the classes of order. Political parties on the Continent have often represented the interests of the various social classes; when those interests have seemed to be about evenly balanced in a parliamentary state, a long and indecisive political tug-of-war has often ensued. For example, let us assume that a revolution from the Left threatens or can be made to seem to threaten. Then the middle classes, so the theory runs, seize power and take refuge in their own form of extremism—fascism, that is, nationalism tricked out with a few radical phrases to win mass support, and draped in mystical garments. This formula can be applied to Mussolini's rise to power in Italy in 1922, to Hitler's rise to power in Germany in 1933, to Franco's rise to power in Spain in 1936-1939, and to many of the eastern European dictators. Yet the formula takes us only so far. Only a study of the different circumstances existing in each of the different countries can give it real body and meaning.

Economic depressions played a role in the rise of almost every dictator: the post-war depression in Italy, and elsewhere the world-wide depression of 1929 and later. We notice, moreover, a certain similarity in the externals of fascism everywhere—colored shirts, private armies, mass hypnotism, special salutes, special war cries and ceremonies, mystical glorification of the nation, and a vast program of conquest. The dictator's program is justified by references to "have" and "have-not" nations; his own nation is always a "have-not," always oppressed.

Fascism is just as violent in its hatred of democracy, liberalism, and parliamentary institutions as in its professed dislike of communism. Indeed fascism shares communism's abhorrence of constitutional procedure, its disregard of the individual human being, and its insistence that the state is supreme. Fascism persecutes its enemies, both real and fancied, with the same ruthlessness we have observed in Stalin's Russia. Censorship, political police, concentration camps, the rule of the bludgeon, the end of legal protection—all these practices are common to both fascism and communism.

When Mussolini ruled in Rome, public buildings everywhere carried the admonition to loyal Italians, "Believe, fight, obey" (*Credere, combattere, obbedire*). Presumably this was intended to be inspiring. Yet all it really means is: Believe (what Mussolini tells you), fight (for Mussolini and his backers), obey (Mussolini). When put this way, the formula is seen to subvert religion and human decency, and to express only a nihilist creed, a belief in nothing but opportunism. Yet many an idealist was taken in by it, under the stress of the unbearable pressures on individuals generated by the tension of the years between the wars.

II: *Italy and Fascism*

The Setting

Although Italy was a member of the victorious Allied coalition, she finished the First World War with a sense of defeat. Six hundred and fifty thousand of her men had been killed and one million wounded. Industry slumped immediately after the war, and within a few months 10 per cent of the industrial workers were unemployed. Prices rose rapidly, and wages failed to keep up. The promised pensions for wounded veterans and families of the killed were long delayed. Strikes and disorders became frequent. Many of the young men released from the armies with no trade but war and no job to go to drifted restlessly and discontentedly, fit prey for leaders with glittering promises.

Perhaps most important, the government itself began almost at once to spread propaganda among the Italian people to the effect that their wartime allies were robbing them of the territories that had been promised them in exchange for their entry into the war. The government hoped to engender a wave of public opinion so violent that it would influence the negotiations for the peace. Although the Allied leaders at the Paris Peace Conference remained unaffected by the storms of protest arising from Italy, the Italian people did come to believe that they had shed their blood in vain. The territories of which they felt themselves deprived were the Slavic lands in Dalmatia, across the Adriatic, promised to Italy by the Secret Treaty of London (see above, Chapter XVIII). This arrangement the Americans had never agreed to, and now would not accept. Popular sentiment in Italy, especially in the army, swung away from the government and toward extremists of one sort or another.

Some Italians hysterically supported Gabriele d'Annunzio, a short, totally bald poet and romantic novelist and long a noisy proponent of the nationalist cause, who formed a band of volunteers. They seized the city of Fiume, the Adriatic seaport over which Croatians and Hungarians had long been in disagreement. Referring to the "stench of peace," and denouncing Woodrow Wilson, d'Annunzio declared that the time for heroic individual action was at hand. Fiume had actually not been awarded to Italy even by the Secret Treaty of London, but d'Annunzio felt that Italy must have it, and that was enough. Consequently, he ran his own gov-

ernment in Fiume until the end of 1920. D'Annunzio patterned his regime there upon that of an imaginary medieval commune in a poem by Italy's romantic poet Carducci (1835-1907). Modeling himself consciously upon the governor of the commune in the poem, d'Annunzio would appear on the balcony of the city hall, address an inspirational harangue to the crowd, and ask for its unanimous consent for whatever he wished to do. This his listeners would grant, raising their right hands high, as the imaginary citizens of Carducci's commune had done. Some of d'Annunzio's followers wore black shirts. When d'Annunzio asked them to whom Fiume belonged they would shout *A noi*, "to us," and when he asked them to whom Italy belonged, they would give the same answer. Indeed, he planned to lead his followers from Fiume to Rome, and thence out into the world to conquer it, presumably with daggers, which he preferred to mechanized weapons.

In November, 1920, the Italian government signed the Treaty of Rapallo with Yugoslavia, by which Fiume was to become a free city. Italian forces drove d'Annunzio out, and into retirement in a villa on the Italian lakes. But the techniques of force, the haranguing of the mob from the balcony, the straight-arm salute, the black shirts, the rhythmic cries, the plans for conquest, and the "corporative" scheme of the Statutes of Fiume (a constitution in line with what D'Annunzio imagined to have existed in medieval guilds and artisans' corporations) served as precedent and inspiration for Benito Mussolini, founder of Italian fascism.

In the first four years after the end of the war, Mussolini created and brought to power a new political force in Italy. In October, 1922, he was summoned to office by King Victor Emmanuel III (1900-1947); from then on he gradually created a totalitarian state of which he was the sole, undisputed ruler. Suppressing all opposition at home, and threatening the peace abroad, the fascist state in Italy served in some degree as model for the Nazis in Germany, for the Falangists in Spain, and for totalitarian regimes in virtually all the European successor states of the Habsburg and Ottoman empires. Eventually, Mussolini was forced, largely by his own propaganda, into an alliance with Hitler. In 1940, this alliance took Italy into World War II, and in 1945 it brought Mussolini himself to an ignominious death, upside down on a communist partisan gallows, with his mistress beside him.

To understand what really happened, we must first consider Mussolini's career before the foundation of fascism; second, the steps by which he came to Rome; and third, the development of the fascist state until the moment of its involvement in World War II.

Mussolini:
Early Career

Mussolini was born in 1883, in the Romagna, a province of central Italy famous for its political extremists, and for the violence with which they express themselves. His father was an ardent socialist who had begun his career as an anarchist under the influence of Bakunin (see above, p. 426). Trained as an elementary-school teacher, Mussolini was already a passionate socialist by the time he was eighteen. He spent some time as an agitator among Italian emigrant laborers in Switzerland (1902-1904), but was twice expelled by the police. He taught school in Italy (1906-1908), then went as socialist journalist and labor leader to Trent, an important center of the Italian minority in Austria, from which he was expelled in 1909. Back in Italy, he was imprisoned for opposing the war against Turkey over Tripoli (1911). In 1912, he became editor of the most important Italian socialist newspaper, *Forward* (*Avanti*).

When World War I began, Mussolini was at first vigorously opposed to Italy's entry. But then, during 1914, he changed his mind.

First he favored "relative neutrality," meaning that socialists should leave themselves free to support Italian entry if such a course seemed likely to prove favorable to them. When the Italian Socialist party refused to follow this idea, he resigned as editor of *Avanti*. Soon afterward (November, 1914), he founded his own newspaper, *The People of Italy* (*Il Popolo d'Italia*) in Milan, and began to advocate an immediate Italian declaration of war on the side of the Allies. For this the Socialist party expelled him.

But these bare bones of a biography reveal only the externals. As a socialist, Mussolini before 1914 was a passionate left-winger. He was an apostle of violent social revolution and a bitter opponent of milder evolutionary and reformist doctrine. He urged that a small, well-knit armed minority should seize power and establish a dictatorship. He loathed militarism, was himself a draft-dodger, and urged soldiers to desert the army. He hated monarchy, and savagely attacked in his writings all the crowned heads of Europe, especially the Italian House of Savoy. He was a vigorous atheist, urged workers to stay away from church, and scorned the teachings of Christ. As an international revolutionary he opposed nationalism, and even referred to the Italian flag as "a rag to be planted on a dunghill."

Yet he was to repudiate almost every one of these positions, and as fascist chieftain to substitute almost the exact opposites. As a fascist, he attacked bolshevism and all left-wing movements; he made his peace with the monarchy and the Church; he became a militant nationalist, a mystic patriot, and a rabid militarist. The repudiation of the views he had held so long and advocated so skillfully is not nearly so astonishing as it seems. From the first, Mussolini did not care for programs; what he wanted was to rule.

A complete opportunist, he could shift his line on any question at a moment's notice if it seemed advantageous. For example, after the war, though he was now a fascist, he at first supported a radical program of social change, indistinguishable from the program he would have advocated had he still been a socialist. He favored the action of the Italian workers in the fall of 1920, when they occupied the factories in a kind of sit-down strike. Yet, within a year, he was using the fears which this strike had aroused in the middle classes to argue that he was the only possible bulwark against "bolshevism." About certain matters, however, he was consistent: he always hated parliaments and he always loved violence.

Mussolini's switch from isolationism to interventionism in the war in 1914 was the first of his important shifts. After his expulsion from the Socialist party, he agitated furiously for war, speaking to groups of similarly minded young men called *fasci* (the image is of a bundle of rods, a symbol of office in the Roman Republic of antiquity). Soon after Italy did enter the war in 1915, Mussolini was conscripted and sent to the front. He was badly wounded in 1917 by an Italian mortar shell that exploded during practice, and he spent several months in the hospital. When he got out, he continued to edit his newspaper, now no longer as a socialist but still as a revolutionary, spewing forth a mixture of extreme revolutionary and extreme nationalist propaganda.

Mussolini: Rise to Power

In March, 1919, Mussolini founded the first *fasci di combattimento* ("groups for combat"). These were not unlike similar groups that urged the seizure of Dalmatia, of which d'Annunzio's was the most important. Mussolini's movement was still very small. There was nothing in March, 1919, to indicate that by October, 1922, the leader of the *fasci di combattimento* would become the most powerful man in Italy. In 1919, he called for every kind of revolutionary violence—seizure of the land, attacks on the factories, shooting of storekeepers who charged high

prices, expropriation of mines and transports, and war by the vanquished "proletarian" nations against the victorious capitalists who had kept Italy from annexing Dalmatia. He now maintained that socialism was too conservative; his movement, far from setting itself against a revolution, was in the vanguard of those who were crying for one.

Yet in Italy a revolution along Bolshevik patterns was most unlikely, if not impossible. The peasants were not very revolutionary, for they already held much of the land except in the extreme south. And the industrial workers, though often discontented, knew that a revolution could be starved out because the country needed to import most of its raw materials. The Socialist party was overwhelmingly in the hands of moderates, and in 1919 Catholics founded the Popular party (*Partito Popolare Italiano*), designed to compete with the Socialists for the votes of the lower classes, who now had universal suffrage.

In the postwar disorders the peasants seized without consent of the landowners less than one-tenth of 1 per cent of the arable land in Italy. The leaders of the Socialist party and the General Confederation of Labor voted down the proposals of anarchist and communist extremists to turn the workers' occupation of the factories into a revolution. The government waited for the workers to grow tired. This they did in less than a month (September, 1920); then they left the occupied factories and went home.

Yet the actual state of affairs is often less important than what influential sections of society persuade themselves to believe is the actual state of affairs. Although the danger of revolution was small, the fear of revolution was great. Thus, during 1920 and 1921 the industrialists and landowners, squeezed by taxation and inflation, became bitter. Shopkeepers and tradesmen wanted street disorders to end, food prices to be regulated, and the co-operative food stores of the socialists and Catholic party to be put out of business as competitors. In particular, professional men and others with fixed incomes suffered as prices and wages went up and salaries lagged behind. The police grew tired of suppressing local disorders and of being repaid with insults. Ex-servicemen, insulted by anarchists and communists for their war records, naturally grew more patriotic.

All these groups identified the forces they did not like as Bolshevik, and accepted as an article of faith the myth of an impending Bolshevik revolution. After a series of fascist-socialist street fights and riots, these "anti-Bolsheviks" began to look to Mussolini's fascist bands as the defenders of their interests. D'Annunzio's defeat left Mussolini as his natural heir. The Left opposition to Mussolini was weakened when the communists split off from the Socialist party in 1921. The *fasci* grew enormously, from 30,000 in May, 1920, to 100,000 in February, 1921, to more than 300,000 at the time of the "March on Rome" in October, 1922. No longer were they merely squads of discontented and idle youths with vaguely revolutionary and nationalist ideas. Now, says one fascist of the period, "the sons and hangers-on of the bigwigs" poured into the organization.

The liberal parliamentary leaders of Italy shared the anti-Bolshevik fears. Instead of attempting to restore order and holding new elections, they felt that the fascist bands were teaching the Left a useful lesson. They encouraged the commanding officers of the army to issue rifles and army trucks and gasoline to the fascists and even assigned army officers to command their operations. The police were encouraged to look the other way during disorders started by the fascists, and local judges were urged to help by releasing fascists who had been arrested. Mussolini himself now proceeded to circulate his newspaper free to the soldiers in the army as a "patriotic" sheet.

A genuine campaign of terror now began against the socialists and Christian Democrats, as the fascist squadrons cruised around Italy in trucks, burning down labor-union offices, newspaper offices, and local Socialist party headquarters, and beating up and sometimes murdering labor leaders or local anti-fascist politicians. The *fasci* forced duly elected officials to resign. The torch, the cudgel, and the famous castor-oil treatment were all characteristic weapons. It is estimated that 2,000 people, anti-fascist and fascist, policemen and innocent by-standers, died by violence between October, 1920, and October, 1922.

The "March" on Rome

In the elections of May, 1921, Mussolini and thirty-four other fascists were elected to Parliament, along with ten Nationalists, their political allies. The momentum of the fascist movement was now too great to be slowed down. Mussolini abandoned his anti-monarchical views, and fascism became a political party (November, 1921) as a necessary step in the drive for power. Too late, the government became alarmed and tried to take measures against the fascists, but the squads were too strong, the police too accustomed to collaborating with them, and the politicians themselves as yet unaware that a tightly directed armed mob could really take over the state. Inside the royal family, the King's cousin, the Duke of Aosta, had become a fascist sympathizer, as had many army generals, the entire Nationalist party, and leading industrialists.

In the fall of 1922 it was clear that the army would not resist a fascist *coup* in Rome itself. When a decree of martial law was presented to the King, he refused to sign it, probably influenced by his knowledge that the army would not fight the fascists and that the Duke of Aosta would gladly take his crown. The refusal of the

Mussolini and fascisti during the "march" on Rome, October, 1922.

King to declare martial law greatly heartened the fascists. Now, as the fascists "marched" on Rome, mostly by storming railroad trains and stealing free rides, the King (October 29, 1922) telegraphed Mussolini in Milan to come to Rome and form a cabinet. Mussolini arrived by sleeping-car the next morning.

Fascism, which had begun as a patriotic anti-Bolshevik movement, and had then turned into an anti-labor movement in the service of the industrialists and landowners, had finally come to power as a conspiracy against parliamentary government in the service of a military clique. Just before taking office, Mussolini announced:

> Our program is simple: we wish to govern Italy. They ask us for programs, but there are already too many. It is not programs that are wanting for the salvation of Italy but men and will-power.*

The Fascist Dictatorship

Mussolini now moved gradually to turn his premiership into a dictatorship. A month after coming to

* Quoted by H. Finer, *Mussolini's Italy* (New York, 1935), 152.

office, he obtained dictatorial powers that were to last only until the end of 1923. Although the constitution theoretically remained in force, Mussolini proceeded to take over the administration. He created a Fascist Militia almost 200,000 strong, which owed complete allegiance to him. He enlarged the regular army, and required its members to take an oath of personal loyalty to him. Before his dictatorial powers expired, he secured from Parliament by pressure a new electoral law. This law provided that the political party which received the largest number of votes in a general election, if that number amounted to at least one-quarter of the vote, should automatically receive two-thirds of the seats in Parliament. The rest of the seats would be divided proportionately. This law made certain the fascists' domination of future parliaments. Indeed, in the election of April, 1924, the fascists actually polled 65 per cent of the vote cast; but this figure reflects a widespread use of intimidation and terrorism at the polls. The first all-fascist cabinet was now appointed. Meanwhile, local administration was made secure by the appointment of fascist prefects and subprefects in the provinces; these officials pursued the enemies of fascism with the same weapons of murder and mayhem that had been used before Mussolini's March on Rome.

Early in 1924, the leader of the opposition to Mussolini, the socialist Giacomo Matteotti, published a book called *The Fascists Exposed*, in which he detailed many of the outrages the fascists had committed on their way to power. It seemed probable that further revelations were in store, exposing some of Mussolini's cabinet members as corrupt. On June 10, 1924, Matteotti was "taken for a ride" in true gangster style and murdered. The crime was traced to members of Mussolini's immediate circle. This scandal rocked Italy, and for a moment it even seemed possible that Mussolini would fall. But he dismissed from office those who were involved, and pledged himself to restore law and order. Actually, he delayed trying the guilty men until March, 1926, and even then they all got off lightly.

What really helped Mussolini over the crisis, ironically enough, was the departure of most of the opposition deputies from Parliament. They declared that they would not return until the Matteotti murder had been solved and the government had been shown to be innocent. Far from making things harder for Mussolini, as they had intended, their departure actually made things easier. Mussolini simply denied his own guilt, imposed a rigid press censorship, and forbade the opposition to meet. Most of the deputies never did return to Parliament, and in 1926 their seats were declared forfeit.

Though the Matteotti crisis continued into 1925, Mussolini simply tightened the screws. A series of laws called the "most fascist laws" (*legge fascistissime*) tightened control over the press, forbade secret societies like the Freemasons, whom Mussolini had loathed ever since his socialist youth, and extended the control of the central government to all the cities and towns by depriving them of their elected officials, who were replaced by officials appointed from Rome. Opponents of the regime were arrested and transported into exile on desolate islands off the Italian coast. Early in 1926, Mussolini was empowered to govern by decree. Three attempts on his life led to a new law providing the death penalty for action against the King, the Queen, or Mussolini. All opposition political parties were abolished in the same year, and the Fascist party was left as the only legal political party in Italy.

More and more the Italian state and the Fascist party were brought into co-ordination. Mussolini was both the *Duce* (leader) of the fascists and the *capo di governo*, the chief of state. At one moment he also held eight cabinet posts simultaneously. The members of the Fascist Grand Council, a "politbureau" numbering roughly twenty of the highest party functionaries, all appointed by Mussolini, held all the important posts in the administration not held by Mussolini himself. In 1928, the Grand Council was given important constitutional duties: preparing the lists of candidates for election to the Chamber, advising Mussolini, and proposing changes in the constitution or the succession to the throne. The Grand Council thus became a kind of third house, above the other two houses of Parliament, the Senate and the Chamber.

The Corporative State

Indeed, Mussolini planned to change the principles of the western parliamentary system. He believed that the interests of labor and capital could and must be made to harmonize with the overriding interests of the state. Instead of a political system as we understand it, he accepted the idea that representation should be based on economic interests organized in "syndicates." Such an idea was not new: the French syndicalist, Georges Sorel, had already argued in this vein. But Sorel believed in class warfare, and in government by syndicates of workers only. Mussolini, following the Italian nationalist syndicalist, Rossoni, believed in capitalism, class-collaboration, and producers' syndicates as well as workers' syndicates.

In 1925, fascist labor unions were recognized by employers as having the sole right to negotiate labor contracts. Then, in April, 1926, the state officially recognized producers' and workers' syndicates in each of six areas—industry, agriculture, commerce, sea and air transport, land and inland waterway transport, and banking—plus a syndicate of intellectuals, making thirteen syndicates in all. Each syndicate could bargain and reach contracts, and could assess dues upon everyone engaged in its own economic field, irrespective of membership in the syndicate. Strikes and lockouts were both forbidden. When labor conditions did not improve, a "charter of labor," promising insurance and other benefits, was issued in 1927. In 1926, the syndicates were put under the control of a special Ministry of Corporations; Mussolini was the minister.

In 1928, the system of parliamentary representation was changed in accordance with fascist syndicalism. A new electoral law provided for a new Chamber of Deputies (400 instead of 560 members). The national councils of the thirteen syndicates could nominate a total of 800 candidates. Each syndicate had a quota, half to be selected by the employers and half by the employees. Cultural and charitable foundations could nominate 200 more candidates. When the total list of 1,000 was completed, the Fascist Grand Council could either select 400 of them, or strike out names and add names of its own, or even substitute an entire new list. The voters would then vote in answer to the question: "Do you approve of the list of deputies selected by the Fascist Grand Council?" They could vote "Yes" or "No" on the entire list, but they could not choose from among the candidates. If a majority voted "Yes," the list was elected; if not, the procedure was to be repeated. Despite the highly touted role of the syndicate, all the power obviously lay with the Fascist Grand Council. Universal suffrage was abolished even for this very limited form of election. Payment of a minimum tax or dues to a syndicate was required of each voter; women could not vote. In 1929, the elections under this system produced a "yes" vote of 8,519,559 and a "no" vote of 137,761.

Between 1930 and 1938 several constitutional steps were taken which seemed to move the syndicates into the center of the stage. Representatives from the syndicates and the government were now formed into a Council of Corporations, which was to act as a co-ordinating committee, settle disputes between syndicates, assist production, and establish the fascist corporations themselves, which had not yet been created. The Council was divided into seven sections corresponding to the seven syndicate areas, and in 1931 each of these sections of the Council was simply declared to be a corporation. In 1933, it was announced that the whole corporate system would be revised; and in 1934 the new elections (which of course returned the Fascist Grand Council's list of candidates) produced a "suicide" Chamber of Deputies, which was expected eventually to put an end to its own existence. Its replacement was to be a new "revolutionary assembly," which Mussolini called into existence in the fall of 1934. The assembly, also called the Central Committee of Corporations, contained 824 members, representing twenty-two newly created corporations. The Fascist party, as well as employers and employees, was represented on each corporation.

But it was not until 1938 that the last step was taken, when the "suicide chamber" ended its existence and replaced itself with the Central Committee of Corporations, which was now called the Chamber of Fasces and Corporations. There was nothing left of the old parliamentary constitution that had been set up by Cavour except the Senate, nominally appointed by the King but actually subservient to Mussolini, who on one occasion had the King appoint forty fascist senators all at once. This new structure, the corporative state, was influenced by d'Annunzio's strange medieval ideas, and by Mussolini's own wish to produce new political and economic forms. The Central Committee of Corporations and its successor body, the Chamber of Fasces and Corporations, were designed to advise the government, to settle labor disputes, and to plan and regulate production. In spite of much oratory by fascist sympathizers about the corporative state and its virtues, the corporations were scarcely the modern counterparts of medieval guilds. It does not appear that they ever had very much to do with running the economic or political life of Italy, which remained firmly under the direction of the fascist bureaucracy.

Other Fascist Domestic Policies

During the thirties, the fascist version of the planned economy made its appearance in Italy. The government issued or withheld permits for factory construction. In agriculture, a concerted effort was launched to make Italy more nearly self-sufficient. This effort was dramatized with the "Battle of Wheat," in which the Italians were treated to contests, prizes, personal appearances by Mussolini, and similar trappings. In 1932, official figures reported that wheat production had risen to a point where it could supply 92 per cent of the nation's normal needs, and the drive was enlarged to include other cereal products. The government subsidized steamship and air lines, encouraged the tourist trade, and protected Italian industries by means of high tariffs on for-

eign products. Marshes were drained and land was reclaimed; the incidence of malaria was reduced. Enormous sums were spent on public works, and great strides were made in the development of hydroelectric power. The trains, at least so thousands of naive American tourists reported, ran on time; as a result, the tourists returned home insisting that "there must be something in this man Mussolini." Yet Italy's weakness in essential raw materials proved to be insuperable.

The state reached into the life of the individual at almost every point. Though Italy was overpopulated, and had for decades relieved the situation only by mass emigration, Mussolini made emigration a crime. He encouraged people to marry and have the largest possible families: he reduced their taxes, extended special loans, taxed bachelors, and extended legal equality to illegitimate children. He hoped in this way to swell the ranks of his armies, and to strengthen his claim that Italy must expand abroad. Children, the future party members, were enrolled in a series of youth movements, beginning at the age of six. The textbooks in the schools, the books in the libraries, the professors in the universities, the plays on the stage and the movies on the screen were all made vehicles of fascist propaganda. The secret police, OVRA (from the initials of the Italian words for "Vigilance Organization against Anti-Fascist Crimes"), endeavored to discover and suppress all opposition movements.

In 1929, Mussolini settled the Roman question (see Chapter XIV) by entering into the Lateran Treaty with the papacy. This treaty recognized the independent state of Vatican City and thus restored the temporal power of the pope, though on a greatly reduced scale. Mussolini also recognized Catholicism as the state religion, and promised to halt anti-papal propaganda. He gave up the right to tax contributions to the Church or the salaries of the clergy, and paid $105,000,000 to compensate the papacy for the Italian occupation of papal territories since 1870. A concordat further regulated the relations between Church and State. Religious marriages were legalized, and religious instruction was extended in schools. The Church agreed not to engage in politics in its newspapers and periodicals.

Yet, despite the fact that many church officials viewed the fascist movement sympathetically, difficulties arose after these agreements had been concluded. In an encyclical, Pope Pius XI (1922-1939) indicated his disapproval of Mussolini's "relentless" economic policies and of the corporations as "serving special political aims rather than contributing to the initiation of a better social order." Mussolini now charged that the Church's "Catholic Action" clubs were engaged in politics, and dissolved them. The Pope denied the charges, and denounced the Fascist party's practice of monopolizing the time and education of the young. In 1931, however, a further agreement was reached, and the clubs were re-opened.

Fascist Foreign Policy and Its Consequences

Since Mussolini's foreign policies form an integral part of the international relations leading up to World War II, we shall discuss them more fully in Chapter XXII. Here we may simply point out that his extreme nationalism, his love of panoply and parades, and his militarism were the logical extensions of his domestic ideas and accomplishments. Mussolini's wish to re-create the glories of ancient Rome impelled him to undertake a policy of adventure in the Mediterranean, which he called *Mare Nostrum* (Latin for "our sea") as a sign that he was the heir to the Caesars. This policy began with the Corfu incident in 1923, and Mussolini's occupation of that Greek island. Details are unimportant, but the entire episode, coming early in the history of fascism and the League of Nations, showed that the fascists would not be bound by international authority. Later, Mussolini's policy of adventure led him to military aggression in Ethiopia, in Spain, and in Albania (which he dominated during the 1920's and occupied in April, 1939). It drove him into an alliance with his fellow-fascist, Hitler, and led him to voice loud claims against the French for Corsica, Tunisia, Nice, and Savoy. And it alienated Italy from her natural allies, France and Britain.

The German alliance was also responsible for a striking new departure in fascist domestic policy. This was the official adoption of anti-Semitism, which took place in 1938. With only 70,000 Jews, most of whom had long been resident, Italy had no "Jewish problem." Italian Jews were entirely Italian in their language and sentiments, and could be distinguished from other Italians only by their religion. Just like the non-Jews of Italy, many of them were prominent in the fascist movement, and many were anti-fascist. There was no widespread sympathy in Italy for the government's adoption of Hitler's racial policies. Yet Hitler's dominating influence led Mussolini to expel Jews from the Fascist party, and to forbid them to teach or attend school, to intermarry with non-Jews, and to obtain new licenses to conduct businesses. The object was to drive the Jews from the economic, cultural, and political life of Italy.

III: *Germany and the Weimar Republic, 1918-1933*

In Germany, where Hitler was eventually to acquire power far greater than Mussolini's, the advent of fascism came later than in Italy. The German experiment with democracy lasted fifteen years after the end of World War I. Two days before the armistice of November 11, 1918, the Social Democrats proclaimed a republic in Germany. On July 31, 1919, this republic adopted a constitution drawn up by a national assembly at Weimar; it is therefore known as the "Weimar Republic." The Weimar Constitution was never formally abandoned, but after Adolf Hitler became chancellor on January 30, 1933, Germany was in fact a dictatorship.

It is convenient to divide the history of Germany between World Wars I and II at 1933, at the moment when Hitler took office as chancellor. Between 1918 and 1933, there are three shorter periods: the period of political threats from Left and Right and of mounting economic chaos, from 1918 to the end of 1923; the period of political stability, fulfillment of the Versailles Treaty requirements, and seeming economic prosperity, from 1924 to late 1929; and the period of economic depression and mounting right-wing power, from late 1929 to January, 1933.

The Impact of Defeat

For the overwhelming majority of the German people, defeat in 1918 came as a great surprise. The military authorities who ran the German Empire during the last years of the war had failed to report to the public German reverses on the battlefield. No fighting had ever taken place on German soil, and the Germans had got used to thinking of their armies as in firm possession of the foreign territories they had overrun. Now these armies came home intact. It is often argued that the Allies committed a grave blunder by their failure to march to Berlin and demonstrate to the German people that they had actually been defeated. Schooled in reverence for their military forces, the Germans could not grasp the fact that their armies had lost the war. Moreover, the Allies, under the leadership of Wilson, simply refused to deal with the Supreme Command of the German armies. Field Marshal von Hindenburg, as supreme commander, was never required to hand over his sword to Marshal Foch, or to sign the armistice. Rather, it was the civilian politicians who had to bear the odium. In this way the Allies unintentionally did the German military caste a great favor.

Before the ink was dry on the armistice agreement, the generals, led by Hindenburg himself, were explaining that the German armies had never really been defeated. This was exactly what the public wanted to believe, and the harsh facts—that Ludendorff and Hindenburg had insisted on surrender because the armies could no longer fight—were never effectively publicized. So the legend that Germany had somehow been "stabbed in the back" by civilians, by liberals, socialists, communists, and Jews, took deep root and became almost an article of faith among many Germans. This legend was widely disseminated by politicians, especially by those who had a stake in the old Prussian system—the monarchists, agrarians, industrialists, and militarists, in short, the nationalist right wing, which still believed in an aggressive Germany. All through the period of the Weimar Republic, these groups remained hostile toward it; their hostility ranged from political opposition to conspiracies to overthrow the government.

The Allies, having made things easier for the worst enemies of peace and democracy in Germany, added another error by including the celebrated "war-guilt" clause in the Treaty of Versailles. The German signatories were obliged to acknowledge what none of them believed, and what subsequent historians would disprove: that Germany alone had been responsible for the outbreak of the war. The war-guilt clause made it harder for the German public to acknowledge defeat and the evils of the past system, to sweep away the militarists, and to bend to the task of creating a virile republic. Instead, it led the Germans to dissipate their energies in denying war guilt, in hating the enemies who had saddled them with the charge, in bewailing the sellout of their generals, and in waiting —many of them, at least—for a chance to show by force that they had been right all the time.

Postwar Political Alignments and Activities

This strengthening of the anti-republican forces of the Right was further increased by the threat to stability from the Left. Responsibility for launching the republic and for preventing disorder fell upon the "majority socialists," made up of Social Democrats and right-wing Independent Socialists, and led by the Social Democrat, Ebert. The Social Democrats were a moderate group. For example, they made no attack on agrarian property, and they allowed the Junkers to maintain intact their estates and the social and political position that went with them. The Social Democrats, true to their reformist tradition, concluded with the industrialists collective bargaining agreements that guaranteed the eight-hour day, when the logic of the situation might rather have dictated the launching of a serious movement for nationalizing German industry.

But to the left of the Social Democrats agitation for a proletarian revolution on the Russian pattern was carried on by the left wing of the Independent Socialists and the "Spartacists" (named for Spartacus, the leader of a slave revolt in ancient Rome). In a congress of workers and soldiers councils (the German equivalent of soviets), the Left was defeated in its attempt to perpetuate these councils. In the winter of 1918-1919, the Left tried to stage its revolution, but Ebert called in the army to stop it. The generals used not only regular units but also newly formed volunteer units, or "Free Corps," made up for the most part of professional soldiers, who were embittered by Germany's recent military defeat and were violently opposed to democracy.

After the bloodshed of December, 1918, even the right wing of the Independent Socialists felt unable to remain in a government which used against the workers soldiers under the command of old-line generals. So they withdrew, and sole responsibility thenceforth rested with the Social Democrats, who put their man Noske into the war ministry. As the civil strife continued, the Spartacists took on the appropriate name of the Communist Party of Germany. In January, 1919, they attempted a *coup*, which Ebert, Noske, and the troops put down. Cavalry officers murdered the two chief leaders of the communists after peace had been restored, at the cost of more than a thousand casualties. Meanwhile, in Catholic Bavaria, disorders led to the brief emergence of a Soviet republic, which was liquidated in May, leaving behind in the middle-class Bavarian population a pathological fear of the Left, and making Bavaria the home of a sort of permanent red-scare. The Bavarian local authorities, throughout the entire life of the Weimar Republic, encouraged the intrigues of monarchists, militarists, and nationalists. It was in Bavaria that Free Corps assassinations were planned, and it was there that Hitler got his start.

In this way the forces of the German Right, ostensibly crushed by the war, were given a powerful new lease on life by the very powers that should have been their most determined enemies—the Allies, who allowed the myth of the stab-in-the-back to grow and who insisted on the war-guilt clause; and the Social Democrats, who made an alliance with the generals and put down the communists and their allies. Meantime, Germany still had an army, the *Reichswehr*, under the able direction of General von Seeckt. Though limited in size to 100,000 men, it consisted chiefly of officer-cadres, magnificently trained and able to take over the command of far larger numbers if and when troops became available.

The political constellation of the new Germany did not consist solely of Social Democrats and extremists of Right and Left. The old parties of imperial Germany (see Chapter XV) reappeared, often with new labels. The right wing of the old Liberals now emerged as the People's party, including the more moderate industrialists, with a platform of private property and opposition to socialism. Its leader was Gustav Stresemann, who had been a chauvinist during the war but had been taught a good deal by Germany's defeat. Former Progressives and left-wing Liberals now formed the new Democratic party, a genuine middle-class republican and democratic group, including many of Germany's most distinguished intellectuals. The Catholic Center party re-emerged with its name and program unchanged. It accepted the Republic, rejected socialism, and favored social legislation under pressure from its left wing of trade-union members, but it opposed far-reaching reform under pressure from its right wing of aristocrats and industrialists. The Social Democrats, the Democrats, the Center, and the People's party represented those groups which, though not all enthusiastic, were willing to try to make the new state work. On the Right, the former Conservatives re-emerged as the National People's party or Nationalists, dominated by the Junkers as before. The Nationalists had the support of some great industrialists, of most of the bureaucrats, and of a substantial section of the lower middle class, which hoped to return to the good old days of the monarchy. The Nationalists did not accept the Republic.

The Weimar Constitution, 1919

When the Germans voted for a national constituent assembly in January, 1919, the parties supporting the Republic won more than 80 per cent of the seats (see table below), with the Social

GERMAN ELECTIONS TO THE WEIMAR ASSEMBLY AND REICHSTAG, 1919-1933

(Number of seats obtained by the major parties, arranged with the Left at the top, the Right at the bottom)

	Jan. 1919	June 1920	May 1924	Dec. 1924	May 1928	Sept. 1930	July 1932	Nov. 1932	Mar. 1933
Communists	—[a]	2	62	45	54	77	89	100	81
Independent Socialists	22	81	—[b]						
Social Democrats	163	112	100	131	152	143	133	121	125
Democrats	74	45	28	32	25	14	4	2	5
Center	71	68	65	69	61	68	75	70	74
People's party	22	62	44	51	45	30	7	11	2
Nationalists	42	66	96	103	78	41	40	51	52
Nazis			38	20	12	107	230	196	288

[a] The Communist party boycotted the elections to the Weimar constituent assembly.
[b] In these and succeeding elections the Independent Socialists had merged with the Social Democrats.

Democrats alone obtaining more than 40 per cent. The assembly met in Weimar, elected Ebert to be President of Germany, and formed a government that reluctantly signed the Treaty of Versailles after a delay of some months. The assembly then adopted the new constitution. The new Germany was still a federative state, but the central government had great authority to legislate for the entire country. The president might use armed force to coerce any of the states which failed to obey the constitution or national laws. The cabinet was responsible to the lower house, or *Reichstag*, which was to be chosen by universal suffrage of all citizens (including women) over twenty.

The president, who was to be elected every seven years by the entire people, was given considerable authority. He was empowered to make treaties, appoint and remove the cabinet, command the armed forces and appoint or remove all officers, dissolve the Reichstag, and call new elections. Further, he could take any measure he deemed necessary to restore order when it was threatened, and might temporarily suspend the civil liberties that the constitution granted. Yet the Reichstag could order such measures repealed. Inside the cabinet, the chancellor was a real prime minister, responsible for planning policy. On the economic side, the constitution provided that the government might socialize suitable enterprises, but guaranteed private property and the right of inheritance.

The powers of the president and the introduction of proportional representation were perhaps the two chief weaknesses of the Weimar Constitution. The powers of the president made dictatorship a real possibility. Proportional representation required that votes be cast for entire party lists of candidates, and thus prevented independent voters from "splitting the ticket," and independent politicians from obtaining office. This system encouraged small splinter parties to multiply.

Right and Left Extremism, 1920-1922

In 1920, pressure from the Right loomed as the most serious threat to the Republic. In March, 1920, a *coup* (in German, *putsch*) was attempted by a group headed by the commander of the troops in the Berlin district and other officers. They wanted to capitalize on military resentment over the disarmament clauses of the treaty, and hoped to bring into power an East Prussian reactionary official named Kapp. Ludendorff and the Free Corps leaders fully supported the movement, which drove the government out of Berlin for several days. Ebert managed to defeat this "Kapp *putsch*" by calling a general strike that paralyzed Germany. It was a measure of the continuity of the old monarchical judicial system that the men arrested and tried for the Kapp *putsch* all got off with extremely light sentences, whereas left-wingers brought before the courts were very harshly punished.

Moreover, as an immediate outgrowth of the strike called by the government, a communist revolt took place in the Ruhr. In pursuit of the communists, German troops entered the area, which had been demilitarized by the Versailles Treaty; this action in turn led to French military intervention and a brief occupation of the Ruhr and Frankfurt (April-May, 1920). In the elections of June, 1920, the electorate began to support the extremists. The Democrats and Social Democrats lost strength. On the Right, the Nationalists and People's party gained, and on the Left the Independent Socialists gained. But the latter group now split; the left-wingers joined the communists, and the right-wingers came back into the Social Democratic party.

In April, 1921, when the Allies presented the bill for reparations, which totaled 132 billion gold marks, the politicians of the Right favored simple rejection of the terms, while the Weimar parties realistically decided that the threat of invasion made this course impossible. Again, the moderates had to take responsibility for a necessary decision that was sure to prove unpopular, and that they themselves did not approve. The minister for reconstruction, Walter Rathenau, a Democrat and a successful industrialist, hoped that a policy of "fulfillment" might convince the Allies that Germany was acting in good faith, and might in the long run lead to concessions. An intensely patriotic German, Rathenau was also a Jew, and drew the particular venom of the anti-Semitic nationalist orators.

The secret terrorist groups of the Right began a campaign of assassination. The first important figure to be murdered (August, 1921) was Matthias Erzberger, the Catholic Center politician who had signed the armistice, and a leading moderate. Next, after some hesitation, the League of Nations awarded to Poland a substantial area of the province of Upper Silesia, containing much wealth and many German inhabitants, which all Germans felt to be rightly theirs. This action aroused the Right still further. Rathenau now became the target, first of a political and press attack, and then in June, 1922, of bullets. His assassins were devout believers in the "stab-in-the-back" theory, and thought that by murdering a Jew they could somehow avenge the "betrayal" of the German army.

Hitler: Early Career

During the months between the assassination of Erzberger and that of Rathenau a new and ominous element had emerged among the welter of right-wing organizations in Bavaria. This was the "National Socialist Party of the German Workers" founded by Adolf Hitler, the son of an obscure, illegitimate Austrian customs official, whose real name had been Schicklgruber. Born in 1889, Hitler early quarreled with his father, and seems always to have felt bitter and frustrated. In 1907, he was rejected by the Vienna Academy of Fine Arts, where he wished to study painting. He became an odd-job man, selling an occasional water color, but always hovering on the edge of starvation. It was during these years that his hatred of the Jews began. As we know (see Chapter XV), lower-middle-class Vienna at the time was deeply devoted to its anti-Semitic demagogue, Mayor Lueger, whom Hitler admired. Because Karl Marx himself had been of Jewish origin and because many Viennese Jews were socialists, Hitler associated socialism with the Jews, and lumped both together as somehow responsible for his own personal troubles and for the ills of the world.

There were plenty of nineteenth-century theorists, German and others, from whose works Hitler drew support for his anti-Semitism: the French Count Joseph Arthur de Gobineau (1816-1882), who had laid the pseudo-scientific foundation for modern anti-Semitism, and for theories of "Nordic" and "Aryan" supremacy, and one of whose most influential readers was the great German composer, Richard Wagner (see Chapter XVI); Wagner's son-in-law, the Englishman Houston Stewart Chamberlain (1855-1927), who wrote a long and turgid book called *The Foundations of the Nineteenth Century*, which glorified the Germans and assailed the Jews—for example, one section was devoted to a "demonstration" that Christ himself had not been of Jewish origin. Chamberlain was furiously opposed to democratic government and, interestingly enough, to capitalism. Thus he provided Hitler with a congenial mixture of racism, nationalism, anti-democratic thought, and radicalism. Hitler was deeply influenced by Chamberlain, and Chamberlain lived to see and hail the foundations of the Hitler movement.

Although Hitler owed much to earlier nationalists and racists, he worked out a twentieth-century adaptation of their nineteenth-century ideas. After he had read their books, he came to hate Vienna as a cosmopolitan and Jewish community, and moved to Munich in 1913. In 1914, he enlisted in the army and fought through the war as a corporal. He won the iron cross for bravery, but was regarded by his commanding officer as too "hysterical" to deserve a commission. After the war, he had come back to Munich, where, as might have been expected, he loathed the new republic and the "Bolsheviks," admired the Free Corps, and made up his mind to become a politician.

When the government put down the revolution from the Left, in 1919 and 1920, the Bavarian military authorities supported the Free Corps. Ludendorff moved to Munich, and became the center of the reaction. Hitler was employed as a political education officer for the troops. While engaged in this work, he discovered a small political group that called itself the "German Workers' Party." This group combined nationalism and militarism with a generous amount of imitation-socialist radicalism. Hitler consequently believed that the party might be able to recruit a mass following. He joined the party in 1919 and soon proved himself to be a far abler politician than any of his colleagues. He stressed as basic the need for intensive propaganda, arguing that all Germans should be united in a greater Germany. He supported the elimination of all Jews from political life, a state guarantee of full employment for workers, the confiscation of war profits, the nationalization of trusts, the encouragement of small business, and a land grant to the peasantry. The seemingly radical character of Hitler's program caused many Germans who were otherwise sympathetic to his ultimate goals to hesitate before turning over any money to him. As early as 1920, he began to reassure them by saying he opposed not "industrial capital" but only "Jewish international loan capital," a clear sign that the nationalization plank in his platform had been abandoned.

Hitler was an extremely successful orator, with almost hypnotic gifts of capturing a crowd. By 1921, he had made himself the absolute leader, the *fuehrer* (compare with *duce*), of the party, and in the same year he strengthened himself by founding the SA (*Sturmabteilung*, or storm troops), brown-shirted units largely recruited from the Free Corps. The storm-troopers wore arm bands with the swastika emblem, patrolled mass meetings, and performed other services for the leader. Their commander was a notorious pervert, Captain Roehm, who was also political adviser to the commander of the infantry stationed in Bavaria. Like the Italian fascists, the German Nazis (so-called from the first four letters of the German word *Nazional*, National, the first word of the party's name) thus had illegal and unofficial access to government supplies of arms through army sympathizers. Besides Roehm, Hitler's closest collaborators included Hermann Goering, a wartime aviator who had shot down twenty Allied planes, but who found himself restless in peacetime, and took on the job of giving the SA a military polish; Rudolf Hess, an Egyptian-born lieutenant and private secretary; and Alfred Rosenberg, a Baltic German who was distinguished for his fanatical hatred of Jews and Bolsheviks, and who served as first editor of the party newspaper.

Hitler and his Nazis were still a very minor political force in 1922 when the middle-of-the-road parties attempted to strengthen the Republic. After the assassination of Rathenau, Stresemann's People's party chose to move away from the Nationalists, who were now tainted by murder, and entered into a collaboration with the Center and the Democrats. So tense had the political situation in Germany become by this time that the presidential elections scheduled for 1922 were postponed until 1925.

The Inflation, 1922-1923

Political maneuvers to meet the increasing threat from the Right, however, were largely nullified by the increasing economic problem posed by steadily growing inflation, which in 1922 and 1923 reached unheard-of extremes. Inflation is a complicated economic phenomenon, and no mere list or description of its causes can really tell the full story. But the single chief cause for the runaway inflation in Germany after 1921 was probably the failure of the German government to levy taxes with which to pay the expenses of the war. The imperial regime had expected to win, and to make the losers pay Germany's expenses by imposing huge indemnities. So it paid for only about 4 per cent of the war costs by means of taxation. As defeat neared, the government borrowed more and more money from the banks. When the loans came due, the government repaid them with paper money that was not backed by gold. Each time this happened, more paper money was put into circulation, and prices rose; each rise in prices naturally led to a demand for a rise in wages, which had to be paid with more paper money. The inflationary spiral was under way. Instead of cutting purchasing power by imposing heavy taxes, the government permitted buyers to compete with each other for goods in short supply, thus speeding up the whole process of inflation.

Many other forces helped inflation along. The German gold shortage, which deprived the government of the gold with which to back its currency, was itself due to several factors. Since Germany had had to pay in gold for goods bought abroad during the war, she had stripped herself of her gold supply; the rich sent great sums out of Germany for fear that the government would attach them to pay reparations. Raw materials were in short supply; industry was disorganized; and credit was curtailed. The armies of occupation had to be maintained at German expense, and reparation payments had to be made. Nationalist Germans maintained that these expenses, especially reparations, were the cause of inflation; but, though reparations certainly helped the process, they were by no means solely responsible for it. The total sums involved in reparations were never great enough to affect the German currency until long after the inflation was under way. Indeed, the inflation was partly due to the industrialists' wish to avoid paying reparations, and to clear their own indebtedness by letting the currency become worthless.

The following timetable shows how bad the situation had become by the end of 1922. When the war was over, the mark, normally valued at 4.2 to a dollar, had fallen to 8.4. In January, 1921, it was 45; by December, 160. By September, 1922, it was 1,303, and at the end of the year it was 7,000. In these months, the government begged for a moratorium on reparations payments and for a foreign loan. But the French were unwilling. They had already paid billions for the rebuilding of areas that the Germans had devastated during the war, and they wanted the Germans to pay the bill. As a guarantee, the French demanded the vitally important German industrial region of the Ruhr. Despite British opposition, the French occupied the Ruhr in January, 1923, after the Germans had defaulted on their reparations payments. The French intended to run the mines and factories for their own benefit, and thus make up for the German failure to pay reparations.

The Germans could not resist with force, but they declared the occupation of the Ruhr illegal, and ordered the inhabitants to embark on passive resistance—to refuse to work the mines and factories or to deliver goods to the French. This order the people of the Ruhr obeyed. Local tension in the occupied area became serious when the French took measures against German police and workers, and when German Free

Corps members undertook guerrilla operations against the French.

But the most striking result of the French occupation of the Ruhr was its effect upon the already desperate German economy. Not only was the rest of Germany cut off from badly needed goods from the occupied area, but the Ruhr inhabitants were idle at the order of the German government and had to be supported at government expense. The printing press struck off ever-increasing amounts of ever-more-worthless marks. Now the exchange went from thousands of marks to the dollar to millions, to billions, and, by December, 1923, well up into the trillions.

Such astronomical figures are meaningless except in terms of the personal and social consequences. A student set off one afternoon for the university with his father's check in his pocket to cover a year's tuition, room, board, and entertainment. When he arrived the next morning after an overnight journey, he discovered that the money he got for the check would pay for one short streetcar ride! Lifetime savings were rendered valueless; people trundled wheelbarrows full of marks through the street in an effort to buy a loaf of bread. Those who lived on fixed incomes were utterly ruined, and the savings of the investing middle classes were wiped out. Real property took on fantastic value. The story is told of two brothers, one frugal and the other spendthrift, who had shared equally in a fortune inherited from their father. The frugal one had invested his money; the spendthrift had bought a fine wine-cellar, which he had proceeded to drink up. When inflation came, all the frugal brother's investments would not buy him a haircut, but the spendthrift found that the empty bottles in his cellar were worth billions on billions of marks apiece, and that he was rich again. Under such circumstances speculation in real estate flourished, and skillful speculators made immense fortunes.

For the German worker inflation did not mean the liquidation of his savings, because he usually had none. It did mean a great drop in the purchasing power of his wages, so great that he could no longer afford the necessities of life. His family suffered from hunger and cold. Since the financial position of the labor unions was destroyed, they were no longer able to help the workers,

Hitler at the time of the beer-hall putsch, Munich, November 1923.

who gave up their membership in droves. The great industrialists, however, gained from the inflation, in part just because it did cripple the labor unions, but still more because it wiped out their indebtedness, and enabled them to absorb small competitors and build giant business combines.

Politically, inflation greatly strengthened the extremists of both Right and Left. The middle classes, although pushed down to the economic level of the proletariat, still possessed the middle-class psychology. In status-conscious Germany, they would not adhere to the working-class parties of Social Democrats or Communists. Disillusioned, they would not adhere to the moderate parties that supported the Republic—the People's party, the Center, and the Democrats. So the Nationalists, and Hitler's Nazis above all, reaped a rich harvest. The hardships of the working class led many workers to turn away from the Social Democrats to the Communists. But Soviet Russian restraint on the leaders of the German party prevented any concerted revolutionary drive until the fall of 1923, by which time poor organization and strong governmental repressive measures had doomed their efforts.

With the country seething in crisis, Stresemann as chancellor in the fall of 1923 proclaimed that because of the economic dislocation Germany could not keep up passive resistance in the Ruhr. He ordered work to be resumed and reparations to be delivered once again. Political troubles multiplied when the Right refused to accept the new policy. At the height of the agitation in Bavaria, Hitler in early November, 1923, broke into a right-wing political meeting in a Munich beer-hall, and announced that the "national revolution" had begun. At gun-point he tried to get other local leaders to support him in a march on Berlin. They agreed, but let him down when they learned that the national government was prepared to put down the Nazis. Although Ludendorff himself joined the Nazi demonstration in Munich, as he had joined the Kapp *putsch* of 1920, troops broke up the demonstration with only a few casualties.

Ludendorff and Hitler were tried in proceedings that have become famous as the most striking example of the Weimar judicial system's partiality for men of the Right. Ludendorff was respectfully acquitted. Hitler was allowed to use the dock as a propaganda platform for his ideas, and was sentenced to the minimum term for high treason: five years. He actually spent eight months in comfortable confinement, during which time he wrote large portions of *Mein Kampf* (*My Battle*), the famous bible of the Nazis.

The End of Inflation, 1923-1924

Communist disorders and the Nazi beer-hall *putsch* marked the last phase of the inflation period. A couple of weeks before Hitler's effort, the government had given extraordinary financial powers to Hans Luther, minister of finance, and Hjalmar Schacht, banker and fiscal expert. All printing of the old currency was stopped. A new bank was opened to issue new marks, which were simply assigned the value of the pre-war mark (4.2 to the dollar). The new currency was backed not by gold but by an imaginary "mortgage" on all Germany's agricultural and industrial wealth, a psychological gesture that won public confidence. It took one trillion of the old marks to equal one of the new. Simultaneously, rigorous economy was put into effect in every branch of the government, and taxes were increased. The public protested loudly, but the measures remained in force until they had accomplished the intended effect. The cure for inflation produced serious hardships too. Prices fell, and over-expanded businesses collapsed. Unemployment rose sharply, wages stayed low, and workers labored long hours.

During 1924, the Allies contributed to the ending of the crisis in Germany by formulating the Dawes Plan, named for Charles G. Dawes, the American financier and later vice-president under Calvin Coolidge. The plan recommended the evacuation of the Ruhr by the French, the establishment of a special bank to receive reparations payments, gradually rising annual payments for the first five years, and an international loan to finance the German deliveries in the first year. The Nationalists violently attacked the proposals as a sinister scheme to enslave Germany to foreign masters. In the Reichstag elections of May, 1924, the Nationalists scored impressive gains, as did the Nazis and the Communists, while the moderate parties all suffered (see table on p. 673). But a coalition managed to win acceptance of the Dawes Plan in August, 1924, by the device of promising the Nationalists representation in the cabinet. When new elections were held in December, the Nazis and Communists suffered losses, and the Social Democrats and moderates gained. A Center–People's party–Nationalist coalition took office early in 1925 and governed Germany. One wing of the Nationalists, however, led by the enormously rich industrial, press, and film magnate, Alfred Hugenberg, who had made a fortune during the inflation, opposed all co-operation with the Republic. Though Germany had moved appreciably to the Right, foreign policy remained in the conciliatory hands of Stresemann, who remained foreign minister through all governments between November, 1923, and his death in October, 1929.

Recovery at Home, 1924-1929

During these less-troubled middle years of the Weimar Republic economic recovery proceeded steadily, until, in 1929, German industrial output exceeded that of 1913. First-rate German equipment, coupled with superb technical skill and a systematic adoption of American methods of mass production, added up to a highly efficient industrial machine. This "rationalization" of industry increased production but brought with it over-borrowing and some unemployment. "Vertical trusts," which brought together in one great corporation all the parts of an industrial process from coal and iron mining to the output of the finished product; and cartels, associations of independent enterprises that controlled sales and prices for their own benefit, were characteristic of the German system. The emphasis was always on heavy industry, which meant that continued prosperity would depend upon a big armaments program.

All through this period, reparations were paid faithfully, with no damage to the German economy. Indeed, the money that flowed out in reparations was greatly exceeded by the money that flowed into Germany from foreign, especially American, investors. Dependence on foreign capital, however, which would cease to flow in time of depression, made German prosperity artificial.

In 1925, after President Ebert died, a presidential election was held in which three candidates competed. The Catholic Center, the Democrats, and the Social Democrats supported the Center leader, Wilhelm Marx. The Nationalists, People's party, and other right-wingers joined in support of Field Marshal Hindenburg, then seventy-seven years old. The Communists ran their own candidate, and thus contributed to the election of Hindenburg, who won by a small plurality. Abroad, the choice of a man so intimately connected with imperial militarist Germany created dismay; but until 1930 Hindenburg acted entirely in accordance with the constitution, to the distress of most of the nationalist groups.

The domestic issues of this period all aroused great heat, but were settled by democratic process. In the elections of 1928, the Social Democrats were returned to power, and the Nationalists and Nazis were hard hit (see table on p. 673). All in all, prosperity encouraged moderation and a return to support of the republic.

"Fulfillment" Abroad, 1925-1930

In foreign affairs, this middle period of the Weimar Republic was one of gradually increasing German participation in the system of collective security. Thus in 1925 Germany signed the Locarno treaties, which took the French armies out of the Rhineland, substituted a neutral zone and a frontier guaranteed by Britain and Italy, and set up machinery for the arbitration of disputes between Germany and her neighbors. These treaties did not, however, guarantee to Poland and Czechoslovakia the eastern frontiers of Germany. In 1926, Germany was admitted to the League of Nations, with a permanent seat on the League's Council. In 1929, Germany accepted the Kellogg-Briand Pact, which outlawed aggressive war (see below, p. 717).

In 1929, a new reparations plan named after the American, Owen D. Young, chairman of the committee which drew it up, substantially reduced the total originally demanded by the Allies. The Young Plan also established lower rates of payments than those under the Dawes Plan and allowed the Germans a greater part in their collection. Before June, 1930, the Rhineland was evacuated by the Allies, four years ahead of the date set by the Treaty of Versailles. Although many of these gains for Germany were accomplished only with so much preliminary difficulty that they were robbed of their sweetness, and although the German Nationalists, Nazis, and Communists thoroughly opposed them all, still German foreign policy was generally designed with the aim of reassuring the rest of the world.

The Impact of the Depression, 1929-1931

But even before the last achievements of this "period of fulfillment," the depression had set in to knock the foundations out from under prosperity and moderation. Unemployment rose during 1929. After the American stock-market crash in October, foreign credits, on which prosperity had so largely depended, were no longer available to Germany. Short-term loans were not renewed, or else were recalled. Tariff barriers were hurting foreign trade. Hunger and want reappeared.

Although unemployment insurance cushioned the first shock for the workers, the lower middle classes, painfully recovering from the inflation, had no such barrier between them and destitution. Their desperation helped Hitler, whose fortunes during the years of fulfillment had fallen very low.

The government fell in 1930 over a disagreement on a question of unemployment insurance benefits. Hindenburg appointed to the chancellorship Heinrich Bruening, a member of the Catholic Center party. Bruening would have liked to support parliamentary institutions and to continue Stresemann's policies of fulfillment, but he was to find it impossible to do either. President Hindenburg, now eighty-two, had come more and more under the influence of General Kurt von Schleicher, an ambitious political soldier who had intrigued himself into the President's favor. Hindenburg was now itching to rule by decree, as the constitution authorized him to in an emergency. By failing to pass Bruening's economic program, the Reichstag gave Hindenburg the opportunity he wanted. Bruening went along, partly because he felt that a genuine emergency existed, but partly because he was determined to keep his bitter political rivals, the Social Democrats, from replacing him in office.

The budget was declared in effect by presidential decree; when the Reichstag demanded that the decree be abrogated, the Reichstag was dissolved and new elections were called. The electoral campaign was notable for a running series of street fights between Communists and Nazis. When the votes were counted (September, 1930), these two extreme parties made great gains at the expense of all the moderates (see table on p. 673). The Nazis' Reichstag representation rose from 12 to 107, and the Communists' from 54 to 77. Bruening had to carry on against the wishes of the electorate; supported only by Hindenburg, he now turned to authoritarian measures, although he had a strong preference for parliamentary methods.

In order to avoid a new government in which Nazis would participate, the Social Democrats decided to support Bruening. When the Reichstag met, Nazis and Communists created disorder on the floor, but they voted together in opposition to government measures. These measures passed only because the Social Democrats voted for them. In 1931, Bruening made an effort to arrange an Austro-German customs union which would co-ordinate the tariff policies of the two countries and help them both fight the depression without affecting their political sovereignty. But the whole project raised in the minds of the Allies, especially the French, the specter of a "greater Germany," and the scheme was vetoed by the World Court. The collapse of the great Austrian bank, the *Kredit-Anstalt*, deepened the depression, despite a British loan to Austria in 1931, and despite the one-year moratorium on reparations payment procured for Germany by President Herbert Hoover.

The Republic in Danger, 1931-1932

After the failure of the Austrian customs union scheme, a right-wing political coalition was formed against the Bruening government. It included Nazis, Nationalists, the veterans organization of the Steel Helmets (*Stahlhelm*), the Junkers' Agrarian League, industrialists, and representatives of the former princely houses. This coalition had great financial resources, and a mass backing, chiefly Nazi. It had its private armies in the SA, in the *Stahlhelm*, and in other semi-military organizations. Because the Left was split, and the Communists in effect acted as political allies of the Right, nothing stood between this new right-wing coalition and a political victory except the person of Hindenburg. The President controlled the army, and by virtue of the Weimar Constitution was able to keep Bruening in office, although the Chancellor was deeply unpopular.

The coalition was further strengthened in early 1932, when Hitler was invited by the great industrialist, Fritz Thyssen, to address a meeting of coal and steel magnates. Hitler warned them against Bolshevism, inveighed against the principles of democratic government, reassured them of his own respect for private property, and won their financial support by convincing them that if he came to power he would be their man. Some of Hitler's followers were now impatient for a new *putsch*, which they were sure would be successful. But Hitler curbed them, believing that the Nazis could come to power legally.

With new presidential elections scheduled for 1932, Bruening tried to avoid the excitement and expense of a campaign by obtaining from the Reichstag an extension of Hindenburg's term. Hitler refused, and the elections were held in March, with Hitler as the candidate of the Nazis. Hindenburg ran as the candidate of the Center, Social Democrats, and other moderate parties. The Nationalists nominated a *Stahlhelm* man, and the Communists of course ran their own candidate. Hitler polled 11,338,571 votes, and Hindenburg polled 18,661,736, only four-tenths of 1 per cent short of the required majority. In the run-off election, the Nationalists backed Hitler, whose total rose to 13,400,000 as against Hindenburg's 19,360,000. The eighty-four-year-old Marshal, re-elected as the candidate of the moderates, was, however, no longer a moderate himself, but the tool of the Junkers and the military.

Although the government now ordered the Nazi SA and SS (élite black-shirted defense corps, *Schutzstaffel*) disbanded, the decree was not enforced. In April, 1932, the Nazis scored impressive victories in local elections, especially in all-important Prussia. Bruening was unable to procure in time either an Allied promise to extend the moratorium on reparations payments or permission for Germany to have "parity" (i.e., equality) in armaments with France. Schleicher, who was now deeply involved in intrigue against Bruening, worked on Hindenburg to demand Bruening's resignation. This Hindenburg did on May 29, 1932, the first time a president had dismissed a chancellor simply because he had lost personal confidence in him. Bruening's successor was Franz von Papen, a rich Catholic nobleman and a member of the extreme right wing of the Center, who installed a cabinet composed of nobles. Papen was Schleicher's man —or so Schleicher thought.

The Center disavowed Papen, who had the real support of no political party or group, but whom the Nazis temporarily tolerated because he agreed to remove the ban on the SA and SS. Papen called new Reichstag elections, on the theory that the Nazis had passed their peak, that they would obtain a decreased vote, and that then they could be chastened and would cooperate in the government. The election of July 31, 1932, gave the Nazis 230 seats and made them the biggest single party in the Reichstag; the Communists gained also, chiefly at the expense of the Social Democrats. The Democrats and the People's party almost disappeared, while the Center scored a slight gain (see table on p. 673). Papen had gained no support in the new Reich-

stag. He wanted to take some Nazis into the government, but the Nazis demanded the chancellorship, which Hindenburg was determined not to hand over to Hitler. Papen now planned to dissolve the Reichstag and to call new elections. By repeating this process, he hoped to wear down Hitler's strength each time, until he brought Hitler to support him and accept a subordinate place. And Papen put pressure on the industrialists who had been supporting Hitler; the Nazi funds began to dry up, leaving Hitler seriously embarrassed. The elections of November 6, 1932, demonstrated the soundness of Papen's theories. The Nazis fell off from 230 seats to 196; and, although the Communists gained substantially and ominously, Papen too won some support (see table on p. 673). Now the Nazis were really desperate. Goebbels wrote in his diary:

Received a report on the financial situation of the Berlin organization. It is hopeless. Nothing but debts and obligations, together with the complete impossibility of obtaining any reasonable sum of money after this defeat.[*]

Hitler: Rise to Power, 1932-1933

Had Papen been permitted to continue his tactics, it is possible that Hitler might have been kept from power. But Papen resigned as a matter of form because he could not count on majority support in the Reichstag. It was generally expected that Hindenburg would reappoint him, but Schleicher, who was jealous of Papen, intrigued against the reappointment. Angry with Schleicher and sorry to lose Papen, Hindenburg forced Schleicher himself to take the office on December 3, 1932. Now the backstairs general was chancellor, but he had no political support whatever, and had alienated even Hindenburg. He lasted in office only about

---

[*] Quoted by S. William Halperin, *Germany Tried Democracy* (New York, 1946), 511-512.

eight weeks before Hitler was appointed chancellor.

Schleicher did score a great diplomatic success by winning a five-power declaration that recognized in principle Germany's right to parity in armaments. At home, he made every effort to appeal to all shades of opinion, except the extreme Left. But this attempt in itself alienated the implacably anti-labor industrialists and the Junkers. The tortuous Papen, eager for revenge, intrigued with these enemies of Schleicher. Early in January, 1933, Papen met Hitler at the house of the Cologne banker, Baron Kurt von Schroeder. The industrialists, who had temporarily abandoned Hitler, now agreed to pay the Nazis' debts. Hitler, in turn, no longer insisted on the chancellorship for himself, thus leading Papen to hope that he would come back into office with Hitler's backing. Hinden-

burg, too, was enlisted. When the President refused to give Schleicher the authority to dissolve the Reichstag at its first new session, which would surely have voted him down, Schleicher had no choice but to resign (January 28, 1933).

But Hitler had now raised the ante and demanded the chancellorship for himself. Papen consented, provided Hitler undertook to govern in strict accordance with parliamentary procedure. Papen was to be vice-chancellor, and still thought he could dominate the government, since only three of its eleven ministers would be Nazis. He therefore persuaded Hindenburg to take Hitler as chancellor. But Papen underestimated Hitler. Though Hitler swore to Hindenburg that he would maintain the constitution, the Weimar Republic was doomed from the moment Hitler came to the chancellor's office on January 30, 1933.

IV: Germany Under Hitler, 1933-1939

The Nazi Dictatorship   Hitler's first weeks in power were devoted to transforming his chancellorship into a dictatorship. He dissolved the Reichstag and called for new elections. During the campaign, opponents of the Nazis were intimidated by violence and threats, and were denied radio time and free use of the press. Yet a Nazi victory in the election still did not seem sure. On February 27, 1933, fire opportunely broke out in the Reichstag building, and Hitler could point to it as a sample of the disorders that the Communists were likely to instigate. Hindenburg issued emergency decrees suspending free speech and the free press, and thus made it even easier for the storm troops to use terror against their political opponents. It is now generally supposed that the Nazis themselves set the Reichstag fire, but they convicted and

condemned to death a Dutch communist named Vanderlubbe, who apparently was mentally deficient.

Despite their campaign the Nazis won only 44 per cent of the votes, which gave them 288 seats in the Reichstag (see table on p. 673). Using the SA as a constant threat, Hitler bullied the Reichstag. Except for 94 Social Democrats (the Communists were denied their seats), its members voted for the famous Enabling Act (March 23, 1933). This act conferred dictatorial powers upon the government, and suspended the constitution. The act was renewed in 1937 by a subservient Reichstag, and again in 1943.

Now Hitler could act as he chose, unimpeded by the laws. He instituted a Ministry of Propaganda under Goebbels. He stripped the state governments of the powers they had had under Weimar, and made

Germany a strongly centralized state (April, 1933) by appointing governors from Berlin who had the power to override the state legislatures. When President Hindenburg died in August, 1934, at the age of eighty-seven, Hitler assumed the office of president as well as that of chancellor, but he preferred to use the title *Der Fuehrer* (the leader) to describe himself. This new move was approved by a plebiscite, in which Hitler obtained 88 per cent of the votes cast.

Political parties which opposed Hitler were forced to dissolve. The government banned Communists and Socialists (May, 1933); the Nationalists dissolved themselves (June, 1933); the government put an end to the Catholic parties (July, 1933), and all monarchist groups (February, 1934). The *Stahlhelm* was incorporated into the Nazi party (June, 1933) and was deprived of its identity (November, 1935). As early as July, 1933, the Nazis were declared to be the only legal political party in Germany.

The appeal of the Nazis to the German people lay in part in their denunciation and repudiation of the "disorderly" parliamentary system. The replacement of the parliamentary bickerings in the Reichstag by a strong man who got things done struck a responsive chord in the public. In the last elections, November, 1933, there were no opposition candidates, 92 per cent of the electorate voted Nazi, and there were only two non-Nazi deputies in the chamber of 661. As in fascist Italy and communist Russia, youth groups fed the party, which soon had a powerful regional organization all over Germany.

The "Blood Purge" of 1934

Within the Nazi party itself, however, a difficult situation was created by those who had believed Hitler's more radical pronouncements on social and economic questions. Many of these Nazis

Hitler and his entourage driving through Hildesheim.

were concentrated in the SA, and its members, most of them from the lower middle classes, were distressed by the way in which Hitler had treated their organization. The SA had made possible his rise to power, but now it was rather an embarrassment to him, no longer quite respectable, and certainly not in favor, as were the SS and especially the army.

On June 30, 1934, Hitler ordered and personally participated in the celebrated "blood purge," or, as he himself called it, "the night of the long knives." Roehm himself, founder and leader of the SA, was shot, and so were, by Hitler's own admission, seventy-three others, including Schleicher and his wife. Other estimates of the casualties run as high as 1,000. In any case, after June, 1934, there was no further opposition to Hitler inside the Nazi party.

Racism

Within a few days after the passage of the enabling law, Hitler struck the first of his many blows against the Jews, whom he had so long denounced. In a country of approximately 60,000,000 people, the Jews counted less than 1 per cent of the population (something under 600,000), not including part-Jewish Germans. The Jews had become leading members of the professions and the arts, and had made outstanding contributions to German culture. Since most Jews were assimilated and deeply patriotic Germans, many of them would probably have become Nazis if they had been permitted. They would have supported Hitler in everything but anti-Semitism. Instead, anti-Semitic doctrines required their ruthless elimination.

The businesses and professions of the Jews were boycotted; they were forbidden to hold office (April, 1933), although a temporary exception was made for veterans of World War I. In the "Nuremberg laws" of September 15, 1935, a Jew was defined as any person with one Jewish grandparent. All such persons were deprived of German citizenship. Intermarriage between Jews and non-Jews was forbidden as "racial pollution." Jews might not fly the national flag, write or publish, act on stage or screen, teach in any educational institution, work in a bank, exhibit paintings or give concerts, work in a hospital, enter any of the government's labor or professional bodies, or sell books or antiques. They were not eligible for unemployment insurance or charity; and the names of Jews who had died for Germany in World War I were erased from war memorials. Many towns and villages, under the spur of government-sponsored propaganda, refused to permit Jews to live inside their precincts.

In November, 1938, a Jewish boy of seventeen, driven to desperation by the persecution of his parents, shot and killed a secretary of the German embassy in Paris. Two days later, organized German mobs looted and pillaged Jewish shops all over Germany, burned and dynamited synagogues, and invaded Jewish homes to beat up the occupants and steal their possessions. The state then compelled the Jews to restore the damaged properties, and to pay an enormous fine. Jews were forced to take special names, to wear yellow stars of David, and to belong to a Reich "Union of Jews." Although some Jews managed to leave Germany, it was usually at the cost of abandoning all their possessions; yet they were the lucky ones. All these measures and many others (for example, "cows purchased from Jews may not be serviced by the communal bull") designed to drive the Jews into ghettos and starvation were but the prelude to the physical extermination in gas ovens to which they were to be subjected by the Nazis during World War II. What distressed many horrified western observers almost more than the actions themselves was the failure of any substantial number of highly educated and "civilized" non-Jewish Germans to register any form of protest.

Enthusiasm for "racial purity" had its positive as well as its negative side. The blond, blue-eyed ideal "Nordic types" were urged to mate with each other early and to have many children. German motherhood was made the object of paeans of praise. And, to keep the race pure, sterilization was introduced, supposedly for the prevention of the inheritance of disease.

Legal and Economic Policies

Hitler entirely revamped the judicial system of Germany, abandoning traditional legal principles, and substituting "folk" justice, which, Hitler said, subordinated the individual totally to the people (*Volk*). So mystic a doctrine meant in practice that whatever Hitler wanted was German law. People's Courts (May, 1934) were established to try all cases of treason, a crime that was now extended to include a wide variety of lesser offenses, such as circulating banned newspapers. Hitler appointed all the judges of the People's Courts. Concentration camps were established for enemies of the regime, who could be immured or executed by the headsman's axe, without appeal. In fact, they could not even have defense counsel of their choice, but had to accept counsel approved by the courts. The Gestapo (*Geheime Staatspolizei*, Secret State Police) was established in April, 1933, in Prussia, and a year later was extended to all of Germany. It had a free hand in opening private correspondence, tapping wires, and spying on individual citizens.

All economic life was brought under the regime. In agriculture, the Nazis aimed at the largest possible measure of self-sufficiency, and, of course, at political control over the peasantry. The Junkers were protected, and no effort was made to divide their vast estates. In 1933, a special law protected farms of less than 312 acres against forced sale and attachment for debt, an act that won the small farmer to Hitler. But the government determined the production required of farms, and fixed farm prices and wages, and fees for distributing farm products. Unused land was put under cultivation, and private citizens were required to grow vegetables in greenhouses. This was part of Hitler's preparation for war. By 1937, Germany was 83 per cent self-sufficient in agriculture, a rise of 8 per cent since the Nazis had come to power.

In industry, taking a leaf out of Stalin's book, Hitler proclaimed a Four-Year Plan in 1933 and a second one in 1936. The first was aimed chiefly at economic recovery and at ending unemployment. Labor camps for men and women helped decrease unemployment, as did rearmament and a program of public works. By 1936, unemployment had dropped from about 7,000,000 to less than 1,500,000. The second plan was designed to prepare for war, and especially to make Ger-

many blockade-proof. Output of raw materials was increased and the materials were distributed first and foremost to armament and other war industries; labor was allocated with similar ends in view; and prices and foreign exchange were controlled. Goering was made boss of the plan.

Under his direction fell the new Goering Iron Works, designed to make up for the loss of the rich iron resources of Alsace-Lorraine, which had yielded three quarters of Germany's iron. To this end, low-content ores were worked, and the government absorbed the higher costs. Output went up in two years more than 50 per cent. Germany's gifted scientists were enlisted to make up for other deficiencies by devising successful but expensive synthetic products. Important in this field were the distillation of motor fuel from coal, and the production of synthetic rubber. The state also built strategic highways, the *Autobahnen*.

The Nazis abolished all labor unions in 1933, and employers' associations in 1934. To replace them, a "Labor Front" was established under Dr. Robert Ley, including all wage-earners, salaried persons, professionals, and employers. Strikes and lockouts had been forbidden. Workers were assured of jobs so long as they quietly accepted the entire system. The Labor Front in one of its aspects was a huge spy organization constantly on the alert for anti-Nazis in the factories; it could reduce their pay, fire them, or put them in jail. An adjunct to the Labor Front was the "Strength through Joy" organization, which provided paid vacation trips for German workers to resorts or tourist centers, and which sponsored concerts and other entertainments.

As the second Four-Year Plan went into effect, the worker found himself increasingly immobile. He had a work-book, detailing his past training and positions held, and he could not get a new job unless the state decided it would be more suitable for him. All graduates of secondary schools had to register with the employment authorities. Men and women of working age were liable to conscription for labor. Just before the war, all agricultural and mining and certain industrial workers were frozen in their jobs. On the side of capital, the big cartel became the all-pervasive feature of German industrial organization—a system of profitable monopoly under state control. The interlocking directorate made the system even tighter than it looked. Six industrialists, for example, held among them one hundred and twenty-seven directorates in the largest corporations, were presidents of thirty-two, and all held government posts besides. The Minister of Economics sat at the top of the economic pyramid, authorizing plant expansion, controlling imports and exports, fixing prices, establishing costs, and allocating raw materials.

Religion and Culture   The Christian churches, both Protestant and Catholic, posed a problem for the Nazis. Extremists among Hitler's followers had always been in favor of a return to paganism and the old German gods celebrated by Wagner's operas. Hitler himself, born a Catholic, had once declared that Germany was his only God. Yet office brought sobering second thoughts, since Germany was after all nominally a Christian country. In the hope of avoiding state domination, the Lutheran ministry in 1933 organized a national synod, which the Nazis almost immediately took over by appointing their own bishop. The efforts of extreme Nazis to purge the Bible and to abandon the crucifix led to discontent. The dissidents, led by Pastor Martin Niemoeller, objected to Nazi theology and efforts at control. But Niemoeller also pledged his loyalty to Hitler, made no objections to Nazi racism, and went to a concentration camp solely out of determination to resist dictation over the Lutheran

Church. When war came, he petitioned to be allowed to command a submarine. The "confessional" movement he led probably did not extend beyond about 15 per cent of the Protestant clergy.

In July, 1933, Hitler and the German Catholics reached a concordat guaranteeing freedom of worship and permitting religious instruction in the schools. Catholics were to be allowed to form youth groups, and to appoint professors of theology. But the Nazis did not live up to these terms. They interfered with the circulation of Catholic magazines, persecuted the youth groups, and insulted Catholic priests in their press as members of the "black international." On the other hand, the Catholic Church found much to oppose in the teachings to which Catholic children were exposed in the Hitler youth groups. Cardinal Faulhaber of Munich denounced the Nazi violation of the concordat in 1933, but his action only intensified the struggle. Thus in the case of the Protestants, a national church sponsored by the Nazis met with some opposition, while in the case of the Catholics, the Nazis acted as Bismarck once had done and conducted a genuine *Kulturkampf* (see Chapter XV). Not that millions of Catholics, both clerical and lay, did not support the regime wholeheartedly, persecutions of the Jews and all. They did; and no voice was raised from among the clergy of either major Christian sect to protest against Nazi racism or militarism.

The Nazi process of *Gleichschaltung* (coordination) was applied in every portion of the national life, including education and the arts. One of the leading Nazi officials once remarked, "When I hear the word culture, I reach for my revolver," a revealing and not untypical reflection of the extreme Nazi attitude. Hitler's own artistic views were simple in the extreme: he preferred nudes, the more luscious and Germanic the better, and this taste he strove to impose on the nation, denouncing most modern and experimental trends in art as non-Aryan. The school curriculum, especially history, could no longer be taught with that "objectivity" which was a "fallacy of liberalism," but had to be presented to the student in accordance with the Nazi doctrine of "blood and soil." Nazi racial doctrines, the great past achievements of Germany, the development of the military spirit, and physical culture—these were the cornerstones of the new education.

The Bases of Foreign Policy

Hitler's foreign policy is discussed in detail in Chapter XXII. But because so much of his domestic policy was geared for war, and because so much of his popular support rested upon his announced aim of restoring Germany's military prestige by expansion abroad, we shall examine some of the theories on which that policy was based. German racism justified the incorporation of all territory inhabited by Germans, including Austria, the western borderlands (Sudetenland) of Czechoslovakia, Danzig, the Polish corridor, and other less important places. And the doctrine of "living-space" (Lebensraum) justified the incorporation of non-German areas—the rest of Czechoslovakia, Poland, and all southeastern Europe, as well as large areas of Russia. Hitler felt that what the Germans needed, they were entitled to take, since they were a superior people.

The notion of Lebensraum stems in part from twentieth-century German intellectuals who looked back with longing upon the Holy Roman Empire of the Middle Ages, the first Reich, and hoped, after the war had ended the second Reich of William II, to behold a third one, incorporating the old territories, no matter who now lived in them. This is the meaning of Hitler's use of the term "Third Reich," to describe the Nazi state, which he proclaimed would last a thousand years. A "scientific" basis for the Lebensraum theory was supplied by the teachers of "geopolitics," chief among whom was Karl Haushofer, professor of geography, retired major-general, and teacher of Hitler's close friend, Rudolf Hess. The geopoliticians supplied a respectable front for Nazi territorial ambitions. Haushofer declared that Britain and France were decadent, that small powers must disappear (except for Switzerland and the Vatican City), that Germany, preserving its master-race pure, must possess the will to power, and expand ruthlessly, occupying the "heart land" of Eurasia, from which the world could be dominated.

Finally, we may point to a school of thought in Germany that is often neglected. An examination of this school will give us a better understanding of the Hitler-Stalin pact of 1939, and also of Hitler's success at home. At one level, this was simply a pro-Russian school. The military members had a theory that Germany's future lay in an alliance with Russia in which Russia's inexhaustible manpower would be joined with Germany's industrial output and military techniques for purposes of conquest. This notion had been strong in German army circles in tsarist days, and continued to exist after the Bolshevik Revolution, especially after the Treaty of Rapallo (see above, pp. 651-652), concluded between Germany and the Soviet Union in 1922. Outside the purely military circles, there persisted also the Bismarckian attitudes of hostility to the West and to Poland and of friendship toward Russia, whatever the color of her regime.

Now that Russia was Bolshevik and the active sponsor of the German Communist party, many German nationalists tried to find some common ground between their nationalism and the ideas of the new Russia. This task was made easier for them by the fact that they had always been violently anti-liberal and anti-parliamentarian in any case, and so were the Stalinists. Thus, during the Weimar Republic, and even after Hitler's triumph, there existed a whole school of extreme German nationalists who were not unsympathetic to communism. Moreover, there also existed among the German Marxists, communists included, a strong nationalistic feeling, which, at its most extreme, brought them quite close to the nationalists. The way in which hundreds of thousands of voters in the last years of the Weimar Republic shifted back and forth between the Nazi and Communist parties is in some measure an evidence of this feeling.

Yet such views were officially combated both by communists, who penalized nationalism among their followers, and among those nationalists who were essentially conservative. It was Hitler who "presented nationalism in a proletarian disguise and captured the imagination of his followers." Where neither communists nor nationalists could attract the support of the all-important lower middle class, Hitler's national socialism succeeded. It succeeded in large part because of its leader's skill in tricking nationalism out in the Marxist phrases that had become part of the general German vocabulary.

V: The Failure of Parliamentarism in Spain and Eastern Europe, 1918-1939

In the troubled years between the wars, authoritarian governments emerged not only in Germany and Italy, but also in Spain, in the succession-states to the Habsburg Empire (with the exception of Czechoslovakia), and in the other states of eastern and southeastern Europe.

Spain: The Background

Spain is so different from the other countries of Europe, and its politics are so complicated, that foreigners are tempted to draw dangerously misleading parallels. The developments leading to the establishment of the Franco regime are meaningless unless we keep in mind the special geographic, economic, cultural, and social background against which they took place. In Spain, local feeling in town and village and province is intense; only occasionally has some common cause united the Spanish people. Politically, this situation has meant that separatism often becomes an issue, particularly in Catalonia and in the Basque provinces of the north.

Second, religion, as the driving force that united Spaniards against the Moslems in the Middle Ages, and against the Protestants in the sixteenth and seventeenth centuries, has played an extraordinarily large part in the national life. But early in the nineteenth century, the Catholic Church in Spain decided to lead against liberalism the same kind of struggle it had led against its earlier enemies, instead of identifying itself with popular causes. So in most parts of Spain the Church became identified with the landowners. Loss of faith became very widespread. Catholic sources report that by the 1930's only minute fractions of the population attended Mass. With the same devotion and passion they had once shown for the Church, the lower classes in Spain adopted one or another of the modern revolutionary doctrines.

Third, though Spain approaches economic self-sufficiency in both agriculture and industrial raw materials, the soil is poor, the system of farming is backward, and the rural areas are heavily overpopulated. Poverty is endemic, which means that discontent is everywhere. Yet the Spanish poor cared less for a higher standard of living for themselves than for freedom from outside interference. Agrarian reform, however, based on expropriation of large estates and the institution of some sort of cooperative farming, has long seemed an essential factor in overcoming poverty.

Fourth, when the Spaniards turned to revolutionary doctrine, it was chiefly in Bakunin's anarchist beliefs and later in Sorel's syndicalism that they found ideas they could cling to. Anarchism (and anarcho-syndicalism) really took hold in Spain, and in Spain alone. The industrial workers of Catalonia and the miserable peasants of Andalusia were anarchist; they wanted to destroy the state utterly rather than conquer and use it. Despite a long history in Spain, anarchism, which at its peak numbered a million to a million and a half adherents, could do no more than create a wish for revolution. It could harass governments but could not overthrow them, and its positive achievements were limited to securing by means of strikes an occasional increase in wages. It was deeply puritanical in tone, and fanatically anti-Catholic. Shrewd observers have likened it to a Christian heresy that takes all too seriously the social teachings of the New Testament. Its adherents turned against the Church with all the fanaticism with which they had once supported it, because they felt that the Church had let them down. The burning of churches and the killing of priests, with which Spanish revolutions have always been marked, have been the work chiefly of anarchists, who "aim at reaching by violence a state from which even the mildest form of compulsion is to be excluded." Anarchist ranks included many professional criminals, drawn only by their love of violence.

But Spanish revolutionary ideas were not confined to the anarchists. Spain also had an increasingly substantial Marxist Socialist party, with its own federation of trade unions paralled to that of the anarchists. The socialists drew their first strength from the urban workers of Castile and from the mining and steel-producing centers of the north. When Spain became a republic in 1931 (see below), the socialists added many rural supporters and the party numbered a million and a quarter in 1934. The socialists were moderates who had refused to adhere to the Comintern in 1920, but who had joined the revived Second International a few years later. Dissidents founded a small Communist party, from which there were soon Trotskyite deviations. Catalonians had their own socialist formation, and the Church also supported labor unions of its own in the north, where it had not become identified with the landlords. The socialist doctrine that each should be rewarded according to his needs fits with the traditional Spanish contempt for success and property. In fact, Spain is essentially a country that has never accepted the capitalist system or the industrial revolution any more than it has accepted the Protestant Reformation.

Carlism, the doctrine of the extreme Right, is another vivid illustration of Spanish maladjustment to the outside contemporary world. Founded in the nineteenth century as a movement supporting Carlos, a pretender to the throne, Carlism is more interesting as a sweeping repudiation of modern society. It calls for the restoration of the Inquisition, regards the railroad and the telegraph literally as inventions of the devil, and rejects the Copernican theory of the universe. Carlism has its lower-class devotees, too, especially among the rebellious farmers of Navarre in the north.

Birth of the Spanish Republic

Over this country there ruled until 1923 King Alfonso XIII, a constitutional monarch strongly ambitious for absolute power. He was supported by a government based entirely on electoral corruption and intimidation, in which "liberals" and "conservatives" took orderly turns at office, and in which the real power rested with the local political bosses. Not having participated in World War I, Spain was spared much of the ensuing anguish. Yet wartime trade with the combatants had built up Spanish industry and had increased the tension between rich and poor.

In this situation a *coup* took place in 1923 led by General Primo de Rivera, acting with the approval of Alfonso. Primo de Rivera proclaimed martial law, imposed censorship, and persecuted political opponents. His dictatorship lasted until 1930, but lost its popularity after 1926. Both its success and its failure are comprehensible in the light of world economic conditions. The regime spent too much on public works, and was caught in the depression. Moreover, it did not fulfill its promises for a constituent assembly and political reform. Rivera did get the socialists to participate in his regime, and put through appropriate labor legislation in the hope of weakening the anarchists. But, since he depended on the army and the landowners, he could not institute agrarian reform. He also alienated the Catalonians, and his repressive measures deprived him of middle-class support.

After Rivera's resignation and death in 1930, King Alfonso soon restored the constitution. Municipal elections (April, 1931) resulted in a victory for the republicans, representing the lower middle classes of the towns, small tradesmen, intellectuals, teachers, and journalists. The King left the country without abdicating. Elections to a constituent assembly in June, 1931, brought in a great republican-socialist majority, and in November the assembly forbade the King's return and confiscated his property. Spain was a republic. The monarchy, having stood only for clergy, army, and aristocracy, had failed.

The assembly went ahead to adopt a new constitution in December. This provided for a single-chamber parliament, a president to be chosen by an electoral college consisting of parliament and an equal number of electors chosen by popular vote, and a responsible ministry. It was clear that the army would rise against the Republic whenever the opportunity was presented, and that the army would have the support of the Church and the large landowners. Moreover, although the Republic temporarily had socialist support, it did not have the support of the anarchists. Thus it was from the first in danger both from the Right and from the Left; its task was to steer between the many extremists of both sides while striving to build up a republican Center.

Crisis of the Republic, 1933-1936

The first crisis arose over a new constitutional statute defining the position of the Church. The assembly rejected a moderate proposal which would have preserved the Church as a special corporation with its own schools, and which might have proved acceptable to most Catholics, even though the Cardinal-Primate of Spain had already denounced the Republic. Instead, a measure was passed that closed church schools and ended state grants to the Church after two years. This hurt education badly, and lost the republicans many supporters, especially among the lower clergy itself. Although the Republic secured much Catalan support by a grant of autonomy, it failed to act decisively on agrarian reform.

The anarchists expressed their dissatisfaction by major risings (1933), which the government put down by force. The jails were full, and unemployment was as high as ever. Repression of the anarchists lost the Republic much Left support, but of course failed to gain it that of the Right, which came back strongly in the elections of November, 1933, as the largest party in parliament. Now the government helplessly swung to the Right, and much of its previous legislation, especially legislation affecting the Church and the working classes, remained a dead letter. The Church and monarchists put forward a young man named Gil Robles as their leader. His views were strongly fascist, and he especially admired Dollfuss, the Austrian chancellor (see below).

On the Left, the socialists no longer collaborated with the government. Grown more revolutionary, they now engaged in strenuous competition with the anarchists for the loyalty of the Spanish workers. Strikes and disorders multiplied. In October, 1934, the socialists called a general strike in protest against the inclusion of three of Robles' followers in the government. Catalonia declared itself a republic, and was deprived of its autonomy. The coal miners of the Asturias in the north staged a revolt, joined in by both anarchists and socialists, which was put down with the loss of more than 3,000 lives. The government's use of Moors (Moslems from North Africa) against Spaniards was deeply resented; the Moors had been dispatched by the new minister of war, General Francisco Franco.

Thus the Right in turn lost its pubilc support; and now the Left, under the impact of the Asturias uprising, and influenced by the line of the Comintern (see above, pp. 653-654), united in a "Popular Front" for the elections of February, 1936. For the first time, anarcho-syndicalists went to the polls and voted for a common list with republicans, socialists, and communists. The Left won a considerable victory, perhaps largely because it promised an amnesty for men involved in past outbreaks. Catalan autonomy, land reform, and anti-clerical measures were of course the first order of business. The moderate Republican, Azaña, was elected president.

But moderation was now out of fashion on the Left. The Popular Front was a coali-

tion *for election purposes only*. Instead of entering Azaña's cabinet, Largo Caballero, leader of the left wing of the socialists, now "played at revolution." He was hailed by *Pravda* as a new Lenin, and acted as if he intended to seize power. Yet he could not have made good this threat, since he had no force with which to back it up. The route to power for left-wing revolutionaries would open up only if the Right attempted a military *coup*, if the government then armed the workers to fight it, and if the workers then won.

On the Left also, and for the first time, the Spanish Communist party in 1936 emerged as a considerable element. Under Primo de Rivera's dictatorship the communists had been so insignificant that he had not even taken the trouble to suppress their newspaper. But their participation in the Asturian uprising and the Popular Front gained them political strength despite their numerical weakness (3,000 members). Oddly enough, they were more moderate in their immediate aims than the socialists, because they felt the need for a long preliminary period of Popular Front co-operation to increase their own power, and because this was Stalin's "respectable" period.

Simultaneously in 1936, on the Right, there emerged, also for the first time, the *Falange* (phalanx), a party founded in 1932 by the son of Primo de Rivera. The founder was an orthodox fascist on the Italian pattern ("harmony of all classes and professions in one destiny") but was not opposed to agrarian reform or other socialist programs. The Falange had the usual paraphernalia. Its symbol was a bunch of arrows; its slogan was *Arriba España* ("Upward Spain!"); its program called for national expansion in Africa, the annexation of Portugal, the building of an empire in South America; it had youth groups and a private army. Although the Falange polled relatively few votes in the election of 1936, most of Gil Robles' right-wing support went over to it after the Popular Front victory. Through the spring of 1936 the Falange worked for a counter-revolution with army, monarchist, clerical, and Carlist groups. Everybody knew a military coup against the government was in the offing. In July it came, under the military leadership of General Franco.

The Spanish Civil War, 1936-1939

The international significance of the Spanish Civil War (1936-1939) as the first act in the conflict that was to ripen into World War II will be considered in Chapter XXII. Decisively aided by Germany and Italy, Franco's forces pushed on to victory, which culminated in their capture of the republican strongholds of Madrid and Barcelona in 1939. During the war, the functions of the weak republican government were usurped by a series of workers' committees, and then a Popular Front regime under Caballero came to office in September, 1936. The rebels named Franco chief of state in November. In government territory, terror reigned. At first the terror was the work of anarchists, but they were suppressed. Their terror was replaced by police terror, the work of the communists, who, with Russia behind them, ruthlessly worked against their rival leftist parties in the regime. On the Franco side, terror also took its toll, as men of all sorts connected with the Republic were killed. After the Franco triumph, the prisons were filled and the executioner was kept busy.

With all its fascist trappings, the Franco regime, the only fascist regime to survive World War II, still depended after the war upon the same classes that had supported the Spanish monarchy—the landowners, the army, and the Church. It was presumably opposed by the poor in city and country alike. But the fear of a new civil war, which lay heavily on all classes, prevented open opposition.

Eastern Europe

The triumph of the Right in one form or another in eastern Europe is explained partly by the lack of a firm parliamentary tradition; partly by the failure to solve grievous economic problems, especially after the great world-wide depression of 1929; and partly by a popular fear of Bolshevism, often quite out of proportion to any serious threat, but skillfully played upon by unscrupulous leaders. Perhaps as important as all the other factors put together was the initial impression created by the successes of Mussolini and Hitler. The way to get ahead in the world, at least after 1935, seemed to be to put on a uniform, proclaim a doctrine of extreme nationalism, and launch a war of nerves against your neighbors by loudly voicing your claims, whatever they might happen to be, and by threatening to make them good by means of the sword.

But it was not only the political example set by the dictators that turned the unstable states of eastern and southeastern Europe toward dictatorship. After the depression, the economic pressures exerted by Germany, whose industrial economy complemented the agrarian economy of these states, enabled her to dominate their foreign trade, especially in the Balkan area. To show how these factors operated, we shall now examine three case-histories— Austria, Hungary, and Yugoslavia.

Austria

The Austria that was left at the end of World War I had an almost purely German population of about 8,000,-000, about 2,000,000 of whom lived in the former imperial capital of Vienna. Long the great market for an enormous hinterland and the supplier of industrial finished goods to the agricultural provinces, Vienna was now cut off from its former territories by political boundaries and tariff walls. Between 1922 and 1925, Austrian finances were under direct League of Nations supervision; a League loan and reconstruction policies brought a measure of recovery. But what might have represented one road to economic salvation—union of Austria with Germany—though voted by the assembly of the new Austrian republic in March, 1919, was forbidden on political grounds by the Allies in the Treaty of St. Germain (September, 1919). These two problems, economic survival and union with Germany, were complicated by the continuation in even more violent form of the basic political struggle of imperial Austria: Social Democrats against Christian Socialists (see Chapter XV). The Social Democrats were a gradualist reformist, but Marxist, party with strong urban support, especially in Vienna itself. The Christian Socialists were a conservative clerical party with a mass following in the countryside and among the urban lower middle classes, and counted many priests among their leaders.

In the mid-twenties, the two hostile parties, usually almost evenly balanced in the parliament, organized private armies: the Christian Socialists, the *Heimwehr* (home guard), and the Social Democrats, the *Schutzbund* (defense league). Their mutual hostility was increased by the relief and workers' housing measures undertaken by the Social Democratic municipal government of Vienna. These measures were financed by taxing the rich. After 1930, when a treaty was signed with Italy, Mussolini more or less overtly supported the Christian Socialists, who grew more and more fascistic in their outlook. The failure of Bruening's plan for a customs union with Germany and the related collapse of the Vienna *Kredit-Anstalt* bank (see above, p. 682) increased tension in 1931, and in September, 1931, the *Heimwehr* tried its first fascist *coup*, which failed. Efforts in 1932 to organize a Danubian economic cooperation scheme—an alternative to Austrian union with Germany, and favored by France—were rendered futile by Italian and German opposition. After Hitler came to power in early 1933, many Christian Socialists became openly Nazi.

The Christian Socialist chancellor, Engelbert Dollfuss, however, strove to curb the Nazis. To this end he suspended parliamentary government in March, 1933, and in effect ended parliamentary democracy. He forbade the wearing of uniforms by political groups, and tried to expel Nazi agitators. In retaliation, Hitler made it prohibitively expensive for German tourists to visit Austria, and thus destroyed one of the most lucrative sources of Austrian income. In the face of Nazi-inspired disorder, Dollfuss banned the Nazi party (June, 1933). But, instead of burying the hatchet and uniting with the Social Democrats against Hitler, Dollfuss pursued them too. He banned all parties except his own "Fatherland Front," a union of all right-wing groups except the Nazis, and raided Social Democratic headquarters, precipitating a workers' riot. The government then bombarded with artillery the workers' new apartment houses, in which the Social Democratic leaders had taken refuge (February, 1934). The Social Democratic party was broken, but the Vienna workmen were permanently alienated and were united in opposition to the regime. Dollfuss had to depend more and more upon Italy to support him against the threat from Hitler. He established himself as a fascist dictator (April 30, 1934), but was assassinated in July by the Nazis. It was only Italian troop concentrations on the frontier that led Hitler to disavow this attempted *coup*.

Dollfuss' successor, Schuschnigg, was committed to the same policies. But Mussolini's desire to win Hitler's support for Italian aggression in the Mediterranean weakened Schuschnigg. The Austrian Chancellor made plans looking toward a Habsburg restoration, tried to concentrate armed power in his own hands rather than those of the *Heimwehr*, and strove to create an understanding with France and her allies

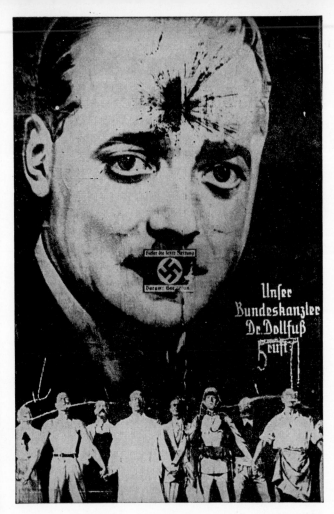

Poster of Chancellor Dollfuss and representative Austrians defaced by Nazis, 1933.

a Nazi chancellor, put Schuschnigg in jail, and began the extension of the Nazi system to Austria by allowing storm troopers to force elderly Viennese Jews to clean the sidewalks with acid under a hail of abuse and blows. In April, 1938, he held the plebiscite on the question of Austrian union with Germany and obtained a 99.75 per cent vote of *Ja*. Mussolini had to bow in 1938 to what he had prevented in 1934, and Austria, increasingly fascist since 1930, had become a mere province of Nazi Germany.

to replace the one with Italy. But he failed in the face of German aggression. In February and March, 1938, Hitler increased the pressure on Schuschnigg, who was subjected to the first of the famous series of grim interviews between Hitler and statesmen of lesser countries. The Fuehrer demanded and obtained privileges for the Nazis in Austria. When the predictable Nazi disorders broke out, Schuschnigg desperately tried to win working-class support, but it was too late.

The final move that precipitated armed German invasion of Austria was Schuschnigg's announcement that a plebiscite would be held on the question of Austrian independence. Hitler marched in, installed

Hungary

In Hungary, the most overwhelmingly important political issue between the wars was "revisionism," the effort to revise the peace treaties that had deprived the Magyars of all territories predominantly populated by Slavic and Rumanian minorities. The Treaty of Trianon (June, 1920) confirmed the loss of a small strip of land to Austria, of Transylvania to Rumania, of Slovakia to Czechoslovakia, and of Croatia and other Serb and Croat territories to Yugoslavia. No tourist who visited Budapest thereafter could escape the huge statue of Hungary mourning the lost provinces, north, east, south, and west, or the great map laid out in flower beds in the public park, showing in different colored blossoms the far-flung territories relinquished but still claimed by the Magyars. The national motto was now *"Nem, nem, soha"* (No, no, never). Revisionist propaganda made a considerable impression in those circles where the Hungarian aristocracy had always had sympathizers, especially among the English upper classes, who had often failed to grasp the great difference in political tradition between themselves and their cultivated and tweedy, horsey, Magyar friends, and who were usually quite ignorant of Hungary's black record in governing her minorities.

The rank and file of Hungarians were relatively indifferent to revisionism as an issue, as they had always been indifferent to the chauvinist questions which agitated their rulers, the great aristocrats and the gentry (see Chapter XV). This unreal and sterile issue continued to dominate Hungarian life after 1920 because the aristocrats and the gentry were able to keep their dominant position. Hungary was one of the few countries of eastern Europe not to experience an effective land reform between the wars. The enormous estates of the great magnates and the smaller properties of the gentry remained almost intact. Behind a thin screen of parliamentary government, an authoritarian dictatorship governed the country on behalf of the old ruling groups. It was helped by a greatly swollen bureaucracy, and it became more and more fascist in character as the years went on. In the troubled days immediately after the war, the Allies paved the way for this triumph of the Right by their failure to support the efforts of Hungarian moderates to create a stable democratic regime. They also permitted a bloody-handed Bolshevik dictatorship to take power briefly. In the reaction against this communist regime, moderation and reform lost out in Hungary and fascism won.

The brief opportunity (if it really was an opportunity) for a moderate regime in Hungary began on October 31, 1918, eleven days before the Armistice, when Count Michael Karolyi became prime minister, after the country had already severed its ties with Austria. Karolyi was one of the richest of the great magnates, but a democrat on the western pattern. He had always been pro-Allied, and was deeply imbued with Wilsonian ideas. Though not a socialist, Karolyi favored social reform. He proved his sincerity by handing over the 50,000 acres of his own estate to be divided among the peasants, and by preparing a land-reform law. He made every effort to reach a compromise with the national minorities, but these groups would no longer

trust any Magyar. The French commander of Allied troops did not assist Karolyi, and demanded a retreat of Hungarian forces from Slovakia. Karolyi resigned in March, 1919, in protest over the loss of Transylvania.

National sentiment and growing radicalism, stimulated by the news of Bolshevik activities brought by Hungarian prisoners returning from Russia, now made possible a left-wing government more and more dominated by Lenin's agent, Bela Kun, a Hungarian-born Jew. Revolutionary nationalization decrees were at once passed and a soviet political system was installed, but land reform was delayed—a delay that alienated the peasants. The Reds used terror in the countryside to overcome opposition. If Hungary had been as large as Russia or as far from the main theater of Allied operations, Kun might have gained time enough to compensate for his lack of trained men, a handicap that it had taken all the genius of Lenin and Trotsky to overcome in Russia.

But the Allies were determined not to let a Bolshevik government rule Hungary. The Rumanians invaded and drove Kun out; they occupied the country during 1919 and part of 1920, and stripped it of everything they could move. Meanwhile, a counter-revolutionary government had been formed under French protection and had returned to Budapest, where Admiral Horthy, a member of the gentry, became regent and chief of state (March 1, 1920). Hungary was now a kingdom without a king, Horthy an admiral without a fleet. Two efforts of the Habsburg King Charles to regain the Hungarian throne were frustrated, largely because of the opposition of the neighboring states. The Hungarian counter-revolution gave free rein to a "White Terror" directed largely against the Jews, but also against Magyar workers and peasants.

For ten years (1921-1931) Count Bethlen as prime minister was the real power in the country, which he ran as if nothing had changed since 1914. The peasants were effectively disfranchised as they had always been; the Social Democrats were tolerated as a trade-union party; and the upper house of magnates was re-established. The League of Nations helped economic recovery by a loan and a reconstruction plan (1923-1926), and in 1927 a treaty with Italy began an intimate relationship between Hungary and Mussolini. The depression and the financial crisis of 1931 drove Bethlen from office. He was succeeded by the strongly nationalist and fascist-minded Gömbös, who was pro-German as well as pro-Italian, and who permitted the first Nazi-like organizations to form. Of these the Arrow Cross was the strongest, but it remained on the fringes of power until almost the end of World War II, largely because Hitler got what he wanted in Hungary without it.

Following Gömbös' death in 1936, his successors were all men of the same stripe. The Italians supplied arms to the Hungarians; Hitler favored their revisionism along with his own. After Austria had fallen to Hitler, he had Hungary in his pocket, and when he broke up Czechoslovakia in March, 1939, the Hungarians seized the extreme eastern portion, Ruthenia, and a small part of Slovakia. To pursue revisionism, the Hungarians had to follow Hitler, since he alone offered the opportunity to re-draw the map as they felt it should be drawn. So, before war broke out, they had withdrawn from the League, and had enacted anti-Semitic laws in the Nazi pattern. But because Hitler needed Rumania too, he would not give the Magyars all of Transylvania. Ironically enough, the price they paid for espousal of revisionism between the wars was the Soviet-dominated regime installed in Hungary after World War II.

Yugoslavia

In the new "Kingdom of the Serbs, Croats, and Slovenes," proclaimed in December, 1918, there came together for the first time in one state the former south-Slav subjects of Austria and Hungary and those of the former independent Kingdom of Serbia. This was in most respects a satisfied state from the territorial point of view; revisionism therefore was not an issue. But, as the name of the new state shows, it faced the serious problem of creating a governmental system that would satisfy the aspirations of each of its nationality groups. Over this problem democracy broke down and a dictatorship was established. The dictatorship was in many respects not of the fascist type, although, as German power waxed, important politicians in the country became convinced that the future lay in Hitler's hands, and responded accordingly. The rank and file of the population, by and large, were peasants deeply devoted to freedom, although unskilled in western forms of parliamentarism. They opposed fascism, and, when they got the chance, ousted the politicians who sought to align them with it.

Serbian political ambitions had helped to start the war. The Serbs were more numerous than Croats and Slovenes together (approximately six million to three and a quarter million Croats and a few over one million Slovenes in 1931). Many Serbs felt that the new kingdom, which their Serbian king ruled from his Serbian capital of Belgrade, should be that "greater Serbia" of which they had so long dreamed. Orthodox in religion, using the Cyrillic alphabet, and having experienced and overthrown Ottoman domination, many Serbs tended to look upon the Croats as effete subjects of the Habsburgs who were lucky to get the chance to live in the same state with them. Roman Catholic in religion, using the Latin alphabet, and having opposed Germans and Magyars for centuries, many Croats felt that the Serbs were crude easterners who ought to give them a full measure of autonomy within the new state. Thus the issue was posed: Serb-sponsored centralism against Croat-sponsored federalism. The

Slovenes, more conciliatory and less numerous, sometimes acted as balance wheel to keep the political machinery moving. But the Serbs forced the acceptance of their answer to the constitutional question. This brought about dictatorship, alienated large numbers of Croats, bred extremism among them, and contributed greatly to the benefit of the country's enemies and to its own sufferings during the second war.

The Croats, under their peasant leader Radich, boycotted the constituent assembly of 1920, and the Serbs put through a constitution providing for a strongly centralized state. In the 1920's both sides generally refused to compromise, although occasionally temporary understandings were reached, as when Radich joined the cabinet briefly in 1925-26. When a Serb deputy shot Radich dead on the floor of parliament in June, 1928, a crisis arose that terminated only when King Alexander proclaimed a dictatorship in January, 1929. Alexander made every effort to settle the problem by wiping out all vestiges of old provincial loyalties. There was to be no more Serbia or Croatia, but new artificially created administrative units named after the chief rivers that ran through them. The whole country was renamed Yugoslavia, as a sign that there were to be no more Serbs and Croats. But it was still a Serbian government, and the Croats could not be made to forget it. Elections were rigged by the government, and all political parties were dissolved. Croat leaders spent much time in jails, which, like most Balkan jails, were highly uncomfortable. This dictatorship of King Alexander passed no racial laws, elevated no one political party to exclusive power, and had no colored shirts, special songs, or other fascist paraphernalia. But it was unmistakably authoritarian and anti-democratic.

One result was the strengthening of Croat extremists, who had wanted an independent Croatia in the days of the Habsburgs, and who now combined this program with terrorism, supported from abroad by the enemies of Yugoslavia—Italy and Hungary. The Croat extremists were called *Ustashi* (rebels), and their leader, Ante Pavelich, was subsidized by Mussolini. He was deeply involved in the assassination of Alexander at Marseilles in October, 1934. Under the regency of Prince Paul (Alexander's cousin) the dictatorship continued. As German economic power in the Balkans increased, leading politicians grew enamored of Germany, and some efforts were made to bring Yugoslav policies into line with those of the Axis. But these policies met with such unconcealed popular opposition that they were never pursued very far. In the summer of 1939, on the very eve of war in Europe, an agreement was finally reached with the Croats that established an autonomous Croatia. But by then it was too late, since the Croats were not satisfied with the boundaries of their own province.

Though the Yugoslavs in 1941 bravely resisted German invasion, they did not have the military power to hold Hitler's armies back. When the conquering Germans and Italians split the country up, they turned Croatia over to the extremist Croat Pavelich, head of the Ustashi, who carried out horrifying massacres of Serbs and Jews. The innocent men, women, and children suffering death and torture at the hands of Pavelich's forces owed some of their anguish to the short-sightedness of Serbian politicians who had failed to solve the problem of Croat autonomy within a peaceful Yugoslavia, and who had thus stimulated the extremists.

Other Authoritarian Regimes

The case-histories we have been considering are unique in detail, yet they furnish interesting parallels to developments elsewhere in eastern Europe. Thus in Poland, Pilsudski led a military *coup* against the democratic government in 1926, and exercised a military dictatorship that became ever more authoritarian, especially after the depression.

In Rumania it was the deep entrenchment of corruption in political life that initially jeopardized the parliamentary system, as the party in power usually rigged elections without shame. In addition, there was widespread anti-Semitism, which was adopted as the chief program of the "Iron Guard," a Rumanian Nazi party. To head off a Guardist *coup*, King Carol of Rumania installed his own fascist dictatorship in 1938. Although the Guardist leaders were "shot while trying to escape," Rumania could not avoid German pressure. After Hitler had acceded to Russian seizure of Bessarabia and Northern Bukovina, and had given Hungary northern Transylvania (August, 1940), Carol had to leave the country, and Hitler's man, Marshal Antonescu, took over, with Iron Guard support.

In Bulgaria, always a strongly pro-Russian country, the genuine threat of communism was a serious problem between the wars, and gave a more or less valid excuse to those who sought dictatorial power. Moreover, Bulgaria, like Hungary, was revisionist because of her failure to gain the Macedonian territory given by the peace treaties to Yugoslavia and Greece. The issue was exacerbated by the presence in the country of thousands of Macedonian refugees, who tended to join revolutionary terrorist societies. Bulgaria, an equalitarian country with no minorities problem, no rich landowners, no aristocracy, and no great industries, none the less produced political cleavages even more violent than those in countries where economic inequality prevailed. In the early twenties, a remarkable agrarian political leader, Stamboliisky gave the country a period (1920-1923) of reasonably popular government. But even he curbed the press and interfered with intellectual freedom, as he strove to control the Macedonian terrorists and the communists both. His imposition of high income taxes alienated the bourgeoisie, and his conciliatory policies toward Yugoslavia infuriated the army.

In 1923, a plot to oust Stamboliisky succeeded, and was followed by his murder and the installation of a strongly authoritarian regime. From then on, communist plots and bomb outrages and Macedonian terrorist strife racked the country. After 1930, the Italian marriage of King Boris led to a rapprochement with Mussolini. In 1934, a military *coup* brought a group of army officers to power; they dissolved the political parties and tried their hands at a dictatorship of their own. But this development was successfully countered in 1936 by King Boris himself, who, like Alexander of Yugoslavia and Carol of Rumania, imposed a royal dictatorship, which lasted from then until his mysterious death during World War II.

In Greece between the wars, the main issues were whether the country should be a monarchy or a republic, and how to overcome the economic difficulties consequent on the transfer of 1,250,000 Greeks from Turkey. On the constitutional question, the population wavered, voting for a monarchy in 1920, for a republic in 1924, and for a monarchy again in 1935, always by enormous majorities. Economic dislocation brought strength to communism among the refugees and in labor groups. The inter-war period was punctuated by a whole series of *coups* by generals, some republican, some monarchist, all more or less authoritarian, but most of them ineffective. The last of these was the most fascist, General John Metaxas, who became dictator in August, 1936. Metaxas abolished political parties, instituted censorship and political persecution of his opponents, launched a program of public works, and imitated the Nazis in other ways. But when the Italian invasion came from Albania in October, 1940,

Metaxas ordered resistance, which was the beginning of Greece's heroic showing in World War II.

Fascism in Review

None of these regimes in eastern Europe was fascist in the full sense of the term. In Italy and Germany the regimes rested, at least initially, upon the popular support of a substantial proportion of the people, even though that support was kept alive by the technique of artificial stimulation. In eastern Europe, on the other hand, the dictatorships rested on the police, the bureaucracy, and the army, and not on the support of the peasant masses. To an eastern European politician of almost any complexion an election was an occasion for bribery, intimidation, and totally absurd promises that he had no intention of trying to fulfill. The hope placed by some western liberals in peasant parties like those of Radich and Stamboliisky proved in the end illusory, either because the original peasant leaders allowed the party to fall under middle-class urban control, as did Radich, or because the Right crushed them, as in Bulgaria and Poland.

Thus the growth of anti-democratic governments of the Right in Europe during the period between the wars strikingly reveals the difficulties in the way of moderate parliamentary regimes in countries without parliamentary traditions. This is not to say that the western liberal tradition is not for export, but only to emphasize that a liberal constitution on paper and a liberal franchise are in themselves no guarantee that a regime on western models can become stabilized. The postwar economic agony had scarcely disappeared before the depression of the late twenties and early thirties struck. Under these circumstances men turned to extremists of the Left and Right. But the fear of communism, combined with the seductive nationalist propaganda of the Right, brought about fascist victories in Italy and Germany. Thereafter, the triumph of the Right elsewhere was assured, and a new world war was inevitable.

Reading Suggestions on the Rise of Fascism

The Roots of Fascism

A. Cobban, *Dictatorship: Its History and Theory* (N.Y.: Scribner's, 1939). Highly suggestive survey, reaching well back into history.

P. Viereck, *Metapolitics: From the Romantics to Hitler* (N.Y.: Knopf, 1941). A survey of the background in German political thought.

C. J. Hayes, *A Generation of Materialism, 1871-1900* (N.Y.: Harper, 1941). Contains a concise and corrosive section on the seedtime of fascism.

Italy

G. Megaro, *Mussolini in the Making* (Boston: Houghton Mifflin, 1938). An unequaled study of Mussolini's early career.

H. Finer, *Mussolini's Italy* (N.Y.: Holt, 1935), and H. A. Steiner, *Government in Fascist Italy* (N.Y.: McGraw-Hill, 1938). Two very solid studies by expert political scientists.

G. A. Borgese, *Goliath: The March of Fascism* (N.Y.: Viking, 1938), and G. Salvemini, *Under the Axe of Fascism* (N.Y.: Viking, 1936). Lively works by important anti-fascist Italians.

G. Salvemini, *Prelude to World War II* (N.Y.: Doubleday, 1954). A survey of Mussolini's foreign policy, by one of his most implacable enemies.

C. Levi, *Christ Stopped at Eboli* (N.Y.: Universal Library). An anti-fascist Italian doctor and painter writes movingly of his exile in a remote and poverty-stricken southern Italian village.

Germany

A. Hitler, *Mein Kampf* (N.Y.: Reynal & Hitchcock, 1939). A complete English translation of the Nazi bible, the basic work for an understanding of the movement.

A. Hitler, *My New Order*, R. de Sales, ed. (N.Y.: Reynal & Hitchcock, 1941). Speeches after the Führer's coming to power.

A. L. C. Bullock, *Hitler: A Study in Tyranny* (London: Oxham's, 1952). The best biography.

S. W. Halperin, *Germany Tried Democracy* (N.Y.: Crowell, 1946). A reliable history of the Weimar Republic, 1918-1933.

R. G. L. Waite, *Vanguard of Nazism* (Cambridge: Harvard Univ. Press, 1952). A good study of the "Free Corps" movement.

J. W. Wheeler-Bennett, *Wooden Titan* (N.Y.: Morrow, 1936) and *Nemesis of Power* (N.Y.: St. Martin's, 1954). Two first-rate studies, the first dealing with Hindenburg, and the second with the role of the German army in politics from 1918 to 1945.

F. L. Neumann, *Behemoth: The Structure and Practice of National Socialism* (N.Y.: Oxford Univ. Press, 1944). The best work on the subject.

K. Heiden, *History of National Socialism* (N.Y.: Knopf, 1935), and S. H. Roberts, *The House That Hitler Built* (N.Y.: Harper, 1938). Two older and still useful studies of the Nazis.

F. von Papen, *Memoirs* (N.Y.: Dutton, 1953). An apologetic autobiography by the scheming right-wing politician.

E. Wiskemann, *The Rome-Berlin Axis* (London: Oxford Univ. Press, 1949). A study of the formation and history of the Hitler-Mussolini partnership.

R. Fischer, *Stalin and German Communism* (Cambridge: Harvard Univ. Press, 1948). A study of the role played by the communist movement in the history of Germany in the twenties.

Other Countries

G. Brenan, *The Spanish Labyrinth* (N.Y.: Macmillan, 1943). A useful study of the Spanish Civil War against its historical and economic background.

C. Bowers, *My Mission to Spain* (N.Y.: Simon & Schuster, 1954); C. J. Hayes, *Wartime Mission to Spain, 1942-1945* (N.Y.: Macmillan, 1945); and

Lord Templewood (Sir Samuel Hoare), *Complacent Dictator* (N.Y.: Knopf, 1947). Three differing views of Franco and the Spanish problem, by three ambassadors, the first two American, the last British.

G. E. R. Gedye, *Betrayal in Central Europe* (N.Y.: Harper, 1939). A careful journalist's account of Austria and Czechoslovakia.

H. Seton-Watson, *Eastern Europe between the Wars, 1918-1941* (Cambridge, England: The Univ. Press, 1946). A useful account dealing with eastern European countries except Greece and Albania.

R. L. Wolff, *The Balkans in Our Time* (Cambridge: Harvard Univ. Press, 1956). A detailed and informative survey reaching back into the era before World War II.

R. L. Buell, *Poland: Key to Europe* (N.Y.: Knopf, 1939). A helpful survey.

R. West, *Black Lamb and Grey Falcon* (N.Y.: Viking, 1941). A highly subjective account of Yugoslavia, loaded with political bias, but fascinating and informative reading.

Historical Fiction

I. Silone, *Bread and Wine* (N.Y.: New American Library), and *Fontamara* (N.Y.: Smith & Haas, 1934). Two good novels on rural Italy under fascism; by a distinguished anti-fascist writer.

H. Fallada, *Little Man What Now?* (N.Y.: Simon & Schuster, 1933), and E. Remarque, *Three Comrades* (N.Y.: Popular Library). Two touching novels of depression-ridden Germany.

E. von Salomon, *"Der Fragebogen"* (*The Questionnaire*) (N.Y.: Doubleday, 1955). One of the plotters against Rathenau, a strong sympathizer with authoritarian movements, tells his life story satirically, against the background of American military government in post-1945 Germany.

E. Hemingway, *For Whom the Bell Tolls* (N.Y.: Scribner's, 1940). A characteristic Hemingway novel, set in the Spain of the Civil War.

CHAPTER TWENTY-ONE

The Democracies 1919-1939

Domestic and Imperial Problems

I: Introduction

The central fact—or irony—of politics between the two world wars is that the war "to make the world safe for democracy" seemed to have made it in effect a difficult and dangerous place for democracy. Idealists like President Wilson had expected that the collapse of the old Romanov, Habsburg, and Hohenzollern empires would automatically insure an increase in the number of democratic states. But instead, as we have just seen, much of Europe came under regimes that were hostile to liberal democracy. Even Italy, which had seemed, superficially at least, to be evolving toward a democratic constitutional monarchy, turned fascist. In the 1920's and 1930's, then, the core of democracy remained in the North Atlantic community (see Chapter XIV), that is, in Britain, France, and the United States.

The upsurge of communism and fascism created grave problems in international relations for the three great democracies. At times in the 1920's it looked as if they might successfully overcome these problems and bring the world back to peaceful habits. But in the 1930's the great worldwide depression, the advent of Hitler, and the aggressions of fascist states in the West and of an expansionist Japan in the Far East rapidly darkened the international scene. With the outbreak of another general war in 1939, it was clear that the two decades since 1919 had been at best a twenty years' truce, a truce broken with increasing frequency by international troublemakers.

Certainly the totalitarian aggressors bore the major responsibility for the unleashing of a second world war. Yet a far from minor factor in the deterioration of the twenty years' truce was the relative weakness of the peaceful democracies themselves. In the 1920's Britain, France, and the United States each became preoccupied to some degree with its own domestic problems. In the early 1930's this preoccupation increased as a result of the urgent crisis of the depression. But this was the very time when international problems demanded equally urgent attention. International trade was steadily shrinking in the face of the drepression and of mounting tariff barriers; the prospects for peace were steadily fading before the saber-rattling and actual saber-wielding of the enemies of democracy. Faced with two equally urgent sets of problems, the democracies turned first to the domestic ones, and then discovered that the international situation was rapidly moving toward war.

Nor was this all. During the twenty years' truce the democracies faced a third set of problems, not as yet so urgent as the other two, but of very great potential importance. This third set involved imperial issues—the relationship between the great democracies and the non-western peoples, many of whom were still under colonial rule or some other form of control by democratic mother countries. Particularly in Asia and the Middle East, the non-western peoples were beginning to assert their nationalism and to voice demands for the loosening of old imperial ties. The nationalist aspirations of the non-western world did not gain full strength until the years immediately following World War II, with the dramatic evolution of old colonies, protectorates, and mandates into newly independent states. The nationalist movements that have brought these newcomers to the family of nations since 1945 grew steadily in the 1920's and 1930's.

The three sets of problems—domestic, foreign, and imperial—faced by the democracies in the inter-war years could not be fully separated. They were interconnected and interrelated in countless ways. We shall underline some of these interrelations, somewhat as we have shown the links between the internal and external policies of the communist and fascist states. But, in order to point up the main issues, we shall also have to separate national, international, and colonial problems in a fashion that may oversimplify the complexities of real life. Our survey emphasizes first the chief domestic problems of the democracies during the twenty years' truce, then moves abroad to the non-western world. In the succeeding chapter we shall analyze the foreign policies of the democracies, as distinguished from their colonial and imperial policies. We begin here with an examination of the crisis confronting Britain on the home front after November, 1918.

II: Great Britain

The Postwar Depression

Save for trifling losses from German Zeppelin raids and coastal bombardments, the British Isles suffered no direct material damage in World War I. But the British armed forces lost about seven hundred and fifty thousand men killed in action, and about a million and a half wounded. The losses of the Empire and the Commonwealth as a whole came to nearly a million killed and over two million wounded. The economic losses of the mother country had been grave indeed—the almost incalculable difference between the actual cost of destructive war and what might otherwise have been productive effort.

The national debt after the war was ten times that of 1914. Many British investments abroad, returns on which had been a great factor in Victorian prosperity, had had to be liquidated. Forty per cent of the great British merchant fleet, the income from which had helped to balance Britain's international accounts and pay for her imports, had been destroyed by enemy action. The whole fabric of international trade on which Britain depended was torn in a thousand places in 1918, and could not be rapidly restored in the unsettled conditions that prevailed in the postwar world. And, finally, to supplement the war production of Britain and France, the industrial plants of the United States, of Canada, and even of India had been called on, and had received a stimulus that made them in peacetime more effective competitors of the British. In the 1920's, the industrial plant of the Germans, nourished in part by loans from newly enriched America, once more took up the rivalry that had so alarmed the British before the war.

In short, victorious Britain faced in an aggravated form the basic economic difficulty that we analyzed in Chapter XIV. The land that had been in Victorian days the "workshop of the world" had now lost its great head start and could no longer give full employment to its millions of workers. And yet those workers were in no mood to accept a lower standard of living. They had made great gains in social security before the war, and they had fought the war in the hope of still better things to come. In the "khaki election" held just after the Armistice of 1918 they had been promised a "land fit for heroes"; they had been promised that the defeated enemy would through reparations pay the costs of the war, and give Britain a new start.

This hope was very early disappointed. No substantial reparations came through, and economic difficulties soon began to accumulate. By 1921 there were already almost a million unemployed. In that same year the British government, faced with the rising cost of living, increased the very meager unemployment payments. These payments, soon given the derogatory name of the "dole," were strictly speaking not old-fashioned poor relief, but payments on unemployment insurance policies that had been part of Lloyd George's social legislation of prewar days. However, large-scale unemployment continued, and some young workers never acquired employment status. Unemployment insurance could not be maintained on a sound actuarial basis, and the payments became in fact a form of poor relief.

The Great Britain of the 1920's experienced no equivalent of the "Coolidge prosperity" that the United States was to enjoy. We must not exaggerate: the British economic decline was not catastrophic.

London, Manchester, and Liverpool did not become ghost cities, though some of the gravely depressed areas, like the coalmining regions of South Wales, did begin to show real signs of decay. What happened was rather a *relative* decline, the comparative slowing up of an economy geared to dynamic growth, with a working population conditioned psychologically to a slowly rising standard of living and a middle class similarly conditioned to traditional comforts. Moreover, this was the twentieth century, the century of the newspaper, the movie, the radio. The British were well aware, for instance, that Americans had automobiles, radios, and a lot else; they, too, wanted those things.

Britain was, then, suffering from ills characteristic of economic old age. The coal industry is a good concrete illustration of these ills. There was still a lot of coal in Britain; but it was costly to mine, since the most easily and cheaply worked seams were being exhausted. The industry was badly organized, with many small and inefficient mines running at a loss, and with machinery and methods that were antiquated in comparison with American and the best continental standards. Productivity per man-hour over the whole industry was low. Worst of all, perhaps, the 1920's saw the rapid rise all over the industrialized world of major competitors to coal—oil, and electricity based on water power—and the consequent decline of British coal exports. The British Isles had no petroleum, and no very great potential in hydroelectric power. Yet coal, the historic basis of British industrial power, simply had to be mined. The workers were unionized and were in no mood to accept cuts in wages; the owners did not want to run their business at a loss. A strike in March, 1921, after the government had rejected Labor party proposals for making permanent the wartime nationalization of the industry, focused national attention on this critical problem. The strike was settled in July, but only by the government's consenting to pay subsidies to cover increased wages.

The Conservative and Labor Programs

Against the background of economic depression, British domestic politics during the twenty years' truce displayed, therefore, a fairly clear class basis. The Conservatives, still often called Tories, tended to get the support of aristocrats and of middle-class people who wanted to attack new problems with traditional methods and with a minimum of government intervention. The Labor party tended to get the support of trade unionists and of intellectuals from all classes who demanded that the government intervene more vigorously in the economic field. We must not exaggerate, however; not every reformer necessarily voted Labor nor every stand-patter Tory. Yet economic issues did sharpen the differences between the two major British parties.

The first casualty in the struggle between Labor and the Conservatives was the old Liberal party, which was ground to a mere husk between the two contending groups. The Conservatives, who had won the lion's share of seats in the "khaki election," decided in 1922 to withdraw their support from the coalition government headed by the Liberal Lloyd George. In the ensuing elections the Conservatives won, and the Liberals, split between the followers of Lloyd George and those of the more orthodox Asquith, lost heavily. Labor won 142 seats—more than the Liberals did—and became for the first time His Majesty's Opposition.

Both Conservatives and Labor realized the underlying difficulties of Britain's position. Both were fully aware that twentieth-century Britain had to sell enough goods and services abroad—enough manufactured goods and shipping, insurance, banking, and tourist services—so that the

THE DEMOCRACIES ~ 707

return on them would buy food for her people and much of the raw materials for her factories. But the parties were not agreed on how to achieve this necessary task. Broadly speaking, the Conservatives wanted to retain private industry, with government and other technical experts helping to make it efficient. But they were thwarted by high tariffs in the United States and elsewhere, by the drive to economic self-sufficiency all over the world, and by the difficulties of trade with the vast area under Russian communist control.

The state of world trade drove the Conservatives more and more to the solution Joseph Chamberlain (see Chapter XIV) had advocated earlier: protective tariffs against competing foreign goods, and the knitting of the Empire and Commonwealth, with their vast variety of resources, into a largely self-sufficient trade area by "imperial preference" agreements. Such agreements would give raw materials from the colonies and dominions preferred treatment in the British market in return for preferred treatment of British manufactures in the colonial and dominion markets. In theory, at least, the scheme could have worked, for the Commonwealth and Empire of the twenties—one-quarter of the world's land and people—had the natural resources and offered a potential market capable of supporting the British Isles in the style to which they were accustomed.

The great snag, of course, was the unwillingness of the constituent parts of the Empire and Commonwealth to accept for themselves the role of producers of raw materials in exchange for British manufactured goods and British services. The self-governing dominions, loyal though they had been during the war, were in no mood to assume a role essentially like that of colonies in the old mercantilistic days. They were looking toward independent nationhood, and they wanted what seems to go with nationhood in our world—their own industries. This was also true of what was

potentially the richest unit in the Empire, India.

The Labor solution was nationalization —that is, government purchase and operation of key industries with just compensation to their private owners, rather than seizure without compensation as in Soviet Russia. The key industries were transportation, power, coal, steel, perhaps even textiles, cutlery, pottery, machine tools—all the industries that seem in these days to thrive best on large-scale organization. A good many Laborites wanted nationalization simply because, as socialists, they believed that profits, rent, and interest paid to "capitalist" private owners were forms of worker-exploitation, and that under nationalization these forms of exploitation would cease. But many of their leaders knew that even nationalized industries would still face the fundamental problem of selling enough goods abroad to keep the economy going. They argued, therefore, that nationalization would enable British industries to produce more cheaply and efficiently. It would do away with wasteful competition and with the inefficient firms so conspicuous in the coal industry, for instance. It would force into productive work both unnecessary managerial and selling staffs, and stockholders and other investors who lived without working.

Moreover, Labor supporters believed that, once nationalization had been achieved, the British workmen would adopt a transformed attitude toward their work. Knowing that they were now the *real* owners of their own industries, they would put their hearts into their work, abstain from feather-bedding, absenteeism, and similar practices, and raise production to a point where the goods of Britain could undersell those of her capitalist rivals in world markets. This belief was reinforced by the somewhat paradoxical faith in free trade that the Labor party had inherited from the Liberals, and by its high hopes for improved international relations. Consequently, Labor was hostile to the Conservative policies of protective tariffs and imperial preference.

Postwar Politics

In the twenty years between the wars neither the Tories nor Labor were able to carry out their full platform. Labor itself, though it came to power briefly in 1924 and in 1929, with its leader Ramsay MacDonald as prime minister, never had a parliamentary position firm enough to nationalize any industry. The Conservatives, by no means unanimous on the degree of economic self-sufficiency they wanted for the Empire, were decisively held up by the unwillingness of the Commonwealth countries to go much further than to accept certain limited imperial preferences.

Despite the wider cleavage between the two parties, British politics still retained many of the amenities of Victorian parliamentary life. The House of Commons, even though it now included workingmen and others who by no means spoke with an "Oxford accent," was still one of the best clubs in the world. For a few weeks in 1926 some 2,500,000 trade-union members attempted a general strike in support of the coalminers, who were already on strike in protest against a cut in their wages. The general strike failed, but during its brief course fundamental British attitudes were revealed. Thousands of men from the middle and upper classes volunteered to keep essential services operating, and in Plymouth a soccer team of strikers played a team of police. Britain, despite mounting tensions, remained a land of general law-abidingness, where the class struggle that the Marxists talked so much about seemed to have come thoroughly under the control of the parliamentary decencies.

In 1928, almost unnoticed, the last step was taken in the political democratization of Britain that had begun in 1832. In 1918, in preparation for the "khaki election," the government had put through a reform bill which eliminated all the old exceptions to universal male suffrage and gave the vote to all men over twenty-one. Culminating a long and spectacular campaign in which "suffragettes" had demonstrated, marched, orated, and even gone to jail in behalf of women's rights, the bill also gave the vote to women. But, with almost a caricature of British caution, it set the voting age for women at thirty years, thus insuring that there would always be more male than female voters. The distinction was too irrational to stand up, especially after experience had demonstrated—as it also did in the United States—that women divide politically about the way men do. In 1928, a bill known irreverently as the "bill for flapper suffrage" gave women the vote at twenty-one.

Although the dole, depressed industries, and other signs of economic ill-health persisted, Britain did experience a measure of recovery in the late 1920's. But then the great depression, the signal for which was given by the New York stockmarket crash in October, 1929, began its spread around the world. Britain, already weakened, was one of the first to be engulfed. Faced by a serious deficit, and unwilling to try to meet it by cutting the dole and other social services, the second Labor government of Ramsay MacDonald resigned in August, 1931.

It gave way to a coalition of Conservatives, Liberals, and right-wing Laborites headed by the same MacDonald. This coalition cabinet put through reductions in the dole and the social services. Late in 1931 it took the decisive step, a hard one in view of Britain's traditional financial leadership and devotion to the gold standard, of going off the gold standard and letting the pound fall in value. In 1932, it took the first step away from free trade by enacting protective tariffs, and in the same year Britain ceased payment on her war debts to the

United States, except for a few "token" payments. These measures did little to help the unemployed or to strike at the root causes of British economic troubles. But they did stem the depression sufficiently to enable the coalition to win two general elections in 1931 and 1935.

Yet the coalition government was in fact dominated by Conservatives, and after the 1935 election the Conservative leader, Stanley Baldwin, took over the post of prime minister. Gradually the British economy pulled out of the worst of the depression, although—some economic theorists might say *because*—Baldwin did nothing beyond keeping the budget in balance. By 1936, however, Mussolini's and Hitler's aggressions were beginning to demand British attention. The economic question and the social question, by no means solved, faded before the threat of another war.

Settlement of the Irish Question

The years between the wars were of great importance for Ireland. The outbreak of war in 1914 put off the threatened revolt against Home Rule in Ulster (see Chapter XIV), but the Irish were hardly reliable partners in the war. In 1916, the faction furthest removed from the Ulster rebels, the Irish nationalists, got German aid and staged an armed rising in Dublin. The British put down this "Easter rebellion," but not before they had created a fresh and effective set of Irish political martyrs. The British government did not dare extend conscription to Ireland until April, 1918, and the attempt made then led the Irish nationalists to boycott the British Parliament and to cease attending its sessions.

In 1919, Home Rule as decreed in 1914 was not enough for the nationalists of Ireland. The Home Rulers of prewar days had yielded to more extreme rebels, the Sinn Fein (meaning in Gaelic, "ourselves alone"), who wanted complete independence. The years 1919-1921 were filled with violence, ambushes, arson, and guerrilla warfare; the Irish, who now had their own illegal parliament, moved into full revolution. The British, tired from their long war, were not in a state of mind to use force effectively; the Irish, on the other hand, were admirably organized and full of fight.

Yet the immediate upshot of the violent phase of the revolution was a compromise, for the Sinn Fein split in two. A moderate wing, led by Arthur Griffith and Michael Collins, was willing to accept a compromise in which Protestant Ulster would remain under direct British rule and the Catholic counties would be given dominion status. A radical wing, led by Eamon de Valera—exceedingly Irish in spite of his Spanish surname—insisted that the whole island achieve complete independence as a republic. The moderates negotiated with the British, and in 1921 obtained for the twenty-six counties of southern Ireland dominion status under the name of the Irish Free State. The Free State had its own parliament, the Dail, and was completely self-governing; it merely accepted the British Crown as symbolic head. The six Protestant counties of Ulster maintained their old relationship with Great Britain, which now became officially the United Kingdom of Great Britain and Northern Ireland.

This settlement was unacceptable to De Valera and the republicans, and the Irish revolution now became a civil war between partisans of the Free State and partisans of a republic, with the old round of burning, ambush, and murder. But the Irish, too, were beginning to tire of violence. When the moderate leader, Michael Collins, a man much closer to earth than De Valera, was assassinated by a republican, public opinion turned away from the extremists. Meantime the Free State was gradually settling down. De Valera, after refusing to sit in the Dail because he would have had to take an oath of loyalty to the king, changed his mind and decided to bring his fellow republicans into the national parliament in 1927.

From then on, almost in the manner of illogical and compromise-loving England, the Irish Free State gradually and peacefully got what the extremists had been killing and burning for. De Valera's party won a plurality in the Dail in 1932, and a majority in 1933; thereupon it proceeded to abolish the oath of loyalty to the Crown and to cut most of the slender threads that still tied the Free State to England. In 1939, Catholic Ireland was so free from British domination that she could declare and maintain her neutrality throughout World War II. In 1949, the final step was taken when Britain recognized her as the fully independent Republic of Eire (Gaelic for "Ireland").

The Commonwealth of Nations

No such secession took place elsewhere among the British possessions in the years between the two world wars. On the contrary, definite constitutional recognition of the essential independence of the dominions seemed to make them more loyal, though at the cost of any central British authority over their economic policies, and, at least in law, over their foreign policies. The capstone of a long process that had begun with the Durham Report nearly a century before (see Chapter XVII) was the Statute of Westminster of 1931. This legislation spelled out the new relations between the dominions and the mother country that had been worked out in an imperial conference five years earlier. The preparatory report of 1926 anticipated the gist of the Statute of Westminster by declaring that Britain and the dominions

. . . are autonomous communities within the British Empire, equal in status, in no way sub-ordinate one to another in any aspect of their domestic or external affairs, though united by a common allegiance to the crown and freely associated as members of the British Commonwealth of Nations.

That phrase "freely associated" means also "able to choose to be freely dis-associated." In other words, the right of a state to secede, which Americans fought a great civil war to decide is *not* a part of the United States Constitution, *is* a part of the constitution of the British Commonwealth of Nations. And the twenty-six counties of Southern Ireland in effect took advantage of this right to set up their republic quite outside the Commonwealth.

The new status acquired by the dominions in 1931 was symbolized by a change in terminology. Henceforward they were no longer to be considered parts of the British Empire but free members of the British Commonwealth of Nations. In this new relationship Britain would have to *negotiate* with Canada or Australia about tariffs, trade conditions, immigration, and the like, just as if they were foreign countries. Although Britain was unable to build a self-sufficient economic unity out of her dominions, still in 1939, as in 1914, the dominions all came into the war on Britain's side. They made this decision even though they had the legal right to follow the example of Ireland and remain neutral.

One dominion, however, came close to remaining neutral: the Union of South Africa. In the 1930's many Afrikanders, the non-English white citizens of the Union, took a sympathetic view of Hitler's activities, partly because his contempt for dark-skinned "races" coincided with their own beliefs. Some even began to press for a separate republic. The great Boer leader, Jan Smuts, on the other hand, was firmly pro-British and anti-Nazi and succeeded, by a fairly narrow margin, in aligning the Union on the British side in World War II. Meanwhile, in the British Empire, as distinguished from the Commonwealth, clouds were gathering; in India particularly, as we shall see, the movement for independence was gaining formidable strength. Yet these problems of Empire and Commonwealth were for the British people during the interwar years of relatively secondary importance compared to the really urgent issues of domestic and foreign policy.

III: *France*

The Impact of the War

In France, both World War I and the postwar difficulties caused more serious dislocation than they did in Britain. In the war itself, France lost proportionately more in human lives and in material damage than did any other major belligerent. Two million Frenchmen in the prime of life were either killed or so seriously mutilated as to be incapable of normal living. In a land of only 39,000,000, and with an already low birth rate, it is likely that this human loss impaired the French potentiality for achievement in all phases of civilization. Many of the men who would have been statesmen, industrialists, scientists, and artists in the 1930's were killed off in 1914-1918. Three hundred thousand houses and twenty thousand factories or shops were destroyed. In a land of conservative economic organization, where work was done slowly and without large-scale automatic machinery, this material setback would be long felt. Psychologically, the feeling of victory by no means compensated for the traumatic losses of the four years of struggle.

France set as her goal the laming of her recent enemy, Germany, in every possible way. She tried to extract reparations to the last possible sum, undeterred by the arguments of economic theorists that Germany could not pay. But she insisted even more on keeping Germany down, isolated in international relations, and without the physical means of warfare. In a pinch, most Frenchmen would probably have been willing to forego reparations in order to keep Germany poor, deprived of the economic plant necessary for modern war. They would have preferred this to collecting reparations from a rich and productive Germany.

In the postwar years, however, French statesmen attempted to follow both policies; they naturally failed in the attempt. The culmination came in January, 1923, under the premiership of the conservative Raymond Poincaré, when French and Belgian troops occupied the great German industrial region of the Ruhr in an effort to make Germany pay full reparations. The Germans replied by passive resistance (see Chapter XX). By 1925, it was clear that the Ruhr occupation had brought no gains to France, and the new French government, chosen after the failure of Poincaré's policy, withdrew the troops.

Meanwhile, the French were undergoing inflation. The inflation resulted in part from the cost of rebuilding the devastated areas—a cost that drained government finances and that was only partly covered by German payments. It resulted also from the high cost of maintaining armed forces—for the French dared not disarm—from the general disorder of international trade, and from the staggering debts piled up during the war by the French government, which, like the imperial German government, had preferred loans to taxes. By the mid-1920's the franc had slipped from its prewar value of 20 cents to a dangerous low of about 2 cents. In the crisis, Poincaré was recalled to power to "save the franc." In 1926, he initiated new taxes and stern measures of economy which, with the gradual restoration of international trade after the French withdrawal from the Ruhr, stemmed the decline of the franc. In 1928, it was officially revalued at 3.92 cents.

The French inflation, though mild compared with the German, nevertheless caused economic and social dislocation. Frenchmen who had lent their government francs worth 20 cents now found themselves deprived of four-fifths of what they had lent. This very considerable repudiation fell with particular severity on the middle class, especially the lower middle class, the *petite bourgeoisie*. The chief sufferers were those living on their savings or on relatively fixed incomes—on pensions, for example, or on the return from bonds, or even on the contents of the wool sock in which the suspicious French peasant traditionally hoarded his cash. Bourgeois people naturally fear pauperization, fear being pushed down into the ranks of the proletariat, and the French were no exceptions. Inflation thus weakened a social class that had long been a mainstay of republicanism in France and added to the social tensions that form the central theme of French domestic history in the period between the two world wars.

Social and Political Tensions

During World War I, the French had temporarily put aside the great political and social conflict they had inherited from the great revolution of 1789. After the war, the "sacred union" of political parties that had carried France through the struggle soon dissolved, and the traditional conflict was resumed. This is sometimes termed the conflict between the "two Frances"—the republican France of the Left, and the royalist, or fascist, France of the Right. The conflict was not quite a simple Marxian class struggle be-

tween rich and poor, capitalist and proletarian, though it was certainly in part such a struggle. On the Right were the wealthier classes, many of them openly hostile to the very existence of the parliamentary state. They were reinforced by conservative peasants and by small businessmen and investors, who were not hostile to the Third Republic as such but who were determined to resist any attempt to extend the social services of the "welfare state." As a result of this right-wing resistance, France lagged behind Britain, Germany, Sweden, and other European states in providing measures of social security.

On the Left were the champions of the welfare state, the Socialists and the Communists, backed by the more radical workers and by many white-collar people, especially in the government service, and by some intellectuals. The effectiveness of the Left was hampered by the postwar split between the Communists, who followed the Moscow line, and the Socialists, who did not, and by a comparable schism within the major trade-union organization, the C.G.T. (*Confédération Générale du Travail* —General Confederation of Labor). Still nominally part of the Left, but actually in the political middle and not anxious to go far toward the welfare state, was the misnamed Radical-Socialist Party, long the political bulwark of the Third Republic. The Radicals were strong among peasants in the south, and among white-collar workers and smaller professional men.

Religious difficulties further embittered French politics. French Leftists, including the Radicals, were anticlerical by tradition. After the war they rashly attempted to introduce anticlerical measures into strongly Catholic Alsace. Alsace, since it had then belonged to Germany, had not been affected by the separation of Church and State carried through in France after the Dreyfus crisis (see Chapter XIV). In the long run, the government had to make compromises on the Alsatian question and

Demonstrators in the Stavisky riots, Paris, February, 1934.

on other clerical issues. After bitter public debate, it finally decided in the mid-1920's to resume diplomatic relations with the Vatican, which had been broken off at the time of the separation.

In the late 1920's, the years of increased prosperity that followed the revaluation of the franc, the Third Republic seemed to be getting the better of its internal difficulties. Indeed, the world economic crisis that began in 1929 was late in striking France, and for a while in 1930 it looked as though the French economy, less devoted to large-scale industry than that of the United States, Britain, or Germany, might weather the crisis much more easily. But France, too, depended on international trade, particularly on the export of perfumes, wines and brandies, Paris gowns, and other luxuries. By 1932, the depression had struck, and the government was in serious difficulties.

The Stavisky Case and the Popular Front

The political crisis came to a head in February, 1934, as a result of the Stavisky case, a financial scandal reminiscent of the Panama scandal of the 1890's. Stavisky, a shady promoter and swindler who had all sorts of connections with important men in the affairs of the Third Republic, was caught at last in a fraudulent bond issue of the municipal pawnshop of Bayonne. The full details have never emerged, but Stavisky's suicide—or murder—in December, 1933, rocked France. On the extreme Right, royalists, enjoying the freedom of a democratic society, had long been organized, notably in a pressure group known as the *Action Française*, and were gaining recruits among upper-class youth. They had a terrorist wing, which went about beating up Communists, who in turn responded by violence. The Right also had near-fascist groups, such as the *Croix de Feu* ("cross of fire"—the reference is to war), organized by Colonel de la Rocque and made up of veterans. Serious riots, unleashed by the Right in the agitation against the government following the Stavisky case, broke out in Paris in February, 1934; they were countered on the Left by a brief general strike. France seemed on the eve of revolution.

Once more, however, as in the time of Dreyfus, the republican forces rallied to meet the threat, and once more after the crisis had been surmounted France moved to the Left. The February crisis itself was overcome by a coalition of all parties save royalists, Socialists, and Communists. But the franc was once more falling, and the conservative premier, Flandin, attempted to retrench government expenditures with measures similar to those that had worked a decade earlier under Poincaré. The forces of the Left joined in the so-called Popular Front, made up of the Radical-Socialist, Socialist, and Communist parties, and backed by the C.G.T., which had temporarily healed the schism between Communists and non-Communists. Their victory in a general election in May, 1936, led to the formation of a Popular Front ministry under the leadership of the Socialist Léon Blum.

The Popular Front came to power in part as a kind of French equivalent of the American New Deal. The workers, the white-collar men, the government employees, even many of the peasants and shopkeepers, were now convinced that the classical formulas of economic retrenchment were not the remedy for the ills of France. They wanted a frontal attack on the stronghold of retrenchment, the Bank of France, still a private institution and, in a substantially correct popular belief, the creature of the "two hundred families" alleged to control the French economy. They wanted more equal distribution of wealth by government spending; in short, they wanted the "welfare state."

Other factors entered into the Leftist victory. Mussolini had begun his Ethiopian adventure, and Hitler his rearmament; many a Frenchman in 1936 voted Left as a protest against the compromises that French politicians had been making with the dictators. Finally, these were the years when Russia, just admitted to the League of Nations, seemed to be pursuing a course of collaboration with the West against the threat of Nazi Germany. Moscow therefore urged the French Communists to give up their old policy of constant opposition and to co-operate with their hated enemies, the Socialists.

It was a bad time for a French New Deal. The nation was bitterly divided between partisans and enemies of the Popular Front; business and farming classes were traditionally reluctant to pay income taxes, which would have to be raised to meet the costs of social services; the economy was not geared to labor-saving devices. The Blum cabinet had an ambitious program—a maximum work week of 40 hours; partial nationalization of the Bank of France, the railroads, and the munitions industry; compulsory arbitration of labor disputes; and other measures of social welfare. Although Blum achieved most of this program on paper, everything conspired to block its successful execution. The Communists did not really co-operate, for they refused to participate in the Blum cabinet and sniped at it from the sidelines in the Chamber and in the press. Businessmen took fright at the mushrooming membership of the C.G.T. and at the "sit-down" or "stay-in" strikes of French industrial workers in June, 1936.

Moreover, as the anti-democratic regimes in Germany, Italy, and Spain went on to new victories, France was driven to expensive rearmament. Capital, however, was rapidly leaving the country to be invested or deposited abroad, and the monied class would not subscribe to the huge defense loans that were essential if the French armed forces were to be put in shape to face the war that began to seem inevitable. Blum was obliged to call a halt in March, 1937. The Popular Front now disintegrated, and the C.G.T. lost millions of its newly recruited members and suffered a new schism between Communists and anti-Communists.

Divided France

Indeed, the morale of the French sagged badly after the collapse of the Popular Front. Under the mounting tensions of 1938 and 1939, the Radical-Socialist premier, Daladier, kept France on the side of Britain in opposition to the Rome-Berlin axis, and various measures of retrenchment—including virtual abandonment of the 40-hour week—kept the French economy from collapse. But the workers took very badly the failure of the Popular Front, and as late as November, 1938, a general strike almost came off, and had to be combated by putting the railway workers under military orders. The possessing classes, on the other hand, were outraged by the fact that Blum's experiment had been made at all; many of them were convinced that their salvation lay in a French totalitarian state—"better Hitler than Blum," as their despairing slogan went. The France that was confronted with war in 1939 was not only inadequately prepared in terms of materials; it was psychologically and spiritually divided, uncertain of what it was fighting for. An American historian of France, commenting on this failure of the French spirit in the 1930's, summarized:

It is a tragedy when a great man loses his strength and his personality; it is a catastrophe when a nation loses its assurance. To me the tragic pathos of the French problem can be summed up in a remark made by my hostess in a Parisian pension in 1937 when she called my attention to the notice about the air-raid shelter for the neighborhood. 'Over there [in Germany],' she said with a choke in her voice, 'the shelters will be safe; ours will be faulty.' She wanted to be proud of the nation for which her husband had given up his life in 1916; she wanted to believe in the community that had given her nurture, but she had lost faith and with it her nerve. These simple words are dramatic evidence of the failure of the *élan vital* of a great people.*

Many Frenchmen before 1940 relied on their great empire to restore the flagging *élan vital* of the mother country. Colonial troops, particularly from Senegal and North Africa, had helped to replenish the diminished ranks of the army during World War I. Enthusiasts spoke of France as a nation not of just the 40,000,000 Frenchmen at home but of 100,000,000 Frenchmen, including the population of the colonial territories. But this was stretching the facts too far. Economically, the Empire as a whole did advance in the 1920's and 1930's, yet only small native elite groups—only relatively few Indo-Chinese or Senegalese or Algerian Arabs, for instance—were assimilated as Frenchmen or desired such assimilation. What they did desire was some sort of home rule or independence. Although some leaders of the French Left urged concessions to native aspirations, few concessions were actually made. French imperial policy in the 1920's and 1930's continued along traditional lines. Perhaps no policy pursued then could have prevented the disintegration of the French Empire that has occurred since World War II, but the old-fashioned policy that was followed certainly did little to reconcile native nationalists to their French overlords.

* J. B. Wolf, "The Elan Vital of France: A Problem in Historical Perspective," *Modern France,* E. M. Earle, ed. (Princeton, 1951), 31.

IV: The United States

Neither the human nor the material losses of the United States in World War I were at all comparable with those of Britain and France. American casualties were 115,000 dead and 206,000 wounded; the comparable French figures were 1,385,-000 dead and 3,044,000 wounded *in a population one-third as large*. Moreover, in purely material terms, the United States almost gained from the war. Heavy industries were greatly stimulated by Allied war orders; the war put the growing financial center of New York at least on equal terms with that of London; the dollar had begun to dethrone the monarch of the nineteenth century, the pound sterling. It is true that the Allies had borrowed from the American government; but until 1933 some interest came in on these loans. Moreover, the stimulation of American industry resulting from these loans exceeded the loss from the final repudiation of war debts in the early 1930's. The United States, then, came out of the war almost unscathed, victorious, and prosperous.

Isolationism

Yet in some cases the American revulsion against the war in 1919 and the years following was as marked as that of Britain, France, and defeated Germany. On the level of party politics, that revulsion helped to unseat the Democrats, who, under President Wilson, had controlled the federal government since 1913. The Republicans won the presidential elections of 1920, 1924, and 1928. Three successive Republicans occupied the White House—Harding (1921-1923), Coolidge (1923-1929), and Herbert Hoover (1929-1933).

On the level of policy and public attitudes, American revulsion against war took the form of *isolationism,* the desire to withdraw from international politics. This isolationism was by no means universal among Americans. Some historians feel that the drives and attitudes of millions of men had already made isolationism certain in 1919. Others feel that a slight shift in the words and deeds of men in high places could have changed the final decision and could have brought America into the League of Nations. If, as we have already seen, the Democratic President Wilson had been willing to meet Republican opposition in the Senate by a few concessions, then perhaps the Treaty of Versailles, League of Nations and all, might have achieved the two-thirds majority in the Senate the Constitution requires for treaties. Or if someone on the Republican side, with skill and prestige, had been able to put through the notion of a bipartisan foreign policy, then with patience and good will the United States might have been brought into the League. Public opinion, say those who take this view, was not against our carrying on the task we had begun in 1917; only a noisy minority in the country as a whole, and the little group of obstinate senators at the top, wanted us to withdraw.

Yet those who remember the years right after 1918 find it hard to deny that the country was swept by a wave of desire to get back to "normalcy," as President Harding later termed it, ungrammatically. A great many Americans felt that they had done all they needed to do in beating the Germans, that further direct participation in the complexities of European politics would simply involve American innocence and virtue that much more disastrously in European sophistication and vice. The not uncommon American reaction against its "strong" presidents took the form of repudiating all of Wilson's work at Paris as that of an un-American tyrant. Furthermore, as the months of negotiation went on with no final decisions reached, Americans, always an impatient people, began to feel that sheer withdrawal was about the only effective action they could take.

The Treaty of Versailles, containing at Wilson's insistence the League of Nations, was finally rejected in the Senate on March 19, 1920. The United States remained technically at war with Germany until July, 1921, when a resolution making a separate peace was passed by Congress and signed under the presidency of Harding. American isolationism was expressed in these years in other concrete measures. The Fordney-McCumber Tariff of 1922 and the Smoot-Hawley Tariff of 1930 set successively higher duties on foreign goods, and emphasized America's belief that her high wage scales needed to be protected from cheap foreign labor.

Yet the United States continued all through the 1920's to insist that the debts owed to her by the Allied powers be repaid. It is true that these were refunded in a series of agreements, and that in the closely related problem of German reparations Americans on the whole cast their weight on the side of a general scaling-down of German obligations. But Congress paid little heed to the argument, so convincing to most economists, that European nations could not repay save through dollars gained by sales of their goods in the American market, and that American tariffs continued to make such repayment impossible. Congressmen tended to reduce the complexities of international debts to President Coolidge's simple dictum: "They hired the money, didn't they?"

The spirit of isolationism also lay behind the immigration restrictions of the 1920's, which reversed the former American policy of almost free immigration. The act of 1924 set an annual quota limit for each country of 2 per cent of the number of nationals from that country resident in the United States in 1890. Since the heavy immigration from eastern and southern Europe had come after 1890, the choice of that date reduced the flow from these areas to a mere trickle.

The Road to Internationalism

Yet during this era of partial isolationism the United States by no means withdrew entirely from international politics. Rather, as an independent without formal alliances, she continued to pursue policies that seemed to most Americans traditional, but that in their totality gradually lined her up against the chief perturbing nations of the years between the two world wars. Even before the drift of her commitments against Germany, Italy, and Japan became clear in the 1930's, Americans had in fact engaged themselves. At what seems to some hardboiled thinkers the level of abstract and meaningless general declarations, they had gone far before the Democratic administration of Franklin Roosevelt in 1933.

In 1928, the Republican Secretary of State Kellogg submitted to the great European powers a proposal for a renunciation of war. Incorporated with similar proposals from the French Foreign Minister Briand, it was formally adopted in August of that year as the Pact of Paris, commonly known as the Kellogg-Briand Pact. It was eventually signed by twenty-three nations, including the United States. It is now the fashion to decry the Pact as futile, and it is certainly true that it did not prevent World War II. And yet by this action the United States expressed a concrete concern over the peace of the world.

In a hundred ways the United States was at work laying the foundations for the position of world leadership it reached after World War II. American businessmen were everywhere; American loans were making possible the revival of German industrial greatness; American motors, refrigerators, typewriters, telephones, and other products of the assembly line were being sold everywhere. In the Far East, the United States as early as 1922 took the lead in the Nine-Power Treaty that committed her and the other great powers, including Japan, to respect the sovereignty and integrity of China. If President Roosevelt in 1941 resisted the Japanese attempt to swallow China and other Far Eastern territory, he was simply following a line laid down under President Harding.

Boom—and Bust

In domestic affairs, the Coolidge era (1923-1929) has now become legendary. These were years of frantic prosperity; everybody played the stock market and the value of stocks rose to fantastic heights. They were the years of "prohibition," the ban on the manufacture and sale of alcoholic beverages, enforced, in theory, by the Volstead Act of 1919 under the Eighteenth Amendment to the Constitution. And so they were also the years of the speakeasy and the bootlegger. They were the years of the short skirt—the shortest, probably, in all western history—of sex appeal, the Charleston, and other forms of sin. They were years which, like the "naughty nineties" of the nineteenth century, we look back on with a sort of reproving envy, years that now look colorful, romantic.

But the Coolidge era was by no means completely summed up in novels of the jazz age, like *The Great Gatsby* of F. Scott Fitzgerald, or even in Sinclair Lewis' half-satirical *Babbitt* and *Main Street*. It was an era of marked industrial progress, of solid advancement of the national plant and productive capabilities. It was an era of the steady spreading in the United States of standards of living heretofore limited to the relatively few, standards of living that seemed to intellectuals vulgar and inadequate, but that were nevertheless a new thing in the world. These were the years when, if you had a servant, you could no longer take her for granted, but had to take some pains to keep her satisfied. They were years for which, at their best, the right symbol is no Hollywood character, no intellectual, no great pioneer of industry, nor even a gangster, but President Coolidge

Apple-sellers in New York during the early years of the depression.

himself, sober, plodding, unimaginative.

At its most glamorous, the era ended with the onset of the great depression in the autumn of 1929. During the preceding year, Wall Street had enjoyed an unprecedented boom. Speculators by the millions were playing the market in the hope of quick resale of stocks at huge profits; they bought shares "on margin," paying only a fraction of their cost in cash, and often borrowing the money to pay that small fraction. Not only stocks but many other purchases were financed on borrowed money. Credit had swollen to the point where it was no longer on a sound basis in a largely unregulated economy. Eventually, shrewd investors began to sell their holdings in the belief that the bubble soon would burst. The result was a disastrous drop in stock values, beginning in October, 1929, and continuing almost without let-up to 1933. Both the speculators and the lenders from whom they had borrowed money were ruined.

The immediate cause of the depression, then, was the stock-market crash. About the more deep-seated causes the economic physicians are not even today wholly agreed. Some of them believe that a capitalist society inevitably produces business cycles oscillating from the highs of prosperity to the lows of depression; that these cycles are of various lengths, short, medium, and long; and that an unusual number of cyclical lows coincided in the late 1920's to make the depression particularly serious. Others, not uninfluenced by Marx, hold that under American capitalism the troughs of a depression are bound to be deeper each time, if only because of the great scale of the American economy.

This much seems certain: Coolidge prosperity was very unevenly distributed among the various parts of the American economy and American society. Agriculture, notably, suffered a kind of permanent depression throughout the 1920's. At the close of World War I, farmers commanded very high prices for their produce and enjoyed an apparently insatiable market at home and abroad. They expanded their production—and borrowed to finance the expansion—often at a reckless rate. Then, as "normalcy" returned in the early 1920's, the foreign market dried up, the home market shrank, farm prices fell rapidly, and the inevitable foreclosure of farm mortgages began. Wage-earning workers, though not hard hit like the farmers, gained but little increase in their purchasing power during the 1920's. The worker did often raise his standard of living, by purchasing a house or a car, but he did it on credit, by assuming the burden of a heavy mortgage or by financing a purchase on installments to be paid over a long period. The "big money" of the Coolidge era went chiefly to business, above all to big business.

The great depression was very severe in many countries throughout the world, but nowhere was it worse than in the United States. Its effects may be measured by the round figure of 16,000,000 Americans unemployed at the low point in the early 1930's —something like one-third of the national labor force. In terms of what economists call the "gross national product" the United States Department of Commerce sets for 1929 the figure of $103,828,000,000; for 1933, the figure set is $55,760,000,000, a little more than half that for 1929.

The most remarkable thing about this grave crisis in the American economy is that it produced almost no organized movements of revolt, no threat of revolution. The intellectuals of the 1930's did indeed turn to "social consciousness," and Marxism made some converts among writers and artists. But the bulk of the population showed no serious signs of abandoning for any revolutionary creed their fundamental belief that the way out lay through the legal means provided by existing American institutions. Even before the election of Franklin D. Roosevelt in 1932, local authorities and private charities, helped out by the establishment early in 1932 of the federal R.F.C. (Reconstruction Finance Corporation) to release frozen assets, did a good deal to soften the worst sufferings of the unemployed. The Republican administration of President Hoover, however, was generally committed to the philosophy of laissez-faire; aside from the R.F.C., it did little to cushion the effects of the depression. People who wanted a more vigorous attack on economic problems voted for the Democrats in 1932; most significantly, they did not vote in very important numbers for the socialist or communist presidential candidates. In the crisis of a great depression the American two-party system evidently continued to meet basic political needs.

The New Deal   The victory of the Democrats in 1932 seemed to give them a clear mandate to marshal all the resources of the Federal government against the depression. The Democratic president, Franklin Roosevelt (1933-1945), took office on March 4, 1933, in the midst of a financial crisis that had closed the banks all over the country. He at once summoned Congress to an emergency session, and declared a bank holiday. Gradually the sound banks reopened, and the New Deal began its course. During its subsequent convalescence, much of the American business community under better conditions turned with great bitterness against Roosevelt and all his works. But in those early months of 1933 the mere fact that a national administration was trying to do something about the situation was a powerful restorative to national morale. The nation emerged from the bank holiday with a new confidence, echoing the phrase from Roosevelt's inaugural address that there was nothing to fear "but fear itself."

The New Deal was in part a series of measures aimed at immediate difficulties and in part a series of measures aimed at permanent changes in the structure of American society. The distinction between its short-term and its long-term measures is in a sense arbitrary, for the men who carried it though were never quite clear in their own minds exactly what they were trying to do. What must chiefly interest us is the implications of their work. In the perspective of western history, the New Deal is the coming to the United States, under the special pressures of the great depression, of those measures—"socialist" to some of their opponents—that we have already seen in European countries like Britain and Germany. They are best summed up in that value-charged term, the "welfare state."

The short-term measures of the New Deal aimed to lower the price of American goods in a world that was abandoning the gold standard by releasing the dollar from its tie with gold. They aimed to thaw out credit by extending the activities of the R.F.C. and by creating such new governmental lending agencies as the Home Owners' Loan Corporation. They aimed to relieve unemployment by public works on a large scale, to safeguard bank deposits by the Federal Deposit Insurance Corporation, and to regulate speculation and other stock-market activities by the Securities and Exchange Commission. The historical significance of many of these measures rested in the fact that they were undertaken not by private business or by state or local authorities but by the federal government. There was one exception to the rule of widening federal activity: the Twenty-first Amendment to the Constitution, repealing the Eighteenth and abandoning increasingly unsuccessful federal efforts to enforce prohibition.

The long-term measures of the New Deal were, of course, more important. The Social Security Act of 1935 introduced to the United States on a national scale the unemployment, sickness, and retirement allowances of the kind that Lloyd George had brought into Britain. Federal taxation, especially income taxes on individual and corporate income, was used to secure a more equal distribution of the national product. Congress passed a whole series of acts on labor relations, the net effect of which has been to strengthen and extend the role of organized labor in American economic life. A series of acts on agriculture, though leaving the business of farming still in the hands of several million individual farmers producing for sale in a cash market, nevertheless regulated crops and prices to a degree that would have been incomprehensible to a nineteenth-century farmer. And finally—the showpiece of the New Deal—a great regional planning board, the Tennessee Valley Authority, has used government power to make over the economic and social life of a relatively backward area by checking the erosion of farmlands, by instituting flood control, and by providing cheap electric power generated at government-built dams.

More than twenty years after the bank holiday of 1933, Americans were still debating the New Deal. It unquestionably left the United States a society very different from that pictured by the classical economists. No real society, indeed, has ever

quite corresponded to the theoretical extreme of free enterprise, in which every man sells and buys what he wants to—or can—and in which the man who cannot "earn" a living quite simply dies. But in the sense in which the United States of, say, 1870 was close to such a society, the United States of the New Deal and after is quite far from such a society.

The rush of free competition has been tempered by government regulation, because it has become clear that in such competition much that men prize would in fact be competed out of existence. If everyone today were free to catch all the trout he wanted to and could, there would soon be no trout left at all. But most Americans accept, and with some help from game wardens observe, the fish and game laws. And in general they have come to see the need for government regulation in the field broadly known as the conservation of natural resources. Even here, however, when it comes to the overgrazing of pasture lands or the farming methods that lead to soil erosion, many Americans are still reluctant to have the government interfere with their "rights."

When the question at stake is the dis-

Franklin D. Roosevelt.

tribution of wealth, rather than its actual exhaustion, Americans are often unwilling to accept limitations on free enterprise. On this issue, even after the New Deal, the champions of government regulation and private initiative still do battle. The Marxist indictment of a competitive society, that under it the rich tend to become richer and the poor to become poorer, is not wholly true. But the last two hundred years of western history suggest that without some government interference the modern scramble for wealth tends to produce a society pyramidal in structure. With a few men of great wealth at the top, the pyramid spreads out through the well-to-do to a broad base of human beings just able to scrape along. In our western society, however, the political power democracy gives to that numerous broad base has over the years been used to alter the very shape of the social pyramid. "Soak-the-rich" taxation and government aid to the poor have flattened it out, cutting it down at the top and pushing it up from the bottom. Indeed, the figure may no longer be a pyramid, but somewhat diamond-shaped, widest in the middle. It is not yet in any human society a straight line, representing absolute social and economic equality.

There is, then, in modern America a leveling, both up and down. The great baronial mansions of the Hudson Valley, of Newport, even of California, are too expensive to maintain, and are being turned into museums or put to institutional use. The worst of the urban slums are being slowly cleaned up to make way for modern housing projects. The very rich still exist, at least in Texas, but the number of the very poor is diminishing. Meanwhile, the total national product has increased. It is not merely that a fixed national income is being more evenly distributed; despite the complaints of conservatives that the leveling process is destroying incentives to hard work and invention, the real national income has increased greatly since the depth of the de-

pression in 1932-1933. There is more to be shared.

It must, however, be noted that the American society that emerged from the New Deal was by no means collectivist; it can by no means be accurately described as "socialistic." The United States of the mid-twentieth century is rather a "mixed economy," in which individual economic activity—that of the worker as well as that of the entrepreneur or manager—is indeed regulated and restricted, but not entirely controlled, by government. The United States still displays an extraordinary range of economic activity, from the "socialistic" Post Office to enormous private industries that are themselves societies, almost governments, with administrative problems and bureaucracies of their own, and on down to small independent businessmen, who are often the best examples of almost pure free enterprise.

Confident America

Although Americans still battle over the New Deal, it seems evident that the measures taken by the Roosevelt administration, combined with the natural strength of American institutions and culture, pulled the United States at least part way out of the depression. They also restored a high degree of confidence to Americans. The intellectuals, whose role in modern America has generally been in opposition to the men of business, in the 1920's had found the United States a hopelessly crass and vulgar society. But in the 1930's, though some intellectuals flirted with Marxism, many turned to support the new American way of the New Deal.

The onset of war in Europe found Americans, as we shall see in the next chapter, anxious not to jeopardize in war their still precarious prosperity, anxious to remain neutral if Europe should persist in going to war. But the United States was not, like the France of 1940, a tired, skeptical land, divided fundamentally into mutually hostile classes. Roosevelt and his Republican opponents had been for some time exchanging insults: the "economic royalists" fought back at "that man in the White House." Yet in the pinch of the international crisis of 1939-1941 it became clear that, although the nation was not completely united, at any rate it was not pathologically divided. As so often in American history, the violence of verbal politics masks a very basic unity. When the war came to the United States in 1941, Americans were largely ready for it psychologically and— what is really remarkable in a western democracy—not too unready for it militarily.

When the war came, moreover, the United States had already made many efforts to enlist the support of the Latin-American states. In 1930, before the so-called "Roosevelt Revolution" in American diplomacy, President Hoover's State Department issued the Clark Memorandum, specifically stating that the Monroe Doctrine does not concern itself with inter-American relations but is directed against outside intervention in the affairs of the Western Hemisphere. The United States was no longer to land the Marines in some Central American republic at the drop of a hat but was trying to strengthen hemispheric solidarity. And so, on the foundations of the Clark Memorandum, President Roosevelt built his celebrated "Good Neighbor" policy toward the other American nations.

Meantime, what may be called American imperial policy was likewise undergoing some liberalization, notably with respect to the Philippines. When the United States had annexed the islands at the close of the Spanish-American War (see Chapter XVII), a stubborn Filipino insurrection broke out in protest, and it took American forces three years (1899-1902) to subdue the rebels. Filipino nationalism, though partially disarmed by the conciliatory measures taken by the United States after the suppression of the rebellion, none the less continued to hope for eventual freedom. In the 1930's American officials undertook negotiations with Filipino leaders with the aim at first of bestowing a rather dilute kind of dominion status on the islands. But by the outbreak of World War II the negotiations had advanced to the point where it was evident that the Philippines would soon gain at least nominal independence.

V: The Loosening of Imperial Ties

The Filipino insurrection of 1899 was a portent. Even before 1914, there were signs that many of the more advanced "colonial" peoples were already chafing under imperialism. Native nationalist movements were creating trouble for the British in Egypt and India, for the French in Morocco and Algeria, and for all the imperial powers in China. The First World War itself speeded up the process of rousing national consciousness among the "natives" of the various empires, and at its end there was no doubt that the hold of the West had been loosened. Psychologically, it seems evident that the experience of the war gave a lift to non-western peoples; they had often rendered important services to their white masters, and their leaders had widened their knowledge of the West. The Arab peoples of the old Ottoman Empire had raised armies of their own and had fought with European aid for their own freedom from Turkey. French colonial troops and British Indian troops had taken part in the conflict, sometimes in Europe itself.

The very spectacle of the masters quarreling among themselves did something to lower the prestige of the West among subject peoples. Moreover, the Allies had fought the war in the name of democratic ideals of self-determination for all peoples, and in their propaganda against the Central Powers they had stressed heavily their opposition to imperialism. The fifth of Wilson's Fourteen Points asserted that in disputed claims to colonial territories "the interests of the populations concerned must have equal weight" with the interests of the colonial powers. It is true that the Allies did not give up any of their territories in 1919, and did indeed add to them under the mandate system (see Chapter XVIII). To many of the subject races, as to liberals in the West itself, the mandate was simply a disguise for the old imperialism; but it is surely significant that a disguise seemed necessary to the imperialist powers. The West was committed now in some sense to a process of at least gradual emancipation of the colonial dependencies.

It was in the Far East that old imperial ties were most clearly loosened during the inter-war years. China, as we shall soon see in more detail, was engaged in a great struggle to free herself from the tutelage of the western colonial powers. The conflict in China, however, was much more than a simple conflict between oriental nationalists and occidental imperialists. Almost from the start it was complicated by two additional elements—increasing communist intervention in Chinese politics, and the increasing threat to Chinese independence from an expansionist Japan. It is scarcely an exaggeration to say that China faced the prospect of simply exchanging one set of imperial overlords for another.

Japan

Alone among non-western peoples, the Japanese experienced the industrial revolution and were able to maintain themselves as a fully independent major political entity during the great age of imperialism (see Chapter XVII). More than that, as the twentieth century opened, it was clear that Japan was a great power, a full but somewhat unwelcome participant in the struggle for imperial position. As we have seen, the Japanese made these impressive accomplishments without radically altering their traditional oligarchical and absolutist political structure.

In the decade after World War I, it looked as though Japan might achieve a gradual liberalization of her political institutions. The cabinets of the 1920's included many men from the business class who favored vigorous expansion abroad but who also granted some measures of cautious liberalism at home. The originally very limited suffrage was gradually extended, and in 1925 all men received the right to vote. For the first time, political parties, western-style, began to put down roots, especially in the urban population, and seemed likely to give new vitality to the Diet, the not very powerful central representative assembly of Japan. Trade unions also took shape and began to win a following.

Japan, however, did not evolve into a parliamentary democracy on the western model during the twenty years' truce. By the early 1930's, political power was falling more and more into the hands of army and navy officers, many of them descended from the feudal *samurai* class (see above, pp. 568-569). This military clique hated the prospect of liberal civilian government and envied and mistrusted the business class. They found a potent political weapon in the office of the emperor, who was supposed to possess the kind of political infallibility that westerners associate with a divine-right monarch. Putting their own words into the emperor's mouth, the admirals and generals used his pronouncements to further their own ends. And, to make doubly sure, they assassinated or terrorized the chief spokesmen of nascent Japanese liberalism.

The consequence was the progressive

clamping of a military dictatorship on Japan during the 1930's. The Diet lost power; popular elections were held and their results were then disregarded. Businessmen supported the new regime out of fear or out of anticipation of the huge profits to be secured from its adventures abroad. A cult of emperor-worship, known as state Shinto, was concocted out of an innocuous traditional Japanese religion in order to focus popular loyalties on the divine mission of the emperor and to insure popular submission to the will of the men who ruled in his name. A corps of ruthless agents, picturesquely named "thought police," hounded anyone suspected of harboring "dangerous thoughts." In short, Japan now had a government that, while exploiting many uniquely Japanese traditions, in its operations showed a striking resemblance to the totalitarian governments of Europe.

Nowhere was the resemblance to European totalitarianism more marked than in the foreign policy of Japan between the two world wars. Like Hitler's Germans or Mussolini's Italians, the Japanese claimed to be a "have-not" nation. They, too, pointed to their steadily growing population—and did all they could to encourage its further growth. They, too, harped on the overcrowding of the homeland, its inadequate resources, and its restricted markets. Behind this lay real economic problems of sustaining the Japanese economy in the face of the depression and the world-wide disruption of international trade, problems of providing food and work for the 60,000,000 Japanese of 1930. In seeking to solve the problems by imperial expansion, the militarists of the 1930's were following a pattern that had already been set by the West. And they were also following the path marked out by the Japanese officers and politicians who had secured Formosa in 1895 and annexed Korea in 1910. During World War I Japan had tried in vain to subjugate China; by World War II she had apparently almost succeeded in doing so. To follow the course of this Japanese imperialism we must turn to the history of its chief victim, China.

China: The Revolution of 1911-1912

By 1900, the Chinese Empire was far gone in political decay. Nominally independent under the rule of its Manchu dynasty, it had lost much of its effective sovereignty through concessions of naval bases and economic and political privileges to the European powers and Japan. Following China's defeat by Japan in 1895, European imperialists engaged in a hectic scramble for further concessions. The Ger-

"Rule Japannia. Very nice, yes!—so long as honourable foreign ladies continue to sit apart." Cartoonist Low comments on Japan's profiting by British and American failure to pursue a co-ordinated Far Eastern policy during the 1930's.

mans leased Kiaochow, the French Kwang-chou Bay, the Russians Port Arthur, and the British Wei-hai-wei (see also Chapter XVII). In 1899, the American Secretary of State, John Hay, sought to end the scramble by getting the powers to accept the principle of the "Open Door," whereby all foreign goods could be marketed in China on equal terms, with no special favors to any one power. Although the interested states subscribed to Hay's policy in principle, the Open Door meant little in practice.

Meantime, a formidable reaction to the outburst of imperial activity was gathering within China itself. The hard-pressed Manchu government encouraged the formation of an anti-foreign nationalist secret society called the Boxers. And the result was the Boxer Rebellion of 1900, in which more than 200 foreigners, mainly missionaries, were slain. The foreign powers, including the United States, used troops to protect their nationals and property against the Boxers. In 1901 they obliged the Manchu government to pay an enormous indemnity and to grant them further rights that, of course, further impaired Chinese sovereignty.

The next Chinese rebellion, the revolution of 1911, was directed against the Manchu regime that had proved so incapable of resisting the encroachments of imperialist states. In this revolution a factor operated that may often be found in the whole process of the loosening of western controls. The movement is directed against the West—against westerners themselves or against native governors who seem to be the agents of the West. But it is a movement inspired at least in part by western ideas and examples, a movement that could scarcely have come into being without the influence of the West.

The Chinese revolution of 1911 was comparatively bloodless in its early stages. It was sealed by the abdication on February 12, 1912, of the six-year-old Manchu Emperor, Pu-yi. From the start, it was inspired by two groups with conflicting ideas of the new society that the revolution was aiming to create. One group soon formed the Nationalist party, the Kuomintang, led by Sun Yat-sen and many young intellectuals who had studied and traveled in the West. Its leaders wanted a democratic parliamentary republic of China modeled on the western political system, though preserving as far as possible the basic Chinese family and village structure, on which western industrial society was to be grafted. The other group, whose leader was Yuan Shih-k'ai, wanted a strong central government basically authoritarian in structure, with authority not in the hands of an emperor and the traditional and highly conservative Chinese mandarin bureaucracy, but in the hands of strong men capable of achieving the modernization of China from above.

A struggle for power broke out between the assembly elected after 1911 and Yuan Shih-k'ai. The party of Sun Yat-sen was defeated, and by 1914, after a "purge" of the Kuomintang members of the assembly, Yuan Shih-k'ai issued a constitutional compact that put him in the presidential office for ten years. Sun Yat-sen and his followers had failed to turn China into a western parliamentary democracy. Sun was, however, a gifted leader, and the ideas for which he stood, though they have never got firmly rooted in China, have never quite disappeared. Sun remains somewhat paradoxically the great hero of the Chinese revolution.

Yuan's subsequent career bears some resemblance to that of another military reformer, Oliver Cromwell. Faced with continuing opposition, not only from the republicans of the Kuomintang but also from the monarchists, Yuan decided to follow the age-old Chinese pattern and set himself up as the first of a new dynasty of emperors to follow the Manchus. A revolt caused him to revoke his plans, and early in 1916 he reorganized the republic with a military cabinet. He died on June 6, 1916, leaving the new republic enmeshed in another age-old Chinese political pattern—the dissolution of all but the shadow of central control and the assumption of real power by regional strong men. A new era of provincial "war-lords" had begun.

In the years of crisis following 1911, China also faced the aggressive attempts of Japan to take over the Far Eastern imperial interests of European powers now at war among themselves. Early in 1915, the Japanese presented in secrecy to the Chinese government the "Twenty-One Demands," which amounted to a demand for something close to a protectorate over China and for all sorts of concrete concessions. The Chinese republic, now at the nadir of its strength, countered by declaring war against the Central Powers, thus securing at least the nominal protection of two of the Allies, Britain and France. The Japanese did not feel able to defy western objections, and so contented themselves with taking over Kiaochow and other German concessions in the Shantung peninsula. At the end of the war, the victorious Allies, with the United States in the lead, acted to check the ambitions of their recent military partner, Japan. At the Washington Conference of 1922 (see also Chapter XXII) Japan was forced to sign the Nine-Power Treaty guaranteeing the independence of China. This rebuff to Japan is one of the first events in the long chain that aggravated the hostility of Japan toward the United States and ended, two decades later, in the attack on Pearl Harbor.

China between
the World Wars

The details of Chinese history between the two world wars are extraordinarily confused and complex. The main elements during this twenty-year period were the Kuomintang, the Communists, and the Japanese invaders. The Kuomintang, after the death of Sun Yat-sen in 1925, came under the leadership of Chiang Kai-shek, an army officer trained in Japan. The Nationalists of the Kuomintang were engaged in a constant and often very unsuccessful struggle to set up an effective central government against the power of provincial "war-lords." They were also often locked in battle with the Communists and the Japanese.

All three of the main forces fought in word and deed for the allegiance—or at any rate for the passive acceptance—of nearly five hundred million Chinese, for the most part peasants, and for the most part illiterate. For the most part, too, the masses of China were so far from sharing western attitudes toward the state that it is hardly an exaggeration to say that they felt toward politics as we westerners feel toward the weather—that it is something beyond human control. In transforming the Chinese into a nation in the western sense, the indispensable step was something more than building railroads and factories or promoting the study of modern science instead of the Chinese classics. It was getting the Chinese peasant to regard himself as an individual Chinese citizen.

This indispensable process was beginning in the 1920's and 1930's. It goes far to explain why the Japanese, when they renewed their aggression in 1931, were virtually beaten from the start in the attempt to become the true masters of China. In an earlier age one can readily imagine the Japanese as military conquerors in China setting up a new dynasty, foreign in origin, but very soon thoroughly absorbed by the Chinese. That this age-old pattern was not followed in the 1930's shows that China herself was changing, that here too the modern expansion of the West, the spread of western ideas, was altering her traditional way of life.

The Japanese attack came in September, 1931, on Manchuria, an outlying northern province of China that was a particularly tempting target for Japanese aggression.

Manchuria had good resources of coal and iron; it adjoined Korea, already a Japanese possession; and it had never been fully integrated into the structure of Chinese government and looked, therefore, as though it could easily be pried loose. Moreover, the Japanese regarded themselves as the natural successors of the Russians, whom they had driven from Manchuria in the Russo-Japanese War of 1904-1905. By 1932, the Japanese were strong enough in Manchuria to proclaim it a puppet state, which they called Manchukuo, under a puppet ruler, Pu-yi, who as a boy had been the last emperor of China.

The Chinese responded to Japan's aggression in Manchuria by a very effective boycott of Japanese goods; the Japanese countered by carrying the war to the great Chinese port of Shanghai. Given the weakness of the Kuomintang government, effective Chinese resistance would have required very full support from stronger outside powers. Neither the western powers nor the League of Nations gave China more than verbal support (for details, see Chapter XXII); the Chinese had to give up their boycott of Japanese goods, and the Japanese remained in Manchuria. Tension between China and Japan persisted, however, and the Japanese soon decided to attempt the absorption of all the rest of China. Their invasion came in July, 1937, without a formal declaration of war.

In a purely military way the Japanese did very well. By October, when the key southern Chinese city of Canton fell, they had taken the strategic points of the coastal area and the thickly peopled lower river valleys. Chiang Kai-shek took refuge with his army and his fellow politicians of the Kuomintang in the interior province of Szechwan. There he set up his capital at Chungking; and there, protected by distance and a ring of mountains, receiving western aid through India by the Burma Road and, when that was closed, by air, the Nationalist government held out until the end of World War II and the collapse of Japanese imperialism.

Yet even at the height of their success, the Japanese had achieved no more than the stretching across China of a string of garrisons, and the control of great cities like Shanghai and Peiping. They held the railroads, subject to guerrilla attacks; they could put their puppets into place in the more important centers; and they could make shift to run the country. But away from the relatively sparse lines of modern communication they were helpless. Many a Chinese village in the area nominally Japanese never changed its ways during the occupation. Nowhere did the Japanese win over the acquiescence, to say nothing of the loyalty, of the Chinese people.

The Nationalists of the Kuomintang led the resistance to the Japanese from the beginning, yet they, too, ultimately failed to win the full loyalty of the Chinese people. This was partly a military matter. Chiang's armies were never able to stand on equal terms with the Japanese. They lacked a good base in modern industrial society, and, as the Japanese early seized the few industrial cities of China, Chiang was always relatively badly off in terms of logistics. In the long exile in Szechwan, moreover, something faltered in the morale of the Nationalists. The ordeal, far from purifying and strengthening them, emphasized their alienation from the masses of the Chinese, their corruption and intrigue, their inability to live up to the early promise of Sun Yat-sen and the Kuomintang. For it was not the Nationalists, but the Communists, who succeeded in capturing and harnessing the human emotions and aspirations, the binding power that will hold men together in society with the tightness modern material culture demands. It was the Communists, not the Nationalists, who apparently came to stand to most Chinese for what made them Chinese; the Communists came to embody Chinese "nationalism."

The Chinese Communists

The Chinese Communist movement began in the early 1920's. It was inspired by direct contacts with the Comintern in Moscow, guided by Soviet agents, and encouraged at first by leaders of the Kuomintang. Sun Yat-sen hoped that the example and advice of the successful Russion party might help to strengthen his own faltering party organization. For a time, the Chinese Communists were no more than a left-wing, fellow-traveling tail to the Kuomintang. Soon, however, the inevitable breach occurred between them and the more conservative elements among the Nationalists, led by Chiang Kai-shek.

The Communists lost out badly in this early struggle for power. In 1926, Chiang's forces began a campaign of persecution and assassination against the Communists; in 1927, the Communists were expelled from the Kuomintang. An important reason for this setback was the failure of the Chinese Communists to get effective support or help from Moscow. The years 1926 and 1927 were the years of the Trotsky-Stalin feud in Russia, and the conflict between these two titans was intensified by their differences over the "correct" Chinese policy of the Soviet Union (see above, p. 652). Stalin, who was rapidly gaining the ascendancy, believed that China was not ripe for a proletarian revolution; therefore, he did nothing to succor his Chinese comrades.

During the next two decades, down to the end of World War II, the relative strength of Communists and Nationalists underwent a gradual and decisive shift. Both parties, it should be noted, were in a sense totalitarian. Both were organized on the pattern of the one-party political system, which left no place for an opposition party; neither of them was geared to the give-and-take of western party politics. The Communists, driven about over much of China during the 1930's, ended up with a base in the region of Yenan in the north; their strategic position somewhat resembled that of Chiang in his southern base of Szechwan. But there was an important difference. In the long years of Japanese occupation, Chiang remained in Chungking with his army and his bureaucracy. The Communists, on the other hand, managed to string their network of organized armies and local councils in and around the Japanese in the north; they extended their apparatus right down to the sea and up through Manchuria. By 1945, the Communists were ready for a successful conflict with the Kuomintang (see Chapter XXIII).

Southeast Asia

The great turning point in the recent history of the Far East has been World War II, with its aftermath of Communist victory in China, of French withdrawal from Indo-China, British from Burma, Dutch from the East Indies, and American from the Philippines. Before World War II there were few clear signs of the spectacular changes to come in Southeast Asia, that part of the Far East stretching east from India and south from China through the islands of Indonesia. But good observers during the twenty years' truce noted the slow growth of nationalist opposition to imperial rule, particularly in Indo-China and the Netherlands East Indies. They saw that the British-controlled Malay peninsula, with its characteristic colonial economy of rubber and tin production, was peculiarly dependent on the economic health of the West and peculiarly vulnerable in a major depression.

India

In India, by contrast to Southeast Asia, World War I was a crucial turning point. India made important contributions to the British armies; indeed the British victory over the Turks could not have been achieved without the Indian army. Her educated classes, growing in numbers and long exposed to the kind of ideas we call liberal and progressive, got the full impact of Allied propaganda in favor of the war to save the world for democracy. Monetary inflation and other war dislocations favored the growing agitation for self-government. Already in the war period the British Viceroy, Lord Chelmsford, and his experts, both British and Indian, were working toward a plan of reform. Public opinion not only in India but throughout the world was sharpened in favor of the Indians by what seemed to be a throw-back to the crude days of imperial force when, in April, 1919, British troops fired on demonstrators at Amritsar (see above, p. 607).

One basic fact about India after World War I, then, was the long and relatively serene British rule, with its attendant slow but steady acclimatization of Indians to western material things like railroads and hospitals and to western ideas like equality and freedom. A second basic fact, growing out of the first, was the growing Indian demand for the termination of British colonial rule. A third basic fact, conditioning the second, was the existence of Hindu-Moslem tension, which we must now examine in some detail.

A large Moslem minority, about a quarter of the total population, had grown up in the seven hundred years since the first invasion of India by Moslem peoples. In the Indus Basin and part of the Punjab in the northwest, and in part of Bengal in the east, the Moslems were actually a majority; elsewhere they lived scattered among the Hindus and other non-Moslems. Though some of the Moslems belonged to the ruling and aristocratic classes, the bulk were peasants, and on the whole the Moslem community was outstripped financially and industrially by the Hindu community. Although some Moslems, especially in the upper classes, were proud descendants of conquering tribes, for the most part the

Moslems and the Hindus were roughly of the same racial mixtures, both really native Indians indistinguishable by any clear ethnological sign.

Yet Moslems and Hindus felt—and feel—toward each other (we are talking in terms of average members of the two communities) in a way exceedingly difficult for most westerners to understand. A friendly British observer has summed it up in this manner:

What are the things which keep Muslims and Hindus apart, which make them feel that they are different races and nations, which keep them permanently potentially on edge with each other? The first perhaps is the doctrinal issue of idolatry. The Muslim has borrowed from the Semitic races both his passionate rejection of polytheism and his passionate hatred of idolatry. . . . The worship of many gods, the portrayal of the divine in human form, is something to him which is less than human, the mark of the beast. It has, I think, no counterpart in the West; for it is far stronger than our ideas of good form or fair play or the behaviour of a gentleman. . . . The ramifications of these emotions are widespread through the whole realm of Hindu-Muslim relations because of the ubiquitous working of the Hindu doctrine of incarnation. So much in Hinduism is divine. The Muslim does not mind a Hindu not eating beef, for example, but he does object to his worshipping the cow. In times of irritation there is consequently a strong urge to kill a cow out of sheer bravado.

On the side of social custom the chief irritant among Muslims is the caste system in general and the claims of the Brahmins in particular. These claims offend the strong Muslim sense of equality and repel by their exclusiveness. The Muslim taboo of pork is another sore point in social relations, for though it is not a food of caste Hindus any more than of Muslims, its defiling effect makes it an easy subject for provocation. So, too, does the Muslim prohibition of music in worship. Pork in the mosque or music outside are certain ways of provoking a Hindu-Muslim riot.

But the mental anguish of mutual relations is not all on the Muslim side. Hindus suffer acutely in the ceremonial sphere. Hindu feelings about the cow are as untranslatable into Western terms as are Muslim feelings about idolatry, and they are no less strong. A Hindu may literally turn sick at the sight or smell of beef. Muslim practice in the matter of food seems to the typical Hindu to be impure, dirty, and degraded, something beneath the level of man. He cannot understand, on the other hand, what he calls Muslim fanaticism on the subject of idolatry. Orthodox Hindu and Muslim individuals can be, and often are, very good friends, but they usually take good care that their intercourse avoids these danger areas.*

It is not surprising, therefore, that after serious attempts to bring Hindu and Moslem into a unified resistance movement against the British, two separate bodies grew up in the twentieth century—the Indian National Congress and the All-India Moslem League. Immediately after World War I the two bodies did often succeed in presenting a common front against the British, but as time went on their mutual opposition, indeed their irreconcilability, tended to increase rather than diminish.

In spite of these difficulties, the Indian drive for self-government and independence went on steadily from the end of World War I. For the Hindus, the effective political organization of the Congress party was held together and given extraordinary influence over the masses by one of the great leaders of the twentieth century, Mahatma Gandhi (1869-1948). Gandhi was not a Brahmin (a member of the highest Hindu caste) but a member of the *bania* or shopkeeping caste. Educated as a lawyer at Oxford and therefore familiar with the West, trained during his youth in politics in South Africa with its Indian minority, Gandhi was admirably equipped to deal with both British and Hindus. Among his own people he appealed by his simple and austere personal life, his fasts, and his exiguous native costume. He worked out the technique of insurrection called "non-violent non-coöperation," which appealed to the fundamental Hindu belief that force is illusory and therefore ineffective. Char-

India on the brink of independence: Gandhi and crowd, 1945.

acteristic measures sponsored by Gandhi were the organized Indian boycott of British goods and the Mahatma's own resistance through hunger-strikes.

Other Congress leaders, especially at the local level, were willing to use more clearly western methods of agitation, propaganda, and, it must be admitted, rather violent non-violence. Concession after concession was wrung from the British, and as the Indians gained political experience in provincial self-government and in the civil service, dominion status appeared to be just around the corner. This was the situation at the outbreak of World War II. By the time the war was over, however, it was evident that the mutual antagonism of Hindus and Moslems might well require the formation not of a single unified India but of two separate states (see Chapter XXIII).

The Middle East

The European powers had a long history of trying to get an imperial stake in the Near East—or Middle

* Percival Spear, *India, Pakistan, and the West* (London, 1949), 89-91.

East, to use the roughly equivalent term made popular by the British in reference to their "Middle East Command" at Cairo during World War II. The Middle East refers essentially to Persia and to the Asian and African lands that were still nominally part of the decaying Ottoman Empire at the opening of the twentieth century. At that time, the Middle East was still a poverty-stricken region. But by 1914 the first discoveries of petroleum had been made, discoveries that have gone on and on until today it is believed that the Middle East contains the largest reserves of oil in the world. The whole of the area was not to share in this new wealth: the major fields were found to be in southwestern Persia, in the river valleys of Iraq (ancient Mesopotamia), and along the Persian Gulf.

Naturally, the new-found riches of the Middle East did not lessen the interest of the European powers in the region during the twenty years' truce. And in the 1930's, as American experts began to worry about the depletion of oil reserves in the Western Hemisphere, the United States entered the Middle East in something more than its older roles of Protestant missionary and benevolent educator at the American colleges in Beirut (Lebanon) and Istanbul. American oil companies joined with British, Dutch, and French companies in developing and marketing Middle Eastern petroleum.

In the inter-war years, then, the Middle East was an area of increased economic imperialism. It was not, however, an area of the cruder sort of political imperialism, although the western powers maintained sufficient control to insure the orderly exploitation of oil resources. As we have already seen, at the close of World War I the Arab territories of the old Ottoman Empire were administered as western mandates, not annexed as western colonies. The French got the mandates for Syria and for Syria's half-Christian neighbor, Lebanon. The British, who already held a protector-

ate over Egypt, got the mandates for Palestine and Iraq. The only Arab state of significance enjoying anything like full independence was Saudi Arabia, which occupied the bulk of the desert Arabian peninsula. It was an essentially medieval state, the personal creation of a remarkable tribal chieftain, a latter-day feudal warrior, Ibn Saud (1880-1953).

The post-war arrangements, which brought so much of the Arab world under a dilute form of imperial control, did not satisfy the aspirations of Arab nationalists. In these nationalist movements the usual ingredients—western education, hatred of westerners, desire to emulate them—were mixed with a common adherence to Islam, and a faint but real feeling of belonging to some kind of common Arab "nation." Arab nationalism was already being focused on the special problem of Palestine, for by the Balfour Declaration of 1917 the British had promised to open this largely Arab-populated territory as a "national home for the Jewish people." The immigration of Jews into Palestine during the years between the wars caused repeated clashes between Arab nationalists and the new Jewish nationalists or Zionists. The seeds were being sown for the Palestine problem of our own day (see Chapter XXIII).

The French made few concessions to Arab nationalism; indeed, they infuriated the Syrians by bombarding their capital of Damascus in the course of quelling an insurrection in 1925 and 1926. The British, by contrast, attempted a more conciliatory policy by granting some of their wards nominal independence and substituting the ties of alliance for the older imperial ties. In 1922, for example, Egypt was proclaimed an independent state under King Fuad, though the British retained the right to station troops in the country and insisted that westerners resident there continue to enjoy special privileges. In 1936, an Anglo-Egyptian agreement provided for the eventual termination of foreigners' privileges and for the eventual withdrawal of British troops; Egypt, however, was to be closely allied with Great Britain. Meantime, the British were following rather similar policies in Iraq and in Transjordan, the half-desert area east of Palestine. Down to World War II, it looked as though this British policy might work. that a happy way had been found of leading the Arabs gradually to the full responsibilities of independence and to lasting friendship with Britain. But the intensification of Arab nationalism in World War II and the subsequent Palestinian war were to blast the hopes that the Arabs would remain grateful and loyal "old boys" of the British imperial school.

Not every Middle Eastern state was Arab or under at least indirect western control. Turkey was a case in point. Reduced to its own national domain in Asia Minor by its losses in World War I, Turkey soon began an ardent nationalist revival, extending the Young Turk revolution initiated shortly before 1914 (see above, p. 589). The leader of this political renaissance was a highly gifted army officer, Mustafa Kemal (1881-1938). The old Ottoman Empire was abolished in 1922, and in its stead the Republic of Turkey was proclaimed, which subsequently began to develop along true parliamentary lines. To point up the new orientation of the republic, Kemal moved the capital from cosmopolitan Istanbul, now on the western edge of Turkish territory, to Ankara in the heart of Asia Minor (see also above, p. 614).

Kemal also imposed rapid, wholesale, and sometimes ruthless measures of westernization. Women received the vote and were, at least in theory though often not in practice, emancipated from traditional Moslem restraints. The whole fabric of social and political life was largely removed, again at least in theory, from the highly conservative influence of Islam. An advanced European law code was introduced; Sunday, not the Moslem Friday, was made the weekly day of rest; even the Turkish language was revolutionized and written for the first time in western letters—a move of major importance, for only a fraction of the Turkish people had ever been able to master the old Ottoman Turkish, with its heavy content of Persian and Arabic words, and with its difficult Arabic script. All Turks were now required to take surnames in the western manner, and Kemal himself aptly took that of Atatürk, "Father of the Turks." He had indeed revolutionized his country, even though westernization was only just beginning to reach down to the grass roots of Turkish society. And he had insured its independence of the West, as Turkish neutrality during World War II was soon to demonstrate.

The example of Turkey was followed, though less sweepingly and less effectively, by the other traditionally independent major state of the Middle East—Persia, or, as it has been officially styled since 1935, Iran, "Land of the Aryans." Beginning in 1906, the medieval political structure of Iran was gradually altered in the direction of a limited monarchy, with an elected parliament and with the Shah as a constitutional monarch. This political transition, however, was far from smooth, and the country did not adapt easily to modern western political institutions. Iran, too, had her counterpart of Atatürk—Reza Shah, an able army officer, and a fevered but unbalanced modernizer, who seized the throne after World War I only to lose it early in World War II. Reza Shah had pro-Nazi sympathies, and in 1941 the British and the Russians both sent troops into Iran to force his abdication and to keep Iran on the anti-Nazi side in the war.

The fate of Reza Shah served as a reminder that the British and Russians preserved their old interest in Iran, where they had often competed for spheres of influence and concessions. It also showed that many seemingly independent nations in the non-western world were not yet strong enough to challenge the military might of the imperial powers of the West. Imperial ties had indeed been loosened, but they were not as yet always severed or dissolved.

Reading Suggestions on the Democracies

Britain and France

R. Graves and A. Hodge, *The Long Weekend* (London: Faber & Faber, 1940). A lively social history of Britain during the inter-war years.

G. E. Elton, *The Life of James Ramsay Macdonald* (London: Collins, 1939); G. M. Young, *Stanley Baldwin* (London: Hart-Davis, 1952); and K. Feiling, *The Life of Neville Chamberlain* (London: Macmillan, 1946). Biographies of three important British statesmen.

C. R. Attlee, *The Labour Party in Perspective*, 2nd ed. (London: Gollancz, 1949). A review of the period by the British Labor leader.

D. Brogan, *France under the Republic* (N.Y.: Harper, 1940), and D. Thomson, *Democracy in France*, 2nd ed. (London: Oxford Univ. Press, 1952). These general studies provide an excellent introduction to French problems in the inter-war years.

E. J. Knapton, *France since Versailles* (N.Y.: Holt, 1952. A Berkshire Study). Handy little manual.

A. Werth, *The Twilight of France, 1933-1940* (N.Y.: Harper, 1942). Condensation of several longer studies by an able foreign correspondent.

The United States

Four volumes in the "Chronicles of America Series" (New Haven: Yale Univ. Press) provide good coverage of the period: H. U. Faulkner, *From Versailles to the New Deal* (1950); D. Brogan, *The Era of Franklin D. Roosevelt* (1951); A. Nevins, *The United States in a Chaotic World* (1950); and A. Nevins, *The New Deal and World Affairs* (1950).

F. L. Allen, *Only Yesterday* (N.Y.: Bantam Books) and *Since Yesterday* (N.Y.: Harper, 1940). Lively social histories of the 1920's and 1930's, respectively.

F. Perkins, *The Roosevelt I Knew* (N.Y.: Viking, 1946); and R. E. Sherwood, *Roosevelt and Hopkins*, 2 vols. (N.Y.: Bantam Books). Perhaps the best of the books about Franklin Roosevelt by the people who worked with him.

F. Freidel, *Franklin D. Roosevelt*. Three volumes of this detailed and careful biographical study have appeared so far. (Boston: Little, Brown, 1952, 1954, 1956).

J. M. Burns, *Roosevelt: The Lion and the Fox* (N.Y.: Harcourt, Brace, 1956). An interesting but rather limited estimate of Roosevelt the politician.

A. M. Schlesinger, Jr., *The Crisis of the Old Order, 1919-1933* (Boston: Houghton Mifflin, 1957). The first volume in a projected extended work on "The Age of Roosevelt" by a prominent young American historian sympathetic to the New Deal.

Economic Developments

J. K. Galbraith, *The Great Crash, 1929* (Boston: Houghton Mifflin, 1955). A well-written study of the Wall Street slump by a prominent American economist.

P. Einzig, *The World Economic Crisis, 1929-1932* (London: Macmillan, 1932); H. V. Hodson, *Slump and Recovery, 1929-1937* (N.Y.: Oxford Univ. Press, 1938); H. W. Arndt, *The Economic Lessons of the Nineteen-Thirties* (London: Oxford Univ. Press, 1944). Other useful books on the great depression.

J. Schumpeter, *Capitalism, Socialism, and Democracy*, 3rd ed. (N.Y.: Harper, 1950); J. M. Keynes, *The End of Laissez-Faire* (London: Woolf, 1926). Thoughtful essays by two major economic thinkers.

Other Topics

E. Fischer, *The Passing of the European Age* (Cambridge: Harvard Univ. Press, 1943). Defense of the thesis that leadership in western civilization has passed from Europe to other continents.

E. O. Reischauer, *Japan, Past and Present*, 2nd ed., rev. (N.Y.: Knopf, 1956). An excellent introductory account.

E. A. Walker, *The British Empire: Its Structure and Spirit, 1497-1953* (Cambridge, England: Bowes & Bowes, 1953). Good survey by a careful historian.

M. Wade, *The French-Canadian Outlook* (N.Y.: Viking, 1946). Perceptive study of a point of view generally ignored, even in North America.

L. Fischer, *Gandhi* (N.Y.: New American Library, 1954). A sympathetic biography.

G. L. Lewis, *Turkey* (London: Benn, 1955). Lively summary of the Atatürk revolution and its consequences.

Fiction

E. Waugh, *A Handful of Dust* (Norfolk, Conn.: New Directions, 1945). Corrosive novel satirizing English society in the inter-war years.

H. Spring, *Fame Is the Spur* (N.Y.: Viking, 1940). A politician is corrupted by ambition; largely parallels the career of Ramsay Macdonald.

W. Holtby, *South Riding* (N.Y.: Macmillan, 1936). Good social novel of industrial England.

A. Gide, *The Counterfeiters* (N.Y.: Knopf, 1927). Mordant study of the French middle class by an eminent novelist.

F. Scott Fitzgerald, *The Great Gatsby* (many editions). A celebrated picture of "flaming youth" in the American Jazz Age.

J. Steinbeck, *The Grapes of Wrath* (many editions). The famous novel about exiles from the Oklahoma "dust bowl" of the 1930's.

E. O'Connor, *The Last Hurrah* (Boston: Little, Brown, 1956). An affectionate portrait of a political boss in a big American city.

E. Hemingway, *The Sun Also Rises* (N.Y.: Bantam Books). Often considered the best novel about the "lost generation" of American expatriates.

A. Malraux, *Man's Fate* (N.Y.: Modern Library, 1936). Excellent novel about Chinese communist revolutionaries in the 1920's.

CHAPTER TWENTY-TWO

The Second

World War

General or world wars in our state-system are usually born of a previous war, or, perhaps better, of a previous peace settlement that fails to solve certain important problems. We have already been obliged in seeking the origins of the First World War to go back to 1870, to Bismarck, to the "rape of Alsace-Lorraine" and the consequent rise of the spirit of revenge among Frenchmen. We shall now have to go back to 1919 and the grave difficulties that arose in the attempt to carry out the settlements of Versailles. So troubled were international relations for the twenty years after 1919, so closely in time did the Second World War follow on the First, that the interval between the two has been christened the "twenty years' truce." And it is not impossible that historians in the future will actually consider the two wars really one war, as they now consider the wars of the French Revolution and Napoleon essentially one war. But for the present, we must use the accepted terms, World War I (1914-1918) and World War II (1939-1945).

I: International Politics, 1919-1932

During the first part of the twenty years' truce, international leadership of the democratic world rested with Britain and France. Though supported in principle and often in practice by the United States, they were increasingly unable to stem the rise of powers hostile to liberal democracy—Italy, Germany, Spain, Russia, Japan. In the end, the beaten perturber of 1918, Germany, once more waged aggressive warfare against the major Allies of 1918. This time Germany allied with two of its former enemies, Italy and Japan, each disappointed with its share of the spoils of victory in 1918.

Why was the peace settlement of 1919 followed in twenty years by a second great war? Why was it so unlike the last great settlement, that of 1815 following the Napoleonic wars, which had inaugurated a long period of general peace, interrupted only by localized wars? Nazi Germany maintained that the second war was the direct and inevitable result of the *Diktat*, the dictated peace of Versailles that ended the first war. Supported by most Germans and many German sympathizers, the Nazis claimed that Germany was humiliated by the war-guilt clause, stripped of territories and colonies that were rightfully hers, saddled with an astronomical and unpayable reparations bill, denied the normal rights of a sovereign state in armaments—in short, so badly treated that simple human dignity made revolt against the *Diktat* and its makers a necessity. Now something of this is true. The settlement of Versailles did saddle the new German Republic with a heavy burden in part dictated by revenge and fear toward the old German Empire. A wiser Allied pol-

icy would perhaps have tried to start the new government off without too great a burden, as the Allies in 1815 did with the France of Louis XVIII (see Chapter XII).

The "Era of Fulfillment"

But the *Diktat* thesis is very far from containing the whole truth. What breaks down the argument that the iniquities of Versailles *alone* explain the second war is the "era of fulfillment." In spite of the Treaty of Versailles, the Germans and their former enemies did manage to come together in the 1920's.

The great landmark of the "era of fulfillment" was the Locarno Treaty negotiated in October, 1925. At Locarno in Switzerland, Germany agreed with France and Belgium on a mutual guarantee of their common frontiers; Britain and Italy agreed to act as guarantors, that is, to provide military aid against the violator if a violation of the frontiers occurred. These agreements made a substantial contribution to the reconciliation of Germany and the Allies. Germany affirmed her acceptance of the western frontier drawn for her at Versailles, and France, for her part, affirmed the new moderate direction that her German policy had taken since the failure of her occupation of the Ruhr.

The "Locarno spirit" of reconciliation endured for the next several years. It was nourished by the general prosperity of both the French and the Germans and by the constructive policies of their respective foreign ministers, Briand and Stresemann. In 1926 Germany was admitted to the

League of Nations, an event that seemed to signify not only the restoration of Germany to international respectability but also German acceptance of the peaceful purposes and duties of League membership. These hopeful impressions received confirmation when Germany signed the Kellogg-Briand Peace Pact of 1928 (see above, p. 717). In 1929, the French consented to withdraw the last of their occupation troops from the Rhineland during the forthcoming year, thus ending the Allied occupation of Germany at a date considerably in advance of the one stipulated in the Versailles Treaty.

Meantime, other international developments were bolstering the "Locarno spirit." The great world-wide organization planned by Wilson, the League of Nations, began its operations in 1920. We shall soon see that the League was never able to impose its will on a determined and defiant aggressor. Yet the record of the League during the 1920's was by no means one of unmitigated failure. In the first place, the League became a going concern. Its Council, dominated by the great powers, and its Assembly, representing all its members, met regularly at the League's "capital," the Swiss city of Geneva. Second, the League played a direct part in the peaceful resolution of two crises that, had they not been resolved, might well have led to little wars —in 1920 a dispute between Sweden and Finland over some Baltic islands, and in 1925 a frontier incident in the Balkans involving Greece and Bulgaria.

The failure of the United States to join the League dealt a hard blow to the organization's effectiveness; the parent had in effect denied the child. But the blow was softened by the major role that the United States took in furthering one of the League's chief objectives—disarmament. Soon after the first war the United States invited the other principal sea powers to consider the limitation of naval armaments. Meeting in Washington during the winter of 1921-1922,

the naval conference achieved an agreement establishing a ten-year "holiday" in the construction of capital ships (battleships and heavy cruisers). The agreement also set the allowed tonnages of capital ships at a ratio of 5 for the United States, 5 for Britain, 3 for Japan, and 1.67 each for France and Italy.

A conference at London in 1930, however, had less success in limiting "non-capital" ships, including submarines. The partial failure of the London naval conference was a portent. Two years later, after long preparation, the League itself convoked a meeting to address the still more pressing problem of limiting military armaments. Not only the League members, but also the United States and the Soviet Union, sent representatives to Geneva. The Geneva conference of 1932, however, accomplished nothing. It was wrecked above all by a renewal of Franco-German antagonism, by the German demand for equality in armaments with France, and by the French refusal to grant the demand.

In 1932, then, the "Locarno spirit" was dead, and the "era of fulfillment" had ended. In the West, Germany, with Italy following suit, was about to abandon negotiation as a way of revising the Versailles Treaty and was about to take Hitler's way of denunciation and defiance. In the Far East, Japan had already upset the balance in 1931 by seizing Manchuria from China. The postwar period had ended; the prewar period was beginning. Thus the genesis of World War II involved many factors in addition to the Treaty of Versailles; we may explore some of them by asking why the promise of "fulfillment" faded so rapidly in the early 1930's.

The Failure of "Fulfillment"

There is one very obvious explanation for the failure of the hopes aroused in the 1920's—the world depression that began in 1929. In Germany itself the depression was a last straw, a decisive factor in putting Hitler into power. In the democracies, too, it had heavy consequences for the peace of the world, for depression sapped their morale and made them less confident.

Another factor that was unsettling to international politics was Soviet Russia. In the eyes of the western nations, Russia was a revolutionary power that could not really be trusted, that could not be fully integrated into the international state-system. The Soviet Union was the center of a revolutionary faith hated and distrusted by the politicians of the West, who feared, by no means without justification, communist agitation among their own peoples. An "eastern Locarno," the acceptance by Russia, Germany, and the lesser states of eastern Europe of the territorial settlements made after World War I, was long talked about and hoped for. The "eastern Locarno," however, never came to fruition. Russia was admitted to the League of Nations in 1934, but the Soviet Union remained an uncertain factor in the balance of power; she was no clear and satisfactory counterweight to the growing power of Nazi Germany.

Still another basic factor that led to the second war was the continuing failure of the three great western democracies, Britain, France, and the United States, to present anything like a united front. Americans of internationalist sympathies have probably exaggerated the results of the sudden American withdrawal into isolationism in 1919. It is hard to believe, especially in light of the rivalry and cross-purposes that Britain and France displayed *within* the League of Nations, that formal American membership in the League would have helped the situation greatly. Still, the isolation of the United States undoubtedly exacerbated French fears and the French sense of weakness, and pushed France toward the sort of intransigence that was illustrated by her disastrous intervention in the Ruhr in the mid-1920's. (See p. 711.)

More serious was the failure of France and Britain to work together effectively. France, exhausted and under-populated, endeavoring to play the part of a first-rate power but supported only by second-rate resources, lived in perpetual fear of a revived Germany. She sought not only to carry out to the full the economic and political measures of the Versailles Treaty that aimed at weakening Germany and keeping Germany weak. She sought also to make up for Russia's defection as her eastern ally against Germany. This she did by making alliances, beginning in 1921, with the smaller states to the east of Germany—Poland, Czechoslovakia, Rumania, and Yugoslavia. All of them wanted French protection against the possible restoration of the Habsburg Empire, from which they had gained so much territory, and all of them except Poland were informally linked together as the "Little Entente."

To a Britain whose statesmen knew well the long story of Anglo-French conflicts from the Hundred Years' War to Napoleon, the France of the 1920's seemed once more aiming at European supremacy, seemed once more an active threat to the traditional British policy of preventing any such supremacy. Although it is now plain that the French were animated rather by fear than by ambition, and that they could never again be aggressors, it is true enough that many of their statesmen seemed to be falling into old ways, or at least old words, of aggression. The mistaken British diagnosis was at least understandable. Moreover, Britain was physically undamaged, and by no means as apprehensive about German recovery as were the French. Indeed, from an economic point of view the restoration of a healthy Germany seemed to British statesmen desirable both as a market for British exports and as an element in the general restoration of international trade. Therefore, as against the French, the

British early adopted a "soft" policy toward Germany, and openly condemned the Ruhr adventure.

Finally, something of the old British isolationism had survived the war, and made the British—and especially their dominions—unwilling to commit themselves firmly to guarantees in continental Europe. Britain did indeed accept Locarno, but in the previous year the dominions had played a large part in her rejection of the more sweeping "Geneva protocol" urged upon her by France, which would have committed its signatories to compulsory arbitration of international disputes.

The difficulties of the Anglo-French partnership also go far to explain the weaknesses of the League of Nations. The effectiveness of any piece of machinery is bound to hinge on the skill and co-ordination of the mechanics who operate it. The League lacked a means of enforcing its decisions. And it was somewhat top-heavy, since the fully representative Assembly counted for less than did the smaller Council, where Britain and France took a preponderant role. When these two mechanics disagreed, therefore, the machinery scarcely operated at all. One example of the way in which the grand purposes of the League suffered from Anglo-French friction is the rejection of the Geneva protocol. Another is the Corfu incident of 1923, when Mussolini for a time defied the League and set a sinister precedent for the later use of gangster tactics by the dictators (see Chapter XX). In the midst of the Corfu crisis the League was crippled by Anglo-French discord over the Ruhr policy of France.

The Aggressors

The Corfu incident underlines the presence of one more element, the most important of all, in the rapid deterioration of the twenty years' truce. This, of course, was the fact of aggressions by Italy, Germany, and Japan. In Chapter XX we saw how the ruthlessly ambitious programs of fascism and Nazism steadily led Mussolini and Hitler to a foreign policy of adventure and aggression. In Chapter XXI we saw how the somewhat similar totalitarian policies of the Japanese militarists led them to begin the seizure of China by their occupation of Manchuria in 1931. With this background of underlying tensions—the punitive features of the Versailles settlement, the disastrous effects of the depression on the Locarno spirit, the continuance of the revolutionary focus in Russia, the defensive attitude of the western democracies and their mutual mistrust, the new aggressive faiths of fascism and Nazism, and the rise of imperialist Japan—we may now proceed to the actual steps along the road to a second world war.

II: The Road To War, 1931-1939

The First Step: Manchuria, 1931

It is now clear that the first step along the road to war was the Japanese seizure of Manchuria in 1931. Stimson, President Hoover's Secretary of State, responded to the seizure by announcing that the United States would recognize no gains made by armed force. Stimson hoped that Britain and the other democracies might follow this American lead, but his hopes were largely disappointed. The League of Nations did send out a commission headed by the British Earl of Lytton, and the subsequent Lytton Report condemned the Japanese act as aggression.

Neither the United States nor the League, however, fortified its verbal protests by effective action; force was not met by force. Japan, refusing to accept the Lytton Report, withdrew from the League of Nations in March, 1933, making the first formal breach in the League's structure.

The Second Step: German Rearmament, 1935-1936

The next breach in the League's structure, and the next step toward war, were made by Germany. In October, 1933, Hitler withdrew from the League, thereby virtually serving notice on the world of his aggressive intentions. On March 16, 1935, he denounced the clauses of the Treaty of Versailles that limited German armaments and set about the open rebuilding of the German armed forces.

The response to this unilateral and hence illegal act set the pattern for the next few years. On April 17, 1935, the League of Nations formally condemned Germany's repudiation of treaty obligations—and Germany continued to rearm. In May, 1935, France hastily concluded with the Soviet Union a treaty of alliance against German aggression—and Germany continued to rearm. In June, 1935, the British, realistically and short-sightedly—for their action seemed like desertion to the French—signed with rearming Germany a naval agreement limiting the German navy to one-third the size of the British, and German submarines to 60 per cent of those of Britain. But this agreement contained the extraordinary proviso that, if the Germans decided that circumstances were "exceptional," they might increase their submarine fleet to 100 per cent of the British!

It is hardly surprising that Hitler's next act drew no more than the customary protests from the signatories of Locarno. This was the "reoccupation" of the Rhineland in March, 1936—that is, the sending of German troops into the western German zone that had been demilitarized by the Treaty of Versailles. Britain and France once more confined themselves to verbal protests.

The Third Step: Ethiopia, 1935

Meanwhile the Italians struck in Ethiopia. In that pocket of old Africa, relatively isolated on its mountains and tablelands, a "sovereign" state had precariously maintained itself, largely because its imperial neighbors, Britain, France, and Italy, would neither agree to divide it nor let any one of the three swallow it. The Italians, who wanted it most, had lost the disastrous battle of Adowa to the native Ethiopians in 1896. This humiliation rankled with the fascists, who felt they had to show the world that there was more than rhetoric in their talk about a revived Roman Empire.

In 1934, a frontier incident at Ualual in desert Italian Somaliland—or in Ethiopia, for both sides claimed the place—put the matter before the international politicians. France and Britain were characteristically quite ready for appeasement of Italy, partly because they hoped to align Mussolini with them against Hitler. They offered him almost everything in Ethiopia, including those concrete economic concessions naive people think are the essence of imperialism. But since Ethiopia was a member of the League, the French and the British insisted that its formal independence be observed. This Mussolini would not accept, and in October, 1935, his troops began the invasion of Ethiopia. Airplanes, artillery, and tanks made the difference between 1896 and 1935. This time the underdog was not the winner. Poison gas finished the task early in 1936, and the King of Italy acquired the coveted title of Emperor of Ethiopia. Once more there was an emperor —of sorts—in Rome!

The League of Nations had already formally condemned the Japanese aggression in Manchuria and the German denunciation of the disarmament clauses of the Treaty of Versailles. In 1935, it at once declared that Italy by invading Ethiopia, a League member, had violated her obligations under the Covenant of the League. Now the League made the momentous decision to test its power to move from words to deeds. In this it had the full and hearty accord of most of its members, and was urged on by the British, and less vocally by the French, and by Haile Selassie, the rightful Emperor of Ethiopia. Haile Selassie made a dramatic appeal in Geneva itself, where Italian diplomats perpetrated the supreme insult of hissing him. On October 11, 1935, fifty-one member nations of the League voted to invoke against Italy the famous Article 16 of the League Covenant, which provided for economic sanctions against a member resorting to war in disregard of its covenants.

The sanctions thus invoked failed. There were loopholes; oil, for instance, was not included in the list of articles barred from commerce with Italy, which had only meager stockpiles of this vital war material. There was much mutual recrimination among members of the League over what articles should be placed on the prohibited list and over the fact that Britain and France did nothing to check Italian movements of troops and munitions through the Suez Canal. Germany was no longer in the League, and was wholly unbound by its decision. Indeed, in the tension and confusion of the Ethiopian crisis, she found a favorable opportunity to reoccupy the Rhineland in March, 1936.

The Ethiopian fiasco was a disastrous blow to the League, which from now on was helpless in high international politics. Its special services as a group of trained international civil servants, its "functional groups," dealing with labor problems, international police matters like the drug traffic, and much else, persisted, however, to be absorbed after World War II by the United Nations. But for the rest of the 1930's the League was hardly even a formal factor in the increasing tensions. No one was surprised or greatly concerned when Italy, belatedly copying Japan and Germany, withdrew from the League in December, 1937.

The Fourth Step: The Spanish Civil War, 1936-1939

The next step after Ethiopia on the road to war is of great psychological interest. No doubt the later direct aggressions of Hitler in Czechoslovakia and Poland were the politically decisive steps. But the Spanish Civil War (for details, see Chapter XX), which broke out in July, 1936, was the emotional catalyst that divided millions of men and women all over the western world. It is still, in spite of the passing of years, a kind of great collective Dreyfus case, a test of conscience and loyalty for our time.

The Spanish Civil War was fought with the great violence and with the consecrated devotion that mark wars of principle. No one can say for sure how the struggle would have ended if it had remained a purely Spanish one, as the American Civil War had remained a purely American one. Certainly the Loyalists would have been in a much stronger position if the democratic powers had followed the usual practice in international law of sending arms to the *de jure* government of Spain. Such speculation, however, is useless. Almost from the very start the Spanish Civil War engaged, not merely the vicarious emotional participation of the West, not merely individual foreign enlistments, but the active though never wholly open intervention of other nations. This intervention was decisive and effective on the part of the fascist powers, Italy and Germany; it was less determined

on the part of communist Russia, and fee-
blest of all on the part of Britain and
France. Early in 1939, with the fall of Barcelona, the Civil War was in effect over.
Once more a fascist group had won.

Meantime, dizzy with success, Mussolini
was going on to other adventures. In October, 1936, he signed a pact with Hitler,
thereby formally establishing the Rome-
Berlin "Axis" and committing fascist Italy
to alliance with Nazi Germany. Mussolini
gave strong support to Franco's rebellion in
Spain. And, late in 1938, he orchestrated a
public outcry in Italy for the French to
hand over certain territories. He wanted
not only Nice and Savoy, which had been
ceded to Napoleon III during Italian unification negotiations almost a century earlier, but also the Mediterranean island of
Corsica, which had been French since the
days of Louis XV in the eighteenth century, and Tunisia, which had never been under Italian rule and had been French since
1881. These outrageous demands came to
nothing, but they did not exactly improve
relations between France and Italy. Finally,
on Good Friday (April 7), 1939, Mussolini
attacked Albania, long coveted by the Italians, and quickly subjugated this backward
little Balkan state. For a few years, Victor
Emmanuel was to be King of Albania as
well as Emperor of Ethiopia.

The Fifth Step: "Anschluss," 1938

The immedi-
ate origins of
World War II lie, however, neither in Italian nor in Spanish fascist aggression, but in
the mounting series of German aggressions.
Hitler had begun the open rebuilding of
German armed forces in 1935. Three years
later, he felt strong enough to undertake
the first enterprise of expansion, an enterprise which, like all he undertook, he insisted was no more than a restoration to
Germany of what the *Diktat* of Versailles

had deprived her of. Austria, German in language and tradition, had been left a mere
fragment by the disruption of the Habsburg Empire. Ever since 1918 there had
been a strong movement among Austrians
for annexation ("*Anschluss*") to Germany
proper. This movement had been strenu-
ously opposed by the victors of the first
war, and especially by France. They
blocked the 1931 project for an economic
Anschluss in the form of an Austro-German
customs union. A year after the Nazis came
to power in Germany, they attempted a
full *Anschluss*. Their 1934 *Putsch* in Austria, though it claimed Chancellor Dollfuss
as a victim, failed because of inadequate
preparations and because of the hostility of
Mussolini's Italy (for details, see Chapter
XX).

Hitler carefully laid the ground for the
success of the next Nazi attempt. The pact
with Italy that formally established the
Rome-Berlin "Axis" (October, 1936) disarmed Mussolini's opposition to *Anschluss*.
Early in 1938 Hitler began what turned
out to be his standard technique of softening his victims for the final blow. He unleashed a violent propaganda campaign by
press, radio, and platform against the alleged misdeeds of the government of independent Austria. In February, 1938, he summoned the Austrian Chancellor Schuschnigg to his Bavarian retreat at Berchtesga-
den, where he let loose a bullying tirade
against the hapless Schuschnigg. In March,
Hitler moved his troops into Austria and
made *Anschluss* a fact. The Nazis met no effective opposition from native Austrian
anti-fascists, by no means a negligible
group, nor any serious international resistance. There was not even a blast from the
League of Nations.

Hitler now had six million more German-speaking nationals in the fold; and in
the union of Austria and Germany he had
achieved something that no Habsburg and
no Hohenzollern had been able to do in

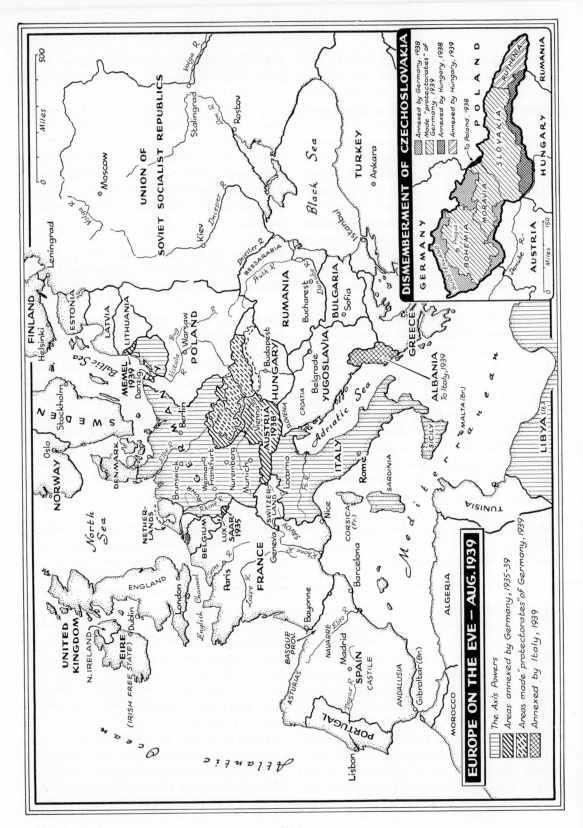

DISMEMBERMENT OF CZECHOSLOVAKIA

Annexed by Germany, 1938
Made "protectorates" of Germany, 1939
Annexed by Hungary, 1938
Annexed by Hungary, 1939

To Poland, 1938

GERMANY
SUDETENLAND
Prague ○
BOHEMIA
MORAVIA
SLOVAKIA
RUTHENIA
POLAND
HUNGARY
Danube R.
AUSTRIA
RUMANIA

Miles
150

EUROPE ON THE EVE — AUG. 1939

The Axis Powers
Areas annexed by Germany, 1935-39
Areas made "protectorates" of Germany, 1939
Annexed by Italy, 1939

Miles
0 500

UNION OF SOVIET SOCIALIST REPUBLICS

Volga R.
Moscow ○
Volga R.
Stalingrad ○
Don R.
Rostov ○
Dnieper R.
Kiev ○

Leningrad ○
FINLAND
Helsinki ○
ESTONIA
LATVIA
LITHUANIA
MEMEL 1939
Danzig
POLAND
Vistula R.
Bug R.
Warsaw ○

Black Sea
TURKEY
Ankara ○
Istanbul ○

BESSARABIA
Dniester R.
Pruth R.
RUMANIA
Bucharest ○
Danube R.
BULGARIA
Sofia ○

NORWAY
Oslo ○
SWEDEN
Stockholm ○
Baltic Sea
DENMARK

North Sea

GERMANY
Berlin ○
Brunswick ○
Weimar ○
Frankfurt ○
Nuremberg ○
Munich ○
Elbe R.
Oder R.
RUHR

Budapest ○
HUNGARY
Vienna ○
AUSTRIA 1938

YUGOSLAVIA
Belgrade ○
CROATIA
SLOVENIA

GREECE
ALBANIA
To Italy, 1939

Adriatic Sea

SWITZER-LAND
Locarno ○
Geneva ○
SAVOY
SAAR 1935
LUX.
BELGIUM
NETHER-LANDS

ITALY
Rome ○
Nice ○
CORSICA (Fr.)
SARDINIA
SICILY
MALTA (Br.)

Mediterranean Sea

UNITED KINGDOM
N. IRELAND
EIRE (IRISH FREE STATE)
Dublin ○
ENGLAND
London ○
English Channel

FRANCE
Paris ○
Seine R.
Loire R.
Rhine R.
Rhône R.
Bayonne ○

Atlantic Ocean

BASQUE PROV.
NAVARRE
Ebro R.
SPAIN
Madrid ○
CASTILE
ASTURIAS
ANDALUSIA
Barcelona ○
Gibraltar (Br.)
MOROCCO
ALGERIA
TUNISIA
LIBYA (It.)

PORTUGAL
Lisbon ○
Tagus R.

modern times. But he showed no signs at all of taking the Bismarckian position of being content with what he had gained. Almost at once he went to work on the acquisition of the Sudeten Germans of Czechoslovakia.

The Sixth Step: Czechoslovakia Dismembered, 1938-1939

The Czechoslovak republic was the only state in central or eastern Europe where parliamentary democracy had achieved a resounding success after World War I. The republic faced a difficult problem of national minorities, but it had the good fortune to inherit most of the best and most highly developed industrial regions of the old Habsburg Empire. Its economy, consequently, was far better balanced between industry and agriculture than was that of the other states of eastern Europe. This healthy economy was mirrored in the social structure, where a working balance was maintained among peasants, middle classes, and industrial workers. The period immediately after the war, as well as the great depression of the 1930's, times of great suffering elsewhere, affected Czechoslovakia very lightly. Yet these advantages could hardly have preserved democracy in the republic had it not been for the enlightened policies of Thomas Masaryk, liberator and president of his country until his resignation at the age of 85 in 1935.

Even the enlightened Czech regime, however, could not keep the country from ultimately being smashed by outside pressures working on its sensitive minorities. The Sudeten German minority of 3¼ millions, feeling, as Germans, superior to Slavs, resisted the new republic at every turn, even when the Prague government made concessions to satisfy their just grievances. Sudeten extremists early turned to Hitler, but even moderates and socialists among the Sudetens were more or less pan-German in their views. From 1933 on, Nazi agitation, supported by Hitler with men and money, became increasingly serious in Czechoslovakia. Early in 1938, having secured Austria, Hitler decided to push the Czech affair next. Henlein, his Sudeten agent, made demands on the Prague government for what amounted to complete Sudeten autonomy. The summer of 1938 was spent in negotiations and in mutual propaganda blasts. The Czechs relied heavily on their allies, the British and the French. Whereas British statesmen now for the first time began to announce publicly that Germany had gone far enough, the British sent out a mediator, Lord Runciman, who seemed inclined to meet Hitler at least halfway.

By the autumn of 1938, Hitler was ready for action. On September 12 he made a violent speech at Nuremberg, insisting on self-determination for the Sudeten Germans. This was the signal for widespread disorders in Czechoslovakia and for the proclamation of martial law by its government. The situation was now a full-fledged European crisis that called for the personal intervention of men at the very top of their states. The British Prime Minister, Neville Chamberlain, made two preliminary visits to Hitler in Germany in an effort to moderate German demands, and finally persuaded Hitler—with the help of Mussolini —to call a full conference of the four great western powers. This conference—Hitler, Mussolini, Chamberlain, and Daladier for France—met in Munich on September 29, 1938. Russia was not invited; her exclusion was to complete her abandonment of the "Popular Front" policy (see Chapter XIX).

Munich was a sweeping victory for Hitler. Czechoslovakia was partially dismembered; her Sudeten rim-lands were turned over to Germany; the Czechs were obliged to hand over Teschen and certain other areas to the Poles; the whole economy and transportation system were lamed; the defense of her frontiers was made impossible by the loss of the border mountains and their fortifications; and Slovakia was given autonomy within a federal state, emphasized by the official change in spelling from Czechoslovakia to Czecho-Slovakia. The Czech leaders had felt it impossible to resist the Germans without the aid of their French and British allies; their people acquiesced bitterly in the settlement of Munich. The Germans had played fully on the differences between the more industrialized Czechs and the still largely agricultural Slovaks. But even had the country been strongly united, the laming blow of Munich would have ruined its morale. Hitler acted quickly. In the very next spring, before the final lines of demarcation set at Munich had actually been drawn, he summoned the Czech President, Hacha, to Germany for another of those ghastly interviews, in which he announced that the fate of the Czech people "must be placed trustingly in the hands of the *Fuehrer*." In March, 1939, Hitler marched his army into the remaining fragments of Czechoslovakia, meeting no real resistance.

The dismemberment of the Czechoslovak republic was now completed. There was no longer even a hyphenated Czecho-Slovakia. Bohemia and Moravia, the Czech areas, became a German "protectorate" under Von Neurath (1873-1956), an aristocrat rallied to Hitler and a former foreign minister. In Slovakia, now quite independent of Bohemia and Moravia, the prime minister, Monsignor Tiso, formally put his country under German "protection." The little easternmost tip of old Czechoslovakia, where the Ruthenian inhabitants had risen up and driven out Czechoslovak officials, enjoyed its independence one day. On the next, the Hungarians, who had already taken a substantial piece of Slovakia in 1938, marched in with Hitler's consent. The Czechoslovakia of Masaryk had fallen victim to the appeasement policies of its democratic allies.

Chamberlain, Daladier, Hitler, Mussolini, and Ciano (Mussolini's son-in-law) at Munich, September, 1938.

The most respectable defense that can be made of Munich and appeasement rests on the argument that the West was buying time to prepare for a war which it knew to be inevitable but for which it was not yet ready. Chamberlain may have thought so; but Winston Churchill and others have pointed out most cogently that the democracies were in a stronger military position relative to that of Germany in September, 1938, than in September, 1939. It also seems likely that Chamberlain and Daladier, as well as millions all over the world, believed, or hoped, that the acquisition of the Sudeten Germans would satisfy Hitler, that after Munich he would behave as Bismarck had behaved after Sedan, and that he would settle down and try to preserve the balance of power. Some westerners even hoped that Hitler would perhaps ally with them against communist Russia or obligingly get himself so entangled in eastern Europe that he would bring on a Russo-German war. Hitler's words and deeds, however, had given no real foundation for the belief that he would now "play ball" with the West. More fundamentally, this was a belief to which the last four hundred years of the European state-system gave no support. Hitler resembled Napoleon far more than he resembled Bismarck; no such strong aggressor had ever been stopped without a general war. History, psychology, sociology, and perhaps even common sense all pointed to the prospect that Hitler would actually be *encouraged* in aggression by Munich, that he would try again soon. And we now know that he had as early as November 5, 1937, announced to his close advisers his unalterable intention of destroying Czechoslovakia and moving on into Poland and the Ukraine.

The actual destruction of old Czechoslovakia in March, 1939, seems not to have surprised anyone. Indeed the curious mixture of resignation, condemnation, and resolution with which this action was greeted in the West marks a turning point. The days of appeasement were over. Hitler's next aggression would not lead to a Munich. We can never be quite sure whether Hitler and his aides thought they could take their next step without bringing on a general war. In public and semi-public, Hitler, Goering, and the other leaders made no secret of their feeling that the British and French were decadent, spineless, inefficient societies, quite unable to summon the courage needed to resist an inspired and rejuvenated Germany. Yet there is good evidence that Hitler expected at least a local war with Poland this time, and that he was quite prepared to face involvement with the French and the British.

The Final Step: Poland, 1939

Poland was almost inexorably his next victim. The Polish corridor dividing East Prussia from the rest of Germany was an affront to great-power psychology. So, too, was the separation from Germany of the Free City of Danzig, on the edge of the Polish corridor. Danzig was thoroughly German in language and tradition. The western regions of the Polish republic, which Hitler now also wanted, had been Prussian for over a hundred years when Poland was set up after World War I. Germans, even quite enlightened Germans, thought of the Poles, as indeed of all Slavs, as inferior people who would benefit from capable German supervision. Hitler began his Baltic adventure in March, 1939, when he took the port town of Memel from Poland's northern neighbor, Lithuania.

The critical issue in the tense half-year that led up to the outbreak of war on September 1, 1939, was not the possibility that Poland, unsupported by Britain and France, would undergo the same fate as Czechoslovakia. The British government publicly supported Poland by signing a pact of mutual assistance with her in April. Indeed, in the midst of the final week of crisis,

Chamberlain's foreign minister, Lord Halifax, sent a telegram to Hitler himself in which he made a rather pathetic appeal to the lessons of history:

It has been alleged that if His Majesty's Government had made their position more clear in 1914 the great catastrophe would have been avoided. Whether or not there is any force in that allegation, His Majesty's Government are resolved that on this occasion there shall be no such tragic misunderstanding. If the need should arise, they are resolved and prepared to employ without delay all the forces at their command. . . . I trust that Your Excellency will weigh with the utmost deliberation the considerations which I have put before you.*

The real critical point was the attitude of Russia. Hitler had an almost obsessive fear of a war on two fronts, a war against major powers to the east and to the west of the kind on which Germany had embarked in 1914. He was in fact drawn within two years into just such a war. Even if he had been faced in 1939 by the united front of Britain, France, and Russia in support of Poland, it is perfectly possible that he could not have restrained himself and his followers. One is tempted to see the Nazi top command as driven on by some abnormal and obsessive motivation and quite oblivious to ordinary considerations of self-interest. Hitler perhaps could no more keep his hands off Poland than an alcoholic can keep his hands off liquor. But, as events developed, Hitler was able to seize Poland without fear of Russian intervention. Indeed, he was able to arrange with Stalin a partition of Poland quite recognizably on the model of the eighteenth-century partitions.

Why did the Russians make their about-face? They had been deeply hurt by their exclusion from the negotiations over the Czechoslovakian crisis of the year before, an exclusion that they blamed primarily on

the British and the French. From the failure of the western powers to stand up to German violations of the Versailles Treaty ever since 1934, the Russians had drawn conclusions at least as disparaging to the western will to fight as those drawn by Hitler. In particular, they deeply distrusted the British Tories under Neville Chamberlain, for they believed that in many ways Tory Britain was more fundamentally hostile to communist Russia than even Nazi Germany was.

The Russians' mistrust of the West was not dispelled by the diplomatic mission that Britain and France sent, belatedly and grudgingly, to negotiate with Russia in the summer of 1939. The western powers proposed a mutual assistance pact, but the efforts of their negotiators were inept and halfhearted. Moreover, Chamberlain's government made a tactless choice of negotiators. One of them, Ironside, had been involved in the British intervention against the Reds at Archangel in the early days of the Bolshevik state—he had, indeed, been made a peer under the title "Baron of Archangel and of Ironside"; another was a mere functionary of the Foreign Office. The Russians like to deal with top people; they like to be made to feel important. Significantly, Hitler, who was also negotiating with Russia at the time, put Foreign Minister Ribbentrop himself on the job. So the Anglo-French overture to Moscow came to nothing. The Russian leaders had apparently reached the conclusion that the West was a broken reed, that if they themselves did not come to terms with Hitler he would attack them anyway.

Finally, the Russians were quite as distrustful of the Polish government as of anyone else. The western, especially the French, policy of encouraging the smaller powers of eastern Europe to act as counterweights to *both* Germany and Russia now bore its natural fruit. The Polish government would not accept Russia as protector; it would not, in these hectic months

* *Documents on British Foreign Policy, 1919-1939*, E. L. Woodward and R. Butler, eds. (London, 1954), 3rd series, Vol. II, No. 145.

of negotiation, consent to the passage of Russian troops in case of war with Germany. The Russians were tempted by the opportunity to recover lands in eastern Poland that they had lost in World War I and its aftermath. To the horror of the West, they signed at Moscow on August 23, 1939, a nonaggression pact with Germany, the famous—or infamous—"Hitler-Stalin pact." A week later, the German army marched into Poland. On September 3, Britain and France honored their obligations, and declared war on Germany. The twenty years' truce was at an end.

Democratic Policy in Review

Intellectuals —the men who write and teach and preach—in the western world have been harsh in their judgment of the foreign policies of the democracies in these twenty years. They have condemned not only France and Britain, but also the smaller states of Europe and the United States. The democracies seem to have stood by in impotence and frustration while in Italy, in Japan, in Germany, and in Spain societies formed and grew strong with the overt intention of destroying democracy on this earth. The democracies were committed by their most fundamental beliefs to the protection of independent nations from aggression. Yet from the Japanese invasion of Manchuria in 1931 to the German invasion of the rump of Czechoslovakia in 1939 there was a steady series of unmistakable aggressions in complete defiance of the existing fabric of international law. No democracy —and this includes the United States, with its long historic interest in the independence of China—did more than protest verbally. By the time the democracies were stung into action, their foes were strong and confident.

Yet it is not really difficult to understand why the democracies behaved as they did in these years. Britain, France, and the United States were the victors of 1918, and by the very fact of their victory they were on the defensive. Wisdom and luck might have made their defense more effective than it was, but nothing could have altered the fact that they were on the defensive. In the long past of our state-system, the defensive has always proved a difficult position, has always been—perhaps from the very nature of western culture with its drives toward change—at a disadvantage against aggression. This disadvantage seems by no means associated with democracies as such. Absolute monarchies have suffered quite as much from the difficulties of the defensive, as the failure of Metternich shows (see Chapter XII).

In the years between the two world wars, the normal tendency of the victors to relax was increased by some of the facts of democratic life. The western democracies were committed to an effort to secure for every citizen some minimum of material comforts; they were committed to the pursuit of happiness. Their normal tendency was to produce butter rather than guns. Their totalitarian opponents may well have been quite as "materialistic" as they, but for them the butter was to be attained in the future, and by means of the guns. In short, the German, Japanese, and Italian governments were able to get their societies to tighten their belts in order to make military preparation possible. It was exceedingly difficult for democratic governments to get such sacrifices from their citizens until war actually broke out.

III: *The Nature of the War*

The first world war of our century had, in its main theater, the Western Front, been one long siege. Since the military experts tended to fight it over and over again in their planning, both France and Germany in the 1930's built two confronting lines of fortifications on their common frontier. The Maginot Line, on the French side, and the Siegfried Line, on the German, were far more formidable than the improvised trenches of the war of 1914-1918. So it is not surprising that on the outbreak of hostilities in September, 1939, most people expected first, that the war would be decided primarily in the area between France and Germany, and second, that it would be a closely confined war of siege in the West, with at most diversional activity in other parts of the world.

But the war itself showed once more the perils of prediction in great human affairs. As Germany was joined by her Axis partners, Italy and Japan, and as the United States entered it, this second world war became much more truly a world war than the first had been. It was decided in Russia, in the Pacific, even in the Mediterranean, quite as much as in the West. And it turned out to be one of the most extraordinarily open wars of movement in history. Indeed, the armies of the British Montgomery and the German Rommel in North Africa moved through the desert with the freedom of nomad hordes of old; but the gasoline engine had replaced the horse.

It was also a war in which for the first time the airplane played a major role, a role foreshadowed in the fighting waged in Ethiopia and Spain during the 1930's. Over the water, the airplane, both land-based and carrier-based, soon established itself as a central factor in naval warfare; in the opinion of many experts, it had made the great warship obsolete. Over the land, the airplane soon established itself as an essential arm of the fire power of land armies, an arm that needed and in the end got careful integration with the ground forces. But even in this war the airplane did not live up to the advanced billing given it by its more imaginative proponents; it did not become the *sole* means of warfare, superseding all others. Air power by itself proved inadequate in the great test of 1940, when the Germans tried to reduce Britain from the air.

Aerial bombardment—toward the end of the war carried on by German pilotless aircraft and rocket missiles—did indeed bring the horrors of warfare back to the civilians of the cities. Military experts had been inclined to believe that civilians could not possibly stand aerial bombardment, and that any country whose cities were subject to a few such bombardments would be obliged to sue for peace. Yet European and Asian civilian populations proved able to stand up to months of bombardment. German civilian deaths from air bombardment have been estimated at about 500,000. Organized systems of shelter, partial dispersal of populations, the obvious but not previously noted fact that much of the space of modern cities is made up of streets, parks, gardens, churches, and other public buildings not used at night (when much of the bombing was done)—all combined to make it possible for the people of heavily bombed cities like Berlin and Tokyo to endure what were in effect front-line conditions.

Yet at the very end of the war a technical innovation was introduced that may indeed have altered radically the character of war, may indeed make any future war so unendurably destructive that it will at least be brief. This was the atomic bomb, developed in secrecy by American and British experts, and first used on the Japanese city of Hiroshima on August 6, 1945. A single bomb destroyed something over half the city. Somewhat less material damage was done by a second and somewhat different bomb dropped on Nagasaki, a hilly city, three days later. But over a hundred thousand people were killed in the two cities by the two bombs, an incidence of death that seems to justify fully the fears that the atomic bomb and its still more frightful hydrogen bomb successors have aroused in our own generation.

IV: Early Successes of the Axis

Polish and Finnish Campaigns

The first campaign of World War II reached a by no means unexpected conclusion. No one had seriously supposed that isolated Poland could possibly stand up for long against the German armed forces, or that Britain and France could possibly get into action rapidly enough to help their Polish ally decisively. Yet the speed of the German conquest surprised almost everyone. The German air force, the *Luftwaffe*, soon gained absolute command of the air, and used it to disrupt Polish communications and to spread terror with its dive bombers. Special German task forces, fully motorized, swept through and around the more primitively armed Poles. This was what the Germans called a *Blitzkrieg*, or lightning war. The German word was later simplified by the English into "blitz," and was used by them to apply to the German air bombardment of Britain in the years 1940-1941.

Hitler's new collaborator, Stalin, hastened to push the Russian armies in from the east on the helpless Poles. He also established Russian military bases in the Baltic republics of Estonia, Latvia, and Lithuania, which had been created out of Russian provinces at the close of World War I. "Mutual assistance" pacts between giant Russia and the tiny Baltic states were to be the entering wedge for their full occupation by Russia in 1940 and their amalgamation, as constituent republics, into the Soviet Union.

Fear of Germany, or an imperialistic desire to expand, or both, also drove the Russian leaders into a war with neighboring Finland for bases in the Baltic (November, 1939). The Russians, who had perhaps miscalculated the strength of their little opponent, did rather badly at first. By March, 1940, however, they had worn down the Finns; they secured their bases and annexed Finnish lands very close to the great Russian city of Leningrad. It seems quite possible that this "winter war" with Finland had a major effect in encouraging Hitler to his fateful decision of 1941 to make war on Russia. The German military experts drew from Russian difficulties in this war conclusions extremely disparaging to Russian capabilities.

"Phony War" and Blitzkrieg in the West

Meanwhile in the west what the British called the "phony war" was pursuing its uneventful course. The French and the British duly mobilized as in 1914, and as in 1914 the British sent a few divisions to the Continent. But the Germans refused to repeat the pattern of 1914. Occupied in Poland, they did nothing in the west. Occasionally a French patrol from the Maginot Line would exchange shots with a Ger-

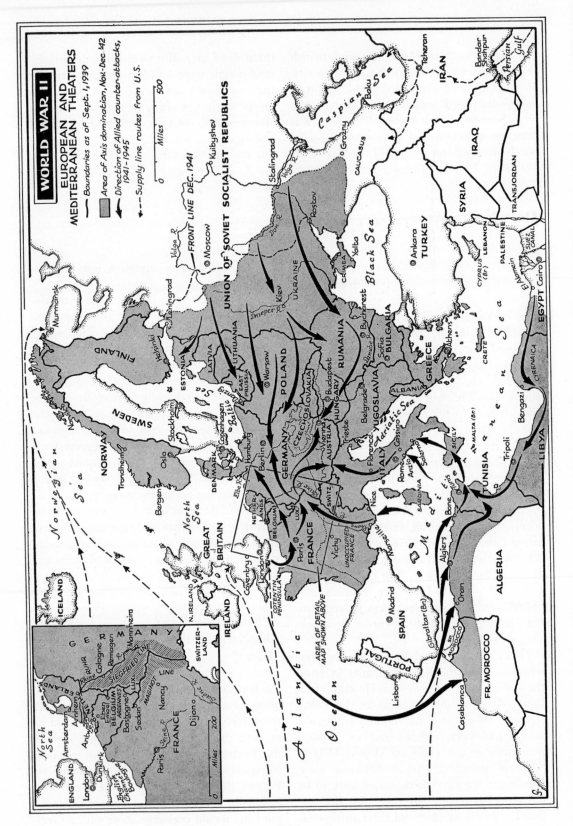

WORLD WAR II

EUROPEAN AND
MEDITERRANEAN THEATERS

— Boundaries as of Sept. 1, 1939

Area of Axis domination, Nov.-Dec. '42

→ Direction of Allied counter-attacks, 1941-1945

--- Supply line routes from U.S.

Miles
0   500

FRONT LINE DEC. 1941

man patrol, but for the most part the troops ate, slept, and went on leave as though they were merely in training.

The Germans, however, had no intention of sitting out a defensive war in the west. But not even modern warfare is wholly emancipated from the weather. The German general staff was not prepared to begin a decisive campaign in the west with the winter ahead. They waited until spring, and in April they made sure of their northern flank, as they had not in 1914, by making a sudden sea and air invasion of neutral Denmark and Norway. Denmark, totally unprepared, was occupied almost without resistance. Norway, also unprepared, made a brave showing. But neither the British nor the French were able to help her with more than token forces, and by the end of April important Norwegian resistance was broken. The Germans now had admirable bases for air and submarine action against the British.

The great blow was struck, without warning, on May 10, 1940, when the German armies, brilliantly supported in the air, invaded the Low Countries. Holland, spared in 1914, was this time invaded so that the Germans might make doubly sure of their northern flank. A carefully planned attack on the key Belgian fort of Eben Emael, an attack that had been rehearsed on a dummy of the fort set up inside Germany, was at once successful, and opened the way into the Low Countries.

In the era of weakness in the 1930's, both the Belgians and the Dutch had been extremely anxious to avoid compromising themselves by planning for joint resistance with Britain and France against a possible German attack. They were now to suffer the full consequences of their own policy of attempting to appease Hitler. For the crucial failure to hold the Germans in actual battle was in the Low Countries. We cannot be sure that a carefully co-ordinated plan among French, British, Belgians, and Dutch would have stopped Hitler. But

clearly the lack of such co-ordination was a major factor in the German success. Indeed, though much has since been written against the "Maginot mentality," it is a fact that the Germans did not take the Maginot Line by frontal assault, but outflanked it at the critical point where it tapered off along the Franco-Belgian border in the hilly region of the Ardennes.

Through the Ardennes the Germans poured their best motorized troops into France. In a Blitzkrieg that once more capitalized on the "lessons of 1914," the Germans resisted the temptation to turn at once on the prize of Paris, but instead drove straight through northern France to the Channel, where the port of Boulogne fell on May 26, a little over two weeks after the start of the campaign. By this stroke the Germans separated the British, Belgian, and part of the French troops from the bulk of the French armies to the south. The British had reacted at once to the German attack by replacing Neville Chamberlain with Winston Churchill as prime minister, and shortly afterward the French replaced General Gamelin with General Weygand as commander-in-chief. The British act was of major importance, comparable to the replacing of Asquith by Lloyd George in World War I. Chamberlain was neither a man of action nor an appealing or heroic figure; Churchill was to prove himself all this and more. Under him the British made a united front in the crisis.

The new leaders, in a desperate last moment, attempted to work out a plan for pinching off the adventurous German motorized thrust by a concerted attack from north and south. But the Belgians, badly disorganized, decided to capitulate, and neither the French nor the British could rally themselves to carry out the movement. In the last days of May and the first days of June the British did indeed achieve the miracle of the successful withdrawal of some 215,000 British and 120,000 French soldiers by sea from the beaches around

Prime Minister Winston Churchill, speaking in 1941.

push the attack on the French homeland at once. Here he was wholly and rapidly successful. The French under Weygand could not rally, and the Germans marched southward almost unopposed. The clear signal to the world that the rally of 1914 at the Marne would not be repeated was given on June 13, when the French declared Paris an "open city" and evacuated it without fighting.

"The Fall of France"

The battle of France was thus decided by mid-June. But the French might yet try to defend the south, or, failing that, use their navy and merchant marine to get as many men as possible across the Mediterranean into French North Africa. There, based on their great empire overseas, they might have continued with British aid the fight against the Germans. Some of the French leaders wished to do this, and in the crisis Winston Churchill made to the French the extraordinary offer of a complete governmental union of the two countries to continue the struggle. His offer was not accepted.

On June 16, Reynaud was supplanted by Marshal Pétain as prime minister, in what amounted to a kind of *coup d'état*. Pétain and his colleagues were determined on peace at any price, and this they got. On June 22, 1940, an armistice was signed at Compiègne at the spot where the armistice of November 11, 1918, had been signed. By this armistice the French withdrew from the war, handed over three-fifths of France, including the whole Atlantic and Channel coasts, to German occupation, and retained under strict German supervision no more than the central and Mediterranean regions. This "unoccupied France" was ruled from the little resort city of Vichy, where Pétain set up a French form of authoritarian, anti-democratic state of which he was "chief." History has labeled his govern-

Dunkirk at the northern tip of France. With useful protection from the Royal Air Force, an extraordinary flotilla of all sorts of vessels, including private yachts and motorboats, got the men off, though almost all their equipment had to be abandoned. Dunkirk was a courageous action, and one that did much to help British morale. But from German documents that fell to the Allies after the final defeat of Germany it is pretty clear that the miracle of Dunkirk was possible only because Hitler himself decided not to press home the destruction of the British forces penned on the coast, on the ground that Britain was no longer a real threat. At the last moment, Hitler too gave in to the lure of Paris, and decided to

ment simply "Vichy France." To most Frenchmen it was a German-imposed rule.

Some few of Pétain's collaborators were pro-German, convinced that totalitarianism was inevitable. But it is now clear that for most of them, even for men like the "collaborator" Laval, a dominant figure at Vichy, and indeed for Pétain himself, the dominant motive in those bewildering June days of 1940 was simply a desire to make terms with the inevitable. They were absolutely sure that Hitler had won the war. They did not believe that Britain had any chance of successfully resisting the German war machine that had crushed France. In this belief they were followed at first by the great majority by Frenchmen.

The new Vichy government attempted to remake France along conservative, indeed monarchist, lines that had not been practical politics since the *Seize Mai* of 1877 (see Chapter XIV). Symbolic of why the Vichy regime failed is its attempt to substitute for the great slogan "Liberty, Equality, Fraternity" a new trinity of "Labor, Family, Fatherland." Even an outsider can see that the new slogan lacked fire. More concretely, the Vichy regime from the start was compromised by its association with the hated Germans; born of defeat, it could do little in the few years it had to live before it died in the Allied victory.

Even in the bad days of June, 1940, a few Frenchmen, led by General Charles de Gaulle, who was flown out to London at the last moment, refused to give up the fight. De Gaulle, with British aid, set up a French National Committee with headquarters in London. A nucleus of French soldiers taken off the beach at Dunkirk, and a stream of refugees who came out of France by all sorts of means in the next few years, made up the "Free French" or "Fighting French." At home in France the "Resistance movement" gradually formed underground to prepare for eventual liberation. North Africa, strongest of the

French colonies, remained under the control of Vichy. But some parts of the colonies rallied to the Free French from the start. Notably in Equatorial Africa, under the leadership of the great Negro governor, Félix Eboué, a most useful base for Allied operations was secured from the first. Weak as these fighting French groups were in the early days, they were at least a rallying point. They were able to set up an effective radio center in England from which they conducted a skillful propaganda campaign against Vichy and the Germans, beamed across the Channel to the homeland, where, we now know, it achieved a large audience.

On June 10, Hitler's ally Mussolini had brought the Italians into the war against France and Britain, too late to affect the outcome of the battle of France. But this "stab in the back" further outraged American opinion, already alarmed by the Nazi successes. And Italy was now irrevocably engaged in the struggle, anxious to secure some kind of success that would offset the great gains of her German ally. The war, up

Hitler's elation after the armistice with France, 1940.

to this time confined to northern and western Europe, now spread to the Mediterranean.

The Battle of Britain

The Germans, for all their miracles of planning and execution, had not really worked out a way to deal with Britain. Hitler seems to have believed that with France out of the war Britain would see the light and make a separate peace, a peace of compromise in which Germany would dominate the continent of Europe and Britain would continue satisfied with her overseas empire. This division of the spoils, Hitler reiterated in public and private, should be eminently satisfactory; he did not threaten the British Empire. Yet for over four centuries Britain had gone to war rather than accept the kind of one-power domination over western and central Europe that Hitler exercised after the fall of France. The British, therefore, paid no attention at all to his peace feelers.

Hitler was counting heavily on the possibility that German submarines could eventually cut off British supplies of food and raw materials from overseas, and thus starve her into submission. But at best this must take a long time, and Hitler was impatient. The obvious thing to do was to attempt a landing in England. But the Germans had made no real preparation for amphibious warfare; they had no specially designed landing craft. Moreover, the German air force and the German navy were at odds over the best way of combining for an invasion across the Channel. A hastily assembled flotilla of miscellaneous vessels was badly damaged by British aircraft, and early in August, 1940, Hitler and Goering, his air marshal, made the fateful decision to try to do the job from the air.

The Battle of Britain that followed had two main phases. First, in August and September the Luftwaffe attempted in daylight bombing attacks to wipe out British airports and fighter planes. The Royal Air Force, admirably organized and directed, and using the new detection apparatus called radar to spot the attackers early, proved just barely strong enough to check the Germans. In the critical actions of September 16, some 185 German planes were brought down, a rate of loss that Goering felt the Germans could not stand. In one of his imperishable phrases, Churchill said of the British fighter pilots, "Never have so many owed so much to so few."

The second phase began in the autumn of 1940. The Germans sought by night bombing of major British industrial centers to destroy British production and to terrify the civilian population so that the government would be obliged to sue for peace. Neither aim was successful. Even at Coventry, an important center of the automotive industry, though grave damage was done, the industry was by no means knocked out. As for civilian morale, it is clear that these bombings strengthened the British will to resist. Civilian defense measures proved adequate to protect both persons and property from that extreme of destruction which might indeed have broken the will to resist. By winter, when the weather gave the British some respite, the Battle of Britain had been won.

Mediterranean and Balkan Campaigns

Hitler now faced the possibility of a long stalemate, something that conquerors like Napoleon in the past have rarely been able to face. Like Napoleon, Hitler turned at first to the obvious strategy of getting at Britain through her Mediterranean lifeline to India and the East. His ally Mussolini, already itching to expand in the Mediterranean, in October, 1940, invaded Greece from Albania—with no success. Just how far Hitler himself wanted to invest in action in this theater is not clear. Certainly he toyed with the idea of a campaign against the British fortress of Gibraltar through Spain, to be coordinated with Axis attacks in the eastern Mediterranean to clear that sea of the British. But the Spanish dictator Franco wanted too high a price from the French for his consent to a German march through Spain, and Hitler was unwilling to risk driving Vichy France, which still controlled French North Africa, too far. In the upshot, the Germans had to be content with backing up Mussolini in Greece and with an attack on Egypt from the Italian colony of Libya. Efforts to rouse native action against the British and French in the Near East were suppressed without grave difficulty by British and Free French action, and Turkey stood obstinately neutral.

Nevertheless, the German commitment to help the Italians in Greece took valuable German divisions away from another task in the spring of 1941, and as the Germans attempted to move overland through Yugoslavia they were involved in a costly guerrilla war. The British did their best to back up their Greek allies, but once more they were not strong enough. German air power crippled British naval power in the waters around Crete, and by June the Axis had conquered the Greek mainland and the islands.

The Invasion of Russia

The other task for which the German forces were to be used in in the spring of 1941 was the conquest of Russia. Hitler had firmly resolved not to repeat what he thought was the fateful mistake of Germany in 1914; he would not engage in a war on two fronts. Yet by his invasion of Russia in June, 1941—an invasion delayed for a perhaps decisive two months by the Balkan adventure—he committed himself to just such a war. Russia was indeed a tempting goal. The Nazi plan had always looked to the fertile areas of Poland and South Russia as the natural goal of German expansion, the *Lebensraum* (see p. 689) of German destiny. With the precedents of successful Blitzkrieg in Poland, western Europe, and now Greece, Hitler and his military experts believed that they could beat the Russians in a single campaign before winter set in. It was quite clear that neither Britain nor the United States—even though the latter should enter the war—could land armies in Europe in 1941. An attack on Russia, then, Hitler seems to have told himself, would not *really* create two fronts. Indeed, once Russia was conquered, as in Hitler's mind it was sure to be, the Germans would have no trouble disposing of Britain, and, if necessary, the United States.

Russia was not conquered in 1941. But it was a very close thing, closer perhaps than the Battle of Britain. Hitler's plan almost worked. There really was a successful Blitzkrieg. Within two months the Germans were at the gates of Leningrad, and in the south they had conquered the Ukraine by the end of October. Hundreds of thousands of Russian troops had been killed or taken prisoner. In sheer distance, the German armies had pushed more than twice as far as they had in France.

Yet, as the Russian winter closed in, the Germans had taken neither Moscow nor Leningrad. Russian heavy industry had been in part transferred to the remote Urals, and existing plants there and in Siberia had been strengthened. The United States was beginning to send in supplies. The vast resources of Russian manpower were still adequate for Russian needs. The government had not collapsed, and national spirit was high. Moreover, the Germans had shown once more, as they had in the Battle of Britain, that their boasted planning was far from perfect. Their troops were not sufficiently equipped to stand the rigors of a Russian winter. Confident that one summer and autumn would be enough to finish the business, the German planners had left the winter to take care of itself. Indeed, between December, 1941, and May, 1942, the Russians regained much useful ground.

American Policy

Meanwhile, the Germans had fallen into a second fatal involvement. Obsessed with what he thought were the disastrous failures of German policy in World War I, Hitler had sought to keep out of war with the United States. Although the United States had a strong isolationist party, and even a handful of Axis sympathizers, American opinion had from the very beginning of the attack on Poland in 1939 been far more nearly unanimous against the Germans and Italians than it had been against the Central Powers in 1914. With the fall of France in 1940, anti-Axis sentiment grew stronger, reinforced by a feeling that if Hitler had his way in Europe the United States would be marked out as his next victim.

Between June, 1940, and December, 1941, the Roosevelt administration, with the consent of the Congress and with the general—though not unanimous—backing of public opinion, took a series of steps "short of war" in aid of Britain and later Russia. By conventional nineteenth-century standards of international relations, these steps were far from being in accord with America's technical status as a neutral; they would have given Hitler ample legal justification for declaring war against the United States. The American government transferred to the British fifty "over-age" destroyers in exchange for Atlantic naval bases in British colonies, supplied the British with all sorts of arms, and used the American navy to help get these supplies across the Atlantic. Above all, in March, 1941, by the so-called "Lend-Lease Act" the United States agreed to supply materials needed for defense, including foodstuffs, to "any country whose defense the President deems vital to the defense of the United States." Supplies at once began rolling into England, and later to other allies in the struggle against the Axis, without the unfortunate complications produced by the war-debt methods of World War I.

Yet Hitler still did not let himself get involved in war against the United States. He had, however, firm commitments to aid Japan. And Japan, controlled by a militarist group, had taken advantage of the fall of France and the Netherlands and the weakness of Britain to speed up vastly the policy of expansion in Asia that she had begun in Manchuria as far back as 1931. She early took advantage of the fall of France to penetrate into French Indo-China. She continued to press her campaign on the mainland of China. The American government, which had never in the days of technical peace in the 1930's been willing to accept Japanese conquests in China, did not now abandon its policy of opposition to what it considered Japanese aggression. It is indeed highly likely that had the American government been willing to allow Japan a free hand to do what she liked in the Far East there would have been no Pearl Harbor. But short of such complete abandonment of the previous American policy in the Far East, it is unlikely that the United States could have kept out of war with Japan.

Pearl Harbor and After

In the summer and autumn of 1941, the American government took steps to freeze Japanese credits in the United States, to close Japanese access to raw materials, and to get the Japanese to withdraw from China and Indo-China. Negotiations toward these ends were going on between the Japanese and the Americans when on December 7, 1941, the Japanese without warning struck with carrier-based airplanes at the American naval base at Pearl Harbor in Hawaii. Grave damage was done to ships and installations, but American power in the Pacific was by no means destroyed. And the consequence was the immediate declaration of war against Japan by the United States. Germany and Italy honored their obligations to their Axis partner by declaring war against the United States on December 11. The war was now literally a world war.

Although the United States was incomparably better prepared than she had been in 1917, she was still at a disadvantage. Against Germany she could for the moment do no more than continue, indeed increase, aid to Britain and Russia by Lend-Lease and take full part in the struggle against the German submarines. Against Japan she was almost as powerless. Her Pacific outposts of Guam, Wake Island, and the Philippines fell in rapid succession to Japanese arms. Nor could the British and the exiled Dutch governments protect their colonies in Southeast Asia. By the spring of 1942, the Japanese had taken Malaya from the British and Indonesia from the Dutch, and had virtual control of Siam and Burma. They seemed poised for an attack on Australia.

V: The Victory of the United Nations

The Turning Points There were several turning points in the struggle. The earliest was a series of naval actions in which Japanese expansion was stopped. In these actions, carrier-based airplanes played a decisive role. On May 7, 1942, in the battle of the Coral Sea in the southwest Pacific, Allied sea and air power halted a possible Japanese invasion of Australia and its protecting islands. In June, American sea and air power dispersed a Japanese fleet that was aiming at the conquest of Midway Island. Although the Japanese landed on American territory in the Aleutians, they never seriously threatened Hawaii or Alaska.

In the West, the Americans and the British were as yet unwilling to respond to Russian pressure for a "second front" on the European mainland. But they were able in November, 1942, to effect a series of landings in French North Africa. Secret negotiations with anti-Axis elements among the French in North Africa were not completely successful, and the landings in Morocco were sharply though briefly resisted by the Vichy French. None the less, the Allies were rapidly established in force in Morocco and Algeria.

The Libyan segment of the long North African coast had been held by the Germans and their Italian allies since the beginning of the war in the Mediterranean, and there had been seesaw campaigns in these desert areas, campaigns that recaptured some of the adventure, even romance, of wars of old. At the time of the North African landings, the British under General Montgomery were holding a defensive line inside the Egyptian frontier, but on October 23, 1942, the British started on an offensive which was planned to co-ordinate with that of General Eisenhower, commander of the Allied forces in French North Africa, in the classic maneuver of catching the enemy in a vise. The Germans responded quickly to the threat, and succeeded in reinforcing their African armies through Tunis, which was delivered to them by the Vichy authorities. The planned expulsion of the Germans and Italians from North Africa was thus delayed, but the vise closed slowly. In May, 1943, Free French, British, and American troops took the last Axis strongholds of Tunis and Bizerte, and accepted the surrender of some three hundred thousand Axis troops.

The North African campaign had clearly

been a turning point. The Allies had successfully made large-scale amphibious landings, and they had annihilated one of the most renowned of Axis forces, commanded by one of the few German generals to strike the imagination of the world, Rommel, the "desert fox." North Africa was by no means a great central operation, but it was nevertheless a major campaign in which the Allies gained confidence and prestige.

The great turning point on land was, however, the successful Russian defense of Stalingrad, a defense that turned into an attack in the same month (November, 1942) that saw the Allied landing in North Africa. After their check in the winter of 1941-42, the Germans had turned their Russian summer offensive of 1942 away from Leningrad and Moscow, and toward the oil-rich regions of southeastern European Russia. The Germans were already beginning to suffer oil shortages, partly because of Allied bombing, but even more because, though they held the oil fields of Rumania, they simply did not have oil enough for the ravenous demands of mechanical warfare. This push toward the Russian oil fields carried the Germans a prodigious distance inside Russia, over a thousand miles from their original starting point. But again it failed, falling just short of the really rich oil fields of Grozny and Baku. Russian distance and Russian manpower, and the Russian ability to take punishment, were too much for these overextended Germans. Their armies were pinched off at Stalingrad, and early in 1943 the Russians started the long march that was to take them to Berlin two years later.

The Battle of Supply

A much less spectacular turning point than the engagements in the Coral Sea, in North Africa, and at Stalingrad was the Allied victory in the battle of supply. Yet this victory was of even greater importance, since naval and military successes ultimately depend on supplies. Even for Russia, an important source of supplies was the United States. But the United States was separated from its allies —and its enemies—by water, and all but the most precious and least bulky supplies, which could go by air, had to move across the seas. If the Germans could stop this movement, or even reduce it greatly, they might still be able to win in spite of the overwhelming resources of the Allies. They made important improvements in their submarines, notably the schnorkel, a device that enabled submarines to travel submerged for great distances. Submarine crews and commanders were well trained and resourceful. But there were not enough submarines, and the countermeasures of the Allies—radar, co-ordination of naval vessels and aircraft, the convoy system, and others—slowly reduced the proportion of sinkings.

Early in 1942, after Pearl Harbor, the rate of sinkings had been really dangerous, and German submarines had operated close to the Atlantic coast of the United States. But by the end of 1942 the statistics showed a turn of the tide, and in the summer of 1943 the Allies were confident enough to announce publicly that the number of sinkings from U-boat action in the first half of 1943 was only a quarter of what it had been in the first half of 1942.

The Axis on the Defensive

In the last two years of the war, the Axis powers were on the defensive. Both in Europe and in Asia the coalition forces attacked with land forces along definite lines of march; these were "campaigns" of the traditional kind. But the way for these armies was made easier by two new factors in warfare, air power and modern propaganda, or "psychological warfare." These new methods did not "win"

the war by themselves, but they were useful adjuncts, and they undoubtedly hastened the process. Air bombardment, at least until the atomic bomb at Hiroshima, was never quite the perfect annihilation that the prophets of air power had preached. The Germans put some of their key production underground. Allied "precision" bombing rarely reached perfection. But as the superior Allied air power grew, as it was used systematically to destroy enemy capabilities in critical materials like ball bearings and oil, and as American airplanes dropped incendiary bombs on the relatively flimsy Japanese cities, it did much to destroy the Axis will and power to resist.

On Germany and Italy the attack by land was pressed in three directions—by the Russians from the east, and by the British, French, Americans, and the smaller Allies from the south and from the west. In the south the Allies moved over to Sicily in a successful amphibious operation (July, 1943) within two months of their final victory in North Africa, and from Sicily they moved in another six weeks across the Straits of Messina to the mainland of Italy. Yet the Italian campaign was never quite the great success the Allies hoped it would be in these earlier days. The Allied victories of the summer of 1943 were, however, sufficient to put Italy itself for the most part out of the war. High officers of the Italian army and others close to the king engineered a *coup* in July which brought about the fall and imprisonment of Mussolini and the beginnings of negotiations between the Allies and the new government headed by Marshal Badoglio.

But the Germans were quite unwilling to abandon the peninsula, as much for reasons of prestige as for military reasons. A detachment of German troops rescued Mussolini from his Apennine prison (September, 1943), and set him up as the head of a "Fascist Republic." The former *Duce* continued in this post until he was executed by partisans in April, 1945. Meantime, Italy had a civil as well as a foreign war on her hands. Her people were for the most part worn out and anxious for peace, but the two minorities, the Fascist-Axis group and the anti-Fascist pro-Allied group, fought on. In June, 1944, the Allies succeeded, after particularly severe fighting around Cassino, in breaking through to Rome, and by August they were in Florence. They did not really penetrate any farther until the final collapse of the Germans in the early months of 1945.

The Defeat of Germany

The great Allied push in the west, it was finally decided at the Teheran conference of Churchill, Roosevelt, and Stalin (December, 1943), would be in France. After meticulous preparation, the long-awaited landings in France began on June 6, 1944. The Allies had chosen the Norman coast at the base of the Cotentin (Cherbourg) peninsula, and seem thereby to have gained some initial advantage of surprise, for the German high command believed the landings would come farther north and east along the Channel coast. The Germans had in their four years of occupancy fortified the French coastline with great thoroughness. But the Allies had also had those four years for study, invention, and planning. In the test, Allied landing craft, amphibious trucks, naval and air support—by now the Luftwaffe had almost been driven from the skies—artificial harbors, and a well-organized supply system proved sufficient to gain a beachhead for the land forces. From this beachhead, a little over a month after "D-Day," they were able to break out at Avranches and sweep the Germans back across the Seine in a great flanking movement led by the American General Patton's Third Army.

A long-planned auxiliary landing on the French Mediterranean coast and a march north up the Rhone-Saône valleys was launched on August 15, 1944, and met very little resistance. Everywhere the French, by now well organized for resistance, welcomed the liberating forces, some of whom were French and French colonials fighting as heirs of the Free French of 1940. Paris, a symbol rather than a mere place, was liberated toward the end of August after its inhabitants had staged an uprising, barricades and all, in the style of 1848, against the German garrison.

The Germans were beaten, but not disorganized. In July, 1944, an attempt to assassinate Hitler and to pave the way for negotiations was made by conservative elements, both military and civilian. But Hitler survived the bomb intended for him, and the Nazis retained their firm grip on the German state. The Allies were encouraged by their rapid successes in July and August to try to destroy the German armies before winter, or to cut them off from their homeland. Patton's mechanized troops ran out of fuel, however; the new German pilotless planes and rockets delayed the full use of Antwerp as a port of supply; and by late autumn it was clear that the Germans had retired in good order to their own Siegfried Line.

From the east, the Russians had been pushing on relentlessly ever since the turning of the tide at Stalingrad. In the campaign of 1943, while the western Allies were busy in Italy, the Russians won back most of their own territories that had been lost in 1941 and 1942. They kept up the pressure during the winter, and started an early spring campaign in the south. By the autumn of 1944, the Russians had been able to sweep through half-hearted resistance from Hitler's Balkan satellite governments to a juncture with the Yugoslav communist guerrillas under Tito, and were ready for the attack on Hungary. In the center and north, they had recovered all their own territory, and were ready to attack Germany itself from the east.

The year 1945 saw the rapid conclusion of the Battle of Germany. The Russians had not stopped for winter, but had pressed on through Poland to menace Berlin early in March. The western Allies broke through the Siegfried Line in February, crossed the Rhine, and entered the heart of Germany. Early in February, 1945, the leaders of the three great Allied powers, Stalin, Churchill, and Roosevelt, met at Yalta in the Crimea and confirmed final plans for the conquest of Germany. It was plain that the Germans, whose key industries had been so riddled from the air that they no longer could support their armies adequately, and whose manpower had been reduced to the very bottom, could not hold out for long. But the Allied planners were anxious to prevent, or at least to check, the race to be the first to arrive in Germany; and they wanted to arrange peacefully for demarcations between the parts of Germany that each ally was to occupy. The decision to give the Russians the honor of taking Berlin is one that, with many other decisions reached in the conference at Yalta, has since been severely criticized in the West. At the time, however, it seemed a natural decision, a legitimate recognition that during the two years of successful offensive against the Germans the Russians had worn down many more German divisions than had the western Allies.

The Russians fought their way into a Berlin already pulverized by the air power of the western Allies. Hitler went down to his death, as he had long promised, in a Germanic funeral pyre at his Berlin headquarters. Though his body was never found and identified, there can be no serious doubt concerning his fate.

The Allied advance into Germany revealed for the first time the full ghastliness of Nazi treatment of slave laborers from

Nordhausen concentration camp. Bodies of Gestapo victims.

conquered lands, of political opponents, and of Jews, Poles, and other German-styled "inferior" peoples. One after another, the concentration camps were liberated—Auschwitz, Belsen, Buchenwald, Dachau, Nordhausen, and others. And the world was appalled at the gas ovens that had claimed so many victims, at the piles of emaciated corpses not yet cremated, and at the pitiful state of the prisoners who had survived. This was one of the horrors of war whose reality exceeded the grimmest expectations of Allied opinion.

By May 8, 1945, Churchill and Truman (who had become the American president on Roosevelt's death in April) were able to announce the end of German resistance, the day of victory in Europe, V-E Day. It was symbolic of difficulties to come that Stalin was offended because the western Allies had accepted from some of the German army leaders a formal surrender at Rheims in France. He chose to announce separately, on Russia's part, the final victory over Germany, and not until the next day.

The Defeat of Japan

V-J Day, the day of victory in Japan, was now the great goal of Allied effort. Russia had carefully refrained from adding Japan to its formal enemies as long as Germany was still a threat. Britain and the United States, on the other hand, were anxious to win Russia as a formal fighting ally against the Japanese. This natural desire—natural in the sense of historical precedent, for coalitions in the past have usually sought to rally as many allies as possible—was responsible for many of the concessions made to Russia in the last months of the German war.

The two years of Allied successes against Germany had also been two years of Allied successes against Japan. The attack on Japan had been pressed home in three main

directions. First, in a process that the American press soon christened "island-hopping," the American navy drove straight toward Japan from the central Pacific. One after another, the small island bases that stood in the way were reduced by American naval forces, which used both air support and the amphibious methods that were being worked out simultaneously in Europe and North Africa. The names of these small islands are now a part of the litany of American arms—Tarawa, Kwajalein, Iwo Jima, Okinawa.

Second, in a series of operations calling for the close co-operation of air, sea, and land forces the Americans and Australians, with help from other British elements, worked their way up the southwest Pacific through the much larger islands of the Solomons, New Guinea, and the Philippines. The base for this campaign, which was under the command of the American General MacArthur, was Australia and such outlying islands as New Caledonia and the New Hebrides. The start of the campaign goes back to the first major offensive step in the Far East, the dramatic and difficult seizure of Guadalcanal in the Solomons by the United States Marines on August 7, 1942. These campaigns involved jungle fighting of the hardest sort, slow and painful work. But by October, 1944, the sea forces had won the great battle of the Philippine Sea and had made possible the successful landing of MacArthur's troops on Leyte and the reconquest of the Philippine Islands themselves from the Japanese.

The third attack on the "Greater East Asia Co-Prosperity Sphere" of Japanese expansion came from the south, in the "CBI" —the China-Burma-India Theater. No brief narrative can do justice to the complex interweaving of events in this theater, where the main effort of the Allies was to get material support in to Chiang Kai-shek and the Chinese Nationalists at Chungking (see Chapter XXI) and, if possible, to damage the Japanese position in Burma, Thailand

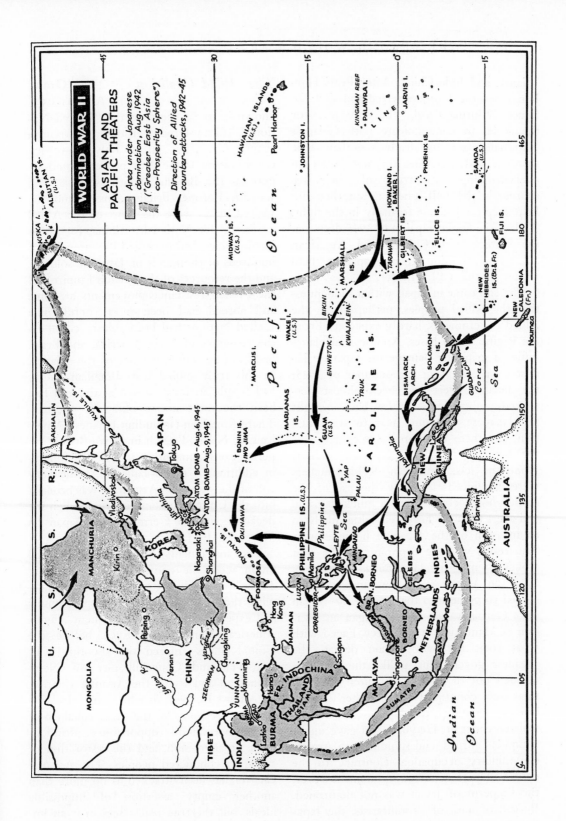

WORLD WAR II

ASIAN AND PACIFIC THEATERS

Area under Japanese domination, Aug. 1942 ("Greater East Asia co-Prosperity Sphere")

Direction of Allied counter-attacks, 1942–45

ALEUTIAN IS. (U.S.)

KISKA I.

MIDWAY IS. (U.S.)

HAWAIIAN ISLANDS (U.S.)

Pearl Harbor

JOHNSTON I.

KINGMAN REEF
PALMYRA I.

JARVIS I.

LINE IS.

PHOENIX IS.

SAMOA (U.S.)

FIJI IS.

NEW HEBRIDES IS. (Br. & Fr.)

NEW CALEDONIA (Fr.)

Noumea

ELLICE IS.

HOWLAND I.
BAKER I.

GILBERT IS.

TARAWA

MARSHALL IS.

BIKINI

ENIWETOK

KWAJALEIN

WAKE I. (U.S.)

MARCUS I.

TRUK

CAROLINE IS.

YAP

PALAU

GUAM (U.S.)

MARIANAS IS.

BONIN IS.

IWO JIMA

Pacific Ocean

Coral Sea

GUADALCANAL

SOLOMON IS.

BISMARCK ARCH.

NEW GUINEA

Hollandia

BORNEO

CELEBES

NETHERLANDS INDIES

Br. N. BORNEO

MINDANAO

LEYTE

Philippine Sea

PHILIPPINE IS. (U.S.)

LUZON

Manila

CORREGIDOR

FORMOSA

Hong Kong

HAINAN

Saigon

FR. INDOCHINA

THAILAND (SIAM)

MALAYA

Singapore

SUMATRA

JAVA

Darwin

AUSTRALIA

Indian Ocean

RYUKYU IS.

OKINAWA

ATOM BOMB – Aug. 6, 1945

ATOM BOMB – Aug. 9, 1945

Nagasaki

Hiroshima

Kobe

Tokyo

JAPAN

KOREA

KURILE IS.

SAKHALIN

Vladivostok

MANCHURIA

Kirin

Peiping

CHINA

Yenan

Chungking

Kunming

BURMA

Lashio

INDIA

TIBET

MONGOLIA

U. S. S. R.

SZECHWAN

YUNNAN

Yangtze R.

Yellow R.

Shanghai

Hanoi

Mandalay

765

(Siam), and Indo-China. After Pearl Harbor, when the Japanese seized and shut the famous "Burma Road," the only way for the Allies to communicate with Chiang's Nationalists was by air. It is perhaps true that the western Allies did not invest an overwhelming proportion of their resources in this CBI Theater, but they did help keep the Chinese formally in the fight. And, as the final campaign of 1945 drew on, the British, with Chinese and American aid, were fighting three Japanese field armies in this CBI Theater.

The end came in Japan with a suddenness that the Allied peoples, perhaps even the Allied governments, hardly expected. From the Pacific island bases, American airplanes inflicted crippling damage on Japanese industry in the spring and summer of 1945; the Japanese fleet had been almost destroyed; submarine warfare had brought the Japanese economy near to strangulation; and there was impressive evidence of the declining morale of Japanese soldiers. None the less, American decision-makers were convinced that only the use of the atomic bomb could bring a quick decision and avert the very heavy casualties likely in an invasion of the Japanese home islands. The result was the dropping of the first atomic bomb, on Hiroshima, August 6, 1945. On August 8, the Russians, who had agreed to come into the war against Japan once Germany was beaten, began an invasion of Manchuria in full force. Faced with what they felt was certain defeat, the Japanese government, unlike the German, decided not to make a last-ditch stand in their own country. On September 2, after brief negotiations, the Japanese made formal surrender at Tokyo. Japan gave up its conquests abroad, and submitted to American military occupation. Contrary to the desires of part of Allied opinion, however, the Emperor of Japan was not dethroned. Purged of most of its militarists, the Japanese government continued to rule under Allied—actually American—supervision.

The Allied Coalition

The "Grand Alliance," known in its last years as the "United Nations," had mustered overpowering strength against Germany, Japan, Italy, and such collaborators as the Axis powers could secure in the Balkans, Southeast Asia, and western Europe. Britain, Russia, and the United States were the heart of the Allied coalition. But Nationalist China, for all its inefficiencies, had occupied the attention of hundreds of thousands of Japanese soldiers, and the resources of the French Empire and the French resistance movements at home and abroad had been most useful. The United Nations had been able to count on the resources of Latin America, and Brazil had been an active member of the alliance. In this truly global war, Brazilian troops had fought in Italy, which at the end had been the most cosmopolitan of theaters. There American (including Japanese-American, or Nisei), French imperial, British imperial, Polish, and other troops had fought, in addition to the Brazilians. At the very end of the war, even Argentina was brought into the United Nations coalition, when she declared war on Germany and Japan on March 27, 1945.

The instruments of continuing Allied union were the conferences of the "Big Three"—Churchill, Roosevelt, and Stalin—with their political and military advisers and experts, and the more frequent Anglo-American conferences. Even before the United States entered the shooting war, Roosevelt and Churchill met off Newfoundland and issued the Atlantic Charter, on August 14, 1941, in which they declared for the freedom of the seas, equality of access to economic opportunity, abandonment of aggression, and the restoration of rights to conquered peoples. The Atlantic Charter has been attacked as no more than another empty assertion of impossible ideals, but the true realist sees in it an important step in rallying world opinion against the Axis. Later, formal conferences

—between Roosevelt and Churchill at Casablanca (January, 1943) and Quebec (August, 1943), and among the "Big Three" at Teheran (December, 1943) and Yalta (February, 1945)—brought to a head consultations that had been steadily carried on at lower political and military levels.

There were always grave military and political matters to be ironed out. It was not easy to maintain even the Anglo-American collaboration, which was perhaps the closest military collaboration between two major sovereign powers ever achieved. For the actual direction of operations in the field, the British and Americans de-

cided to set up, not just the sort of supreme command the Allies painfully achieved late in World War I under Foch (see p. 595), but a complete intermeshing of staffs. All down the line, an American in command always had a Britisher as his second, and a Britisher in command always had an American as his second. In the pinch, and in spite of normal national jealousies, the arrangement worked. An anecdote about General Eisenhower from North African days relates that he sent an American officer home, not because he called his immediate superior a so-and-so, but because he called him an *English* so-and-so. At the

Hiroshima, after the atomic bomb hit. The center of the blast was near the building in upper center.

highest level, the Combined Chiefs of Staff, in close touch with top American and British government officials, did the over-all planning. The Russians were never brought into such close military co-operation, and in the field the Russians always fought on their own.

Political Issues

A political issue that bulked large at the time with liberals seems not to have seriously divided the Allies during the war itself. This is the issue of "unconditional surrender." Here recent history had an overpowering influence on the policy adopted. Hitler had simply followed widespread German opinion in insisting that in World War I Germany had not really been defeated in the field, but had been betrayed by the false promises of Wilson's Fourteen Points into surrendering while still undefeated. This time the Allied leaders were determined to give the Germans no excuse for a future rallying point of this sort. The Germans must be beaten unmistakably, and Allied troops must enter Berlin as conquerors. There must be no political negotiation at all, simply unconditional military surrender. There was some opposition to this policy during the war, at least in lands of free political expression like Britain and the United States. This opposition rested partly on humanitarian grounds, but also on the belief that the prospect of unconditional surrender would inevitably stiffen the German will to resist, and would unite the nation behind Hitler instead of allowing Allied psychological warfare its full effect by promising anti-Nazi elements some reward for deserting the Nazi cause. In retrospect, it does not seem that Hitler would ever have negotiated with the Allies; and after the failure of the attempt to kill him with a bomb in July, 1944, there was little chance that the Germans themselves would overthrow the Nazi government.

Another political problem made a much clearer rift between the British and the Americans. The underlying issue was just how far anti-German elements in France, Italy, and other occupied lands must go in proving that they were good honest democrats in order to secure the backing of the democratic western powers. Here the difference in the underlying tone of American and British policies was evident in the views of Roosevelt and Churchill. Roosevelt was convinced that if the Allies did not interfere to support scheming conservatives and reactionaries in the occupied lands, but instead allowed their peoples to choose their form of government freely, then they would choose democracy. Churchill was much less idealistic. He was eager to use any elements that were hostile to the Germans, even if their hostility was quite recent, and he had little faith in the capacity or desire of peoples like the Italians for Anglo-Saxon democracy. Therefore he was quite willing to back Badoglio and the monarchists in Italy; Roosevelt kept insisting that the Italians wanted and needed a republic.

In French politics the issue was further complicated by Roosevelt's suspicions of De Gaulle, whose firm resistance in June, 1940, had made him the inevitable leader of the French movement for liberation. To Roosevelt, De Gaulle seemed a potential man on horseback, no better than Boulanger or Napoleon III. To Churchill, De Gaulle seemed indeed difficult, a man obsessed with the need to restore the greatness of France, but an indispensable ally. As it turned out, the Gaullists, in collaboration with the organized French resistance in the homeland, did take over the civilian administration of French territory as it was liberated, and France by free popular vote restored in the Fourth Republic a form of government essentially like that of the Third. In Italy, the liberated people voted the establishment of a republic. What had threatened at one time to be a serious difficulty between the idealistic American policy and the realistic British policy was resolved by the action of the liberated people themselves.

But the political issue that has bulked largest since World War II was by no means so clear an issue during the war itself. This is the problem of Russian domination in eastern and southeastern Europe. It is easy to say that at Yalta the western powers took much too soft a line with the Russians, allowed them to push their armies much too far westward, and relied foolishly on Russian promises to permit free elections in Poland, Hungary, Czechoslovakia, and the Balkans. This criticism may be supplemented by the old British motif of the "soft under-belly," by maintaining that the western powers should have struck as soon as possible, perhaps in 1943, from the Mediterranean into the Danube Valley in order to have arrived there ahead of the Russians. Proponents of these criticisms present us with an Iron Curtain that would then have been drawn far to the east of where it now is, with an eastern and a southeastern Europe that would now be democratic and on the side of the West rather than on the side of the Russians.

The chief trouble with this argument is that it fails to take into account two basic facts. First, most of the small eastern European countries had no real tradition of western-style democracy; most of them had moved toward fascist totalitarianism before World War II (see Chapter XX).

Second, during the war itself it was by no means clear to western leaders, or to western public opinion, that the Germans and the Japanese would be beaten so readily. Even leaders like Churchill, who seems never really to have trusted the Russians and who was to coin the phrase "the Iron Curtain" soon after the war, did not dare risk losing the aid of Russian manpower and material resources during the war itself. Even in 1945, at Yalta, with Japan still very much in the fight, appeasement of the Russians seemed absolutely essential.

In the Far East, political problems seemed less serious—at least in wartime. There was general agreement that the Chinese Nationalists, however corrupt and inefficient their government was, had to be supported against the Japanese. Nor did the final decision to accept the continuance on the throne of the Japanese emperor arouse serious opposition in the West. The critical decisions on the Far East were rather the work of the troubled period after V-E and V-J days, when to the bitter disappointment of most western peoples it became clear that the peace was likely for some time to be no more than a continuation of war. Indeed, there was no peace, and these years deserve a term that was soon coined, the years of "cold war." The once "colonial" peoples throughout the world were now roused against "imperialism." It is to the many problems that these people set for the triumphant western powers that we now turn.

Reading Suggestions on the Second World War

General Accounts

W. S. Churchill, *The Second World War*, 6 vols. (Boston: Houghton Mifflin, 1948-1953). Magisterial account by a chief architect of Allied victory, the first volume reviews international affairs between the wars.

Q. Howe, *A World History of Our Own Times*, Vol. II (N.Y.: Simon & Schuster, 1953). Survey by a capable and opinionated American publicist.

E. H. Carr, *The Twenty Years' Crisis* (London: Macmillan, 1946). A stimulating review of inter-war diplomacy by a capable and opinionated Englishman.

J. F. C. Fuller, *The Second World War* (N.Y.: Duell, Sloane, and Pearce, 1949); and C. Falls, *The Second World War*, 2nd ed. (London: Methuen, 1948). Two succinct and very useful military accounts. Both are written from a British viewpoint.

Special Studies

F. Gilbert and G. A. Craig, eds., *The Diplomats, 1919-1939* (Princeton: Princeton Univ. Press, 1953). A helpful symposium.

A. Wolfers, *Britain and France between Two Wars* (N.Y.: Harcourt, Brace, 1940). A solid analysis of the foreign policies of the two powers.

S. R. Smith, *The Manchurian Crisis, 1931-1932* (N.Y.: Columbia Univ. Press, 1948). Monograph on the crisis that marked the watershed between the post-war and the pre-war periods.

J. W. Wheeler-Bennett, *Munich: Prologue to Tragedy* (London: Macmillan, 1948); and L. B. Namier, *Diplomatic Prelude, 1938-1939* (London: Macmillan, 1948). Good studies of the last international crises before World War II.

W. L. Langer and S. E. Gleason, *The Challenge to Isolation, 1937-1940* (N.Y.: Harper, 1952), and *The Undeclared War, 1940-1941* (N.Y.: Harper, 1953). Solid studies of America's role.

C. C. Tansill, *Back Door to War: The Roosevelt Foreign Policy* (Chicago: Regnery, 1952). Representative work of the school of writers who castigate Roosevelt for allegedly pushing America into war.

H. F. Armstrong, *Chronology of Failure* (N.Y.: Macmillan, 1940); "Pertinax" (André Géraud), *The Gravediggers of France* (Garden City: Doubleday, 1944); M. Bloch, *Strange Defeat* (N.Y.: Oxford Univ. Press, 1949). Three perceptive studies of the French defeat in 1940.

A. J. Liebling, ed., *The Republic of Silence* (N.Y.: Harcourt, Brace, 1947). Excellent collection of materials pertaining to the French resistance movement.

C. Wilmot, *The Struggle for Europe* (N.Y.: Harper, 1952). Important statement of the thesis that the Allies should have struck at the "soft under-belly" of the Axis powers, thereby saving eastern Europe from communism.

A. Weber, *Farewell to European History; or, the Conquest of Nihilism* (London: Kegan Paul, Trench, Trubner, 1947). A German sociologist reviews—and regrets—his country's part in the crises of World War II.

In addition, many detailed histories of special aspects of World War II have been published, as have the memoirs of some of the leading participants. The following examples of particular interest to American readers may be cited: In the first category, the multi-volumed *United States Army in World War II* (Washington: Department of the Army, 1947—), and the dozen volumes of S. E. Morison, *History of United States Naval Operations in World War II* (Boston: Little, Brown, 1947—); in the second category, D. D. Eisenhower, *Crusade in Europe* (N.Y.: Doubleday, 1948).

Historical Fiction

N. Mailer, *The Naked and the Dead* (N.Y.: Bantam Books, 1954); I. Shaw, *The Young Lions* (N.Y.: New American Library). Characteristic examples of the American novel of World War II.

H. P. M. Brown, *A Walk in the Sun* (N.Y.: Knopf, 1944). Unusually good novel about the Italian campaign.

N. Monsarrat, *The Cruel Sea* (N.Y.: Pocket Books); H. Wouk, *The Caine Mutiny* (N.Y.: Doubleday). Two justly popular novels about the naval aspects of World War II.

A. J. Guérard, *Maquisard* (N.Y.: Longmans, Green, 1948). Good novel about the French resistance.

Fitzroy Maclean, *Escape to Adventure* (Boston: Little, Brown, 1950). Not fiction, but true adventure; an antidote to Mailer's book above.

CHAPTER TWENTY-THREE

The Revolt against Imperialism

I: Introduction: Causes and Nature of the Revolt

As Chapter XXI has already shown, the First World War had brought a gradual loosening of the imperial ties binding many non-western peoples to the great colonial powers of the West. The Second World War greatly accelerated and intensified this process. In many cases, during the decade after 1945, imperial ties were more than loosened: they were cut to shreds. Not only were the empires of van-quished Italy and Japan liquidated; the great world empires of the supposed victors in the war—the British, the French, the Dutch, and even the Americans—suffered drastic amputations. In Asia, the Middle East, and Africa a long list of newly independent states appeared—India, Pakistan, Burma, Indonesia, the Philippines, Syria, Lebanon, Israel, the Sudan, Tunisia, Morocco, and still others. States like China,

Iran, and Egypt, that had long been free in name but had often been subject to some western imperial control, now asserted more practical independence of the West.

What caused this great revolt against imperialism after World War II? One important answer is provided by the war itself. In the Second World War, as in the First, the western democracies often relied on colonial troops, with a consequent boost to the self-esteem of the peoples providing the troops. In both wars the propaganda of the democracies to show the justness of their cause naturally promoted new ambitions for the basic democratic rights of self-government and self-determination. In both wars inflation and other economic hardships like rationing, shortages, the enjoyment of war profits by the few rather than the many, heightened these ambitions and swelled the sense of grievance on the part of non-western peoples.

But the second war, unlike the first, destroyed the magic invulnerability of the West, for the western possessions in the Far East did fall before the attacks of non-western conquerors, the Japanese. The final defeat of Japan apparently did little to offset the immense damage done to western prestige. Moreover, two of the great imperial powers, the French and the Dutch, were only by courtesy numbered among the victors of World War II, with almost fatal consequences for their prestige in the non-western world. Nationalist leaders in the non-western world also knew that British power had been seriously weakened by the tremendous drain of the war, and that the outcome of the British election of 1945, in which the somewhat anti-imperialist Labor party defeated the resolutely imperialist Conservatives, promised a rapid liberalization of British policy. Nationalist leaders further knew that the real victors in the war were the United States and the Soviet Union, each in its very different way outspokenly anti-colonial.

In the long perspective of history, however, the Second World War was the immediate, not the ultimate, cause of the colonial revolt. The deeper causes must be sought in the five-hundred-year record of western expansion, and in the western tradition itself. The mainsprings of western culture—Christianity and the secular faiths of progress, democracy, and nationalism—provided little nourishment for imperialist policies. The West could not conceal from the educated natives its own great ethical and political writings. Indeed, it often laid before them with pride the Christian Bible, the American Declaration of Independence, the French Declaration of the Rights of Man, even the Communist Manifesto. It was hardly possible to keep on telling the natives indefinitely that "all men are created equal" really meant that "white men are created the superiors of colored men." In terms of ideals and ideology, western imperialism carried within itself the seeds of its own failure—or, from another point of view, its own transfiguration into self-determination for all peoples.

The great instrument for the spread of western ideas to non-western peoples was the education, both formal and informal, provided the natives by the West itself. In the nineteenth century, this education owed a great deal to the efforts of Christian missions, though toward the end of the century it became rather a secular education inspired by the deliberate efforts of the governing power. Broadly speaking, formal education at least was almost everywhere limited to a comparatively small class among the natives. In India, the sons of rajahs went to Oxford, but so too did bright boys from the slowly rising middle classes; by the twentieth century, western education in India itself had begun to take on something of the form of the western "career open to talents." Some non-Europeans turned against this western education and took refuge in a reaffirmation of the old values of their culture, of

Hinduism or Islam, for example. But for the most part the educated natives came to feel that their lands could have true independence only by imitating the West, by learning its industrial, technological, and military skills.

The new educated classes throughout the world of western imperialism emphatically wanted independence. They were by the twentieth century revolutionists, often very well acquainted with the long tradition of revolution in the West itself. Some became great admirers of the Bolshevik revolution in Russia, and a few received training in the techniques of revolution in Moscow itself. A great many westerners made the mistake of assuming that these nationalist revolutionaries were a totally unrepresentative minority of the native populations, that the great colonial masses, illiterate and poor, did not really follow their own native educated class but asked nothing better than to be ruled by the kindly whites. Of course the subject races have always had their share of "Uncle Toms" (a term used as one of scorn by American Negroes for those of their number who appear too submissive toward the whites). But the "Uncle Toms" have not given their stamp to non-western populations. The urban masses, and slowly after them the peasant masses, began to share the feelings of nationalism, began to feel that the foreigner must go.

The ripening of nationalism was also greatly aided by the imperialist powers themselves. Almost everywhere they penetrated they brought enough sanitary engineering, enough medicine, enough law and order to lower the death rate and to enable the native population to grow as it had never grown before. But that very growth made more mouths to feed, and the fact of population pressure became increasingly obvious to the educated and uneducated alike. Furthermore, education gave the natives some of the white man's special magic, his control over material things and over the elaborate machines of the modern world. The natives began to learn something of the scientific knowledge and engineering skills that made these things possible. By the very acquisition of these skills, they came to feel more and more the white man's equal, less and less willing to accept a subordinate position in things of the spirit now that, in material things, they were drawing even.

Any westerner who tries to comprehend the new political forces in the world outside the West must understand that in that world things of the spirit have often counted for more than material things. It has been said that nationalism is a kind of secular religion, and the validity of this judgment has been borne out time and again in the Turkey of Atatürk and his successors, in the India of Gandhi and Nehru, in Communist China, and in many, many other lands. Resistance to foreign imperialism, real or imagined, and exaltation of one's own native land have become articles of faith, commanding the kind of unswerving devotion that a religion demands of its followers. We shall see that when the Iranian nationalist, Mossadeq, nationalized the properties of the Anglo-Iranian Oil Company, he sacrificed the material to the spiritual, as it were, for he sacrificed vital oil royalties to obtain nationalistic satisfaction.

In Iran and elsewhere, many westerners have been bewildered by the apparently irrational behavior of ultra-nationalists, and have refused to believe that the "extremists" were the only substantial political group they could deal with. There must be "moderates" who would in good season subdue the extremists and turn to the sweet reasonableness of compromise. With some exceptions, this western faith in moderation has proved thoroughly illusory: in a crisis, the "moderates" have vanished, for they have joined the ranks of the "extremists." No westerner should really be surprised by this, for the moderate is often an early victim of revolution. The moderates were soon swept aside in the France of 1793 and the Russia of 1917.

The extremism of the nationalist revolutionaries of our own day is, then, by no means without historical precedent. Indeed, the Turks of the 1920's and 1930's devised a "new" history which sought to demonstrate, on extremely flimsy evidence, that everything ancient and worthwhile, including the alphabet, came from the Hittites and Sumerians and other very early peoples who were, of course, really Turks. But the extremes to which non-western nationalism may go are not always merely picturesque. Very recent history has recorded the Mau Mau terror in Kenya, the recurrent outbreaks between Hindu and Moslem in India, the many outrages against French individuals in Morocco and Algeria, the implacable hatred of Arab for Israeli —this catalogue of violence could be made much longer.

The reader may well have concluded that the movements he is about to study in more detail have been the *most* nationalistic in all history. And, in a sense, the conclusion is correct. But it must also be pointed out that these nationalisms often express ambitions and ideals far more than they reflect the actual facts. In other words, these are nationalisms striving to create nations, not to preserve nations already well developed. To cite merely one example: there has been much talk since 1945 of an Arab "nation" stretching across the whole of North Africa and the Middle East. The reality is that the Arab world is fragmented into more than a dozen separate political units, and that in most of them traditional loyalties to religious sects, to family or tribe, and to social class are still very strong. Yet it is also clear that loyalties to entities outside religion, family, and class are beginning to grow. This forging of new loyalties to young nation-states, this very immaturity of non-western nationalisms, is one more reason why the revolt against imperialism is indeed a revolution.

II: Asia

Defeated Japan Our survey of the world outside the West begins with the Far East, where the Second World War witnessed the spectacular rise and fall of imperialist Japan. At its height, Japan's "Greater East Asia Co-Prosperity Sphere" had many very obvious analogies with Napoleon's system of satellite states and even more with that of Hitler. Japanese methods seem to have been strikingly unoriginal, directly patterned on western precedent. The Japanese relied chiefly on the time-honored device of setting up puppet or satellite native governments, and exploiting for their own benefit the economic resources of the conquered lands. Their empire disintegrated in the atomic blast of Hiroshima. It was never cemented by the loyalty of its component parts.

Yet the Japanese started with at least one very great asset: they were an Asian people, a colored people, not westerners with the burden of white supremacy to carry. They could come as the emancipators of Asians and Pacific islanders, and in their propaganda they did indeed sound this note vigorously. And they made converts, but only a minority in each conquered land. Asians though they were, they did not endear themselves to their fellow Asians. Their armies looted and committed atrocities. The Japanese abroad behaved like any other master race; they showed that they felt superior to the natives. Time might have taught the Japanese a lesson in social psychology, and they might have been able with time to consolidate their grandiloquently named "co-prosperity sphere"; but time they did not have.

The end of World War II saw Japan reduced to her own islands, stripped of her overseas possessions. The overwhelming extent to which the military defeat of Japan was due to American efforts insured that the occupation and indeed the peace terms of 1952, whereby Japan regained formal independence, would be almost wholly an American concern. Though there was a strong current in American opinion that demanded the deposition of the Emperor, he was left on his throne, deprived of his divine status, and subjected to the close control of General MacArthur and the forces of occupation. Americans found to their astonishment that on the surface at least the Japanese people, far from taking the occupation with hostility, seemed almost to admire their occupiers. They seemed not to understand what democracy meant—apart from baseball and some other American folkways—but they seemed very anxious to learn. Their behavior roused a good deal of rather loose speculation about national group psychology, some of which appealed to the rigorous early toilet-training of Japanese children to explain the national willingness to obey a master.

We are dealing here not only with history, but also with a very problematic and uncertain present. The Japanese have certainly not had a democratic society or a democratic political organization in the past, and it is unlikely that they can set up a democracy of the western type in short order. If a well-developed industrial economy is an indispensable base for the development of democracy, the Japanese have already a great start over all other non-western peoples. We must, however, beware of the simple conclusion that, because Japan took over industrialism from the West, she will automatically become thoroughly westernized. Sir George Sansom, a wise western observer who knows Japan well, writes:

Thus, while it may be said that the introduction of power-driven machinery brought to bear upon Japanese life a strong influence of Western origin, this is true only with qualifications. . . . Printing and binding machinery, for example, increases the number and circulation of books and newspapers, of which the contents may well be such as to spread ideas critical of foreign countries. . . .

It is true that Western clothing, food, transport, and communications, as well as Western ideas, have enlarged and diversified Japanese life, but they have not necessarily changed its essential character. The cumulative effect of industrialization upon a people whose material culture is simple must destroy much of what is indigenous; but the impact of an advanced Western culture upon an advanced Eastern culture may, despite far-reaching superficial changes, succeed in producing resistance, or even hostile reactions in matters of vital import—in the totality of a people's feelings about life and society.[*]

Poor though the Japanese peasant and laboring classes are by American standards, they are far ahead of other non-western peoples. And grave though the population problem is, with some 90,000,000 people living in 147,000 square miles, it is not as desperate as it is in the crowded farmlands of India or Java or Egypt. Japan must, however, find foreign markets for her industrial production if she is to maintain and improve her national standard of living. Her position is singularly like that of Britain: she must export or die.

Finally, the growth of the tension between the United States and Russia has made Japan an American ally, an island outpost off the eastern edge of the Communist land-mass. If Japan is to be an effective ally, the United States must find a way to help her obtain in the free world the markets she needs. But, when the Japanese have recovered their strength, they may well try

---

[*] G. B. Sansom, *The Western World and Japan* (New York, 1949), 497-498.

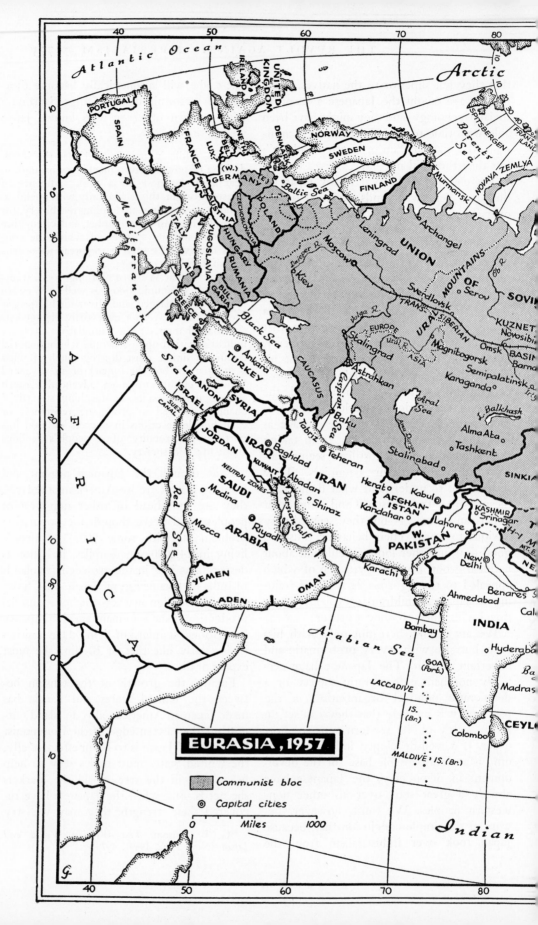

EURASIA, 1957

Communist bloc

◎ Capital cities

Miles
0   1000

to recover their old markets in China, even though it is now Communist, and may even renew their imperial aspirations.

Communist China

The Second World War produced a major shift in the balance of power in the Far East. As Japan went down, China arose, a Communist China, antagonistic to the "imperialists" of the West, particularly Americans. As we have already seen, in Chapter XXI, by the late 1930's the Communists were engaged in a struggle for power, a virtual civil war, with the Nationalists of the Kuomintang, headed by Chiang Kai-shek. During World War II, the United States backed the Nationalist government at Chungking and, when the war ended, hoped to be able to reconcile the Nationalists and the Communists and make China a democratic, pro-American state. In such a state the Communists would have been a legal party and a large one, as in France or Italy, but not a majority group. In 1946, the American negotiator, General Marshall, however, failed in his attempt to bring the two parties to a working agreement.

After Marshall's return to the United States in January, 1947, the result of the renewed Chinese civil war was never seriously in doubt. The Communists now received very effective support from the Soviet Union, including war material that the Japanese had surrendered to the Russians in Manchuria. The Kuomintang government was weakened by its own ebbing morale, by its dwindling popular support, and by an ever-mounting inflation that had gathered force during the war and further ravaged an economy already ruined by the long Japanese occupation. Late in 1949, the Nationalists, driven from the mainland, transferred their government to the island of Formosa, which Japan had relinquished in 1945. The Communists, lacking naval strength, could not pursue Chiang and the Nationalists.

China, then, by 1950 had gone Communist and formed part of the great Soviet bloc. Americans, in the face of the total failure of their China policy, began a bitter debate over the reasons why the Communists had been able to unite China under their control. This controversial question is clearly not yet a historical question, since no one can command all the documents or the partial detachment necessary to a fair appraisal. The historian can, however, warn against any explanation of the Communists' success that rests on the notion that a few conspirators, a few wicked men, with perhaps a few misled ones, brought about the Communist victory. Wicked men and conspirators were indeed active in China, but they were powerless to accomplish anything on the scale here involved without the assistance of what we call "social forces," "economic needs," and "morale." These may be vague terms, but they represent millions upon millions of human beings. We must now try to spell out their meaning in China.

The Communists had used the long struggle against Japan from 1937 to 1945 to broaden their base of operations and to widen their popular appeal. They made a successful effort to bring their soldiers into good relations with the peasants, and to make soldiers and peasants alike aware that they could act together. China was a land where the soldier was traditionally regarded as the lowest of human beings, a destructive force like a flood or a typhoon, natural but most unpleasant. Against such a traditional view the Communist slogan—"the soldiers are fish and the people water" —came as a really revolutionary stroke. This characteristic Chinese aphorism was at once understood to mean that the army rested on popular support and confidence.

Again, the Communists were able to bridge the traditional gap in China between the intellectual and the ordinary person. Communist success here was facili-

THE REVOLT AGAINST IMPERIALISM ~ 779

tated in the 1940's by the uprooted state of mind of Chinese intellectuals, who were searching for new beliefs and seeking fresh hope. They seemed to find what they sought in the program of the Communists. An American expert on China, Professor Fairbank, writing soon after the close of World War II, concluded that the struggle with Japan revolutionized the outlook of the Chinese intellectual:

> The encouragement of popular participation in cultural, economic, and political programs, according to most observers, created a new psychological atmosphere or morale in those wartime areas where the Communist program became effective. . . . This religion of the common man embraces the revolutionary ideal that modern technology and a new social organization may be used to remake and enrich the life of the peasant. . . . In order that the revolution may draw perpetual sustenance from the masses, the party workers must live in the villages, work with the peasant, eat his food, lead his life, think his thoughts. Only thus can the party cadres lead the peasant masses in their regeneration.
>
> This almost religious concept of liberation is the most dynamic spiritual element in the modern Chinese scene; and by a seemingly inexorable logic of events it has become the sanction for a new party dictatorship.*

The historian, of course, cannot predict with any confidence what will come of the Communist experiment in China. After World War II all legal traces of subjection to the West went by the boards, notably extraterritoriality—the right of certain European states to try their own nationals in China by their own courts and their own law. The old ties between China and the West have been replaced by new ties with Soviet Russia. Many westerners believe that this development marked a defeat for Chinese nationalism, that China has simply moved out of the imperial orbit of the West and of Japan and into that of the Soviet Union. Many Chinese, on the contrary, apparently find in their Communist regime

* J. K. Fairbank, *The United States and China* (Cambridge, Mass., 1948), 268-269.

the fulfillment of their national aspirations. They seem to view Russia as a partner rather than as an overlord, to believe that the Soviet Union can supply western technology without imposing western imperial controls.

The Communist regime in China has often followed policies closely paralleling those marked out earlier by Russia, notably the concentration of real authority in the hands of the dictatorial few at the top. A significant difference in emphasis, however, early developed in social and economic policy, where the Communists in China have focused on satisfying peasant hopes for the breakup of large private holdings and an end to landlordism. This focus is at odds not only with Marxian theories of the industrial proletariat as the major revolutionary class but also with the Soviet policy of creating larger and larger collective farms.

But there have also been signs that the Communist leaders of China are adjusting their social and economic policies to the tradition of Marx, Lenin, and Stalin. Certainly they are more than simple agrarian reformers, for they have launched the equivalent of the Russian Five-Year Plans for industrialization. To release manpower from farms for industrial jobs and at the same time to maintain the agricultural production required for an ever-growing population will be a formidable undertaking indeed. The Soviet Union accomplished a similar undertaking—but only at a very high price in human misery—with a more modern economy as a base, and with a population better educated and more familiar with the rudiments of the economic revolutions of modern times.

The Korean War

The outbreak of the Korean War in June, 1950, introduced an intense phase of the "cold war" between communism and the free world (see Chapter

Communist China: measuring out the land for redistribution.

XXIV). The scene of the fighting, Korea, is a peninsula at the eastern extremity of Asia, bordering on Manchuria and Siberia, and close to Japan. Tsarist Russia had hoped to penetrate the area, but these hopes withered with the Russo-Japanese War and Japan's subsequent annexation of Korea in 1910. In 1945, at the close of World War II, Russian troops occupied the northern part of Korea and American troops occupied the southern part. The country was divided in the middle by a line along the 38th parallel of latitude; a communist-inspired North Korean People's Republic was set up on one side, and an American-inspired South Korean Republic on the other. When all American forces except for a few specialists were withdrawn from South Korea, the North Koreans marched in to unite the nation under communist control.

Instead of appeasement, in the tradition of the 1930's, America at once moved troops into Korea. It was a close call, but American troops got there soon enough to halt the North Korean drive and then to push the enemy back well north of the 38th parallel toward the frontier of China. At this point, Communist China, apparently alarmed by events, entered the war, and the fighting moved southward. By 1951, the line of battle had been roughly stabilized along the old boundary between North and South Korea. To end the stalemate, negotiations were begun; they dragged on for two years, but an armistice was finally concluded in July, 1953.

The government of the United States carried on its defense of South Korea in the name of the United Nations, and received small but valuable detachments of troops from some of its allies. The American government was firm in its effort to limit the war to resistance to aggression at a given spot. The United Nations commander in Korea, however, the American General MacArthur, concluded that it was necessary to press the war into Communist China. American officials, and in particular America's allies, feared that such a step would bring Russia actively in on the Chinese side, and would unleash the much-dreaded World War III. In consequence, General MacArthur was recalled by order of President Truman in April, 1951.

The Korean settlement by no means ended the tension between Communist China and the United States. The American government continued its refusal to recognize Red China, and serious friction developed over Formosa, which the Communists seemed determined to capture and the United States seemed equally determined to keep out of Communist hands. Antagonism between China and the United States also arose over the question of Southeast Asia, where the Communists sought to turn native nationalism and anti-colonialism to their own advantage.

Southeast Asia World War II set off a really major political explosion in Southeast Asia. The Japanese conquest and occupation destroyed belief in the invincibility of the white nations, and in 1945 the western powers were by no means able to pick up where they had left off. Moreover, the United States was in the process of granting independence to its own imperial wards, the Filipinos. In the years after World War II, consequently, the East Indies obliged the Dutch to give them independence; they became the Republic of Indonesia. Britain gave Burma independence outside the Commonwealth, and in the Federation of Malaya and the great port of Singapore at its southern tip made concessions toward eventual self-government. The French made similar concessions to the various states of Indo-China—Vietnam, which included the populous and relatively rich

U.S. Marines in Korea watching an American plane pull up after dropping a bomb on a Communist concentration.

coastal areas; and Cambodia and Laos in the more primitive hinterland. But the French did not go far enough or fast enough to prevent a chronic Indo-Chinese war, in which the native rebels got Chinese Communist support.

This political revolution has by no means solved the problems of Southeast Asia. One great problem is economic. This area, so long cast in the colonial role of producing raw materials, will find it hard to achieve economic independence without western assistance. Politically, it is natural that many of these peoples should suspect the aid offered by their former masters, yet if they do not take it, they may simply drift into economic chaos and facilitate their own capture by the Communists. In 1954 the French, increasingly hard pressed in Indo-China, agreed to partition Vietnam; the northern half of this important state went Communist, and the southern half went to a weak native government under the protection of France and the United States. Elsewhere in Southeast Asia the Communists scored no spectacular gains, but it was not for want of trying. In the newly independent Philippines they supported a troublesome guerrilla rebellion, and in Malaya, profiting by the jungle terrain and by the sympathy of part of the large Chinese population, they waged a chronic guerrilla war.

By 1957, it was not at all certain that the new nations of Southeast Asia could maintain stable governments and continue to defend themselves against such Communist infiltration. Native leaders, long accustomed to damning western imperialism, showed some signs of realizing that Communist imperialism posed the greater immediate threat. Significantly, however, only three Asian states—Pakistan, Thailand (Siam), and the Philippine Republic— joined SEATO (the Southeast Asia Treaty Organization), sponsored by the West in 1954 as a counter to Communist penetration. Most of the Asian states preferred a policy of neutrality (see also Chapter XXIV).

India and Pakistan

At the end of World War II, the victory of the British Labor party, pledged to grant India self-government, made Indian emancipation a certainty. But the deep-seated tension between Moslems and Hindus (see Chapter XXI) now assumed critical importance. When the Hindus' Congress party and the All-India Moslem League faced the need to make a working constitution for India, they found themselves up against a blank wall of complete disagreement. The Moslems had long been working for a partition into separate Hindu and Moslem states, and this was in the end reluctantly accepted by the Hindus. In 1947, Hindu India and Moslem Pakistan were set up as self-governing dominions within the British Commonwealth.

Pakistan is a state divided into two parts, widely separated by intervening Hindu territory—the larger, West Pakistan, in the northwest, and the smaller, East Pakistan, in East Bengal (the great city of Calcutta, in West Bengal, went to India). The rest of the former British Indian Empire became by its constitution of 1950 the Republic of India. Pakistan, with its 75,000,000 people and its relatively poorly developed industry, is weaker than India with its over 350,000,000, and at first kept closer political ties with the British Commonwealth. Even India has not, however, sought like Ireland to break all such ties. The independent Republic of India is still a part of what it calls the "Commonwealth of Nations"—without that adjective "British." Indeed, with independence a reality, Indian-British relations seem to have entered on an era of good feeling that would have been unthinkable before 1940.

The partition was not achieved without violence. In view of the way races and religions are geographically mingled in the subcontinent, it could not result in a complete separation of Hindus in one state and Moslems in another. The line of partition between India and West Pakistan evoked bitter fighting between members of the two communities, and thousands of lives were lost. It resulted in a wholesale transfer of populations as Hindus moved from Pakistanian territory into India and Moslems moved from Indian territory into Pakistan. Still a source of trouble between India and Pakistan is the mountainous region of Kashmir, which is ruled by a Hindu reigning house but has a population in the majority Moslem. The Indian army has held it in occupation, to the great economic disadvantage of Pakistan, a nation still struggling to balance its budget. The United Nations sought to determine the fate of Kashmir by arranging a plebiscite, but down to 1957 it failed to secure the needed approval from both parties.

India and Pakistan have in any event got a start as independent nations. Partition has at least been accepted, reluctantly by India, joyfully by Pakistan. Both have undergone some difficulties as a result of the political inexperience of their leaders, but, thanks to their British training, not on the scale apparent in some of the new nations of Southeast Asia. Both are getting down to the hard task of solving their pressing internal problems, and both have done very well in the business of international politics. India in particular, led by Nehru, has undertaken the difficult and risky task of setting up as mediator not only between East and West, but between Communism and the democratic world—a task flattering to national self-esteem.

Both countries have had to cope with formidable economic problems—Pakistan with poverty and lack of industry, and India with poverty and lack of sufficient agricultural output to sustain her enormous population. India, indeed, faces in an acute form the population pressure that bears so heavily on many other non-western coun-tries. There are now more than 350,000,000 people in the Republic of India, 4,000,000 are added annually, and this population is periodically threatened by famine and by actual death through starvation. In 1950, the government of Nehru launched a Five-Year Plan for economic development, and, on its successful completion in 1955, initiated a second one. These plans rely more heavily on private enterprise than the echo of Soviet planning in the title might suggest, and western experts have helped in their execution. Under them, irrigation and flood-control works have been started, transport and communication improved, and employment opportunities and average incomes modestly increased. Experts estimate, however, that even an India with a greatly modernized economy will have grave difficulty in supporting a population much in excess of its present numbers. Although birth control is abhorrent to the traditional ways of Hinduism, the government of Nehru is sponsoring a campaign for its adoption.

Hinduism is a unique and all-important element in the new Indian republic More than that, it throws much light on the essential differences between East and West, and in particular on the kind of traditional setting in which the great drama of non-western political awakening is being played. Hinduism is an immensely complex and ancient way of life for which the word "religion," in its western sense at least, is not adequate. (See also Chapters V and XXI.) It has no church organization in the Christian sense, no clear-cut theology, no established Bible. Of the three major developed ways of life or cultures that the West has encountered in its expansion over the world, Hinduism is furthest from ours. In comparison, Islam is actually a relative of Christianity, and Chinese society, in spite of its quite un-western family structure, has affinities with what one may call the utilitarian or worldly strain in the West.

For Hinduism, this world of sense-experi-

Indian village. Boys' school in background, village elders sitting in the center.

ence is an illusion, but an illusion that has somehow to be overcome. Death is essential to the overcoming, but death is not enough. Each living man, indeed each living thing, is a soul alienated by the very fact of living from the ultimate, universal soul which is peace, absence of struggle and desire, ineffable non-being. The holiest of men by turning away entirely from the world, by living without desire—but not by any such simple solution as suicide—can perhaps attain this non-being in the end. But most human beings are now living out in this world the consequences of a sinful life as another personality in the past. Indeed, the most sinful of men who have lived in the past have been punished by reincarnation as animals or even as insects (which is why the most orthodox of Hindus will harm no living thing). And even among men, their sins in past incarnations are reflected by their status, their *caste.* The poor, the humblest, are such because their sins have been

greater; they cannot improve their lot in the western sense, for they can only slowly in subsequent incarnations redeem their wickedness by living as holy a life as possible.

Hindu society, with its caste system, its lack of any basis for belief in material progress and in what we call "welfare," its innumerable tabus, found grave difficulties in the way of adopting western culture. That the Hindus have adopted as much as they have is another proof of the penetrating power of the West. For instance, it is quite impossible to preserve literal untouchability in modern India. The lowest Hindu group, actually below and outside the caste system, were called "untouchables" because even their shadow would corrupt a caste-Hindu. No one can keep untouchable in an Indian railroad car. Many Hindu intellectuals have indeed been so far westernized that they have no real intellectual basis for calling themselves Hindus; but even for westernized intellectuals, and much more for the uneducated, the long accumulation of habits, feelings, and ingrained attitudes cannot be quickly altered.

The brave new Republic of India, then, is trying hard to mold a modern nation out of this often intractable Hindu material. The difficulties here are often prodigious. For example, there is the problem of language. English is the only tongue commonly understood by most educated Indians, since the country contains ten major linguistic regions, each with its own distinctive tongue; yet the use of English is often attacked as an ignoble concession to "colonialism," and regional pride in matters of language leads to regional pride in matters of politics. That the national government has continued resolutely to pursue the twin goals of political centralization and social and economic betterment is a tribute to the firmness and skill of its leaders. So far, these leaders have succeeded well enough to prevent any obvious "softening-up" of India for eventual penetration by the Communists.

III: *The Middle East*

The Middle East, too, has experienced revolutionary changes since 1945. These changes have been first and foremost political: the increasing assertion of national independence by the Middle Eastern states, and their mounting antagonism to the West. Other major issues have arisen, all linked to the central fact of the Middle Eastern political revolution—oil, communism, the common Arab hostility to the new Jewish national state of Israel, and the possibility of Arab unity. We shall survey each of these problems in turn.

Political Changes

The Middle Eastern mandates obtained by France and Britain after World War I (see Chapter XVIII) collapsed after World War II. Syria and Lebanon won their full independence from the French, and the British withdrew from Palestine. The new state of Israel took over western Palestine, and the eastern part was annexed by Transjordan, which now styled itself, after its ruling dynasty, the Hashemite Kingdom of Jordan. The Sudan, an African state by location but linked by language and interests to the Arab world, emerged into independence after a half-century of joint administration by Britain and Egypt. Old imperial ties were often destroyed in the Middle East during this postwar decade from 1946 to 1956. Jordan, its meager resources badly strained by the influx of Arab refugees from Palestine, and its Arab Legion dependent on British subsidies, nevertheless expelled the British chief of its legion in 1956. In Iran, a revived nationalism chose as its target the Anglo-Iranian Oil Company.

Egypt, above all, starting in 1952, experienced a political revolution that, it now seems clear, was an event of major importance. This revolution was directed both against the British and against the traditional ruling groups among the Egyptians themselves. Although Britain had taken real steps toward freeing Egypt from her control before World War II (see Chapter XXI), she did not move fast enough to satisfy Egyptian nationalists. During the war, furthermore, she offended them deeply by threatening to use force against King Farouk in order to secure his dismissal of a cabinet sympathetic to the Nazis. After the war, Farouk himself, once a highly popular monarch, rapidly lost prestige both because of his well-publicized appetite for high living and because of his own involvement in a scandal concerning the provision of defective supplies to the Egyptian army. From Farouk and his palace clique, the odor of corruption and scandal spread through the upper levels of the government.

The revolution, when it came in July, 1952, was the work of a group of young army officers, whose closest historic relatives would seem to be such westernizing military revolutionaries as the Young Turks of the early twentieth century and the Russian Decembrists of 1825. In some of its policies the revolutionary government of Egypt's strong man, Gamal Abdul Nasser, followed a path paralleling that marked out by another Middle Eastern strong man, Atatürk (see Chapter XXI). The revolutionary regime in Egypt has abolished the monarchy, drawn up a republican constitution (which has more than a tinge of totalitarianism), pared down the traditionally large role of courts of religious law, and encouraged the emancipation of women.

But the Egypt of Nasser, unlike the Turkey of Atatürk, is confronted with a single overriding economic fact: it is probably *the* most overpopulated state in the world, struggling to support 22,000,000 people in a land that is 95 per cent desert. Experts believe that Egypt is one of the very few countries in the world where the standard of living of the common man has actually declined over the past generation. The revolutionary government, accordingly, started an ambitious program of social and economic improvement. To increase agricultural output it projected new irrigation schemes, including a high dam across the Nile in southern Egypt; to provide more jobs—and to bolster Egyptian national pride—it accelerated the pace of industrialization; it lowered the high death rate by expanding welfare services, and has sought, so far with little success, to check the phenomenally high birth rate (approximately double that of the United States)

by promoting the practice of birth control.

In 1955 and 1956, though these pressing domestic problems were very far from being solved, the government of Nasser kept itself in world headlines by a series of spectacular moves in foreign policy—"deals" with communist states for arms and for the sale of Egypt's chief export, cotton; bids for leadership of the Arab world; and open defiance of the West by nationalizing that great international waterway, the Suez Canal. There seems little doubt that these measures greatly appealed to Arab nationalists inside—and outside—Egypt: in their eyes, Nasser was playing the game of power politics in proper style. Yet the most sympathetic observer must also doubt that all this commotion is really contributing to the betterment of Egypt's economy. It may well be, however, that in the present climate of opinion in the Middle East—and elsewhere in the non-western world for that matter—people are more interested in showy displays of nationalism than in gradual and unspectacular social and economic improvement.

Not every Middle Eastern state moved along such flamboyant lines after World War II. Iraq, too, produced a pro-Nazi government during the war and was forced by Britain to change her ways. But after the war Iraqi leaders eventually decided that there was more to be gained by cooperating with the western powers than by defying them. In the postwar decade, Turkey remained the most reliable of the West's allies in the Middle East. Fortified by American military and economic aid against possible Russian designs on her eastern provinces and the Straits, she settled down to work out the full consequences of the great Atatürk's reforms. By 1950, when the Turks enjoyed their first really free election, it looked as though Turkish democracy had come of age. Later developments, however, such as the muzzling of the press and of opposition spokesmen, blurred this impression. Perhaps more important, postwar Turkish governments have expanded industry, built roads and schools, and begun the essential task of bringing the Atatürk spirit of westernization to the peasants, who make up some 80 per cent of the population. Some of the aggressively secularist policies of Atatürk have been dropped to propitiate the large element of conservative Moslem opinion. Religious instruction has been restored in the schools, and the call to prayer, banned under Atatürk, is sounded once more in Arabic from the minarets (and often amplified by loudspeak-

ers!). Turkey remains, by western standards, a poor country, incompletely westernized. By Middle Eastern standards, however, the achievement of the Turks is remarkable: they have rejuvenated their nationalism and at the same time adjusted it both to their new western ideals and to their own Moslem past. This cheerful conclusion must now be modified by noting that, in recent years, Turkey has found increasing difficulty in paying for the imports demanded by her expanding economy, notably oil.

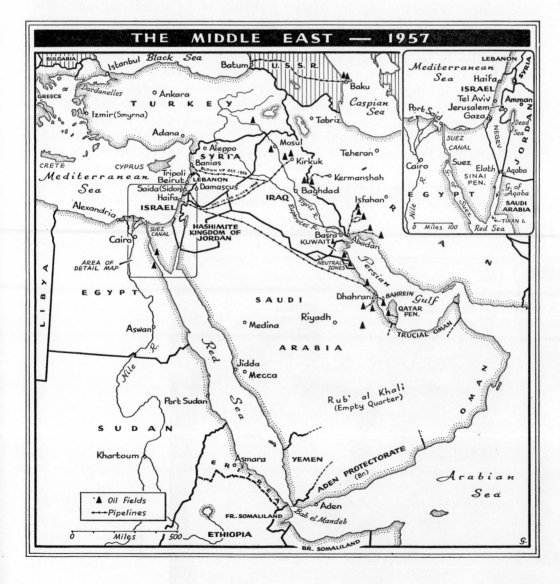

Oil

Oil, the lack of which has in a sense impoverished the Turks, has by contrast greatly enriched some of the Middle Eastern states, notably Saudi Arabia, Iraq, and Kuwait, a stretch of British-controlled desert near the head of the Persian Gulf, which in the 1950's became the largest single producer in the whole area. The oil resources of the Middle East have been developed by European and American companies, operating under the close supervision and protection of their national diplomatic services. Westerners have not simply taken the oil, as the Spaniards took the precious metals from the New World. They have paid for it, perhaps not what they would have paid at home, but still they have paid, and at mounting rates.

But this rapidly increasing development of Middle Eastern oil has created all manner of problems. First, the Middle East after World War II became far and away the most important supplier of oil to the countries of western Europe. Whence the alarmed concern of Britain, especially, lest Egypt's nationalization of the Suez Canal disrupt the vital flow of oil from the Persian Gulf to Europe, and lest, too, it set a precedent for the eventual nationalization of the oil companies operating in the Middle East. Second, the division of profits between western companies and the oil-producing countries has also created an international issue. This issue arose in an acute form in Iran, where the Anglo-Iranian Oil Company and the Iranian government had a long history of mutual antagonism and bitter negotiations. In 1951, under the leadership of an ardent nationalist, Mossadeq, the Iranian government nationalized the properties of Anglo-Iranian. Mossadeq's policy won wide support among his countrymen for its bold defiance of the West, but the sudden cessation of oil revenues soon produced an economic crisis. The issue was finally resolved after a *coup* in Teheran, the Iranian capital, had driven Mossadeq from office into jail (1953). Iranian oil remains nationalized, but a consortium of western companies participates in its exploitation and in the profits thereof.

Egyptian President Nasser, Indian Premier Nehru, and Yugoslavian President Tito on the Isle of Brioni, June 19, 1956.

Third, who benefits by the revenues oil brings, the rulers or the ruled? In Saudi Arabia, much of the money goes to the very numerous royal family and its retainers; the kindest estimates put at 30 per cent the portion spent on projects for public improvement, while the less charitable ones go as low as 5 per cent. In Iraq, by contrast, 70 per cent of oil revenues in recent years have gone into such long-range improvements as flood-control dams on the Tigris and Euphrates, power stations, and irrigation works. It is not clear, however, whether these projects in turn will greatly benefit the masses or simply enrich the wealthy landholders who have traditionally dominated Iraqi society and politics.

Communism

The nationalistic ferment of the Middle East and the question of dividing oil-brought wealth are important factors in the potential appeal of communism in the area. Other factors are also involved. One is the Soviet continuation of the old tsarist drive into the area. A second factor is the readiness of some Moslems to accept communism: in the Middle East, as in Indonesia, Islam has not proved to be the bulwark against communism many westerners naïvely assumed it would be. Communism appeals particularly to a social class that may be broadly termed the intellectuals—students, teachers, lawyers, journalists, bureaucrats in routine jobs. These are men who feel themselves the natural leaders of their countries but are frustrated by the entrenched position of the traditional ruling groups, and frustrated still more because they are in a sense educated beyond the social and economic capacities of their countries to assimilate them.

All of this, however, does not mean that communism will inevitably engulf the Middle East. So far, most governments there have actively, often ruthlessly, repressed local communist groups; so far, native na-tionalism has been a far more powerful force than communism. It is possible that the governments of these newly independent states will succeed in enlisting the allegiance of the intellectuals. Finally, the Russians themselves, in their dealings with Iran since World War II, have proved to have as heavy a hand with the natives, to be as crude imperialists, as any of the western nations.

Israel

A more obvious danger to the peace of the Middle East has been the chronic warfare, both "cold" and "hot," between the Arabs and Israel. In the course of the half-century preceding World War II, many (though by no means all) Jews came to support Zionism, that is, Jewish nationalism. The Zionist hopes of creating a new state on the site of the ancient Jewish homeland received a great lift from the Balfour Declaration of 1917 and the subsequent British policy of admitting Jewish immigrants into Palestine (see Chapter XXI). Hitler's persecutions and World War II made the problem of increased Jewish immigration to Palestine critical. At the same time, Britain, the mandatory power, wished to protect its great interest in the Middle East by cultivating the friendship of the Arab states. But within Palestine itself the flooding Jewish tide was submerging the Arabs, who had long settled there and felt that this was *their* homeland.

Worn out with fruitless efforts to secure a compromise between Arabs and Jews, the British withdrew from Palestine in 1948, and the Jews at once proclaimed the new state of Israel and secured its recognition by the United Nations. The Israelis now had to fight to maintain their state. In the ensuing war, the total resources in manpower of the Arab states were far greater than those of Israel, but the inability of the Arabs to put a united army in the field, their military inefficiency, and the better technical equipment and morale of the Israelis resulted in a victory for the Jews. A truce, but not a formal peace, was patched up under the auspices of the United Nations. Israel did not secure the whole of Palestine, but did obtain the better part, a long, narrow strip along the Mediterranean, with some eastward projections, one of which took in part of Jerusalem, the spiritual capital of Judaism. The "old city" of Jerusalem, however, including the Wailing Wall and the site of Solomon's temple, remained in the hands of Jordan and thus under the control of the Arab enemy.

In the course of the Arab-Israeli struggle, some million Arabs fled from Israel into the surrounding Arab states, which were either unable or unwilling to absorb the refugees. Although the United Nations has organized a special agency to give relief to the refugees and arrange for their permanent resettlement, this program has not worked out well, largely because many of the refugees resist resettlement. To many refugees, any improvement in their material status is an abandonment of their conviction that the Israelis will soon "be pushed into the sea," and that they themselves will return to their old homes. This problem of the dispossessed Palestinian Arabs has, of course, sharpened the hostility between Arab and Jew, as has also the sizable minority of Arabs within Israel. The upshot since 1948 has been a most uneasy truce, frequently broken by both sides, notably by Israel's massive retaliation against Egypt and Egyptian frontier raids in October, 1956.

Israel faces not only a grave problem in external relations but also grave internal issues, quite apart from that of its Arab minority. Independent Israel has continued to admit as many Jewish immigrants as possible, some of them of advanced western culture, but others, from North Africa and Yemen, still largely living in the Middle Ages. The forging of these disparate human elements into a single nationality is a formidable task. Furthermore, immigration has greatly swollen the total population of Israel, which now contains about a million more people than it did before World War II and in an area not much bigger than Connecticut. Much of that area is mountainous, with a thin rocky soil and inadequate rainfall, and some of it is sheer desert. The Israelis have applied talents and training derived from the West to make the best use of their limited resources, but they have not been able to attain a balanced economy, particularly a balanced trade. They must still depend on outside aid, especially from their many sympathizers in the United States.

The dependence of Israel on western support, indeed the very existence of Israel, have profoundly affected relations between the Arab states and the West. In the view of Arab nationalists, Israel is a western creation, deliberately set up in their midst to spite them and to thwart their own economic development. It is hard for anyone who has not heard an Arab plead his case to imagine the passion with which he argues it or the overwhelming influence that he ascribes to Jewish voters and Jewish financiers in the shaping of American policy. In such an atmosphere, it has been difficult indeed for the western nations, particularly the United States, to retain cordial relations with Arabs who are in any case very sensitive nationalists.

Arab Unity
—and Disunity

The Arab states are united in their hatred of Israel. They are also formally united in the Arab League, an organization created in 1945 and having as its members the full roster of independent Arab states—Syria, Lebanon, Iraq, Jordan, Saudi Arabia, Yemen, Egypt, and Egypt's newly independent neighbors, Libya and the Sudan. This league gives its members some sense of common purpose, and many

Arab intellectuals, and some Arab politicians like Nasser of Egypt, have nursed Pan-Arabic schemes and dreamed of a great Arab nation united from Morocco to the easternmost tip of the Arabian peninsula.

Realization of this Pan-Arabic dream seems a long way off. The word "Arabic" is clear and exact only in reference to a language, and even there it applies both to the classical written language of the Koran and to a variety of modern colloquial tongues. There is no Arabic "race," for the inhabitants of North Africa and the Middle East are an extraordinary mixture developed over thousands of years of history in this racial melting pot. Moreover, Arabic is not completely coincidental with Islam: the Arab world contains an extraordinary range of Christian minorities. Within Islam itself, there is a great gap between the ardent puritanism of Saudi Arabia and the relatively mild devotion of urban Moslems in Egypt and elsewhere, or between the broad-minded Sunni Moslems and the narrow, gloomy adherents of Shi'a Islam in the single country of Iraq. In cultural and economic life, the Arab world covers a wide range from Saudi Arabia, where twentieth-century oil flows in a medieval land, on up to Egypt and Lebanon, the richest and most advanced of the Arab states.

Events since World War II have often revealed the competing political ambitions of individual Arab states. Jordan, for example, with its refugee-swollen population, feeble economy, and shaky administration, has become the "sick man" of the Arab world; Egypt, Syria, and Iraq would all apparently like to be its heirs. Egypt, most populous of the Arab states, its great city of Cairo the one acknowledged metropolis of the Arab world, its revolutionary government bursting with dynamic nationalism, would seem to be the natural architect of Arab unity. But Egypt's pretensions have been challenged by Iraq, which, unlike Egypt, is a truly undeveloped country, free from population pressure and rejoicing in the oil revenues that the accidents of nature have denied to Egypt.

Even the greatest crisis in the Middle East since the Palestinian War of 1948 did not apparently forge a greater Arab unity. In October, 1956, Britain and France undertook armed intervention in support of Israel and with the aim of recovering control of the Suez Canal, recently nationalized by Egypt. They were forced to withdraw not as the result of any great concerted Arab pressure but because so much of world opinion, including American opinion, was exerted against them in the United Nations. The immediate result of the Anglo-French intervention, most ironically, was the closing of the Suez Canal through Egyptian acts of sabotage—precisely the situation that the intervention had aimed to prevent in the first place.

IV: Africa

Outside the Middle East, India, and the Far East, there are many other areas in the world where non-western peoples are struggling with the kinds of problems that we have been considering in this chapter. On the mainland of the Americas south of the Rio Grande most of the Latin-American republics face the problem of lifting the cultures of their Indian and mixed populations to the modern western level. The Caribbean remains a problem area, beset with overcrowded islands like Britain's Jamaica and the United States' Puerto Rico. Americans, British, Dutch, and French are trying to solve the difficulties of their Caribbean possessions in a generally

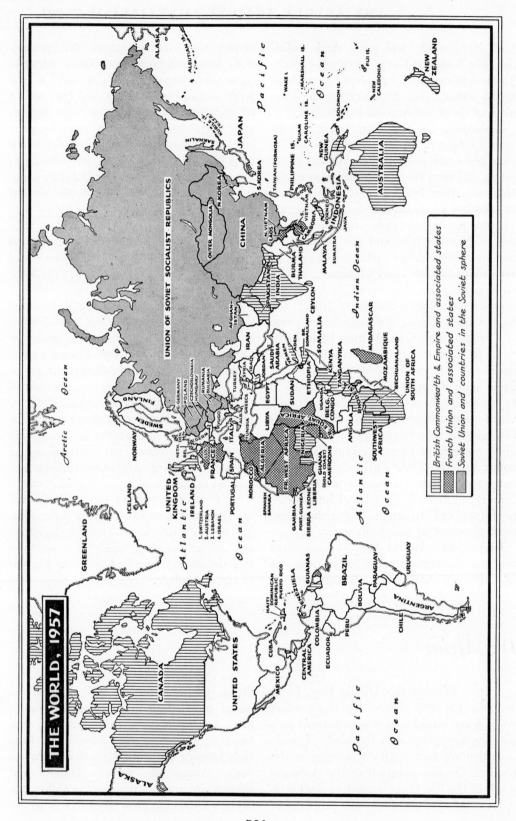

THE WORLD, 1957

British Commonwealth & Empire and associated states
French Union and associated states
Soviet Union and countries in the Soviet sphere

co-operative and democratic spirit. Since World War II the British, for instance, have made political concessions to their West Indian islands that may eventually secure them something like dominion status. In the islands of the Pacific, the decline of the native Polynesian peoples has by no means been arrested. A bright spot exists in the Hawaiian Islands, where the American melting pot seems to be working to assimilate a most extraordinary mixture of Chinese, Japanese, Polynesians, and whites into a common western culture.

"Black" Africa

There remains Africa. Here, too, events since 1918 have made old-fashioned imperialism, based on comfortable notions of white supremacy, very outdated. Negro Africa at the beginning of European expansion was everywhere at a far lower stage of culture, as culture is conventionally rated, than were the Chinese, East Indians, and the peoples of the Near East. It was also at a far less efficient level of economic and political organization. Yet so fast have events moved that all over Negro Africa since World War II there has been a demand for increased self-government and for fairly rapid attainment of independence.

In the mid-twentieth century the Nigeria we studied in Chapter XVII, for instance, has reached a stage where Lugard's formula of "indirect rule" no longer fits. Nineteenth-century indirect rule meant that at bottom the natives would rule in those matters where traditional tribal customs still held, while whites would apply the rules of the modern world, the complex techniques of sanitation, engineering, and western law. What has happened in no more than two generations is that the natives— at least the considerable minority of natives educated in western schools—now want to apply the western rules themselves. What is known as the "Africaniza-

tion" of the civil service has already gone far in British West Africa; there are already Negroes appointed to important administrative posts.

The policy does not stop with the civil service. It involves also the adoption of western parliamentary government, with elected legislatures, freedom of the press and of assembly, all the apparatus of western democracy. In the early 1950's one British possession in West Africa, the Gold Coast, obtained sizable grants of self-government. But these were not sufficient for native nationalists who demanded complete national independence and declared dominion status to be outmoded. Accordingly, negotiations were undertaken with the result that in March, 1957, the Gold Coast emerged as the state of Ghana, enjoying both independence and membership in the framework of the British Commonwealth of Nations. It was also to be admitted into the UN.

The road to political emancipation in tropical Africa, however, is by no means completely smooth. The other imperial powers with colonies there—the French, the Belgians, the Portuguese—have lagged behind the British in the matter of political concessions. Furthermore, tensions have arisen in "black" Africa between the educated natives of town and city and their fellows of the tribal villages. To the villagers the Negro civil servant who has risen in the service is often a most objectionable character, a man who is blocking the advancement of his fellows. Finally, in a society still economically colonial—that is, with raw materials still produced by a labor force barely emancipated from slavery or something like it, still uneducated and with very low standards of living—there is a real danger that political reform will get ahead of economic growth. The politically emancipated masses under these conditions then become ripe for agitation that is bound to look communistic, and indeed often is communistic.

"White" Africa

Over the past century or so, the whites in Africa have pushed northward from the Cape of Good Hope for several thousand miles as true settlers. On the plateaus and highlands of South and Central Africa they live—or try to live—as their more fortunate fellow Europeans who settled the relatively empty continents of North America and Australia live. They have tried to make new homes as farmers, grazers, businessmen, professional men. But there is this great difference: in South and Central Africa they have not been able to push aside the natives, as Americans pushed aside the Red Indians, and as the Australians pushed aside the Blackfellows.

Kenya. Young Kikuyu suspected of Mau Mau terrorism.

Everywhere the whites are in a minority. Though in a few regions they have adopted the nineteenth-century American method of putting the natives in "reservations," they have for the most part used the natives also as a cheap labor force on farms and in mines. The living conditions of the black masses were and are bad, as in the fearful Negro slums around the South African metropolis of Johannesburg. But what happened everywhere else, except among the Polynesians, happened in South and Central Africa: the native population has increased substantially in numbers.

Kenya

We may take as one example a region that has been very much in the public eye in the mid-twentieth century. This is Kenya, a British crown colony in East Central Africa. Kenya is on the Equator, but through it runs the mountain spine of Africa; there are thousands of square miles of rolling grass and forest lands with an excellent climate for Europeans. Realizing this was white-man's country, the British government followed ample imperial precedent and decided to reserve some five million acres for European settlement. The Europeans came, a few tens of thousands of them, and largely with native labor developed big farms.

There remain something over five million natives in Kenya. Those living in the highlands were pushed aside into native reserves that they have now outgrown. The lands that they sold to the British they could not have realized they were alienating forever, for their whole land system was quite unlike the white man's. (This is a familiar pattern in American dealings with Red Indians, too.) The natives have made extraordinary progress in fifty years. Now they too wanted *tyledees* (title deeds); they wanted the land back.

The main native tribe in the highland regions, the Kikuyu, has responded to the growing pressure by developing a secret society known as the Mau Mau into an instrument of terror directed not only at the whites but at the more peaceful and conservative of their own fellow tribesmen. There is no doubt that the Mau Mau have been a minority among the Kikuyu, a daring and fanatical minority capable of the most cruel deeds, and that their goal has been the extermination or at least expulsion of the whites. There is no doubt that some Kikuyu at least were honestly opposed to the methods and ends of the Mau Mau.

Among uneducated tribesmen the Mau Mau could not use the methods of direct propaganda familiar among pressure groups in the West. What they did was spread terror by murder, not only of occasional isolated white farmers, but of their own tribesmen who stood against them. Here we may see the great difficulty of eliminating in a few years customs and folkways of old standing. The Mau Mau forced reluctant fellow tribesmen to take an oath backed by full tribal fear of the gods of the oath; if a man goes back on the oath, the Kikuyu believe, the gods will take vengeance not only on the foreswearer himself but also on those closest to him, his family. Many moderate Kikuyu have indeed been emancipated on the surface from the tribal religion, but not enough at heart to risk the Anglo-Saxon procedure of reporting to the police an oath extracted from them by force. A few really convinced Christian Kikuyu held out against Mau Mau at the risk of their lives; a few still loyal to the old pagan religion held out quite as courageously, for they, too, were morally outraged by the unscrupulousness of the Mau Mau campaign.

Caught in the Mau Mau net, however, was the great mass of the tribe. These were Kikuyu who were torn between the old and the new, no longer secure in the complex institutions of the tribe (primitive people have complicated, not simple, institutions), and yet by no means secure in the competitive individualistic life of the West, and indeed fundamentally handicapped in that life by the lack of economic opportunity. It was the "average" Kikuyu who supported the Mau Mau. It was the young Kikuyu who needed but could not afford a motor bike with a seat behind for the girl whom he was courting (they did not court that way in the old days); it was the tenant Kikuyu who, lacking land of his own, saw no possibility of surviving in old age; it was the Kikuyu who wanted his children to be educated but could not afford the school fees.

Late in 1952, the Kenya government declared a state of emergency, and help was flown from Britain. Two years later, the immediate crisis was apparently surmounted, and Kenyans were once again calling attention to the tourist attractions and economic opportunities of their land. But Mau Mau feeds on underground methods and has operated in a way that has struck terror into the heart of the white man.

South Africa

In the long run, what happens in Kenya, and in the regions to its south and west—Tanganyika (old German East Africa), Uganda, and Rhodesia—will be powerfully affected by what happens in the Union of South Africa. The Union is today the most dramatic center of race conflict, the place where the old, unregenerate feeling of white supremacy comes up most clearly against subject peoples already stirred by western institutions, western machines, western ideas and ideals. According to the census of 1951, there were in the Union of South Africa over 10,000,000 non-Europeans and a little over 2,500,000 Europeans, a ratio for the whole Union of four non-Europeans to one European. The non-Europeans include eight and a half million Bantu Negroes, nearly a million and a half "Colored" persons—that is, of mixed European and non-European blood—and 365,000 Asians, mostly Indians. The census, no doubt for reasons of political tact, does not break "Europeans" down into "British" and "Afrikaners" (the older term for these descendants of the Dutch and Huguenots was "Boers"). Political parties in South Africa, however, are organized by nationality, and to judge by party votes the Afrikaners outnumber the British everywhere in the Union except Natal.

These five elements—Afrikaners, British, Bantu, Asian, Colored—exist as quite self-conscious, propaganda-making groups, sometimes mutually exclusive in their aims. Their practice is not quite so extreme as their claims. They do indeed live in some sense together; to date, at least, life goes on in South Africa without actual civil war or revolution. Not even the Afrikaners, the most ardent believers in racial superiority, can bring themselves to undertake the extermination of Bantus and Colored. The cynic might add that the Afrikaners with out the blacks would have to do a lot of unpleasant work that the blacks now do for them. But the difficulties of South Africa go deeper into the human heart than economics can ever go.

During the 1930's, as we have seen in Chapter XXI, the Afrikaners developed pro-Nazi sympathies. In World War II, the Union came close to declaring its neutrality, as many Afrikaners would have wished; and its actual participation was comparatively limited. After the war, in 1949, the Union annexed the former German colony of Southwest Africa, for which it had been given the mandate following World War I. It made this annexation after refusing to convert its League of Nations mandate into a United Nations trusteeship. Politically, Southwest Africa supports the Nationalist Afrikaner party, since it has attracted Afrikaner rather than British immigrants. Meanwhile, the gap between British and Afrikaner increased; in the province of Natal, the only one where the British are in a majority among the whites, there were vigorous threats of secession from the Union.

This Afrikaner-British hostility, this return after the hopeful first years of the Union to the emotions that made the Boer War, is puzzling. If ever two groups "ought" to get together against a threat to their common position, it is the out-numbered Europeans facing the great mass of non-Europeans in South Africa. Yet the fact is that Afrikaner and British are mutually hostile. To the Afrikaner majority, the British are not sufficiently firm toward the blacks, are too soft and "liberal." Yet the average Britisher is by no means without his sense of what he calls the "color bar," by no means anxious to turn the Union over to a black majority.

The Negroes now do not have the vote. The voting rights of the Colored, that is, those of mixed blood, are still debated, but the defenders of white supremacy are against any participation in politics by anyone with any colored blood. The Afrikaner majority is resolutely segregationist in almost all possible fields of human relations—though they know they must have black workers.

The native policy of the Afrikaners is known as *Apartheid*—literally, apartness, separation. Behind *Apartheid* there is simple race prejudice of a kind familiar to Americans. Yet the Afrikaners also believe, as some Americans believe, that whites and blacks can develop in separate but adjacent groups, intertwining but never mingling. They believe that the whites can dominate political life, while the blacks get some of the benefits of modern economic and technological progress and continue to live in their own very separate quarters. In South Africa the policy of *Apartheid* is more rigorously separatist than the corresponding policy of segregation in the United States. It has been tightened in recent years, in contrast to the loosening of the American policy of segregation. Above all, *Apartheid* is set as an aim in a land where, unlike the United States, the blacks outnumber the whites almost four to one. It is quite clear that the South African non-Europeans, and especially the great Bantu majority, do not accept *Apartheid* as a blueprint for the future. Their extremist leaders at least, like the Mau Mau in Kenya, would like to get rid of the whites, and of Asians too, would

Top. *Slums near Johannesburg, Union of South Africa.* Bottom. *Adderley St., Capetown, Union of South Africa.*

797

like to sweep them out of South Africa altogether.

French North Africa

In the years since World War II perhaps the most serious outbreaks of violence on the African continent have occurred in the French North African possessions—Morocco, Tunisia, and Algeria. Here the main elements in the situation have sometimes resembled those in the Middle East—growing nationalism on the part of Arabic-speaking natives, greatly influenced by the general political ferment in the Arab world; threats of communist penetration; unsuccessful attempts by the imperial power to pursue old policies and maintain its old position. The situation has been complicated by two additional elements. One has been the presence of an important minority of Frenchmen and other European settlers, the *colons* or colonists. The *colons* have an important economic stake to protect, they cling to the old nineteenth-century imperial outlook, and they have therefore rigidly opposed, sometimes by violence, any significant concessions to native nationalism. The second element is that, while Morocco and Tunisia were often treated as colonies, they were legally French protectorates and retained at least shadow native governments under French domination. Algeria, however, has been treated as more than a colony and has actually been considered—most unrealistically, it would now seem—as a part of France herself.

This difference in status has helped the French to relax their hold on Morocco and Tunisia. Faced by mounting native unrest in these possessions and at the same time by a deteriorating situation in Indo-China, the French government attempted repression at first and then, in the mid-1950's, overrode violent objections by the *colons* to give the Moroccan and Tunisian governments virtual independence in domestic affairs and to declare them "interdependent" with France in matters of foreign policy and defense. The new position of Morocco and Tunisia appeared to be something less than dominion status on the British model, but it was a revolutionary advance over their earlier position. Although it may not satisfy all native hopes, the leaders of the freshly emancipated governments have shown more moderate statesmanship and less vindictiveness against the old imperial master than has been common in the Arab states of the Middle East.

In Algeria, however, lying between Morocco and Tunisia, there have been few suggestions of moderation or compromise down to 1956. Instead, there have been chronic rebellions by natives, chronic intransigence by *colons*, and finally a full-scale war, proving as costly for the French as the earlier one in Indo-China. The more Algerian nationalism was put down, the more its followers turned to bloody reprisals and to other forms of extremism.

V: The British Commonwealth

Canada

Within the British Commonwealth of Nations, aside from South Africa, domestic history has produced no striking novelties since 1939. Canada, as we shall see in the next chapter, is in the mid-twentieth century in the midst of an economic boom exceeding even that of the United States, and supported to a large extent by American capital. Politically, contrary to an opinion not still wholly rooted out of the American mind, Canada is in no sense ruled by Great Britain. She is, in short, an independent state tied to Great Britain by no juridical bonds, though an active and loyal member of the British Commonwealth. Those who determine her national consciousness by no means feel themselves a mere appendage of the United States, but think of themselves rather as an influential and independent mediator between the United States and Great Britain.

It is true that Canada is not all of one piece. The French Canadians, who are increasing in numbers slightly but not overwhelmingly faster than the rest of the Canadians, still speak their own language, and still in their Province of Quebec possess special privileges, in education for example, for which the United States affords no real parallel. There are French Canadians who cherish the kind of irredentist national feelings that cause so much trouble in other quarters of the world. To judge by the extremist French-Canadian periodical press and by some campaign speeches, one might well believe that in Canada the problem of nationality is as acute as it is between Afrikaners and British in South Africa, or between Ulstermen and the men of Eire in Ireland. In neither world war have the French Canadians been exactly enthusiastic for the Allied cause, and in both they have had to be very carefully managed by the federal government. But the majority of French Canadians are loyal to the existing government, and anxious to work with the English-speaking majority. They cannot sensibly hope to make all Canada French; as devout Catholics, they cannot want reunion with a France that since 1789 has had so strong a republican and anticlerical cast; and from a possible partition of Canada into separate English-speaking and French-speaking nations they are held back by a fear of absorption into the United States, which they know would make an end to their special group privileges.

New Zealand and Australia

In New Zealand, smallest of the dominions, the advance of social legislation has continued, capped as early as 1941 by a national scheme for socialized medicine, anticipating that of the mother country by several years. New Zealand still has a partly colonial economy, exporting wool, frozen meat, and other raw materials, and importing finished goods, still for the most part from Britain itself. But it has enough home industry to preserve its self-respect. The islands, with their 100,000 square miles, are not yet crowded by their 2,000,000 total population, and the original natives, the Maoris, are by no means in the position of straitened peoples like the Kikuyu in Kenya, or the Navahos in the United States. They have produced military and political leaders and professional men, and seem to be in the midst of as successful a process of peaceful and dignified westernization as has yet been recorded.

In Australia, there are no minority problems. The Commonwealth has had to overcome some provincial separatism (railroad gauges vary from province to province, for instance), but Australian states are hardly more basically differentiated than are, say, those of the American West. Twentieth-century Australia too is in a large degree a welfare state. Organized labor has worked, as it did in England, through a political Labor party which has had its terms of power in the federal as well as in state governments. But Australia today is well short of full socialism. Australia, a society even newer than the United States, has still a greater touch of frontier boisterousness. In both world wars, American troops seemed to neutral observers positively quiet and disciplined, positively devoted to spit-and-polish, in comparison with their Australian allies.

Modern Australia shares with New Zealand a very serious problem indeed. The two together are but a handful of whites on the edge of a Far East with a rapidly growing population for whom there are no good lands left at home. Both have maintained rigorous policies of excluding all save white immigration. Both are relatively thinly settled, having together a population but little over 10,000,000. Both fear the rise of a power in Asia that might reach out and overwhelm them. The decisive defeat of Japan in World War II has quieted their worst fears, but the threat remains a very real one. In terms of international relations, this means that both must rely on the United States as ultimate defender. But this by no means implies that they will cut themselves off from Britain, a step for which emotionally and even economically they are not prepared.

The Nature of the Commonwealth

The British Commonwealth as a whole has had a very important development in recent decades. Its constitutional structure was fixed in 1931 by the Statute of Westminster (see Chapter XXI). Its membership was enlarged in the late 1940's by the addition of India, Pakistan, and Ceylon, lands that are certainly unlike the other dominions and not British in any ordinary sense of the word. The statement in the Statute of Westminster that the members of the Commonwealth are "autonomous communities" is not mere rhetoric and is, if anything, an understatement. A member can set up tariffs against other members, regulate immigration by citizens of other states in the Commonwealth, have its own diplomatic services, make treaties with states both inside and outside the Commonwealth, raise and use its own armed forces, have its own flag, and much else.

Yet surely the Commonwealth itself is not just an imaginary entity? In juridical language, the "Crown" remains as a stated link among the dominions. But this term is an extraordinarily rarefied abstraction. Canadians may dutifully put the Queen on their postage stamps. They do indeed cheer visiting British royalty; but in these days so do Americans. The Canadians now legally, and very carefully, call themselves "Canadian citizens" and not "British subjects." In India, the Crown seems to be nothing as flesh-and-blood as a Queen, but a complete abstraction. Yet the Commonwealth has held together in two great wars, and has to date managed to retain India with its past of bitter rebellion. Perhaps nothing more than convenience and habit holds the Commonwealth together. These are, however, powerful forces, especially when they take the form of economic and strategic convenience and democratic habits.

The Commonwealth nations have expressed their democratic habits and traditions in the shape of actual institutions. They have a solid backlog in law, in the practice of parliamentary and party government, in education and in political ideas, in the unspoken assumptions and folkways of their peoples. This obviously applies to the older dominions, the white ones. On the surface, especially in terms of folkways, it might appear obviously *not* to apply to a country like India. Yet British ways have sunk deep roots into Indian life, especially among the new ruling classes. To take one example from recent history: the Indian commander of the forces supervising the repatriation of prisoners under the terms of the 1953 truce in Korea looked, to judge from the press photographs, very much like a well-tanned English general, who might be named Cholmondely or Massingham.

The British Commonwealth has no common federal organ of government. "Imperial Federation"—a scheme for the establishment of a true federal government with executive, legislative, and judicial branches —was much talked and written about in the late nineteenth and early twentieth centuries. Nowadays Imperial Federation is hardly even seriously considered. The business of the British Commonwealth, however, does get done, despite the lack of formal central institutions. Regular conferences among British and dominion prime ministers and their staffs, and among administrators and experts of all sorts, have become the established procedure. Such conferences are the meetings, not of mere diplomats, but of conscious political part- ners. Hopeful men, especially in the Commonwealth, like to believe that this rather informal type of association not only has proved its strength but also can be expanded to include other colonies when they are ready for self-government, as Ghana has already suggested. And there are some who believe that the British Commonwealth can set a better pattern for a possible world federation than can any other scheme yet devised.

VI: Conclusions

In the brief period since World War II, the status of colonial peoples has altered more than in any period since the modern expansion of Europe began in the fifteenth century. As a result of this revolution, the size of western colonial empires has shrunk dramatically. The British have given up Burma, Ceylon, India, Pakistan, and Palestine, and have started to make concessions elsewhere. The Dutch have given up Indonesia reluctantly, and the Americans have liberated the Philippines voluntarily. Out of the wreckage of Mussolini's empire, Ethiopia has regained her old independence and Libya has won hers for the first time. The French, next to the British the most important colonial power, still retain some of their old imperial possessions, notably in Madagascar and in Equatorial and West Africa. But they have already lost Syria, Lebanon, and part of Indo-China, and their influence in North Africa is visibly waning.

Meantime, events in Asia have driven home the fact that the once-despised orientals are in warfare virtually the equals of western powers, with almost equal chances of success. Witness the Japanese victory over Russia in 1905 and the damage inflicted by the Japanese on American warships at Pearl Harbor in 1941. And the West has also experienced such effective types of resistance as the nonviolence of Gandhi, the savage terror of the Mau Mau, and the guerrilla tactics of communist-led rebels in Indo-China and Malaya. This dramatic equalizing or near-equalizing of westerner and non-westerner in the test of physical force has revolutionized the international balance. It has enlarged the communist bloc, notably by the addition of China, and it has created a new neutral bloc, centered on India, to which many of the new Asian and Middle Eastern nations seem to be gravitating. The implications of this change we shall discuss in the next chapter.

The revolution against imperialism that we have just examined is an unfinished revolution. It is almost certain to spread further in the coming years; how rapidly we can only guess. In the later 1950's, however, western imperialism, though certainly in retreat, is not finished or dead. Even in terms of old-fashioned imperialism —that is, the colony in which ultimate decisions are made by the mother country— the British, French, Belgians, and Portuguese have great territories that are still in varying degrees of tutelage. The United States has a few Pacific outposts, Guam and the islands taken from the Japanese in World War II, that are still colonies in the old sense; Spain and Holland have their fragments of empire.

Most colonies, and some of the newly self-governing territories, still have essentially colonial economic status; they still supply raw materials and receive finished goods. Finally, it is by no means clear that the great experiment in a new kind of tie between the western homeland and former dependencies, the British Commonwealth, is foredoomed to failure. The loose tie that binds the Commonwealth is not much like the old imperial tie, but it may still be sufficient to keep it together as a going concern.

In any case, it is evident that western imperialism has already profoundly changed the non-western states. Even the former imperial preserves that have won full independence have been shaped anew by the expansion of the West. They could not escape the influence of the wide movements of western men, western things, and western ideas. The West will not inherit the earth; but it has already set its stamp upon the future.

Reading Suggestions on the Revolt against Imperialism

General Accounts

V. M. Dean, *The Nature of the Non-Western World* (N.Y.: New American Library, 1957). Informative general introduction to the newly independent and significant states.

R. Linton, ed., *Most of the World* (N.Y.: Columbia Univ. Press, 1949). A good survey of the peoples of Africa, Latin America, and Asia.

H. J. Morgenthau, *Politics among Nations: The Struggle for Power and Peace*, 2nd ed. (N.Y.: Knopf, 1954). An excellent survey from a tough-minded, realistic standpoint.

F. S. C. Northrop, *The Meeting of East and West* (N.Y.: Macmillan, 1946). A philosophic discussion of the problems of One World.

A. J. Toynbee, *Civilization on Trial* (N.Y.: Oxford Univ. Press, 1948). Essays treating the contacts between civilizations.

Special Studies: Asia

R. I. Crane, *Aspects of Economic Development in South Asia* (N.Y.: Institute of Pacific Relations, 1954); C. Dubois, *Social Forces in South East Asia* (Minneapolis: Univ. of Minnesota Press, 1949). Two solid works on a little-known area.

C. Wolf, *The Indonesian Story* (N.Y.: Day, 1948); and G. McT. Kahin, *Nationalism and Revolution in Indonesia* (Ithaca: Cornell Univ. Press, 1952). Two useful accounts of the young republic.

T. G. Spear, *India, Pakistan, and the West*, 2nd ed. (N.Y.: Oxford Univ. Press, 1952. Home University Library); R. Symonds, *The Making of Pakistan*, 3rd ed. (London: Faber & Faber, 1951). Useful introductions to the new states of the Indian subcontinent.

E. O. Reischauer, *The United States and Japan*, new ed. (1957); J. K. Fairbank, *The United States and China* (1948); W. N. Brown, *The United States and India and Pakistan* (1953). Three instructive surveys by American experts in the useful series, "American Foreign Policy Library," D. C. McKay, ed. (Cambridge: Harvard Univ. Press).

F. Low, *The Struggle for Asia* (N.Y.: Praeger, 1955). A survey focused on communist attempts to penetrate the area.

G. Wint, *The British in Asia*, rev. ed. (N.Y.: Institute of Pacific Relations, 1954). A scholarly survey.

H. S. Quigley and J. E. Turner, *The New Japan: Government and Politics* (Minneapolis: Univ. of Minnesota Press, 1956). Up-to-date account by American experts.

K. S. Latourette, *The American Record in the Far East, 1945-1951* (N.Y.: Macmillan, 1952); H. Feis, *The China Tangle* (Princeton: Princeton Univ. Press, 1953). Two admirable attempts at a balanced approach to the vexed problem of American policy toward China during and after World War II.

W. W. Rostow and others, *The Prospects for Communist China* (Cambridge: Technology Press of M.I.T., 1954). An ambitious and suggestive survey of the potentialities of Red China.

Special Studies: The Middle East

The Middle East: A Political and Economic Survey, 2nd ed. (London: Royal Institute of International Affairs, 1954). A most useful reference book.

G. Lenczowski, *The Middle East in World Affairs*, 2nd ed. (Ithaca: Cornell Univ. Press, 1956). An informative survey.

L. V. Thomas and R. N. Frye, *The United States and Turkey and Iran* (Cambridge: Harvard

Univ. Press, 1951). A good introduction by two American experts.

G. Antonius, *The Arab Awakening* (Beirut: Khayat's College Book Coöperative, 1955). The classic study of the formation of modern Arab nationalism.

H. Z. Nuseibeh, *The Ideas of Arab Nationalism* (Ithaca: Cornell Univ. Press, 1956). A revealing analysis by an American-trained Arab.

C. Issawi, *Egypt at Mid-Century* (N.Y.: Oxford Univ. Press, 1954). A first-rate detailed study; perhaps the most informative single volume in English concerned with the modern Arab world.

Gamal Abdul Nasser, *Egypt's Liberation* (Washington: Public Affairs Press, 1955). The leader of the Egyptian revolution writes about its philosophy.

S. H. Longrigg, *Oil in the Middle East* (N.Y.: Oxford Univ. Press, 1954). An excellent study, decidedly pro-western in tone.

N. A. Faris and M. T. Husayn, *The Crescent in Crisis* (Lawrence: Univ. of Kansas Press, 1955). An informative evaluation of modern Arab problems by Arab scholars.

W. Z. Laqueur, *Communism and Nationalism in the Middle East* (N.Y.: Praeger, 1956). An instructive detailed study.

Special Studies—Africa and the British Commonwealth

J. H. Hofmeyr and J. P. Cope, *South Africa*, 2nd ed. (N.Y.: McGraw-Hill, 1952); L. Marquard, *The Peoples and Policies of South Africa* (N.Y.: Oxford Univ. Press, 1952); G. H. Calpin, ed., *The South African Way of Life: Values and Ideals in a Multi-Racial Society* (N.Y.: Columbia Univ. Press, 1953). Three useful introductions to the South African problem.

C. W. de Kiewiet, *The Anatomy of South African Misery* (New York: Oxford Univ. Press, 1957). A balanced survey by a leading American educator, himself of South African background.

A. Campbell, *The Heart of Africa* (N.Y.: Knopf, 1954). The native problem as seen by a competent journalist.

R. Wright, *Black Power* (N.Y.: Harper, 1954). Self-government in the Gold Coast viewed by an American Negro intellectual.

L. S. B. Leakey, *Mau Mau and the Kikuyu* (N.Y.: Day, 1954). The indispensable book on the subject.

G. Grady, *Democracy in the Dominions*, 2nd ed. (Toronto: Univ. of Toronto Press, 1952). Attacks an important subject seldom treated: the comparative institutional history of the various dominions.

Fiction

A. Paton, *Cry, the Beloved Country* (N.Y.: Scribner's, 1948). The famous novel about the plight of the South African Negroes.

R. Godden, *Breakfast with the Nikolides* (Boston: Little, Brown, 1942), and *The River* (Boston: Little, Brown, 1946). Two sensitive novels about India by an Englishwoman.

N. Saghal, *Prison and Chocolate Cake* (N.Y.: Knopf, 1954). Informative novel about India by an Indian.

G. Greene, *The Quiet American* (N.Y.: Viking, 1956). Satirical portrait of an American "do-gooder" trying to modernize Indo-China.

P. H. Newby, *The Picnic at Sakkara* (N.Y.: Knopf, 1955). A balanced novel about a British professor who becomes involved with revolutionary students in Egypt.

CHAPTER TWENTY-FOUR

The Western World

Since 1945

I: The "Cold War"—The International Aftermath

The French still call their national history since 1789 "contemporary history." Behind this usage, which must seem strange to an American, there lies a principle valid for us: the French feel that the great issues, the great problems, stemming from the events of 1789 have still not received even the compromises, the partial solutions, we expect here on earth for such problems. If the term "contemporary" be so understood, it is clear that events all over the world since 1945 must be considered "contemporary history"—and indeed are likely to have to be so considered for some time. For in international politics alone, the two great problems of the revolt of former "colonial" peoples that we have just considered and the continuing rivalry between coalitions led respectively by the United States and the Soviet

Union, which we noted briefly at the end of Chapter XXII, are still very critical problems, still apparently far from the kind of solution that enables the historian to set up a landmark, an end of a period. We must now trace further the history of international politics since 1945, a history that is dominated by the rivalry of the United States and Soviet Russia, a history that, just because it is so very "contemporary," just because we are all so immersed in it, cannot be treated with the completeness, the relative accuracy, the objectivity, the historian strives for.

The Aftermath of War

By now the reader will realize that the great ills of general war take many years to clear up, that they are never neatly cured by a formal peace. As we have seen in earlier chapters, it took a long time to repair the damage done to European nations by World War I. In France, for instance, the human losses were so great that full recovery was impossible. The damage of World War II greatly exceeded that of the earlier war because of its far-flung battlegrounds, the mass executions in Nazi concentration camps, the casualties suffered by civilians through air attacks, starvation, and disease. The total number of human deaths resulting from the war has been estimated at 22,000,000, more than half of them civilians, a total at least double that of World War I. It should, however, be noted that if the deaths from influenza among civilians in 1918 are counted as part of the casualties of World War I, the total human losses in the two wars are much more nearly equal. No major epidemic accompanied World War II; and even in theaters of war of relatively primitive sanitation, new medical knowledge kept deaths from disease at a low figure. Material damages to property, however, have for the Second World War been estimated in excess of

$2,000,000,000,000 (two thousand billion), many times that for the First. These tragic losses cannot in our time be fully repaired. But they were at least offset in many countries during the decade following 1945 by a high birth rate and by brisk programs of economic reconstruction and modernization.

Of all the problems created by modern wars, perhaps the knottiest is that of reconstructing international politics. As we have just seen, after 1945 a widespread revolution swept the colonies and dependencies of the European states. Imperial ties were severed or loosened, and new independent states appeared in many areas formerly under western control. In the world as a whole, a new international alignment developed after the defeat of the Axis aggressors. The rival states of the United States and Soviet Russia faced each other in a struggle that has been called the "cold war."

These troubles are not unprecedented. An aftermath of political turbulence followed World War I and the Versailles Treaty of 1919. Even the Vienna settlement of 1815, which seems in retrospect a generally satisfactory peace, was not without its aftermath, the revolutions of 1820-1821 that Metternich tried so hard to suppress (see Chapter XII). It may be, however, that the aftermath of World War II will seem even to future historians, with more perspective than we now have, to have been more than usually severe.

New Elements and Old

New elements of course entered into the postwar situation. The atomic bomb, guided missiles, the very real possibility of bacteriological warfare and other horrible weapons for the first time made concrete and plausible the threat that a new general war might wipe out the human race—or at the very least might destroy the physical and the moral bases of civilization, and reduce what is left of mankind to something like another Stone Age. This amounts to the statement that the age-old balance between attack and defense, and, more important, between human ability to destroy and human ability to build and repair, has in fact been so altered that attack and destruction will be paramount. The experts in physics and allied fields are by no means in agreement as to whether the new weapons, if used without restriction, would set up such lethal reactions—from, for instance, radiation—that human life on earth would be wiped out. The experts in human relations are in even less agreement as to the likelihood that such weapons will actually be used without restriction. But the fear that they will be so used is undoubtedly widespread, especially among educated westerners.

Further, the existence of only one system of states related in international politics—the actuality of One World—was new. Ever since Columbus, civilization had been building up to this One World, and after 1945 what had once been rhetoric became fact. There were still out-of-the-way pockets on the earth where the inhabitants had no direct concern with international politics, but by and large all organized political units were either in the western camp or in the Russian, or else they were wavering between the two.

The actual leaders of the rival camps were new to that position. In the world wars of Napoleon and the Kaiser, Britain and either France or Germany had been the centers of the opposing groups. Now the United States and Russia became the unquestioned focal points of world power. Although Russia had been an important element in international politics since Peter the Great, and although the United States had been active in international politics in spite of strong isolationist theories ever since it had been founded, neither state assumed leadership until the 1940's.

But it is a grave mistake to simplify the situation, as some publicists do, into one where only the United States and Russia count as superpowers, and where all the rest of the world can be neglected. Great as these two states are in manpower and in production, actual and potential, the two together have no more than an eighth of the total population of the globe. And, although, thanks especially to the extraordinary productive capacity of the United States, the two together have a much greater proportion of the world's present productive capacity, they still have less than the potential of the rest of the world combined. Neither state is, in fact, materially autarkic, self-sufficient. The leaders of both have shown by their actions that they do not regard their rivalry as a simple duel of rival autarkic units, but rather as a competition for the active allegiance of the rest of the world. Each is in fact the head of a great coalition, which each has sought to extend, or at least strengthen. And neither coalition is a perfect monolithic block; members of each coalition can and do try to go their own way.

Indeed, if their rivalry breaks into a general war, that war will probably be decided in favor of the side that does win the allegiance of the strongest combination of countries. In short, any such war will be a war of coalitions. In a sense, then, the future of the world depends on whether those who are neither Russian nor American decide that the Soviet Union or the United States is in fact the aggressor. The present rivalry between these two states is indeed a rivalry for the heart and soul of mankind.

This kind of rivalry, we repeat, is not new. It has in its current form, however, a depth and intensity attributable to a new combination of elements. Eighteenth-century wars, for instance, were largely struggles for sheer power, sheer territorial and other material gains, with perhaps a touch

of emotional nationalism as an added incentive. With the wars of the French
Revolution and the nineteenth century,
nationalism entered in more forcefully, and
remains, along with the struggle for power,
a major element in the present situation.
But the present struggle between the
United States and Russia seems even more
deep-seated than the nationalist wars of
old. It is a struggle to make prevail over
this earth one way of life, one set of ideals
and basic beliefs, to the exclusion of the
other. This profound struggle, we must
note, is underestimated and vulgarized if
it is called a struggle over "ideologies."

To sum up: there are both in Russia and
in the United States, and among the peoples lined up with each, many who feel
strongly that at least *in the long run* Russian communism and western democracy
cannot as actual going societies live together on this earth. The historian will
not by any means conclude from this analysis that war between the two coalitions
is inevitable; he must conclude that adjustments between the two systems will be
difficult to make, that something like an
"armed truce" or a "cold war" is likely to
last for some time, and that the threat of
a World War III is by no means unreal, by
no means the work of neurotic alarmists.

The Communist Bloc in Europe

Concretely,
the years fol-
lowing the end of the war in Germany and
Japan saw the alignment of most of the
world either on Russia's side or on that of
the United States. After Yalta, the Russians disregarded what western statesmen
believed were firm commitments to allow
the countries of eastern Europe and the
Balkans to choose freely their own form
of government—and presumably to align
themselves with the West if they wished.
The Russians built up, by familiar methods
of one-party politics, with rigged elections,

proscriptions, pressures of all sorts, the
solid bloc of satellite lands that we know as
the Iron Curtain countries. Beginning early
in World War II, the Russians simply absorbed, as constituent republics of the
U.S.S.R., part of Finland, the whole of
Estonia, Latvia, and Lithuania, and parts of
Poland and Rumania as well as the extreme
eastern end of old Czechoslovakia. At the
close of the war, they annexed part of East
Prussia, so that Königsberg, sacred to Germans as the home of the great philosopher
Kant, was now Kaliningrad, renamed for a
high Soviet official. In eastern and southeastern Europe they organized "people's
republics," dependent states with communist governments, in Poland, Czechoslovakia, Rumania, Hungary, Bulgaria, and Albania.

Their troops formally occupied about
one-third of Germany, roughly between
the Elbe and the Oder rivers, where they
also organized a satellite East German Republic. The parts of Germany lying east of
the Oder, save for the sections of East
Prussia directly annexed to the U.S.S.R.,
they handed over to their Polish satellite.
Here apparently a wholesale transfer of
population removed the Germans into
either East Germany or exile, and the Germans were replaced with Poles. Finland became part of the Russian system, but has
subsequently enjoyed distinctly more autonomy than the other satellites and has
retained its pre-war political institutions.
Austria, divided between the occupying
forces of East and West, was detached from
Germany, and Hitler's first major territorial gain, the *Anschluss*, was undone.

Berlin, to the east of the dividing line
between the Soviet and the Allied zones
in Germany, was occupied in separate zones
by Russia, the United States, Great Britain, and France, but was left completely
surrounded by Soviet-dominated German
territory. The lack of any western-con-
trolled connection between Berlin and West
Germany was serious, for here on April 1,

EUROPE, 1957

A NATO countries { North Atlantic Treaty Organization

Communist bloc

◉ Capital cities

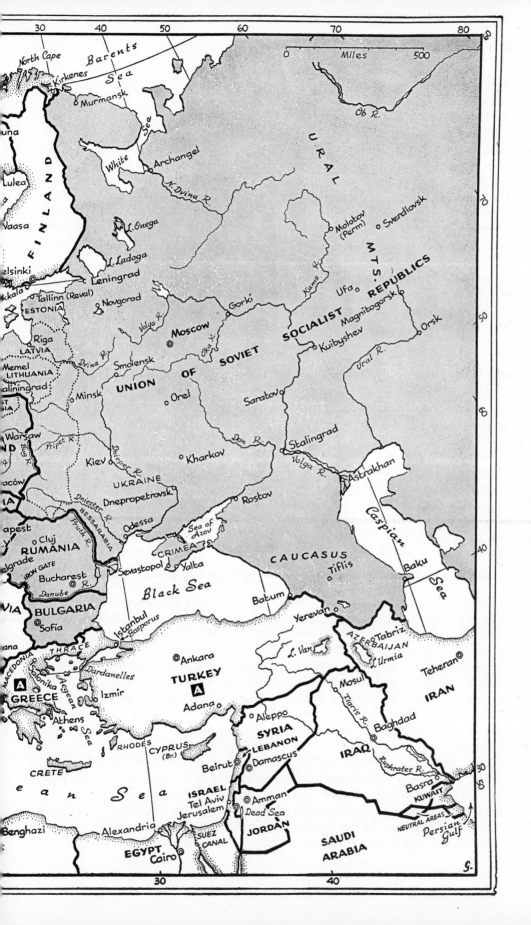

1948, the Russians began one of the most bitter phases of the "cold war." By shutting off the land routes from the west into Berlin, they attempted to force the western Allies to turn Berlin wholly over to them. The Allies stood firm, however, and achieved the almost incredible feat of supplying a great metropolitan area wholly by air. In the six months of the blockade, Allied aircraft flew over 2,300,000 tons of coal, food, and other necessities into western Berlin. They also set up their own counterblockade of eastern Berlin. On September 1, the Russians gave up, and Berlin returned to its sufficiently abnormal status of joint occupation.

Yugoslavia

One anomaly developed in this great bloc of Russian satellites in eastern Europe. Yugoslavia, which had refused to go over to the Germans in 1941, remained throughout the war a theater of intense guerrilla action. There were two main groups, the Chetniks, led by General Mikhailovich, representing the conservative Serb domination of the south Slav kingdom, and the Partisans, led by Joseph Broz, better known by his underground communist name of Tito. As the war went on, the communist-inspired Partisans gained ground against the Chetniks, who seem to have preferred to compromise with the Germans and Italians rather than continue a war on the communist side. By 1943, the western Allies, their eyes fixed on the paramount need of beating Hitler, decided to support Tito with supplies; when the Russians entered Belgrade in October, 1944, they found their fellow communist Tito in control.

Yugoslavia seemed a natural satellite. Yet in June, 1948, the world learned with some surprise that the Tito regime had been expelled from the propaganda union of communist states known as the Cominform (Communist Information Bureau),

successor to the Comintern. Soon relations between Yugoslavia and the Russian satellite system were terminated amid mutual recrimination. Yugoslavia remained a communist state, though after 1948 Tito slowed down the process of land collectivization and sought to gain support from the West. In our present perspective, Yugoslavian nationalism seems to have proved stronger than communism. The break between Tito and Stalin, though furthered by the unwillingness of a strong personality like Tito to take orders from Moscow, seems to have been at bottom an expression of the strength of Yugoslav national feeling.

But whether the break was a matter of personalities at the top, or of national feelings widely held, or—and this is most likely—of both, the successors to Stalin, who died in 1953, set about mending it. They made public gestures of reconciliation, and got communist leaders in their various satellites to assume in public part of the blame for the original break. By 1956, Tito had swung back somewhat away from the West and toward the communist orbit, though without a clean break with the West. The whole behavior of Yugoslavia since 1945, however, is a reminder that we still have a balance-of-power world in international politics.

This reminder was strengthened by events in Poland and Hungary in the fall and winter of 1956-1957. In Poland, strikes and demonstrations against Russian direct control sufficed to put into power without serious bloodshed a nationalist-communist government headed by Gomulka. Poland, like Yugoslavia, remained communist, but secured somewhat more national freedom, even in religion. The Hungarian experience was more tragic. In a bloody urban revolt, reminiscent of the days of 1848, the people of Budapest, sparked by university students, rose and drove out the Russians, setting up a multi-party free government under Imre Nagy. The Russians returned in force within a few days, however, and put down the revolt, placing a typical puppet government under Kadar in office. Some 140,000 Hungarians fled into Austria to freedom and resettlement in various western lands; but no western power felt able to interfere directly in Hungary. The Russian "system" of satellites, though threatened, remained on the surface intact.

China

To the east, the Russians shortly after the end of the war added to their bloc the most populous nation on earth, China with its half-billion inhabitants (for details, see Chapter XXIII). A land with which the United States in the past had had most friendly relations, a land she had for years sought to protect from European and Japanese aggression through her policy of the "Open Door," was now formally enrolled among America's enemies. Inevitably, this turn of events aroused great bitterness in the United States. The bitterness was expressed not only in the refusal of the United States to recognize Communist China, but also in the reproach that the American government, and particularly the Department of State, had so bungled relations with China that the Reds won by default—if not by the positive encouragement of fellow-traveling Americans.

These events are so recent that it is foolish to hope that they can be judged with detachment. But this much can be affirmed: once the negotiations of the American General Marshall for a Communist-Nationalist understanding had failed after the close of World War II, the Chinese Nationalist government could have been maintained on the mainland of China only by all-out American support, including almost certainly the use of American troops. It is most unlikely that in 1948-1949 any American government would have felt it had the support of American public opinion

in committing the country to an active war in China.

Since then, however, the United States has supported with her navy and with economic aid the Chinese Nationalist government on the island of Formosa, retroceded to China by Japan, which had seized it in 1895. The United States has also successfully opposed all efforts to gain for Communist China admission to the United Nations, where in 1957 the seat for China was still held by the Formosa government. American support of this Chinese Nationalist government, a support quite logical in cold-war politics, has, however, somewhat strained Anglo-American relations, for the British have recognized Red China. Finally, as we have seen in Chapter XXIII, after actual "hot war" in two former colonial areas, Korea and French Indo-China, compromise settlements divided these lands into a northern, communist-dominated section and a southern section still under western influence.

Stresses within the Communist Bloc

The communist bloc is a vast area, a set of contiguous states, occupying the "heartland" of the great Eurasian continent, from Leipzig to Vladivostok and Peiping. How solid a bloc it will prove to be is one of the great unsolved problems of our time. It survived intact an event that some observers believed might bring on a major internal crisis—the death of Stalin. After Stalin died, early in 1953, there were clearly strains within the top leadership (for details, see below, p. 832), but there was no repetition of the Stalin-Trotsky duel that followed Lenin's death. Soviet foreign policy continued its great efforts to hold the communist bloc together, and to undermine western influence in the former colonial areas, in India, in Southeast Asia, in the Middle East.

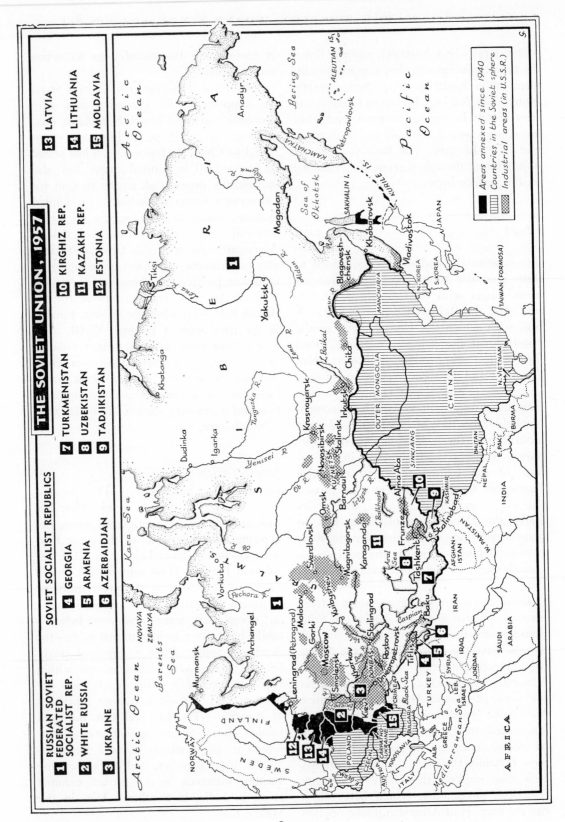

THE SOVIET UNION, 1957

RUSSIAN SOVIET FEDERATED SOCIALIST REP.
1
2 WHITE RUSSIA
3 UKRAINE

SOVIET SOCIALIST REPUBLICS
4 GEORGIA
5 ARMENIA
6 AZERBAIDJAN

7 TURKMENISTAN
8 UZBEKISTAN
9 TADJIKISTAN

10 KIRGHIZ REP.
11 KAZAKH REP.
12 ESTONIA

13 LATVIA
14 LITHUANIA
15 MOLDAVIA

■ Areas annexed since 1940
▤ Countries in the Soviet sphere
▨ Industrial areas (in U.S.S.R.)

Yet the communist bloc since World War II has been subject to two interrelated stresses. First, all its constituent states, including the two giants, Russia and China, have faced the internal problems set by the communist revolutions of which they are the children. The study of revolutions in the past suggests that, after the initial enthusiasm of the great common effort to establish the new society, there is a period of stress and adjustment. Russia may already have weathered successfully the Soviet equivalent of Thermidor (see Chapter XIX). But communism also makes very great promises to men—promises of peace, material abundance, the good life for all, not in another world after death, but right here, now, or at least very soon. In the communist states these promises have not yet been fulfilled. Perhaps they can be partially fulfilled, enough to maintain the populations in a reasonable state of content; perhaps they can be softened and compromised; perhaps the populations can be made to accept such substitutes as the absurd nationalistic claims that the Russians were the first to invent virtually everything worth inventing. And perhaps not. It is significant that, though the Soviet Union continued after the war the pre-war Five-Year Plans, some emphasis was placed on consumers' goods, the sort of things that the ordinary person purchases for his own use.

We may be somewhat more certain of a second possible weakness in the communist bloc. The units of the bloc are after all nation-states, some of them with long histories as self-conscious, independent states and societies. Publicists who take the word for the deed have sometimes echoed the Marxist word that communism has now destroyed entirely the sentiment and fact of nationalism. But the historian will be very cautious here. He will incline to believe that not even the magic of communism can at once master the nationalistic forces that in the past prevented the merging of such self-conscious states and societies into perfectly unified blocs. It would be rash to predict that Rumania, Czechoslovakia, or China will go "Titoist" and follow the Yugoslav example of breaking with Moscow in some future crisis; Poland, however, seems to have broken off part way. It would be simple historical common sense to assert that the present Russian communist coalition is by no means immune from the stresses and strains that have always made coalitions hard to hold together. The events of the autumn of 1956 in Poland and Hungary underlined these stresses. Moreover, an eventually industrialized China, with a population more than twice that of the U.S.S.R., might well consider itself entitled to occupy a more significant power position in the communist coalition than at present.

Communists outside the Russian Bloc

Beyond the U.S.S.R. itself and its bloc of communist countries, communism under Russian inspiration has been at work, in varying degrees of strength, all over the world. That strength is hard to measure country by country for the period since 1945. In some parts of the world, such as Malaya and Indo-China, the communists soon became organized fighting groups with partisan armies in the field. In other parts, such as Spain, the communists have been outlawed, but they most certainly exist as an active underground movement. In still other areas, as in France and Italy, they are a legally organized party taking part in elections for legislative bodies. Here a yardstick of their strength is the popular vote and the number of seats they have obtained in the national legislatures. The yardstick, however, may often be misleading. In France, for example, the communists secured a bit more than a quarter of the popular vote in the national elections of 1946 and 1951. Yet students of the French scene believe that of the communist votes only a small fraction represented party militants; the bulk formed a "protest" vote, workers protesting the high cost of living, intellectuals and others protesting the do-nothing policies of postwar French cabinets and the alleged American threat to French cultural and political independence.

Broadly speaking, communism as an internal movement in the non-communist world can be divided for convenience into two broad categories. There are the communists in lands of darker-skinned people who have until recently, or who are still, in a colonial relation to the West; and there are the communists in the western states themselves.

In the first group, communist policy has naturally been to try to exploit hostility to the West, and especially to former imperial masters, British, French, Dutch, and —in the Philippines—American. There are in these countries, as we have seen, vast masses who by western standards are miserably poor, underfed, living on the margin of existence. They should in simple logic be ripe for communist propaganda. Yet many good observers hold that in so far as these masses are politically conscious, they are inspired by nationalism, and by the kind of nationalism that feeds on hatred of the whites. The typical communist converts in these countries are not "proletarians" but educated intellectuals who are at once frustrated nationalists and frustrated aspirants to well-paid white-collar jobs. In the Middle Eastern states, for instance, they are lawyers, teachers, journalists, or minor government officials, all resentful of the fact that their social, economic, and political status is not as high as they feel it should be. They are an *avant garde* as yet without a mass army behind them.

In the second group, politically a significant one in France and Italy, very small elsewhere in western Europe, the existence of a labor movement with a long radical past insured that the discontented intellectuals of the communist *avant garde* would have at least some support from the workers. In most of Latin America the communists are outlawed, and resemble rather those of the Middle East than those of Europe—that is, they are for the most part disgruntled intellectuals. Only in Guatemala did a communist-oriented regime hold power for a brief period in the early 1950's.

The "Free World"

After World War II, the United States assumed the leadership of the "free world," the coalition opposed to the great Russian coalition. On this western side are the British Commonwealth and Empire, France and the French Union, western Europe generally, West Germany, Greece, Turkey, parts of the Middle East, Latin America, and the recent enemy Japan. In organized productive activity, in potential material resources, even in actual population, this coalition is stronger than the Russian bloc. Even in geopolitical terms, though the solid land mass of the communists may at first glance seem to have the advantage over the scattered lands of the free world, modern sea and air power has helped to knit the free world together in a military sense.

Soon after 1945, in fact, the United States took the lead in developing measures to strengthen the non-communist states, particularly in Europe, against possible communist aggression from without or subversion from within. Notably, in 1947 America sponsored the Marshall Plan (named for the Secretary of State, General Marshall) to accelerate economic recovery from the damage and disruption of World War II and thus to rectify conditions on which communists might otherwise have thrived. In 1949, the United States sponsored the North Atlantic Treaty Organization, "NATO," a defensive alliance including not only the states on the European and American shores of the North Atlantic but also Iceland, Italy, Greece, and Turkey.

The central problem of the free world since 1945, however, has been not so much military as political: whether the free world really is united against the communist bloc, whether it has the political and moral resources to hold together. The "free world" is by no means uniformly free. Doctrinaire liberals in the West complain that some of the states lined up with them —Franco's Spain, Portugal under the milder dictatorship of Salazar—are totalitarian and anti-democratic; that the Argentine Republic, though no longer under Perón, is still, as are some other Latin-American countries, a dictatorship, and a military one at that; that throughout the Middle East it is not the miserably oppressed people, but only the exploiting "effendi," who support the West; that throughout Africa America's allies, the British, French, Portuguese, and Belgians, still hold the Negroes in colonial subjection; that semi-feudal Ethiopia is a caricature of a free country. To this liberal indictment the candid observer has to reply that it is in large measure true. If he is content to take a simple realistic position, the observer can remark that in an international crisis like the "cold war" the enemy of your enemy is in fact your friend. The important thing is that Franco, Salazar, and other dictators are at least bitterly opposed to the communists.

This brings us to another central aspect of the problem of international relations since World War II. The war thrust the United States into a position of leadership. How well equipped has she shown herself for that position? Events since 1945 have shown that Americans lack the kind of experience that peoples like the Romans and the British acquired over the long years of their leadership. Americans are idealistic, impatient, anxious for quick results; they could learn much wisdom from the old

French proverb—"The best is often the enemy of the good." But events have also shown the assets of Americans. Though they have continued to have difficulty with the color line in the United States, they have also done much since World War II toward ending the segregation of Negroes in schooling, in the armed services, and elsewhere. In relations with peoples of darker skin overseas, further, the Americans seem to be rather less overbearing than their British predecessors. They are not, like the Germans, burdened with a belief in crude racist theories. Though they find it hard to understand the religious views of people like the Hindus, for instance, they are used to the practice of religious toleration.

The enemies of the United States, for obvious reasons, paint Americans as simply another aggressive conquering nation, out to dominate just as conquerors have always dominated. Americans do not recognize themselves as so painted. Their success in helping make the world a better place will depend on whether they can convince the rest of the human race that they are not the usual sort of conquerors.

The democratic coalition led by the United States of course has been subject to nationalistic stresses and strains—the pride, the economic interests, the long traditions that make Englishmen or Frenchmen or Germans or Luxemburgers want some things that other members of the coalition do not want. But we have already seen that the Russian bloc suffers from comparable stresses. Communist difficulties, however, cannot really come out into the open, save for such an exceptional instance as the break between Tito and Stalin, or in actual rebellion, as in East Germany in 1953 or Hungary in 1956. Western difficulties can and do come out steadily into the open.

In most of the free world it is possible for ordinary interested citizens to consider in public, in the schools, in the press, in political meetings, the problems that confront them. They can attempt to assess their weaknesses objectively, in the firm democratic conviction that they can understand and overcome these weaknesses. This, it is clear even from our incomplete knowledge of what goes on behind the Iron Curtain, the communists cannot do. Rigorously controlled from above, they cannot learn the truth about the West—or about themselves. The experience of two world wars has shown that, in spite of the inconvenience and dangers of such openness of disagreement, in the long run full and fair discussion leads to better results than does suppression. The freedom of the free world is an asset, not a liability.

Old international tensions and disputes involving free nations have been settled, or at least eased, by difficult and sometimes painful negotiations. For one example, in 1954 the Italian Republic and Tito's Yugoslavia agreed to partition the area of Trieste, so long disputed between Italians and Yugoslavs (see above, p. 611). Another strategic and hotly disputed territory had its status defined in 1956. This was the Saar (see also Chapter XVIII). At the close of World War II, the French had occupied—and hoped to annex—this important coalmining area lying on their northeastern frontier, even though its population was largely German. West Germany disliked this prospect, and in 1956, after prolonged negotiations, and after it had become clear that the Saarlanders wanted to return to Germany, the French agreed to hand back the Saar. This Saar settlement marked a step toward the easing of traditional Franco-German bitterness, a bitterness that had only recently been exacerbated by the brutal Nazi conquest of France.

In some ways, however, the West is handicapped by the fact that the Russians have a new, aggressive, revolutionary faith with special appeal to underdog groups everywhere. They have something of the proselyting strength that helped Napoleon as the heir of the great French Revolution.

They can and do promise the downtrodden something new. All this need not mean that the West should be driven into a kind of conservative defensiveness, like Metternich after 1815 or the western democracies after 1918. It does mean that the western nations must be constantly aware of such a danger, that they must not let themselves appear, especially in the less advanced countries of Asia and Africa, to be backing up the established order at all costs, to be resisting all social and economic changes. Underdeveloped countries have applauded statements like that of President Truman in his inaugural address in 1949, when he promised backward areas help in the task of raising their standard of living. Since 1945, the western states have begun to understand that they must make their own democratic faith in reality what it has always been in ideal, a gospel of advance all along the line.

The Neutrals

We have hitherto written as though the contemporary world were *either* communist *or* democratic, at least in sympathy. Actually such a division is sharper and more extensive than has been usual in modern history, but even so, the formula *either-or* is not quite accurate. There are neutrals in this world, though the mere fact that ardent pro-westerners have coined a new, depreciatory term for them, "neutralists," is surely significant. There are always, even in advanced countries, the politically indifferent individuals who simply don't care about politics; and in large parts of the world there are millions too poor and too ignorant to be able to share political emotions. But among the politically conscious, we may distinguish two groups of neutrals. First, in France, England, and indeed throughout the free western world, there are those who refuse to line up either with the United States or

Prince Wan Waithayakon of Thailand addresses the opening session of the eleventh United Nations General Assembly.

with Russia. They are not by any means all motivated in the same way. Some are idealist intellectuals, often old-fashioned socialists, who feel, like Mercutio in *Romeo and Juliet*, "a plague o' both your houses"; for them, both the United States and the Soviet Union are on a bad track, both expansionists, both vulgar materialists. Some are men who remember when France, or Britain, or Germany was a first-rate power. They cannot bring themselves to accept leadership from either the United States or Russia; they still hope to bring back leadership to *their* nation. But so far, these neutrals have not swung the balance away from the western bloc in Europe or in Latin-America.

The other group of neutrals seems now a much more important force in the world. They are centered in the world of non-European stock, and in that world they are centered in India. Indeed in the Indian leader Nehru the neutrals have a figure who in the 1950's attained world stature. To the leaders of western policy, Nehru has often seemed an enemy, a difficult, prideful man, who is really playing the Russian game. Yet it is not impossible that, if some day historians get access to Russian documents, it will be found that the leaders in the Kremlin felt that Nehru was not really on their side. Meanwhile, we can but note that in India, and to a degree throughout the non-European world, there are many who refuse to line themselves up either with Russia or with the United States.

The United Nations

In spite of the open clash between communists and the free world in Korea, in spite of guerrilla warfare elsewhere in the East, in spite of the Iron Curtain, there has existed since World War II an international organization in which both communist and non-communist countries meet in at least nominally peaceful discussion. This is the United Nations. Formed of active opponents of the Axis during World War II, the United Nations was broadened and endowed with a charter in a great general meeting at San Francisco in 1945. By 1950, it had sixty member-nations, including Russia (with extra votes for the Ukrainian and White Russian republics of the U.S.S.R.), the Soviet satellites of Poland and Czechoslovakia, and the maverick communist state of Yugoslavia. The former enemy nations were denied entrance, as were Rumania, Bulgaria, Albania, Spain, and Ireland, since either American or Russian opposition prevented their admission.

In 1955, however, a most complex bit of maneuvering occurred in which countries like Canada took an important part, thus proving that the U.S.A. and the U.S.S.R. did not monopolize international politics. This resulted in the admission of sixteen new members to the United Nations, raising the total membership to seventy-six. Some of the new members were clearly sympathetic with the western bloc—Austria, Ireland, Italy, Portugal, and Spain; some were Russian satellites—Albania, Bulgaria, Hungary, Rumania; and others, many of them former imperial wards of the West, generally belonged to the ranks of the neutrals—Ceylon, Jordan, Libya, Nepal, Finland, and two components of old French Indo-China, Cambodia and Laos. This membership "deal" was a typical compromise not wholly satisfactory either to the United States, which vainly sought to secure the admission of Japan, or to Russia, which vainly sought to bring Mongolia in. By 1957, admission of the Sudan, Morocco, Tunisia, and Japan brought membership to eighty, nearly covering the world. Ghana (formerly Gold Coast) was a sure eighty-first.

The United Nations is the direct successor of the League of Nations, and its structure is almost the same as that of the League. Like the League, the U.N. represents a conference of sovereign states, a meeting of diplomats, not a world government in any way. The U.N. has a General Assembly, which can make recommendations on many issues of international interest; here each member-state has an equal voice. And it has a Security Council to deal primarily with threats to the security of states. This council has eleven members, five of whom—Nationalist China, France, Great Britain, the U.S.S.R., and the U.S.A.—are permanent members; the other six are elected for two-year terms by the General Assembly.

The key fact about the organization of the U.N., the fact that has made it for the most part simply a great international forum, is the veto power of the permanent members of the Security Council. For all save matters of procedure, the five permanent members must be unanimous if a vote is to pass the Security Council. Thus any one of the "Big Five" has the right of absolute veto in the Council. This veto was incorporated in the charter of the U.N. primarily in deference to the U.S.A. and the U.S.S.R., both of whom sought to safeguard their independence of action and to avoid being forced by the U.N. to follow policies of which they did not approve. The veto, however, was employed almost exclusively by Russia. The result was to cripple the effectiveness of the Security Council, but a by-product was the increased significance of the General Assembly, which became, in the phrase of the late Senator Vandenberg, "the town meeting of the world."

Like the League of Nations, the U.N. has special functional councils and agencies. The list of these agencies is very long and includes, among many others, the Trusteeship Council to supervise former mandated colonial territories, the Economic and Social Council, the International Court of Justice or "World Court," UNESCO (the U.N. Educational, Scientific, and Cultural Organization), the World Health Organization, the Food and Agriculture Organization, and the International Bank for Reconstruction and Development (the World Bank). The U.N. has its own permanent staff of civil servants, and has its headquarters in a dramatic new building on the East River in New York City. Many critics hold that this transfer of the world capital from neutral Switzerland, the home of the League, to the greatest city of the most powerful member-state was a mistake. It gives color, they hold, to the accusation that the U.N. is simply a device to further American imperialism.

The Record of the United Nations

It is still far too early to appraise the value of the U.N. Impatient advocates of a world-state are fond of pointing out that the U.N. is no more than a diplomatic gathering, that it has no "teeth" of its own, that it had to borrow the American army in the Korean crisis, that it must be transformed into a real government with the power to act directly on individuals, not just on states. These advocates of world government make much of the parallel with the United States Articles of Confederation from 1781 to 1789, in which the thirteen states were loosely organized under a Congress that had no taxing power, no police power, and no judicial power over the member-states. They call for an international duplicate of the American Constitution of 1789, which set up a federal government with these direct powers over citizens of the United States. In 1789, however, the thirteen former colonies had a common language, common political institutions and traditions, obvious common interests of many kinds. The eighty nations of the U.N. today have hardly the beginnings of such things in common. It looks as if a world government today may be quite impossible unless it is imposed by force.

But the United Nations does exist, and its very existence is for all but the most impatient idealist a promise of something better. In its first decade of operations, the U.N. was not able to solve big problems like the "cold war" or the international control of atomic weapons. But it did arrange the partition of Palestine and keep the Israeli-Arab "little war" from becoming a major conflict (see Chapter XXIII). It did act forcefully, with United States help, against the aggression of North Korea in 1950—a single achievement quite surpassing any achievements of the League of Nations. It did put its own force in 1956 into Egypt to intervene between the Egyptians and the Israelis (see Chapter XXIII).

Finally—a major accomplishment of the U.N. too often overlooked—some of its special agencies have made a most promising start in aiding the underdeveloped, disease-ridden, famine-threatened countries of the globe. The World Bank gave them loans to finance basic projects like electric generating stations. The World Health Organization mobilized the medical resources of the world to nip in the bud a cholera epidemic menacing Egypt. And W.H.O. also launched campaigns to immunize European and Asian children against tuberculosis and to curb malaria in Italy, Greece, and many other lands. Experts from the Food and Agriculture Organization have gone to overcrowded states like Italy and India to advise farmers in ways to increase their output and make more food available. In these and dozens of other ways the U.N. has executed its charter's pledge "to promote social progress and better standards of living."

International Relations in Perspective

To summarize: in the long perspective of this book, and especially in the perspective of the Enlightenment of the eighteenth century, it has to be written that in the second decade after the defeat of Germany and Japan in 1945, there is not yet what men commonly have called peace. The reader will of course know that peace in 1713, or 1815, or even 1926 (after Locarno) did not mean there were no international rivalries, no armaments, no alliances, no threats of possible war. But peace did mean then at least a lessening of tension; it did mean that men could relax, could use such a phrase as the one that President Harding made famous in 1920: "back to normalcy." How far the world still is from such a relaxing of tension can be very concretely symbolized: in two of the great cities of western tradition, Berlin and Jerusalem, barbed wires and sentry boxes separate one section from another, set up within each city as barriers to circulation. Or, in more general terms, the very existence of the phrase "Iron Curtain" suggests a world in which, though technology has made travel rapid and communication almost instantaneous, one part of that world is in actual fact largely shut off from the other and from the travel and communication technology has made possible.

Yet the state of international politics must not be painted in too black colors. If, as westerners must believe, the aggressor since 1945 has been the communist bloc, then at least the western democracies have not given the aggressor the freedom of play which all too often in the past such aggressors—and notably in the very recent past Hitler, Mussolini, and the Japanese imperi-

alists—have been given by the powers they were seeking to undermine. The leading nations of the West, the United States, Britain, France, West Germany, Italy, all do have a very great degree of freedom of the press. A complete outsider sampling that press might well be bewildered, for somewhere he would find almost all conceivable judgments on western policy in international relations since World War II. He would find that policy described as outright militarism, as an attempt by the United States to conquer the world; and he would find that policy described as the rankest kind of "appeasement," as complete failure to stand up to the Russians and the Chinese and their satellites; and he would find many judgments in between these extremes. But it looks as though a fair-minded observer would conclude that the West had so far succeeded in "containing" the communist bloc, as, once the fact of Russian aggression became clear in 1946-47, the West under American leadership set out to do. This is surely not "appeasement."

Moreover, the United Nations, where representatives from both blocs must by its very constitution meet periodically, is still in being, and still offers a means of arriving at those compromises which are as essential in international as in domestic politics. And, as we have already noted briefly, and shall see more clearly in the next section, the purely *material* damage of World War II had ten years later been more than made up. There were still poverty, malnutrition, shocking material conditions in many parts of the world; there were domestic problems that the conscientious man of good will could feel to be at least as horrendous as was the threat of World War III in international politics; and yet in general the economist would have to say in the second decade of the "cold war" that men generally were more "prosperous" than they were in 1939.

II: The Postwar History
of the Major American and European States

If one could look at the history of the various nations of the western world since 1945 with a mind wholly free from concern with international relations, one might even dare use a nineteenth-century word like "progress." In command over nature, over material resources, that great leap forward that began with the modern age, and was hastened in the economic revolutions, has since 1939 actually accelerated. In our political and social life, where progress is not so readily measurable, at the very least our democratic ways of life display continuity with those of our fathers. Concretely—and again omitting the fears suggested by the atomic bomb and the possibilities of World War III—the child born almost anywhere in the free democratic West since World War II can look forward to a longer life span than that of his parents, to a longer time in formal education, to a higher real income, to more leisure, to more continuous employment, to greater security in illness and old age. We may spell all this out in a brief survey of the major nations of the West.

The United States

The most apparent fact about the United States since 1945 is its long and great economic prosperity. But perhaps the most important, and to some observers the most surprising, development in recent history has been the way in which the American people have been willing to assume the responsibilities, the burdens, that have come their way in international politics. At the end of World War I we cut ourselves as free of "foreign entanglements" as we could, and some of our European allies feared at the end of World War II that we might do so once more. But we have on the contrary, after a rather abrupt cutting off of Lend-Lease in 1945, continued to render substantial economic aid to our allies. And we have taken on treaty obligations, notably in NATO (North Atlantic Treaty Organization), which are basically old-fashioned alliances. In 1919 we refused to join the League of Nations; in 1945 we were the heart and soul, the organizers, of its successor, the United Nations. It is not that isolationists were suppressed; indeed they still exist, and command great newspapers and a solid representation in Congress. But they are in a minority, a minority that has hardly been able to block a single measure of foreign policy.

All in all, this change from isolationism to full international leadership is one of the most remarkable changes of our time. A well-organized movement against any of our numerous treaty commitments since the Marshall Plan of 1947, *if it had had the majority of the American people behind it,* could have succeeded in spite of the fact that since the end of World War II official Republican and Democratic party policies have been on the whole in "bipartisan" agreement on our participation in international politics. The informed commentator on American politics will guess that the leaders of both parties know well that the isolationists are actually a minority.

Indeed, the political history of the United States since 1945 is a good confirmation of what we have already said (see above, pp. 436, 464) about the basic agreement that must be shared by both parties in the two-party system that prevails in the English-speaking countries. Harry Truman, Democrat, who as vice-president had succeeded to the office on the death of Franklin Roosevelt in 1945, was elected over the Republican Thomas Dewey in 1948 in an election that caught the experts by surprise, for the advance polls indicated the election of Dewey. In 1952, however, General Eisenhower, Republican, with his immense personal popularity, was elected president over the Democratic candidate, Adlai Stevenson, and carried his party to a majority in Congress. Now by tradition the Republicans are (comparatively) conservative, the party of business; and the Democrats are (comparatively) liberal or radical, the party of the working man, the "little fellow." Those parentheses are important. In fact, the victorious Republicans after 1952 left intact the essentials of Democratic legislation since Franklin Roosevelt's victory in 1932: the system of social security, which the Republicans actually extended, the Tennessee Valley Authority, and a whole complex set of federal agencies, the main task of which was to "intervene" in the economic life of the nation. The Republicans did this, even though their official philosophy stressed free enterprise and condemned government regulation. And they also retained the great armed forces—including the draft—we had had to build up since 1940, and the foreign policy we have outlined above.

In 1954, the Supreme Court of the United States handed down a decision that is sure to figure as a major one in the history books of the future. Segregation in public schools—specifically, the existence of separate schools for whites and for Negroes in the southern and border states and in the District of Columbia—was declared contrary to the law of the land. Notably in the District of Columbia, in Maryland, Kentucky, Missouri, and in a few districts elsewhere, like the "atomic city" of Oak Ridge in Tennessee under federal control, steps were taken at once to implement this decision. In the rest of the South, the decision evoked an opposition that carried the historian's mind back to the long struggle over Reconstruction after 1865. Significantly, not even the bitterest southern opponent of desegregation talked about secession; but there was much talk about what amounted to nullification (the right claimed by South Carolina in 1832, when it declared unconstitutional the tariff acts of Congress). The majority of southerners were clearly determined to "get around" the decision somehow or other, and such American precedents as the Volstead Act implementing the Eighteenth Amendment suggest the likelihood that they will for the time succeed. It is possible, however, for those who believe our democracy must some day achieve full racial equality in such matters as education to take heart from other precedents. The Supreme Court decision has already eliminated segregation in several hundred school districts, has made the kind of step forward the history of social reform in the West shows to be the safest and surest, a step that will permit reformers to gather strength to make another.

Relatively unnoticed, another innovation has been made in the structure of the American political society. The United States, regretting its experiment in "imperialism" after the Spanish-American War of 1898, had taken up a firm position in foreign policy in favor of the emancipation of dependent peoples everywhere. Not unmindful of world opinion and of proverbs like "practice what you preach," we freed the Philippines, which on July 4, 1946, became a sovereign state, though still rather in the American orbit. Our relatively small Pacific island possessions we could justify on the grounds of military necessity. Hawaii and Alaska, though denied by federal "politics" the statehood they were anxious to get, were still territories with a legal status, and not, in spite of some editorial commentators, exactly oppressed colonies.

There remained the large and populous

island in the Caribbean we used to call Porto Rico, which was in fact a colonial dependency, in a singularly anomalous relation to the United States. Only a minority of its inhabitants really wanted independence on the Philippine model, if only because the economic advantages of free trade with and free immigration to the United States were so great for the island, which had a very high birth rate. We arrived at a compromise that probably owed something to British precedents in their Commonwealth. Porto Rico, now Puerto Rico in good Spanish, in 1952 became an *Estado Libre Associado*, or *Commonwealth*, with its own constitution, its own self-government, but still a part of, or "associated with," the United States. Under its popularly elected Governor Muñoz-Marin, the island began an encouraging but difficult campaign to industrialize its economy to take better care of its large and generally poverty-ridden population.

The economy of the United States, which had proved more than equal to the task of carrying on the Second World War, continued its upward course in the years after 1945. There were mild "recessions" in 1948 and 1953, but nothing the most pessimistic commentator could call a depression. Indeed, by the mid-fifties even a few Marxists were beginning to express their doubts about the inevitable "bust" their theories told them must always follow a capitalist "boom." And on the other side, orthodox western economists were beginning to assert that the United States had in fact licked the problem of the business cycle, that we had so many "built-in safeguards" in our social insurance, our banking and corporation laws, our ability—and willingness—to undertake public works at the first sign of depression, that though we should have recessions, we should never have a depression like that of the thirties. The historian, by training and disposition cautious, can hardly yet pronounce on this question; he can merely record the fact of the great prosperity, and its extension to almost all parts of the nation, and to almost all social classes.

Socially, the American drive towards some very concrete forms of equality has continued since the Second World War. It is not quite true that in the traditional sense of the word there are no "classes" in the United States in mid-twentieth century, but it is almost true. In polls, the overwhelming majority of Americans refuse to call themselves "upper class" or "lower" or "working class"; if they *must* use a label, something like 90 per cent will choose "middle class." In terms of sheer income, we still have some very rich men in spite of graduated income taxes and inheritance taxes. And we still have, in part but not wholly because of the low economic status of many Negroes, some very poor, who are not well fed or well housed. Indeed, in terms of actual real income, some nations of western Europe are closer to rough equality than are we. And yet both in terms of the career open to talents—the absence of barriers to social mobility—and in terms of what we may loosely call the social atmosphere, the United States remains the land where the social ideals of democracy are most nearly realized. The Negroes are indeed an exception, though not wholly so; in the arts, in the field of entertainment, and within their own community in all fields, the gifted Negro can rise.

As we shall see in the last section of this chapter, democracy in the United States has by no means been accepted by intellectuals inside and outside the country at the values given it in our last few paragraphs. The commonest of complaints against the atmosphere, the "style" set by mid-twentieth-century democracy in the United States, is foreshadowed in the fears of men like J. S. Mill (see Chapter XIII) about the "tyranny of the majority." Americans, so it is claimed, tend to be actually more and more *alike*, conformists instead of equals; they tend to eat the same frozen and packaged foods, look at the same television programs, ride in the same cars (all with too much chromium), live in the same ranch houses, and so on at great length. They have even made their part of this great continent of such a sameness that a French or English traveler can write that if you have seen one American city you have seen them all. And, worse from the point of view of the intellectual critic, they have, he says, jealously tried to keep down individuals and groups who do not conform to the general standards of mediocrity. The historian trying to be objective must insist that the reality is not quite so simple. Above all, he must point to the rich and varied group life in contemporary America. The very intellectuals who so dislike the "average" American are wholly free to attack him, wholly free to avoid him—with a little effort, perhaps—wholly free to eat their own unfrozen foods, and read their own "little magazines," and avoid looking at television.

The historian must also record what can now be seen as one of the crisis-provoked periods of partial suppression of "civil rights" in the 1950's, a period that will always be associated with the name of Senator McCarthy of Wisconsin. The cold war had inevitably made the existence of believers in communism in the United States difficult. The pattern for dealing with such problems had been set in our own history as early as the era of the French Revolution (the Jacobins frightened the possessing classes in those days at least as much as communists did in the twentieth century). What opponents of the process called "witch-hunts," and proponents called "security measures," were undertaken against individuals in responsible positions, especially in education, defense industries, and government, who might be pro-communist —that is, pro-Russian.

We are still much too near the McCarthy episode to judge its place in American history; and indeed the average liberal will regard the term "episode" as an underesti-

mate of the importance of a crisis he considers to have been a threat to American democracy. But it must be insisted that when the gifted and irresponsible English publicist Lord Russell wrote of a "reign of terror" in the United States in the early 1950's he was grossly exaggerating, from the point of view of a historian. Grave injustices were indeed done to many individuals who were in no sense traitors. The term "communist" was unfairly extended by McCarthy and his imitators and admirers to include many barely "left of center." McCarthy himself was an unscrupulous demagogue. But if one compares the French reign of terror in 1792-1794 or the Russian "purge" trials of the 1930's, one is struck with the really enormous differences. No blood was shed in this country, the prisons were not filled, and the ordinary citizen went on his way just as he always had. McCarthyism was a bad symptom in the American body politic; but it has apparently not proved chronic. In 1957, McCarthy no longer even made the headlines.

Finally, and more positively, it must be repeated that the "tyranny of the majority" has hitherto not prevented a really amazing proliferation of all sorts of groups in the United States. The intellectual critic, who can sometimes manage to attack what he has just claimed does not exist, complains that we are a "nation of joiners." Clearly, we don't all join the same groups. Even at the level of "serious" organizations, and discounting the innumerable ones based on hobbies, sports, artistic interests and the like, one is struck with the evidence of what must be called American "multanimity." The gamut of "pressure groups" alone, from say the Anti-Saloon League to the organized distillers or brewers, from the antivivisectionists to the prestigeful American Medical Association, from organized labor through organized farmers to the National Association of Manufacturers, is sufficient to bewilder observers from abroad. In religion, our multanimity is even more striking; somewhere in the United States—in the Los Angeles area if nowhere else—there must be gathered together representatives of almost all of what William James called the "varieties of religious experience." In the arts, the conventional, the average, the thing that satisfies the man in the street—and it isn't by any means always the same thing—exists side by side with the wildest extremes of "modernism." Indeed, the observer who takes the trouble to look at the whole of American culture is likely to worry rather over how such a huge assemblage of varied human beings can hold together than over the tendency toward a "tyranny of the majority."

Canada and Latin America

As in the First World War, Canadian troops fought in the Second World War from the start, and proved a most important factor in the great coalition against the Axis. Since 1945, Canada has enjoyed an economic growth and prosperity proportionately even greater than that of the United States. A great deal of capital from the United States poured in, and much was raised at home. Canada, though still producing vast amounts of raw materials from farm, mine, and forest, came in these decades to be a great industrial nation, exploiting her remarkable hydroelectric resources and her oil and mineral wealth. In the mid-fifties Canada took the lead in carrying out a long-discussed plan for a canal from the Great Lakes to the lower St. Lawrence, a canal deep enough to accommodate ocean-going ships, and producing in addition important hydroelectric power. In the United States, vested interests along the Atlantic seaboard, foreseeing competition from the new seaway in the lucrative midwest trade, had long succeeded by typical pressure-group lobbying methods in preventing American participa-

tion in the scheme. It is indicative of Canada's independent nationhood that she was able to announce her intention of going ahead with the scheme—which could be done, though imperfectly, entirely on Canadian territory—without the United States if necessary. Faced with this prospect, the United States joined Canada in a collaborative development and work began in 1954.

Politically, postwar Canada has been one of the stablest of western nations. Although in the provinces other parties have held power, in the federal government the Liberals, first under Mackenzie King, who died in 1948, and then under Louis St. Laurent, were in power from 1935 on without a break. Canadian politics provide an interesting example of the power of left-of-center sentiments in a great modern democracy—or perhaps merely of the unfavorable connotations of the old word "conservative," for the Canadian Conservative party changed its name to the "Progressive Conservative party," without thereby gaining federal power. In its socio-economic structure the Dominion conforms to the general western pattern in that it preserves great freedom of the press, the "career open to talent," and in terms of the contrast of laissez-faire *versus* government regulation, a mixed economy in which the mixture perhaps is somewhat stronger on the side of private enterprise than on that of government participation and regulation. The English-speaking and the French-speaking peoples of this bilingual nation continued in relations essentially unchanged since the war (see Chapter XXIII).

In Latin America, the spotlight since the end of World War II has been most conspicuously on the Argentine Republic, a large nation (16,000,000 population in 1950) of European immigrant stock, which had until the middle of the twentieth century a typical colonial economy, exporting beef and grain and other raw materials to Europe and importing manufactured goods. The economy was based on a social system which gave power to a small landlord class. The beginnings of industrialization, and especially the growth of Buenos Aires into a great metropolis (a metropolitan area of nearly 5,000,000 people) brought a middle class and a working class into an already unstable social mixture. There had been in many circles in the Argentine admiration for both Mussolini and Hitler; and though there were democratic elements, these were generally oriented to France and the French radical tradition. The United States was, to put it mildly, rather envied than admired. The republic sat out the war, coming in on the Allied side only at the very end.

After a bitter campaign, the coalition called "Democratic Union" was beaten by a new figure in Argentinian politics, Colonel Juan Perón, in a national election in 1946. Perón became a dictator on the old European model—that is, he contrived to hold power by the kind of appeal and by the methods we have analyzed in Chapter XX for Mussolini, Hitler, and Franco. Perón, however, went down before a characteristic Latin-American military *coup d'état* in 1955, and a somewhat uneasy series of "caretaker" governments under the leadership of army officers succeeded. It is clear at least that Perón fell basically because he was driven more and more to appeal to the poorer masses, the *"descamisados"* or "shirtless," and thus lost his support among the conservative upper classes. Moreover, after the death of his theatrical wife, Eva, who seems to have been much brighter than he, Perón let himself get into a quarrel with the Roman Catholic Church. Finally, Perón never solved the grave economic and financial problems that arose from Argentina's "colonial" status as a supplier of raw materials to industrial nations. His fall suggests—though any transfer from Latin-American to other political systems is dangerous—that the great weakness of the Nazi-fascist formula was its attempt to solve the social problem by a modern form of the old Roman "bread

and circuses," which simply won't work in a modern economy. Moreover, his fall without outside interference suggests that dictators can be unseated from within, even in modern times of mass propaganda and miracle weapons, if they lose the support of the military.

In the important country of Mexico, as populous as the Argentine, the years since 1945 have seen increasing economic prosperity as the nation gradually "modernized" itself. In terms of general western standards, Mexico had a long way to go; and she had a heritage of distrust of her great northern neighbor, the United States, a distrust sharpened by the definitely socialist and anticlerical character of the revolutionary movements that she experienced in the 1910's, twenties, and thirties. This revolution, it seems to an outside observer, has recently lost, as do most such revolutions in the West, much of its extremism, its radical dogmatism, its determination to realize for all the promises of "liberty, equality, fraternity." Mexico is in part at least reconciled to the need for foreign capital, for the good opinion of North Americans, for patience in the long task of raising the standards of her masses.

For the rest, Latin America in the 1950's presents a picture not too unlike earlier ones. North Americans and West Europeans who hold absolute standards of "democracy" or, better, "modernity," are still likely to be a bit patronizing toward these lands of dictatorships, revolutions, general backwardness. Yet with all their difficulties, these Latin-American states—including those of the Caribbean—have shared in the very great material progress of the twentieth century, and, in particular, since World War II. The statistics of population, per capita income, literacy, life span, and so on all rise for these lands—but they rise from much lower levels than those of Europe and the United States, and more slowly. Finally, in spite of the heritage of hatred of "Yankee imperialism" and envy of North American successes, the Latin-American countries have on the whole held to the side of the western democracies in the cold war. Russians, and pro-Russians, have insisted that these republics are in fact dependencies of the United States, are in our "sphere of control." A fair-minded observer would not concur with this verdict. There is no doubt that the wealth and power of the United States give it predominant influence in this hemisphere. But the observer who has studied the record of the Pan-American Conferences and other devices by which the republics of this hemisphere are brought together for consultation would be obliged to conclude that in the perspective of history North American "guidance" is as strong a word as need be used. We have not in any crisis since World War II made use in Latin America of any form of force. The Marines, who before 1934 often landed south of the border, have not done so since in that year they were withdrawn from Haiti.

Western Europe

The old geographical term "Western Europe" has by the development of the cold war been turned into a political, indeed a cultural, term. It was used fairly freely in the 1950's to indicate those nations of Europe outside Russian domination, outside the Iron Curtain, some of which, like Greece and Turkey, are certainly not geographically part of Western Europe. We must take up some of the postwar developments in the most important of these countries. But first it must be noted that, although the form of the "sovereign" state and many of the bundle of sentiments we call "nationalism" have been preserved in the region, there have been since 1945 real attempts to bring some sort of functional unity to the region. There have been, in short, attempts to organize a "Europe" on a level above the nation-state. To date, the most far-reaching in actual practice has been the realization of the so-called Schuman Plan. Under this plan, France, West Germany, Italy, and the three "Benelux" nations of Belgium, the Netherlands, and Luxembourg have in effect created for their coal and iron industries a free market area in which a joint administrative body can make certain final and binding decisions *without the participation of any governmental agency of any one of the six nations*. At least on paper, this Coal and Iron Union means that *some* part of the sacred "sovereignty" of each nation has been given up.

On various other levels, this kind of cooperation has gone on, short of theoretical abdication of "sovereignty," but actually involving the give-and-take of compromise well beyond the older, purely diplomatic, ways. Such in military affairs is NATO, the North Atlantic Treaty Organization, which, however, was threatened by the increasing tendency of Europeans to believe that post-Stalin Russia did not intend to make war. Such in economic affairs is the Organization for European Economic Cooperation, which began in 1947 to implement the American Marshall Plan for economic recovery. And such in general politics is the Council for Europe, which has indeed no "teeth," no power of making law, but is a kind of federal consultative parliament for western Europe, to which governments send official representatives. It meets at Strasbourg, a city delicately poised between France and Germany. In summary: for the "whole-hog" European federalist who wants a United States of Europe on the American model, what has been done toward European unity since 1945 is very little; for the historian who knows how deep-seated are the nationalist habits of thought and mind in Europe, what has been done since 1945 toward transcending the limitations of those habits is a very great deal. Indeed, there was a prospect in 1957 that a great free market would be created in West Europe,

Great Britain The United Kingdom of Great Britain and Northern Ireland seemed to many, especially to Americans, to have undergone a revolution late in 1945. A general election held in July, 1945, gave results exactly opposite to those of the famous "khaki election" of 1918 (see Chapter XXI). Though Churchill was far more of a national hero than even Lloyd George had been, a nation that was determined on radical changes threw out Churchill and his Conservative party and returned a Labor party pledged to a measure of "socialism" —not, be it carefully noted, communism. The new prime minister was Clement Attlee, himself by no means a proletarian, but a middle-class British gentleman and social worker. Under the Labor cabinet, the government proceeded to take over, with due compensation to the owners, the coal industry, the railroads, and some parts of commercial road transportation, and began to nationalize the steel industry. Britain already had a well-developed system of various social insurances; this was now capped by a system of socialized medical care for all who wished it, a system strongly opposed at first by the medical profession. The educational system was partly reformed in an effort to make education more democratic, and to lengthen the required period of compulsory education. In accordance with Labor party philosophy, various parts of the old empire were given independence, like Burma, and others were granted dominion status—that is, national independence within the extraordinary British multinational system (see Chapter XXIII).

Yet the nature and extent of this British "revolution by consent" were greatly misunderstood, especially by American conservatives. We can now see clearly that the new Britain was more like than unlike the old one and the rest of the free West. What came out of the changes after the Labor party victory of 1945 was an economy pushed a little more toward collectivism than before, but still very much indeed a "mixed" economy. Coal and railroads, nationalized, did not become great state trusts run by bureaucrats on the Russian model, but rather public corporations with a structure not unlike that of great private industries in the West, and run by a board not by any means wholly under either bureaucratic or political thumbs. Great sectors of the economy remained in private hands, under no more than the kind of government regulation common even in the United States, which itself had a "mixed economy." Proof of the essential moderation of this British revolution is afforded by the conduct of the Conservatives, who with Churchill still at their head were returned to power in 1951. The nationalization of steel, which had begun, was indeed stopped; but otherwise the victorious Conservatives kept intact the "socialism" of their opponents, including the national health scheme of socialized medicine, to which even the medical profession had become pretty well reconciled. There are of course Englishmen who think that their country has taken quite the wrong track since 1945, and who would like to restore the old ways of private enterprise and laissez-faire; but there are not enough of them, apparently, to win elections and dominate Parliament.

In American—and, it must be added, in German—eyes, the British have not since the war proved resilient enough to keep up with the extraordinary pace of economic improvement through technological innovation. A symptom: the British motor-car industry, which immediately after the war was in a good position to gain a big share of the world market, in the 1950's saw its lead reduced, until the Germans, especially with their inexpensive, standardized light car, the *Volkswagen*, took over the lead. In all the various indices of production, the British are definitely behind the Germans and the Americans. But they are still a great industrial people, suffering from the fact that just because they were the *first* to industrialize in the modern manner their plant tends toward obsolescence, and, more important, their ways tend to be set, hard to change rapidly. The British, for instance, are often ineffective salesmen.

The British were the last of the major nations to feel themselves able to give up rationing and other belt-tightening measures the war had made necessary. Britain, more than any other great nation, had completely outgrown its ability to raise enough food to supply its fifty million inhabitants. Britain had to export manufactured goods to get money to import the food it needed; but it also had to limit those imports, to raise all it possibly could on home lands. The British people therefore put up with many restrictions—for example, on chocolate, which had to be imported—in what they rather mildly called an "austerity program." By the mid-fifties most of these restrictions had been lifted. Yet the British people still faced a kind of chronic fear that in this harsh world they could not quite compete with younger peoples, that they could not sell enough to buy enough in the world market for their crowded population which—this is of major importance—was not, like the masses of Asia, used to a bare minimum of existence, but on the contrary to a high standard of living.

To all these troubles was added a widespread awareness of the fact that Britain, which only a lifetime ago was the leading nation of the world, now saw herself stripped of some of her empire, with the rest uncertain, playing what American editorial writers liked to call "second-fiddle" to her former colonial possession, the United States. No wonder the British felt they were suffering undeservedly, and had what a witty commentator called a "Job complex." British leaders can still hardly forget their former supremacy, and still, quite naturally, cannot accept deferring to the United States. Yet in spite of all these psychological difficulties, the British have been true, often under much strain, to the American alliance. The Franco-British invasion of Egypt in 1956 (see Chapter XXIII) looked at first like a complete break between Britain and the United States; but though the alliance was surely badly strained, it seems to have survived.

France

If to the British the events of the last war and its aftermath seem to have been hard on their pride, on the French these years inflicted what the psychologists call a trauma. Complete defeat by the Germans; occupation by the hated foe; economic exploitation by the Germans to the point where the French government was almost bankrupt; liberation which, in spite of the admirable part played in it by the Fighting French and the French Resistance movement, was still clearly the work of American and British arms; the grave postwar difficulties of trying to hold together an empire whose peoples were in revolt—all these were elements in a picture of drastic decline. To complete the picture must be added the fact that France had not since the mid-nineteenth century kept pace with the leading industrial nations in production, in finance, above all in population. American editorial writers, if they tended to rub in British weaknesses, were much shorter with the French; even "second-rate power" seemed to many of them an exaggeration—France, according to them, had ceased to count in international affairs, was a "tenth-rate power." This was, of course, grossly exaggerated, for in the first postwar decade (1946-1956) France made a striking economic recovery.

For the French themselves, the hopes, and especially the political hopes, of the Liberation had been high, and their rapid disappointment was a crowning blow. The German occupation, which had never been completely oppressive, if only because the Germans could not spare the manpower to make it so, had grown less and less efficient; the French Resistance after 1942 was able to discuss the future of France, make plans, and even publish underground books and pamphlets. They make pathetic reading today. France was to have a new constitution, indeed a new republic, the Fourth Republic, with none of the weaknesses of the Third, no splinter parties, no rapid overturns of ministries, no corrupted journalists, no really poor people, no bitter hatreds between Catholics and freethinkers, and so on. The Fourth Republic turned out to be almost undistinguishable from the Third, especially in matters that call attention from abroad, like frequent falls of ministries. France after 1945 continued to be an interesting and lively country, a country in some ways as "democratic" as any on earth; but it had not become the dream-country of the Resistance intellectuals.

But there were signs that the French, who had a not undeserved reputation for touchy nationalism, had begun to feel that nationalism was not enough. It was a Frenchman, Robert Schuman—he came by his German name naturally enough, for he was born an Alsatian—who fathered the plan for a Coal and Steel Union. Another Frenchman, Jean Monnet, from the impeccably French town of Cognac, has been a mainstay of plans and actual work for the economic union of Europe. Just how far from the intransigent nationalism of Clemenceau (see Chapter XVIII) the France of the 1950's had come is evident from French willingness to give up trying to make the Saarlanders French, and to accept their political and cultural union with Germany in return for some of the unsentimental coal of the Saar. France is perhaps the clearest example of an abated nationalism in the modern world. She may well prove to be the leading state in the uniting of Europe.

The Other Western Countries

In Italy, a plebiscite in 1946 showed 54.3 per cent of the voters in favor of a republic, and with its establishment the House of Savoy ceased to rule. This is a close and rare thing among plebiscites, an honest vote. It might seem that so close a division would augur ill for the stability of the new republic, and so in the long run it may. But the history of Italy since World War II has been encouraging for those who hope for the spread of democracy in the West. It is true that the Communist party was strong in Italy in those years, true also that the old heritages (see Chapter XIV) of backwardness in the South, of parliamentary splinter groups and squabbling, of tension between Catholics and anti-Catholics, were not written off at once. Still, Italy shared in the postwar economic revival, enjoyed a cultural upswing especially marked in the novel and in the cinema, and managed to "contain" her own communists. Most Italians seem relieved that they no longer had to aspire to imperial greatness.

For the rest, Spain under Franco and Portugal under Salazar survived the fall of the Rightist totalitarian dictators at the end of the war. Under pressure of the cold war, the United States, in spite of strong protests from liberals and radicals at home, granted economic help to Franco in return for air bases in Spain. It seems clear that the standard of living of the Spanish masses remains low, that they have not shared the economic advances of the last few decades to the extent usual in the West. It seems clear that there is much suppressed opposition to Franco in Spain. Yet beyond a few student demonstrations, there was little actual evidence of the always threatened fall of the dictator. The problem of succession to Franco, who was born in 1892, would seem still unsolved.

Germany in the second decade after the end of Hitler's aggression remained one of the great enigmas of our time, if only because, in the sense in which we had got used to thinking of Germany, there was no such land. Eastern Germany and a good deal of the heartland of Germany in Thuringia and Saxony was a satellite "people's republic" inside the Iron Curtain; there was Berlin, divided between American, British, and French zones of occupation, within which there was full freedom of movement, and a Russian zone; and there was West Germany, a federal republic with its capital at the old university town of Bonn, and by the early 1950's fully integrated as an independent state into the western coalition. These divisions seemed unnatural and unstable, a state of affairs that could not possibly last. Yet the western powers and Russia had in some twelve years been unable to come to any agreement on the terms under which Germany could be re-united. There was no formal joint treaty of peace.

The western powers, convinced that in a free vote of all Germans a united nation on the western side would emerge, have attempted to get a great plebiscite. The Russians, aware that they would lose out under such conditions, refuse. Their East Germany is in population and resources notably inferior to West Germany. Added to these difficulties is the fact that Russia annexed to herself part of old East Prussia, and compensated her new Polish satellite with the rest of the old regions won by the Germans from the Slavs in part centuries ago. Poland as resuscitated reaches west as far as the Oder-Neisse line, and includes the big city of Stettin, which became the Polish Szczecin.

If it could be considered merely in itself, as a finality, the West German Federal Republic would be set down as one of the great successes of the postwar period. West Germany was not badly treated by the Allied occupiers, if only for the reason that these powers knew as early as 1946 that they would need the Germans on their side against the Russians. An innovation in international procedure was the postwar trial of Nazi leaders for "war crimes." Goering, second to Hitler, was convicted and condemned to death, as were eleven other leaders; others received lesser penalties. Many westerners, including the distinguished American Senator Robert Taft, held that these trials were not legal, were based on *ex post facto* "law," and were nothing more than the thinly disguised "woe to the vanquished" of old. Nevertheless, the Nuremberg trials seem not to have burned deeply into the souls of Germans. Similarly, the whole process called "de-Nazification"—that is, the elimination of ardent Nazis of the lower echelons from public life—though it gave rise to a great deal of discussion in Germany and outside, though on the whole it appeared to western liberals to have erred on the side of clemency, seemed after a decade to have left no major wounds. There were of course in Germany "irreconcilables," but the temper of West Germans was, most observers concluded, surprisingly free from bitterness toward the West.

Very great economic prosperity no doubt helped create this state of mind. Great numbers of refugees came into West Germany from the Russian occupied areas. Indeed, after twelve years they continued to come from East Germany in smaller numbers. At first, these refugees added to the woes of West Germany, and the camps and relocation centers for the refugees taxed everybody concerned. But in the long run these refugees have added to a productive labor force which comes closer to the Americans in actual performance than that of any other great nation, and in some fields exceeds American productive standards. The government of the Federal Republic, first set up in 1949 with a democratic "fundamental law" greatly influenced by the western powers, but apparently acceptable to the Germans, became wholly "sovereign" in the 1950's. In Konrad Adenauer, who became Chancellor in 1949, the West Germans have had a political leader of great firmness and moderation, who managed to remain acceptable to all but the extreme German nationalists and the extreme Left, and yet enjoyed the increasing admiration of the western powers. Beaten West Germany, like beaten Japan, has become an ally of her conquerors.

Soviet Russia

The contemporary historian endeavoring to single out the most important features of Soviet development since the end of World War II faced formidable problems, not the least of which was the so-called Iron Curtain, through which the Soviet region permitted to leak out only such data as reflected favorably on itself. One thing at least seemed clear: Stalin's death in March, 1953, had already become a landmark. Up to the moment of his death, Soviet politics at home continued in the pattern he had made familiar in the years before the war: a tight, one-man dictatorship, run by Stalin in the name of state and party both, where the rhythm of terror and tension, temporary relaxation and renewal of terror, kept even the most important functionaries of the regime awake at night. As Stalin grew older, it became a favorite game in the West to speculate on his succession and the forces that would be released at the moment of his death. Would the Communist party, or the Secret Police, or the army—which seemed to be the agencies in the U.S.S.R. with power of their own—emerge as supreme? Would it be some combination of two of the three against the other one? Was this or that member of the Politburo identified with one or another of these three chief agencies? Would there be a bitter personal rivalry that might disrupt the whole machinery of Soviet government, something comparable to the struggle between Stalin and Trotsky for the succession to Lenin?

When the great moment actually came,

there was at first no evidence of disunity or personal rivalry within the Politburo. Georgi Malenkov, personally close to Stalin, succeeded him as Premier, but surrendered his Communist party secretaryship to Nikita Khrushchev. It was thus clear from the beginning that nobody would immediately inherit all of Stalin's power, and the fact that it would be shared was underlined almost at once by the pronouncements that came from the regime, denouncing the "cult of personality" (i.e., Stalin's former one-man rule), and proclaiming a "collegial" system (i.e., government by committee). But before the end of 1953 there came the official announcement that the dreaded chief of the Secret Police, and Politburo member, Beria, always regarded as a potential heir of Stalin, had been executed for treason. The observer might interpret this move, so reminiscent of the purges of Stalin's own era, as an indication that the members of the Politburo were circling around each other with their knives out, or that the Communist party and the army had indeed united to thwart a bid for power on the part of the Secret Police. The emergence of the war hero, Marshal Zhukov, into positions of some political importance gave color to this view, as, perhaps, did the rise to even higher eminence of the "political" general, Bulganin.

But all expectation that a "free-for-all" among the remaining members of the inner circle would ensue, or that the regime might be shaken by personal rivalries, was in error. True, Malenkov vanished from the top post of Premier, to be succeeded by Bulganin, but Malenkov, though he admitted grievous errors, was simply demoted to a lower cabinet post, and remained in the Politburo. Some indication as to the real locus of power might perhaps be found in the fact that the errors confessed by Malenkov (especially the effort to concentrate collective farms into enormous "agrogorods" or agricultural towns, which

Premier Nikolai Bulganin and Party Secretary Nikita Khrushchev.

had indeed failed) were actually Khrushchev's errors, for which Malenkov now had to take responsibility. Yet, though Khrushchev was certainly very powerful, his fellow-members of the Politburo had great influence, and showed no outward signs of fearing him as all had feared Stalin. On the whole, it appeared that the transfer of power had actually gone quite smoothly in the U.S.S.R., and that among the rulers, in the happy phrase of George Orwell's *Animal Farm*, "all were equal, but some were more equal than others."

At a Party Congress, held early in 1956, Khrushchev made a speech in which he not only carried the attack on the "cult of personality" to new heights, but openly denounced Stalin by name, emotionally detailing the ghastly acts of personal cruelty to which the psychopathically suspicious nature of the late dictator had given rise. Khrushchev thus echoed what western ob-

servers of the U.S.S.R. had been saying for years. As the details of the speech were leaked out to the Soviet public, there was of course some distress at the smashing of the idol they had worshiped so long; but a good many of them had no doubt all along suspected that Stalin was something less than god-like. So the widespread disorders that some observers were predicting failed to materialize.

With the new regime came a perceptible relaxation of internal tension. Many thousands were released from labor and prison camps, an amnesty affecting literally millions of Russian families. Foreigners again were permitted to travel to Russia, though under restrictions. Russian scientists and scholars appeared once again at international conferences. The scientists in particular were well fed, well housed, and apparently content; the level of their work seemed high indeed to their colleagues from the West. So did the technical education made available for the talented potential engineer and research physicist or chemist in the U.S.S.R. American newspapers pointed out how far the Russians were out-distancing the West in the number of tech-nicians in training and trained. Though the Russians denounced American atomic experiment, they themselves detonated one experimental bomb after another.

Moreover, the annual increment in So-viet industrial production was impressive in-deed. And now, perhaps, real wages were be-ginning to rise as well. In 1956, André Philip, a French Socialist, gave as his estimate a rise from the index figure of 100 for 1913 to 123.6 in 1950. Philip, who is by no means an uncritical admirer of the United States, estimates the comparable American figures to be 100 in 1913 and 308 in 1950. It can be seen that Russia remains in this respect very far behind us, even in terms of relative progress.

The broad lines of Russian economic de-velopment in recent times are clear enough. Under government ownership and adminis-tration, heavy industry and in general the whole capital structure of the nation have been built up relatively rapidly. This accu-mulation has in fact been carried out by ab-staining from consumption, which ac-counts for the fact that Russian average real income per capita is still so low. Finally, collectivization, which has at least pro-duced the goods in heavy industry, has in agriculture not worked nearly so well, an-other factor that has tended to keep down national real income per capita. Western stereotyped thinking, either of the kind wholly hostile to "socialism" or wholly friendly to it, cannot claim justification from the Russian experience. The West in the 1950's was far ahead of Russia in eco-nomic terms. But the West had a great head start, and the Russia of the Soviets has clearly advanced, at an increasingly rapid rate.

There is little sound evidence that the mass of Russians are effectively hostile to the regime. Certainly, however, there is a good deal of discontent with material con-ditions of life in Russia; lack of consumers' goods, incredibly crowded urban housing, peasant dissatisfaction with the conditions of collectivized farming—and with the new "kulaks" who administer the collectives and run the tractor stations—all this adds up to an undercurrent of discontent more powerful than is common in the modern West. On the other hand, it is clear that most Russians, brought up in the new re-gime, are proud of much that it has done. They are, in short, good patriots, and they "identify," as the psychologist has it, with the Russia they know and love. Although the influx of travelers and the loosening of the protective bands Stalin tried to keep around the nation have no doubt confirmed their belief that westerners are really a great deal "better off" than they are, they seem unshaken in their fundamental loyalties.

One more word. We shall, in the final sec-tion of this book, say something about the state of mind, the "temper" of the modern West in mid-twentieth century. The culture of the Soviet Union has in actual fact had very little to do concretely with contemporary western art, culture, ways of life. Even among West European admirers of Communist Russia, Soviet art and letters do not figure very large. Some Soviet music, that of Shostakovich for in-stance, an occasional novel, such as Sholok-hov's *And Quiet Flows the Don,* and the beautiful performances of traveling ballet artists: this is about all that has come through to the West. Distance, language difficulty, and lack of political sympathy cannot altogether explain this. After all, the giants of the Russian nineteenth cen-tury—Tolstoy, Dostoevsky, Chekhov—are household words among cultivated peo-ple in western Europe and America. No dis-passionate future historian of culture seems likely to record the first forty years of the Soviet regime as a flowering time of

Russian culture. The well-disposed observer will explain this fact as the result of the diversion of all Russian energies to the building up and maintenance against a hostile world of the communist society; the less well-disposed will insist that the atmosphere of a totalitarian dictatorship—especially when headed by a man so little educated in his tastes as Stalin—is bound to stifle cultural initiative in all fields.

The Soviet Satellites   Despite the repeated violent denunciations of so-called western "colonialism" in which the Soviet leadership indulged for propaganda purposes in the years after the end of World War II, the fact remained that the U.S.S.R. alone among the United Nations had acquired a new empire. All the lands that lay between the 1939 Soviet frontiers and the western portion of Germany, with the exceptions of Greece and Finland, were reduced to the level of Soviet satellites, at different times and by various combinations of force and chicanery. Greece was saved only by the armed support of the western Allies against two communist-led uprisings (1944-1945 and 1946-1949), while Finland received especially mild treatment and was permitted to stay free under a non-communist regime. But Poland, Hungary, Czechoslovakia, Rumania, Bulgaria, Albania, and East Germany were all turned over to native communists backed by Russian arms. Only the national tradition of resistance to outside domination, combined with its geographic position, enabled Yugoslavia under a native communist regime to defy Stalin, and to establish for itself, for a while at least,

a unique position in the postwar world.

Elsewhere—and to a considerable degree in Yugoslavia as well—the single-party state, with single-list elections, the dictatorial central regime, with interlocking state and party functions, the huge bureaucracy familiar to students of the U.S.S.R., became the typical features of political life. Collectivized agriculture (often in the face of furious peasant opposition), nationalized industry, over-ambitious industrial planning, the lowering of already low standards of living, religious persecutions, total educational conformity, a new militarism, slavish copying of Soviet cultural models—these were characteristic. That the regimes were bitterly unpopular could be seen not only from the flow of refugees who risked their lives to escape across the closely guarded frontiers but also from an occasional explosion of popular discontent, such as that in East Germany in the summer of 1953 and that in Poland and Hungary in the autumn of 1956.

Since the death of Stalin, some relaxation of totalitarian methods could be detected in the satellites, especially in Poland, where readers of the press discovered more free criticism of the regime than had previously been tolerated. As in the U.S.S.R. itself, moreover, industrial production was up. Despite inefficiency and cruelty, despite exploitation of satellite resources for the benefit of the U.S.S.R., the fact remained that the drastic methods of communist economic activity in many cases got results. No westerner could afford to write off the satellite states as stagnant or directed by idiots. Their contribution to the Soviet economy was great and growing. They were clearly not oriented to the West.

III: *The Temper of the Western World*

We have seen that the western world is in mid-twentieth century materially better off than it has ever been before. Yet, to judge from random sampling of "serious" writing, philosophy, criticism, the novel, and especially that big vague category that may be described as writing about man's fate, we are held to be spiritually worse off than were our nineteenth-century predecessors. Admittedly, it is difficult to assess the temper of an age, above all of one's own age. There can be no doubt, however, that few serious modern poets are capable of writing the modern equivalent of Browning's

> God's in His Heaven—
> All's right with the world!

Most of the very popular philosophers of history, led by Toynbee, to whom we shall come in a moment, believe we are really in for a hard time, even though eventually we may win through to a better society. The newest "school" of philosophy, the Franco-German existentialists, seem to ordinary human beings more than gloomy—to be actually neurotic. Surely it is symptomatic that pat phrases have been coined for our time—"The Age of Anxiety," "The Aspirin Age," "The Age of Longing," "The Age of Suspicion," and perhaps a new one, "The Age of Tranquillizers."

Clearly the menace of a coming World War III fought with all the wonders of modern science and technology accounts for some of this sense of doom. Clearly also the gap between the intellectuals—writers, teachers, preachers, artists—and ordinary people, a gap that began to be conspicuous in the Romantic movement (see Chapter XI), has if anything widened in our time. This gap, this feeling of alienation on the part of intellectuals, adds to their sense of doom. And, of course, some degree of intellectual pessimism, some belief that the world is going to pot, is our long inheritance from the "cradles of civilization," if not from our prehistoric ancestors.

The Prophets of Doom

Nevertheless, the underlying pessimism of our age must be examined, for it is very real among the educated classes in the West. First of all, in a book on history, we must examine that particular contemporary attitude sometimes called "historicism," the effort to use our knowledge of the "curve" of the past to extrapolate, so to speak, the immediate and even the distant future. The historicists of our own day are almost unanimous in extrapolating a very gloomy immediate future indeed. From the German Spengler, who died in 1936, down to the Englishman Toynbee and the American Sorokin, the philosophers of history feel bound to compare our fate with that of previous civilizations, and in particular with that of the Greco-Roman world of antiquity. They do not agree on just how far down the road to final destruction we have come, and indeed on whether the direction we seem to be taking is irreversible. Many of them seem to feel that even though our western civilization is doomed, the human race as a whole is not. Our descendants may win their way through to a new dawn, a new civilization.

Now in the few thousand years for which written historical records are available, it is quite clear that man—biological man, *homo sapiens*—has as a species maintained himself, and indeed in the last few centuries has markedly increased in numbers. But the various groups he has formed, most strikingly the political groups, have lived and died. The Babylonian state, the Athenian *polis*, the Roman Empire, the Inca Empire, no longer exist, though something of their culture may survive. The German philosopher of history Spengler claimed that the higher cultures have a normal life-cycle of about a thousand years. This span he maintained is an objective fact, just as the seventy-year life span is an objective fact for *homo sapiens*. Since Spengler had conveniently decided that our own western culture was "born" about 1000 A.D., he was able to decide automatically that in the late twentieth century we should be very near our inevitable end. But most historians would maintain that western culture was "born" somewhere around the fourth or fifth century A.D., with the triumph of Christianity in the West, the fall of Rome, the beginnings of the German succession states. If this really is our birth date, then our culture has lived 1700 years, the equivalent for *homo sapiens* of an impossible life span of 160 years.

Actually, we cannot prove scientifically that a given political and cultural group is dying; we do not understand what determines the life-cycles of these groups. We have a reasonably clear historical knowledge, however, of the growth and decay in the Mediterranean of a great culture, the Greco-Roman, and especially of its culmination in the Roman Empire. It is from this classic cycle that most of our modern philosophers draw their conclusions about our approaching end. Toynbee has brought out the comparisons between the dying classical world and our own—an art and literature overelaborated, imitative, and lacking freshness, a widespread sense of the decadence of culture, very great centralization in government, perhaps even a new proletarian religion over against the established one, then Christianity against paganism, now communism against Christianity. But no natural scientist would dare make

prophecies on the strength of one case. And there are obvious differences between the world of declining Rome and our own, most conspicuous of which is our modern science and technology and our command over the material things they give us. Besides, to take a modern painting like that by Picasso, illustrated on p. 838: this art is perhaps strange, and it is experimental, building on the new theories of late-nineteenth-century painters (see Chapter XVI); but it can scarcely be called overelaborate, imitative, or stale.

The cautious historian looking at the world today will content himself with saying that the twentieth-century West has lost some of the Victorian faith in progress, shows a tendency toward pessimism about the immediate future of civilization, shows a feeling of insecurity. But even in making this statement, the historian will add qualifications. First, prophecies of doom are nothing new in the West. The notion of the end of the world and the second coming of Christ in a Day of Judgment goes back to the beginnings of Christianity, and keeps returning. In recent centuries the pessimistic view has often taken the form of belief in the badness of the times, the rottenness of civilization, the need and therefore the inevitability of destruction and rebirth. Rousseau himself (see Chapter IX) was a prophet of doom two hundred years ago.

Second, the historian will ask himself whether or not, especially today, these prophets of doom are good mirrors of ordinary men and women. It seems pretty clear, for instance, that in the United States since World War II there has been a gap between the pessimism of the intellectuals and the optimism of the people. Most Americans still believe in progress, and even in western European nations like France, where there is a kind of national fatigue, one may doubt whether the man in the street is in fine existentialist despair. Still, it would be absurd to maintain that even in the United States the two world wars,

Picasso, "Girl before a Mirror," 1932.

the great depression, and the threat of a third world war have left men in the optimistic frame of mind of their fathers.

The Optimism of the Enlightenment

The important aspect of modern thought for us at the end of our long survey of modern history is not the fashionable "historicism" but the more general public attitude toward our special inheritance from the Enlightenment of the eighteenth century. As we have pointed out, there grew up among western men in the early modern centuries, and there came to full bloom in the eighteenth and nineteenth centuries, a view of man's fate here on earth which was essentially new. This is the view that all men may rightly expect to be happy here on earth. As St.-Just, the youthful colleague of Robespierre in the French Revolution, put it, "Happiness is a new idea in Europe"; or as Jefferson, with his gift for phrasing, put it, one of the rights of man is the "pursuit of happiness." Of course men have presumably always sought happiness here on earth. In historic Christianity, however, they did not really expect it here on earth, but only in an afterlife in heaven; indeed, Christianity had an overtone of belief that happiness in heaven was in part at least a reward for suffering here on earth.

The *philosophes*, the eighteenth-century thinkers who set the broad terms of this modern optimistic world-view (see Chapter IX), meant by happiness a condition or state in which each man had at any given moment what he wanted, a state in which each man—each woman, and, incredibly, even each baby—was not aware of being thwarted. To the inner state of this happiness there would conform an outer state of material plenty in which everyone would have what he wanted to eat, would be well-housed, would have a satisfactory sex life,

and would of course enjoy good health, both mental and physical. The matter may indeed be put in terms of modern psychology. Men can rightfully expect in this world a life of perfect adjustment, a life without conflict, aggression, insecurity.

Broadly speaking, the *philosophes* held that such perfect happiness had not yet been attained on earth—an obvious fact—because there had grown up a whole set of institutions, habits, and beliefs that had brought evil into human life. Men in 1750, the *philosophes* believed, were not following the *natural laws* that would make them happy, but the *unnatural laws* that made them unhappy. The formulators of the new idea of happiness believed that the unhappy state of the world could be traced to a combination of the privileges unnaturally acquired over the centuries by the few rich and powerful together with the unnatural ignorance and prejudices the few had imposed on the many. They therefore concluded that the solution lay first in depriving the few of their unnatural privileges and, second, in disclosing to the many by a natural system of education and government the key to their own happiness. In short, they believed that men are by nature good not evil, reasonable not foolish, intelligent not stupid.

This, then, though put oversimply, is the essence of what may be called the democratic dream of the eighteenth-century philosophers, the dream of a heavenly city here on earth. But two hundred years later the dream has not come true. Some men still persist in it, holding that we have not yet conquered the privileged classes, not yet opened men's minds, not yet really tried full democracy. Marxism, for example, in its simplest outline is the eighteenth-century formula all over again: the bad institutional environment under which men cannot help being miserable is capitalism; the good institutional environment under which men cannot help being happy is socialism. Needless to say, the Soviet Russian experiment has not yet brought this socialism to earth.

But the failure of the dream has caused many more men to question its very basis, the doctrine of the natural goodness and reasonableness of man. Such men hold that something profoundly rooted in human nature, and not merely in man's institutions or in his environment, makes a measure of unhappiness the natural lot of mankind. The modern western world, in consequence, has witnessed a process of reaction and adjustment to the contrast between the high hopes of the Enlightenment and the continuing evils of the world. We may distinguish three broad classifications of these reactions and adjustments.

Repudiation or Revision of the Enlightenment

First, there is the reaction of complete repudiation of all the Enlightenment stood for. This reaction takes many forms. One of them, limited largely to some emotional intellectuals, is the sense of doom we have just discussed, the feeling that in trying to make this earth a heaven man has in fact made it a hell. More commonly, this reaction takes the form of denying all the premises of democracy. It is maintained that most men are wicked or stupid or foolish, that they need to be ruled by their betters, who are always few in number, and that therefore we must return to divine-right monarchy or to the feudal-clerical aristocracy of the Middle Ages, or follow the "new conservatism," or devise some new authoritarianism.

Second, there is the Christian view that men must return to the basic Christian concept of a mixture of good and evil in humanity. In this view, life on earth must always demonstrate the conflict between the divine and the animal in man, a conflict tragic and profound, not mean and vile as the mere pessimist sees it, and, above all, not for the individual a ceaseless "existential-ist" conflict, but a conflict that has an end in heaven or hell, and that takes place in a universe dominated by *purpose*, not by *accident*. For some of these Christians the desirable earthly society is indeed rather an aristocracy than a democracy. But many of them, like the American theologian and moralist, Reinhold Niebuhr, may be described as moderate democrats. Though they believe that the democratic dream in its radical eighteenth-century form is impious nonsense, they none the less hold that a balanced democratic society is the best way of attaining justice on earth, the best earthly reflection of man's dual nature.

Third, there are those who accept the aims of the *philosophes* and even in part the eighteenth-century estimate of human nature. But they find that the Enlightenment went wrong in its time-sense, wrong in its hope that its claims could be attained in a generation or two. These thinkers are essentially chastened children of the Enlightenment. They share the view that men are made to be happy, but are convinced by the events of the last two generations that wickedness and unreason are not, as the *philosophes* believed, rooted shallowly in a few bad institutions. On the contrary, they believe that evil, prejudice, and stupidity are deeply rooted in very complex institutions, in tradition, and perhaps even in man as a biological organism.

These thinkers have been greatly influenced by the emphasis that modern psychology has put on the irrational character of the human personality, on the subconscious and the unconscious, and on the consequent difficulty of the actual task of "enlightenment." They now think the task of making the world better will be long and difficult. But it is a task they believe can and must be continued. And they differ basically from the Christians in that they refuse to accept the Christian tension between this world and the next. They hold that man is a product of nature, and that the supernatural does not exist.

The important thing for us to note at the end of this long historic record is that between the second and the third groups we have been discussing, between the Christians and the chastened children of the Enlightenment, a practical accord is possible. It is indeed being worked out in the West. In this accord is the possibility that the men of the first group, the enemies of democracy, may be defeated, and that democracy may live on to give the lie to the prophets of doom. In such an accord we may preserve the willingness to put up with restraints, with imperfections, and with suffering without losing the hope, the dream, that is still alive for us in "liberty, equality, fraternity." We may thus avoid the illusions and retain the ideals of our heritage.

Reading Suggestions on the Western World Since 1945

The World

H. W. Gatzke, *The Present in Perspective: A Look at the World since 1945* (Chicago: Rand McNally, 1957). An excellent brief survey of our "grave new world."

A. J. Zurcher, ed., *Constitutions and Constitutional Trends since World War II*, 2nd ed. (N.Y.: New York Univ. Press, 1955). A very good, up-to-date collaborative account.

G. Myrdal, *An International Economy: Problems and Prospects* (N.Y.: Harper, 1956). An able study by a professional economist with wide international experience.

L. Fischer, *This Is Our World* (N.Y.: Harper, 1956). A subjective and most suggestive journalist's survey of the trouble spots of the globe.

E. Wilson, *Red, Black, Blond, Olive* (N.Y.: Oxford Univ. Press, 1956). Interesting studies of four societies—a New Mexico Pueblo, Haiti, Russia, Israel.

The Democracies

The following volumes in the "American Foreign Policy Library" series, D. C. McKay, ed. (Cambridge: Harvard Univ. Press), provide good introductions to the areas treated: C. Brinton, *The United States and Britain*, 2nd ed. (1948); D. C. McKay, *The United States and France* (1951); H. S. Hughes, *The United States and Italy* (1953); F. D. Scott, *The United States and Scandinavia* (1950); D. Perkins, *The United States and the Caribbean* (1947); A. P. Whitaker, *The United States and South America: The Northern Republics* (1948) and *The United States and Argentina* (1955).

G. Kennan, *Realities of American Policy* (Princeton: Princeton Univ. Press, 1954). By a thoughtful exponent of a realistic policy.

F. L. Allen, *The Big Change* (N.Y.: Harper, 1952). Perceptive essay on American social history since 1900.

C. Brinton, *The Temper of Western Europe* (Cambridge: Harvard Univ. Press, 1953). A cautiously optimistic evaluation.

F. Williams, *Socialist Britain* (N.Y.: Viking, 1949); and C. Palmer, *The British Socialist Ill-Fare State* (Caldwell, Idaho: Caxton, 1952). A defense and a critique of Labor's postwar reforms.

G. Wright, *The Reshaping of French Democracy* (N.Y.: Reynal & Hitchcock, 1948). Lively study of constitution-making in 1946.

A. Werth, *France: 1940-1955* (London: Hale, 1956). An informative though not always balanced analysis by a journalistic expert.

H. Luethy, *France against Herself* (N.Y.: Praeger, 1955). Perceptive study of divided France by a Swiss.

J. P. Warburg, *Germany: Key to Peace* (Cambridge: Harvard Univ. Press, 1953). An instructive survey.

W. Fleisher, *Sweden: The Welfare State* (N.Y.: Day, 1956). An objective examination of a small democracy.

Communism and the Cold War

D. J. Dallin, *The New Soviet Empire* (New Haven: Yale Univ. Press, 1951). Survey from an anti-Soviet standpoint.

G. A. Almond, ed., *The Appeals of Communism* (Princeton: Princeton Univ. Press, 1954). An interesting symposium.

M. Einaudi and others, *Communism in Western Europe* (Ithaca: Cornell Univ. Press, 1951). A very illuminating examination of French and Italian communists.

R. L. Wolff, *The Balkans in Our Time* (Cambridge: Harvard Univ. Press, 1956). An informed account of an important area.

A. B. Ulam, *Titoism and the Cominform* (Cambridge: Harvard Univ. Press, 1952). A study of the communist heresy.

Henry L. Roberts, *Russia and America: Dangers and Prospects* (N.Y.: Harper, 1956). A valuable summary.

The Prospect before Us

L. Mumford, *The Transformations of Man* (N.Y.: Harper, 1956). A philosophy of history in only 249 pages!

C. G. Darwin, *The Next Million Years* (Garden City, N.Y.: Doubleday, 1953); R. Seidenberg, *Posthistoric Man* (Chapel Hill: Univ. of North Carolina Press, 1950). Two stimulating attempts to chart the future of the human race.

H. Brown, *The Challenge of Man's Future* (N.Y.: Viking, 1956. A Compass Book). Most realistic of the books on "Whither Mankind."

C. T. Chase, *The Evolution of Modern Physics* (Princeton: Van Nostrand, 1947); and L. Barnett, *The Universe and Dr. Einstein* (N.Y.: New American Library, 1952). Two good popular treatments of a difficult and most important subject.

P. Geyl, *From Ranke to Toynbee* (Northampton, Mass., 1952. *Smith College Studies in History*, Vol. 39). Lectures on Spengler and other important philosophers of history.

S. Hughes, *Oswald Spengler: A Critical Estimate* (N.Y.: Scribner's, 1952). On a characteristic prophet of gloom.

A. C. Valentine, *The Age of Conformity* (Chicago: Regnery, 1954). A good example of the criticism of modern American democracy from the worried conservative standpoint.

C. Frankel, *The Case for Modern Man* (N.Y.: Harper, 1956). An admirable restatement of hopeful belief in democracy and "progress"; antidote to the prophets of gloom.

R. Niebuhr, *The Children of Light and the Children of Darkness* (N.Y.: Scribner's, 1944), and *The Irony of American History* (N.Y.: Scribner's, 1952). Characteristic works by an important American theologian who argues that Christian pessimism offers a good working basis for democracy.

K. R. Popper, *The Open Society and Its Enemies* (Princeton: Princeton Univ. Press, 1950). A major work on the problems of modern democracy.

W. Kaufman, ed., *Existentialism from Dostoevsky to Sartre* (N.Y.: Meridian, 1956). Instructive selections from the existentialists, together with helpful critical comment.

A series of brief, clearly written books on the problems of man's fate, seen from varied contemporary angles, will be found listed under Ruth Nanda Anshen, ed., *World Perspectives* (N.Y.: Harpers, 1954—).

Fiction

A. Camus, *The Plague* (N.Y.: Knopf, 1948). A good novel about the human predicament; by a leading intellectual of post-war France.

L. Trilling, *The Middle of the Journey* (N.Y.: Viking, 1947). Enlightening novel about an American ex-communist.

A. Huxley, *Brave New World* (N.Y.: Bantam Books, 1953). One of the first and one of the best nightmarish accounts of utopia.

G. Orwell, *1984* (N.Y.: New American Library). A classic tale of a "brain-washed" world.

O. F. Skinner, *Walden Two* (N.Y.: Macmillan, 1948). A psychologist's utopia of "cultural engineering."

S. de Beauvoir, *The Mandarins* (Cleveland: World, 1956). A novel analyzing contemporary French intellectuals.

Illustrations

Reindeer from Cavern at Font-de-Gaume, *Courtesy of the American Museum of Natural History* — 7

Queen Nefertiti, *Courtesy of the Metropolitan Museum of Art* — 10

The Parthenon, *TWA* — 12

Cathedral of Notre Dame, *TWA* — 28

Venice in the Sixteenth Century, *from Civitates Orbis Terrarum, 1573, by G. Braun, New York Public Library, Reserve Division* — 35

House of Jacques Coeur — 37

Erasmus, by Dürer — 54

Botticelli, "Primavera" — 57

Masaccio, "Expulsion of Adam and Eve from Eden" — 58

Leonardo da Vinci, "The Madonna of the Rocks" — 59

Michelangelo, "Creation of Adam" — 60

Titian, "Vendramin Family in Adoration," *Reproduced by Courtesy of the Trustees, the National Gallery, London* — 61

Donatello, "Mary Magdalen" — 63

Michelangelo, "Pieta" — 64

St. Peter's, Rome, *The Bettmann Archive* — 66

Martin Luther, by Cranach, *Courtesy of the Metropolitan Museum of Art* — 76

Emperor Charles V, by Titian — 80

Classroom Sketches of Calvin, *from Iconographie calvinienne by Emil Doumergue, New York Public Library* — 84

Loyola, *The Bettmann Archive* — 94

El Greco, "Burial of the Count of Orgaz" — 122

Francis I of France, *Courtesy of the John G. Johnson Collection, Philadelphia* — 125

Henry VIII, by Holbein — 128

Elizabeth I, *Courtesy of the National Portrait Gallery, London* — 131

Ma Yüan, "A Sage Under a Pine Tree," *Courtesy of the Metropolitan Museum of Art* — 144

Departure of an Exploration Trip to America, *The Bettmann Archive* — 150

Indian Village Near Roanoke, *New York Public Library* — 155

Jesuit Missionary in China, *The Bettmann Archive* — 160

A Fifteenth-century European's Conception of People in Unknown Lands, *New York Public Library, Prints Division* — 164

Louis XIV, by Rigaud, *The Bettmann Archive* — 171

The Palace of Versailles — 180

King Charles I, by Van Dyck — 187

The Baldachino, St. Peter's — 202

Rubens, "Rape of the Daughters of Leucippus by Castor and Pollux" — 203

Rembrandt, "The Night Watch" — 204

Mohammed, *The Bettman Archive* — 210

Mihrimah Mosque, Constantinople, *New York Public Library Picture Collection* — 211

A Russian Ikon, *Sovfoto* — 221

Building the Uspensky Cathedral in the Kremlin, *New York Public Library* — 225

Peter the Great, by Falconet, *Sovfoto* — 230

Metal-planing and Metal-cutting Factory in the Eighteenth Century, *The Bettmann Archive* — 253

One of the Giant Soldiers of Frederick William I of Prussia, *New York Public Library Picture Collection* — 262

The Battle of Culloden, *The Bettmann Archive* — 266

Thirteen Glimpses of Voltaire, *New York Public Library Picture Collection* — 281

Emperor Joseph II of Austria Working a Plow, *Austrian Information Service* — 290

Catherine the Great, by Lampi — 297

"Shortly after Marriage," by Hogarth, *Reproduced by Courtesy of the Trustees, the National Gallery, London* — 309

An English Commentary on the Boston Tea Party, *Courtesy of the Metropolitan Museum of Art* — 315

The Bastille, July 14, 1789, *French Embassy Press and Information Division* — 325

Execution of Louis XVI, *Spencer Collection, New York Public Library* — 333

Sketch of Marie Antoinette on Her Way to the Guillotine, by David, *New York Public Library Picture Collection* — 335

Napoleon, Sketched at the Theater, *The Bettmann Archive* — 347

"The Battle of Trafalgar," by Turner, *The Bettmann Archive* — 351

Gillray, "Tiddy-Dolly, the Gingerbread-Baker, Drawing Out a New Batch of Kings," *New York Public Library Picture Collection* — 355

"And They Are Like Wildcats," Etching by Goya, *Courtesy of the Metropolitan Museum of Art* — 359

Constable, "Dedham Mill," *Courtesy of the Victoria & Albert Museum. Crown Copyright.* — 365

The Houses of Parliament, London, *Pan American World Airways* 366

Delacroix, "The Massacre at Scio" 381

Daumier, "The Uprising," *Courtesy of the Phillips Collection, Washington* 391

Metternich, *New York Public Library Picture Collection* 397

Industrial Marvels at the Great Exhibition, London, 1851, *New York Public Library Picture Collections* 402

London Slums. Woodcut after Doré, *The Bettmann Archive* 408

Steel Works at Pittsburgh, 1876, *The Bettmann Archive* 411

Sketch of Robert Owen's Unity Village, 1817, *London Times, August 9, 1817* 420

The Paris Commune, 1871, *The Bettmann Archive* 450

Meeting of Garibaldi and King Victor Emmanuel, *The Bettmann Archive* 458

Civil War Ruins at Charleston, South Carolina, *The Bettmann Archive* 463

Bismarck, *The Bettmann Archive* 473

"Dropping the Pilot," William II Dismisses Bismarck, *New York Public Library Picture Collection* 480

Emperor Francis Joseph, *The Bettmann Archive* 483

Ceremony during Emancipation of Russian Serfs, *The Bettmann Archive* 316

Workers Fighting on the Barricades in Moscow, 1905, *Sovfoto* 508

Claude Monet, "La Grenouillière," *Courtesy of the Metropolitan Museum of Art* 528

Edouard Manet, "The Death of Maximillian," *Courtesy of the Boston Museum of Fine Arts* 529

Cézanne, Landscape with Mont Sainte Victoire in Background, *Courtesy of the Metropolitan Museum of Art* 530

Maillol, "La Mériterranée" 531

Daumier, How the Public Feels after Listening to the Music of Wagner, *The Bettmann Archive* 533

Sigmund Freud, *The Bettmann Archive* 538

Disraeli Purchases the Suez Canal, *Punch, February 26, 1876* 557

Chinese Painting of the Arrival of One of the First English Steamers at Canton, about 1840, *The Bettmann Archive* 560

Execution of Mutineers after the Sepoy Rebellion in India, 1857, *New York Public Library Picture Collection* 562

President Theodore Roosevelt and Panama, *The Bettmann Archive* 568

Berlin Crowds Singing "Deutschland Über Alles," 1914, *The Bettmann Archive* 584

Princip, Immediately after the Assassination at Sarajevo, *The Bettmann Archive* 591

Two Advertisements about the *Lusitania*, 1915, *The Bettmann Archive* 593

Aerial Dogfight during World War I, *The Bettmann Archive* 602

French Troops at Verdun, *The Bettmann Archive* 603

Lloyd George, Clemenceau, and Wilson in Paris, 1919, *The Bettmann Archive* 610

Tsar Nicholas II and His Family, 1917, *The Bettmann Archive* 623

Lenin, *The Bettmann Archive* 625

Machine Guns in Action against Revolutionaries in Petrograd, *The Bettmann Archive* 628

The New Soviet Industrial Center of Magnitogorsk, *Sovfoto* 643

Low Cartoon Comment on the Hitler-Stalin Pact, August, 1939, *Copyright Low All Countries. Reproduced by Permission of the Artist* 655

Stalin, *United Press* 656

Mussolini and Fascisti during "March" on Rome, October, 1922, *United Press* 666

Hitler at Time of Beer-hall Putsch, Munich, November, 1923, *FPG* 678

Hitler and his Entourage Driving through Hildesheim, *The Bettmann Archive* 685

Poster of Chancellor Dollfuss Defaced by Nazis, 1933, *United Press* 696

Demonstrators in the Stavisky Riots, Paris, February, 1934, *United Press* 713

Apple-sellers in New York, *Wide World Photos* 718

Franklin D. Roosevelt, *United Press* 721

Low Cartoon, "Rule Japannia," *Copyright Low All Countries. Reproduced by Permission of the Artist* 725

Gandhi and Crowd, 1945, *Information Service of India, New York* 731

Chamberlain, Daladier, Hitler, Mussolini, and Ciano at Munich, September, 1938, *United Press* 746

Prime Minister Winston Churchill, *United Press* 754

Hitler's Elation after Armistice with France, 1940, *United Press* 755

Stalingrad, *Sovfoto* 761

Nordhausen Concentration Camp, *United Press* 763

Hiroshima after the Atomic Bomb Hit, *Brown Brothers* 767

Measuring Land for Redistribution in Communist China, *Eastfoto* 780

U. S. Marines in Korea, *Wide World Photos* 781

Indian Village, *FPG* 784

Nasser, Nehru, and Tito on Brioni, June 19, 1956, *United Press* 788

Mau Mau Suspects in Kenya, *British Information Services* 794

Slums Near Johannesburg, *United Press* 797

Adderly St., Capetown, *South African Government Information Office, New York* 797

Prince Wan Waithayakon Addresses the UN General Assembly, *United Press* 817

Premier Bulganin and Party Secretary Khrushchev, *United Press* 833

Picasso, "Girl before a Mirror," 1932, *Courtesy of the Museum of Modern Art. Gift of Mrs. Simon Guggenheim* 838

Index

A

Aachen, 22 (see also Aix-la-Chapelle)

Aborigines (Australian), 5

Absolutism (see also Divine-right monarchy): Age of, 118-119; English, 184-185; French, 46, 124-127; Spanish, 119-120

Abyssinia, 552 (see also Ethiopia)

Académie des Sciences, 196

Academy, French, 170, 277

Academy at Dijon, 284

Acadia (Nova Scotia), 173

Act of Settlement of 1701, 195

Acton, Lord, 79

Adages and Colloquies (Erasmus), 55

Addresses to the German Nation (Fichte), 357

Adenauer, Konrad, 831-832

Adowa, battle of, 459, 552

Adrianople, Treaty of, 382

Aehrenthal, Count von, 492, 589

Africa: after World War II, 791-798; Belgian Congo, 567; Boer War, 553-557; British in South, 552-557; European posts in, 159; French imperialism in, 564-566; French North Africa after World War II, 798; Kenya, 794-795; Negro states, 793; Portuguese explorations in, 140; 1914, map, 556; nineteenth-century imperialism in, 551-552; in Seven Years' War, 270; South (see South Africa; Union of South Africa); whites in, 794; World War II in North Africa, 759-760

Afrikaners: after World War II, 795-796; settling of, 159

Agrarian League, 481

Agriculture: collectivized in Russia, 639-641; in first American settlements, 154, 156; improved by Frederick the Great, 287; Mussolini's "Battle of Wheat," 669; New Deal and, 721

Agricultural revolution, 251-252, 406-407

Air warfare: World War I, 601, 602 (illus.); World War II, 750, 756, 761

Aix-la-Chapelle, Treaty of, 172, 267

Alaska, 822

Albania: attacked by Mussolini,

743; Russian absorption of, 807; Soviet satellite, 835

Albuquerque, Alfonso de, 141

Alexander the Great, 14, 16, 141

Alexander, King of Greece, 599

Alexander, King of Yugoslavia, 699

Alexander I, Tsar of Russia, 298, 299-301, 350, 354, 358, 359, 369, 372, 382, 383, 386, 387

Alexander II, Tsar of Russia, 500-502; assassination of, 505; foreign policy, 505; reforms, 497

Alexander III, Tsar of Russia, 497, 505-507

Alexander VI, Pope, 41, 71

Alexandra, Empress of Russia, 622

Alexis, son of Peter the Great, 235-236

Alfonso the Magnanimous, 41

Alfonso XIII, King of Spain, 691-692

Algeciras, conference at, 589

Algeria: after World War II, 798; French colony, 564; Ottoman Turks in, 241

All Quiet on the Western Front (Remarque), 603

Alphabet, 9

Alsace-Lorraine, 46, 47: after World War I, 585; Alsatian question in 1920's, 712-713; obtained by Bismarck, 477; re-won by France, 613

Alton Locke (Kingsley), 428

Alva, Duke of, 110

Alvarado, Pedro de, 150

Alvensleben convention, 473-474

America: colonies, 154-157; discoveries by Spaniards, 121, 147-148; English settlements, 154-156; English, Spanish, French colonies compared, 157; institutions of colonies, 156-157; naming of, 148; settlement of colonies, 154-156

American Indians: destroyed by settlers, 161-162; Indian village (illus.), 155

American Revolution, 271, 313-318: background, 314-316; and George III, 313-314; implications, 316-318

Amiens, Peace of, 350

Amish sect, 86-87

Amritsar massacre, 607, 730

Amsterdam, Bank of, 111

Anabaptists, 83, 86-87, 91-92

Anarchism: anarcho-syndicalism, 426-427; defined, 426; and

Proudhon, 427-428; in Spain, 691

Anatolia, 209, 210

Andrássy, Count Gyula, 484

Andrussovo, Treaty of, 222

Angevin family, 41

Anglican Church, 83, 88-89: after Restoration, 193; Book of Common Prayer, 130; in Ireland, 442, 443; Thirty-Nine Articles, 89, 130; in Virginia, 156

Anglo-Dutch War of 1664-1667, 193

Anglo-Saxons, 21, 23

Annals of Agriculture (Young), 313

Anne, Empress of Russia, 292-293

Anne, Queen, 194, 195

Anschluss, 743

Anticlericalism: in Bismarckian Germany, 477-478; in England, 85; and Enlightenment, 280-281; in French Revolution, 328; Joseph II and, 289; of Renaissance, 69, 70; in Third Republic, 454; in united Italy, 458-459

Anti-Machiavel (Frederick II, the Great), 287

Antinomianism, 86, 87-88, 90

Anti-Semitism: of Alexander III, 506; in Austria, 493, 494, 512, 696; in France, and Dreyfus case, 453-454; of Frederick the Great, 287; of Hitler, 675-676, 686, 688; in Hungary, 495, 512, 697, 698; of Mussolini, 670; in Poland, 222; in Rumania, 700; in Russia, 509, 512; Spanish Inquisition, 50; in Weimar Germany, 675; in Yugoslavia, 699

Antonescu, Marshal, 700

Aosta, Duke of, 665

Apartheid, policy of, 796

Appeal to the Christian Nobility of the German Nation, The (Luther), 77, 78

Aquinas, St. Thomas, 89

Arab League, 790-791

Arab Legion, 785

Aragon, dynasty of, 41, 49

Arakcheev, Count, 300, 383

Arc de Triomphe, 366

Architecture: of Dark Ages, 22; of early nineteenth century, 366-367; of Enlightenment, 308-309; Gothic, 19; Gothic and Renaissance compared, 65; origins, 9; Minoan, 11; of Renaissance, 56, 65-67; in sixteenth-century France, 124; Tudor and early Stuart, 132; Victorian Age, 531-532

Areopagitica (Milton), 192

Argentine Republic: after World War II, 815, 825-826; and World War II, 766

Armada, Spanish, 111, 131

Armed forces: British in eighteenth century, 255; in colonial system, 145; French in eighteenth century, 257; of modern states, 104; of Ottoman Turks, 238; of Prussia, 262 (*illus.*), 263; of sixteenth-century Spain, 110

Arnold, Matthew, 439, 527

Arsenal, Venetian, 34, 36, 43, 44, 104

Artel, 640

Arts (see also Architecture, Literature, Music, Painting, Sculpture): Baroque, 201-204; in Dark Ages, 22; in Elizabethan England, 132-134; of Enlightenment, 308-309; of early Greece, 12-13; Minoan, 11; of Muscovite Russia, 220-222; of Near East, 9-10; during Reign of Terror, 336-337; in Renaissance, 39, 55-67; of Romantic movement, 365-367; in seventeenth century, 199-205; in sixteenth-century France, 127; in Spain, 120, 123; Victorian Age, 528-534

Artois, Count of (see Charles X, King of France)

Asiento privilege, 173-176, 265

Asquith, Herbert, 445, 606

Assignats, 328, 330, 331, 338, 339

Astronomy: advances of seventeenth century, 197-198; Renaissance, 68-69

Aswan dam, 558

Atatürk (see Kemal, Mustafa)

Athens, 11

Atlantic Charter, 766

Atomic bomb, 750-751, 766

Attlee, Clement, 828

Auerstädt, battle of, 351

Augsburg, 37, 38: Peace of, 107, 112; War of the League of, 172-173

Augustus the Strong, Elector of Saxony, 230, 231, 264

Augustus III of Poland, 264, 301

Aurangzeb, Emperor of Moguls, 158

Ausgleich, 484, 485, 492, 495, 496

Austerlitz, battle of, 351, 354

Australia: aborigines, 5; after World War II, 799-800; dominion status, 576-577; European settlements in, 574

Austria: annexation by Hitler, 743; and Congress of Vienna, 369, 372; Diplomatic Revolution, 268; divided by Iron Curtain, 807; dual monarchy, 484-485; enlightened despotism of Maria Theresa and Joseph II, 288-290; expansionist wars, 264; fascism in, 694-696; Habsburg Empire, 105-111, 112, 113-118 (see also Habsburg Empire); minorities in *1867-1914*, 485-489; parliament, 511; revolutions of *1848*, 395-398; Schleswig-Holstein problem, 474, 475; Seven Years' War, 269; society and politics, *1867-1914*, 492-494; in War of Polish Succession, 264; war with Prussia, *1866*, 474-475

Austrian Succession, War of the, 266-267: Russia and, 301-302; results for Austria, 288

Austro-Turkish War, *1716-1718*, 264

Autobiography (Mill), 416

Avanti (*Forward*), 663

Azaña, Manuel, 693

Azov, 228, 231

Aztec empire, 149

B

Babeuf, Gracchus, 338

Babbitt (Lewis), 418

Babylonian Captivity, 41

Bach, Johann Sebastian, 309, 310, 311

Bach system, 483, 484

Bacon, Francis, 133, 196

Badoglio, Marshal, 761, 768

Bagehot, Walter, 433, 544

Baghdad, 241, 242

Bakewell, Robert, 251

Bakunin, Michael, 426, 503, 504, 691

Balance of power, 11, 102: Charles VIII and, 105; Crimean War and, 441-442; and eighteenth-century Italy, 260; Grand Alliance, 173; Philip II and, 109; prior to World War II, 739; and War of Polish Succession, 265; and World War I, 582-583; Yugoslavia and, 810

Balboa, Vasco Nuñez de, 148

Baldachino, the (St. Peter's Rome), 202 (*illus.*)

Baldwin, Stanley, 709

Balfour, Arthur, 444

Balfour Declaration, 600, 732

Balkans, *1878, 1914, maps*, 590

Balkan Wars, 589

Balzac, Honoré, 524

Baner, General, 114

Banking: industrial revolution and, 401, 404-405; origins, 36; in Renaissance, 36-38

Bank of Amsterdam, 111

Bank of England, 250, 251

Baptists, 86-87, 92

Barbusse, Henri, 603

Barcelona, 49

Bardi banking family, 37, 56

Barents, Willem, 161

Barings of London, 405

Baroja, Pio, 526

Baroque style, 201-204

Bartholdi, Frédéric Auguste, 531

Basel, Treaty of, 343, 344

Bastille, fall of, 325 (*illus.*), 326, 342

Bate's case, 186

Battle of the Nations, 359

Bavaria: ambitions of Elector of Bavaria, 266; attacked by Joseph II, 290; Catholicism in, 107; soviet republic in, 606; and Weimar Republic, 672-673

Bazaine, General François, 449

Beck, Governor, 161

Beauharnais, Josephine de, 343, 347, 355

Bebel, August, 479

Beccaria, Cesare, 279-280, 289, 296

Beethoven, Ludwig van, 364

"Beggars'" League, 109

Beggar's Opera, The (Gay), 310

Behaim, 147

Belgium: gains of Paris Conference, 613; Hitler's invasion of, 753; imperialism of, 549, 552, 567; invasion of, in World War I, 592; revolution of *1830*, 385-386, 409

Belgrade, 241

Belgrade, Treaty of, 301

Bellamy, Edward, 534

Belle Hélène, La (Offenbach), 533

Bengal, Nawab of, 269, 270

Bennett, Arnold, 526

Bentham, Jeremy, 414-415, 416

Bergson, Henri, 535

Beria, Lavrenti, 832

Berlin airlift, 807-810

Berlin, Congress of, 491

Berlin Decree, 356

Berlioz, Louis Hector, 364

Berri, Duke of, 384

Bessarabia, 614, 656

Bessemer, Henry, 404

Bestuzhev-Ryumin, 301, 302

Bethlen, Count, 697-698

Bethmann-Hollweg, Chancellor, 592, 605

Beust, 484

Bible: and Darwin, 516, 517-518; King James' Version, 187

Bidault, Georges, 452

Biglow Papers (Lowell), 527

Bill of Rights, 194, 317

Biren, 293

Bismarck, Otto von: attack on Catholic Church, 478-479; dismissal of, 480 (*illus.*); domestic program, (*1878-1890*), 478-480; German Empire, 477-480; and German imperialism, 567; 473 (*illus.*); and Napoleon III, 449; North German Confederation, 475-476; rise to

power, 473-474; Schleswig-Holstein question, 474, 475; seeds of World War I, 585-586; unification of Germany, 470, 472, 511; war with Austria, *1866*, 474-475; war with France, 476-477
"Black Hole" of Calcutta, 269-270
Black, Joseph, 276
Black Partition, 504
Blanc, Louis, 390, 401, 421
Blenheim, battle of, 173
Blitzkrieg, 751, 753, 757
Bloody assizes, 194
Blücher, Gebhard Leberecht, 360
Blum, Léon, 714, 715
Bobadilla, Francisco, 147
Boccaccio, Giovanni, 52-53
Bodin, Jean, 127
Boer Republics, 442
Boer War, 481-482
Boers, 553, 577
Bohemia: and Austria-Hungary, 485-486; and Czechoslovakia, 613; February Patent, 484; revolutions of *1848*, 397; Thirty Years' War, 112-113
Boileau, Nicolas, 195, 199
Boleyn, Anne, 84-85
Bologna, Concordat of, 84, 125
Bolsheviks and Bolshevism, 497, 506, 509: after World War I, 606; in Communist Russia (*1917-1941*), 621-658; in Hungary, 697; Lenin and, 625-626; Russian revolution of *1917*, 623, 625-626, 627, 628, 629; and World War I, 598
Bonaparte, Jerome, 355
Bonaparte, Joseph, 354, 357, 378
Bonaparte, Louis, 355-356, 361
Bonaparte, Louis Napoleon (*see* Napoleon III)
Bonaparte, Lucien, 345
Bonapartists, 390
Booth, John Wilkes, 464
Borelli, 197
Borgias, 41, 57
Boris, King of Bulgaria, 700
Borodin, Michael, 652
Bosanquet, Bernard, 534
Bosnia-Herzegovina, 491-492; annexed by Austria, 589; Russian war for, 505
Bossuet, Bishop, 179, 195
Boston Tea Party, 315 (*illus.*), 316
Bosworth Field, battle of, 48
Botticelli, 57 (*illus.*), 58, 59
Boulanger, General, 452-453
Bourbon, Constable de, 106
Bourbon kings, 126, 259, 264, 267
Bourgeois Gentilhomme, Le (Molière), 199
Bourges, Pragmatic Sanction of, 46, 69, 125
Bouvard et Pécuchet (Flaubert), 526
Bouvines, battle of, 23

Boxer Rebellion, 726
Boyne, battle of the, 172-173, 195
"Boy Patriots," 265, 270
Bradley, F. H., 534
Brahmin caste, 142
Brahms, Johannes, 532
Brandenburg, 115
Brandenburg-Prussia, 172, 260, 261-263
Brazil: independent, 379; Portuguese explorations in, 140-141; Portuguese settlements in, 149, 153; World War II, 766
Brest, Union of, 222
Brest-Litovsk, Peace of, 598, 599, 631-632, 633
Brethren of the Common Life, 70
Breughel, Pieter the Elder, 62
Briand, Aristide, 452, 455, 717, 737
Bridgewater, Duke of, 248
Brieux, Eugene, 526
British Commonwealth of Nations, 575-577: after World War II, 798-801; between world wars, 710-711; Canada, 798-799; nature of, 800-801; New Zealand and Australia, 799-800
British North America Act of *1867*, 576
Broglie, Duke of, 451
Brook Farm, 420
Browne and Brownist movement, 130
Browning, Robert, 836
Bruening, Heinrich, 681, 682, 683
Brumaire *coup*, 339
Brunswick, Duke of, 331, 332, 342
Brusilov, General, 598
Buddha, Gautama, 142
Buddhism, 142-143
Bukharin, Nikolai, 636-637, 639, 645, 646, 653
Bulgaria: authoritarian government, 700; Congress of Berlin and, 505; Ottoman rule, 244; Russian absorption of, 807, 835
Bulletin of the Opposition, The (Trotsky), 645
Bundesrat, 476
Bunyan, John, 200
Burckhardt, Jacob, 433
Burgesses, 48
Burgoyne, General, 316
Burgundy, Duchy of, 46, 106
Burgundians, 22
Burke, Edmund, 341-342, 345, 361, 368-369, 536
Burleigh, 131
"Burma Road," 764
Burne-Jones, Edward, 528
Burschenschaft, 387
Bute, Lord, 314
Butler, Samuel, 526
Byng, Admiral, 269
Byron, Lord, 362, 368
Byzantine Empire: conquered

by Turks, 211; Greek heritage, 21; origins, 17; Russian debt to, 208, 209; tradition of, 209
Byzantium, 32

C

Caballero, Largo, 693, 694
Cabot, John and Sebastian, 153
Cabral, Pedro, 140
Cadillac, Antoine, 157
Caesar, Augustus, 16
Caesar, Julius, 16
Cahiers, 322
Cajetan, Cardinal, 77, 79
Calas, Jean, 282
Calcutta, 158
Caldwell, Erskine, 526
Calonne, Charles Alexandre de, 102
Calvin, Jean, 83-84: execution of Servetus, 87; sermon quoted, 91; sketches of, 84 (*illus.*)
Calvinism (*see also* Huguenots): in Netherlands, 109; in New England, 156; Peace of Augsburg and, 107, 112; predestination, 90-91
Campoformio, Treaty of, 344
Canada: after World War II, 798-799, 825; American invasion of, 462; background of *1837* revolt, 575; dominion status, 576; Durham Report, 575-576
Canals, first, 248
Candide (Voltaire), 282
Canning, George, 379, 380, 434
Canterbury Tales (Chaucer), 51
Cape La Hogue, battle of, 172
Cape of Good Hope, 140, 159
"Capitulations," 241
Capuchins, 93
Carbonari, 378
Carducci, 662
Carlism, 691, 694
Carlos, Baby (*see* Charles III)
Carlsbad Decrees, 387
Carlyle, Thomas, 439
Carnot, President, 426
Carol, King of Rumania, 700
Carolingian Renaissance, 22
Carpetbaggers, 464
Carthage, 14
Cartier, Jacques, 153
Casa de Contratación, 121
Caste system, 142, 164
Castiglione, Baldassare, 66, 67, 71-72
Castile, 49
Castlereagh, Robert Stewart, 369, 372: Quadruple Alliance, 373-374; and Troppau Protocol, 379
Cateau-Cambrésis, Treaty of, 107
Catherine of Aragon, 84-85
Catherine I, Empress of Russia, 228, 292
Catherine II, the Great, 292, 293-294, 295-298, 297 (*illus.*), 302-304, 342

Catholic Emancipation Act of *1829*, 442
Catholic League, 112, 126
Catholic Reformation, 93-96: Council of Trent, 95-96; Inquisition, 94-95; Jesuits, 93-94
Cavaignac, General, 391, 392
Cavaliers, 156, 189-190
Cave paintings, 7 (*illus.*), 8, 9
Cavour, Camillo Benso di, 456-457
Cellarius, 19
Cervantes Saavedra, Miguel de, 53, 120, 123
Ceylon, 159, 800
Cézanne, Paul, 530 (*illus.*)
C.G.T., 712, 714, 715
Chaadaev, 502
Chamberlain, Austen, 445
Chamberlain, Joseph, 443, 444, 445, 707
Chamberlain, Neville, 445: and Churchill, 753; Czechoslovakian crisis, 745; Russian distrust of, 748
Chamberlain, Stewart Houston, 675
Chambord, Count of, 451
Champlain, Samuel de, 153
Champollion, Jean François, 344
Charlemagne, 22
Charles, Bonnie Prince, 267
Charles, King of Hungary, 697
Charles I, King of Spain (*see* Charles V, Emperor)
Charles I, King of England, 184, 185, 187-190, 187 (*illus.*)
Charles II, King of Spain, 173
Charles II, King of England, 190, 191, 193, 196
Charles III, King of Spain, 290-291
Charles V, Emperor, 47, 61, 78, 80 (*illus.*), 84-85, 106-107, 119, 241 (*illus.*)
Charles VI, Emperor, 176, 260, 264
Charles VII, King of France, 45-46, 100, 101
Charles VIII, King of France, 105-106
"Charles X, King," French pretender, 126
Charles X, King of France, 384, 385
Charles XII, King of Sweden, 230-231, 232, 258, 264
Charles Albert, King of Piedmont, 393
Charles the Bold, of Burgundy, 47
Charter of *1814*, French, 384, 385
Chartism, 441, 446
Chaucer, Geoffrey, 51, 53-54
Cheap Clothes and Nasty (Kingsley), 428
Chekhov, Anton, 526, 834
Chelmsford, Lord, 730
Chetniks, 810
Chiang Kai-shek, 637, 652-653, 727, 728, 729, 764, 765, 778
Chicherin, Gregori V., 651

China: between world wars, 727-728; communism in, 729; communist government in, 778-779, 811; European attempts to settle, 159-160; Japanese imperialism in, 569, 570, 726; Opium War, 559; resistance to West, 143-145; revolution of *1911-1912*, 725-727; social organization, 143-145; treaty with Russians, 224; World War II, 758, 766
Chippendale, Thomas, 308
Choiseul, Duke of, 272, 278
Christian IV, King of Denmark, 113, 114
Christianity: characteristics of early, 18; and decline of Roman Empire, 17; Eucharist, 83, 89, 112-113; and history, 18; in Japan, 160; Jesus (*see* Jesus Christ); in New World, 162; origin, 18; in Ottoman Empire, 237, 240, 243-244
Christian Socialism, 493, 494
Chronometer, 248
Church of England (*see* Anglican Church)
Churchill, John, General, 173
Churchill, Winston, 599, 600, 602, 753, 754 (*illus.*), 756, 762, 763, 764, 766, 768, 828
Cisalpine Republic of Lombardy, 344
Cities: in Middle Ages, 26; origins of, 7
Citizen, origin of concept, 12
City-states: in Italian Renaissance, 39-44; and Macedonians, 14; origins, 11-13; religion in, 12
Civil Constitution of the Clergy, 328, 329, 330
Civilization, origins of, 8
Civil War: American, 463-465; English, 188-192; Russian, 632-633; Spanish, 742-743
Clarendon Code, 193
Clarissa Harlowe (Richardson), 307
Clark Memorandum, 723
Clark, Michael, 709
Clemenceau, Georges, 455, 605, 606, 610 (*illus.*), 613, 616
Clement VII, Pope, 106
Clement XIV, Pope, 281
"Clermont," steamboat, 404
Cleves, Duke of, 107
Clive, Robert, 267, 270, 344, 561
Clough, Arthur Hugh, 527
"Cloth of Gold, Field of the," 127
Coal mining, Great Britain: in depression of *1920's*, 706; in eighteenth century, 253
Cobden, Richard, 439
Code of Hammurabi, 9
Code Napoléon, 346-347, 360
Coeur, Jacques, 37, 46
Coffee houses, 248
Cognac, League of, 106
Coke, Sir Edward, 186
Colbert, Jean Baptiste, 169, 181, 182-183, 196

Cold war, 769, 779-781, 805, 806-807, 810, 830
Coleridge, Samuel Taylor, 163, 362, 364, 367, 368, 439
Coligny, Gaspard, 125
Collins, Michael, 709
Colonialism (*see* Imperialism)
Colosseum, 17
Columbus, Christopher, 50, 139, 147-148
Combination Acts, 409, 433, 434
Comines, Philippe de, 46, 47
Cominform, 810
Comintern, 621, 651-653
Commercial revolution, 247-249
Common law, 29, 157
Commonwealth of Nations (*see* British Commonwealth of Nations)
Communion (*see* Eucharist)
Communist International (*see* Comintern)
Communist League, 423
Communist Manifesto, 398, 423-424, 425
Communism: in China, between world wars, 727, 728, 729; in China, after World War II, 778-779; Communist bloc in Europe, 807-810; in France (*1919-1939*), 712, 713, 714, 715; in Hitler's Germany, 653, 690; Marx, 421-426; outside Russian bloc, 813-814; Russia (*1917-1941*), 621-658; in Southeast Asia, 781; stresses within communist bloc, 811-813; in United States (*1930's*), 719
Compagnie des Indes Orientales, 159
Compass, 138
Comuneros, revolt of, 119
Conciliar Movement, 41, 69
Concordat of Bologna, 84, 125-126
Concordat of *1801*, 348
Concordat of *1855*, 483
Concord, battle of, 316
Condition of the Working Class in England, The (Engels), 423
Condorcet, Marquis de, 275-276, 332, 334, 337
Condottieri, 41, 42
Confederation of the Rhine, 355
Confucius, 145
Congregationalists, 156
Congress of Berlin, 491
Congress of Vienna, 301, 359, 369-373, 470
Conservative party, Great Britain, 436, 443, 444, 706-709
Conspiracy of the Equals, 338
Constable, John, 365 (*illus.*)
Constantine I, Emperor, 17, 18, 21
Constantine, Archduke of Russia, 383
Constantine, King of Greece, 599
Constantinople, 211
Constitution: French of *1791*,

329, 330; French of *1795*, 338; French of *1852*, 447; French of *1875*, 451-452; Second French Republic, 345-346; Prussian of *1850*, 395, 472; of United States, 317-318; Weimar Republic, 673-674
Consubstantiation, doctrine of, 83, 89
Continental Congress, 316
Contract theory of government, 284-285
Coolidge, Calvin, 716, 717, 718-719
Copernicus, Nicholas, 68-69
Corfu incident, 740
Corinth, 11-12
Corneille, Pierre, 199
Corn Laws, 407, 408, 439
Coronado, Francisco Vasquez, 149
Corporatism, thesis of, 118-119
Cortés, Hernando, 149
Cortes, of Spain, 49, 50, 119
Così Fan Tutte (Mozart), 310
Cossacks, 222-223, 224, 235, 296
Cotton gin, 402
Coulson, Samuel, 410-411
Council for Europe, 827
Council of Blood, 110
Council of Castile, 50
Council of Ferrara-Florence, 212
Council of Five Hundred, 338
Council of Trent, 95-96
Council of Troubles, 110
Counter-Reformation (*see* Catholic Reformation)
Courtier, The (Castiglione), 67, 71, 72
Crane, Stephen, 526
Cranmer, Archbishop, 85, 130
Crete, 243
Crimea: annexed by Catherine the Great, 303, 304; Ottoman Turks and, 240; Tartars in, 214
Crimean War: background, 241; and Bismarck, 472; effects in Russia, 497; France in, 448; Francis Joseph and, 483; Great Britain in, 441; Russia in, 499-500
Croatia and Croats: and Hungary, 489, 490-491; and Yugoslavia, 614, 698, 699
Croce, Benedetto, 535
Croix de Feu, 714
Cromwell, Oliver, 189, 190-191
Cromwell, Richard, 191
Crusades, 21
Cuba, 551, 567
Cubism, 530
Culloden, battle of, 266 (*illus.*), 267
Culture: of Elizabethan Age, 132-134; of Enlightenment, 304-311; of fifteenth century, 33; Florentine, 42; Greco-Roman, 13-14; under Hitler, 688-689; influence of eastern on western, 163-165; of Middle Ages, 27-30; in Muscovite

Russia, 220-222; nineteenth-century intellectual revolution, 515-545; of Peter the Great, 234-235; of Renaissance, 39, 50-67; of present-day Soviet Russia, 834-835; Russian (*1825-1881*), 502-503; of seventeenth century, 195-205; of Spain's Golden Age, 123-124
"Curial" system, 484, 486
Curzon, Lord, 633
Custozza, battle of, 393, 397
Cyprus, 241
Cyrus, 11
Czechoslovakia, 484, 485-488: created by Paris Conference, 613-614; dismembered by Hitler, 745-747; Russian absorption of, 807, 835

D

Dacia, 304
Dail, 709-710
Daily Telegraph affair, 481-482
Daladier, Edouard, 715, 745
Dalmatia, 490, 491
D'Annunzio, Gabriele, 662, 669
Dante Alighieri, 33, 51-52
D'Antin, Duc, 179
Danton, Georges Jacques, 331-332
Darby family, 253
Dark Ages, 11, 21-22, 24
Darius, 11
Darwin, Charles, 516-517 (*see also* Darwinism)
Darwinism, 516-523: effect on social and economic attitudes, 518-519, 520-521; Darwin's theories, 516-517; effect on philosophy, 535; effect on theology, 517-518; eugenics, 519-520; new historical determinism, 522-523; origin of species, 516; and racism, 520-521
Darwin, Sir Charles Galton, 522
Daumier, Honoré, 391 (*illus.*), 530, 533 (*illus.*)
David, Jacques Louis, 335 (*illus.*), 365, 366
Da Vinci, Leonardo, 42, 56, 57, 59 (*illus.*), 60-61, 67, 602
Davis, Jefferson, 464
Dawes, Charles G., and Dawes Plan, 680
"Day of the Barricades," 126
Deák, Francis, 484, 490, 495
Debussy, Claude, 533
Decameron, The (Boccaccio), 52-53, 70
Decembrist Revolution, 382-383
Decembrists, 497, 498
Declaration of Independence, 317
Declaration of Indulgence, 193
Declaration of the Rights of Man, 327, 329
Declaratory Act, 315
Decline and Fall of the Roman

Empire, History of the (Gibbon), 308
Defenestration of Prague, 113
Defense of the Realm Act, 604
Defoe, Daniel, 200
De Gaulle, Charles, 755, 768
De Humanis Corporis Fabrica (Vesalius), 68
Deism, 281-282
Delacroix, Ferdinand, 365-366, 381 (*illus.*)
De Las Casas, Bartholomew, 152-153
Delcassé, Theophile, 452, 589
De León, Ponce, 148
De Maupassant, Guy, 526
Denikin, General, 633
Denmark: Hitler's invasion of, 753; Schleswig-Holstein question, 474; in Thirty Years' War, 113-115
Deputies, Chamber of, 384, 451-452
Depression of *1929*: in France, 713; in Great Britain, 708-709; and international situation, 704; in United States, 718-720; unsettling of world politics, 738-739
De Revolutionibus Orbium Coelestium (Copernicus), 68
Descartes, René, 197, 198
De Soto, 150
d'Esperey, Franchet, 599
Despotism, enlightened, 286-291
De Vaca, Cabeza, 150
De Valera, Eamon, 709-710
Devolution, Right of, 172
Devolution, War of, 172
Dewey, Thomas, 822
Diaz, Bartholomew, 140
Dickens, Charles, 524
Dickinson, Emily, 528
Dickinson, Lowes, 582
Diderot, Denis, 277, 295
Dido and Aeneas (Purcell), 204
Diet of Japan (*1919-1939*), 724, 725
Diggers, 192
Diktat, the, 610, 617, 737
Diplomatic Revolution, 268, 302
Directory, the, 338-339, 343, 344, 345
Discourse on the Moral Effects of the Arts and Sciences (Rousseau), 284
Discourses on the First Ten Books of Titus Livius (Machiavelli), 44, 45
Disraeli, Benjamin, 411, 435, 436, 439, 442, 557-558, 561
Divine Comedy (Dante), 51
Divine-right monarchy: clergy in, 179; of Louis XIV, 177-178; in Muscovite Russia, 215; nobility in, 178-179; theory of, 118, 177-178
Dolgoruky family, 292-293
Dollfuss, Engelbert, 693, 695, 743
Doll's House (Ibsen), 526
Domestic system, 252
Donatello, 63 (*illus.*)

Don Giovanni (Mozart), 311
Don Quixote (Cervantes), 123
Donskoi, Dmitri, 649
Dostoevsky, Feodor, 834
Drake, Francis, 110, 153-154
Drang nach Osten, 260
Dreiser, Theodore, 526
Dreyfus case, 453-454
Drogheda, Statute of, 132
Dryden, John, 200
Duma, 300, 469, 501, 509-511, 622, 623-624
Dumouriez, Charles François, 334, 342
Dunkirk, 754
Dupleix, Joseph François, 267
Dürer, Albrecht, 56, 62
Durham, Earl of, 575-576
Dutch East India Company, 112, 158-159
Dutch Republic (*see* Netherlands, United)
Dutch revolt, 109-110

E

Eastern Orthodox Church, 209, 212
"Easter rebellion," 709
East Germany, 831, 835
East India Company (Dutch), 112, 158-159
East India Company (English), 158, 249, 251, 267, 315-316, 561
East India Company (French), 158
East Indies, Netherlands, 159
Ebert, Friedrich, 672, 674, 680
Eboué, Félix, 755
Ecclesiastical reservation, problem of, 107, 112, 118
Eck, John, 77, 79
Economic Consequences of the Peace, The (Keynes), 611
Economic revolutions, 247-254, 400-430
Edict of Nantes, 126-127, 169-170, 176, 179, 204
Edict of Restitution, 113
Education: advanced by *philosophes*, 280; Alexander II, 501; in Austria under Joseph II, 289; in Great Britain since World War II, 828; under Napoleon, 348-349; under Nazis, 689; under Nicholas I, 498; under Peter the Great, 234-235; reforms in Great Britain in nineteenth century, 411, 440-441; and revolt against imperialism, 772-773; in Russia (*1934-1941*), 649-650
Edward VI, King of England, 129-130
Egypt: after World War II, 785-786, 791; annexed by Ottoman Turks, 240; attacked by Napoleon, 344; between world wars, 732-733; and British imperialism, 557-558; cradle of civilization, 8; Franco-British invasion (*1956*), 829; Hitler's attack on, 757

Eighteenth Brumaire of Louis Napoleon, The (Marx), 425
Eire, Republic of, 710
Eisenhower, Dwight David, 759, 767, 822
Elders, Council of, 338, 345
Elgin, Lord, 576
Eliot, John, 162
Eliot, Sir John, 187
Elizabeth I, Queen, 130-134: and Anglican Church, 89; for the Dutch, 110; 131 (*illus.*); and Ivan the Terrible, 215; and Parliament, 129; war with Spain, 131
Elizabeth, Empress of Russia, 268, 292, 293, 294
Elizabethan Poor Law, 184
Emile (Rousseau), 280, 284, 286, 306
Ems telegram, 476-477
Enabling Act, 684
Enclosures, 38, 252
Encyclopédie, 277-278
Enemy of the People (Ibsen), 526
Engels, Friedrich, 422-423, 425
Enghien, Duke of, 347
England to *1707* (*see* Great Britain *for references after 1707*): African posts, 159; balance of power politics, 102; Bloody Mary, 130; Charles I, 185, 187-190; Charles II, 190, 191, 193, 196; Church of (*see* Anglican Church; Henry VIII); civil war (*1642-1649*), 189-190; civil war reviewed, 191-192; constitutional tradition in seventeenth century, 183-184; Cromwell and the Commonwealth, 190-191; Edward VI, 129-130; Elizabeth I, 89, 130-134; English Reformation, 84-86; explorers and settlers, 153-157; fight for India, 158-159; Glorious Revolution, 194-195; Great Britain, formal union of, 195; growth of statute law, 29; Henry VII, 48-49; Henry VIII, 84-85, 127-129; James I, 185, 186-187; James II, 172, 193-195; later Stuarts and Catholic problem, 193; Parliament's role, 47-48; Parliament in seventeenth century, 183-186, 187; Peasants' Revolt, 69; Protestantism in, 84; Renaissance in, 132-134; Restoration, 192-194; road to civil war, 188-189; Scotland united with, 195; seventeenth-century, 183-195, 200; sixteenth-century, 127-134; Spanish Armada, defeat of, 111; during Thirty Years' War, 115; Tudor Parliaments, 128-129; during War of Spanish Succession, 173; Wars of the Roses, results, 47; William III of Orange, 172
English Reformation, 84-86, 128
English Renaissance, 132-134

Enlightenment, Age of, 272, 274-311: art, 308-309; attitude toward Middle Ages, 19; Austria, 288-290; basic principles and traits, 247, 274-278; culture of, 304-311; current attitude toward, 839-841; education, 280; enlightened despotism, 286-291; evangelical revival, 306-307; and George III, 313; literature, 307-308; Locke and Newton and, 275-276; Montesquieu, 283-284; music, 309-311; and Napoleon I, 349; *philosophes*, 274, 275, 276, 277, 278-286; philosophy, 305-306; political thought, 283-286; religious attitudes, 280-282; Rousseau, 284-286; Russia, 292-304; Spain, 290-291; Sweden, 290-291; Unitarianism, 87
Eoliths, 11
Erasmus, Desiderius, 53, 54 (*illus.*), 55, 67, 70
Erastus and Erastianism, 89, 126
Erfurt Union of Princes, 472
Erzberger, Matthias, 675
Escorial, palace of the, 111
Essay concerning Human Understanding (Locke), 275
Essay on Crimes and Punishments (Beccaria), 279, 296
Essay on Population (Malthus), 412, 516
Essex, Earl of, 132
Esterhazy, Major, 453
Estonia: created by Paris Conference, 614; seized by Stalin, 656; Russian absorption of, 807; World War II, 751
Ethiopia: after World War II, 801, 815; Italian attempts to seize, 459; Mussolini's invasion of, 741-742
Eucharist: Anglican Church, 89; consubstantiation, doctrine of, 83, 89; transubstantiation, 83; Utraquist practice, 112-113; Zwingli's doctrine of the, 83
Euclidean geometry, 13
Eugene, Prince of Savoy, 173
Eugenics, 519-520
Eugénie, Empress, 449
European expansion (*see also* Imperialism): ancient and modern contrasted, 137-138; economic record, 162-163; effects on West, 163-165; fifteenth through seventeenth centuries, 136-165; and mercantilism, 182; motives of modern, 138-139
Evelyn, John, 229
Evolution (*see* Darwinism)
Ezterhazy family, 311

F

Fabianism, 445, 544
Factory system, 252-253, 254
Factory Acts, 439-440
Faerie Queene (Spenser), 133

Fairbank, J. K., 779
Fairy Tales (Grimm Brothers), 357, 363
Falange, 693-694
Falconet, 230 (*illus.*)
Farnese, Elizabeth, 259, 264
Farouk, King of Egypt, 785-786
Fascism (*see also* Hitler; Mussolini; Nazism): in Austria, 695-696; common characteristics, 660-661; Hitler's Germany, 684-690; in Hungary, 697-698; in Italy (*1918-1939*), 661-670; reviewed, 701; in Spain, 794
Fascists Exposed, The (Matteotti), 667
Fashoda, battle of, 588
Fathers and Sons (Turgenev), 503
Faulhaber, Cardinal, 688
Faulkner, William, 526
Faust (Goethe), 362
February Patent, 484, 485
Fedor, son of Ivan the Terrible, 218
Fehrbellin, battle of, 172, 261
Fenian Brotherhood, 443
Ferdinand I, Emperor of Austria, 396, 397
Ferdinand I, King of the Two Sicilies, 378
Ferdinand II, Habsburg Emperor, 112, 113
Ferdinand VII of Spain, 378, 379
Ferdinand of Aragon, 41, 50, 80, 105, 107, 241
Ferrara-Florence, Council of, 212
Fertile crescent, 10
Feudalism, 21, 23-24: Church and, 26-27; definition, 24; feudal contract, 24-25; towns, 26
Fichte, Johann Gottlieb, 357, 358, 363
Fief, 24
Fielding, Henry, 307, 308
Filaret Romanov, 220
Finland: after World War II, 835; Alexander I and, 301; Russian absorption of, 807; war with Stalin (*1939*), 656, 751
First International Working-men's Association, 425
Fitzgerald, F. Scott, 718
Fiume, 611, 662
Five Hundred, Council of, 345
Five-Mile Act, 193
Five-Year Plans: in India, 783; in Russia, 641, 642, 643, 647
Flandin, Pierre E., 714
Flaubert, Gustave, 524, 526
Fleury, Cardinal, 258
Florida: acquired by England, 271; discovered by de León, 148; returned to Spain, 316
Flying shuttle, 254
Foch, General, 595, 602
Fontainebleau, chateau of, 124
Forain, Jean Louis, 530
Fordney-McCumber Tariff, 717
Formosa: Chinese Nationalists

in, 778, 780, 811; Dutch post on, 159; taken by Japan, 569
Forster, William, 440
Fort Christiana, 154
Fort Duquesne, 267, 270
Foundations of the Nineteenth Century (Chamberlain, H. S.), 675
Fourier, François M. C., 418-419, 420, 537
Fourteen Points, 608-609, 610, 724
Fox, Charles James, 342
Fox, George, 192
France (*see also* French Revolution; Gallican Church): after World War II, 829-830; American colonies, losses in, 270-271; armies, 104; arts in seventeenth century, 199-200; arts in sixteenth century, 127; Boulanger and Panama, 452-453; Charles VIII, 105; communists in, 813-814; Congress of Vienna, 373; Constitution of *1791*, 329-330; Constitution of *1795*, 338; Constitution of *1875*, 451-452; *coup d'état* of *1851*, 446-447; De Gaulle, 768; Diplomatic Revolution, 268; Dreyfus case, 453-454; and Duchy of Burgundy, 46-47; Estates General, 46, 180, 318, 322, 323-324; First Coalition against, 342-343; legacy of Revolution and Napoleon, 360-361; eighteenth-century, liabilities, 257-258; explorers and settlers, 153; in fifteenth century, 45-47; First French Republic, 331-339; Francis I, 106-107, 124; Gironde and Mountain, 332-335; Henry IV, 126-127; Hitler's invasion, 753; imperialism in Africa, 159, 557, 564-566; imperialism in Asia, 566; imperialism in Middle East, 732; imperialism in nineteenth century, 549, 551, 552; July Monarchy, 389-391; June Days, 391, 408; leadership of Enlightenment, 276-278; Louis XII, 105; Louis XIV, 168-169, 170-173; Louis XVIII and Bourbons restored, 359-360; Napoleon (*see also* Napoleon Bonaparte; Napoleon III), 341-374; National Assembly, 324, 325, 326, 327-328; National Convention, 342; New France, 157-158; domestic and imperial problems (*1919-1939*), 711-715; Paris Conference gains, 616; Philip II and, 109; Popular Front, 714-715; Protestantism in, 84; revolution of *1830*, 384-385; revolution of *1848*, 389-392; rule of Milan, 42; Second Empire (*1852-1870*), 447-449; Second French Republic, 391-392; Seven Years' War, 269, 270-271; Stavisky case and Popular Front, 713-

715; Thermidorean reaction, 337-339; Third Coalition, 351-354; Third Republic, 449-455; in Thirty Years' War, 114-115; treaty with Ottoman Empire, 241; Vichy, 754, 759; war with Britain (*1739*), 265, 266; War of Polish Succession, 264; wars of religion, 125-127; World War I, 585, 711-712; World War II, 754-755
France, Anatole, 526
Franche Comté, 172
Francis I, King of France, 57, 84, 124, 125 (*illus.*), 127
Francis II, Emperor of Austria, 264, 267, 288, 331, 351, 358
Francis II, King of the Two Sicilies, 457
Francis Ferdinand, Archduke of Austria, 580, 581, 591
Francis Joseph, Emperor of Austria, 397, 482, 483, 484, 485, 486: Bosnia-Herzegovina, 492; and Croatia, 490; 483 (*illus.*); and Kossuthists, 496; and Napoleon III, 457
Franco, Francisco, 654, 815, 830: Civil War, 694; fascism of, 661; Minister of war, 693
Franco-Prussian War of *1870*, 505
Frankfurt Assembly, 394, 395, 472
Frankfurt, Treaty of, 477, 585
Franklin, Benjamin, 276, 318
Franklin, Sir John, 148
Franks, 22
Frederick I, King of Prussia, 261-262
Frederick II, the Great, King of Prussia, 263, 277, 302: Diplomatic Revolution, 268; enlightened despotism of, 286-288; and Joseph II, 290; partitions of Poland, 302-303; Seven Years' War, 268-269; War of Austrian Succession, 266-267
Frederick III, King of Prussia, 480
Frederick William, the Great Elector, 261-262
Frederick William I, King of Prussia, 262-263
Frederick William III, German Emperor, 354, 387, 388
Frederick William IV, King of Prussia, 394, 395, 398, 472
Frederick V, Elector of the Palatinate, 113
Frederick the Wise, Elector of Saxony, 78
Freedom of speech: English civil war and, 192; repressed by Napoleon, 347
Freemasons, 382, 667
Freischutz, Der (von Weber), 364
French and Indian War, 270
French language: in Louis XIV's time, 277; in Russia, 294-295
French Revolution, 318-337: and

Catherine the Great, 298; causes of, 318-324; confiscation of church property, 327-328; Constitution of *1791*, 329-330; dissolution of monarchy, 325-331; Estates General, 323-324; execution of Louis XVI, 333; fall of Bastille, 326; financial crisis, 322-323, 325; first and second estates, 319-320; First French Republic, 331-339; Gironde and Mountain, 332-334; Legislative Assembly, 330-331; National Assembly, 327-328; National Convention, 332-334; monarchy, 318-319; popular uprisings, 325-327; Reign of Terror, 334-337; Revolutionary Tribunal, 334, 338; Rousseau and, 284; "September massacres," 332; third estate, 320-322

French East India Company, 267
Frescobaldi, 201
Freud, Sigmund, 538-540
Freudianism, 540-541
Friedjung, Heinrich, 491
Friedland, battle of, 351
Fronde, the, 170
Frontenac, 157
Frontier theory, 165
Fuad, King, 732
Fugger family, 37-38
Fulton, Robert, 404
Fundamentalism, 10: and Darwinism, 518
Furnace, blast, 403
Fur trading, 157, 161

G

Gabelle, 321
Galicia, 488
Galileo, 196, 198
Galitsyn family, 292-293
Gallican Church, 46: after Dreyfus, 454; causes of French Revolution, 319; Civil Constitution of the Clergy, 328; Concordat of Bologna, 84; Concordat of *1801*, 348; Council of Trent, 96; under Louis XIV, 179; property confiscated, 327-328
Gallipoli campaign, 599
Galsworthy, John, 526
Gama, Vasco da, 140
Gamelin, General, 753
Gandhi, Mahatma, 730 (*illus.*)
Garibaldi, Giuseppe, 457, 458 (*illus.*)
Gastein, Convention of, 474
Gauguin, Paul, 530
Gay, John, 310
General Confederation of Labor (C.G.T.), 712, 714, 715
General Directory of Prussia, 263
Geneva, 83
Geneva protocol, 740

Genoa, Ligurian Republic of, 344
George I, King of England, 195, 255
George II, King of England, 255, 267
George III, King of England, 255, 270, 313-314, 316, 317
George V, King of England, 445
George, David Lloyd, 445, 605, 606, 610 (*illus.*), 616, 706
German Confederation, 372 470-473, 474-475
German language, 79
Germany: after World War II, 828, 830-832; Constitution of *1919*, 673-674; depression of *1929*, 681-682; divided by Iron Curtain, 807-810; eighteenth-century, 259-263; (*1850-1914*), 469, 470-482; Empire, 477-482; fifteenth-century, 32-33; under Hitler, (*1933-1939*), 684-690 (*see also* Hitler); imperialism of nineteenth century, 551, 552, 566-567; inflation, (*1922-1923*), 677-679; Knights' War and Peasants' Rebellion, 81-82; and Napoleon, 350; Nazism (*see* Hitler); North German Confederation, 475-476; Protestant Reformation in, 80; rearmament of, 741; revolutions of *1830*, 387-388; revolutions of *1848*, 393-395; Romantic Age in, 361-362, 363; Schleswig-Holstein problem, 474, 475; Thirty Years' War, 112-118; unification of, 582; unification of Germany, (*1866-1871*) (*map*), 471; war with Austria, *1866*, 474-475; war with Napoleon III, 476-477; Weimar Republic, (*1918-1933*), 671-684 (*see also* Weimar Republic); World War I aspirations, 583-584; World War I, effects of defeat, 671-672; World War I, losses and reparations, 613, 616-617; World War II, 741-764
Gerson, Jean, 84
Gestapo, 687
Ghana (Gold Coast), 793
Ghibellines, 39, 42
Gibbon, Edward, 308
Gibraltar, 316
Gilbert, Sir Humphrey, 154
Gilbert and Sullivan, 436, 533
Gioberti, Vincenzo, 392, 398
Giolitti, Giovanni, 460
Giotto, 56, 57
Girondins, 330, 331, 332-334, 335, 338
Gladstone, William Ewart, 435, 442, 443, 553
Glinka, Mikhail Ivanovich, 364-365
Glorious Revolution, 194-195, 255, 275
Gluck, Christoph, 310

Gobineau, Joseph Arthur de, 675
Godunov, Boris, 218
Goebbels, Paul Joseph, 683, 684
Goering, Hermann, 676, 687, 747, 756, 831
Goethe, Johann W. von, 362, 364
Gold Coast (Ghana), 793
Golden Book of Venice, 43
Gömbös, Gyula von, 698
Gomulka, 810
"Good Neighbor" policy, 723
Gordon, General, 442
Goths, 22
Goya, Francisco José de, 359 (*illus.*), 365
Grand Alliance, 173
Grand Army of Napoleon, 358-359
Grand Trianon, 606
Grant, Madison, 521
Gravitation, law of, 197, 275
Great Britain, after *1707* (*see* England *for references before 1707*): after World War II, 772, 828-829; Battle of Britain, 755-756; Boer War, 553-557; Bourbons and, 264, 267; British Empire, 552-563; Canada and, 575-577; Chartism, 441; Commonwealth of Nations, 575-577, 710-711; depression following World War I, 705-706; Diplomatic Revolution, 268; and Egypt, 557-558; (*1815-1914*), 433-446; eighteenth-century, 254-257; in First Coalition, 342, 343; foreign policy, (*1815-1914*), 441-442; free trade, 439, 444; George III, 313-314; imperialism between world wars, 729-733; imperialism of nineteenth century, 442, 549, 551, 552; improvements for labor, (*1815-1914*), 439-440; in India, 559-563, 729-731, 782; British India (*map*), 555; industrialization in nineteenth century, 400-406; Irish problem, 442-444, 709-710; Labor party, 445-446, 706-708; and Middle East, 732-733; (*1919-1939*), 705-711; parliamentary reforms, 433-436; politics between world wars, 706-709; and South Africa, 552-557; two-party system, 436-438; Seven Years' War, 269-271; Utilitarian reforms, 438-439; War of Austrian Succession, 267; War of Jenkins' Ear, 265-266; war with France, *1739*, 265; welfare state, 444, 445; World War I aspirations, 584-585; World War I, entry into, 592; World War II, 753-754, 766-768
Great Century, The (Latourette), 571
Great Elector (*see* Frederick William I)

Great Fear, the, 326, 327
Great Gatsby, The (Fitzgerald), 718
Great Northern War, 230-232, 246, 263, 264
Great Protestation, 186
Great Schism, 41
Great Wall of China, 142
Greco, El, 122 (*illus.*), 123, 201
Greece: after World War II, 835; arts in ancient, 12-13; ancient, 11-14; between world wars, 700-701; Greeks in Ottoman Empire, 243-244; Minoan civilization, 11; Mussolini's invasion, 756, 757; mythology of, 13; slavery in early, 25; war of independence, (*1821-1829*), 380-382
Greek Orthodox Church, 209, 212
Greeley, Horace, 420, 425
Green, T. H., 534
Greenwich Mean Time, 248
Grévy, Jules, 451
Grey, Sir Edward, 592
Grey, Lady Jane, 130
Grey, Lord, 434, 436
Griffith, Arthur, 709
Grimm brothers, 357, 363
Guadalcanal, 764
Guatemala, 814
Guelfs, 39, 42
Guilds, 36, 38, 42
Guinegate, battle of, 105
Guise family, 126
Guizot, François, 385, 389, 390
Gumbinnen, battle of, 597
Gunpowder, 27, 68
Gustavus III, King of Sweden, 290-291
Gustavus Adolphus, King of Sweden, 114
Gutenberg, Johann, 67

H

Habsburg Empire, 33, 102, 105-111, 112, 113-118: and Catholicism, 93; Charles V, 80; domains in eighteenth century, 260; dual monarchy, 484-485; dynastic state, 103; (*1850-1914*), 469, 482-496; Ferdinand I, 396, 397; in First Coalition, 342, 343; in Hungary, 243; Maria Theresa and Joseph II, 288-290; Maximilian, 47, 105; Paris Conference, 613-614; parliament, 511; Philip II, 37-38, 61, 107-111, 119; possessions (*map*), 108; Napoleon *vs.*, 343, 344; revolutions of *1848* in, 395-398; rule of Italian States, 259; treaty with Ottoman Turks, 242
Habsburg-Valois wars, 41, 241
Hacha, Emil, 746
Hakluyt, Richard, 163
Halifax, Lord, 748
Hall of Mirrors, 201
Hamlet (Shakespeare), 133
Hampden, John, 187-188, 189

Hampton Court, conference of, 186-187
Handel, George Frederick, 309-310, 311
Hannibal, 14
Hanover, House of, 195, 255, 267, 270, 313-314, 316, 317
Harding, Warren G., 716, 717, 718
Hardy, Thomas, 525-526, 537
Harems, Turkish, 238, 240
Hargreaves, James, 254
Harvey, William, 197
Hastings, Battle of, 23
Hastings, Warren, 561
Hats and Caps, 258, 291
Haushofer, Karl, 689
Haussmann, 447
Hawaiian Islands, 567, 793, 822
Hawkins, John, 110, 153
Hay, John, 726
Haydn, Joseph, 310, 311
Hegel, Georg W. F., 367-368, 422, 535, 695
Heimwehr, 695
Heine, Heinrich, 387
Henlein, Konrad, 745
Henry II, King of France, 107, 124
Henry III, King of France, 126
Henry IV of Navarre, King of France, 126-127, 169, 178
Henry VII, King of England, 45, 48-49
Henry VIII, King of England, 84, 105, 127-129, 128 (*illus.*)
Henry, Colonel, 453, 454
Henry, Prince of Portugal, 140
Herder, Johann Gottfried von, 363
Herzen, Alexander, 503
Hess, Rudolph, 676, 689
Hessians, 255
Hidalgos, 121, 122
Hinayana, 142-143
Hindenburg, Paul von, 597, 671, 680, 681, 682, 683, 684, 685
Hinduism, 783-785
Hippocratic medicine, 13
Hiroshima, 766, 767 (*illus.*)
Historicism, 522-523, 836
History of Civilization (Guizot), 385
History of the French Revolution (Thiers), 384
Hitler, Adolf (*see also* World War II): *Anschluss*, 743-745; anti-rationalism of, 537; and Austria, 695-696; armistice with France, 756 (*illus.*); beerhall *putsch*, 679; "blood purge" of *1934*, 685; death of, 763; dictatorship of Germany, (*1933-1939*), 684-690; early career, 675-680; elections of *1932*, 682-683; foreign policy, 689-690; 678 (*illus.*); invasion of Russia, 620, 654; legal and economic policies, 686-688; on Karl Lueger, 494; *Mein Kampf*, 679; nature of fascism, 661; Nazi dictatorship, 684-685; pact with Mussolini,

670; pact with Stalin, 655, 749; and peace conference of *1919*, 610; racism, 686, 689; rearmament of Germany, 741; religion and culture, 688-689; rise to power, 683-684; and Russia, 689; Third Reich, 689
Hlinka, Father, 489
Hobereaux, 320, 321
Hobson, J. T., 548
Hoffman, General von, 597
Hogarth, William, 308, 309 (*illus.*)
Hohenzollern, House of, 89, 260-263, 268
Holbach, Baron, 282
Holbein, Hans, 62, 128 (*illus.*)
Holland (*see* Netherlands)
Holstein, Baron von, 586
Holy Alliance, 372, 373
Holy League of the Papacy (*see* Papal States)
Holy Roman Empire, 102: dissolved by Napoleon, 355; in eighteenth century, 260; end of, 118; *vs.* Louis XIV, 172; (*map*), 108
Home Rule movement, 443-444, 709-710
Homer, Winslow, 528
Hong Kong, 559
Homo sapiens, 5
Hood, Thomas, 527
Hooker, Richard, 89
Hoover, Herbert, 716: Clark Memorandum, 723; the depression, 720; and German reparations, 682
Hopkins, Gerard Manley, 528
Horthy, Admiral, 697
House of Commons, 48: under Henry VIII, 128-129; (*1919-1939*), 708
House of Lords: in *1815*, 434; in *1885*, 436; under Henry VIII, 128; Parliament Act of *1911*, 445
House of Trade, 121
Howells, William Dean, 524-525
Hubertusburg, Peace of, 269
Hudson, Henry, 153, 161
Hudson's Bay Company, 161
Hugenberg, Alfred, 680
Hugo, Victor, 363-364, 524, 527
Huguenots, 125: churches, 84; Edict of Nantes and, 126-127; Great Elector and, 262; repressed by Louis XIV, 179; siege of La Rochelle, 170; in South Africa, 159
Hugues Capet, 23
Humanism, 51-55, 75-76
Humbert, King of Italy, 426, 459
Hume, David, 305, 361
Hundred Years' War, 37: in England, 47; in France, 45; "Second," 265
Hungary: after World War II, 810-811, 835; communist control after World War I, 607; dual monarchy, *1867*, 484-485; Habsburgs and Ottomans

fight in, 243; independent republic, 398; minorities in, 489-492; (1918-1939), 696-698; October Diploma, 483-484; parliament, 511; Protestantism in, 84; Ottoman Turks' attacks on, 241; revolt against Russians, 810-811; revolutions of 1848, 396; Russian absorption of, 807; society and politics, (1867-1914), 494-496; Unitarianism in, 87
Hus, John, 69, 77
Hussite movement, 69
Hutten, Ulrich von, 81
Hutter, Jacob, 92
Hutterites, 86-87, 92

I

Iberville, Sieur d', 157
Ibsen, Henrik, 433, 526
Idylls of the King (Tennyson), 527
Ikons, Russian, 220-222, 221 (illus.)
Immigration, to U.S., 717
Imperialism (see also European expansion): Anglo-German rivalry, 574; anti-imperialist arguments, 571-572; arguments for and against, 570-572; of Belgium, 567; British Empire, 441, 442, 552-563; causes and nature of revolt against, 771-774; colonies of settlement, 574; economic aspect, 548-549; fifteenth through seventeenth centuries, 136-165; of France, 257, 455, 564-566, 715; of German Empire, 481, 566-567; of Italy, 567; of Japan, 568-570, 724-725, 727-728; and mercantilism, 182; motives of modern, 138-139; movement in general, 547-552; new and old types, 547-548; (1919-1939), 723-734; nineteenth-century, 547-577; of Portugal, 140-141; powers involved, nineteenth century, 549-551; results of, 573-577; revolt against, after World War II, 771-802; Social Darwinists for, 570; of Spain, 259; of United States, 467, 567-568, 723; "White Man's Burden," 570-571
Imperialism (Hobson), 548
Imperialism as the Latest Stage of Capitalism (Lenin), 548
Impressionists, 529-530
Inca empire, 149
Independence, American War of (see American Revolution)
Independence, Greek War of (see Greece, War of Indpendence)
Independents, 204 (see also Congregationalists; Puritans)
Index, the, 96
India: about 1715, map, 159; after World War II, 782-785,

800; aftermath of World War I, 607; between world wars, 729-731; "Black Hole of Calcutta," 269-270; British India, map, 555; caste system, 142, 164; East Indian companies, 158-159; European influence on, 561-563; French and English contest for, 158; neutralism of, 817; partition, 782-783; political organization, 559-561; Portuguese explorations, 140-141; rivalries of princes, 267; Seven Years' War, 269-271; ways of life, 141-143
Indians, American, 155 (illus.)
Indo China: after World War II, 781; communists in, 813; French, 566
Indo-European languages, 11
Indonesia, Republic of, 781
Indulgences: theory of, 76-77; Council of Trent on, 95-96
Industrial Revolution, 165, 400-406: and agricultural revolution, 406-407; banking and capital, 404-405; beginnings of, 252-254; Catholic response to, 429-430; in central and eastern Europe, 512; coal and iron, 403-404; economic and social consequences, 406-411; English and French industry compared, 183; in Japan, 724; the machine, 402-403; middle-class aspirations, 408-409; population changes, 407-408; transport and communication, 404; in United States, 465-466; working class grievances, 409-411
Influence of Sea Power Upon History (Mahan), 467
In Memoriam (Tennyson), 527
Inquisition, 50, 94-95, 378
Institutes of the Christian Religion (Calvin), 83
Instrument of Government, 191
Insular Cases, 567-568
Intendants, 180, 181, 319
International Workingmen's Association, First, 425
International, Second, 425-426
International, Third (see Comintern)
International law, 103
"Intolerable Acts," 316
Iran, 733, 788, 789
Iraq: after World War II, 786, 791; between world wars, 732, 733; oil in, 788, 789; held by Ottoman Turks, 241
Ireland: background of Irish problem, 131-132; Grand Remonstrance, 188; in Glorious Revolution, 195; Home Rule, 443-444, 709-710; Irish Free State, 709-710; Irish problem in nineteenth century, 442-444; kindom under English rule, 131-132; potato famine, 407; rebellion and Cromwell, 190; uprising of 1597, 132

Irish Land Act (1870), 443
Iron Curtain, 769, 832: communist bloc, 807-810; division of Germany, 831; stresses within communist bloc, 811-813
Iron law of wages: disciples of Ricardo, 413; and Marx, 422; rejected by Mill, 416
Ironside, 748
Irredentist issue, 585, 592, 609, 613
Isabella of Castile, Queen, 49-50, 147
Islam, beliefs of, 210
Isolationism: of Britain, before World War II, 740; of United States, after World War I, 716-717
Israel, 600, 789-790
Italo-Turkish War, 567
Italy: after World War II, 768, 830; assets and liabilities of unification, 458-460; banking in Renaissance, 36-37; Cavour and complete unification, 456-458; Charles V, 106; Charles VIII, 105; city-states, 32; communists in, 813, 830; corporative state, 667-669; (1848-1914), 455-460; eighteenth century, 259-260; fascism, 661-670; foreign policy of fascist rule, 670; imperialism of, 549, 552, 567; Mussolini (see Mussolini); and Napoleon III, 448; and Philip II, 109, 120; revolutions of 1820's, 377, 378, 379; revolutions of 1830, 387; revolutions of 1848, 392-393; territory gained in Paris Conference, 613; unification of, 429, 582; in World War I, 593, 598; in World War II, 755; 761-762
Ivan III, Tsar, 214-215
Ivan IV, the Terrible, Tsar, 215, 217-218, 223, 225, 649
Ivan VI, Tsar, 292, 293
Ivanhoe (Scott), 363
Ivry, battle at, 126
Iwo Jima, 764
Izvolzki, 589

J

J'Accuse (Zola), 453
Jacobins: influence of, 329-330; and Napoleon, 344, 345, 360; National Convention, 332, 334; organization closed, 338; Paris insurrection, 331; Reign of Terror, 335, 336
Jacobites, 255, 256, 267
Jacquard loom, 405
Jacqueries, 81, 321
Jamaica, 190
James I, King of England, 113, 185, 186-187, 225
James II, King of England, 172, 193-195
James, William, 534, 535
Jameson Raid, 481, 553

Jamestown colony, 154
Janissaries, 238, 242
Jansenists, 204, 205
Japan: after World War II, 774-778; European settlements in, 160; imperialism in nineteenth-century, 568-570; imperialism (1919-1939), 724-725; invasion of China (1931), 727-728; Manchurian invasions, 569, 727-728, 740-741; Paris Conference gains, 616; Pearl Harbor, 758-759; Portuguese trade, 141; Russo-Japanese War, 497, 507, 569; Stalin pact, 657; World War I, 593; World War II, 758-759, 764-766
Jefferson, Thomas, 277, 323, 460, 839
Jehovah, 10
Jellachich, Joseph, 397
Jena, battle of, 351, 354
Jenkins' Ear, War of, 265-266, 272
Jesuits, 93-94: dissolved by Clement XIV, 281; expelled by Bismarck, 478; expelled from Spain, 291; in France, and Charles X, 384; missionaries in China, 146, 159-160; missionaries in New France, 157; missionaries in Paraguay, 153; missionary in China, 160 (illus.); re-establishment, 367, 378
Jesus Christ, 18
Jesus, Society of (see Jesuits)
Jewelry, origins, 8
Jews: (see also Anti-Semitism; Israel; Palestine): Alexander III and, 506; in Austria, 289, 493, 494, 696; Balfour Declaration, 600, 732; Concordat of 1801, 348; Dreyfus case, 453-454; Frederick the Great, 287; Hitler and, 675-676, 686, 688; in Hungary, 495, 697, 698; Israel, 789-790; monotheists, 10; and Mussolini, 670; in Netherlands, 111; Palestine, 614, 732, 785; in Poland, 222; in Prussia, 262; in Roman Empire, 16; in Rumania, 700; in Russia, 509; Spanish Inquisition, 50; in Weimar Germany, 675; in Yugoslavia, 699; Zionism, 732
John, Don, of Austria, 111
Johnson, Dr. Samuel, 316
Joliet, Louis, 157
Jordan, 785, 791 (see also Trans-Jordan)
Joseph II, Emperor of Austria, 288-290, 290 (illus.), 304, 311
Journey from St. Petersburg to Moscow (Radishchev), 298
Juarez, Benito Pablo, 448
Julius II, Pope, 41, 61, 70, 105
June Days, 391, 408
Junkers, 262, 288, 358, 472, 673
Jutland, Battle of, 601

K

Kadar, 811
Kadets, Russian, 507, 509, 510, 512, 624
Kamenev, Sergei Sergeivich, 638, 646
Kant, Immanuel, 306, 367
Kapital, Das (Marx), 425
Kapp, Wolfgang, 674
Karageorge, 380
Karlovitz, Peace of, 230, 243
Karolyi, Count Michael, 697
Kashmir, 783
Kaunitz, Count Wenzel Anton von, 268
Keats, John, 362
Kellogg-Briand Pact, 681, 717, 738
Kemal, Mustafa, 600, 614, 733
Kenya, 794-795
Kerensky, Alexander, 624, 627, 628
Keynes, John Maynard, 611, 617
"Khaki election," 705, 706, 708
Khmelnitsky, 222
Kievan Russia, 209, 214
Kikuyu tribe, 794-795
King, Mackenzie, 825
King James Bible, 187
Kingsley, Charles, 428-429
Kipling, Rudyard, 527, 571
Kirov, Sergei, 645, 646
Kolchak, Aleksandr Vasilievich, 633
Kolkhoz, 640, 641, 644, 649
Königgrätz (Sadowa), battle of, 475
Köprülü family, 243
Koran, 210
Knights' War, 81
Knox, John, 84
Korea, 569
Korean War, 779-781
Kornilov, Lavr Georgievich, 627, 629
Kossuth, Louis, 396, 398, 485
Kossuthists, 495, 496
Kotzebue, August F. F., 387
Kremlin, 215, 225 (illus.)
Kronstadt movement, 634
Krüdener, Baroness von, 300, 372
Kruger, S. J. P., 481, 556, 587
Kruger telegram, 481, 556, 587
Krupp family, 487
Khrushchev, Nikita, 832, 833 (illus.)
Kubla Khan (Coleridge), 133
Kulturkampf, 477, 479
Kun, Bela, 607, 633, 697
Kuomintang, 778: between world wars, 727, 728; and Borodin, 652; and Chinese Communists, 729; revolution of 1911, 726
Kurbsky, Prince, 215
Kutchuk Kainardji, treaty, 303
Kutuzov, Mikhail, 359, 649
Kuwait, 788
Kwajalein, 764

L

Labor (see also Guilds; Labor unions; Welfare state): in Germany, 1880's, 479-480; protection in United States, 465-466; in Second French Empire, 447
Labor party, British, 445-446, 706-709, 828
Labor unions (see also Guilds): abolished by Hitler, 687; Catholic, 430; Catholic, in Germany, 478; general strike in Britain, 1926, 708; banned by July Monarchy in France, 389-390; in French Third Republic, 455; in Japan, 724; Le Chapelier Law, 328; in nineteenth century, 409; and Social Democratic Party, 481
Lafayette, Marquis de, 390
Laffitte, 385
Laissez-faire: Frederick the Great vs., 287; and liberalism, 413, 414; policy defined, 278-279
Lamballe, Princesse de, 332
Lancaster, House of, 47
Land and Liberty society, 504
Laos, 782
Laplace, Marquis Pierre Simon de, 276, 337
La Rochefoucauld, François de, 200
La Rochelle, siege of, 170
La Salle, Sieur de, 157
Lassalle, Ferdinand, 475, 479
Lateran Treaty, 669
Latin America (see also names of individual countries): colonial empire in, 150-153; after World War II, 825-827
Latin language, 17, 51
Latourette, Kenneth, 571
Latvia: created by Paris Conference, 614; Russian absorption of, 807; seized by Stalin, 656; in World War II, 751
Laud, William, 188
Lausanne, Treaty of, 614
Laval, Pierre, 755
L'Avare (Molière), 199
Lavoisier, Antoine Laurent, 276, 337
Lavrov, Pëtr Lavrovich, 504
Law, John, 249-251, 257
Lawrence, Colonel T. E., 600
Laws of Ecclesiastical Polity (Hooker), 89
League of Augsburg, War of the, 172-173
League of Cambray, 105
League of Cognac, 106
League of Nations, 609, 611-613, 617: and Austria, 695; and China, 728; Ethiopian invasion, 742; Germany admitted, 681, 738; Germany's withdrawal, 741; Hungary, 698; Japan's withdrawal, 741; Jewish state, 600; mandates, 616; record summed up, 738;

Russia's entry into, 653, 739; Russia expelled, 656; United States and, 716, 717, 739; weaknesses, 740
League of the Three Emperors, 586
League of Torgau, 107
Lebanon, 732, 785
Lebensraum, 689, 757
Le Chapelier Law, 328, 349
Leeuwenhoek, Anton van, 196
Lefort, François, 228
Leibniz, Gottfried Wilhelm von, 197
Leif the Red, 8
Leipzig, battle of, 114
Lend-Lease Act, 758, 759, 821
Lenin, 506, 627, 628, 629, 636, 638, 639: and Bolshevism, 625-626; civil war, 632; dissolution of assembly, 629, 630; on imperialism, 548; and Marxism, 497; NEP, 635; revolution of *1905*, 509; and Stolypin, 510; 625 (*illus.*)
Leo X, Pope, 70, 78, 79, 93
Leo XIII, Pope, 429-430, 452
Leopold II of Austria, 330-331
Leopold II of Belgium, 567
Leopold of Saxe-Coburg, 386
Lepanto, battle of, 111, 241
Lesseps, Ferdinand de, 421, 453
Leszczynski, Stanislas, 231, 264, 301
Levellers, 192
Lewis, Sinclair, 527, 718
Lexington, battle of, 316
Ley, Dr. Robert, 687
Leyden, John of, 86, 90, 91
Liberalism: classical economists, 412-413; democratic, of Mill, 415-417; in German revolutions of *1848*, 393, 394; in Habsburg revolutions of *1848*, 396; in Italian revolutions of *1848*, 393; political parties, 512; responses to industrial revolution, 412-417; in revolutions of nineteenth century, 377, 378, 389
Liberal party of Great Britain, 436; and Free Trade, 444; and Irish Home Rule, 443; and Labor party, 445, 446; losses of *1922*, 706; for welfare state, 445
Liberal party of Hungary, 496
Liberum veto, 222
Libya, 460, 801
Liebig, Justus von, 407
Liebknecht, Wilhelm, 479
Light Brigade, charge of the, 499
Ligurian Republic of Genoa, 344
Lincoln, Abraham, 464
Linnaeus, 276
Lissauer, Ernst, 584
Lit de justice, 181
Literature: effects of colonial expansion on western, 163; of Enlightenment, 307-308; in Elizabethan England, 132-134;

in Muscovite Russia, 220; naturalistic novel, 524-525; poetry of Victorian Age, 527-528; realistic novel, 524; in Renaissance, 33, 50-55; of Romantic Age, 361-364; of seventeenth century, 199-201; of Victorian Age, 523-528; World War I, 603
Lithuania: created by Paris Conference, 614; invaded by Hitler, 747; seized by Stalin, 656; World War II, 751; Russian absorption of, 807
Lithuanian-Polish state, 214
"Little Englanders," 572
"Little Entente," 739
Litvinov, Maxim M., 651, 653, 655
Lloyd, Edward, 248
Lloyd's List, 248
Locarno Treaty, 737, 681
Locke, John, 200, 274, 275, 284, 317
Lombardy: Austrian Habsburgs in, 259; Cisalpine Republic of, 344
London, City of, 254, 256
London, Treaty of, 598, 662
Longobards, 22
Looking Backward (Bellamy), 534
Lorentz, Hendrik Antoon, 433
Louis XI, King of France, 45, 46
Louis XII, King of France, 57, 105-106
Louis XIII, King of France, 169-170
Louis XIV, King of France, 168-169, 246; arts during reign, 199; divine-right monarchy, 177-178; effects of wars, 182-183; failures of, 172-173; Palace of Versailles, 180; royal administration of, 179-181; successes of, 171-172; *vs.* Dutch, 172; *vs.* Spain, 172; War of Devolution, 172; War of the League of Augsburg, 172-173; wars reviewed, 176-177; 171 (*illus.*)
Louis XV, King of France, 246, 257-258: and causes of French Revolution, 318; and the *Encyclopédie*, 277; and Kaunitz, 268
Louis XVI, King of France, 23, 318-319, 331: and Estates General of *1789*, 323, 324; execution of, 333-334, 333 (*illus.*); financial crisis, 322-323; flight from Paris, 330; "King of the French," 329; and popular uprisings, 325, 326, 328
Louis XVIII, King of France, 360, 384
Louisburg: Seven Years' War, 270; War of Austrian Succession, 267
Louisiana: French colony, 157; sold to United States, 350

Louis Philippe, King of the French, 385, 390
Louvois, 182
Louvre, the, 124, 201
Low Countries: Calvinism in, 83, 84; revolt of Netherlands, 109-110; under Philip II, 120, 121
Lowell, James Russell, 527
Loyalists, American, 317
Loyola, Ignatius, 93-94, 94 (*illus.*), 120
Lübeck, Treaty of, 113
Ludendorff, Erich F. W., 597, 598, 671, 674, 676, 679
Lueger, Karl, Mayor of Vienna, 494, 675
Luftwaffe, 751, 756
Lugard, Sir Frederick, 558
Lully, Jean Baptiste, 204
Lunéville, Treaty of, 350
Luther, Hans, 679
Luther, Martin (*see also* Lutheran Church), 68, 75-80, 76 (*illus.*): revolt of, 77-79; Ninety-Five Theses, 76-77; opposition to, 79-80; Peasants' Rebellion, 82; translation of Bible, 79
Lutheran Church, 80-81, 88, 89-90: Nazi control of, 688; Peace of Augsburg, 107; in Prussia, 262; spread in Europe, 82
Lützen, battle of, 114
Luxemburg, Rosa, 548
Lvov, Prince, 624
Lyautey, Marshal, 565
Lyell, Sir Charles, 516
Lyrical Ballads (Coleridge and Wordsworth), 362
Lytton, Earl of, 740
Lytton Report, 740, 741

M

Mably, Abbé, 305
Macadam, John Loudon, 404
MacArthur, General Douglas, 764, 775, 780-781
McCarthy, Senator Joseph, 824
McCormick, Cyrus, 406
MacDonald, Ramsay, 652, 708
Macedonians, 14
Machiavelli, Niccolò, 43, 44-45
Machines: origins, 13; and industrial revolution, 402-403
Mackensen, General von, 599
Mackenzie, William L., 575
McKinley, William, 426
MacMahon, Marshal, 451
Madagascar, 159
Madame Bovary (Flaubert), 524
Madras, 267
Maeterlinck, Maurice, 433
Magellan, Ferdinand, 148-149
Magenta, battle of, 448, 457
Magic Flute, The (Mozart), 311
Maginot Line, 750, 751, 753
Magna Carta, 29
Mahan, Alfred T., 467
Mahayana, 142-143
Maillol, Aristide, 531 (*illus.*)

Maine, sinking of the, 567
Main Street (Lewis), 418
Maintenon, Madame de, 180
Malaya, 782, 813
Malenkov, Georgi, 832, 833
Mallarmé, Stéphane, 528
Malplaquet, battle of, 173
Malta, Knights of, 345
Malthus, Thomas, 412, 413, 414, 516
Mamelukes, 344
Man and Superman (Shaw), 526
Manchu dynasty, 143, 725, 726
Manchuria: seizure by Japan, *1931*, 727-728, 740-741; Russo-Japanese War, 507, 569
Mandarins, 143-144
Mandates, system of, 614-616
Manet, Edouard, 529 (*illus.*), 530
"Manifest destiny," 462
Manorialism (*see also* Feudalism): position of peasants in, 25-26; Peasants' Rebellion, 81-82; in sixteenth-century, 38
March Laws, 396, 397
Marco Polo, 8
Maria Theresa: enlightened despotism of, 288-289; and Pragmatic Sanction, 260; War of Austrian Succession, 266, 267
Marie Antoinette, 318-319, 323, 326, 332, 335 (*illus.*)
Marie-Louise, wife of Napoleon, 355
Marne, Battle of the, 595
Marquette, Père, 157
Marriage of Figaro (Mozart), 310-311
Marseillaise, 298
Marshall, George C., 778, 811
Marshall Plan, 814, 821, 827
Marston Moor, battle of, 189
Marx, Karl, 367, 421-426: basic principles, 421-423; *Communist Manifesto*, 423-424; later career, 424-426; and Proudhon, 427; and Russian revolutionism, 657-658
Marx, Wilhelm, 680
Marxism: in Austria, 695; basic principles, 421-423; and imperialism, 548; and Lenin, 497; and March revolution, 623; Paris Commune of *1871*, 450; and *philosophes*, 839; in Russia, 506, 509; and Russian industrialism, 642; Social Democratic parties, 512; in Spain, 691
Mary of Burgundy, 47
Mary I (Tudor), Queen of England, 130, 131, 132
Mary II, Queen of England, 194
Mary (Stuart), Queen of Scots, 130, 131
Maryland, colony of, 156
Masaccio, 58-59, 58 (*illus.*)
Masaryk, Thomas, 488, 745
Massachusetts, settlement of, 154-155
Mathematics, advancements of seventeenth century, 196-197

Matteotti, Giacomo, 667
Matthias, Count of Thurn, 113
Mau Mau, 794-795
Mauritius, island of, 159
Mavrogordato, Dr. Alexander, 243
Max, Prince of Baden, 609
Maximilian, Archduke of Austria, 448
Maximilian, Habsburg Emperor, 47, 105
Maximilian of Bavaria, 112
Mazarin, Jules, 170, 171
Mazepa, 231
Mazzini, Giuseppe, 388-389, 392, 393, 398
Medici family, 37, 42-43
Medici, Catherine de', 124, 126
Medici, Cosimo de', 42
Medici, Lorenzo de, the Magnificent, 43, 57
Mehemet Ali, 380, 382, 499
Mein Kampf (Hitler), 679
Melanchthon, 79
Mendel, Gregor, 517
Mendoza, Pedro de, 150
Menelek, Emperor, 552, 567
Mennonites, 86-87, 92
Mensheviks, 506, 623, 626
Menshikov, 228, 229, 233, 292
Mercantilism: aims of, 109; and British leadership, 254; British *vs.* Bourbons, 272; in eighteenth century, 248, 249; and European explorations, 141; Physiocrats *vs.*, 278; of Portuguese, 141, 145; in practice: Colbert, 182-183; of Spain, 121; in theory, 181-182
Meredith, George, 581
Mesopotamia, 8, 614, 616
Messiah, The (Handel), 310
Mesta, 49
Metallurgy, 253
Metaxas, General John, 700-701
Methodists, 307
Metternich, Prince Clement: at Congress of Vienna, 369, 372; Habsburg revolutions of *1848*, 394, 396; revolutions of *1820's*, 379; and revolutions of *1830*, 387, 388; and Russia, 382; 397 (*illus.*)
Metz, battle of, 449
Mexico: Aztecs conquered by Cortés, 149; Maximilian in, 448; since World War II, 826; viceroyalty of Spain, 151
Michelangelo, 56, 57, 60, 61: as architect, 65; as sculptor, 63-65; *Creation of Adam*, 60 (*illus.*); *Pietà*, 64 (*illus.*)
Middle Ages: architecture, 19; class structure, 23-26; economic expansion, 27; education in, 26; factors in transition to modern state, 26, 27; feudalism, 23-24; geographic divisions, 19-20; influences on Renaissance, 33; invasions of Scandinavians, 23; survival in modern times, 29-30; towns,

26; trade, 34; transition to High Middle Ages, 23
Middle East (*see also names of individual countries*): Arab unity and disunity, 790-791; after World War II, 785-791; art of ancient, 9; communism in, 789; debt to, 9; early civilizations of, 8; early religions of, 10; great period of early, 11; imperialism in, (*1919-1939*), 731-734; Israel, 789-790; nineteenth-century imperialism, 551; oil, 788-789; political changes after World War II, 785-787
Mikhailovich, General, 810
Milan: in Renaissance, 41-42; claimed by Francis I, 106-107; won by Habsburgs, 107, 109
Milan Decree, 356, 357
Mill, John Stuart, 415-417, 544, 823
Milton, John, 33, 192, 200
Mind and Society, The (Pareto), 542
Minin, Kuzma, 218-219
Mining: in eighteenth century, 253; and industrial revolution, 403-404
Minoan civilization, 11
Mirabeau, Comte de, 324
Missionaries: Jesuits as, 94; Jesuits in New France, 157; in Latin America, 153; in nineteenth-century expansion, 571; Portuguese, 146
Mississippi Bubble, 249-251
Mississippi Company, 249-251
Mogul Empire, 158-159
Mohács, battle of, 241
Mohammed, 21, 210 (*illus.*)
Mohammed II, 240
Mohammed III, 238
Molière, 195, 199, 204
Molotov, Viachislav M., 655, 657
Moltke, Helmuth von, 595
Monasteries: closing of, in England, 85, 128; reformed by Joseph II, 289; in Russia, 220
Monet, Claude, 528 (*illus.*), 529
Monk, General, 191
Monmouth, Duke of, 194
Monnet, Jean, 830
Monroe Doctrine, 379-380, 467, 551
Montagu, Lady Mary, 258
Montesquieu, Charles de, 276: and American Constitution, 317; and Catherine the Great, 296; and French Constitution of *1795*, 338; political philosophy, 283-284
Monteverdi, Claudio, 201, 203
Montgomery, Marshal, 750, 759
Moravia, 613
Moravian Brethren, 306
More, Thomas, 82, 85
Morocco, 564-565, 798
Morris, William, 534
Morse, Samuel, 406
Moslems, in Spain, 50

Mossadeq, Mohammed, 773, 788
Mountain, 332-334, 336, 338, 360
Moussorgsky, Modest, 532
Mozart, Wolfgang Amadeus, 310-311
Muckrakers, 466
Muftis, 239
Munich conference, 745, 746 (*illus.*), 747
Münnich, Marshal, 293, 301
Muñoz-Marin, Governor, 823
Murad IV, 242-243
Murat, Joachim, 354
Murray, Gilbert, 13-14
Music: Baroque, 201, 203-204; in eighteenth-century Naples, 259-260; in Elizabethan England, 132-133; of Enlightenment, 309-311; in Lutheranism, 89; operas, Baroque, 201, 203-204; Renaissance, 66-67; of Romantic movement, 364-365; Victorian Age, 532-533
Mussolini, Benito: alliance with Hitler, 670; and Austria, 695; and Bulgaria, 700; Corfu incident, 740; early career, 663-664; corporative state, 667-669; domestic policies, 669-670; fascist dictatorship, 666-667; foreign policy, 670; imprisonment of, 761; invasion of Ethiopia, 741-742; "march" on Rome, 665-666; nature of fascism, 661; rise to power, 662-663, 664-665; and Russia, 652; territorial demands in *1930's*, 743; and Vatican City, 459; and Yugoslavia, 699; 666 (*illus.*)

N

Nagy, Imre, 810
Nanking, Treaty of, 559
Napier, John, 197
Naples: won by Habsburgs, 105, 107, 109; in eighteenth century, 259-260; procured for "Baby Carlos," 264-265
Napoleon Bonaparte, 337, 339, 341-374: 346 (*illus.*); administration, 345-347; *Arc de Triomphe*, 366; Brumaire *coup d'état*, 344-345; *Code Napoléon*, 346-347; Continental System, 356-357; Congress of Vienna, 301, 359, 369-373; downfall, 357-360; early career, 343-344; economics of, 349; education under, 348-349; Emperor, 346; Empire (*1807-1812*), 354-366; enlightened despot, 318; First Coalition against, 342-343; *Grande Armée*, 358-359; Hundred Days, 374; and Josephine, 343, 347, 355; legacy to France, 360-361; religion under, 347, 348; rise of, 341-342; Second Coalition against, 345; Third Coalition against, 351-354; wars with Tsar Alexander I,

299, 300; war (*1800-1807*), 349-354; Napoleonic Europe, *1812*, 352-353 (*map*)
Napoleon II, 355
Napoleon III, 446, 447, 499: and Bismarck, 472, 474-475; and Cavour, 457; domestic developments of Second Empire, 447-448; foreign policy, 448; "Liberal Empire," 449; as President of Second Republic, 392, 398, 449-451; Second Empire, 446-449; war with Bismarck, 476-477
Narva, battle at, 230-231
Naseby, battle of, 189
Nasser, Gamel Abdul, 786, 788 (*illus.*)
National Assembly, French: beginning of Revolution, 324, 325, 326; Constitution of *1791*, 329-330; Constitution of *1875*, 451; (*1789-1791*), 327-328; Third Republic, 446, 450
National Insurance Act of *1911*, 440
Nationalism: Bohemian, 113; French, 830; in French North Africa, 798; of Germany, 393, 394; of Habsburg Empire, 395-396; of Italy, 392, 393; in Middle East, 785, 786; and Protestantism, 98-99; and revolt against imperialism, 773-774; revolutions of *1848*, 388-389, 392, 393, 394, 395-396; Romantic movement and, 363-364; in Southeast Asia, 781
National Workshops, 390, 391, 416
Nation-states: beginnings of modern, 23, 100-101; divine-right monarchy in growth of, 178; and dynastic state defined, 103; in sixteenth and early seventeenth centuries, 118-119; sovereignty defined, 101
Navies: British, eighteenth-century, 254-255; French, eighteenth century, 257; improvements in eighteenth-century, 248; modern, 104; of Portuguese, 145; role in European expansion, 138-139; sea battles of World War I, 600-601; Spanish Armada, 111; Turkish, 109
Navigation Act of *1651*, 190
Nazi party (*see also* Hitler, Adolf): anti-rationalism of, 536, 537; in Austria, 695-696; beginnings of, 676; concentration camps, 763-764, 763 (*illus.*); dictatorship of Germany, 684-690; and the *Diktat*, 737
Near East (*see* Middle East)
Necker, Jacques, 325
Nefertiti, Queen, 10 (*illus.*)
Nehru, Pandit Jawaharlal, 783, 788 (*illus.*), 817
Nelson, Horatio, 344, 350

Nemours, Duke of, 386
Neo-Guelfs, 392, 393
Neolithic Age, 7-8
Netherlands: and Belgian revolution of *1830*, 385-386; claims in Africa, 159; colonization in America, 154; in eighteenth century, 258-259; in First Coalition, 342; Hitler's invasion, 753; Louis Bonaparte as King, 355-356, 361; and Peter the Great, 228; and Philip II, 109-110; post on Formosa, 159; posts in Japan, 160; revolt of, 109-110; *vs.* Louis XIV, 172; United, 111-112; war with Cromwell, 190
Netherlands East Indies, 159
Neuilly, treaty of, 606
Neurath, Baron Konstantin von, 746
Nevsky, Alexander, 649
New Amsterdam, 154
Newcastle, Duke of, 256
New Deal, the, 720-722
New Economic Policy, of Russia, 634-635, 639
New England: settlement of, 156; and War of Austrian Succession, 267
Newfoundland, 154
New France, 157-158
New Harmony, Indiana, 420
New Model Army, 189, 190
News From Nowhere (Morris), 534
New Stone Age, 7-8
Newton, Isaac, 197, 198, 274, 275, 317
New York Tribune, 425
New Zealand, 577, 799-800
Next Million Years, The (C. G. Darwin), 522
Nicholas I, Tsar of Russia, 383, 387, 388, 398, 483, 497-500, 502
Nicholas II, Tsar of Russia, 497, 508-509, 511, 592, 622, 623 (*illus.*), 624
Nicholas V, Pope, 41
Niebuhr, Reinhold, 840
Niemoeller, Martin, 688
Nietzsche, Friedrich, 521, 533, 534, 535, 541-542
Nigeria, 598, 793
Nightingale, Florence, 499
Nihilism, in Russia, 503-505
Nijmegen, treaties of, 172
Nikon, Patriarch, 220
Nile Valley, 8, 10
Nine-Power Treaty, 718, 727
Nineteen Propositions, 189
Ninety-Five Theses, 76-77
Nivelle, General, 604
Noailles, Viscount de, 327
Nobel, Alfred, 433
North Briton, 314
North, Lord Frederick, 314, 315, 316
North Atlantic Treaty Organization, 814-815, 821, 827
North German Confederation, 475-476
Northern Society, 383

Northwest Passage, 148
Norway, 753
Noske, Gustav, 672
Notables, Assembly of, 323
Notre Dame, Cathedral of, 28 (*illus.*)
Novgorod, 212
Novikov, Nicholas, 298
Nuremberg trials, 831
Nystadt, Treaty of, 232

O

Obrenovich, Milosh, 380
O'Connell, Daniel, 442
October Days, the, 326, 327
October Diploma, 483, 484
October Manifesto, 509
Octobrists, 512
Offenbach, Jacques, 533
Okinawa, 764
"Old Believers," 226, 227
"Old Pretender," 195
Old Stone Age (*see* Paleolithic period)
Ollivier, Emile, 449
Olmütz, "humiliation of," 472
Olympic games, 12
O'Neill, Hugh, 132
On Liberty (Mill), 416-417
On the Origin of the Inequality of Mankind (Rousseau), 284
"Open Door" policy, 552, 726
Opera: Baroque, 202-204; in Enlightenment, 310-311; of Romantic movement, 364-365; Wagner, 532-533
Opium War, 559
Oprichnina, 217
Orange, William the Silent, Prince of, 110
Oration on the Dignity of Man (Pico), 54
Oratory of Divine Love, 93
Organization for European Economic Cooperation, 827
Organization of Labor (Blanc), 421
Origin of Species, On the (Darwin), 516
Orlando, Vittorio E., 610
Orléans, Duke of, 249, 257-258
Orwell, George, 833
Osmanlis, 236-244 (*see also* Ottoman Empire)
Ostermann, 293, 301, 302
Ottoman Empire: abolished, 733; administration (*1453-1699*), 238-239; and Bosnia-Herzegovina, 491, 492; Byzantine heritage, 208, 210-212; in Crimean War, 499-500; decline of (*1566-1699*), 241-243; expansion to *1566*, 240-241; (*1453-1699*), 236-244; treaty with France, 241; debts to Greece, 211; Greek War of Independence, 380-382; Habsburg wars, 264; imperialism in (*1919-1939*), 731-734; Napoleon and, 354; Peter the Great *vs.*, 228-229; Republic of Turkey, 614 (*see also* Tur-

key); first Russo-Turkish War (*1768-1774*), 302-303; second Russo-Turkish War (*1787-1791*), 304; slave system, 236-238; subject peoples, 243-244; uprisings of Young Turks, 589; war with Poland and Russia (*1686*), 223; weaknesses of system, 239-240; before World War I, 469; World War I results, 614, 616; (*1725-1914, map*), 590
Otto the Great, 22
Oudenarde, battle of, 173
Owen, Robert, 419-420: plan of Utopian village, 420 (*illus.*)
Owen, Wilfred, 603
Oxenstierna, Chancellor, 114

P

Pact of Paris (Kellogg-Briand Pact), 717
Painting: Baroque, 201-204; cubism, 530; Dürer, 56, 62; of Enlightenment, 308; Holbein, 62; impressionism, 529-530; Masaccio, 58-59; in Middle Ages, 27; in Muscovite Russia, 220-222; Northern European Renaissance, 62; origins, 9; Renaissance, 56-62; Romantic Movement, 365-366; Victorian Age, 528-530
Pakistan, 781, 782-785
Palatinate, 113
Paleolithic Age, 7
Palestine (*see also* Israel): Balfour Declaration, 607; between world wars, 732; mandate to Britain, 614
Palestrina, 66
Palmerston, Lord Henry John Temple, 436, 441, 457
Panama, 567
Panama Canal, 467, 567
Pan-Germanism, 493-494, 512
"Panopticon," 414, 415
Pan-Slav Congress, 397
Pan-Slavism, 505, 512
Papal States, 41, 392, 393, 429
Papen, Franz von, 683, 684
Paper money, 249
Papineau, 575
Paradise Lost (Milton), 200
Pareto, Vilfredo, 542-543, 544
Paris Commune of *1871*, 450 (*illus.*)
Paris, Count of, 451
Paris, Peace of: *1763*, 270-271, 314; *1783*, 316; *1856*, 499-500
Paris Peace Conference (*1919*), 610-613
Parkman, Francis, 157
Parliament, British: analyzed by Montesquieu, 283; architecture of, 367; Bill of Rights, *1689*, 194; constitutional tradition of seventeenth century, 183-184; dissolved by Charles I, 187-189; compared with Estates General, 48; dissolved

by Cromwell, 190-191; dissolved by James I, 186; English and continental traditions compared, 184; Grand Remonstrance, 188; Great Protestation, 186; and Hanoverians, 255-257; role of the crown, 184-185; in Middle Ages, 29; Nineteen Propositions, 189; Petition of Right, 187; religious sides in seventeenth century, 185-186; and religious uniformity, 130; Root and Branch Bill, 189; Rump Parliament, 190; Short, 188; Six Articles, 85; and early Stuarts, 185-186; Thirty-Nine Articles, 89; reforms (*1815-1914*), 433-436; separation of powers, concept of, 283; supremacy of, in eighteenth century, 255-267; Triennial Act of *1640*, 188; Tudor and Continental, 129; under Tudors, 128-129; 366 (*illus.*)
Parliament, German, 475, 476
Parliament (Dail), Irish Free State, 709-710
Parliament (Diet), Japanese, 569
Parliament, Russian, 509-511
Parliament, Swedish, 129
Parliament Act of *1911*, 436, 443, 445
Parma, Duke of, 110
Parnassians, French, 528
Parnell, Charles, 443
Parsifal (Wagner), 533
Partisans of Yugoslavia, 810
Partition, Treaty of, 173
Party of National Work (Hungary), 496
Party system: British, 436; two-party and multi-party contrasted, 436-438; in United States, 464
Pascal, Blaise, 197, 205
Passarovitz, Treaty of, 264, 265
Passing of the Great Race, The (Grant), 521
Patkul, 230, 231
Patton, General, 762
Paul I, Tsar of Russia, 298-299, 344-345, 349-350
Paul III, Pope, 96
Paul, Prince of Yugoslavia, 699
Pavelich, Ante, 699
Pavia, battle of, 106, 124
Pavlov, Ivan Petrovich, 537-538
Pearl Harbor, attack on, 758-759
Peasants' Revolt (England), 69
Peasants' Rebellion (Germany), 81-82
Peel, Robert, 434, 436, 438, 439
Peel, the elder, 439, 440
Peloponnesus, 243
Peninsular War, 357, 359 (*illus.*)
Penn, William, 154
Pensées (Pascal), 205
People's Budget of *1909*, 445
People of Italy, The (Il Populo d'Italia), 663

People's Will, 504-505
Perón, Juan, 826
Perry, Matthew Calbraith, 160, 552
Persia (see also Iran): Empire, 11; Moslems in, 210; Peter the Great vs., 232
Peru, 149, 151
Peruzzi banking family, 37, 56, 57
Pestalozzi, Johann Heinrich, 280
Pétain, Henri Philippe, 754-755
Peter I, the Great, Tsar of Russia, 226-236: administration, 232-233; character of, 227-228; contest with Sophia, 227; 230 (illus.); innovations from West, 229-230, 234-235; rule of, estimated, 235-236; vs. Ottoman Turks, 228-229; wars, 230-232; western trip, 228-230
Peter II, Tsar of Russia, 292
Peter III, Tsar of Russia, 269, 292, 293-294, 302
Peterloo massacre, 434
Petrarch, 52
Phalanxes, theory of, 418-419
Philhellenic movement, 382
Philip II, King of Macedon, 14
Philip II, King of Spain, 37-38, 61, 107-111, 119
Philip IV, the Fair, King of France, 201
Philip V, King of Spain, 173, 259
Philip the Good, Duke of Burgundy, 46-47
Philip, Duke of Parma, 267
Philip of Hesse, 79
Philip, André, 834
Philippine Islands: acquired by United States, 567; anti-communist pact, 782; claimed by Spain, 149; communists in, 782; Republic, 822; relations with United States, 723; Spanish-American War, 551; under Philip II, 120; World War II, 759, 764
Philosophes, 274, 275, 276, 277, 278-286, 304-305: after French Revolution, 342; and American Constitution, 317-318; and bourgeoisie, 321; concept of justice, 279-280; contrasted with Methodists, 307; Declaration of Rights of Man, 327; and modern thought, 839-840; reform program of, 278-286; and Romantic movement, 363
Philosophic Radicals, 415, 438
Philosophy: Anti-rationalism, 536; contemporary, of history, 836; in Enlightenment, 305; idealism and realism, 534-535; of late nineteenth century, 534-537; origins of formal, 12; Oxford school of, 534; pragmatism, 535-536; rationalism in, 198-199; Romantic movement in, 367-368; in seventeenth century, 195, 198-199; utilitarianism, 414-415

Philosophy of Poverty, The (Proudhon), 427
Physics and Politics (Bagehot), 544
Physiocrats, 278, 279, 286
Picasso, Pablo, 837, 838 (illus.)
Pico della Mirandola, 53, 54-55, 58, 70
Picquart, Colonel, 453
Pietists, 306, 361
Pilgrim's Progress, The (Bunyan), 200
Pilsudski, Józef, 652, 699
Pinzon family, 147
Piracy, 145
Pirenne, Henri, 23
Pitt, William, 270, 314
Pitt, William, the Younger, 316
Pitti Palace, Florence, 65
Pius V, Pope, 96
Pius VII, Pope, 348
Pius IX, Pope, 393, 429
Pius XI, Pope, 459, 670
Pizarro, Francisco, 149
Plains of Abraham, battle of, 270
Platonic Academy, Florence, 54, 58
Platt Amendment, 567
Plehve, Vyacheslav, 508
Plymouth colony, 154
"Pocket" boroughs, 256
Poincaré, Raymond, 711-712
Poland: after World War II, 807, 835; and Alexander I, 301, 372; authoritarian government, 699-700; and Catherine the Great, 302, 304; demonstrations against Russians, 810; Hitler's conquest of, 747-749, 751; liberum veto, 222; partitions of, 302, 304, 342, 469; Protestantism in, 84; restored by Paris Conference, 613; revolution of 1830, 386-387; Russian absorption of, 807; in seventeenth century, 222; Unitarianism in, 87; War of the Polish Succession, 264, 265, 301
Pole, Cardinal, 130
Polignac, Prince of, 385
Politiques, 127
Poltava, battle of, 231
Polytheism, 10
Pompadour, Madame de, 278
Pompeii, discovery of, 308
Poniatowski, Stanislas, 302
Pontiac, Chief, 314
Poor Law: Elizabethan, 184; New (1834), 438-439
Pope, Alexander, 282, 308
Popular Front, France, 714-715
Populism, Russian, 504, 512
Portsmouth, Treaty of, 507
Portugal: after World War II, 815, 830; claim on Macao, 159; Empire, 145-146; explorers, 140-141; imperialism of nineteenth century, 551, 552; and Ottoman Turks, 241; under Philip II, 111; Prince Henry, the Navigator, 140; revolu-

tions of 1820's, 377, 378-379; settlements in Brazil, 153
Potemkin, Grigori Aleksandrovich, 304
Poverty of Philosophy, The (Marx), 427
Poyning's Act, 132
Pozharsky, Dmitri, 218-219
Pragmatic Sanction of Bourges, 125, 260, 266
Pragmatism, 535-536
Prague, Peace of, 475
Pravda, 627, 636
Predestination, doctrine of, 90-91
Prehistory, 5-7
Prelude, The (Wordsworth), 527
Presbyterianism, Scotland, 188
Pressburg, Treaty of, 351
Pride, Colonel, 190
Pride's Purge, 190
Primogeniture, 24
Prince, The (Machiavelli), 44-45
Princip, 580, 591 (illus.)
Principles of Ethics (Spencer), 519
Principles of Political Economy, The (Mill), 416
Printing, 200
Progress of the Human Mind (Condorcet), 275
Prohibition era, 718
Protestantism: Anabaptists, 86-87; Anglicanism, 88-89; beliefs and practices, 87-92; Biblical foundations for, 86; Calvinism, 83-84, 90-91; common beliefs, 87-88; French Wars of Religion, 125; in history, 97-99; Lutheranism, 89-90; and nationalism, 98-99; orgin of term, 76; and progress, 97-98; Puritans, 130; radical sects, 91-92; Unitarianism, 87; Zwingli, 82-83
Protestant Reformation, 75-99: consequences for Habsburgs, 107; English Reformation, 84-86; in Germany, 241; impact on progress, 98; Knights' War, 81; Luther (see Luther, Martin); Luther's Revolt, 77-79; Peasants' Rebellion, 81-82; in Sweden, 114
Protestant Union, 112, 113
Proudhon, Pierre Joseph, 427-428
Prussia: Bismarck's rise to power, 473-474; Congress of Vienna, 369, 372; Diplomatic Revolution, 268; eighteenth century, 247, 260-263; in First Coalition, 342-343; Frederick II, the Great, 286-288; German Confederation (1850-1859), 470-473; growth of, (map), 261; Lutheranism in, 89-90; North German Confederation, 475-476; revolutions of 1830, 387; revolutions of 1848, 394, 395; Russian ab-

sorption of East, 807; Schleswig-Holstein question, 474, 475; Seven Years' War, 268-269; Treaty of Tilsit, 354; wars with Austria, 266-267, 474-475

Pruth, battle of, 244

Psychology: Freud, 538-541; Pavlov, 537-538

Puerto Rico, 567, 823

Pugachev, Emelyan Ivanovich, 296

Punic Wars, 14

Purcell, Henry, 204

Puritans, 130: and Cromwell, 189; in Massachusetts, 156; seventeenth-century England, 185-186

Pushkin, Alexander, 364

Pu-yi, Emperor, 726, 728

Q

Quadruple Alliance, 373-374, 379

Quakers (Religious Society of Friends): and Indians, 162; origins, 87, 92; in Pennsylvania, 156; practices and beliefs, 192, 204

Quebec, 157, 158

Quebec Act, 316

Quesada, Jiminez de, 149

Quesnay, François, 278, 289

Quietists, 204

R

Rabelais, François, 53, 54, 70

Racine, Jean Baptiste, 195, 199, 277

Racism, 520-521

Radical-Socialist Party of France, 712, 714, 715

Radich, Stepan, 699

Radishchev, Alexander, 298

Railroads: and industrial revolution, 404; Trans-Siberian, 506, 507, 509

Railways Servants Act, 491

Raison d'état, policy of, 169-170

Raleigh, Sir Walter, 154

Ramillies, battle of, 173

Rapallo, Treaty of, 652, 662, 689

Rasputin, Gregory, 511, 622

Rathenau, Walter, 675

Razin, Stenka, 220

Reconstruction Finance Corporation, 720

Red Sunday, 508

Reflections on Violence (Sorel), 427

Reflections on the Revolution in France (Burke), 341, 368

Reform Bill of 1832, 409, 434-435

Reform Bill of 1867, 435

Reformation (see Protestant Reformation)

Reichstag: and Bismarck, 476, 477; and Hitler, 674; in Weimar Republic, 674

Reign of Terror, 275, 334-335

Reinach, Joseph, 453

Religion: in Austria (Joseph II), 289; of China, 145; in Enlightenment, 280-282, 306-307; under Hitler, 688; Christianity, 18, 83, 87-92, 112-113; of India, 142-143; Islam, 210; under Napoleon, 347, 348; national lines in sixteenth century, 96; Near East, 10; Protestant beliefs and practices, 87-92; schism in Russian Church, 226; in seventeenth century, 204-205; in sixteenth-century France, 125-126

Religious toleration: in American colonies, 156; in Austria (Joseph II), 289; conformity under James I, 186-187; Deists, 281-282; Declaration of Indulgence, 193; Edict of Nantes, 126-127; effects of English Civil War on, 192; Frederick the Great, 287; ideal of, 92; under Napoleon, 347; in Netherlands, 111; Ottoman Turks, 236; the Quakers, 192; in Sweden (Gustavus III), 291; Thirty Years' War, 118

Remarque, Erich Maria, 603

Rembrandt van Rijn, 201, The Night Watch, 204 (illus.)

Renaissance, 32-72: architecture, 65-66; arts, 39, 55-67; banking, 36-38; cities, 38; class divisions, 39; economic background, 34-39; England, 47-49, 132-134; Florence, 42-43; Humanism, 51-55; industry and trade, 34-36; Italian States, 39-45; literature and thought, 50-55; Milan, 41-42; music, 66-67; political background, 39-50; religion, 69-71; science, 67-69; sculpture, 62-65; Spain, 49-50; "style" of, 71-72; Venice, 43-44

Renner, Karl, 494

Rerum Novarum (Leo XIII), 429-430

Restoration of Stuarts, 192-194

Revanchards, 572

Revisionist movement, 581: in Bulgaria, 700; in Hungary, 696-697, 698

Revolutionary Tribunal, 334, 338

Reynolds, Sir Joshua, 308

Reza Shah, 733

Rhine, Confederation of the, 355

Rhode Island, 156

Rhodes, Cecil, 520, 553, 570, 571

Rhodes, island of, 240, 241

Ribbentrop, Joachim von, 748

Ricardo, David, 412-413, 414

Richardson, Samuel, 307-308

Richardson, Henry Hobson, 531

Richelieu, Cardinal, 114, 169-170, 171, 179

Riego, Colonel, 378

Rigaud, 171 (illus.)

Rime of the Ancient Mariner (Coleridge), 362

Rimsky-Korsakov, Nikolai, 532

Ring of the Nibelungen (Wagner), 533

Rise of Silas Lapham (Howells), 524

Rivera, General Primo de, 692

Robespierre, Maximilien, 333, 334-337, 338

Robinson Crusoe (Defoe), 200

Robles, Gil, 693

Rockefeller, John D., 466

Rocque, Colonel de la, 714

Roderick Random (Smollett), 307

Rodin, Auguste, 531

Roehm, Ernst, 676, 685

Roger-Ducos, 345

Roman Catholic Church: Bismarck and, 477-478; Catholic Reformation, 93-96; Conciliar Movement, 41; Concordat of Bologna, 84; Concordat of 1801, 348; Concordat of 1855, 483; Council of Trent, 95-96; and Crimean War, 499; in Dark Ages, 21; and Darwin, 518; and Eastern Orthodox Church, 211-212; in feudal-manorial system, 26-27; in France, 41, 125-126 (see also Gallican Church); government of, 18; Great Schism, 41; and Habsburgs, 512; Hitler and, 688; in Hungary, 495; and industrial revolution, 429-430; and Italian unification, 458, 459; Joseph II and, 289; Lateran Treaty, 669-670; Luther and, 78-80; in Middle Ages, 19, 28, 29; missionaries (see Jesuits); papal infallibility, 478; papal inquisition, 94-95; Peace of Augsburg, 107; in Renaissance, 39, 41, 69-71; Scholasticism, 82; Six Articles repealed, 129-130; in Spain, 50, 690, 691, 692-693; Union of Brest, 222

Romance languages, 51

Roman Empire: and Christianity, 17, 18; decline of, 11, 17; relation to feudalism, 24; summed, 16-18

Romanov, Tsar Alexis, 219, 220

Romanov, Fedor, 218, 219, 220

Romanov, Tsar Michael, 219, 220, 225

Romantic Age: arts, 365-367; and Elizabethan era, 133; literature, 361-364; and Middle Ages, 19, 25; music, 364-365; religion and philosophy, 367-368

Rome, 12, 14, 41, 106

Rommel, General, 750, 760

Roon, Albrecht von, 473

Roosevelt, Franklin Delano, 719. Atlantic Charter, 766; and Far Eastern policy, 718; idealism of. 768; 721 (illus.); New

Deal, 720-723; World War II, 758, 762, 763
Roosevelt, Theodore, 466, 467, 568 (illus.); argument for imperialism, 571; Russo-Japanese War, 507
Root and Branch Bill, 189
Rosenberg, Alfred, 676
Rosetta Stone, 344
Rossetti, Dante Gabriel, 528
Rossoni, 668
Rothschilds, 405
Rotten boroughs, 434, 435
"Roundheads," 156, 189, 190
Rousseau, Jean-Jacques, 306, 361, 837: educational theories, 280; legacy to Owen, 419; political thought, 284-286
Royal Academy, 308
Royalists (Cavaliers), 189-190
Royal Society for Improving Natural Knowledge, English, 196
Royce, Josiah, 534
Rubens, Peter Paul, 201, 203 (illus.), 366
Ruhr: Dawes Plan, 680; French and German rivalry, 677-678; French occupation (1923), 711, 712, 739, 740
Rumania: authoritarianism in, 700; Paris Conference gains, 614; Ottoman rule, 244; Russian absorption of, 807; Soviet satellite, 835; in World War II, 656
Rump Parliament, 190
Runciman, Lord, 745
Ruskin, John, 439
Russell, Lord, 824
Russia: after World War II, 832-835; Alexander I (1801-1825), 299-301; Alexander II and reform, 500-502; Alexander III (1881-1904), 505-507; autocracy (1725-1762), 292-294; and Byzantine Empire, 208, 209, 215-216; Catherine the Great (1762-1796), 295-298; civil war, 632-633; collectivization, 639-644; Communist, 620-658; conquest of Siberia, 160-161; Crimean War, 499-500; Decembrist revolt, 382-383; Dumas (1906-1914), 509-511; 1825-1914, 469, 496-511; expansion of, 217-218, 222-224, 263-264, 549, 551; foreign policy (1725-1796), 301-304; foreign policy of Alexander II, 505; foreign policy (1918-1941), 651-657; and Hitler, 689, 749; intellectuals (1825-1914), 502-505; Ivan III, 214-215; Ivan IV, the Terrible, 215, 217-218; Kievan, 209, 214; Muscovite, 212-226; nobles and serfs, 216-217, 294-295; New Economic Policy, 634-635, 639; Nicholas I (1825-1855), 497-500; Nicholas II, 497, 508-509, 511; Paris Conference losses, 614; Paul (1796-

1801), 298-299; Peter the Great, 226-236; purge trials, 645-647; revolution of 1905, 507-509; Romanov dynasty, 219-220, 292; in Second Coalition, 345; 1725-1825, 292-304; Soviet satellites, 835; Time of Troubles, 218-219, 225; Stalin (see Stalin, Joseph); war communism, 630-634; World War I, 585, 598; World War II, 655-657, 757-758, 760, 762-763, 764
Russian Orthodox Church, 512: and Council of Ferrara-Florence, 212; and Crimean War, 499; and imperial family, 215-216; and Muscovite state, 214, 220-222; Nicholas I, 498; and Peter the Great, 234, 235, 236; schism in, 226; Stalin and, 650-651
Russian Revolution of 1917, 622-630: background, 622-623; Constituent Assembly, 629-630; March revolution, 623-624; November revolution, 627-629; provisional government, 624-625
Russlan and Ludmilla (Glinka), 364-365
Russo-Japanese War, 497, 507, 569
Russo-Polish conflict, 222-223
Russo-Turkish wars: (1768-1774), 302-303; (1787-1791), 304; (1877-1878), 586
Ruthenians: in Austria, 488; and Czechoslovakia, 613
Ryswick, Peace of, 173

S

Sacraments, 88
Sadowa, battle of, 475, 484
St. Bartholomew's Day, 125
St. Francis Xavier, 160
St. Germain, Treaty of, 606, 695
St.-Just, 839
St. Laurent, Louis, 825
St. Lawrence seaway, 825
St. Nicholas, 221 (illus.)
St. Paul's Cathedral (London), 201
St. Peter's (Rome), 57, 65, 66 (illus.)
St. Peter's Square (Rome), 201
St. Petersburg, 231, 234, 235
Saint-Simon, Henri, Count of, 408-409, 418, 420-421
St. Stephen, lands of the Crown of, 485
St. Wenceslaus, lands of the Crown of, 485
Salammbô (Flaubert), 524
Salazar, 815, 830
Salisbury, Lord, 587
Salons of Paris, 277
Salutary neglect, policy of, 254, 314
Samsonov, 597
Samurai, 568-569

Sansom, Sir George, 569, 775
San Stefano, peace of, 505
Sarai, 214
Sarajevo, assassination at, 580, 581, 583, 591
Saratoga, battle of, 316
Sardinia, 176
Sargent, John Singer, 528
Sassoon, Siegfried, 603
Saud, Ibn, 614, 732
Saudi Arabia: between world wars, 732; independent state, 614; oil, 788, 789
Savonarola, 58, 71
Saxons, 22
Saxony, 107
Schacht, Hjalmar, 679
Scharnhorst, General, 358
Scheer, Admiral, 601
Schleicher, General Kurt von, 681, 683-684, 685
Schleswig-Holstein, 474, 475
Schlieffen plan, 595
Schönbrunn, treaty of, 358
Schopenhauer, Arthur, 535
Schroeder, Baron Kurt von, 684
Schubert, Franz, 364
Schuman, Robert, 452, 830
Schuman Plan, 827
Schuschnigg, Kurt von, 695-696, 743
Schwarzenberg, Prince Felix, 397-398, 482
Science: agriculture, eighteenth century, 251-252; Darwinism and, 516-517, 519-520; earliest, 9; in early Greece, 13; eighteenth century advances, 276; and European expansion, 137, 163-164; inductive, 196-197; and industrial revolution, 400-404, 405-407; in Middle Ages, 27, 28-29; psychology, nineteenth century, 537-541; Renaissance, 67-69; scientific method, 196; seventeenth century advances, 195-198
Scotland: Charles I and, 188; vs. Cromwell, 189-190, 191; formal union with England, 195; Mary Stuart, Queen, 130
Scott, Sir Walter, 25, 363
Sculpture: Donatello, 63 (illus.), Michelangelo, 63-65; origins, 9; Renaissance, 62-65; Victorian Age, 531
Second Coalition, 345, 349
"Second Hundred Years' War," 265
Second International, 425-426
Seeckt, General von, 673
Segregation, U.S. Supreme Court decision on, 822
Selassie, Haile, 742
Selim, Sultan, 240
Senegal, 159
Sepoy Rebellion, 561, 562 (illus.)
September massacres, 332
Serbia and Serbs: annexation of Bosnia-Herzegovina, 589; assassination of Francis Ferdinand, 580, 591; in Bosnia, 492; in Croatia, 490, 491; in Hun-

gary, 490; under Ottomans, 244; and Yugoslavia, 614, 698, 699

Serfdom: abolished in Hungary, 396; abolished in Prussia, 358; emancipation ceremony (Russia) 500 (*illus.*); Frederick the Great, 288; and Joseph II (Austria), 289; French, abolished, 327, 355; in Poland, 222; in Russia, 216-217, 220, 232, 233, 235, 294-295, 296, 297, 298, 299, 496; Russian emancipation statute (*1861*), 500-501; Russian rebellion of *1601*, 218, 219

Servetus, 87

Seven Years' War (*1756-1763*), 257, 268-271, 272, 302, 314

Sèvres, Treaty of, 606, 614

Sextant, 248

Sforza, Francesco, 42

Sforza, Il Moro, 42, 57, 105

Shaftesbury, Lord, 411

Shakespeare, William, 33, 133, 134, 163, 362, 364

Shaw, George Bernard, 445, 526, 535

Sheikh-ul-Islam, 239

Shelley, Percy Bysshe, 362, 367, 368, 382

Shinto state (Japan), 725

Ship money, 187-188

Sholokhov, Mikhail, 834

Short Report on the Indies (de las Casas), 152

Shostakovich, Dmitri, 834

Shuisky, 218

Sibelius, Jan, 433

Siberia, Russian conquest of, 223-224

Sickingen, Franz von, 81

Siegfried Line, 750, 762, 763

Siemens, 404

Siéyès, Abbé, 324, 345

Silesia, 266, 267, 268

Silk, manufacture of, 169

Simon, Jules, 451

Singer, Isaac, 403, 406

Sinn Fein, 709

Sino-Japanese War (*see* Russo-Japanese War)

Sistine Chapel, 60 (*illus.*), 61

Six Articles, 85, 129-130

Sixtus IV, Pope, 70

Skoda armament works, 487

Skyscraper, first, 532

Slavery: abolished in British Empire, 553; and American Civil War, 463, 464; the Asiento, 173; in Athens, 12; in Brazil, 151; disappearance of, in Europe, 25; in Roman Empire, 17; trade, 153, 161; in Spanish Empire, 152; "triangle trade," 268; in Ottoman society, 25, 236-238, 240

Slavophiles, 502, 503

Slovakia and Slovaks, 489, 613

Slovenes, 489, 614, 698, 699

Smith, Adam, 278-279, 413, 422

Smollett, Tobias, 307, 308

Smoot-Hawley Tariff, 717

Smuts, Jan, 710

Social Contract, The (Rousseau), 284-286

Social Democratic party: Austrian, 494, 695; German, 480, 481, 482, 672-674; Russian, 506, 508, 509, 622, 625-626

Socialism, Blanc, 421; Christian, 428-429; *defined*, 417-418; Fourier, 418-419; in France between world wars, 712, 714; Marxian, 401, 421-426; Owen, 419-420; Saint-Simon, 418; Utopian, 401, 417-421

Social Revolutionary party of Russia, 506, 512, 622, 623

Social Security Act of *1935*, 720

Socinus, 87

Sokols, 487

Solemn League and Covenant, 188

Solferino, battle of, 448, 457

Somerset, Duke of, 129

"Song of the Shirt" (Hood), 527

Sophia Romanov, 227

Sorel, Georges, 427, 535, 668, 691

Sorokin, 836

Sorrows of Young Werther (Goethe), 362

South Africa: Boer War, 553-557; British in, 552-557; Union after World War II, 710, 795-798; Union of, 557

South America, *1914*, (*map*), 550

Southern Society, 383

South Sea Bubble, 249-251

Sovkhoz, 640, 641

Sozzini, 87

Spain: after World War II, 830; Armada, 111; armies of, 104; authoritarianism in, 690-694; Charles III, 290-291; Charles V, 119, 120; Civil War, 654, 694, 742-743; communists, in, 813; in eighteenth century, 258, 259; Empire, 149-153; explorers and discoverers, 147-151; Ferdinand and Isabella, 49-50; in First Coalition, 342; Golden Age, 119-124; Joseph Bonaparte as King, 357; Treaty of Vervins, 127; under Moslems, 49; Philip II, 107-111, 119-120, 121; Renaissance, 49-50; Republic, 691-694; revolutions of *1820*'s, 377, 378, 379; War of Jenkins' Ear, 265-266; War of Polish Succession, 264-265; World War II, 757

Spanish-American War, 467, 551, 567

Spanish Succession, War of the, 173, 176

Sparta, 11

Spencer, Herbert, 519, 545

Spengler, Oswald, 836, 837

Spenser, Edmund, 133

Speransky, Michael, 299-300, 498

Spinning jenny, 254, 402

Spirit of the Laws, The (Montesquieu), 283-284, 296, 317

Spiritual Exercises (Loyola), 93

Spitsbergen, 161

Stalin, Joseph, 621, 832: and Chinese communists, 729; as Commisar, 628; *vs.* Trotsky, 635-637; foreign policy, 653-655; internal affairs, 639-651; pacts with Baltic republics, 751; pact with Hitler, 655; pact with Japan, 657; World War II, 655-657, 762, 763, 766-768

Stamboliisky, Alexander, 700

Stamp Act of *1765*, 315

Stamp Act Congress, 315

Star Chamber, 48, 188

Statue of Liberty, 531

Statute of Drogheda, 132

Statute of Westminster, 710, 800

Stavisky case, 713-714

Steam engine, 13, 254

Stein, Baron, 358

Stephenson, George, 404

Stevenson, Adlai, 822

Stevin, Simon, 197

Stimson, Henry L., 740

Stock companies, 249-251

Stolypin, Peter, 510, 621, 626

Strauss, Johann, 533

Strauss, Richard, 532, 533

Streltsy, 227, 229

Stresemann, Gustav, 673, 676, 679, 680, 737

Stroganov family, 223

Stroganov, 299

Strossmayer, Bishop, 490

Stuarts (*see* James I, James II, Charles I, Charles II)

Sturm und Drang movement, 361-362

Suez Canal, 557: British control, 442; De Lesseps, 421, 453; Egyptian nationalization of, 786, 791; transport of oil, 788

Suffrage: in Austria and Hungary, 495; eighteenth-century English limitations, 256; under Henry VIII, 128; Italy, nineteenth century, 456; Reform Bill of *1832* (Great Britain), 409, 435; Reform Bill of *1867* (Great Britain), 435; universal, in Britain, 708; universal, in Russia (*1905*), 509; universal male, in France, 409; universal male, in Japan, 724; women's, in Turkey, 733

Suffragettes, 708

Sugar Act of *1764*, 314-315

Suleiman the Magnificent, Sultan of Turkey, 107, 241

Sully, Duc de, 169

Sumner, William Graham, 545

Sun Yat-sen, 652, 726

Supremacy, Act of, 85

Suvorov, General, 345

Sweden: eighteenth-century, 258; Gustavus III, 290-291;

Parliament of, 129; Peter the Great vs., 230-232; Prussians vs., 261, 263; Russia's chief rival, 223; settlement in America, 154; in Thirty Years' War, 112, 114-115
Swift, Jonathan, 195
Swiss confederation, 47, 118
Switzerland, 83
Syllabus of Errors (Pius IX), 429, 477-478
Symbolists, 528
Syria, 732, 785

T

Taft, Robert, 831
Talleyrand, 369, 372, 385
Tamerlane (*see* Timur)
Tannenberg, battle at, 597
Tarawa, 764
Tariff Reform League, 444
Tartars, 209, 214, 223, 227
Tartuffe (Molière), 199
Teheran conference, 762
Telegraph, 404
Telephone, 404
Tennessee Valley Authority, 721
Tennis-Court Oath, 324
Tennyson, Alfred Lord, 527
Test Act, 193, 434
Tetzel, Johann, 76-77, 78
Thailand, 782
Theatines, order of, 93
Thebes, 11-12
Theocracy, 98
Thermidorean Reaction, 343
Thiers, Adolphe, 384-385, 390, 451
Third Coalition, 351-354
Thirty-Nine Articles, 89, 130
Thirty Years' War, 112-118: Bohemian period, 112-113; compared with French Wars of Religion, 125; Danish period, 113-114; effects on Germany, 115; effect on Ottoman Empire, 242; nature and causes of, 112; Peace of Westphalia, 115-118; and Richelieu, 170; Swedish-French period, 114-115; Swedish period, 114
Thyssen, Fritz, 682
Tigers (Hungary), 495, 496
Tisza, Colomon, 495
Tisza, Stephen, 496
Tilly, Johann, Count of, 113
Tilsit, Treaty of, 354, 358
Timur, 211
Tindal, William, 85
Tirpitz, Admiral, 481
Tiso, Monsignor, 746
Titian, 56, 60, 61 (*illus.*) 61-62, 80 (*illus.*)
Tito, 762, 788 (*illus.*), 810
Tkachev, 504
Tocqueville, Alexis de, 360-361, 389
Tokugawa family, 160
Toledo (Spain), 119
Tolstoy, Leo, 834
Tom Jones (Fielding), 307

Tordesillas, Treaty of, 140-141, 149
Torgau, League of, 107
Tories: (Conservatives) in Britain after World War I, 706-709; and Conservatives, 436; in Glorious Revolution, 194; and Hanoverians, 255
Torricelli, Evangelista, 196
Torstenson, General, 114
Toscanelli, 147
Townshend, General, 600
Townshend duties, 315
Townshend, Viscount, 251
Toynbee, Arnold, 561, 836, 837
Trade: growth of, eighteenth century, 248; role in European expansion, 139
Trade unions (*see* Labor unions; Guilds)
Trading companies, 159, 249
Trafalgar, battle of, 350-351, 351 (*illus.*)
Transjordan, 733, 785
Transmigration of souls, doctrine of, 142
Trans-Siberian Railroad, 506, 507, 509
Transubstantiation, doctrine of, 83
Transvaal, 553, 556
Trent, Council of, 95-96
"Triangle trade," 268
Trianon, Treaty of, 696
"Tribute of Children," 237
Triennial Act, 188
Triple Alliance, 582, 586, 592
Triple Entente, 582, 586-588, 592
Trieste, partition of, 816
Tripoli (Libya), 460, 801
Tristan and Isolde (Wagner), 533
Trollope, Anthony, 524, 534
Troppau Protocal, 379, 388
Trotsky, Leon, 626, 627, 628, 638, 639, 645, 646, 652, 653: civil war, 632; and Kronstadt movement, 634; *vs.* Stalin, 635-637
Truman, Harry S., 764, 821-822
Tsushima, battle of, 507
Tudor dynasty, 48, 84-86, 127-129 (*see also* Elizabeth I; Henry VII; Henry VIII; Mary Tudor)
Tull, Jethro, 251
Tunisia, 564, 798
Turenne, General, 172
Turgenev, Ivan, 503, 524
Turgot, 279, 319, 322-323
Turkey: after World War II, 786-787; between world wars, 733; in World War I, 593; Republic of, 614
Turner, Joseph M., 351 (*illus.*), 529
Tuscany, Grand Duchy of, 43, 264
"Twenty-One Demands," 727
Two Sicilies, Kingdom of the, 41

Two Treatises of Government (Locke), 275
Tyler's Revolt, 81
Type, movable, 67-68

U

Uccello, Paolo, 59-60
Ukraine, 222
Ulema, 239
Ulm, battle of, 351
Ultras, 384, 385
Under Fire (Barbusse), 603
Underhill, Captain John, 162
Uniates, 489
Union Act of *1840*, 576
Union of Brest, 222
Union of Soviet Socialist Republics, 637-638 (*see also* Russia)
Union of South Africa, 710, 795-798
Union of Utrecht, 110
Unitarianism, 87
United Nations, 818-820: Communist China, 811; Israel, 789, 790; Kashmir, 783; Korean War, 780-781; organization, 818-819; record, 819-820
United Netherlands, 111-112 (*see also* Netherlands)
United States (*see also* America; American Revolution): after World War II, 821-825; Asian affairs, 780, 781; Civil War and Reconstruction, 463-465; Constitution, 317-318; depression of *1929*, 718-720; domestic problems (*1919-1939*), 716-723; economic and social development, 465-467; entry into World War I, 593; federal union, 460-463; imperialism of nineteenth century, 549, 567-568; imperialism of twentieth century, 732; international affairs after World War II, 814-816; road to internationalism, 717-718; isolationism, 467, 716-717; and Mexico, 448; New Deal, 720-722; Spanish-American War, 567; War of *1812*, 575; War of Independence, 313-318 (*see also* American Revolution); World War II, 758-759, 760, 766-768; growth of continental (*map*), 461
Unkiar Skelessi, Treaty of, 499
U.S.S.R., 637-638 (*see also* Russia)
Utilitarianism, 414-415, 438-439
Utopian socialism, 401, 417-421: Blanc, 421; Fourier, 418-419; Owen, 419-420; Saint-Simon, 418
Utraquists, 112-113
Utrecht, Union of, 110
Utrecht, Peace of, 246, 247
Utrecht, treaties of, 173-176, 261
Uvarov, 498

V

Vaihinger, Hans, 535
Valdivia, Pedro de, 150
Valmy, battle of, 342
Valois, House of, 45, 105-107, 124-127
Vandals, 22
Vandenberg, Arthur, 818-819
Vanderbilt, Cornelius, 466
Vanderlubbe, 684
Van Dyck, Anthony, 187 (*illus.*)
Van Gogh, Vincent, 530
Vatican City: library, 53; Mussolini and, 669-670; relations with France, 713; as sovereign state, 459
Velasquez, Diego Rodriguez de Silva y, 201
Venice, Republic of: diplomacy in, 103; eighteenth-century, 259; *vs.* League of Cambray, 105; in Renaissance, 43-44; trade during Renaissance, 34; in sixteenth century, 35 (*illus.*)
Venizelos, 599
Ventôse, Laws of, 336
Verdi, Giuseppe, 532
Vereeniging, Treaty of, 557
Vernacular languages, 50-51
Verrazzano, Giovanni da, 153
Versailles, Palace at, 180 (*illus.*), 201
Versailles, Treaty of, 581, 606, 611, 616-617, 671, 672, 674, 681, 716, 717, 737, 738, 741
Vervins, Treaty of, 127
Vesalius, 68
Vespucci, Amerigo, 148
Victor Emmanuel II, King of Italy, 457, 458 (*illus.*), 665-666
Victor Emmanuel III, King of Italy, 460, 662, 743
Victoria, Queen, 400, 433, 442
Victorian Age: literature and the arts, 523-534; political and social thought, 541-545
Vienna, Congress of, 301, 359, 369-373, 470
Vienna, sieges of, 241, 243
Vikings, 23
Villeneuve, Admiral, 350
Virginia, settlement of, 154, 156
Visconti family, 42
Viziers, 238-239
Volstead Act, 718
Voltaire, François Marie Arouet, 276, 283, 308: on Cardinal Fleury, 258; and Catherine the Great, 295; and causes of French Revolution, 319; as deist, 281; and Frederick the Great, 286, 288; 281 (*illus.*)

W

Wagner, Richard, 532, 533, 675
Waldseemüller, Martin, 148
Waldteufel, 533

Wallenstein, General, 113, 114
Walpole, Horace, 308-309
Walpole, Robert, 251, 255, 265, 266
Walsingham, 131
Wan Waithayakon, Prince, 817 (*illus.*)
War of the Austrian Succession, 266-267
War of *1812*, 575
War of the League of Augsburg, 172-173
War of the Polish Succession, 264-265
War of the Spanish Succession, 173
Wars of the Roses, 47
Wars of the Three Henries, 126-127
Warsaw, Grand Duchy of, 354, 355, 358
Washington, George, 267, 316
Waterloo, battle of, 360
Watt, James, 254
Watts, George Frederic, 528
Way of All Flesh, The (Butler), 526
Webb, Walter P., 164-165
Wealth of Nations, Inquiry into the Nature and Causes of the (Smith), 278-279
Webb, Sidney J. and Beatrice, 445
Weber, Karl Maria von, 364
Weber, Max, 98
Welfare state: in Britain, 445, 828; in Egypt, 786; in France, 712; in Germany, 480; National Insurance Act of *1911* (Great Britain), 440; New Deal, 720-722; in New Zealand and Australia, 799; in United States, 465, 466, 822
Wellesley, Sir Arthur (Duke of Wellington), 357, 360
Wellington, Duke of, 357, 360
Wells, H. G., 445, 526
Wentworth, Thomas, Earl of Strafford, 188
Wesley, John, 306-307, 361
"Westerners," theses of, 502, 503
West Indies: colonization of, 158, 268; early American trade, 154; Seven Years' War, 270, 271
Westminster, Statute of, 576, 710, 800
Westphalia, Peace of, 111, 115-118, 260
Weygand, General, 633, 753, 754
Wheel, invention of, 7
Whigs: in Glorious Revolution, 194; under Hanoverians, 255-256; and Liberals, 436
Whistler, James, 529
Whitehead, Alfred, 196
White Mountain, battle of, 113
White Russia. 303
White Terror: under Louis XVIII (*1814*), 360; of Thermidorean Reaction (*1794*), 338

Whitney, Eli, 402, 406
Whittier, John Greenleaf, 420, 527
Wiclif, John, 69
Wilkes, John, 314
William I, King of the Netherlands, 386
William I, King of Prussia and Emperor of Germany, 473, 476, 477, 479, 480
William II, Emperor of Germany, 470, 480-482, 567, 571, 583-584, 586, 587, 588, 591-592
William III of Orange, 172, 176, 194, 195
William IV, King of England, 434
William the Conqueror, 23
William the Silent, Prince of Orange, 110
Williams, Roger, 156
Will to Believe (James), 535
Will to Power (Nietzsche), 535
Wilson, Daniel, 453
Wilson, Woodrow, 466, 716, 717: after World War I, 607; alliance with Britain, France, 617-618; elected to second term, 605; Fourteen Points, 608-609, 610; idealism of, 703; and imperialism, 724; Paris Conference, 610, 611, 613; and ratification of Versailles Treaty, 617; with Clemenceau and Lloyd George, 610 (*illus.*); World War I, 593
Windischgrätz, Prince and Princess, 397
Witte, Sergei, 510: Trans-Siberian Railroad, 506, 507; revolution of *1905*, 509
Wolfe, James, 270
Wolsey, Cardinal, 85
Worcester, battle of, 190
Wordsworth, William, 362-363, 367, 368
World War I, 580-618: aftermath, 606-608; Allied victory, 601-602; and Allies' imperialism, 723-724; balance of power, shift in, 582-583; Balkan and Turkish Fronts, 598-600; Balkan Wars and, 589; Bismarck and, 585-586; causes, 582-593; course of the war, 594-606; diplomatic alignments before *1914* (*map*), 587; Eastern Front, 597-598; effect on France, 711-712; effects on defeat in Germany, 671-672; effects on Italy, 661-663; effects on United States, 716; Fourteen Points, 608-609, 610; German aspirations, 583-584; home fronts, 604-605; Italian Front, 598; Italo-Turkish War, 567; mandates, 614-616; morale on fighting fronts, 603-604; naval war, 600-601; in Near East, 600; peace, the, 606-618; political repercussions, 605-606; role of propaganda, 605; public opinion

and, 583; punishment of Germany, 616-617; resources of belligerents, 594-595; settlement evaluated, 617; territorial settlement, 613-614; Triple Entente, 586-588; weapons, 601-602; Western Front, 595-597

World War II, 736-769: aftermath, 805-820; allied coalition, 766-768; allied victory, 759-769; American policy, 758; Asian and Pacific theaters (*map*), 765; Axis on defensive, 760-762; Battle of Britain, 755-756; Blitzkrieg, 752-754; Czechoslovakia dismembered, 745-747; defeat in Germany, 762-764; defeat of Japan, 764-766; German rearmament, 741; invasion of Russia, 757-758; Italy, 755; Mediterranean and Balkan campaigns, 756-758; nature of the war, 750-751; Pearl Harbor and after, 758-759; "phony war," 751-752; Polish and Finnish campaigns, 751; political issues, 768-769; road to war (*1931-1939*), 740-749; Russia in, 655-657; supply, battle of, 760, turning points, 759-760

Wrangel, Baron, 633
Wren, Sir Christopher, 201
Wright brothers, 601
Writing, first, 9

X

Xerxes, 11
Xerxes (Handel), 310
Ximines, Cardinal, 50

Y

Yalta conference, 763, 769
Yermak, 223
York, House of, 47
Yorktown, surrender at, 316
Young, Arthur, 251-252, 313, 320-321
Young, Owen D., and Young Plan, 681
Young Turk Revolution, 492, 733
Ypsilanti, 380
Yuan Shih-k'ai, 726
Yudenich, General, 633
Yugoslavia: created by Paris Conference, 614; *1918-1939*, 698-699; World War II, 757; after World War II, 810-811, 835

Z

Zagreb trials, 491
Zarathustra (R. Strauss), 533
Zemski sobor (land assembly), 217, 218, 219-220, 222
Zeppelins, 601
Zhukov, Marshal, 832
Zinoviev, 638, 639, 646, 651
Zinoviev letter, 652
Zinzendorf, Count, 306
Zionism, 493, 789
Zola, Emile, 453, 525
Zollverein, 394, 473
Zwingli, Ulrich, 82-83, 86

1853 "Opening" of Japan by U.S. Commodore Perry

1859 *Origin of Species* by Darwin, and *On Liberty* by J. S. Mill: landmarks in history of scientific and liberal thought, respectively

1861 Outbreak of Civil War in United States
Emancipation of Russian serfs by Tsar Alexander II

1867 British North America Act: begins transformation of Empire into Commonwealth
Ausgleich (compromise): Habsburg Empire reorganized as Dual Monarchy

1870 Outbreak of Franco-Prussian War: leads to German and Italian unification and to French Third Republic

1882 Triple Alliance of Germany, Austria-Hungary, Italy

1891 *Rerum Novarum* by Pope Leo XIII: basic document of modern Catholic social philosophy

1898 Zola's *J'Accuse*: agitation over Dreyfus affair in France
Spanish-American War: United States emerging as world power

1904 *Entente Cordiale* of Britain and France

1905 Japan victorious in Russo-Japanese War; partly successful revolution in Russia

1911 Beginning of revolution in China

1914 (June 28) Assassination of Archduke Francis Ferdinand at Sarajevo precipitates World War I

1917 (March 8) Riots in Petrograd usher in Russian Revolution

1919 Peace conference of Paris after World War I: Treaty of Versailles

1922 (October 30) Fascist "march" on Rome: Mussolini in power